PATTERSON SMITH SERIES IN
CRIMINOLOGY, LAW ENFORCEMENT, AND SOCIAL PROBLEMS

A listing of publications in the SERIES *will be found at rear of volume*

MEMOIR OF THE LIFE

OF

ELIZABETH FRY.

Engraved by J.J. Hinchcliff

From a Portrait by Mrs Charles Pearson,

with her kind permission.

*My attached and
obliged friend
Elizth Fry*

PUBLICATION No. 187: PATTERSON SMITH SERIES IN
CRIMINOLOGY, LAW ENFORCEMENT & SOCIAL PROBLEMS

MEMOIR OF THE LIFE

OF

ELIZABETH FRY

WITH

EXTRACTS FROM HER JOURNAL AND LETTERS

EDITED BY HER DAUGHTERS
KATHARINE FRY AND RACHEL ELIZABETH CRESSWELL

TWO VOLUMES IN ONE
REPRINTED WITH THE ADDITION OF
GENEALOGICAL TABLES AND AN INDEX

Second Edition
REVISED AND ENLARGED

MONTCLAIR, N.J.

PATTERSON SMITH

1974

98491

First published 1847

Second edition, revised and enlarged
published 1848 by John Hatchard & Son, London

Second edition reprinted 1974 by
Patterson Smith Publishing Corporation
Montclair, New Jersey 07042

New material copyright © 1974 by
Patterson Smith Publishing Corporation

Library of Congress Cataloging in Publication Data

Fry, Elizabeth (Gurney) 1780-1845.
Memoir of the life of Elizabeth Fry, with extracts from
her journal and letters.

(Patterson Smith series in criminology, law enforcement
& social problems. Publication no. 187)
Reprint of the 1848 ed. with genealogical tables and
index added.
1. Fry, Elizabeth (Gurney) 1780-1845. I. Fry, Katharine, 1801-1886, ed. II. Cresswell, Rachel Elizabeth (Fry)
ed.

HV8978.F7A3 1974   365′.92′4 [B]   70-172597
ISBN 0-87585-187-8

I. ELIZABETH FRY'S GURNEY ANCESTRY, AUNTS, UNCLES, AND COUSINS

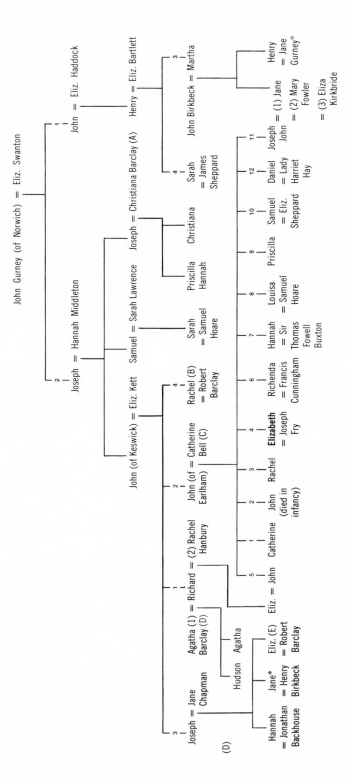

Letters in parentheses designate persons also found in Table II. * indicates identity within this table.

II. ELIZABETH FRY'S BARCLAY ANCESTRY AND RELATIVES

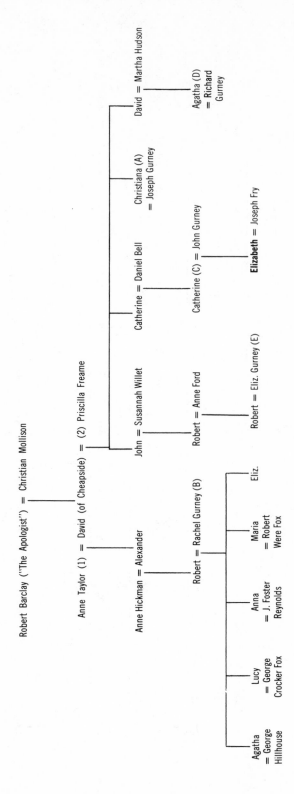

Letters in parentheses designate persons also found in Table I.

III. NEPHEWS AND NIECES OF ELIZABETH FRY

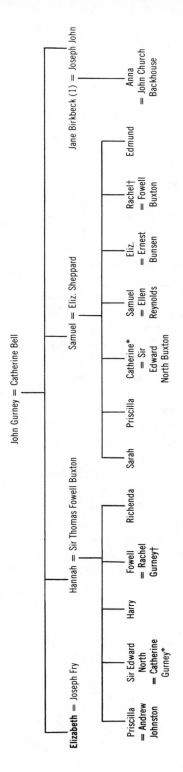

*, †, indicate identity within this table.

IV. THE CHILDREN OF JOSEPH AND ELIZABETH FRY

Katharine (b. 1801)

Rachel (b. 1803)
    married (1821) Francis Cresswell

John Gurney (b. 1804)
    married (1825) Rachel Reynolds

William Storrs (b. 1806)
    married (1832) Juliana Pelly

Richenda (b. 1808)
    married (1828) Foster Reynolds

Joseph (b. 1809)
    married (1834) Alice Partridge

Elizabeth (1811—1815)

Hannah (b. 1812)
    married (1832) William Champion Streatfeild

Louisa (b. 1814)
    married (1835) Raymond Pelly

Samuel Gurney (b. 1816)
    married (1838) Sophia Pinkerton

Daniel Henry (b. 1822)
    married (1845) Lucy Sheppard

INTRODUCTION.

"Blessed are the dead which die in the Lord, yea saith the Spirit, for they rest from their labours and their works do follow them." Very cheering is it to the pilgrim on his weary path, to mark the history of those who have gone before, and to trace the power by which they have been enabled

> To " labour up the hill of heavenly truth"
> And " fill their odorous lamps with deeds of light."

He may draw from it increased courage in endurance and fresh motives for exertion, for the path is not always easy, nor the way plain. When a Christian traveller therefore is taken from the earth, the question arises whether any thing in his history would encourage others, or exalt the cause of righteousness and truth. Should the labours of the departed have assumed a peculiar aspect, or have been in any respect uncommon ; the importance of this enquiry will be only enhanced. The motives of conduct, the secret springs of action must then be known, before the character can be fairly contemplated, or a just estimate formed of the individual.

Elizabeth Fry was one who formed the bright exception, not the rule, in the history of woman. Her numerous friends and associates desire to know her better, and to possess a more detailed account of her life. And how can the truth be so well told, as by her own journal, her letters, and those incidents in her life which illustrate her character.

Elizabeth Fry's family feel that their mother's memory belongs to others as well as to themselves—nor dare they withhold this record from the many, who have observed her proceedings with interest, and have considered but scarcely comprehended her career.

Two of her daughters have undertaken the office of preparing her papers for publication ; and, with the sanction of their father, selecting to the best of their judgment, such parts as may elucidate the subject, and interest the general reader. They are aware of the disadvantages under which they labour, from such an office being altogether new to them, but if the memory of their mother should not suffer through their means, they shall be well content to endure their own feelings of short coming. They owe deep thanks to many, who have lent them assistance ; returned letters, furnished materials, and helped in arranging them. But there is one point they anxiously wish to impress upon those who may peruse this Memoir ; that Elizabeth Fry never could have accomplished her works and labours of love, had not faithful and zealous associates been raised up to her help. Their unwearied energy, their skill, and their important assistance will be continually perceptible in the following pages. Many of these have ceased their labours upon earth ; many are advancing into the evening of life. To mention them as they deserve, and to raise a memorial to them also, though from the nature of the case impossible, would be to the writers most gratifying. There is another subject, connected with the life of Elizabeth Fry, on which her daughters would especially ask the forbearance of the public. It is the very difficult one of representing their mother as she was, and can only truly be represented " a Minister of the Society of Friends." This peculiarity was the strongly-marked feature

in her life. Here they anticipate, that many will not understand her course; whilst to that section of the church of Christ
to which she belonged, it will probably be the most interesting portion of the whole. It is not their intention, as Editors,
to enter into any discussion on the subject of the ministry of
women; but, deeply impressed with the unlimited nature of the
operations of the Holy Spirit, they dare not doubt, but that
under His influences, their mother went forward in the path
marked out before her—and that she was as a fine and well-
tempered instrument in the hand of the Great Head of the
Church, to effect certain purposes of His will, in which her
connexion with the Society of Friends, and adoption of their
views, became an important auxiliary. But far beyond any
sectarian, or peculiar tenets, would they earnestly endeavour
to bring before the reader the development of her Christian
character, the expansiveness of her charity, and the unity she
felt with all those whom she believed to be followers of the
Lord Jesus Christ; desiring, that though dead she may yet
speak, and that others may be stimulated by her example to
follow her, as she desired and endeavoured to follow Christ.

The extracts from her Journal and Correspondence display
the nature of her religious mind—her absolute dependence upon
the Highest influences for guidance and direction; her unremitting study of the written word, and the spirit of prayer in
which she carried on all her domestic duties and her objects of
benevolence. To adorn the doctrine of God her Saviour, to obey
his precepts, and in every thing to give Him alone the glory,
was unceasingly before her mind; emphatically did she express
this during her last illness, when she thus spoke to one of
her children:—" I can say one thing—since my heart was
touched, at the age of seventeen, I believe, I never have
awakened from sleep, in sickness or in health, by day or by
night, without my first waking thought being, how best I might
serve my Lord."

Let no one therefore attribute too much of the remarkable

success that attended her undertakings, to her natural gifts, to her winning manner, her harmonious voice, her gentle firmness of purpose, or quickness of perception ; but rather to the fact— that she was called by God to His own service, and that He saw meet eminently to fit her for it, and to work in her both to will and to do of His good pleasure.

KATHARINE FRY.

RACHEL ELIZABETH CRESSWELL.

Plashet, April, 1847.

INTRODUCTION

TO THE SECOND EDITION.

WHEN the first Edition of this Memoir was presented to the Public, it was a question how far it would be approved by that stern, and in the end, unerring judge, and whether the character and career of Elizabeth Fry would be generally understood and appreciated.

Very few months have elapsed since the work was completed, a large edition has been exhausted, and no small number of critics and reviewers have come forward to express their opinions, to sketch the picture with their own pencils, and colour it as their taste or preconceived opinions dictated. The Editors would acknowledge that they have been kindly, most kindly treated; nor have they been unmindful of the counsel given in preparing the present Edition.

But it is not with themselves that they have here to do; as has been beautifully said for them, " The fame of such a mother, is not only an inheritance but a trust." It is of her that they would speak;—of her natural character—the faith she possessed,—and the times she lived in. To attempt this was not originally their intention, but the varieties of opinion that have been broached induce them to alter this decision, and to add their own testimony to those already given.

Her natural Character.—This was a combination of great
decision, even resoluteness of purpose, exquisite tenderness
and power of loving, and timidity to an extent scarcely con-
ceivable by those unacquainted with her in the closest relations of life. Had qualities so opposite been abandoned to
the guidance of human reason, traits of devoted affection and
determination in effecting the desired end, might have been
discernible; but counteracted or misdirected by the extreme of
fearfulness, they must have failed in effecting any uniform
good. The possessor would probably have been a victim to
unrest and unsatisfied desires,—those dependent upon her
exposed to caprice and uncertainty. The amalgamating power
of religion combined the opposing elements; it directed her
decision in her long protracted efforts for the good of others;
it controlled and sanctified her natural affections; it exalted
her powers of loving, and raised them to that which could
satisfy the desires of her heart. It became her *delight* to do
the will of her Heavenly Father; her fearfulness blended with
it, and gave her courage in all things according to the faith
that was in her, to " obey God rather than man."

She possessed a quality eminently calculated to gladden and
adorn life, a taste for the beautiful in nature and art, the
former especially,—but all was offered on the altar of her heart
to retain and indulge only in accordance with the service of
her great Master.

There was another feature in her character which greatly
assisted her in her dealings with her fellow men,—her delicate
tact and rapid perception. It was by a sort of intuition she
arrived at the knowledge of the opinions and feelings of others.
This also became a means of good, guiding her in her intercourse with the various persons of all ranks and conditions,
with whom she held communication. But it was not alone by
religious truth in the aggregate that she was so wonderfully
benefited,—the peculiar form in which religion came to her

was precisely that which appears to have been the best calculated to her temperament, disposition, and circumstances.
Had the " water of life" been brought to her through any
other channel ; had a Scott, a Newton, or a Wesley, been the
appointed messenger to say to her, ' Believe and live,' very
different would have been the career of Elizabeth Fry. How,
any other dispensation would have affected her can only be
matter of speculation. One thing is however obvious, that
she as an individual, and the peculiar career allotted to her,
serve as no common illustration of the adaptation of the guiding providences of God to the circumstances and the required
duties of man ; for without the habits, the garb, the address,
and the protection of the Society of Friends, and above all,
without the fullest reception of the doctrine of the unlimited
nature of the operations of the Holy Spirit, it would have
been impracticable for her to accomplish the work allotted her
to do.

The Faith she possessed.—Gradually and through obscurity
she made her way from vague and indistinct opinions to the
fullest reception of the great doctrine of the Atonement. She in
no manner mystified or confused it with the offices of the Third
Person of the Godhead, but simply and absolutely believed in
Jesus Christ as her Redeemer, and looked to His Sacrifice
alone for salvation. She believed in the Holy Spirit as one
with the Father and the Son, and as being the Enlightener,
Sanctifier, and Guide of the Elect people of God; by which
word (Elect) she understood those without distinction of
sect or party, who having received the Lord Christ into
their hearts, are in the language of Scripture, renewed or born
again.

She believed that salvation is fully and freely offered to all
mankind. The letter U is continually to be found in her
Bible against those texts which she considered indicative of the

universality of Divine Grace.* Here she planted her foot, here with matured judgment, and advanced experience, she took her stand, and with all who united with her in these essentials of religion, whatever their denomination might be, she was capable of close communion. So far the teachings of our Lord and his disciples were in her estimation clear and unquestionable. But as if to adapt religion to all countries and conditions of men, no minute directions are left for the arrangement of Church Discipline, although that there are to be authorities and orders to maintain discipline and enjoin obedience, is continually implied. To suppose that any one form of religion as now established upon earth, contains in itself exclusively, in its doctrine, in its ritual, in its practice, the essence of vital Christianity, is to treat all other institutions only as more or less removed from error,—or approximate to truth as they approach to, or recede from, the imagined standard of perfection.

Elizabeth Fry, whilst she urged the need of devotedness of heart and purity of conduct upon all, asked not who was

---

* The following texts on this subject were written out by herself, and carried with her in one of her long journeys :

For as in Adam *all* die, even so in Christ shall *all* be made alive. 1 Cor. xv. 22.

Therefore as by the offence of one judgment came upon *all* men to condemnation ; even so by the righteousness of one the free gift came upon *all* men unto justification. Rom. v. 18.

God our Saviour. Who will have *all* men to be saved, and to come unto the knowledge of the truth. For there is one God, and one Mediator between God and man, the man Christ Jesus ; who gave himself a ransom *for all*, to be testified of in due time. 1 Tim. ii. 3, 4, 5, 6.

We trust in the living God who is the Saviour of *all* men, specially of those that believe. 1 Tim. vi., part of verse 10·

That he by the grace of God should taste death for *every* man. Heb. ii. part of verse 9.

And he is the propitiation for the sins : and not for ours *only*, but for the sins of the *whole* world. 1 John ii. 2.

a Lutheran, or Calvinist, or Roman Catholic abroad, a member of the Church of England or a dissenter at home. Fully conscious of the imperfection even in holy things to which all church administration is liable, passing as it does through a human medium, and affected by the feelings and opinions of men, she would not unfrequently compare it to water pure in itself, tainted by the channel through which it flows. But this arose not from indifference to her own religious convictions, it was not occasioned by indifference to the convictions of others; although delivered from undue dependence upon the secondary points of religion, she firmly adhered to her own principles, and to the form of doctrine which she considered to be right.

She believed that there was a distinct path, a path of right for every individual, she did not look upon the choice of a religious profession as a matter left to the devious imaginations of man, but one of solemn responsibility, affecting the stability of his Christian character, and his preparedness for an eternal state of being. Nor did she undervalue the weight of outward circumstances; of birth, education, country, position, or the creed inherited from forefathers, for whilst she had no sympathy with the spirit that would arrogate perfection to itself, she was none the less alive to the evil of undervaluing the privileges of church polity and church fellowship.

The danger is undeniable to which the unprejudiced truth-seeker is exposed, of taking refuge in the conclusion that if no one religious community is absolutely in the right, and consequently of universal adaptation, as a sequence every professing body of Christians must be more or less in error. From the scriptures of truth, and from the analogy to be observed between God's outward and spiritual government of the world, far different results are obtained. The former teach us that whilst secondary points are left for adaptation to country, political institutions, and the varying eras of the world, some system of church government is indispensable for all

Analogy proves, that man, habituated to receiving ideas through the medium of his outward senses, needs the help of such a staff as this to sustain him in the journey of life. Not mistaking the means for the end, that he should rest satisfied in the possession of that which is given as a support only, *along* the road of life, nor on the contrary that he should fling it from him as useless and cumbersome, and attempt unsupported and alone a path so fraught with danger and beset with temptation.

Elizabeth Fry was one of those who desired for herself and others, in the wisdom of humility, to mark the accidents of life by which each individual is surrounded, to note well his position as a citizen of the world that is, whilst he forgets not his calling as an inheritor of the world to come,—ever mindful of the fact, that a God of Grace is also a God of Providence, and that he who would speed well on his way, must be mindful of outward circumstances, whilst he listens with reverential attention to the guiding voice of inward conviction.

The Times she lived in.—Elizabeth Fry entered life at a period, when principles were developing and opinions forming unknown before. The French Revolution, and the writers which preceded it, had filled the social atmosphere with new elements. Produced by the struggle between tyranny and bigotry on the one hand, infidelity and licentiousness on the other, its lessons were written in blood, but as it swept over Europe, to all who were prepared to learn it taught wisdom. Thought, before in fetters, became free—but time and results were requisite to prove the tendency of the theories in vogue, to show that laxity is not liberty, and that honest truth-seeking is compatible with faith and devotedness of heart.

When Elizabeth Gurney came to an age of reflection, this yet remained to be discovered. To dare to doubt was almost synonymous with courage, and to believe in nothing not unfrequently mistaken for truth.

Glorious exceptions there undoubtedly were, and not a few

who clung the closer to the religious faith of their fathers, and to the institutions of their country, for the strife and uprooting around them.

Of ministers of religion it was expected, that with the pen as from the pulpit, they should urge their own opinions, and recommend the doctrines and commands of the Bible. The public was accustomed to the name of Hannah More, and of some writers of a similar stamp ; but when a young and gifted member of the legislature, endowed with talent, fortune, and most rare attainments in social life, came forward with a sound and simple exposition of Christian life and Christian conduct, its reception proved the degeneracy which had crept into English society.

A book which now represents the opinions of a vast proportion of the educated classes was received at that time by the thoughtful with astonishment, by the worldly-minded with displeasure, and by the careless with contempt. Elizabeth Gurney had tasted the charms and the dangers of unbridled thought, but her conscience once aroused, and her judgment satisfied that these things ought not so to be, she parleyed not with the enemy; not alone taking her stand on the broad basis of Christian truth, she sheltered herself behind the minute observances of the sect to which she belonged.

Had she not been led in a path so narrow when laxity and indifference to secondary things was the prevailing cry around her, the Christian liberality she displayed, when in after years a spirit of intolerance and adherence to party obtained general ascendancy, would have failed in teaching the intended lesson. Alarmed at the carelessness and contempt for holy things observable during the early part of her life, she bore her testimony to the necessity of a close and conscientious observance of the externals of religion ; equally fearful of the intolerant spirit which she saw in later years, she endeavoured by example and advice to enforce the principle of Christian love and unity between professors of every denomination who are servants of the same Lord. This posture of passive mental resistance tended unquestionably to the strengthening of her own faith and courage, and to her fitness for the work appointed her to do.

In another point of view, the times she lived in were essentially fitted for the career of Elizabeth Fry.

Before the beginning of the present century almost all good was accomplished by individual and insulated exertion, and, except in cases of endowment, ceased with him who originated the idea.

The last fifty years have brought with them a principle of Christian fellowship and association, unknown before—as a helping element, of indescribable value to the world and the Church.

Had Elizabeth Fry lived but one half century earlier she might have ministered to the necessities of some particular set of prisoners, or superintended one or more prisons in her own vicinity. She might, like Howard, have travelled and taught and brought to light crying evils to the harrowing up of men's souls, but the good gained would have been circumscribed and died with herself.

So far, however, from such being the case, it pleased Almighty Wisdom to raise her up at a moment when England, in an attitude of listening attention, was prepared to learn and profit. When light-bearers had arisen to illumine the prevailing darkness, and to enforce the doctrine, that without abandoning the circumstances of life allotted by Providence, there is a duty incumbent on each individual to perform by his fellowmen ; a debt to be discharged proportioned to the talents entrusted to him of wealth, power, intellect, example, and love. It was a whisper at the first, but it was rising louder and louder ; it was heard in the saloon, it was acknowledged in the hall of commerce, and might no longer be scouted in the senate-house !

Elizabeth Fry lived to find herself one amongst many. At

the outset of her course, minds kindred to her own were comparatively rare, but as she advanced on her pilgrimage wonderful joy was occasioned her by the variety and extent of Christian benevolence which she witnessed around her.

She has passed to her rest! but the spirit by which she was actuated exists and advances. Not alone from the middle ranks of society, nobles and princes, legislators, philosophers, and divines, have given in their adherence to the principle that man is bound to spend and be spent in the service and for the well-being of his fellow-men. Nor is this confined to England, men of many climes and differing in the externals of religion, have enrolled themselves in one vast crusade against misery and sin. Man in his strength, woman in her weakness, may be found there. They serve under one Captain, and whatever their distinguishing badge may be, there is emblazoned but one motto on the banner which floats over them all—" Glory to God in the highest, on earth peace, good will towards men."

MEMOIR OF THE LIFE

OF

ELIZABETH FRY

WITH

EXTRACTS FROM HER JOURNAL AND LETTERS

EDITED BY TWO OF HER DAUGHTERS

VOL. I

CONTENTS.

CHAPTER I.

CHAPTER II.

CHAPTER III.

CHAPTER IV.

CHAPTER V.

CHAPTER VI.

CHAPTER VII.

CHAPTER VIII.

CHAPTER IX.

CHAPTER X.

CHAPTER XI.

MEMOIR

OF THE

LIFE OF ELIZABETH FRY.

CHAPTER I.

1780—1792. Birth—Parentage—Descent—Her Mother, her character —Memoranda by her—Removal to Earlham—Death of Mrs. Gurney —Recollections by Elizabeth Fry, of her own early life.

ELIZABETH FRY was born in Norwich, on the 21st of May, 1780. She was the third daughter of John Gurney, Esq., of Earlham, in the county of Norfolk, and Catherine, daughter of Daniel Bell, a merchant in London; whose wife Catherine, daughter of David Barclay, was a descendant of the ancient family of the Barclays of Ury, in Kincardineshire, and granddaughter of Robert Barclay, the well-known apologist of the Quakers.

The name Gurney, or Gournay,* is of great antiquity in the county of Norfolk, and is derived from the town of Gournay en Brai, in Normandy. The Norman lords of which place, held fiefs in Norfolk, as early as the reign of William Rufus. Two younger branches of this Norman race existed for some centuries.

---

* See Burke's History of the Commoners of Great Britain and Ireland, vol. i. p. 484.

The one which was the most distinguished, was seated in Somersetshire ; the other at Hingham Gurneys, and West Barsham, in Norfolk, where it continued till 1661 ; when it became extinct in the direct male line, and the estates devolved on co-heiresses.

John Gurney, or Gournay, of Norwich, merchant, descended from a younger son of the West Barsham branch, was the immediate ancestor of the present family of Gurney.* He was born in 1655, and in early life embraced the tenets of the Society of Friends, on their first appearance, under George Fox their founder.

Joseph Gurney his son, purchased Keswick ; which continues to be the residence of the head of the family. John Gurney, of Keswick, his son, died in 1770 ; leaving three sons, of whom John Gurney, of Earlham, the father of Elizabeth Fry, was the second. She was thus by many generations of both descents, an hereditary member of the Society of Friends.

John Gurney of Earlham, the father of the subject of this Memoir, was born in 1749, and was educated in the principles of the Society of Friends. As he advanced in life, his pursuits led to intercourse with persons of various denominations; this, with a naturally social disposition, induced unusual liberality of sentiment towards others. He was a man of ready talent, of bright discerning mind, singularly warm-hearted, and affectionate, very benevolent, and in manners courteous and popular.

His marriage with Catherine Bell took place in 1775.

Mr. and Mrs. John Gurney established themselves in a roomy quadrangular house in St. Clement's parish, Norwich, which belonged to that branch of the family; where for some years they passed the winter months, spending the summer at Bra-

* See Burke's Commoners.

merton, a pretty village about four miles from Norwich, in an unpretending cheerful dwelling on the Common.

Mrs. Gurney was a person of excellent abilities, and of considerable attainments, as well as much personal beauty. She was disposed to scientific and intellectual pursuits, and singularly delighted in the charms and beauties of nature, imbuing her children, almost in infancy, with tastes that have remained with them through life. She preferred society that might be termed literary, to such as merely resulted from local circumstances.

At the period of which we speak, talent was frequently allied to scepticism, and the highest attainments in human learning were too often unaccompanied by soundness of religious faith. Many persons doubted; even more were indifferent to the great truths of Christianity; and so general was this state of things, that individuals of personal piety, who moreover earnestly desired the prosperity of the kingdom of Christ, too little considered the opinions entertained by others, and associated freely with those whose religious belief was essentially at variance with their own. We cannot doubt, but, that to a certain extent, such was the case with Mr. and Mrs. Gurney; or that it had an injurious effect upon their family, especially after the death of Mrs. Gurney; who laboured faithfully for the good of her children, reading the Bible with them, and urging upon them the necessity of prayer and personal piety. She watched minutely over the formation of character and habit, and planted in their young minds seeds, of which, they long afterwards reaped the excellent fruits.

Her own words, in memoranda found after her death, are so descriptive of her, that they find a fitting place here.

Bramerton, April 1788.—In the morning endeavour, at first waking, to bring the mind into a state of silent waiting and worship, preparatory to the active employment of the day; when up, visit the several apartments of the children, and, if leisure permit, before breakfast read the scriptures, if not, it should not be afterwards omitted; forget not the kindest attentions to my dearest companion before parting for the day. After walking with the little ones, and endeavouring to enjoy each individually, begin with the necessary instructions for Catherine and Rachel; then attend to the kitchen and all family regulations, and to the claims of the poor. When S. B. (the governess) has completed John's lessons, he may be suffered to play abroad with Peter (the coachman) or the gardener, but occasional admonition should be given, as to their conduct before him; visit the nurseries, with a view to arrange all matters to the advantage of the children : from thence repair to S. B.'s apartment, to attend from twelve to two o'clock, to assist in the education of the three eldest girls, who, as S. B. begins at ten o'clock with Kitty, are supposed to have advanced considerably in their lessons, before they are joined by me ; endeavour after patience and forbearance in this most important affair, which when completed for the day, may be succeeded by a walk, dressing, and again attending the nurseries before dinner; at which time, forget not the excellent custom of grateful, pious acknowledgment for blessings bestowed. The introduction of the children after this meal, generally affords my dear husband and myself an opportunity of the united enjoyment of our domestic comforts. A short afternoon may either be devoted to the company of my dear husband, or to writing letters, reading, or instructing the children alternately; particularly in the knowledge of the scriptures; also in the superintendence of S. B.'s apartment. Before tea, or immediately after, to assemble the little ones, to take particular and individual leave of each other ; and the few remaining hours of the evening to be devoted to the promotion of my husband's enjoyment, and, if possible, to blend instruction and amusement for the elder children, who are our constant companions till the time of rest. Then being quiet and uninterrupted with my best friend, be not unmindful of the religious duties of life; which consideration, may, I hope, lead to that trust in Providence, that gives spiritual tranquillity and spiritual support.

Remember, that these desultory remarks are designed, first, to promote my duty to my Maker—secondly, my duty towards my husband and children, relations, servants and poor neighbours.

Earlham, 1792.—" If in conversation we studied rather to avoid whatever may in its nature be reprehensible, than to search for approbation or admiration, would not associating with our friends become more innocent if not more profitable ? If our piety does not appear adequate to supporting us in the exigencies of life, and I may add, death ; surely our hearts cannot be sufficiently devoted to it. It may be encouraging to the poor traveller through life to consider, that as he recedes from vice he approaches towards virtue ; and as he despises the one, he will become enamoured with the other. Modern authors on religion and morality, describe perhaps very well what human nature ought to be, but do they sufficiently point out the means of becoming so ? Do they direct the inquirer to the still small voice within ?

Books of controversy on religion are seldom read with profit, not even those in favour of our own particular tenets. The mind stands less in need of conviction than conversion.

REMARKS ON EDUCATION.

As our endeavours in education, as in every other pursuit, should be regulated by the ultimate design ; it would be certainly wise, in those engaged in the important office of instructing youth, to consider, what would render the objects of their care perfect, when men or women ; rather than what will render them pleasing as children. These reflections have led me to decide upon what I most covet for my daughters, as the result of our daily pursuits. As piety is undoubtedly the shortest and securest way to all moral rectitude, young women should be virtuous and good, on the broad firm basis of Christianity ; therefore, it is not the opinions of any man or sect whatever, that are to be inculcated in preference to those rigid but divine truths, contained in the New Testament.

As it appears to be our reasonable duty to improve our faculties, and by that means to render ourselves useful ; it is necessary and very agreeable, to be well informed of our own language, and the Latin as being the most permanent ; and the French as being the most in general request. The simple beauties of mathematics appear to be so excellent an exercise to the understanding, that they ought on no account to be omitted, and are perhaps scarcely less essential, than a competent knowledge of ancient and modern history, geography, and chronology. To which may be added, a knowledge of the most approved branches of natural history, and a capacity of drawing from nature, in order to promote that knowledge, and facilitate the pursuit of it. As a great portion of a woman's life ought to be passed, in at least regulating the subordinate affairs of a family; she should work plain work neatly herself, understand the cutting out of linen; also, she should not be ignorant of the common proprieties of a table, or deficient in the economy of any of the most minute affairs of a family. It should be here observed, that gentleness of manner is indispensably necessary in women, to say nothing of that polished behaviour, that adds a charm to every qualification; to both of which, it appears pretty certain, children may be led without vanity or affectation, by amiable and judicious instruction.

As children are not without some latent sense of their duty to their Maker, perhaps the following observations would not be amiss to offer, when they first go to a place of worship. Since we know that He, who gave us life, health, and strength of body, has given us an understanding mind, which will shew us what is reasonable and right to do, we ought to consider, whether it is not right to love and obey that excellent Being, who has certainly placed us here on earth and surrounded us with blessings and enjoyments, that we may become as He would have us; that is, good; and that we should adore and love Him at all times; but as many things happen to lead the mind from this adoration and love of God, which is His due, and our truest enjoyment, it is necessary to retire with our friends and neighbours from hurry and business, that we may think of Him who delights to bless us, and will consider us as His children, if we love Him as a heavenly Father. Do not, then, my dear child, suffer thy thoughts to wander, or to dwell upon trifles, when thou art most immediately before Him, whom thou must strive to love, with all thy heart and soul.

In the year 1786, Mr. and Mrs. Gurney removed to Earlham Hall, a seat of the Bacon family, about two miles from Norwich. Mr. Gurney subsequently purchased an adjoining property, thus adding to the range and variety afforded to his large young party, by that pleasant home. Earlham has peculiar charms from its diversified scenery. The house is large, old, and irregular; placed in the centre of a well-wooded park. The river Wensum, a clear winding stream, flows by it. Its banks, overhung by an avenue of ancient timber trees, formed a favourite resort of the young people; there, in the summer evenings, they would often meet to walk, read or sketch. On the south-front of the house extends a noble lawn, flanked by groves of trees growing from a carpet of wild flowers, moss and long grass. Every nook, every green path at Earlham tells a tale of the past, and recalls to those, who remember the time when they were peopled by that joyous party, the many loved ones of the number, who, having shared with one another the pleasures of youth, the cares of maturer age, and above all, the hope of Immortality, are now together at rest!

Of the twelve children of Mr. and Mrs. Gurney, nine were born before their removal to Earlham; one of them died in infancy. The three youngest sons were born after their settlement there.

The mode of life at Bramerton was continued with little alteration at Earlham, till November, 1792, when it pleased God to remove from this large family, the kind mistress—the loving wife—the devoted mother. She died after an illness of three weeks leaving eleven children, the eldest scarcely seventeen, the youngest, not two years old. During a period of comparative leisure, Elizabeth Fry occupied herself in perusing her early journals. She thought it well to destroy all that were written before the year 1797, and to substitute the following sketch of their contents, assisted by her own recollections.

Dagenham, Eighth Month 23rd, 1828.—My earliest recollections are, I should think, soon after I was two years old. My father at that time had two houses, one in Norwich, and one at Bramerton, a sweet country place, situated on a Common, near a pretty village ; here, I believe, many of my early tastes were formed, though we left to reside at Earlham, when I was about five years old. The impressions then received remain lively on my recollection ; the delight in the beauty and wild scenery in parts of the Common, the trees, the flowers, and the little rills, that abounded on it, the farm-houses, the village school, and the different poor people and their cottages ; particularly a poor woman with one arm, whom we called one-armed Betty ; another neighbour, Greengrass, and her strawberry beds round a little pond ; our gardener, who lived near a large piece of water, and used to bring fish from it ; here, I think, my great love for the country, the beauties of nature, and attention to the poor, began. My mother was most dear to me, and the walks she took with me in the old-fashioned garden, are as fresh with me, as if only just passed ; and her telling me about Adam and Eve being driven out of Paradise : I always considered it must be just like our garden at Bramerton. I remember that my spirits were not strong ; that I frequently cried if looked at, and used to say that my eyes were weak ; but I remember much pleasure and little suffering, or particular tendency to naughtiness, up to this period. Fear about this time began to show itself, of people and things : I remember being so much afraid of a gun, that I gave up an expedition of pleasure with my father and mother, because there was a gun in the carriage. I was also exceedingly afraid of the dark, and suffered so acutely from being left alone without a light after I went to bed, that I believe my nervous system was injured in consequence of it ; also, I had so great a dread of bathing, (to which I was at times obliged to submit,) that the first sight of the sea, when we were as a family going to stay by it, would make me cry ; indeed, fear was so strong a principle in my mind, as greatly to mar the natural pleasure of childhood. I am now of opinion, that it would have been much more subdued, and great suffering spared, by its having been still more yielded to ; by having a light left in my room, not being long left alone ; and never forced to bathe ; for I do not at all doubt that it partly arose from that nervous susceptible constitution, that has at times, throughout my life, caused me such real and deep suffering. I know not what would have been the consequence, had I had any other than a most careful and wise mother and judicious nurses, or had I been alarmed, as too many children are, by false threats of what might happen.

I had, as well as a fearful, rather a reserved mind, for I never remember telling of my many painful fears, though I must often have shown them by weeping when left in the dark, and on other occasions: this reserve made me little understood, and thought very little of, except by my mother and one or two others. I was considered and called very stupid and obstinate. I certainly did not like learning, nor did I, I believe, attend to my lessons, partly from a delicate state of health, that produced languor of mind as well as body; but, I think, having the name of being stupid really tended to make me so, and discouraged my efforts to learn. I remember having a poor, not to say low opinion of myself, and used to think that I was so very inferior to my sisters, Catherine and Rachel. I believe I had not a name only for being obstinate, for my nature had then a strong tendency that way; and I was disposed to a spirit of contradiction, always ready to see things a little differently from others, and not willing to yield my sentiments to theirs.

My natural affections were very strong from my early childhood, at times almost overwhelmingly so; such was the love for my mother, that the thought that she might die and leave me used to make me weep after I went to bed, and for the rest of the family, that notwithstanding my fearful nature, my childlike wish was, that two large walls might crush us all together, that we might die at once, and thus avoid the misery of each other's death. I seldom, if I could help it, left my mother's side, I watched her when asleep in the day with exquisite anxiety, and used to go gently to her bed-side to listen, from the awful fear that she did not breathe; in short, I may truly say, it amounted to deep reverence, that I felt for my father and mother. I never remember, as a little child, but once being punished by my mother; and she then mistook tears of sorrow for tears of naughtiness, a thing that deeply impressed me, and I have never forgotten the pain it gave me. Although I do not imply that I

10

had no faults, far from it, as some of the faults of my childhood are very lively in my recollection ; yet from my extreme love and fear, many of these faults were known almost only to myself. My imagination was lively, and I once remember, and only once, telling a real untruth with one of my sisters and one of my brothers. We saw a bright light one morning, which we represented far above the reality, and upon the real thing being shown us that we had seen, we made it out not to be it. My remembrance is of the pleasure of my childhood being almost spoiled through fear, and my religious impressions, such as I had, were accompanied by gloom : on this account, I think the utmost care needed, in representing religious truth to children, that fearful views of it should be most carefully avoided, lest it should give a distaste for that which is most precious. First show them the love and mercy of God in Christ Jesus, and the sweetness and blessedness of his service ; and such things in scripture, for instance, as Abraham's sacrifice, should be carefully explained to them. I think I suffered much in my youth from the most tender nervous system ; I certainly felt symptoms of ill health before my mother died, that I thought of speaking to her about, but never did, partly because I did not know how to explain them ; but they ended afterwards in very severe attacks of illness. I have always thought being forced to bathe was one cause of this, and I mention it, because I believe it a dangerous thing to do to children. What care is needful not to force children to learn too much, as it not only injures them, but gives a distaste for intellectual pursuits. Instruction should be adapted to their condition, and communicated in an easy and agreeable way.

How great is the importance of a wise mother, directing the tastes of her children in very early life, and judiciously influencing their affections ! I remember with pleasure my mother's beds for wild flowers, which, with delight, I used, as a child, to attend to with her ; it gave me that pleasure in observing their beauties and varieties, that though I never have had time to become a botanist, few can imagine, in my many journeys, how I have been pleased and refreshed, by observing and enjoying the wild flowers on my way. Again, she collected shells, and had a cabinet, and bought one for Rachel and myself, where we placed our curiosities; and I may truly say, in the midst even of deep trouble, and often most weighty engagements of a religious and philanthropic nature, I have derived advantage, refreshment, and pleasure, from my taste for these things, making collections of them, and various natural curiosities, although, as with the flowers, I have not studied them scientifically.

My mother also encouraged my most close friendship with my sister Rachel, and we had our pretty light closet, our books, our pictures, our curiosities, our tea things, all to ourselves; and as far as I can recollect, we unitedly partook of these pleasures, without any of the little jealousies, or the quarrels of childhood.

My mother, as far as she knew, really trained us up in the fear and love of the Lord; my deep impression is, that she was a holy devoted follower of the Lord Jesus; but that her understanding was not fully enlightened as to the fulness of gospel truth. She taught us as far as she knew, and I now remember the solemn religious feelings I had whilst sitting in silence with her after reading the scriptures, or a Psalm before we went to bed. I have no doubt that her prayers were not in vain in the Lord. She died when I was twelve years old; the remembrance of her illness and death is sad, even to the present day.

CHAPTER II.

AMONG the vast changes of the last century, there was no change greater than that which took place in the education of women.

Addison, and his coadjutors, were among the foremost to teach the women of modern England, that they possessed powers of mind, and capabilities of usefulness. Many, as they sipped their coffee, with the Spectator of the morning in their hand, were awakened to the consciousness of a higher destiny for woman, than the labour of the tapestry frame, or pursuits of an entirely frivolous nature. A taste for reading became more or less general. The heavy wisdom of Johnson, the lighter wit of Swift, the satire of Pope, the pathos of Gray, and the close painting of Goldsmith, found among women not only those who could enjoy, but who could appreciate their different excellencies. Mrs. Montague, Mrs. Carter, Mrs. Chapone, with a group of gifted friends and associates, proved to the world the possibility of high literary attainments existing with every feminine grace and virtue. The stimulus was given, but like all other changes in society, the opposite extreme was reached, before the right and reasonable was discovered. Infidelity was making slow, though sure advances upon the Continent. Rousseau and

Voltaire were but types of the state of feeling and principles in France. The effects gradually extended to our own country, and England has to blush for the perversion of female talent, the evil influence of which, was only counteracted by shewing as a beacon light, to warn others from shipwreck. Science and philosophy, so called, advanced and flourished, but by their side flourished also the Upas tree of infidelity, poisoning with its noxious breath the flowers and the fruits, otherwise so pleasant to the eye, and so good for the use of man. The writings of Hannah More were well calculated to enlighten and improve her sex; she spoke as woman can alone speak to women; but she was then only rising into celebrity, and as an author little known.

Norwich had not escaped the general contagion. On the contrary, at the period of which we speak, it was noted for the charm, the talent, and the scepticism of the society of the town and neighbourhood. The death of Mrs. Gurney, had left her seven daughters, unprotected by a mother's care, to pursue the difficult path of early womanhood. They appear to have been rich in attraction and talent, lively and original, possessing a peculiar freshness of character, with singular purity of purpose, and warmth of affection. But their faith was obscure, and their principles necessarily unfixed and wavering. They appreciated the beauty and excellence of religion; but it was natural, rather than revealed religion with which they were acquainted.

There was something of mysticism amongst the Quakers of that day, and by no means the clear and general acknowledgment of the doctrine of the "*Trinity* in *Unity*," as revealed in the New Testament, which is now to be met with amongst the greater part of the Society of "Friends." To the present time, that expression, as designating the Deity, is not in use among them, from its not being found in the Bible. The family of Mr. Gurney, thus left to their own resources, unaccustomed to the study of the scriptures, and with no other sources of information from which to learn, for a time were permitted to " stumble upon the dark mountains, seeking rest and finding none."

These remarks apply especially to the three elder daughters, as they gradually advanced into life. The four younger ones, sheltered in the school-room, were comparatively spared the difficulties through which their sisters were pioneering the way. Mr. Gurney's occupations, both public and private, and his naturally trustful disposition, prevented his seeing all the dangers to which they were exposed. They formed many acquaintances, and some friendships, with persons greatly gifted by nature, but fearfully tainted by the prevailing errors of the day. Great pain and bitter disappointment resulted from these connexions ; but demanding only an allusion here, as they indirectly affected Elizabeth through the sufferings of others, and the experience gained to herself.

To the gaieties of the world, in the usual acceptation of the term, they were but little exposed. Music and dancing are not allowed by Friends ; though a scruple, as to the former, is by no means universal. Mr. Gurney had no objection to music : they had all a taste for it, though almost uncultivated ; some of them sang delightfully. The sweet and trilling pathos of their native warblings are still remembered with pleasure by those who heard them, especially the duets of Rachel and Elizabeth. They danced occasionally in the large anti-room leading to the drawing-room, but with little of the spirit of display so often manifested on these occasions. It was more an effusion of young joyous hearts, who thus sought and found an outlet for their mirth. When her health permitted it, no one of the party entered with more zest into these amusements than Elizabeth. Her figure tall, and at that time slight and graceful, was peculiarly fitted for dancing. She was also an excellent horsewoman, and road fearlessly and well ; but she suffered much from delicacy of constitution, and was

liable to severe nervous attacks, which often impeded her joining
her sisters in their different objects and pursuits. In countenance, she is described as having been as a young person very
sweet and pleasing, with a profusion of soft flaxen hair, though,
perhaps, not so glowing and handsome as some of her sisters.

She had much native grace, and to many people was very
attractive. Elizabeth was not studious by nature, and was, as a
child, though gentle and quiet in temper, self-willed and determined. In a letter, written before she was three years old, her
mother thus mentions her :—" My dove-like Betsey scarcely
ever offends, and is, in every sense of the word, truly engag-
ing." Her dislike to learning proved a serious disadvantage to
her after she lost her mother; her education, consequently,
being defective and unfinished. In natural talent, she was
quick and penetrating, and had a depth of originality very uncommon. As she grew older, enterprise and benevolence were
two predominant features in her character. In contemplating
her peculiar gifts, it is wonderful to observe the adaptation of
her natural qualities to her future career ; and how, through the
transforming power of divine grace, each one became subservient to the highest purposes. Her natural timidity changed to
the opposite virtue of courage, but with such holy moderation
and nice discretion, as never failed to direct it aright. The
touch of obstinacy she displayed as a child, became that finely
tempered decision and firmness, which enabled her to execute
her projects for the good of her fellow-creatures. That which
was in childhood something not unlike cunning, ripened into
the most uncommon penetration, long-sightedness, and skill in
influencing the minds of those around her. Her disinclination to the common methods of learning, appeared to be connected with much original thought, and a mind acting on its
own resources ; for she certainly always possessed more genius
and ready quick comprehension, than application or argument.

Such were the circumstances, and such the characteristics of Elizabeth Gurney and her sisters, after the death of their mo- ther : and years passed on, with few changes, but such as ne- cessarily came with the lapse of time, and their advance in age. But He who had purposes of mercy towards them ; in His own way, and in His own good time, was preparing for them eman- cipation from their doubts, and light for darkness. Won- derful is it to mark how, by little and little, through various instruments, through mental conflicts, through bitter experi- ence, He gradually led them, each one, into the meridian light of day—the glorious liberty of the children of God.

At a time when religion in a more gloomy form might not have gained a hearing ; when the graver countenance of rebuke would probably have been unheeded, a gentleman became ac- quainted with the Earlham family, of high principle, and culti- vated mind. With him the sisters formed a strong and lasting friendship. He addressed himself to their understandings, on the grand doctrines of Christianity ; he referred them to the written word as the rule of life ; he lent them, and read with them, books of a religious tendency. He treated religion, as such, with reverence ; and although himself a Roman Catholic, he abstained from every controversial topic, nor ever used his influence, directly or indirectly, in favour of his own church. There was another individual who proved an important instru- ment, in leading the sisters to sound views of religion, though, when first acquainted with them, herself wandering in the wilderness of doubt, if not of error. This was Marianne Galton, afterwards Mrs. Schimmelpenninck.* Being a highly educated person, of great mental power, and accustomed to exercise her abilities in the use of her reason and an honest search after truth; she acquired considerable influence over

* Authoress of a Tour to Alet and the Grande Chartreuse, &c., &c.,

them.   As the truth of revelation opened upon her own understanding, and her heart became influenced by it, they shared in
her advance, and profited by her experience.   There were other
individuals with whom they associated, whose influence was
desirable, but less powerful, than that of either Miss Galton or
Mr. Pitchford.

They appear also to have derived advantage, at times, from
the religious visits of Friends to Earlham.   The family of Mr.
Gurney were in the habit of attending no place of worship, but
the Friends' meeting.   The attendance of Elizabeth was continually impeded by want of health, and it is difficult to know
when the habit of absenting herself might have been broken
through, but for her uncle, Joseph Gurney; who urged the
duty upon her, and encouraged her to make the attempt.   He
was a decided Friend, and had much influence with her, both
then, and during her future life.   She was ready, indeed, to
essay any thing, that might tend to satisfy her conscience, or
meet the cravings of her heart, for a something which as yet
she had not obtained.   There is occasionally to be met with in
the character of fallen man, a longing after perfection—after
that which can alone satisfy the immortal spirit; this she experienced in no common measure.   Her Journal is replete with
desires after " virtue" and " truth."   She seeks and finds God
in His works, but as yet she had not found Him, as He stands
revealed in the page of inspiration.

January, 1797.—My mind is in so dark a state, that I see
everything through a black medium.

April.—Why do I so much wish for the Prince* to come ?
Pride, alas ! is the cause.   Do such feelings hurt my mind ?
they may not in this instance, but if given way to, they are
difficult to overcome.   How am I to overcome them ?

* H. R. H. William Frederick, afterwards Duke of Gloucester, then
quartered at Norwich.

April.—Without passions of any kind how different I should be! I would not give them up, but I should like to have them under subjection; but it appears to me, as I feel, impossible to govern them, my mind is not strong enough, as I at times think they do no hurt to others. But am I sure they will hurt no one? I believe by not governing myself in little things, I may by degrees become a despicable character, and a curse to society; therefore, my doing wrong is of consequence to others, as well as to myself. "As the beams of the sun irradiate the earth, and yet remain where they were, so it is, in some proportion, with an holy mind, that illustrates all our actions, and yet adheres to its original."—*Seneca's Morals.*

April 25th.—I feel by experience, how much entering into the world hurts me; worldly company, I think, materially injures, it excites a false stimulus, such as a love of pomp, pride, vanity, jealousy, and ambition; it leads to think about dress, and such trifles, and when out of it, we fly to novels and scandal, or something of that kind, for entertainment. I have lately been given up a good deal to worldly passions; by what I have felt I can easily imagine how soon I should be quite led away.

29th.—I met the Prince, it showed me the folly of the world; my mind feels very flat after this storm of pleasure.

May 16th.—There is a sort of luxury in giving way to the feelings! I love to feel for the sorrows of others, to pour wine and oil into the wounds of the afflicted; there is a luxury in feeling the heart glow, whether it be with joy or sorrow. I think the different periods of life may well be compared to the seasons. First, we are in the spring, only buds are to be seen, next, our characters are blown, and it is summer; autumn follows, and there are then many remains of summer, and beautiful ones too; there springs also the best fruit from the summer flower. Winter must come, it will follow in its course; there is not much more pleasure then, than collecting a few solitary berries, and playing with the snow and ice.

I like to think of everything, to look at mankind; I love to "look through Nature up to Nature's God." I have no more religion than that, and in the little I have I am not the least devotional, but when I admire the beauties of nature, I cannot help thinking of the source from whence such beauties flow. I feel it a support. I believe firmly that all is guided for the best by an invisible power, therefore I do not fear the evils of life so much. I love to feel good—I do what I can to be kind to everybody. I have many faults which I hope in time to overcome.

18*th*.—Most likely about a hundred years from this time, neither one person, nor anything that has life, will be alive. What is still more wonderful is, that all should be so continually changing, almost without our observation.

Monday, 21*st*.—I am seventeen to day. Am I a happier or a better creature than I was this time twelvemonths ? I know I am happier ; I think I am better. I hope I shall be much better this day year than I am now. I hope to be quite an altered person, to have more knowledge, to have my mind in greater order ; and my heart, too, that wants to be put in order as much, if not more, than any part of me, it is in such a fly-away state ; but I think if ever it were settled on one object it would never, no never, fly away any more ; it would rest quietly and happily on the heart that was open to receive it, it will then be most constant ; it is not my fault it now flies away, it is owing to circumstances.

30*th*.—It is a great comfort to me that life is short, and soon passes away—yet, it is certainly a pleasure or blessing to exist. I think I have now no reason to wish to die, I am so well; but I must own with ill health, such as I used to have, life is a burden; perhaps I now think worse of it than I did when I had it, for the imagination increases evils at a distance, as it does every thing else; I was supported through it, whilst it lasted : though I was very unhappy, I could not call myself a miserable being. Ill health is certainly a deprivation of the powers of life ; we do but half live when ill : my fate is guided by an all-wise and all-virtuous Director, I shall not be ill, unless it is right I should be so.

Monday, June.—I am at this present time in an odd state ; I am like a ship put out to sea without a pilot; I feel my heart and mind so over burdened, I want some one to lean upon.

(Written on a bright summer's morning.)

Is there not a ray of perfection amidst the sweets of this morning? I do think there is something perfect from which all good flows.

20th.—If I have long to live in this world, may I bear mis-fortunes with fortitude; do what I can to alleviate the sorrows of others, exert what power I have to increase happiness; try to govern my passions by reason, and adhere strictly to what I think right.

July 7th.—I have seen several things in myself and others, I have never before remarked; but I have not tried to improve myself, I have given way to my passions, and let them have command over me. I have known my faults, and not corrected them, and now I am determined I will once more try, with re-doubled ardour, to overcome my wicked inclinations; I must not flirt; I must not ever be out of temper with the children; I must not contradict without a cause; I must not mump when my sisters are liked and I am not; I must not allow myself to be angry; I must not exaggerate, which I am inclined to do. I must not give way to luxury; I must not be idle in mind, I must try to give way to every good feeling, and overcome every bad; I will see what I can do; if I had but perseverance, I could do all that I wish, I will try. I have lately been too sa-tirical, so as to hurt sometimes; remember! it is a fault to hurt others.

8th.—A much better day, though many faults.

10th.—Some poor people were here; I do not think I gave them what I did, with a good heart. I am inclined to give away; but for a week past, owing to not having much money, I have been mean and extravagant. Shameful! Whilst I live, may I be generous; it is in my nature, and I will not overcome so good a feeling. I an inclined to be extravagant, and that leads to meanness, for those who will throw away a good deal, are apt to mind giving a little.

11th.—I am in a most idle mind, and inclined to have an

indolent dissipated day ; but I will try to overcome it, and see how far I can. I am well, oh, most inestimable of comforts ! Happy, happy I, to be so well ; how good, how virtuous, ought I to be ! May what I have suffered be a lesson to me, to feel for those who are ill, and alleviate their sorrows as far as lies in my power ; let it teach me never to forget the blessings I enjoy. I ought never to be unhappy ;—look back at this time last year, how ill I was, how miserable ;—yet I was supported through it ; God will support through the suffering He inflicts ; if I were devotional, I should fall on my knees and be most grateful for the blessings I enjoy ; a good father, one whom I dearly love, sisters formed after my own heart, friends whom I admire, and good health, which gives a relish to all. Company to dinner ; I must beware of being a flirt, it is an abominable character ; I hope I shall never be one, and yet I fear I am one now a little. Be careful not to talk at random. Beware, and see how well I can get through this day, without one foolish action. If I do pass this day without one foolish action, it is the first I ever passed so. If I pass a day with only a few foolish actions, I may think it a good one.

25th.—This book is quite a little friend to my heart ; it is next to communicating my feelings to another person. I would not but write in it for something, for it is most comfortable to read it over and see the different workings of my heart and soul.

30th.—Pride and vanity are too much the incentives to most of the actions of men, they produce a love of admiration, and in thinking of the opinions of others, we are too apt to forget the monitor within. We should first look to ourselves and try to make ourselves virtuous, and then pleasing. Those who are truly virtuous not only do themselves good, but they add to the good of all. All have a portion entrusted to them of the general good, and those who cherish and preserve it are blessings to society at large ; and those who do not become a curse. It is wonderfully ordered, how in acting for our own good, we promote the good of others. My idea of religion is, not for it to unfit us for the duties of life, like a nun who leaves them for prayer and thanksgiving ; but I think it should stimulate and capacitate us to perform these duties properly. Seeing my father low this evening, I have done all I can to make him comfortable, I feel it one of my first duties; I hope he will always find in me a most true friend and affectionate daughter.

August 1st.—I have done little to day, I am so very idle; instead of improving I fear I go back; I think I may improve, being so young, but I also think there is every chance of my disimproving; my inclinations lead me to be an idle, flirting, worldly girl. I see what would be acting right, but I have neither activity nor perseverance in what I think right. I am like one setting out on a journey; if I set out on the wrong road, and do not try to recover the right one before I have gone far, I shall most likely lose my way for *ever*, and every step I take, the more difficult shall I find it to return, therefore the temptation will be greater to go on, till I get to destruction. On the contrary, if now, whilst I am innocent of any great faults, I turn into the right path, I shall feel more and more contented every step I take, and if I do now and then err a little from the proper path I shall not find it so hard to return to it, for I I shall by degrees find the road to vice more and more unpleasant. Trifles occupy me far too much, such as dress &c., &c. I find it easier to acknowledge my vices than my follies.

6th.—I have a cross to-night. I had very much set my mind on going to the Oratorio, the Prince is to be there, and by all accounts it will be quite a grand sight, and there will be the finest music; but if my father does not like me to go, much as I wish it, I will give it up with pleasure, if it be in my power, without a murmur.—I went to the Oratorio, I enjoyed it, but spoke sadly at random; what a bad habit!!

12th.—I do not know if I shall not soon be rather religious, because I have thought lately, what a support it is through life; it seems so delightful to depend upon a superior power, for all that is good; it is at least always having the bosom of a friend open to us, (in imagination) to rest all our cares and sorrows upon, and what must be our feelings to imagine that friend perfect, and guiding all and everything, as it should be guided. I think anybody who had real faith, could never be unhappy ; it appears the only certain source of support and comfort in this life, and what is best of all, it draws to virtue, and if the idea be ever so ill founded that leads to that great object, why should we shun it ? Religion has been misused and corrupted, that is no reason why religion itself is not good. I fear being religious, in case I should be enthusiastic.

15*th.*—For a few days past I have been in a worldly state, dissipated, a want of thought, idle, relaxed and stupid, all outside, no inside. I feel I am a contemptible fine lady. May I be preserved from continuing so, is the ardent prayer of my *good* man, but my *evil* man tells me I shall pray in vain. I will try. I fear for myself, I feel in the course of a little time I shall be all outside flippery, vain, proud, conceited ; I could use improper words at myself, but my *good* man will not let me. But I am good in something, it is wicked to despair of myself, it is the way to make me what I desire not to be, I hope I shall always be virtuous ; can I be really wicked ? I may be so, if I do not overcome my first weak inclinations. I wish I had more solidity and less fluidity in my disposition. I feel my own weakness and insufficiency to bear the evils and rubs of life. I must try by every stimulus in my power, to strengthen myself both bodily and mentally, it can only be done by activity and perseverance.

19*th.*—Idle and relaxed in mind, greatly dissipated by hearing the band, &c. &c. Music has a great effect on me, it at times makes me feel almost beside myself.

30*th.*—"Come what, come may, time and the hour run through the roughest day," a very sad and trying day. Tried by being poorly, by others, and by myself : very far from what I ought to be.

Sept. 3*rd.*—There is much difference between being obstinate and steady ; I am obstinate, when I contradict for the sake of contradiction ; I am steady, when I keep to what I really think right. I am too apt to contradict, whether I should or not. If I am bid to do a thing, my spirit revolts ; if I am asked to do a thing, I am willing.

December.—A thought passed my mind, that if I had some

religion, I should be superior to what I am, it would be a bias
to better actions; I think I am by degrees, losing many excellent qualities. I am more cross, more proud, more vain, more
extravagant. I lay it to my great love of gaiety, and the
world. I feel, I know I am falling. I do believe if I had a
little true religion, I should have a greater support than I have
now; in virtue my mind wants a stimulus; never, no never
did mind want one more: but I have the greatest fear of religion, because I never saw a person religious, who was not
enthusiastic.

January, 1798.—I must die! I shall die! wonderful, death
is beyond comprehension. To leave life, and all its interests,
and be almost forgotten by those we love. What a comfort
must a real faith in religion be, in the hour of death; to have
a firm belief of entering into everlasting joy. I have a notion
of such a thing, but I am sorry to say, I have no real faith in
any sort of religion; it must be a comfort and support in
affliction, and I know enough of life to see, how great a stimulus is wanted, to support through the evils that are inflicted,
and to keep in the path of virtue. If religion be a support,
why not get it?

14th.—I think it almost impossible to keep strictly to principle, without religion; I don't feel any real religion; I should
think those feelings impossible to obtain, for even if I thought
all the Bible was true, I do not think I could make myself
feel it: I think I never saw any person, who appeared so
totally destitute of it. I fear I am by degrees, falling away
from the path of virtue and truth.

16th.—My mind is in a state of fermentation, I believe I am
going to be religious, or some such thing.

18th.—I am a bubble, without reason, without beauty of
mind or person; I am a fool. I daily fall lower in my own
estimation. What an infinite advantage it would be to me, to
occupy my time and thoughts well. I am now seventeen, and
if some kind, and great circumstance does not happen to me, I
shall have my talents devoured by moth and rust. They will
lose their brightness, lose their virtue, and one day they will
prove a curse instead of a blessing. Dreaded day!!

I must use extreme exertion to act really right, to avoid idleness and dissipation.

It was on the 4th February, 1798, at the Friends' Meeting at Norwich, that Elizabeth Gurney appears for the first time, to have had her understanding opened to receive the gospel of Christ. The appointed instrument of this, to her most happy and wonderful change, was William Savery an American Friend, who had come to England, to pay what is termed in the language of Friends, a religious visit to this country. He appears to have been sound in the Christian faith, and to have laid due stress on the great doctrine of the atonement. He was a strict Friend ; earnest in urging a faithful obedience to the immediate guidings of the Spirit of God, yet careful, lest from any want of watchfulness and humility the youthful mind should be led into error.

From the time of their founder, George Fox, it has been the habit of Friends to travel occasionally, as ministers or preachers, in their own and other countries. There is needed but a glance at their origin and tenets, to perceive, that this must have formed an integral part of their principles.

When George Fox entered upon his remarkable career, the horizon in these realms was dark indeed ; but lowering as were the clouds which threatened the state, over the church of Christ, still heavier ones appeared to be impeding. The work of the Reformation had been by many considered as incomplete ; though, throughout the reign of Elizabeth they had patiently waited, hoping that her successor, trained in the school of Knox and the Scottish Reformers, would complete the work which they conceived to be but just begun. So far from their expectations being realized, James, on many occasions, shewed an obvious leaning to the religion of his mother ; and the same spirit was still more clearly displayed by his successor, Charles.

Under the counsels of Archbishop Laud, the King permitted, if he did not encourage the attempt, to restore many Romish rites and superstitions. Great laxity, even license, was allowed the people in habits and manners ; whilst stringent laws were enforced, to bind men's consciences and produce uniformity of opinion. There were persons, who, though they deplored this state of things, were yet content to pursue a course of personal piety and virtue. Some individuals found in Puritanism, a religion consonant to their feelings. Many embraced the doctrine of the Anabaptists, but others remained dissatisfied, shrinking from papal darkness, which again threatened to cover the land ; distrustful of the harsh and exclusive spirit of the Puritans, and alarmed at the excesses of the Anabaptists, they sought a deeper life in religion, and a more spiritual worship of Almighty God. Apparently to this juncture, and to this state of feeling, may be attributed the origin of Quakerism.

The parents of George Fox were members of the Established Church of England ; and for a time he conformed to the external religious observances in which he had been educated ; but his soul panted for the "waters of life," nor could he obtain rest until, to use his own expression, "He who hath the key did open and the Father of Life drew him to His Son by His Spirit." * Having thus been led himself into experimental acquaintance with vital godliness, he desired that others might partake with him in this glorious privilege ; and from that time, he devoted a large portion of his life ·to travelling from place to place, to declare " the truth " as presented to his own mind. This chiefly consisted in urging upon his hearers, that the Light of Life was within them, and by obedience to its dictates, man might be brought to the saving knowledge of God ; hence, he was led to the conviction, that he was called

* George Fox, Folio Journal, p. 7. Third Edition. London, 1765.

to bear testimony to the great and neglected Truth, that the
" light that lighteneth every man that cometh into the world "
must be sought by each individual in the recesses of his own
bosom, in silence, in patient waiting, in pureness, in abstrac-
tion from outward things; and that he was to make a consistent protest and passive opposition to every thing that proceeded from the world, and had no saviour of Christ.   That
his dwelling so much upon the doctrine of Christ, being come
in the Spirit, was not intended to the disparagement of the
doctrine of Christ, having come in the flesh, was proved by the
answers he gave to the following questions: he was asked
why Christ cried out on the cross, "My God, my God, why
hast Thou forsaken me:" and why He said, "If it be possible
let this cup pass from me, yet not my will, but Thine be done."
George Fox replied, "That at that time, the sins of all mankind were upon Him, and their iniquities and transgressions
with which He was wounded, and which He was to bear, and
be an offering for, as He was man; but that He died not as
He was God.   So in that He died for all men, tasting death
for every man, He was an offering for the sins of the whole
world."*   Many gradually united in the views and objects of
George Fox; not that from him they learned the opinions,
which they afterwards assisted in promulgating.   They, like
himself, desired a something, which they found not in the persuasions or lofty professions around them.   Politics, and prejudice, and party feeling were rife in the land.   Godliness as
the great concern between man and his Maker, independent of
human motive, was scarcely to be met with.   Men of observation and earnestness perceived that the pure gold of devotion
was everywhere alloyed by selfishness or design, and strove to
find in a higher guidance, and the influence of the Divine

* George Fox, Folio Journal, p. 4.   Third Edition.   London, 1765.

Light, a spiritual power capable of controlling alike, individuals and nations, and bring them under obedience to the Law of Christ.

To such men, the message of George Fox, was but an illustration or echo of their own sentiments, their own hopes, and expectations. They held, that man is able to obey the Divine will, without the help of outward law or ordinances. They looked upon salvation as a free gift, offered to all men. They believed that many would be saved by the Sacrifice of Christ, whose outward ears had never heard his name, through following the guidance of that, which St. John describes as "the light shining in darkness, but the darkness comprehending it not." They insisted on the importance of the Bible, as the rule of life; but maintained that, until the mind of men be illumined by the life-giving Spirit, it is not able to receive and comprehend its deep realities. Frequently, with their Bibles in their hands, they exhorted or persuaded, enforcing from this source instruction and reproof; but their general mode of worship consisted in silent waiting upon God; and believing in the immediate teaching of the Holy Spirit, one or another as he considered himself called to do so, addressed those assembled, in exhortation, or raised his voice in prayer. Among the persons who entertained these opinions, were to be found men, of almost every situation and position in society. The first to proclaim their principles in London were Edward Burrough, and Francis Howgill; the former died in Newgate, under hard and lengthened imprisonment. The Secretary of Milton was a Friend, named Thomas Ellwood; he had been born a gentleman, and educated as a scholar; his life is a curious history of the spirit and manners of that time. His account of a visit, before his own change of principles, to the house of Isaac Penington, an eminent writer amongst Friends, is very characteristic.

"I mentioned before, that during my father's abode in London, in the time of the civil wars, he contracted a friendship with a Lady Springett, then a widow, and afterwards married to Isaac Penington, Esq., to continue which, he sometimes visited them at their country lodgings, (as at Datchet and at Causham Lodge, near Reading). And having heard that they were come to live upon their own estate at Chalfont in Buckinghamshire, (about fifteen miles from Cowell,) he went one day to visit them there, and to return at night; taking me with him. But very much surprised we were, when being come thither, we first heard, then found, they were become Quakers; a people we had no knowledge of, and a name we had till then scarce heard of. So great a change from a free debonair and courtly sort of behaviour (which we formerly had found them in) to so strict a gravity as they now received us with, did not a little amuse us, and disappoint our expectation of such a pleasant visit as we used to have, and had now promised ourselves. Nor could my father have any opportunity by a private conference with them, to understand the ground or occasion of this change; there being some other strangers with them, (related to Isaac Penington) who came that morning from London to visit them also.

"For my part, I sought, and at length found means to cast myself into the company of the daughter, whom I found gathering some flowers in the garden, attended by her maid; who was also a Quaker. But when I addressed myself to her after my accustomed manner, with intention to engage her in some discourse which might introduce conversation on the foot of our former acquaintance; though she treated me with a courteous mein, yet, (young as she was) the gravity of her look and behaviour struck such an awe upon me, that I found myself not so much master of myself as to pursue any further converse with her. Wherefore, asking pardon for my boldness

in having introduced myself into her private walks, I withdrew; not without some disorder (as I thought at least) of
mind. We staid dinner, which was very handsome, and lacked
nothing to recommend it to me, but the want of mirth and
pleasant discourse, which we could neither have with them, nor
by reason of them, with one another amongst ourselves ; the
weightiness that was upon their spirits and countenance keeping down the lightness that would have been up in us. We
staid, notwithstanding, till the rest of the company took leave
of them ; and then, we also doing the same, returned, not
greatly satisfied with our journey, nor knowing what in particular to find fault with."*

The name of William Penn belongs to history ; as founder
of the colony of Pennsylvania, and the personal friend of
James II., and as having united in himself, the qualities of
Legislator and Philanthropist. Happy would it have been for
the Children of the Soil, had the practical lessons he taught, in
his humane and enlightened treatment of the Aborigines of
North America, been pursued by Lawgivers and Colonists in
later days !

The early Friends were exposed to much persecution, by imprisonment, personal ill-usage, and the seizure of their property. Whether prelacy or puritanism prevailed, all who
differed from those in power, were liable to oppression. During the Protectorate, there were at one time, no less than 4000
Friends imprisoned, for their religious opinions, some for assembling to worship God in the mode which they believed to
be right ; many for not taking off their hats before Magistrates ; others for refusing to take the oaths of Allegiance and
Supremacy, all swearing being by them considered as forbidden
in our Saviour's command, " Swear not at all." But inde-
pendently of this scruple against taking any oath, that of

* Thomas Ellwood's Life, p. 44, printed 1714.

supremacy was peculiarly repugnant to their habit of viewing the Church exclusively under its spiritual aspect, the claim to exercise temporal authority in a spiritual community, seeming to them a profane and carnal intrusion. Some Friends suffered severely, for refusing to fight. Their patient endurance, and unflinching kindness and attention to one another, through personal risk and difficulty extorted from their persecutors, a similar testimony to that borne to the brotherly kindness displayed in the primitive church; " See how those Christians love one another." It is inconsistent with the declarations of George Fox, or with the line of conduct he pursued, to suppose, that in the first instance, he entertained the idea of drawing together any separate body of men under a denomination of their own: but spiritual, as were the views entertained by himself, and those, who were of one mind with him, high and holy as was the standard they desired to uprear; as the number of Friends increased, it became necessary, in order to effect unity of purpose, and co-operation in action, to establish amongst themselves, a system of Discipline, or Church Government, which, with slight alterations, extends in its ramifications at the present day throughout all parts of the world, where the Society exists.

It embraces a close and minute superintendence of their members, as to moral conduct and religious duties; integrity in monetary dealings; the education of their children; adherence to certain principles peculiar to themselves, but which they deem becoming fruits of the Christian character, and liberal care for the necessities of their own poor. Nor does the benevolence of Friends end here; they frequently, as a body, have presented addresses to Government, in behalf of the distressed and oppressed, and have raised considerable sums for their assistance. As individuals, they are active in promoting Schools, and in supporting the Bible Society. They were faithful adherents of Wilberforce and Clarkson in their lengthened efforts to abolish the slave-trade ; nor was it a novelty to Friends to espouse this cause;—George Fox himself wrote upon the subject of the kind and christian treatment of slaves, to Friends in Barbadoes, " to prepare them for freedom." John Woolman and Anthony Benezet laboured in America, to convince Friends of the sinfulness of holding slaves ; many joined in these endeavours with such success, that in the latter days of the Society, Friends universally emancipated their slaves, and a law amongst them was established, by which no Friend was permitted to be a slave-holder, on pain of forfeiting his Membership. In the last great struggle for the Abolition of Slavery itself, the voice of the Society of Friends arose, as that of one man, they spared neither expense nor exertion to effect the desired object. They united with Sir T. Fowell Buxton and those Christian Philanthropists, who had bound themselves neither to rest nor surrender, till every slave in the British dominions, had obtained in his liberty, the inalienable right of man.

Hospitals, workhouses, and prisons, share the attention of Friends ; and that not only in their own, but in other countries. William Allen, though pre-eminent, was but one of many, who have travelled and laboured for the good of mankind ; inculcating the benefits of education, of religious tolerance, and a more enlightened system of Penal Justice. Others have extended their missionary journeys to remote countries: within the last few years, we find one, (Daniel Wheeler) visiting the Polynesian islands and Australia, and another (James Backhouse) continuing for nearly seven years to labour among the settlers and convicts in that colony, besides a long tarriance in Southern Africa. But, whether those journeys are undertaken amongst their own Society, or more extensively pursued, no one is authorised to travel in the " work of the ministry," who has not been acknowledged by Friends as an approved preacher.

Even then, the individual is not permitted to travel, until the "concern" has been laid before the Monthly Meeting, to which he belongs. Should it meet with the approbation of the Meeting, a certificate is given to that effect, signed by the Clerk of the Meeting, and those of the members who incline to annex their names.

Should the journey be likely to prove a long one, or to occupy much space of time, "the Friend under concern," has again to bring the matter before the Quarterly Meeting, to which he belongs, and to obtain the concurrence of that larger body, consisting of many Monthly Meetings. If the projected journey be intended to extend beyond his own country, the matter is again laid before the Yearly Meeting of Ministers and Elders, and the countersign of the Clerk of that Assembly is needed to render the document complete.

In the present day proselytism enters little, if at all, into the views of Friends. Their labours are chiefly directed among their own body, to arousing the careless, consoling the afflicted, and stimulating the advanced Christian to press forward on his way. Towards those, not Friends, their errand is somewhat different. It is by no means their custom to introduce their peculiar tenets in their religious discourses, but in general terms to urge upon their hearers the dangers and temptations of the world, to recommend a life of holiness, and to set forth the great truths of Christianity as revealed in the Scriptures.

It was on such a mission that William Savery visited this Country. He travelled through Great Britain and Ireland, and some parts of the Continent. He was absent from his own country above two years. Elizabeth Gurney was not the only person, to whom his influence was signally beneficial. He possessed considerable natural powers, a cultivated mind, and a heart eminently devoted to the work in which he was engaged. In his own Journal William Savery mentions his visit to Norwich:—

" *Norwich, First-day, 4th of the month.* Attended their
Meeting; some not members stepped in, and there were about
two hundred under our name; very few middle aged or young
persons who had a consistent appearance in their dress, indeed,
I thought it the gayest Meeting of Friends I ever sat in, and
was grieved to see it. I expected to pass the Meeting in silent
suffering, but at length believed it most for my peace to express
a little, and through gracious condescension was favoured to
relieve my mind, and many were tendered. Had a meeting in
the evening, in a large Meeting-house, in another part of the
town: there seem to be but few upright standard-bearers left
among the members in this place, yet they are not entirely
removed. Attended the Public Meeting, and the house, though
very large, could not contain the people by several hundreds,
but considering their crowded situation, many being obliged to
stand, they soon became settled, and through mercy it proved a
remarkably open, satisfactory Meeting, ending in prayer and
praise to the Author of every blessing. The marks of wealth
and grandeur are too obvious in several families of Friends in
this place, which made me sorrowful, yet I saw but little
opening to relieve my mind; several of the younger branches,
though they are enabled through divine grace, to see what the
Truth leads to, yet it is uncertain whether, with all the alluring
things of this world around them, they will choose the simple,
safe path of self-denial."*

Elizabeth's sister, Richenda, thus describes this eventful
day :—

On that day, we, seven sisters, sat as usual in a row, under
the gallery at Meeting; I sat by Betsy. William Savery was
there — we liked having Yearly Meeting Friends come to
preach; it was a little change. Betsy was generally rather

---

* William Savery's Journal, published by Gilpin, 1844, pp. 27-8.

restless at meeting; and on this day, I remember her very smart boots were a great amusement to me; they were purple, laced with scarlet.

At last William Savery began to preach. His voice and manner were arresting, and we all liked the sound; her attention became fixed: at last I saw her begin to weep, and she became a good deal agitated. As soon as Meeting was over, I have a remembrance of her making her way to the men's side of the Meeting, and having found my father, she asked him if she might dine with William Savery at the Grove,* to which he soon consented, though rather surprised by the request; we went home as usual, and, for a wonder, we wished to go again in the afternoon. I have not the same clear remembrance of this Meeting; but the next scene that has fastened itself on my memory, is our return home in the carriage. Betsy sat in the middle, and astonished us all by the great feeling she showed. She wept most of the way home. The next morning, William Savery came to breakfast, and preached to our dear sister after breakfast, prophesying of the high and important calling she would be led into. What she went through in her own mind, I cannot say, but the results were most powerful, and most evident. From that day her love of pleasure and of the world seemed gone.

How deep the impression, made upon the mind of Elizabeth, her own journal pourtrays.

Sunday, February 4th, 1798.—This morning I went to Meeting, though but poorly, because I wished to hear an American Friend, named William Savery. Much passed there of a very interesting nature. I have had a faint light spread over my mind, at least I believe it is something of that kind, owing to having been much with, and heard much excellence

---

* The Residence of her uncle, Joseph Gurney.

from one who appears to me, a true Christian. It has caused me to feel a little religion. My imagination has been worked upon, and I fear all that I have felt will go off. I fear it now; though at first I was frightened, that a plain Quaker should have made so deep an impression on me; but how truly prejudiced in me to think, that because good came from a Quaker, I should be led away by enthusiasm and folly. But I hope I am now free from such fears. I wish the state of enthusiasm I am in may last, for to-day I have felt *that there is a God;* I have been devotional, and my mind has been led away from the follies that it is mostly wrapt up in. We had much serious conversation; in short, what he said and what I felt, was like a refreshing shower falling upon earth, that had been dried up for ages. It has not made me unhappy: I have felt ever since humble. I have longed for virtue. I hope to be truly virtuous; to let sophistry fly from my mind; not to be enthusiastic and foolish; but only to be so far religious as will lead to virtue. There seems nothing so little understood as religion.

6*th.*—My mind has by degrees flown from religion. I rode to Norwich, and had a very serious ride there, but meeting, and being looked at, with apparent admiration, by some officers, brought on vanity; and I came home as full of the world, as I went to town full of heaven.

In hearing William Savery preach, he seemed to me to overflow with true religion, and to be humble, and yet a man of great abilities; and having been gay and disbelieving only a few years ago, makes him better acquainted with the heart of one in the same situation. If I were to grow like him, a preacher, I should be able to preach to the gay and unbelieving better than to any others, for I should feel more sympathy for them, and know their hearts better.

Sunday, 11th.—It is very different to this day week (a day never to be forgotten whilst memory lasts). I have been to Meeting this morning. To-day I have felt all my old irreligious feelings—my object shall be to search, try to do right, and if I am mistaken, it is not my fault; but the state I am now in makes it difficult to act. What little religion I have felt has

been owing to my giving way quietly and humbly to my feelings; but the more I reason upon it, the more I get into a
labyrinth of uncertainty, and my mind is so much inclined to
both scepticism and enthusiasm, that if I argue and doubt, I
shall be a total sceptic; if, on the contrary, I give way to it,
and as it were, wait for religion, I may be led away. But I
hope that will not be the case ; at all events, religion, true and
uncorrupted, is of all comforts the greatest; it is the first
stimulus to virtue ; it is a support under every affliction. I
am sure it is better to be so in an enthusiastic degree, than not
to be so at all, for it is a delightful enthusiasm.

15th.—My mind is in a whirl. In all probability I shall go
to London. Many, many are the sensations I feel about it,
numbers of things to expect. In the first place, leaving home,
how truly I shall miss my best of friends, and all of them.
(Meaning particularly her brothers and sisters). In the next
place, I shall see William Savery most likely, and all those
plain Quakers. I may be led away, beware ! my feelings are
far more risen at the thought of seeing him than all the play-
houses and gaieties in the world. One will, I do not doubt,
balance against the other; I must be careful not to be led
away; I must not overdo myself. I dare say it will not be half
so pleasant as the Earlham heartfelt gaieties in the Prince's
time ; I must be very careful not to get vain or silly, for I fear
I shall. Be independent, and do not follow those I am with,
more than I think right. Do not make dress a study, even in
London. Read in the Bible, when I can ; but if I see William
Savery I shall not, I doubt, be over fond of gaieties.

16th.—We went to hear the band, which I am sorry for, as
I cannot get courage to tell my father, I wish I had not gone ; I
will not go again without his knowing it beforehand.

CHAPTER III.

Visit to London, gaiety there—Return to Earlham—Decision between religion and the world—Letter from William Savery—Gradual development of opinion—Journey into Wales and the South of England —Intercourse with Friends—Colebrook Dale—Increasing tendency to Quakerism.

In this peculiar and awakened state of mind, Elizabeth, with the consent of Mr. Gurney, visited London, that she might become acquainted for herself with those amusements and fascinations that the world offers to its votaries; that she might have the opportunity of " trying all things," and choosing for herself that which appeared to her " to be good." Her father took her to London; and there, with an old and faithful attendant, left her for some weeks, under the protection and kind care of a relation. She was often interested and amused with the objects that were presented to her notice, but seldom satisfied or approving. The result was, that she returned home entirely decided:—the way of religion chosen, the way of the world rejected; and from that time, most steadily though gently, did she continue to advance in the path in which she believed it to be her duty henceforth to walk.

February 24th.—At last landed safely here (London); it is very pleasant in some things, very unpleasant in others. On Monday, I do not think it unlikely I shall go to the play. Tuesday, I expect to spend quietly with Dr. Lindoe and Mrs. Good. On Wednesday, I hope to see the Barclays, and to have a dance. On Thursday, I expect to be with Amelia Opie, and so on for different days.

25th.—Although I told William Savery my principles were not Friendly, yet I fear I should not like his knowing of my going to the play. I think such religion as his must attract an atheist; and if there were many such Quakers as he is, the Society would soon increase.

Monday, 26th.—I went to Drury Lane in the evening. I must own I was extremely disappointed; to be sure, the house is grand and dazzling, but I had no other feeling whilst there than that of wishing it over. I saw Banister, Mrs. Jordan, Miss Dechamp. I was not at all interested with the play, the music I did not much like; and the truth is, my imagination was so raised that it must have fallen, had the play been perfect.

Tuesday.—I went to the play at Covent Garden, I still continue not to like plays.

Wednesday, 28th.—We were out this morning; I felt proud, vain and silly. In the evening, we had a dance.

Thursday, March 1st.—I own I enter into the gay world reluctantly. I do not like plays. I think them so artificial that they are to me not interesting, and all seems so—so very far from pure virtue and nature. To-night I saw Hamlet and Bluebeard; I suppose that nothing on the stage can exceed it. There is acting, music, scenery to perfection, but I was glad when it was over; my hair was dressed and I felt like a monkey. London is not the place for heartfelt pleasure, so I must not expect to find it.

4th.—I feel uncharitably towards —— I said uncharitable things of them, and gave way to inclination, for I own I love scandal, though I highly disapprove of it; therefore it is the more commendable if I overcome it.

5th.—I took a lesson in dancing, and spent the day quietly.

7th.—I went to Meeting in the evening. I have not enough eloquence to describe it. William Savery's sermon was in the first part very affecting, it was from the Revelations; he explained his text beautifully and awfully, most awfully I felt it; he next described the sweets of religion, and the spirit of prayer. How he did describe it! He said, the deist, and those who did not feel devotion looked at nature, admired the thunder, the lightning and earthquakes, as curiosities; but they looked not up through them to nature's God. How well he hit the state I have been in, I trust I may not remain in it; his prayer was beautiful, I think I felt to pray with him.

17th.—May I never forget the impression William Savery has made on my mind, as much as I can say is, I thank God for having sent at least a glimmering of light through him into my heart, which I hope with care, and keeping it from the many draughts and winds of this life, may not be blown out, but become a large brilliant flame, that will direct me to that haven, where will be joy without a sorrow, and all will be comfort. I have faith, how much, to gain, not all the treasures in this world can equal that heavenly treasure. May I grow more and more virtuous, follow the path I should go in, and not fear to acknowledge the God whom I worship; I will try, and I do hope to do what is right. I now long to be in the quiet of Earlham, for there I may see how good I can be, and so I may here, for the greater cross the greater crown; but I there can reflect quietly and soberly on what has passed, there I hope to regulate my mind, which I know sadly wants it. May I never lose the little religion I now have; but if I cannot feel religion and devotion, I must not despair, for if I am truly warm and earnest in the cause, it will come one day. My idea is, that true humility and lowliness of heart is the first grand step towards true religion. I fear and tremble for myself, but I must humbly look to the Author of all that is good and great, and I may say humbly pray, that He will take me as a sheep strayed from His flock, and once more let me enter the fold of His glory. I feel there is a God and Immortality; happy, happy thought! May it never leave me, and if it should, may I remember I have felt that there is a God and Immortality.

26th.—This morning I went to Amelia Opie's and had a pleasant time. I called on Mrs. Siddons, who was not at home; then on Doctor Batty; then on Mrs. Twiss, who gave me some paint for the evening. I was painted a little, I had my hair dressed, and did look pretty for me. Mr. Opie, Amelia, and I went to the Opera concert. I own, I do love grand company. The Prince of Wales was there; and I must say, I felt more pleasure in looking at him, than in seeing the rest of the company, or hearing the music. I did nothing but admire his Royal Highness ; but I had a very pleasant evening indeed.

27th.—I called with Mrs. H——, and Amelia, on Mrs. Inchbald. I like her vastly, she seems so clever and so interesting. I then went to Hampstead, and staid at our cousin Hoare's, until the 12th of April. I returned to Clapham. My uncle Barclay, with great begging, took us to the Opera. The house is dazzling, the company animating, the music hardly at all so, the dancing delightful. H—— came in in the middle of the Opera, I was charmed to see him, I was most merry, I just saw the Prince of Wales. Tuesday.—My dearest father came to London, we dined at the ——, and went to a rout in the evening. Friday.—I had a pleasant merry day, with Peter Pindar (Dr. Walcot). Monday.—I went with my father and the Barclays to Sir George Staunton's.

April 16th.—I arrived at home with my father, after paying a few more visits.

Thirty years afterwards she thus reviews this important period of life.

Dagenham, Seventh Month, 1828.—Here ended this important and interesting visit to London, where I learned much and had much to digest. I saw and entered various scenes of gaiety ; many of our first public places ; attended balls and other places of amusement. I saw many interesting characters in the world, some of considerable eminence in that day ; I was also cast among a great variety of persons of different descriptions. I had the high advantage of attending several most interesting meetings of William Savery, and having at times his company, and that of a few other Friends. It was like the casting die in my life; however, I believe it was in the ordering of Providence for me, and that the lessons then learnt are to this day valuable to me. I consider one of the important results was, the conviction of these things being wrong, from seeing them and feeling their effects. I wholly gave up on my own ground, attending all public places of amusement, I saw they tend to promote evil ; therefore even if I could attend them without being hurt myself, I felt in entering them, I lent my aid to promote that, which I was sure from what I saw, hurt others; led many from the paths of rectitude and chastity, and brought them into much sin; particularly those who had to act in plays, or sing in concerts. I felt the vanity and folly of what are called the pleasures of this life, of which the tendency is not to satisfy, but eventually to enervate and injure the heart and mind; those only are real pleasures which are of an inno-cent nature, and used as recreations, subjected to the cross of Christ. I was in my judgment much confirmed in the infinite importance of religion, as the only real stay, guide, help, and comfort in this life, and the only means of our having a hope of partaking of a better. My understanding was increasingly open to receive its truths; although the glad tidings of the gospel of Christ were little, very little, if at all understood by me, I was like the blind man; although I could hardly be said to have attained the state of seeing men as trees. I obtained in this expedition a valuable knowledge of human character, from the variety I met with; this I think was useful to me, though some were very dangerous associates for so young a person, and the way in which I was protected among them, is in my remembrance very striking; and leads me to acknowledge, that at this most critical period of my life, the tender mercy of my God was marvellously displayed towards me; and that His all-powerful, though to me then almost unseen and unknown hand, held me up and protected me. Can any one doubt, that it was His Spirit which manifested to me the evil in my own heart; as well as that which I perceived around me, leading me to abhor it, and to hunger and thirst after Himself and His righteousness, and that salvation which cometh by Christ.

Earlham, April 30*th,* 1798.—To-day the children brought me a letter from William Savery: I cannot well express what I felt at receiving it. I do not know the course I am to run, all is hid in mystery, but I try to do right in every thing. I feel he gives me a stimulant to virtue; but I fear by what I expressed in my letter, he suspects that I am turning plain Quaker. I hate that he should estimate me falsely. I must remember that on the foundation of the doctrine I believe we agree. I must look to One higher than he ; and if I feel my own mind satisfied I need not fear. Look up to true religion as the very first of blessings, cherish it, nourish, and let it flourish and bloom in my heart ; it wants taking care of, it is difficult to obtain. I must not despair or grow spectical, if I do not always feel religious. I have felt God as it were, and I must seek to find Him again.

The letter referred to is as follows :—

" 13th of Fourth Month, 1798.

" DEAR FRIEND,

     " As I left thee unwell, and without having it in my power to take thee affectionately by the hand, as I was much inclined to do ; it gave me great pleasure to receive thy kind letter, which brings no complaint of thy present want of health ; for, I assure thee, I feel interested in thy welfare and happiness every way. My attachment has not been more cordial or agreeable to any young Friend in England, and my heart leaped with joy to find thou art willing to acknowledge a state of hunger and thirst after righteousness, which if thou cherish and dwell in, thou never need to doubt, my dear friend, will eventually be crowned with the enjoyment of the heavenly promise, " thou shalt be filled." Thou art favoured with amiable and benevolent dispositions, which I hope thou hast wisely determined shall not be eclipsed by a conformity to the god of this world ; nor enslaved by its rudiments and maxims, its philosophy and vain deceit, but rather with a holy magnanimity, regardless of the world's dread laugh, thou wilt resolve to implore the Omnipotent hand that formed thee for Glory, Immortality, and Eternal Life, to finish the glorious work He has begun, by creating thee anew in Christ Jesus unto every good word and work ; bringing thee under the dominion of His own power and spirit, the fruit of which is love, joy, peace, long-suffering, gentleness, goodness, faith, meekness, temperance.

" I know, my dear, thou hast and will have many temptations to combat with ; thou wilt, doubtless, be frequently importuned to continue with thy gay acquaintance in pursuit of that unsubstantial and false glare of happiness, which the world in too bewitching and deceitful colours holds out to the poor young, unwary traveller, which if he be ensnared with, most certainly ends in blinding the intellectual eye, from discerning the uncontaminated source of soul-felt pleasure, resulting from a humble heart at peace with its God, its neighbour, and itself. Thou asks my advice, my dear friend, and without any premeditation when I sat down, I find I have been attempting it; but it is very evident, thou art under the especial care of an infinitely better Instructor, who has already uttered his soft and heavenly voice to teach thee that the first step towards religion is true humility; because, in that state only we can feel the need we have of an arm stronger than human to lean upon, to lead us out of, and keep us from polluting things, which hinder our access to, and confidence in that boundless source of purity, love, and mercy; who amidst all the vicissitudes of time is disposed to be our invincible Shepherd, Guardian, and Friend, in whom we may trust and never be afraid; but this blessed confidence is not, cannot be enjoyed by the gay, the giddy, proud, or abandoned votaries of this world.

" It is the peculiar privilege of those, who are sincerely endeavouring to wash their hands in innocency, that they may compass the altar of God availingly. I have experienced what it is to be under the imperious and slavish dominion of my own uncontrolled passions; and I know that such a state is abundantly mixed with the wormwood and the gall, and I have been, through adorable mercy, convinced there is an infinitely more happy one to be attained, even in this life; an enjoyment, under the perfect law of liberty, of that serene state of mind wherein there is no condemnation, as Paul speaks, the law of the spirit of life in Christ Jesus setting the soul free from the law of sin and death. I do not pretend, my dear friend, to boast myself as having attained such an uninterrupted state, yet the transient foretaste which we partake of, in proportion to our obedience to revealed duty, is enough to inspire the soul of every Christian soldier, so to run through God's mercy and grace, that we may obtain the full and complete enjoyment of it. There are many formal professors of religion, who think to obtain peace with God, by a critical exactness and even rigid austerity in outward observances, and outside formalities, as well as many who from constitution or habit are always exhibiting the dark and gloomy side of religion, not having, in my humble opinion, their minds sufficiently expanded by just conceptions of the adorable love and mercy of God; and both of these spread a discouraging report of the good land, or of the way which our Heavenly Father has appointed for us to obtain possession of it. I speak only my own experience, dear Elizabeth, when I say, that whenever I have found my way more than usually strewn with thorns, I have generally discovered on a deep scrutiny of my heart, it has been the fruit of some open or secret departure from the paths of obedience and virtue, so that I am confirmed it is in our own ways we are corrected; but the ways of the Lord are ways of pleasantness, and all His paths peace. I know very well that the most virtuous, being children of frail humanity, and this world not designed to be the place of their undisturbed rest, but a school of discipline to prepare them for a better, are subject to afflictions as well as others; still there is this difference in the midst of them all, that while the votary of this world is overwhelmed with murmuring and repining, and agitated with sorrow which worketh death, under the afflictive dispensations, that all, more or less, in the wisdom of Providence for our good must pass through in this life; the humble Christian, believing that even afflictions from His sovereign hand are mercies in disguise, and that all things shall work eventually for good to them that love and fear Him, are strengthened through the Lord's love and mercy to say, " The cup that my Heavenly Father hath blessed, shall I not drink it ?" " for our light affliction which is but for a moment worketh for us a far more exceeding and eternal weight of glory, while we look not at the things which are seen, but at the things which are not seen, for the things which are seen are temporal, but the things which are not seen are eternal." On the other hand, the temporal enjoyments of this life being sanctified to us by the hand that gave them, and the world used without abusing it, the peace, comfort, and rational enjoyment of them is doubly tasted by the religious and grateful soul. My dear child, my heart is full towards thee, I have written a great deal more than I expected ; but I fain would take thee by the hand, if I were qualified so to do, and ascend, as our Heavenly Father may enable us together, step by step, up that ladder, which reaches from earth to heaven ; but, alas ! my weakness is such, I can only recommend both myself and thee to that good hand, that is able to do more abundantly for us than we can either ask or think ; and bid thee, for the present, in much christian affection, farewell.

" WILLIAM SAVERY."

April 21*st.*—I am so glad I do not feel Earlham at all dull, after the bustle of London ; on the contrary, a better relish for the sweet innocence and beauties of Nature. I hope I may say, I do look " through Nature up to Nature's God." I go every day to see poor Bob, (a servant in a decline, living at a cottage in the Park,) who I think will not live. I once talked to him about his dying, and asked him if he would like me to read to him in the Testament. I told him, I felt such faith in the blessings of Immortality, that I pitied not his state ; it was an odd speech to make to a dying man. I hope to be able to comfort him in his dying hours. I gave some things to some poor people to-day ; but it is not there that I am particularly virtuous, as I only am following my natural disposition. I should be far more so, if I never spoke against any person, which I do too often. I think I am improved since I was last at home ; my mind is not so fly-away. I hope it never will be so again. We are all governed by our feelings ; now the reason why religion is far more likely to keep you in the path of virtue, than any theoretical plan is, that you feel it, and your heart is wrapt up in it ; it acts as a furnace on your chaacter, it refines it, it purifies it ; whereas principles of your own making are without kindling to make the fire hot enough to answer its purpose. I think a dream I have had so odd, I will write it down.

Before I mention my dream, I will give an account of my state of mind, from the time I was fourteen years old. I had very sceptical or deistical principles. I seldom, or never thought of religion, and altogether I was a negatively good character, having naturally good dispositions, I had not much to combat with ; I gave way freely to the weakness of youth. I was flirting, idle, rather proud and vain, till the time I was seventeen, I found I wanted a better, a greater stimulus to virtue, than I had, as I was wrapt up in trifles. I felt my mind capable of better things ; but I could not exert it, till several of my friends, without knowing my state, wished I would read books on Christianity ; but I said till I felt the want of religion myself, I would not read books of that kind; but if ever I did, would judge clearly for myself, by reading the New Testament, and when I had seen for myself, I would then see what others said. About this time, I believe, I never missed a week or a few nights without dreaming, I was nearly being washed away by the sea, sometimes in one way, sometimes in another ; and I felt all the terror of being drowned, or hope of being saved ; at last I dreamt it so often, that I told many of the family what a strange dream I had, and how near I was being lost. After I had gone on in this way for some months, William Savery came to Norwich. I had begun to read the Testament with reflections of my own, and he suddenly, as it were, opened my eyes to see religion ; but again they almost closed. I went on dreaming the dream. The day when I felt I had really and truly got true and real faith, that night I dreamed the sea was coming as usual to wash me away, but I was beyond its reach ; beyond its powers to wash me away ; since that night I do not remember having dreamed that dream. Odd ! It did not strike me at the time so odd ; but now it does. All I can say is, I admire it, I am glad I have had it, and I have a sort of faith in it ; it ought, I think, to make my faith steady, it may be the work of chance, but I do not think it is, for it is so odd not having dreamed it since. What a blessed thought to think it comes from heaven ! May I be made capable of acting as I ought to act ; not being drowned in the ocean of the world, but permitted to

mount above its waves, and remain a steady and faithful servant to the God whom I worship. I may take this dream in
what light I like, but I must be careful of superstition; as
many, many are the minds that are led away by it. Believe
only in what I can comprehend or feel; don't, don't be led
away by enthusiasm; but I don't fear. I feel myself under
the protection of One, who alone is able to guide me to the
path in which I ought to go.

29th.—The human mind is so apt to fly from one extreme to
another; and why is not mine like others ? I certainly seem to
be on the road to a degree of enthusiasm, but I own myself at
a loss how to act. If I act as they would wish me, I should
not humbly give way to the feelings of religion; I should dwell
on philosophy and depend more on my own reason than any
thing else. On the contrary, if I give way to the religious
feelings to which I am inclined, (and I own I believe much in
inspiration), I feel confident, that I should find true humility
and humble waiting on the Almighty the only way of feeling
that inward sense of the beauties, and of the comforts of religion; it spreads a sweet veil over the evils of life; it is to me
the first of feelings; that state of devotion, that absolutely
makes you weep, is most fine! I own my dream rather leads
me to believe in, and try to follow the path I would go in. But
I should think my wisest plan of conduct would be to warmly
encourage my feelings of devotion, and to keep as nearly as I
can to what I think right, and the doctrines of the Testament;
not at present to make sects the subject of my meditations, but
to do as I think right, and not alter my opinions from conformity, to any one gay or plain.

May 8th.—This morning being alone, I think it a good
opportunity to look into myself to see my present state, and to
regulate myself. At this time the first object of my mind is
religion. It is the most constant subject of my thoughts and
of my feelings; I am not yet on what I call a steady foundation. The next feeling that at this present fills my heart, is
benevolence and affection to many, but great want of charity,
want of humility, want of activity; my inclinations lead me, I
hope, to virtue; my passions are, I hope, in a pretty good

state; I want to set myself in good order, for much time is lost and many evils committed by not having some regular plan of conduct; I make these rules for myself:—

First,—Never lose any time; I do not think that lost which is spent in amusement or recreation, some time every day; but always be in the habit of being employed.

Second,—Never err the least in truth.

Third,—Never say an ill thing of a person, when I can say a good thing of them; not only speak charitably, but feel so.

Fourth,—Never be irritable nor unkind to any body.

Fifth,—Never indulge myself in luxuries that are not necessary.

Sixth,—Do all things with consideration, and when my path to act right is most difficult, feel confidence in that power that alone is able to assist me, and exert my own powers as far as they go.

19th.—Altogether I think I have had a satisfactory day. I had a good lesson of French this morning, and read much in Epictetus. Saw poor Bob, and enjoyed the sweet beauties of nature, which now shine forth; each day some new beauty arrives. I love the beauty of the country, it does the mind good. I love it more than I used to do. I love retirement and quiet much more since my journey to London. How little I thought six months ago, I should be so much altered; I am since then, I hope, altered much for the better. My heart may rise in thankfulness to that omnipotent power, that has allowed my eyes to be opened in some measure to see the light of truth, and to feel the comfort of religion. I hope to be capable of giving up my all, if it be required of me, to serve the Almighty with my whole heart.

21st.—To-day is my birth-day. I am eighteen years old! How many things have happened to me since I was fourteen; the last year has been the happiest I have experienced for some time.

23rd.—I have just been reading a letter from my father, in which he makes me the offer of going to London, what a temptation! but I believe it to be much better for me to be where I am, quietly and soberly to keep a proper medium of feelings, and not to be extravagant any way.

24th.—I wrote to my father this morning. I must be most careful not to be led by others, for I know at this time I have so great a liking for plain Friends; that my affections being so much engaged, my mind may be so also by them. I hope as I now find myself in so wavering a state, that I may judge without prejudice of Barclay's Apology.

27th.—I must be careful of allowing false scruples to enter my mind. I have not yet been long enough a religionist to be a sectarian. I hope by degrees to obtain true faith; but I expect I shall lose what I gain, if I am led to actions I may repent of; remember and never forget my own enthusiastic feeling nature. It requires caution and extreme prudence to go on as I should do. In the afternoon I went to St. Peters, and heard a good sermon. The common people seemed very much occupied, and wrapt up in the service, which I was pleased to see; afterwards I went to the cathedral, then I came home and read to the Normans and little Castleton.

29th.—I feel weak in mind and body. If I go on approving revealed religion, I must be extremely careful of taking the idle fancies of the brain, for anything so far superior. I believe, many mistake mere meteors for that heavenly light, which few receive. Many may have it in a degree, but I should suppose few have it, so as to teach others with authority.

June 1st.—I have been great part of this morning with poor Bob, who seems now dying. I read a long chapter in the Testament to him, the one upon death, and I sat with him for some time afterwards. Poor fellow! I never saw death, or any of its symptoms before; sad to see, it truly is; I said a few words to him, and expressed to him how happy we should be in expectation of immortality, and everlasting bliss. Father of mercies, wilt Thou bless him, and take him unto Thee? Though my mind is flat this morning, and not favoured with Thy Spirit in devotion; yet I exert what I have, and hope it will prove acceptable in Thy sight. Almighty God, Thy will be done and not ours. May I always be resigned to what Thou hast ordered for me; I humbly thank Thee, for allowing my eyes to be opened, so as even to feel faith, hope and love towards Thee. First and last of everything infinite, and not to be comprehended except by Thy Spirit which Thou allowest to enlighten our hearts.

12th.—This evening I have got myself rather into a scrape; I have been helping them to beg my father for us to go to the Guild-dinner, and I don't know whether it was quite what I approve of, or think good for myself; but I shall consider, and do not intend to go, if I disapprove of it. How strange and odd! I really think I shall turn plain Friend; all I say is, search deeply; do nothing rashly, and I then hope to do right; they all, I think, now see it—keep up to the duties I feel in my heart, let the path be ever so difficult; err not at all if I can avoid it, be humble and constant. I do not like to appear a character I am not certain of being. For a few days past, I have at times felt much religion for *me*: humility and comfort belong to it. I often think very seriously about myself. A few months ago, if I had seen any one act, as I now do, I should have thought him a fool; but the strongest proof I can have that I am acting right at the present time is, that I am certainly a better, and I think a happier character. But I often doubt myself, when I consider my enthusiastic and change-able feelings. Religion is no common enthusiasm, because it is pure, it is a constant friend, protector, supporter, and guardian; it is what we cannot do well without in this world; what can prove its excellence so much as its producing virtue and happiness? How much more solid a character I am, since I first got hold of religion! I would not part with what I have for anything; it is a faith that never will leave my mind, I hope most earnestly. I do not believe it will, but I desire always to be a strictly religious character.

13th.—I have some thoughts of by degrees increasing my plan for Sunday evening; and of having several poor children, at least, to read in the Testament and religious books for an hour. I have begun with Billy; but I hope to continue and increase one by one. I should think it a good plan; but I must not even begin that hastily. It might increase morality

among the lower classes, if the Scriptures were oftener and
better read to them.   I believe I cannot exert myself too much,
there is nothing gives me such satisfaction as instructing the
lower classes of people.

24th.—I persevered in going to Meeting this afternoon.
Coming home, I saw a scene that indeed interested me, my
father jumping into the water at the New Mills, after a poor
boy whom I thought drowned; my feelings were great indeed,
both for my father and the boy.   I believe I should have
leapt in afterwards, if my father had gone out of sight; he did
it delightfully, with such activity and spirit, it was charming to
see him.   Poor little boy!   I took him as soon as he was out
of the water; it agitated me extremely.

July 9th.—How little is the mind capable of really feeling
that we are all in the presence of God, who overlooks every
action.   Should we not tremble when we think of it?   How
many faults do we commit?   It is impossible, without the
assistance of His almighty power, to comprehend it.   We
could never be wicked, while we felt ourselves in the presence
of the Almighty.   Virtue alone can make this thought a happy
one.

20th.—I suppose we shall go off to-morrow on our journey.
We expect the Opies and Bartlett Gurney to dinner.   It is my
wish to do my lesson with Le Sage, and the first thing afterwards attend to my father; read to Mrs. Norman; see nurse
Norman; walk to Colney about Billy; came home, set my
things in the greatest order.   Evening.—I have been confused
by the thoughts of going and company.   How much do I fear
for myself this journey.

During the summer, Mr. Gurney, with his seven daughters,
took a journey into Wales and the south of England.   Elizabeth delighted in nature, and dwelt with pleasure on the beautiful scenery they passed through; but to the works of man,
however imposing, she was comparatively indifferent.   She
visited cathedral cities; she saw scenes of high historic interest;
castles, whose walls could reveal dark tales of bye-gone days;

but she scarcely mentions them, and if she notices them at all, it is but to draw some moral inference. In visiting the Dock-yards, at Plymouth, and beholding one of the noblest instances of man's power and skill, a first-rate man-of-war, in perfect order, and equipped for sea, she considers the effects of war, and its influences on the human race. But by far the greatest interest, afforded her by this journey, was the prospect of seeing different Friends, and becoming better acquainted with them and their principles. The travellers paid a visit to Colebrook Dale, the residence of the well-known Christian philanthropist, Richard Reynolds, there she was left for some days, with her cousin, Priscilla Hannah Gurney. This lady was cousin to the Gurneys of Earlham, by both their father and mother, her father being Joseph Gurney, and her mother Christiana Barclay. She was exactly the person to attract the young; she possessed singular beauty and elegance of manner, a figure small, but perfect, her eyes of great brilliancy and expression. She was of the old school, and tinged with its forms and dignities; her costume partook of this, and her long retention of the black hood, gave much character to her appearance. She early renounced the world and its fascinations, left Bath, where her mother and sister Christiana Gurney resided, became eventually a minister among friends, and found a congenial retreat for many years at Colebrook Dale. The influence of this visit upon Elizabeth was very powerful. A place more likely to interest her, persons more suited to her state of mind, could not have been, than Colebrook Dale, and the residents there. Richard Reynolds, at that time advanced in years, was a patriarch among his family, his friends, and dependents. He devoted a large proportion of a noble fortune, acquired by honourable industry, to objects of benevolence. His extensive iron-works were carried on with careful attention to the moral good of those employed in them.

Several valuable Friends resided at Colebrook Dale, connected with each other in business, or by marriage, or the
stronger bond of similarity of taste and principle. They were
a happy, united band, Christian love prevailing among themselves, and towards others. It is sad to think among the
changes of life, how many of this pleasant community have
passed away.

Farnham, July 26*th.*—To night I am much tired, quite
fagged, body and mind, and the text comes strongly before me,
" Blessed are they that mourn, for they shall be comforted," for
though I feel weak in body, I have truly support in mind. God
is a merciful Father, and when His children (though evil like
me) mourn, He will comfort them, and preserve them, if they
will exert their own powers also, to serve Him in spirit and
in truth. How often I˜fail! He is never-failing, no, never!
He makes the sun to rise on the just and on the unjust, and
we acknowledge not His blessings, but lament over the few
clouds that shade its brightness : and sometimes murmur at the
Lord that made us. Weak mortals! and I am weak indeed.
But I feel I have to deal with a merciful Father.

Weymouth, 29*th.*—We dined here, and after dinner went on
the sea. I always feel rather afraid when there, for I consider
that if the least accident were to happen, I should be drowned ;
and I do not know if it be right only for pleasure to run the
risk of one's life. I always feel doubtful of ever seeing land
again ; but I believe it to be partly unwise cowardice ; if
duty led me to it, I do not think I should fear. Some minds,
by nature, are more cowards than others, and require more
faith to overcome it. This evening I am sorry to say, I feel
a hankering after the world and its gaieties : but what real
satisfaction is there in being admired ? I am uncertain about
going to the Rooms to-morrow. I should not object, I think,
if no expense follow it ; but if I can keep away I will do
so ; I have been considering, and believe this subject requires real thought. I hear there is to be a ball, and I don't
doubt we may go : if I go, I shall enter the world and fall

very likely into some of its snares. Shall I feel satisfied in
going, or most satisfied in staying at home ? I believe in
staying at home. The worst of all will be, I shall have to
contradict the will of all the others, and most likely to disappoint my father by not going ; there is the rub, if I don't go
perhaps he will not let the others go. I think I shall leave it
on these grounds ; if I can stay at home in any way, do—but
if I cannot without vexing my father I must go, and try not
to be hurt by it.

Dawlish, August 3rd.—This morning Kitty came in for us
to read the Testament together, which I enjoyed : I read my
favourite chapter, the 15th of Corinthians, to them. Oh ! how
earnestly I hope that we may all know what truth is, and follow its dictates. I still continue my belief that I shall turn
plain Quaker. I used to think, and do now, how very little
dress matters ; but I find it almost impossible to keep up to
the principles of Friends without altering my dress and speech.
I felt it the other day at Weymouth. If I had been plain, I
should not have been tempted to have gone to the play, which
at all events I would not do ; plainness appears to be a sort of
protection to the principles of Christianity in the present state
of the world. I have just received a letter from Anna Savery,
and have been answering it, and have written rather a religious
letter, which I mean to show them, though it is to me a cross,
as I say in it I think I am a Quaker at heart. I hope it will not
hurt them ; but it is better to be on clear grounds with my
best friends, upon that which so nearly interests me. I know
it hurts Rachel and John the most. Rachel has the seeds of
Quakerism in her heart, that if cultivated, would grow indeed,
I have no doubt. I should never be surprised to see us all
Quakers.

4th.—I have been having such a morning with Chrissy Gurney, I do really love her ; she makes me more of a Quaker than
any one I ever was with. She certainly is the most interesting
woman I ever met, quite one after my own heart ; she is to me
indescribable. It is odd to me, and I believe it is to herself,
that she is not a Quaker. But she is good without it, not

but what I think she would be happier with it. I have very little doubt I shall gain from her; I quite feel leaving this place.

Plymouth Dock, 8th.—After a good night, as soon as breakfast was over, we went to see the ropes made at the Docks, which was a most curious sight. How thankful I should be, that for all my constant erring from the path of truth, I am yet sometimes allowed to feel I have an Arm to lean upon, superior to human, that will support me in time of trouble. After leaving the Dock-yards, we went on board a ferry-boat, and I felt rather afraid, to my shame. We then went to see a Review, which I feel rather uncertain if it were right for me to go to, as I so highly disapprove of war; but I believe whilst I appear as as other people, I must act as they do unless with the greatest difficulty. I do not alter from conformity, but from conviction. Afterwards we went to Lord Mount Edgecumbe's, a very fine place, but I was not in the mind for it. Am I right or not? They have just been to say, an officer has come for us to hear a very famous Marine Band; and I do not go, because I have some idea it is wrong, even to give countenance to a thing that inflames men's minds to destroy each other; it is truly giving encouragement, as far as lies in my power, to what I most highly disapprove, therefore I think I am right to stay at home. I will now go on with an account of the day. We went on board a man-of-war with Judd (their maid) and the men-servants; it was a fine but melancholy sight. I may gain some information by it, but it is not what I quite approve of, the same as the band; my heart feels most anxious this night that I may go right, for strait and narrow is the path that leadeth to eternal life, and broad is the way that leadeth to destruction. I must remark, before finishing this journal, that I feel much satisfaction attending my not going to the Review, a thing my heart is so much set upon as military music; as soon as I determined, in my own mind, to give it up, inclination vanished, and now would lead me to stay at home. If I look at it, my path is clearer than I think; for it ought to give me comfort and hope, that in so small a thing

I feel so much satisfaction it should help me forward in my journey to that haven, where alone comfort is to be found.

Ivy Bridge, 9th.— The first thing we undertook this morning was to see the Dock-yards, which is a sight too astonishing to describe. But after all the art, expense and trouble, that men put themselves to, what do they gain, but the destruction of their fellow-creatures? After that we went by water to Plymouth, and saw many Friends; but one very plain, who was agreeable to us all, even interesting. As I left Plymouth, my mind felt deeply hurt on account of the poor sailors and women, of whom I have seen a sad number, and longed to do them good, to try one day to make them sensible of the evil state they appear to be in. Just at that time, I read or thought of that passage in the Testament, where it says, we are to look upon all men as greater than ourselves. Christ truly taught humility, and I reflected that, in all probability, if I had had the same temptations, I should have been equally wicked; for I am sorry, indeed, to say, I fear I mostly give way to temptation, when it falls in my way. Ah! much, much have I to do, much to strive for, before I shall be able to feel my house is built upon a rock. I know how weak is its present foundation; but this night my mind is cheered by the brightening light of religion.

Clifton, 15th.—This morning I have seen much beautiful country about Clifton. I think it very likely we shall go to the Welch Half-Yearly meeting, where I expect we shall meet most of the Colebrook Dale Friends, whom I quite long to see. We have been a pleasant excursion this afternoon, to a Mr. Harford's; I had an interesting drive home, and thought about serious subjects. I often think of home with a longing heart, to set off once more quietly in my career.

Ross, 16th.—We have travelled far to-day; I set out rather thinking I should have Mrs. B——'s company, which I had, and enjoyed at times much; experience teacheth knowledge. I think her in all respects not sufficiently practical, but too theoretical. I don't like her theories, she appears to me to think too highly of bringing the things of this world (that do not in my opinion lead to happiness) to perfection. If too much attended to, I think it loss of time; and of course I believe, though she has much religion, that this prevents her enjoying it as much as she would otherwise do ; for, those who depend too much on this world, are apt not to depend sufficiently on the one to come. Some sweet and beautiful scenes we saw from Gloucester to Ross, by moonlight, which I enjoyed.

Abergavenny, 18th.—We went one stage before breakfast from Usk to Pontypool ; as soon as we got there, we met two plain Friends, they both preached ; my mind had some devotional feelings, which I felt a blessing. I remained and dined with them, and a little of that peculiar love, I feel towards plain Friends sprung up in my heart for them. Before the afternoon Meeting, I went with Mrs. B——— to call on Lady M———. I own I felt very uncomfortable, I felt as if I were too much a Friend with Friends, and too worldly with other people. I then went to Meeting and had a very serious reflecting time. I thought I should be acting a better part to say thee instead of you, to other people when I could, for I felt myself to-day, one minute saying thee, the next you ; it appeared hypocritical. I had an argument in my own mind, which I will try to remember ; I first thought how there could be any difference, in Christian virtue in saying you or thee to people. I considered there were certainly some advantages attending it ; the first, that of weaning the heart from this world, by acting in some little things differently from it. But I then thought, is it not better to be remarkable for excellence of conduct, than for such little peculiarities ? I find that in a perfect state, such things would not signify, but we are in an imperfect state ; and our virtue is hard to maintain, without some fortress to support it ; we must combat with imperfection, and at times be obliged to make great things of little things, and use them as arms to defend us from the many wiles and snares of the world.

Landaly, 21st.—A gentleman dined with us, to whom I did not attend, till I discovered he was Lord ———. Oh pride, how it does creep in upon me !

Aberystwith, 23rd.—Is dancing wrong? I have just been dancing ; I think there are many dangers attending it, it may lead to vanity and other things. But I think, in a family party,

6

and in an innocent way, it may be of use by the bodily exercise; it animates the spirits, and produces good effects. I think dancing and music the first pleasures in life. The more the pleasures of life are given up, the less we love the world, and our hearts will be set upon better things; not but that we are allowed, I believe, to enjoy the blessings Heaven has sent us. We have power of mind sufficient to distinguish the good from the bad; for under the cloak of pleasure, infinite evils are carried on. The danger of dancing, I find is throwing me off my centre; at times when dancing, I know that I have not reason left, but that I do things which in calm moments I must repent of. I went and bathed, which required much exertion of courage. After dinner we went to the Devil's Bridge. I was much pleased with the beautiful scenery; but as we were climbing down the rocks, which appeared almost perpendicular over the fall of water, I was taken with the most painful sensation of fear, and dared not go another step, but sat down and thought I should have fainted; if I had, I must have fallen to the bottom. After we arrived safely home to a sort of little inn, where we slept, we had a very happy evening; for we were wet, and were obliged to put on our dressing gowns, and sit over a fine turf fire, in the public-house; singing, and being sung to, by the interesting Welsh inhabitants.

Caernarvon, 27th.—After a good breakfast, we set off on our journey. The first few miles I shall find very difficult to describe, for such a scene I had not an idea of; all surrounded with rocky mountains, lost in the clouds as they passed over them. Sometimes we were on the edge of a precipice, sometimes on the borders of a river, where the road was cut out of the rock, and high mountains on each side, now and then the wild goats straying over them. We were obliged to walk part of the way, which was trying to me, as I had the tooth-ache. Since I have been here, I have had a Welsh harper, which I was not quite sure was right, as it was giving, or at least causing money to be given, that might have been spent much better.

28th.—My mind is in an uncomfortable state this morning; for I am astonished to find I have felt a scruple at music, at

least I could not otherwise account for my feelings ; but my
mind is rather uneasy after I have been spending time in it.
These cannot be sensations of my own making, or a contriv-
ance of my own forming, for I have such happiness when I
overcome my worldly self ; and when I give way to it, am uneasy;
not but what I think feelings are sometimes dangerous to give
way to ; but how odd, yet how true, that much of human reason must be given up. I don't know what to think of it, but I
must act somehow, and in some way ; yet do nothing rashly or
hastily, but try to humiliate myself to true religion ; and
endeavour to look to God who alone can teach me and lead me
right ; have faith, hope, and if little things are to follow to
protect greater ones, I must, yes, I must do it. I feel certainly happier in being a Quaker, but my reason contradicts
it. Now my fears are these, lately I have had Quakerism
placed before me in a very interesting and delightful light ; and
is it unlikely that inclination may put on the appearance of
duty ? Now my inclination may, before long, lead me some
other way ; that is a sad foundation to build the fortress upon
which must defend me through life ; but I think I am wrong in
one thing, though it is right to doubt myself ; yet do I not
make myself more uneasy, for fear I should be a ridiculous
object to the world, and some of my dear friends. I believe I
can give myself a little advice, not to promote anything leading
to unquakerism ; but try if it make me happy or not, and then
take greater steps if I like.

Colebrook Dale, 31*st*.—Cousin Priscilla's room. This evening I am at Colebrook Dale, the place I have so much wished
to be at. I had rather a comfortable drive here from Shrews-
bury ; read in the Testament, and got by heart one or two
verses. I felt it a great pleasure to see cousin Priscilla ; but
my heart has not been enlarged towards this sweet set. We
have taken a long walk this afternoon. It brings me into a
sweet state, being with plain Friends like these, a sort of humility. I expect to be here some days, which I delight in. I feel
this evening in a calm, and rather religious state of mind. I
am blessed a little to feel the existence of my Father who is in
heaven ; and I have some hope I may one day be confined in

7

the sheep-fold, and not stray from the flock. I hope I shall, and I may ; for thanks be to the Almighty, He has formed us for eternal glory, if we will be sufficiently melted down to be moulded into the right form.

September 2nd.—I cannot easily describe that which I would, for I know not in my own mind what my feelings exactly are. This morning when breakfast was over, I had some talk with Priscilla, and then we sat down to read the account of a young woman of the name of Rathbone, to me striking and interesting ; how well she was assured of Immortality, how clearly did she see her path to Heaven ! Happy, happy woman ; blessed, ah blessed is thy fate ! may we also be permitted to accompany thee to glory, immortality and eternal life, with our God and our Saviour ; shall I ever be sensible of deserving immortal glory ? too great a blessing I fear for me and my weak self ever to obtain. For hard is the task and narrow is the road that leadeth thereunto. We then went to Meeting, my mind was clouded, but now and then a small ray enlightened it. Between the two Meetings, I read again with cousin Priscilla, and all my sisters, that account of the young woman. Hard is the task of dedicating the heart unto God ; I fear, yet I hope I may with His assistance one day so fortify it, as to become a defender of truth and religion. After the afternoon Meeting, we drank tea at Deborah Darby's ; I felt much love towards her, and her friend Appleby particularly ; I felt gratified when she said William Savery had mentioned me to her, and that Rebecca Young, who was out, was sorry she could not see me ; there is little, ah little indeed in me ! When we came home this evening, my father took me aside and gave me some good advice ; to beware of passion and enthusiasm, which I hope I do most earnestly pray I may be, for truly they are snares of the enemy.

3rd.—Got up late. Heard Deborah Darby was here, and went down ; during breakfast, I felt my heart beat much ; as soon as it was over, Deborah Darby preached in a deep, clear, and striking manner. First, she said, God would visit us all, and did visit us, that God was a father to the fatherless, and a Mother to the motherless ; my mind felt deeply oppressed by it. She then addressed me in particular ; I do not remember her words, but she expressed, first, I was, as I am, sick of the world ; and looked higher (and I believe I do,) and that I was to be dedicated to my God, and should have peace in this world, and glory everlasting in the world to come. Could more satisfaction be given ? let me be thankful, I really cried, and I think never felt such inward encouragement. Let me be a worthy servant of my Master who is in heaven. May I, Oh ! may I do right. My father has given me leave to stay till Fourth-day morning, kind he truly is. He spoke to me again this morning. I feel myself highly favoured is all I can say, and may my heart bow before its Maker now and evermore ! After they all went, I came and wrote my journal, and sat with cousin Priscilla, and we read till dinner. After that we sat again together with the children, and went on with some letters interesting to me, from that young woman to Richard Reynolds. This afternoon I was at the Darbys. I have felt as it were tinctured with the goodness of those I have been with ; but little I own. Oh my inward temptations, shall I ever overcome you ! Priscilla Gurney I feel my constant little friend, dearly indeed do I love her.

4th.— After tea, we went to the Darbys, accompanied by my dear friend Richard Reynolds, and still dearer Priscilla Gurney. We had spent a pleasant evening, when my heart began to feel itself silenced before God, and without looking at others, I found myself under the shadow of His wing, and I soon discovered that the rest were in the same state : I was persuaded that it must be that which I felt. After sitting a time in awful silence, Rebecca Young spoke most beautifully, she touched my heart, and I felt melted and bowed before my Creator. Deborah Darby then spoke; what she said was excellent, she addressed part of it to me; I only fear she says too much of what I am to be. A light to the blind ; speech to the dumb ; and feet to the lame ; can it be ? She seems as if she thought I was to be a minister of Christ. Can I ever be one ? If I am obedient, I believe, I shall.

Merridon, 5th.—I rose this morning about five o'clock, I did not feel so much as I expected leaving Colebrook Dale. There is a mountain for me to climb over, there is sacrifice for me to make ; before I am favoured with faith, virtue, and assurance of immortality. I feel it would appear so like conformity to the opinions of others, to alter just after being with these Friends, but I think that it is a time to do so, for strength and courage have been given me. This day I have said thee instead of you; but still go on soberly and with consideration.

Coventry, 6th.—I rose in good time to write to Priscilla Gurney, and felt in a state of darkness and discouragement about my language, but I am happy to say my mind again feels clear. I dare not draw back. I hope to continue in the habit with spirit, and if by yesterday week I have kept up to it, and then feel discouraged, I may give it up. I felt saying thee very difficult to-day to Mrs. ——, but I perceived it was far more so after I sang to them. I altogether get on pretty well, but doubts came into my mind this morning; yet were I not to persevere I should, I believe, feel unhappy in it. How shall I say thee to H—— in Norwich! It will I think make me lose all my dissipation of character, and be a guard upon my tongue.

Earlham, 9th.—My father, Kitty, and myself set out early this morning for Newmarket. When I was there, I saw Henry B——; my sensation was odd when I saw him, for I took to my heels and ran away. I thought I could not get courage to address him in the plain language; but after I collected myself, I did it without much difficulty. How easy it has been made to me! By what nice degrees I have entered it, but I believe the hardest part is to come; I have felt the advantage of it, though at times in a dark and discouraging state. It makes me think before I speak, and avoid saying much, and also avoid the spirit of gaiety and flirting.

CHAPTER IV.

Mr. Gurney and his family returned home in September, 1798; Elizabeth, undoubtedly strengthened in her desire to become a plain Friend, though scrupulously careful not to advance one step hastily, or to oppose the wishes of her brothers and sisters on any point, in which she could yield to them with an easy conscience. She resumed her usual habits of self-occupation and usefulness to others; visiting and relieving the poor, both at Earlham and in Norwich, especially the sick; reading the Bible to them and instructing their children. Her school too, gradually increased from the small beginning of one little boy, to so great a number, that her teaching them in the house became inconvenient, and a vacant laundry was appropriated to this purpose. She had at last above seventy scholars without assistance, without monitors, without even the countless books and pictures of the present day; how she controlled the wills and fixed the attention of so many unruly children, must ever remain a mystery to those who have not the gift she possessed, of influencing the minds of others.

Nor was her attention confined to the poor, where any little kindness seemed needed, there she delighted to offer it. A circumstance marking this trait in her character, was related a few years ago to one of her family, by a lady, the widow of an officer, who was living alone in a small house near Norwich, about 1798, during her husband's absence. Her income was limited; she was young, and had few acquaintances. It was during her confinement with her first child that she was surprised by a loud ring at the bell. Her servant came running up stairs with a basket in her hand, and in the broad dialect peculiar to Norfolk, informed her mistress that it had been left by " a beautiful lady on horseback, in a scarlet riding habit," whose servant had told her it was Miss Elizabeth Gurney. The basket contained a chicken and some little delicacies; and the same attentions were repeated, although she personally was a stranger to Elizabeth and her family.

We have no exact knowledge of the time when the scarlet riding habit was abandoned; nor is it easy to ascertain by what gradations she became a Friend in outward appearance. She was slow in adopting the costume; she first laid aside all ornament, then she chose quiet and inconspicuous colours, and had her dresses made with perfect simplicity. As late as the spring of 1799, an eye-witness describes her in a plain slate-coloured silk dress; but a black lace veil twisted in the turban fashion of the day with her long blonde hair, the ends hanging on one side.

Earlham, 10th September.—We arrived last night from our long, and in some respects, delightful journey. So far from hurting me, I hope it will act as a fresh stimulus to virtue and religion, at least it should; I have had some bright and clear times that should not be forgotten. I felt quite in a flutter, expecting H—— and Dr. Alderson to dinner; they came, and I had little difficulty in saying, thee;—so do such evils vanish, if duty support us. In the afternoon, I had a very serious talk with Kitty about my being a Friend. She thinks that my judgment is too young and inexperienced to be able to take up any particular opinions; she may be right. I am willing to give up the company of Friends and their books, if she request it; but I do firmly believe my mind will never be easy or happy unless I am a Quaker.

14th.—I know I am not able to judge, and all I pray for is, faith, humility and patience; and I hope, if ill or well, to do the will of God. May, Oh may I! is the inmost prayer of my heart. I must try not to fear; what will not faith do for us! It would lead us to all happiness, but works are required, and I believe true faith hardly attainable without them.

27th.—This evening I have been doing exercises, and singing with them; my mind feels very clear to-night and my body much better. I have been thinking about singing, I hope in that, as in every thing else, to do what is right. I cannot say I feel it wrong to sing to my own family, it is sweet and right to give them pleasure. I do not approve of singing in company, as it leads to vanity and dissipation of mind; but that I believe I have no occasion to do, as dear Rachel does not request it, for she does not like it herself. I should be sorry quite to give up singing as the gift of nature, and on her account; as long as it does not lead me from what is right, I need not fear.

29th.—I have much enjoyed the company of my dear boy Sammy this evening, I think we shall always feel much love for each other; young as he is, I love him particularly. Afterwards we received a letter from dear Priscilla Gurney.

October 5th.—In the evening a fiddler came, we all had a dance, I had the tooth-ache, and so from its making me merry, it made me grave. I do not feel satisfaction in dancing.

6th.—This morning I awoke not comfortable, the subject of dancing came strongly before my mind. Totally declining it, as a matter of pleasure I do not mind, only as I am situated with the others I find it difficult; the question is, if these may not be scruples of my own forming, that I may one day repent of? The bottom of my heart is inclined to Quakerism, and I know what imagination can do. I believe the formation of my mind is such, that it requires the bonds and ties of Quakerism to fit it for immortality. I feel it a very great blessing being so little in the company of superior fascinating Quakers; because it makes me act freely and look to the only true Judge, for what is right for me to do. The next question I ask myself is, am I sufficiently clear, that dancing is wrong, to give it up? because I know much precaution is quite necessary. I believe I may if I like, make one more trial, and judge again how I feel; but I must reflect upon it, determining to give it up, if I think right. I wish to make it a subject of very serious reflection, hoping, as usual, to do right; it will hurt them much I fear, but time I believe will take that off, if they see me more happy and better for it. Let me redouble all kindness to them. Catharine seems to wish I would give up my correspondence with Anna Savery, which I think I may do. This day has been very comfortable in most respects, though I have not done much. I have finished my letter to my dear cousin Priscilla, and that to Mrs. —— ; but I cannot feel quite easy to send it, without first speaking to my father, for I do believe it is my duty to make him my friend in all things, though I think it probable, he will discourage me in writing to my friend Sophy, yet never keep any thing from him ; but let me be an open, true, kind, and dutiful daughter to him, whilst life is in my body.

12th.—I have many great faults, but I have some dispositions I should be most thankful for. I believe I feel much for my fellow-creatures ; though I think I mostly see into the minds of those I associate with, and am apt to satirise their weaknesses ; yet I don't remember ever being any time with one who was not extremely disgusting, but I felt a sort of love for them, and I do hope I would sacrifice my life for the good of mankind. My mind is too much like a looking-glass—objects of all kinds are easily reflected in it whilst present, but when they go, their reflection is gone also. I have a faint idea of many things, a strong idea of few ; therefore my mind is cultivated badly. I have many straggling, but not many connected ideas. I have the materials to form good in my mind, but I am not a sufficiently good artificer to unite them properly together, and make a good consistence; for in some parts, I am too hard, in others, too soft. I hope and believe the great Artificer is now at work, that if I join my power to the only One who is able to conduct me aright, I may one day be better than I am.

17th.—My journal has not gone on well of late ; partly owing to my going out, and having people in this room, now there is a fire ; I dislike going out, what my mind wants, is peace and quiet. The other night, as I was alone in a carriage, a fine starlight night, I thought, what is it I want ? how I overflow with the blessings of this world; I have true friends, as many as I wish for; good health, a happy home, with all that riches can give, and yet all these are nothing without a satisfied conscience. At times I feel satisfied, but I have not reason to feel so often; oh, that I could! perhaps this night, with constant exertion all day, I may feel that first of feelings. It is now afternoon.—I woke in a bad mind, but I am happy to say I overcame it, by doing as I thought right, which appeared at once to turn the scale from dulness to liveliness; from a bad mind to a good one. This afternoon I have much to correct, I feel proud, vain and disagreeable; not touched with the sweet humility of Christianity; nor is my heart enlightened by its happy doctrines. I have now two things heavily weighing on my mind—dancing and singing, so sweet and so pretty do they seem; but as surely as I do either, so surely does a dark cloud come over my mind. It is not only my giving up these things, but I am making the others miserable, and laying a restraint upon their pleasures. In the next place, Am I sure I am going upon a good foundation? if I am doing right, God will protect me and them also; If I am doing wrong, what foundation do I stand upon? None: then all to me is nothing. Let me try to take my thoughts from this world, and look to the only true Judge. I believe singing to be so natural, that I may try it a little longer: but I do think dancing may be given up. What particularly led me to this state, was our having company, and I thought I must sing; I sang a little, but did not stay with them during the playing. My mind continued in a state of some agitation, and I did not sleep till some time after I was in bed.

19th.—My mind feels more this morning, if any thing, than it did last night. Can such feelings be my own putting on? they seem to affect my whole frame, mental and bodily; they cannot be myself, for if I were to give worlds, I could not remove them; they truly make me shake. When I look forwards I think I can see, if I have strength to do as they direct, I shall be another person: sorrow, I believe, will remove to be replaced by joy; then let me now act! My best method of conduct will be to tell Rachel how I am situated in mind, and then ask her what she would advise; and be very kind and tell her the true state of the case. Is it worth while to continue in so small a pleasure for so much pain ? The pleasure is nothing to me, but it is a grand step to take in life.—I have been and spoken to Rachel, saying, I think I must give up singing. It is astonishing the total change that has taken place, from misery I am now come to joy; I felt ill before, I now feel well—thankful should I be for being directed, and pray to keep up always to that direction. After having spoken to my darling Rachel, where I fear I said too much, I rode to Norwich after some poor people ; I went to see many, and added my mite to their comfort. Nothing I think could exceed the kindness of my dear Rachel. Though I have no one here to encourage me in Quakerism, I believe I must be one before I am content.

7th December.—Yesterday evening, I went to the Eidoranion. I have had a letter to say my dear friend William Savery is arrived safely in America. Kitty and I have been having a long talk together this evening upon sects; we both seem to think them almost necessary. It is long since I have what I call truly written my journal ; writing my journal, is to me expressing the feelings of my heart during the day ; I have partly given it up from the coldness of the weather, and not having a snug fire to sit by. I wish now, as I have opportunity, to look a little into the present situation of my heart; that is the advantage of writing a true journal, it leads the mind to look inwards. Of late I do not think I have been sufficiently active, but have given rather way to a dilatory spirit. I have been reading Watts's Logic, it tells me how ill-regulated are my thoughts, they ramble truly ! Regularity of thought and deed is what I much want; I appear to myself to have almost a confusion of ideas, which leads to a confusion of actions ; I want order ; I believe it difficult to obtain, but yet with perseverance attainable. The first way to obtain it, appears to me, to try to prevent my thoughts from rambling, and to keep them as steadily as possible to the object in view. True religion is what I seldom feel, nor do I sufficiently try after it by really seeking devotion ; I do not warmly seek it, I am sure, nor do I live in the fear of an all-wise Being who watches over us; I seldom look deep enough, but dwell too much on the surface of things, and let my ideas float. Such is my state. I can't tell how I feel exactly :—at times all seems to me mystery; " when I look at the heavens the work of Thy fingers, the moon and the stars which Thou hast ordained, what is man that Thou art mindful of him, or the Son of Man that Thou visitest him ?" Thou must exist, oh God ! for the heavens declare Thy glory, and the firmament showeth Thy handy-works.

8th.—Since dinner I have read much Logic and enjoyed it; it is interesting to me, and may, I think, with attention, do me good. Reading Watts, impresses deeply on my mind how very careful I should be of judging; how much I should consider before I speak or form an opinion; how careful I should be not to let my mind be tinged throughout, with one reigning subject, to try not to associate ideas; but judge of things according to the evidence they give my mind of their own worth. My mind is like a pair of scales that are not inclined to balance equally; at least when I begin to form a judgment, and try to hold the balance equally, as soon as I perceive one scale is at all heavier than the other, I am apt at once to let it fall on that side; forgetting what remains in the other scale, which though lighter should not be forgotten. For instance, I look at a character, at first I try to judge calmly and truly; but if I see more virtues than vices, I am apt soon to like that character so much that I like its weaknesses also, and forget they are weaknesses. The same if evil may preponderate, I forget the virtues.

12th.—This day finished with a dance. If I could make a rule never to give way to vanity, excitement or flirting, I do not think I should object to dancing; but it always leads me into some one of these faults; indeed, I never remember dancing without feeling one, if not a little of all the three, and sometimes a great deal. But as my giving it up would hurt many, it should be one of those things I part with most carefully.

30th.—I went to Meeting in the morning and afternoon; both times rather dark; but I have been a little permitted to see my own state, which is the greatest favour I can ask for at present; to know what I should do, and to be assisted in my duties : for it is hard, very hard, to act right, at least I find it so. But there is the comfortable consideration, that God is merciful and full of compassion, he is tender over His children. I had a satisfactory time with my girls and boys.

January 4th, 1799.—Most of this morning I spent in Norwich seeing after the poor ; I do little for them, and I do not like it should appear I do much. I must be most guarded, and tell those who know I do charity that I am only my father's agent. A plan, at least a duty, that I have felt for some time, I will now mention. I have been trying to overcome fear ; my method has been to stay in the dark, and at night to go into those rooms not generally inhabited ; there is a strange propensity in the human mind to fear in the dark, there is a sort of dread of something supernatural : I tried to overcome that, by considering that as far as I believed in ghosts, so far I must believe in a state after death, and it must confirm my belief in the Spirit of God ; therefore if I try to act right, I have no need to fear the directions of Infinite Wisdom. I do not turn away such things as some do ; I believe nothing impossible to God, and He may have used spirits as agents for purposes beyond our conceptions ; I know they can only come when He pleases, therefore we need not fear them. But my most predominant fear is that of thieves ; and I find that still more difficult to overcome, but faith would cure that also, for God can equally protect us from man as from spirit.

8th.—My father not appearing to like all my present doings, has been rather a cloud over my mind this day ; there are few, if any, in the world I love so well, I am not easy to do what he would not like, for I think I could sacrifice almost any thing for him, I owe him so much, I love him so much.

I have been reading Watts on Judgment this afternoon ; it has led me into thought, and particularly upon the evidence I have to believe in religion. The first thing that strikes me, is the perception we all have, of being under a power superior to human. I seldom feel this so much as when unwell ; to see how pain can visit me, and how it is taken away. Work for ever, we could not create life. There must be a cause to pro-

duce an effect. The next thing that strikes me, is good and
evil, virtue and vice, happiness and unhappiness—these are acknowledged to be linked together ; virtue produces good ; vice
evil ; of course the Power that allows this shows approbation
of virtue. Thirdly, Christianity seems also to have its clear
evidences, even to my human reason. My mind has not been
convinced by books ; but what little faith I have, has been confirmed by reading the holy writers themselves.

26th.—The thoughts of the evening occupied me, yet thinking I might dance. —— was here, who showed me a great
deal of attention. I have not been enough on my guard ; yet
I feel more satisfied than I mostly am after such occasions. I
was in very high spirits, for me.

27th.—I have had, in many respects, comfortable Meetings ;
only my thoughts too giddy dwelling too much on what pleased
me yesterday ; they have, I am sorry to say, been occupied with
old subjects, such as dress and a little flirting, I fear. I have
enjoyed my little party as usual, who are now, when complete,
fifteen in number. What path I shall go in life is hidden from
my view. May I go in that in which I ought to go ! Do not
forget how much more tempting it is to choose the easiest, and
yet do not enter difficulties for difficulty's sake. Try to be led
by no person, but by my own conscience.

29th.—I am in a doubtful state of mind. I think my mind
is timid, and my affections strong, which may be partly the
cause of my being so much inclined to Quakerism ; in the first
place, my affections were worked upon, in receiving the first
doctrines of religion, and I loved them through a Quaker ;
therefore it is likely they would put on that garb in my mind.
In the next place, my timidity may make me uncomfortable, in
erring from principles that I am so much inclined to adopt ; so
far I should be on my guard, and I hope not to forget what I
have just mentioned. But yet, I think the only true standard
I can have to direct myself by, is that, which experience proves
to give me the most happiness, by enabling me to be more virtuous : I believe there is something in the mind, or in the heart
that shows its approbation when we do right. I give myself
this advice : do not fear truth, let it be ever so contrary to in-

clination and feeling. Never give up the search after it; and let me take courage, and try from the bottom of my heart to do that which I believe truth dictates, if it lead me to be a Quaker or not. The last and the best advice I can give myself, is; as far as I am able, to look up to the God who is unitedly worshipped by the whole earth, who has created us, and who we feel has power over our thoughts, words and deeds.

February 7th.—I read much this morning in St. Basil, which is to me excellent, interesting and beautiful. He advises a constant thanksgiving for the many blessings we enjoy, and that we should not grumble at the evils we are subject to ; how much more cause have I for thankfulness than sorrow ! I seldom give thanks for the many blessings that surround me. St. Basil beautifully says, " we should not eat, we should not drink, without giving thanks to God."

14th.—I hope, I have from experience gained a little. I am much of a Friend in my principles at this time, but do not outwardly appear much so ; I say " thee " to people, and do not dress very gay, but yet I say " Mr." and " Mrs.," wear a turban, &c., &c. I have one remark to make ; every step I have taken towards Quakerism has given me satisfaction.

18th.—I feel I must not despair ; I consider I first brought sceptical opinions upon myself, and it is only what is due to me that they should now hurt me. I hope I do not much murmur at the decrees of the Almighty ; and can I expect, who am so faulty, to be blessed with entire faith ? Let me once more try and pray, that the many evil roots in my own mind may be eradicated. I had altogether a pretty good day, rather too much vanity at being mistress at home, and having to entertain many guests.

24th.—What feeling so cheering to the human mind as religion; what thankfulness should I feel to God ! I have great reason to believe Almighty God is directing my mind to the haven of peace, at least I feel that I am guided by a Power not my own. How dark was my mind for some days ! How heavy ! I saw duties to be performed that even struck me as foolish. I took courage and tried to follow the directions of this voice; I felt enlightened, even happy. Again I erred, again I was in a cloud ; I once more tried, and again I felt brightened.

25th.—This time last year, I was with my dear friend William Savery, at Westminster Meeting. I can only thankfully admire, when I look back to about that time, the gentle leadings my soul has had, from the state of great darkness it was in; how suddenly did the light of Christianity burst upon my mind. I have reason to believe in religion from my own experience, and what foundation so solid to build my hopes upon; may I gain from the little experiences I have been blessed with, may I encourage the voice of truth, and may I be a steady and virtuous combatant in the service of God. Such I think I may truly say is my most ardent prayer. But God, who is omnipresent, knows my thoughts; knows my wishes, and my many many feelings; may I conclude with saying, "cleanse thou me from secret faults."

28th.—We have had company most part of the day. I have had an odd feeling. Uncle Joseph and many gay ones were here; I had a sort of sympathy with him. I feel to have been so much off my guard, that if tempted I should have done wrong. I now hear them singing. How much my natural heart does love to sing : but if I give way to the ecstacy singing sometimes produces in my mind, it carries me far beyond the centre ; it increases all the wild passions, and works on enthusiasm. Many say and think it leads to religion; it may lead to emotions of religion, but true religion appears to me to be in a deeper recess of the heart ; where no earthly passion can produce it. However, music may sometimes be of use : and I think our earthly feelings are made use of to lead us to much better things. I think music and dancing the first pleasures in life, not happiness ; they elevate too high. They may be right, but I do not feel quite free to enjoy them ; I will now leave it, as my judgment is not clear.

March 1st.—There is going to be a dance—What am I to do ? As far as I can see, I believe, if I find it very necessary to their pleasure, I may do it, but not for my own gratification. Remember, don't be vain ; if it be possible, dance little.

I began to dance in a state next to pain of mind ; when I had danced four dances, I was trying to pluck up courage to tell Rachel I wished to give it up for the evening ; it seemed as if she looked into my mind, for she came up to me at that minute in the most tender manner, and begged me to leave off, saying she would contrive without me ; I suppose she saw in my countenance the state of my mind. I am not half kind enough to her, I often make sharp remarks to her, and in reality there are none of my sisters to whom I owe so much ; I must think of her as my nurse ! she would suffer much to comfort me ; may she, oh God ! be blessed ; wouldest Thou, oh wouldest Thou, let her see her right path whatever that may be, and wilt Thou enable her to keep up to her duty, in whatever line it may lead. Let this evening be a lesson to me, not to be unkind to her any more. I think I should feel more satisfaction in not dancing ; but such things must be left very much to the time. How very much do I wish for their happiness ; that they may be blessed in every way, is what I pray for to the Great Director ; but all is guided in wisdom, and I believe, as a family, we have much to be thankful for all ways, both for bodily and mental blessings.

4th.—I hope the day has passed without many faults. John is just come in to ask me to dance in such a kind way,—oh dear me ! I am now acting clearly differently from them all. Remember this, as I have this night refused to dance with my dearest brother, I must out of kindness to him not be tempted by any one else. Have mercy, oh God ! have mercy upon me ! and let me act right, I humbly pray Thee ; wilt Thou love my dearest most dear brothers and sisters, wilt Thou protect us ? Dear John ! I feel much for him, such as these are home strokes, but I had far rather have them, if indeed guided by Supreme Wisdom ; for then I need not fear. I know that not dancing will not lead me to do wrong, and I fear dancing does ; though the task is hard on their account, I hope I do not mind the pain to myself. I feel for them ; but if they see in time I am happier for it, I think they will no longer lament over me. I will go to them as soon as they have done, try to be cheerful and to show them I love them ; for I do most truly, particularly John. I think I might talk a little with John, and tell him how I stand, for it is much my wisest plan to keep truly intimate with them all ; make them my first friends. I do not think I ever love them so well as at such times as these. I should fully express my love for them, and how nearly it touches my heart, acting differently to what they like. These are truly great steps to take in life, but I may expect support under them.

16th.—I know I want correction, for these few days past I have not gone on well, a sort of coldness, darkness, and uncertainty that will sometimes take possession of the mind; it is I believe much owing to a want of vigilance and activity on my part, and it does not always please the Almighty to enlighten us equally. I am a very negligent being. If, as Deborah Darby said to me, I will do as far as I know to be right, I may one day be a light to the blind, feet to the lame, &c., &c. Shall such a state ever be mine? if there be any chance of such a thing, I should labour for it. I think the time I spent at Colebrook Dale one of the happiest, if not the happiest time of my life. I think my feelings that night, at Deborah Darby's, were the most exalted I ever remember. I, in a manner, was one of the beginners of the Meeting; suddenly my mind felt clothed with light, as with a garment, and I felt silenced before God; I cried with the heavenly feeling of humility and repentance. Then, when I was in this awful state, there were two sermons preached, one telling me to get the pearl of great price; and the other telling me what I might expect, even happiness in this world, and everlasting happiness in the one to come. But that silence, which first took possession of my mind exceeded all the rest.

Fourth month, 6th.—I have not done a great deal to-day, and yet I hope I have not been idle : I try to do right now and then, but by no means constantly. I could not recover the feeling of being hurt at rejecting, I suppose, the voice of my mind last night when I sang so much ; they were not I believe feelings of my own making, for it was my wish to enjoy singing without thinking it wrong. I have written to Hannah Hoare to-day : the remembrance of the kind affection of that family is very sweet to my mind, I feel a real love for them and interest in their welfare. They understand better than almost any people I ever saw, the true method of being kind; they seem to feel for others, and therefore understand what will most please them, I hope not to forget their attentions to me, and

have a strong desire that our friendship may be lasting, and
not subject to be blown away by the first wind that comes ; I
have seen so much of the fickleness of young people's friendships, I do not feel the dependence upon them I formerly did.
I am inclined to think the time will come, when I shall not be
quite so dear to my gay friends, but I have a great hope they
will keep steady ; I heartily wish they may.

7*th.*—I have hopes the day may come when Norwich Meeting
will prosper and be enlivened again, from a state of cloudiness.
In the afternoon, I went with them to hear a person preach at
the Baptists' Meeting : I felt afraid of setting my own opinions
up and being uncharitable. It did not seem to suit me like our
silent method of worship, and the prayers and sermon did not
make their way into the heart as those of our Friends do ; but
it is likely I should feel that, as I have much love for my own
Society. Uncle Joseph was here in the evening, and he seemed
rather surprised at my going to hear Kinghorn. I had an interesting time with my young flock, I fear I might say rather
too much to them ; mayst Thou, oh Father ! preserve them, for
without Thy aid my efforts are ineffectual ; mayst Thou make
me an instrument in leading them to true virtue, and may the
day come when Thou wilt call them to everlasting joy.

15*th.*—I had for my poor wandering thoughts a satisfactory
Meeting ; partly owing to being nervous, for it leads me to
cast my care upon the Lord. I went to Bedlam, and felt glad
to see the poor Melton woman going on well. If comfort be
once permitted to enter her heart, it will be a cause of true
pleasure to me, and I hope of gratitude to the all-wise Director ; but He knows better than I what is for her good. To-
day, at Meeting, I felt such a relief in the thought that God
knows all our thoughts, all our temptations, and that He knows
also how much power we have to overcome them : for I felt I
could not have a just estimate of my own self.

22*nd.*—I have read a good deal of Lavater's journal, and have
felt sympathy with him. I like the book, as it reminds me of
my duty. I hope that I shall have more steady reliance upon
God ; more regularity of mind ; less volatility of thought. To
have my heart pure in the sight of Thee, who knowest and seest

all my weaknesses, all my defects ; God have mercy on me, I pray Thee ! mayst thou find in me a faithful servant, abounding in good works; may my whole heart say truly, Thy will be done! may I ever with all my heart say the Lord's prayer. Thou knowest my wishes, oh God ; Thou knowest them !

24th.—I awoke with good resolutions, wishing to obtain that peaceful state of mind, of feeling myself humbly trying to do the will of the Almighty ; I took good resolves, but my nature seems not in the mind to act up to them. I feel to have too much volatility of thought to keep that watch so necessary about my thoughts, words and actions. I do not think this has been a bad day ; part of it very satisfactory, particularly teaching three little girls. How little the feelings of my heart seem under my own power ; I feel them like my body, under another power ; yet mankind do not seem willing to allow that God is the Governor and Director of the heart, though they mostly acknowledge, it is He who guides all outward circumstances ; we find we have inward and outward evil to combat, but we have a power within ourselves, that will much alleviate the many evils we are subject to.

28th.—I then had a very satisfactory evening with my dear Sam ; how do I love that dear boy—may he do well ! I am inclined to think the day will come, when we shall see him a religious character.

Fifth Month, 1st.—Even acting right will sometimes bring dissensions in a family, as it says in the Testament; we must not be discouraged even when that is our lot, for whatever may be our situation, if we strictly adhere to that which we believe to be our duty, we need not fear, but rest steadily upon Him who can and will support us. I often observe how much weakness of body seems to humble the mind ; illness is of great benefit to us, as I have found from experience, if we try to make good use of it; it leads us to see our own weakness and debility, and to look to a stronger for support. So I believe it may be with the mind ; dark and gloomy states are allowed to come upon it that we may know our own insufficiency, and place our dependence upon a Higher Power.

16th.—I have not done much to-day, partly owing to taking

a walk to Melton, and company this afternoon. I am sorry to
say, imperceptibly my mind gets wrapped up in the Election.
I must take care, or I think I shall be off my guard, and I do
think if I become so warm in it, I shall find it better to go out
of the way; and may perhaps go to London Yearly Meeting.
But why not try to command my mind at home ? I intend to
try, but in such cases as this, it is difficult to act a negative
character; for even such a body as I am, might, I believe, get
many votes amongst the poor: but yet I feel as if it were giving
to the poor with an expectation of return from them to ask for
their votes. Still, if the cause be such, as may be of use in
tending to abolish the war (for every member in the House carries some weight), is it not right to be anxious to get any one,
who opposes war, into it ? " many a little makes a mickle."

27th.—At last this long wished for expected day has arrived ;
it has been one of real bustle. Before we went to Norwich, I
was much affected to hear of the death of poor Betty Pettet,
and it moved me. Let death come in any way, how very affecting it is ! We went to Norwich, and then entered its tumults. I
have not been so very very much interested ; I might have acted
pretty well, if pride, vanity, and shame had not crept in ; we
lost the Election, which is certainly a very great blank, but we
soon get over such matters, and it convinces me, the less public
matters are entered into the better, they do not suit us ; keep to
our own sphere, and do not go out of its bounds.

Seventh Month, 12*th.*—This day has not been idle, but not
religious. I was most part of the morning at Norwich ; in the
afternoon, I settled accounts ; and in the evening, cut out
clothes for the poor. I don't think I have looked into the Testament, or written my journal to-day ; it leads me to remember
what uncle Joseph said to me the other day, after relating or
reading to me the history of Mary, who anointed our Saviour
with the precious ointment, and His disciples said she might
have sold it, and given to the poor, but Christ said, " The poor
ye have always with you, but me you have not always ;" now I
thought as uncle Joseph remarked, I might this evening have
spent too much time about the poor, that should have been
spent about better things.

In July, Mr. Gurney travelled into the North of England, accompanied by his daughters Elizabeth and Priscilla, and his son Samuel. They attended the General Meeting at the Friend's Public School at Ackworth : this interested Elizabeth, from bringing her into communication with several Friends. Among others, there was one from America, named Hannah Barnard, a person of talent and much plausibility; but who was strongly suspected of being unsound in that essential article of faith, the divinity of Christ; to prove this was however no easy matter ; but after much difficulty and delay, the Friends in England declined her further religious services, and advised her to return home, where she was shortly afterwards disunited, as a member of their religious body, by Friends of that country. It appears that Elizabeth Gurney was not attracted by this person, although at that time her own opinions were by no means clear or decided ; she felt in her communications with her the want of that unction, which alone could satisfy her mind ; for however imperfect and shortcoming the true believer may be, there is a reflection of the Master's image to be perceived in every instance, where, in His offices of Prophet, Priest, and King, the Saviour has been received into the heart of man. The Institution at Ackworth is for the maintenance and education of 300 Friends' children ; it is partly supported by contributions, partly by a moderate payment on the part of the parents. There is a Provincial Committee appointed by the Ackworth General Meeting, held in London, at the time of the Yearly Meeting. Once in the year, the members of this Committee are met at Ackworth, by a deputation from the Yearly Meeting ; and any other Friends who are disposed to join them. A minute investigation then takes place of the religious state of the children, their advance in learning, their health, and domestic comfort.

The travellers afterwards visited Sheepwash, an estate on the beautiful banks of the Wanspeck, at that time belonging to Mr.

Gurney. Elizabeth's histories of their rambles among the woods and scenery there, often delighted her children in after life; they extended their journey to Edinburgh, and returned home, paying a few visits on their way.

Lynn, Seventh Month, 28th.—This was one of the very bustling mornings, to which Earlham is subject̩on any of the family leaving home. We had a quiet sort of a journey here, and though I felt sorry, yet I am glad to be away from home, as we have lately had so much bustle, and I know I have so little cultivated or encouraged a religious state of mind; indeed I have been in a darkish state of late, sadly erring from the path of right: and I appeared to have gone so far out of it, that I could not get into it again, till temptation was a little lessened, which I hope it will be this journey. I think it probable, I shall be more stimulated in the right, than the wrong path.

Peterborough, 29th.—We went to Meeting this morning; and since have been travelling.

30th.—We had a long day's journey; I hope it has been my object at least to try to act right. The propriety of saying "thou" has lately struck me: if I think it right to say it I hope I shall be able, though any alteration of speech is very difficult to make.

Ackworth, Eighth Month, 1st.—To-day what is called the General Meeting began; we first had a meeting of worship, which was rather agreeable: after which, we dined with a very large party in the boy's dining-room at the School; as I was wandering about in the bustle, I went into the plain Friends' room,(which I often did)where I had not been very long, before I felt myself fall into silence before God, which the rest of the party appeared to do also; we had not sat long before William Crotch began to preach to me. I was much affected; then old Friend Hustler said something to me; may I profit by such refreshing times. At four o'clock, the Women's Meeting met; I amongst a great number was chosen one of the Committee to examine the children, school and household: Hannah Barnard appeared to me to hold rather too high a hand. After Meeting, we examined the bed-rooms, which I thought in good order, and talked a little to Hannah Barnard.

2nd.—I arose about six to go to the School to hear the girls spell, which I was pleased with, but should have liked to have questioned them more myself. After that, we breakfasted ; then met in the Committee, to fix a little the plans we should go upon. I and Sarah Cockfield were mentioned to go and attend to the Grammar School ; I said that I had only a slight knowledge of grammar. We then went to the Grammar School ; the writing, ciphering, working, mending, spinning, knitting, and sewing, all which I liked much, and thought upon the whole they did very well indeed ; we then examined parts of the house ; after which we dined, and at three o'clock met to hear the report of the Committee ; I forgot that before dinner, we met at twelve o'clock to draw up the report of what we thought of the proceedings of the school. It was some time before any one would speak ; Friends were begging the Committee to say what they thought, but in vain, till I think Hannah Barnard broke the ice, and encouraged the young people to say what they thought ; for they had been requested before. As it appeared to me it was delaying the Meeting, I took courage (as I thought it was more right than wrong) to speak ; and said what I thought of the grammar and ciphering ; I felt glad I had done it, though I trembled at doing it, not a little. Towards the latter part of the sitting, I was pointedly asked what I thought of their spelling, which I said ; and also that I did not think they attended to the words of one, so well as to those of many syllables. After the Meetings, I was encouraged in what I had done, by salutations from the Friends, Hannah Barnard and Elizabeth Cogshall. After dinner, we met again and heard the report they had written to bring in to the men. I thought the Meeting paid rather too much deference to Hannah Barnard, in delaying the Meeting, because she was not come in. The Meeting concluded, after long waiting to choose a sub-committee, which after all was not done, and we took the report to the men ; I own my body and mind longed impatiently to have Meeting over. After tea, I had a few interesting minutes with Hannah Barnard, to whom I had longed to speak about my beloved friend William

Savery; I met her standing against the wall in the long passage, by Dr. Binn's door. I went up to her, took hold of her hand and entered into talk with her; I mentioned dear William Savery : we went and sat in the Doctor's room, where was Thomas Scattergood, whom, though I do not think he spoke, yet I liked.

3rd.—I arose in a bustle and hurried about till the "cold victuals" were given to the poor, which plan I did not much like, as it seemed like showing off. William Crotch preached to them very agreeably, after which Thomas Scattergood called us aside, and in a little Meeting expressed the great love he felt for me yesterday, which made it appear to me, as if there were a sympathy of soul, and we both were guided by the same spirit; he expressed how much he felt for me at the time I came into Doctor Binn's room, and had then felt it on his mind to say something to me; I also had felt a silent inclination to hear. We then set off on our journey to York. I have not sufficiently dwelt on the kindness of some Friends to me during our stay at Ackworth. First, dear Christiana Hustler and her daughter; Friend Messer, and many others. May I really profit by this time. We arrived at York to a late dinner, and drank tea at Lindley Murray's, whom though I hardly spoke to, I really loved; there was also B—— F——'s daughter, who seemed sweetly under the guidance and influence of religion; she was to me truly interesting, but I think I was too forward with her; I felt my own inferiority.

4th.—This morning we walked about York, and saw its wonders. We saw the Friends' Retreat for crazy people, which my father thought extravagantly carried on. The Minster is a beautiful building; how much people spend about a pious building! would they spend as much time and trouble about their own souls? We got to Darlington to night. This morning, I was much pleased by a note and present from Lindley Murray, of one of his English Readers; it renewed my feelings of love towards him.

5th.—We were at both Meetings, at Darlington, to-day; I was much pleased with the Friends there, and their appearance of unity and hospitality. We reached Durham to-night; I was much pleased with the beautiful scenery entering the town.

6th.—Arrived at Newcastle in a hard rain. Was in a bad storm of thunder and lightning, at the Glasshouses; altogether my mind was calm.

7th.—Much bustle and fatigue in walking about Newcastle, seeing different sights; we arrived at Sheepwash to-night.

8th.—This morning, we spent in riding about my father's estate, which is a beautiful place; I had rather an exertion of courage in riding an unruly horse. We walked out again in the evening; I had much of the toothache.

9th.—Walked with R—— C—— to Broom Park. I must beware of my proud, vain self.

10th.—We spent the day, till about five, at Broom Park; I do not like myself in that sort of company, I am almost sure to lose ground by a sort of foolish wish to please every body; I do not absolutely deviate from my character; but I enter as far as I can into the character of those I am with, and unintentionally give up more than I should. We went from thence to Alnwick Castle, belonging to the Duke of Northumberland, a very magnificent place; but seeing such places, never leads me to wish for high life, for, after all, are the possessors happier, if so happy as others? the only true and lasting source of happiness is an easy conscience.

Edlington, Scotland, 11th.—We saw to-day a very beautiful view, Peese Bridge, nature and art are so finely united; there is sea, land, wood, waterfall, mountain, valley, and a bridge, I should say more than two hundred feet high.

Shields, 19th.—I am sorry it is so long since I wrote my journal. We have been to Edinburgh, which is a city well worth seeing, for its beauty and curiosity. There was an American Friend who put me much in mind of dear William Savery. We again went to Broom Park, where we were most hospitably received. On Second-day evening, on our way from Edinburgh, I was rather nervous. I feel, I am sorry to say, little progress in the path of virtue: keeping up that watch and dependence upon God is so difficult; it is hard work to look only to the true Source in our hearts, we are so apt to wish to save ourselves that trouble, and to look to inferior sources. I believe talking much on the subject has not a good effect, for it leads us to an outward rather than deeply inward feeling; it is hard work really to dig deep; I seem to have so many faults or errors encamped round about me, they are out of my power to overcome alone; but can I not do it with looking to God for assistance?

Earlham, 29th.—On Third-day evening, we arrived safely at home, after altogether a pleasant journey.

Ninth Month, 13th.—This morning I awoke with a cloud over me, and so I must expect both to wake and sleep, if I do not try more completely to do the will of God. I dare not take resolutions, as I know now I cannot keep up to them.

17th.—This evening, I feel a comfortable state of mind, not so inclined to be off my guard as sometimes, I know it is not owing to myself; but being so, should be a cause of gratitude. This evening I did a thing I felt I had to repent of, but it has at least made me clear upon the subject; as they were singing and playing, they begged me to sing, and I did it, but I felt far more pain than pleasure from doing it. A really uneasy mind was my portion the rest of the evening.

18th.—This morning I went to Meeting, and fully felt my weakness; but I have found myself to-day and yesterday, a little under the influence of religion, which is a blessed thing. I had much palpitation at the Meeting of Discipline, because I saw some things so clearly, but being mentioned by others, I thought I might get off giving an opinion. I was proposed to be representative, and said I had no objection, indeed I felt no objection on my own part, because though I know how weak I am, yet even the weak should not fear to exert the little power they have; and I do feel interested for the Society, and for the most part, approve its principles highly.

Tenth Month, 1st.—I feel in a state of much mental weakness, real and true discouragement; I have little faith and little hope, and almost fallen so as not to be able to rise. But if there be a God and a Saviour I need not fear; for though I know and find my state of corruption, yet I believe the warmest wish of my heart is, to do the will of God, and to act right: I do most truly hunger and thirst after righteousness. I find one thing very hard to overcome, which is pride and vanity in outward religious matters. True religion, I believe, will not admit of pride and vanity. Another temptation is, that I have too much formed in my own mind what I think I am to be ; which may outwardly encourage me in a path, that nothing but the dictates of conscience should lead me into. I am really weak in faith, and in works ; I believe at least I have a hope that if I exert the little power I now have given me, the day will come when I shall feel the power of God within me.

13*th.*—Narrow is the path that leadeth unto life eternal, and few there be that find it. There are many called, but few chosen —for though we are blessed with being called, yet if we follow not when we are called, and that strictly, we do not deserve to be called the children of God, for, as it says in the Revelation, " He that overcometh shall inherit all things, and I will be his God and he shall be my son."

24*th.*—I feel this morning as I have felt lately, quite in a hurry about what I have to do ; and I do not think that that is the way to do it well ; it is better to go soberly and quietly to work about it, and not to flurry and bluster. I think this day has not been quite so idle, and I hope in a little degree I may have done well. I put some things in proper order, read history and grammar, wrote letters and worked. I feel in rather a flat, silent state of mind. May I be thankful that opportunity is offered me to spend my time in doing something. May pride and vanity be cast far from me. May doing Thy will, be my constant object, oh God ! I see Thee not for Thou art invisible, yet I have reason to believe, I am not invisible to Thee ; therefore look upon my weakness with pity, and deign to strengthen my lukewarm faith.

26*th.*—I am rather in a volatile mind this morning, and that state which requires care. I still feel as if I could not act really and minutely well ; a sort of lukewarmness that leads to forgetfulness ; and a flying off from the centre in my inmost heart. But weak as I am, if I exert my powers, and in times of need pray for more, and try to turn out worldly ideas, till I receive strength by waiting in stillness upon God ; to let His will be done in me ; I then shall find if the arm of the Lord be sufficient for me. But I feel and know it is much easier to write than practise ; for it is hard, a very hard matter, to wait quietly upon God ;

it is for the time, giving up the world to follow Him. For though I seldom or ever have found more than darkness in my own endeavours to wait, (and how seldom I do it?) yet remember, "Ask and it shall be given thee, seek and thou shalt find, knock and it shall be opened unto thee." If I continue steady in seeking, and will try and pray to seek more and more, the day will come when I shall find ; let me remember this. I believe at times the door has been in mercy opened, when at the moment I have not been knocking, for I have now and then tasted the beauties of holiness ; but it appears as if it had mostly been through others, or with others, I have felt it. But how humbly thankful should my soul be, that my path of conduct has so far been shown me, when I have sought after it, and that I have had my eyes anointed to see the difference of right and wrong in my conduct ; that, perhaps, is enough for me for the present ; may I be sufficiently thankful for it, for does it not show that the Most High has not forsaken me ?

Eleventh Month, 17th.—In the evening, with my children, I had in some respects a very comfortable time ; it was at least my wish to act right with them. In part of one of the chapters, I seemed carried through to explain something to them in a way I hardly ever did before. It was striking the difference in my power this evening, and this day week. This day week I tried and tried to explain, and the more I tried the more I seemed to blunder ; and this evening I was determined not to attempt it, unless I felt capable, and that I did, suddenly and unexpectedly to myself ; I had a flow of ideas come one after another, in a sweet and refreshing way. The rest of the evening was principally spent with Hannah Scarnell, talking about my poor mother, who died this day seven years.

26th.—Towards the latter end of yesterday evening I had some uncomfortable mental feelings, and this morning they really amounted to pain of mind. I believe they were deep and inward temptations of the imagination ; silent waiting upon God seemed my only resource, and it was difficult to do so ; it was like a trial in my mind between the two powers. My imagination, I think, was partly set at work by being nervous, rather more so than usual : and it requires spiritual strength to overcome the painful workings of a nervous imagination. There are few temptations, I believe, so hard to overcome, as those that try to put on the appearance of duties. They are willing to represent the spirit of truth in our hearts ; at such times before I act, try quietly to wait upon God ; look to Him for help, and when things at all appear in the light of duties, the thought of which produces agony to the soul, it requires much deliberation before we act.

Twelfth Month, 11*th.*—In the afternoon I was rather industrious. I was uncertain whether to go to the Grove or not, but at last I fixed to go. In going there, I observed the sweet states I had experienced for being obedient. My path seemed clear, and my heart acknowledged, "I have sought, and have found, I have knocked and it has been opened unto me ;" it also appeared to me in how beautiful a manner things work together for good. After all this, again, Myself got the victory, and I came home with a degree of remorse, for saying upon some subjects more than I should have said ; how great a virtue is silence, properly attended to !

At this time, Elizabeth Gurney wore the cap and close hand-kerchief of Friends, and with the dress, had adopted their other peculiarities ; this added to her comfort, and spared her many difficulties. Of their principles she had been long convinced, and had deliberately chosen Quakerism as the future religion of her life.

Her mind being thus established on matters of the first importance, was better prepared to entertain a subject which now claimed her consideration. Proposals of marriage from Mr. Joseph Fry : at that time engaged with his brother Mr. William Fry, in extensive business in London. Her timid sensitive nature shrunk at first from so momentous a question, and for a time she seemed unable or unwilling to encounter the responsibility. Gradually, with individual preference, her mind opened to the suitability of the connexion. Her habits and education had rendered affluence almost essential to her comfort ; whilst entering

Mr. Fry's family, and the prospect of residing among Friends, offered great and strong inducements to her feelings. Her anxious desire to be rightly guided in her decision, is marked in the following letter to her cousin, Joseph Gurney Bevan. He was to her a kind relative, and wise counsellor; he had been the chosen associate of her father's early manhood, and the friend of his mature years. Being himself a decided Friend, he was the better able to enter into the peculiar circumstances of Elizabeth Gurney, and the difficulties she had to encounter.

Twelfth Month, 12*th*.—I believe the true state of my mind is as follows. I have almost ever since I have been a little under the influence of religion, thought marriage at this time was not a good thing for me; as it might lead my interests and affections from that Source in which they should be centred, and also, if I have any active duties to perform in the church, if I really follow as far as I am able the voice of Truth in my heart; are they not rather incompatible with the duties of a wife and a mother? And is it not safest to wait and see what is the probable course I shall take in this life, before I enter into any engagement that affects my future career? So I think, and so I have thought. But to look on the other side. If Truth appears to tell me I may marry, I should leave the rest, and hope whatsoever my duties are, I shall be able to perform them; but it is now at this time the prayer of my heart, that if I ever should be a mother, I may rest with my children, and really find my duties lead me to them and my husband; and if my duty ever leads me from my family, that it may be in single life. I must leave all to the wisdom of a superior Power, and in humble confidence pray for assistance both now and for evermore, in performing His will.

Clapham, *Fourth Month*, 1800.

My dearest Cousin,

It is not pleasant to me, having a subject that now is of no small importance to me, unknown to thee, for I feel thee to be, and love thee as my kind friend. Some time ago, Joseph

Fry, youngest son of William Storrs Fry of London, paid us a visit at Earlham, and made me an offer of marriage. Since our stay in this neighbourhood, he has renewed his addresses. I have had many doubts, many risings and fallings about the affair. My most anxious wish is, that I may not hinder my spiritual welfare, which I have so much feared, as to make me often doubt if marriage were a desirable thing for me at this time, or even the thoughts of it; but as I wish (at least I think I wish), in this as in other things, beyond every thing else to do the will of God, I hope that I shall be shown the path right for me to walk in. I do not think, I could have refused him with a proper authority, at this time. If I am to marry before very long, it overturns my theories, and may teach me that the ways of the Lord are unsearchable; and that I am not to draw out a path of right for myself, but to look to the One who only knows what is really good for me; but the idea of leaving my station at home is to me surprising, as I had not thought that it would have been the case, and perhaps it may not now happen, but it does not seem improbable. How anxiously do I desire I may through all, strive after the knowledge of God, and one day, if it be right, obtain it. Excuse this hasty scrawl, and believe me, my dear cousin, thy very affectionate,

E. GURNEY.

First Month 1*st*, 1800.—This has not been one of the clear and bright days of life: little has been done, and that little as in a nightmare; not feeling able to get forward, and discouraged. None but one Being knows how I spend my time, and how little I really do in the service of God; but I cannot quite judge myself, and I feel I have complained too much to-day of the burdens of life to other people. My uncle Joseph was here, and I felt my own weakness by his side. I had my children, and found them a great burden; at least I thought that I was making more show than reality. So are my down sittings and my up-risings. Have mercy on me, if Thou existest, oh God! forsake not one who does wish to trust in Thee, and be Thy servant in the way Thou mayst see meet for her.

7*th*.—This morning, at Meeting, I had rather a trying time in

some respects, at least I fully felt the disobedient state of my
own heart. I think, as far as I can judge from past experience,
my feelings were not those of imagination. I felt, supposing it
was my duty to speak in that Meeting, what would it not be to
me ? and I don't think I felt perfectly clear of that awful duty;
not that I now believe it will be at this time required of me, but
it appears to me a devotion of heart that I must try to attain;
or else my lamp will not be prepared, that I may go when my
Master calleth. I have felt, and still feel, " I cannot do it,"
when required of me. Almost as much as that : though I yet
believe, if I were sure it was required by God, it should be done,
if I had power ; but in our present state of weakness, we are to
see so far and no farther, and we can only act as far as we, in our
great weakness, think is the best way for us. My faith is as a
grain of mustard-seed. But we may all judge from experience;
and I think I may truly say, that when I have followed the direction of this Voice in my heart, (those feelings that may be enthusiasm or what else) yet I never have failed to feel content in
doing so ; even to be amply rewarded, and never to have repented
following its dictates, but the more I have been wholly and humbly given up to obey, the more I have found my foundation a
stable one ; and trying as it has been sometimes, yet after I have
gone through the trial, reason and inclination and all have applauded. But reason and inclination often leave us in the day
of trouble. However, to go on with my tale. I continued most
of the Meeting in this state, not clear of this awful duty, and yet
by no means seeing it right to act; but as for that, I believe I
would hardly let it come into my mind, and in my thoughts ; I
wished William Crow to preach, as I do sometimes, and when
he rose my heart seemed to feel, it was right for him to do so.
He began to speak of the state of some one present, and did take
me surprisingly home to mine ; he mentioned how the ministry
had come before that mind ; but seemed to think it was not an
immediate duty, but was to be tried. So I leave it. I am unwilling to think any thing of the kind would be at present required of me. I believe it would be a greater trial than I can
describe, my whole appearance being so different from those
who are generally ministers among us. But yet I hope if

ever duty really requires it of me I may do it, let it be early or
late.

At this time she thus writes to a young Friend :—

True religion seems a subject of that great importance, that
we must not play with it, either mentally or in word; perhaps
thou wilt think it odd, but at seasons I am not a friend to too
many religious thoughts; for thoughts are apt to wander, and
border on imagination. Religion is a deep inward working of
the feelings, and of the heart; we must not look too much for
bright light on the surface of things, but we must humbly and
quietly try to seek deep; attending to the day of small things,
trying to be faithful in the little, or we cannot expect to be rulers
over more. Seek for these little feelings of the heart; watch that
thou mayst know truly the voice of thy Shepherd. I feel this
advice may be received by us both; I cannot tell how thou findest
it, but this voice has at times led me into trials; but where I have
followed, truly I may say I have had my reward; where I have
not, then I have felt the good part within me weakened. I
believe our temptations may be different, but the deeper I dig in
my own mind, the clearer I see how I am surrounded with them;
I can hardly bear to feel them, and to observe them; but that
light which I deeply sought has shown me the danger; and as
a friend of mine wrote to me the other day, "in vain is the
snare laid in the sight of the bird." By thus seeking, may we
truly find the road that leadeth unto salvation. Fare thee well!

Second Month, 9*th*.—In the evening, my father brought two
friends with him and Lawrence Candler. As I was reading to
my children in the laundry, my father brought them all in;
when I had finished reading in the Testament we were all silent,
and soon John Kirkham knelt down in prayer and we all rose up;
it was a very solemn time; my heart was not much moved, but I
believe many of my dear children were much affected by it; he
then preached to them, and it was surprising to me to see how
much it seems the same spirit that works in all; and how solemn
a thing it is to preach and pray only from authority, and how

very different an effect it has on the mind to other advice; however, it was an encouraging thing, and I hope it will not be passed over by me or the children.

11*th*.—How much I wished, almost prayed, I may one day be a perfect sacrifice, wholly given up to the service of God.

18*th*.—Time will tell, if what "Friends" have told me will be true, that I shall one day be different from what I am; indeed, taste of the beautiful comfort and support of true religion, and not only receive myself, but be an instrument in giving to others; and that my own beloved family will feel support in me, and in a degree do as I may have done, or that my principles will spread. None but One knows my heart, and my most deep wishes, nay, I may almost say prayers, that I may, in whatever way it may be, do to my utmost the will of God; may I not faint in the day of trial and tribulation; and may self not be exalted in the day of prosperity.

Fifth Month, 30th.—I have written lately many melancholy journals, and I seem rather inclined this morning gratefully to mention the calm and sweet state I feel in. Even if the feelings be but for this time, it is a blessing to have them. My feelings towards Joseph are so calm and pleasant, and I can look forward with so much cheerfulness to a connexion with him.

Sixth Month, 6th.—I felt rather nervous and weak this morning. I wrote to Eliza Fry, and worked and talked. I might talk too much. I received a letter I liked from Joseph, and answered it this afternoon. I felt unwilling to represent my own faults to him, although I told him how faulty I was, yet it is much more unpleasant to acknowledge any real fault committed, than the natural inclination to faults. Christiana Gurney has a droll effect upon me, and leads me to feel as if she thought me a lukewarm Quaker. I believe I am so, in some respects; because, deeply interested as I am in the Society, and much as I approve some of its scruples, yet my limits are great, and I do not feel little scruples of that importance some other persons do.

9*th*.—I have been busy to-day without doing much. They all went out about twelve. I then put my poor people's things in a little order, and cut out linen till dinner, and from dinner till tea. I am slow in what I do. I have thought seriously upon becoming mistress of a house. I look in that, as in other things, that principle may be my support, for it leads and supports in the smallest occurrences of life. The preparations of clothing, &c., &c., as they lead me into the little things for which I have a taste, if I do not take care may hurt me, and yet they are both pleasant and interesting to me.

17th.—My state is a truly comfortable one this morning, such peace of mind and body. I seem to have at present no cloud over me—so calm, so easy—partly owing to having lately felt so much bodily pain, ease and rest are peculiarly pleasant ; let it be an encouragement to me, next time pain or sorrow surround me, that even when heavily clouded, the sun may not be far off; may enjoying this sort of peace lead me to long for a more durable and lasting one, and may it stimulate me with more vigour to seek after it, by more frequent patient waiting upon God, and may I experience an increasing willingness to take up the cross when called to do so.

Eighth Month, 4th.—This has been a comfortable day to me. I have been busy, and a little gone on in my old plans ; I have great hopes of leaving all things in good order, which is a relief to me. It is a blessing indeed to feel thus healthy in mind and body; for I think we are subject to mental diseases, that are not in our power any more than bodily ones, and that require our patience ; although it is our duty in both mental and bodily maladies, to do our utmost to overcome them.

13th.—This morning the Fellowe's were here ; nothing particular happened till evening, when all my poor children came ; it was rather a melancholy time to me. After having enjoyed themselves with playing about, I took them to the summerhouse and bade them farewell ; there were about eighty-six of them, many of them wept ; I felt rather coldly when with them, but when they went away, I shed my tears also ; and then my desires took the turn of anxiously longing for the spiritual welfare of all of us, as a family.

CHAPTER V.

THE marriage of Joseph Fry and Elizabeth Gurney took place
on the 19th of August, 1800, at the Friends' Meeting House in
Norwich; her own description of the day is :—

I awoke in a sort of terror at the prospect before me, but soon
gained quietness and something of cheerfulness; after dressing
we set off for Meeting; I was altogether comfortable. The Meeting was crowded; I felt serious, and looking in measure to the
only sure place for support. It was to me a truly solemn time;
I felt every word, and not only felt, but in my manner of
speaking expressed how I felt; Joseph also spoke well. Most
solemn it truly was. After we sat silent some little time, Sarah
Chandler knelt down in prayer, my heart prayed with her. I
believe words are inadequate to describe the feelings on such an
occasion; I wept good part of the time, and my beloved father
seemed as much overcome as I was. The day passed off well,
and I think I was very comfortably supported under it, although
cold hands and a beating heart were often my lot.

Leaving the home of her childhood was a great effort to her.
Driving through Norwich for the last time, " the very stones of
the street seemed dear" to her. On the 31st of the same month,
she says:—

We arrived at Plashet about three o'clock; it was strange to me. I was much pleased with the place, and admired the kindness of its inhabitants.

Her home, however, was for some years to be in scenes far less congenial to her early habits, than Plashet House, in Essex ; then, the residence of her husband's parents. It was a much more prevailing custom in that day, than it is now, for the junior partner to reside in the house of business. In conformity with which Mr. and Mrs. Joseph Fry prepared to establish themselves in St. Mildred's Court, in the city of London. The house was large, airy, commodious, and what in the city is a still more rare advantage, quiet ; and continued to be an occasional residence of different members of the family, till it was pulled down in consequence of alterations in London.

Elizabeth Fry was, by her marriage, brought into completely new circumstances ; her husband's family had been members of the Society of Friends, since an early period after its foundation. In this, it resembled her own ; but unlike her own parents, her father and mother-in-law, were " plain and consistent Friends ;" she was surrounded by a large circle of new connexions and acquaintance, who differed from her own early associates, in being almost exclusively strict Friends. Thus she found herself the " gay, instead of the plain and scrupulous one of the family." This for a time brought her into occasional difficulty and trial. She often painfully felt the incongruity of the parties assembled at her house, formed of her own family and nearest connexions, whom she so tenderly loved, and those with whom she was in strict religious communion, but whose habits and sentiments differed from theirs ; and she feared for herself, lest in the desire to please all, she should in any degree swerve from the line of conduct she believed right for herself.

George Dilwyn, from Philadelphia, a Friend engaged in religious service in London, became their guest, on the 7th of

November, only a week after the young married pair had arrived at their home ; he remained with them upwards of a month, and his company appears to have been useful and agreeable to them ; although his presence brought the bride into difficulty, on a point that at the present time seems almost inconceivable, that of reading the Holy Scriptures aloud in the morning. Family devotion, amongst all persuasions, was much less common at that period than it is now; and the habit of assembling the household at a stated hour daily, for domestic worship, was almost unknown.   Mr. and Mrs. Fry's servants were not partakers of this privilege, except on Sunday evenings, until some years after their marriage.

Plashet, Ninth Month, 8th.—From continued change of scene, and the great deal that I am obliged to talk, I seem of late to be continually letting out, and taking nothing in ; of course much weakened by it.

28th.—I had rather a serious evening Meeting. I first wept, I believe, with thinking of them at home ; however, I afterwards began to pray as far as my weak spirit could, for I am weak indeed, and even my good wishes are so surrounded with worldly inclinations, that it seems to require much strength to get through ; and my faith is weak, and without faith it is a hard matter to act, but I believe I may find enough for action, if I will seek for it.

Tenth Month, 3rd.—I went to town this morning, and walked about some time, ordering plate, &c., &c.   My inclination is to have every thing very handsome, but I do not think it right to have things merely for ornament, unless there be some use attached to them.

5th.—I do not remember ever wishing for worldly good of any kind, as I have for spiritual : but actions show how much the love of the world still remains ; indeed, I seem chained down to the world and worldly things, and my habitation seems in the dust.   May it ever rise higher.

Earlham, 8th.—Here I am once more sitting in the music-room, writing my journal; how often I have written it here, and with how many feelings!

St. Mildred's Court, 30*th*.—After breakfast, my husband and I set off from Plashet in my father's coach with nurse Barns, for Mildred's Court. I felt rather low at the prospect before me, and more so when I saw the state of the house; confusion in every part. I had a bed-room turned into a sitting-room, put in order, and then went and put myself in order for dinner; our brother William dined with us. I spent rather a pleasant afternoon, which is to me quite a rarity. Joseph and I had a comfortable evening. Both I believe feeling the true comfort, I may say blessing, of being at last quiet in our own house. All seemed to shine upon us. May we mutually endeavour to hold all in subservience to that Being, to whom all our thoughts, wishes, and actions, are known. I sometimes feel the self-interestedness of wishing to be good, for after all what earthly enjoyment is like it? may we not stop short in our career, but try to run the race that is set before us.

Eleventh Month, 7*th*.—George Dilwyn came to-day; I feel almost overcome with my own weakness, when with such people.

11*th*.—After breakfast, I believed it better to propose reading in the Bible, but I felt doing it, particularly as my brother William was here; not liking the appearance of young people, like us, appearing to profess more than they who had lived here before us. However I put off and put off till both William and Joseph went down; I then felt uneasy under it, and when Joseph came back I told him, as I did before, what I wished; he at last sat down, having told George Dilwyn my desire. I began to read the 46th Psalm, but was so overcome that I could hardly read, and gave it to Joseph to finish.

12*th*.—I rather felt this morning it would have been right for me to read the Bible again, and stop George Dilwyn and Joseph reading something else. Now stopping G. D. was a difficult thing; for a person like me to remind him! however, I did not fully do as I thought right, for I did not openly tell G. D. we were going to read, but spoke to my husband, so as for him to hear; then he read, I knowing I had not done my best.

14*th*.—I again felt some difficulty at reading the Bible, however, I got through well. George Dilwyn encouraging me, by

8

saying, he thought I portioned the reading well. After a little bustling we set off for Hampstead. I was there told by ——, he thought my manners had too much of the courtier in them, which I know to be the case, for my disposition leads me to hurt no one, that I can avoid : and I do sometimes but just keep to truth with people, from a natural yielding to them in such things as please them. I think doing so in moderation, is pleasant and useful in society. It is amongst the things that produce the harmony of society : for the truth must not be spoken out at all times, at least not the whole truth. I will give an instance of what I mean. Suppose any one was to show me the colour of a room, that I thought pretty, I should say so, although I thought others more so, and omit saying that; perhaps I am wrong, I do not know if I be not, but it will not always do to tell our minds. This I have observed, and I am sorry for it, that I feel it hard when duty dictates to do what I think may hurt others. I believe this feeling of mine originates in self-love, from the dislike of being myself the cause of pain and uneasiness.

15th.—George Dilwyn said, for our encouragement this morning, that he had seen, since he had been with us, the efficacy of reading in the Bible the first thing, he thought it a good beginning for the day.

19th.—Dear Kitty and Priscilla came this afternoon ; I felt a good deal at seeing them. How dear they are to me ! George Dilwyn came home this evening ; and it was rather odd, but we fell into unusually interesting conversation.

22nd.—I think I have tried to do better to-day, and a bad cold has prevented my saying much, which is so often a stumbling-block, for that little member, the tongue, is very hard to command ; until the root be mended, I cannot expect the branches to flourish, or to bring forth much fruit. Thoughts, words and actions, appear to spring from a corrupt source. I feel my sisters a lesson to me, they seem so much more virtuous.

Twelfth Month, 1st.—We dined at the Barclays to-day; I felt it pleasant being at Clapham, although the change of society I have, is at times a trial ; it requires much strength to be on one's guard.

5th.—To-day, we had the W——s and C——s to dinner.

We provided handsomely, but I much disapprove of a luxurious table ; as superfluity at table appears to me as bad, if not worse, than in other things.

8th.—I value being alone with my husband ; it is a quiet I have not lately enjoyed, and it does seem to me, at this time, one of the great blessings of life : talking of blessings, am I not ungrateful, when thus surrounded with them, to be wishing for more ? it is a pity !

9th.—Anna Savery drank tea here ; we had not sat long after tea before we fell into silence. During the time, I first felt a sort of anxiety for the welfare of us young travellers, and it came strongly across my mind, Is it not my duty openly to express it ? this put me into an agitation not easily to be described ; and I continued in this state, which was a truly painful one, nearly feeling it my duty to pray aloud for us ; oh, how hard it did seem ! I tried to run from it, but I found the most safety in trying to wait upon God ; hoping, if it were imagination, to overcome it ; if it were duty, that I might be obedient. Towards the latter end, I felt more inclined towards obedience. But what an obstacle is my not holding my will in subserviency to that of my Maker; for perhaps after all it was only a trial of my obedience, that would not have been called for, but to show me how far I was from a resigned state of heart. I felt oppressed the rest of the evening.

10th.—I awoke in a burdened state of mind ; I thought it better to relieve it to my dear husband, and found comfort in doing so ; he warned me against imagination. I must try to trust in the Lord, and I hope to find safety. I felt quite in a state of agitation till we went to Meeting ; it made me feel almost ill in body, both last night and this morning ; however, my mind was sweetly calmed in the Meeting, and I felt vastly relieved from my terrors, and a little love and trusting in the Heavenly Master. I was almost ready to do whatever might be right for me. Oh ! may I give up to what is called for at my hand, and may I not be deceived, but follow the true Shepherd, for my feet seem much inclined to wander !

14th.—I attended both Meetings as usual, and as usual I came from them, flat and discouraged. To attend our place of worship and there spend almost all the time in worldly thoughts, is, I fear, too great a mark of how my time is mostly spent; indeed, my life appears at this time to be spent to little more purpose than eating, drinking, sleeping, and clothing myself. But if we analyze the employment of most, what do they more than in some way attend to the bodily wants of themselves or others? What is our work, the good we do to the poor, &c., &c., but for the body!

In reply to the letter of a Friend, Elizabeth Fry at this period thus describes her own state of mind and anxiety for spiritual advance :—

Mildred's Court, *First Month,* 1801.

In referring to thy former letter, I remembered thou there hailed me as a fellow-traveller towards a better country; and I remember feeling encouragement from it : I am doubtful how far thou couldest now do so, but I trust, although I see little and feel hardly any thing of good in my own mind, that I am not yet quite forsaken as one dead to good works. I am at times ready to feel, what shall I do? for if I were sure this state was out of my own power, I need only quietly rest, hoping for better times; but my fear is, that, from want of more watchfulness, I am so continually devoted to things of this world, as to blind my spiritual sight from observing things belonging to the other. There are times when my anxiety for good is great indeed, and for a short time, it is my endeavour to seek strength where I hope to find it; but alas! my good wishes and good endeavours are of short, very short duration. I often remember that part of Scripture (more particularly at Meeting) where our Saviour says to Simon, " Couldest thou not watch with me one hour?" I feel able to draw some consolation from what I here read, when I see that others so great and good have found it hard to do so; but I experience the force of the question. I have at times great fears that I may be led astray in matters of the first importance, for there is a power that will at times deceive the unwary mind, for we may remember it can even put on the appearance of an angel of light. It was my lot, in very early life, to be much in company with Deists, and to be rather a warm advocate for their doctrines. I now in many shapes feel myself touched with these early imbibed opinions: for it appears to me that, unless I be, by a very superior power, really lifted above these opinions, my poor weak nature is apt to doubt almost every thing. How poor is the enjoyment, how dark is our prospect, when the enlightening rays of true religion are taken from us! I did not expect thus to have opened my heart to thee, but one thing led on to another. I now and then remember a remark of thine, that thou believed a soul was still living to that which is good, whilst it partook of that unity that the poor travellers Zionward are favoured to feel towards each other; I have sometimes hoped, when thinking of it, that I am not yet quite dead to such things; as I feel my heart nearly drawn towards some of those whom I believe to be truly making progress in this blessed journey, and while I at times so peculiarly love the disciple, I hope I am not an enemy to the Master.

First Month, 11*th*, 1801.—I attended both Meetings; what wishes I had at moments for good! and how surprisingly ineffectual they were!

15*th*.—I set off early for Newington, to see J. G. Bevan, who I heard was poorly. I think my visit answered. I met with a very kind reception, and he appeared pleased to see me. He proposed to me reading with the family on First-day evening; which is what I have often thought of, but do not wish to practise until my husband and I are unitedly clearer on the subject.

Second Month, 3*rd*.—This morning, after writing notes, &c., &c., I walked out and went to see a poor woman who I half like and half do not, as there is something in her very odd; however, I spent much time about her. I then read the letters from home, which were comfortable and satisfactory. I was just dressed for company; we had a rather pleasant visit, but I think of late I more and more dislike society of every kind, I really wish for a more retired life; my present constant liability to company seems too much for my weak mind.

4*th*.— I went to Meeting as usual: Sarah Lines mentioned to the Meeting the manner in which she had accomplished her late journey, and the feelings of reward she experienced; her account struck me very much; her influence was, on me at least, truly pleasant and satisfactory. She afterwards named her concern to visit some Meetings in the City of London, which was also done with remarkable simplicity, and I may say, almost humility. I longed for her continued good, and almost prayed she might be kept in a state of humility. For striking is it how liable, at all stages, we are to fall. I almost longed for the good of the religious, as of some far distant from me. Before the Monthly Meeting finished, Mary Bevan got up and addressed herself to the young women, saying we were not to be discouraged at not being called like her (Sarah Lines), but that all who endeavoured to perform their duty, should and would equally meet with their reward. I felt much, and longed for good. I think myself at this time on rather dangerous ground, for retirement of mind, or that necessary watchfulness which keeps us poor mortals out of danger, is what I am nearly a stranger to; and in the state of deadness to religion, that has lately been my experience, I am also tried by great fears about what duty may call me to. If these be fears of my own imagination, how much is truth wanted to overcome them. Seek, seek, until I find, and do not give up till the last!

Third Month, 15*th*.—I felt really better this morning (alluding to previous indisposition) and went to Meeting, but all my small efforts to quiet my thoughts were ineffectual; the same in the afternoon; it is very serious. Really when I awake in the morning I feel a flatness; when I find my great object of the day no longer appears to be even to wish to do the will of my Creator. But I am as one who has in some measure lost his pilot, and is tossed about by the waves of the world. But I trust that there is yet a power that will prevent my drowning; I draw some consolation from my dreams of old, for how often was I near drowning, and yet at last saved!

17*th*.—Mary Ann Galton arrived to day, every room in our house was full, and altogether, with the tooth-ache, I have hardly had spirit to go through it comfortably.

18*th*.—We had a large dinner-party; I felt unusually poorly and nervous at dinner, being fagged with tooth-ache and the numbers around me.

21st.—This morning I proposed to my father to take us to
Richmond Hill, as we had never been there.   After some doubting we agreed to go, and we set off; before we left London it
rained violently, but we persevered, I was fully of the mind it
was better to do so ; but hardly expressed it enough, for I make
myself appear almost weak by my fear of other people.   I feel
with my father almost always a difficulty in boldly doing what I
think right.   One great pleasure in the day has been being so
much with him, and I have quite enjoyed his company.   The
views and country were delightful ; it appeared to do me good
once more to look at the beauties of nature, and to see the little
lambs and all was very pleasant.

25th.—I feel almost overcome with the multiplicity of visit-
ings and goings out.

Fourth Month, 9th.—We set off this morning on our journey
to Norfolk.   I felt leaving my dearest husband.   The beauties
of nature were striking—violets and primroses quite decorated
the hedges.

Fifth Month, 8th.—Of late I have been cumbered with the
little things in life that are not worth being worried about.

I have fixed dinners for the Yearly Meeting with Jane King.

During the fortnight occupied by the Yearly Meeting, St.
Mildred's Court was, according to a very general custom among
the Society, an open house for the reception of the Friends
assembled in London on that occasion, from all parts of the
kingdom : some were inmates there during the time, whilst the
parties at dinner were generally very numerous.   A most curious
remnant of a by-gone generation, was the appearance of the old
and orthodox Friends in the early part of this century.   The
head-dress of the women often consisted of a plain cap, fitting
closely to the head, and over this the black silk hood so well
known in pictures, to which, when abroad, was added a low
crowned broad beaver hat : the voluminous folds, long-peaked
waists, and stiff formality of the drab-coloured camlet gowns,
contrasting far more strangely with the light and classic drape-
ries then worn, brought into vogue during the French Revolu-

tion, than they would have done with the modern-antique fashions now prevailing.

Fifth Month, 15*th*.—We went in the evening to see a Friend (Joseph Lancaster), who kept a school for poor children. I felt a wish that the young man might be preserved in humility ; for I know, from experience, it is a hard matter, when we have the apparent approbation of many, and more particularly of those whom we esteem.

16*th.*—I was rather busy this morning. After dinner, our dear cousin Priscilla arrived, I felt seeing her, I love her very much : being with such, has a great effect on me, where they interest me as she does ; but may I not be led by man, but by his Maker.

22*nd.*—They had a religious opportunity, they begin I think to lose their solemnity from their frequency.

27*th.*—I went to Gracechurch Street Meeting this morning, and to the Meeting of Discipline in the afternoon, which tired me.

29*th.*—After dinner, we attended our Women's Meeting, at four o'clock, which lasted till nearly eight o'clock, it was to me very long and very tedious; indeed it may be, and I doubt not is in great part my own weakness, but to hold fast my faith, I found in this Yearly Meeting, no instrument ought to be looked to. I am afresh come to this conclusion, that only the clear dictates of duty should lead us to act, even in matters of religion ; that we should be very careful in expressing even a religious sentiment, without great clearness, and more particularly where others are concerned. How exceedingly cautiously should religious advice be given to others ! it should not be done, without strong and clear feelings of duty, for I know from experience, such things are apt, even if they be given as encouragement, to discourage or weaken the feeble mind, if out of place ; I believe it better to do too little than too much in them. Notwithstanding the many remarks that I have made, I trust I shall in the end be better for this time, for I have seen much to love and admire in the instruments, and I trust the principle is not weakened within me. May it lead me to seek deeply to serve my Maker in singleness of heart, for that appears the only way to rectitude of conduct ;

and not to forget the numerous rocks there are to split upon, on every side. These observations should teach me the necessity of keeping a constant watch and dependence on my Creator.

Sixth Month, 5th.—I had most of this morning in quietness' which was quite a treat to me ; I wrote my journal, settled my accounts, and was not destitute of a wish to do right : we had many to dinner, which rather vexed me, as I had set my mind on quiet.

15th.—If I can with truth acknowledge it to be my first wish to do my best, although I may not feel the sensible gratification of doing my duty, I may yet be really doing it. If I do all I can, I have no occasion to fear sooner or later meeting with my reward. I was rather disappointed at our having company, indeed we have now little time alone : it is quite a serious thing, our being so constantly liable to interruptions as we are. I do not think, since we married, we have had one fourth of our meals alone. I long for more retirement, but it appears out of our power to procure it ; and therefore it is best to be as patient under interruptions as we can, but I think it a serious disadvantage to young people setting out in life.

Plashet, Seventh Month, 9th. We are so much from home and in such continual bustles, that really when I am here, I feel at a loss for regular employment. I just have time enough to keep things in order ; engagement follows engagement so rapidly, day after day, week after week, owing principally to our number of near connexions, that we appear to live for others, rather than ourselves : our plan of sleeping out so often, I by no means like, and yet it appears impossible to prevent it ; to spend one's life in visiting and being visited seems sad. Joseph Lancaster came in after breakfast, I had some talk with him about poor people ; he enlightened me about his school plans, but not generally about the poor.

10th.—I had to fix with Jane King about the nursery, and to reprove a servant for something I did not approve, which kept me in a state of agitation for some time, it is so trying to me to reprove any one ; it is so very trying to my natural disposition, partly I suppose from a feeling of self-love that does not like being the cause of pain ; partly I suppose from feeling for others.

I mostly feel satisfaction when I take courage to act the mistress, as it is so much out of my nature.

11*th*.—It now and then strikes me to how little end are all these employments that occupy us; we seem principally occupied in clothing, feeding and taking care of our bodies, and yet I trust if even that be done in a right spirit, we still are doing our duty, and it is in these actions about our bodies that our minds and principles act also, if it be our object to do all things to the glory of God. But we are apt rather to do things in subserviency to our own will, rather than the will of our Maker; we therefore devote ourselves to these outward and bodily things. Now, when such things are done, which I believe they may be, under a devotional spirit, we are not injured by being occupied with such trifles.

Eighth Month, 5th.—I feel that when I do my part towards really performing my duty, it sheds a sweet and sober colouring over all my occupations ; but when I do not, it appears to cast a mist that I am obliged to find my way as well as I can, without my guide.

15*th*.—I have had an interesting talk with my dear sister Rachel ; she appears to me to have perceived that, which will direct her steps. But how hard it is deeply, strictly, and for a long time together, to have our first object to serve our Creator —for at first there is a natural glee, as for something new, and then we feel we have to pass through lukewarmness, which is a dangerous state ; I believe one, where many are lost. May I be carried through it !

It is evident that the circumstances in which Elizabeth Fry was placed at St. Mildred's Court, were too fatiguing for her, then approaching her first confinement, so as to depress, not merely her bodily powers and her natural energy, but also in a degree her spiritual liveliness. In anticipation of this event, her active mind had already occupied itself in forming nursery arrangements.

Her eldest child was born in August, and to this event succeeded the pleasures and anxieties of a young mother ; upon

which no one could have entered with a more lively sense, either
of their enjoyment or responsibility.

" My thoughts are now very often in my nursery, fixing plans
for children. I am very full of castles about my good management ; but all must be, should be, held in subserviency to a
great and divine Power, who alone knows what is best for them
and us ; and it is to be hoped He will, in His mercy, guide the
hands of the parents to lead them in the right path in every
way. I am a great friend to close and constant attention to
early education, even the very first years of a child's life."

Ninth Month, 12*th.*—I have hardly had time or strength as
yet to describe the events I have lately passed through. I did
not experience that joy some women describe when my husband
first brought me my little babe, little darling ! I hardly knew
what I felt for it, but my body and spirits were so extremely
weak, I could only just bear to look at those I loved. I felt
the dear baby at first a quiet source of pleasure, but she early
became a subject for my weakness and low spirits to dwell upon,
so that I almost wept when she cried; but I hope, as bodily
strength recovers strength of mind will come with it.

20*th.* —I have now pretty much recovered. I was at Meeting this
morning ; there appears great cause for my being thankful to
have got through so great a trial, and to have a dear little living
girl; but we are not always sensible of the blessings we enjoy.

23*rd.*—Certainly I am ignorant about the management of
such young infants, but I do not feel uneasy about the charge of
her body, from my self-confidence I fear ; but I believe if we
endeavour to do our duty, even in such things, we shall find the
way. I much wish to avoid my mother-in-law's very " cotting"
plan, for a degree of hardiness I think most desirable—I think
being too careful and tender really makes them more subject to
indisposition.

Tenth Month, 1*st.*—My present feelings for the babe are so
acute as to render me at times unhappy, from an over anxiety
about her, such an one, as I never felt before for any one. Now
it appears to me, this over anxiety arises from extreme love, weak
spirits and state of health, and not being under the influence of

principle, that would lead me to overcome these natural feelings, as far as they tend to my misery. For if I were under the influence of principle, I might trust that my dear infant was indeed under the care and protection of an infinitely wise and just Providence, that permits her little sufferings for some good end, that I know not of. How anxiously do I hope this poor dear baby may be held in resignation by me to the Divine will. Oh ! that I might feel dependence on that Almighty arm about her and about other things. Beyond every thing else, I wish to do my duty, idle and relaxed as I am, in performing it.

Mildred's Court, 10*th*.—I here sit hearing the great noise and bustle of the Illumination for Peace ; my dearest babe is sleeping in the room ; my husband and the rest of the party are gone out to see it. This evening I am very tired, and the noise of the mob nearly makes my head ache. This is the way in which they show their joy ! it does not seem to me the right manner of showing our gratitude, as it appears to lead to drunkenness and vice. I think true gratitude should lead us to endeavour to retain the blessing, or to make good use of it by more virtue in ourselves, and encouraging others to the same.

Earlham, 21*st*. —We have had a comfortable journey, meeting them at Thetford was very pleasant, they appeared so delighted to see us. I altogether entered this place in much agitation, our reception was delightful ; my father and all so much admire our little darling, and seemed to love her so dearly that it was delightful to me : it was indeed a striking sight to see them all meet her, so much real interest was shown. Yesterday I went once more to Norwich Meeting, my reception was very warm.

Mildred's Court, Eleventh Month, 25*th*.—My cough has been so poorly that my husband called in Dr. Simms. I asked his advice about our little one being inoculated, he strongly recommended the cow-pox, and said that he would undertake the care of her if we liked : I think highly of his judgment, and I believe it to be our duty to avoid evil, both bodily and mentally. So trifling a complaint as the cow-pox, being likely to prevent so dreadful a disease as the small-pox at least it appears justifiable to try it ; although the idea is not pleasant, it almost looks like taking too much on ourselves to give a child a disease. But I

altogether was easy to do it. I felt a good deal about the operation, which was very little and easily performed.   What a wonderful discovery it is, if it really prevent the small-pox !

30*th.*—I went to see a poor woman, it is always a cross to me
leaving my child, but going over the bridge I enjoy ; the air, sky
and water look so sweetly.

Twelfth Month, 5*th.*—I was up in pretty good time, dressed by
eight, and after reading, settled my great housekeeping accounts.
I wrote to cousin Priscilla, my uncle Barclay and my father.
This evening I feel very flat, rather in a low state, partly perhaps
bodily weakness. I feel almost ready to pant after the courts of
the Lord.

First Month, 26*th,* 1802.—It is more than a month since I
wrote my journal; I am sorry for it, but I have been Martha-
like, and so much engrossed in the affairs of this life, that little
time has been spent in reviewing my conduct; indeed I appear
very much to have taken my flight from spiritual things.   It is
not my feeling bereft of the comforts of religion that alarms me,
it is my not sufficiently seeking after them I fear ; for I hardly
ever am on the watch for the Master's coming.   I may say my
heart has now and then been full, almost to prayer, for my husband, child, and myself ; particularly for my little infant, that we
may not prove stumbling-blocks in its way to salvation ; if it
please God it should live to an age of understanding.   I believe
it would be better for me if I were in a more constant habit of
daily retirement ; for it would afford me time for self-examina-
tion, which I am so unaccustomed to, and if I only sit quietly,
I believe I may find it useful, although I feel of myself I can do
nothing.

28*th.*—I do heartily enjoy our being alone, and falling into
some plans, not being interrupted, I appear naturally to fall into
employment ; and it is so sweet to have quiet plans at my own
dear home.   How much I think my marriage tends to my outward comfort ; it is wonderful to me to observe how every act of
mine has prospered, that has been done under the anxious wish
of serving my Creator in it.

Second Month, 13*th.*—My poor baby has been so poorly,
that we took her to Dr. Willan's ; she has had a cough and is

really unwell. I felt much tired and longed for resignation and patience.

20th.—I felt our dearest child in great danger, as did many besides me, indeed I believe all of us. This was indeed a trial, but I was supported with some resignation of soul, feeling the weight of that part of the prayer, " Thy will and not mine be done."

21st.—As the morning advanced, my little infant began to change from a very feverish state to an almost deadly languid one, that I believe most present, thought might be the beginning of a more awful change. She sat on my lap, I happened to be also very faint at the time; I think I may say, I felt resigned to the all-wise dispensations of Providence, which was a great blessing ; my mind felt depending on that Power that alone can support in the day of trial. I desire to feel that of myself I can do nothing, and that I may remember the blessing of being able to say, " Thy will and not mine be done."

23rd.—Our little one appears mending, although very poorly, faint, and weak : her recovery seems more than I can enter into at present with a joyful heart. But I feel rather as if quietly waiting for the will of her Maker to be done. Some would perhaps call me insensible to the blessing. May I continue to look to the all merciful fountain of Good, and hold my submission to His will, and properly estimate the numerous blessings afforded me : and may I be thankful for my little one. My prayer seems to have been heard, that whether she lived or died she might not suffer very much.

Fourth Month, 19*th.*—Oh ! may my obedience keep pace with my knowledge, at this time ; my knowledge of good appears small ; my longings to be better are only known by a Superior Power, who I trust will in time have mercy on me. I have this day prayed, that in this day of darkness I may not prove an obstruction in the way of others ; truly a South Land is my portion, I only long for the wells of living water.

Fifth Month, 18*th.*—The sight of my uncle Joseph this morning rejoiced me ; he is to me, in every point of view, so dear, I love him as a religious character, and as my near and dear relation. We had many friends to dinner and many to supper.

19*th.*—This day Yearly Meeting began generally. I was in my usual lukewarm flat state, full of the wanderings of imagination ; but I believe, as a spectator, Meetings were more satisfactory than last year. We had a very large number to dinner.

31st.—Yearly Meeting is now, I am happy to say, finished. I attended all the Meetings but one. In some of them I was much more interested than last year, and felt for the interest of the Society. We have seen a good deal of Friends, and I think I admire them more than I did last year. I have had a few more serious feelings than usual, I have been always devoted to the world, except now and then, when my heart has anxiously hoped for something better. I have felt very much how we are all surrounded with continual temptations, and how very hard it is to hold fast that which is good ; I see so many faults in myself, that I fear there are many I know nothing of, from not sufficiently seeking for them ; for I observe faults in others who are better than myself, that I believe they know nothing of.

Earlham, Sixth Month, 7th.—I have felt and enjoyed the beauties of nature ; I am so unused to quiet time, I hardly know how to spend it to advantage. I have feared they would think me trifling in my pursuits, I read so much less than they do.

Mildred's Court, Eighth Month, 19th.—To-day we have been married two years : time slips through quickly, trials and pleasures before unknown, have indeed been felt by me, trials and joys of many kinds. The love of a husband, the unity experienced ; the love of a child, the maternal feelings, when under subordination, are real and great sources of enjoyment, they are apt to occupy the mind perhaps too much. My family is to me in more comfortable order than it was, at least I feel more mistress of it. My forgetfulness I find a material hindrance to me in many such concerns. In the afternoon, I was a good deal with my dearest Joseph.

Ninth Month, 11th.—In the evening my husband and I went to Vauxhall, to see a person who sent to beg of us, and to my surprise, found her dress, house, and furniture, almost like a gentlewoman's. Beggars of this sort I cannot understand, not being accustomed to them : they are people difficult to serve, as they ask to so large an amount. Now this person wants £30, to clear her only of debt ; and I have other reasons for not wishing to have too much to do with them, they live so far off. We went and returned by water.

13*th.*—I had a very interrupted morning. In the afternoon, I went to see after a poor woman, and also to get a place for the little black girl, which took me some time, so that I was out till late.

At this time, Elizabeth Fry took a long journey into the North of England with her husband; a few entries respecting it are presented to the reader.

Coventry, Tenth Month, 2nd.—We were up in good time, and went to see Shakspeare's monument, at Stratford-upon-Avon; a sweet country churchyard; in the Church we saw the monument. We breakfasted at Warwick, and saw the Castle and Church; the outside of the Castle I liked very much, the inside pretty well. We are at an unpleasant inn here; but I have learnt one lesson —that I do not think in travelling we are sufficiently cautious in our behaviour to inn servants, but hurry them and worry them too much : I hope to be more cautious in future. I went to see D—— L—— and his wife, and by accident went to the wrong house; I made several droll blunders, and became confused.

Wolverhampton, 6th.—During our journey here, I was very low and anxious on account of our little baby, who appeared so uneasy, and in much pain. She seemed suddenly really unwell. I wish my heart not to be too much set on her or her health; for I should endeavour to remember, she is taken care of by One infinitely wiser than I am. All medicine, gum-lancing, &c., is one of my trials, for I do not like or approve putting children to unnecessary pain, unless I have good ground for believing it right to do it; and yet I fear my cowardice improperly preventing my doing it.

Colebrook Dale, Tenth Month, 7th.—We had an early tea at Shifnal, a nice place, and then went forward to the Dale. The thoughts of going there were strange, after having felt so much as I had before at that place.

Rock Ferry, 10th.—We admired Chester, the town is so extraordinary; from the walks on the walls the country is beautiful. We could not prudently go over to Liverpool on account of the rain, therefore we remained here, which I believe we all enjoyed; the quiet within was so pleasant, when the storms without were so violent, and I enjoyed my beloved husband's company; what earthly pleasure is equal to the enjoyment of real unity with the nearest of all ties, husband and children.

Liverpool, 12*th*.—Our patience was rather tried, by waiting from breakfast time till twelve o'clock, for a passage over. My fears of the water are surprisingly gone off, I hardly felt any fear, although the wind was high and we sailed. I believe as we grow older, and have greater and more serious things to occupy us, those little feelings go off; I do not think I am nearly such a coward about some little things, as I was before I married.

Manchester, 17*th*.—We drank tea at John Thorp's; I really admire and love that man, I think we seldom see so much of good, united with a cultivated understanding, and the sweet simplicity of religion, as in him. I long for help to penetrate the clouds that surround me, for I feel that of myself I can do nothing.

Keswick, 25*th*.—This morning we went in the rain to see a very fine waterfall, it was a grand and beautiful sight; but I do not much like this country, at this time of the year, it looks so barren and dreary. This evening I went with Joseph on horseback to see some fine waterfalls. There is too much water in this place, and about here, to please my taste, too much lake, and too much of barren mountain; too little snugness, and too few fine trees.

26*th*.—This would have appeared to me some time ago, rather a fearful day; we first took a long ride, part of it over rather frightful roads, on the edge of a precipice, without any wall or guard to it. This evening, my husband and I climbed Skiddaw, when we arrived at the top, after some pain and fatigue, we were almost in a whirlwind, and so extremely cold and damp, being in the midst of a cloud, and the wind so violent, that it appeared almost impossible to stand against it: however we got down safely.

Mildred's Court, Eleventh Month, 18*th*.—We have had a prosperous journey, and have at last arrived at our comfortable home. It really looks quite sweet and nice; it is a great thing to have gone so far and returned home safely.

Their family was at this time increased by her brother Samuel Gurney coming to London, to learn the details of business there. He resided for some years at St. Mildred's Court. The shelter of such a residence, in that great and depraved Metropolis, can hardly be too highly estimated, but besides this, he had the advantage of his sister's close and watchful care. She had been much attached to him, when young ; and it was an interest and pleasure to her to have him for an inmate. Her labours were eminently blessed to him—and in his faithful love through life, she reaped a rich reward.

First Month, 5th, 1803.—I feel hardly willing to begin this year without observing how very numerous my blessings are ; as far as outward blessings go, I believe I want nothing : may I endeavour to be aware of it, and may it stimulate me afresh to strive to serve that Power which has conferred them on me My secret trials and temptations are known by no man, that inclination to lukewarmness of mind, and also forgetfulness of what is good are powerful temptations. They do not, like some others, make a very conspicuous appearance ; but they undermine our strength, for want of sufficient effort and sufficient watchfulness; I look forward with much hope, that I may be supported in the day of expected trial. But if I seek so little for a close acquaintance with what is good ; if I cannot now endeavour humbly to place my confidence in the Power that alone can deliver, is it likely that in such emergency I shall be able to do it. I believe if rightly influenced, I might in some small measure rejoice, if I could feelingly believe, that these afflictions which are but for a moment work for us a far more exceeding and eternal weight of glory. Suffer we must in this world :—and the less we kick against the pricks, the happier for us.

She thus records the birth of her second child, which took place, March 25th.

Fourth Month, 12th.—My heart abounded with joy and gratitude when my dear little girl was born perfect and lovely. Words are not equal to express my feelings, for I was most mercifully dealt with, my soul was so quiet and so much supported.

Plashet, Fifth Month, 21*st.*—I have been long prevented writing my journal, by a severe attack of indisposition. It is difficult exactly to express what I have gone through, but it has been now and then a time of close trial ; my feelings being such at times, as to be doubtful whether life or death would be my portion. One night I was I believe very seriously ill ; I never remember feeling so forcibly how hard a trial it was in prospect to part with life. Much as my mind, as well as body, was then tried in this emergency, still I felt forcibly an inward support, and it reminded me of that text of Scripture, " Can a woman forget her sucking child, yea they may forget, yet will I not forget thee." And then I told those around me, that I was so ill, I could almost forget my child ; but I felt the existence of a Power that could never forget. I have gone through much since, in various ways from real bodily weakness, and also the trials of a nervous imagination : no one knows but those who have felt them, how hard they are to bear, for they lead the mind to look for trouble, and it requires much exertion not to be led away by them ; nothing I believe allays them so much as the quieting influence of religion, and that leads us to endeavour after quietness under them, not looking beyond the present. But they are a regular bodily disorder, that I believe no mental exertion can cure or overcome, but we must endeavour not to give way to them.

Mildred's Court, Sixth Month, 5*th.*—Since I last wrote, I have been gradually becoming better, but still I feel not in usual health ; my nerves are in an irritable state, I am soon overcome and overdone. I have been at Meeting, and am now once more entering upon my usual occupations : I fear I am not so much benefited as I ought to be by the illness I have lately gone through ; for I have so forcibly felt—What am I, without a hold on something beyond this life ?

Earlham, Seventh Month, 30*th.*—I went to Norwich this morning with my husband, and when there, we received a letter from William, expressing a desire for Joseph's immediate return. The account rather vexed me ; and also the gloomy appearance about the French coming, cast a gloom over the party ; John came in

8

the evening, and it was truly pleasant, all twelve of us, and the two children being here together. But partly owing to circumstances, the uncertainty of human events so deeply impressed me, that I could not avoid feeling the doubt of our all meeting again.

The fear of a French invasion, and the daily expectation of their landing, took such hold of people at this time, that Mr. Joseph Fry was summoned by his brother, " to be at his post." On his return, he found preparations had been made for flooding the marshes of the river Lee, and breaking down the bridges on the Essex road ; whilst his father-in-law was also prepared, so soon as the French should land, to convey his daughters into the Isle of Ely ; still regarded by the East Anglian portion of England as a " Camp of refuge."

Mildred's Court, Eighth Month, 22nd.—My brother William came to town in haste, to say my mother was come home very ill. I went with Dr. Willan to Plashet, to see her. I was quite sorry to find her so ill, and felt real love for her. My time is very much occupied with other people, indeed I find it has a very dissipating effect ; and it is difficult to keep my mind in its right centre, when it is so often diverted from it.

Tenth Month, 4th.—After reading a little, I went some way off to see a poor woman. After searching a long time in one of the disagreeable parts of London, I could not find her, but I was directed to another poor person who lived near the place, and although I believe the first woman had deceived me, it led me to serve two others that I have reason to think really wanted. I felt quite in my element serving the poor, and although I was much tired with looking about, it gave me much pleasure, it is an occupation my nature is so fond of ; I wish not to take merit to myself beyond my desert, but it brings satisfaction with it more than most things.

Upton, Third Month, 15th, 1804.—Since I last wrote, I have more closely witnessed the scene of death, than I ever did before. Last First day morning, about three o'clock, my mother died ; I was with her at times on Seventh day, and although I have every reason to believe she died happily, I did not experience those awful, sweet feelings, I should have looked for, at so serious a time. On First day morning, I went into the room, and sat some time with the corpse : it was very affecting to me to see it, and I was a good deal overcome, and felt it much. I have been surprised how little this event has led me into a serious state of mind, I fear it has not had so profitable an effect upon me as it ought.

The death of her mother-in-law, a woman of powerful mind and understanding, united Elizabeth Fry still more closely with her husband's father ; to whom she had been always much attached.   From the time of her marriage, he had treated her with uniform kindness and attention : and now in his affliction, it was her pleasure as well as her duty, to unite with his own children in soothing his declining years ; more time was consequently passed at Plashet with him, and his only daughter, Elizabeth.

At this period of her life, the poor shared much of her attention, and notwithstanding the impediments offered by a great Metropolis, to a young and delicate woman personally visiting them, she persevered occasionally in this habit, until withdrawn from it, by resideuce in the country, and the increase of more important duties.   Her energy and courage in pursuing this object were great, as is proved by the following anecdote.

One cold winter day she was accosted by a woman asking charity, in the street, with a half naked little child in her arms, very ill with the hooping-cough ; grieved at the appearance of the child, and her suspicions excited by the evasive answers of the woman, Mrs. Fry offered to accompany her home, and there relieve her necessities : this the woman tried to elude, but determined on her purpose, she succeeded in following her into a low, back street, where, in a wretched, filthy house, the melancholy spectacle presented itself, of a number of sick and neglected infants, not only without comforts, but with the aggravations of misery. The next day, when the medical attendant of her own children went at her request to assist the little sufferers, the room was empty, woman and children gone, nor was any trace ever found of them. On inquiry among the neighbours it was discovered that these were parish children, put to this woman to nurse, who kept them in this condition not merely to assist her purposes of mendicity but with the intention of shortening their lives, and then, by concealing their death, receiving the pittance allotted for their maintenance.

It has already been shown, that in 1801, her attention was called to Joseph Lancaster, who, struggling under difficulties and embarrassments, had assembled around him a large school of very poor children in an upper chamber in Southwark.

She had also formed some valuable friendships with superior and excellent people. Of this number was her cousin Joseph Gurney Bevan, her father's early friend, whom she especially esteemed ; John Hull of Uxbridge, and Rachel Smith, a Friend living in London, all judicious counsellors and her frequent companions.

During the next few years, she was permitted to pass through many illnesses and much suffering ; but her soul appears to have been elevated and purified in the furnace ; deep conflict was often her portion, until her bonds were burst, and she was enabled " to rejoice in the Lord, and joy in the God of her salvation." Earnest desires for the religious good of others, sprang up in her heart. As secondary things were swallowed up in spiritual, her mind became deeply impressed with the belief, that it would be required at her hands, publicly to advocate the cause of God her Saviour, as a minister. This was an awful prospect, from which her whole nature recoiled.

Seventh Month, 10*th.*—Since I last wrote I have gone on pretty comfortably in most respects ; at times a degree of lowness, but I

have altogether been much more encouraged than I was, and feel
at present able to leave my fears, trusting in the mercy of Him
who may afflict.   Oh! may I be ready to bear!   I have had
many desires after good, and I think reading a little of " No
Cross, no Crown," has been rather a stimulus to me, to endeavour after more strictly attending to that voice that instructs us
how to take up the daily cross, in overcoming our natural pro-
pensities.   I was reading in Jeremiah to-day, " Cursed be they
who serve the Lord deceitfully," and I hoped that might not
be my case.   What I long for is, to serve the Lord with strict
integrity, keeping self-love in subserviency.

Her eldest son was born in July ; her confinement was followed
by a trying and tedious illness.

Eighth Month, 19*th.*—I have been confined three weeks to-
day, and I have a nice little boy.   I at present feel body and
mind very weak ; and so I have done most of the time.

Bath, Ninth Month 24*th.*—Since I last wrote, I have been
very unwell, and passed through great suffering, owing to great
sickness, faintness, and nervous irritability : however, each trial
has had its alleviation ; I have not once quite sunk ; I have experienced, that though at times it has been rather hard to bear,
I do not think it has been too much for me ; for although I
have felt the wounding hand, yet I have also soon found that
the same Power could, and did, make whole.

Mildred's Court, First Month, 14*th,* 1805.—A new year
begun—one of my first desires upon waking was, that I might
improve in it.

Plashet, Second Month, 5*th.*—Since I last wrote, I have been
much occupied with many things : rather more than usual about
the poor.   I have been desirous that attending to them as I do,
may not prove a snare to me, for I think acting charitably
leads us often to receive more credit than we deserve, or at
least to fancy so ; it is one of those things that give my nature pleasure, therefore I believe I am no further praiseworthy
than that I give way to a natural inclination.   Attending the
afflicted is one of those things that so remarkably brings its

reward with it, that we may rest in a sort of self-satisfaction which is dangerous; but I often feel the blessing of being so situated, as to be able to assist the afflicted, and sometimes a little to relieve their distresses.

11th.—We ought to make it an object in conversation and in conduct, to endeavour to oblige those we are with, and rather to make the pleasure of others our object than our own ; I am clear it is a great virtue to be able constantly to yield in little things, it begets the same spirit in others, and renders life happy.

Fifth Month, 7th.—Yesterday, my sister, Eliza Fry, was here; we were saying something about the children's dress ; and she remarked that for the sake of others, (she meant the fear of not setting a good example,) she would not do so and so. I said it struck me that those who do their duty with integrity, are serving others as well as themselves, and do more real good to the cause of true religion, than in looking much outwardly, either to what others do or think. I think that conscience will sometimes lead us to feel for others, and not act so as materially to hurt a weak brother; but I believe we should seldom find that we hurt those whose opinion would be worth caring for, if we kept close to the witness in our own hearts. If I were going to do a thing, I should endeavour to find whether it appeared to me in any way wrong, and whether I should feel easy to do it ; looking secretly for help where it is to be found, and there I believe I should leave it ; and if it led me to act rather differently from some, I should probably be doing more good to society, than in any conformity, merely on account of others, for if I should be preserved in the way of obedience in other things, it would in time show from whence such actions sprung, and I think this very spirit of con- forming in trifles to the opinion of others, leads into forms that may one day prove a stumbling-block to the progress of our Society; whereas, if we attend to the principle that brought us together, it will lead us out of forms, and not into them.

Earlham, Sixth Month, 7th.—There is quite a change since I last wrote, I have passed through much illness among the chil- dren ; the Yearly Meeting, and since that, coming here. After my return from Plashet, dear little Rachel was very poorly, and poor John ; all these things tried me, but I endeavoured to bear

them with patience and cheerfulness. The Yearly Meeting was
very interesting to me, I felt a good deal about it; in the first
place, I am struck afresh with the beauty of our principles :
but so am I also with the great want of simplicity and integrity
in us who profess them ; for I am willing to believe, that if we
more closely attended to. it, there would be more unity, more
clearness, and more promptness in our manner of attending to
the business of the Society. I used to fear that a selfish principle frequently rose up amongst us, rather than the simple love
and fear of God, which spirit I think alone should rule in the
management of the discipline intended to protect our religious
principles. The dread I had over me, in Plaistow Meeting, of
saying something, impressed me in most of the Meetings. I had
such clear ideas in some of the Meetings ; but I did not believe
it necessary for my salvation to do it, and I believe hardly any
motive short of that could induce me. Once in hearing the
queries answered, How many were negligent in attending Week-
day Meetings ? it struck me, it arose from allowing the business
of the world to stand too much in competition with the things
of God, and of how much more importance one was than the
other; for a right attention to religious duties, enables us much
better to perform our temporal ones. I have enjoyed coming
here, and being with them.

Seventh Month, 3rd.—It appears to me, that we who desire to
be the servants of Christ, must expect to do a part of our Master's
work; which no doubt is to bear with the weaknesses and infirmities of human nature, and if we be favoured to feel them, and
not sink under them, we may be enabled in time to help others
to bear their burdens ; and it appears to me, that all Christian
travellers must expect to pass through, in their measure, the
temptations and trials their Master did on earth.

Mildred's Court, 19th.—Yesterday, and the day before, I
have been driven from one thing to another, and from one person to another, as is usual in this place. I have feared my attention being quite diverted from good. But I have also thought
that doing our duty is most effectually serving the Lord. May
I therefore endeavour to do mine, and not be impatient at my
numerous interruptions, but strive to centre my mind in a

humble desire to do the will of my Creator, which will through
all create a degree of quietness.

Mildred's Court, Second Month, 15th, 1806.—I have been confined nearly all this week with a bad cough, and still continue
poorly. I have particularly felt the vacancy of all outward help,
or consolation, or protection ; neither reading good books, writing journals, nor anything else, will, or can do : but placing
our dependence on the Power, that calls us out of darkness into
light, and that alone can lead us and point out to us the rocks
on which we are likely to split, for though we may certainly profit
by the experience of others, yet there is a new way as it were for
each to tread in : and they are not the same temptations which
assail all travellers Zionward, but different natures are differently
tried ; all must first seek for light to guide them (individually),
that will teach them in the right time what to do, and what to
leave undone, and prove in the end their strong tower, and
preservation from all harm.

Earlham, Third Month, 8th.—These words of Haggai strike
me, i. 5, 6, " Now therefore thus saith the Lord of hosts ; consider your ways. Ye have sown much, and bring in little ; ye
eat, but ye have not enough ; ye drink, but ye are not filled
with drink ; ye clothe you, but there is none warm ; and he that
earneth wages earneth wages to put them into a bag with holes."
Whether they may not be applied to myself and some others,
who go on as it were, saving seed not of the best sort, too much
mixed with our own desires, our own gratifications, and therefore we bring forth little ; instead of saving that pure seed of
doing the will of our Heavenly Father for His sake, that would
truly increase and bring in much to us, even more than we should
want for ourselves, but we might even have to spare for others.
Truly we eat, but have we enough ? we taste how good the Lord
is, but do we satisfy the hungry part within us ? In the same
way we drink, but do we seek with sufficient earnestness to
be filled with drink ; we clothe ourselves, but do we not want
warmth of clothing ? do we not want in zeal, in good works ;
and that warm love that would lead us nearer and nearer to
that pure fountain of life, that alone can satisfy poor, hungry,
seeking souls.

Plashet, Seventh day Morning.—Feeling myself going on, as it were driven by the current of the world; I desire, if possible, to stop myself, and examine for what end am I thus busy? Is it to gratify self-love, or is my motive, that all that I do, should be done in the service of Him whom I desire to serve?

Fifth Month, 13th.—There is One only who knows my heart, and its great wants. To Him then I look, even to Him who has borne our infirmities. Teach me Thy way, lead me in the paths of righteousness for Thy name sake; give me strength in weakness, if thou seest meet, O Lord! that I may overcome temptation. O Lord! teach me to do Thy will towards those nearly connected with me: may I be a faithful steward of what may be committed to my trust.

Elizabeth Fry having been appointed by the Friends of Grace-church-street Meeting, a visitor to the school and workhouse belonging to the Society at Islington, entered upon the employment with no little interest as congenial to her former tastes and habits. She visited the school as often as her other engagements would permit, always to the general pleasure of the children, who soon learned to appreciate her interest in them, and desires for their good.

Fifth Month, 15th.—Yesterday I went to the workhouse to spend the evening with the children; a prospect I have had in view some time, almost ever since I have been on the appointment. I took them things for tea: I dreaded going on many accounts, fearing I should not feel at liberty to make any remarks I might wish to the children during their reading, which it was my principal object in going to attend. I did not exactly see my way; however, I thought I would (as Friends say) make my way. I found after tea, they did not read till nearly eight, and I could not remain later than a little past seven. I spoke to the governess about it, and she was quite willing to alter the hour, and so was the stewardess. I proposed reading a little pamphlet that has lately come out by Frederick Smith, to children. There was a solemnity during reading it, so that Ann Withers was in tears most of the time, and some of the children were disposed that way; afterwards, when we had finished, I endeavoured to weigh whether I really had anything to say to them or not; I thought that I had, and therefore took up the book as if to explain it; making my own remarks which appeared to affect the children and the governess, so that those who were on the point of tears really wept. Now this event has made me feel rather odd; it is marvellous to me how I got courage to do it before Ann Withers. I have felt so desirous not to stamp such a thing too highly, for I am ready to believe, though the party appeared to feel what I said so much, it was principally owing to their great tenderness, as that which I said seemed rather to flow naturally from my heart and understanding, than anything really deep from the living fountain. I have desired that this little event may not encourage me too much, for hard things seemed made quite easy. Oh! that in anything like a religious duty, I may never go beyoud the right Guide, nor ever give self the praise. Keep me humble and dependent on Thee, O Lord! even if self suffer in being made so.

Mildred's Court, 21*st.*—The Yearly Meeting has been begun for us for some days, as we have had company here very often since Seventh day. On Second day, we had rather a choice party to dinner, and to me a very solemn opportunity after : I can hardly describe what passed, but it was of that nature, that I considered it as an increase of talent committed to our charge ; and ought indeed afresh to stimulate to seek after and depend upon Him, who alone can protect us. How much I desire that Friends may at this time get beyond the natural part, that is indeed corruptible ; and get down to the spiritual part, that will unite us in the love of Christ, and lead us to endeavour in meekness and forbearance one towards another to come at the right thing. I know well the harmony of Friends is great ; but my fear is, lest the natural part should be disposed to take a part in spiritual things, and sometimes lead us to judge from externals one of another, and so mar that spiritual beauty that would otherwise show itself, and perhaps beguile some into the way of godliness.

Her fourth child was born June 1st, 1806.

Sixth Month, 8th.—This day week I was confined with a sweet boy. How much do I now desire, that I may be able to leave all things to the Allwise Disposer of events, trusting in his wisdom and mercy; so far indeed I have abundant cause for thankfulness, and though my poor mind has at times passed through a little of the depths; yet I have felt the delivering power near at hand : may I hope that in the right time it will again come to my help !

Seventh Month, 4th.—Once more so occupied with life and its concerns, that last night I could not write; I felt it a cause of thankfulness being able to get through the day.

6th.—It struck me this morning at Meeting, that in states when we appear to have no power of our own, no energy, and no capability to do any good thing, our cry is heard, and our petitions come in a more acceptable form, than sometimes when full of power, vigour and life. How much do I desire that above all things, I may have a life in doing the will of my Creator. I am ready to believe that I had rather suffer affliction to be what I ought to be, than to enjoy the pleasures of life, if less profitable.

Mildred's Court, Eleventh Month, 10th.—I have received a very sweet and encouraging letter, from my beloved cousin J. G. Bevan. This led me for many hours in the day, to be in a craving state for spiritual food, and led me to anxious desires that the work might be perfected in me, and that nothing of the creature may ever stand in competition with the will and the work of the Creator.

Early in December, Mr. and Mrs. Fry, went to Earlham, to be present at the marriage of her sister Louisa, to Samuel Hoare, the son of Samuel Hoare, Esq., of Hampstead, Middlesex.

Earlham, Twelfth Month, 6th.—On Fourth day morning, the 24th, our dear Louisa was married at Tasborough Meeting. A very serious and interesting time to us all. My father, all of us eleven, my husband and Samuel Hoare. The Meeting was very solemn, and did to me sweetly license them in their solemn engagement, it was like a seal set to it. There was testimony upon testimony, and blessing upon blessing, from the ministers present; and what was better than all to me, a sweet inward covering over the Meeting.   All appeared unity and love ; rather remarkable to see so large a family all so nearly sympathizing, and closely united.   My dear brother John was sweet indeed, and deeply feeling; may it last in him, and may he truly find the pearl of great price.

Newmarket, Twelfth Month, 31*st.*—The last day of this year, looking forward to the next.   Thou who knowest what our trials and temptations are, keep us faithful unto Thee ; preserve us from the snares of the enemy, be with us all as a family ; and bless the dispensations of Thy Providence to us, by drawing us nearer to Thyself through them !

First Month, 6*th,* 1807.—My dear brother John, I believe this morning will marry our dear cousin Elizabeth Gurney, may they truly prove blessings to each other, and to both families.

Among the papers of Elizabeth Fry was found the following letter, but whether ever sent to her brother and sister, there are now no means of ascertaining ; it is however too valuable to omit here.

My very dear John and Elizabeth.

I leave off writing my journal, to write to you ; for whilst I was expressing in it my feelings, the love I then felt and now feel for thee, dear John, came so powerfully before me, that instead of writing it in my journal, I wish to express it to you both.   My interest and sympathy is great in your present undertaking ; and my desire, sincere, that in your union you may indeed obtain the Divine blessing.   What is the Divine blessing, but in the first place to be cleansed from our sins and weaknesses so fully, that we may in innocency compass the altar of God availingly. And secondly, to live under the protection of Him, who is able to save us from every hurtful thing, and turn all the circumstances of our lives to good account ; so as in them to bless us and draw us nearer to Him, who can do all things for us, both inwardly and outwardly.

It is hardly likely that I shall see you before, or soon after you marry, you have, you know, my good wishes for your prosperity in every way, but you must expect some bitter mixed with the sweet cup ; for without it we should rest too much in the enjoyments of life. I think you will be a very devoted couple to each other ; therefore I advise you to be on your guard, and to remember that all natural things, and natural affections amongst the rest, are corruptible. That there is something better that must be loved first, and that we must hold all things in subjection to this Power, that alone must be worshipped, and that alone can sanctify all other things to us, and so make them partake of the enduring, powerful, heavenly nature. This is what I desire all my affections to be tinged with ; that I may love those who are near to me, not alone with my own natural feelings, but that a better love may be felt in me towards them ; a love that is not affected by the separations and trials of life.

Mildred's Court, First Month, 27th.—Do with me as Thou wilt, only let me be Thine ! This is in measure my desire this morning, and that whether it be in heights or depths, I may spend my life to Thy glory.

Mrs. Fry again travelled into Norfolk to attend the wedding of her sister Hannah.

She was married to Thomas Fowell Buxton, Esq., afterwards Sir T. Fowell Buxton, Bart.

Fifth Month, 20th.—I have been deeply interested in my beloved Hannah's marriage, which was satisfactory ; I desire their good every way. Now I am again entering Yearly Meeting : this leads me to various feelings and some desires after the good of the whole body, more particularly that we may rest in no form, and not make too much of it. How very poor I feel, but I admire at the merciful hand that still appears extended to help me.

Sixth Month, 22nd.—To day I have been to try to draw a poor young woman from her evil course : I felt my own incapability to help her, and my lukewarmness. But I desire that if it be right I may receive a little help, and be enabled in some measure, to assist in drawing a poor sinner into a better path, and if such should be the case, may I give the glory where it is due.

Plashet, Seventh Month, 20th.—I have been, I think I may say very ill, with something of an intermittent fever. I desire to express a little, what I have gone through. I have certainly at times been very closely pressed, bodily and mentally : but for all that, I have no cause to complain, but indeed to give thanks. I very soon found I had but one place to fly to, but one sure place of refuge, and that was, humbly to endeavour with all my power, wholly to give myself up to God, knowing His dispensations were allwise : as for my poor soul, I could only look to His mercy and forgiveness ; for he can pardon in mercy, little as I deserve it. I could offer few words on behalf either of soul or body, but the desire was to be wholly given up to Him, who could do all things for me ; I desired to leave all. Oh, how do I crave that I may, in sickness and in health, and under every dispensation, be wholly given up, body, soul, and spirit, and no longer falter as between two opinions.

Eighth Month.—At Meeting, Richard Philips spoke on the necessity of faith, I felt tendered and refreshed, and so well altogether that health appeared quickly returning ; but, not unlike the events of life, the next morning I awoke ill ; in a suffering state, and very faint. I had two days of considerable trial from such very deeply painful feelings of bodily weakness and sinking, then a day of comparative rest. The next day a return of my old complaint, the fever, and one more since then. It was of a very suffering nature to me whilst it lasted ; but still I may say with truth, I once more have only cause to give thanks, for the burden did not appear too hard, and there was a merciful and healing power open to my cry, for I was helped, and my prayers appeared to be granted. But I found that looking back to the help that I had before experienced would not do ; the manna of yesterday was not for to-day !

QUESTIONS FOR MYSELF.

First,—Hast thou this day been honest and true in performing thy duty towards thy Creator in the first place : and, secondly, towards thy fellow-creatures ; or hast thou sophisticated and flinched.

Second, —Hast thou been vigilant in frequently pausing in the hurry and career of the day, to see who thou art endeavouring to serve ; whether thy Maker or thyself ? And every time that trial or temptation assailed thee, didst thou endeavour to look steadily to the Delivering Power ; even to Christ who can do all things for thee.

Third,—Hast thou endeavoured to perform thy relative duties faithfully : been a tender, loving, yielding wife, where thy own will and pleasure were concerned ; a tender, yet steady mother with thy children, making thyself quickly and strictly obeyed, but careful in what thou requirest of them : a kind, yet honest mistress, telling thy servants of their faults, when thou thinkest it for their or thy good, but never unnecessarily worrying thyself or them about trifles : and to every one endeavouring to do as thou wouldest be done unto ?

Mildred's Court, First Month, 1st, 1808.—A new year begun —and to me, with some weight at my heart ; oh, for my beloved's welfare, as well as my own and our dear lambs, spiritually. May none of us prove an injury to the principle we profess ; and may we in all our undertakings, that originate in evil, be marred and stopped in our course : oh ! I can say, if Thou seest meet, lead us not into temptation, but deliver us from evil. I know how frail we all are, may we not be utterly cast off ; may we in the end prove our integrity, and all be given up to follow the good alone, in the newness of life. How grievous to serve the evil one ; and how sweet to follow Him, the Shepherd of Israel ; and lead others, in ever so small a measure to do so. O Lord ! I pray for mercy, give us not up to the will of the enemy : may we live to show forth Thy praise ! I am favoured in some small measure to hope in the Lord, and to rejoice in the power of His salvation ; for indeed He can deliver from evil.

15th.—I yesterday felt a good deal about Mary Ann D—— coming to teach the children and live here, fearing for the peace of our nursery establishment ; and I did desire that as far as was right, I might in these matters receive the Divine Blessing : for to me it is no light matter to direct my household and children ; and I feel in that, as in all other things, without Divine assistance what can I do ?

Second Month, 18*th.*—Oh, that my faith fail not, but that I may be enabled to look to the right place for support!

Her fifth child was born February 19th.   In the May following Elizabeth, wife of her eldest brother John, and daughter of her uncle, Richard Gurney of Keswick, died, after a lingering illness.   She was cut off in the bloom of youth, and the height of human happiness ; at a period when the large family of which she was a member, were in the enjoyment of this world.s brightest prosperity.

They possessed health, affluence, and rather uncommon endowments of person, disposition, and talent.   Little acquainted with the trials of life, and intimately connected with each other ; the shock occasioned by the early death of this interesting and beautiful young woman, vibrated with a sort of surprise as well as sorrow, to the utmost limits of their extensive circle.   Death with its melancholy accompaniments was strange to them; for this was their first affliction since the loss of their mother.   It was the cause of arresting the hitherto unchecked stream of their prosperity; yet in the overruling Providence of God, it was singularly blessed to them, from the effect produced upon their minds, and the circumstances that arose out of it.

By the desire of their widowed brother, the sisters sought for him in his extreme affliction, the visits and counsels of the Rev. Edward Edwards, Lecturer of Saint Margaret's, Lynn.   This gentleman, an early friend of Venn, acquainted with Scott and Newton, and at the time we speak of, in habits of intimacy with Mr. Simeon, of Cambridge, and other clergymen of similar sentiments, proved indeed, a messenger of good to the Gurney family ; who were all more or less awakened to the importance of a reli-

gious life,—but were making their way through many difficulties
and doubts—not one of them established in any form or sect
excepting Elizabeth Fry ; the others tending more or less to the
Church of England or to Friends, but all anxious and alive to
the subject. Mr. Edwards directed them in their affliction to
the wisdom and the mercy of the hand that had smitten them ;
and as time permitted them to turn their attention to controversial subjects, he supplied them with books, and assisted them in
becoming acquainted with the differences existing in the Christian
Church, and by leading them to study these subjects upon
Scriptural grounds, enabled them to decide for themselves. It
was not without pain, that she, who had so decidedly chosen the
path of Friends, saw others so dear to her, as decidedly choosing
another way and uniting themselves with the Church of England ; but, as each one became established in his own course,
some one way, some the other, a wonderful union and communion sprang up among them, so that their bond in natural
things , was not stronger, than that, which united them, as devoted worshippers of the same Lord.

Fifth Month, 27*th.*—Since I last wrote, I have gone through
much trouble. Last Seventh day week, an account was received
of the death of our much loved sister, Elizabeth Gurney. I felt it
deeply; during her illness my heart cried unto the Lord for mercy,
and He would take her unto Himself, and that her transgressions might be blotted out. Being still so much inclined to
trying nervous feelings, made me feel it in a more painful way :
not finding any rest away from them all, Joseph and I went to
Lynn—an afflicting time. On Third day morning, I had a
most affecting meeting with dear John, yet felt myself far too
week, poor, and in too painfully nervous a state, to afford him
comfort; but rather needed it myself. It was a very melting
interview : the remainder of the day being spent in the house
with the dear remains was really sweet to me ; I had comfort in

my sorrow.   Fourth day, we left Lynn for Earlham.   The next
morning was the funeral at Norwich, and poor I, hardened and
almost entirely devoted to my own nervous feelings.   This was a
trial to me, when I had hoped to have been enabled to seek after
the best help for the dear afflicted ; and also to feel on account
of our much loved lost Elizabeth.   But I desired that this humiliating dispensation might be for my good.

Earlham, Eighth Month, 20th.—I have been married eight
years yesterday.   Various trials of faith and patience have been
permitted me ; my course has been very different to what I had
expected, and instead of being, as I had hoped, a useful instrument in the Church Militant, here I am a care-worn wife and
mother, outwardly nearly devoted to the things of this life.
Though at times this difference in my destination has been trying to me, yet, I believe those trials (which have certainly been
very pinching) that I have had to go through have been very
useful, and brought me to a feeling sense of what I am ; and at
the same time have taught me where power is, and in what we
are to glory ; not in ourselves nor in any thing we can be, or
do, but we are alone to desire that He may be glorified, either
through us or others, in our being something or nothing, as He
may see best for us.   I have seen, particularly in our spiritual allotments, that it is not in man that walketh to direct his steps ;
it is our place, only to be as passive clay in His holy hands,
simply and singly desiring, that He would make us, what He
would have us to be.   But the way in which this great work is
to be effected, we must leave to Him, who has been the Author,
and we may trust will be the Finisher of the work : and we must
not be surprised to find it going on differently, to what our
frail hearts would desire.

I may also acknowledge that through all my trials, there does
appear to have been a particular blessing attending me, both as
to the fatness of the land, and the dew of Heaven ; for though
I have been at times deeply tried inwardly and outwardly, yet I
have always found the delivering Arm has been near at hand, and
the trials have appeared blessed to me.   The little efforts or small
acts of duty I have ever performed, have often seemed remarkably
blessed to me ; and where others have been concerned, it has

also I think been apparent in them, that the effort on my part, has been blessed to both parties. Also, what shall I say when I look at my husband and my five lovely babes. How I have been favoured to recover from illnesses, and to get through them without material injury in any way. I also observe, how any little care towards my servants appears to have been blessed, and what faithful and kind friends to me, I have found them. Indeed I cannot enumerate my blessings; but I may truly say, that of all the blessings I have received, and still receive, there is none to compare to believing that I am not yet forsaken, but notwithstanding all my deviations, in mercy cared for. And (if all the rest be taken from me) far above all, I desire, that if I should be led through paths I know not of, which may try my weak faith and nature, I may not lose my faith in Thee; but may increasingly love Thee; delight to follow after Thee, and be singly Thine; giving all things up to Thee, who hast hitherto been my only merciful Protector and Preserver.

Again, sickness and death were permitted to enter her immediate circle. Henceforward, Elizabeth Fry was frequently called upon to witness the last moments of some, and largely to sympathize in the afflictions of others. She was now to partake personally in the solemn scene of death, on occasion of the decease of her father-in-law William Storrs Fry; this event took place at St. Mildred's Court, where she had nursed him assiduously during some weeks' illness. To the latest period of her life, she dwelt with pleasure on the satisfaction and privilege of having been permitted to be a comfort and assistance to him, during his passage through the dark valley. He was a man of piety and amiability of disposition, and had endeared himself to her by gentleness, and affectionate attention. He was in the habit of frequently driving to London from Plashet. The heavy coach with its bear-skin hammer-cloth, and black horses was a pleasant sight; for he brought with him an atmosphere of kindliness and love; nor did he fail to be the bearer of flowers or fruit or some fresh productions of the country so welcome to dwellers in a city. His decease produced an important change in her circumstances, causing the removal of the family to Plashet.

Mildred's Court, Tenth Month, 17*th.*—We have had my poor father Fry here for five weeks, very ill indeed; and last Seventh day morning, at a little before two o'clock, he died. This was to me a very affecting time, not so much so on his own account, as we had reason to hope and believe it was well with him; but the awful sight of death was very overcoming to me, never having witnessed such a scene before. But I often had very sweet and refreshing moments by his bed-side; and from his own expressions, we had great reason for hope—at one time he said, he had no fear, and indeed it appeared a well-grounded feeling. During the first part of his illness, while at Mildred's Court, death appeared to him in an awful and almost dreadful point of view, though he could not help feeling a degree of comfort in his innocent life, yet he desired life for a little longer to prove his further dedication; this he often expressed. After he was confined up-stairs, he seemed more powerfully to feel the necessity of an interest in that Power which can alone do all things for us, and prove indeed our salvation, for it is only through the redeeming power of Christ, we can look for salvation. He said, he felt himself, " a poor repentant nothing;" and " alone depended upon mercy." Some days after that, he said he had " no fear:" and one morning when we thought him dying, he said, we " need not be afraid, for he was comfortable, comfortable, comfortable." I, with many others wept, I believe with thankfulness. I felt little less than joy, as I did at one or two other times in the room. There was such sweetness attending him. It is certainly an encouraging consideration, for it shows to me that it does much signify what talent is committed to us, if we be but faithful with it. My dear father was not one that had great things required of him apparently; but being faithful in the little, we need not doubt, he now possesses more. I loved him very dearly, and his memory is sweet to me; I have a pleasure in considering I was able to nurse him in his last illness. There is one remark I make, that I believe it is through Christ we are saved, but I would not have that lessen our diligence to work out our own salvation, for I believe those who endeavour to follow Him, are enabled to have faith, and have an interest in that power that can save.

Eleventh Month, 10*th.*—I have hardly settled at home since my dear father's death. Last First day, I was sent for to see my dear sister Hannah, who was very poorly; it proved to be the scarlet fever, and being the only sister at liberty, I have nursed her. This I consider a great privilege to be able to do; though I have felt it a very serious thing, with a young babe, and the mother of so many little lambs, to enter so catching a disorder. I have desired I might not enter it in my own will, or simply to gratify inclination, which leads me to enjoy nursing those I love so dearly : circumstances appeared to bring me into it, indeed I had hardly an option, as I was in the first instance brought into it, not knowing what the complaint was; and in the second, there was no one else that I thought proper to fill my place, as my sister Louisa was prevented. I have desired that what is really best for me may occur, even if it be to pass through trouble. But if my merciful Creator sees meet to preserve me and my family from any further suffering on this account, may I be enabled to give the praise where it is due, and may it afresh stimulate me to seek with renewed vigilance, to dedicate myself and all that belongs to me, to Him, whom my poor weak unworthy soul loves; I could think beyond every thing, though I know the world has a strong hold, and perhaps my heart is more devoted to it than to its Creator. I feel thankful for my beloved sister being better.

Plashet, 20*th.*—Though I have been but very delicate in my health the last week, yet I have been favoured with sweet and precious moments. I have felt sweet peace, not exactly the peace arising from any act of obedience in particular; but unmerited, unlooked for quietness of soul, so that I could say, my peace flows as a river! not that my natural spirits have been high, far from it; but there has, at times, been an enjoyment in the low valley far above any feeling of exhilaration, and I have been reminded of that text, " I will keep him in perfect peace, whose mind is staid on me." Though, as I said before, I am conscious that this is quite an unmerited state; and also how little I have done, towards trying to stay my mind in the right place. No one as yet has taken the complaint of my sister, which I consider a great outward blessing; may I be enabled to give thanks, and to prove my thankfulness, by more and more endeavouring to give up body, soul and spirit to the service of my beloved Master, if I dare say so of Him whom my soul delights to serve.

Fragment that occurs at this part of the Journal.

Children should be deeply impressed with the belief, that the first and great object of their education is, to follow Christ, and indeed to be true Christians : and those things on which we, the Society of Friends, differ from the world in general, should not I think be impressed on them, by only saying, as is often done, " because Friends do it;" but singly and simply as things that the Christian life appears to us to require, and that therefore they must be done. They should also early be taught that all have not seen exactly the same ; but that there are many equally belonging to the church of Christ, who may in other respects be as much stricter than ourselves, as we are than they in these matters. But this does not at all lessen the necessity of our employing a simple mode of expressing ourselves, who are permitted to see the consistency and propriety of it.

(Signed)   ELIZABETH FRY.

30th.—At this time there is no set of people I feel so much about as servants :—I do not think they have generally justice done to them ; they are too much considered as another race of beings, and we are apt to forget that the holy injunction holds good with them, " Do as thou wouldest be done unto," and I believe in striving to do so, we shall not take them out of their station in life ; but endeavour to render them happy and contented in it, and be truly their friends, though not their familiars or equals, as to the things of this life, for we have reason

to believe the difference in our stations is ordered by a wiser
than ourselves, who directs us how to fill our different places;
but we must endeavour never to forget, that in the best sense we
are all one, and though our paths here may be different, we have
all souls equally valuable and have all the same work to do;
which, if properly considered, should lead us to great sympathy
and love, and also to a constant care for their welfare, both here
and hereafter.

Mildred's Court, Second Month, 14th, 1809.—The thought
of forming a new establishment at Plashet, with servants, &c., is
to me a very serious one. I find it so difficult fully to do my
duty towards them, and even when I do, to give them satisfaction. My mind is often much burdened on this subject ; I
long to make them my friends, and for us all to live in harmony
and love. We greatly (I mean servants and their heads in
general) misunderstand each other ; I fully believe partly from
our different situations in life, and partly from our different
educations, and the way in which each party is apt to view
the other. Masters and mistresses are greatly deficient, I think
in the general way, and so are most servants towards them :
it is for both to keep in view strictly to do unto others, as they
would be done unto ; and also to remember that we are indeed
all one with God.

Oh, that I may keep watchful and near my Guide ; and that
if it be consistent with the Divine will, I may be enabled to say,
" As for me and my house, we will serve the Lord," and delight
to do His commandments.

CHAPTER VI.

In the spring of 1809, Joseph and Elizabeth Fry removed to Plashet.

To one who was alive to every sound and every object in nature, it was indeed a change, from the smoke and din of a crowded city to the calm tranquillity of the country. It was a renewal of early tastes and pleasures, not the less appreciated because years had passed over her in sunshine and in storm, leaving traces of hard-earned experience. She had remarkably the talent of throwing aside graver objects, and for short intervals divesting herself of care. She would enjoy her garden and flowers, generally with some of her children about her, and then as quickly resume her employments. Although these occupations appeared different, there was unity of purpose in the whole. She desired to serve God in the fulfilment of her daily duties; she offered to Him the sacrifice of thanksgiving, by the spirit in which she accepted and enjoyed His beauties in creation. Her brow would relax, and her countenance beam with intelligence, as she explained to her children the wonders of the Heavenly bodies, the structure of an insect, or the growth and beauty of a flower.

Soon after their removal to Plashet, Mr. Fry made considerable alterations in the grounds. During her permitted intervals
of relaxation, she gradually filled the plantations with wild
flowers. Followed by her little ones, with their baskets and
trowels, their old Norfolk nurse, whose love of primroses almost
equalled her own, and Dennis Regan the Irish gardener, she
would set forth to transplant seedlings, or deck fresh spots with
that pale yellow flower, so profusely found in every copse, and
on every green bank, not only at Earlham, but throughout her
native county.

Happy is it, that in the dealings of God with man, there is so
marvellous an adaptation to the respective powers and circumstances of each individual. When He demands unusual service,
or peculiarly active devotion to the cause of religion upon
earth, He frequently bestows with it, a power in proportion, of
receiving refreshment and delight from the outward blessings of
life. That many refuse to enjoy, and deny themselves the good
things that He has provided for His children, proves nothing
against the bounty and indulgence, of the hand, which proffers
them. After the deepest conflicts of spirit, amidst heavy and
peculiar sorrows, she, whose character we desire to pourtray,
would turn with a thankful heart to the blessings granted ; her
courage raised, her faith strengthened, by thus dwelling on His
wonderful goodness to the children of men.

Plashet, Third Month, 8th, 1809.—My dearest little Rachel
has been seriously unwell for some time past, so as to make me
very low at times ; but I have not suffered much from painful
anxiety, as in mercy I may say I have been screened from
that feeling. I desire with regard to my dear lambs to be
ready to give them up if called for at my hand ; for we know
not what is best for them : and I believe we should seek to look
upon them, as charges committed to our stewardship, and not
as our property.

18*th.*—I do not think I have ever expressed the pleasure and enjoyment I find in a country life ; both for myself and the dear children. It has frequently led me to feel gratefully, for the numerous benefits conferred ; and I have also desired that I may not rest in, or too much depend on any of these outward enjoyments. It is certainly to me a time of sunshine. All I desire is a heart more truly devoted ; both inwardly and outwardly, I have lately experienced great sweetness and tranquillity of mind.

Earlham, Fifth Month, 6th.—We arrived here yesterday, after a very comfortable journey ; I feel being here very much, principally on account of my beloved sisters being led in so different a path to myself. I desire to be enabled to feel as I ought about it, and not selfishly on account of their differing from me, so long as the truth prospers with them.

Plashet, Sixth Month, 13th.—After having gone through so much since I last wrote, it is difficult for me to express all, but more particularly from rather unusual and repeated causes of thankfulness, in having experienced the Divine Arm held out for my encouragement and help. I had one or two very striking times during the Yearly Meeting, as if meant to confirm my poor feeble faith. Once, when dear Ann Crowley and John Hull dined with us ; before a word was spoken, or the cloth was removed from the table, my soul was brought from a dry, flat, insensible state, to be humbly prostrate before Him, whom it has at times desired to serve. So much so, that I felt that this was enough without words from others : but it was not long before dear Ann Crowley had to express the same, and told me the very thoughts and feelings of my mind and heart. It was indeed a wonderful confirmation ; almost like seeing face to face in a glass. What a blessing to be under such a living ministry, that speaks to and reveals the innermost soul ! Since the Yearly Meeting, I have been greatly helped and supported through the trial of my dear sister Elizabeth Gurney's confinement, which at one time, I felt no strength to encounter ; but power and courage were given me sufficient for the day.

Seventh Month, 3rd.—I have as usual to acknowledge many mercies received by me ; I have been greatly occupied in attending my sister Fry, who has been dangerously ill, from breaking a blood-vessel. I have felt her patient conduct an example to me.

Ninth Month, 13*th.*—Time runs on apace. I desire my imagination may not dwell on that which is before it. Every outward thing appears nearly, if not quite ready; and as for the inward preparation, I cannot prepare myself.

Her sixth child was born on the 20th September.

23*rd.*—On Fourth day, my lovely boy was born, a willing mind to suffer was hard to get at: I longed to have the cup removed from me. I had to acknowledge present help in trouble, so that I could only give thanks; indeed I have renewed cause for thankfulness and praise, which my poor unworthy mind has felt little able to render since, being weak at times, tempted and tried; but I desire to abide near, and cling to that power, that can pardon and deliver.

Tenth Month, 5*th.*—Yesterday I was much affected by an account of poor dear nurse at Earlham, being dangerously ill of scarlet fever, at Lynn, and not likely to live. Sweet love and unity I have towards her, accompanied by a feeling belief that it will be well with her, in life or in death; for I could almost say, she bore the mark of her high calling, being a living example in the house; not a talker, but a doer of the work; at least so she appeared to me. This awfully brings death home, which indeed I feel hardly able to look at in my own power, but it is one of those subjects upon which I do not desire often to dwell, I had rather look to the work of each hour as it comes: and oh, when it please the Master to call me hence, may he find me watching!

6*th.*—The account of dear nurse's death arrived yesterday; in her, we have all lost a most valuable friend.

Tunbridge Wells, 16*th.*—Since I last wrote, I have had much to feel on account of my dear father, who has gone through a similar operation to the one which he underwent in London; but it has been cause of gratitude that he has so far gone on well; dearest Priscilla has also had the scarlet fever. I have felt all these things: but not in a distressing way, having more hope than fear, and both of them going on well has been a comfort to me. With regard to myself, my health has altogether continued finely ; a little more nervous trial the last day or two. But I desire to be submissive and quiet if I can, under whatever may come, if it be right that I should be tried. Having no Meeting here, we yesterday sat silently together in the family ; and I have to relate what has pained me with regard to myself. There appeared on our first sitting down so solemn a covering, but, notwithstanding all my covenants, and all my good desires, I flinched in spirit and turned my mind from it, instead of feeling, " Speak Lord for thy servant heareth ;" my great fear was, lest I should have to acknowledge, that I believed the promise was verified with us, that " where two or three are met together in My name, there am I in the midst of them."

Now, I think it very likely I should not have found myself thus called upon ; but my fear was so great, that I dare not ask whether it were the right call or not, but turned from it. This has renewedly led me to see what I am, and humbly to desire, feeling my own extreme weakness and rebellious heart, that He who has in mercy begun the work in me will be pleased still to carry it on, and to grant ability to do that which He may require at my hands. I could almost have said, yesterday, " Let not Thine hand spare, nor Thine eye pity," until thou hast made me what Thou wouldest have me to be ; and yet afterwards I was more disposed to say, "Be pleased to mix mercy with judgment." I had a sweet little encouragement during my confinement ; being one morning rather remarkably led to feel for a young woman whom I believed to be devoted to the world ; and that very person calling a few hours afterwards, though I did not know she was coming, I was enabled to express what I felt to her, and had to experience the truth of that text, " in the day of my power my people shall be made a willing people :" it appeared as if this were granted to help me through it, in my very weak state: may I show my gratitude by further obedience, when power is less manifested.

Earlham, 30th.—I hardly know how to express myself :— I have indeed passed through wonders. On the 26th, as we were sitting quietly together,_(after my dear sister Richenda had left

us, and my soul had bowed on my beloved father's account, of
whom we had daily very poor reports,) an express arrived bringing Chenda back, saying our most dear father was so ill, that
they did not expect his life would be spared. Words fall short
to describe what I felt, he was so tenderly near and dear to me.
We soon believed it best to set off for this place, on some accounts under great discouragement, principally from my own
bodily weakness, and also the fever in the house ; but it did not
appear as if we could omit it, feeling as we did, therefore, after
a tender parting with my beloved flock, my dearest Joseph,
Chenda, and I with the baby, set off. We arrived at Mildred's
Court the first night, where our dear sister left us in hopes of
seeing our parent alive. In very great weakness I set off the
next morning, and had at times great discouragements ; but
many hours were comforting and sweet. Hearing on the road at
the different stages that my dearest father was living, we proceeded till we arrived at Earlham, about twelve o'clock that night.
We got out of the carriage, and once more, saw him who has
been so inexpressibly dear to me through life, since I knew
what love was ; he was asleep, but death was strongly marked on
his sweet, and to me, beautiful face. Whilst in his room all was
sweetness, nothing bitter, though how I feel his loss is hard to
express : but indeed, I have had abundant cause to rejoice on
his account. After very deep probation, his mind was strikingly visited and consoled at last in passing through the valley
of the shadow of death. He frequently expressed that he
feared no evil, but believed that through the mercy of God in
Christ, he should be received in glory ; his deep humility, and
the tender and loving state he was in, were most valuable to
those around him. He encouraged us, his children, to hold on
our way ; and sweetly expressed his belief, that our love of
good (in the degree we had it) had been a stimulus and help to
him.

The next morning he died, quite easily ; I was not with him,
but on entering his room soon after it was over, my soul was
bowed within me, in love, not only for the deceased, but also for
the living, and in humble thankfulness ; so that I could hardly
help uttering (which I did) my thanksgiving and praise, and

also what I felt for the living, as well as the dead. I cannot understand it; but the power given was wonderful to myself, and the cross none — my heart was so full that I could hardly hinder utterance.

The words were the same as afterwards at the funeral, " Great and marvellous are Thy works, Lord God Almighty ; just and true are thy ways, thou King of saints." Her sister Rachel thus describes it—" Dear Betsey uttered thanksgiving, and a song of rejoicing, for mercy that had been so richly extended to our beloved father ; and a prayer, that it might be continued to us all."

I have desired since to leave this event ; but it was a glorious time, such an one as I never before passed through, all love, all joy, all peace, or the nearest I think to that state, that I ever experienced. I had the first night, of coming, a few nervous and painful moments about the scarlet fever, on account principally of my beloved flock at home ; and a fear, whether in my weak state of body, it might not to be too much for me. But love so powerfully drew me to them, that I believe I could not properly have staid away ; and indeed I have felt in my place, as far as I could tell. Should I forsake my beloved family in the day of trouble ? I hope, and believe not ! we have had most valuable and sweetly enlivening times together, all love, I believe I hope each of our hearts quickened, to feel fresh and renewed desire to be dedicated to His service, who has thus shown Himself in mercy to our beloved father. What can we render for all these benefits ?

Eleventh Month, 3rd.—We attended our beloved father's funeral. Before I went, I was so deeply impressed at times, with love to all, and thanksgiving, that I doubted whether it might not possibly be my place to express it there ; but I did, the evening before, humbly crave not to be permitted to do so, unless rightly called to it. Fear of man appeared greatly taken away. I sat the Meeting under a solemn quietness, though there was preaching that neither disturbed nor enlivened me much ; the

same words still powerfully impressed me, that had done ever
since I first entered the room where the corpse was. Upon
going to the grave this still continued ; under this solemn quiet
calm, the fear of man appeared so much removed, that I believe
my sole desire was, that the will of God might be done in me.
Though it was unpleasant to me, what man might say, yet I most
feared it was a tempation, owing to my state of sorrow ; but
that, I fully believe was not the case, as something of the kind
had been on my mind so long; but it had appeared more ripe
the last few weeks, and even months, I had so often had to " rejoice in the Lord, and glory in the God of my salvation ;" that
it had made me desire, that others might partake, and know, how
good He had been to my soul, and be encouraged to walk in those
paths, which I had found to be paths of pleasantness and peace.
However after a solemn waiting, my dear uncle Joseph spoke,
greatly to my encouragement and comfort, and the removal of
some of my fears. I remained still, till dearest John began to
move to go away; when it appeared as if it could not be
omitted, and I fell on my knees, and began, not knowing how I
should go on, with these words, " Great and marvellous are Thy
works, Lord God Almighty, just and true are all Thy ways,
Thou King of Saints ; be pleased to receive our thanksgiving ;"
and there I seemed stopped, though I thought that I should
have had to express, that I gave thanks on my beloved
father's account. But not feeling the power continue, I
arose directly : a quiet, calm, and invigorated state, mental and
bodily were my portion afterwards, and altogether a sweet day,
but a very painful night, discouraged on every side, I could believe by him who tries to deceive. The discouragement appeared to arise principally from what others would think, and
nature flinched, and sank, but I was enabled this morning to
commit myself in prayer. May I be preserved in future, if my
life be spared, from taking Thy holy name in vain ; enable me
if Thou seest meet, to follow hard after Thee, that I may know
Thy voice, Thou Shepherd, and Bishop of souls, and be as one
of Thy sheep. It was my prayer this morning, to be able to turn
from the subject, as my poor weak mind felt hardly able to look
at it, which was in some measure the case. This day has alto-

6

gether been a comfortable one, though very low at times, and having to walk in the valley; may I be enabled, if it be right for me, to trust and not to fear. I have greatly felt my beloved father's loss to-day; and yesterday, though calm, yet I suffered much on his account; he was in some things, like my heart's delight, I so enjoyed to please him and was so fond of him, that to hear of the sufferings he passed through, before he came to a state of reconciliation, greatly affected me to-day; but I have had more comfort on his account, than anything else. The great love and kindness I have received from them all, and my uncle Joseph, has been encouraging to me; and my husband has been a true helpmate, and sweet counsellor.

Some account of this scene of bereavement, and yet of great consolation, is extracted from the journal of her sister, Rachel Gurney.

" *Monday, October* 23*rd*, 1809.—To-day my dear father expressed to me his conviction, of the necessity of preparing for another world, whilst health and strength were ours; he said, that he trusted mercy would be extended to him, for all his past errors, and infirmities, and acknowledged thankfully, how he had been blessed with spiritual support; although discouragement and heaviness had been at times his portion.

" A paroxysm of pain, attended with great anguish of mind, caused him to speak despondingly of his condition, and the text, ' If any man say he is without sin, he is a liar, and the truth is not in him,' recurred painfully to him, until reminded of the ensuing verses, ' If any man sin, we have an Advocate with God the Father, Jesus Christ, the righteous,' &c., which gave him some comfort, although his mind was burdened, and his spirit oppressed, by the remembrance and consciousness of sin. My sister Catherine pointed out to him the precious promise, ' To him who forgave much, shall much be forgiven,' as applying particularly to his case. This was to him a beaming consolation, and he replied, ' Few men, have, I believe, forgiven more than I have.'

" *Wednesday, October* 25*th.*—We are now brought (as far as we can judge) to the awful crisis of approaching death !

"On Monday night, a very interesting conversation took place. My dear father spoke of the purity of the law laid down by our Saviour, extending even to the thoughts and desires, and lamented his frequent failings and short comings. He acknowledged that the love of religious truth, and the conscientious practice which characterized his children, had been the means of blessing and instruction to him; and he sought their prayers in the present hour of extreme trial.

"I was composedly observing a holy peace shedding its radiance on his countenance, as he sank that night to rest; and I sat by his bed-side, in the full assurance of faith, that the Lord was present with him, notwithstanding the doubts and fears which had oppressed him. Tuesday was a mournful day. Deep probation of spirit, and grievous depression from bodily illness were his portion, but he wrestled with God in prayer, and grace and help were given him. On Wednesday morning, his mind shone forth in wonderful brightness, and although the spasms of pain, which he endured were agonising, grace appeared to triumph, and his spirit seemed to rise out of the fiery furnace, purified by the Great Refiner. With simplicity and ardour he laid hold on the hope set before him ; trusting only in the satisfaction that has been made for sinners, by the blood of Christ. The consolation attendant upon this change in his mind was the greater, from the sore conflicts he had had to pass through in his illness, and the anguish of mind he had endured.

"He was comforted by the presence of his children, who had assembled around him, and expressed to us with tenderness and humble thankfulness, his deep and grateful sense, that he owed more to us than he had been able to give us, and that we had indeed been to him a strength and stimulus in all good things. He continued in the possession of joy and peace until his death which took place on Saturday morning, the 28th of October when he entered (we humbly trust) that region, where the redeemed ones rejoice in the view, as well as feel the influence of their God."

Plashet, Eleventh Month, 16th.—We arrived here on Third day evening ; though plunged into feeling before I arrived, I felt flat on meeting my tenderly beloved little flock. I was enabled coming along to crave help; in the first place, to be made willing either to do, or to suffer, whatever was the Divine will concerning me. I also desired that I might not be so occupied with the present state of my mind, as to its religious duties, as in any degree to omit close attention to all daily duties, my beloved husband, children, servants, poor, &c.; but if I should be permitted to enter the humiliating path, that has appeared to be opening before me, to look well at home, and not discredit the cause I desire to advocate. Last First day morning, I had a deeply trying Meeting, on account of the words, "Be of good courage, and He will strengthen your hearts, all ye that hope in the Lord," which had impressed me towards Norwich Meeting before I went into it; and after I had sat there a little time they came with double force, and continued resting on my mind until my fright was extreme; and it appeared almost as if I must, if I did my duty, utter them. I hope I did not wholly revolt, but I did cry in my heart, for that time to be excused, that like Samuel, I might apply to some Eli to know what the voice was that I heard, my beloved uncle Joseph, I thought was the person; on this sort of excuse or covenant, as I may call it, a calmness was granted the rest of the Meeting, but not the reward of peace. As soon as Meeting was over, I went to my dear uncle, and begged him to come to Earlham to see me. The conflict I had passed through was so great, as to shake my body as well as mind, and I had reason to fear and to believe, I should have been happier and much more relieved in mind, if I had given up to this little service; I have felt since like one in debt to that Meeting. My dear uncle came, and only confirmed me by his kind advice, to walk by faith and not by sight; he strongly advised a simple following of what arose, and expressed his experience of the benefit of giving up to it and the confusion of not doing so. How have I desired since, not to stand in the fear of man; but I believe it is the soul's enemy seeking whom he may devour, for terrible as it was, as then presented to me, and as it often has been before, yet, when some ability was granted to get through, that same enemy would have had me glory on that account. May I not give way either to one feeling or the other, but strive to look to the preserving power of God.

Twelfth Month, 4th.—When I have given up in the morning only to make an indifferent remark to the servants, on our reading, sweet peace has been my portion ; but when it has been presented to me and I have not followed, far different has been the case. In Meeting it is such an awful matter, for the sake of others as well as myself. If it be Thy work in me, be pleased, O Lord ! to grant faith and power sufficient for the needful time ; I long to serve Thee, and to do Thy commandments, but I believe if I be faithful in the little, Thou wilt be pleased to make me ruler over more.

9th.—Soon after sitting down in Meeting (on Fourth day,) I was enabled to feel encouraged by these words, " Though the enemy come in like a flood, the Spirit of the Lord will lift up a standard against him." This appeared my experience, for soon the storm was quieted, and a degree even of ease was my portion. About eleven o'clock, these same words that had done so in Norwich Meeting, came feelingly over me, " Be of good courage, and He will strengthen your hearts, all ye that hope in the Lord." And that which had hitherto appeared impossible to human nature, seemed not only possible, but I believe I was willing ; simply desiring, that in this new and awful undertaking I might not lose my faith, and that the Divine will might be done in me. Under this sense and feeling, as if I could not omit, I uttered them. Though clearness still continued, nature in a great measure seemed to sink under the effort afterwards, and low feelings and imaginations to have much dominion, which in mercy were soon relieved, and I have gone on sweetly and easily since, often even rejoicing.

11th.—Surrounded with numerous outward occupations, weak in body, and at times tossed in mind, so that the wall of preservation appears almost broken down, yet my heart says, I will not fear but that I shall at last praise Him, whom I desire to be " the health of my countenance and my God." I feel a wish and great necessity, of pressing hard after Him, who alone can preserve me, for when the enemy appears, to whom can I flee, but to Him, whom I desire to call Father ? and who has hitherto proved my merciful Protector. Be pleased to keep me in this hour, make me, O Lord ! what Thou wouldest have me to be ; enable me to become passive in Thy holy hand, mayst Thou be glorified, even if it be through my suffering ; and preserve me from ever taking, what is only Thy due, to myself.

22nd.—Again on Fourth day, I have dared to open my mouth in public : I am ready to say, What has come to me ? Even in supplication—that the work might be carried on in myself and others, and that we might be preserved from evil. My weight of deep feeling on the subject, I believe, exceeded any other time ; I was, I may say, brought into a wrestling state, that the work of the ministry in me might, if right, be carried on if not, stopped short. I feel of myself, no power for such a work ; I may say, wholly unable ; yet, when the feeling and power continue, so that I dare not omit it, then what can I do ?

23rd.—Giving up, to make a little remark after reading to the servants, has brought sweet peace ; indeed so far, it has appeared to me, that prompt obedience has brought me the most peace. The prospect of the Meetings next week, more particularly the Quarterly Meeting, already makes me tremble, I can hardly say why, but it is very awful to be thus publicly exposed in a work that I feel so little fitted for ; yet, I believe, it is not my own doing, nor at my own command.

Plashet, First Month, 1st, 1810.—It is rather awful to me entering a new year, more particularly when I look at the alterations the last has made—most striking the last three months or a little more ! First, a child born ; second, the loss of nurse ; third, my beloved father's death ; fourth, my mouth being opened in Meetings. My heart says, What can I render for having been so remarkably and mercifully carried through these various dispensations of Providence ? I think I never knew the Divine Arm so eminently extended for my comfort, help, and deliverance ; and though of late I may in a degree have had to pass through the valley of the shadow of death, yet it has not lasted long at a time, and oh, the incomings of love, joy, and peace, that have at other periods arisen for my confirmation and consolation ! But the manna of yesterday I find, will not do for to-day.

9th.— In the evening of First day, I expressed what I had long on my mind to the servants, on entering a new year, which brought sweet peace. Yesterday, we dined at my brother and sister Samuel Gurney's—we met there my brother and sister, Hoare, and my brother, Fowell Buxton; I felt afterwards, as if I had not been enough on my guard, in conduct and conversation, indeed I awfully feel my conduct with regard to others, as well as to myself; for it appears strange for those to preach, who do not practice. Oh, for a double watch over thought, word, and deed!

11*th.*—It has been strongly impressed on me, how very little it matters, when we look at the short time we remain here, what we appear to others; and how much too much, we look at the things of this life. What does it signify, what we are thought of here, so long as we are not found wanting towards our Heavenly Father? Why should we so much try to keep something back, and not be willing to offer ourselves up to Him, body, soul, and spirit, to do with us what may seem best.unto Him, and to make us what He would have us to be? O Lord! enable me to be more and more, singly, simply, and purely obedient to Thy service!

Second Month, 5th.—The first part of last week I was much occupied in arranging my new household; at least, two new servants, housekeeper and cook. I much felt the weight of filling my place rightly towards the servants, whom I may say, I love; how did I desire to help them, in the best sense, and that I might feel, that, as for me and my house, we will serve the Lord; I may say, there is nothing I desire so much; and the more I know, and the more I wish to follow Him in the way of His requirings, the more sweet do I find the path, and the more desirable does it appear.

19*th.*—Yesterday was an awful, and to me instructive day at Plaistow Meeting. I had not sat very long, before I was brought into much feeling desire that the darkness in some minds might be enlightened; however, no clearness of expression came with it, but under a very solemn covering of the spirit of supplication, a few words offering, I, after a time gave way to utter them; but that which appeared greatly in the cross to me, was having some words presented, to speak in testimony * afterwards, which I did, I believe, purely because I desired to serve my Master, and

---

* An expression frequently made use of in the Society of Friends to imply preaching.

not to look too much to the opinion of my fellow-servants; and
there was to me, a remarkable solemnity, and something like an
owning, or accepting, of this poor little offering. I have desired,
and have been in a degree enabled to feel a little on that sure
foundation; that although the wind may blow, and the rain
descend, yet whilst I keep on this Rock, they will not be able
utterly to cast me down. What a mercy, amidst the storm, to
feel, ever so slightly, something of a sure foundation! Thus
much I know, that even if I be mistaken in this awful undertaking, my desire is to serve Him in it, whom my soul, I may
truly say, loves and delights to please. O Lord! I pray Thee,
preserve Thy poor handmaid in the hour of temptation; and
enable me to follow Thee in the way of Thy requirings, even if
they lead me into suffering, and unto death.

Third Month, 23rd.—A small scruple arose in my mind
yesterday, with regard to dress; I was almost surprised to find,
how unwilling I was to yield to it, not so much from the love of
the thing, but disliking to appear so foolish to myself and others,
as to mind such trifles. This morning it did not appear, as far
as I could judge, to be necessary for me to give up to it; but I
believe I may learn a useful lesson from what I experienced
yesterday, to feel more for others, for I am too apt to rejoice in
the liberty I have in little matters, and it may lead me not to
feel enough for those who are more particular. When any little
matter arises as a duty on the mind, we should be most cautious
in rejecting it; but I think something like trying the fleece wet
and dry may be permitted, for such things may be only to see
whether we are willing to part with all, even our wisdom, for
our beloved Master's sake. Be pleased, O Lord! when Thou
seest meet, to call for any proof of my love, to enable me
to prove to Thee, to myself, and to others, that indeed I love
Thee, and desire to follow Thee, whithersoever Thou mayst
lead me.

31st.—My little —— has been very naughty; his will I find
very strong: oh, that my hands may be strengthened rightly to
subdue it. O Lord! I pray for help, in these important duties!
I may truly say, I had rather my dear lambs should not live,
than live eventually to dishonour Thy great cause; rather may

7

they be taken in innocency, but, if Thou seest meet, O Lord! preserve them from great evils, and be pleased in Thy abundant mercy, to be with them, as thou hast been, I believe, with their poor unworthy parents; visit them, and revisit them, until Thou hast made them what Thou wouldest have them to be. Oh, that I could, like Hannah, bring them to Thee, to be made use of as instruments in Thy Holy Temple! I ask nothing for them in comparison of Thy love; and above all blessings, that they may be vessels in Thy House; this blessing I crave for them, that they may be employed in Thy service, for indeed I can bow and say what honour, what joy so great, as in ever so small a measure, to serve Thee, O Lord!

Early in April, Mr. and Mrs. Fry took a journey into the West of England; from thence was written the following letter to her children at home.

Cowley Bridge.

I suppose my sweet little flock will be glad to hear of the adventures of their dear papa, mamma, Sarah, and baby, and therefore I mean to make as good a story as I can, of what has happened to us in our journey from Mildred's Court to Cowley Bridge. In the first place, we admired the grand houses, and saw the Queen's Palace, and before we had gone much further, we passed near one belonging to the King: but much as I should have liked it, we neither saw King nor Queen.

Of the first day's journey, I do not remember much, except that I often thought of you, who were left at home. There were some beautiful deer feeding in a park, that I think you would have liked very much to see. I almost longed for my little gardeners with our trowels, &c., to get some of the many primroses and violets there were in the hedges. In some places, almost like a carpet of green, blue, and yellow, and the further we have gone, the more we have seen.

On Sixth day night, we slept at Andover, and I felt rather low. I hope, my dear children, you will each try to give me the pleasure when I come home, of hearing you have been going on as I should like.

On our second day's journey, we went up and down a great many hills, till we arrived at Dorchester, where we met dear Anna Buxton, and went with her to a Friend's house at Bridport, who had fourteen children, and one nearly the age of each of you ; and they quite enjoyed to hear of you.

To day, we arrived here to dinner, and I hope I find your dear aunt not worse than when we parted from her. The place is very beautiful, hills, vales, and water.

My love to Harriet and Mary Ann, and kind remembrance to all the servants. Yours in tender love,

ELIZABETH FRY.

Soon after her return ; to her valued friend, the Rev. Edward Edwards, she expressed her desires and anxieties on account of her children.

Plashet, *Fourth Month*, 20*th*, 1810.

My dear Friend,

I hope thou art aware that the reason I have not before congratulated thee on thy dear wife's safety, was my absence from home. We do not often feel a stronger call for gratitude than on the birth of a child, not only as it releases from suffering, but also for the sake of the precious charge committed to our trust. I sometimes wish that like Hannah, we may indeed (as it is in Scripture expressed) lend them to the Lord, that they may from their youth, like little Samuel, be devoted to His service. The more we can live under this desire, the better I believe for them, as they should early find there is nothing we desire for them, in comparison to their being servants to Him, whom we may indeed acknowledge, as far as our experience goes, is no hard Master, but that his yoke is easy, and his burden light; and his paths are indeed paths of pleasantness and peace. May we that are fathers and mothers increasingly keep this first and great object in their view, that neither riches, nor knowledge, nor any other thing should be held in competition with it, but that they should early learn that whatever they do, it should be done to the glory of God. I do not doubt that we unite in these desires, but at times, I greatly feel my own weakness, in fulfilling my duty towards them, and desire to look for help, where I believe it is only to be found. Priscilla has just been here, and appears rather tired after her journey; it is sweet to see her amongst us again, she appears very much to have enjoyed her time at Lynn, and says much of your tenderness and feeling towards her. I think, my dear friend, thou wilt believe me, when I say there are none of our particular scruples, if I may so call them, more hard to bear, than those which prevent our uniting with those we nearly love, and esteem highly as examples of the religious life, in their forms of worship, but although it appears safest for us not to unite in the form, yet I hope and believe we do all spiritually unite, and bow before the great footstool in sweet harmony. I should like, if we could have found time and suitable opportunity, to tell thee a little how I have felt some of these things, and perhaps we may one day be more together.

I am glad to hear continued good accounts of thy dear Anne, and with much love to her and thyself,

I remain, thy affectionate friend,

ELIZABETH FRY.

Mildred's Court, Sixth Month, 1st.—Yesterday I attended the funeral of our beloved Anna Reynolds, whose death has been deeply felt by me. We had, I think, I may truly say, a glorious time, for the power of the most High, appeared to overshadow us : a belief of her being in safety, has bowed my soul prostrate, in humble thankfulness, and renewedly led me to desire to prove my gratitude for such unspeakable mercy, as has been showed my near and beloved relations, by my love and entire dedication. I uttered a few words in supplication, at the ground ; my uncle Joseph, my cousin Priscilla, and many others beautifully ministered ; after Meeting, I might truly say, my cup ran over, such sweetness covered my mind. After a solemn time in the family, with dear cousin Priscilla, and Ann Crowley, I ventured on my knees, praying, that His Holy Hand would not spare, nor His eye pity, until He made us, what He would have us to be ; only I craved, that He would not forsake us, but, let us be made in some small measure sensible, that He was with us, and that it was His rod, and His staff, that we depended upon. Through heights, and through depths, through riches, and through poverty ; may it alone be my will, to do the will of the Father !

Plashet, 2nd.—I have found it pleasant and refreshing, being again with my beloved family in this sweet place. I have desired that the time spent in the Yearly Meeting, and what I have received there, may return as bread cast upon the waters.

Eighth Month, 10*th.*—I have thought this morning, I may in a measure adopt the language of the blessed Virgin, " My soul doth magnify the Lord, and my spirit hath rejoiced in God my Saviour." May my being led out of my own family, by what appear to me duties, never be permitted to hinder my doing my duty fully towards it, or so occupy my attention, as to make me in any degree forget or neglect home duties. I believe it matters not where we are, or what we are about, so long as we keep our eye fixed on doing the great Master's work, and that whatever we do, may be done to His glory. When I feel as I do to-day, what a glorious service it is, though we may have at times, to pass through great trial and poverty, and remember how in these little religious services, I have been helped and carried through, and that as I expressed before, my soul hath in a measure been able to magnify the Lord, and my spirit to rejoice in God its Saviour ; I fear for myself, lest even this great mercy should prove a temptation, and lead me to come before I am called, or enter service I am not prepared for ; but in all these things, I have but one place of safety, to take refuge in. Be pleased, then, O Lord ! Thou who knowest my heart, and all its temptations ; be pleased to preserve me, and enable me if Thou seest meet, to do Thy will, in strength and in weakness, when it leads to the hardest crosses as well as into the way of rejoicing.

To an early friend, and guest at St. Mildred's Court, she writes describing her outward circumstances and mental exercises about this time.

Plashet, Seventh Month, 1810.

My beloved Friend,

As I have been much with thee in mind this morning, I feel inclined to tell thee how sincerely I love thee ; I believe in that

love which neither time nor distance can affect. Looking back
to some account of what I passed through when thou wast at our
house long ago, and how nearly I felt united to thee, has
brought thee to my remembrance. I have often felt disposed to
write to thee, since thou left England, but did not feel my letters worth sending so far ; many changes have taken place, since
we were together, perhaps more remarkably to me ; we have now
six little children, three girls and three boys, all well and lovely,
and much enjoyment they give us, though at times in looking
to their best interest, we are ready to tremble for them : may we
do our part, so that we can in faith and humble confidence, look
to Him who can alone bless our endeavours. All our beloved
parents are taken from us, the loss of my own father, as thou
mayst suppose, was a close trial, but I am ready to believe and
hope, it brought its blessings to many of us ; the great mercy
he received at last, from his having a sweet hope and confidence,
that through the mercy of his Redeemer, it would be well with
him, proved to my mind, I think, the strongest excitement to
gratitude I ever experienced, so much so, that it appeared to
break the ice for me, and on my knees I publicly expressed my
thankfulness. This matter of publicly exposing myself, in this
way, has been for many years struggling in my mind, long before
I married, and once or twice when with thee, in London, I
hardly knew how to dare to refrain. The past I must leave, but
I am ready to think extreme unwillingness to give up to this
matter, has kept me longer than I need have been in a lukewarm, and at times wilderness estate, however, since a way has
thus been made for me, it appears as if I dare not stop the
work ; if it be a right one, may it go on and prosper, if not
the sooner stopped the better. I can hardly doubt that if I am
only enabled to cling fast to Him, whose work I believe it is,
that I shall experience preservation, though I find my state a
new one : I do not understand myself, and find I must walk by
faith and not by sight ; at times I am permitted to abound and
to feel power that I cannot but believe to be beyond myself, at
others, brought very low, poor, weak, and almost miserable ; my
faith tried as to a hair's breadth, yet through all, I have found
abundant cause for thanksgiving and praise.

Earlham, Ninth Month, 1st.—Yesterday I had much conversation with my beloved sisters Rachel and Richenda, upon
their religious experience, and present belief. At the time I felt
very fully strengthened, to express my mind, and not to shrink,
and I believe I did no hurt ; but I have felt and still feel very low,
much pressed down ; why, I cannot tell, they represent their case
clearly, but can I, after what I have felt, known, and experienced,
doubt the truth of this blessed principle ; the sensible and constant direction of the Spirit of God in man ? The head and judgment of man, is most frail, or it would not twist so many ways ;
the work of religion, must be in the heart, and if that become
sanctified by the great "I Am," and brought low before Him,
and our wills be brought into subjection to the Divine will, and
He become our all in all ; then the great work, appears to me
accomplished in us.

Plashet, 10th.—I desire gratefully to acknowledge, my being
once more returned home to my beloved family, my little ones
appearing to have prospered in my absence, and I hope all going
on well. And also I think, with abundant cause to be grateful,
that on leaving Earlham, and my tenderly beloved brothers and
sisters, my mind felt very clear, trusting that I had been enabled
to accomplish that which came to hand to do amongst them ; and
I hope without hurting the great cause. How very near and dear
they are to me. On First day, I attended Ipswich and Colchester
Meetings ; I believe I was helped in the ministry, in both ; if
any praise be due, may it be given both by me and others, to the
great Author. Spent an interesting evening, with dear old John
Kendal.

13th.—It is my great wish, that being engaged in these awful
and important duties, may not, in any degree, lessen my attention
to the smaller concerns of life ; but rather prove a stimulus to do
all well : I wish, if right, still to feel a life in them, and not have
my mind so occupied by the greater, as not to enter with spirit
into the smaller. How much does gratitude call for at my hands
at this time ? My beloved husband, a true helpmate and sympa-
thizer with me ; my health and natural spirits very good ; my
sweet children going on comfortably and well.

Tenth Month, 5th.—I had yesterday a very narrow escape of

my life, from falling out of a whiskey upon my head, owing to a
violent jolt ; if it had gone on, I believe it must have gone over
my head ; many have been either killed or materially injured by
such a fall.   I was at the time favoured with clearness, and knew
what to do, and by immediately applying cold water to my head
from a pond just by, my suffering was in a great measure relieved.
I wonder I have not felt this event more seriously, but I did not,
even at the time, feel much frightened, or overcome : I believe I
was thinking, only about a minute before, that in case of my
sudden death, I had nothing to look to but mercy.

24th.—I feel self-love and pride are hidden, very, very deep
in me, and may sometimes rise, under specious appearances : I
cannot root them out myself; but may I more often than the
day, look to Him, who can do it for me.

26th.—This day year, a day I think never to be forgotten,
whilst memory lasts, my beloved father died! and I first opened
my mouth as a minister.

30th.—I crave to be in all things doing the will of Him, whom
I desire to feel my Master ; this is at times hard to come at ;
I do not feel by any means, a ready and willing servant ; still,
not willing either to speak a word before meals, or after our
reading.   My very frequent speaking in Meeting, is very awful
to me.   Be pleased, O Lord! still to be with Thy poor child,
preserve her, if Thou seest meet from right hand as well as left
hand errors : increase my faith, and renew a right spirit within
me.   May neither heights nor depths ; riches nor poverty ;
health or sickness ; be permitted to overcome me, and separate
me from Thy love ; and be pleased, O Lord! to enable me
always to give Thee the glory, and not to take it to myself.
May I more faithfully do my duty towards Thee, towards my
neighbour, and towards myself: when called upon publicly to
advocate Thy cause, be pleased to grant me faith sufficient!
Create in me a more willing mind, to express whatever may
arise, as in the newness of life ; whether in public or in private,
that the short time of my continuance here, I may in life, conduct, and word, live to Thy glory.   Amen, saith my poor soul.

In December, she travelled into Gloucestershire, taking three of her children, to visit Mr. and Mrs. William Fry ; her sister Mrs. Fry, was in seriously delicate health, they were residing at that time at Hill House, Rodborough, a very beautiful place, which Mr. Fry had hired, hoping that his wife might derive benefit from the air.

Rodborough, Twelfth Month, 22*nd.*—I enjoy being here, and the company of those I am with. I trust not in myself, in my own weak and disobedient heart, but I trust in Thee, O Lord ! before whom the mountains skip like rams, and the little hills like lambs.

Plashet, 28*th.*—I may indeed acknowledge a way has been to me wonderfully made, for even my disobedient heart has been brought down, and made willing to submit ; may I never forget it, or to whom the power and praise belongs ; who capacitated me to do, what to human nature felt impossible, on First day, at Meeting, at Nailsworth. When evening came, after passing through little short of distress of soul, I was enabled, after their reading, to kneel down and offer my little sacrifice, which I felt abundantly helped in, both as to power and utterance ; my beloved sister Eliza seemed to feel it extremely, so much so, that I was afraid it might overcome her, and make her ill ; but she soon revived, and told me how much she had felt it, and united with me, which was sweet and encouraging. I was enabled to leave that place with a clear and peaceful heart, knowing of no burden.

Plashet, First Month, 5*th,* 1811.—I find it no easy matter to serve the poor, I desire to do right towards them ; but it is very difficult either to turn them away, or to give to all, without doing as much hurt as good. I desire a right spirit about them, and ability to know what is best to be done.

6*th.*—In the evening the servants and children read with us, and much in the cross to human nature, I believe I may say, my will was subdued for me, and power given to crave a blessing upon us and our household ; I felt abundantly helped, and a sweet feeling has been my portion since ; like abiding under the shadow of His wing, whom I desire to be my Lord, and my God, my all in all.

11th.—Felt very low yesterday evening, rather unusually so for me, partly from the children being naughty and trying. I also feel how poorly my duties are performed towards all. If I be clearer in one description of duty than another, I think it is towards servants ; but in that I often have to mourn over my defects. I have felt a little encouragement this morning, and am at times brought to leave others, and their interests, and look and depend upon Him, who can help them, and even listens to the cry of His little ones. As for my beloved children, I had rather they should not be, than have them live to go greatly astray ; but let me not forget that if they, like myself, should go astray for a time, there is that Power which can bring them back. Oh, that this may be the case ; may they eventually become redeemed from the world, and advocates or valiants in the great cause ! It is almost my single desire for them ; all others are small in comparison—and as for my beloved husband, oh ! that we may be preserved, going hand in hand, and bowing before the Holy One in sweet unity ; not turning aside to any other gods, or making to ourselves graven images, and worshipping them.

Second Month, 7th.—Yesterday was to me an awful and affecting day ; there came up a minute from the men, desiring the women to meet them after the next Monthly Meeting, to consider the subject of acknowledging me as a minister. Friends felt so kindly for me, as to call me out of meeting to tell me, lest hearing it should overcome me ; this was unnecessary, for though I felt and feel it deeply, that was not likely to be the case. It brings me prostrate before the great " I am ;" but I have little or nothing to say for myself: certainly, it is cause of humble gratitude, to believe my little offerings in the ministry have not burdened, but been acceptable to the church. O Lord ! if it be Thy will to preserve my life yet a little longer, and continue me in this service, preserve me, even if it be through chastisement, from ever hurting Thy great and holy cause, and enable me to walk worthy of the vocation whereunto I am called.

8th.—I have thought this morning, whether we, as a Society, do not suffer more than we need, by expecting too much of ourselves; whether our hope and reliance is sufficiently on Him whom we desire to become our all in all; experience has taught me, that Christ in me, or His saving and anointing power in me, is indeed my only hope of glory. I look not to myself, but to that within me, that has to my admiration proved my present help, and enabled me to do what I believe of myself I could not have done. Under a sense of my own unsubjected will, I do not desire too much to give way to the spirit of mourning, or judging myself, but at once endeavour to turn to Him, and wait upon Him, who can alone strengthen for every good word and work, and will I believe undoubtedly arise, in His own time, for the help of His little dependent ones, and make a way for them, where they see no way. Enable me, O Lord! increasingly to put my whole trust and confidence in Thee.

Her seventh child Elizabeth, was born at St. Mildred's Court rather unexpectedly, on the 20th of February.

*St. Mildred's Court, Second Month,*26*th.*—Though confined to a lying-in-room, and not actively engaged, may I seek in all things to be acting in conformity to the Divine will; for this state has its temptations. May the day's work, whatever it be, keep pace with the day.

The Meeting of which she was a member being satisfied with her ministry, and feeling unity with it, acknowledged her at this time in the character of a minister amongst them. Her course, as such, consequently became more easy to her, from having received the sanction of the Society for such religious services, as she felt herself called upon to perform.

Third Month, 14*th.*—My husband brought me word in the evening, that Friends had agreed to acknowledge me as a minister. This mark of their unity is sweet, and I think strengthen-

M 2

ing, and I believe will have advantages, as wells as trials attending it.   I feel and find it is neither by the approbation, any
more than by the disapprobation of man, that we stand or fall ;
but it once more, leads me only to desire, that I may simply
and singly, follow my Master in the way of His requirements,
whatsoever they may be.   I think this will make a way for me
in some things, that have been long on my mind.

Plashet, Sixth Month, 3rd.—Yearly Meeting is finished :
I have renewed evidence that there yet remains a God, hearing
prayer, as my inward cries, as well as outward, appear to have
been in some instances rather remarkably heard and granted.   I
have also had renewed evidence, that there yet remains a Gospel
ministry, as I have been ministered to, and have known the
same with others, and have been I believe enabled a little to
minister myself ; I could almost believe from the living Source.
I have not had much to do in this way, but a little at times, in
private and public.   I find it an awful thing to rise, amongst a
large assembly, and unless much covered with love and power,
hardly know how to venture.

19*th.*—I feel at times deeply pressed down, on account of my
beloved children.   Their volatile minds try me, but amidst my
trials I have a secret hope concerning them, that all will end
well ; and a blessing attend them, if they bow to the blessed
yoke, (for so I feel it,) in their youth.   May you, if ever you read
this, my beloved little ones, hearken to the advice of your tenderly
affectionate mother.   Submit to the cross of Christ in small
matters and in great, there is no way like it ; the crown, is in a
measure partaken of even here.   That no enemy of your souls be
permitted to overcome you, or turn your feet into another path,
is the sincere desire, nay, prayer of her, who feels your souls' welfare very near to her own ; may we all so live, that when time to us
here shall be no more, we may unite, and sing praises in eternity.
Look at it, what folly, for the sake of self-gratification for a few
years, to forfeit even the chance of such a prospect! ah, my
children, press forward through all opposition ; walking by faith,
rather than by sight, for in that alone you will find strength and
safety ; looking too much out, loses time and creates confusion,

whilst humbly looking within, with the eye of faith, and following whatever that may lead into, or out of, tends to confirm, stablish, and strengthen. May the God of peace be with, bless, and preserve you, saith my soul, Amen. O Lord! be pleased to have mercy on them, win them over to Thy love, and teach them that there is no way like Thy way, no joy like Thy joy!

Earlham, Seventh Month, 21*st.*—I am come with my beloved husband, to attend my dear uncle Gurney's funeral. I cannot easily express my feelings this day, the state of the souls of the family, is so deeply interesting to me. My soul has been laid low, and brought very prostrate, feeling for the various conditions of my beloved family, who are brought together on this awful occasion ; desiring for those who have at times to advocate the great cause, that we may get deep enough, and not speak from outward knowledge and observation, but alone move in the great service, as the pure life may lead us into it : may we be enabled to say enough, and preserved from saying too much. Be pleased, O Lord ! to grant us tongue and utterance, to show forth Thy praise, that those afar off, may be induced to come, taste, and see, how good Thou art. Be pleased also to anoint their eyes, and their ears, both to hear and see for themselves, that there is none like unto Thee ; but that Thou art worthy both now and for ever, to be praised and exalted above all. Amen !

30*th.*—I was weak and low, when tried with bodily pain, and felt my great fearfulness about having my tooth drawn. How very weak I am, but I still hope, if I had believed it my duty, I should have had it done ; but none know, but the timid, what a fearful mind has to pass through, even about trifles : whenever strength is granted me, whether about outward or spiritual things, it appears indeed a gift ; fearfulness is so much my nature.

Plashet, Eight Month, 23*rd.*—We had three clergymen and their wives, besides another neighbour and his wife here yesterday ; I believe good men, and I hope good women also ; I felt love, and I think that sort of unity with them, that I have with good Friends. From a great fear of hurting others, I feel, though I believe it is not very apparent, a bowing to their opinions, and not openly professing my own, which tries me. There, no doubt, are advantages, as well as disadvantages, in associating with people of different descriptions; especially in being with the Good, we are increasingly led to estimate the good in all, and also to observe, how the mercy of our heavenly Father is extended towards us, and how He sees meet to accept us in our different ways. But at the same time, there is safety in keeping within our narrow enclosure, more particularly for young people not established in principle. It may induce them to make the example of others a plea for more liberty, instead of rightly stimulating them to look at home and examine how far they are doing the work committed to them, which should be the effect of seeing others zealously pursuing their course. It is also important, as children become marriageable, with whom they associate, and parents should in this, as in other things, keep on the watch, and seek the best direction how far to go and where to stop. But my feelings of love would lead me almost to encourage an intimacy with one of these clergymen and his wife: but I desire to be rightly directed, and if we are likely to lose more than we gain by not holding fast the profession of our faith without wavering, then I hope not to encourage it; I leave it, thinking it will make its own way, which I trust will be the right one, but Friends being so much united with others, and brought so forward in works of benevolence, may prove a snare by flattering them and taking them off their guard. It is on account of schools that we have been thus brought together.

In establishing herself at Plashet, Mrs. Fry had formed various plans for the benefit of her poorer neighbours, which she gradually brought into action. One of her early endeavours, was to establish a girls' school for the Parish of East Ham ; of which Plashet is a hamlet. Immediately opposite the gate of Plashet House, there stood a dilapidated dwelling, picturesque from its gable end and large projecting porch; it was inhabited by an aged man and his still more aged sister ; they had seen better days, and eked out a narrow income with the help of the

7

brother's labours in a small garden, and the sale of rabbits, of which they kept a vast quantity. Like persons fallen in life, they were reserved; the sister almost inaccessible. But by degrees Mrs. Fry won her way to the old lady's heart; she might be seen seated in an upper chamber, on one side of a fire-place lined with blue Dutch tiles, opposite the invalid, who, propped by cushions leaned back in an easy chair, in a short white dressing-gown over a quilted petticoat, her thin wrinkled hands resting on her knees, and her emaciated refined countenance brightening under the gentle cheering influence of her guest, as she endeavoured to raise her hopes and stimulate her desires after that country, where it shall be no more said, " I am sick." Annexed to this old building was a spacious and comparatively modern room, which appeared suitable for a school room, and Mrs. Fry's persuasions succeeded in obtaining the consent of the old people to use it as such.

A young woman named Harriet Howell, who was much occupied at that time in organizing schools on the Lancasterian system, came to Plashet. The excellent clergyman of East Ham (alluded to in the journal) Mr. Anlezark, with his lady united with her in the object. A school of about seventy girls was established, and, although afterwards removed to a more central situation continues to the present day.

The bodily wants of the poor, especially in cases of sickness or accident, claimed her careful attention. There was a depôt of calico and flannels always ready, besides outer garments, and a roomy closet well supplied with drugs. In very hard winters, she had soup boiled in an out-house, in such quantities, as to supply hundreds of poor people with a nourishing meal. Nor was her interest confined to the English poor in East Ham. About half a mile from Plashet, on the high road between Stratford and Ilford, the passer by will find two long rows of houses, with one

larger one in the centre, if possible more dingy than the rest. At
that time they were squalid and dirty. The windows generally
stuffed with old rags, or pasted over with brown paper, and the
few remaining panes of glass refusing to perform their intended
office from the accumulated dust of years; puddles of thick
black water before the doors; children without shoe or stocking;
mothers, whose matted locks escaped from the remnants of caps,
which looked as though they never could have been white; pigs,
on terms of evident familiarity with the family; poultry, shar-
ing the children's potatoes—all bespoke an Irish colony.

It was a pleasant thing to observe the influence obtained by
Mrs. Fry, over these wild but warm-hearted people. She had
in her nature a touch of poetry, and a quick sense of the droll;
the Irish character furnished matter for both. Their powers of
deep love and bitter grief excited her sympathy; almost against
her judgment, she would grant the linen shirt and the boughs
of evergreen to array the departed, and ornament the bed of
death.

One clear frosty morning, Mrs. Fry called her elder children to
accompany her on a visit to one of these cottages. A poor woman,
the mother of a young family, had died there, she had been well
conducted as a wife and mother, and had long shown a desire for
religious instruction; the priest, a kind-hearted, painstaking
man, liberal in his views and anxious for the good of his
flock, thought well of the poor woman, had frequently visited
her in her illness, and was in that as in many other cases, very
grateful, to Mrs. Fry for the relief and nourishment she had
bestowed, which it was not in his power to give.

On the bed of death lay extended the young mother, her features which were almost beautiful stiffened into the semblance
of marble. Her little children were on the floor, the husband,
in a corner leaning on a round table, with his face buried in

his hands. A paper cross laid on the breast of the corpse ; the sun shone into the room, and mocked the dreary scene. The apartment was close, from the fumes of tobacco and the many guests of the wake, which had been held during the night, contrasting strangely with the fresh air which blew in through the half-opened door way. Mrs. Fry spoke soothingly to the husband, she reminded him of his wife's desires for his good, and for that of his children ; she slightly alluded to the uselessness of the cross as a symbol, but urged the attention of those present to the great doctrine of which it was intended to remind them. Again, she offered solace to the mourner, promised assistance for his little ones, and left the room.

Some of the scenes in Irish Row were very different, " Madam Fry," as she was called by them, being so popular as to produce some inconveniences and many absurdities. She enjoyed giving pleasure, it was an impulse as well as a duty with her to do good ; gathering her garments round her, she would thread her way through children and pigs, up broken stair-cases, and by narrow passages to the apartments she sought ; there she would listen to their tales of want or woe, or of their difficulties with their children, or of the evil conduct of their husbands. She persuaded many of them to adopt more orderly habits, giving little presents of clothing as encouragements ; she induced some to send their children to school, and with the consent of the priest, circulated the Bible amongst them. On one occasion, when the weather was extremely cold, and great distress prevailed, being at the time too delicate herself to walk, she went alone in the carriage, literally piled with flannel petticoats for Irish Row ; the rest of the party walking to meet her, to assist in the delightful task of distribution. She made relieving the poor a pleasure to her children, by the cheerful spirit in which she did it ; she employed them as almoners when very young, but expected a minute account of their giving, and their reasons for it. After the establishment of the Tract Society, she always kept a large supply of such as she approved, for distribution.   It was her desire never to relieve the bodily wants of any one, without endeavouring in some way, more or less directly, to benefit their souls.   She was a warm advocate for vaccination, and very successful in performing the operation ; she had acquired this art from Dr. Willan, one of its earliest advocates and most skilful practitioners.   At intervals, she made a sort of investigation of the state of the parish, with a view to vaccinating the children.   The result was, that small-pox was scarcely known in the villages over which her influence extended.

In a green lane, near Plashet, it has been the annual custom of the Gypsies to pitch their tents, for a few days in their way to Fairlop fair.   The sickness of a gipsy child, inducing the mother to apply for relief, led Mrs. Fry to visit their camp ; from that time, from year to year, she cared for them whenever they came into her neighbourhood ; clothing for the children and people, and a little medical advice she invariably bestowed ; but she did far more than that, she sought to influence their minds aright, she pleaded with them on the bitter fruits of sin, and furnished them with Bibles, and books the most likely to arouse their attention.

But though thus abounding in labours for the good of all around her, she was liable to deep inward discouragements, undoubtedly increased by her sensitive nature and delicate frame, but arising chiefly from her intense desire in nothing to offend Him whom her soul loved and whom she so entirely de-sired to serve.

Ninth Month, 5th.—I have lately been so much hurried by an almost constant change of company and employments, as to be at times a good deal tried, and I am fearful my temper will be made irritable by it.   I think I may truly say, my desire is, to do

my duty fully and faithfully to all connected with me, nearly and
remotely, rich and poor ; but I find I cannot satisfy all, and often
feel to myself doing almost every thing very imperfectly ; a little
like the old man and his ass, trying to please every body, and
pleasing nobody, and losing his own approbation into the bargain.
This I believe is in a measure the case, though not altogether
so ; perhaps I may one day spend my time to an apparently better
account. Be pleased, O Lord ! to bless the small feeble endeavours of Thy poor child, to do her duty to others, for without Thy
blessing, they are all ineffectual, and with Thy blessing, I need
not doubt but they will tend to my own good, and to the good of
those I desire to serve, more particularly at home. With my dear
little ones I often feel myself a poor mother, but my hope is not
in myself, for I am sensible I do not apparently manage them
so well as many others do their children ; but, O Lord ! Thou
knowest my heart, and its desires for them, and that I may not
be found wanting towards them. I neither ask health nor
riches, nor any thing for them in comparison with this, that as
they grow in years, they may grow in favour with Thee, and
with those who love Thee, by walking in humility and in Thy
fear. My feeling of my own great deficiencies towards them
and others, at times leads me to take great comfort from the
shortness of life, if I be but ready, and have done faithfully the
work committed. I fancy I could willingly leave them and all,
trusting that better instruments might be raised up for their
help ; but poor as I am, if it please the Lord to make me an instrument of good to them and others, and to bless my small
efforts to serve Him, I believe I should rejoice in keeping alive
for some time longer. I feel every week that is pretty well run
and towards the end of the Race, that it is well, and a cause of
gratitude.

In September, Mrs. Fry visited Earlham. On the 10th of that
month was held the first meeting of the Norwich Bible Society ;
it was very largely and generally attended. Mrs. Fry who was
warmly interested in the Bible Society, from its commencement
to the close of her life, was present with her brother Joseph John

Gurney and other members of the family. Mr. Gurney, then in
the prime of early manhood, on this occasion first took his stand
in public life, as an advocate for the general circulation of that
sacred volume, which he had chosen as the guide of his youth,
and which has proved the stay of his advancing years.

Earlham, Ninth Month, 10*th.*—I think a more deeply exercised state, that has at times bordered on distress of soul, I hardly
ever remember, than I feel this morning going to Meeting; in the
first place, with the Edwards' and my own family, in their various
states ; in the next place, my prospect of going into the men's
Monthly Meeting; and in the last, an idea having passed my mind,
whether I may not have, amongst the very large companies who
are likely to be here, consisting of many clergymen and others,
to say something either before meals, or at some other time. The
words that (I believe) have arisen for my encouragement, are
these, " The Lord is my Shepherd, I shall not want." Yes, I will
try not to fear, for if God be with me, who can be against me ?

12*th.*—What can I render for all his benefits ? In the first
place, I went to the Meeting of worship with the Edwards'. I
had not long been there, before I felt something of a power
accompanying me and words arose, but my exercise of mind was
so great, that it seemed like being " baptized for the dead :"
though not that I know of, from any particular fear of man ; I
was helped (I believe I may say), as to power, tongue, and
utterance. That Meeting might be said to end well.

Yesterday was a day indeed :—one that may be called a mark
of the times. We first attended a General Meeting of the Bible
Society, where it was sweet to observe so many of various sentiments all uniting in the one great object, from the good Bishop
of Norwich (Bathurst) for so I believe he may be called, to the
dissenting Minister, and young Quaker (my brother Joseph). We
afterwards, about thirty-four of us, dined here, I think there were
six clergymen of the Establishment; three dissenting Ministers ;
and Richard Philips, besides numbers of others. A very little
before the cloth was removed, such a power came over me of love,
I believe I may say, life, that I thought I must ask for silence

after Edward Edwards had said grace, and then supplicate the
Father of mercies, for His blessing—both of the fatness of the
earth, and the dew of Heaven, upon those, who thus desired to
promote His cause, by spreading the knowledge of the Holy
Scriptures ; and that He would bless their endeavours, that the
knowledge of God and His glory might cover the earth, as the
waters cover the sea ; and also for the preservation of all present, that through the assistance of His grace we might so
follow Him, and our blessed Lord in time, that we might eventually enter into a glorious eternity, where the wicked cease from
troubling, and the weary are at rest. The power and solemnity
were very great. Richard Philips asked for silence, I soon knelt
down, it was like having our High Priest amongst us ; inde-
pendently of this power, His poor instruments are nothing, and
with His power, how much is effected ! I understood many
were in tears, I believe all were bowed down spiritually. Soon
after I took my seat, the Baptist minister said, " This is an act
of worship ;" adding that it reminded him of that which the
disciples said, " when He walked with us, did not our hearts
burn within us ?" A clergyman said, " We want no wine, for
there is that amongst us, that does instead." A Lutheran
minister * remarked, that although he could not always understand the words, being a foreigner, he felt the Spirit of Prayer,
and went on to enlarge in a striking manner. Another
clergyman spoke to this effect; How the Almighty visited
us, and that neither sex, nor any thing else stood in the way of
His grace. I do not exactly remember the words of any one, but
it was a most striking circumstance, for so many of such different
opinions, thus all to be united in one spirit ; and for a poor
woman to be made the means, amongst so many, great, wise, and
I believe good men, of showing forth the praise of the great
" I Am." After reading last evening, the dear Lutheran minister,
Dr. Steinkoff, said a few words in prayer. This morning,
my desire, indeed I may say prayer, is, that this may not
degenerate into a form amongst us, and I should not be surprised, if I had to express as much ; however, that I leave.

* The Rev. Dr. Steinkoff.

Be pleased, O Lord! still to preserve me on the right hand, and on the left, and let me in no way do contrary to Thy will ; and if called upon to testify that I can only unite in prayer, where I apprehend Thy Spirit leads into it, enable me I beseech Thee to do it so, as to strengthen, rather than weaken the love that I feel so sweetly to unite me with those who differ from myself.

In a letter from Mr. Hughes, one of the Secretaries of the Bible Society, he thus describes this occasion :—

" On the Monday after my return, I proceeded with my excellent colleagues for Norwich, where a numerous and respectable meeting was held on Wednesday, in a very spacious and commodious hall ; the Mayor presided, the Bishop spoke with great decision and equal liberality; and the result of the whole was, the establishment of the Norfolk and Norwich Bible Society ; about £700 was subscribed, and one happy amiable sentiment appeared to pervade the company.   My colleagues and myself adjourned to Earlham, two miles from Norwich, where we had passed the previous day, and where we witnessed emanations of piety, generosity, and affection, in a degree that does not often meet the eye of mortals.   Our host and hostesses were the Gurneys, chiefly Quakers, who, together with their guests, amounted to thirty-four.   A clergyman, at the instance of one of the family, and I presume with the most cordial concurrence of the rest, read a portion of the Scriptures, morning and evening; and twice we had prayers, I should have said thrice, for after dinner on the day of the Meeting, the pause encouraged by " the Society of Friends," was succeeded by a devout address to the Deity, by a female minister Elizabeth Fry, whose manner was impressive, and whose words were so appropriate, that none present can ever forget the incident, or ever advert to it, without emotions alike powerful and pleasing.   The first emotion, was surprise ; the second, awe ; the third, pious fervour.   As soon as we were readjusted at the table, I thought it might be serviceable to offer a remark, that proved the coincidence of my heart with the devotional exercise in which we had been engaged ; this had the desired effect.   Mr. Owen and others suggested accordant sentiments, and we seemed generally to feel like the Disciples, whose hearts burned within them as they walked to Emmaus.

"The days passed in this excellent family were opened with joy and closed with regret; few such days will occur again ; yet when devotion shall cease to be measured by days, pleasure far more intense shall spring up for ever fresh ; and all the members of the vast *Household of Faith* shall behold each other, in a scene where purity is unblemished, and harmony uninterrupted, and bliss complete and everlasting."

" When shall I wake and find me there ?"

Plashet, Tenth Month, 3rd.—In the evening, after reading at Earlham, I was greatly helped in prayer for my brothers and sisters, who were all present ; it was in thanksgiving and prayer; acknowledging our many blessings, particularly that of being so united with each other, which blessing I craved might increase, that we might increasingly dwell in God and He in us. I also prayed for our little ones, that they with us might have the knowledge of God, and of our blessed Lord Christ Jesus, that we might eventually obtain a habitation not made with hands, eternal in the heavens. It was a very solemn time, many, I believe, wept, and I trust all felt it, and united in prayer. I think I may say I went away rejoicing, which appeared marvellous to me, my season of discouragement had at times whilst there, been so great ; but I believe these things tend to keep me low and preserve me, or I might, when so uplifted, be tempted to take my flight. I find on my return much cause for gratitude.

The personal and particular providence of God, in His dealings with men, is never more proved than in the varied and apparently contrary means by which He brings them to a saving knowledge of Himself. In the case of Mrs. Fry, we observe results consonant to her peculiar circumstances, and to the instruments used to awaken her from the sleep of death to a life of righteousness. It is impossible to doubt, but that God Himself, by His Holy Spirit, opened her heart to receive the

glad tidings of salvation ; although at the time, her knowledge
of the great scheme of man's Redemption, appears to have been
obscure and indistinct. She was like a mariner, who, not fully
acquainted with the chart and compass by which to pursue the
voyage, is yet guided by an invisible hand into the Harbour of
Refuge. Her heart was dedicated with that reverential love, so
conspicuous in her character. Her becoming a minister, awful
to her nature, terrible to her as a delicate and timid woman, she
yet received with thankfulness ; inasmuch as she considered it a
token of being owned by Him, and employed in His service.
Far different to those, who well versed in the theory of religion,
and observant of its outward forms, have not given their hearts
to the Lord. The time had however arrived, when He who
had great things for her to perform in the world and the Church,
so willed it, that this devoted servant should be furnished with
all knowledge, as well as spiritual understanding, and having
proved the grounds of her confidence, should be able, from the
great treasury of Biblical Truth, to give a reason for the hope
that was in her.

Some of her sisters having joined the Church of England,
from conviction, and at the same time adorning their profession
by an eminently spiritual and self-denying life, had its effect
upon her ; and prepared the way for further intercourse and
union with others, who differed from herself in the externals of
religion.

In her intercourse with them, she was frequently driven to the
defence of her own opinions ; and to do this, it became necessary that they should not only be clearly defined to her own
mind, but that she should be able so to express them, as to
render them intelligible to others.

With Mr. Edwards, Mr. Simeon, Mr. Francis Cunningham,
(afterwards her brother-in-law,) and many persons of similar
sentiments, she had frequent intercourse. Whilst in some things

they differed ; as the stream from which they drank diverged into various channels,—she learned to acknowledge that it flowed from the same fountain of everlasting truth. The Bible Society bringing her into contact with many excellent and devoted Christians of other denominations, tended to the same result, and to induce those liberal and expansive feelings towards all whom she believed to love the Lord Jesus Christ in sincerity, which from that time became marked and growing features in her character.

CHAPTER VII.

SOON after Mrs. Fry's return from Norfolk, her baby became seriously ill; scarcely was this anxiety removed, before one of her sisters had the affliction of losing an infant daughter, just the age of Mrs. Fry's little Elizabeth. The event was very affecting to her, and touched her tenderest feelings ; her exceeding love of her own little children, extending in an unusual degree to those of her brothers and sisters.

Plashet, Tenth Month, 17th.—I was enabled, on First day evening, to pray for my dear children in their presence ; since then I have felt more cheerful and easy about them, having committed them to His keeping, who alone can protect them. I am but a poor instrument in His holy hand, His they are ; though He may have appeared to give them to us, my heart's desire and prayer is, that like as Hannah with Samuel, they may all be lent unto the Lord. My dear baby is poorly, I desire not to be too anxious about her ; but that the Divine will may alone be done in all things, and that I may be enabled to commend her to His holy keeping ; not that I feel compunction for naturally desiring her life, and that she may be saved from much suffering.

21st.—Much occupied night and day, by the illness of my sweet babe ; I was so low in the night, that I shed many tears, a mother's feelings are strong in me ;—Oh, that I may be granted a submissive and resigned spirit, and that imagination may not colour the dark side, may I in all my various allotments be

enabled to bow in faith, before Him, who orders all things well ;
even amidst the risings of natural feeling, which, rightly modified,
I do not believe to be wrong.   I desire, above all, that not my
will, O Lord ! but Thine be done.   Amen, saith my soul.

25th.—My dear babe much better ; it appears as if my prayer
had been heard.

Eleventh Month, 18*th.*—(The day of the funeral of her little
niece.)   To whom can I go in moments of trial, but to Him
who hath hitherto helped me ?   Be pleased, O Lord ! to be with
us, and bless the present occasion to us ; may it draw us nearer
to Thee, and make us increasingly willing to become Thy servants, and Thy handmaids ; if any thing should, as a minister
come to my hands to do, may I be helped by Thy power, and
anointed by Thee, who can alone savingly help us.   May the
state of my heart be such, that I may with truth say, here am I,
Lord, do with me what Thou wilt, only make me what Thou
wouldest have me to be.   May this event be of lasting benefit
to us all ; but more particularly to the dear parents.   Grant me,
O Lord ! wisdom and power to proclaim Thy power and Thy
praise, that if made use of at all, others as well as myself, may
be drawn nearer to Thee, and wholly give Thee praise, never
taking or giving that glory to the creature, which alone belongs
to the Creator.

Afternoon.—The funeral of dear little Susannah Buxton, has
taken place to-day. The event of her death has been very affecting to me, and most unexpected to us all, this day week, she only
appeared to have a cold ; she was one of the loveliest, sweetest,
and most lively of little babes.   She appeared to suffer little in
her illness.   I was not there at her death, but comfort was then
near to her dear mother, and faith that strengthened her to believe it was well, and that her spirit had ascended unto God,
who gave it.   This was very much the case with me when there
after her death ; but naturally it has been a close stroke, the
child was very dear to me, but consolation has been near.

We have had to-day a very solemn, and I trust in the best
sense, an encouraging time, the remembrance of it is sweet and
reviving to me.   I was helped in prayer, greatly as I think, and
in a few words afterwards ; but may self pass unobserved, for

there was a better than man present with us. Words fall very short of expression : Oh, that all would come, taste and see how good the Lord is, for blessed is the man that trusteth in Him, —although like others, he may be afflicted !

Henry Hull, a valuable Friend and Minister from America, was at this time frequently a guest at Plashet. Early in the winter, Mrs. Fry believed it her duty to unite with him in a religious visit to some of the Meetings near London. Her sister, Priscilla Gurney, accompanied them ;—they were absent about a fortnight.

Twelfth Month, 28th.—My heart is very full this morning at the prospect of this journey ; the tears rise in my eyes, for it appears probable that we shall be out longer than I at first expected. I have something of a confidence that my beloved family will be cared for in my absence. My prayer for myself is, that I may not run without being sent ; and if the gift in me grows and increases with exercise, may I ever be preserved from decking myself with the Lord's jewels.

Plashet, First Month 13th, 1812.—I returned safely home yesterday, and to my great comfort found all my beloved children well and good. My beloved husband is gone into Wales ; all my household appear in very comfortable order ; and so far from having suffered in my absence, it appears as if a better blessing had attended them than common ; thus much for them, now for myself—I may, I trust, with gratitude acknowledge, that I have in my religious duties, experienced the Lord to go before me, and to prove my rear-ward, I have naturally been in a low estate, much felt my absence from home, and have not been well in my health. I have also in a spiritual sense been often brought low, under a peculiar feeling of some of my infirmities, and great fear of the power of the tempter. I have felt much increased value and love for Henry Hull, and dear Priscilla has been a sweet, kind, and valuable companion ; may our union be farther cemented. My desire for myself on my return is, that I may walk within my house with a perfect heart.

Second Month, 1st.—On reading over my old journals yesterday, it has led me to admire how some of my early prayers and desires have been answered ; how gradual has been the arising and opening of Divine Power in my heart. How much has occurred to strengthen my weak faith, and doubting, fearful heart ; how much has been done for me, and how little have I done myself ; how much have I rebelled, except in the day of power ; how often unwatchful, yet in mercy, how has help been administered, even a willing heart, which I consider an unspeakable gift : but I think I should have flourished better, and grown stronger by this time, had I more fully and more faithfully followed the Lamb whithersoever He goeth. My heart's desire and prayer for myself, above everything else, is, that this may be more entirely done by me. O Lord ! be pleased still to carry on Thy own work in me, until Thou hast made me what Thou wouldest have me to be ; even entirely Thy servant, in thought, word and deed ! Thou only knowest my weakness and fear of suffering ; when in Thine infinite wisdom, Thou mayst see meet to afflict, be pleased to mix mercy with judgment, and uphold me by Thine own power ; I thank Thee for all Thy benefits towards me, and desire to prove my gratitude by my love and good works. O Lord ! enable me so to do ? Amen.

3rd.—The prospect I have had for some months of going into Norfolk, to attend the Monthly and Quarterly Meetings, is now brought home to me, as I must apply to my next Monthly Meeting for permission. It is no doubt a sacrifice of natural feeling, to leave the comforts of home, and my beloved husband and children ; and to my weak nervous habits, the going about, and alone (for so I feel it in one sense without my husband) is, I have found from experience, a trial greater than I imagined ; and my health suffers much, I think, from my habits being necessarily so different. This consideration of its being a cross to my nature, I desire not to weigh in the scale ; though no doubt for the sake of others, as well as myself, my health being so shaken is a serious thing. What I desire to consider most deeply is this :—Have I authority for leaving my home and evident duties ? What leads me to believe I have ! for I need not doubt but that when away, and at times greatly tried, this query is likely to arise. The prospect has come in that quiet, yet I think powerful way, that I have never been able to believe I should get rid of it; indeed hitherto I have hardly felt anything but a calm cheerfulness about it, and very little anxiety. It seems to me as if in this journey I must be stripped of outward dependences, and my watchword appears to be, "My soul wait thou ONLY upon God; for my expectation is in Him."

6th.—My beloved little ones have been ill with a severe cold, and my sweet babe has so very serious an attack, and one that has now lasted some days, that I believe her life is thought to be in danger. I have suffered a good deal, the most in the night; my desire for myself is, to be enabled to submit to the dispensations of Almighty wisdom, and that faith may be granted me, to drink the cup, whatever it may be, as coming from the Lord's holy hand; nothing doubting but that it will be ordered in infinite wisdom and mercy. Natural feelings I do not desire to be without, for I had rather have them, if under proper subjection. Jesus wept, may not we? I feel much gratitude that her sufferings appear comparatively small, and rather to decrease; if I could have a prayer on her account outwardly, it would be that she might be spared much suffering; but I desire and pray above all things, that I may leave all to Him, who has dealt with me and my little ones in unspeakable mercy, that He will yet watch over us for good, and not permit us to suffer more than is best for us. How much better to have her life cut short in innocency, than for her to live to that state in which her sins should have separated her from her God. Be pleased, O Lord! to grant Thy poor servant and her little one, strength sufficient for the day, and whether mourning or rejoicing be my portion, may it work together for my good, and make me a better servant to Thee. Amen, and Amen.

7th.—A few hours after I last wrote, a change took place in the dear babe for the better, and the amendment has been gradual since. I have not found it easy to feel this great relief rightly; I desire to receive it as from the blessed hand that makes sore and binds up, that wounds and make whole.

20th.—My sister, Elizabeth Fry, means to go with me into Norfolk; my uncle Joseph is likely to go another way: it appears as if I could not mind much who is to go with me. But I feel disposed to a very single dependence, and if I be rightly put forth to this service, may He who puts me forth be with me, if I have to administer food to others, may it be that which is convenient for them, and that will tend to their lasting nourish- ment. I have often thought that, in this little prospect, I must go like David, when he went to slay the giant. I am ashamed of the comparison ; but I only mean it in this respect, I go not trusting in any power, or strength of my own; I feel I dare look to no helper outwardly. I feel young and a stripling, without armour, yet I trust the Lord will be with me, and make the sling and stone effectual, if He please to make use of His poor child to slay the giant in any one.

Earlham, Third Month, 14*th.*—Have I not renewed reason for faith, hope, and confidence in the principle which I desire to follow. In the night I had to acknowledge that the work must be Thine, O Lord! and that it is to me wonderful. My fears and causes of discouragement were many, for some little time before I set off, my own poor health, and my little ones ; then my lowness and stupidity. In the first place, my health and the dear children's improved so much, and I inwardly so brightened, that I left home very comfortably. As I went on my way, such abundant hope arose, that light, rather than darkness appeared to surround me. I have now attended the Monthly Meetings, and three other Meetings. I have also had frequent opportunies of a religious nature, in families ; the most remark- able, were, one in a clergyman's family, in supplicationf or him and his house, and another, where he had to supplicate for my help. May I ever remember how utterly unfit I am in myself for all these works : unto me alone belongs abasedness. I can take nothing to myself. As Thou hast seen meet, O Lord! Thou who art strength in weakness, thus to make use of Thy poor handmaid, as an instrument in Thy service, be pleased to keep her from the evil, both in reality and appearance, that she never may in any way bring reproach upon Thy cause !

16*th.*—I expect my beloved brother, John, may be here to- day; may I be enabled so to walk before him, in humility and godly fear, (not the fear of man,) that he at least may be enabled to believe I am not following cunningly devised fables, or ima-

ginations of my own, but rather seeking to follow a crucified
Redeemer, in the way in which He leads me.

In a letter to her cousin, Joseph Gurney Bevan, she thus enlarges on the duties in which she was engaged :—

May I now be enabled to attend to my own vineyard, and
after having been made instrumental thus to warn and encourage
others, may I not become a cast-away myself. I hardly understand what Friends mean by reward for such services, for I do
not feel the work mine, and no reward is due ; as for reward, is
it not enough to feel a Power better than ourselves influencing
and strengthening us to do the work that we humbly trust is His
own ? for what honour, favour, or blessing so great, as being
engaged in the service of Him whom we love, in whatever way
it be, whether performing one duty or another, and having a
little evidence granted us, that we are doing His will, or endeavouring to do it. I peculiarly feel in ministerial duties that I
have no part, because the whole appears a gift,—the willing
heart, the power, and every thing attending it ; the poor creature
has only to remain as passive as possible, willing to be operated
upon.

Plashet, Third Month, 28*th.*—I will first mention how it was
with me in the Norwich Quarterly Meeting. I went, looking to
Him who has hitherto helped me ; my beloved uncle Joseph said
a few words, as a seal to what I had expressed, and it was, I
believe, a peculiarly solemn and favoured time : much blessed in
a few words of supplication, at the Grove, before dinner. In the
adjourned Meeting, I felt it safest to go the Men's Meeting,
where I had to bid them farewell in the Lord ; after I had been
helped with a few words of tender love and encouragement,
Sarah Bowly said a little, and then my dear sister Elizabeth
arose, and said, " She hoped what had passed that day, would
not be attended to as a tale that was told, but as everlasting
truths ;" which appeared to me to bring great solemnity and
sweetness with it. In the Women's Meeting, we also had a very
solemn time at parting, in which I bade them farewell ; desiring

that we might all ascend, step by step, that ladder which reaches from earth to heaven. Before we set off, I had, after reading, in heart-felt and heart-rending supplication, to pray for the preservation of the family, and our support in the day of trial; and amidst all the various turnings and overturnings of the Holy Hand upon us. Here I once more am, surrounded by outward blessings and well in health; yet I hardly know how to return thanks, or to rejoice in Him who has helped me, being poor, low, stripped, the tears come into my eyes. Though cast down, I love the Lord above all, and desire, through the saving redeeming power of Him, who came to save that which was lost, and has, I believe, proved a Saviour to me *in part*, that I may draw nearer and nearer to the most high God, and become in all things, more completely His.

No one can read the expression, " in part," as applied to the Saviour's complete and finished work, without having his attention arrested by it; a letter which is here introduced to the Rev. Edward Edwards, explains that her use of these words arose not from any mistrust of the saving power of Christ, but from her consciousness that the great work of sanctification in her heart was incomplete and unfinished.

My beloved Friend,
Thy letter is one I do not desire lightly to answer, as I wish to receive it and attend to it with the seriousness it deserves, as coming from one, who I believe desires the prosperity of truth individually and generally, and in this desire, has with love addressed me for my own good, and also the good of the body to which I belong. I hope to profit by it; I am spiritually but a child, " I think as a child, I speak as a child, and I understand as a child." I do not believe that the great mysteries of the gospel are by any means fully opened to me; but my dependence is on Him who has so far opened my eyes, that He will in His own time further enlighten me, confirm, settle, and strengthen me in that faith which is the substance of things hoped for, the evidence of things not seen. Thus far I believe, from having experienced

what it is to feel alienated or separated from my God, no doubt
by corruptions and sin. I experienced the state of being under
the law ; I may truly say, " I know that in me, that is, in my
flesh, dwelleth no good thing; for to will is present with me,
but how to perform that which is good, I find not; for the good
that I would I do not ; but the evil which I would not that I do.'
Thus I have experienced and do yet experience, that it is not
in me, or my fleshly nature, to do or to will any good thing.
Then how naturally do these words arise, " O ! wretched man,
(or woman,) that I am, who shall deliver me from the body of this
death ?"   Then comes the Saviour, then comes the Deliverer, to
whom can I go, but to Him, who alone has the words of eternal
life ?   I feel ashamed of now bringing my experiences forward, as
it is with humility and confusion of face that I may acknowledge,
I have also felt what it is in a measure to be in Christ Jesus ;
" for the law of the spirit of life in Christ Jesus, maketh us free
from the law of sin and death ; for what the law could not do,
in that it was weak through the flesh, God sending his own Son
in the likeness of sinful flesh and for sin, condemned sin in the
flesh, that the righteousness of the law might be fulfilled in those
who walk not after the flesh but after the Spirit."   I have thus
quoted Scripture, because I know no other way of so clearly expressing my own faith, and experience in measure, and also what
I believe to be the faith of the body, (though there may be unbelievers amongst us as well as others,) that we lay aside all our
own works, and believe we neither will nor do of ourselves, but
that it is God, or the saving power of Christ, that worketh in us
to will and to do ; that we desire alone to give all the glory to
Him, of whatever is done to his praise, believing Him to be the
author and finisher of our faith, and our only hope of glory.
The work of regeneration is a gradual one, and I feel, if alive
at all, only a beginner, therefore do not understand that I feel
free from the law of sin and death ; but I believe if the spirit of
Christ in us be permitted to operate, and is not resisted by our
wills, we may experience a being made free from the law of sin
and spiritual death, even here below.

Fourth Month, 4th.—Since I last wrote, I have been afflicted inwardly and outwardly ; I have had a more serious attack of illness than I have had for many months.   It led me to consider, if taken hence, where would be my hope ?   To feel an operative faith, of being accepted through the mercy of God in Christ, is a gift which we cannot command.   Oh ! that my soul may be more deeply anchored in this faith, that nothing may be permitted to shake it : I also find, that without the present gift of faith, I cannot commit my beloved husband and children to His holy keeping, who can alone preserve them.

16*th.*—I am poorly, and I believe five of my dear children have the hooping-cough ; but all appears light, nay, more than light, such sweetness has covered my mind, little short at times of joy and peace, as if no alloy were permitted to take hold ; so are we dealt with, not according to our merits, but to His mercy, who careth for His poor dependent ones, and enlivens them when He seeth meet.

This letter to her brother, John Gurney, undated, was obviously written during this spring, not long after her Norfolk journey.

My dear John,

I feared thou wouldest almost think me forgetful of thee in not having expressed my near interest in thy welfare for so long ; but feeling very low this morning, to whom can I write better than to one who mourns, and can sympathize with me, though our causes for suffering may be different.   I hope my last letter did not hurt dear Catherine and Rachel.   I have felt fearful how far it was right for me to touch upon their present state, lest I should hurt the cause I most desire to advocate ; I am therefore cautious of saying much, but I very deeply feel the state of the family, believing it not unlikely they will leave a path that has to me appeared a remarkably blessed and safe one ; and not only to so weak an instrument as I am, but surely there have been many in our family, that in the same path have done credit to the Christian cause.   However, I desire to leave it, if in ever so small a degree my tears and prayers, (when enabled to offer them,) may prove effectual in desiring preservation for you all, that after trying all things, you may indeed be enabled to hold fast that which is good, even if it lead you into a different path from me ; but I acknowledge it has been sweet to me, whenever I have had a hope that the day might come, when we should fully unite in spiritual things ; but if it never should, may true charity and love be our portion; I mean that spirit of charity that comes from above, and unites all true and sincere travellers Zion-ward. I should much like soon to hear from you ; with regard to thee and Rachel I have no fear about your love for me, for I could believe, much as we have differed, we have never been separated; indeed, dear John, when thou lived to the world, how did my soul pant after thee, what tender solicitude have I felt on thy account, and now I do indeed rejoice in thy experience. I cannot think, if when we felt so very differently, we loved so much, now that we desire to be following the same Master, and to be devoted to the same cause, we shall be separated)—I believe it cannot be.

Fragment found between the leaves of her journal, about this date.

Plan to try for children. Boys sent to tutor, after our reading. Little ones with me till nearly ten o'clock ; again from two to three ; from after dinner till seven. See the elder girls at lessons twice during the morning, and have them with me from one till two ; boys and girls from seven till eight, together ; besides their being at meals now and then.

Plashet, Fourth Month, 24th.—To whom can I go when brought into straitened places, but to Him who has hitherto succoured me, in His own way? Snares are apt to beset me on every hand ; for there are left, as well as right hand errors. I expected to remain pretty quietly at home, but I have been four times to Meeting this week. Seldom have I had to move much more in the cross than on Third day; how did I naturally flinch, how did I recoil at a prospect which came unexpectedly upon me, of going into the Men's Meeting at Plaistow. In the Meetings for Discipline, I sought Him to whom power belongeth, and in His power, His people are made a willing people ; I believe my prayers were heard ; and may I, as need to be the case with all pilgrims, who seek to go Zion-ward, not turn from any thing, from unwillingness and impatience. May we rather seek Him, who " giveth power to the faint, and to him that hath no might He increaseth strength."

Sixth Month, 16*th.*—It now appears too late to give much account of the Yearly Meeting. The prospect of going into the Men's Meeting, naturally was so awful, nay, almost dreadful, that as I sat at breakfast, fears arose lest my understanding should fail ; however, though in great measure taken from me, upon first sitting down in Meeting, yet after a time the concern arose with tranquillity, and with a powerful, though small voice, at least with power sufficient to enable me to cast my burden upon the Meeting ; this brought, I thought, great solemnity, I appeared to have the full unity of Friends, dear Rebecca Bevan went with me ; I felt myself much helped when there ; matter, tongue, and utterance were all given in testimony and supplication. I think the calm frame I enjoyed, upon returning into the Women's Meeting, must almost be a foretaste of that rest which the soul pants after.

Sixth Month.—My press of engagements has been very great, in the first place, the deep affliction of our much-loved friend, Henry Hull. He having received letters, to say, that his wife, son, mother, and brother-in-law, were all dead of a contagious fever, and the lives of the rest of the family very uncertain ; much as he suffered, he bore it like a man and a Christian, so as to encourage, rather than try my faith ; it of course took up my time and attention, to wait upon, and care for him. We have had a very large family party, my brother and sister Fry, three children, and servants ; my sister Elizabeth, and cousin Sarah, besides many Friends backwards and forwards : also much illness in the house, my sister and her nurse, and also her baby, very dangerously ill. These have all been objects of care, and interest, so that I am sorry to say, I have been at times so weighed down, and panting for rest, that I have been almost irritable, and

I fear not enough estimated the value of their company, or the comfort of being able to serve them ; but I hope my health may be some excuse for me, for they are very dear to me.   I think my temper requires very great watchfulness, for the exercises of my mind, my very numerous interests, and the irritability excited by my bodily infirmities, cause me to be in so tender and touchy a state that the " grasshopper becomes a burden." In this, as in all my infirmities, I have but one hope ; it is in the power of Him who has in mercy answered my prayers, and helped me in many of my difficulties, and I humbly trust yet will arise for my deliverance.   As to the ministry, I have been raised up and at times cast down, but my heart and attention have been mostly turned to rigidly performing my practical duties in life, which is my object by night and by day.   I have felt, as if I could rest in nothing short of serving Him whom my soul loves, but I desire to watch, and am fully aware that with regard to myself, I have nothing to trust to, but mercy ; but leaving myself, I long whilst permitted to remain in mortality, not to be a drone, but to do every thing to the glory of God.   I think I desire to do all things well, more for the cause sake, than for the sake of my own soul, as my conviction of the mercy and loving-kindness of Him who loveth us, and who is touched with a feeling of our infirmities, is so great, that whilst my heart is seeking to serve Him, (full as I am of defects,) I am ready to trust that, that mercy which has hitherto compassed me about, will be with me to the end of time, and continue with me through eternity.   The fear of punishment hardly even arises, or has arisen in my mind, it is more the certain knowledge that I have, of the blessedness of serving our Master, and the very strong excitement of love and gratitude, and desire for the promotion of the blessed cause upon earth.   Through all my tried states, I have one unspeakable blessing to acknowledge ; and that is, an increase of faith.

Seventh Month, *3rd.*—We have for the last week been alone, which appears greatly to have recruited soul and body ; I much wanted this time with my dear husband and children, it has enabled me to turn my attention to my home duties, and I trust I may rest pretty easy in believing things are generally in good order, as to servants, children, &c., &c. The poor may want a little further investigation ; I feel thankful in thus being enabled to stop and examine the state of my family and house. How much have I to be thankful for, though all may not be quite what I wish ; how many valuable dependants I have : those who I believe love us, and that which is good ; some I hope will remain our friends for life. My beloved children who are come almost to an age of understanding, I long to see more under the Cross of Christ, and less disposed to give way to their own wills; I sometimes indulge them too much when young, I mean very little, and perhaps their nurses do so too. I could desire, though it appears asking a great deal, as to things temporal, that if right for us, we may be able through life to live in the open liberal way we do now, endeavouring to make all around us comfortable, and that we may be able to continue generous friends to the poor· I fear to be much limited would be very difficult to me, I desire that my attention being so much turned to things temporal, may not hinder my progress in things spiritual ; I do not believe it injurious to have the natural part occupied in natural things, provided all be done under subjection, and with a single eye to the service of our great Master.

Plashet, Eighth Month, 14th.—Eighteen, in addition to our own family, slept here last night ; we passed a comfortable, and, I hope, not an unsatisfactory day. When surrounded by many of my own family, I desire to be preserved from the spirit of judgment, but I find it difficult not to be on the watch with those who have been outwardly baptized ; how far the living baptism shines forth in them, and enables to renounce the devil and all his works, the pomps, lusts, and vanities of this present world. Surely, saith my soul, there is but one saving baptism, even that which redeems from the world ; and I more and more, think I see the danger of the outward form or ordinance, lest any should deceive themselves that they are baptized into Christ, when in reality they know little about it; not that I judge those before alluded to, but there is need of further washing, I believe, in them and in me.

Ninth Month, 2nd.—This morning our poor servant who has

for some weeks kept his bed very seriously ill, died. I feel that I have cause for humble gratitude, in having been at the awful time strengthened by faith, and I believe, I may say, having experienced the Divine presence near; I have often sat and watched by his bed-side, desiring to know whether I had any thing to do or say, as to his soul's welfare. I found neither feeling, faith, nor ability, to say or do much more than endeavour to turn his mind towards his Maker, but I think never more than once in anything of the anointing power. Yesterday morning I found him much worse, a struggle upon him, that appeared breaking the thread of life, and his sufferings great, mentally and bodily. The first thing I found in myself was, that a willing mind was granted me, and in sitting by him, the power and spirit of supplication and intercession for him arose, to which I gave way; it immediately appeared to bring a solemn tranquillity, his pains and restlessness were quieted; his understanding I believe was quite clear, he thanked me, and said once or twice, " God bless you, ma'am," as if he felt much comfort in what had passed. Faith, love, and calmness, were the covering of my mind. He had, I believe, only one or two more slight struggles after I left him; after that I was sent for, and found that the conflict appeared over, and he breathed his last in about a quarter of an hour. There was peculiar sweetness, and great silence and solemnity in the room. I had to acknowledge that I believed the mercy of our Heavenly Father was then extended towards him, and to express a desire, that it might in the same awful moment be extended towards us, feeling how greatly we stood in need of mercy. The rest of the day passed off as well as I could expect; I feared lest the servants and others should attribute that praise to me, with which I had nothing to do, for I could not have prayed, or found an answer to prayer, without an anointing from the Most High. It led me to feel it a blessing to be entrusted with this sacred and precious gift; for though ministers may have much to pass through, and many crosses to take up, for their own good and that of others, yet, it is a marvellous gift when the pure life stirs, operates, and brings down strongholds. My nerves were rather shaken, so as to make me naturally fearful, at times, the rest of the day. I have a great desire, that this event may be blessed to the household, more particularly the servants, that it may humble and bow their spirits, that they may live more in love, and grow in the knowledge of God, and of our Lord and Saviour Jesus Christ.

It will be difficult for those who knew Mrs. Fry only in later life, and her zealous endeavours to obtain for all within her reach religious instruction, and the hearing or reading of the Bible, to comprehend her not affording a member of her own household, under serious protracted illness, more regular instruction on matters of such vast importance. The dispensation into which she had been brought, acting upon her timid nature, induced extreme fear of "running before she was sent," or treading " unbidden upon holy ground;" when, on the contrary, she believed that it was the Master's voice which called, there was neither place nor circumstance that could arrest her steps.

After a time, it pleased Him, who was guiding his servant according to the purposes of His own will, by an increased acquaintance with human nature, and more general association with all sorts of men, to teach her, that the Omnipotent works by outward providences and second causes, and that whilst the Holy Spirit can alone bless and fructify the seed, it is none the less the duty of man in simple obedience to the written word, to use every opportunity in his power to sow the good seed, trusting to God to give the increase.

The funeral of the servant was fixed for the following Sunday ; as the time approached, Mrs. Fry felt an earnest desire arise in her heart, that the occasion might be one of benefit to others as several of his friends were to be present ; some from the immediate neighbourhood.

She proposed that in the evening all the assembled guests should be invited to attend the family reading with her own household, but before the hour arrived for the performance of a duty, which was to her exceedingly weighty, she was summoned to visit Eliza, the newly married wife of her cousin Mr. James Sheppard, who was rapidly sinking into the grave. The afflicted husband and sister were deeply needing the skilful tenderness with which she could meet such exigencies. At Meeting, in the morning, her heart had been strengthened, and apparently prepared for the duties of the day. By the bed of languishing we find her, waiting for that unction, without which she was sensible that her services could avail nothing; and the same evening, in her own dwelling, when surrounded by about forty besides her children, she speaks in exhortation and prayer. Her address was closely suited to the state of some persons present, and unflinchingly did she impress upon them, that the " way of transgressors is hard." The occasion was long remembered by individuals who were there, and who attributed their permanent improvement to the solemn truths they then heard ; and for the first time, effectively received into their hearts. Her own journal of the day, written the following morning, pourtrays the workings of her mind.

Plashet, Ninth Month, Second day.—Yesterday was rather a remarkable one. I rose very low and fearful, though I am almost ashamed of acknowledging how it was, and has been with me after so many deliverances ; but my spirit appeared overwhelmed within me, partly I think from some serious outward matters, but principally from such an extreme fear of my approaching confinement, feeling nothing in myself to meet it, and knowing that it must come unless death prevent it. I went to Meeting, but was almost too low to know whether I should go or not ; however, being helped in testimony to show the blessedness of those who hope in the Lord, and not in themselves, appeared to do me good, as if I had to minister to myself as well as to others ; I had a trust that my help was in the Lord, and that therefore I should experience my heart to be strengthened. A message came requesting my immediate attendance on poor dear Eliza Sheppard, who appeared near her end, of course I went. These visits are very awful; to sit by that which we believe to be a death-bed; to be looked to by the afflicted and others, as a minister from whom something is expected, and the fear at such a time of the activity of the creature arising, and doing that which it has no business to do. After sitting some time quiet, part of which she appeared to sleep, and part to be awake, a solemn silence covered us, and words of supplication arose in due time; when I believed her to be engaged in the same manner, by her putting her hands together, I knelt down and felt greatly helped, but had not so much to pray for her alone, as for all of us there present with her. I had a few words also to say in taking leave; the visit appeared sweet to her by her smiles, and her whispering to her sister expressing this. Thus ended this solemn scene, her husband, her own sister and brother, and dear Elizabeth Gurney were present; dear Eliza Sheppard's mind appeared in a truly calm, resigned state. I returned home in rather more than an hour, when the prospect of the evening felt very serious to me. After poor John's funeral, I wished the servants, and those who attended it and were disposed to do so, to be present at our reading. The party were in all about forty, many young people, and others. We first read two chapters in Matthew; after a pause, I knelt down, and had to supplicate, first, for all the party; afterwards, for our own household, more particularly for the servants; in all which I was helped, and a very solemn silence followed. The party broke up; I think I found myself strengthened, rather than weakened, by the day's work, mentally and bodily, though my own great weakness soon returned upon me, and it appeared striking that such an one should have been so engaged, but painful as these feelings of depression are to bear, I know "it is well," as it keeps me humble, at least I hope so, lowly and abased. Oh! saith my soul, after thus ministering to others, may I not become a castaway myself, and neither in trouble, or rejoicing, bring discredit on the cause that I love, or on His name whom I desire to serve.

Plashet, 10*th*.—A hopeful, and I trust thankful frame of spirit, may the praise be wholly and entirely ascribed where the praise is due, for neither in myself, nor in any outward thing or person, can I at times receive consolation, unless the Divine blessing attend. Enable me, O Lord! to rejoice in Thee, and to give Thee thanks, that Thou hast so far seen meet to relieve me from my fearfulness, and the captivity I have been in. Oh! it is a blessed thing to know that there yet lives a Saviour, ready to help our infirmities, blessed be His holy name for ever. In Him do I trust, not in myself; be pleased, O Lord! to confirm, establish and strengthen my feeble heart, that I may rightly and fully ascribe glory, honour and power to the Father, Son, and Holy Spirit; yet feeling all as one, and but as mighty parts of the same eternal, invisible, and invincible power. Whatsoever be taken from me, may this faith live, grow, and increase abundantly!

Her eighth child was born September 12th, 1812. Writing very soon afterwards to her cousin, Joseph Gurney Bevan, she thus records her thankfulness.

Plashet, Fourth day.

My beloved Cousin,

I am safe, and I have a sweet little girl. What can I render? My heart feels this morning rather overwhelmed within me. I hope not without love to the great Master; but how sweetly has it flowed towards many, whom I believe to be more or less His followers. I have particularly felt it towards my much-loved Friends in Gracechurch-street Meeting. My spirit has felt amongst you; I hope you do not forget me, for I do not forget you; with what love have you as a body been brought to my remembrance, many individually. May we each fill our respective ranks, none drawing back, but stepping forward in the cause of righteousness. Though I have been long out of sight, yet I trust I am not quite out of the minds of many, but I desire the prayers of the church, for preservation, and more full dedication and resignation in all things to the Divine will. It would be very pleasant to see thee, or any of those whom I feel so near (though so unworthy of it yet I could hope) in the covenant of life. My heart has also been so filled with love towards the

Friends of my own Quarterly Meeting, that I could have written them a letter of love.

17*th.*—It appears due for me to acknowledge the tender mercies and loving-kindness of a long-suffering God, in my late safe deliverance, though at times tried by various feelings of weakness, yet I have been permitted to find the healing virtue near, keeping soul and body, the calming influence of which has at times been very sweet ; at others, my heart has had to flow with love towards many.   No doubt my late confinements have been precious seasons wherein the love of the Father has been present with me ; though occasionally at others, brought very low, and tried by bodily and mental infirmities.   Enable me, O Lord ! to render all the praise to Thee, and yet to trust and not be afraid.

Plashet, Ninth Month, 28*th.*—When my spirits are low, I am apt to feel leaving the country, which is proposed for the winter.   I am almost surprised at myself, the tears have often risen ; very few indeed, I believe none know, how sweet the quiet and the beauties of the country have been to me ; it takes hold of some of my tender feelings.

Mildred's Court, Eleventh Month, 24*th.*—I arrived here last evening to settle for the winter, after a very encouraging Public Meeting, with dear William Forster, at Plaistow, which I believe did me good ; I felt the Power near, it appeared to cover us and the assembly, though I passed through much in the Meeting, so as to shake me very much ; but truth appeared to me to come into dominion, which was cause for humble gratitude. May I be enabled to perform my duties, at home and abroad.

Mildred's Court, Twelfth Month, 11*th.*—Yesterday, I experienced liveliness of spirit, without any apparent cause ; nothing but free mercy and grace, for I think, as far as I was concerned, I was rather rebellious after reading, than otherwise.   It is an unspeakable source of gratitude, to feel alive spiritually, even to feel condemnation ; for without that, how can we understand what justification is ? these spiritual dispensations, are, indeed, like the wind that bloweth where it listeth : yet my belief is, amidst them all, whatever they may be, whether abounding or suffering be our portion, that it is infinitely important to be found doing the will of God, if we expect our houses to stand, amidst the various storms and trials we are brought into ; for although we may appear to ourselves dry, sterile, and " unfruitful as the barren sand ;" yet, there is the conviction granted of being founded on a rock that nothing can shake. Not that I desire to boast of the works of obedience, for after all they will not do alone, for even in them, how much do we fall short ! our dependence must be, after having even done our best, on the mercy of God in Christ Jesus, on the merits of Him, in whom was perfect obedience.

As this tarriance in London was to be a very short one, it was not thought necessary to remove the clerks and servants usually residing at St. Mildred's Court, the size of the house admitting their continuance without interfering with the arrangements of the family. The circumstances of so many young men being thus under the same roof with themselves, in Mrs. Fry's estimation involved the duty of including them in the family worship, though she found it not a matter easy to arrange.

Mildred's Court, First Month, 12th, 1813.—At last I have been enabled to accomplish my desire in having the greater part of our family here, present at the Scripture reading in the morning, it has been to me a very humbling thing, and I may say trying ; the difficulty, reluctance, and lukewarmness about it, that appeared to exist, so that I was obliged to beg my beloved husband to ask it for me. It was very exercising on the First day morning when we met; but through all, unusual peace has been my portion, in giving up to it. It has been entered into more by faith than by sight, as it appeared so very discouraging, others not uniting in what seems to me so important a duty; but I have a secret hope and belief, that good will come of it, if the Lord will be pleased to bless and strengthen me in it. Oh ! saith my soul, may it tend to our sanctification and redemption. Be pleased, O Lord ! so to bless it, that it become not a dead form, but may it enliven our hearts towards Thee ; and enable Thy poor hand-maid to be a faithful minister of Thy word amongst them, so as to be made instrumental in drawing some nearer to thee. I am thankful, for being so far helped on my way, and for a little peace within, when discouragement was without.

Mildred's Court, Second Month, 5th.—The subject of visiting the Monthly Meetings, has been very present with me. Grant, O Lord ! I beseech Thee, strength and ability to do Thy will, and promote Thy cause in the hearts of others ; I know I am little and weak, yet Thou canst cause one to chase a thousand, and two to put ten thousand to flight. I feel little doubt but that my way will be made in this matter, and that this concern is not of my own appointment. Let me commit myself as much as I can into better hands, there leaving it, seeking in all things a humble mind and resigned will. I have felt and still feel, if the armour of the Lord be put on, which I humbly trust it will be ; that I shall be enabled to fight valiantly. Be with me, O Lord ! then I need not fear, what any man or any power can do unto me. See and cleanse me, if there be any wicked way in me, and lead me in the way everlasting, make this visit instrumental of still more closely uniting me in Gospel love, and fellowship to all scattered here about, yet preserve the poor creature from ever being exalted, or taking that glory that is not its due.

Mildred's Court, 11th.—I feel fresh cause for thankfulness, in being helped through yesterday at our Monthly Meeting, in mentioning my concern to Friends, to visit the Monthly Meetings, &c., of our Quarterly Meeting ; I was unusually exercised in doing it, it appeared such a very pressing matter, as if I must do it, though some of my best and most valued friends advised me against it, thinking that I might safely go without any minute, which I did not feel to be the case, as I apprehended the concern to be more extensive than it at first appeared. I have seldom experienced greater relief in any thing. I could hardly help rejoicing yesterday, with the feelings of thankfulness, that the thing was got through so much to my satisfaction and comfort. Oh, how I loved my friends, 1 even felt it sweet their participating with me, as I believe they did, though little was said, in what I have felt so awful and important, yet, enough was said to satisfy me, and even in one instance, in stronger terms than I quite approved, more than I dared myself say of the concern. I felt a fear yesterday, and also feel it to-day, of taking any thing like my rest in this sweet feeling that has attended me, and so becoming unwatchful, not devoted and circumspect enough. I believe I may truly say my desire is that this event may be blessed to me, and be instrumental in making me better in all things. The Minute granted me is this—" The Women Friends being now present; Elizabeth Fry laid before us a concern, which she had weightily felt, to pay a religious visit to the Monthly Meetings, within this Quarterly Meeting, the same being solidly considered, this Meeting feels unity with her, in her said concern, and recommends her to the sympathy of her friends.'

When a Friend applies for leave from the Meeting to which he belongs, to travel in the work of the Ministry, it is customary, after the Meeting for worship, on the day of the Monthly Meeting, for the men and women to remain together, instead of separating as they usually do for the Meetings of Discipline, in order to receive the communication of the Friend under concern, and to afford it their joint and serious deliberation. When a Woman Friend is in the case, arrangements are carefully made to provide for her comfort and suitable protection, whilst engaged in these labours.

Mildred's Court, Second day, 15*th.*—My fear for myself the last few days is, that I should be exalted by the evident unity of my dear friends whom I greatly value, by being, as I feel I am, in degree looked up to, by those less experienced than myself in the gift, (small as my own is) ; and also my natural health and spirits being good, and being engaged in some laudable pursuits, more particularly seeing after the prisoners in Newgate. Oh, how deeply, how very deeply, I fear the temptation of ever being exalted or self-conceited. I cannot preserve myself from this temptation, any more than being unduly cast down or crushed

by others. Be pleased, O Lord ! to preserve me, for the deep
inward prayer of my heart is, that I may ever walk humbly before Thee ; and also before all mankind. Let me never in any
way take that glory to myself which alone belongs unto Thee, if
in Thy mercy Thou should ever enable one so unworthy either
to do good or to communicate.

16*th.*—Yesterday we were some hours at Newgate with the
poor female felons, attending to their outward necessities; we had
been twice previously. Before we went away, dear Anna Buxton
uttered a few words in supplication, and very unexpectedly to
myself, I did also. I heard weeping, and I thought they appeared much tendered ; a very solemn quiet was observed ; it
was a striking scene, the poor people on their knees around, in
their deplorable condition.

Thus simply and incidently, is recorded Elizabeth's Fry's first
entrance upon the scene of her future labours, evidently without
any idea of the importance of its ultimate results.

In January of this year, four members of the Society of
Friends, all well known to Elizabeth Fry, had visited some persons in Newgate who were about to be executed. Although no
mention is made of the circumstance in the journal, it has
always been understood that the representations of these gentlemen, particularly those of William Forster one of their number,
first induced her personally to inspect the state of the women,
with the view of alleviating their sufferings occasioned by the
inclemency of the season.

At that time, all the female prisoners in Newgate, were confined in that part, now known as the untried side. The larger
portion of the Quadrangle was then used as a state prison. The
partition wall was not of a sufficient height to prevent the state-
prisoners from overlooking the narrow yard, and the windows of
the two wards and two cells, of which the women's division consisted. These four rooms comprised about one hundred and

10

ninety superficial yards, into which, at the time of these visits, nearly three hundred women with their numerous children, were crowded; tried and untried, misdemeanants and felons, without classification, without employment, and with no other superinten- dence than that given by a man and his son, who had charge of them by night and by day. In the same rooms, in rags and dirt, destitute of sufficient clothing (for which there was no provi- sion) sleeping without bedding on the floor, the boards of which were in part raised to supply a sort of pillow, they lived, cooked, and washed.

With the proceeds of their clamourous begging, when any stranger appeared amongst them, the prisoners purchased liquors from a regular tap in the prison. Spirits were openly drunk, and the ear was assailed by the most terrible language. Beyond that necessary for safe custody, there was little restraint over their communication with the world without.

Although military sentinels were posted on the leads of the prison, such was the lawlessness prevailing, that Mr. Newman the governor, entered this portion of it with reluctance. Fearful that their watches should be snatched from their sides, he advised the ladies, (though without avail,) to leave them in his house.

Into this scene, Mrs. Fry entered, accompanied only by one lady, a sister of Sir T. F. Buxton. The sorrowful and neg- lected condition of these depraved women and their miserable children, dwelling in such a vortex of corruption, deeply sank into her heart, although at this time, nothing more was done than to supply the most destitute with clothes. A vivid recol- lection of the green baize garments, and the pleasure of assisting in their preparation for this purpose, is still retained in her family. She carried back to her home, and into the midst of other interests and avocations, a lively remembrance of all that she had witnessed in Newgate; which within four years induced that systematic effort for ameliorating the condition of these poor outcasts, so signally blessed by Him who said, "That joy shall be in heaven over one sinner that repenteth, more than over ninety and nine just persons which need no repentance."

CHAPTER VIII.

NOT only did a considerable space of time elapse after Elizabeth Fry's first visits to Newgate before she renewed them, but
in the interim many events occurred of deep import to herself.
He who "sits as a Refiner and Purifier of silver," saw well to
exercise her in the school of affliction, before raising her up for
the remarkable work she had to do. Long and distressing indisposition ; the death of her brother John Gurney, that of her pa-
ternal friend John Gurney Bevan ; the loss of a most tenderly
beloved child ; considerable loss of property ; separation for a time
from all her elder children, were among the means used by Him,
who cannot err to teach her the utter instability of every human
possession, to draw her heart more entirely to Himself, and to
prepare her for His service. The rare combination in her natural character, of the extremes of courage and timidity were not
more remarkable, that in her spiritual course, her holy boldness
and confiding love contrasted with her dread of in anything of-
fending her " Holy Helper," as she loved to designate Him to
whom her heart was given.

Mildred's Court, Second Month, 19*th.*—I feel very unworthy this morning, though the day appeared to begin well, in a few words of solemn supplication. After reading, yesterday, I think I was too much off my watch, and did not keep that bridle over my tongue, which is so important ; too much disposed to bow the knee of my soul to mortals, rather than to the living God alone. In consequence, I felt this morning at reading, unwilling to take up the cross. In how very many ways is my soul beset, no mortals know, or I believe, even suspect, how much so ; at times my hands appear ready to hang or fall down. Alas ! may it not be so.

To the Reverend Edward Edwards.

Mildred's Court, *Third Month, 2nd,* 1813.

My dear Friend,

I have been questioning whether to write to my dear sister Richenda or thyself, for my heart is full towards you; but as I had thought of writing to thee before, I think thou hast the first claim. Words fall short of expression when the heart is very full ; this is my case at present. I feel you all very near and dear to me, and there are times when I cannot help longing to have all differences and distinctions done away, that we may have one heart and be of one mind ; this was brought home to me by the desire I have for your sympathy and prayers in my steppings along, that you may be able, as it were, to go with me heart and hand ; I feel this because you are so near to me (I trust) in the covenant of love and life, but amidst these cogitations a sweet thought has arisen, that although in time we may not experience all walls of separation to be broken down, yet, we may look forward to a blessed eternity, where with one accord and one heart, we may join the heavenly host in ascribing glory and honour, wisdom and power unto our God, and the Lamb for ever.

Even here the sweet love and unity of which we at times are permitted to partake, appears like a foretaste of that which is to be enjoyed. If any of you should feel disposed to write me a few lines, I hope you will do so ; and if any hint or caution arises,

I beg that you will freely give it; for it is well to watch over one
another for good. The sense of my own weakness, infirmity and
utter insufficiency to promote the glorious cause, also a natural
flinching from such an exposure, and so far taking up the cross,
at times make my heart feel sick and my spirit ready to faint
within me; then again arises for my help and consolation, a faith
in Him who gives power to the faint, and to him who has
no might increases strength; indeed my confidence is not in
myself but in the power of a Saviour and Redeemer. My desire
is, through the ability given, or grace afforded, that I may attend
to the blessed injunction of " Continue ye in my love. If ye
keep my commandments, ye shall abide in my love, even as I
have kept my Father's commandments and abide in his love."
May it be under the constraining influence of this love, that I
ever dare to advocate the cause that I love, and be preserved
from my own willings and runnings. I find my dear friend thou
hast lately been afflicted, and tried; unto such how many precious
promises are offered, yet there are times when the heart feels
unable to receive them, and we can hardly believe ourselves of
the number to whom they apply.   Is this ever thy case? perhaps we can sympathize in the feeling of at times walking in
darkness, and having no light; may we then " trust in the Lord,
and stay ourselves upon our God." My dear love to thy wife,
dear Richenda, and my brother, D——— G———, and remember
me affectionately to our friends, the Hankinsons. Believe me
thy affectionately interested friend,

ELIZABETH FRY.

Mildred's Court, Third Month, 22*nd.*—Began the day poorly,
by not doing what came to hand at our family reading; and now I
am going to set out to visit the sick and sorrowful belonging to
Westminster Meeting. O Lord! have mercy on me, and pardon
my transgressions, and enable Thy poor unworthy one to speak
a word in season to the afflicted and tried. Thou only knowest
my heart and its many fears; preserve me from evil, and keep
the gift pure I beseech Thee, and unalloyed by the dross of my
nature, as I fear for it, lest being so very often called forth, I
should ever stir in my own strength; help Thy poor dependent

child, O Lord! I pray Thee have mercy on me, be with me in the way that I should go, preserve me from undue fear of man, yet keep me open to the caution, reproof, or advice of those further advanced; keep me humble, lowly and obedient, walking in Thy fear, and in Thy love. Amen. Enable me to walk before thee this day, with a watchful, circumspect and faithful heart. Thou hast blessed, be yet pleased to bless!

Fourth Month, 2nd, Mildred's Court.—Richard Phillips called here to day, and I really think I stand too much in awe of his and John Hull's opinions, as regards my religious movements, for I believe they may err; it is far better to look to that Power that cannot err, and whom I know to teach as no man can teach. I think I am far too much a slave to the opinions of the good; I mind it far more than the laugh of the world. May I be preserved from spiritual pride; and yet, I trust, I may live in unity with the good, as long as I live. I feel my own infirmity very much, and see how needful it is for the vessel to be kept clean that contains a gift to hand to others, even if it be through humiliation and crosses. I have been to-day too much engaged trying to serve others; in these duties there is danger of pride creeping in; I have found it in myself, being so consulted and pressed upon. May I watch, and trust in my Redeemer, who is yet able and willing to cleanse and to save.

Plashet, 8th.—Yesterday I gave up my minute. I was helped to acknowledge how it had been with me, that way had been made for me inwardly and outwardly, to accomplish that which I had in view; and although I before had deep humiliation to pass through, and had to bear the cross greatly in some things, also to feel much abased, under a sense of my own infirmity and unworthiness, yet that I had experienced a power better than myself helping me; even that which I believed to be the power of an endless life strengthening me to do things which I could not of myself have done; I had learned afresh that to the creature nothing belongeth but confusion of face but to the Holy Helper, who alone is worthy; glory, honour, power, thanksgiving, and praise. Sweet quietness and peace, was felt after this acknowledgment to the women and men. I also expressed my desire, that whenever weakness or infirmity had shewn itself, it might be laid to the creature, but whenever good, however small, had appeared, that it might by myself and others be attributed to the Creator.

Plashet, 28*th.*—Dear Edward Edwards and his wife are staying here, which has been pleasant to me.

Fifth Month, 1*st.*—So one month passes away, and another comes. A sweetness and power enlivens my heart this morning· I pray Thee, O Lord! Thou who hast hitherto helped me, be with me this day, preserve me humble and lowly in spirit, enable me to do Thy will ; if Thou grantest ability to Thy poor handmaid to speak in Thy name, enable her and all to give wholly unto Thee the glory and honour of Thy own work. We had a very striking time yesterday evening, before our dear friends Edward and Anne Edwards left us, when sitting with them, my sister Priscilla and some others. Dear Edward Edwards knelt down, and to my feelings expressed himself in a very lively manner ; others were led to speak both in testimony and supplication ; afterwards, I had to pour forth a little of my soul ; there appeared to flow a current of life and love, as if we were owned by the Most High ; I felt my own like a song of praise, and have in my misgiving nature feared that those present might think it done in the impetuosity of the creature, which I believe was not the case, being naturally very flat and low. What I experienced I can hardly express, a little like him who thought he could go on till midnight, expressing the goodness of the Lord to him. I certainly was much raised spiritually, and so I believe were all the party, and that we were united together in Christ. I do not think I ever believed so much as I have done since last Third day Meeting, and last evening, that the hand of the Almighty is in the changes that have taken place in our family ; one going one way, one another ; for it has in so remarkable a degree opened a door of spiritual unity with those who differ in some points from each other. It has a tendency to spread that blessed principle, which we uphold as a Society, of the anointing Power, leading us into all truth—the Spirit of Christ in man, as his only hope of glory. May we each faithfully keep our places, and do the work committed to us, whatsoever it may be. I also trust, we Friends may receive benefit by this intercourse increasingly opening our hearts in love to all, and enlarging us in the gift of charity; and that it may tend not only to our believing, but more openly declaring our faith in Christ, as our Saviour, our Redeemer, and our only Hope of Glory.

Sixth Month.—I am likely to attend dear Mary Dudley, to the families of this Monthly Meeting, which appears a suitable opening for me, and one which seems lively and desirable to my spiritual sight, though the cross is not so great in it, as a concern of my own; but I believe that I may thankfully receive the blessing that things are at times made so sweetly easy to me, and that I need not seek for painful baptisms for what cannot the Lord do ? can He not make hard things easy, for do I not know as to the outward, how He once permitted me to have a child born comparatively without suffering, may it not be so spiritually ?

Plashet, 24th.—Enabled publicly, after reading, to cast my case upon my Holy Helper, and I have since found much comfort and relief to my before tried mind, so as to know a degree of that precious feeling of my peace flowing as a river, and being in measure enabled to do that which I have to do, as unto the Lord. How much more ought such an internal evidence to strengthen and comfort me, than any little discouragement of man really to hurt !

Plashet, Tenth Month, 14th.—Clouds a little dispersed—my health and natural spirits good—no particular cause of trial that I know of, but a want of a more devoted heart, this want I deeply feel; but I fear I do not constantly and fervently enough seek Him, who can bring all things into subjection unto Himself. I flinch from the cross, and also fear I am not diligent, and do not strive enough to enter the kingdom. I do not mean in creaturely impetuosity, but in humble fervour, and watchfulness, and lowliness of heart. I woke under this feeling, as I very often do, like one athirst, and it came across me like a gleam, that what I could not do, the Redeemer wonld do for me, even grant the willing mind to submit in all things; this gave me hope. Words of doctrine I do not pretend to understand, or to enter into; one thing I do know, that Christ in me, or that ever blessed power that I have felt, do feel, and I trust ever may feel even unto the end of time,

when time to me here will be no more, is my *only hope* of glory—
my *only hope* of salvation.   It is in knowing what this ever
blessed, saving, healing, and strengthening power can do and has
done, that I have a hope of being saved in eternity, as well as in
time, and having an entrance granted me into that kingdom, where
the " wicked cease from troubling, and the weary are at rest."
Though a great and wonderful mystery, yet I do here heartily and
fully acknowledge, that as far as I know a coming unto God, it
is through and by Christ ; and I doubt not there are numbers
who never knew, and never consequently acknowledge by whom
they come unto God, and by what means they are saved ; (though
this may he made more manifest to some of us, even the " power
and mercy" of God in Christ Jesus reconciling the world unto
himself:) who may experience a being reconciled, without
knowing by whom they are reconciled ; though their lives, and
their deeds prove an abiding in the saving and anointing power
of their Redeemer and the Saviour.

Plashet, 15*th.*—My original intention in writing this journal,
has been simply and purely the good of my own soul, but if
after my death, those who survive should believe that any part
of it would conduce to strengthen others in the faith, and to
encourage them in righteousness, by manifesting the loving-kindness of the Almighty to His unworthy child, or to the comfort of
any mourner in Zion, I am willing that it should be exposed,
even if my weaknesses are acknowledged ; so long as they lead
to the love of Him, who has in tender mercy manifested Himself to be strength in my weakness, and a present Helper in
every needful time.

Eleventh Month, 12*th.*—I am likely to set off early to-morrow
without my husband, to go into Norfolk ; this prospect I feel
pleasant and painful ; pleasant, the idea of being at Earlham,
painful, leaving home, and more particularly my husband. May
I be enabled there faithfully to do my duty, in whatever way I
may be led, in Meeting, or out of Meeting ; may the time
spent there be to our mutual comfort and edification, and
may those left be cared for, and preserved soul and body, by
Him who careth for us ; this I humbly trust will be the case.
Amen.

Plashet, 25th.—I returned safely home to my beloved family, on Second day evening, the 22nd, I trust I may say in thankfulness of heart, finding all well, and going on altogether very comfortably. I returned by Ipswich, accompanied by my sister Priscilla and my brother Joseph, and spent all First day there ; but I was unusually low, almost distressed, on account of little Betsy, as I heard she was unwell, and knew not the extent of it ; so that my natural impatience to get home was great; but I felt kept there, and as if I could not go away, and though thus deeply tried in myself, was greatly helped from one service to another during the day, being variously and often engaged. It was a day of natural tribulation as far as fears went ; and may I not say almost of spiritual abounding ? So it is ! and so I often have found it, that I have to be brought as to the dust of the earth, before I am greatly helped. Out of the depths, we are raised to the heights. Dear Priscilla, before we parted, prayed for my safe and peaceful return home, which prayer has been remarkably granted. Third day, my beloved husband with our children attended the Monthly Meeting, where our certificate was received.

This was from Gracechurch Street Meeting to that of Plaistow, in accordance with the discipline of Friends to recommend Joseph and Elizabeth Fry and their children, as members of that Meeting ; their removal to Plashet having brought them within its compass.

I should say that the day was begun by returning thanks in my own family, amongst my children, husband, and servants, to my peace ; the rest of the day passed in much domestic comfort, with my husband at home. This was one of the very bright days of life ; blessings are abundantly granted, and sometimes even a blessing upon the blessings, that makes us all feel sweet and lovely !

Plashet, Twelfth Month, 13th.—I do think at times that it is by far my first desire to be brought into conformity to the Divine will, but at other times I am ready to fear that I deceive myself ;

but I am thankful in believing that the secret intents and purposes of my heart are known, though at the same time I am sensible that there is much infirmity, and evil propensity which must be known; yet even of that I am glad, for it is well the physician should know the extent of the malady, as he alone can rightly apply the remedy. Thou knowest me, O Lord! much better than I know myself; Thou knowest the intents and purposes of my heart; bring that under which in any way opposes itself to Thy will being done in me, by me, and through me; be with me unto the end, O Lord! I pray Thee, and in Thine own time subdue all that rebels against Thee; do for me that which I cannot do for myself; even carry on Thine own work in me to Thy own praise; make me willing at all times to speak in Thy name, when it is according to Thy will, yet more and more manifest Thine own power in Thy poor unworthy child, that if not inconsistent with Thy holy will, her beloved husband, children and servants, may be drawn nearer unto Thee, and be encouraged to abide in a meek and quiet spirit; that others seeing their good works, may also glorify Thy great and glorious name. Amen.

First Month, 24th, 1814.—I feel affected by the distresses of the poor, owing to the very sharp weather; and hardly know how to serve them, but I mean to go after them, and desire a blessing may attend my small efforts to relieve them, for it appears very little we can do for them, so as thoroughly to assist them; but I trust a better than ourselves is near to help and support them under their many trials.

Plashet, Second Month, 4th.—I am low, under a sense of my own infirmities, and also rather grieved by the poor. I endeavoured to serve them, and have given them such broth and dumplings as we should eat ourselves; I find great fault has been found with them, and one woman seen to throw them to the pigs; however, I truly desire to act in this with a Christian spirit, still persevering to do my utmost for them, and patiently bear their reproach, which may be better for me than their praises.

Plashet, 11th.—Tried by my servants appearing dissatisfied by what I believe to be liberal things; I feel these things when

I consider how false a view we may take of each other, and how different my feelings towards them are from being ungenerous, which I fear they think. I know no family who allows exactly the same indulgences, and few who give the same high wages, and yet I do not know of any one so often grieved by the discontents of servants as myself. I believe I had rather go without indulgences myself, (if I thought it right) than curtail theirs; but the lavish way in which most of their description appear to think things ought to be used, is a trial to me, and contrary to my best judgment; but a constant lesson to myself, is the ingratitude and discontent which I think I see and feel in many, because I doubt not it is the same with myself. How bountifully am I dealt with, day by day, and yet if there be one little subject of sorrow or apparent discontent, do I not in my heart dwell upon that, and not by any means sufficiently upon the innumerable mercies and blessings that surround me. Feeling that I am so infirm, can I wonder at the infirmities of others ? Far from it, and though tried at times by my domestics, yet my belief is, that my small labour of love has not been lost upon all, and that I have amongst them, faithful, valuable, and conscientious servants, who, through all love us, and are in reality our friends, though they may at times mistake and misconstrue our conduct towards them, and show us their weakness, as well as we may show ours.

Third Month, 20*th*.—The craving of my soul for preservation is almost past expression: feeling as I am permitted to do, at times, the goodness of the Lord, how fervent is my desire, how inexpressible my prayer, that I may ever be His in and through all things; that I may dwell nearer in spirit to my Redeemer, that increased humility, watchfulness, patience and forbearance, may be my portion; that I may not only be saved myself, but that I may not stand in the way of others' salvation, more particularly in that of my own household and family; and that I may, if consistent with the Divine will, be made instrumental in saving others. Now in the time of my retirement from the world, from being unwell, my soul craves in deep prostration, preservation from Thee, O God ! There are seasons of deep prostration, when my

soul is overwhelmed within me, under the feeling of Thy goodness, Thy power, and in love towards Thyself, Thy ever blessed
cause, and those that fear Thy name. This morning my heart
recommends numbers, who are assembled for the solemn purpose of worshipping Thee, to Thy grace and good keeping;
animate them by Thy love, keep them in Thy fear; yet be with
and keep Thy poor unworthy handmaid, be it unto her according
to Thy will, or Thy word: yet in Thy abundant mercy permit
her soul to magnify Thee, O Lord! and her spirit to rejoice in
God her Saviour, which she has been permitted to do of late,
even in seasons of deep humiliation, or when coming out of the
depths.

25th.—May I spiritually and temporally this day be enabled
to give myself up to my Master, not looking upon myself as my
own, or feeling anxious as to what I suffer, or may suffer, but
rather resigning myself unto Him who knows what is best for me;
but this is not in my own power. Keep me, O Lord! near unto
Thyself, and Thy own preserving power, and let me not wander
from Thee, either in word, deed, or desire, or be over anxious as
to what may await me, but strengthen me, if consistent with
Thy will, to trust in Thy mercy towards one so poor, so weak,
and so frail.

Fourth Month, 16*th.*—I may acknowledge the help and
comfort I have found in my beloved sister Rachel, through this
time of trial she has been a great support; I have also received
much kindness from my dear sisters, Elizabeth Gurney and
Elizabeth Fry. My dearest sister Rachel one evening knelt down,
and prayed that we might be enabled to trust in the Lord, as He
only knew what was best for us; it came with great weight and
solemnity. Sweet as the encouragement given has been, yet
there have been seasons when I have been too low to take it, or
to feel it; but in abundant mercy a little help, has been administered to my very unworthy soul from the Fountain Head,
and my fears have been greatly quieted.

Plashet, 30*th.*—None know but those who suffer from them,
the deep humiliations such disorders create, as those I have lately
had; I mean great bodily weakness, accompanied by nervous

lowness of spirits, and much mental fear. In the first place, how deeply do they try us, being in their own nature so painful; in the next, from the difficulty of doing strictly right in them, how far to endeavour to divert by cheerful amusement, or by taking such things as may soonest relieve them: and added to these, I think many are apt falsely to accuse themselves, and to mistake the painful restlessness and fear occasioned by them, for impatience and mistrust ; I have sometimes a hope that this is not my case, though at others great fear arises, lest I should in any degree let go my hold, or be impatient after having so abundantly known the goodness, and loving-kindness of the Almighty. Oh, saith my soul, may He once more revive the spirit of His poor unworthy one, and breathe upon these dead bones, that they may live.

In great weakness and infirmity. Gracious and Almighty Father, permit Thy poor child to come unto Thee, her God and Saviour, that if consistent with Thy holy will, she may once more be healed and revived, through Thy Almighty saving power; give her not over to the will of her soul's enemies, and permit not temptation or weakness to overcome her, but in Thine own unspeakable and unmerited mercy, be Thou yet unto her, her Lord and her God, her Saviour and Redeemer, her present help in trouble, and her only hope of glory. Amen.

Plashet, Fifth Month, 16th.—Humbled under a sense of being not in a sweet temper, of which I truly repent ; but I ever feel it a favour to be clear when I am doing wrong, and to feel repentant for it, for my greatest fear is of imperceptibly falling away, and becoming insensible to the errors of my ways.

Plashet, 24th.—My soul followeth hard after Thee, O Lord! enable Thy poor child to follow after Thee, preserve her from letting in want of faith, mistrust or fear, but enable her to cleave very close unto Thee, and through all her trials, that nothing may in any degree separate her from Thy love.

Plashet, Sixth Month, 13th.—Though clouds may be permitted to overshadow me, before the real trial comes, yet I cannot but have a hope that help will marvellously be extended in the needful time. Help, dearest Lord, or I perish ; permit me neither to let go my hold in times of trial, nor deny Thee in

thought, word or deed, but to acknowledge Thy goodness to
Thy very greatly favoured but unworthy child.   These words
arise ; be still, and thou shalt see the salvation of God.   Be it
so, saith my soul.

The birth of her ninth child, took place on the 14th of June.

Plashet, 17th.—I think I may say, I have sought to be still,
and have indeed seen the salvation of God.   I passed the remainder of the day, till about eight o'clock, in much quietness
and tranquillity generally speaking.   In the evening, I felt ill,
with great disposition to faint, so that for a very short time my
sight was nearly gone, but my mind was quiet.   I did not feel
easy to settle for the night, without asking them all to sit quietly
by me, that I might have an opportunity of pouring out my soul
in prayer to my great and ever blessed Helper.   This I was
enabled to do ; the thing which I think I most prayed for, was
strength, and that I might not be overwhelmed in body, soul, or
spirit—a calmer state was afterwards my portion.   I feel now a
poor insensible creature ; may I in due time be sensible of what
the Lord has done for me, so as to stimulate me abundantly to
love and good works, if consistent with His ever blessed will ;
but without the assistance of His power, I can no more by doing
than in suffering show forth His praises, therefore I pray Thee,
O Lord ! yet be with and help Thy poor child, in this the
moment of her prosperity, as well as in her adversity ; enable
her so to hold fast on Thee, whom she desires far above all to
love and to serve, and to prefer above her chiefest joy, neither
to deny Thee in thought, word, or deed.   Enable me, O Lord,
I pray Thee, in everything that I do to prove myself more completely devoted to Thee, in all my relative, as well as in all my
other duties, that I may be thine, and that Thou mayst be
glorified, not only by me, but by those whom Thou hast given
me, that these dear lambs may in due time show forth Thy praise,
as well as all those to whom, in Thy unspeakable mercy Thou
hast made Thy poor child in any degree an instrument of
help.

Plashet, 20th.—As I lay this morning, these words occurred to me, Lackest thou anything ?   The answer of my heart was, Nothing Lord, Thy mercies abundantly overflow, only enable me and mine to keep a still closer covenant with Thee, and to remember Thy commandments to do them ; and may my soul ever make her boast in Thee her God and Saviour, and never, no never, take that to itself that in no degree belongs to it. Under a fear of too freely approaching Thy sacred footstool in word, as Thou Lord knowest my heart, and its secret purposes, do that for me that I cannot do for myself ; and may I day by day, yet experience Thy grace to be sufficient for me, whether in mourning or in rejoicing.

21st.—My soul cannot help feeling greatly bound in gratitude for the many and great benefits received ; thanksgiving is the voice of my heart, though something of anxiety and disquietude has been my portion, more particularly on account of my beloved husband, and children. I also desire to settle my household aright, to walk before them with an upright, humble, and perfect heart, fulfilling the Law and the Gospel. I desire to be scrupulously nice as to my conduct towards servants ; if they revile, revile not again, not even in heart ; I am not tempted in word to revile them, but I may speak too freely of them, for they at times grieve me by their apparent ingratitude, and want of consideration ; but may I bear as I desire to be borne with. In some instances, I am amply rewarded by their gratitude and love ; in others much wounded by them. I thought if not saying too much for myself, that I have wept as between the porch and the altar on their account, and on that of my beloved family altogether ; I feel it cause for much thanksgiving, so far to be restored to them again, but my natural spirits at times are overcome. Grant wisdom and grace, O Lord ! I pray Thee, to Thy poor child, to order her steps aright before them all, being wise as the serpent and harmless as the dove.

Elizabeth Fry had held on her way, though " faint yet pursuing," through this long and peculiarly distressing state of illness and suffering. Now she was enabled to rejoice in the blessing given, and the possession of another infant, always so welcome to her motherly and loving nature ; but in the mingled cup of life, it was to be expected that bitter would follow the sweet, if it did not accompany it, she received tidings of the critical illness of her beloved friend and relative, Joseph Gurney Bevan. In the fulness of her heart she addressed him.

Plashet, *Sixth Month,* 20*th.*

My tenderly beloved Cousin,

I hear thou art very ill, which I feel a good deal. I should have been pleased had it been ordered so that I could have assisted in waiting on thee ; but though absent in body, I believe I shall be very often visiting thee in spirit, indeed, before I heard of thy being so poorly, this has been frequently the case with me. I have once more had to rejoice, in tender mercy and abundant loving-kindness having been again graciously manifested to me, helping me, strengthening me, and carrying me through my time of trial, and then granting me the sweet blessing of a dear little lamb added to our flock. As for thyself, what can I say ? for thy own sake, we hardly dare ask that thou mayst very long be continued amongst us, amidst the attendant trials of time, fully believing, that through the mercy of God in Christ Jesus, sooner or later, an entrance will be ministered unto thee abundantly, into the everlasting kingdom of our Lord and Saviour Jesus Christ. I know a little of thy low opinion of thyself, that perhaps thou canst hardly take precious promises home, but remember, " Eye hath not seen, nor ear heard, nor hath it entered into the heart of man to conceive the things that the Lord hath prepared for them that love Him." And most surely thou *hast loved* Him, and not only so, but sought *to prove thy love,* and hast thou not done it by feeding the lambs ? If enabled, let us remember one another for good. I feel selfishly anxious that this may not prove a very serious attack ; but I desire to leave it in better hands. I am inclined, before I leave off, just to express what a feeling of love and gratitude I have towards thee, for thy kindnesses to me have been many and great. Believe me thy nearly attached cousin, and I trust I may, in another sense, say *child*.

ELIZABETH FRY.

As soon as her health was sufficiently restored to admit of it, Mrs. Fry took a journey to Earlham, to see her brother John Gurney, who was then rapidly declining. He had never recovered the shock of his wife's death six years before, and the bodily fatigue which he had undergone in his attendance upon her. As the things of this world failed him, he laid hold of more enduring realities ; he who had been eminent for beauty of person and fascination of manner became as remarkable for the graces of the Christian life ; and the spirit of deep submission with which he endured his infirmities, was alone surpassed by his childlike faith in his Redeemer, and the joy and peace he knew in believing.

Plashet, Eighth Month, 15th.—Once more arrived at my sweet home, and truly thankful in having finished my visit to my much-beloved brothers and sisters with satisfaction. I feel most tenderly for all, and I humbly trust, all are pressing Zion-ward, though I cannot say that I fully understand or enter into the activity of the creature appearing to show itself so much in things belonging to the soul's salvation ; but this I know, inasmuch as it is of God, it will stand, but inasmuch as it is of man, it will fall. It is not for a poor unworthy fellow-mortal like myself to say what is of God, and what is not, though I may apprehend that there is a mixture, not only in them, but in myself, and in us as a body, though our belief and profession is, that nothing short of the Holy Spirit can really help forward the cause of righteousness on the earth, whether it be immediately or instrumentally ; and that we can only do good when influenced by this Spirit, and therefore desire to wait for its stirrings. I parted from my beloved sister Rachel, who has for months past been to me a tenderly beloved friend, a most watch-

ful and valuable nurse, and a most loving sister; I felt parting
from her a good deal.

Plashet, 29*th.*—My heart has been much affected by the
accounts of my beloved brother, who appears sinking into the
grave, step by step ; but his soul most mercifully cared for, and
also his body greatly shielded from suffering.

Earlham, Ninth Month, 9*th.*—I trust I have been enabled to
do what I ought in this matter ; after writing the above, a letter
arrived that quite confirmed me in the propriety of making ready
to set off early on the Third day morning, but I could not feel
easy to do it till that time.   I felt bound in spirit to offer up my
family to the care of a protecting Providence publicly, after our
reading in the morning, before I set off, which I was enabled to
do ; and also to pray for my beloved brother, that in passing
through the valley of the shadow of death, he might fear no evil
(this prayer appeared fully answered). I left home after this with
a peculiarly happy, may I not say cheerful mind ? I mean free
from burden. I have seldom had a more comfortable journey in
small things as well as great, I saw the kind hand of Providence.
May it afresh teach me to trust, and not be impatient when
things outwardly appear to go cross, there may be good in it.
I could not but admire, when travelling the last stage, how little
fatigue I felt, so that I thought I could go on much further,
(truly the back is fitted to the burden,) I had just stopped long
enough to have a good supper, when an express arrived, to say
that my beloved brother's decline was so rapid, as to make my
seeing him doubtful, I felt no doubt about going forward, and
arrived here about four in the morning.

The scene closed the following day; she describes it in a letter
to her family at home.

> Earlham, *Ninth Month,* 8*th,* 1814,
> (by the remains of my beloved brother.)

My much loved Husband and Children,

Believing you will feel with me in what so nearly concerns me
and not only me, but you also, I sit down to tell you as nearly as

I can what has happened since I came here. I believe you know I arrived about four o'clock yesterday morning. I was then led into the room where my tenderly beloved brother lay in bed ; he was awake, but some feared he would not know me, instead of which, upon seeing me, his words were, " My dear sister, come and kiss me," then he expressed his great pleasure at our being together—he looked very sweet, quite easy, may I not say, like one redeemed. After staying some time by him, I went to bed; but I did not rest much, feeling low, burdened, and rather poorly. My dear sister Priscilla, came to me a little past nine o'clock, and advised me to come, he was so very bright, his powers of mind appearing much clearer than any dying man I ever witnessed, except our poor servant John. Upon going into his room, he kissed us each again, and again said he wished for all his sisters together, appearing clearly to recollect each, for upon one saying, " Now there is no exception, all the sisters are with thee," he at first misunderstood, and said, " Did you say there is one exception, for there is not," or to that effect; he said it was delightful how we loved one another. It appeared my place to return thanks for such unspeakable blessings. He then said, " What a sweet prayer !" and afterwards, " I never passed so happy a morning ; how delightful being together and loving one another as we do." As the day further advanced, he said, " What a beautiful day this has been !" My dear uncle and aunt Joseph came a little before dinner: Charles Brereton, William Wilkinson and his wife, Hannah Scarnel, nurse Norman, and his own man, were our companions. Dr. Alderson called in the morning, and D. Dalrymple, each much affected, he expressed himself so kindly to them ; he desired his love to Amelia Opie ; he enjoyed our dear sister Richenda, singing hymns to him ; he took leave of most of the old servants ; to one whom he used not much to like, he spoke the most kindly, said he was glad to see him, and shook him warmly by the hand, and bade him " farewell ;" he appeared deeply impressed with his many blessings and the mercy shown him. About half an hour after it was over, we had once more to approach the sacred footstool (for ability) to bless the Sacred Name, both for His giving and taking away. Thus closed such a day as I never passed ; may we not say, "blessed are the dead that die in the Lord ?" Oh, my beloved children and husband, may we not only feel, but profit by this striking event. . . . . .

Earlham, Ninth Month, 13*th.*—My heart feels very full ; my body I believe has trembled ever since I rose, to meet the party, now assembled, and likely to assemble here. My own corrupt dispositions, I found showed themselves to myself yesterday, which I believe tended to lay me very low ; may I not say the feeling of my heart is, that I am lying prostrate in the dust ? I have been greatly tendered in spirit with love to those here, whom I believe to love the *Lord ;* united to them in a manner inexpressible in my inmost heart—all barriers being broken down. Yet I feel it needful to be very watchful, very careful ; to be faithful to the testimony, that I apprehend myself called upon to bear, not only for my own sake, but also for the sake of the younger ones about me ; Lord, be pleased to help me, to guide me, to counsel me, that from my own will and prejudice, I wound not a beloved brother or sister in Christ, but so keep me in Thy fear, in Thy love, and under a sense of Thy presence ; that I act in these most awful and important duties, according to Thy most Holy and blessed will. During these few days, when so surrounded by many of various descriptions, keep my eye, I fervently pray Thee, single unto Thyself, doing whatever Thou wouldest have me, either to do or to suffer—not bowing the knee of my heart to any mortal or seeking to gratify or even satisfy self—but, O Lord ! let Thy will be done in me, by me, and through me ; permit our souls to be united in sweet and precious unity with all who fear Thy name, and not only those ; even animate the hearts of others, who may not yet know Thee, that they also may be touched by Thy love, and united together in Thy fear. Let Thy good presence be with us, that the feeble be strengthened, the discouraged animated by hope, the luke-warm stimulated, and the backslider turned from the error of his ways, even so, if consistent with Thy holy will. If Thou seest meet to make use of Thy unworthy children to speak in Thy name, be unto them tongue and utterance, wisdom and power, that through Thy grace and the help of Thy Spirit, sinners may be converted unto Thee. Amen, Amen.

6

Plashet, 22nd.—My beloved brother's funeral, was a very solemn and humbling day to me, whilst we sat at Earlham round the body, my uncle Joseph, my sisters Catherine Rachel and Priscilla, and I, each had something to say ; also Edward Edwards. I had to finish the sitting with these words, " There are different gifts, but the same Spirit. And there are differences of administrations, but the same Lord. And there are diversities of operations, but it is the same God which worketh all in all. But let us earnestly covet the best gifts." It certainly was a striking occasion. Were not all in a measure leavened into one spirit ? It was a very solemn time at the ground, and I trust an instructive one, very affecting to our natural feelings, thus to leave the body of one so tenderly beloved, to moulder with the dust. Upon my return, I heard of the sudden death of my long loved cousin, J. G. Bevan. My spirit was much overwhelmed within me, but there was a stay underneath ; blessed be the name of the Lord. I bid them all farewell, at Earlham, in near unity. Oh, may my children love, as we love—this has been the prayer of my heart !

30th.—Another month nearly gone, how much has passed in it ; how awfully has death been brought to my view. I have felt it a good deal, on my own account ; and cannot say, that at present death appears to have no sting for me, or the grave no victory. May that blessed state ever be mine, of knowing the sting of death to be altogether removed.

Letter to her cousin, Priscilla Hannah Gurney.

Plashet, *Tenth Month,* 19*th*, 1814.

My beloved Cousin,

I regret not answering thy letter before, but almost constant engagements have prevented me. I believe few can more feelingly sympathize than myself, in thy great loss in this our tenderly beloved cousin Joseph Gurney Bevan ; he was indeed to me a sure and tried friend and counsellor, how have I admired to see him a friend and a sure friend in the needful time, I used to observe none were able to move him. When under much discouragement, he helped to lift up my head in hope.

He was indeed a true friend, a wise counsellor, and is an inexpressible loss to me, I feel a real and great deprivation, and a vacancy that I know not who can fill. Dear John Hull's state is also very affecting, but he yet remains not only alive, but lively in spirit, I have once been to see him, and may be thankful that he is yet spared to us, but it is a blessing I do not expect long to enjoy ; dear Rachel Smith's loss is also present with me. Now for my tenderly beloved brother ; words fall very short of expression. I do not know that I can feel grateful enough on his account; we may truly say that his end appeared blessed indeed, love, joy, and peace were the covering of his spirit, "Blessed are the dead that die in the Lord." No evil nor sorrow appeared to be permitted to come near him, no pain, mind, or body, that we could perceive, what a favour! He was buried in the Friends' Burying Ground at Norwich, by his wife.

Plashet, Eleventh Month, 2nd.—My beloved husband and girls returned from France, on Second day ; my heart was rather overwhelmed in receiving them again. I also had to feel the spirit in which some persons took my having allowed them to go, making what appeared to be unkind remarks. Oh, how do I see rocks on every hand ; thus almost all persons who appear to pride themselves upon their consistency, are apt to judge others ; whilst some, who no doubt yield to temptations greatly suffer, and weaken themselves by it. How weak, how frail are we on every hand ; my heart was much overwhelmed, seeing the infirmities of others, and feeling my own.

Mrs. Fry was always very jealous over herself, lest her avocations as the head of a family, should be neglected, from her time and attention being so greatly occupied by those duties, which she believed herself called to perform in the Church; but she was even more alive to the danger of carrying on the business of life, in dependence upon her own strength and power ; her heart's prayer was,

> "Whate'er I do in any thing,
>   To do it as to Thee."

In a letter to one of her sisters in Norfolk, on the subject of hiring a cook, she says—

—— My late letters savour much of the Martha, but whilst here, cooks appear a very important, if not a necessary part of our comfort, as our food must be dressed.   I am, and have been for many weeks past, in my best health ; what a comfort is this, may I not be unmindful of it; but how prone we are to cleave to the things of the earth, rather than in heart to cleave to a better spirit !   I sometimes feel like an earth-worm, though at times raised above it, which is an unmerited mercy ; but I find we may be employed in arranging laundries, kitchens, and such things, until our heart is too much in them.   Does not all call for watchfulness, that even in the performance of our duties, however small, they become not a temptation, and we go not astray ; lest the seed become choked, and no fruit brought to perfection ?

It would not be true to say, that Mrs. Fry naturally cared much for outward appearance, or that she took pleasure in domestic concerns.   She loved a simple liberality, and unostentatious comfort ; her element was hospitality, and whilst Christian moderation was observed, her taste was gratified, by an open, generous mode of living ; but she would not have chosen for her own pleasure, the oversight of either house or table, and when in later life, circumstances rendered care and economy a duty, it was a great relief to her, to be able to depute the charge of household affairs to one of her daughters.   She was always most correct in account-keeping; the distinct heads of House, Garden, Farm, Charity, with many others, marked the pains-taking care with which she performed her self-imposed task.   As the mistress of a family, if she erred, it was upon the side of indulgence ;

scarcely liking to exert that power over the wills and feelings of others, which is so conducive to their good, and so infinitely in favour of those governed, as well as those in the more arduous position of governing others; but she was aware of this herself, and a " firm hand with a household," was among the maxims she impressed upon her daughters as they advanced in life.

During the infancy of her children, she was singularly devoted to them, by night as well as day. She attended to their minutest ailments, and was distressed by their sufferings; in health and happiness they refreshed her by their smiles. She had the gentlest touch with little children, literally and figuratively. She would win their hearts if they had never seen her before, almost at the first glance; and by the first sound of her musical voice. As her children grew older, her love was undiminished, but her facility was less than before the sinfulness of the human heart had developed itself in positive evil; this especially applies to the elder ones. She had not a talent for education, if that word be used for imparting knowledge, probably, because her own had been interrupted and unfinished; nor did she appreciate, till the experience of life had taught her, the necessity of exerting minute, continued and personal influence over the minds of children. She had to learn that if the golden harvest of success is to be reaped, the husbandman must exert both industry and skill. The genial sun to ripen, and the refreshing shower to moisten the ground, are indeed needful; but the soil must be turned up, and the seed sown by the labour of man.

Mildred's Court, First Month, 16*th,* 1815.—We came here for a little change of air, on account of our poor babe, who has been, and continues seriously ill. Instead of her sweet smile, her countenance mostly marks distress; the cause appears greatly hidden; my mind and heart are oppressed, and my body fatigued, partly from losing so much sleep. I have felt my infirmity during this affliction, and also having betrayed it to others, which I have I apprehend, to judge by my touchy feelings; but, I trust, I repent. Oh, what am I? very poor, very unworthy, very weak, but through all I trust that the Lord will be my stay; and even when brought thus low, I have known a little of being at seasons clothed with that righteousness which cometh from God; I found it was well so feelingly to have been brought to a knowledge of what I am *in myself*, as I could more fully testify from whence the good comes, when brought, in measure, under its calming, enlivening and loving influence. Preserve me, O Lord! from hurting the little ones, more particularly those before whom I have to walk; and permit me yet to encourage their progress Zion-ward.

25th.—A time of anxiety about things temporal has lately been my portion, but much deliverance has so far been granted; my sweet baby is much better, though other matters are still pressing, yet it appears, as to things temporal, that prayer has been heard and answered. From one cause or another, how much my heart, mind, and time have for more than a year past, been engaged with the cares of this life; alas! may the pure seed not be choked; but I fear it creates at times an irritability of temper, that has tried others as well as myself, and a disposition to something of a murmuring spirit, which I truly desire to be preserved from, I so highly disapprove it. I think I shall see some of my heavy burdens removed in due season; how do I desire that I may be enabled rightly to bear them, and that the pure and ever blessed cause may not suffer, in me, by me, or through me. I find it more difficult to act well in adversity, than in prosperity, the temptations of my mind being rather of a low cast; affliction appears both to irritate and enervate me, yet I trust it also casts me on the Foundation that cannot be shaken, and through all humbles me, and in the end does me good.

Plashet, Second Month, 6th.—Infirmity brought home in many ways, in myself and others. Oh, if right, for a little help; but I sometimes fear that I am too anxious for more perfect righteousness, perhaps from some selfish motive, or to be seen of men, but I know not myself as I am known, and He who knows the ill best knows how to apply the remedy. My heart has this morning been melted within me, in love to our blessed Lord, and I have found great consolation in looking at his sufferings previous to his crucifixion ; how deeply and acutely He appeared to feel! This affords great comfort to His feeble ones; oh, that by His stripes we may be healed!

27*th.*—I have a religious concern in prospect, which I am likely to lay before Friends to-morrow; but believing that to be the Lord's work, I am enabled to leave it, trusting in Him.

This entry in Elizabeth Fry's journal, alludes to some Meetings she attended on her way into Norfolk. She spent a few days at Earlham, before her return home.

Erith, Third Month, 23*rd.*—Yesterday morning commenced our little journey, our friends the Steinkoffs and Rebecca Christy with us, as I did not like the Steinkoffs should leave us, believing them to be fellow-disciples. My heart felt very full, with my husband, children, and household around me, it almost overwhelmed me, I had to cast my whole care upon my holy and blessed Helper, who has hitherto kept me, and cared for me and mine. Oh, saith my soul, may He preserve us, now separated, as well as together. I have had to speak to them all in testimony, in these words, " If ye love me, keep my commandments," believing that we poor fellow mortals might address that language to each other. Then upon sitting down to breakfast, I had to return thanks for bread being broken to us spiritually and temporally, and to pray for more. I deeply felt parting, most particularly with my sweet dear little babe, but I believe we parted under the canopy of divine love, and blessing. We travelled well, and comfortably here, but in the night I had a deep plunge, making me exceedingly low and nervous. The enemy appeared to come in like a flood ; I sought after quietness and patience, and in due time, felt a standard to be lifted up against him, for which mercy, may I not say, " Bless the Lord, oh, my soul, and all that is within me, bless his holy name." I believe baptisms are necessary for our preparation and refinement for such awful services, therefore I desire not to flinch, but to pray that, if consistent with the Divine will, fears may not have dominion over me. Oh, for preservation on every hand, and be pleased, righteous Father, to be with and bless my husband and children, as well as thy poor unworthy handmaid ; enable her so to keep the word of Thy patience, that Thou mayst keep her from the hour of temptation. Amen, and Amen. Be with us, O Lord ! this day and night, that we may know our poor bodies and souls to be a little strengthened, if consistent with Thy holy will.

Plashet, Fourth Month, 15th.—I may acknowledge being carried through the seventh trouble, even by an uplifted and stretched out arm. A sweetly uniting time at Earlham, surrounded with many disciples of different descriptions—cousin P. H. Gurney, S. Nash, W. Forster, Edward and Anne Edwards, Henry Tacy, Francis Cunningham and Charles Brereton ; all the four last, clergymen. It appeared that I had to go amongst them, to encourage those whom I believe to be advanced far before myself; I was enabled to hold up their hands, my soul felt with them, and rejoiced over them in a way I can hardly describe, my own brothers and sisters also ; it was a time of great union, and much dominion of the truth. Many appeared glad to have me amongst them, and being enabled to cheer them, (or some of them,) gave me a place in their hearts that I felt required much watchfulness and fear, lest I should be exalted, but I remember that we must bear evil report and good report. Since my return, though I have rejoiced and returned thanks for again being here, for our general preservation, for our many deliverances, and for our strength in weakness, yet a degree of lowness and humiliation covers my spirits ; home brings many cares, many great and important weights. Keep me, O Lord ! I pray Thee fervently, keep me watchful, keep me faithful, keep me humble, that through Thy unmerited mercy, and through the merits of my Redeemer, I may not only be saved myself, but be made instrumental in Thy holy hand, to help those so very near and dear : enable me to watch continually unto prayer, for myself and for them, that we take not

our flight from Thee, who hast manifested Thyself to be so
good, so gracious, so full of tender mercy and loving-kindness.

Towards the end of the summer, which had been passed in
tranquil enjoyment at Plashet, she believed it her duty to join
her friends William Forster and Rebecca Christy in a visit to
the families of Kingston Monthly Meeting.

Plashet, Ninth Month, 9th.—I think I may acknowledge,
that although much stripping and deep poverty has at times
been my portion, during my visit to the families of Kingston
Monthly Meeting, with dear William Forster and Rebecca
Christy; yet power, consolation and sweetness have also been
felt at times, and I think our way has been remarkably made
in the hearts of those we have visited. I came home with
the feeling, that he that waters is also watered. The prospect of
not having finished and leaving home again, is serious; but oh,
for preservation and strength to do the will of God at home and
abroad.

15th.—I returned home last evening, having just finished
my engagement with William Forster and Rebecca Christy.
Being at home again, and having some heavy clouds, a little,
indeed, a good deal dispersed, is a great comfort and relief.
We have been much favoured in our goings along; help being
granted from season to season, much unity of the Spirit and
general sweetness and openness amongst others. But I have
felt since my return, this morning, in our frail state, how difficult it is, even when engaged in religious services, to prevent
our infirmities creeping in and showing themselves, something
like the iniquity of our holy things. Great as is the honour and
favour of being employed in the Master's service, and the peace
and consolation which attend the remembrance of it; yet I am
so much aware of the evil seed not being eradicated from my own
heart, that my present feeling is this, " Who can understand his
errors; cleanse Thou me from secret faults, keep back Thy
servant also from presumptuous sins, let them not have dominion

over me ;" and how anxiously do I desire that I may not only be as a vessel washed and cleansed from impurities, contracted in being used, but also if these have shown themselves, that the most precious and blessed cause of truth and righteousness, may not have been hurt by me, but that our little labours of love, may be blessed to ourselves and others ; and now that I am come home, oh, may I labour and not faint.

Tenth Month, 14*th*.—I have been of late, principally occupied at home, which has its peculiar exercises, as well as being abroad; having to govern such a large household, where the infirmity and evil propensity of each one, old and young, too often show themselves and deeply try me in many ways. It confirms me in a feeling of my infirmity ; it humbles me ; yet I trust through all the discipline of the cross may be found amongst us, and through its subjecting influence, the wrong thing in measure is kept under.   However, I have my consolations, and great consolations, but I find, I am not to rest even in the ruling and order of my household. Many changes in our family circle, among others, my dear sister Richenda is likely to marry Francis Cunningham.

Mrs. Fry had known many trials during the two preceding years, but an acute sorrow, and one unlike any which she had hitherto experienced, now awaited her. The death of one of her children, Elizabeth the seventh child, nearly five years of age. She was lovely, and of much promise, with her mother's name she possessed much of her nature, and more of her general appearance, effect and manner, than any of her other children. Her disposition was tender and affectionate, but like her mother's in early life, inclined to resist authority, though amenable to gentleness and love.   The seeds of piety had appeared to take strong root in her heart, and she delighted in religious instruction adapted to her tender years.

Her illness was short, scarcely one week, and her suffering slight. Apprehension was only beginning to be felt, before the messenger was heard at the door. A few hours' unconsciousness followed, and the scene closed. She had been carried into her mother's room the day before, and had become too ill to leave it. Her parents, the greater part of the last day, sat over her; her mother's countenance betraying the emotions within, exquisite pain, even anguish was depicted there, and yet there was a calmness, an expression of unshaken confidence which prevailed over all. When the last sigh had been breathed, perfect stillness reigned in the chamber of death. It was broken by the thrilling voice of her mother, as she uttered the deep thankfulness of her heart. She had besought from Him who heareth prayer, that if consistent with His holy will, her little one might in mercy be spared suffering. That fear was ended, pain could not reach her now. For this her soul overflowed with gratitude; but infinitely beyond this, was her thanksgiving, that sin could no more " have dominion over her," that her child had " entered through the pearl gates into the city," and was for ever with her Lord.

Plashet, Eleventh Month.—It has pleased Almighty and Infinite Wisdom, to take from us our most dear and tenderly-beloved child, little Betsy—between four and five years old. In receiving her, as well as giving her back again, we have, I believe, been enabled to bless the Sacred Name. She was a very precious child, of much wisdom for her years and I can hardly help believing, much grace ; liable to the frailty of childhood, at times she would differ with the little one, and rather loved her own way ; but she was very easy to lead, though not one to be driven. She had most tender affections, a good understanding, for her years, a remarkably staid and solid mind. Her love very strong, and her little attentions great to those she loved, and remarkable in her kindness to servants, poor people, and all animals, she had much feeling for them ; but what was more, the bent of her mind was remarkably towards serious things.

It was a subject she loved to dwell upon; she would often talk of "Almighty," and almost every thing that had connexion with Him. On Third day, the 21st, after some suffering of body from great sickness, she appeared wonderfully relieved, and I may say raised in spirit; she began by telling me how many hymns and stories she knew, with her countenance greatly animated, a flush on her cheeks, and her eyes very bright, a smile of inexpressible content, almost joy—I think she first said with a powerful voice,

> "How glorious is our Heavenly King
> Who reigns above the sky."

And then expressed how beautiful it was, and how the little children that die stand before Him, but she did not remember all the words of the hymn, nor could I help her; she then mentioned other hymns, and many sweet things; she spoke with delight of how she could nurse the little ones and take care of them, &c. her heart appeared inexpressibly to overflow with love. Afterwards she told me one or two droll stories, and made clear and bright comments as she went along; then stopped a little while, and said, (as in the fulness of her heart, and the joy of a little innocent child who feels very good, for she indeed appeared under the influence of her Redeemer), "Mamma, I love every body better than myself, and I love thee better than every body, and I love Almighty much better than thee, and I hope thee loves Almighty much better than me." I believe my answer was, "I hope or believe I do," which she took up and said, "I hope thee does, if not, thee are wicked." Afterwards I appeared to satisfy her that it was so. This was expressed on the Third day morning, and she was a corpse on the Fifth day evening; but in her death, there was abundant cause for thanksgiving; prayer appeared indeed to be answered, as very little, if any suffering seemed to attend her, and no struggle at last; but her breath grew more and more seldom and gentle, till she ceased to breathe. During the day, being from time to time strengthened in prayer, in heart, and in word, I found myself only led to ask for her, that she might be for ever with her God whether she remained much longer in time or not, but that if it pleased Infinite Wisdom her sufferings might be mitigated, and as far as it was needful for her to suffer, that she might be sustained. This was marvellously answered beyond anything we could expect, from the nature of the complaint; which the doctors thought would terminate in Water in the Head. I desire never to forget this favour, but if it pleases Infinite Wisdom to be preserved from repining, or unduly giving way to lamentation, for losing so sweet, so kind a child, for her little attentions were great, and her love strong to her father, to me, and to all near to her. I have been permitted to feel inexpressible pangs at her loss, though at first it was so much like partaking with her in joy and glory, that I could not mourn if I would; only rejoice, almost with joy unspeakable and full of glory. But a very very deep baptism was afterwards permitted me, like the enemy coming in as a flood; but even here way for escape has been made, and my supplication answered, the healing virtue at times much felt, the bitter cup sweetened, but at others (I doubt not permitted in mercy) my loss has touched me in a manner almost inexpressible; to awake, and find my much and so tenderly beloved little girl so totally fled from my view, so many pleasant pictures marred. As far as I am concerned, I view it as a separation from a sweet source of comfort and enjoyment, but surely not a real evil; abundant comforts are left me, if it please my kind and Heavenly Father to give me power to enjoy them, and continually in heart to return Him thanks on account of His unutterable loving kindness to my tenderly beloved little one, who had so sweet and easy a life, and so tranquil a death; and that, in her young and tender years, her heart had been animated with love and desires after Himself, and also that, for our sakes, she should so often have expressed it in her childish innocent way. My much loved husband and I have drank this cup together, in close sympathy and unity of feeling. It has, at times, been very bitter to us both, but as an outward alleviation, we have, I believe, been in measure each other's joy, and helpers in the Lord. The sweet children have also tenderly sympathised; brothers, sisters, servants, and friends, have been very near and dear in shewing their kindness, not only to the darling child, but to me, and to us all.

My dear sister Richenda being here, I have looked upon almost as providential. Sarah Tatum's presence, a particular comfort to my poor lamb. So we find, outwardly and inwardly, the "Lord doth provide."

Extract from a letter of Richenda Gurney's, to her sister Rachel at Rome, dated Plashet, November 26th :—

"I never witnessed stronger faith, more submission, more evidences of the power of grace in any one than in our beloved sister at that time; I felt it a mercy to be a humble sharer in the rich portion granted her in this hour of need ; never was I more impressed with the blessedness which is experienced by those who have served the Lord Jesus, who have preferred Him above all things, who have been willing to take up their daily cross to follow Him. He is not a hard Master ; He never leaves nor forsakes His own, and will show himself strong, in behalf of those whose hearts are perfect towards Him. After a few minutes, we retired with our dear sister into the next room. She was desirous that children and servants, (especially the nurses) and all her friends who had been present, should come to her; when thus surrounded, as she lay on the sofa, she poured out her heart in thanksgiving and prayer, in a manner deeply affecting and edifying ; for myself, I felt it highly valuable, and would not but have been there for a great deal. Whilst memory lasts, I think and hope I never shall forget the scene, or the impression it made.

From among many letters of sympathy and affection received at this period of deep sorrow, the following extract is taken from one written by her beloved brother Joseph John Gurney.

"Norwich, *Eleventh Month*, 24*th*.

" My dearest Sister,

" I think it right to send a few lines of acknowledgment in return for the affecting account received to-day of thy beloved child. Thou wilt not doubt the sympathies of Earlham, nor can we doubt, that thou, dearest Betsy wilt have to acknowledge, under these painful circumstances, whatever may be the result, the tender mercies of Him, whose fostering hand is over thee and thine, for good. May we all be enabled to place a still more sure confidence in Him, life calls loudly for it."

Plashet, Eleventh Month, 27*th.*—Man is not to live by bread alone, but by every word of God. It appears now my case, in my deep sorrow; I am not, indeed, to live by bread alone, but to be nourished, and kept alive by that inward powerful word, that cometh from God, and by every word being renewed in the needful time; I feel no other sure source of consolation, abundant mercy has indeed been shown me, my weaknesses met, and my prayers answered, even about smaller things. Although it pleases my Heavenly Father thus to chastise me, yet I am permitted to feel that He doth love those whom He chasteneth. I feel His love very near, and like a tender parent, that may see right to inflict the rod, rather, perhaps, than spoil the child; yet the same hand administers the salve to the wound, and cherishes the more tenderly after it, and makes manifest to His poor child that although a deep wound, it is in mercy, and to the unspeakable gain of one most tenderly beloved, having taken her from the conflict of time, and (I humbly trust) permitted her an entrance into the enduring joys of eternity ; and that, through the blood and power of her Redeemer, she has been washed and made clean. Though from her tender years, and good and innocent spirit, we believed her remarkably ready, still I saw and felt need of a Saviour, even for such a little child ; for of course, she had some childish trangressions, or little deviations, but I believe that they were all washed away, and that indeed reconciliation was obtained, as far as there ever had been any separation. So I cannot help hoping that she was ripe for glory.

6

28th.—Dearest Lord, be pleased to arise a little in Thy own power, for the help of Thy poor unworthy servant and hand-maid; and if consistent with Thy holy will, to dispel some of her distressing feelings, and make her willing to part with and com-mit to the earth her beloved child's body, and once more to grant an evidence that her soul is at rest with Thee in heaven, and that this awful trying occasion of her funeral, may, in the end, be like balm to the wound.

30th.—Once more my supplications were answered—the bitter conflict that I was permitted to feel during the night, and the morning previous to the funeral of my beloved child, was in the needful time mitigated, and strength granted to give up her remains to the grave, I hope without a murmur ; but although faith tells us that the spirit is indeed fled from its earthly house, yet the distress felt in parting with the body, I can hardly describe ; for the body of little children, their innocent and beau-tiful faces and forms, we are prone to delight in; and there is a sort of personal attachment towards little children, that partakes of the nature of animal life, which I believe is hardly to be described, but only fully known to parents. This perhaps would make us cling more, even to the poor body—which I felt certainly wonderfully vacant after its blessed inhabitant was fled—yet partly perhaps from nervous weakness, my remaining love to the body, its sweet looks, and some thinking we might keep it longer ; also feeling that the last relics of my much loved, kind, and to me beautiful lamb, were then about to leave us here for ever, was a pinch to the natural part not to be told : I felt really ill. But I may indeed return thanks unto Him who has given us the victory, through our Lord and Saviour Jesus Christ. This I have been permitted to feel, for my child's death at the time had lost its sting, and the grave its victory—for my soul was upheld in the needful time, though so great had been my dread, that I was enabled to pray for help before I left the house, and also to return thanks at the grave for the tender mercy shown to her, and to me, and to all; and afterwards in the room at the Meeting-House, to encourage others to serve the Most High, seeing how great was His loving kindness and tender mercy ; and that the uncertainty of time called for standing prepared. This morning, my poor soul has felt refreshed in once more being enabled, before my household, to cast my care upon my Holy Helper, and to pray for fresh ability in performing the duties of life, and indeed that this event might be sanctified to us all.

Plashet, Twelfth Month, 1st.—I have been enabled in measure to arise and attend to the business of life, but a cloud appeared to rest over me, in remembrance of what we have lost; but when enabled to view her with her Heavenly Father, and out of the reach of all harm, then I can go more cheerfully on my way, and enjoy my remaining blessings; particularly my children, though every thing of the earth has been made I think increasingly to shake, in my view. But I desire that this feeling may increase in my mind; she cannot return to me, but I may go to her. Ah! may I not say, how hast Thou helped her that is without power! How savest Thou the arm that has no strength. May I be more willing to be faithful in the gift at all times, in all places, in weakness and in strength.

Plashet, 2nd.—I am brought into some conflict this morning, respecting my attending the Dorsetshire Quarterly Meeting. I had looked to it before the illness of our dear lamb, and not feeling clear of it, and yet not much light shining upon it, my poor soul is tried within me; for under my present circumstances, I appear much to want the help of faith to leave my other sweet lambs; but ought I not rather to feel renewed stimulus, seeing how short time is, to do what comes to hand, and after all that I have experienced, should I not rather trust than be afraid, for was the hand of Providence ever more marked, even as it related to outward things. I believe I am fully resigned to go, if it be the Lord's will, for I do believe for all my many and great infirmities, my flinching nature, my want of faith and patience, yet it remains my first desire, to do or to suffer according to the Divine will. If consistent with Thy Holy Will, dearest Lord, if I ought to go be pleased to throw a little light upon the subject, and if not, somehow make it manifest; and if Thou should think fit to call Thy poor child into Thy service, be pleased to be with her in it, and bless her labours of love, where her lot may be cast, that others may be made sensible how good a God Thou art, how great is Thy tender mercy and loving kindness, and that these may be encouraged yet to serve Thee, more with the whole heart ; also be pleased, dearest Lord, if Thou should so order it that I go, to keep my beloved husband, children and household in my absence, that no harm may come to them spiritually nor bodily. Thou hast in abundant mercy regarded the weak estate, and infirm condition of Thy handmaid, and hitherto answered her cry, and even met her in her weakness, that if not asking in her own will, she could supplicate Thee, that their poor bodies as well as their souls, may be preserved from (much) harm in her absence; but, dearest Lord, let me not go, if my right place be at home ; but if Thou callest me out, be pleased to grant a little faith, and a little strength, that I may go forth in Thy power, trusting in Thee, as it relates to them, as well as to myself.   Be pleased also if I be called from home at such a time, not to let it try or weaken the faith of others ; but rather may it tend to confirm and strengthen it.

Plashet, 11th.—Truly I went forth weeping, and my sweet Louisa being poorly much increased my anxiety, and it is difficult to say the fears and doubts that crept in, on my way to Shaftesbury, though through mercy the enemy's power appeared limited, and my fears gained no dominion over me, but they were soon quieted, and I had mostly quiet, comfortable nights, though it was wading through deep waters, and in great weakness ; yet help was from season to season administered.

Plashet, 14th.—It is the opinion of medical men that the scarlet fever, in a mild form, is the complaint in the house ; it is most probable that it will appear again amongst us, but that, I desire to leave.   They also think our dear Rachel has a very serious hip complaint, but this I also feel disposed not to be very anxious about.   With regard to my tenderly beloved little Betsy, she is in my most near and affectionate remembrance, by night, and by day ; when I feel her loss, and view her little (to me) beautiful body in Barking burying-ground, my heart is pained within me : but when, with the eye of faith, I can view her in an everlasting resting place in Christ Jesus, where indeed no evil can come nigh her dwelling, then I can rest even with sweet consolation ; and I do truly desire that when her loss is so present with me as it is at times, that I cannot help my natural spirits being

much overwhelmed, that I may be preserved from any thing like
repining or undue sorrow, or in any degree depreciating the
many blessings continued; particularly so many sweet dear
children being left us, for through all, I feel receiving them a
blessing, having their life preserved a blessing, and in the sweet
lamb who is taken, I have felt a blessing in her being taken away;
such an evidence of faith has been granted that it is in mercy,
and at the time such a feeling of joy on her account. It is now
softened down into a very tender sorrow, the remembrance of her
is inexpressibly sweet, and I trust that the whole event has done
me good, as I peculiarly feel it an encouragement to suffer whatever is appointed me ; that being (if it may ever be my blessed
allotment) made perfect through suffering, I may be prepared
to join the purified spirits of those that are gone before me ; and
having felt so very deeply, I am almost ready to think has a
little prepared my neck for the yoke of suffering.

Plashet, First Month, 11*th,* 1816.—The turning a new year
I felt very much, more particularly the change in the last, in
our beloved Betsy being taken from us. I little expected so
soon upon entering this, to have one so deeply beloved as my
brother Samuel, so seriously ill ; I have from his early years
prayed for him, and interceded with strong intercession of
spirit that he might not be hurt by evil. I hardly knew how
to give him up, and my soul has craved, that if right, he may
live to continue to be a blessing to his family, an ornament to
the Church, and to show forth the praise of his Great Lord and
Master.

Plashet, Third Month, 10*th.*—I returned home, after being
at Stamford Hill for change of air ; but my cough, &c., &c., continues very poorly, but through abundant mercy, a calm, and not
unfrequently a cheerful spirit is my portion ; though I do not
feel dwelling so evidently near the fountain and source of all
good, as I desire, at least fears arise for myself, though it
appears due to acknowledge that the fountain and source of all
good dwells near me, so that some things which would at times
have ruffled and troubled me a good deal, have passed quietly,
nay, comfortably by; as if in this time of weakness of body, I was
shielded in degree from the storms. My views of these trials con-

tinue at times to be rather unusually calmed, at least not often so dreadful as at some former periods. I feel, although I expect to get through my approaching confinement, my life more concerned in my present lung complaint, than it often has been in more painful and trying attacks ; but at present, unworthy as I am, this does not excite uneasiness, though perhaps it might, if I believed it more serious than I do ; but at times I have that hope in my Redeemer, not in myself, but in Him who has already visited and cared for me, in Him whom my soul has loved, and at seasons rejoiced in, in Him to whom in weakness I have sought to prove my love, by serving Him through His own help, that I am ready to believe, nay, to trust, that He will be with me to the end ; that He will not leave nor forsake his unworthy one, that He will yet sustain her, in doing and in suffering, as far as He may be pleased to call into either ; that after carrying her through all the remaining conflicts of time, He will even continue to be with her to all eternity ; and where He lives and reigns, there she expects to find everlasting rest and peace. Thou hast, gracious Lord, been a merciful God to me, that hast granted me help and strength, in the name of Thy beloved Son, Thou hast visited and anointed my unworthy soul.

Plashet, Fourth Month, 3rd.—Since writing the last journal, much feeling of illness and lowness of spirits have been my portion ; but how much do I desire quietness and patience, in this straitened place, where the waves and billows are in measure permitted to pass over my head. It is indeed like a cloud resting over the tabernacle, so that I cannot perceive clearly the comforts and blessings that surround me. I felt a little ray of comfort this morning, in these words, " My King and my God," for however tried, however afflicted, however clouded, we may be, in this there is indeed hope and consolation, (if it please Almighty loving-kindness to permit us to see it,) even to feel that the Most High is our King and our God; that He hath in abundant mercy manifested Himself to be so, and that now and then, through the help of our Redeemer, we have been enabled to prove that we have sought to serve Him, and desired that He alone should be our King and our God. Dearest, kindest Lord, Thou who hast regarded me, and dispersed many clouds for me, be pleased yet to regard me whatever be my state, however low I may be brought before Thee, and in Thine own time disperse my clouds, let the sun arise as with clear shining after rain, and if consistent with Thy Holy Will, let not fear nor irritability gain dominion over me; but be Thou my King and my God, from season to season, scattering all mine enemies before my face that they overcome me not; and if consistent with Thy Holy Will, permit no conflict, either before, at, or after my confinement, really to overcome body, soul or spirit; but as my day is so may my strength be. I believe my present indisposition may be increased by my long confinement to two rooms for my cough, now nearly a month; and not a little from sorrow and distress. I have known much this winter; the loss of my lovely child—the frequent illnesses in the house amongst the family—loss of property—my own long cough; yet I know hardly any trial, except indeed real evil, that appears so greatly to undermine comfort outwardly and inwardly, as a nervous state of body and mind; it calls for watchfulness on the part of those who have it, not unduly to give way to it, though I believe few things are really less in our power. It also calls for the most tender compassion and sympathy in others, even if it makes the poor sufferer appear impatient and cross; for it affects the whole frame nearly as much as a bad fever—indeed, my experience leads me to think, that such are attacks of low fever, that come under a less conspicuous form than some, and therefore do not attract so much attention, though I fully believe they often occasion greater and more acute internal suffering, than where disease shows itself more distinctly. I think these complaints are more or less general, and bring into so much conflict of mind, as well as body, that they should be received as refining trials from the Great Head, the Author of all good, and treated as such by ourselves and others.

15th.—I was favoured to feel much relieved and comforted yesterday in pouring forth my soul in supplication before my family after dinner; a sweet calm followed, help appearing to be very near. After all other remedies fail, what a stronghold is prayer; how has my poor soul and body been helped in answer to my supplications, more particularly those called for before others; it is, I think, a very striking evidence that such sacrifices are acceptable in the Divine sight, and called for at His hand, even in publicly committing ourselves to Him. Oh, that I were not so faithless, but more believing, then I think fear never would take the place it does ; yet this is my infirmity, perhaps permitted for my good, that I may more and more know what I am, and what the Power is that we alone desire to rest upon us.

Her tenth child was born April the 18th.

Fourth Month, 27*th*.—Thanks, I may say, be unto my God who has proved Himself an all-sufficient Helper. A heavy cloud passed over—but fears now arise for my spiritual preservation ; and my desire is great in word and in deed, to be enabled to testify of the gracious goodness of my Holy Helper. Family cares also come upon me, which my great weakness hardly knows how to encounter. The remembrance of my little Betsy has been very present with me by night and by day. Be Thou pleased, O Lord God Almighty ! yet to look down upon us, and bless us, and if Thou seest meet to bless our loved infant, to visit it by Thy grace, and Thy love, that it may be Thine in time, and Thine to all eternity ; we desire to thank Thee for the precious gift. I have also had a fresh trial in the dangerous illness of my beloved brother, Daniel, since his return from the Continent.

In June, her children went to Pakefield, for the benefit of sea air, where they were under the care of their aunt, Mrs. Francis Cunningham. Their parents followed them, and for a short period remained with them. It was a new position for her, to be the guest of an active devoted clergyman, and that clergyman her brother-in-law. She remained some weeks in Norfolk, and at last returned without her four elder children. Mr. and Mrs. Fry had determined upon passing the ensuing winter in London, a situation in many respects so disadvantageous for her daughters, that she left them with her loved and valued relatives. She deeply felt their being thrown amongst those who were not Friends, but the advantages of the wise care and oversight of her sister Rachel Gurney, and the privilege of associating with the brother who invited them to be his guests, overcame her objections, and she agreed to an arrangement which appears to have given the complexion to their future lives, and more or less directly to have influenced every member of the family.

Her boys remained at Earlham till nearly Christmas, when their parents had arranged to send them to school; her two children the next in age became inmates with their uncle and aunt, Mr. and Mrs. Samuel Gurney, and joined the school-room party at Ham house, which was then conducted by the kind friend and governess of their elder sisters, who has since at different periods successively laboured with them all.

Earlham, Sixth Month, 27th.—Much has passed since writing the above,—dear John Hull's death, a matter of real importance to me,—the children all gone to the sea-side, except the baby—but home was sweet to me, though much hurried by business there. We attended Barking Meeting, to visit the grave of our beloved little Betsy; it brought many tears, but I afresh remembered she was not there, but is indeed utterly gone from this transitory scene. I often pant after a resting-place with her—may it in due season be granted me, but I also at present feel strongly tied and attached to life, and have much to endear it to me.

Seventh Month, 4th.—I have been at Pakefield with my beloved brother and sister; my soul has travailed much in the deeps, on many accounts, more particularly with them, that in keeping to our scruples respecting prayer, &c., &c., the right thing might be hurt in no mind. Words fall very short of expression, of how much my spirit is overwhelmed within me for us all: our situation is very peculiar, surrounded as we are with those of various sentiments, and yet, I humbly trust, each seeking the right way; to have a clergyman for a brother, is very different to having one a friend; a much closer tie, and a still stronger call for the sake of preserving sweet unity of spirit, to meet him as far as we can,

to offend as little as possible by our scruples, and yet for the
sake of others, as well as ourselves, faithfully to maintain our
ground, and to keep very close to that which can alone direct
aright.

Earlham, Eighth Month, 17*th.*—I have a fear lest delicate
health, and being wearied by the cares of life, and the kind care
of others, should induce my indulging the flesh too much, in
eating, drinking, and sleeping, which I do not desire, far from
it; but sometimes the words addressed to the Church at Ephesus,
as it respects the first love and first works, come home to me,
when I remember how much, in the day of my first love, I
watched over myself in these respects; but my constitution, for
many years of my life has had such a stress upon it, that I am
fearful in my own will of giving up those indulgences, that appear so evidently to have contributed and yet to contribute to
its support; but I desire to be watchful and careful in this respect, which I trust I have in a measure been, but I often feel
as if I were too much living to the flesh, and yet I know not
exactly how or in what to alter.   May I in these and all other
things, be helped and guided by the Holy Spirit, for my heart's
desire and prayer is, that I may offend neither in thought,
word, or deed.

This letter to her two eldest daughters, Katharine and
Rachel, was written after her almost solitary return to Plashet.

Plashet, Ninth Month, 1816, *Evening.*

My dearest Girls,
    After drinking tea alone in your father's little dressing-room,
and taking a solitary walk, and sitting in the rustic portico at
the end of the green walk, I am come to write to you, as I
cannot have your company.   Only think! this evening I have
neither husband nor child to speak to, little Hannah being gone
to tea at the Cottage.   I found it even pleasant to go and stand
by poor old Isaac the horse, and the cows and sheep in the
field, that I might see some living thing to enliven poor Plashet.
The grounds look sweetly, but the cherry tree by the dining-

10

room window is cut down, which I think quite a loss. The poor little school children, when I see them, look very smiling at me, and I suppose fancy that they will soon see you home. Poor Jones's little boy is still living ; such an object of skin and bone I have hardly ever seen. I fear she is greatly distressed. Our house looks charmingly, as far I think as a house can—so clean, neat and lively—but it wants its inhabitants very much.

Your most nearly attached mother,

E. F.

A few days later she again addresses them.

Plashet, *Ninth Month*, 27th, 1816.

My much loved Girls,

Your letters received last evening gave us much pleasure. I anxiously hope that you will now do your utmost, in whatever respects your education, not only on your own account, but for our sake. I look forward to your return with so much comfort, as useful and valuable helpers to me, which you will be all the more, if you get forward yourselves. I see quite a field of useful service and enjoyment for you, should we be favoured to meet under comfortable circumstances in the spring. I mean that you should have a certain department to fill in the house, amongst the children and the poor, as well as your own studies and enjoy-ments; I think there was not often a brighter opening for two girls. Plashet is after all such a home, it now looks sweetly, and your little room is almost a temptation to me to take it for a sitting-room for myself, it is so pretty and so snug ; it is newly furnished, and looks very pleasant indeed. The poor, and the schools, I think, will be glad to have you home, for help is wanted in these things. Indeed if your hearts are but turned the right way, you may, I believe, be made instruments of much good ; and I shall be glad to have the day come, that I may in-troduce you into prisons and hospitals. " Therefore, gird up the loins of your mind and be sober." This appears to me your present business—to give all diligence to your present duties ; and I cannot help believing, if this be the case, that the day will come when you will be brought into much usefulness ; and

I also hope, what follows the text I quote will be your blessed experience. Read the first chapter of first Peter, from the 13th verse———

Early in December Mrs. Fry went into Norfolk, in consequence of heavy affliction befalling the family of her uncle Joseph Gurney, in the death of Joseph his only surviving son. She staid at Earlham, where her two eldest boys under the care of their aunts, were pursuing their education with the clergyman of the village. She then visited her brother Daniel Gurney at North Runcton, with whom her daughters were residing. Whilst she rejoiced in the peculiar advantages enjoyed by her children, she foresaw the probable effect of their circumstances and the influences they were under.

Mildred's Court, Twelfth Month, 13*th.*—I returned yesterday from attending poor dear Joseph's funeral at Norwich, the son of my uncle Joseph Gurney. I have gone through a good deal, what with mourning with the mourners, the ministry, &c., &c. I think I was in this respect, at the funeral, helped by the Spirit and the Power that we cannot command; though I left Earlham with a burdened mind, not having any apparently suitable opportunity of relief, hurrying away, to my feelings prematurely, of which I find even the remembrance painful; my sweet dear girls and boys I much feel again leaving, seeing their critical age and state. What I feel for the children I cannot describe. Oh! may they be sheltered under the great Almighty wing, so as not to go greatly astray.

First Month, 1*st,* 1817, *Evening.*—This has been rather a favoured day, the commencement of another year,—so far sweet and easy, and enabled to commend us and ours, to the best keeping, which brought consolation and comfort with it. Afterwards a very comfortable Meeting at Gracechurch Street; indeed it is like being at home returning there, and I cannot but hope that I am here in my right place.

Second Month, 13*th.*—I yesterday left my dearest boys, John

7

and Willy, at Josiah's Forster's school; it has been a very important step to take, but I trust it is a right one, as we could
not comfortably see any other opening for them. I was enabled
to commend them in supplication to the Lord for His blessing and providential care. It is indeed a very serious thing
to me, thus permitting them to enter the world and its temptations, for so I feel it, it caused me great lowness at first, but
afterwards, having committed them to the best keeping, my soul
was much comforted and refreshed, and much enlarged in love
towards them, as well as the kind friends whose house I was at.
Oh may it please Almighty Wisdom to bless the boys, and keep
them by His own preserving power from any great sin, and may
He pardon the follies of their youth.

She wrote and gave to each of her sons, the following Rules
for a Boy at a Boarding School :—

1st. Be regular, be strict in attending to religious duties; and
do not allow other boys around thee to prevent thy having some
portion of time for reading, at least a text of scripture, meditation and prayer; and if it appears to be a duty, flinch not from
bowing the knee before them, as a mark of thy allegiance to the
King of kings, and Lord of lords. Attend diligently when the
Holy Scriptures are read, or to any other religious instruction,
and endeavour in Meeting to seek after a serious waiting state
of mind, and to watch unto prayer. Let First day (the
Sabbath) be well employed in reading proper books, &c., but
also enjoy the rest of innocent recreation, afforded in admiring
the beauties of nature, taking exercise in the garden, &c., for
I believe this is right in the ordering of a kind Providence,
that there should be some rest and recreation in it. Show a
proper, bold, and manly spirit in maintaining amongst thy play-
fellows a religious character, and a strict attention to all the religious duties ; remember these texts to strengthen thee in it—
"For whosoever shall be ashamed of me and of my words, of
him shall the Son of Man be ashamed, when He shall come in
His own glory, and in his Father's, and of the holy angels."—
Luke ix. 26. "But I say unto you, whosoever shall con-

fess me before men, him shall the Son of Man also confess before the angels" of God : but he that denieth me before men, shall be denied before the angels of God. Now the sooner the dread laugh of the world loses its power, the better for you. This strengthens principle in ourselves and others. Remember these words;—"All that will live godly in Christ Jesus shall suffer persecution."—2 Tim. iii. 12.

Strongly as I advise thy thus faithfully maintaining thy principles, and doing thy duty, I would have thee very careful of either judging or reproving others ; for it takes a long time to get the beam out of our own eye, before we can see clearly to take the mote out of our brother's eye. There is, for one young in years, much greater safety in preaching to others by example than in word ; or doing what is done in an upright manly spirit unto the Lord, and not unto man. I conclude this part of my advice by this short exhortation : "Be sober and watch unto prayer, and do all to the glory of God."

2ndly. I shall not speak of moral conduct, which, if religious principles be kept to, we may believe will be good, but I shall give certain hints that may point out the temptations to which schools are peculiarly liable. I have observed a want of strict integrity in school-boys, as it respects their schoolmasters and teachers, a disposition to cheat them, to do that behind their backs which they would not do before their faces ; and so having two faces. Now this is a subject of the utmost importance —to maintain truth and strict integrity upon all points. Be not double-minded in any degree, but faithfully maintain, not only the upright principle on religious grounds, but also the brightest honour according even to the maxims of the world. I mourn to say I have seen the want of this bright honour, not only in school-boys, but in some of our highly professing Society ; and my belief is, that it cannot be too strictly maintained, or too early begun ; I like to see it in small things, and in great, for it marks the upright man. I may say that I abhor any thing like being under-handed or double-dealing; but let us go on the right and noble principle of doing unto others as we would have others do to us ; therefore, in all transactions, small or great, maintain strictly the correct, upright, and most honourable prac-

tice.   I have heard of boys robbing their neighbours' fruit, &c.,
&c.   I may truly say, that I believe there are very few in the
present day would do such things ; but no circumstances can
make this other than a shameful deviation from all honest and
right principles : and my belief is, that such habits begun in
youth, end mostly in great incorrectness in future life, if not in
gross sin, and that no excuse can be pleaded for such actions ;
for sin is equally sin, whether committed by the school-boy or
those of mature years, which is too apt to be forgotten, and
that punishment *will* follow.

CHAPTER IX.

> One, I beheld! a wife, a mother, go
> To gloomy scenes of wickedness and woe;
> She sought her way through all things vile and base
> And made a prison a religious place:
> Fighting her way—the way that angels fight
> With powers of darkness—to let in the light.
> Tell me, my heart, hast thou such victory won,
> As this, a sinner of thy sex, hast done,
> And calls herself a sinner! what art thou?
> And where thy praise and exaltation now?
> Yet, she is tender, delicate and nice,
> And shrinks, from all depravity and vice;
> Shrinks from the ruffian gaze, the savage gloom,
> That reign where guilt and misery find a home;
> Guilt chained, and misery purchased, and with them
> All we abhor, abominate, condemn—
> The look of scorn, the scowl, th' insulting leer,
> Of shame, all fixed on her who ventures here,
> Yet all she braved; she kept her stedfast eye
> On the dear cause, and brushed the baseness by.—
> So would a mother press her darling child
> Close to her breast, with tainted rags defiled.*

When death has set his seal on the past, and stamped his sacred impress on the motives and actions of the departed Christian, we find a solemn pleasure in contemplating his deeds; but when those deeds are recorded by one, who has himself put

---

* The Maid's Story.—Tales of the Hall, by The Rev. George Crabbe.

off mortality, our interest becomes deepened, and we can but dwell upon the marvellous consideration of their present state of being—their thoughts—their feelings—their probable interchange of sentiment—now that, the veil of the flesh removed they see no longer as in a glass darkly, but face to face.

These lines were written by Mr. Crabbe in allusion to Mrs. Fry; his acquaintance with her was slight, but his deep reading of the human heart enabled him to appreciate her undertakings, and the personal sacrifices at which they were made.

Mildred's Court, Second Month, 24th.—I have lately been much occupied in forming a school in Newgate, for the children of the poor prisoners, as well as the young criminals, which has brought much peace and satisfaction with it; but my mind has also been deeply affected in attending a poor woman who was executed this morning. I visited her twice; this event has brought me into much feeling, attended by some distressingly nervous sensations in the night, so that this has been a time of deep humiliation to me, thus witnessing the effect and consequences of sin. This poor creature murdered her baby; and how inexpressibly awful now to have her life taken away! The whole affair has been truly afflicting to me; to see what poor mortals may be driven to, through sin and transgression, and how hard the heart becomes, even to the most tender affections. How should we watch and pray, that we fall not by little and little, become hardened, and commit greater sins. I had to pray for these poor sinners this morning, and also for the preservation of our household from the evil there is in the world.

Extract from a letter to her sister, Rachel Gurney:—

Mildred's Court, *Third Month,* 10*th and* 11*th.*

My heart, and mind, and time, are very much engaged in various ways. Newgate is a principal object, and I think until I make some attempt at amendment in the plans for the women, I shall not feel easy; but if such efforts should prove unsuccessful, I think that I should then have tried to do my part and be easy. My own Monthly Meeting, though absent from it, is rather a weight, and Gracechurch Street I am also much interested about. I have gone besides to only one London Meeting, all the time that I have been here. The poor occupy me little more than at the door—as I cannot go after them, with my other engagements; the hanging at Newgate does not overcome me as it did at first, and I have only attended one woman since the first. I see and feel the necessity of caution in this respect, and mean to be on my guard about it, and run no undue risk with myself.

I have felt in thy taking care of my dearest girls, that thou art helping me to get on with some of these important objects, that I could not well have attended to, if I had had all my dear flock around me.

The disgraceful state in which many of the prisons of the British empire were found thirty years ago, excites our astonishment, and we naturally seek to account for the continuance of so crying an evil.

That the sceptical philosophy which prevailed towards the end of the last century, was unfavourable to questions of moral and religious reform, we cannot doubt. Whether the startling events of the French Revolution—the tremendous wars that followed it—the rise and fall of empires—had so engrossed the attention and drained the resources of the English nation, that improvement at home was neglected; or whether looking to a still deeper source, it may be attributed to that tendency to degenerate inherent in all human institutions, the fact is indisputable. Howard and his humane exertions appear to have been forgotten, and Acts of Parliament to have become a dead letter; some, if not all the provisions of those acts, being in the vast majority of gaols, openly violated. For Counties as well as Boroughs, an old gate-house, or the ancient feudal castle, with its dungeons, its damp, close and narrow cells, and its windows overlooking the street, often formed the common prison of offenders of either sex, and of all grades of crime. The danger of escape was provided against, by heavy irons and fetters. Dirt and disease abounded : and even where the building contained wards and yards, the women were imperfectly separated from the men, whilst idleness, gambling, drinking, and swearing, were habitual amongst them. These evils were magnified by the crowded state of the prisons; for crime had enormously increased, and convictions more than doubled within the ten preceding years. Of the prisons for the counties, those of Bury, Ilchester, Gloucester, with a few others formed honourable exceptions to the general rule; and in the Metropolis, the Penitentiary at Millbank, which had been recently erected.

The moral contamination produced by the disorderly state of prisons, was beginning to be perceived, and the necessity for stricter discipline and better regulations to be acknowledged.

In the United States of America, and in a few instances on the continent of Europe, the experiment had been tried, and with such success as to establish the principle, that classification, employment and instruction tended to the reformation of the criminal, and to the decrease of crime. A deputation of the Gaol Committee of the Corporation of London was appointed in 1815, to visit several gaols in England, especially that of Gloucester, with a view to the amelioration of those under their own jurisdiction. From this resulted some improvements in Newgate. The women from that time occupied the whole of the quadrangle, now called the "women's side;" including what were formerly the state apartments ; mats were provided for them to sleep on. Double gratings, with a space between, were placed to prevent close communication with their visitors, who were of both sexes, and many of them as vile and desperate as themselves ; but to overcome the difficulty thus presented, in receiving the contributions of those whose curiosity brought them to the spot, wooden spoons fastened to long sticks were contrived by the prisoners, and thrust across the intervening space. Notwithstanding these improvements, they remained in an unchecked condition of idleness, riot, and vice of every description. They were of the lowest sort—the very scum both of the town and country—filthy in their persons, disgusting in their habits, and ignorant not only of religious truth but of the most familiar duties of common life.

At the suggestion of her brother-in-law the late Samuel Hoare, Esq., Mrs. Fry had, in the interval between 1813 and 1816, accompanied him on a visit to the women in Cold Bath Fields House of Correction, whose neglected state had much impressed him. Mr. Hoare, with another of her brothers-in-law, the late Sir T. F. Buxton, and some of her personal friends, were at this time occupied in forming a society for the reformation of the juvenile depredators, who infested London, in gangs. This object led them into different prisons, where their attention was soon attracted to the subject of prison discipline. Although not originating in this cause, it may be presumed, that the conversation and influence of these gentlemen would tend to keep alive in the mind of Mrs. Fry, the interest awakened in 1813 for the female prisoners in Newgate. As in that instance, so at this time, her journal fails to convey any explicit information respecting her visits there. We are indebted to other sources, for the fact, that they were recommenced about Christmas, 1816.

On her second visit, she was, at her own request, left alone amongst the women for some hours; and on that occasion, she read to them the parable of the Lord of the vineyard, in the 20th chapter of St. Matthew, and made a few observations on the eleventh hour, and on Christ having come to save sinners, even those who might be said to have wasted the greater part of their lives, estranged from Him. Some asked who Christ was; others feared that their day of salvation was passed.

Their children, who were almost naked, were pining for want of proper food, air, and exercise. Mrs. Fry, on this occasion, particularly addressed herself to the mothers, and pointed out to them the grievous consequences to their children, of living in such a scene of depravity; she proposed to establish a school for them, to which they acceded with tears of joy. She desired them to consider the plan, for without their steady co-operation she would not undertake it; leaving it to them, to select a governess from amongst themselves. On her next visit, they had chosen as schoolmistress, a young woman, named Mary Connor, recently committed for stealing a watch. She proved eminently qualified for the task, and became one of the first-fruits of Christian labour in that place; she was assiduous in her duties, and was never known to infringe one of the rules. A free pardon was granted her about fifteen months afterwards; but it proved an unavailing gift, for a cough, which had attacked her a short time before, ended in consumption. She displayed, during her illness, much patience and quietness of spirit; having, as she humbly believed, obtained everlasting pardon and peace, through the merits of her Lord and Saviour. She died in this hope " full of immortality."

Mrs. Fry's views were received with cordial approbation, by the Sheriffs of London, the Ordinary, and the Governor of Newgate; although they looked upon the experiment as almost hopeless. An unoccupied cell was, by their permission, appropriated for the school-room. On the day following this arrangement, Mrs. Fry, accompanied by her friend, Mary Sanderson, and with the poor prisoner Mary Connor, as mistress, opened the school, for the children and young persons under twenty-five years of age; but from the small size of the room, they had the pain of being obliged to refuse admission to many of the women, who earnestly entreated to be allowed to share in their instructions. Mary Sanderson then visited a prison for the first time, and her feelings were thus described by herself to Sir T. F. Buxton.

" The railing was crowded with half-naked women, struggling together for the front situations with the most boisterous violence, and begging with the utmost vociferation. She felt as if she were going into a den of wild beasts, and she well recollects quite shuddering when the door closed upon her, and she was locked in with such a herd of novel and desperate companions."

Something similar must have been the effect on that faithful co-adjutor in this work, Elizabeth Pryor, at rather a later period, upon seeing the women, "squalid in attire and ferocious in countenance, seated about the yard." From the prison door one issued, "yelling like a wild beast;" she rushed round the area with her arm extended, tearing everything of the nature of a cap from the heads of the other women. The sequel too is important; for this very woman, through the grace and mercy of God, became humanized under the instruction of the ladies. After having obtained her liberty, she married; and for years came occasionally to see Mrs. Pryor, who considered her a well-conducted person, her appearance being always most respectable.

A few other ladies gradually united themselves to those already engaged in the work, and the little school in the cell of Newgate, continued for many weeks their daily occupation.

" It was in our visits to the school, where some of us attended almost every day, that we were witnesses to the dreadful proceedings that went forward on the female side of the prison ; the begging, swearing, gaming, fighting, singing, dancing, dressing up in men's clothes ; scenes too bad to be described, so that we did not think it suitable to admit young persons with us."*

The ladies thought some of the existing evils could be remedied by proper regulations ; but in the commencement of the undertaking, the reformation of the women, sunk as they were

* Mrs. Fry's evidence before the House of Commons.

in every species of depravity, was scarcely thought of, much less anticipated. By degrees, however, the heroic little band became convinced that good   might be effected even amongst these, for intercourse with the prisoners had inspired them with confidence. The poor women were earnest in their entreaties, not to be excluded from the benefits, which they began to perceive would result to themselves, from improved habits. But whilst thus encouraged on the one side, every sort of discouragement presented itself on the other. The officers of the prison, as well as the private friends of these ladies, treated the idea of introducing industry and order into Newgate, as visionary. Even some the most interested in the attempt, apprehended that it would fail, from the character of those for whose good it was intended, from the unfavourable locality, in the midst of a great metropolis; and from the difficulty of obtaining a sufficiency of labourers for such a work. It was also urged that even if employment could be procured, the necessary materials for work would be destroyed or stolen. In recalling this period, one of those engaged in it thus writes : " But amidst these discouraging views, our benevolent friend evinced that her heart was fixed ; and trusting in the Lord, she commenced her work of faith and labour of love."

Mildred's Court, Third Month, 7th.—My mind and time have been much taken up with Newgate and its concerns. I have been encouraged about our school, but I find my weak nature and proneness to be so much affected by the opinions of man, brings me into some peculiar trials and temptations: in the first place, our Newgate visiting could no longer be kept secret, which I endeavoured that it should be, and therefore I am exposed to praise that I do not the least deserve ; also to some unpleasant humiliations—for in trying to obtain helpers, I must be subject to their various opinions ; and also, being obliged to confer at times with strangers, and men in authority, is to me a very unpleasant necessity. I have suffered much about the hanging of the criminals, having had to visit another poor woman, before her death ; this again tried me a good deal, but I was permitted to be much more upheld, and not so distressed as the time before. May I, in this important concern, be enabled to keep my eye singly unto the Lord, that what I do may be done heartily unto Him, and not in any degree unto man. May I be preserved humble, faithful, and persevering in it, as far as it is right to persevere. And if consistent with the Divine will, may the blessing of the Most High attend it, that it may be made instrumental in drawing some out of evil, and leading and establishing them in the way everlasting, where they may find rest and peace.

The woman here alluded to, was Elizabeth Fricker ; she was executed for robbing, or being accessory to robbing in a dwelling-house. The following memorandum was written by Mrs. Fry, March 4th, 1817, the day preceding the execution.

I have just returned from a most melancholy visit to Newgate, where I have been at the request of Elizabeth Fricker, previous to her execution to-morrow morning, at eight o'clock. I found her much hurried, distressed, and tormented in mind. Her hands cold, and covered with something like the perspiration preceding death, and in an universal tremor. The women who were with her, said she had been so outrageous before our going, that they thought a man must be sent for to manage her. However, after a serious time with her, her troubled soul became calmed. But is it for man thus to take the prerogative of the Almighty into his own hands ? Is it not his place rather to endeavour to reform such ; or restrain them from the commission of further evil ? At least to afford poor erring fellow-mortals, whatever may be their offences, an opportunity of proving their repentance by amendment of life. Besides this poor young woman, there are also six men to be hanged, one of whom has a wife near her confinement, also condemned, and seven young children. Since the awful report came down, he has become quite mad, from horror of mind. A strait waistcoat could not keep him within bounds—he had just bitten the turnkey, I saw the man come out with his hand bleeding, as I passed the cell.

I hear that another, who had been tolerably educated and
brought up, was doing all he could to harden himself, through
unbelief, trying to convince himself that religious truths were
idle tales. In this endeavour he appeared to have been too
successful with several of his fellow-sufferers. He sent to beg
for a bottle of wine, no doubt in the hope of drowning his misery
and the fears that would arise, by a degree of intoxication, I
inquired no further, I had seen and heard enough.

In a published letter, by the Honourable H. G. Bennett,
addressed to the Common Council and Livery of London, on
the abuses existing in Newgate, he says, in allusion to Fricker's
case :—

"A man by the name of Kelly, who was executed some
weeks back for robbing a house, counteracted by his conversation, and by the jest he made of all religious feelings, the labour
of Dr. Cotton to produce repentance and remorse amongst the
prisoners in the cells ; and he died as he lived, hardened and
unrepenting. He sent to me the day before his execution ; and
when I saw him, he maintained the innocence of the woman
convicted with him, asserting, that not Fricker, but a boy concealed, opened the door, and let him into the house. When I
pressed him to tell me the name of the parties concerned,
whereby to save the woman's life, he declined complying without
a promise of pardon ; I urged as strongly as I could, the crime
of suffering an innocent woman to be executed to screen criminal
accomplices; but it was all to no effect, and he suffered, maintaining to the last the same story. With him was executed, a
boy of nineteen or twenty years of age, whose fears and remorse
Kelly was constantly ridiculing."

Mildred's Court, Third Month, 11*th.*—My mind too much
tossed by a variety of interests and duties—husband, children,
household, accounts, Meetings, the Church, near relations,
friends, and Newgate—most of these things press a good deal
upon me. I hope I am not undertaking too much, but it is a
little like being in the whirlwind, and in the storm ; may I not

be hurt in it, but enabled quietly to perform that which ought to be done; and may it all be done so heartily unto the Lord, and through the assistance of His grace, that if consistent with His Holy Will, His blessing may attend it, and if ever any good be done, that the glory of the whole work may be given where it is alone due.

19*th.*—I yesterday applied to our Monthly Meeting for liberty to join William Forster, in paying a religious visit to the families of Gracechurch Street; I think I had reason to be encouraged, from the solemn covering over us, and also the unity expressed by Friends. I thought it a great mercy and favour to have the unity of all; but I desire not to place undue dependence even on this, though it is sweet, and I esteem it a great blessing to have it. My dear sister Elizabeth was particularly favoured in what she said. If permitted to enter this service, may the Lord be with us in it, and bless us. I have not at present felt much burdened by the prospect; I consider it an honour, favour, and blessing to be engaged in the service of our great Master, even if humiliations, trials and crosses attend it.

20*th.*—Thou Lord, who knowest my heart and my wants, be pleased to help me under them; also permit Thy poor child to ask Thee, yet to look down upon her husband, children, brothers and sisters for good, upon all those most near and dear to her, and particularly those who are in trial.

Fourth Month, 12*th.*—I have found in my late attention to Newgate, a peace and prosperity in the undertaking, that I seldom, if ever, remember to have done before. A way has very remarkably been opened for us, beyond all expectations, to bring into order the poor prisoners; those who are in power are so very willing to help us, in short the time appears come to work amongst them. Already, from being like wild beasts, they appear harmless and kind. I am ready to say, in the fulness of my heart, surely "it is the Lord's doing, and marvellous in our eyes;" so many are the providential openings of various kinds. Oh! if good should result, may the praise and glory of the whole, be entirely given where it is due by us, and by all, in deep humiliation and prostration of spirit.

In the month of April, 1817, the wife of a clergyman, and
eleven members of the Society of Friends, formed themselves
into "An Association for the Improvement of the Female
Prisoners in Newgate." The object they had in view is stated
to have been, "To provide for the clothing, the instruction, and
the employment of the women; to introduce them to a knowledge of the Holy Scriptures, and to form in them, as much as
possible, those habits of order, sobriety and industry, which may
render them docile and peaceable whilst in prison, and respectable when they leave it." On comparing these intentions with
the existing state of things, it is easy to believe that the scheme
was viewed by those in authority as highly desirable, but almost
impracticable. Still to their honour be it spoken, they promised and gave their warmest co-operation.

The concurrence of the sheriffs and city magistrates was asked
and obtained. But the doubt still remained, how far the women
would submit to the restraints, which it would be needful to
impose upon them, in order to effect this change. To ascertain
this, the sheriffs met the ladies one Sunday afternoon at Newgate; the women were assembled, and in their presence, as well
as that of the ordinary and governor, they were asked by Mrs.
Fry, whether they were willing to abide by the rules, which it
would be indispensable to establish amongst them, for the accomplishment of the object so much desired by them all. The
women, fully and unanimously, assured her of their determination to obey them strictly. The sheriffs also addressed them,
giving the plan the countenance of their approbation; and then
turning to Mrs. Fry and her companions, one of them said,
"Well, ladies, you see your materials."

How they used these "materials," and the blessing permitted
to attend their exertions, is demonstrated by a letter received in
1820, from one of the prisoners then present.

"To Mrs. Fry.

"Parramatta, New South Wales, *July* 10*th*, 1820.

"Honoured Madam,

"The duty I owe to you, likewise to the benevolent Society to which you have the honour to belong, compels me to take up my pen to return to you my most sincere thanks for the heavenly instruction I derived from you and the dear friends, during my confinement in Newgate.

"In the month of April, 1817, how did that blessed prayer of your's sink into my heart; and as you said, so have I found it, that when no eyes see, and no ears hear, that God both sees and hears, and then it was that the arrow of conviction entered my hard heart, and in Newgate, it was that poor Harriet S——, like the prodigal son, came to herself, and took with her words, and sought the Lord ; and truly can I say with David, ' Before I was afflicted I went astray, but now have I learned Thy ways, O Lord !' and although affliction cometh not forth of the dust, yet how prone have I been to forget God my Maker, who can give songs in the night; and happy is that soul that when affliction comes, can say with Eli, ' It is the Lord,' or with David, ' I was dumb, and I opened not my mouth, because Thou didst it,' and Job, when stripped of every comfort, ' Blessed be the Lord who took away, as well as gave'—and may the Lord grant every one that is afflicted, such an humble spirit as theirs. Believe me, my dear madam, I bless the day that brought me inside of Newgate walls, for then it was that the rays of Divine truth shone into my dark mind ; and may the Holy Spirit shine more and more upon my dark understanding, that I may be enabled so to walk, as one whose heart is set to seek a city whose builder and maker is God. Believe me, my dear madam, although I am a poor captive in a distant land, I would not give up having communion with God one single day for my liberty ; for what is the liberty of the body, compared with the liberty of the soul ? and soon will that time come, when death will release me from all the earthly fetters that hold me now, for I trust to be with Christ, who bought me with His precious blood. And now, my dear madam, these few sincere sentiments of mine I wish

you to make known to the world, that the world may see that
your labour in Newgate has not been in vain in the Lord.
Please to give my love to all the dear friends, and Dr. Cotton,
Mr. Baker, Simpson and all, the keeper of Newgate, and all the
afflicted prisoners ; and although we may never meet on earth
again, I hope we shall all meet in the realms of bliss, never
to part again.   Please give my love to Mrs. Stennett and Mrs.
Guy.

" And believe me to remain,
" Your humble servant,
" HARRIET S——."

The remainder of the history will be better told in the words
of Sir T. F. Buxton.   It is true that his description of the early
labours of the Ladies' Newgate Association has been repeatedly
before the public ; but there will probably be some into whose
hands this book may fall, who may not have perused it, and
others, from whose memory it may have passed.   We do not
hesitate, therefore, to make use of details so graphic, narrated as
they are by one whose exertions to benefit these " outcasts of the
people," were only excelled by her's, of whom he wrote.*

" Having succeeded so far, the next business was to provide
employment.   It struck one of the ladies, that Botany Bay
might be supplied with stockings, and indeed all articles of
clothing, of the prisoners' manufacture,   She therefore, called
upon Messrs. Richard Dixon and Co., of Fenchurch Street, and
candidly told them, that she was desirous of depriving them of
this branch of their trade, and stating her views begged their
advice.   They said at once, that they should not in any way
obstruct such laudable designs, and that no further trouble need
be taken to provide work for they would engage to do it.   Nothing
now remained but to prepare the room: and this difficulty was
obviated, by the sheriffs sending their carpenters.   The former

* An Enquiry whether crime and misery are produced or prevented
by our present system of Prison Discipline.   Third Edition, 1818,
page 109.

laundry speedily underwent the necessary alterations, was cleaned and white-washed, and in a very few days, the Ladies' Committee assembled in it all the tried female prisoners.   One of the ladies, Mrs. Fry, began by describing to them the comforts to be derived from industry and sobriety, the pleasure and profit of doing right; and contrasted the happiness and peace of those who are dedicated to a course of virtue and religion, with that experienced in their former life, and its present consequences ; and describing their awful guilt in the sight of God appealed to themselves, whether its wages, even here, were not utter misery and ruin.   She then dwelt upon the motives which had brought the ladies into New-gate ; they had left their homes and their families, to mingle amongst those from whom all others fled ; animated by an ardent and affectionate desire to rescue their fellow-creatures from evil, and to impart to them that knowledge, which they, from their education and circumstances, had been so happy as to receive.

" She then told them, that the ladies did not come with any absolute and authoritative pretensions ; that it was not intended they should command, and the prisoners obey, but that it was to be understood, all were to act in concert ; that not a rule should be made, or a monitor appointed, without their full and unanimous concurrence ; that for this purpose, each of the rules should be read and put to the vote ; and she invited those who might feel any disinclination to any particular, freely to state their opinion.   The following were then read :—

Rules.

" 1. That a matron be appointed for the general superinten-dence of the women.

" 2. That the women be engaged in needlework, knitting, or any other suitable employment.

" 3. That there be no begging, swearing, gaming, card-play-ing, quarrelling, or immoral conversation.   That all novels, plays, and other improper books, be excluded ; and that all bad words be avoided; and any default in these particulars be reported to the matron.

" 4. That there be a yard-keeper, chosen from among the women : to inform them when their friends come ; to see that they leave their work with a monitor, when they go to the grating, and that they do not spend any time there, except with their friends. If any woman be found disobedient, in these respects, the yard-keeper is to report the case to the Matron.

" 5. That the women be divided into classes, of not more than twelve ; and that a monitor be appointed to each class.

" 6. That monitors be chosen from amongst the most orderly of the women that can read, to superintend the work and conduct of the others.

" 7. That the monitors not only overlook the women in their own classes, but if they observe any others disobeying the rules, that they inform the monitor of the class to which such persons may belong, who is immediately to repeat to the matron, and the deviations to be set down on a slate.

" 8. That any monitor breaking the rules shall be dismissed from her office, and the most suitable in the class selected to take her place.

" 9. That the monitors be particularly careful to see that the women come with clean hands and face to their work, and that they are quiet during their employment.

" 10. That at the ringing of the bell, at nine o'clock in the morning, the women collect in the work-room to hear a portion of Scripture read by one of the visitors, or the matron ; and that the monitors afterwards conduct the classes from thence to their respective wards in an orderly manner.

" 11. That the women be again collected for reading, at six o'clock in the evening, when the work shall be given in charge to the matron by the monitors.

" 12. That the matron keep an exact account of the work done by the women, and of their conduct.

" And as each was proposed, every hand was held up in token of their approbation.   In the same manner, and with the same formalities, each of the monitors was proposed, and all were unanimously approved.   When this business was concluded, one of the visitors read aloud the twenty-first chapter of St. Matthew the parable of the barren fig tree, seeming applicable to the state of the audience ; after a period of silence, according to the custom

of the Society of Friends, the monitors, with their classes, withdrew to their respective wards in the most orderly manner.
During the first month, the ladies were anxious that the attempt
should be secret, that it might meet with no interruption; at
the end of that time, as the experiment had been tried, and had
exceeded even their expectations, it was deemed expedient to
apply to the Corporation of London. It was considered that the
school would be more permanent, if it were made a part of the
prison system of the City, than if it merely depended on individuals. In consequence, a short letter, descriptive of the progress already made, was written to the sheriffs.

"The next day, an answer was received, proposing a meeting
with the ladies at Newgate.

"In compliance with this appointment, the Lord Mayor, the
Sheriffs, and several of the Aldermen attended. The prisoners
were assembled together; and it being requested that no alteration in their usual practice might take place, one of the ladies
read a chapter in the Bible, and then the females proceeded to
their various avocations. Their attention, during the time of
reading, their orderly and sober deportment, their decent dress,
the absence of everything like tumult, noise or contention; the
obedience and respect shown by them, and the cheerfulness
visible in their countenance and manners, conspired to excite the
astonishment and admiration of their visitors. Many of these
knew Newgate, had visited it a few months before, and had not
forgotten the painful impressions made by a scene, exhibiting,
perhaps, the very utmost limits of misery and guilt.

"The magistrates, to evince their sense of the importance of
the alterations which had been effected, immediately adopted the
whole plan as a part of the system of Newgate, empowered the
ladies to punish the refractory by short confinement, undertook
part of the expense of the matron, and loaded the ladies with
thanks and benedictions. About six months after the establishment of the school for the children, and the manufactory for the
tried side; the committee received a most urgent petition from
the untried, entreating that the same might be done among them,
and promising strict obedience. In consequence, the ladies made
the same arrangements, proposed the same rules, and admitted in

6

the same manner as on the other side, the prisoners to participate in their formation. The experiment has here answered, but not to the same extent. They have had difficulty in procuring a sufficiency of work, the prisoners are not so disposed to work, flattering themselves with the prospect of speedy release; besides, they are necessarily engaged, in some degree, in preparation for their trial. The result of the observations of the ladies, has been, that where the prisoners, from whatever cause, did no work, they derived little, if any, moral advantage ; where they did some work, they received some benefit, and where they were fully engaged, they were really and essentially improved."

A gentleman well known to Mrs. Fry, who was desirous of seeing and judging for himself of the effects of this singular experiment, visited Newgate just one fortnight after the adoption of the new rules. We give his own words.

" I went and requested permission to see Mrs. Fry, which was shortly obtained, and I was conducted by a turnkey to the entrance of the women's wards. On my approach, no loud or dissonant sounds or angry voices indicated that I was about to enter a place, which I was credibly assured, had long had for one of its titles, that of ' Hell above ground.' The court-yard into which I was admitted, instead of being peopled with beings scarcely human, blaspheming, fighting, tearing each other's hair, or gaming with a filthy pack of cards for the very clothes they wore (which often did not suffice even for decency) presented a scene where stillness and propriety reigned. I was conducted by a decently-dressed person, the newly appointed yards-woman, to the door of a ward, where, at the head of a long table sat a lady belonging to the Society of Friends. She was reading aloud to about sixteen women prisoners, who were engaged in needlework around it. Each wore a clean looking blue apron and bib ; with a ticket having a number on it suspended from her neck by a red tape. They all rose on my entrance, curtsied respectfully, and then at a signal given resumed their seats and employments. Instead of a scowl, leer, or ill suppressed laugh, I observed upon their countenances an air of self-respect and gravity, a sort of consciousness of their improved character, and the altered position in which they were placed.   I afterwards visited the other wards, which were the counterparts of the first."

Encouraged by many concurring circumstances, the newly formed Ladies' Committee, now for the first time introduced a matron into Newgate.   The prisoners were divided into classes, and placed under her superintendence.   She was eventually paid in part by the Corporation ; and received in addition twenty pounds a-year from the funds of the Ladies' Association. They furnished the rooms appropriated to her, and she was regarded as their servant.   The yards-woman was also appointed and paid by them.

Previous to the appointment of the matron, and until she was thoroughly established in her office, some of the ladies spent the whole day in the prison amongst the women ; taking a little provision for themselves in a basket, or remaining without any ; and for a long time afterwards, one or two of them, never failed to spend some hours daily in this important field of labour.

From the manuscript journal of one of their number, Sophia de C——, we are permitted to present to the reader some extracts descriptive of this period : —

" *Fifth Month,* 1*st,* 1817.—After nearly a sleepless night, spent in anticipation of the scenes of the morrow, I called on Dorcas Coventry, who had promised to introduce me to inspect the important labours which the Ladies of the Prison Committee had engaged in, for the reformation of the women in Newgate, for some time past.   We proceeded to the felons' door, the steps of which were covered with their friends, who were waiting for admission, laden with the various provisions, and other articles which they required, either as gifts, or to be purchased, as the prisoners might be able to afford.   We entered with this crowd of persons, into an ante-room, the walls of which were covered with the different chains and fetters, suspended in readiness for the culprits : a block and hammer were placed in the centre of it, on which the chains were rivetted. The room was guarded with blunderbusses, mounted on moveable carriages. I trembled, and felt sick, and my heart sunk within me, when a prisoner was brought forward to have his chain lightened, because he had an inflammation on the ankle. I spoke to him, for he looked dejected, and by no means ferocious. The turnkey soon opened the first gate of entrance, through which we were permitted to pass without being searched, in consequence of orders issued by the sheriffs. The crowd awaited until the men had been searched by the turnkeys; and the women, by a woman stationed for that purpose in a little room by the door of entrance. These searchers are allowed, if they suspect spirits, or ropes, or instruments of escape to be concealed about the person, to strip them to ascertain the fact. A melancholy detection took place a few days ago. A poor woman had a rope found upon her, concealed for the purpose of liberating her husband, sentenced to death for highway robbery, which sentence was to be put into execution in a few days. She was of course taken before a magistrate and ordered into Newgate to wait her trial. She was a young and pretty little Irish woman, with an infant in her arms. After passing the first door into a passage, we arrived at the place where the prisoners' friends communicate with them, it may be justly termed a sort of iron cage : a considerable space remains between the gratings, too wide to admit of their shaking hands. They pass into this from the airing yard, which occupies the centre of the quadrangle, round which the building runs, and into which no persons but the visiting ladies, or the persons they introduce, attended by a turnkey, are permitted to enter. This door is kept by a principal turnkey, and was opened to our attendant by his ringing a bell. A little lodge, in which an under turnkey sleeps, is also considered necessary to render the entrance secure. This yard was clean, and up and down it, paraded an emaciated woman, who gave notice to the women of the arrival of their friends. Most of the prisoners were collected in a room newly appropriated for the purpose to hear a portion of the Sacred Scriptures read to them, either by the matron, or by one of the Ladies' Committee ; which last is far preferable. They assemble when the bell rings, as near nine o'clock as possible, following their monitors or wards-women, to the forms which are placed in order to receive them.   I think I never can forget the impression made upon my feelings at this sight.   Women from every part of Great Britain, of every age and condition, below the lower middle rank, were assembled in mute silence, except when the interrupted breathing of their sucking infants informed us of the unhealthy state of these innocent partakers in their parents' punishment.   The matron read; I could not refrain from tears, the women wept also ; several were under the sentence of death.   Swain, for forging, who had just received her respite, sat next me ; and on my left hand, sat Lawrence alias Woodman, surrounded by her four children, and only waiting the birth of another which she hourly expects, to pay the forfeit of her life ; as her husband had done for the same crime, a short time before.

" Such various, such acute, and such new feelings passed through my mind, that I could hardly support the reflection, that what I saw was only to be compared to an atom in the abyss of vice, and consequently, misery of this vast metropolis. The hope of doing the least lasting good, seemed to vanish ; and to leave me in fearful apathy.   The prisoners left the room in order. Each monitor took charge of the work of her class on retiring. We proceeded to other wards, some containing coiners, forgers, and thieves ; and almost all these vices, were ingrafted on the most deplorable root of sinful dissipation.   Many of the women are married ; their families are in some instances permitted to be with them, if very young; their husbands, the partners of their crimes, are often found to be on the men's side of the prison, or on their way to Botany Bay.

" Some of these poor women are really beautiful, and healthy, and even modest-looking; their figures fine, and their countenances not disfigured by the expression of sin.   The greatest number appeared to me Irish, a very few Scotch, the former are always ignorant, and preserve the peculiarities of their national character, even in this abode of sorrow and captivity ; for to them privation and hardship are well known, and their Roman Catholic profession places their responsibility to God, in the keeping of their priests, so that life is deprived of its heaviest burden, and they expect to be finally happy, if they attend even in that place, to the private ceremonies which their form of worship enjoins. I felt much more interested during my momentary glance, for some of these poor creatures, than for others. I was warned by my friend not to place too much dependence on expression of countenance, or on what they might say, as deception is the ruling temptation while here, and without much care, would produce mischief and injustice. They appear to be aware of the value of character, to know what is right, but to forsake it in action ; finding this feeling yet alive, if properly purified and directed, it may become a foundation on which a degree of reformation can be built. In appealing to this statement in their breasts, and cultivating their own knowledge of it, many of the causes of former misbehaviour are crushed. Thus they conduct themselves more calmly and decently to each other, they are more orderly, more quiet, refrain from bad language, chew tobacco more cautiously, surrender the use of the fire-place, permit doors and windows to be opened and shut, to air or warm the prison, reprove their children with less violence, borrow and lend useful articles to each other kindly, put on their attire with modesty, and abstain from slanderous and reproachful words.

"It is to be hoped that by and by, a deeper and purer sense of the truths of religion may be found the cause of a real reformation. None amongst them was so shocking as an old woman, a clipper of the coin of the realm, whose daughter was by her side, with her infant in her arms, which had been born in Bridewell; the grandfather was already transported with several branches of his family as being coiners. The old woman's face was full of depravity. We next crossed the airing-yard, where many prisoners were industriously engaged at slop-work, for which they are paid, and after receiving what they require the rest is kept for them by the Committee, who have a receipt book, where their earnings and their expenditure may be seen for any time, by the day or week. On entering the untried wards, we found the women very different from those we had just left, they were quarrelling, and very disorderly, neither knowing their future fate, nor any thing like subordination amongst one another. It resembles the state of the women on the tried side, previous to the formation of the Visitors' Committee; not a hand was employed except in mischief. One bold creature was ushered in for committing highway robbery. Many convicts were arriving just remanded, from the Sessions House; and their dark associates received them with applause, such is the unhallowed fellowship of sin. We left this revolting scene, and proceeded to the school-room, situated on the untried side of the prison, for want of room on the tried. The quiet decency of this apartment was quite a relief, about twenty young women rose on our entrance, and stood with their eyes cast to the ground.

"A young woman of respectable appearance, named Mary Connor, had offered herself as mistress, for keeping the young children in order; who were separated from their parents' wards, and placed in this room. I gave those who wished it, permission to read to me, several could both read and write, some could say their letters, and others were in total ignorance, they wept as I asked them questions, and I read to them the parable of the prodigal son, as being peculiarly applicable to their present situation, they then resumed their needle-work. We next proceeded to the sick ward, (it was in good order,) and took a list of the additional clothes wanted there, and read a chapter from the New Testament, we then bade adieu to this dismal abode.

"*2nd*—Rose early and visited Newgate, (accompanied by Elizabeth Pryor,) where most of the Committee met to receive the Lord Mayor, the Sheriffs, several Aldermen, among whom were Sir William Curtis, Atkins, and some of the Gaol Committee, who had visited Elizabeth Fry the preceding day, in order to learn what had been done, what remained to be improved, and to lend the assistance they deemed needful in this important work. The wisdom and integrity of her purpose was made apparent to them, and the plans gradually expanded before each of them; nothing was precipitated, caution marked every step, and even the irritable state of City politics does not interfere with this attempt at improvement. The women were assembled as usual, looking particularly clean, and Elizabeth Fry had commenced reading a Psalm, when the whole of this party entered the already crowded room. Her reading was thus interrupted for a short time. She looked calmly on the approaching gentlemen, who, soon perceiving the solemnity of her occupation, stood still amidst the multitude, whilst Elizabeth Fry resumed her office, and the women their quietude. In an impressive tone she told them, she never permitted any trifling circumstance to interrupt the very solemn and important engagement of reading the Holy Scriptures ; but in this instance it appeared unavoidable from the unexpected entrance of so many persons, besides which, when opportunity offers, we should pay respect to those in authority over us, those who administer justice : she thus, with a Christian prudence, peculiar to herself, controlled the whole assembly, and subdued the feelings of the prisoners, many of whom were but too well acquainted with the faces of the magistrates, who were themselves touched and astonished at being thus introduced to a state of decorum so new within those walls, and could not help acknowledging, how admirably this mode of treatment was adapted to overcome the evil spirit which had so long triumphed there. The usual silence ensued after the reading, then the women withdrew. We could not help feeling particularly glad that the gentlemen were present at this reading; the prisoners crowded round the Lord Mayor and Sheriffs, to beg little favours. We had a long conference with these gentlemen relative to this prison and its objects, the wisest regulations for Prison Discipline, and the causes of crime; indeed we could not have received more kind or devoted attention to what was suggested. Elizabeth Fry's manner seemed to awaken new trains of reflection, and to place the individual value of these poor creatures before them in a fresh point of view. They talked of building a school-room, but as it would encroach on the area of the yard, the scheme was unanimously abandoned. Regulations for cooking, washing and dining were promised ; but everything at present that involves expense to the city is relinquished. Economy, not parsimony was the theme of the Lord Mayor ; private benevolence has up to this time, supplied every extra expense, besides what is termed the

6

Sheriffs' Gift. The Sheriffs came to our Committee-room,—
they ordered a cell to be given up to the Committee for the
temporary confinement of delinquents; it was to be made appear as formidable as possible, and we hope never to require it.

"12th.—The soldiers who guarded the interior of Newgate,
were, at our request dismissed; they overlooked the women's
yard and rendered them very disorderly.

"23rd.—I found poor Woodman lying-in, in the common
ward, where she had been suddenly taken ill; herself and little
girl were each doing very well. She was awaiting her execution, at the end of the month. What can be said of such sights
as these.

24th.—I read to Woodman, who is not in the state of mind
we could wish for her, indeed so unnatural is her situation, that
one can hardly tell how or in what manner to meet her case.
She seems afraid to love her baby, and the very health which is
being restored to her, produces irritation of mind."

That the scene described by Sophia de C——, was satisfactory to the City authorities, is proved by a document which Mrs.
Fry and her colleagues had the gratification of receiving a few
days afterwards. But before introducing copies of these papers;
it is due not only to the gentlemen whose names are appended to
them, but to other members of the Corporation, to recall the
cordial manner in which they accepted the services of the ladies,
and acknowledged the extent and importance of the improvements effected. They had themselves experienced insurmountable difficulties in the attempt to control, or to introduce order
amongst the women in Newgate, and appear to have relinquished the task as hopeless. When therefore this new system
and its unlooked for success was exhibited before them, they
did not start aside mistrustful of the agency, or the novelty of
the proceedings, but without hesitation gave the weight of their
influence and authority to uphold those efforts, which without

their support, would probably have been of short duration, and of comparatively unimportant results.

Saturday, 3rd of May, 1817.

Committee of Aldermen to consider all matters relating to the Gaols of this City.

PRESENT :

THE RIGHT HON, THE LORD MAYOR.

SIR WILLIAM CURTIS, BART.

MR. ALDERMAN JOSHUA JONATHAN SMITH.

MR. ALDERMAN CHRISTOPHER SMITH.

MR. ALDERMAN ATKINS.

MR. ALDERMAN GOODBEHERE.

GEORGE BRYDGES, ESQ., and ALDERMAN, } Sheriffs.
ROBERT KIRBY, ESQ.,

The committee met agreeably to the resolution of the 29th ultimo, at the Keeper's house at Newgate, and proceeded from thence, attended by the Sheriffs, to take a view of the Gaol of Newgate.

The committee on viewing that part of the gaol appropriated to the female prisoners, were attended by Mrs. Elizabeth Fry, and several other ladies, who explained to the committee the steps they had adopted, to induce the female prisoners to work and to behave themselves in a becoming and orderly manner, and several specimens of their work being inspected, the committee were highly gratified.

(Signed)   WOODTHORPE.

Saturday, 10th of May 1817.

Committee of Aldermen to consider all matters relating to the Gaols of this City.

PRESENT :

THE RIGHT HON. THE LORD MAYOR.

SIR WILLIAM CURTIS, BART.

MR. ALDERMAN JOSHUA JONATHAN SMITH.

MR. ALDERMAN CHRISTOPHER SMITH.

MR. ALDERMAN ATKINS.

MR. ALDERMAN GOODBEHERE.

GEORGE BRYDGES, ESQ., ALDERMAN, and one of the Sheriffs.

The committee met at the Mansion House, and were attended by Mrs. Elizabeth Fry, and two other ladies; who were heard in respect of their suggestions for the better government of the female prisoners in Newgate.

" Resolved unanimously, that the thanks of this committee be given to Mrs. Elizabeth Fry, and the other ladies who have so kindly exerted themselves, with a view to bettering the condition of the women, confined in the Gaol of Newgate ; and that they be requested to continue those exertions, which have hitherto been attended with such good effect.

(Signed)   " WOODTHORPE."

From a paper found among Mrs. Fry's other writings, we are enabled to give the heads of the suggestions alluded to in the minute of the Gaol Committee.

1st. Newgate, in great want of room. Women to be under the care of women matron, turnkeys, and inspecting committee.

2nd. As little communication with their friends as possible. Only at stated times except in any very particular cases.

3rd. They must depend on their friends for neither food nor clothing ; but have sufficiency allowed them of both.

4th. That employment should be a part of their punishment, and be provided for them by Government. The earnings of work to be partly laid by, partly laid out in small extra indulgences, and if enough, part go towards their support.

5th. To work and have their meals together, but sleep separate at night, being classed, with monitors at the head of each class.

Religious instruction.

The kind attention we have had paid us.

Great disadvantages arise from dependence upon the uncertainty and fluctuations of the Sheriffs' fund. Neither soap nor clothing being allowed without its aid ; and the occasional help of Grand Juries, or other charitable people.

The different arrangements of the ladies, together with the purchase of clothing for the prisoners, entailed considerable expenses ; which soon proved beyond their private resources ; a

subscription was therefore opened to meet them, to which the
Sheriffs added the sum of eighty pounds. Mrs. Fry, at an after
period, related to one of her coadjutors, that at this time she
applied to some of her own relations for assistance in this object,
for she perceived the work before her to be great, and the opening
for usefulness beyond her expectation, but that to follow it up, she
required the command of more money, than she could conscientiously ask from her husband.   Her application was most cordially responded to by them ; especially by her cousin, Hudson
Gurney, Esq., and her uncle, Robert Barclay, Esq.; they gave
her help, and encouraged her to persevere in her important
objects, desiring her to apply freely to them whenever their
assistance was required.

The following extracts are from letters of Mr. Barclay's.

Bury Hill, *November 25th*, 1817.
"Dear Niece,

"I received by this day's post, thy interesting communication
of yesterday, touching the present state of Newgate. As to the
excellent plan of reform of the female convicts under the care of
thyself and the committee. I freely authorize thee to send to
my sons, D. and G. B——, for twenty-five to fifty pounds, as
in thy own opinion the case may now require.

"ROBERT BARCLAY."

"Bury Hill, *December 27th*, 1818.
"I wish thee to consider, that all my circle sympathise with
thee in thy very arduous and successful pursuits of a public as
well as private nature ; and in any case that wants thy support
in a pecuniary line, do depend on my will and ability to give thee
assistance by writing me a report of thy wishes.

"ROBERT BARCLAY."

But far beyond any other assistance was that she received
from her own brothers ; who not only entered warmly into her

objects of interest, but were unfailing in the generous support
they afforded them. From that time, until her labours of love
were ended upon earth, not one year elapsed in which they
did not most liberally contribute, as occasion required, to her
various purposes of benevolence, leaving the division to her own
judgment. Thus did He, who had called her to this work, open
the hearts of persons in various circumstances, each to contribute
of that which he had, some in personal exertion, and cheerful
consecration of time and strength ; some the countenance of
their authority and official dignity, whilst others poured in the
needful supply of silver and gold.

Plashet, Sixth Month, 16*th.*— I found the prison going on
in a very encouraging manner, so much quietness and order,
quite like a different place to what it used to be. We may
humbly trust from the fruit produced, that the blessing of the
Most High has given the increase to the scattered seed.

Extracts from a letter to her two eldest daughters.

Plashet, *Third day Evening*.
(Post mark) 11 June, 1817.

My dearest Girls,

We have been daily watching with some anxiety for a letter,
to say, when we were to expect you and your dear aunt, for our
hearts are not a little set upon seeing you again ; indeed, we
long to have you all once more around us. We are a little like
children at school, counting the days till the holidays. But I
thought it might be well to remind you before your return, of a
few needful things. You are, indeed, on your way to a sweet
and happy home. But such is now your situation there, that
you must, my loved girls, industriously do your part ; you are
young, but under present circumstances, you must be *very* industrious, very persevering, you must rise early ; remember there
is no governess. Then I shall expect of you diligence in your
own education, and in some other things, I may want you to do ;

we must, none of us, be idle ; and as you are now come to an age of some understanding, I hope to find you real helpers, and at times rejoice in this hope. My dear children, remember if you wish to be real helpers to me, and to your dear father, you must take heed to yourselves, and seek to keep your eye single to Him, who can alone enable you to do your duty towards yourselves or towards us. For I am more and more convinced, that unless what we do, is done heartily unto the Lord, it profiteth little, and availeth nothing. I cannot tell you, for I have not language to express it; the longing that I have, that you my sweet dear children may go on in the right way. How far before all other things do I ask it for you. That whilst here, you may be " guided by His counsel, and afterwards received into glory." I may tell you, that your home-prospect is very bright, your little room, school-room and bed-room, all to yourselves ; you must set a sweet example amongst the others, for this is exceedingly important. We hope this week will not pass without seeing you ; my very dear love to your uncles and aunts. Yours very dearly,

ELIZABETH FRY.

A year had elapsed since her daughters had left home, the greater part of which time they had been the guests of their uncle Daniel Gurney, at North Runcton, under the maternal care of their aunt Rachel. It was joy to be at home again; but that home was altered; the brothers were gone to school. Life which had to them seemed play before, now, had become earnest.

Plashet, Sixth Month, 20th.—My dearest boys are returned from school, and the girls I expect this evening. To be once more surrounded by our sweet flock, is pleasant, and appears cause for much thankfulness. May a blessing attend us amongst them, so that in word and in deed we may preach Christ; and O gracious Lord ! be pleased so to let Thy blessing attend our labours of love, that they may all grow in grace, and in the knowledge of Thee and Christ Jesus whom Thou hast sent.

Seventh Month, 21*st.*—I seem kept almost always, by night and by day, going again and again to the mercy-seat; I can hardly express what I have felt at times—groanings unutterable, for the children upon their getting out of childhood, in their many temptations : some seem more beset than others, but I do trust in Him, who has done marvellous things for me, and I humbly believe will do so also for them ; this is the language of faith in my heart, so that I can hardly help consoling myself with the hope that sooner or later it will be verified, " I will pour my Spirit upon thy seed, and my blessing upon thy offspring, and they shall spring up as among the grass, as willows by the water-courses. One shall say, I am the Lord's ; and another shall call himself by the name of Jacob ; and another shall subscribe with his hand unto the Lord, and surname himself by the name of Israel." Once in a very low time, I opened at this Scripture ; and it appeared to come so seasonably when depressed about my children, some years since, from Esdras, " My hands shall cover thee so that thy children shall not see Hell."—Esdras ii. 29—32.

28*th.*—I am alone at home with my nine children, a great and very precious charge ; at times they appear too much for me, at others I greatly enjoy them ; I desire that the anxiety for their welfare, and to have them in order, should not prevent my enjoying thankfully, the blessing of being surrounded by so sweet a flock. I sometimes think of these words, " The fruit of the womb is his reward ;" and having borne them through much fear, and at times much tribulation, I believe I should thankfully enjoy them ; not improperly resting in the precious gift. How I delight to see the springings of goodness in them, the blessed seed appearing, as well as mourn when the evil shows itself. Most gracious Lord, be pleased to be with them and bless them; strengthen the good I beseech Thee, and weaken the evil in their hearts.

Eighth Month, 4*th.*—My having been brought publicly forward in the newspapers, respecting what I have been instrumental in doing at Newgate, has brought some anxiety with it; in the first place, as far as I am concerned, that it may neither raise me too high, nor cast me too low, that having what may appear my good works, thus published, may never lead me or others to give either the praise or glory where it is not due. And that being brought thus forward in a way I do not like, and by a person whom I do not quite approve ; I may in this, and in all other things, experience preservation, for indeed, I cannot keep myself, and that this labour, if consistent with the Divine Will, may continue to be blessed, and to make progress. And for myself, that I may be kept humble, watchful, faithful, and persevering.

The change that had taken place in Newgate, was noticed for the first time in the public journals, during the autumn of this year, by a man, who has since been distinguished for his wild and theoretical views. This was Robert Owen of New Lanark. He published in all the newspapers a long letter on his system of education, in which, in order to adduce an additional proof of the effects of kindness and regular habits on characters the most abandoned, he briefly noticed what had been done in Newgate. This was, to Elizabeth Fry and her companions, a painful and unpleasant circumstance, notoriety being far from their inclination. It immediately arrested public attention, Prison Discipline having become an object of inquiry and general interest.

Plashet, Eighth Month, 28th.—I was yesterday at Newgate with Sheriff Brydges, &c., &c. I have felt of late, fears, whether my being made so much of, so much respect paid me by the people in power in the city, and also being so publicly brought forward, may not prove a temptation, and lead to something of self-exaltation or worldly pride. I fear, I make the most of myself, and carry myself rather as if I was somebody amongst them ; a degree of this sort of conduct appears almost necessary —yet oh ! the watchfulness required not to bow to man, not to seek to gratify self-love ; but rather in humility and godly fear, to abide under the humiliation of the cross. Lord, be pleased so to help and strengthen me in this, that for Thine own cause' sake, for my own soul's sake, my beloved family's, and the

Society's sake, I may in no way be a cause of repreach ; but in my life, conduct, and conversation, glorify Thy great and ever excellent name. In all my perplexities be pleased to help me, and make a way where I see no way.

On the 10th of September, her brother, Joseph John Gurney, of Earlham, married Jane, daughter of John Birkbeck, Esq.

Plashet, Ninth Month, 19th.—I returned from attending my dearest brother Joseph's wedding, with Jane Birkbeck, yesterday; they were married on the 10th; a meeting very conspicuously owned by the great and good Shepherd of Israel, so that we could but look upon it as a token for good ; the ministry flowed ; but the immediate visitation of Divine love was a still better thing. My brother said a few words in supplication to my great comfort and refreshment, not doubting but that the Holy anointing was poured upon him ; therefore I believe that he will be a great instrument in his Heavenly Father's hand, if he only keep very near to His guidance in heights and in depths; but I could *naturally* feel fears for his very sensitive and tender mind—the conflicts necessary for the service are so great and deep. His dear wife I believe will prove a true helper to him. I saw them afterwards settled at Earlham.

The same day, in connexion with this marriage, she wrote to her sister Richenda Cunningham.

Plashet, *Ninth Nonth*, 19th, 1817.

My dear and tender love is with you. It is my anxious desire that you may all find Earlham the same sweet home that it ever has been to you, although the mistress is changed ; and that the same refreshment, comfort and liberty of spirit that we have all enjoyed there, may be continued just the same. I wished to have been there at the time you all met, that if I had had any part to take, it might have been to have encouraged all to serve their Master, in the way that they believed was acceptable in His sight, and yet, to do all that we each could to make each other's path easy and to encourage one another in the right way of the Lord.

To her brother, Joseph John Gurney.

Plashet, Tenth Month, 16th, 1817.

My dearest Joseph,

It is rather odd to myself that I should not have written to thee before, who hast been the frequent subject of my most tender interests. My heart has been raised for thy support and preservation under every circumstance.

Perhaps, my dear brother, thou wilt like to hear a little of me, though thou hast so much to occupy thy heart and mind. Few, perhaps, can acknowledge more of the abundant loving kindness of the Almighty, who in a remarkable way has dealt with me. But in blessing He has been pleased at times to permit some deep sorrows in the cup ; some known to my fellow mortals, and some remarkably hidden ; but this, I doubt not, has been for good. At times, even though there are so many whom I love, so many near and dear to me, " I watch and am as a sparrow alone upon the house-top," like " the owl in the desert, or the pelican in the wilderness ;" but I believe " when no man seeth me, God seeth me, and when no man pitieth me, God pitieth me." I have felt also what the blessing is of having Him on our side ; how doth He comfort those that mourn, and administer to all our wants. In short, though cast rather down in some things, I have felt much raised up in others, as if the power of the Endless Life shone strong in me through all ; so that I may say, " though sorrowing, yet always rejoicing." This is a most private letter, as such an acknowledgment is almost like boasting, but I believe I may say it is not so, for all I desire to convey is, that amidst all my cares, sorrows, and perplexities, through His gracious power who strengthens me, I do rejoice.

Let me hear from you soon, and believe me in near and tender love, thine and thy dear Jane's,

Very affectionate sister,

E. F.

Mildred's Court, Twelfth Month, 17th. — A remarkable

blessing still appears to accompany my prison concerns ; perhaps the greatest apparent blessing on my deeds, that ever attended me. How have the spirits of both of those in power, and the poor afflicted prisoners appeared to be subjected, and how has the work gone on ! most assuredly the power and the glory is alone due to the Author and Finisher of every good work : things in this way thus prosper beyond my most sanguine expectations, but there are also deep humiliations for me. My beloved children do not appear sufficiently under the influence of religion. I am ready to say ; oh ! that I could prosper at home in my labours, as I appear to do abroad. Others appear to fear for me, that I am too much divided, but alas ! what can I do, but follow the openings. I think that I do also labour at home ; but He who searcheth the heart, who knoweth all things, He knows my faith, my goings out, and my comings in ; He knows the desires of my heart towards Himself—indeed the deep inward travail of my spirit has been unutterable and indescribable ; but my humble trust and strong confidence is, that He who hears and answers prayer, listens to my cry, hearkens to my deep inward suppli- cations for myself, my husband, children, brothers, sisters, and household, my poor prisoners, and all things upon which I crave a blessing ; and that being breathed in the faith, and I humbly trust through the power of the Redeemer, access will be granted them, and He who has been with me, will be with me even unto the end. Amen, and Amen, saith my unworthy, sorrowful, and yet in another sense, rejoicing soul ; as I do, at seasons through all, in a marvellous manner, in all my sorrows and cares greatly and unspeakably rejoice in God my Saviour, my Redeemer, and my only hope of glory.

Mildred's Court, 23rd.—My spirit is much overwhelmed within me, this morning, but may I be enabled to look to the Rock that is higher than I. O Lord ! I beseech thee, sustain me, and grant me cheerful resignation to Thy will, whatever Thou mayst be pleased to do with my little one, who is sick ; either in life, or in death, may she ever be Thine, and be com- forted by thy love, and life-giving presence. Amen.

Mildred's Court, 1818.—Lord, be pleased to grant the bless· ing of preservation which is above every blessing. It is very

striking and wonderful to me, to observe how some things have
been verified, that in times of great lowness and unutterable distress, I have been led to believe would happen ; in reading the
142nd Psalm, these words particularly, " The righteous shall
compass me about, for Thou shalt deal bountifully with me."
Has not this been, and is it not now remarkably verified, by
those filling almost the highest stations in life, to the lowest ; by
persons of almost all denominations, have I not been compassed
about ?   My prison concerns have thus brought me, a poor and
very unworthy creature, into public notice, and I may most
humbly adopt this language in the 71st Psalm, " I am as a
wonder unto many ; but Thou art my strong Refuge.   Oh ! let
my mouth be filled with Thy praise and Thy honour all the
day ;" but, O Lord ! merciful and gracious, Thou who knowest
the heart and its wanderings, and also its pantings after Thyself,
be pleased yet to manifest Thyself to be a God hearing and
answering prayer.   Thou hast in times of deep adversity, and of
great affliction, when the heart of Thy handmaid has been ready
to say, Refuge failed her, Thou hast then been her Stronghold,
her Rock, and her Fortress ; so that she has not been greatly
moved nor overcome by her soul's enemy.   Be pleased, most
merciful and gracious Lord God Almighty, now to keep her in
the day of prosperity, when the righteous compass her about, and
she may be for a time even as a wonder unto many.   Keep her,
O Lord ! even as in Thine own Almighty hand, that no evil
befall her, nor any plague come nigh her dwelling ; and as Thou
hast so far in Thine abundant mercy and lovingkindness, delivered her soul from death ; Oh, be pleased to keep her feet from
falling, hold up her goings in thy paths that her footsteps slip
not, but increasingly enable her at all times, under all circumstances, in heights and in depths, in life and in death, to
show forth Thy praise, to walk faithfully and circumspectly
before Thee, obeying Thee in all things, in Thy fear and in
Thy love ; abounding in the true faith as it is in Jesus, ever
giving Thee, O Lord God on High, with Christ Jesus our Lord,
and Thy Holy Spirit our Comforter, one God, blessed for ever,
the glory due unto Thee, now in time, and in an endless eternity.
Amen, Amen.

During this winter, Mrs. Fry's time was occupied to an extent, of which none but those who lived with her can form any idea. The letters she received from all parts of the country to inquire the particulars of the system pursued in Newgate, were numerous. Ladies wished to form associations to visit the prisons, or magistrates to improve the state of the prisoners under their control ; these letters required long and careful answers, too much was at stake to send them off without seriously considering their contents. Some of the most distinguished and influential people in the kingdom, were anxious to witness, for themselves, what had been done in the prison ; and there was rarely a morning, part of which was not spent in accompanying such parties there. Poor people, thinking her purse as boundless as her goodwill, wrote innumerable petitions, " humbly praying" for assistance, others sought for counsel, or desired employment, which they imagined she could obtain for them : these letters required to be read and considered, and, although far the greater number were laid aside, others were of a nature, that she could not feel satisfied to pass unnoticed. Time was necessary to do any real good in extricating deserving families from difficulties. Her benevolence was of that cast, that she hardly could endure to know that others wanted the necessaries of life, whilst she was herself surrounded by superfluities and luxuries ; and it was always with pain that she refused the request of any of these applicants. The cases of many of the prisoners also, demanded much time and attention. The whole of this press of business was accomplished, with no other help than that given her by the young people of her own family, who constantly employed under her direction, were able to prevent its greatly accumulating ; and in general the communications of each day, were attended to as they were presented.

Comparatively small as her knowledge was, at this time, of Prison Discipline, Mrs. Fry had already arrived at some conclu-

sions with respect to this important subject, which future observation and more enlarged experience tended only to confirm. The
idea of a prison exclusively for women was already entertained
by her, and she made some attempts to induce the authorities to
adapt the College of Physicians to this purpose.   It is exactly
behind Newgate, and was said to be likely to be sold.   The
necessity of female officers, being placed over female prisoners,
also greatly impressed her; which with other similar points are
so clearly developed in the minutes of her evidence before the
Committee of the House of Commons " On the Prisons of the
Metropolis," that we present some portions of the evidence to the
reader.   This examination took place on the 27th of February,
1818, and the results of the efforts of the Ladies' Association,
up to that date are also recorded in Elizabeth Fry's own words.

" You applied to the Committee of the Court of Aldermen ?
Not at first ; I thought it better to try the experiment for a
month, and then to ask them whether they would second us, and
adopt our measures as their own ; we therefore assembled our
women, read over our rules, brought them work, knitting, and
other things, and our institution commenced ; it has now been
about ten months ; our rules have certainly been occasionally
broken, but very seldom ; order has been generally observed ; I
think I may say we have full power amongst them, for one of
them said, it was more terrible to be brought up before me, than
before the judge, though we use nothing but kindness ; I have
never punished a woman during the whole time, or even proposed
a punishment to them ; and yet I think it is impossible, in a well
regulated house, to have rules more strictly attended to, than
they are, as far as I order them, or our friends in general. With
regard to our work, they have made nearly twenty thousand
articles of wearing apparel, the generality of which is supplied
by the slop shops, which pays very little.   Excepting three out
of this number of articles that were missing, which we really do
not think owing to the women, we have never lost a single thing.
They knit from about sixty to a hundred pair of stockings and

socks every month ; they spin a little. The earnings of work, we think, average about eighteenpence per week, for each person. This is generally spent in assisting them to live, and helping to clothe them. For this purpose they subscribe, out of their small earnings of work, about four pounds a month, and we subscribe about eight, which keeps them covered and decent. Another very important point is, the excellent effect we have found to result from religious education ; our habit is constantly to read the Scriptures to them twice a day ; many of them are taught, and some of them have been enabled to read a little themselves ; it has had an astonishing effect : I never saw the Scriptures received in the same way, and to many of them they have been entirely new, both the great system of religion and of morality contained in them ; and it has been very satisfactory to observe the effect upon their minds ; when I have sometimes gone and said it was my intention to read, they would flock up stairs after me, as if it were a great pleasure I had to afford them.

" You have confined yourself to reading the Scriptures, and pointing out generally the moral lessons that might be derived from them ? Yes, generally so.

" Without inculcating any peculiar doctrine ? Nothing but the general Scripture doctrine ; in short they are not capable of receiving any other.

" Nothing but the morals of the Scripture ; the duties towards God and man ? That is all ; we are very particular in endeavouring to keep close to that ; we consider, from the situation we fill, as it respects the public as well as the poor creatures themselves, that it would be highly indecorous to press any peculiar doctrine of any kind ; any thing beyond the fundamental doctrines of Scripture. We have had considerable satisfaction in observing, not only the improved state of the women in the prison, but we understand from the governor and clergyman at the Penitentiary, that those who have been under our care are very different from those who come from other prisons. We also may state, that when they left Newgate to go to Botany Bay, such a thing was never known in the prison before, as the quietness and order with which they left it ; instead of tearing down every thing and burning it, it was impossible to leave it more

peaceably. And as a proof that their moral and religious instruction had had some effect upon their minds, when those
poor creatures were going to Botany Bay, the little fund we
allow them to collect for themselves, in a small box under our
care, they entreated that might be all given to those that were
going, those who remained, saying, that they wished to give up
their little share of the profit to the others.

" Do you know anything of the room and accommodation for
the women in 1815 ?   I do not; I did not visit it in that year.

" What was it in 1817 ?   Not nearly room enough ; if we had
room enough to class them, I think a very great deal more might
be accomplished ; we labour very much in the day, and we see
the fruit of our labour ; but if we could separate them in the
night, I do think that we could not calculate upon the effect
which would be produced.

" At present, those convicted for all offences pass the day
together ?   Very much so ; very much intermixed, old and
young, hardened offenders with those who have committed only
a minor offence, or the first crime ; the very lowest of women
with respectable married women and maid servants. It is more
injurious than can be described, in its effects and in its consequences. One little instance, to prove how beneficial it is to
take care of the prisoners, is afforded by the case of a poor
woman, for whom we have obtained a pardon (Lord Sidmouth
having been very kind to us whenever we have applied for the
mitigation of punishment since our Committee has been formed).
We taught her to knit in the prison ; she is now living respect-
ably out of it, and in part gains her livelihood by knitting ; we
generally endeavour to provide for them in degree when they go
out.   One poor woman to whom we lent money, comes every
week to my house and pays two shillings, as honestly and as
punctually as we can desire.   We give part and lend part, to
accustom them to habits of punctuality and honesty.

Is that woman still in Newgate whose husband was executed ;
and she herself condemned to death, having eight children ?
She is.

Has not her character been very materially changed since she
has been under your care ?   I heard her state to a gentleman

going through the other day, that it had been a very great blessing to her to be at Newgate, and I think there has been a very great change in her ; her case is now before Lord Sidmouth, but we could hardly ask for her immediate liberation.

" What reward or hope of reward do you hold out?   Rewards form one part of our plan.   They not only have the earnings of their work, but we endeavour to stimulate them by a system of marks.   We divide our women into classes, with a monitor every class, and our matron at the head ; it is the duty of every monitor to take up to the matron every night, an account of the conduct of her class, which is set down ; and if they have a certain number of what we call good marks, at the end of any fixed period, they have for rewards such prizes as we think proper to give them, generally small articles of clothing, or bibles and testaments.

" Be so good as to state, as nearly as you can, what proportion of the women, without your assistance, would be in a state of extreme want?   It is difficult to say; but I think we average the number of eighty tried women ; perhaps out of that number twenty may live very well, twenty very badly, and the others are supported by their friends, in some degree ; when I say twenty who live very well, perhaps I mention too large a number; perhaps not above ten.   I think their receiving support from out doors, is most injurious, as it respects their moral principle, and everything else as it respects the welfare of the city.   There are some very poor people, who will almost starve at home, and be induced to do that which is wrong, in order to keep their poor relations who are in prison : it is an unfair tax on such poor people ; in addition to which, it keeps up an evil communication, and, what is more, I believe they often really encourage the crime by it for which they are put into prison ; for these very people, and especially the coiners and the passers of bank notes, are supported by their associates in crime, so that it really tends to keep up their bad practices.

" Do you know whether there is any clothing allowed by the city ?   Not any ; whenever we have applied or mentioned any thing about clothing, we have always found that there was no other resource but our own, excepting that the sheriffs used to clothe the prisoners occasionally. Lately, nobody has clothed them but ourselves; except that the late sheriffs sent us the other day a present of a few things to make up for them.

" There is no regular clothing allowed ? It appears to me that there is none of any kind.

" Have you never had prisoners there who have suffered materially for want of clothing ? I could describe such scenes as I should hardly think it delicate to mention. We had a woman the other day on the point of lying-in, brought to bed not many hours after she came in ; she had hardly a covering, no stockings, and only a thin gown. Whilst we are there, we can never see a woman in that state, without immediately applying to our fund.

" When they are brought in they come naked almost ? This woman came in, and we had to send her almost every article of clothing, and to clothe her baby ; she could not be tried the next sessions ; but after she had been tried, and when she was discharged, she went out comfortably clothed ; and there are many such instances.

" Has it not happened, that when gentlemen have come in to see the prison, you have been obliged to stand before the women who were in the prison in a condition not fit to be seen ? Yes ; I remember one instance in which I was obliged to stand before one of the women to prevent her being seen. We sent down to the matron immediately to get her clothes.

" How long had the woman been in goal ? Not long ; for we do not, since we have been there, suffer them to be a day without being clothed.

" What is the average space allowed to each woman to lie upon, taking the average number in the prison ? I cannot be accurate ; not having measured ; from eighteen inches to two feet, I should think.

" By six feet ? Yes. I believe the moral discipline of a prison can never be complete, while they are allowed to sleep together in one room. If I may be allowed to state it, I should prefer a prison where women were allowed to work together in companies, under proper superintendence ; to have their meals together, under proper superintendence, and their recreation also; but I would always have them separated in the night; I believe it would conduce to the health, both of body and mind. Their being in companies during the day, tends, under proper regulations, to the advancement of principle and industry; for it affords a stimulus. I should think solitary confinement proper only in very atrocious cases; I would divide my women for a few weeks till I knew what they were; but I would afterwards regulate them as I have now mentioned.

" Has gaming entirely ceased ? It has of late; they have once been found gaming since we had the care of the prison; but I called the women up, when I found that some of them had been playing at cards, and represented to them how much I objected to it, and how evil I thought its consequence was, especially to them; at the same time, I stated, that if it were true that there were cards in the prison, I should consider it a proof of their regard, if they would have the candour and the kindness to bring me their packs. I did not expect they would do it, for they would feel that they betrayed themselves by it; however, I was sitting with the matron, and heard a gentle tap at the door, and in came a trembling woman, to tell me she had brought her pack of cards, that she was not aware how wrong it was, and hoped I would do what I liked with them; and, in a few minutes, another came up, and in this way, I had five packs of cards burnt. I assured them, that so far from its being remembered against them, I should remember it in another way. I brought them a present of clothing for what they had done; and one of them, in a striking manner, said, she hoped I would excuse her being so forward, but if she might say it, she felt exceedingly disappointed; she little thought of having clothing given to her, but she had hoped I would have given her a Bible, that she might read the Scriptures herself. This had been one of the worst girls, and she had behaved so very badly upon her trial, that it was almost shameful. She conducted herself afterwards in so amiable a manner, that her conduct was almost without a flaw. She is now in the Penitentiary, and I hope will become a valuable member of society.

" You have stated three things, which to your mind are essential to the reformation of a prison ; first, religious instruction ; secondly, classification ; thirdly, employment; do you think any reformation can be accomplished without employment ? I should believe it impossible ; we may instruct as we will, but if we allow them their time, and they have nothing to do, they naturally must return to their evil practices.

" How many removals of female prisoners have you had in the last year, in Newgate ; how many have gone to Botany Bay ? Eighteen women; and thirty-seven to the Penitentiary.

" Can you state, out of what number of convicts these have been in the course of a year ? I do not think I can ; but of course out of many hundreds.

" In fact, there has been but one regular removal within the last year ? But one.   There is one very important thing which ought to be stated on the subject of women, taking care of women. It has been said, that there were three things which were requisite in forming a prison that would really tend to the reformation of the women ; but there is a fourth, viz : that women should be taken care of entirely by women, and have no male attendants, unless it be a medical man, or any minister of religion ; for I am convinced that much harm arises from the communication, not only to the women themselves, but those that have the care of them.

" In the present arrangement, is it not so with regard to the women ?   It is very nearly so : but if I had a prison completely such as I should like, it would be a prison quite separate from the men's prison, and into which neither turnkeys, nor any one else should enter but female attendants, and the Inspecting Committee of Ladies; except, indeed, such gentlemen as come to look after their welfare.

" In what does the turnkey interfere now with that prison ? Very little; and yet there is a certain intercourse which it is impossible for us to prevent, and it must be where there is a prison for women and men, and there are various officers who are men in the prison ; it is impossible that they should be entirely separate.   In the present state of Newgate, such a plan as I have in my mind respecting the proper management of women prisoners, cannot be put into execution. We must have turnkeys, and a governor to refer to ; but I should like to have a prison which had nothing to do with men, except those who attended them medically or spiritually.

" Do you believe men to be as much excluded from all communication with the women now as is possible in the present state of Newgate? Yes; I think very nearly so. My idea, with regard to the employment of women, is that it should be a regular thing, undertaken by Government; considering (though I perhaps am not the person to speak of that), that there are so many to provide for ; there is the army and navy, and so many things required for them; why should not Government make use of the prisoners ? But I consider it of the utmost importance, and quite indispensable for the good conduct of such institutions, that the prisoners should have part of the earnings of their work for their own use; a part they might be allowed to take for tea, sugar, &c., but a part should be laid by, that there may be some provision for them when they leave the prison, without their returning to their immoral practices. This is the case, I believe, in all prisons well regulated, both on the continent of Europe, and in America. In a prison under proper regulations, where they had very little communication with their friends, where they were sufficiently well-fed and clothed, constantly employed and instructed, and taken care of by women, I have not the least doubt that wonders would be performed, and that many of those, now the most profligate and the worst of characters, would turn out valuable members of society ———. After having said what I have respecting the care of the women, I will just add, that I believe if there were a prison fitted up for us, which we might visit as inspectors, if employment were found for our women, little or no communication allowed with the city, and room given to class them, with female servants only; if there were a thousand of the most unruly women, they would be in excellent order in one week ; of that I have not the least doubt."

In the report of this committee, the following sentence occurs. " The benevolent exertions of Mrs. Fry and her friends, in the

female department of the Prison, have indeed, by the establishment of a school, by providing work and encouraging industrious habits, produced the most gratifying change. But much
must be ascribed to unremitting personal attention and influence.

CHAPTER X.

After the arduous exertions and interests of the winter of
1817—18, it was no small relief to Mrs. Fry and her family, to
find themselves in the retirement of Plashet.

Plashet, Fourth Month, 29*th.*—I desire thankfully to acknowledge our return to this sweet place, and all the dear children
alive and well. May we more evidently *live* in the best sense,
even unto God. Since I last wrote, I have led rather a remarkable life ; so surprisingly followed after by the great, and others,
in my Newgate concerns ; in short, the prison and myself are
become quite a show, which is a very serious thing in many
points. I believe, that it certainly does much good to the cause,
in spreading amongst all ranks of society, a considerable interest in the subject; also a knowledge of Friends and of their principles: but my own standing appears critical in many ways. In
the first place, the extreme importance of my walking strictly,
and circumspectly, amongst all men, in all things ; and not
bringing discredit upon the cause of truth and righteousness.
In the next place, after our readings there, the ministry is a
most awful calling, thus, publicly amongst men to be in season
and out of season. I desire to live, (more particularly in these
things,) in the fear of God rather than of man, and that neither
good report nor evil report, the approbation nor disapprobation
of men, should move me the least, but that my eye should be
kept quite single to the great and good Shepherd and Bishop of
souls; this is my continual prayer for myself.

Yesterday, I had a day of ups and downs, as far as the opinions of man are concerned, in a remarkable degree. I found that there was a grievous misunderstanding between Lord Sidmouth and myself, and that some things I had done, had tried him exceedingly ; indeed, I see that I have mistaken it, in my conduct in some particulars, respecting the case of poor Skelton, and in the efforts made to save her life, I too incautiously spoke of some in power. When under great humiliation in consequence of this, Lady Harcourt, who most kindly interested herself in the subject, took me with her to the Mansion House, rather against my will, to meet many of the Royal family at the examination of some large schools. Amongst the rest, the Queen was there. Much public respect was paid me, and except the Royal family themselves, I think that no one received the same attention. There was quite a buzz when I went into the Egyptian Hall, where one to two thousand people were collected ; and when the Queen came to speak to me, which she did very kindly, there was I am told a general clap. I think I may say, this hardly raised me at all, I was so very low from what had occurred before, and indeed, in so remarkably flat a state, even nervous.

Plashet, Fifth Month, 2nd —My mind has not recovered this matter of Lord Sidmouth's ; and finding the Bank Directors are also affronted with me, added to my trouble ; more particularly as there was an appearance of evil in my conduct ; but I trust no greater fault in reality, than a want of prudence in that which I expressed. I fear, however, that it has been construed into almost an untruth : these things are very trying to human nature and even more so for the cause sake; but I do trust that I may be enabled to stand my ground under it, and to remove these opinions. I am ready to believe that my great and good Master, will make a way for my deliverance, where I see no way.

Before explaining the cause of misunderstanding between Mrs. Fry and Lord Sidmouth; it is needful to glance at the subject of Capital Punishment, as it presented itself to her mind, at the existing state of the law, its practical execution, and the feeling of the public on the subject. Crimes of almost all grades and descriptions were then punishable with death. Almost every variety of robbery or fraud, although unattended with personal violence, could be treated as a capital offence. With respect to forgery, this was so absolutely the case, that Sir Thomas Edlyne Tomlins, in his Law Dictionary, published 1820, says, (after a long list of all manner of possible and impossible cases,) " By these, and other general and special acts and provisions, there is now hardly a case possible to be conceived, wherein forgery that tends to defraud, whether in the name of a real or fictitious person, is not made a capital crime." Such was the state of the law : so sanguinary, as to prevent the possibility of its own execution. Had it been carried into effect, it was calculated that an average of above four executions daily would have taken place, exclusive of Sundays, in Great Britain and Ireland ; the Old Bailey alone furnishing an average of above one hundred victims yearly. To lessen so monstrous an evil, every possible expedient was permitted, if not encouraged. The police, by bribery, or compassion arising from a touch of old fellowship, being themselves often, but thieves turned thieftakers, connived at the escape of those whom they pretended to seek ; juries shrunk from a word which brought death to the wretched culprit before them, and seized with thankfulness any extenuating circumstance to satisfy their consciences, and enable them to return a verdict of " Not Guilty." Judges inclined to the side of mercy ; respites and reprieves were continually granted, when the cases left for death were considered in Council ; but with all these openings for escape, the doomed were still too many, and some further expedient for lessening their number had to be discovered. The enormous increase of population, the vast and growing amount of wealth, and the multiplication of monetary transactions, added to the number and variety of forgery cases. The circulation of small notes

gave great facility both to forgery itself, and uttering
forged notes ; and the law recognized no distinction between
the systematic forger—the well-dressed utterer, passing hundreds in the day ; and the foolish lad or confiding female, who
misled by vanity, confounded by sophistry, or simply in obedience to the will of their betrayers, became at once their dupes
and victims.

There was a system, (now but a tale of the past, and only
worthy of notice as depicting the evils from which our country
has been delivered, of arranging for such as *were not to die,* to
plead " Guilty to the minor Count." The Bank solicitors in
conjunction with some of the Old Bailey authorities, thus selecting certain individuals for deliverance from death.*

For those who pleaded " Not Guilty," there was still the
chance of some failure in evidence, or some favourable circumstance coming to light upon the trial ; besides the last hope of
a reprieve, when the last report came down from Council. Instances there were, where " calculating chances," the accused
would decline the proffered boon, and put in the plea of Not
Guilty, on the possibility of entirely escaping punishment.

But besides all these contingencies, there was another cause
of impunity, arising from punishment being disproportioned to
crime. A humane man could not endure to prosecute for robbery or fraud, however great the injury to his possessions or loss
of property might be ; the life of a fellow-creature had to be
weighed in the balance—the perishing things of time against the
immortal spirit. Innumerable were the offenders who from this
cause continued not only unpunished, but in an unchecked
career of fresh offences and increasing guilt. Such was the
criminal law in word, and such in practice ; when men began to
rouse them, and awake to the fact that crime was rapidly on the

* The Bank of England had this power by an Act, 41 Geo. III. c. 39.

7

increase ; whilst the laws were no longer applicable to the existing state of things, nor such as could be enforced, without a
sacrifice of human life, too fearful to contemplate. Ten years
before, as early as the commencement of 1808, Sir Samuel
Romilly had directed his attention to the severity of the criminal
code, and brought the subject before Parliament ; but it appearing to him that he "had no chance of being able to carry through
the House, a Bill to expunge at once all these laws from the
Statute-book, he determined to attempt the repeal of them one
by one, and to begin with the most odious of them, the Act of
Queen Elizabeth, which makes it a capital offence to steal privately from the person of another."*   It was in May that he
gave notice of his intention to bring in this Bill ; but we find
in the Journal of William Allen, dated April 12th, allusion to
an association already in existence.

" Luke Howard went with me to Basil Montague's, Lincoln's
Inn.   Met Frederic Smith there, and agreed to join a little
society, formed to endeavour to diminish the number of capital
punishments."†

Again, July 1st,

" Basil Montague, Thomas Furley Forster, and B. M. Forster, R. Philips, F. Smith, J. G. Bevan, and Luke Howard, dined
with me, to converse on the subject of our little society, when
several resolutions were agreed to, and we have now taken a
regular form.   Its title is, ' A Society for Diffusing Information on the Subject of Punishment by Death.'   They are to
dine with me again on Second day, the 10th, when S. Woods is
to join us, and for the next six months, are to dine at Plough
Court, on the first Second day (Monday) in the month, in order
that we may be in time for the publications.   Basil Montague

---

* The Memoirs of the Life of Sir Samuel Romilly, edited by his Sons,
vol. ii. edition ii. p. 245.

† Life of William Allen, vol. i. p. 92.

is to open a communication with Sir Samuel Romilly, and it appears as if we should go on with spirit."*

From that time, every succeeding Session, till his lamented death, in 1818, Sir Samuel Romilly renewed his attacks upon the state of the Criminal Code; he changed his plan of operations as circumstances required, but though for many years, almost single-handed, he never abandoned his design. Dr. Parr, Jeremy Bentham, and Dugald Stewart, addressed him in strong terms of encouragement. That Dr. Parr's ultimate views extended even further, is implied by the counsel which he offered Sir Samuel Romilly, *"for the present,"* to confine his " Plan of Reform to crimes unaccompanied with violence." The association already alluded to, continued its operations, circulated tracts and other papers, and diffused general information on the subject. In the House of Lords, amongst the few supporters of Romilly's measures, Lord Holland was the foremost, and the Marquis of Lansdowne supported the same side. In 1810, we find the Dukes of Sussex and Gloucester, united with these noblemen in signing a protest, when the Peers rejected Sir Samuel's Bill, to remove the penalty of death for shoplifting.

" Dissentient.—1st, Because the statute proposed to be repealed appears to us unreasonably severe, inasmuch as it punishes with death the offence of stealing property to a very inconsiderable amount, without violence, or any other aggravation.

" 2ndly, Because, to assign the same punishment for heinous crimes, and slight offences, tends to confound the notions of right and wrong, to diminish the horror atrocious guilt ought always to inspire, and to weaken the reverence in which it is desirable that the laws of the country should be held.

" 3rdly, Because severe laws are, in our judgment, more likely to produce a deviation from the strict execution of justice, than to deter individuals from the commission of crimes ; and our

* Life of William Allen, vol. i. p. 104.

apprehension that such may be the effect is confirmed in this instance, by the reflection, that the offence in question is become more frequent, and the punishment, probably on account of its rigour, is seldom or never inflicted.

" 4thly, Because, the value of money has decreased since the reign of King William, and the statute is consequently, become a law of much greater severity than the legislature which passed it, ever intended to enact.

" WILLIAM FREDERICK.
" AUGUSTUS FREDERICK.
" VASSAL HOLLAND.
" LANSDOWNE."

When a party theory, or visionary scheme occasions even strong excitement, a little time and reality dispels it. Not so, when justice and humanity claim conjointly to be heard. The history of the last fifty years has taught us, that their success may be delayed by prejudice, impeded by difficulties, and opposed by selfishness ; but in the end they triumph. Mrs. Fry's visits to Newgate had brought her in close communication with the condemned criminals in that prison, and had furnished her with an intimate knowledge of the effects of an execution, and the circumstances attendant upon it, nor was it Mrs. Fry alone, who, on this important subject was acquiring knowledge from personal observation.

At that time Newgate had become almost a show ; the statesman and noble, the city functionary and the foreign traveller, the high-bred gentlewoman, the clergyman and the dissenting minister, flocked to witness the extraordinary change that had passed over the scene. From time to time, the condemned cell on the female side was occupied. The visitors to Newgate were informed, that on such a day, and at such a time, some poor woman, whose name and offence were told them, was to die, and that her few remaining hours were being there past in comparative seclusion. They heard of the same things on the men's

side of the prison, and perhaps visited the culprits ; but invariably some females were to be seen with their fellow-prisoners
seated at the Bible reading, under sentence of death : they occupied the front bench. These were persons who had received
sentence at the Old Bailey, but were awaiting their final doom
from the decision of the Council. A newspaper announcement
that such a person or persons were this morning executed in
front of Newgate may cause a sensation, but it is quickly gone.
To look upon persons full of life and strength and capacity,
and to know that they are doomed to die by their fellow-mortals, occasions another and a very different feeling. One woman,
the day before her execution, said to Mrs. Fry, " I feel life so
strong within me, that I cannot believe that this time to-morrow I am to be dead !" Nor was this confined to those who
saw : the tale was repeated, the scene described, and the event,
became a topic of general discussion. The statesman viewed it
more especially as a political question, in its tendency to increase or diminish crime : the philanthropist considered it
chiefly, as it affected the individual offender : the merchant and
the man of business interested himself in a question so closely
affecting the security of property.

The following rough memoranda, in the form of question and
answer, were found in Mrs. Fry's writing among her papers :—

Does capital punishment tend to the security of the people ?
By no means. It hardens the hearts of men, and makes the
loss of life appear light to them : and it renders life insecure,
inasmuch as the law holds out, that property is of greater value
than life. The wicked are consequently more often disposed to
sacrifice life to obtain property. It also lessens the security of
the subject, because so many are so conscientious, that they had
rather suffer loss and sustain much injury, than be instrumental
in taking the life of a fellow-creature. The result is, that the
innocent suffer loss, and the guilty escape with impunity.

Does it tend to the reformation of any party ?

No ; because in those who suffer it leads to unbelief, hypocrisy, and fatalism ; in those who remain, to discontent, dissatifaction with the laws, and the powers which carry them into execution ; to hardness of heart, unbelief and deceit.

Does it deter others from crime ?

No ; because the crimes subject to capital punishment are gradually increasing. Punishment is not for revenge, but to lessen crime and reform the criminal.

Newspaper paragraphs were written—pamphlets were circulated ; the public mind became excited, and the voice of the people made itself heard.

On February the 17th, two women were executed for forgery, Charlotte Newman and Mary Ann James. The morning of their execution, Newman addressed the following letter to Mrs. Fry ; and James wrote one to her fellow-prisoners; these letters found their way into the public prints. The calm and submissive tone in which they were written, astonished those who know not of the fearful opiate administered to the soul, in the universal belief of criminals under sentence of death for forgery—that they were more sinned against than sinning—that they were martyrs to a harsh and uncertain law, by which property was held of greater value than the life of man—and that thus, being in the position of the injured parties, they had but to meet their fate with fortitude and submission, and heaven would be their just reward.

"Honoured Madam,

" As the only way of expressing my gratitude to you for your very great attention to the care of my poor soul ; I feel I may have appeared more silent than perhaps some would have been on so melancholy an event; but believe me, my dear madam, I have felt most acutely the awful situation I have been in. The mercies of God are boundless, and 1 trust through His

grace this affliction is sanctified to me, and through the Saviour's
blood my sins will be washed away.   I have much to be thankful for.   I feel such serenity of mind and fortitude.   God, of
His infinite mercy, grant I may feel as I do now in the last
moments.   Pray, madam, present my most grateful thanks to
the worthy Dr. Cotton and Mr. Baker, and all our kind friends
the ladies, and Mrs. Guy.   It was a feeling I had of my own
unworthiness, made me more diffident of speaking so brief as
was perhaps looked for.   I once more return you my most
grateful thanks.   It is now past six o'clock, I have not one
moment to spare; I must devote the remainder to the service
of my offended God.

> "With respect, your humble servant,
> "(Signed)   CHARLOTTE NEWMAN.

"Tuesday morning, six o'clock, February 17th, 1818, James
joins with me, and feels all I have expressed, I hope."

> "Condemned Cell.

"My dear fellow-prisoners,

"Impressed with the deepest sense of your feelings for me
under my awful situation, I am sure was I to ask any thing of
you it would be granted.   Then, was I to ask one particular
favour of you all, I would flatter myself, as my last dying word,
it would be granted.   I would wish to impress on your minds the
true light of the Gospel, and, by informing you how I found an
interest in Christ; in the first place, God gave me the spirit of
humility, you must feel a love and affection for those that so
kindly visit this prison.   Then pray to the Lord to give you the
grace of His Holy Spirit, and I am sure our dear beloved friends,
will acquaint you by what way that is to be found.   I was dark
when I first came into these walls, and what must you all suppose
the love, the gratitude I feel now, I am going but a short time
before you.   God can call you in a moment.   Then pray, I
entreat you, do not neglect the great work.

"Go up stairs rejoicing as if to a bridal feast.*   Keep every

* The daily Bible reading in the Ladies' Committee Room.

10

rule. Oh, should the Lord deliver you from these walls, think on me, and remember the end of sin is death. You all have my prayers. Oh, lay hold of Jesus. He is my refuge and my strength. Look up to Him ; and may the Lord be with you and keep you all. To-morrow morning I shall be with my heavenly Father in Paradise.

"I am your fellow-prisoner,
"Wishing every blessing, your affectionate,
(Signed)   "MARY ANN JAMES."

The same day that brought poor Newman's letter, Mrs. Fry received one from a very different correspondent, from William Wilberforce, Esq.

"Kensington Gore, *Tuesday, 17th February,* 1818.

"My dear Madam,

"I think I need not assure you that I have not forgotten you this morning. In truth, having been awake very early, and lying in peace and comfort and safety, the different situation of the poor women impressed itself strongly on my mind.

"I shall be glad, and Mrs. Wilberforce also, I assure you, to hear that your bodily health has not suffered from your mental anxiety, and I will try to get a sight of you when I can, to hear your account and remarks on the effects of the events of the last few days, both on the poor objects themselves and their prison companions.

"With real esteem and regard,
"I am, my dear Madam,
"Yours, very sincerely,
"W. WILBERFORCE."

During this spring there were continual executions; they were, however, no longer passed over as matters of course, but became a prominent topic of discussion, both as to the individual cases, and the general principle involved. Within the prison, the report from the Council was expected with even more than

X 2

usual anxiety. It was always a time of excitement and fearful anticipation to all but those, who were so hardened by crime as to scoff alike at the laws of God and man.

There were no data by which to form any conclusion ; no reasons to be discovered for the selections made ; every one knew that he might suffer, and every one alike hoped to escape. Among the rest was a woman named Harriett Skelton ; a very child might have read her countenance, open, confiding, express- ing strong feeling, but neither hardened in depravity, nor capa- ble of cunning ; her story bore out this impression. Under the influence of the man she loved, she had passed forged notes : adding one more to the melancholy list of those, who by the finest impulses of our nature uncontrolled by religion, have been but lured to their own destruction.

She was ordered for execution —the sentence was unlooked for—her deportment in the prison had been good, amenable to regulations, quiet and orderly ; some of her companions in guilt were heard to say, that they supposed she was chosen for death, because she was better prepared than the rest of them.

The condemned cell for females was a narrow apartment, with two windows, one commanding the inner quadrangle, where were the tried prisoners, the other looking into a long passage, with iron grating on either side, dividing the tried from the untried side of the prison, across which the convicts were per- mitted to communicate with their friends.   There she was taken to pass her few and numbered days on earth ; two women were in attendance upon her, according to the usual custom on these occasions. She might receive the visits of the Ordinary, or any friend admitted by the Governor, but by her the cell was not to be again quitted, till she left the prison for the scaffold.

There was a white-headed old man, who might be seen at those times in frequent attendance upon these poor captives ; having for years devoted much time and attention to unostentatious

but invaluable visits in Newgate.   He rejoiced with no common
joy when Mrs. Fry and her associates undertook their labour of
love ; but, never did he show more of his Master's spirit, than
in his treatment of the prisoners sentenced to die ; he appeared
skilled in imparting to them something of his own humility,
and though he could not, nor did he endeavour to persuade them
in all cases to acquiesce in the justice of the sentence, he led
many of them to the knowledge of being but miserable sinners
themselves, and to some acquaintance with that Saviour, who
had experienced in his own person a malefactor's death.

But Skelton had other visitors besides Mr. Baker ; dwellers in
places and lordly halls were to be found in her desolate abode ;
it was a new scene for them ; the dark vaulted passages—the
clanking fetters—the damp smell—the grating sound as the
heavy key was turned—the massive bolt drawn back—and the
iron-sheathed door forced reluctantly open.

Her case excited the strongest compassion : Mrs. Fry was
urged even vehemently, to exert herself in behalf of the unfortunate woman ; there were circumstances of extenuation, though
not of a nature to alter the letter of the law.   Amonst other
attempts she made one through the Duke of Gloucester.   They
had not seen each other for many years ; not since the days of
the scarlet riding habit, and the military band, at Norwich.
How differently did they meet now—on what altered ground
renew their acquaintance.   Life has been tried by them both—
the world and its fascinations.   The Duke of Gloucester came to
Newgate ; and his former companion in the dance, led him with
sober if not solemn brow, through the gloom and darkness of
that most gloomy of prisons.   He made a noble effort to save
Skelton by an application to Lord Sidmouth, he accompanied
Mrs. Fry to the Bank Directors, but all was in vain ; the law
took its course, and she was hanged.

Mrs. Fry had strongly expressed herself with respect to the

Bank of England cases, and probably had insisted on circumstances, which, though true in fact, were difficult distinctly to
prove. She had applied to Lord Sidmouth herself, and through
others, and had been the indirect means of causing much excitement on the subject of Capital Punishment.   Government was
becoming embarrassed.   To touch so complicated a machine
as the criminal code of England appeared an undertaking too
vast and dangerous to attempt, and yet such was the pressure
from without, that something must be yielded to popular feeling.   Lord Sidmouth was seriously annoyed, and expressed his
annoyance in a mode so distressing to her, that with all her
gentleness and forbearance, Mrs. Fry was compelled to acknowledge that she could hold no further direct communication
with one, who assumed to doubt her veracity, unless some explanation was offered.   The question at issue related to the
power lodged in the Bank of England to select such persons as
they considered fit subjects to plead "guilty" to the minor
count, and so to escape the extreme penalty of the law.*

Mrs. Fry never was shaken in the belief that Skelton had had
the offer so to do, but most unwisely, as it proved, had rejected
it, and that through this error in judgment she had paid the
forfeit of her life.   Here terminated their intercourse, deeply to
her regret, after the kindness and consideration with which Lord
Sidmouth had treated her, and until that period listened to her
suggestions.   Mrs. Fry had not abandoned all hope of reconciliation, without endeavouring by a personal interview to remove
his impressions, and to convince him, that although she might
be mistaken, and have erred in judgment her intentions had
been upright, and her desire sincere not to oppose his wishes.
The Countess Harcourt, who proved herself a kind and faithful friend on this, as on many other occasions, accompanied her.

* 41 Geo. III., c. 29.

Nothing but pain resulted from the visit. Wounded and grieved she quitted the Home Office, to go by command of Queen Charlotte to the Mansion House, still under the protection of Lady Harcourt. There it was intended that she should be in the drawing-room presented to her Majesty, but, by some misunderstanding Lady Harcourt and Mrs. Fry were conducted at once to the Egyptian Hall, and placed on the side of the platform to await the arrival of the royal party. After a time, the Queen perceived Mrs. Fry, and, at the close of the examination advanced to address her. It was a subject for Hayter—the diminutive stature of the Queen, covered with diamonds, but her countenance lighted up with an expression of the kindest benevolence; Mrs. Fry, her simple Quaker's dress adding to the height of her figure, though a little flushed, preserving her wonted calmness of look and manner, several of the bishops standing near her; the platform crowded with waving feathers, jewels, and orders, the noble hall lined with spectators, and in the centre, hundreds of poor children brought there to be examined, from their different schools. The English nation may be slow in perceiving the beauty of a moral sentiment, but when perceived, none appreciate it more highly. A murmur of applause ran through the assembly, followed by a simultaneous clap, and a shout, which was taken up by the multitude without, and died away in the distance. They hailed the scene before them; they saw in it not so much the Queen and the Philanthropist, as royalty offering its meed of approval at the shrine of mercy and good works.

The Christian observer who has thus far followed the career of Mrs. Fry, will read in this day's history an instructive lesson. The humiliation of the morning contrasted with the exaltation of the latter part of the day. Even her humility might have suffered, her well-poised mind have lost something of its equilibrium, had not the balance been thus held, and impressions so opposite been permitted, one to counteract the other—for how striking the lesson taught of the vanity of human applause, or human disapprobation—the futility of labouring to serve any other Master than Him, who reads the hearts and knows the thoughts of the children of men.

To Lady Harcourt, soon after the Queen's visit to the Mansion House, Mrs. Fry addressed this letter :—

My dear Lady Harcourt,

Would it be asking too much of thee to let me know particularly how the Queen is after her great exertions the other day? I rejoice to think what a sweet impression her visit appears to have made upon the people. I feel very unworthy of the kind attention that she paid me, and my heart is warmed with the desire that a blessing may attend her, and her family, in time and in Eternity. Our poor dear King has often had my prayers —may the Lord be his "Everlasting light, and his God his Glory." I regretted that the favour done me by the Queen was mentioned in the public papers, and more particularly from political reasons that I was said to be leaning on Alderman W——'s arm. I had much rather, my dear Lady Harcourt, I had been mentioned as being in thy company, and I hope prudence influences the wish rather than pride, as I believe I feel for the cause' sake ; it requires great care who I make my prominent friends. I think the fact should be contradicted by those who knew it to be false, but not in the public prints. I can assure thee, gratified as I could not but feel in the kind attentions that I received that day from the Royal Family, and from thyself; that I felt much too low at heart, and too much grieved at the misunderstanding with Lord Sidmouth, to be capable of much pleasure, as he is one that I have really esteemed, and what is more, I should think few had been to him so faithful as a friend. I have pleaded his cause privately and publicly, when I have heard anything said against him. From my peculiar situation, I have had it in my power with numbers of people, to strengthen his reputation as to his having much mercy mixed with his views of justice. I think he would pity me, if he knew what I have suffered day and night—for it is my principle, and I trust I may say practice, to hurt no one, not even the lowest; I could not rest if I pained my menial servant, therefore, canst thou wonder that this misunderstanding has deeply wounded me? I hope that it will be in my power once more to obtain his regard and confidence. Some day when perfectly agreeable to thee, I will call upon thee to represent some further particulars respecting our little Association. I remain, my dear Lady Harcourt, with much regard and respect,

Thy obliged,

ELIZABETH FRY.

The answer to this letter does not exist; but one of a later date, conveys an interesting account of the last illness of Queen Charlotte, which was at the time attributed to the great fatigue she underwent in her visit to the city, from which she never recovered—and may therefore be suitably introduced here.

COUNTESS HARCOURT TO MRS. FRY.

St. Leonards, September 7th, 1818.

" My dear Friend,

" I have just received a letter from Kew, stating the poor Duchess of Gloucester's inability, under her present affliction, to acknowledge your letter : but she has desired I will do it for her, and thank you for the justice you do her, in being sensible of the satisfaction she feels, at the proof, the enclosed letter gives, of the infinite good that is done by the system, you have established by your meritorious exertions. Indeed, my good friend, the letter from the poor woman, must have been a great gratification to you, it makes one feel with still more regret, that the same system is not followed in the country, and that the men have no such blessed advantage. Surely the time will come, when the eyes of Government will be open to the necessity of doing something for the male convicts. But it is painful to think any time should be lost, as every soul is of equal value, and perhaps they are perishing daily for want of such assistance as might save them.

" We are at present in great anxiety on account of the poor Queen, and look forward with constant apprehension to the last fatal account. I wish she had had the advantage of knowing you earlier and more intimately. But I believe her opinions on religious subjects, are what you would highly approve, and Mrs. Bendorff who never leaves her, reads and prays with her constantly, and has done so, at all periods. The conduct of the two Princesses, is most exemplary, but I much fear Princess Augusta's health is declining, and her nerves are very much shook. If the Duke of Gloucester had not kindly suffered the Duchess to remain, and share this painful duty with Princess Augusta, she must have sunk under it. Princess Sophia is also very ill, at Windsor, from her extreme anxiety. The distressed state of the Royal Family, should prove that there are none of those circumstances, that are called advantages, that can even alleviate, much less exempt the possessors from the misfortunes common to mortality. The lesson is a useful one, and so is the patience and resignation with which the Queen bears her sufferings ; and her family bear their sorrows. I am told the Queen shows a particular gentleness and gratitude to all around her, making no complaints, even when in agonies of pain. Her strength of constitution which is very great, is probably the cause of the protraction of her sufferings, and the period may still be prolonged some days, or it may terminate in a moment.

" I hope whenever you have it in your power, you will let us have the pleasure of seeing you at St. Leonards, it would give me great satisfaction, and I would contrive that my good friend Dr. Pope, should meet you if possible ; but I hope if ever you are so good as to come, you will let me know, lest I should be absent ; and it would gratify me also to see those sweet girls, who I met in your house. Since I wrote the above, I hear the Queen's sufferings have been less, the last two days. I earnestly hope that it may please God to make her latter end more easy, than she has been for some time past. I believe she has not been able to go to bed for near a week, but has passed the night in

her chair. With my best wishes for your health, and that of
your family, I beg to assure you that I am, my dear Madam,
                  " Your sincere friend,
                     " And affectionate Servant,
                        " MARY HARCOURT."

A fresh object of interest now opened upon the attention of
the Ladies' Newgate Association. The removal of the female
convicts for transportation : and the circumstances under which
those whom they so anxiously desired to benefit, were to pass
the long and dreary months of confinement on ship-board.

It was a practice amongst the female transports to riot, previous
to their departure from Newgate, breaking windows, furniture,
or whatever came within their reach. They were generally conveyed from the prison to the water side in open waggons, went
off shouting amidst assembled crowds, and were noisy and disorderly on the road and in the boats. Mrs. Fry prevailed on
the Governor to consent to their being moved in hackney coaches.
She then promised the women, if they would be quiet and orderly,
that she and other ladies would accompany them to Deptford,
and see them on board ; accordingly when the time came, no
disturbance took place ; the women in hackney coaches, with
turnkeys in attendance, formed a procession, which was closed
by her carriage, and the women behaved well upon the road.
When on board the ship, the ladies were distressed to see so
many women and children herded together below deck. They
were to be divided into messes of six each, and as each woman
must of necessity associate the most with those of her own mess,
it seemed to be a good opportunity to class and number them.
This was no sooner proposed, than accepted by all concerned in
the arrangement ; they were divided into classes of twelve, including the monitor, chosen from the number by the women
themselves. As far as possible, those whose ages or criminality
were similar were placed together, each class contained two

messes.   The superintendence thus became as complete, as the
nature of the case would permit.   There were one hundred and
twenty-eight convicts, besides their unhappy children.

Employment and instruction were still wanting; the women
complained of having nothing to do.   To procure work for a
hundred and twenty-eight persons, during so long a voyage,
appeared to be a hopeless endeavour ; and even if it could be
obtained from Government or individuals, that it would be
useless to give it to them, with no responsible person to take
charge either of its execution or appropriation.   The ladies were
told, that patchwork and fancywork found a ready sale in New
South Wales.   They accordingly made it known that they required little pieces of coloured cotton, for this purpose ; and
in a few days, enough were sent from the different Manchester
houses in London, fully to supply them with work, aided by
some knitting.   The time and ingenuity required in patchwork,
rendered it a particularly suitable occupation ; and as the convicts
were to have the things when done, to sell for their own profit
on arrival, it was evidently their interest to turn their skill to
the best account.   By this means, another important good was
effected ; for at that time, no factory or barrack of any description existed, for the reception of the women when landed in the
colony ; not so much as a hut in which they could take refuge, so
that they were literally driven to vice, or left to lie in the streets.
The proceeds of their industry on board ship, though small,
would enable such as desired it, to obtain shelter until engaged
as servants, or until they could find some respectable means of
subsistence.   A fact that occurred the following year, in the
Wellington female convict ship, showed the correctness of this
opinion, and how well patchwork had answered the intended purpose, for when that ship touched at Rio de Janeiro, the quilts
made by the women were there sold for a guinea each.   Bibles,
prayer-books, and religious tracts, were placed under the care of

each monitor, for the use of her class ; arrangements were also made, that those who could not read and wished to learn, should have the opportunity of doing so.

But though some provision was thus made for the necessities of the women, the poor children were still in misery and igno rance, fourteen of them were of an age to receive instruction ; with some difficulty, a small space towards the after part of the vessel was set apart for a school, there, during the greater part of the day, the children were taught to read, knit, and sew; one of the convicts undertook to be school-mistress, for whom a reward was placed in the hands of the Captain, provided she persevered in her duties to the end of the voyage. During the five weeks that the ship lay in the river, some of the ladies engaged in the prison work, devoted much of their time to making these arrangements. The expense of £72 10s. was incurred in working materials, aprons for the women, and additional clothing for the most destitute. The good effects of these regulations were speedily seen, but none were sanguine as to their continuing in force after the ship had fairly put to sea, and there would be no longer any stimulus or inducement to persevere. The Captain, a very respectable man, died suddenly at Calcutta, on the voyage home, which prevented its being ascertained with certainty, how long, or to what extent the plans were beneficial. The only person who could give or enforce an order, was the surgeon-superintendent, appointed by Government to the care of the women. In this instance, the appointment had fallen on a man, who did not take the least interest in the moral organisation of the convict-ship. The last time that Mrs. Fry was on board the Maria, whilst she lay at Deptford, was one of those solemn and interesting occasions that leave a lasting impression on the minds of those who witness them. There was great uncertainty whether the poor convicts would see their benefactress again. She stood at the door of the cabin, attended by her

friends and the Captain; the women on the quarter-deck facing
them. The sailors anxious to see what was going on, clambered
into the rigging, upon the capstan, or mingled in the outskirts
of the group. The silence was profound—when Mrs. Fry opened
her bible, and in a clear audible voice read a portion from it.
The crews of the other vessels in the tier, attracted by the novelty
of the scene, leant over the ships on either side, and listened
apparently with great attention; she closed the bible, and after
a short pause, knelt down on the deck, and implored a blessing
on this work of Christian charity from that God, who though one
may sow and another water, can alone give the increase. Many
of the women wept bitterly, all seemed touched; when she left
the ship they followed her with their eyes and their blessings,
until her boat having passed within another tier of vessels, they
could see her no more.

Plashet, Seventh Month, 1st.—Since I last wrote, much as
happened to me; some things have occurred of an important
nature. My prison engagements have gone on well, and many
have flocked after me, may I not say of almost all descriptions,
from the greatest to the least; and we have had some remarkably favoured times together in the prison. The Yearly
Meeting was a very interesting one to me, and also encouraging.
I felt the unity of Friends a comfort and support. I had to
go into the Men's Meeting, which was a deep trial of faith,
but it appeared called for at my hand, and peace attended
giving up to it. The unity the women expressed at my going,
and the good reception I found amongst the men were comforting to me, but it was a close, very close, exercise. Although
I have had much support from many of my fellow-mortals,
and so much unity expressed with me both in and out of our
Society—yet I believe many Friends have great fears for me and
mine; and some not Friends, do not scruple to spread evil reports, as if vanity or political motives led me to neglect a large
family. I desire patiently to bear it all, but the very critical
view that is taken of my beloved children, grieves me much.

8th.—My heart is too full to express much ; yesterday I had a very interesting day at Newgate with the Chancellor of the Exchequer, and many other persons of consequence ; much in the cross to myself, I had to express a few words in supplication before them, but the effect was solemn and satisfactory. After this I felt peaceful and comforted; sometimes I think after such times I am disposed to feel as if that day's work was done, and give way to cheerful conversation, without sufficiently waiting for the fresh manifestations of the Spirit, and abiding under the humiliations of the Cross.

It is needful now to revert to the excitement produced in the public mind, when the knowledge of the remarkable transformation effected in Newgate began to be spread abroad. The visits of Mrs. Fry were the theme of conversation in all circles, and the accounts circulated of the interesting and imposing scenes which were to be witnessed there, brought a strange variety of persons to that abode of sorrow. It would be too much to say that all, who then or in after times attended the readings in Newgate, were actuated by high and holy feelings in desiring admittance; but if a list of the names of the visitors could be published, it would prove how strong was the sympathy felt among the nobly born, and richly endowed with intellectual as well as worldly wealth. A letter, written at this time, is so descriptive of this, that we are grateful to the surviving members of the writer's family, for their concurrence in its insertion here.

Extract of a letter from Lady MACKINTOSH to Mrs. FRY.

" I have had a note from Sir James, in which is the following passage, I cannot resist copying it, in the hope of your pardon for doing so. 'I dined Saturday, June 3rd, at Devonshire House. The company consisted of the Duke of Norfolk, Lords Lansdowne, Lauderdale, Albemarle, Cowper, Hardwicke, Carnarvon, Sefton, Ossulton, Milton, and Duncannon, &c. The subject was Mrs. Fry's exhortation to forty-five female convicts, at which Lord ——— had been present on Friday. He could hardly refrain from tears in speaking of it. He called it the deepest tragedy he had ever witnessed. What she read and expounded to the convicts, with almost miraculous effect, was the 4th chapter to the Ephesians. Coke (of Norfolk) begged me to go with him next Friday; I doubt whether, as that is the day of my motion, I shall be able to go, and whether it be prudent to expose myself to the danger of being too much warmed by the scene, just before a speech in which I shall need all my discretion.'

" As the above extract was only intended for my eye, I am sure you will so consider it. My motive for submitting it to you is twofold; that you may not be ignorant how much your great work of mercy contributes to inspire good feelings, and to supply pure and edifying subjects of conversation at the tables of the most illustrious persons in the country, for rank and talents. And also to know if you will have the kindness to inform me, whether there is not some mistake in the day to which Lord ——— alludes."

Among the visitors were to be found persons, who as friends of humanity came to ascertain the truth of all that they had heard; actuated by the same motives, bishops, clergymen, and other ministers of religion resorted thither. It will be at once seen how the concurring testimony of individuals distinguished in such various ways, must have influenced public opinion in favour of a mode of treatment which, in the course of a few weeks, had struck at the root of the more glaring evils, so lately existing in the principal metropolitan prison of England. Nor can it be doubted that the influx of visitors, objectionable as it must be considered in itself, and injurious as it would be, in a well-ordered prison, was then an important means of spreading knowledge and exciting interest, and thus assisting to prepare the way for the improvements in Prison Discipline subsequently effected. It appears highly probable that the rapidity and ease, with which legislative enactments on these subjects were afterwards carried, may be in part attributed to what had been seen and learnt in Newgate.

On Wednesday, June 3rd, 1818, the Marquis of Lansdowne moved an address to the Prince Regent, on the state of the prisons of the United Kingdom. In his speech, after stating appalling facts as to the increase of crime within the preceding ten years, attributing it to various causes, especially to the vicious and deplorable condition of the prisons themselves, his lordship made this observation in reference to Newgate :—

" It was impossible from the manner in which it was constantly crowded to apply any general system of regulations. There, it was necessary to place several felons in the same cell, and persons guilty of very different descriptions of offences were mixed together. The consequences were such as might be expected, notwithstanding all the efforts of that very meritorious individual, (Mrs. Fry) who had come like the Genius of Good into this scene of misery and vice, and had by her wonderful influence and exertions, produced, in a short time, a most extraordinary reform among the most abandoned class of prisoners. After this great example of humanity and benevolence, he would leave it to their lordships how much good, persons similarly disposed, might effect in other prisons, were the mechanism, if he might use the expression, of those places of confinement better adapted to the purposes of reformation. The institution of the great Penitentiary-house was likely to be attended with great advantages, though he did not approve of all the regulations. That establishment was a great step taken in the important work of reformation. He was aware there were persons who considered all expense of this kind as useless, who thought that all that could be done was to provide for the safe custody of prisoners, and that attempts to reform them were hopeless. Let those who entertain this notion, go and see what had been effected by Mrs. Fry and other benevolent persons in Newgate. The scenes which passed there, would induce them to alter their opinion. There were moments when the hardest hearts could be softened and disposed to reform.

After reading this sentence, delivered in the House of Lords, and published in all the journals of the day, it can astonish no one, to find that admittance into Newgate was sought with eager curiosity by all sorts of persons ; to many of whom, admission could not with any propriety have been refused by either magistrates, officers, or ladies. Inconveniences arose from it, but at this juncture of prison reformation, they were infinitely outweighed by its effects in diffusing information and calling attention to the subject.

The ladies of the Committee had at this time effected several minor arrangements to lessen the temptations, and increase the reasonable comforts of the prisoners. In the early part of the year, they took measures to prevent the introduction of an unlimited quantity of beer into the prison. They engaged a submatron or gate-keeper, who assisted in the lodge, and amongst other duties, superintended a little shop, which had been established, as it is quaintly expressed in their minute book, " between gates," where tea, sugar, a little haberdashery and other equally harmless articles were sold to the prisoners. The communication between them and their friends outside the prison being so much restricted, lessened their supplies from that quarter, and the prison allowance being scarcely sufficient, this plan was resorted to, in order to meet their necessities and ensure their portion of the earnings being expended in a proper manner.

Plashet, Seventh Month, 24th.—I have many causes of deep anxiety at this time. What to do with our boys, for the best, has occupied much of my consideration, and at present I see no other way than continuing them at school ; but I do not acknowledge too much, if I say that it is the prayer of my heart that a kind Providence may open the way for their going to the best place for them, wherever it may be, and deep is the craving of my spirit, that they may in the end go on well. O Lord! I beseech Thee, whatsoever Thou mayst be pleased to do with them, whether to grant them health or sickness, riches or poverty, long life or short life, oh, for Thy beloved Son's sake, give them not over to the will of their enemies, but establish their goings in Thy paths ; put a new song into their mouths, even praises to Thee their God. And seeing, gracious Lord, that in a very marvellous manner, Thou hast been pleased to make a way for Thy child and servant, where she could see no way—how in a wonderful manner Thou restored her in early life, showed Thyself to be on her side, when spiritually her enemies appeared ready to overcome and destroy her, and how also in many and various seasons, " Thou hast made darkness light before her, and crooked paths straight," how Thou hast been pleased to raise her from season to season, from the bed of languishing; how Thou hast temporally cared for her, and answered her prayer, when it appeared likely even that she would be scarcely provided for, how Thou hast helped her in spirit at seasons to do Thy will, to see into the glorious mysteries of Thy kingdom, how Thou hast aided her in her weakness, and enabled her to overcome the extreme fear of man ; and to declare Thy doings amongst the people, and to show Thy marvellous works to the children of men, even from princes and prelates, to the poorest, lowest, and most destitute ; so as in a remarkable manner to bring to pass what she saw for herself in early life, though as through a glass darkly, which others more clearly saw for her, and had to declare unto her ; and seeing gracious Lord, and Almighty God and Saviour, how Thou hast been pleased to deal with Thy unworthy servant, to increase in her even at seasons, mightily and powerfully the knowledge of Thee her God, and Christ Jesus her Lord.——Be pleased to help her in the like precious faith, and preserve her from the many snares of the enemy; let not the spirit of the world or its applause ever again entangle her; nor the reproach of any, not even of the good unduly discourage her, but let her be increasingly Thine own, and at all times, at all seasons, and in every place, by whoever surrounded, give unto Thee the glory due unto Thy name, and worship Thee in the beauty of holiness, and let neither heights, nor depths, life, nor death, nor any other thing, ever separate her from Thy love, but enable her, O Lord ! at all times, and at all seasons, and in every place, and by whomsoever surrounded, to glorify Thy great and ever excellent name, with Thy beloved Son Christ Jesus our Lord. And with regard to her beloved family, be unto them, what Thou hast been unto her ; even their Guide, and their Guard, their God and their Saviour ; and make a way for them, where their poor mother sees no way for them, Amen, says my unworthy soul, cast down but not destroyed, afflicted but not in despair, at times almost comfortless, but not forsaken ; at other times abounding in the joy, and blessing of my God.

In August, Mrs. Fry left home to visit Scotland, and the North of England, accompanied by her brother Mr. Joseph John Gurney, Mrs. J. J. Gurney, and one of her own daughters.

Belford, Northumberland, Eighth Month, 25th.—For some time I have looked to attending the General Meeting in Scotland, but it appeared almost impossible, my home-claims being so very strong—indeed the Monthly Meeting before the last, it came with great weight so as to frighten me ; but I neither saw outward way for it, nor did I feel the heart made willing ; but as I have so often found when there is a real " putting forth," way is made within and without; so it has been now, all my sweet flock are I trust, carefully provided for ; Katharine and the three little ones at Earlham, Joseph and Chenda at Runcton, John and William at school, and Rachel with me. My beloved husband means to meet me on my journey ; not only outward way has been made, but the willing heart also granted, and I had remarkably sweet peace and relief in being willing to give up to it, such an evidence that I think it remains undoubted in my mind. Friends appeared to feel much unity with me, which was a help. My beloved brother Joseph and sister Jane, joining me has been much cause for humble thankfulness, it has made what would have been very hard to flesh and blood comparatively sweet and easy ; we are a sweet united band in spirit and in nature ; Joseph a very great help in the ministry. I think he is, and will yet be more abundantly an instrument of honour in his Master's hand. We have sat four Meetings, visited several families of Friends, and inspected many prisons, which is one of our objects. In our religious services, our gracious Helper has appeared very near ; we have gone on in them with much nearness and unity ; we know the blessed truth that as we abide in Christ we are one in Him. I have felt at seasons as leaving all for my Master's sake, and setting out without much of purse or scrip ; but how bountifully I am provided for, internally and externally ; the Great Shepherd of the sheep has been near to me in spirit, as strength in my weakness, riches in my poverty, and a present helper in the needful time ; I may say,

> " Are these thy favours day by day,
>   To me above the rest,
> Then let me love Thee more than they,
>   And try to serve Thee best."

Conflicts have attended, and no doubt will attend me ; but I look upon it as an honour, a favour and a blessing, even to suffer in the Lamb's army ; if we may but be of the number of his soldiers, who fight the good fight of faith, and are in any degree permitted to promote the cause of truth and righteousness upon earth.

Aberdeen, 29*th.*—I have felt low upon arriving here ; five hundred miles from my beloved husband and children ! but a good account of them is cause for thankfulness, still it is a deeply weighty thing, and I have to try my ground again and again. In almost every new place, the language of my spirit is, Why am I here ? At this place we find several other Friends, also travelling in the ministry, which makes me feel it the more ; but as my coming is not of my own choice, or my own ordering I desire to leave it, and to commit myself, my spirit and body, and all that is dear to me, absent and present, to Christ my Redeemer. We visited the old Barclay seat, at Ury, where our mother's forefathers once lived. How great the change from what it once was !

Stonehaven, Ninth Month, 2nd.—We left Aberdeen this
afternoon, having finished our services there, and at Kilmuck,
where several Friends reside. Other Friends besides ourselves,
being at Aberdeen, certainly tended to increase my exercise, for
fear of the ministry not going on well, or by not keeping in our
ranks ; but I think that we were enabled to do so, and although
much passed, yet we had cause for thankfulness, inasmuch as
there appeared to be harmonious labour for the advancement of
truth, and the spreading thereof. I had to go into the Men's
Meeting, and my brother Joseph came into the women's Meeting. I do not know what Friends thought of us, as our exercises are certainly of rather a peculiar nature, so very often
bending the knee in prayer; and the nature of our testimonies
so much alike, though Joseph appears to me the most highly
gifted young minister I ever remember, as to power, wisdom,
tongue, and utterance. What an unspeakable cause of thankfulness to have him thus brought forth as a bright and shining
light ! Our General Meeting at Aberdeen was ended under a
feeling of quiet peace ; but fears crept in for myself, that I had
fallen away a little as to life in the truth, and power in the
ministry, for I did not experience that overflowing power which
I have sometimes done at such seasons; still gracious help was
granted me from season to season. The day after the General
Meeting, we went to Kilmuck, about fifteen miles north of
Aberdeen, a short time after our arrival there, before I went to
Meeting, such a feeling of suffering came over me as I can
hardly express, it appeared only nervous, as I was so well in
body that I could not attribute it to that, it continued exceedingly upon sitting down in Meeting, and led me into deep strong
supplication, that the enemy might by no means deceive us, or
cause our ministry to be affected by any thing but the holy
anointing. I feared if this awful state had to do with those
present, that I should have something very close to express ; if
only with myself, I considered that it might be a refining trial.
However, Joseph knelt down, in the beginning of the Meeting,
as well as myself, and afterwards he spoke as if he felt it necessary to warn some to flee from their evil ways, and from the
bondage of Satan. This tended to my relief ; but it appeared

as if I must follow him, and rise with these words, " The sorrows
of death compassed me about, the pains of hell gat hold upon
me ;" then enlarging upon the feeling I had of the power of the
enemy, and the absolute need there is to watch, to pray, and to
flee unto Christ, as our only and sure refuge and deliverer; I had
to show that we might be tried and buffeted by Satan, as a
further trial of faith and of patience, but that if we did not yield
to him, it would only tend to refinement. After a time I felt
greatly relieved, but what seemed remarkable was, that neither
Joseph nor I dared leave the Meeting, without once more bowing
the knee for these dear Friends; but after all this very deep
and remarkable exercise, a solemn silence prevailed, really as if
truth had risen into dominion ; and after my making some such
acknowledgment in testimony, that our low estate had been
regarded, that our souls could then magnify the Lord, and our
spirits rejoice in God our Saviour, that light had risen in obscurity, and darkness had in measure become as the noon-day, and
the encouragement it was for us to run with patience the race that
was set before us, &c., the Meeting concluded; and I think upon
shaking hands with the Friends, there hardly appeared an eye
that had not been weeping amongst those that were grown up.
This whole exercise was very remarkable, in a nice little country
Meeting, and the external so fair ; but afterwards we heard of
one or two painful things, one in particular ; we visited nearly
all the families, were much pleased with some of them ; their
mode of living truly humble, like our cottagers. The next day
we had a Meeting with the few Friends in Aberdeen, where the
exercise was not very great, and the flow in the ministry sweet,
and I trust powerful. We parted from our beloved old friends,
John and Elizabeth Wigham, their children, and children's children, and are now on our way to Edinburgh.

Hawick, 13th.—I may thankfully acknowledge being so far
upon our way, but our journey through life is a little like a
common journey, we may after a day's travelling, lie down and
rest, but we have on the morrow to set off again upon our travels:
so I find my journey in life, I am not unfrequently permitted to
come for a short time to a sweet, quiet resting place; but I find
that I soon have to set forth again. I was glad and relieved in

leaving Aberdeen, and then a fresh work begun in Edinburgh ;
on Seventh day, we visited the prisons, accompanied by some
gentlemen, the Lord Provost and others. Here we were much
interested, we had to dine out with several gentlemen; we went
in the morning to Meeting, and were favoured to do well, many
were there not Friends; and what were my feelings, in the evening.
to find a considerable number of people, quite a Public Meeting.
It gave me a great deal of alarm, but we had a good Meeting,
and I trust the cause was exalted ; people flocked much after us.
Our being there was mentioned in the newspapers which accounted
for this ; but it was to my own feelings a low time. The morning before we came away, about eighteen gentlemen and ladies
came to breakfast with us, amongst them Sir George and Lady
Grey, good people, whom I have long wished to know : we had,
after breakfast, a solemn time. Alexander Cruickshank read,
and afterwards I knelt down, and I think we were drawn together in love and unity of spirit. We arrived at Glasgow that
evening, and the next day visited the prisons, and formed a
Ladies' Committee. We visited some families the next day,
and accompanied by several gentlemen, magistrates and others,
we again went to the Bridewell and Prison, where I had to start
the Committee in their proceedings ; it was awful to me, having
to bow the knee for a blessing, before so many who were strangers
to our ways, but blessed be the Lord, the power of truth appeared
to be over all, so that I remembered these words, "rejoice not
that the spirits are made subject unto you, but rather rejoice
that your names are written in heaven." We had two Meetings,
one in the morning for Friends but many others came, and one
to my deep humiliation in the evening for the public; awful
work as it was, we were favoured to get through well, and to
leave Glasgow with clear minds. We have since travelled
through great part of Cumberland, attended many Meetings
there, some very important ones, and some highly favoured
by the Presence and the Power of the Most High ; thence to
Kendal.

At Liverpool was the next Meeting we attended, it was a
large public one, and so it has been in many places. I deeply
felt it, I hardly dared to raise my eyes because of the feathers

and ribbons before me, however, best help was afforded, to my very great relief and consolation ; truth appeared to be in great dominion.   After a sweet uniting time with the Benson family, we left Liverpool for Knowsley, the seat of the Earl of Derby, as we had had a pressing invitation from Lady Derby ; we were received with the utmost kindness and openness by all this very large household ; a palace was now our allotment; a cottage has been so during our journey, my internal feeling was humiliation and self abasement.   Yet I rather enjoyed the no-velty and cheerfulness of the scene, there were nearly thirty of their family and guests, cordial kindness was shown us ; our scruples most particularly attended to, and every effort made to promote our comfort.

Knowsley, 24th.—Here we are, all the family about to be collected for a religious opportunity ; Lord, be pleased to be with us, to own us by Thy life-giving presence, and help us by Thy Spirit, for it is a very awful time.   Make us, Thy unworthy children, fit for Thy service, and touch our lips as with a live coal from Thy altar, for we are unworthy to take Thy great and ever-excellent name into our mouths ; Thou Lord only knowest the state of Thy unworthy servant, help her infirmities, blot out her transgressions, and enable her to show forth thy praise, if con-sistent with Thy Holy Will, that all may be more abundantly converted unto Thee, and brought into the knowledge of Thy beloved Son Christ Jesus our Lord.

Sheffield, 26th.—After writing the above, I was summoned into the dining-room where the family were assembled—I should think in all nearly a hundred.   My beloved brother read the third chapter of John ; there was then a solemn pause, and I found it my place to kneel down, praying for a blessing upon the house and family, and giving thanks for the mercies bestowed upon them ; particularly in the time of their affliction, in having been supported by the everlasting Arm ; and prayer arose for its being sanctified to them. The large party appeared humbled and tendered—then dearest Joseph arose, and was greatly helped by the power of the Spirit—I followed him with a few words. Many of the party were in tears ; some exceedingly affected.   Joseph then knelt down, greatly helped ; the service principally fell upon

him, dear fellow. After he rose, I reminded them of the words
of our blessed Redeemer, " that whosoever giveth a disciple a cup
of cold water in the name of a disciple, shall receive a disciple's
reward;" this, I said, I humbly trusted would be their case. I
also alluded to their servants' kindness in the same way. Thus
ended this memorable occasion. It was like what we read of
in Friends' journals formerly, when the power appeared to be
over all in a very extraordinary manner. I remember in John
Richardson's journal some such an account. So it is,—and this
is not and cannot be our own work, surely it is the Lord's
doing, and marvellous in our eyes!

Earlham, Tenth Month, 6th.—Once more arrived at this
interesting place, that has so long been a home to me. I will go
back to where I left off. Our visit to Sheffield was an important
one; I had so deeply to feel for a beloved Friend, who has long
been a mother in Israel, under heavy family affliction. Oh, what
I felt for her in Meeting, and out of Meeting, I cannot describe;
my spirit was in strong intercession for her preservation and
support, under these deep tribulations. We had a favoured
Meeting in the morning, though I had indeed to go through the
depths before I ascended the heights. By the desire of my dear
brother, we had a public Meeting in the evening, which was well
got through, but not without suffering. We then proceeded to
York; I can hardly express how deeply I felt entering that
Quarterly Meeting; " fears gat hold upon me," still hope arose
underneath, that this end of our services as to our northern
journey would crown all—and so I think it proved—not only from
service to service, and from Meeting to Meeting, did the Holy
blessed anointing Power appear to be abundantly poured forth
upon the speakers, but upon the hearers also ; that where I feared
most I found least to fear ; such unity of spirit, such a flow of
love and of life, as quite refreshed, encouraged, and comforted
my soul. I was much rejoiced to find so many fathers and
mothers amongst them. " Bless the Lord, O my soul ! all that is
within me bless His holy name."—" Praise and exalt Him, above
all for ever," might then have been the language of my soul.

We travelled on to Lynn, and there my brother left me to
remain over First day, with his dear Jane. At the Meetings

there, I felt as if I had to minister almost, without the power, and yet that I must yield to the service ; but I was so fearful and weak, at both Meetings, that truth did not appear in dominion, perhaps I found the change after York, and I missed my dear brother Joseph.   I often minister as if in bonds, this is very humbling, so many fears, so many doubts arising ; this was the case in nearly all my services during the day.   My Aunt Birkbeck truly sweet and kind.   Here I had the comfort and delight yesterday, of meeting six of my tenderly beloved children, and many of my dearest sisters and brothers.   How thankful do I feel for their having been kept in my absence, it would have been such a trial to my weak faith, if they had not gone on well.   Oh ! may I prove my gratitude by my love.

The principal object of this journey was connected with the concerns of the Society of Friends ; but Elizabeth Fry and Joseph John Gurney also made a point of visiting the prisons of the towns through which they passed.   As the Notes* made on this occasion were published the following year, by Mr. Gurney, it is unnecessary to do more in the present work than to record some of the most striking scenes they met with, disgraceful in their nature and injurious in their effects ; and to introduce his sketch of the general results of the whole.   They felt themselves much indebted to the magistrates of the towns and districts through which they passed, for the kindness and openness with which they received them.   They rejoiced that the views entertained by these gentlemen were correct and benevolent ; few evincing any disposition to adhere to the old system, fraught as they had found it to be with accumulated errors and evil consequences.   In many places, the expediency of erecting prisons

* Notes on a Visit made to some of the Prisons in Scotland and the North of England, in company with Elizabeth Fry.   By Joseph John Gurney.   London : Printed for Archibald Constable and Co., Edinburgh, 1819.

8

on an improved plan was under consideration ; and in some they were already in course of building.

Durham old Gaol and House of Correction ; and the Gaols at Haddington, Aberdeen, Glasgow, and Carlisle, as well as many in the smaller Borough towns, were of the worst possible description. Of Dunbar Gaol and Haddington visited August 26th, and Kinghorn in Fifeshire the next day, Mr. Gurney writes :—

" Dunbar Gaol.

" You ascend a narrow dirty staircase, into two small rooms, of which this little Borough gaol consists. These two rooms, one of which is for debtors, the other for criminals of all descriptions, are kept in a state of extreme filth, and are severally furnished with a little straw, and a tub for every dirty purpose. There is no court nor airing ground in the prison, nor any other accommodation whatever. Happily there was no one confined here.

" Haddington County Gaol.

" Very different was the case with this gaol; for in consequence chiefly of a riot, which had taken place in the neighbourhood, we found it crowded with prisoners; and seldom indeed have we seen any poor creatures so wretchedly circumstanced. That part of the prison which is allotted to criminals and vagrants consists of four cells on the ground floor, measuring respectively thirteen feet by eight, and one on the second story, measuring eleven feet by seven. It is difficult to conceive any thing more entirely miserable than these cells. Very dark—excessively dirty—clay floors—no fire-places—straw in one corner for a bed, with perhaps a single rug—a tub in each of them, the receptacle of all filth. In one of the cells, we observed three men who had been engaged in the riot; in another, a woman (the wife of one of them) and two boys; in the third, two more men and a woman (the wife of one of them). We understood that one of these women was a prisoner, the other a visitor ; but have since been informed by the jailor, that they were both visitors. None of the prisoners were ironed, except one man who had attempted to break prison. This unfortunate person was fastened to a long iron bar. His legs, being passed through rings attached to the bar were kept about two feet asunder, which distance might be increased to three feet and a half, at the pleasure of the jailor. This cruel and shameful mode of confinement, which prevented the man from undressing, or from resting with any comfort to himself during the night, and which by the constant separation of the legs, amounted to positive torture, had been continued for several days. We earnestly entreated for his deliverance, but apparently without effect.

" Another scene of still greater barbarity was in reserve for us. In the fourth cell—a cell as miserable as the rest—was a young man in a state of lunacy. No one knew who he was, or whence he came ; but having had the misfortune to frequent the premises of some gentleman in the neighbourhood, and to injure his garden seats, and being considered mischievous, he was consigned to this abominable dungeon, where he had been, at the date of our visit, in unvaried solitary confinement, for eighteen months.

"No clothing is allowed in this prison; no medical man attends it ; no chaplain visits it. Its miserable inmates never leave their cells, for there is no change of rooms, and no airing-ground; nor can they be under any one's constant and immediate care, for the jailor lives away from the prison. They can, however, keep up an almost unchecked communication with the people of the town, as the small grated windows of their cells look upon the streets. We observed a lad on the outside of the prison, seated on a ledge of the wall, in close conversation with the three men who had been committed for rioting. The prisoners were at this time, allowed nothing but water, and four pennyworth of bread daily. I have since learned from the jailor, that this was a short allowance, by way of punishment for refractory conduct, and that they usually have eightpence a day. Those who were in the gaol, when we visited it, appeared in a remarkably careless and insensible state of mind. This we could not but attribute, partly, to the hardships and neglect which they here experience.

" I have yet to describe the most objectionable point of this terrible prison, namely, its accommodations for those debtors

who are not burgesses.   There were at this time three men of
that description in the prison : shortly before, there had been
five ; and at one time, seven.   These unhappy persons, innocent
as they are of any punishable offence, be they many or be they
few, be they healthy or be they sick—are confined day and
night, without any change or intermission whatsoever, in a
closet containing one small bed, and measuring not quite nine
feet square.

" As we passed through Haddingtonshire, we were struck with
the richness and fertility of the country, and with the uncommon
abundance of the crops which it produces.   It is considered one
of the wealthiest counties in Scotland.   Surely, then, we may
indulge the pleasing expectation, that the inhabitants of this
county, and especially its very liberal magistrates, will no longer
suffer it to continue without such a prison, as will tend to the
reformation of offenders ; such a one, at any rate, as will not,
like their present gaol, violate the common principles of justice
and humanity.

" KINGHORN, FIFESHIRE.

" In this little Borough, there is a small prison, now disused ;
and in a state of great dilapidation.   We were informed by the
people, who, wondering at our strange curiosity, crowded after
us into the building, that in one of the wretched rooms upstairs,
had been confined for six years, in miserable solitude, a young
Laird, who was in a state of lunacy ; and who at length terminated his suffering by swallowing melted lead.   The death of
this afflicted young man is said to have happened about twenty
years ago.   I introduce this story, (for the truth of which,
though I had no reason to doubt it, I cannot vouch,) for the
purpose of once more drawing the attention of the public, to the
cruel practice still prevalent in Scotland, of confining deranged
persons in prisons."

The following extract from Mr. Gurney's work, well describes
the aggregate state of the Scotch prisons.

" There are certain peculiarities in the construction and
management of many gaols in Scotland, which, in the first place,

deserve a distinct notice. They may be shortly enumerated, as follows :—No airing grounds ; no change of room ; tubs in the prisoners' cells for the reception of every kind of filth ; black-holes ; no religious service ; jailors living away from their prisons ; consequently an impossibility of any inspection, and an almost total absence of care ; free communication through the windows of the cells with the public. The three last mentioned particulars, have an obvious tendency to encourage disorder; the others, as evidently entail a dreadful degree of wretchedness. To the particulars in Scotch gaols, which are productive of unnecessary suffering, may also be added the long iron bar which is fixed in the floor, and through which the legs of the prisoner are fastened by rings. This, as far as we have observed, is the most usual method of chaining, adopted in Scotland, and a more cruel one could not easily have been devised ; for it not only keeps the legs of the prisoner constantly apart from each other, but prevents his undressing or going to bed. It is indeed a happy circumstance that so many of the prisons in Scotland are without any inhabitants. Certainly, when any unfortunate person does become the inmate of some of these dreadful abodes, his situation is truly pitiable. He probably finds himself in a damp, dark and filthy cell ; it may be, with only straw for his bed ; assailed by the most noisome smells ; entirely solitary, without any possibility of change, exercise, or relief. If he had been imprudent enough to attempt his escape from his misery, that misery will be doubled by his being chained to the iron bar, or consigned to the yet more terrible dungeon, denominated the black-hole. Amidst all this suffering, no religious instructor visits him, and even his appointed keeper lives entirely out of his reach. Can it be justifiable that any human being, and more especially the un-tried prisoner, who is innocent in the eye of the law, should be exposed to sufferings so multiplied, and so little alleviated, and for a length of time together ?

" There are two points, to which it appears necessary once more to advert, before I leave the subject of ' misery in Scotch prisons ;' the first is, the treatment of debtors; the second, that of lunatics.

By the law of Scotland, if a debtor escapes from prison, the jailor, and through the jailor, the magistrate, who issued the warrant, becomes responsible for the debt.   It is necessary, of course, that the jailor and the magistrate should protect their own interest ; the consequence is, that the Scotch debtor is consigned to the closest and most severe confinement.   He has no yard to walk in, no means of taking exercise or changing the air : if there be a yard in the prison, he is probably not allowed to make use of it : he is kept like the vilest criminal, perhaps with numerous companions, in some close, and miserable and fetid apartment, which he is permitted on no occasion to quit, even for a moment. His health is exposed to the most serious injury ; and there is actually nothing to alleviate his distress, but the lethargy of a despondent mind.   Let it be remembered, that respectable and virtuous persons may frequently be subjected, by circumstances which they cannot control, to all this wretchedness ; and let the question then be answered, whether enactments productive of so much unmerited cruelty ought to be any longer tolerated by a civilized and Christian community."

But that which most deeply affected Mrs. Fry, and excited sorrowful recollections, which she retained almost to the close of her life, was the condition of the poor lunatics confined in those prisons.   Not the wretched prisoner fastened to the iron bar at Haddington ; not those chained to the bedstead at Forfar ; nor to the wall of their cells, as at Berwick ; nor to a ring on the floor, as at Newcastle, left such a melancholy impression on her mind, as the state of the poor lunatic in the cell at Haddington. But happily, this evil also was in progress of remedy, through the erection of Lunatic Asylums.

The frequent appeals made by Mrs. Fry in behalf of the insane, and the tenderness with which she treated them when she came in personal contact with those afflicted ones, in prisons or other places, proved how powerfully her heart was touched with compassion for that heaviest of human maladies; "the worst of evils" as she once expressed it, " to the individual and those connected with him, except sin."

It was with pleasure the travellers found the Bridewell at Aberdeen, and the House of Correction at Preston, approaching to what was then considered a standard of excellence.

To such persons as were interested in Prison Reform, Mr. Gurney's Book afforded much matter for reflection. Whilst they deplored the evils he described, they rejoiced that they should be brought to light—as the first step towards their being remedied. Not so with those, who, from indifference or neglect, had endured their continuance without at least any availing effort to alter a state of things both impolitic and unchristian. Attempts were made to contradict some of the facts he asserted, but entirely failed.

The beginning of the present century, though marked by strong political feeling and national excitement, presented the same apathy as to questions of Moral Benevolence, which from the time of the Commonwealth had pervaded all ranks and conditions of men. But a new era was approaching—a better day begining to dawn. Many were prepared to hail any advance towards improvement; and whilst they shrank from alteration for the sake of change, were yet capable of appreciating the fact, that with the progress of civilization, the increase of population, and the altered state of society, institutions adapted to a former day had become inapplicable; and that measures suited to the darker ages would not bear investigation and the increasing light of knowledge. But far beyond these considerations of expediency, was the growing influence of Religion, she raised her voice to proclaim that Reformation, not revenge, is the object of Punishment—to be a " terror to evil doers, and a praise to those who do well;" whilst in the words of her Great Master, she was heard to say, "Neither do I condemn thee, go and sin no more."

Mr. Gurney and Mrs. Fry received many letters after the "Notes" were published—many opinions and suggestions were offered—some objections were raised—but there were individuals, and they were not few in number, nor unimportant in influence, who simply encouraged them in their researches, and expressed warm desires for the eventual success of the cause they espoused. Among these letters, two from the Countess Harcourt, are introduced here.

"My dear and most respected friend,

"It is impossible to have read the excellent publication, giving an account of your tour with Mr. Gurney, without being most anxious to express the satisfaction Lord Harcourt and I received from the work. He read it to me, and there was scarcely a page at which we did not stop, to exclaim our admiration of the justness of the remarks, and our earnest wishes that they might prove the means of ameliorating the system of our prisons. We felt that each word gave conviction to our minds; and the beauty of the style, certainly added to the gratification of reading it. Oh! my good friend, what a blessed tour you have made, and may Heaven reward your wonderful exertions, by making them effectual to the purpose intended.

"I ought not to use the word envy, but I cannot help feeling the great difference between the manner in which your life is spent and my own. You ought indeed to be thankful that it has pleased God 'to put into your mind good desires,' and to have given you health to go through such arduous undertakings. I hope I shall know that your health has not suffered, but I shall not be in London to witness it for some time to come, and I dare not ask you to visit St. Leonard's, at this season of the year. Happy should I be to see you here, if this place proved to be in your road and Mr. Gurney's, at any period, either now, or in summer; and though I shall not be in town immediately, yet I must go there with Lord Harcourt in April, when I shall hope to see you. I shall recommend every friend I have to read your admirable book ; and when the Duchess of Gloucester returns to Windsor, I shall entreat her to read it, and to send the Duke (to whom she writes constantly) an account of it ; as it may be useful in France as well as in England.

"And now, dear Mrs. Fry, accept, I entreat of you, Lord Harcourt's best wishes and regards, as well as those of

"Your sincere and affectionate friend,

"MARY HARCOURT.

THE COUNTESS HARCOURT TO ONE OF MRS. FRY'S CHILDREN.

"St. Leonard's, *5th of February*, 1819.

"My dear young friend,

"Your letter has given me the greatest concern; that your excellent mother should be so unwell, grieves me to the heart, and that she should be disabled from continuing her useful exertions. But I hope and trust it will please God in his mercy to restore her health, and I beg you will have the goodness to write me an account of her state, after a short period is passed. Pray tell her, that as soon as we had finished reading the beautiful account of her tour, I sent it to the Duke of Gloucester, who is at Paris, hoping that it might be the cause of ameliorating the situation of our fellow-creatures in that yart of the continent of Europe. Benevolence should never be exclusive, and we ought to wish equally well to mankind, in whatever part of the world they may be placed.

"The Duke of Gloucester is in high repute at Paris, and probably has the means of communication with the most philanthropic part of the nation. If I can get a copy down in time, I will send it to the Duchess of Gloucester, who does not leave Brighton till Monday; or perhaps you had better send one by the coach, the moment you receive this, as it may be the means of the Regent reading it, from his great affection for, and opinion of his sister. I told Princess Augusta yesterday, I should send her a copy. Those Princesses will be happy to see dear Mrs.

z 2

Fry, whenever she is well enough, but I now fear that cannot happen soon. Pray give my affectionate regards to her,
"And believe me, my dear young friend,
"Yours very sincerely,
"MARY HARCOURT."

After her Scotch journey, Mrs. Fry's return home from Earlham, was hastened by an accident occurring to her husband; but although she found him recovering the effects of it, other anxieties awaited her.

Plashet, Tenth Month, 15th.—I have had the comfort of finding my beloved husband mending. My first arrival for a few hours was sorrowful; my dearest Kate being seriously ill, but I am thankful to say she soon recovered. My Louisa is now poorly, but I hope not materially so. My prison concerns truly flourishing: surely in that a blessing in a remarkable manner appears to attend me; more apparently, than in some of my home duties. Business pressed very hard upon me; the large family at Mildred's Court, so many to please there, and attend to—the various accounts—the dear children and their education,—my husband poorly—the church—the poor—my poor infirm aunt whom I have undertaken to care for—my public business, and my numerous friends and correspondents. I have desired to keep my mind quiet and lifted up to my Redeemer, as my Helper and my Guide; inwardly, I have felt helped, even He whom my soul loves has been near, but I have also had some perplexity and discouragement, thinking that some of those very dear, as well as others, are almost jealous over me, and ready to mistrust my various callings; and are open both to see my children's weaknesses, and almost to doubt the propriety of my many objects. Such are my thoughts! Indeed I too much feel the pain of not being able to please every one; but this cannot be, and if I only may please my Master, I trust that His servants will not greatly disapprove me. I certainly at times feel pressed almost out of measure; but then I do not think that I have brought myself into all this service, therefore I humbly hope that I and my family may be kept in it. I sometimes wish I had more order in my pursuits, but this appears almost impossible. Oh! for a little help daily and hourly to press forward towards the mark, until the prize be obtained through good report, and evil report through perplexities and cares, joys and sorrows. Thou hast helped in a marvellous way, O Lord! be pleased to continue to help and to be very near thy poor unworthy child and servant, and make a way for her where at seasons she may see no way. Amen.

Plashet, 22nd.—I was thinking this morning, amidst all my business, my many engagements, my numerous cares, and the little time I have for reflection and quiet; what I should do if my dependence was not placed upon the Eternal word of life? which is with me in every place. I could not but feel this an invaluable gift; the Scriptures that testify of it are truly valuable, but though proceeding from it, they are not it. I think it a blessing to feel the operative power of this word of life, and through abundant mercy, it leads me at seasons, sometimes at very low seasons, to feel it my meat and my drink to do the will of my Heavenly Father.

Plashet, 28th.—Entering my public life again is very serious to me, more particularly my readings at Newgate. They are to my feelings too much like making show of a good thing, yet we have so often been favoured in them to the tendering of many hearts, that I believe I must not be hasty in putting an end to them, or hindering people coming to them ; it is the desire and prayer of my heart, that way may rightly open about them, and that when engaged in them, I may do what I do heartily unto the Lord, and not unto man, and look not either to the good or evil opinions of men. The prudent fears that the good have for me, try me more than most things, and I find that it calls for Christian forbearance, not to be a little put out by them. I am confident that we often see a Martha-like spirit about spiritual things. I know by myself what it is to be over-busy. O Lord! enable us to keep our ranks in righteousness, and pardon the iniquity of even our holy things, of our omissions and commissions ; and be pleased to enable Thy poor unworthy child and servant, to cleave very close to Thee in spirit, and if it should please Thee, that she should again be brought forth even as a spectacle among the people, Oh! be pleased to keep her from ever hurting or bringing discredit upon Thy ever blessed cause; but enable her to do justly, love mercy, and walk humbly before Thee, and so to abide in the light and life of Christ her Saviour and Redeemer, that many may be led to glorify Thee, her Father who art in heaven. Amen, and Amen.

Plashet, Eleventh Month, 7th.—This week I have been at seasons tossed with tempest. The death of poor Sir Samuel Romilly, took rather painful hold of me, as such things are apt to do; hardly any thing appears to me so dreadful, as thus taking the work into our own hands, and shortening the precious gift of life; a more awful crime surely cannot be, but it is thought he was deranged from the sorrow of losing his wife. Certainly in times of deep anguish and distress, it calls for all our watchfulness and constant prayer, that our spirits be not overcome within us; for we cannot keep ourselves, but by depending alone upon Him who can keep us, we may humbly trust that we shall be kept. Thou Lord, who searchest the heart, and art touched with a feeling sense of our infirmities, keep us, we pray Thee, not only from blood-guiltiness, but from such a state as would lead to our being overcome by any of the changes that await us here below; that we may indeed know our establishment to be upon the everlasting Rock of Ages, so that nothing may have power greatly to shake us.

Plashet, 17th.—My spirit is brought deeply prostrate within me, my flesh and my heart at seasons feel ready to fail—sorrows have compassed me about. Among other distresses, finding how powerful the enemy is, and how even those I fully believe to be servants of the Most High, give way to what appears to be a gossiping slanderous spirit; so that that which may be imagined by themselves and others to be a spirit of watching over one another for good, degenerates into a spirit of watching over one another for evil, and savours not of that charity which "thinketh no evil," and "rejoiceth not in iniquity"—not going in love to the parties implicated, but expressing their judgment and their fears to others; this I have deeply felt, more

8

particularly as it relates to things said of Ministers, for it is a fearful thing to lessen the weight of the instruments of the Lord, lest their services should also be lessened. Another sorrow just now is, fearing that I have not one child much under the influence of grace, or that appears really bending to the cross, and this is not only serious for themselves, but brings me into many straits. It is difficult to know how in all things to conduct myself towards them, to be neither too strict, nor too much the reverse. Still I have a humble hope that the work of grace is manifest in some of them, and I trust that it will grow and increase. Perhaps, I am hardly tender enough over the temptations of youth, O Lord! make me more so, a better wife and mother, more calculated to bring them all to Christ their Redeemer. As for myself, innumerable fears creep in, I find myself so much more at liberty than many, so little bound by scruples, and so many weak feelings in my heart, that I am ready to fear whether I am not also falling away. Then, what will become of us? Yet sweet hope and strong confidence arise in Him, who has hitherto helped me, and as I do most deeply and most sensibly feel that I have no confidence in the flesh, as far as I know myself, but that my whole confidence, reliance, and hope are on Christ my Redeemer. I cannot, dare not, mistrust. However numerous my temptations, however deep my trials, however great my perplexities, still the everlasting Shepherd of the sheep is able and willing to care for me, to deliver me, and in his love and pity to redeem me. Lord enable me so to hear Thy voice, and to follow Thee, that I may ever be of the number of Thy sheep, and Oh! in Thine own time, visit my dear children by Thy love, Thy grace, and Thy power, that they may serve Thee, that Thou mayst be their God, and that they may be of the number of Thy people; and may an entrance ever be granted us into Thy everlasting kingdom of rest and peace. The 40th and 42nd Psalms spoke comfort to me this morning; I may say they express the language of my spirit at the present time.

CHAPTER XI.

Mildred's Court, First Month, 17th, 1819.—I returned home yesterday from leaving my dearest boys at Darlington. My journey was certainly a favoured and an encouraging one. The situation for my beloved boys appears very safe and desirable. I had abundant kindness and unity shown me, particularly by my dearest sister Rachel. I came home to many troubles and anxieties, also certainly to many comforts and blessings; but ah! gracious Lord, be pleased to conduct me safely through the difficulties that surround me, and give neither me nor mine over to the will of our enemies.

Second Month, 7th.—I am confined almost to my room; a time of not much trial, but at times a little worried and per-plexed as to my state. I think that some of the minor trials of life, are in some respects as difficult to bear with a real Christian spirit, as those that may appear greater; for under them we do not so absolutely feel the necessity of the Rock of Ages being our support, but are more apt to lean to outward help, and to look one to another for counsel and comfort. I seldom remem-ber being less able to come at Divine consolation. The Bible is in measure a sealed book to me, and other religious books all flat; outward sources also appear shut up. Not without inward comfort, yet many fears have arisen for myself. Am I separated in heart more from my Lord ?   Have my public engagements diverted me from the life of self-denial, of daily taking up my cross ?   If this be the case, I cannot heal myself, I cannot help myself, I cannot bring myself back—therefore, O Lord ! Thou who graciously carest for Thy children, and those who through all their unworthiness love Thee, and desire to follow Thee, be pleased to heal my backslidings, to help me, and as far as I have wandered from Thee, to bring me back. It may be well now and then (as I am now) to be removed from nearly all outward means of help or excitement in the religious life—no joining in worship with those whom I love in the truth—no assembling with my family ; and even in my private reading and retirement, little or no sensible edification—may it lead me to more entire dependence on the Invisible Arm of Strength, that I may know my Redeemer, even if his face be hidden from me, to be my only Helper, Counsellor and Comforter.   Enable me, dearest Lord, to commit myself and my all into Thy keeping; do with us as Thou wilt, only keep us Thine own, and be Thou our help and our strength.   Amen.

Plashet Cottage, 13*th.*—Here I am, surrounded with every thing that this poor body can wish for, for its comfort and indul- gence, and I am quite in a state to enjoy my many surrounding comforts, especially the kindness of my beloved friends, of which I feel very unworthy.   I hope that the length of my indisposi- tion will not tire them.   I am ready to think that perhaps this state of bodily infirmity is permitted for my mental rest— that I may retire a little from the world and its business.   I suffer little pain of any kind.   I desire quite to leave it in better hands, and to be enabled to turn this time of rest to a good account ; so that body, soul, and spirit may be helped by it, and if I should be restored to the active duties of life, may I be better fitted to perform them all heartily, as unto the Lord—and to go forward in His strength.   If, on the contrary, long suffering be my prospect, and perhaps even my time shortened here—may it please Infinite Wisdom that none of those things should suffer in which He has seen fit that I should be engaged ; but that if consistent with His Holy Will, other instruments may be raised up to carry on these works, and those who are already engaged in them, may have their hands strengthened to labour with fresh diligence; and oh! may the same kind Power that has been with me and done wonders for me in health, be with me and do all for me in sickness and in death.

Mildred's Court, Third Month, 5th.—Fears indeed have compassed me about in this illness. I never remember before, the fear of dying taking so much hold of me; though as far as I know, neither reason nor faith have led me to believe death near. I believe these fears to arise from the nature of my complaint, in great measure; and therefore that it is well to turn from them by innocent and amusing reading, and other things that would divert my attention from myself. It is not well to be influenced in conduct by these fears; for I have experienced, as far as I know, that the Spirit of the Lord shows itself by love, by power, and by a sound mind, rather than by nervous apprehensions. Where the nervous system is weak, no one should be discouraged by dark clouds for a season overshadowing the best things. This is our infirmity, that we often see as through the medium of this frail tabernacle. But without any nervous feelings, I know my state to be a serious one, and when favoured by the clouds being a little dispersed, and a more quiet and cheerful mind, I desire to examine my ownself, to prove my ownself, that if any thing stand between me and my God, it may be removed; for surely I am unfit to come and appear before God! Yet I have a strong confidence, that He who has in so marvellous a manner been with me through this wilderness travel, will be with me even unto the end, and accomplish His own work, by washing my garments and making them white in His blood—and so fitting me for an entrance into His kingdom. Although I feel the consolation in my small measure of having sought to prove my love to Him in my life, yet when I look at the corruption of my heart, my unworthiness and disobedience, my many transgressions, what hope can I have of entering the kingdom, but through the merits of Christ my Redeemer, who is willing and able to save to the very uttermost, those who come unto God by Him, seeing that He ever liveth to make intercession for them. It has been the desire and prayer of my soul for many years, thus to come unto Him, whom indeed I have loved, and that I might fully experience the power of His salvation, both now and for ever. Lord, Thou only knowest my weakness—my temptations—my unworthiness—be pleased to regard me in my low estate, to accomplish that which concerneth me, and in Thine unmerited mercy, not only to sustain me through the conflicts of time, but so wash me in Thine own blood, that an entrance may be granted me into Thy kingdom, " where the wicked cease from troubling and the weary are at rest."

Mildred's Court, 10*th.*—I do not know that I have language to express my thankfulness for the relief of having passed the night, and this morning, with some feeling of returning health, though very weak, and greatly shaken. The first night I spent here, after leaving Plashet Cottage, was an awfully trying one, conflicts and fears within, great suffering from great irritation of stomach without; all that could be shaken appeared to be shaken. I could not even pray ; I felt I had neither faith nor power, and I dared not call upon the Lord for deliverance in my own will or way, but felt that I must wait until power was given me in my low estate. " I remembered my God on my bed, and was troubled, for He hid His face from me," but this very close conflict did not last long, though it continued in some degree till the next evening, when I was enabled to pray : since then I have taken nourishment, and what is above all, spiritually, I have found near access in inward prayer. " The mountains have skipped like rams, and the little hills like lambs, at the presence of the Mighty God of Jacob." O Lord ! be with me, I pray thee, to the end, whatever Thou mayst have in store for me. Amen.

14*th.*—My faith is strong, respecting my dearest children, that in the end they will have in various ways to glorify the God of their fathers, though all may not be led into conspicuous or public services.

24*th.*—I have had another very deep plunge of illness, pain and suffering of body, and much lowness of spirits. The cry of my heart however, once more has been answered. Help and a little strength has been granted, and considerable relief from great faintness and illness, so that I have yet sweet hope and belief that my Redeemer, who has shown Himself on every side, will not

give me over to the will of mine enemies, but will more and more
arise for my help spiritually and naturally. Oh ! Most gracious
Lord, still help me, keep me near to Thyself, send health and
cure, when consistent with Thine holy and ever blessed will ;
and grant Thy poor child, a humble, quiet, and resigned spirit.

Mrs. Fry had now been confined to the house, nearly to her room,
for some months ; and her long-continued state of suffering and
illness, having become a cause of much solicitude to her family,
change of air, and gentle travelling were recommended ; she accordingly left home, the end of March, for a short journey into
Sussex and Kent. She was in so weak a state, as to be taken
upon a bed in the carriage ; she travelled by easy stages, and
passed slowly on from place to place, through Petworth, Arundel,
and Worthing, to Brighton, thence through Hastings to Tonbridge Wells, pausing at each place, refreshed and cheered by
the change, and the charming country scenes, amongst which
she found herself. The travellers arrived in London, in May,
after an absence of five weeks.

Petworth, Sussex, Third Month, 30th, 1819.—I am so far
on my journey, with my beloved husband, Katharine, Chenda,
and servants, for my health. I feel comfortable, my spirits very
tranquil, and what is more, at seasons I have been permitted to
hold something like sweet communion with my Lord.

Brighton, Fourth Month, 8th.—I have once more been to
Meeting—on First day morning, on Third day, the first meeting
of the Quarterly Meeting on Fourth day, and also to the
Monthly Meeting. It was sweet and refreshing, once more to
assemble with some of the outward church. In abundant mercy,
strength was granted in my great weakness, yet once more to
show forth the praise of Israel's Shepherd ; deep as my late conflicts have been, yet all appears intended renewedly to stimulate
and encourage myself as well as others, to run with fresh diligence the race that is set before us. The language of my heart
is, " Though he slay me, yet will I trust in Him." A wonderful

calm has been granted me after a very awful, and to my fearful nature, terrible storm. I have, through unmerited mercy, had such a sweetness and serenity over me, that the cares and sorrows of life have been almost hidden from my view, and I have hardly felt able even to look at them. These are the dealings of a kind Providence to an unworthy child, He has shown His power in casting down and raising up, in wounding and making whole, blessed be His name for ever. And Oh! dearest Lord, whenever Thou mayst be pleased to lay me low again, lift up I beseech Thee a standard against the enemy of my soul, that he overcome me not; and when I cannot help myself, be Thou my help and my strength. And I reverently return Thee thanks, that Thou gracious Lord, hast manifested Thyself to be my deliverer, that Thou hast once more broken my bonds asunder, brought my poor soul out of prison, and not given me over to the will of my enemies; but in Thine abundant mercy, delivered me from my fears, and I humbly trust, established my goings, and put a new song into my mouth, even praises to Thee, my God; Amen, and Amen.

During her stay at Brighton, Mrs. Fry had the gratification of receiving from the female prisoners in Newgate, these letters:—

"Honoured Madam,

"Influenced by gratitude to our general benefactress and friend, we humbly venture to address you. It is with sorrow we say, that we had not the pleasure of seeing you at the accustomed time, which we have been always taught to look for; we mean Friday last. We are fearful that your health was the cause of our being deprived of that heartfelt joy, which your presence always diffuses through the prison ; but we hope through the mercies of God, we shall be able personally to return you the grateful acknowledgments of our hearts, before we leave our country for ever, for all the past and present favours so benevolently bestowed upon what has been termed, the 'most unfortunate of Society,' until cheered by your benevolence, kindness and charity ; and hoping that your health, which is so dear to such a number of unfortunates, will be fully re-established before we go, so that after our departure from our native land, them who are so unfortunate as to fall into the same situation as them who now address you, may enjoy the same blessings both spiritually and temporally that we have done before them ; and may our minds be impressed with a due sense of the many comforts we have enjoyed, whilst under your kind protection.

Honoured and worthy Madam, hoping we shall be pardoned for our presumption in addressing you at this time; but our fears of not seeing you before the time of our departure, induces us to entreat your acceptance of our prayers for your restoration to your family ; and may the prayers and supplications of the unfortunate prisoners, ascend to heaven for the prolonging of that life, which is so dear to the most wretched of the English nation.

" Honoured Madam, we beg leave to subscribe ourselves with humble respect, your most grateful and devoted,

" THE PRISONERS OF NEWGATE."

" *Monday, March 8th*, 1819."

From some women who had made a disturbance in the prison.

" Honoured Madam,

" With shame and sorrow we once more humbly beg leave to address you, in duty and respect to you, and in justice to the greater number of our fellow-prisoners, who through our misconduct have fallen in the general disgrace which our behaviour has brought upon us all ; for which we are sincerely sorry, and entreating our sorrow may be accepted and forgiveness granted, by her, who we look up to as our most respected friend and benevolent benefactress. We are not only called by justice to this submission and acknowledgment of our fault ; but by gratitude to you, honoured Madam, and the rest of the worthy ladies who have interested themselves in our behalf. We hope what is past may be forgotten, and through your great goodness, be no hindrance to the great and many blessings, (to use the same language we have on a former occasion,) we have enjoyed since under your kind, shall we dare to say, your maternal love : blessings both spiritual and temporal, which so many unfortunates have enjoyed, and which is at present misused through our misconduct. Entreating you to impute it to our being led away by the passion of the moment, and humbly hoping this acknowledgment may prove successful in restoring us to your good opinion, and contradicting the bad one impressed on the public mind.

"With sincere regret and penitence for what is past, we beg leave to subscribe ourselves, with very humble respect, your very humble servants,

"Signed by eleven women, and witnessed by
"Mary Guy, Matron."
"Friday, March 26th, 1819, Transport-side, Newgate.

Answer to the two letters from the female prisoners, in Newgate, 1819.

Brighton, Fourth Month, 4th, 1819.

To the female prisoners in Newgate, more particularly to those who are likely to leave their native land, perhaps never to return to it.

Although it has pleased the Almighty, that for some time I should be separated from you by illness, yet you have often been in my affectionate remembrance, accompanied with anxious desires for your good. I am fully sensible that many of you claim our pity and most tender compassion, that many have been your temptations, many your afflictions, and what we may most pity you for is, that in the time of temptation you have yielded to what is wrong, and so given yourselves over to the will of the enemy of your souls! But mournful as your state is, yet you may have hope, and that abundantly; if you only seek to repent, to return from the error of your ways and live unto God. Remember these words, "Christ came into the world to save sinners," and that "He is able to save to the very uttermost those who come unto God by Him, seeing that He ever liveth to make intercession for them." Therefore, let me entreat you before it is too late, to come unto Christ, to seek Him with your heart, and to submit yourselves unto Him and His righteous law—for He knows all your thoughts and all your desires, and is willing and ready to receive you, to heal your backslidings, and to love you freely. He was said to be the Friend of sinners, and those will indeed find Him their friend, who look to him and obey Him—He will enable such to forsake the evil of their ways, and to do that which is acceptable in His sight. Do you not remember in the parable of the Prodigal Son, that when he was yet *afar off*, the Father saw him, had compassion on him, and even went out to meet him. So I doubt not, you would find it, even some of you who are now afar off from what is good, if you are only willing to return, you would find yourselves met by your Lord, even with great compassion, and He would do more for you than you could ask or think. I feel much love for you, and much desire for your own sakes,, for the sake of others, and for our sakes, who are willing to do what we can to serve you, that you would thus in heart seek the Lord, and prove your love to Him, and your repentance, by your good works and by your orderly conduct. I was much grieved at the little disturbance amongst you the other day, but I was pleased with the letter written me by those who were engaged in it, and I quite forgive them. Let me entreat you whatever trying or even provoking things may happen, to do so no more, for you sadly hurt the cause of poor prisoners by doing so, I may say all over the kingdom ; and you thus enable your enemies to say, that our plans of kindness do not answer, and therefore, they will not let others be treated kindly. Before I bid you farewell, I will tell you that I am not without a hope of seeing you before long, even before the poor women go to the Bay, but if I do not, may the blessing of the Lord go with you when on the mighty deeps, and in a strange land. What comfort would a good account of you give us, who are so much interested for you, and in case I should not see you, I have two things particularly to mention to you and guard you against— things, that I believe have brought most of you to this prison. The one is giving way to drinking too much, the other is freedom with men. I find I can most frequently trace the fall of women to these two things, therefore let me beseech you to watch in these respects, and let your modesty and sobriety, appear before all, and that you may grow in these and every other Christian virtue and grace, is the sincere desire and prayer, of your affectionate friend, and sincere well-wisher.

ELIZABETH FRY.

Mildred's Court, Third Month, First day.—I am at home from Meeting, as I felt easy to be here, it being wet, and my cough bad, though still favoured to feel surprisingly better. But as I return to health and life, so do I return to its cares; yesterday brought several mortifying and discouraging things with it, principally as to my public services, my private cares and sorrows I am also more sensible of, from being less occupied by my own suffering and infirmity. In coming out of this illness (for so I appear to be) I am rather awfully struck with the remembrance of how little I appeared to feel either willing or prepared to die; or as to my illness, fully resigned to suffer according to the will of God, so that the whole has been a deeply humbling dispensation. I cannot say I much depended upon my feelings, for I was in so nervous a state that I do not think I saw things through a right or just medium, I should think much more of it, if there had not been a cloud over me about every thing—however, it is awful and serious to be subject when poorly to such nervousness—yet, surely, through all, the Everlasting Arm was underneath, and the Lord was my stay and surety; He will not leave nor forsake me just in the needful time, even in death He will be my help and my strength. The difference of last winter and this has been striking, though I then had my deep conflicts, I was, as it were, marvellously raised up—the holy anointing oil appeared freshly poured forth. How did the righteous compass me about, from the Sovereign, the Princes, and the Princesses, down to the poorest, lowest, and most destitute; how did poor sinners of almost every description seek after me, and cleave to me—What was not said of me? What was not thought of me? may I not say in public and in private, in innumerable publications, &c. This winter the bed of languishing—deep, very deep prostration of soul and body—the enemy coming in at seasons like a flood, sorrows compassing me about, instead of being a helper to others, ready to lean upon all, glad even to be diverted by a child's book. In addition to this, I find the tongue of slander has been ready to attack me. The work that was made so much of before, some try to lessen now. What shall I say to all this—that in my best judgment, in my soundest faith (if I have this faith) it is the Lord's doing, by His permission, and marvellous in my eyes. He raiseth up and casteth down, He woundeth and maketh whole, and though now cast down in myself, my faith is, that He will again raise me up ; that even once more the righteous will compass about His unworthy child ; that He will not give me over to the will of my enemies, or let me be utterly cast down, but that in deed and in truth I may say, " Great and marvellous are Thy works, Lord God Almighty, just and true are all Thy ways, Thou King of saints." Deeply as my spirit may feel to have been wounded within me, yet the first desire of my heart is, I believe for myself and for all, that we may run with fresh alacrity the race that is set before us, looking unto Jesus, as the Author and Finisher of our faith, not so much from slavish fear, as from filial love ; I long, yea I pant after serving my Master with a perfect heart, the short time of my continuance here.

Plashet, Fifth Month, 7th.—Rather serious symptoms once more come on—What can I say, what can I do ? Lord enable me to come unto Thee, that I may be helped spiritually and naturally ; be pleased, O Lord ! to strengthen me, if the bed of languishing should again be my portion, and lift up the light of Thy countenance upon me, whether in health or sickness.

Sixth Month, 5th.—It is the desire and prayer of my spirit, now that I am decidedly better, that I may be enabled to set and keep my house in order, inwardly and outwardly. Dearest Lord, be pleased to help me by Thy presence and Thy good Spirit.

The return of the family to Plashet, was followed by the restoration of Mrs. Fry's health. During the holidays, all her children were assembled there. Soon after her sons went back to school, she wrote to one of them as follows :—

To WILLIAM STORRS FRY.

Plashet, Seventh day Morning.
Eighth Month, 14th, 1819.

My dearest William,

I anxiously hope that thou art returned with fresh diligence to all thy employments; pray try to be a learned man. I trust that the modern languages will not be neglected by thee, they are so important in the present day, when we have so much intercourse with the Continent. My darling William, how anxiously do I desire your all being happy. I do not think I have language to express my desires for your good, and comfort, in every way; be encouraged, my dear boy, in every thing to do right; remember what is said, " He that cometh to serve the Lord must prepare his soul for temptation." Temptations, we must expect to meet with, and many of them, but the sin is not in being tempted, but in yielding to temptation. I am sorry about your fruit, but have had two cakes made for you instead. Pray, my dearest William, write to me very often, for I feel such a most tender and near interest in you all.

Thy most affectionate and loving mother,

E. FRY.

Ninth Month, 6th.—Since I last wrote, I parted from my beloved boys for school, John, William, and Joseph. I felt a good deal in giving them up, but at the same time believing it to be a right thing, I humbly trust that the blessing of the Most High will be with them. My dearest sister Priscilla has been very dangerously ill, raising blood from the lungs, which has brought me into great feeling and conflict. As I mostly find the case in nursing, it has caused me afresh to see my own unworthiness; so little do I feel able to administer spiritual help, so hard is it to my nature, particularly when under discouragement, to wait upon my gift or to give it its free course; but I may thankfully acknowledge, that I appeared to be a great comfort, help, and strength to her, indeed her dependence was so close upon me, that I could not leave the house night or day, for any length of time. Her state appeared to be indeed a bright and a very blessed one; so calm, so gentle, so humble, and so much resigned to live or to die. Since I have left her sick room, sorrow and deep discouragement have been my portion, from the extreme difficulty of doing right towards those most near; it does appear at times impossible for me, but most likely, this arises from want of more watchfulness and more close abiding in the Light and the Life of our Lord. When I exercise a watchful care from seeing the dangers that attend some, it seems to give the greatest pain, and so causes me the deepest discouragement. Still, yesterday, in the great, in the bitter sorrow of my heart, I found in a remarkable manner the power of my Redeemer near, even helping by His own good Spirit and presence. When I felt almost ready to sink—and my footsteps indeed ready to slip—then the Lord held me up. In the first place, after a very little while, from having been deeply wounded, my heart overflowed with love and forgiveness towards the one who had pained me; I felt what would not I do for the individual? and a most anxious desire, if I had missed it, to make it up by every thing in my power. Thus, when I had feared discouragements would have almost overwhelmed my spirit, there was such a calming, blessed, and cheering influence came over my heart, that it was like the sick coming to our Saviour formerly, and being immediately healed; so that I was not even able to mourn over my calamity. It appeared as if the Holy One who inhabiteth Eternity would not give me over to the will of my enemies.

Mildred's Court, Tenth Month, 23rd.—We left Broadstairs last Sixth day after a pleasant time there, and I may thankfully acknowledge, much more strengthened and revived in health, than when we went to it; in short, the air, quiet, and comparative rest, I think have been very useful to me. I have not before mentioned the serious illness of my sister, Eliza Fry, which took us to London for some time. Her life certainly seemed to be in considerable danger; but through great mercy, our prayers appeared to have both been heard and answered, and we have now the comfort of seeing her mending. One day when she had every symptom of bringing up blood again, and we were all in great distress round her bed, I felt called upon (I may say powerfully) to kneel down, and ask for her revival, if consistent with the Divine Will; the prayer appeared to be answered, which is a cause for thankfulness, and an encouragement spiritually; as if the same Almighty ear was yet open to hear our cry. Re-entering our London life is certainly a serious thing. Much as I have to attend to, and very numerous as my calls are, yet I have belived that these words should be my motto, Phil. iv. 6, 7, "Be careful for nothing; but in every thing by prayer and supplication with thanksgiving let your requests be made known unto God. And the peace of God, which passeth all understanding, keep your hearts and minds through Christ Jesus." Now, though I may have many trials of faith and of patience, the more I can be without too much carefulness, and cast all my care on my Lord and Redeemer, the better I believe it will be for my body and soul; and the better also for all those with whom I have to do. Dearest Lord, I pray Thee, help me to abide in this state, that I may dwell near to Thee in spirit, and amidst all the perplexities of life, that I may feel Thee to be my Helper, my Comforter, my Guide, and my Counsellor. Amen.

Among other anxieties, Mrs. Fry was often doubtful whether the variety of association, arising from her public engagements, was beneficial to herself and her children.

To her brother, Joseph John Gurney, whose opinion she highly valued, she applied for counsel; his reply exists, and marks the view he took of her peculiar circumstances and calling.

"Earlham, *Sixth day night, Twelfth Month,* 31*st,* 1819.

"My dearest Sister,

"I am so very closely occupied, that I find it by no means easy to snatch half an hour to answer thy letter. My deliberate opinion is, that thy introduction to the great ones of the earth, is in the ordering of Divine Providence; and this decides the question at once—as to thy being endangered by it I think nothing of it. With regard to the dear girls, though it is not exactly what one would have chosen, we must trust that it is for the best; if they are but kept humble, knowledge will not do them harm."

To HER SONS.

Mildred's Court, *First Month,* 19*th,* 1820.

My dearest John, William and Joseph,

I am sorry that I have not written to you before, to tell you how much I rejoice in your father's excellent account of you. I believe no words can express the deep interest I take in your welfare, and how pleasant it is to me to have such good accounts of your conduct and learning. I cannot help hoping that my sons will be my comfort, and may I not say by their goodness and learning, that they may become my glory. My London life is now a very busy one, it is almost like living in a market or a fair; only that I have not merchandize to sell. We see a great variety of company, principally people who are interesting and occupied by subjects of importance. We lately had a gentleman, an East Indian Missionary, who told us many particulars about the poor Indians : I think in one province, about seven hundred poor widows burn themselves every year, when their husbands die. We expect soon to see the Persian Ambassador, and I mean to give you an account of him. It is now two o'clock, and I have been trying to write you a nice long letter ever since a little after ten ; and now I am so tired with the numerous people, that have been here, &c, &c., that I fear I cannot finish it. I much enjoy long letters from you, telling me every particular about yourselves; I like having your poetry. Believe me your nearly attached mother.

E. Fry.

To her Cousin, Priscilla Hannah Gurney.

Mildred's Court, *Second Month,* 23*rd,* 1820.

My very dear Cousin,

I have for some time past wished to write to thee, but it is very seldom that I can get any quiet opportunity. I wish much to hear particulars of thee ; I feel that confidence in our near tie to each other, that I believe communication is not necessary to keep it up, but I cannot help sometimes regretting that I have not more opportunity of opening my heart to one, whom I feel so particularly near and dear to me, and who I am sure so tenderly sympathizes in all my sorrows, and joys also. I have been favoured with health this winter, except being at times a little overdone, and having some cough. My engagements, as usual, are very numerous. I have, from being on a committee of our Quarterly Meeting visited some of our Monthly Meetings, but

I have had no other engagements of that sort. Our prisons continue to prosper, and Newgate goes on well; it does not require much of my time, though the many things it introduces me into, occupy me a good deal. And now for my beloved family; I think that they are going on much the same as when thou left us; I long to see more of the advancement of the blessed Truth amongst us, but I still hope, that that day will come. I anxiously desire to be enabled to do my part, and to walk before my household with a perfect heart, but this is a great attainment, almost too much for so weak and unworthy a person to look for; my sweet little ones go on charmingly. We have good accounts of our boys, this is a great comfort for us. I have a little favour to ask of thee, the children and myself are collecting English shells, and as I know my aunt made so fine a collection, we want to know what is the best book for us to procure to direct us in our search, and where, and from what coast, we are most likely to procure the finest; we have written to know whether we cannot buy some in Devonshire. I think this such a good object for the children, and nice amusement for us all in London, where we have not the garden and flowers to enjoy, that I endeavour to cultivate it. My dearest husband is now by me, and desires his love. I hope thy reply to this will be as full of thy concerns as this is of mine. Believe me, thy nearly attached Cousin.

ELIZABETH FRY.

From this period the entries in her journal are only occasional, frequently at intervals of some months; and then seldom more than her reflections on passing events, with little or no direct information respecting the events themselves. Earnest desires for good, and petitions for Divine assistance, constituting the greater part of them. After the arduous exertions, and varied interests of this winter, it was no small relief to Mrs. Fry to find herself again with her family in the retirement of Plashet; although her enjoyment was soon to be clouded by peculiar and touching family sorrows, in which she could not but bear a large part, both in exertion and tender sympathy.

Plashet House, Fourth Month, 26th.—My time has been so exceedingly occupied as to prevent my writing, but I have gone through a great deal. My dearest brother and sister Buxton being so heavily afflicted, has brought me into very deep conflict, in short almost inexpressible ; still, through all, we may acknowledge that we have found the Lord to be gracious, for assuredly He has been very near to help and support. Dearest Lord, we pray Thee, continue to have mercy upon us all ; and at this time of great sorrow, to regard us in our low estate, and to increase our faith according to its trial. Amen.

Fifth Month, 3rd.—Hard, very hard, as this trial has been, and is ; yet there is abundant cause to bless, praise, and magnify the great and excellent name of our Lord, both for having given these precious children, and then taking them through His redeeming love into His Kingdom of Light, Life, Peace, and Glory. But what a proof, that our hearts must not be set upon any temporal things.

In pursuing her labours at Newgate, Mrs. Fry had gradually learned many particulars of the Penal Colony of New South Wales. She found that in point of fact, all the labours of her coadjutors, and her own; all systems of Prison Discipline ; all efforts to reform the offender ; were absolutely null and void, and but a wasteful expenditure both of time and money, so long as the female convicts were without shelter, without resource, and without protection, on their arrival in the land of exile. Rations, or a small allowance of provisions, sufficient to maintain life, they certainly had allotted them daily : but a place to sleep in, or the means to obtain one ; or necessary clothing for themselves, and when mothers, for their children, they were absolutely without. It was worse than useless ; it was only an aggravation of their misery to inculcate morality, and to raise the tone and improve the tastes, of these unhappy ones, and above all to prove to them, that, " without Holiness no man can see the Lord," whilst they were placed in circumstances, where existence could only be maintained, at the price of virtue. Much of this was learned from the prisoners themselves, but every inquiry made upon the subject, confirmed their accounts; still data were required, and more detailed information was wanted, when Mrs. Fry received this letter from the Rev. Samuel Marsden, Chaplain at New South Wales. Some passages are of necessity omitted, from the fearful nature of the details given.

" Parramatta, February 23rd, 1819.

" Honoured Madam,

" Havin₃ learned from the public papers, as well as from my friends in England, the lively interest you have taken in promoting the temporal and eternal welfare of those unhappy females who fall under the sentence of the law; I am induced to address a few lines to you respecting such as visit our distant shores. It may be gratifying to you, madam, to hear that I meet with those wretched exiles, who have shared your attentions, and who mention your maternal care with gratitude and affection. From the measures you have adopted, and the lively interest you have excited in the public feeling, on the behalf of these miserable victims of vice and woe, I now hope the period is not very distant when their miseries will in some degree be alleviated. I have been striving for more than twenty years to obtain for them some relief, but hitherto have done them little good. It has not been in my power to move those in authority, to pay much attention to their wants and miseries. I have often been urged in my own mind, to make an appeal to the British nation, and to lay their case before the public.

" In the year 1807, I returned to Europe. Shortly after my arrival in London, I stated in a memorial to His Grace the Archbishop of Canterbury, the miserable situation of the female convicts; to His Majesty's Government at the Colonial Office, and to several members of the House of Commons. From the assurances that were then made, that barracks should be built for the accommodation of the female convicts, I entertained no doubt, but that the Government would have given instructions

to the Governor to make some provision for them. On my return
to the Colony, in 1810, I found things in the same state I left
them ; five years after my again arriving in the Colony, I took
the liberty to speak to the Governor as opportunity offered on
the subject in question, and was surprised to learn, that no
instructions had been communicated to His Excellency from His
Majesty's government, after what had passed between me and
those in authority at home, relative to the state of the female
convicts ; at length I resolved to make an official statement of
their miserable situation to the Governor, and if the Governor
did not feel himself authorized to build a barrack for them, to
transmit my memorial to my friends in England, with his
Excellency's answer, as a ground for them to renew my former
application to Government for some relief; accordingly I forwarded my memorial, with a copy of the Governor's answer home,
to more than one of my friends. I have never been convinced
that any instructions were given by His Majesty's Government
to provide barracks for the female convicts ; on the contrary,
my mind is strongly impressed, that instructions were given :
if they were not, I can only say, that this was a great omission
after the promises that were made. I was not ignorant that the
sending home of my letter to the Governor, and his answer,
would subject me to censure as well as the displeasure of my
superiors. I informed some of my friends in England, as well
as in the Colony, that if no attention was paid to the female
convicts, I was determined to lay their case before the British
nation, and then I was certain, from the moral and religious
feeling which pervades all ranks, that redress would be obtained.
However, nothing has been done yet, to remedy the evils of
which I complain. For the last five-and twenty years, many of
the convict women have been driven to vice, to obtain a loaf of
bread, or a bed to lie upon. To this day, there never has been
a place to put the female convicts in, when they land from the ships.
Many of these women have told me with tears, their distress of
mind on this account, some would have been glad to have returned
to the paths of virtue, if they could have found a hut to live in,
without forming improper connexions. Some of these women
when they have been brought before me as a magistrate, and I

have remonstrated with them, for their crimes, have replied, ' I have no other means of living, I am compelled to give my weekly allowance of provisions for my lodgings, and I must starve, or live in vice.' I was well aware that this statement was correct, and was often at a loss what to answer. It is not only the calamities that these wretched women and their children suffer, that is to be regretted ; but the general corruption of morals that such a system establishes in this rising Colony, and the ruin their example spreads through all the settlements. The male convicts in the service of the crown, or in that of individuals, are tempted to rob and plunder continually, to supply the urgent necessities of those women.

" All the female convicts have not run the same lengths in vice. All are not equally hardened in crime. And it is most dreadful that all should alike, on their arrival here, be liable and exposed to the same dangerous temptations, without any remedy.

I fear, madam, I have taken up much of your time, but I wished to prepare the way, if I should at any future period have occasion to solicit your aid. Mrs. B—— who came from Newgate in the Friendship, often mentions your kindness ; she lives near me with her husband ; they are well, and doing well, and conduct themselves with much propriety, will be useful members of society, and are getting forward very fast in worldly comforts.

> " I have the honour to be, Madam,
> " Your most obedient humble servant,
> "SAMUEL MARSDEN."

Plashet, Eighth Month.—I may indeed say, dearest Lord, help me in all my difficulties, regard me in my low estate, and let me see the lightings up of the light of Thy countenance on my beloved children. Though I am deeply sensible in bringing to the knowledge of Thyself, Thy ways are not our ways, and that Thou mayst even permit the poor mind to wander in darkness and in unbelief for a season, that it may be more fully prepared to see the beauty of Thy light, to rejoice in the appearance of the day-star from on high, and to feel the excellency of faith; yet if, in Thy tender mercy and compassion, Thou wouldest permit Thy unworthy one to see some fruit of the working of Thy Spirit in her children, that she might still rejoice and be glad in Thee; but above all, Lord strengthen and enable her to cast all her care upon Thee, and to commit herself, and those most near and dear to her, to Thy grace and good keeping. I desire not to forget all Thy benefits, which are many and great, naturally and spiritually; we are all of us favoured with health, still day by day provided for, and some desires spiritually raised in our hearts after Thyself; and I am also thankful that Thy blessing is in so remarkable a manner resting on the prison cause, and on our labours for these poor destitute creatures, that have come under our care. O Lord! be pleased to bless the work of our hands, even in these things establish Thou it, and if consistent with Thy holy will, be pleased to bless the labours of Thy poor child at home, as well as abroad. Amen.

I think before I conclude this journal, I should express amongst my many blessings, how much I am enabled to take pleasure in the various beauties of nature, flowers, shells, &c., and what an entire liberty I feel to enjoy them; I look upon these things as sweet gifts, and the power to enjoy them as a still sweeter. I am often astonished, when my mind is so exceedingly occupied, and my heart so deeply interested, how I can turn with my little children to these objects, and enjoy them with as great a relish as any of them; it is a wholesome recreation, that I fully believe strengthens the mind. I mention it as a renewed proof that the allowable pleasures of life, so far from losing their zest by having the time and mind much devoted to higher objects, are only thereby rendered more delightful.

19th.—I have this day been married twenty years; my heart feels much overwhelmed at the remembrance of it—it has been an eventful time. I trust that I have not gone really backwards spiritually, as I think I have in mercy certainly increased in the knowledge of God, and Christ Jesus our Lord; but this has been through much suffering. I doubt my being in so lively a state as ten years ago, when first coming forth in the ministry; but I believe I may say, that I love my Lord above all—as far as I know, far above every natural tie; although in His infinite wisdom and mercy, he has been pleased at times to look upon me with a frowning Providence. If I have lately grown at all, it has been in the root, not in the branch, as there is but little appearance of good, or fruit, as far as I can see. In the course of these twenty years, my abode has often been in the valley of deep humiliation; still the Lord has been my stay, and I may say through all, dealt bountifully with me, assuredly He has raised me up from season to season, enabled me to speak well of His name, and led me to plead the cause of the poor, and those that are in bonds, naturally and spiritually.

Ninth Month, 2*nd.*—Since writing my last journal, I have had a Minute from my Monthly Meeting, and have been visiting two Essex Monthly Meetings. I have passed through deep exercise and travail of spirit in doing it, but thanks be unto my God, I found help in the needful time, and when least expected, in unmerited mercy, the holy anointing oil was once more freely poured forth upon me, so that I was enabled boldly to declare His doings amongst the people, and to show forth His marvellous works to the children of men. I am to-day likely to set out again—Lord be with us, I pray Thee help us, guide us, strengthen us, uphold us, and comfort us, and enable me to leave all with peace and comfort at home. We are now likely to break up housekeeping here for many months, how and when we shall meet together again in this place, and whether ever— our Lord only knoweth.

4*th.*—I returned yesterday from finishing visiting the Monthly and Quarterly Meetings in Essex. I was carried through the service to my own surprise, I felt so remarkably low, so unworthy, so unfit, and as if I had little or nothing to communicate to them, but I was marvellously helped from Meeting to Meeting; strength so arose with the occasion, that the fear of man was taken from me, and I was enabled to declare Gospel truths boldly. This is to me wonderful, and unbelievers may say what they will, it must be the Lord's doing, and is marvellous in our eyes—how He strengtheneth them that have no might, and helpeth those that have no power. The peace I felt after the services, for some days seemed to flow like a river, for a time covering all my cares and sorrows, so that I might truly say, " There is even here a rest for the people of God." I am sure from my own experience, there is nothing whatever in this life, that brings the same satisfying, heart-consoling feeling. It is to me a powerful internal evidence of the truth of revealed religion, that it is indeed a substantial truth, not a cunningly devised fable. My sceptical doubting mind, has been convinced of the truth of religion, not by the hearing of the ear, but from what I have really handled, and tasted, and known for myself of the word of life, may I not say the power of God unto salvation ? I visited my most dearly beloved brothers and sisters at Earlham, towards whom I feel united by bonds inexpressible. My sweet dear sister, Priscilla, continues very seriously ill, which much melted my heart, but her establishment on Christ the Rock of Ages, consoled us under every sorrow.

The Newgate Association having become established ; and three years having tested the success of the plans pursued there, a Corresponding Committee was formed to answer inquiries and communicate information. Ladies' Associations were established in several places, and in others one or two individuals undertook the work of prison visiting; but some degree of classification, employment, and moral influence, were all that their unassisted endeavours could effect. To carry out Mrs. Fry's views, solitude by night, complete classification, unceasing superintendence, compulsory occupation, regular instruction, and religious influence were necessary to give any chance of reformation of character ; and to obtain these advantages, larger prisons, embracing more extensive districts, and conducted on a system of strict surveillance were required.

But Newgate had proved that something might be effected under the most unfavourable circumstances. As applications for information became more numerous, and her interest in the subject increased, with her husband and her two elder daughters she undertook a journey, which would include visits to many of the most important prisons in England. They left Plashet in September; Mrs. Fry joined her fellow travellers at Nottingham, they having preceded her to visit Oxford and Blenheim. Her method in visiting prisons was much the same in every instance, though of course modified by circumstances. She had generally letters from official persons, or private friends, to the Visiting Magistrates of the prison she desired to see. There she would go, generally accompanied by the officers of the prison, any magistrates who disposed to accompany her, or private individuals interested in it; frequently ladies would be of the party. She would go from yard to yard, from one ward to another, addressing the most minute inquiries to the jailor or turnkey; and calculating the capabilities of the building for the greatest possible degree of improvement. The result of her observations she almost always stated afterwards, in a letter addressed to those of local authority. Besides this, she endeavoured to form a Committee of Ladies, to visit the female prisoners, or she strove to induce at least one or two to undertake this Christian duty. She convinced the judgment of some—she touched the feelings of others—but seldom failed to bring to her purpose such of her own sex as she had selected, from being, in her opinion, suitable for the undertaking.

Mrs. Fry visited the prisons at Nottingham, Lincoln, Wake-field, Doncaster, Sheffield, Leeds, York, Durham, Newcastle, Carlisle, Lancaster, and Liverpool, besides many others; and in the greater number established Ladies' Committees, for visiting the female prisoners. This journey led to important results, from the increased experience and knowledge it gave her, and also tended to the diffusion of both interest and information on the subject of Prison Discipline. But overburthened as she already was with correspondence, the increase of letter writing which resulted from it, was a serious evil, notwithstanding the valuable assistance she received from the Corresponding Committee of the Ladies' Newgate Association.

Southend, Darlington, Ninth Month, 5th.—I left home, after parting with my sweet Chenda, and dearest little ones, last Sixth day week. I had a quiet peaceful journey by myself, and met my beloved husband and children at Nottingham. We have, generally speaking, been sweetly united, and enjoyed our journey so far very much. I had much weighty service in Nottingham, and established a Ladies' Association for visiting prisoners. Numbers followed me, particularly to Meeting; but I was helped through, finding grace sufficient in time of need. I was called away from Sheffield, to attend the funeral of dear little Jonathan Backhouse, who died rather suddenly—a sweet boy, about eight years old; a great and deep trial to his father and mother; but their Lord has been their stay, and I think I may say, we have had to rejoice together in Him, whose tender mercies are over all His works; indeed the more we see, and the more we know, may we not say, " blessing, and glory, and honour, and power, thanksgiving and praise belongeth to God, and the Lamb for ever and ever," and this in times even of deepest sorrow and privation naturally, when helped by the influence of the Spirit.

Swinton, near Hackfall, Yorkshire, 29th.—We are here staying at a beautiful place, with a brother of Lady Harcourt's. He and his wife, and all the family are exceedingly kind to us; they indeed make too much of us. However much such visits may be to the taste, they always bring me into considerable exercise of mind; in the first place, for fear of not faithfully standing my ground in Christian humility, simplicity, and faithfulness; and in the next, from the fear of not making proper use of such providential openings for promoting the blessed cause of truth and righteousness. O dearest Lord! if Thou callest for any thing at my hands, I pray Thee open my way outwardly, and strengthen me spiritually :—

Extract from a letter to her little children.

Kendal, *Tenth Month,* 21*st,* 1820.

We are now nearly three hundred miles from you. It would make me very sorrowful, did I not know that there is every where the same kind Providence to take care of us, and I hope He will permit us to meet again. We much enjoyed the dear boys' company, and had them with us for a little while by the sea-side. I have a large basket of shells, which I mean to divide amongst our collections when I come home, and now I am trying to make a beautiful collection of spars, which I think will delight you. I mean to give you each one piece. How much surprised I think you would have been, to see the country we have lately passed through. Mountains, covered at the top with clouds and some with snow; then such beautiful lakes and rivers, quite different to ours, running over rocks, and making such a noise; some of them with salmon and trout in them; and then the waterfalls, fine streams flowing from the tops of the mountains, over the rocks, that I think we may hear them miles off. How much I should like to show them to you. I hope some of you may see these wonderful and beautiful sights, and that it will lead you to love Him who made them.

Mildred's Court, Eleventh Month, 5th, First day evening, (*alone.*)—We returned from our journey on Sixth day evening, a day or two sooner than we expected, from the very serious illness of my beloved sister Fry, who is rather better now. I might say much of what has passed on this journey; having gone through heights and depths; in some instances great help and deliverance, particularly spiritually, but I am at this time more disposed to examine my heart, and try my ways, and also endeavour rightly to look at and feel my present circumstances. I believe, as far as I know my heart, its first desire continues to be to dwell in conformity to the will of God; my soul thirsteth after Him, and His righteousness. I am at times favoured to get so near in spirit to Christ my Redeemer, as to feel his healing virtue cleansing me from sin; giving rest to my at times weary soul, and enabling me to rejoice in Him, and the power of His salvation, also knowing His holy anointing to be poured forth

so that I feel as if I could do all things through Him who
strengtheneth me ; and am enabled to cast aside fear, and declare
His word with power, and a heart overflowing with His love
towards my fellow-mortals. Then, at other times, I feel much left
to myself, whether the cause is my own transgression, I am not
quite sure; one thing I know, in the secret of my heart, I feel
myself a sinner before my Lord, and I am deeply sensible of
corruption. I do not feel exalted by the approbation of men,
though being greatly cast down by their disapprobation, leads
me to think that I like it. I feel full of love to others, particularly those near me, but I have not towards them that
patience and forbearance that I ought to have, and I think
I am too easily provoked—not sufficiently long-suffering with
their faults. I do not sufficiently remember that the wrath
of man worketh not the righteousness of God. I am not
willing to speak the truth in love to my neighbours, but
too prone to a flattering spirit ; being naturally so afraid of
man, that it even affects my conduct to my servants, &c., &c.
There are many other sins I could state, to which I am very
prone, when not under the immediate influence of grace, but I
desire, and in some measure endeavour, not to give way to
them. Now for my circumstances—my husband and myself
have had a very uniting journey ; I deeply feel the separations that attach to this place, and desire to make pleasing
him one of my first objects. My children are not likely to be
much with me this winter, but they in their various situations
claim much of my mind and time. My household cares at
times a weighty burden, which peculiarly cast me down, and
appear as if they must swallow up much of my powers. It is
what I have no natural taste or power for, and therefore it is so
difficult to me ; however, I believe that I feel it unduly, and I
desire to be enabled to do my duty in it. My public field of
service in the prison cause, affords a wonderful opening for usefulness ; if I had time I should have enough to do without
attending to almost any thing else ; and what is more, the
attention paid to this subject brings so much fruit with it. My
heart is also very full towards the members of my own Society,
and others ; that there appears a large field for service, if I could

attend to it—but I have (though enjoying so much of the unity of my friends) many deep discouragements and perplexities—particularly in our outward circumstances; and some nearest to me not more decidedly showing their allegiance to their Lord! I truly desire to receive counsel and direction as to what to do, and what to leave undone, and in the simplicity of faith, to cast all my care upon my Lord, and then I may trust that I shall be sustained, and led and kept in the way everlasting. Continue, O Lord! I beseech Thee, to help me by Thy Spirit, to guide me by Thy counsel, to sustain me by Thy power, and above all, to keep me by Thy grace, that the enemy of my soul gain no dominion over me.

Letter to two of her Daughters.

Mildred's Court, *Twelfth Month*, 13th, 1820·

It was pleasant to hear of your safe arrival at Earlham, after your journey with your dear uncle. Our London life is so very busy, and one event puts another so much out of mind, that it is difficult to relate exactly how time passes; but I will try to tell you as far as I remember, how we have been engaged. On Seventh day morning, I was much occupied till about one o'clock, in settling accounts. So one more year is passed, and have we wanted any needful thing or indulgence? Afterwards, I visited the eight poor men under sentence of death, their wives, some of their families and friends, and a very affecting time it was. We read together, and appeared to be under the merciful influence of that blessed Spirit, that manifests itself to be from Him who remains to be "Lord God on high, mightier than the noise of many waters." On Third day, I went to Sophia Vansittart, and had a satisfactory interview with her; she is willing to join a Ladies' Committee in Westminster, and to visit Tothill-fields prison, if way can be made in it.

The interest of Elizabeth Fry was not confined to the prisons of her native country. She opened a correspondence with St. Petersburg, through the medium of the late Walter Venning,

Esq., who devoted himself to visiting and instructing the prisoners in that city. The Princess Sophia Mestchersky, and other ladies, had formed themselves into a committee with the most happy success, to visit the women confined in the five prisons of that capital. In a letter written by the Princess to Mr. Venning, on the 2nd of August, 1820, she says :—

"Though I acknowledge myself completely unable to write in English, as you wish me to do, for to shew your friends in England the state of our prisons, such as the Ladies' Committee found it to be in the beginning, and such as it is now, eight months after the establishment of the society ; yet when you told me it would prove a token of our regard and high esteem for Mrs. Fry and her fellow-labourers, I readily comply with your request, and shall try to overcome all the difficulties which ignorance of your language and the novelty of the subject, present to me. Not I alone, Sir, but all the Ladies of our Committee, expressed a hearty wish that something of our public exertions, and of our efforts to follow the example which that lady gives us, might be communicated to her, as a proof that her labours are blessed from above, and that a spark of that love which animates her generous heart, has also reached our distant country, and influenced many hearts with the same Christian feelings for suffering humanithy. May this prove a comfort to her soul, and a new encouragement for her to continue her labours in that large and important field of usefulness, in which she is called to serve our Lord. We will all endeavour to follow her according to the strength and abilities granted us, looking for help and hoping for success to and from Him, from whom we receive every blessing, and whose strength is made perfect in weakness."

From Elizabeth Fry to the late Walter Venning, Esq., of St. Petersburg.

Respected friend,

Though personally unknown to thee, I am confident, from the interest we both feel in one cause, that thou wilt excuse the

liberty I take in writing to thee, to express my heartfelt satisfaction at the interesting and important accounts, thou hast given
my brother Hoare of the proceedings of the Gentlemen and
Ladies' Prison Associations in Petersburg. Most warmly do I
desire their encouragement in this work of charity and utility,
for the more I am acquainted with the subject, and the more
extensive my observation of the effects of prison discipline is,
the more confident I feel of its importance ; and, that although
the work will be gradual, yet through the Divine blessing, its
result will be sure. Not only that many will be stopped in their
career of vice, but some truly turned from their evil ways, and
the security and comfort of the community at large increased,
by our prisons, that have been too generally the nurseries of
vice, and scenes of idleness, filth, and debauchery, being so
arranged and so attended to, that they become schools where the
most reprobate may be instructed in their duty towards their
Creator and their fellow-mortals ; and where the very habits of
their lives may be changed.

It will be found in this, as in every other good work, that
some trials and some discouragement will attend it ; but the
great end in view must induce those engaged in it to persevere,
and use increased diligence to overcome them, doing what we
do to the Lord, and not unto man, and then we shall do it well.

We continue to have much satisfaction in the results of our
efforts in Newgate—good order appears increasingly established,
there is much cleanliness amongst our poor women, and some
very encouraging proofs of reformation in habit, and what is
much more, in heart. This, in a prison so ill arranged, with no
classification, except tried from untried, no good inspection, and
many other great disadvantages, is more than the most zealous
advocates of prison discipline could look for.   We find the same
favourable result follows the labours of other Ladies' Associations in this kingdom ; as I have the pleasure to state that in
England, Scotland, and Ireland, many are now established.   It
may not be unseasonable to observe a few of the regulations
that appear most important in maintaining good and orderly
habits among female prisoners. In the first place, keeping them
as much as possible under the care of women ; more particularly

having a head matron appointed who is not a prisoner; for desirable as we find it to have monitors under the matron from amongst the women, yet there should be one, at least, who they feel has not broken the laws of her country, and who is an impartial representative of the Ladies' Committee, both by night and day. Monitors from amongst themselves should superintend the different classes; daily giving an account of their conduct to the matron or visitors, which should be entered in a class book. The ladies here find much advantage in meeting once a month, to settle any business that may come before them. They then arrange their attendance for the month; generally two visiting every day except on the First day, (Sunday), when other persons attend to them. After reading the Scriptures, if there be time, the ladies look over the register of the conduct of the women, and attend to their particular department; some to the children and adult schools; others to the accounts, clothing, or different sorts of work; for each has her particular business, by which means order is preserved amongst ourselves. The engagement is thus so much lightened, that hardly any of the Newgate Association attend more than one morning in the week. As part of the women's earnings are allowed them, they have a little money to spend; a shop is therefore provided for them, where they may buy things at a fair market price, which prevents imposition and also communication with those who are out of the prison.

I take the liberty of stating these facts, as some of them may be useful to those who have not quite so much experience as we have had. If at any time the ladies at Petersburg would like to correspond with us, it would give us pleasure to render them any assistance in our power, and we should be much interested to hear of their proceedings. We would gladly send them specimens of the work, but our great want of room in Newgate prevents our bringing it to the perfection we otherwise might do.

I lately had the pleasure of seeing the Duchess of Gloucester, who is our Patroness; she desired me to express how much gratified she was with thy account of what you are doing in Petersburg, and her wish that the ladies may be encouraged in their good work.

It is now more than three years since we first began our operations in Newgate, and how encouraging it is, that the experience of every year should increase our hopes and diminish our fears as to the beneficial result of these exertions. Indeed it is wonderful to observe the effects of kindness and care upon some of these poor forlorn creatures—how it tenders their hearts, and makes them susceptible of impression. I am of opinion, from what I have observed, that there are hardly any amongst them so hard, but that they may be subdued by kindness, gentleness, and love, so as very materially to alter their general conduct. Some of the worst prisoners have, after liberation, done great credit to the care taken of them. In two particular instances, young women who had sunk into almost every depravity and vice, upon being liberated conducted themselves with much propriety, as far as we know, and after long illnesses died peacefnl deaths. They were striking instances; through a blessing upon the care taken of them, they in a remarkable manner were turned from Satan unto God, and we humbly trust, through the mercy of Redeeming love, they are received into Glory. Some are settled in service, others we hope are doing well in different situations. We wish it were in our power to attend more to the prisoners upon leaving the prisons, as we think this an important part of the duty of such associations; but in London the numbers are so very great that it is almost out of our power to do it, as we desire, though we endeavour to extend a little care over them.

How delightful it is to hear of the interest that the Emperor, Prince Galitzin, and ladies of such high rank take in the cause of the poor prisoners. May the best of blessings rest upon them, for thus manifesting their care over the destitute of the earth.

We also feel gratefully sensible of their kindness to our friends William Allen and Stephen Grellet. I hope thou wilt let us know before long how you go on. I am much obliged for the book thou kindly sent me; and believe me, with much regard and esteem,

Thy friend,
ELIZABETH FRY.

After the death of Mr. Venning, the correspondence then

commenced was long continued with his brother. From this gentleman the following communication has been received, which is so interesting, that Mrs. Fry's original letters to him being inaccessible, can hardly be considered cause of regret.

" I cheerfully comply with your desire to be furnished with some of the most striking and useful points contained in your late beloved mother's correspondence with myself in Russia, relative to the improvement of the Lunatic Asylum in St. Petersburg. I the more readily engage in this duty, because I am persuaded that its publication may, under the Lord's blessing, prove of great service to many such institutions on the Continent, as well as in Great Britain. I wish indeed that I could give you the letters themselves, but unfortunately they are inaccessible to me, being left behind in Russia, together with other important documents, under the care of a friend who is now unable to find them; I have however recorded the substance of them in my journal, so that I shall be able to describe them without much difficulty.

" I begin by stating that her correspondence was invaluable as regarded the treatment and management of both prisoners and insane persons. It was the fruit of her own rich practical experience communicated with touching simplicity, and it produced lasting benefits to those institutions in Russia. In 1827, I informed your dear mother, that I had presented to the Emperor Nicholas, a statement of the defects of the Government Lunatic Asylum, which could only be compared to our own Old Bedlam in London, fifty years since, and that the Dowager Empress had sent for me to the winter palace, when she most kindly, and I may say joyfully, informed me that she and her august son, the Emperor, had visited together this abode of misery, and were convinced of the necessity not only of having a new building, but also of a complete reform in the management of the insane; and, further, that the Emperor had requested her to take it under her own care, and to appoint me the governor of it. I must observe that in the meantime the old asylum was immediately improved, as much as the building allowed, for the introduction of your dear mother's admirable system. Shortly after, I had the pleasure of accompanying the Empress to examine a palace-like house, (Prince Sherbatoff's,) having above two miles of garden, and a fine stream of water running through the grounds, only five miles from St. Petersburg. The next day an order was given to purchase it. I was permitted to send the plan of this immense building to your dear mother for her inspection, and hints for improvement. Two extensive wings were recommended, and subsequently added, for dormitories. The wings cost about £15,000., and in addition to this sum from the government, the Emperor, who was always ready to promote the cause of benevolence, gave himself £3,000 for cast-iron window frames recommended by your dear mother; as the clumsy iron bars which had been used in the old Institution, had induced many a poor inmate, when looking at them, to say with a sigh, ' Sir, prison ! prison !' Your dear mother also strongly recommended, that all except the violent lunatics should dine together at a table covered with a cloth, and furnished with plates and spoons.

"The former method of serving out the food was most disgusting. This new plan delighted the Empress, and I soon received an order to meet her at the Asylum. On her arrival, she requested that a table should be covered, and then desired me to go round and invite the inmates to come and dine, sixteen came immediately and sat down; the Empress approached the table, and ordered one of the upper servants to sit at the head of it, and to ask a blessing; when he rose to do this, they all stood up: the soup with small pieces of meat was then regularly served; and as soon as dinner was finished, they all rose up spontaneously, and thanked the Empress for her motherly kindness. I saw the kind Empress was deeply moved, and turning to me she said, ' Mon Cher, this is one of the happiest days of my life.' The next day, the number increased at table, and so it continued increasing. After your dear mother's return from Ireland, where she had been visiting, among other Institutions, the Lunatic Asylums, she wrote me a letter on the great importance of supplying the lunatics with the Scriptures. This letter deserved to be written in letters of gold, I sent it to the Imperial Family, it excited the most pleasing feelings, and marked approbation. The Court Physician, His Excellency Dr. Richl, a most enlight-

ened and devoted philanthropist, came to me for a copy of it.
It removed all the difficulty there had been, respecting the
giving the Holy Scriptures to the inmates.   I was therefore permitted to furnish them with copies, in their various languages.
It may be useful to state the result of this measure, which was
considered by some, to be a wild and dangerous proceeding; I soon
found groups collected together, listening patiently and quietly
to one of their number reading the New Testament.   Instead of
disturbing their minds, it soothed and delighted them.   I have
witnessed a poor lunatic, a Frenchman, during an interval of
returning reason, reading in his bed-room, the New Testament,
with tears running down his cheeks ; also a Russian priest, a
lunatic, collect a number together, while he read to them the
Word of God.

" On one occasion, I witnessed a most interesting scene, on
entering the Institution, I found a young woman dying, her eyes
were closed, and she was apparently breathing her last breath, I
ordered one of the servants of the Institution, to read very loud
to her, that verse, ' For God so loved the world, that he gave
His only begotten Son, that whosoever believeth in Him should
not perish, but have everlasting life.' Dr. K—— observed, ' Sir,
she is almost dead, and it is useless.' On my urging its being done,
Lo ! to the astonishment of all present, she opened her eyes, and
smiled, I said, ' Is it sweet, my dear ?' she nodded assent. ' Shall
it be read to you again ?' a smile and nod of the head followed.
She evidently possessed her reason at that moment, and who can
trace or limit the operations of the Holy Spirit, on the reading
of God's own word even in her circumstances ?

" When I received a letter from your mother, I always wrote it
out in French, and presented it in that language to the Empress,
and when she had read it, it was very encouraging to see with
what alacrity she ordered one of her secretaries to translate it
into Russian, and then deliver it to me to be conveyed to
the Asylum, and entered into the journal there for immediate
adoption. I remember, on one occasion, taking a list of rules, at
least fourteen in number, and the same day they were confirmed
by the Empress ; and these rules introduced the following important arrangements, viz. : the treating the inmates, as far as

possible, as sane persons, both in conversation and manners towards them—to allow them as much liberty as possible—to engage them daily to take exercise in the open air—to allow them to wear their own clothes, and no uniform prison-dress— also to break up the inhuman system of permitting the pro- miscuous idle curiosity of the public, so that no one was allowed to see them without permission ; a room on entering the Asylum was prepared for one at a time, on certain days to see their relations.   The old cruel system drew forth many angry expres- sions from the poor lunatics, ' Are we then wild beasts to be gazed at ?'

"The Empress made a present to the Institution of a piano- forte, it had also a hand organ, which pleased exceedingly the poor inmates ; and on one occasion, the Empress, on entering the Asylum, observed that the inmates appeared unusually dull, when she called them near, and played herself on the hand organ an enlivening tune.   Another important rule of your mother's was, most strictly to fulfil whatever you promise to any of the inmates, and above all, to exercise patience, gentleness, kindness and love, towards them ; therefore, to be exceedingly careful as to the character of the keepers you appoint.   These are some of the pleasing results of your mother's work.   The Dowager Empress on one occasion, conversing about your mother, said, ' How much I should like to see that excellent woman Madame Fry in Russia,' and often did I indulge that wish, and what a meeting it would have been between two such devoted philanthropists as your mother and the Dowager Empress, who was daily devoting her time and fortune to doing good, daily visiting in person the various institutions of her own forming, and who once observed to me, ' We must work while we can, the time is short.'   In the second volume of the life of that beloved and devoted phi- lanthropist, William Allen, is the lovely character of this extraordinary Princess truly delineated, she possessed the rare secrets of doing acts of love, with love.   Although the Empress was in her sixty-ninth year, I had the felicity of accompanying her in no less than eleven of her personal visits to the Lunatic Asylum, say, from the 29th of February, to the 11th of October, 1828.   On the 24th of October, thirteen days after, she died, to the deep-felt regret of the whole empire. Rozoff, a young lunatic, as soon as he heard it, burst into tears ; she would visit each lunatic when bodily afflicted. and send an easy chair for one, and nicely dressed meat for others, and weekly send from the Palace, Sauterne wine, coffee, tea, sugar, and fruit for their use.

" Among the many striking features in your mother's correspondence, her love to the word of God, and her desire for its general circulation, were very apparent; and evidently that sacred Book was the Fountain whence she herself derived all that strength and grace to carry on her work of faith and labour of love which her Divine Master so richly blessed. As the result of my own observation and experience in foreign countries, I can fully bear witness, relative to very many deeply interesting instances of spiritual good attendant on the free distribution of that inspired word ; nor shall I ever forget the solemn charge made by his late Highness Prince Charles Lieven, to the Metropolitan of the Greek Church Seraphin, at the last meeting of the Russian Bible Society, held at the St. Alexander's Monastery in St. Petersburgh. Dr. Paterson, myself, and two or three other members were present, seated on one side of the table, and opposite the dignitaries of the Church, when, after much discussion, the pious Prince said most seriously to the Metropolitan, ' How will you be able to answer at the day of judgment, for the awful conduct of impeding the free circulation of the Scriptures to the people ?' and further observed, that there never was a Tzar of Russia, who forbad the Bible to the people ; we all perceived that His Eminence was deeply affected. I can most fully corroborate this statement in reference to the Emperors Alexander and Nicholas, both of whom were desirous that the Bible should be freely circulated.

" In December, 1827, when accompanying the Emperor Nicholas through the New Litoffsky Prison, he not only was well pleased in finding every cell fully supplied with the Scriptures, the rich result of his having confirmed the late Emperor Alexander's orders, to give the Scriptures gratis to all the prisoners ; but on seeing some Jews in the prison, he said to me, ' I hope you also furnish these poor people with them, that they may become Christians, I pity them.' I witnessed a most touching scene, on the Emperor's entering the Debtor's Room, three old venerable grey-headed men feel on their knees, and cried, ' Father, have mercy on us;' the Emperor, stretched out his hand in the peculiar grandeur of his manner, and said, ' Rise, all your debts are paid, you are at this moment free; without knowing the amount of the debts, one of which was considerable. I hope this feeble attempt to detail a little of your dear mother's useful work, may be acceptable, leaving you to make what use of it you may think proper.

" I remain, my dear friends,

" Yours most sincerely,

" JOHN VENNING.

" Surrey House, Norwich, *March*, 1847."

St. Petersburg was not the only continental city, with which communication on the subject of ladies visiting prisoners had now been opened.

At Turin, La Marquise de Barol née Colbert was assiduously occupied in this important work. This lady was a Roman Catholic, and had entered upon it, from a sense of duty. The Rev. Francis Cunningham, when travelling through that place, had obtained permission to see the prison, had there become acquainted with her, and opened a correspondence for her with his sister-in-law Mrs. Fry, which was maintained for many years. Letters were also received from Amsterdam, where those interested in the reformation of prisoners, were endeavouring to form a Prison Discipline Society, and Committees to visit the prisoners.

Mildred's Court, First Month, 1st, 1821.—Having poured forth my soul in prayer, and having exhorted my household to live in the love and fear of the Lord, I have obtained some relief upon entering a new year, and finishing another. I opened my Bible at these words, so consonant with the feelings of my heart, I quote them here, " Hear my prayer, and be merciful unto thine inheritance; turn our sorrow into joy, that we may live, O Lord, and praise Thy name."

There are few things more sad than to enter a new year with coming sorrow on the heart, to see an affliction that appears inevitable casting its dark shadow on the future. From 1792, the year of Mrs. Gurney's death, her daughters had continued an unbroken band; but the time was approaching when a breach was to be made amongst them. Priscilla, the youngest of the seven sisters, had been long in declining health, and the rapid increase of consumptive symptoms now foreboded that "the silver cord was to be loosed, and the bowl be broken at the cistern." To Mrs. Fry's nature, the loss of those she loved was peculiarly sorrowful. Had her faith not been proportionably strong, she could hardly have endured the trial. Her sister, Priscilla, having, like herself, become a Friend from conviction, and like herself being involved in the solemn and arduous calling of the ministry, had added another link to their close natural tie; one probably which from their disparity in years, would hardly have existed as it did, but for this circumstance.

Priscilla Gurney was gifted with a singular finish and completeness of character, very gentle, yet very bright, effective, and accurate in all that she undertook; she possessed fine sense, with exquisite taste and tact, and appreciation of the beautiful; she had assiduously cultivated her intellectual powers; she was gifted in the use of the pencil, and excelled in that graceful and feminine but rare accomplishment, skill in useful needle-work. In person she was slight, and rather below the middle stature, without regular beauty she was singularly pleasing, and refined in countenance; with a bright complexion and sunny brown hair. Beautifully descriptive are some lines written by a young lady in Ireland, upon becoming acquainted with her, when she visited that island in the character of a minister among Friends.

" Did such a mind beam thro' a homely face,
Beauty were not required to lend a grace,
Did such a face veil an unworthy mind,
Our partial eyes would be to error blind,
Sweet minist'ring spirit, with delight we see,
Inward and outward graces, joined in thee!"

As the Earlham family were led into different dispensations in religion, she believed that Quakerism was the appointed one for herself, and gradually adopting their views and opinions, she became a decided Friend. This was not done hastily ; nor did it in the least interfere with the strong bond which bound her to those of her family who had taken a different course ; and yet it is easy to understand, especially after she became a minister, what a deep mutual interest must have subsisted between her and her sister Elizabeth Fry. Earlham was her residence with her other unmarried sisters and brothers; nor did it cease to be their home, at the marriage of their brother, Joseph John Gurney, in 1817. His adoption of the principles of Friends had been a great satisfaction and support to her, in her own course. In July, 1814, she thus writes to her sister Elizabeth Fry.

" Earlham.

" I am very comfortably settled again, and feel it a privilege to be at this sweet home. We are quite a cheerful, and I may say often a happy party. Catherine has been such a support and help to us, that I very much feel the comfortable effect of having her again at the head of the family, I sometimes have secretly my low times to pass through, but neither expect nor wish it to be otherwise, and when there is much to feel, I fully believe it is generally best ' not to appear unto men to fast.' Our dearest brother Joseph is truly a strength and help to me."

And again in the autumn of the same year.

"Earlham, *Fourth day*.
" My dearest Betsy,

" As I have many hours to myself just now, I think I may treat myself with writing a little to thee. Except a cough, I am

6

quite well again, and indeed this has been a very slight attack of
my old complaint, not sufficient to make confinement necessary,
although prudent. It is like having my wings clipt once more,
and gives a check to the objects which I had in view, but I
think (at least I hope) I have felt this beneficial; every such
check ought to teach us submission, and to make us more willing
to be, not what we should like or choose, but what is best for us
to be. There are few lessons so hard for me to learn as to be
nothing—this has been a little my experience the last few days,
that of living as a nothing to anybody, and as very poor in myself;
but I believe this is peculiarly good for me, for such is our situation here, we have so many excitements, that I may confess to
thee, my dearest Betsy, that a true resignation to the cross, and
to this state of nothingness in myself is at times very hard to
my nature to attain—and yet how needful it is to our safe standing! It is sometimes my earnest desire to be preserved in a
willing and humble frame of mind, willing to walk in the way of
the cross, in the path of self-denial.

" I am sometimes almost surprised at myself, that I do not more
often write intimately to thee; but, perhaps I am increasingly,
and sometimes too much inclined to keep silence, and meditate
on the various dispensations of Providence towards us. I feel
how little there is to say, and I hope we may each more and more
simply desire that His will may be done by us, and in us.

" Our intercourse with some of the clergy lately has been very
interesting. In this I have had my share, and I really hope I
have derived benefit from it; but of course there are limitations
with me, and I often feel close exercise and even conflict of mind,
which is little known to others. It is sometimes difficult to
abstain from what appears such a source of comfort and enjoyment to them; but I have often been permitted to feel a sweet
and encouraging degree of unity with those not entirely agreeing
with me, and no real peace but in endeavouring to keep stedfast
to that way which has appeared right for me. I may write
freely to thee, because we can but feel together, and can pretty
well understand one another, and our particular situation
amongst the different members of the family. Upon the whole,
I have felt more encouragement than any thing else, as to the

ultimate good of our treading in rather different paths ; a sweet hope often prevails that all may work together for our good. In reviewing the last two years of my life, a period in many ways so important to me; I am truly glad that I have been at home, and that my present path has been brought to so close a test as it has. I may say that it is often marvellous to me how the way has been made for me, and how obstructions have been removed. I do not know how it may be with thee, but I have felt this *calling* (for such, I think, we cannot but feel it,) increasingly interesting to me, and increasingly an engagement of deep feeling.

" Thy truly affectionate sister,
" P. GURNEY."

From the Isle of Wight, where she had passed the winter preceding, on account of her declining health, she wrote, in 1820 :—

"Thou hast been much in my thoughts lately, my beloved sister, and I can hardly describe to thee, the flow of love and of deep interest which sometimes arises towards thee, there is a certain understanding which I feel with thee, that I can hardly feel in the same way with any other mortal, except, perhaps, it may be with our dearest brother Joseph. We three do, I believe, intimately understand one another's paths—we know one another's conflicts—we have partaken in the same depths—we have been mercifully permitted, according to our different measures (for I feel my measure small indeed compared with thine), to partake of the same kind of spiritual consolations, and of the same deliverance from depths into heights. What a support, and stay, and refreshment, in short, what a mother hast thou been to us both ! I must confess my heart often turns towards thee with joy and with thankfulness, though thy path has been strewed with many crosses and many afflictions, yet so in proportion has I firmly believe been the victory, which has been given thee through Christ our Saviour, to the great comfort and encouragement of many, as well as to thy own present, and may we not humbly trust, eternal peace and salvation! how fervently do I desire, that the blessing which has so eminently attended thee, may be in all things thy crown, thy rejoicing—that it may prosper thee in all thy ways!"

The summer of that year, Priscilla Gurney passed at Earlham. As the autumn advanced, she was removed to Cromer Hall, then the abode of her brother-in-law, Mr. Buxton ; and with him, and her sister, Mrs. Buxton, she passed the few remaining months of her life, nursed, with the most assiduous care, by her sister Rachel, who had been devoted to her through the latter stages of her prolonged decline.

Cromer Hall, Second Month, 9th.—Here I am, with my dear brother Samuel Gurney, come to visit our dearest sister Priscilla in her declining state. The sweet and peaceful state of her soul is cause for much thankfulness and rejoicing, but the low valley is my own abiding place ; and my desire for myself and mine, I may say, my prayer is, O dearest Lord ! give us not over to the will of our enemies. My feeling for my dearest brothers and sisters is ; in the first place, thanksgiving, particularly for their spiritual state ; and secondly, desire that grace may be found sufficient for them, and that no snare of the enemy, however gilded by apparent holiness, may ever hurt or ensnare them ; and for my dearest sister Priscilla,—O Lord ! Thou who hast been with her, be with her to the end, and in Thine own time burst all her bonds asunder and bring her into the abundant and glorious liberty of Thy children. And also permit Thy unworthy child, through all her trials to acknowledge how truly marvellously Thou hast provided for her, and abundantly loaded her with benefits. Cause us, dearest Lord, to hear, to feel, and to acknowledge Thy loving kindness and Thy tender mercies not only now but for ever. Amen.

Cromer Hall, Third Month, 11th, First day.—Dearest Priscilla said to this effect, that the experience of her illness had greatly confirmed and deepened her in the foundation and principles of Friends, more particularly as it respected the ministry ; though she most truly found her boundaries enlarged towards all ; and upon my saying thou feelest all one in Christ, "yes," she said, "just so." She expressed how entirely she felt her dependence on the Lord alone, and how little she felt the want of outward ministry, though what came in the life was refreshing and sweet. She yesterday expressed her love for silence, how she found it tended to strengthen body as well as soul, and it was one reason she wished to be alone at night. She also expressed this morning, great desire for the Friends of the family, that they should hold fast their principles.

Extracts of a letter to her daughter Richenda :—

Cromer, Third Month, 6th.

Thy dearest aunt Priscilla continues much the same, and I propose staying here for the present. Now dear, I have an afflicting peace of news for thee ; poor Thomas P—— died last First day ; what a family he has left ! I find thy aunt Eliza is much worse. So it is—one is taken and another left. May we who are left make use of our remaining time. Thy sweet aunt Priscilla asked for thee ; she is so weak she can hardly speak. I hear most encouraging accounts of thy going on ; what a comfort for thy poor mother, now in the time of her sorrow. Continue, my beloved child, to try to please thy Heavenly Father, and then as thou " grows in stature, thou wilt grow in wisdom, and in favour with God and man."

Cromer Hall, Third Month, 25th, 1821.

My dear Husband and Rachel,

About nine o'clock this morning the scene closed, and our most tenderly beloved sister went to sleep in Jesus. The conflict of death was long upon her ; I think it may be said from Third or Fourth day, to this morning. She has been sensible, evidently so, till late last evening, and her calm, quiet and patient state continued. I think every day her conflict diminished, she had nearly lost the power of speech ; but when we were all collected round her last evening, about nine, she was heard by several to say, " Farewell, Farewell," several times. Some one heard her add, " My love is with you," and the last

c c 2

thing we could hear was, " O Lord !"   In the morning, she appeared very full of love—put out her hand to several of us—showed much pleasure in your uncle Buxton's being here, and tried to speak to him, but could not be understood—expressed her wish for reading, and from her feeling of love and fondness for the chapter and some signs, we believed she meant the thirteenth of 1 Corinthians, and we had a very sweet animating time together, and afterwards our dear brother Fowell spoke very sweetly to her ; and besides the Bible, she appeared to have some satisfaction in hearing other books read, as it has been her habit during her illness, just like mine when ill. She appeared to have finished her work, and have nothing to do but to die ; her sweet spirit was quite at liberty to pass away the time in reading, and having I believe no headache, she could bear it, though she confined it to religious books, yet many of these were of an interesting nature ; her hymns* interested her much—she liked Samuel Scott's Diary—Piety Promoted—Accounts of the Missions—Watts and How—and many other books of that description. I write thus particularly, because I thought you would wish to hear. I think her object in reading was gentle amusement, and at times edification—she was very particular not to read the Bible except she felt herself in rather a lively state. We were all by her when her prepared spirit left the body, and a sweet time it was ; no struggle. After commending her to her Lord, and for His name's sake into glory, my brother Joseph quoted these words—

> " One gentle sigh the fetters breaks,
> We scarce can say they're gone,
> Before the willing spirit takes
> Its station near the throne."

Catherine expressed her firm belief that she was one of the blessed who died in the Lord.

Rachel after a time, uttered a few words in thanksgiving for her, and prayer for us who remain.

Thy letter, my dearest Rachel, gave me much satisfaction, and

---

* Selection of Hymns, by Priscilla Gurney.

my opinion is, though death loses its sting of sin to the righteous, yet they equally, or very nearly so, have the natural conflict to pass through; and death certainly is a very great conflict, generally speaking; but it has struck me again and again, what this would have been to a sensitive mind, feeling at the same time the sense of condemnation and the sting of sin; but my beloved child, there is much in thy remarks, and I think the death of the righteous is often represented as too easy, for human nature is the same in all, and how much did our blessed Lord go through who took upon Himself our nature. Ah! my child, I think of thee and thy birth-day. May the Lord be with thee in it, opening thy eyes to behold the beauty of holiness, and enlarging thy heart by His own power to make thee willing " to lay aside every weight and the sin that may so easily beset thee, and to run with patience the race that is set before thee, looking to Jesus the Author and Finisher of our faith."

In much near and dear love farewell,

E. FRY.

A near connexion and dear friend of the family, at the request of Mrs. Fry, wrote to one of her daughters, with some additional particulars of the closing scene.

" I at night retired to North Repps, so that I was not much of a burden to any, and the comfort it was to partake with them, and to be in the room with their most precious charge, I can never forget, or express. Thursday and Friday were not, that I recollect, particularly striking days, though so affecting; it was like being in the room with a peaceful, new-born babe—scarce a sound was heard, and little of what this world could give needed. The critical seasons of nursing over, a little liquid at intervals most gently and abstemiously administered, was all her tender state could bear—your mother was the most successful in getting that down—in compliance with her wishes, she took it to the last, even after her own mind had ceased to feel the duty or necessity of trying to do so; the light of a small fire was all that was admitted on her side of the room; the window was closely

shaded, so that the reader, (and she was continually read to,)
more often helped herself by fire light than from any aperture
in the foldings of the window curtains; your uncles Francis
Cunningham and Joseph John Gurney, and your aunt Catherine,
as I understood, scarcely ever entered without her pointing to the
reading seat, she seemed always to expect that they would have
a Bible in their hands, and begin; they considered that she was
soothed by reading, to the last night of her existence here: that,
of course those alone could know, who were in the deepest
sympathy with her, and who hung over her with devotedness of
heart beyond my power of describing.

   "I never can lose sight of that group, the cluster of sisters,
the perfect stillness, the sacred and assured peace,—not a sob
arrested the ear, but exquisite tenderness pervaded the whole:
your mother prayed, returned thanks to the Saviour, and committed her, and then the family, fervently and unreservedly into
His care. Joseph prayed in the same strain—a pause, and
Fowell wished that text to be repeated to her, ' When Thou
passest through the waters I will be with thee, and through the
rivers they shall not overflow thee, &c., for I am the Lord thy God
the Holy One of Israel, thy Saviour;' your mother also repeated
some of the most animating promises of God concerning the
blessedness of a future state. ' Thou canst not conceive my love,
the joys that will soon be thine, the glories that are prepared for
thee; be encouraged to bear meekly the few remaining feelings
of weakness and infirmity. Thy affliction will last but a moment
longer, and endless happiness is in store for thee, and we will
pray to the Saviour in his mercy to prepare us to follow thee,
not to separate us long, but speedily to receive us all, and reunite
us in His Kingdom.' "

   First day, Fourth Month, 14*th.*—I returned from Norfolk
—my second visit, after being from home about six weeks,
where I had attended my much-loved sister to the last, almost
constantly devoted to her in the day, for four weeks before her
death, and then staying her funeral, &c. For the first fortnight,
tenderly as I felt for my beloved sister's sufferings, yet there
was so much sweetness in being with her, such inexpressible

unity with her spirit in its redeemed state, that it was not a
distressing time. I was also greatly favoured with excellent
health, as the sea air appeared to revive me so much; but the
last fortnight, my health sunk a good deal, and my beloved
sister's great reduction, with, no doubt, some suffering, was almost
too much for me; still I may acknowledge, that rather marvellously, every day help, strength, and sufficient consolation
have been granted. I was certainly impatient at my darling
sister being so long passing through the valley of the shadow
of death; but how did I perceive my folly when I saw how
gently she was led through it, and how I might observe the kind
hand of Providence making her way naturally and spiritually;
and I do believe, deeply as we felt for her, it was to herself
greatly sweetened, and a renewed cause for us to return thanks
on her account.

Mrs. Fry's return from Norfolk was shortly followed by new
and very different interests to those which had occupied her by
the death-bed of her sister. The subject of Capital Punishments had become one of increasingly general interest and discussion, opinions differed and opposing views were entertained;
but it was no longer looked upon with indifference.

The Society " for the Improvement of Prison Discipline, and
Reformation of Juvenile Offenders" was also actively at work.
Many persons of influence had joined it, and zealously supported the plans of the committee. Mrs. Fry's experience at
Newgate was considered as an exemplification of the effects of
moral discipline and control, combined with Christian kindness.
She believed it to be a positive duty to use the influence this
circumstance gave her, to the utmost of her power, and to avail
herself of every opportunity for communicating the results of
her personal observation. Nor was her attention confined to this
branch of the subject; she was too keen an observer not to know,
that her experiment, though so successful, could not be universally tried, and that nothing short of a complete change in the

spirit and practice of the criminal legislation of the country, carried on by systematic government regulation, could effect permanent and general good. She considered that the religion we profess to obey; that the humanity implanted even in the natural heart of man, should induce individuals suited for the office, to visit prisons, hospitals, and other public institutions; although this was to her mind a matter wholly independent of their construction and arrangement. In a letter on the subject of female convict ships, in which she urges the necessity of certain measures being adopted by government, she adds :—

"I am anxious that a few things which would greatly tend to the order and reformation of these poor women, and protect their little remaining virtue, should become established practices, authorized by government, and not dependent upon a few individuals, whose life and health, and every thing else, are so uncertain."

Few persons ever possessed so little speculativeness of character, combined with such extraordinary quickness of perception as Mrs. Fry. She perceived, that whereas the greater part of persons had hitherto been content to take no heed of passing circumstances, and to allow abuses to continue, scarcely recognizing their existence, the time was come, when the rights of humanity would make themselves heard. Men of reflection had begun to investigate the causes, and the probable results, of the facts around them. Enormous errors were committed, incalculable mistakes made, as must ever be the case, when finite man leans to his own finite understanding; yet the good preponderated; and where philosophy had learned in the school of Christ, undeniable truths were proclaimed, and peace and good will extended to mankind.

Mrs. Fry perceived that light had dawned, she was persuaded that it could never be again extinguished; but she saw, that to direct the mental energies of the people aright, general education, combined with scriptural instruction, and the unlimited circulation of the Holy Bible were absolutely requisite. She also saw a growing sympathy between all ranks and conditions of men, which, while it trenched not on the " powers that be," nor touched that beautiful order providentially arranged in their diverse ranks and positions, yet breathed a spirit of tenderness and consideration towards those in the humbler sphere, of respect and fitting reverence towards those in the higher. She never troubled herself with politics; all were her "kind friends," who listened to her representations, or supported measures, tending, as she believed, to the increase of religion and morality. She used to mention Dr. Porteus Bishop of London, having expressed the opinion that judging from the existing aspect of things, the time was not far off when men would rank themselves more and more on either side of the great arena of life—that the mass of mankind who had looked on, and scarcely heeded the battle would diminish in number; that though many might be mistaken, and, and with the best intentions support the wrong, whilst others would uphold the right from selfish or worldly motives ; yet that indifference would cease to be the prevailing and oppressing sin, and a lively participation in feeling if not in fact, with the subjects of the day would become general. Mrs. Fry would often remark the truth of these observations as years passed on ; and great measures were mooted, struggled for, and at last obtained.

On the 23rd of May, Sir James Mackintosh brought forward his motion, " for mitigating the severity of punishment in certain cases of forgery, and the crimes connected therewith." Sir Samuel Romilly had with the exception of Lord Nugent, and a very few others, stood almost unsupported in the Lower House ; now, the contest had become nearly equal, and Sir James Mackintosh's Bill was lost by a very small majority. It was on this occasion, that Mr. Buxton delivered his admirable speech upon Capital Punishment. Many had gone that night, doubtful as to the expediency of the measure proposed, but were convinced by Mr. Buxton's arguments, based as they were upon incontrovertible facts, varied calculations, and unquestionable evidence. Some had taken their seats, indifferent as to the question at issue; his warm appeal to their humanity, and the responsibility of legislating for the lives of thousands, without having weighed the merits of the case, or considered the practical effects of punishment, aroused them from their apathy ; others from a dread of change, and a certain sort of adherence to the opinions of a party, unconnected with the merit or demerits of the opinions themselves, were startled by the delicate irony, with which he shewed the impracticability of the laws, and the strange devices resorted to, to evade their literal fulfilment. Excellently did he generalize the subject, when he said, " There is no one who will deny, that the laws of the land ought to be congenial with the feelings of the people. There was a time, we may suppose, in which this happy sympathy prevailed. But that period is long passed. During the last century, they have each fled from this point of concurrence ; the law in its enactments, and the people, in the tenor of their feelings. The people have made enormous strides in all that tends to civilize and soften mankind, while the laws have contracted a ferocity, which did not belong to them in the most savage part of our history, and to such extremes of distance have they proceeded, that I do believe there never was a law so harsh as British law, or so merciful and humane a people as the British people. And yet, to this mild and merciful people, is left the execution of that rigid and cruel law!"

Although the 23rd of May brought a defeat, it was a defeat so nearly approaching to victory, as to afford Mrs. Fry heartfelt satisfaction. She had again cause to rejoice, when early in June, she witnessed the Freemasons' Hall filled on occasion of the Meeting for the Improvement of Prison Discipline, and the Reformation of Juvenile Offenders. The *Times* of the 4th of June, gives an account of the Meeting. She was mentioned by many of the speakers in terms of high eulogium, and was loudly applauded, when she quitted the Hall; but not an allusion to this is made in her journal, or in any letters that have been found.

The Duke of Gloucester presided, supported by Lord John Russell, Lord Stanley (Earl of Derby), Lord Belgrave, (Marquis of Westminster), Lord Calthorpe, the Bishop of Gloucester (Ryder), Sir James Mackintosh, Sir Thomas Baring, and many other inviduals of rank and talent. Nobly was the cause advocated which had brought them together. Lord John Russell was almost prophetic in expectation, when he concluded a short but brilliant speech by expressing his belief, that our country was about to " become distinguished for triumphs, the effect of which should be to save, and not to destroy ;" and that "instead of laying waste the provinces of our enemies, we might begin now to reap a more solid glory in the reform of abuses at home, and in spreading happiness through millions of our own population."

CHAPTER XII.

THE death of Mrs. Fry's sister Priscilla Gurney, was followed by another domestic interest, the marriage of one of her daughters, a circumstance which excited all her maternal feelings. The connexion was one in which she would cordially have rejoiced, had she not known that it would separate her child from that body of Christians to which she was herself so closely united. The rule of the discipline amongst the Society of Friends is, to disunite from membership those who marry persons not members of the Society. It is very strictly enforced, and to promote such connexions is looked upon as an act of delinquency on the part of parents or guardians.

Plashet, Seventh Month, 5th, 1821.—I have been favoured to return home in peace, and what is more, with the very consoling hope and belief that I have done right in leaving Rachel at Runcton, to judge for herself in this most important affair; I cannot help thinking that, in tender mercy, a kind Providence has permitted it, and that it will be for good, should it take place. I have indeed had some awful plunges, and deep wadings about it, but have never in any of them believed it right to alter our determination respecting our dear child. I have certainly felt encouraged by the help of a better than myself, which has appeared peculiarly near, enabling me remarkably to commit the cause to Him ; as if very near access was granted to Himself

7

even the Fountain of all our sure mercies. And when most cast down, under the inexpressible fear that I was giving her up too soon ; or that I should get involved by it, so as to act either inconsistently with my high religious profession, or be thought to do so by others, and so to hurt my services in the church; even at these times, I have felt a power within me, like oil upon the waters, quieting every storm, consoling and helping me. In the low, the very low state I have been brought into, with an acute sense of the reproach of man, so that I almost expected my mouth would have been shut in Meetings, I have been encouraged and naturally surprised to find that I have seldom known the power of the Spirit more near to help, and to be unto me tongue and utterance, wisdom and power. May it be a lesson to all, not too much to judge others for acting a little out of the usual course.

I can hardly express the peace, comfort, and sense of blessing I have had this day. Lord, continue to be very near unto thy unworthy servant, and to her children, and if this dear friend be united to her family, let him be unto her as a son and brother in Thee, O Lord ! and as a true helper amongst us.

Plashet, 7th.—Something of a sweet hope and strong confidence, that however for a season I may be deeply tried, and not see. the fruit I desire produced, yet that I can, and may adopt these words, " Although the fig-tree shall not blossom, neither fruit be in the vines, the labour of the olive shall fail, and the fields shall yield no meat ; the flock shall be cut off from the fold, and there shall be no herd in the stalls : yet I will rejoice in the Lord, I will joy in the God of my salvation."—" The Lord God is my strength, and He will make my feet like hind's feet, and cause me to ride upon mine high places." Oh, how unspeakably precious to know the Lord to be our helper, our strength and our comforter ; unworthy as I am of it, I have found it to be peculiarly the case in my late anxiety. Surely there are times when we are enabled experimentally to acknowledge that Christ is to be felt in us, as a well of water springing up unto everlasting life. How marvellous is the power and principle of God's salvation in the soul of man !

Plashet, Eighth Month, 4th.—I have lately been hopeful and tranquil about my beloved child ; trusting that all will end well. I have been much devoted to my other children. I feel this rest cause for much thankfulness, but from one cause and another, I have for the last few months gone through so much that I find my general health shaken. I am not so strong, I think, as I used to be ; at times the prospect of going down the hill of life is awful, and the natural powers decaying, still it is accompanied by a sweet hope, that my last days may be my best days, and perhaps my brightest days, that, however, I must leave, only may I be ready to live or to die. Better prepared, if I live, to live more entirely to God; and if I die, to die in the Lord. Lord, grant that it may be so with me, and that those most near and dear to me, may be partakers also of the joys, glories, and power of Thy salvation. Amen.

Plashet, 29*th.*—My beloved daughter Rachel, was married last Fifth day, the 23rd, at Runcton, by my brother-in-law, Francis Cunningham. Great as the trial certainly has been, and is, to my natural feelings of her leaving the Society of Friends, yet I am of opinion that whatever she may eventually settle into, we have done right in not preventing this connexion; for my secret belief is, that it is for good, and a providential opening for her ; though I am fully alive to the pains and disadvantages attending her marrying out of the Society of Friends.

30*th.*—" For we are made partakers with Christ if we hold the beginning of our confidence stedfast unto the end." Lord, grant that Thy unworthy child hold fast her confidence stedfast unto the end, and not only so, but hold fast the profession of her faith without wavering; and if, as some fear for her, she has not stood her ground in her conduct in her child's marriage, make it manifest, that she never may act so again. And so, dearest Lord, take Thine own work into Thine own hands, with this beloved child, that as Thou turnest the stream in its course, so turn this event into good and into blessing to her and to us ; as we have desired to do right in Thy sight respecting it, and have early committed the cause to Thy guidance and to Thy disposal, Oh, gracious Lord, protect as well as bless us and them in it.

Plashet, Ninth Month, 3*rd.*—I doubt not but that my late

tendency to depression of spirits is caused not only by the sorrow which I certainly feel, and great disappointment, from a child not keeping to the principles that I have brought her up in, and also from the deep sense I have of their intrinsic value ; but, moreover, that I have to bear my conduct in the affair being misconstrued by others. I have certainly met with much kindness, great love and sympathy, and from quarters where I should have least expected it, also particularly from the Friends of my own Monthly Meeting.

O Lord ! Thou knowest that I love Thee and Thy cause above all things. I desire to serve Thee, and if Thou art pleased to continue to make use of me, may I be kept clean and bright by Thy power and fit for Thy service ; and Oh, as Thou hast been pleased to enlarge the heart of Thy handmaid towards those who love and fear Thy name of other denominations, and that she dared not *prevent* her child being united to one of these— Oh, sanctify Thyself this union, strengthen them by Thy might in the inner man, to do Thy will, whatever it may lead them into ; that their light may so shine before men, that they, seeing their good works, may glorify Thee, our Father, who art in heaven. Amen, and Amen.

Plashet, Tenth Month, 18*th.*—I have lately been called into various engagements. I attended the Quarterly Meeting of Kent to much comfort and satisfaction, surprised to find so much openness, so little obstruction in the way, and not a little consoled to feel the anointing, afresh and fully poured forth to my great relief ; and I believe I may say enabled to declare the word in that power that tendered and refreshed many minds. Afterwards visited Lord and Lady Torrington, at Yotes Court ; Maidstone Barracks and Gaol, and the Noels at Barham Court to satisfaction. The love of the gospel appeared much over us towards all amongst whom our lot was cast ; our dear sister, E. Fry, was with us throughout. Since this, I attended the Quarterly Meeting for Sussex and Surrey, but not to the same relief and satisfaction.

I had one very important Meeting at Brighton, so many came that it rendered it a Public Meeting, it was a fearful time, but the best help was granted, to my peace and consolation, and a

8

hope that it was not without good to others. Since my return home, last Seventh day, the 13th, I have been enabled to enjoy and estimate my blessings, particularly my delightful quiet home, garden, and little children.

Plashet, Eleventh Month, 17*th.*—Francis Cresswell and Rachel returned home last Sixth day week, 9th. Rachel's external change has of course been much felt by me, and at times I have been overwhelmed, but I consider it a mercy, that even when discouragements have most prevailed, I have been (I think) confirmed in the belief that what I did in the affair was not wrong, and that good will in the end spring out of it to my beloved child, and I trust to her dear husband also ; and through all I see many causes for thankfulness in it. I feel it a time of much discouragement when cast in the way of Friends, kind as they are to me, feeling as if a cloud hung over me in their view. I am at times ready to be astonished, after having so loved their principles and made many sacrifices for them, that all these things should be. I desire to examine myself whether it is my fault, my omissions or commissions, or what is the cause; but it at times brings great humiliation, and I am ready to feel as if I never could again labour out of my own house or in my own Society ; but this, I cannot, I dare not give way to ; I never sought in my own will to be brought forward publicly as I have been, or could I have prospered in my public labours as I have prospered, had such been the case. It appears to me, that however deep my discouragements, I must follow on to know my Lord in any way that He may require, and put my whole trust in Him, who already has done wonders for me, more than I could either think or ask ; and, who through all my trials, I believe will in spirituals and temporals prove Himself to be a wonder-working God, and that I shall yet know the mountains to flow down at His presence. I cannot but believe there will be those of my own house who will magnify His great and ever excellent name. Be it so, saith my soul, it would be more to me than the increase of corn, wine, or oil. I certainly have a strong confidence that spiritually and naturally help will arise, and that it is laid upon One that is mighty.

First Month, 9*th,* 1822.—My brother Buxton, Patty Smith,

and I, went to town. She and I visited Cold Bath Fields
and Clerkenwell Prisons, with the magistrates, and applied for
a matron to be appointed.

Second Month, 8*th*.—A very busy town morning; visited
Newgate, Milbank Penitentiary, and Tothill Fields Prison ; our
friends the Vennings and William Allen dined here.

Plashet, 13*th*.—Since I last wrote, I may say that my desires
have been renewed to live under the cross, and not to flinch
from it ; in one instance, a want of prompt obedience, led me
to withhold a few words of prayer, that rose in my heart, when
my beloved sisters, and my dear brother, Samuel Hoare, were
here, and I felt afterwards, that we suffered loss, but I desire to
take warning, and at three different times afterwards, under
rather trying circumstances to myself, I endeavoured to be
faithful, and peace accompanied with humiliation, followed.   I
have desired to be watchful over personal indulgences, as my
fatiguing life and often delicate health has given me a liberty in
these things, that now I am better I desire to curtail, as far
as it is right for me ; but I find I do not serve a hard Master,
nor one that would lead me into any extremes, for sometimes,
when in my own will, for appearance sake, economy, &c., I
have wished to leave off indulgences, I have not felt easy with
it, and as far as I know, the right thing in my heart has warranted my using a sufficient supply of what I require, though of
course limited by Christian moderation.   But I may thankfully
acknowledge my present needs being unusually small.   I certainly find my bounds enlarged a little, as Job Scott expressed
himself near his end, whatever is not criminal appears nearly
alike to me, (or words to that effect).   That which I believe the
Spirit of Truth led me into, continues dear and valuable, and
confirmed ; though I do not certainly now feel small things of
so much importance, as when they were peculiarly the seasonable and called for sacrifices, as I fully believe they were ; such
as dress, food, and perhaps some other things ; in speech I think
I have in no degree altered, never having seen it my place to conform to all the idiom of some Friends.   The only thing that I
know of the least alteration in, is in calling places after Saints ;

I think I now and then do it, and as far as I remember, used not to do so. I am rather doubtful as to the scruple being now called for, as the word saint, has so much lost its original meaning, and simply describes the place; but I certainly could not conscientiously call my poor fellow-mortals saints; we know too little of each other, and have, I believe, no right to such titles, either on earth or after we are gone. I am not in the least shaken about our general language, on the contrary, quite confirmed from experience, as it respects the single language, titles to each other, except titles in law which I approve, as marking classes in society appointed by a wise and kind Providence. The names of the days and months, as used by Friends, I much prefer as more consistent with Scripture, and the Christian life; and I believe that the day is come, that even the names of the heathen gods are better not in our mouths as was prophesied would come to pass. Thus far, as it respects the cross in our peculiar views—may we, as a people, never conform to each other, but simply conform to the cross of Christ, as manifested to us individually; and keep to that manifestation, unless the same light and same power clearly lead out of it after it has effected its purpose, or remove it, which may at times be the case with further experience; and if this be the case, that we each follow the Spirit of Truth for ourselves, we shall continue to be in a measure, and become in a very increased measure, a lively and a spiritual body, showing forth the praise of the Most High. But to return to myself, I trust I endeavour to bear my cross as to temper, for I think my many cares, my sorrows, and also perplexities have made my natural temper much more irritable, and I too often feel condemned for a hurried, and at times provoked spirit, but I desire not to give way to it, and to watch against it, though occasionally I fear, it catches me unawares. I have great dread for myself, of dwelling in any degree in my ministry on good works, or being influenced in life by the good opinion of men, as I feel I naturally like to have it, and my timid and discouraged mind much feels their disapprobation; I do not think I am such a slave to the opinion of others as I was, for I have anxiously desired and endeavoured to serve my Lord, and not my fellow-mortals; and have suffered much from running the risk of their displeasure, in doing what I believed my duty. I trust, though I know it to be a temptation, it does not really influence my conduct more than it ought to do, in ministry, or in works of charity, as I never remember entering either service to please any mortal. My heart says, God forbid that I should do so; though after having obtained their approbation, (perhaps when least expected,) there may be some danger of desiring and endeavouring too much to maintain it. Dearest Lord, preserve me, even from this, that whatever I do, may be done purely to Thee, and to Thy glory. Amen.

My mind is much engaged by temporal things, managing my house, farm, &c., &c., from a duty this has become quite a pleasure; I desire to be thankful for it, but yet not to have my heart in the earth or the things of it; my mind feels so peculiarly qualified just now to enjoy the beauties of nature, from my children and our various animals, down to vegetation and minerals. May these things lead me upwards, and not draw me downwards. The prayer of my heart is, that in whatever I do I may be enabled to bring my deeds to the light, that it may be made manifest they " are wrought in God," and that my gracious Lord and Redeemer would see, if there be any evil way in me, and lead me in the way everlasting.

15th.—I went early to town, visited Newgate, Giltspur Street Compter, and Clerkenwell Prison.

Plashet, 21st.—Yesterday, we attended the wedding of Cornelius Hanbury and Mary Allen. It was a very solemn and comforting day.

Third Month, 9th.—Since I last wrote, we have visited almost every family belonging to Ratcliff Monthly Meeting, Elizabeth Copeland, my sister Elizabeth Fry, and myself. I may say that we have found what we believed to be the best help near us, as we went from house to house, enabling us to speak well for our Master, and to encourage the feeble travellers in their way to Zion. Some of the visits were poor and low times, with such as appeared to have their hearts more in present things than in those that are to come, which produces great flatness; but we were rejoiced to find many whom we could not doubt were humble-minded Christians, seeking to dwell near the Spirit of truth in their hearts. How do I rejoice in the prosperity of Zion, and the enlargement of her borders! (the true church, under all denominations, may be called Zion,) and in our small body, I love to see it spiritual and consistent with our high profession. I have felt it an honour and favour to be once more thus engaged in my dearest Master's cause, it has at times brought that sweet peace with it, that nothing else can give.

Hampstead, Fourth Month 11th.—We have been staying here a few days with my beloved brother and sister Hoare, as I wish to cultivate that love which is so precious between our two families. The excellent order of her children I rejoice to see, but it makes me low about mine, I fear that I am not equally doing my part towards them. Lord, make up my many deficiencies!

16th.—The day to me rather disturbed. I attended Newgate. Visited Sophia Vansittart, came home by four, and got ready to receive Lord and Lady Torrington, and the Benjamin Shaws, also my brother Buxton.

17th.—After reading, I knelt down in prayer. Lord and Lady Torrington went to Meeting with us; it was a very solemn one.

Plashet, Fifth Month, 2nd.—I am favoured with general health of body, and cheerfulness of mind; a good deal occupied by temporal things, though I trust not resting in them. My readings in Newgate at this time of year, are peculiarly exercising to me, so many attend, and often such a variety; and some of such high rank, I should think so little accustomed to hear the truth spoken. The prospect of them is sometimes really awful to me, and if I know the desire of my heart respecting them it is this—that the cause of truth and righteousness may be exalted, my Lord glorified, and living faith in Him promoted; and for myself and those engaged in the work, that we may dwell low before Him who hath helped us, abide in His fear, and not the fear of man; seek His pleasure, and not our own pleasure, and if in unmerited mercy, He is pleased to help us and to own us by His presence, that we may ever remember, that to us belongs nothing but confusion of face, but to Him alone, glory, honour, power, thanksgiving and praise. Amen. Lord, be pleased to bless these seasons, that we have been brought into, we humbly trust by the ordering of Thy providence; so that they may tend to good, and that they may be to some, as "bread cast upon the waters, that will return after many days."

Plashet, 28th.—Since writing the above, I have had fresh cause to raise up my Ebenezer; help having been granted, and to my own feelings way marvellously made for me, in things that I exceedingly dreaded. In the first place, I felt very low, and peculiarly under discouragement, partly from my sense of weakness both of body and mind, and partly from the idea that Friends might not feel unity with me after my child's marriage. In the first place, I had in the meeting of Ministers and Elders to pray for direction and help for myself and others during the Yearly Meeting, which appeared as if owned by the Great Head of the church. The next thing was our Ladies' Prison Meeting, which I dreaded, and had many misgivings about; however, this was got through quite beyond my expectation; the accounts of many instances of reform from different prisons were truly encouraging and comforting, and the whole feeling was as if a blessing were in it; dear Mary Dudley prayed, and several of us had to acknowledge the kindness of the Most High in it, and to Him alone, in all things, did we desire to give the glory. This Meeting gave me a little hope and encouragement, still, when I found that my awful concern to visit the Men's Meeting remained, fear was indeed my portion, and such a dread lest I might not know the voice of the great and good Shepherd; however, I found amidst all my fears, no way of relief for my mind, but in laying my views before the Women's Meeting; they were met with much unity and encouragement, quite beyond what I expected. My beloved sister, Elizabeth Fry went with me, Sarah Benson, and my aunt Jane Gurney. We entered the Men's Meeting, trembling. What an awful service it is for a poor weak woman to go amongst so many hundred men. After being seated, I soon found the spirit of prayer poured forth ; I knelt down, and found myself greatly strengthened to offer up my supplications for ourselves, and for the body then present ; Elizabeth Fry then spoke, in much calmness and power, which I doubt not would deeply impress those who heard her ; I followed her, and it was marvellous to me the unction that I felt to deliver what opened to me, principally to the young people, and to the sorrowful and perplexed, especially from outward causes ; there was great solemnity over the Meeting, and very many appeared to be in tears ; therefore what can we say, but that our merciful God was on our side, and He became our Helper. Surely it is the Lord's doing, and marvellous in our eyes.

Much comfort and satisfaction were expressed after Meeting, by different Friends, and so my fears vanished. May this afresh lead me in doing and in suffering to commit my cause to my most Gracious Helper, Saviour, and Redeemer, and fully to trust in Him.

Sixth Month, 10*th.*—Obliged to go to town to meet the Prince and Princess of Denmark, at the Borough Road School ; afterwards received a very poor account of dearest Jane. A low day.

Plashet, 13*th.*—Accounts came that our dear sister Jane, the wife of my much-loved brother Joseph, died at Earlham on Second day the 10th, a little before six o'clock, and that my dearest brother, thanks be to Him who helped him, was enabled to give her up with a resigned spirit. Heavenly love and support were very manifest to them both ; and she appeared greatly prepared for it, notwithstanding the short notice she had. She was I believe, one who loved and feared the Lord, and who proved her love by her humble dedication, and watchful and circumspect conduct ; she was an excellent wife, mother, daughter, and sister, a great friend to the poor, and remarkably generous. May her loss be fully made up, to our poor brother, by that gracious Power that has thus bereaved him of one so dear and so lovely to him.

Earlham, 16*th.*—After weighing the matter the best I could, such were my inexpressible drawings of love to Joseph and the others, that I believed it best for my body and mind to come here, though I left home really poorly ; but I found the change of air useful, till last evening after arriving here, when I felt very unwell, which took sad hold of my nerves, and I had a painful night. Still I may acknowledge my true and deep consolation in seeing my dearest brother Joseph, my aunt Birkbeck, and the rest of the family so greatly even marvellously supported.

Earlham, 21st.—Day by day strength is granted to us, to my beloved brother and his poor mother-in-law, though the late afflicting event casts a cloud over all temporal things; some of the party appear wonderfully raised in spirit and strong in faith. I rejoice and am glad for them, for myself I feel peculiarly unworthy, and as if far behind some others in spiritual advancement, and true dedication ; I am ready to be reminded of that text, " The first shall be last, and the last first." Still I trust there is a following on to know the Lord amidst many infirmities.

Earlham, 22nd.—I feel brought low before the Lord ; what can I say and what can I do, but beseech Thee, oh, our Lord ! to care for us, present and absent, to undertake for us, to show us the sufficiency of Thy grace, and the power of Thy salvation. We beseech Thee, through Him that hath loved us and given Himself for us, that Thou wouldest draw us all, whether now far from Thee or near unto Thee, by the powerful cords of Thy loving kindness, out of darkness into Thy marvellous light, that we may ever dwell in Thy light and in Thy love, and know the fulness of Thy power, Thy glory, and Thy majesty. Amen.

We were favoured to get through the first Meeting of the Quarterly Meeting to great satisfaction, the truth arose even into something of dominion ; many of the Lord's servants had to minister in His name, and even I unworthy as I am, was greatly helped.

Plashet, Seventh Month, 1st.—I was just set off for town, when I had to return, to receive the Princess of Denmark ; it was a satisfactory visit. Several Italian noblemen and others to dinner. My brother and sister Hoare and many besides slept here. My fatigue great.

4th.—I hope it is with much thankfulness that I can acknowledge being safely at home. I expect to-morrow to have all our family with us, our ten children with dear Rachel's husband. There is to my feelings a great blessing in being thus surrounded by our numerous family; and I have real pleasure, and at times joy in it, though I must also say that my longings are beyond expression to have all more devoted to the best of Masters—to see them more under the influence of the Holy Spirit—more under the discipline of the cross of Christ, that it might be more fully, more clearly, and more decidedly manifest, that as for us and our house we serve the Lord. The best of things, the best of causes, not being sufficiently uppermost with us, my soul is brought to cry unto the Lord for help. What can I do ? A poor unworthy servant; I am fearful of doing too much, and fearful of doing too little. Oh, that I may be enabled to seek and find counsel of God. I believe there is a good root of principle in all of my children, of an age of understanding, but I long for them to show themselves more decidedly upon the Lord's side, and more openly to profess Christ before men; I trust there is an increase of this work in some of them. Lord work in them in Thine own way, only let none rest till they experience the power of Thy salvation for themselves. Amen.

31st.—We propose in a few days, breaking up our interesting party. My husband, myself, and little Hannah and Louisa mean to go to Runcton, and then to the sea at Hunstanton, with our beloved brother Joseph, our sister Rachel, and his dear little children. We trust that this is a right arrangement, and we hope that it may strengthen my health, previous to my confinement. In a day or two after our dear boys are gone to school, we mean to set off, therefore we know not whether it may ever please the Lord that we should all meet again, two of us particularly; however, we must seek to leave it entirely to Him, whose tender mercies are over all His works, and who alone knows what is best for us. When our families are scattered in different parts, may our Lord be near unto us, and may He preserve our goings out and our comings in before Him.

Hunstanton, Eighth Month, 16*th.*—My husband, myself, Hannah and Louisa, arrived here this day week to dinner; where we have met with a most kind and hospitable reception at our dear aunt Birkbeck's, herself and our kind friend Maria Sewell, doing all they can to make us happy and comfortable. We had a peculiarly pleasant and satisfactory journey here; we arrived at Runcton on Third day, and staid there, till Sixth day; my dear brother's kindness was abundant to us, and our beloved Frank and Rachel, whom we found there much enjoyed seeing us. It was a very uniting, peaceful time, but by far my greatest comfort on the journey, has been my dearest husband's company.

20th.—Yesterday was our wedding-day, we have been married twenty-two years; how many dispensations have I passed through since that time, how have I been raised up and cast down! How has a way been made in the depths, and a path in the mighty waters; I have known much of good health, and real sickness; great bodily suffering, particularly in my confinements, and deep depression of spirits.

I have known the ease of abundance of riches, and the sorrow and perplexity of comparative deprivation; I have known to the full I think, the enjoyment of domestic life; even what might be called the fulness of blessing, and also some of its most sorrowful and most painful reverses. I have known the aboundings of the unspeakable, soul-satisfying, and abounding joy of the Lord; and I have been brought into states, when the depths had well nigh swallowed me up. I have known great exaltation amongst my fellow-mortals, also deep humiliation. I have known the sorrow, of some most tenderly beloved, being taken from me by death; and others given me, hitherto more given than taken.

What is the result of all this experience? It is even, that the Lord is gracious and very merciful, that His compassions fail not, but are renewed every morning; and may I not say, that His goodness and mercy have followed me all the days of my life ? Though He has at times permitted me amidst many and unspeakable blessings to pass through unutterable sorrows; known only to the full extent by Him and my own soul, yet He hath been an All-sufficient helper ; His right hand hath sustained me and held me up, blessed be His name for ever, He hath never forgotten to be gracious, nor hath He shut up His tender mercies from me. May I not indeed raise up my Ebenezer, and acknowledge that there is indeed "no God like our God," and that it is indeed a most blessed thing to serve Him, even if it be by the way of the cross, for He is indeed worthy to be served, worshipped and obeyed, now and for ever. Above all, I pray for myself, that whatever dispensations I may yet pass through, nothing may separate me from His love, or hinder me from His service, but that I may be increasingly and entirely devoted to Him in heart, mind, and spirit ; through the help of my most dear and blessed Redeemer.

Plashet, Ninth Month, 6th.—I arrived at home to dinner last Third day, after being absent four weeks and a day.

We left Lynn on Second day morning in much love and peace. My dearest brother Joseph, my sister Rachel, and my little Hannah to Earlham ; ourselves to return home.

To HER BROTHER JOSEPH JOHN GURNEY.

Plashet, *Ninth Month, 6th,* 1822.

My dearest Joseph,

I believe thou wilt rejoice to hear, as well as Catherine and Rachel, that I never remember arriving at home, and finding the whole aspect of things so peaceful, and according to my desire ; my reception has been most cordial. I am more and more of the opinion, that there is an arising of light amongst us, that I humbly trust and inexpressibly crave may in due season disperse all the darkness. I paid a very satisfactory visit to Frank and Rachel, and there found much cause of comfort and satisfaction. I feel finely myself, and I hope truly thankful for this time of rest from trial, for so I think I must call it : indeed in all states my Lord has been abundantly gracious to me, and is pleased just now in a peculiar manner to manifest it to me. I believe the quiet and refreshment of Hunstanton, and some of your dear company, has greatly tended to my present degree of health, and even in measure to the capacity of enjoying my home comforts.

Thy nearly attached sister,

ELIZABETH FRY.

Plashet, 16*th.*—I believe it right once more to make an acknowledgment of the mercy of my God. Although I feel in a very sensitive state of mind and body, yet my soul is in great mercy kept calm, quiet, and generally cheerful, before the Lord ; I speak thus because through the grace and free mercy of my God, I feel in measure living unto Him ; and as if His power and His presence were near, to calm the storms that would naturally arise, and also as if what I did, I was enabled to do in reference to His will.   Most assuredly He is no hard Master ; how truly can I speak to this ! although in wisdom He has led me by the way of the cross, very greatly so, to flesh and blood, both in doing and in suffering ; yet there is abundant liberty in the gospel, how do I at times find that the very same Spirit leads into rest and refreshment and consolation—how far from requiring what we are not able to perform ! May those, for such there are, I do believe, even tender ones, who desire to do right in the sight of the Lord ; who from their own activity go beyond His requirings, and therefore misinterpret His word inwardly and outwardly, and make religion appear a gloomy and rigid path, may these be brought to feel the rest, refreshment and even right liberty (not in evil) which the gospel of light and salvation really brings into.   I think I know what it is when a fearful mind, or looking to the opinions of others, or a judgment of myself has led to a sort of self-denial, that the best witness in my heart has neither warranted nor led into, though I most fully acknowledge also that too great laxity is my more prevailing temptation, as it respects myself and others—but enough

do I know of the true liberty of the gospel, however at seasons
we may indeed have to bear our cross in doing and in suffering—
enough do I know of it, to long for all to be brought into it, from
the most worldly to the most rigid formalist, under every denomination, for such I believe there are amongst all ; and though
I feel for these, in what appear to me bonds of their own making,
yet I doubt not, but that in tender mercy they are accepted, and
that their state is safe indeed, compared with that of the worldly-
minded.

Plashet, 24*th.* — Dined at Ham House, to meet Dr.
Chalmers.

On the 1st of November, her eleventh and youngest child was
born, and on the same day her eldest grandchild.

Plashet, Eleventh Month, 7*th.*—Words fall utterly short of
expression of the unmerited mercy which has been shown us. On
the night of the 30th, I had to pass through a very deep conflict of spirit, comfort appeared to fail, deep discouragement and
great fear took hold of me ; I felt I had a baptism to be baptized with, and how was I straitened until it was accomplished,
(if the servant dare allude to drinking even at seasons of the cup
the Master drank of) but after a time the conflict ceased, sweetness, trust, love and confidence, took place of it.   I felt bound
to have my husband, children, my dear sister Gurney, and Susan
Pitchford, besides such of the maids as liked to join us collected
together, when, after reading I poured forth my soul in fervent
prayer, for my dearest Rachel and myself in our time of conflict, for help spiritually, and naturally for tender mercy.   And
how striking to me it was, in little more than twenty-four
hours—only fourteen hours apart—Rachel and myself had each
a darling boy born.   Both of us very graciously and wonderfully helped.

Plashet, 13*th.*—I write this journal in the midst of my
lying-in with my eleventh child, in a very tender delicate
state of body, and unworthy state of soul, after having (of late
peculiarly) received many and great blessings, spiritually and
naturally.   I cannot feel thankful enough for all my many

blessings ; so weak has been my state that the very grasshopper has become a burden, and I think I have shown my infirmity to others, as well as felt it myself, though I may say that I have sought after a quiet and patient spirit.   In a serious and trying attack of spasms in my side, I found in tender mercy, that Power to be near, which helped me ; although I was seriously alarmed about myself, I felt my pleasant pictures marred, and was even much affected at the idea, that perhaps I should be taken from my beloved family, still I think it was principally nervous fear ; for when such a call really comes, strength will be given for the time, and the same help administered, that has so marvellously been displayed in many of the deep conflicts of time.

My soul feels utterly unworthy, and deeply prostrate before Thee, dearest Lord, at my utter inability fully to return Thee thanks for all Thy benefits.   Make me fit to receive them ; enable me to acknowledge them ; strengthen me to walk more circumspectly before Thee in thought, word, and deed   Thou knowest that I love Thee, that, above all things, I believe my desire is, to serve Thee, love Thee, and obey Thee.   Thou hast manifested, and canst manifest Thyself to be all-sufficient, to be " strength in weakness, riches in poverty, and a present helper in every needful time."   Grant a little help, if Thou seest meet to bring me again into life ; that I may serve Thee better, love Thee more, and as a wife, mother, mistress, and member of Thy church, and of society at large, may more perfectly keep my eye single unto Thee, and do all to Thee, and through Thee, to the praise of Thy holy name.   And continue to grant if it please Thee, a blessing on those labours of love, that Thou hast permitted me to be brought into in the prisons, and that the work may not stop till much more be accomplished in it. Amen.

First day, 17*th.*—My body recovering, though weak.   My spirit tendered before the Lord for His great and unspeakable benefits.   My naturally too-insensible heart softened before Him, who I may say is the delight of my soul, my Lord and my God, my Saviour and Redeemer.   I remember those that are worshipping, as worshipping with them, and my spirit feels sweet

unity with the Church Militant, and perhaps, though utterly
unworthy of it with the Church Triumphant, as if I could unite
with both, in the everlasting song of high praises, even to our
God, and to His Lamb, who hath shown such tender mercy
towards us, and made Himself manifest to us as our Saviour
and Redeemer. Blessed for ever be His name.

27th.—Peace and sweetness appear to rest upon me in entering life. Oh! for my sweet infant, if life be granted him,
may he be indeed devoted to the Lord. We neither circum-
cise nor baptize, but may he be baptized by the saving baptism
of Christ! and be in spirit circumcised unto the Lord! I have
(perhaps in weakness) much set my heart upon this child,
rather expecting he may be a comfort to us in our old age, and
not only so, but above all, that he may prove a devoted servant
of Christ. May this blessed work not be hindered by any false
indulgence in us; but may it be truly promoted by example,
precept, and the true discipline of love and wisdom.

Twelfth Month, 2nd.—Yesterday, at Meeting, the Truth rose
into much dominion, blessed be the name of the Lord. I was
enabled to supplicate and minister to my own relief, and I trust
to the refreshment of others, also my dearest brother Joseph,
Rebecca Christy, and my sister, Elizabeth Fry, in prayer. It
appeared a solemn time. The day, generally speaking, a
favoured time; but in the night I was deeply brought to a sense
of my own weakness. If the beautiful garments spiritually
were put on in the morning, surely they were taken off at night.
What are we but instruments, however, for a season decorated
with our Lord's ornaments; self cannot boast, when left to ourselves, and our decorations taken off! How wonderful is the
work of the Spirit—how it heals, and raises up body and soul,
when they are to be brought into service; none can tell, but
those who have experienced something of it, how the anointing
is poured forth from on high. It is an honour I am unworthy
of, to be thus helped spiritually, particularly in the ministry.
But how deeply doth my spirit crave that I may also be aided
in all the practical duties of life.

14th.—I yesterday went to London, and visited Newgate.
My greeting there was warm from the prisoners, the committee,

and others. I felt peaceful there, and afresh sensible that the work was not ours, that we had first been brought there ; and I had to crave a blessing upon our labours, and also to acknowledge the tender mercy of our God as our Saviour and Deliverer. I was low in myself, but felt renewedly the great importance of the prison cause ; and if those who espouse it, are enabled to persevere, what good may be done, in preventing much crime that has been both plotted and perpetrated in prisons.

During the visit to England of the Prince and Princess Royal of Denmark, they inspected many of the public institutions and charities, and took a lively interest in objects that conduced to the moral and religious welfare of the people. It was therefore a particularly gratifying circumstance to Mrs. Fry, that one morning, when paying her respects at Gloucester House, Her Royal Highness the Duchess of Gloucester presented her to the Princess, who was also there. A few days afterwards, the family at Plashet were surprised by an intimation, that the Princess would that morning, honour them with her company to breakfast. She came, and remained some hours ; this occasion was the commencement of that intercourse which continued at intervals till the close of Mrs. Fry's life.

To the Princess Royal of Denmark.

Plashet House, *Eleventh Month*, 23rd, 1822.

Dear and respected Friend,

Allow me to call thee so, for such I feel thee, as thou art truly both loved and respected by me. According to thy kind and condescending wish, expressed when here; I take up my pen to inform thee, that upon the first of this month, through the tender mercy of my God I was safely delivered of a sweet boy, and to add to our cause of joy and thanksgiving, my dear daughter had also one born on the same day, so that twenty-four hours added a son and grandson to our already numerous family; we have, both of us, with our infants, been going on well, and with the exception of some illness, that I passed through in the early part of my confinement, and my habitual delicacy at such times, I am as well now as I can expect to be.

I have often thought of thy kind visit with deep interest, and strong desires are raised in my heart for thy welfare and preservation in every way, that the God of Peace may be with thee continually, guiding thee by His counsel, helping thee by His Spirit, comforting thee by His love, during thy continuance here; and afterwards, when He may be pleased to take thee hence, to be seen of men no more, through His mercy in Christ Jesus, receiving thee into glory. I also feel real interest and best desires for the Prince Royal,—may you both be encouraged in every good word and work. I remember the words of Paul, in the 15th chapter of the 1st of Corinthians, 58th verse. " Be ye stedfast, unmoveable, always abounding in the work of the Lord, forasmuch as ye know that your labour is not in vain in the Lord."

It would give me great pleasure and satisfaction to hear from thee, or if that be asking too much, perhaps the lady whom we had the pleasure of seeing here, will let us know many particulars respecting your welfare, and how you go on in Denmark, as it respects the prisons, schools, and other works of charity and love. I should also be pleased to know whether the books and the other things we sent to Count Moltke, and also some of the work of the prisoners, ever came safely to thy hand, as we were prevented sending them quite so soon as we hoped to have done. I should be glad to be very respectfully and affectionately remembered to the Queen, and also to the Prince Royal, thy consort; and believe me, with much respect and regard,

Thy attached and obliged Friend,
Elizabeth Fry.

Plashet, First Month, 2*nd,* 1823.—" Our years pass away as a tale that is told." Upon concluding one, and beginning another year, my heart has been brought low before the Great I Am ; and I have desired, after a renewed searching of heart, to see how my accounts stand spiritually, and in what I can more fully serve my Lord, and bear the fruits of the Spirit. I have inwardly prayed for help, as well as vocally, for myself, my family, my household, and those most near and dear to me; above all, that there may be known amongst us more of the light, life, and spirit of religion; and beyond every other blessing, more knowledge of the truth as it is in Jesus. In looking back to the last year, I see an unusual portion of blessing to have been granted us, as it respects my unworthy self, I have, I think, been permitted to be once more established in the unity of my friends, which I fancied was a little shaken respecting my conduct in Rachel's marriage; and had their real unity proved in a remarkable manner, on my going into the Men's Yearly Meeting, deeply in the cross to myself, but eventually to my great edification and abundant consolation.

Outwardly, we have received much of blessing. In the first place, a sweet child and grandchild granted us. Our whole family being in health. In things temporal, enough and more than enough for our real comfort; residing in the pleasant country, I esteem a blessing; and besides all this much capacity to enjoy has been our portion, much more so, since the best things have been more uppermost. One of my deepest sorrows has been in sympathy with my most tenderly beloved brother, in the loss of his sweet and valuable wife. What another year may produce we must leave; but I desire beyond all, that spiritual blessings may more abound amongst us, that grace, mercy, and peace may dwell within our borders, also within the borders of those most near and dear to us. With regard to things temporal, I desire to commit our cause to Him who knows what is best for us; humbly praying a continuance of His mercy and goodness, and that in each of our trials His grace may be sufficient for us.

Amongst the strongest interests of the opening year was the marriage of Mrs. Fry's youngest brother Daniel Gurney Esq., of North Runction, to the Lady Harriet Hay, one of the daughters of the Earl of Erroll. The contrast of his circumstances of prosperity, with those of his brother, Joseph John Gurney, treading the lonely path of widowhood, touched her closely; and after writing to one brother, she thus addressed the other.

To her brother Joseph John Gurney.

Plashet, *First Month*, 8*th*, 1823.

My dearest Joseph,

Having just written to one dear brother, feeling and expressing my sympathy in his joys; I think I shall better conclude my morning's work, by also telling thee how much I have been with thee in mind in thy low estate. I feel for thee and sympathize with thee, but if a poor fellow-mortal feels so tenderly for another, how must it be with Him, whose love, pity and tender compassion are unbounded. Surely thy Lord and His Comforter, will be found very near to thee, in His own time healing thy wounds. I believe, as we may rejoice and return thanks for our dear brother's present fulness of enjoyment, so we may also for thee in thy privations; because all is permitted in tender mercy and loving-kindness. I doubt not that thou hast many pains to bear, by night and by day, as the desolation produced by thy loss would naturally occasion; but I trust patience will have its perfect work, and so tend further to purify and redeem and fit thee for thy Master's work. I wish in any way we could help or comfort thee; wouldest thou like Kate to pay thee a visit for two or three weeks, or is there any thing we could do to cheer thee?

We are going on comfortably here; my darling baby a considerable object of interest. I am once more moderately launched in public as well as private life, I am therefore much engaged, and although often fagged, yet not really overdone, I take so much care of myself. There has been a feeling of peace in entering Meetings and the prison cause again, as if the calling to these things was continued: how I desire a simple, faithful, watchful walking, with my eye single to the Lord. My path calls for cautious steppings, and peculiarly needs the best light —may it be granted me.

7

Many begin to come here after me, as I cannot leave my babe to go to them.

Farewell, my much loved brother,
Thy nearly attached sister,
E. FRY.

Plashet, First Month, 8th.—A deep feeling of infirmity has been my portion. Yesterday, my mind was so much engrossed in temporal things, that I did not get rid of them even at Meeting ; and the day before some inattention in a servant annoyed me too much in mind, which in degree was shown, so as to be followed by condemnation, and being thus brought, through my omissions and commissions to the feet of Jesus, the prayer of my heart is to Him for justification and purification, that I may know my transgressions to be forgiven, and that I may be afresh fitted and prepared by His Spirit, for a more watchful and circumspect walk before Him, whom my soul loves, and pants after; and I believe desires above all things to serve, worship, and obey.

22nd.—On the 16th, I was sent for to Hampstead, to my beloved sister Hoare, (who was ill). Such seasons are to me times of real conflict spiritually and naturally ; spiritually, to know what in the way of religious service may be required at my hand, and also close sympathy with those in trouble, naturally, from my acute sense of suffering, and my excessive love for my sisters. I know few things that occasion me a deeper feeling of impotence and unworthiness, than attending the sick. I may say, it always brings home to me very deeply the unworthiness of my own heart; indeed, I do not much think nursing is my allotment, though often in it, for my acute feeling for those near to me is such, that however I may maintain a cheerful countenance, my heart is affected so as painfully to shake my nerves.

The sentiments here expressed respecting her attendance on the sick, are very different from those entertained of her by other people. Mrs. Fry displayed in such cases, great presence of mind ; a quick perception of the changes taking place in the patient, singular readiness in expedients to meet them, much judgment and skill in the administration of remedies ; and the whole combined with a quiet cheerful manner, and most tender sympathy, so as to inspire complete confidence and dependence on herself in the sufferer, as well as the assistants.

I attended Westminster Meeting which I have looked to for some time as well as others of our Quarterly Meetings. I believed when there, that if I were well carried through that, to the relief of my own mind, and if best help then felt near, I should have to visit most of the Meetings in our Quarterly Meeting, held on First day mornings. It so proved that I felt help very near, so that the language of my spirit was, " It is the Lord's doing and marvellous in my eyes." In nothing has the work of grace been so marvellous to me as in the ministry ; it surely is not my own work—I know enough of myself to believe it to be quite impossible. Oh, what an unction I now and then feel, it is as much to be felt strengthening the soul, as the body is felt to be refreshed after wholesome and good food. The work of the Spirit is a wonderful work, and to my naturally doubting and sceptical mind astonishing. I have been permitted to know more of it than I could have either asked or thought. I believed it best to lay my prospect of a general attendance of these Meetings, before our dear Friends at the Monthly Meeting yesterday, which was to my peace ; sweet unity and sympathy were expressed in it, and my beloved sister E. F. proposed to join me, which is a comfort to me. It is cause of much thankfulness to have such a companion.

Plashet, Second Month, 13*th.*—I attended Tottenham Meeting on the 2nd. I went low and under deep exercise of mind ; I returned in great measure relieved, though naturally upset with many fears ; I hardly ever remember being engaged in a service where doubts and fears beset me to an equal extent. On First day, the 9th, we were at Devonshire House ; it was an extraordinary Meeting. I desire in more simplicity of faith to attend the other Meetings. I think I have been too anxious, too fearful ; if the work be not ours, why worry and perplex myself about it ?

19*th.*—Since writing the above, I attended the Peel Meeting on First day, which was to the great relief of my mind : since that time my bonds have appeared wonderfully broken, my spirit has had to rejoice and be glad, and my fears have been removed, so that I can indeed say, how marvellous is the work of the Spirit !

On Second day, I dined at the Mansion House, with my husband ; a change of atmosphere spiritually, but if we are enabled to abide in Christ, and stand our ground, we may by our lives and conversation glorify God, even at a dinner visit, as well as in more important callings. Generally speaking, I believe it best to avoid such occasions, for they take up time, and are apt to dissipate the mind ; although it may occasionally be the right and proper calling of Christians, thus to enter life; but they must then keep the eye very single to Him, who having placed them in the world can alone keep them from the evil.

24*th.*—We were helped through the service yesterday at Ratcliff Meeting. It really appeared a favoured time, and peculiar harmony and power in the ministry generally prevailed, with great solemnity in the silence. I may say that I had afterwards a cheerful, peaceful day with my family.

Third Month, 5th.—I have lately been remarkably full of occupations, and yet they have appeared right, and almost unavoidable. On First day, I attended Southwark Meeting ; mercy and peace eventually accompanied it. On Fifth day, I went to town, to meet the Secretary of State (Sir Robert Peel) and the Speaker of the House of Commons, at Newgate, with my brother Fowell Buxton and my husband; I trust the time was blessed to the good of the cause.

Sixth day in town again to Newgate, one of the bishops and many others there ; it was a solemn time—a power better than ourselves seemed remarkably over us. I visited another prison and then returned home; besides these out of door objects, I am much engaged in nursing my babe, which is a sweet employment, but takes time ; the rest of the children are comfortably settled in with dear Mary Ann Davis, who is now once more with us. Upon sitting down to write, and looking round me, surrounded as I am with my family, supplied with so many temporal comforts, spiritual blessings not withheld; for I trust that there is rather an increase than decrease of the best thing amongst us; I thought as the query arose in my heart, "Lackest thou any thing?" I might indeed say, "Nothing, Lord," except a further establishment for us all, in the ever blessed truth, as it is in Jesus. What can I render to Thee for all thy benefits? Grant, dearest Lord! in Thy child and servant, a heart fully and entirely devoted to Thee and Thy service. Amen.

29th.—Since I last wrote, I have attended Winchmore Hill Meeting to satisfaction, together with my dear sister Elizabeth, William Allen, and my brother Samuel, whose company I enjoyed. My husband has engaged Leslie, the painter, to come and take likenesses of him and me, to which, from peculiar circumstances, I have appeared obliged to yield; but the thing, and its effect on the mind are unsatisfactory to me, it is not altogether what I like or approve; it is making too much of this poor tabernacle, and rather exalting that part in us which should be laid low, and kept low; I believe I could not have yielded the point, had not so many likenesses of me already appeared, and it would be a trial to my family, only to have these disagreeable ones to remain. However, from one cause or another, this has not been a satisfactory week, too much in the earth and the things of it, too little in the spirit; though not without seeking to take up my cross, deny myself, and follow my Lord and Master. I feel particularly unfit and unworthy to enter again upon my religious engagement; we propose going to Uxbridge this evening. My only hope is in Him, who can alone cleanse, fit, strengthen and prepare for his own work; under a deep feeling of my short comings, may I not say, dearest Lord, undertake for me!

Fourth Month, 7th.—We went to Uxbridge, though naturally rather a low time, yet it ended to my real comfort. The Morning Meeting was a very solemn one, a deep feeling of good, and the anointing of the Spirit appeared freely poured forth. The

Evening Meeting was satisfactory; and in several religious opportunities in the families, my heart was enlarged in much love to the dear Friends there, whom I think I may say, I love in the Lord.

12th.—Since I last wrote, we have been engaged in various ways, particularly in the sale of work done by the poor prisoners in Newgate; this has been a considerable public exposure, but I trust not without profit. I deeply felt upon entering it, the danger of the pollutions of the world, and the desire that we, who are seeking in this way to promote the cause of truth and righteousness might maintain the watch on this point. I trust no harm was done ; but I feel after being with so many, and associating with so many, much brought down in myself, under a feeling of great infirmity. I think in looking back the two last days, I do not feel condemned, but rather that I have been in my right place, and that some good may result from the whole thing. Still as a poor instrument, I fear greatly for myself; knowing my inclination to stand in awe of men, and greatly to mind their displeasure, although I am not so sensible of being exalted by their approbation. I also fear for myself, lest the enlargement of heart I feel towards all, particularly the members of the Church of Christ, of every denomination, and the sort of liberty I feel, which I apprehend to be " in the gospel," should lead me to outstep my bounds, and give myself a liberty beyond that which I have attained unto ; or that in abounding love and good-will to others, I should be induced to cover, bear with, or acknowledge that, which should be decidedly testified against. I long to stand my ground in all things, at all times, and in all situations, faithfully to bear the cross of Christ ; at the same time proving what I so abundantly feel, the liberty, joy and glory of that salvation that cometh by Christ. How perfectly true it is, that His followers find His yoke to be easy, and His burden light. I have the comfort to feel, notwithstanding my many fears on the subject, particularly for myself; a considerable portion of peace, hope and belief, that the remarkable manner in which we have been brought forward in these services, is not of our own ordering, but that we may acknowledge in deep humility of heart that it is the Lord's doing—to Him alone can we look, and upon Him alone depend for help and preservation. Lord, continue to be near unto us in this work, in the various situations into which it may introduce us, may we experience the blessing of preservation, may our labours be blessed in checking the power of evil, and in turning the sinner from the error of his way, unto Thee, our Lord, our Saviour and our Redeemer !

The quantity of work executed by the prisoners in Newgate was considerable. In order to dispose of it, a sale was occasionally resorted to. It was held in some public room in London, the ladies of the Newgate Association selling, at different tables the various proceeds of the prisoners' industry. It was conducted very much on the same plan as the sales of fancy work, since so common for the benefit of charities. On the present occasion, the sum of three hundred and nineteen pounds was realised.

In addition to Newgate, the Borough Compter, and Giltspur Street Compter were regularly attended by members of the Ladies' Association; Whitecross Street prison was also occasionally visited by them. The arrangements first made by Mrs. Fry had now borne the test of six years' experience, and the results were highly satisfactory, not only in those prisons which may be supposed to have been under her personal superintendence, but also in the many prisons in the different parts of this kingdom, and on the continent, where ladies had formed committees to visit the female prisoners. At the time of which we are writing, the subject of prison discipline was but imperfectly understood; though it was generally acknowledged that classification was necessary, that the most abandoned characters might not associate with the comparatively uncontaminated. Employment and instruction were considered essential for every class of prisoners, and it was with peculiar pleasure, Mrs. Fry saw the principle admitted, and ultimately become the law of the land, that women, when in prison, were to be placed under the charge of female officers. She was anxious that the same system should be carried out by the appointment of matrons on board the convict ships; where, with the exception of the Naval Surgeon Superintendent, the women were placed under the care of *sailors*. The masters of these vessels, as well as their crews had the power of free communication with them, not only during the voyage, but whilst the vessel lay in the River Thames, which was frequently the case for weeks together. To separate one class of prisoners effectually from another, was impossible in these floating prisons ; if they did not meet when below, nothing could prevent them from associating with whom they pleased when on deck. There was no one to teach them to read—no religious instruction. There was no adequate provision for the preservation of cleanliness, and their clothing was insufficient.

Since the Maria had been visited in 1818, as each successive season brought the sailing of a female convict ship, the subject obtained a large share of Mrs. Fry's attention. Amongst those who assisted her in her efforts to improve the condition of these ships, the late Mrs. Pryor was one most especially devoted to the work; with the exception of one ship, (the unfortunate Amphitrite), she visited every transport which sailed from England with female convicts, until prevented by the sickness, which terminated in her death, in 1841.

This was not done without much fatigue and inconvenience; frequent exposure to weather in open boats, and occasionally to danger. On one occasion, Mrs. Pryor and Mrs. Fry were placed in a situation of considerable alarm, from which they were relieved, by the interposition of the present Harbour Master at Ramsgate. Both the objects of his kind consideration having passed hence, and the particulars of the circumstance being imperfectly retained in the memory of those to whom they related it; we are indebted to him for the following account:—

" It was on a fine sultry day, in the summer of 1821, that I was racing up the River Thames, in the command of the Ramsgate Steam Packet, Eagle, hoping to overtake our Margate competitors, the Victory, and Favourite steamers, and bringing them nearer to view as we rounded the points of the Reach of the river. It was in the midst of this excitement, that we encountered one of those sudden thunder squalls, so common in this country, and which passing rapidly off with heavy rain, leave behind them a strong and increasing northerly gale. I was looking out ahead, pleasing myself with the reflection that we were the fastest vessel against a-head wind, and should certainly overtake our Margate friends; when upon entering Long Reach, about two miles below Purfleet, I saw a boat labouring with very little effect against the gale, and with a whole ebb-tide just making to add to their difficulties; in this boat were two ladies, in the close habit of the Society of Friends, evidently drenched with the heavy shower which had overtaken them. I was then a dashing, high-spirited sailor; but I had always a secret admiration of the quiet demeanour of that Society, and occasionally had some of them passengers with me, always intelligent and inquiring, and always pleased with any information a seaman could extend to them. Well, here was a dilemma! To stop, would spoil my chase, in which most of my passengers were as eager as myself, but to go on, and pass two ladies in such a situation! I passed the word softly to the engineer; desired the mate to sheer alongside the boat carefully; threw the delighted rowers a rope, and before the passengers were fully aware that we had stopped the engines, the ladies were on board, the boat made fast astern, and the Eagle again flying up the Thames. I have those two persons strongly, nay, indelibly stamped upon my mind's eye. The one I had last assisted on board, still held my hand, as she thanked me, with dignified but beautiful expression: ' It is kind of thee, Captain, and we thank thee. We made no sign to thee; having held up our handkerchiefs to the other packets, we did not think we should succeed with thee.' I assured them that I could not have passed them under such circumstances, and called the stewardess to take them below into the ladies' cabin and see to their comfort. They had been well cloaked, and had not suffered so much as I had anticipated.

" The gale had cleared away the rain, and in a very short time they came upon deck again, one of them was Mrs. Fry, and she never lost an opportunity of doing good. I saw her speaking to some of my crew who were looking very serious as she offered them tracts, and some of them cast a side glance at me for my approval or otherwise. I had some little dislike to sects then, which I thank God left me in riper years,—but who could resist this beautiful persuasive, and heavenly-minded woman. To see her, was to love her; to hear her, was to feel as if a guardian angel had bid you follow that teaching which could alone subdue the temptations and evils of this life, and secure a Redeemer's love in eternity! In her you saw all that was attractive in woman, lit up by the bright beams of philanthropy; devoting the prime of life, and health, and personal graces, to her Divine Master's service; and I feel assured that much of the success which attended her missions of mercy, was based upon that awe which such a presence inspired. It was something to possess a countenance which pourtrayed in every look the overflowings of such a heart, and thus as a humble instrument in the hands of Divine Providence, she was indeed highly favoured among women.

" She told me that her companion Mrs. Pryor and herself had been down to Gravesend to take leave of the unfortunate women (convicts) on board a ship bound to the settlements, and gave me so touching a description of their behaviour, that I volunteered to take charge of any thing for her at any time, or render her any service in my power in my voyages. When about to land, her anxiety to make some pecuniary recompense was very great, but I would not allow her to do so. Mrs. Fry never forgot me when she came near our locality; I saw her from time to time, the earthly tabernacle failing, but the same spirit lighting

up with animation her untiring energies. It was an honour
to know her in this world; may we follow her to the society of
the accepted and blessed in that which is to come.

"K. B. MARTIN."

"Ramsgate, *February*, 1847."

On another occasion, Mrs. Fry reached Deptford late in
the afternoon of a very tempestuous March day. A female convict ship was under sailing orders for the next morning, and
it being after office hours, she went to the private house of
Admiral Young, to request him to send her off to the ship. By
the time she returned on shore, it was quite dark, and the wind
and rain to which she had been exposed seemed to make a little
rest and refreshment almost indispensable before she set off homewards. But she resisted all the invitations of Admiral Young
and his family to remain with them; assigning as a reason that
she had left one of her children seriously ill, to whom she was
anxious to hasten back. This little incident left a deep impression on their minds; "that such a claim on a mother's
heart, had not been permitted to interfere with that, to which
she had pledged her best energies and powers."

The sphere of labour in which Mrs. Fry and her friends were
embarked, required not merely the exercise of womanly tenderness, but also of courage and energy; but they found that He,
who had so wonderfully cleared a path for them in Newgate,
did not desert them in the still more difficult work which was
now before them. There was a remarkable adaptation of talents
and ability for the execution of the various branches of the
undertaking in different members of the Committee; and many
who have not come so prominently forward, as those just named,
then began their equally useful, though less conspicuous exertions, and may still be found at their posts, with untiring
energy, notwithstanding the lapse of time and increase of years,
preparing that portion of the convicts' outfit, which is entrusted

to the Committee to provide, and carrying out the regulations framed so long ago.

Soon after the ladies first visited these ships, the women ceased to be received on board at Deptford ; but the ships were moored for this purpose in a less frequented part of the river, below Woolwich. The mode in which they were brought on board, long continued to be highly objectionable ; they arrived from the country in small parties, at irregular intervals, having been conveyed on the outside of stage coaches, by smacks, or hoys, or any conveyance that offered, under the care of a turn-key ; often have the ladies, when engaged in their interesting occupation, seen a person of this description come alongside in a wherry with a group of unfortunate creatures under his charge wayworn, and ill, or perhaps a solitary outcast brought upon deck, lamenting her misfortunes in the broad dialect of some far distant county—a small bundle of insufficient clothing being frequently the only preparation for the long voyage before her. In some instances, their children, equally destitute as themselves, accompanied them ; in others, their sufferings were increased by sudden separation from their young infants. Often did Mrs. Pryor and her friend and companion, Lydia Irving, quit these scenes, in which they had passed nearly the whole day, not to return to their homes, but to go to Whitehall, to represent such cases, that the necessary letters should be dispatched without the loss of a post, ordering the restoration of these poor nurslings to their mothers, before the ship should sail.

In addition to these evils, the women were almost invariably more or less ironed, sometimes cruelly so. On board the Mary Ann, in 1822, Mrs. Pryor complained that " the prisoners from Lancaster Castle arrived, not merely handcuffed, but with heavy irons on their legs, which had occasioned considerable swelling, and in one instance, serious inflammation." There is in existence a list of the names of women, received in irons, on board the Brothers, which sailed in 1823 ; it was taken down at the time, by direction of Mrs. Fry, in order that a represention might be made upon the subject to the Government.   By this list, it appears that twelve arrived on board handcuffed.   Eleven women from Lancaster were sent to the ship " iron-hooped round their legs and arms, and chained to each other.   The complaints of these women were very mournful, they were not allowed to get up or down from the coach without the whole being dragged together ; some of them had children to carry, they received no help, or alleviation to their suffering." A woman from Cardigan travelled with a hoop of iron round her ancle, until she arrived at Newgate, where the sub-matron in-sisted on having it taken off.   In driving the rivet towards her leg to do so, it gave her so much pain, that she fainted under the operation.   She stated, that during a lengthened imprison-ment, she wore an iron-hoop round her waist ; from that a chain connected with another hoop round her leg above the knee, from which a second chain was fastened to a third hoop round her ancle : in the hoop that went round her waist were, she said, two bolts or fastenings in which her hands were confined when she went to bed at night, which bed was only of straw.

Such were a few of the scenes, into which Mrs. Fry was intro-duced, in this department of her important labours for the good of the suffering and the sinful of her own sex.

A simple tribute of affectionate remembrance, from a convict who was transported in 1823, on board the Brothers, should be recorded, in referring to that ship : a calabash from the garden of Hester ———.   The present referred to has reached Mrs. Fry's family, since she was taken from them ; it was accom-panied by a message of gratitude.   The donor recalled herself to their memory as having been school-mistress in Newgate, and that when she left the prison, Mrs. Fry had given her a pound of lump sugar, and half a pound of tea.   Hester ——— has been married twenty years, in New South Wales, is very comfortably established ; and wished her former benefactress to be informed, that she has "plenty of pigs and fowls, buys her tea by the chest; and that the patchwork quilt which now covers her bed, was made of the pieces given her by the ladies when she embarked."

The women on board the Brothers seem to have been orderly and well conducted. The Surgeon afterwards wrote as follows :

"Port Jackson, *May*, 1824.

"How steady is the pace of those who have forsaken the evil of their ways ; such are the females (at least a great number) who have been under moral discipline in Newgate. I have every reason to be pleased with their exemplary conduct ; they submit to restraint, and conform themselves to discipline.

"The force of example and the value of moral discipline have been admirably shown in this voyage ; and when I shall lay before you the proofs, you will become more sensible, perhaps, than you have been of the value of the labours in which you and your friends are employed, and may urge others to join in the same good work."

A Missionary, who sailed in the same vessel, confirmed this pleasing statement.

"For your comfort and encouragement, I beg leave to report to you the good conduct and decent behaviour of the Newgate women. That the kind instructions you have given them were not in vain, was very evident from their conduct during the voyage."

On board the convict ships, as at Newgate, the ladies had to contend with difficulties which were integral parts of the system, and which they were wholly unable to remove ; it was in both instances, a simple practical endeavour on their part to do what they could under existing circumstances, to obviate evils and promote order and good conduct. In this they were indebted to Admiral Young, of the Dockyard at Deptford, for much kind co-operation and assistance in his department, of fitting out the convict ships. The introduction of patchwork, as an employment for the women, was the happy suggestion of this gentleman, when conversing with Mrs. Fry on the difficulty of supplying them with employment during the voyage, he thought it would furnish the largest amount of occupation in the smallest compass.

She had also frequent communication with Admiral Sir Byam Martin, Comptroller of the Navy from 1813 to 1832. This was an important and onerous office, but one which in consequence of alterations in the constitution of the Admiralty, no longer exists. From him she received courteous and unfailing attention ; he appreciated her motives, and considered the arrangements proposed by her, to be not only humane but judicious.

The first advances towards improvement in the female convict ships were made under Sir Byam Martin's direction, and very much was accomplished during the time he continued in office. Amongst the many rough drafts of letters that remain among her papers, the following were addressed to him. One of them refers to an attempt that had been made by a naval surgeon, to discourage the Navy Board from carrying out plans conducive to good order on board convict ships, under the plea that such " comforts," as he called them, did not exist in troop ships.

To ADMIRAL SIR THOMAS BYAM MARTIN, COMPTROLLER
OF THE NAVY.

Mildred's Court, *Third Month*, 2nd, 1820.

Elizabeth Fry cannot feel satisfied that Sir Byam Martin should leave town, without her expressing how much obliged she feels for his prompt and kind attention to the wants of the female convicts, in allowing them more soap and towels for the

voyage. It is no small gratification to observe the great attention paid by the Commissioners of the Navy Board to the welfare
and reformation of the poor convicts. Elizabeth Fry is glad
to find that the building for the women in New South Wales is
begun; she wonders that Samuel Marsden, as Chaplain, and
Deputy Commissary General A——, should not have been
better informed respecting it. Elizabeth Fry has been sorry to
find that the Newgate women, on board the Janus, were not
orderly. It is not improbable that after the gentle government
they had been accustomed to and subdued by ; the change to
rather a different system, and being some of them the most
hardened offenders, may in some degree account for their conduct. It is a fresh proof of the necessity of patience and
perseverance ; for experience proves that some trials and discouragements must be expected in all our undertakings, even
when they are accompanied by the desire of promoting the
cause of righteousness, mitigating the sorrows, and lessening
the temptations of our fellow-creatures. But in these things, we
must endeavour to do our best, and then commit the cause to
Him, who can alone grant a blessing upon our labours, and
change the heart of man.

To Admiral Sir Thomas Byam Martin.

Plashet, *Seventh Month,* 1820.

Respected Friend,

I trust thou wilt excuse my not returning Doctor ——'s
letter before, or answering thy note accompanying it ; but numerous engagements have prevented me. Although it has occasioned me some anxiety, as it has led me to fear, that most
kindly as thou hast seconded our views, thou hast a little mistaken them. I believe, I may say for all the ladies of our Association, that we do not desire indulgences or increased comforts for
convicts, except so far as good and orderly conduct may conduce
to it. Some of our prisons we think decidedly too comfortable ;
and our great wish is, that by employment and instruction, with
habits of cleanliness and order, the time of their imprisonment

may be a time of reformation, not of indulgence. There is one great encouragement to persevere in the care of prisoners, and in forming proper arrangements for them, that in the best regulated gaols the returns are small indeed in comparison of what they are in others; and even in Newgate, as far as we have been able to calculate from the information received from the former Governor of the Prison, a very small proportion return to the women's side, in comparison to the number before we had the care of them. I believe kindness does more in turning them from the error of their ways than harsh treatment; and that many a poor creature claims a compassion and a tenderness that is little known, but to those who visit prisons, as there are many of whom it may be said, that they were driven into guilt, and only want the way to be made open, to return with joy into the paths of virtue.

With respect to convict ships, government appears to us most liberal in its supplies for the poor convicts, more so indeed than would be right for those under punishment, did not the great length of the voyage, and the frequently delicate state of the health of women and children render it almost necessary; and we are of opinion, that having such arrangements made amongst the women as tends to their good order and reformation would render the voyage less agreeable, and of course less tempting to the profligate, though no doubt more safe to the well-disposed, as it would be instrumental in protecting their remaining innocence and virtue; I believe no female convict ship sails without some of this description in her. Surely, for the welfare of such, both here and hereafter, and the hope that even the worst may be preserved from further evil; as well as the important consideration, that for the sake of the colony, the women's morals should be protected on the voyage, it is worth the effort to make even a convict-ship a place for industry, instruction, and reform. I do not doubt thy kindness of heart on this subject; but we so often find in every good work, that enemies arise, some of them perhaps for want of understanding the subject, that I have feared lest any should discourage either thyself, or any other gentlemen who are interested in the cause of prisoners, from adopting such arrangements as are most likely to promote their good, with that of society at large and the security and safety of the community.

I remain, &c.

E. FRY.

Her efforts to ameliorate the condition of these objects of her care, were not confined to the period of the voyage. A letter written by her to the Right Honourable R. Wilmot Horton, explains her views on the arrangements to be made for them on their arrival in the colonies.

Respected Friend,

In compliance with thy obliging proposal, I take the liberty of stating in writing our views relative to the female convicts in Van Diemen's Land ; in order that they may be submitted to the consideration of Lord Bathurst ; as we cannot but fee anxious that the care we extend to this degraded class of the community not only in the different prisons, but also on the voyage, should be rendered permanently beneficial, through the co-operation of government in the colonies. In the first place, we deem it expedient that a building be erected at Hobart Town for the reception of female convicts. The building, if raised by the male convicts, and composed of such materials as the country affords, would, it is supposed, be completed greatly within the present estimate. That a respectable and judicious Matron be there stationed, to superintend the whole establishment under the direction of the Governor, or some magistrate appointed by him for that service. That part of the building be appropriated to the use of an adult and girls' school, and that school-mistresses be selected by the Matron from among the reformed prisoners, provided they be sufficiently qualified for the office. That immediately on the arrival of a ship, after it has been visited, either by the Governor, or by some other person appointed by him, for the purpose of inspecting its general condition ; the convicts be quietly (and as privately as possible) conducted from the ship to the said building, where the deportment of every prisoner

F F 2

shall be scrutinized with exactness. If the Secretary of State
for the Home Department were to direct, that the Surgeon-
superintendent should be furnished by the magistrates, with a
written account of the general conduct and character of every
individual, even previously to their commitment, together with
the nature and extent of their offence; we think it would greatly
aid the Governor in his decision with regard to the proper dis-
posal of the prisoners in the colony. That those who merit a
favourable report be selected, and allowed to be taken into
service, by the respectable inhabitants, under such restraints and
regulations as may be considered needful. The others to remain
confined ; receiving at the same time suitable instruction, and
employment, until they evince sufficient amendment in habits
and dispositions, to warrant the grant of a similar indulgence ;
and we conceive that much benefit might result, if some of the
regulations mentioned in the new Act of Parliament, relative to
prisons were enforced in this colony, and in New South Wales.
We would also propose that a sufficient supply of strong ard
decent clothing, (not parti-coloured) be provided for them during
the voyage, to be put on when they enter the ship, in exchange
for their own ; of which an inventory shall be immediately taken
by a female officer, and given with the clothes to the Surgeon,
(in the presence of their respective owners,) who shall carefully
keep them in reserve, and deliver them to the Matron of the
prison, to which they are destined, who shall receive the same
in presence of the prisoners, and shall at the same times, see,
if they tally correctly with the inventories. And upon their
discharge from prison, but not before, she shall restore them to
their proper owners. We consider that it would be a great
advantage in the voyage, and more especially whilst lying in the
river, that the women should wear a simple uniform dress, and
we think it *indispensable* for establishing order, and for enforcing
the needful regulations on board the ship, that a Matron be
stationed constantly there, whilst they remain in the river—to
attend to their clothing, &c., and to search their female visitors,
in order that no spirituous liquors, or any thing else that is
improper be introduced. Could a person in that capacity
accompany them during the voyage, it would no doubt be

highly useful.   We are pleased to understand, that the Factory in Paramatta, has more than cleared its expenses, during the last year ; as the interest we feel in the welfare of the colonies, induces us, not only to desire the religious and moral improvement of the population at large, but in all our plans we wish to keep in view such a system, as shall eventually prove the most economical to government, as well as the most beneficial to the Colonial States.

In consequence of thy friendly encouragement, I have ventured thus freely to offer with submission our sentiments ; we are fully aware that much has been accomplished, that many of our requests have been granted with obliging readiness, and we shall feel our sense of gratitude much increased, if Lord Bathurst will condescend to peruse these remarks, and to act in compliance, as far as his judgment can approve, and his authority enforce.

Believe me, to remain
With respect and regard,
Thy obliged friend,
ELIZABETH FRY.

To these, and similar communications, prompt and polite consideration was almost invariably paid ; and in many instances, the suggestions they contained, met with the cordial support and co-operation of those to whom they were addressed. It was not for the sinners and outcasts alone that Mrs. Fry pleaded ; whatever she believed likely to promote the real good of the people, and the cause of religion upon earth, found in her a ready advocate.   To the poor and needy her ear was always open, and she would " humble herself," for so she felt it, to ask that for them of her family and friends, which it was not in her own power to bestow.   All classes found in her a kind adviser and a warm sympathiser in their sorrows and their joys.

The Duchess of ———— to Mrs. Fry.

"*June* 28*th*, 1823.

" You, dear madam, were so kind as to call upon me some
days ago, I was most unfortunately out, and missed you ; will
you not have the kindness to try again ?   I cannot express in
writing, half the pleasure your last visit gave me. The poor are
not the only beings to whom you bring hope and comfort, whom
you strengthen, when you hope they are in the right ; and whom
you would assist to recover the way of life, did you see (which
their own feelings, prejudices, temper, or sufferings might blind
them to,) that they were going wrong. If you would let me
have a line, to tell me when I might hope to see you, I would
take care not to be again disappointed.   I leave town the last
week in July.

" Believe me, your most truly obliged,

" ———————— "

Plashet, Fifth Month, 3*rd.*—There are times of encouragement and building up, and of discouragement and treading down.
I remarkably experienced the latter state yesterday, as it respects
the prison cause; I met with ingratitude amongst the prisoners
such as I never remember before, for generally their gratitude
has been quite remarkable.   It called for patience, yet candour
and firmness.   Some reflections also that I found had been cast
upon it, by one who understood the subject, tried me much.
Still, on the prison subject, I have this secret feeling which
wonderfully upholds me under the difficulties that may arise ;
in the first place, I believe I have been providentially brought
into it, not of my own seeking ; and secondly, that if He, who
in a remarkable manner, has hitherto appeared to bless the
work, should be pleased for a season to permit a cloud to pass
over it, that is nothing to me.   I have always considered the
work not mine, and have desired that self may have no reputation in it ; if trials of this kind come they may be for our good
who are engaged in it, and for our humiliation, and for an exercise of charity towards those whom we have sought to serve.
I had also the sorrow, yesterday, of seeing dear Priscilla Buxton

who was here, taken ill. I took her home, with real anxiety on her account, and with some on account of my own children, as the medical man said her complaint was very catching. I desire to cast my care upon the Lord and to submit my cause to Him, and to His tender mercy and loving kindness, trusting that He will still bless our labours amongst the poor prisoners, and quiet their perturbed spirits ; also that dearest Priscilla will soon revive again, and our dear children not materially suffer.

8th.—The poor prisoners quite come down, and very sorry for what they have done. Priscilla better—it proved no serious illness. But from various causes my spirit is much pressed down within me ; partly from an unusual press of very weighty engagements, and discouraging circumstances at the same time arising. Still I repine not, but put my trust in Him who can alone help me, and has hitherto made a way for me. Lord, undertake for Thy unworthy servant, and make way for her, where she may at present see little or no way. Continue, if it be consistent with Thy holy will, to be with her, and bless her in her deeds.

Plashet, 31st.—Since I last wrote, I have passed through a scene of deep affliction, in attending dear Mary Hanbury. I was called to her on Third day, the 6th ; after great illness, she died on the 16th, leaving her beloved father (William Allen), husband, and helpless infant. I had to drink the bitter cup with the afflicted in an unusual degree, so as to bring me very low in myself, out of which state I have not fully risen, but am rather sunk in mind and body. I have, however, the consolation of believing, that I was a help and comfort to my sweet and dear young friend, whose remembrance is precious to me, so was her company, I think I may say to the last, her spirit appearing to overflow with love, joy, and peace. She having, I believe, kept the faith, finished her course, and fought the good fight. I have since attended great part of the Yearly Meeting, and the Prison Meeting; in all, to me a low time. The Prison Meeting and cause, more in a valley to my view, than I think I have yet known since I entered the work, yet I have faith that it will again rise. The Yearly Meeting also, a low time, as it respects myself. But the pressure of engagements that I have had, together with the sorrow I had partaken in, and my almost innumerable occupations have been as if they hurried, and almost overwhelmed my natural mind. I am ready to say, spiritually, Where am I? What am I about? Am I sick or in health? Going backwards or forwards? Lord! Thou knowest that the desires of my heart are still living after Thyself, and that nothing satisfies it, but being filled with the fulness that cometh from Thee.

Plashet, Eighth Month, 7th.—We have lately had much company, which leads to handsome dinners, and that sort of excitement which I feel painful on account of my family; but I find it very difficult to act rightly under some of these circum‑ stances. Oh! for more ability, in the power, and in the spirit to maintain the standard of truth and righteousness in my own house, in all things; so that others may be induced to do the same.

Earlham, Tenth Month, 1st.—My beloved husband left me this morning for London, and I am here with nine children and my little grandson. Since I last wrote, the face of things brightened. I went to Bristol to attend the Quarterly Meeting there, accompanied by my brother, Joseph John Gurney, and my sister E. F.; we left home on Sixth day, the 11th of last month, and returned on Fifth day, the 17th. In this short time we travelled about two hundred and eighty miles, visited the Meeting at Bath, and the Bristol Quarterly Meeting, held two Public Meetings, visited the prison, attended to the magistrates and committee; visited Hannah More, my cousin Priscilla H. Gurney, and several more. Much was accomplished in a short time, although not without deep exercise of spirit, and considerable fatigue of body. We were treated with the utmost kindness wherever our lot was cast; and what was above all, in our various engagements, we have reason humbly to trust that the presence of our Lord was with us. I returned home very poor in spirit, and things pressed so hard upon me that I felt almost ready to give up coming here. But since my arrival, I have been comforted in being with my tenderly beloved brothers and sisters. They are, indeed, near to my heart, their kindness has com‑

forted me, and it has been refreshing to be with them. The last few days, my husband and I have been at Cromer, and paid an interesting visit to my much-loved brothers and sisters there. I was at different times engaged religiously amongst them, and help was granted me in these services. I feel unworthy and unfit, and find that there is need of close, cleansing, baptisms of spirit, to make me in any degree ready thus to espouse the best of causes. I am much struck in having all my children, but one, now here; several of them grown up ; what marvellous changes have I witnessed since I first knew this place ; wonders indeed, have been done for me spiritually and naturally—how have I been raised up, as out of the dust ! I am surrounded by a numerous, fine, and healthy offspring ; one only taken from me, and that one with a peculiar evidence of going to an everlasting and blessed inheritance. Spiritually also how has mercy been shown me ; has not the beloved of my soul said, "live," and how has He been with me in many tribulations, and sanctified many blessings. Indeed, I have found that my Lord is a wonder-working God, and has manifested himself to be to my soul, " Wonderful, Counsellor, the Mighty God, the Everlasting Father, and the Prince of Peace." What can I render for His unspeakable benefits ? Lord, in Thy unmerited mercy continue to be with and bless Thy servant, whose hope is in Thee. Grant also Thy grace to her children, to love, serve, and obey Thee, that her God may be their God, her Saviour their Saviour, and her Comforter their Comforter. Be with, visit, and bless her husband, brothers and sisters, and children's children yet unborn, as well as the sweet grandchild, now granted her. Amen.

Plashet, 18th.—I can hardly express through all, what a sweet, and cheering feeling has covered my heart, upon once more being here, surrounded by most of my family.

27th.—Although under some oppression and sorrow of spirit, I believe it right for me to make a stir in our parish, about the Bible Society, for the sake of the rich and the poor. I do not do this, supposing that I can do much in it myself, but thinking that others may be set to work. I am quite convinced that this sort of intercourse between the rich and poor is very profitable, and that, uniting together, in any degree, to promote the one great object, the real good of others, is in itself beneficial ; and

breaks down many walls of partition between the two classes.
If, dearest Lord, it promote Thy cause, make it manifest to be
Thy work, and bless our labours in it, to the good of this parish
and neighbourhood.

Plashet, Eleventh Month, 24th, 1823.—Since I last wrote, I
have been much engaged in the parish, amongst the poor, which
is certainly satisfactory to me, and I have met with much encouragement amongst them.   I have also met with unexpected
difficulty, discouragement, and opposition, to my real surprise.
Yet I trust this may be blessed to myself, in making self of no
reputation in the work, and leading me to feel the foundation
upon which I act, that all may be simply done as a duty to my
neighbour called for from me by the Lord. It is rather difficult
even in these laudable works (for so they are in themselves), to
be unruffled by the various views of our fellow mortals ; and to
maintain the spirit of love and charity towards those, who not
only view things differently from ourselves, but show towards us
an improper feeling.   I truly desire to be kept in the spirit of
love ; and to endeavour by the meekness of wisdom, as far as it
is granted to me, to win over my neighbours to what I believe
to be a right thing for our parish. Ah, for a little help, dearest
Lord, in this, as well as many other callings, and let this labour
of love tend to establish some in the ways of righteousness, and
to lead others to turn from the evil of their way.   Preserve thy
servants engaged in it in a humble, patient, diligent, and persevering frame of mind.

Plashet, 10th.—Upon reading the second chapter of Deute-
ronomy, I felt this verse so much the acknowledgment of my
heart, that I transcribe it : " For the Lord thy God hath
blessed thee in all the works of thy hand, he knoweth thy
walking through this great wilderness, these forty years the
Lord thy God hath been with thee, thou hast lacked nothing."
Although all the works of my hand may not yet fully have
appeared blessed; yet upon many, may I not say most, a peculiar
blessing seems to have rested.   Lord, continue to be with Thy
unworthy servant, that trusteth in Thee, and let her not want
that which may be needful for body, soul, or spirit.   Grant this
petition, dearest Lord, not on account of any merit of her's, but
for the sake of Him who gave Himself for her.   Amen.

CHAPTER XIII.

Plashet, Second Month, 7th, 1824.—I have once more a few minutes to express my feelings, and present situation here. My mind and time are very much absorbed at home, where many things deeply occupy my heart and head. To do right in my many relative duties is very difficult; how deeply I feel my short comings in them ! and yet I fervently desire to do my best. —————— has my prayers much more often than the day. Lord, help this dear child by Thy Spirit, guide him by Thy counsel, and save him by that salvation that cometh by Christ. And for my sweet dear William, so visit him, and influence him by Thy anointing, that he may become a vessel of honour, fully calculated and prepared to show forth Thy praise. Ah! dearest Lord, bless the lads ; and above all things I ask of Thee, far above all temporal good, sanctify them and fit them to exalt and magnify Thy great and ever-excellent name. Although my prayers may now be raised, particularly for my two sons, feeling them more exposed to the world than many of the others, yet my fervent petitions are very often raised for all my children. My household also has my anxious solicitude ; desiring amongst them all, to do justly, to love mercy, and walk humbly, and also to act the part of a really kind mistress, by not countenancing their faults, and by keeping up a proper authority. My public concerns are at this time very pressing, for I have to remove prejudices in the minds of many, which prevent ladies visiting

7

prisons; other things also press at times, almost too much upon me ; so that my mind feels really worn.   Indeed it is my faith, that were there not a principle that enlivens, strengthens, and calms my soul, I could not possibly attend to all that comes before me, without being really confused and brought down by it. I may truly say it is often astonishing to myself, how help is laid upon One who is mighty; who is willing to assist His dependent children, and enables them to get through that, which I believe to their natural powers alone would be impossible.   How remarkably do I at times know my spirit to be refreshed, and instead of being worn down, " my youth renewed like the eagles;" all fresh and lively again and ready to " go forward."

21st.—My mind continues almost too full; at times I fear that it will be overstrained.   Oh! for a quiet spirit and humble dependence ; remembering that I am but a frail instrument, and however others may estimate my services, and therefore require them of me, yet I must recollect Him, who can equally well carry on His work with them, or without them.   The burden and perplexity of the opposition to improvement in prisons, is almost too much for me ; it is so much against my nature to take my own defence, or even that of the cause in which I am interested into my own hands.   Oh ! for a little of the best wisdom, and influence of the Holy Spirit to walk circumspectly amongst all men ; wise as the serpent, harmless as the dove, and however I may be treated, to be myself full of charity.

Plashet, Third Month, 11*th.*—I am now, thanks be to my gracious Lord and Master, nearly recovered from a short, though severe, attack of illness.   I have felt for some little time past very delicate, as if I were really overdone, and as if I could not go on much longer; these feelings increased so much, that it was with difficulty I rose, and came down to breakfast on Second day morning.   I sat the reading, and a few minutes afterwards fainted quite away.   I was completely laid low, and hardly able to keep awake half an hour all day, accompanied with other unpleasant symptoms.   I could but feel how soon we are brought very low ; it was I think the most sudden plunge into real illness that I ever experienced.   It brought many things home to my mind.   First, a desire that I might be more willing to suffer, and to die ; also more ready.   Secondly, a fear lest my heart was too much occupied *in doing*, and with the things of this life. Thirdly, the want of more constant, more deep and living faith. As to the prospect before me, of paying a religious visit to Friends of Worcester and Birmingham, it did not harass me, although, with my sister Elizabeth, I had obtained a certificate from our Monthly Meeting for that purpose.   I was enabled to commit this cause, and then leave it.   It appeared that I had to make this sacrifice of my will, to be ready to leave all, for my dear Master's sake; and I am glad I was enabled to do it, whether the sacrifice be accepted or not.   I have a very low estimate of our instrumentality, for I know that there is a Power that can equally work with or without His instruments.   And even if He may be pleased to draw their hearts in love to some afar off, and try their willingness to attend to His call ; yet he may fulfil all without them, equally visit His people, and equally as He may see meet, grant the reward of peace.

14th.—If I should go, I think I never left home for such a service in a state of greater, if so great reduction.   Still I believe I must go in faith, trusting in Him, who I humbly hope has put me forth, and will go before us, if this offering be required at our hands, which I cannot help believing that it is through all our discouragements, and the many clouds that have obscured the prospect.

LETTER TO ONE OF HER DAUGHTERS.

Warwick, *Third Month*, 19*th*, 1824.

My Dearest Katharine,

Here we are so far on our way; it is wonderful to me how we have gone on.   On Third day evening, when we arrived at Worcester, I was faint, but still went to the Meeting of Ministers and Elders, where I felt help very near, but I was in a delicate state of health.   We went to Dr. D——'s, where we were most kindly cared for.   On Fourth day, I passed through deep and great exercise of mind, and weakness of body, but that Power that has so often helped me and strengthened me, enabled me to go through all, to the great relief of my mind; but in the evening I felt very unwell, so much so, that I thought if better

in the morning it would be surprising; however, I was rather
better, but there was such a party to meet us at breakfast,
clergy, methodists, &c., &c. We had after breakfast a solemn
reading, my brother Samuel read, he has been a comfort indeed
to me. We then proceeded to the prison; I should think thirty
or forty with us, magistrates, and others. After going over the
prison, it was proposed we should have all the prisoners, men and
women, and the company, collected in the chapel, which we dared
not refuse. Picture us in a large chapel, full of almost all descriptions of people. Samuel, Elizabeth, and I, besides two clergymen and magistrates at the upper end. Samuel read the
fifteenth chapter of Luke. Then I spoke to them, afterwards
my dear sister. It finished in prayer, and was a very solemn
time; much satisfaction was expressed by all parties. I think
I am really better, but far from my usual health. We have had
two Meetings to-day. I am sorry to say I find the post is
gone; but I must say farewell, in much very near and dear
love. I long to tell you much more.

I am thy nearly attached mother,

ELIZABETH FRY.

Plashet, Third Month, 29*th.*—We returned home last Fifth
day, having accomplished the duty we had in prospect, to our own
peace, and I trust to the edification of those amongst whom
our lot has been cast. I continued very unwell the whole
journey, and what with exercise of mind, and real illness of
body, I think I have seldom known such a time; nor do I ever
remember being so helped through the different services that I
was brought into. Visiting gaols, attending two Quarterly
Meetings, and many not Friends; one occasion in Worcester
gaol; one large Public Meeting, the first I ever had of that
description; and many other Meetings: but the way I was
raised up, as from the dust, was wonderful to myself, enabled to
speak with power, and in the Quarterly Meetings to go from
service to service. It was indeed a remarkable evidence, that
there is in man something beyond the natural part, that when
that is in its lowest, weakest state, helps and strengthens; none
can tell what its power is but those who submit to it. I now

feel fully called to rest. I gratefully remember the abundant kindness shown me upon my journey. Greater enlargement of my heart in love do I never remember, or to have met more from others. I have been permitted to feel throughout this illness, at times, very sweet consolation. A state of rest, as if the sense of pain and sorrow was taken away from body and mind, and now and then almost like a peep into the joys of the King-dom.

Plashet, Fourth Month, 10th.—I feel remarkably unable to enter any active service. I know that power spiritually and naturally are not at my command, and if in mercy it should be again granted me, may I in humility, simplicity, and faithful-ness, let my day's work keep pace with my day.

Blackheath, Fifth Month.—I have a dear son and daughter willing and ready to take me in, and do every thing they can for me, and who so well accommodate me.

How tender mercy is shown to me spiritually, strength suffi-cient given to bear the burden of my illness, although at times heavy. How my pains have been mitigated, when at times they have felt too much for me, and my secret prayers answered, by relief coming in the needful time.

First day, 15th.—Yesterday, after a very weak and faint morning, I attended our Ladies' British Society Meeting;* it was surprising, even to myself, to find what had been accom-plished! How many prisons are now visited by ladies, and how much is done for the inhabitants of the prison-house, and what a way is made for their return from evil. It is marvellous in my eyes, that a poor instrument should have been the apparent cause of setting forward such a work. Deep as my interest has certainly been in the destitute and forlorn ; yet how much more, both in time and heart, have I been occupied with my own family. I fancy that my natural affections are very acute, and that if it had not pleased a kind Providence to lead me into some other services, and in His tender mercy to bless me in them, I think there would at times have been great danger of my being pressed down out of measure by home cares.

* Ladies' British Society for Promoting the Reformation of Female Prisoners.

The Meeting alluded to, was the third anniversary of the " Ladies' British Society for Promoting the Reformation of Female Prisoners." It had been formed as a central point for communication, and for mutual assistance between the various associations engaged in visiting female prisoners in different parts of England; also for the purpose of corresponding with those persons on the continent, who interested themselves in these subjects.

The Duchess of Gloucester honoured the Society with her patronage ; many distinguished names were found amongst its vice-patronesses—some of these ladies had visited the prisons in their own neighbourhoods ; and the Duchess of Gloucester when on a journey with the Princess Augusta, had condescended personally to inspect the state of a prison on their way. On the present occasion, Mrs. Fry and her friends were encouraged by the fact, that some of the arrangements which had been adopted by them, and found to be peculiarly useful, had become the law of the land, and were enforced in the principal prisons of the kingdom, in consequence of an Act of Parliament passed during the preceding session. The most important of these regulations was, the appointment of female officers ; increased means afforded for religious instruction ; and compulsory employment.

The Convict Ship Committee was, and still is, a branch of this Society.

The necessity of asylums for the reception of discharged prisoners claimed at this time the attention of the Ladies' Association. The report of the year 1824, mentions the Shelter for this purpose, at Dublin, and a Refuge at Liverpool. The establishment of similar institutions quickly followed in Great Britain, and on the continent of Europe.

In 1822, a small house for sheltering some of the most hopeful cases of discharged prisoners, was opened in Westminster, under the name of Tothill Fields Asylum. It owed its existence to the Christian benevolence of one lady—Miss Neave. She has consecrated her time and purse to this important object, which was first suggested to her mind during a drive with Mrs. Fry, thus related by herself :—" A morning's expedition with dear Mrs. Fry made me at once resolve to add my help, if ever so feebly, to the good cause. I distinctly remember the one observation made. I can call to mind at this moment, the look, and tone, so peculiar, so exclusively her's who spoke—' Often have I known the career of a promising young woman, charged with a first offence, to end in a condemned cell! Was there but a Refuge for the young offender, my work would be less painful.' That one day's conversation upon these subjects, and in this strain, laid the foundation of our prisoners' home."

The inmates, at first, were only four in number; in 1824, they had increased to nine; at the present time, under the name of " The Royal Manor Hall Asylum," it contains fifty young women ; and since its first establishment, six hundred and sixty-seven have been received within its walls.

There was another class of persons who claimed the attention of the ladies of the British Society at this meeting. The vicious and neglected little girls, so numerous in London, early hardened in crime, who, whether they had or had not been imprisoned, had no chance of reformation at home; yet were too young to be placed with advantage in any existing asylum. Before the next anniversary, a School of Discipline, for the reception of such children was opened at Chelsea, where, withdrawn from their former associates, they might be trained to orderly and virtuous habits. The idea first occurred to Mrs. Fry, when conversing in the yard at Newgate, with her friend Mrs. Benjamin Shaw, on the extreme difficulty of disposing of some very juvenile prisoners about to be discharged. She then begged Mrs. Shaw to consider the subject, and to draw up some plan for the purpose. This lady immediately applied herself to the important work, nor did she relax in her exertions, until she had seen the School of Discipline firmly established, and its value tested by the experience of years.

Mrs. Fry was anxious that Government should adopt this Institution, for receiving abandoned female children, and addressed Sir Robert Peel, then Secretary of State, on the subject. He warmly encouraged the design as one " capable of effecting much good." He recommended its being supported by the subscriptions of individuals unconnected with public establishments, and enclosed a liberal donation from himself.

Both these Institutions continue to be very important auxiliaries of the British Ladies' Society, receiving considerable pecuniary assistance from its funds, in consideration of the many individuals placed in them, by its sub-committee for the Patronage of Discharged Female Prisoners.

But neither these, nor any existing establishments, adequately meet the needs of the many applicants discharged from the London prisons ; and until some further refuge for such is established, the labour bestowed upon them, during their imprisonment, must remain, in too many instances, an incomplete work, whether begun by the chaplain, the officers of the gaol, or the ladies of the Visiting Association. Earnestly and unflinchingly did Mrs. Fry urge this topic. She grieved to know, that persons not utterly hardened, not wholly given over to depravity, who desired to retrace the downward road along which they had travelled, continually found themselves without resource, without encouragement, exposed to the condemnation of the world, or renewed temptations to vice. She felt, that until every unhappy fallen one, without exception, had the opportunity afforded her of repentance and amendment of life, England, as a Christian country, had not fulfilled the injunction of our blessed Lord : " *As* I have loved you that ye also love one another."

Brighton, Fifth Month, 18*th.*—We arrived this evening,

my health continuing very delicate. I have been induced to come here, partly by finding my weakness increase, and partly to oblige my husband, and others; although it is on many accounts much to my regret, leaving my dear children at Blackheath, where I was just arrived with great part of my family. I have also much felt leaving the dear Friends at the Yearly Meeting; still I trust we have done right in coming, and can now, only commend myself and my all, absent and present, to Him who alone can keep and preserve us; and if it please Him to bless this measure for my recovery, may thankful hearts be our portion.

First day, 23rd.—I am once more away from Meeting on this day; but my strength does not appear sufficient, to venture to sit one. It certainly has, until the last few days, been upon the decline; I cannot but feel how unworthy I am of the many comforts that surround me, I am indeed most abundantly and agreeably supplied. It is a favour to be able so greatly to enjoy the beauties of nature as I do; seldom so ill, but I receive pleasure, and I trust profit from them; the sea is now an almost hourly source of pleasure to me, when I am awake, as is my garden when at home. I feel this the most when from being in a weak state, important things and the business of life do not occupy me so much, and my mind and body appear called upon to rest. I felt this morning as I sometimes have before, about the time people generally assemble to worship, (when I have been sitting in solemn silence poorly, and alone;) *peculiar unity* with, and sweet love for, the members of the Church of Christ, not only that part of it to which I belong, but to others also. I do believe there is a communion of spirits, that neither separation of person, nor difference of sentiment can obstruct, if we abide in a watchful waiting state, and that so many of the members of the living Church, being engaged in waiting upon, and worshipping our God, through Christ Jesus our Lord, spreads a good and refreshing influence which extends even to those who are absent.

Sixth Month, 6th.—Having passed through a time of deep distress, oh may I profit by it! May I now in real simplicity of heart trust Him in all things, who knows what is best for me,

and seek to turn from myself, and keep my eye single to my
Lord and Saviour; may it be my meat and drink, to do and
suffer, according to His ever blessed will.

Seventh Month, 9th.—Through fluctuations, I have been
favoured gradually to recover my health in great degree;—
the cause of thankfulness in being relieved from so painful an
illness, has been much more than I can express, or I fear,
properly estimate. I have several times attended Meeting to
my peace and satisfaction. I have very much entered life again,
and been a good deal occupied in endeavouring to form a charity,
for the good of the poor. I have feared for myself in it, lest it
should overdo me; and I have feared for my best welfare, in so
soon being brought into contact with so many persons and once
more taking a prominent part in the world; but if the thing be
right, I trust that I shall not suffer, and that it will prosper to
the good and comfort of the poor, and to the real advantage
and edification of those, who are willing to give up their time
and money for their advantage. How does it require to dwell
low in spirit, for self, to take neither part nor glory in things
of this kind.

During her stay at Brighton, Mrs. Fry was often distressed by
the multitude of applicants for relief. This was not confined to
beggars by profession, who infested the streets, following carriages and foot-passengers with clamorous importunity, but
extended to the resident poor, many of whom had acquired the
habit of asking assistance at the houses, not only of the inhabitants, but the visitors to the place. It was difficult for the
former, but almost impossible for the latter, to discover their
true condition, whether their poverty was real or assumed; and
if real, whether caused by improvidence and idleness on their
own part, or whether the result of misfortune and providential
infliction.

Not long before, she had made the acquaintance of Dr.
Chalmers, and had learned something of his views as to the best
method of assisting the lower classes, and encouraging them in

habits of self dependence, industry, and forethought. He had explained to her his experience of Provident Societies, and the advantage of small deposits being made by the working classes when earning any thing beyond a bare sufficiency, for the time of sickness or old age. This subject had arrested her attention, as one of great importance; for she saw that very much might be done towards ameliorating the condition of the lower orders, by arousing them to exertion, and teaching them how to assist themselves. But whilst she perceived all the advantages that would arise from such a system, she was not prepared to yield one point to those political economists, who theorised on the wants of the poor, as a mechanical principle, which should be left to find its own level. Her heart was solemnly impressed with the duty of almsgiving—of " providing for the sick and needy," in the literal acceptation of the words. " The poor" were, to her feelings, a sacred trust committed to the faithful and obedient, to receive at their hands, tenderness, consideration, and relief, as the case might be. She considered the commands of Scripture to be imperative ; and the privilege to be a high one, which permitted him to whom the Lord had given more abundantly, " to do good, and to communicate, for with such sacrifices God is well pleased."

Her mind being occupied by this subject, and she in a re-markable manner possessing the quality of bringing good into action, and practically applying principles, the truth of which had commended themselves to her own mind ; it was but a pro-bable result of the mendicancy, poverty, and imposture, she witnessed at Brighton, that the information she had acquired from Dr. Chalmers should occur to her as affording a probable remedy for these evils.

In a country village, we generally find the squire, the clergy-man, and their families to be the medium of almsgiving. Chil-dren are educated, clothing clubs established, and the sick sup-

plied with those little comforts so important to them. In suburban districts the resident gentry frequently unite in caring
for their poorer neighbours. Of later years, field-gardens, or
allotments, have been introduced; arrangements by which time
is available for profit, and the hours of the labourer, which he is
entitled to employ for his own advantage, may produce to him
a species of capital.

In most towns, in manufacturing districts, and where masses
of people congregate, the case is different. There the most
importunate, the least diffident—the mother of a family, who
prefers gossiping and wandering about, to the care of her home
and children, obtains the almsgiving of the more wealthy.
Encouragement is held out to begging and improvidence, for
the giver, satisfied in having "relieved the poor," asks not
whether his charity has tended to good, or increased evil. Some
may inquire into the circumstances and character of the appli-
cant, before extending relief, but this is the exception, not the
rule; and the same thing may occur, as in a case of absolute
imposture, the most intrusive obtain assistance, whilst the sufferer,
who shrinks from begging, who struggles to exist upon his own
resources, has nothing beyond the coarse hard fare of poverty,
unfit for illness, and unlikely to induce restoration to health.

Brighton appeared exactly the field for working a District
Visiting Society. There was no lack of benevolent feeling, and
abounding affluence was to be found there; but the former was
frequently misdirected and the latter misapplied. A Provident
Society had been in operation for some years, but this touched
only one part of the evil.

It was no easy matter to unite in the same object, persons
wholly differing in opinion, especially on religious matters; but
without co-operation the desired end could not be effected, and
after some delays, and much discouragement, the Brighton
District Society was established, under the patronage of the

8

Bishop of Chichester.   The Earl of Chichester President; the Dean of Salisbury, the Rev. H. M. Wagner, Viscount Molesworth, Sir Edward Kerrison, and Mr. Kemp, amongst the Vice-Presidents.   The objects of the Society were stated to be, " The encouragement of industry and frugality among the poor, by visits at their own habitations; the relief of real distress, whether arising from sickness or other causes; and the prevention of mendicity and imposture."

In January, 1835, the First Annual Report was given to the public.   The Society embraced two objects: " The relief of real distress, and a system of small deposits, upon the plan of Savings Banks, which was encouraged by a present premium, in order to induce the labouring classes to try to lay by a little store for their own necessities."   To accomplish the desired ends, Visitors were found or offered themselves to go from house to house, and become acquainted personally with the character and circumstances of their occupants.

" The smallest pittance, as a deposit for rent, or clothing, or fuel, by being often repeated, may prove to the poorest, that it is within their power effectually to help themselves, by such habits of frugality and resolution."   The personal intercourse of the Visitors with the poor, is a most important branch of the subject, it tends to good-will on both sides; it induces order and cleanliness amongst the visited, and a feeling of kindness and interest in the heart of the Visitor.

A subscription was raised for assisting cases of distress, and for the purpose of adding something to the savings of the depositors.   This premium upon the savings of the poor must be considered as a very doubtful measure, and only to be tolerated in the out-set, to induce them to begin the habit.   To be permanent, any institution of this nature must be self-supporting; and the lesson is not taught, unless the depositor finds the advantages of his own saving and economy, without help or assistance from others.

To enable the Visitors to afford judicious relief where really required, and to become in this manner the almoners of those, whose circumstances preclude the possibility of personal investigation is a very different question, and one which recommends itself to the approval of every reflecting mind. In a town, divided amongst District Visitors, relief is equalized. A few are not relieved by many, but the many by the whole. Five years afterwards, an active member of the Committee, amongst other particulars, says :—" *Brighton, November* 10*th*, 1830.—The families visited are improved in habits of cleanliness. This and similar things, follow from the regular intercourse of ranks. The higher are not degraded, but the lower are raised." From this period, District Societies and the benefits they confer, became a subject of great interest to Mrs. Fry, she assisted in their formation in many places, and as opportunity offered, recommended them as useful and desirable in towns and populous districts.

In Mrs. Fry's illness at Brighton she was liable to distressing attacks of faintness, during the night and early morning, when it was frequently necessary to take her to an open window for the refreshment of the air. Whether through the quiet grey dawn of the summer's morning, or by the fitful gleams of a tempestuous sky, one living object always presented itself to her view on these occasions ; the solitary blockade-man* pacing the shingly beach. It first attracted her attention, and soon excited her sympathy, for the service was one of hardship and of danger.

In the course of a drive, passing near a station, she stopped the carriage and spoke to one of the men ; he civilly informed her, they were not allowed to hold any communication with strangers, and declined further conversation. Afraid that by

* Now called the " Coast Guard," or " Preventive Service," for the detection of smuggling.

having spoken to him, she might, inadvertently, be the means of bringing him into difficulty, she gave him her card for his commanding officer ; desiring that he might be informed she had spoken to the man, in order to inquire a few particulars respecting the state of the men, and of their wives and children, whom she saw about their dwellings. This little occurrence had almost passed from her mind, when a few days afterwards the subject was renewed by a visit from the Naval Lieutenant in command of the Station where she had stopped. He came to answer her inquiries in person. The service was one that entailed much privation, both on officers and men ; the stations were often placed in dreary and inaccessible places. From the very nature of the service they were precluded from communication with the inhabitants, amongst whom it was exceedingly unpopular; constantly harassed with nocturnal watching, exposed to danger, both from weather and affrays with smugglers, they might almost be said to be in a state of blockade themselves. What Mrs. Fry heard, only confirmed her desire to do something for their moral and religious good. The lieutenants in command of several of the neighbouring posts warmly seconded her views. Considering the nature and regulations of the Coast Blockade, almost the only thing that could be done, was to supply the people with Bibles and useful books. In furtherance of this purpose, she applied to the Bible Society, whose liberal response was conveyed in the following letter from one of its Secretaries :—

THE REV. DOCTOR STEINKOPFF TO MRS. FRY, BRIGHTON.

"Savoy, *July* 12*th*, 1824.

" My Esteemed and Dear Friend,

" I have received your truly kind and affectionate letter this morning, and immediately communicated its contents to the

Printing Sub-Committee of the British and Foreign Bible Society, which happened to meet at Earl Street. They have unanimously resolved to transmit fifty Bibles and twenty-five New Testaments to the Brighton Auxiliary, with a request to place them at your disposal, for distribution among the men employed in the Preventive Service. In general, we have found cheap sale preferable to gratuitous distribution, but if in consideration of all the peculiar circumstances of the above-mentioned men, you should judge it most desirable to present the copies as a donation to them, you are at liberty so to do.

" Mrs. Steinkopff and myself, thank you most cordially for every expression of kindness, and every assurance of Christian affection. We rejoice most sincerely to hear that your health is improving, and we unite with the members of your dear family, as well as with all your friends, in the humble prayer that it may please the Great Disposer of all human affairs, long to spare your useful life, and soon to restore you to perfect health and strength. But whatever He may be pleased to send—health or sickness, prosperity or adversity, life or death, this we know, that God is love ; and that all things must work together for good to them that love God. May His love be shed abroad into our hearts by the Holy Ghost. May it be our delight as His redeemed people to serve Him without fear ; in holiness and righteousness before Him, all the days of our life.

" We live in most important and eventful times ; the work of God is enlarging, His kingdom is advancing ; far distant nations hear the joyful sound, sinners are converted, the people of God provoke each other to love and good works, one Christian and benevolent institution is rising after the other, great good is accomplished ; but Satan is also stirred up, his emissaries are busy, he is sowing the tares of discord, fanatics arise, the Roman Catholic Hierarchy endeavours to regain its lost ground ; a new Papal rescript has appeared against Bible societies, yet, let this be our motto, ' If God be for us, who can be against us.'

" I remain my dear friend,
　　　" Yours respectfully,
　　　　　" C. F. A. STEINKOPFF."

The distribution of these books was a welcome office to her, to whom it was intrusted ; it brought her into agreeable and interesting communication with some of the officers as well as men stationed in the neighbourhood of Brighton. Her endeavours to serve them were received with openness, and responded to with the warmth and simplicity of the sailor character—a communication a few months afterwards proved that the benefit was likely to be lasting.

FROM LIEUTENANT C——, R. N.

"Salt Dean Watch-House, March 22nd, 1825.

"My dear Madam,

"Happy am I in being able to make you acquainted with the unexpected success I have met with, in my attempt to forward amongst the seamen employed on the coast, your truly laudable and benevolent desire, the dissemination of the Holy Scriptures. I have made a point of seeing Lieutenant H——, who has promised me, if you will extend your favours to Duchmere, he will distribute the books, and carefully attend to the performance of Divine Service on the Sabbath day. Also Lieutenant D——, who will shortly have a command in this division. I trust, Madam, I shall be still further able to forward those views, which must to all those who embrace them prove a sovereign balm in the hour of death, and in the day of judgment. With respectful compliments to the ladies, allow me to remain dear Madam, your devoted servant,

"——— ———."

A copy of the following letter was enclosed.

TO LIEUTENANT C——, R. N.

" Salt Dean Naval Watch-House, near Brighton,
" March 21st, 1825.

" Sir,

" We, the seamen of Salt Dean Station, having the pleasure to announce to those ladies, whose goodness has pleased them

to provide the Bibles and Testaments for the use of us seamen that
we have received them.   We do therefore, return our sincere and
most hearty thanks for the same, and we do assure the ladies
whose friendship has proved so much in behalf of seamen, that
every care shall he taken of the said books ; and at the same
time great care shall be taken to instruct those who have not the
gift of education, and we at any time shall feel a pleasure in
doing the same.

" We are, Sir,

" Your most obedient and dutiful servants,

" WILLIAM BELL,

" D. STRINGER,

" in the name of the Salt Dean party."

We have seen Mrs. Fry for many years, pressed by domestic
duties, and by cares from without, seldom, for more than a few
hours enjoying rest or mental repose, scarcely enough, to recruit
her for coming exertion.   We are now to look upon rather a
different scene, and find her enjoying a lengthened period of
comparative leisure.   Between the river Thames, and a large
piece of contiguous water, called Dagenham Breach, stand two
cottages, surrounded by trees, mostly willows, on an open space
of lawn, with beds of reeds behind them and on either side
covering the river bank.   They are open to the south-west, and
are only to be attained by a rough and circuitous cart-road, or
by crossing the water in front of the cottages.   A narrow dyke
led from the Tilbury Fort Road to the Breach waters.   There a
boat would meet the comer and convey him to that secluded
watery world.   Before this year, Dagenham had been but an
occasional resort for fishing; now the repairs of the house at
Plashet, induced the family to try it as a temporary abode.
The experiment answered, and for some years, many summer
weeks were passed by them in that singular retreat.

The life led there was one of real enjoyment ; boating, fishing, the beautiful views of the Thames, and its opposite banks of Erith and Belvidere, the absence of form, the almost living in the open air, were pleasant and refreshing. Mrs. Fry delighted in the repose it afforded—her exquisite love of Nature was indulged, her children lived around her; the busy world seemed left behind. Some of those summer evenings are graven on the memory of the survivors. The glorious sunsets, the shipping on the river, the watery sounds, the freshness of the air, the happy groups of childhood, the pleasure of the parents, but above all, the calm bright look and spirit with which she enjoyed the whole. How pleased she was at the happiness around her, how entertained at the little adventures incident to boats and boating, how ready to unite in expeditions amongst the upland lanes and heaths of Beacontree and Hornchurch, and to encourage that gladness of heart which has its origin in the beautiful and the true.

Dagenham, Seventh Month, 30*th.*—We left Brighton last Sixth day, the 23rd, and after what I passed through in suffering, and afterwards in doing in various ways, I may acknowledge that I have no adequate expression to convey the gratitude due to my merciful and gracious Lord. I left it after a stay of nearly ten weeks, with a comparatively healthy body, and above all, a remarkably clear and easy mind ; with a portion of that overflowing peace, that made all things natural and spiritual appear sweet, and in near love and unity, not only with Friends there, but *many, many* others. I felt as if, although an unworthy instrument, my labours there had not been in vain in the Lord, whether in suffering or in doing. It has not been without a good deal of anxiety, fatigue, and discouragement, that this state of sweet peace has been attained, as I am apt to suffer so much from many fears and doubts, particularly when in a weak state of health. The District Society, in which I was interested, I left, I trust, in a way for establishment; and likely to be very useful to the poor and to the rich. Also an arrangement to supply the Blockade men on the coast with Bibles and other books: and I hope they will be put in the way

of reading them, instead of losing their time. But in carrying
out these plans, and particularly for the District Society, there
were many discouragements, no person, at one time, believing
them to be practicable from the great difficulty of bringing
parties together, who, through their peculiar religious views,
and other causes, never would co-operate ; indeed, at one time,
the thing appeared to come to an end, but it unexpectedly rose
again, and as far as I can judge, is in a fair way of establishment. Some of the poor Blockade men seemed much affected
by the attention paid them, as also did their officers ; and I am
ready to hope that a little seed is scattered there. In Meetings
I passed through much, at times going when I feared I should
faint from weakness ; but I found that help was laid on One
who is Mighty, and I may indeed say, in my ministerial services, that out of weakness I was made strong. The Meetings
were generally largely attended by those not Friends, of course
without invitation, but I trust that they were good ones, and
that we were edified together. This was through deep humiliation, and many, many fears. It certainly calls for great care
and watchfulness in all things that we enter, to find that they
be not of ourselves, but of our Master, whose servants we are ;
for He alone should point out our work.

The end, in an uncommon manner, appeared to crown all.
Upon my way home I spent a few days at my uncle Barclay's, at
Bury Hill. I much feel my uncle's great liberality in helping
me so much with the poor. May he not lose his reward !

I was a little overwhelmed in once more arriving in my own
neighbourhood ; and upon visiting Plashet, on my way here,
my heart felt tendered at the remembrance that I had left that
place twelve weeks that day, and then begun my wandering
life ; how much I had passed through since that time, and what
a blessing to be so much better. I expect that it will be long
before my return home, as the repairs of the house are not nearly
completed.

EXTRACT OF A LETTER TO ONE OF HER DAUGHTERS.

Plashet House, *Tenth Month,* 8*th,* 1824.

—— The vallies at present are in measure my portion. A cloud has in degree certainly rested upon us, which I do not feel removed, although broken. But I think my weak state adds much to this feeling, a sort of incapacity fully to arise, and a tendency to sink under circumstances, as if my power naturally was hardly equal to the many demands upon me. I am certainly a very different person ; I would do, but I cannot do that which I would. Yesterday I dared not go to Newgate, nor the Sixth day before : I have only been once. But if the work be as I trust it is, of the Lord, it will go on without a poor creature like me. The dispensations that I have been under for many months past, have been very humbling. May they truly profit, and further, do that for me which I most desire, even draw me nearer to my God and Saviour ; and may He who has, in so marvellous a manner, led me through this wilderness, prevent my being cast down too low, and enable me to estimate my many blessings, spiritual and temporal ; which I am very sensible have been unusually granted me in many ways, though I believe that remarkable depths as well as remarkable heights have, in the ordering of Infinite wisdom, been my portion, but through all, I may indeed say, " The Lord be magnified," and may I bless His holy name for ever. I have unexpectedly been led to say so much.

I am thy very loving mother,

ELIZABETH FRY.

Plashet, First Month, 6*th,* 1825.—Since I last wrote, I have visited Norfolk, altogether satisfactorily. My beloved sister Rachel being unwell, and my dear brother Joseph wanting me, induced me to go ; though I felt indeed a poor, short-coming, unworthy one amongst them, and rather low in spirit, yet I believe that it was all well being there. Besides Earlham, I was at Runcton, and enjoyed my dear brother and sisters' kindness. I hope ever gratefully to remember his kindness and help in times of trouble—may the better blessing rest upon him and his.

My dearest daughter Rachel has been very unwell, which has taken up much of my time and attention. The unfinished state of our house has continued to produce much disorder and confusion, which has tried my mind, its effect being very undesirable upon the household generally. The last day of the last year, I lost a dear valuable Friend, who had just become an elder of our Meeting. After a few days' illness he was taken away from us no doubt in mercy and wisdom, but it is a great loss to those that are left. He was one of whom I believe, that after passing through the fire, he came out double refined, and fitted to join, not only the militant, but the triumphant church. My dear sister Catherine has been very ill the last few days, which has closely brought home to me the uncertainty of all things here.

I now wish to look back upon the year that has just passed, and to endeavour to examine my present standing. As for outward circumstances, I have lost none *very* near to me, but we have known more than common sorrow from illness. I might say I was seriously unwell, from the beginning of the Third Month to the autumn. I passed through many very painful hours, and some peaceful ones, a few of deep suffering ; I question, whether in my life comfort and hope were more, if so much, extinct in my mind. Still, "a prayer-hearing, answering God," delivered me out of my distresses, I may say, " plucked my feet out of the mire and clay, and set them upon a rock, again established my goings, put a new song into my mouth, even praises to my God." This has been a year of much increase of property, so as to remove many of those fears that I have had upon the subject. As for myself I have not much to say, still deeply sensible of great unworthiness, many short-comings, the world too uppermost, too great a tendency to bow to man, rather than purely serve the living God ; not what I would be as wife and mother. Yet through all, there is a living desire to serve my Lord acceptably ; at times in suffering, not repining ; and in doing, although I may flinch, yet taking up the cross ; continuing to speak well of the Lord amongst the people, engaged in heart in the prison cause, Bible Society, and other things of the kind ; being made use of in them is an honour I feel and know I am unworthy of, and if ever, through grace, I am enabled to promote the cause of truth and righteousness, may I never take glory to myself, but give it altogether to Him who alone is worthy. And now, on entering another year, grant, dearest Lord, to Thy servant who trusteth in Thee, more patience, more trust, more watchfulness, more humility, more quietness of mind, and above all, more reliance and faith in Thee, her God and Saviour, and in the influences of Thy Spirit. Be pleased to bless not only her, but all near to her, with Thy presence and Thy good Spirit.

26th.—I returned from a short expedition to Brighton last evening. A very interesting and I trust not unimportant one. My object was the District Society that I was enabled to form there, when I was so ill, or rather recovering from that state. Much good appears done, much more likely to be done; a fine arrangement made, if it be but followed up ; and I humbly trust that a blessing will attend the work, and has already attended it. I feel that I have not time to relate our interesting history, but I should say that the short time we spent there was a mark of the features of the present day. A poor unworthy woman, nothing extraordinary in point of power, simply seeking to follow a cru-cified Lord, and to co operate with His grace in the heart; yet followed after by almost every rank in society, with the greatest openness for any communications of a religious nature ; numbers at Meeting of different denominations, also at our own house, noblemen, ladies in numbers, clergy, dissenters, and Friends of course; we had most satisfactory religious opportunities toge-ther, where the power of the endless life appeared to be in great dominion. Our dear Lord and Master Himself appear-ing remarkably to own us together. William Allen was there, a great helper; we were at dear Agatha and Elizabeth Barclay's, whose kindness, love, and sweetness were abundant towards us. Two of my daughters were with me. When I see as I did at Brighton, how remarkably I appear raised up, so that " the righ-teous compass me about," I cannot help feeling, that in my case the cross has " humbled to exalt," and also that inasmuch as I have sought to follow my Lord, when I have feared that in doing so, I should lose the good opinion, and even the love, of

almost every body, the good as well as others, how has it proved
my experience that "he that honoureth me I will honour." I
passed through great exercise of spirit lest I should be exalted,
or the truth suffer through me, but my belief is, that if no suffering or humiliation prevents my keeping close to my Lord, no
flinching of mine, that *close* under His banner I shall be safe,
whether He be pleased to raise me up and honour me, or cast
me down and afflict me.   On my return home I find all well,
but cares flow fresh in upon me, with something of a rush. Oh,
for a quiet spirit and a mind not easily agitated by the worries
and perturbations of the cares of life !

Third Month, 3rd.—I hope I am thankful for being really
better, though delicate in health. I wish I did not dread illness
so much, it is a real infirmity in me ; may grace be granted to
overcome it.   I think strange to say I felt, and I fear appeared
to those about me to be irritable.   Certainly I had some cause
to be so, but after what I have known of the power that is able
indeed, to help us, I never ought to give way to anything of the
kind ; all should be meekness, gentleness, and love.   Perhaps I
said too much about some pictures and various ornaments that
have been brought from France for us ; much as I love true
Christian simplicity, yet if I show a wrong spirit in my desire to
maintain it in our house and furniture, I do wrong and harm the
best of causes. I far prefer moderation, both from principle and
taste, although my experience in life proves two things ; first,
that it is greatly for the good of the community, to live according to the situation in which we have been placed by a kind
Providence, if it be done unto the Lord, and therefore done
properly ; then I believe that by so doing we should help others
and not injure ourselves.   Second, I have so much seen the
extreme importance of occupation, to the well-being of mankind, that many works of art, that tend to our accommodation,
and even the gratification of our taste, may be innocently partaken of, may be used and not abused, and kept in their proper
places ; as by so doing, we encourage that sort of employment
that prevents the active powers of man being spent in things
that are evil.

But to return to myself, "Ah ! for a closer walk with God !"

I long for it ; a more constant dwelling near in spirit to my Lord
and Saviour, being altogether His, guided by His counsel,
strengthened by His grace, animated by His love, obedient,
faithful, humble, watchful, patient, prompt in His service. If I
know myself this is my first desire for myself and others.

The contrition so frequently expressed in the course of Mrs.
Fry's journal, for irritability of temper, is calculated to mislead
a stranger, who would naturally suppose that it must occasionally have betrayed itself in conduct. To those who intimately
knew the never failing gentleness, forbearance, and Christian
meekness of her deportment, that such feelings ever ruffled her
mind, is almost inexplicable. Those most closely connected
with her, in the nearest and most familiar relations of life, can
unhesitatingly bear their testimony to the fact, that they never
saw her in what is called a pet, or heard an angry or passionate
expression of displeasure pass from her lips. Her tender conscience and fear of offence towards God and man, can alone
account for these outpourings of the hidden evils of her heart.

Plashet, Fourth Month, 6th.—The state of our house keeps
my mind very much occupied by trifles and temporal things. It
is very important with my very numerous objects to have outward
things in order ; indeed I go so far, as not to like to sit down in
a room, even for my time of reading and retirement, without
having it neat, and things in their places. I think some people
are not sensible how greatly some of these smaller matters conduce to the healthy state of the mind, and even in degree to the
prosperity of the soul. I often greatly suffer from the great
press upon me, making it nearly impossible not to be in confusion both as to my things and papers, and even what is more,
in my mind. How I long for a quieter and better regulated
mind, and to have all more in order ; as to outward things I
hope a few weeks will accomplish this. The delightful weather
and season ; the innumerable beauties of nature, now showing
themselves, have, I may say, refreshed my soul, and led it to

"look through Nature, up to Nature's God." To my mind the
outward works of creation are delightful, instructive, and edifying. I am, I hope, thankful for so much capacity to admire
and rejoice in them. How important to cultivate this taste in
youth ! It is an advantage through life, in many ways.

Plashet, Fourth Month, 21st.—My occupations are just now
multitudinous. The British Society, and all that is attached to
it, Newgate as usual. Forming with much fear, and some misgivings, a Servants' Society, yet with a hope, and something of
a trust, that it will be for the good of this class of persons for
generations to come. I have felt so much for such, for so many
years, that I am willing to sacrifice some strength and time for
their sakes. It is, however, with real fear that I do it, because
I am sensible of being at times pressed beyond my strength of
body and mind. But the day is short, and I know not how to
reject the work that comes to hand to do.

Plashet, 25th.—I have had some true encouragement in my
objects since I last wrote. The British Society meeting was got
through to much satisfaction. To myself, (the poor humble instrument amongst women in this country,) it is really wonderful
what has been accomplished in the prisons during the last few
years. How the cause has spread, and what good has been done,
how much evil prevented, how much sorrow alleviated, how many
plucked like brands from the burning ; what a cause for deep
thanksgiving, and still deeper humiliation, to have been in any
degree one of the instruments made use of to bring about these
results, I have also received a delightful account of the effects
of my labours for the poor at Brighton ; it appears that the
arrangements made, have greatly prospered amongst both rich
and poor; also for the blockade-men on the coast. This is cause
for fresh thankfulness of heart. I may say, that I there sowed
in tears, and I now reap in joy.

The Servants' Society appears gradually opening as if it would
be established according to my desire. No one knows what I go
through in forming these Institutions, it is always in fear, and
mostly with many misgivings ; wondering at myself for doing
it. I believe the original motive is love to my Master, and love
to my fellow-creatures ; but fear is so predominant a feeling in

my mind that it makes me suffer, perhaps unnecessarily from
doubts. I have felt something like access in prayer, before making the regulations of the Servants' Society. Sometimes my
natural understanding seems enlightened about things of that
kind, as if I were helped to see the right and useful thing. This
I remarkably found in the prisons,—in the Brighton District
Society, and in my youth a good deal about schools for the poor,
before they were so general as they now are. My dearest sister
Rachel continues really unwell, her state makes me anxious. I
wonder I am so calm about it, for she is in some respects beyond any other person to me, and I certainly think I owe more
to her than to any one else ; my natural tie to her is inexpressible, and if she should be taken from us, one of my strongest
interests in life will be gone.

Fifth Month, 23*rd.*—I think that I am under the deepest
exercise of mind that I ever experienced, in the prospect of a
Meeting to be held this evening, for all the young people assembled at the Yearly Meeting. It is held at my request, my
brother Joseph uniting in it. In a remarkable degree it has
plunged me into the depths, into real distress, I feel so unfit, so
unworthy, so perplexed, so fearful, even so sorrowful, so tempted
to mistrustful thoughts, ready to say, " Can such an one be
called to such a service ?" I do believe that " this is my
infirmity ;" and I have a humble hope and confidence, that out
of this great weakness I shall be made strong. As far as I know
it has been in simple obedience to manifested duty, that I gave
up to this service, and went through the ordeal of the Yearly
Meeting. If I know my own deceitful heart, it has been done
in love to my Lord and to His cause. Lord preserve me through
this depth, through this stripping season : if it should please
Thee to grant me the garments of Thy salvation, and the help
of Thy Spirit, further enable me wholly to give unto Thee the
glory, which is due unto Thy name. If Thou makest use of
Thy handmaid to speak in Thy name, be Thou Thyself her help
and her strength, her glory and the lifter up of her head. Enable her to rely on Thee, on Thy might and on Thy mercy, to
commit her whole cause unto Thee, and keep in the remem-

brance of Thy handmaid, that the blessed cause of truth and
righteousness is not *her's* but *Thine*.

Plashet, Sixth Month, 2nd —The awful and buffetted state of
my mind was in degree calmed as the day advanced. I went to
town with my beloved brother Joseph, who appeared to have been
in something of a similar depth of unusual suffering—we went
into the Meeting together; the large Meeting-house was soon so
crowded, that no more could get in ; I suppose from eighteen
hundred to two thousand persons, principally youth. All my
children were there except little Harry. I heard hundreds went
away who could not get in. After going in and taking my seat,
my mind was soon calmed, and the fear of man greatly, if not
quite taken away. My beloved brother, Joseph, bowed the knee
and poured forth prayer for us. I soon after rose and expressed
what was on my mind, towards the assembly : First, that all
were acceptable who worked righteousness and served the Lord.
Secondly, that the mercies of our God should induce this service
as a debt due to Him. Thirdly, that it must be done by following
a crucified Lord, and faithfully taking up the cross. Fourthly,
how important, therefore, to the church generally and to our religious Society, for us so to do individually and collectively : for
that if this were done, there would be from amongst that company, those who would be as lights to the world, or as a city set
on a hill that cannot be hid ; I had to conclude with a desire
that an entrance might be abundantly ministered unto them,
into the everlasting kingdom of our Lord and Saviour Jesus
Christ. I then sat down but did not feel to have fully relieved
my mind. Joseph rose, and stood more than an hour, he
preached a very instructive and striking sermon on faith and
doctrine. Then my dear sister Elizabeth Fry, and my uncle
Joseph, said something. Afterwards I knelt down in prayer,
and thought I found no common access to the Fountain of all
our sure mercies; I was enabled to cast my burden for the youth
and my own beloved offspring amongst the rest, upon Him who
is mighty to save, and to deliver. I had to ask for a blessing
upon our labours of love towards them, and that our deficiencies might be made up; that the blessing of the Most High

7

might rest upon them from generation to generation, and that cross bearers and standard bearers might not be wanting from amongst them. I felt helped in every way, the very spirit and power appeared near, and when I rose from my knees I could in faith leave it all to Him who can alone prosper His own work. A few hints that impressed me I afterwards expressed, which were to encourage the youth in the good works of the present day; but to entreat them when engaged in them to maintain the watch, lest they should build up with one hand, and pull down with the other. Secondly that it was never too soon to begin to serve the Lord, and that there was nothing too small to please Him in. Then commending them to His grace and bidding them farewell, the Meeting concluded in a very solemn manner; it lasted about two hours and a half, and general satisfaction appears to have been felt. When it was over, I may say we rejoiced together, I hope, in the Lord: so that my soul did magnify the Lord, and my spirit rejoiced in God my Saviour.

Plashet, 6th.—The death of my dear aunt Gurney, obliges me to go into Norfolk; I therefore set off to-day, accompanied by my sister Elizabeth. I propose also attending the Essex Quarterly Meeting in going, and the Suffolk in returning. It has been a sacrifice giving up to go, but I desire to do it in simplicity of faith as unto my Lord; trusting that it will prove for edification and refreshment. My beloved William, also sets off from home, for a journey on the Continent with Dr. Pinkerton; I have desired to do right in letting him go and feel satisfied in it. I have been enabled this morning to commit him, and all of my children, to the everlasting Shepherd and Bishop of souls, particularly for him, dear fellow! that the Almighty may be with him, and that he may become more established in the ever blessed faith, as it is in Jesus. I leave home, and give up my dear son in faith, humbly trusting through the tender mercy of my Lord, that all will be well.

EXTRACT FROM A LETTER TO HER FAMILY AT HOME.

Earlham, *Sixth Month,* 11*th,* 1825.

I wonder almost that I have not written to you before, but my engagements have been, I think I may say, hourly and constant. On Fifth day, the funeral, and yesterday, Norwich Monthly Meeting; we dined at the Grove. I have felt a good deal in this visit. The changes that take place in these parts are very affecting. I paid a quiet visit to the grave-yard the other morning, and there sat first upon my mother's, then my father's, then Priscilla's and John's graves; and, as you may suppose, wept at their sweet remembrance. I could not but meditate upon the probability of all our heads being before very long placed under the "green grass turf." These were my cogitations, and I trust not without some of a higher nature; it is a fearful thing not to be ready, for the change may come very unawares : but I may say, as it respects my own, I have lately felt increasing hope that "all will be well."

Plashet, 18*th.*—I am returned home after attending my dear aunt's funeral, and two Quarterly Meetings. I paid a very interesting visit to Earlham. I have passed through much deep feeling, and been in various ways much engaged as a minister, of which service I am wonderfully unworthy, but out of weakness I often experience help and strength to my own admiration.

Since I returned home, a great press of company every day, Lord Bexley and Sophia Vansittart, Lord Suffield, Lord and Lady Torrington, and many others. Lord, grant a little help, quiet and enlighten my heart, that I may see what to do, and what to leave undone, and that which I find to do, enable me to perform in simplicity of faith, unto Thyself, and Thy glory; and, Lord, be pleased to keep Thy very frail and unworthy servant on the right hand, and on the left, that evil overcome her not.

Seventh Month, 14*th.*—I think of late my engagements have been more numerous than ever, so as at times to overwhelm and overdo body and mind. I have deeply felt my uncle Hoare's death. Twice in the week I have visited that family in their affliction, to my inward peace.

The kindness and attentions received from Mr. and Mrs. Hoare, in early life, had left a grateful impression on Mrs. Fry's mind. The intercourse then begun had been maintained from that time, and was rendered even more interesting and intimate by the marriage of her sister Louisa, into their family, and the congenial sentiments of her brother-in-law, Samuel Hoare, Esq., on the subject of Prison Discipline, in which he took an active and important part.

LETTER FROM HER SISTER, MRS. SAMUEL HOARE.

"Hampstead, *July* 29*th*.

" My dearest Betsy,
" I have much wished to communicate again with you. I have felt your presence and aid and ministry amongst us, so peculiarly valuable during our late time of trial. It is indeed blessed to be the appointed and willing instrument in aiding the weak, and consoling the sorrowful, and this has been most remarkably the case with you. I have found the last few weeks a time of discipline, not without humiliation, as well as sorrow to me ; but we have been very quiet and tranquil since the day we passed together.
" Dearest Betsy,
" Your most affectionate,
" L. HOARE."

From the scene of mourning at Hampstead, she passed successively to the bedsides of two of her near connexions; in both instances, she was actively engaged in nursing.

Plashet, Eighth Month, 3*rd.*—I regretted these calls, because I particularly wished to have my mind calm and at liberty with my beloved family, before the very interesting and important event of my son's marriage.

Dagenham, Eighth Month, 10*th.*—On Fifth day, the 4th of this month, my dear eldest son was married. Upon the previous evening, with a few of the family present, I was enabled to commend him to his God, for direction, and for protection; it was a very serious time. The next morning, we all, in our wedding garments, proceeded to London; my beloved husband and myself alone in the chariot, deeply feeling the weight of the occasion. Upon our arrival at the Meeting House, in Westminster, we found the party generally assembled. Soon after our sitting down in the Meeting there was that which quieted our spirits, and said, " Peace, be still." We sat more than half an hour, when dear Rebecca Christy knelt down, and, in a powerful manner, prayed for the young people, that a blessing might be with them, above all a spiritual blessing; my heart went with her, and I poured forth my tears before the Lord on their account; there was a very solemn feeling over us, a little as if the Master owned the wedding company by His presence. I had to offer fervent petitions for their good, naturally and spiritually, and for grace for them to keep their solemn covenant with each other, and to make fresh covenant with their Lord. We had an elegant and hospitable entertainment afterwards; my dear uncle Barclay was there, he is grandfather to the bride, and great uncle to the bridegroom.

The day after the wedding we came here, which I have much enjoyed, being so quietly with my beloved husband and children, and so much devoted to them. The refreshing air and change of scene appear really to have invigorated me.

27*th.*—Since writing the above our bride and bridegroom returned. It has been to me really a time of rejoicing. Lord, bless them together, and grant them Thy love, Thy peace, and Thy joy. We have very satisfactory accounts of our beloved William from abroad, for which I trust I am thankful. Our dear son and daughter Cresswell are likely to live in Norfolk. I much feel parting from them and my sweet grandchildren. I think all our bonds of love strengthen. My sister Rachel's continued indisposition is, perhaps, my greatest outward trial at present, but, as it respects her, in the most important things, " all is well," therefore my anxiety about her is not of the

deepest or most sorrowful kind. In short, at this time, it seems
as if in every thing I must return thanks, and like the disciple,
formerly, might answer to the query, " Lackest thou any
thing?" Nothing, Lord, except more of Thy grace and good
Spirit in all our hearts, to make us thankful receivers of Thy
unmerited, innumerable, and unspeakable gifts.

Plashet, Ninth Month, 8th.—The ministry of my brother
Joseph, William Allen, and Cornelius Hanbury, were delightful to me on First day. How I rejoice over those who love the
Lord. There have been times lately, when I could say, I was
happy.

The period of rest and refreshment at Dagenham was only
preparatory to fresh exertion. Mrs. Fry again believed it her
duty to leave home, and travel into Devonshire and Cornwall,
accompanied by her sister-in law, Elizabeth Fry.

Dagenham, 21st.—Yesterday we laid our concern before our
Monthly Meeting. I believe we had the sympathy, unity, and
near love of our Friends, which was really encouraging and comforting. How truly do the living members of the militant
church help one another ; surely it is well now and then to have
their feeling for each other excited. I was enabled, in the
Meeting to commend those who go, and those who stay, to the
keeping of the Unslumbering Shepherd, and found near access
to Him in prayer, being strengthened to cast my care upon Him
on whom help is laid. I have felt happier since. This morning,
in our family, I had to return thanks for the time of rest and
refreshment that we have had here, and also to pray for preservation for all.

Kingsbridge, 29th.—Here we are, so far on our journey ; we
left Plashet on Seventh day, and I felt in no common degree
easy and peaceful, although a little low at leaving home, and
parting from those dear to me ; but still in a cheerful state of
mind, and able in going along to cast my care in no common
degree upon my Holy Helper, so that anxiety on account of those
left and about our future engagements appeared taken from me.
I much enjoyed passing through the abundant beauties of the

country. I have here felt the weight of the service we are engaged in, and found both my body and mind shaken by the deep exercise of my mind. I think we got well through the Quarterly Meeting. I earnestly desired to be altogether conformed to my blessed Master's will, without any reserves, and in this feeling I believed it right to have a Meeting appointed for this evening. It has cost me a good deal to give up to such a service, but I am more comfortable since I have done so; although I feel very unfit for such services. Ah! dearest Lord, anoint us with fresh oil for this service, that it may tend to the exaltation of Thy name, and the unity, edification, comfort and strength of Thy people of every denomination.

Plymouth, Tenth Month, 1st.—I trust that I am thankful to be able to say that the Meeting (at Kingsbridge) was very satisfactory, and to my feelings, brought almost unspeakable peace. I thought we were favoured in a remarkable manner to feel sweet unity of spirit, with those present, of various descriptions, and we might say, like the disciples formerly, " Did not our hearts burn within us as He talked with us by the way ?" At first, deep poverty of spirit, with many fears on my own account beset me, but as the Meeting advanced, power increased ; these were allayed, and we might rejoice in the feeling, that the Lord God Omnipotent reigneth, God over all, blessed for ever !

Liskeard, 8th.—Another week is now past, and much has been gone through. At Plymouth, we attended several Meetings, but one was most important to me ; it was one that I had appointed at Devonport. I first felt the concern when a girl travelling with my father, I then believed, that if ever I became a minister I must hold a Meeting there ; and the time now appeared come for it. My attraction was to the lowest and worst classes. It was indeed an act of faith ; I have a feeling of unfitness and unworthiness for such services, beyond what I can express. The day passed tolerably, I attended two regular Meetings, but as the time for this Meeting drew near, my heart was ready to fail ; fears got hold of me, and almost had dominion over me. On entering the assembly, I hardly dared look up, when I did, I thought there must be fifteen hundred people present, mostly poor ; I may, I think say, it was before it ended a glorious time ;

10

much solemnity prevailed amongst us, the power of the great and good Spirit appearing to reign over all. I cannot help humbly trusting that the fruit will remain. We had an interesting Meeting with the youth, and another the next morning at a wedding; we were much united to many dear friends. We have since visited three Meetings in Cornwall. The beautiful country delights me, when my mind is at liberty. My heart is often with those dear ones, far away, particularly my daughter Rachel, and my sister Rachel; but I feel that I have left all for my Master's sake, therefore can trust them to Him.

Plashet, Eleventh Month, 7th.—We returned home last Sixth day, where I had the unspeakable comfort of finding all going on well. To return to my journal of our journey; from Liskeard, we proceeded to a place called St. Austle, and then to Falmouth. We attended two Monthly, one Quarterly, and other Meetings amongst Friends; also had public ones at Falmouth and many other places. I do not wonder that Friends write about their Meetings, as I believe none but ministers can tell how deeply they are to be felt, the great weight before them, and the necessary preparatory baptisms. The act of faith in appointing them, not knowing whether we shall have any thing to say in them or not and the sense of the infirmity of the instrument to my fearful, nervous mind, is almost overwhelming; then when help has been granted, the thing well got through, the burden taken off, peace does certainly at times flow; and rejoicing in the Lord, our Holy Helper, is in no common degree experienced, to the unspeakable refreshment and consolation of the soul. So we found it in many instances. Our visit to Falmouth, and the round we took in Cornwall, with my beloved cousins, Lucy and Maria Fox, and their husbands, was highly interesting, naturally and spiritually. We visited some of the striking and wonderful scenery on the coast of Cornwall; saw much of the people and of Friends, they are an interesting, enlightened people, and our Meetings drew us together in religious communion. We paid an important, though short visit to Exeter; I fear a little hurried, yet liberty seemed granted me not to tarry by the way. We had a good Public Meeting, also one with Friends, visited many of their families, and formed a Prison Committee. We con-

cluded our visit to Devonshire at a sweet little Meeting at Spice-
land. Many dear friends, on our journey, were like fathers and
mothers, brothers, sisters, and children to us ; may I long gratefully remember it. We returned home by Wellington, Bath,
Melksham, and Bury Hill. My dearest cousin, Priscilla H.
Gurney's state, appeared to be that of the Pillar in the Temple,
to go no more out. And now what shall I say ? This long
looked for and important journey finished, and I safely and
happily at home. The first feeling is, what can I render unto
the Lord for His unspeakable gifts and providential care over us,
permitting us all, including dear William after his continental
journey, to meet again in safety and peace ? Also for having
been " out of weakness made strong " in so remarkable a manner,
enabled to " wax valiant in fight," and for such services as
we were called into, being anointed with fresh oil.

Plashet, Twelfth Month, 15*th.*—Several large banking-houses
in London, and many in the country, have stopped payment; a
great many are in danger, strong as well as weak ones ; what
will yet occur none can tell.

19*th.*—The country is in a very awful state, the press upon
bankers is so very great, that throughout the kingdom many
are stopping payment.

31*st.*—The last day of this year, in many respects a memorable one to me. In the beginning of it, I experienced, in outward things, the flow of great prosperity. In the close of it,
great anxiety. I have seen my eldest son married. I have been
favoured with the lives of those nearest to me, and with a few
exceptions, their health.

Spiritually, I have been enabled to make some sacrifices,
which have cost me dear, particularly the Meeting for Youth,
during the Yearly Meeting; and the Public Meetings on my
journey in the west of England, which were to me greatly taking
up the cross; but in doing and in suffering help has been
granted me, and whether spiritually or naturally, I have much
cause for thanksgiving and praise !

CHAPTER XIV.

THE storm that had prevailed in the money world, during the latter part of 1825, subsided as 1826 advanced; but it did not pass away without leaving fearful traces of its course. Many mercantile houses were entirely overthrown ; amongst them, some, involving much-valued friends of Mrs. Fry, whilst others were so shaken, as never to recover the shock. These things made it a very anxious time to her, and called forth much of her sympathy towards the sufferers.

First Month, 28*th*, 1826.—The principle of justice cannot be too deeply impressed upon the youthful mind, also, the greatest uprightness in all money transactions. How do I desire for myself that, however it may be my duty to be occupied about temporal things, my treasure be not in them, but that my heart and soul may be raised above them. This morning, I think I have had a glimpse of those possessions that cannot be shaken by the ups and downs of life. I see temporally also, that there are innumerable blessings in the outward works of creation, open to all, whether rich or poor. The same glorious sun to enlighten, and other bright and beautiful things made in common for every one.

Thinking over these subjects, those words in Ecclesiasticus struck me much, chap. xi. 21, 22:—" Marvel not, at the works of sinners; but trust in the Lord, and abide in thy labour: for it is an easy thing in the sight of the Lord on the sudden to make a poor man rich. The blessing of the Lord is in the reward of the godly, and suddenly he maketh his blessing to flourish." I may say the Lord doth provide, the Lord hath provided, and my humble trust is that the Lord will provide.

Third Month, 29*th*.—Yesterday, I attended the Quarterly Meeting, where I think there was to be felt something of celestial showers on thirsty land, partly through the ministry of others, partly from what I trust was an immediate ministration from the Great Minister of ministers. A dear relation, a clergyman, was at meeting, I felt sweetly united to him. After all, however we may differ as to the means of grace, our end in view is the same, and we feel at times that we have but one Lord, one faith, and one baptism. I increasingly find, that whoever love the Lord Jesus, are without distinction, as brothers, sisters, fathers, and mothers to me; although I know that I am a very unworthy partaker of this foretaste of that, for which we may look in the heavenly inheritance.

In reply to a slight request, at that time addressed by Elizabeth Fry to Hannah More, she received this gratifying reply:—

My dear Friend,

Any request of yours, if within my very limited power, cannot fail to be immediately complied with. In your kind note, I wish you had mentioned something of your own health, and that of your family.

I look back with no small pleasure to the too short visit with which you once indulged me, a repetition of it would be no little gratification to me. Whether Divine Providence may grant it or not, I trust through Him who loved us, and gave himself for us, that we may hereafter meet in that blessed country, where there is neither sin, sorrow, nor separation.

Believe me, my dear friend, with true esteem and warm affection, to remain yours sincerely,

H. MORE.

Barley Wood, 15*th of April*, 1826.

Mrs. Fry entertained the highest appreciation of this lady's character, and of the benefits she had conferred upon her country, especially upon her country-women. She always referred with great pleasure to her visit to Barley Wood, and the impresion made upon her by the mingled sweetness and dignity of Mrs. More's countenance and manner.

In a letter to a friend Mrs. More thus mentions the circumstance :—

" To own the work of nonconformity in lesser things and of perfect conformity in heart and mind. Yesterday the long-desired meeting took place between Mrs. Newgate (oh, that that name should ever become an honour !) Fry and myself; we were ready to eat one another up. Her appearance and manner reminded me of what I have often said, that I should like to have her picture as Deborah judging Israel under the palm tree ! She is indeed delightful. At parting she knelt down, and put up a feeling prayer for unworthy me."

In a copy of her " Practical Piety," given by Mrs. More to Mrs. Fry, is this inscription.

TO MRS. FRY,

Presented by HANNAH MORE,
As a token of veneration
Of her heroic zeal,
Christian charity,
And persevering kindness,
To the most forlorn
Of human beings.
They were naked and she
Clothed them;
In prison and she visited them;
Ignorant and she taught them,
For *His* sake,
In *His* name, and by *His* word,
Who went about doing good.

Barley Wood, June 17th, 1818.

Fourth Month, 20*th.*—I look forward with some anxiety to
the British Ladies' Society Meeting, to-morrow; I desire preservation for myself in it, that what I do, may be done unto the
Lord and not unto man, with true Christian courtesy.   There is
a respect due to those, who are placed by a kind Providence in
high stations as to this life, but I also feel that there is a bold
Christian character to maintain, as we are all one in Christ, and
children of one heavenly Parent.   May none of us engaged in
the work, suffer loss ; but may the cause in which we are interested be really promoted, and the whole be done to the glory
of God our Saviour, and His doctrine be adorned by it.

22*nd.*—The meeting was a very interesting one ; much good
appears to be doing by those who visit prisons.   Many places
of refuge are also formed.   I had a good deal to say at different
times in the meeting, and concluded with a little general advice to
a very numerous assembly of ladies.   At first, I was very peaceful,
and really believed that the best of causes had been promoted in
that meeting ; but during the night and this morning, I was
nervous and low, deeply impressed with the extreme difficulty of
acting right in conspicuous places, and the danger on every
hand that attends being brought into them, as I at times am.
I may say, that I have earnestly sought the Lord for help and
preservation.   I fully unite in the Christian duty of true simplicity in dress; I think it rather too much dwelt upon by us,
as a Society, but much too little by many in the religious
world.

Fifth Month, 27*th.*—We are in the midst of the Yearly
Meeting ; to me a very important time, as I am greatly interested in the welfare of the Society.   I do most fully unite in
most of its practices and principles ; but still I may say, I have
somewhat against it, I see that we may improve as we go on, if
that which first led us to be a peculiar people, be kept to by us.
I think in our Meetings for Discipline, too much stress is laid
on minor parts of our testimonies, such as " plainness of
speech, behaviour, and apparel," rather than on the greater and
weightier matters of the law ; these (lesser things) are well, and
I believe should be attended to ; but they should not occupy
an undue place.   I do not like the habit of that mysterious, am-

biguous mode of expression, in which Friends at times clothe their observations, and their ministry. I like the truth in simplicity, it needs no mysterious garment. I also can hardly bear to hear Friends make us out to be a chosen people, above others.

I have very much kept silence amongst them, being generally quite clear of any thing to do; but as a spectator, I have rejoiced in the love, the sweetness, and the power of good amongst us, and the evidence that our great High Priest is owning us for good.

Sixth Month, 3rd.—Our Yearly Meeting concluded yesterday. I can hardly express the sweetness of the remembrance of the time. We have at seasons, I may truly say, rejoiced together in the Lord, and partaken of that, which as evidently comforts and delights the soul, as outward refreshment does the body, when hungry, thirsty, and faint. I have been really refreshed in spirit.

Dagenham, Seventh Month, 20th.—I am once more come to this quiet abode, and cannot but enjoy its refreshing influence, more particularly, as my soul has of late been too much disquieted within me; a good deal, I think, from the perplexed state of the business world. Also, I have been, perhaps, too anxious respecting the well-being of my children, and too prone to fret myself in spirit about them. I have been frequently tried by many fears respecting myself, whether I might not have done, and might not do, more for my children. I do not think I am naturally gifted with the talent of education, as some of my sisters are. I have had some doubts whether our peculiar views, in many little things, much in the cross to young people, do not in measure turn them from religion itself; on the other hand, I see in others how imperceptibly the standard lowers, when these minor scruples are given up. I am persuaded, in the education of youth, there are two sides to the question. I have no doubt whatever of the utility of these things, when adopted from conviction; my doubts are, how far they should be pressed upon young persons, through education. However, I see no other way for myself, and believe, that I must bring my children up, as, I have seen with such indubitable clearness, to be right for myself, which has been so wonderfully blessed to my own soul. That happy day may arrive, when, on their own ground, I may see some of my beloved children walking in the same way; if this would too much gratify me naturally and spiritually, then I am indeed ready to say, by any means, or in any way, so they but come to the knowledge of Christ their Saviour, and be saved through Him, I should be satisfied. It is certainly very sweet, for those who are united by natural ties, also to choose the same path in spiritual things, but experience has proved, in the case of my beloved brothers and sisters, that much of the unity of the spirit and the bond of peace may be experienced, when we may not see eye to eye.

24th.—Yesterday was so very wet and windy, that we spent a quiet First day here. Serious as it is, not to attend our places of worship, yet it is not without its advantages, to find, that the same worship can be performed in private as in the public assembly; and that it is not the place, or the people, but (if in a right spirit) an acceptable worship may be offered every where. All our family assembled twice in the day, I think to real edification, so that it proved neither dull nor unpleasant, though we were all shut up for a long day in this little house.

Plashet, *Eighth Month,* 3rd.

We have had our dearest brother and Lady Harriet here the last few days; I have felt nearly united to them, and, desire to return thanks, that such sweet unity exists amongst us. He is a dear and most kind brother to me, and I see the hand of a merciful Providence in his heart being so open towards us; he warmly and steadily does all he can to help us. To my other dear brothers, also, I feel deeply grateful, and still more so, I trust, to Him who hitherto has helped us, and inclines their hearts towards us.

To her Sister Rachel Gurney.

Dagenham, *Eighth Month,* 12*th,* 1826.

My dearest Rachel,

It appears rather too long since we have had any communication. I am now very desirous of hearing again of you, and how thou art.———We are comfortably settled here, for which I already feel better, and am revived by the fresh air and beautiful views, for the river and the Kentish hills are to my taste delightful. The longer I live, the more I enjoy quiet and real retirement; I think my inclination would dictate withdrawing very much from the world,—I desire to be thankful that I am enabled to partake of this enjoyment, although, I believe, the time is not yet come for me really to withdraw from the bustle of life.——— We have begun to read my brother Joseph's Essays together, in the morning, we hope to read them through, whilst we are here. We think of getting Pepys' Memoirs, to read in the afternoon. The close contact that we are brought in with each other, and so often having my beloved husband join us, is really valuable ; he means to read the Essays with us.

I have time here to think of my friends, as well as to love them.

I am, indeed and in truth thine and Catherine's nearly attached sister,

E. F.

Dagenham, 29*th.*—I returned from Rochester, yesterday. We went to Gravesend in the steam-packet, which was refreshing ; a beautiful calm evening, the river and its banks in great beauty, and nothing in the people on board, to hurt my mind. I distributed a few tracts, but in other respects I fear I did no good. We proceeded to Rochester, where we met with a most kind and cordial reception. I feel watchfulness very necessary with those, who, from our outward situation in life, are prone to estimate us above our desert, and in doing things that may appear humble, the danger of pride taking advantage and being gratified. On the other hand, I felt a little encouraged that my earnest desire to do justice to my servants, and to watch over them for

6

good, had not been in vain ; for Sarah T——, whose wedding
I went to attend, and who, with her family, was so delighted to
have me and some of my children there, lived with me nine
years as upper nurse, and in that time, I never remember having
the least real difference with her. I am a great friend to doing
full justice to servants, and bearing as much as we can with their
infirmities, remembering the many disadvantages that they
labour under. To proceed with my narrative—we went with the
company to the wedding, and had a satisfactory meeting. As
soon as the meeting was over, a gentleman came to beg me to
attend a Bible Meeting about to be held, which I afterwards
understood was a Naval and Military one. On which account,
some dear Friends doubted the propriety of our going ; but my
heart was full of zeal, I felt clear, that of all people, as promoters of peace, we should show ourselves willing and glad to aid
them in such an object, as the most likely means of advancing
that day, when they " shall beat their swords into plough-shares
and their spears into pruning-hooks." Lord Bexley, who came
to attend the meeting, called upon me twice at the T——'s, to
beg me to go. I made up my mind to do so, and was delighted
to see so many naval officers, particularly young men, coming
forward to espouse so great and good a cause. I feared for myself being in any degree exhilirated in spirit by the kindness
and marked attention shown me, and by the honour conferred
on me ; wholly unworthy as I am of being instrumental in encouraging others in works of righteousness.

We returned home by the steam packet. I believed it right
to enter a little into conversation with most of the passengers,
and to give them tracts ; also, as the way opened for it, to throw
a little weight into the right scale. We then had a boat to meet
us, and visited the two female-convict ships now in the river.
Their order, cleanliness, and general appearance, delighted me ;
I was struck with the wonderful change, since we first undertook them. Elizabeth Pryor has been greatly blessed in her
labours, and it is a true consolation to see what has been
accomplished. Joseph, Richenda, and Louisa, returned with
me here safely by boat, just in time to dine with my husband,
and the rest of my children. I have thus minutely entered into

the particulars of this expedition, as, some day when my head is laid low, it may interest my children, and children's children, to know how it fared with me at such times. This morning, my soul was so deeply prostrated in prayer, that I had to pour it forth after reading. I feel, more particularly after being engaged in service, like a vessel that wants fresh washing ; and to whom can I go but to Him, who ever remains the fountain open for the uncircumcised and the unclean ?   I found, I believe, access to the throne of grace. Oh! what need is there of the washing of regeneration, and the renewings of the Holy Ghost. It is as necessary to the soul, as daily washing and food are to the body; and if by this means any of us are fitted for any good word or work, to us, truly belongs nothing but humiliation and confusion of face ; but to our Lord and our God, glory, honour, power, thanksgiving, and praise.

30*th.*—Since I last wrote, a good deal has passed, and I have been reminded of a saying of Cecil, " We are to follow and not force Providence." Last week, I expected much quiet, except a visit to the convict-ships, instead of which, all my plans for myself were altered by circumstances.   At Hampstead, we met a gentleman, Cæsar Malan, from Geneva, who appeared in deep concern for our souls ; he seemed to feel our meeting remarkably in the ordering of Providence. His belief is, that we are, as believers, not sufficiently sure of salvation, and that we admit too many doubts and fears, upon the subject; as the promises of God are sure, and that, in not feeling confident, and expressing ourselves to be so, we do harm to the cause. What he said, savoured too much of " once in grace, always in grace ;" still, I hope I received a good lesson, which may make me less fearful, and more hopeful. Very likely, I look too much to my own infirmity, and to the power of temptation to separate me from the love of God in Christ Jesus and too little up to Him, through whom we are called to become more than conquerors.

Dear William Wilberforce, his wife, and children, dined with us. I think I may say, he is one whom I love in the Lord; and highly " esteem for his work's sake."

This day, though not great in its events, was instructive to

me ; teaching me, where things do not go on in my way, to be
quiet, and trust in small things as in great; that "our steppings
are ordered of the Lord," though unworthy of such a favour.
I returned to Stamford Hill, through a storm and with some
difficulty, because I thought it right to persevere, in case my
sick brother and his family should want me. The next morning
I had a time in thanksgiving and prayer with them; also, I
visited another family, and endeavoured to encourage them in
the way of the Lord. The young man, the master of the house
told me that I had been made, in days past, a remarkable instrument of good to him, in a religious visit paid to him when
visiting families, with William Forster, in Gracechurch Street.
I returned home to my beloved family after this expedition, in
peace.

I find much advantage and pleasure in rising early in this
place. I am dressed about seven, read, meditate, &c., till half-
past, then breakfast, and attend to my husband and sons before
their going to London. After this, our family reading; it being
here more convenient after breakfast than before. Then a devotional reading with the children, and, in the course of the
day, I read them one of my brother J. J. Gurney's Essays on
Christianity. When quietly here, I often write on the prison
cause, also letters of business and friendship, and very much
enjoy the rest, and the sweet refreshing beauties of the river and
country, so that I find the sort of life we lead useful and pleasant. I have been favoured, at times, with feelings of almost
inexpressible peace and love, in the enjoyment of natural and
spiritual things.

The return of the season had brought with it, the interest of
the annual transportation of female convicts. This year, five
ships had been taken up for that purpose. There had been two
every year from 1823. In 1827, five ships, as well as in 1826.
Four, five, six, were the numbers employed the three following
years. Of course, this endeavour on the part of Government to
increase the female population in New South Wales, occasioned

great expense to the British Ladies' Society, with much additional trouble and fatigue.

Though kind friends and assistants undertook the laborious
task of minute preparations for the voyage, Mrs. Fry encouraged
them by her presence and example, as far as was compatible with
her numerous avocations at home and abroad.   She met with
much kindness from Admiral (then Captain) Young, Principal
Resident Agent of Transports on the River Thames, and his
family.   Their recollections are vivid of many scenes and transactions, and go far to supply the place of that valuable information which Admiral Young, had he been living, could have
himself furnished.

Mrs. Young has often recurred to a farewell visit to a female
convict-ship, on the point of sailing, in which she accompanied
Mrs. Fry, saying, that she could " scarcely look upon her as
any other than an angel of mercy, calmly passing from one to
another of the poor wretched beings around her, with the word
of counsel, comfort, or reproof, that seemed suited to each
individual case, as it presented itself to her notice. With several
kind assistants, she was arranging work for them during the
voyage; in itself no trifling matter.   But many a point of
deepest interest and anxiety brought to her ready ear, met with
such response as could only be looked for from a devoted follower of Him, who ' went about doing good.' "

On the mind of Miss Young the circumstance was strongly
impressed, of accompanying her father (Captain Young) to the
female-convict ships, lying off Woolwich, to meet Mr. Wilberforce and Mrs. Fry.   " On board one of them, between two and
three hundred women were assembled, in order to listen to the
exhortation and prayers of, perhaps, the two brightest personifi-
cations of Christian philanthropy that the age could boast.
Scarcely, could two voices, even so distinguished for beauty and
power, be imagined united in a more touching engagement—as

indeed was testified by the breathless attention, the tears and the suppressed sobs of the gathered listeners. All of man's word, however there heard, heart-stirring as it was at that time, has faded from my memory; but no lapse of time can ever efface the impression of the 107th Psalm, as read by Mrs. Fry, with such extraordinary emphasis and intonation, that it seemed to make the simple reading a commentary; and, as she passed on from passage to passage, struck my youthful mind, as if the whole series of allusions might have been written by the pen of inspiration, in view of such a scene as was then before us. At an interval of twenty years, it is recalled to me as often as that Psalm is brought to my notice.

" Never, in this world, can it be known to how many hearts its solemn appeals were that day carried home, by that potent voice."

Dagenham, Ninth Month, 4th.—I paid a very interesting visit to two female convict-ships, with my dear sister Elizabeth Fry, and cousin Sarah, last Third-day. We there met William Wilberforce, Sophia Vansittart, and many others. The exercise of my mind was deep, and the trial of body considerable, from the inconvenient situation in which I had to read below deck, surrounded by the poor prisoners and the company. What I feel on such occasions is difficult to describe; that it should all be done unto the Lord—that it should be a time of edification— that none may in any way be hurt by it—that my natural great fear of man, and of his judgment, should in no way influence me; and, lastly, that self may neither glory, if helped, nor be unduly mortified if a cause for humiliation arise. It was a uniting time, I trust; many of the poor prisoners seemed to feel it so, several of them wept. It is an interesting, important service; may it not be neglected when our heads are laid low.

Since I last wrote, I have attended the Quarterly Meeting, at Leighton Buzzard, with my dear brother Samuel Gurney, and my sister Elizabeth Fry. I also paid a visit to the prison at St.

Albans. I can hardly say how sweet were some of the moments I passed in this little journey. It appeared as if I were to go partly for my own sake to be refreshed, and so it proved. The religious services I was called into hardly were a cross, I found my Master's yoke so very easy, even pleasant. I could say, " I delight to do thy will, oh God." I can hardly express the unity of spirit, and the bond of peace, that I felt amongst those who were nearly strangers to me. Oh ! what blessings, and what privileges, do the meanest servants of our dear Lord and Master partake of. There is no joy, and no peace, to be compared to the peace and joy attendant upon doing the will of God : it is meat and drink indeed !

To one of her daughters, who had consulted her on the establishment of a Visiting Society.

Plashet, *Tenth Month*, 13*th.*

I hope thou didst not think me inattentive to thy wishes in not writing to thee respecting the District Society, but I was very busy at the time, and I hoped that the papers I forwarded would answer the same purpose. I think much advantage will result from its establishment ; I only fear it will rest too much upon thee, and in time become a burden with thy other duties, cares, and delicate health. I think thou art like me, in having rather a calling to the care of the poor, and I rejoice in the belief that thou mayst be a blessing to many of them ; but the more thou canst privately be the mover in these good works, the better. I know the pain and difficulty attached to filling foremost places in public works, and DUTY only sustains under it ; I also know how apt persons are to push those forward, who are able and willing, even beyond what is desirable for them.

Now for a very particular message to our dear friend Edward Edwards ; I have not written to him, for I know that I am but a poor scribe, but I have remembered him and his dear family in their affliction and great privation. I have been glad to hear of the support granted them in the time of trial ; I feel for them in the nature of dear Anne Edwards' illness, but I remembered

what Job Scott said on this subject, that it is our finite view
that makes it painful to us, when disease, as in the case of fever,
clouds the mind and affects mental power ; it certainly adds to
the pain of parting with those we love, but how great the consolation to believe, as in this case, that she, whose loss they
mourn, had nothing to do but to die.; I trust they will all find
the best help near to them.   As for dear Edward Edwards, I
believe the same goodness and mercy that has hitherto followed
him will follow him to the end, until he enters the house of his
Lord for ever, to join those who have gone before him, who have
washed their garments and make them white in the blood of the
Lamb.   As for his children, how encouraging it is to observe
what a Providential care we see extended to the fatherless and
motherless.   I think he may indeed trust for his family ; they
also know where to look for protection, direction and blessing.

My very dear love to thy uncle, and dear Lady Harriet. What
a sweet impression their visit has left on our minds, excepting
the sorrow about their baby's illness.   I am, my beloved child,
your tenderly attached mother.

E. F.

P. S.—Though not mentioned, thy darling boys are near my
heart, and often thought of by me.

Plashet, Tenth Month.—I have had to attend much to the
sorrowful in our congregation at Plaistow.   One Friend had her
husband die away from her, amongst strangers on the continent ;
other dear friends of mine had their eldest son drowned in a
very distressing manner.   I have truly sympathised with them,
indeed the last case gave me real pain, and brought me into much
conflict of mind.   I have deeply felt the weight of being the
instrument to minister to them, and for them, in these awful dispensations, that I might not hinder, but promote the intention
of Infinite Wisdom and Mercy in permitting them. The poor boy
was buried yesterday, the other mourners were present part of
the time.   My sister Elizabeth Fry, and Cornelius Hanbury
were there to aid in the ministry.   The anointing for religious
service appeared freely poured forth.

Eleventh Month, 13*th.*—I am now enjoying a little quiet before breakfast, and a beautiful morning. What a delightful relish does religion give to the beauties of creation, and to the blessings granted us of every kind. Indeed, the longer I live, the more ardent is my desire for all, particularly those nearest to me, to partake of this unspeakable gift. The sting and misery of sin in all its forms, with my observation and experience in life, is increasingly evident to me, so that at times my heart is sore pained within me, because so many forget His law; but the text I desire to attend to is this, "I will hope continually and yet praise thee more and more."

18*th.*—I have for some weeks past believed that I must accompany my beloved brother Joseph to Ireland, in the spring to visit Friends, and also the prisons. It is weighty indeed, and my most earnest desire is to be rightly directed in it; that if I ought to go, my way may be made manifest step by step, and that if I ought to stay, it may altogether be obstructed. What am I at home or abroad, unless my Lord be with me to bless my labours? therefore, I can only seek to be altogether passive before Him, praying that He would in His mercy make known His will concerning me, and carry on His own work in me to His own praise. I am very unworthy of being engaged in His service, and always look upon it as an honour that is not my due.

In a letter from Lynn to one of her sisters, Mrs. Fry expresses her anxious desire for right guidance and direction.

Twelfth Month, 15*th.*

My mind is very weightily impressed with the prospect before me, of which my dearest brother and sister can tell thee; I have thought right to speak of it to them, and Frank, and Rachel; they feel much for me in it, and I think are not able really to discourage me from it. I do not feel in high spirits, although I trust that I am sensible of my many causes for thankfulness. My first desire for myself and those I love is, that whatever our circumstances may be, we may be conformed to the Divine Will, and fully experience the salvation which comes by Christ. I hope you will all three, (and dear Francis also if with you,) remember me for good just now, and desire my safe direction in all things.

I am nearly and devotedly yours all,

ELIZABETH FRY.

Mrs. Fry was cheered soon after her return home, by an encouraging letter from her sister, Rachel Gurney, who whilst she saw not with her in all things, nor believed herself called into a similar course, was yet capable of the closest appreciation of her motives of action, and sympathy with her in the pains and efforts involved.

My dearest Betsy,

Thy letter has interested us much to-day; with such a prospect as lies before thee, there must be ups and downs, and close straits to go through, and these will bring thee into some low feelings; but I cannot doubt that the way will in due time be made straight and plain. I am sure thy concerns will be most nearly interesting to us, and I trust we may be enabled to bear them in mind, so as to be good for ourselves, as well as some comfort and help to thee! Aunt Jane invited me to stay at the meeting, whilst our dear brother Joseph laid his concern to accompany thee before it. This was done with much feeling and humility on his own part, and a strong expression of unity from those present. It was a pain to me that he went off to Ipswich, to attend a funeral there, without my seeing him afterwards; but I think the meeting would be altogether encouraging to him. By this we lose him for nearly a week, which has come in as a real blank, from having been unexpected, and having taken him off just as Francis Cunningham and our dear friends the Hankinsons were here. It is a real loss; but we need more willing spirits in the cause of truth and righteousness! This will I trust find thee safely at home again, with our dearest sister Chenda by thy side; I hope thou wilt not be too much overdone to enjoy her company. It is no small thing to have met as we have done!

Thus adds her sister Catharine Gurney :—

"My dearest Betsy,

"I must add a line of sympathy under these weighty concerns, and, as far as I understand the case, of encouragement. I am for thy going, notwithstanding the importance of thy calls at home. I cannot but think the expedition will be made the instrument of great good, probably to yourselves and others. Francis entered warmly into it; he seemed to have no other feeling. This, I think, will give thee satisfaction."

Twelfth Month, 27th.—Last Third-day week, I believed it my duty to lay my concern to visit Ireland, before my Monthly Meeting; at the close of the meeting for worship. We told our dear friends what we had in view, and, feeling the great weight of leaving my family, made me doubt a little, whether Friends could unite in my going; but for all these things, I think I hardly ever felt a more solemn covering over a meeting, both before and after we spoke; and a very unusual number expressed their sympathy, unity, and desire to encourage us; not only the elders and ministers, but the very babes in Christ. There was testimony upon testimony. I felt uncommon peace and relief afterwards, as if the thing was right; many expressed a belief that the Lord would be with us, and preserve us, that He would be our shield and exceeding great reward, that He would go before us, and be our rear-guard.

Dear W. Allen believed "that those who stayed by the stuff would partake of the spoil." I never remember feeling the blessing of Christian love, and unity of spirit, more than at this time, and how truly the members of the Christian Church bear one another's burdens, and so fulfil the law of Christ.

Yesterday, we laid it before our Quarterly Meeting. The certificate having been signed on First-day, to my rejoicing, by all those who I thought might possibly have been somewhat against it, as well as those who I knew heartily united with us. I had, in both the Men and Women's Meeting, to express something, particularly to the youth, that for all the humiliations and deep baptisms attending it, I considered it an honour and favour

8

that I was unworthy of, to be thus made use of in my Master's
service; for I could in deed and in truth testify, that there are
no ways like His ways, no service like His service, and no joys
to be compared to the joys of His salvation.   I also addressed
the wives and mothers amongst us, on parting from our women
Friends, asking not only their sympathy, but their prayers ; as
" the prayer.of the righteous availeth much ;" and not only for
me, but in a particular manner for those who stayed behind.
To-day, my mind feels lightened and peaceful, and I have a
confirming hope that this calling is of the Lord, utterly unworthy
as I know I am, to do the least thing for such a Master ; as for
the outward sacrifices attending this step, I count them as
nothing, if I may but humbly trust that my most gracious Lord
and Master will, through His own power, and His own mercy,
keep those who stay, as well as those who go, near to Himself.
The pain of leaving my most tenderly beloved family, my comfortable and commodious home, with my delicate bodily frame, is
a sacrifice most willingly made by me, if those left do not suffer
harm by it.   I believe I must go in faith, nothing doubting ;
trusting all to Him, who knows the deep, earnest petitions of my
heart, for them and for us, and who can work with or without
instrumentality. The certificate granted us, by our Quarterly and
Monthly Meeting, was this :—

"To Friends of the Nation of Ireland.

" Dear Friends,—Our beloved Friend, Elizabeth Joseph Fry,
has, in a weighty manner, informed this Meeting, that her mind
has been for many years impressed with a belief, that it would be
required of her to offer to pay a religious visit to the Meetings
of Friends in Ireland, pretty generally; and, also, to stand
resigned to further religious service, both amongst Friends, and
those not of the Society, as truth might open the way, and that
she apprehended the time was nearly come for her to enter
thereon.   Our beloved Friend Elizabeth Fry, also informed the
Meeting, that she believed it right to offer to accompany her
sister in the said visit, as her mind had been somewhat similarly
impressed for many years past. The said proposals, having had
our deliberate and solid consideration, and much unity and sym-

pathy having been felt and expressed with our dear friends, we think it right to set them at liberty to perform the same : informing you that they are ministers of the gospel, in unity and good esteem with us.   We commend them to the affectionate care of those amongst whom their lot may be cast.   We desire their preservation in a humble dependence on the great Head of the Church, for daily supplies of wisdom and strength, that they may thereby be enabled to perform the work assigned them, to the promotion of the cause of truth and righteousness, and to the peace of their own minds.   We remain, in love, your friends. Signed in Radcliff and Barking Monthly Meeting, held at Plaistow, by adjournment, the 24th of Twelfth Month, 1826.

" Signed by forty men, and thirty women."

At a Quarterly Meeting, for London and Middlesex, held the 26th of Twelfth Month, 1826—

" Our beloved friends, E. J. Fry, and E. Fry, have attended this Meeting, and in a feeling manner opened before it the concern described in the foregoing certificate.   This Meeting, after a time of solid consideration, and under a feeling of much unity and sympathy with them, in reference to the arduous prospect before them, unites in setting them at liberty ; desiring, that they may experience the preservation and guidance of the Shepherd of Israel, and be permitted, when the service allotted to them is performed, to return with the reward of peace.

" Signed in, and on behalf of, the Meeting, by
" PETER BEDFORD, *Clerk.*
" Signed in, and on behalf of, the Women's Meeting,
"HANNAH MESSER, *Clerk.*"

This important point obtained, and the unity of her friends officially expressed ; Elizabeth Fry prepared, with her companions, for their departure, after making various arrangements to ensure the comfort of her family during her absence.

To her Sisters, Catherine and Rachel Gurney.

Plashet, *First Month*, 3rd, 1827.

My dearest Catherine and Rachel,

It appears too long since I wrote to you, and since I received your welcome letters. I was rejoiced at our brother Joseph's good account of you. I got through the Quarterly Meeting most satisfactorily. I hardly ever remember such a current of love and unity poured forth on such an occasion ; which was particularly comforting, under my peculiar home circumstances. We have had Dr. Pinkerton, his wife, and three of his children, here since Second day : I have valued their company. We had, last evening, a large party of young people to meet them, and a very cheerful time they had ; but, I think, a very innocent one. I like to see young persons happy and merry; it reminded me of some of our days, that are not only passed, but appear now quite in the distance. I felt a little doubtful whether to have it, but I yielded the point to the children, and am glad to say, I see no cause to repent it. I suppose I shall have many farewell visits; indeed, we are full of engagements. I have been deeply interested about the poor woman who was hanged yesterday, in Newgate. Her end, I trust, was happy. I have had much to feel about her ; it is such awful work, thus prematurely to have a fellow-creature launched into eternity !

On Second-day, we had a very long British Society committee; that cause, I think, yet prospers much. It was a solemn time, and an encouraging one to us to go forward. My curious book, I hope, will be useful, and promote the cause.* The children are now generally well and comfortable. My dearest husband talks of going to Dublin with us, or else meeting us on our return.

I write this flat letter in haste : it is hardly worth your having ; but, as I have so little time for writing, I should like it forwarded to my dearest Rachel, at Lynn. I am sorry to hear of dear Sarah B.'s trying accident; express my dear love and

* Observations on the Visiting, Superintending, and Government of Female Prisoners. By Elizabeth Fry. 1827.

sympathy to her. Our brother Joseph appeared well and comfortable ; he dined, and spent a valuable evening with us here, on First-day.

In abundance of love to you, and at Lynn, I am your nearly attached

E. F.

To HER DAUGHTER, MRS. FRANCIS CRESSWELL.

Plashet, Second Month, 1st.

My dearest Rachel,

As the time for my departure for Ireland is now drawing near, I feel bound, in this way, in the most tender manner, to bid thee FAREWELL, in every sense of the word. May the Almighty be with, and bless thee and thine, my much-loved child ; and, above all things, increasingly manifest Himself, in His own power, to your souls, to your edification and consolation, your help and strength. I feel as if my family must increasingly show themselves on the Lord's side, simply, humbly, and faithfully, holding up His standard of truth, and of righteousness; in which belief I include thee and thy husband. The time is short; we can none, therefore, too soon give ourselves up wholly to the Lord, for our own sakes, and the sake of others.

I feel peaceful in my prospect of departure, though deeply unworthy, and naturally unfit for such a service ; but my hope is in this, that "help is laid upon One that is mighty," who alone can enable me to do all things to His praise.

I have abundance to do ; therefore in near love, once more, I say to thee and the boys, farewell in the Lord.

Thy loving, tender mother,
E. F.

On the 4th of February, Elizabeth Fry, with her brother Joseph John Gurney, commenced their journey towards Ireland. They were joined on the road by her sister-in-law. Acutely did she feel leaving her family, and most painful was it to them to part with her ; nor was the trial lessened by some of her children as they advanced in life, not being altogether satisfied as to these engagements, or able to comprehend how a career so peculiar, could be consistent with their mother's domestic duties. It required the wonderful results of her exertions, and the practical effects of these journeys, to convince them, that it was by the great Head of the Church, that she was "put forth" for such services.

Her last sabbath at home she thus describes:—

The First-day preceding my leaving home, was most interesting. In the first place, I had all the servants collected at the morning reading, and expressed very fully my desires for them, and their preservation in the right way, which they appeared to feel a good deal, and it was a heart-tendering time. My beloved John and his Rachel were staying with us, and their sweet babe. Before meeting, I had the children a little while alone, and the meeting was in no common degree solemn. The afternoon meeting, if any thing, was still more so, the ministry very lively and refreshing. My dearest sister, Louisa Hoare was with us to my real comfort; my brother, William Fry and his children were at both meetings. In the evening, we had a large number to tea, and at our evening reading. It was very interesting taking leave of my most dearly beloved family. The presence of the Most High appeared to overshadow us; prayer was offered again and again, and testimony upon testimony was given. One Friend expressed his full belief that we should return in peace and safety, and that no harm would come nigh my dwelling; a general feeling of the rectitude of our going was no small comfort. The next morning, I bid my darling children farewell in their beds. I left home about six o'clock, accompanied by my sons William and Joseph. My natural pain in parting with those most tenderly beloved, was mitigated by a portion of that peace the world cannot give, in making what I trust was a sacrifice well pleasing to the best of Masters.

Extracts from her own letters, furnish not merely the history of her journey, but an account of her natural fears, and her spiritual consolations—the difficulties that appeared before her, and the power by which she was enabled to surmount them. Written in haste, and often when greatly wearied, these letters have nothing to recommend them but their truth, simplicity and earnestness of feeling; but those who wish to follow her through the journey of life, not only in what she did, but what she thought and felt in doing, will prefer them, such as they are, to a more laboured history related by others.

Melksham, Second Month, 6th.

My much-loved Husband, Children, Brothers and Sisters,

I now commence the journal of my journey, which I desire regularly to keep until I may be favoured to return home. This, it is my expectation that I shall do; but if in the ordering of Infinite Wisdom, it should not be the case, may all concerned, be enabled to bow to the dispensations of the Most High; for in all He doeth, He doeth well.

On leaving my sweet dwelling, and my much-loved family, I felt very quiet, as if after all the deep feeling of the day before, I had only to rest, and could almost have thought myself insensible to what I was doing. After a refreshing breakfast at Mildred's Court, we set off, leaving William and Joseph; I felt, dear fellows, as if I had not in parting nearly enough expressed my abounding love, and my sense of their kindness in accompanying us there. We had a pleasant journey; the company of my beloved husband and brother delightful. We were received here with great kindness and hospitality. I have just been refreshing myself by a walk in a farm-yard, with an old farmer, and have bought a nice cheese for Plashet, which I hope you will like; it should be kept several months before it is eaten. The most important feature of this day, so far, has been parting with my dearest husband. I was enabled to commend him unto Him, who can alone bless and preserve us, whether together or separate. How very, very near you feel to my heart, and how sweet it is, as time advances, to find that our spiritual, as well as our natural bonds increase in strength, which I may thankfully acknowledge I believe to be our case.

Fourth day, evening, Worcester.—My brother Joseph and I left Melksham after breakfast, this morning. I passed a comfortable night, more so than I could have expected, but there is a power that makes up our losses, particularly when in the way of our duty; surely bearing our cross in small and great things, for what we believe to be, the sake of the cause of righteousness, brings peace with it. We travelled through a beautiful country : the Vale of Rodborough affectingly reminded me of days that are passed; we saw, at Malmsbury, some most beautiful Saxon or ancient gothic architecture. Our distribution of tracts on the road has been really entertaining, it was pleasant to see how gratefully received. We are now in excellent quarters, so fare-well for to-night.

We left H. Newman's, after a most hospitable reception, before eight this morning, and have been travelling all day, except stopping at Colebrook Dale to dinner, where I was reminded of very interesting and important days of my youth; some very sweet ones that were passed in this black-faced country. We met a pleasant party of the Darby family to dinner, many of them I think you know, and a very interesting party of the youth, both boys and girls, young men and maidens : whilst my dear companions gave them a little good advice, I went up stairs, and had some rest. Several little things have given me pleasure on the journey; the good appearance of the poor, and I should hope their general prosperity; the animals also,—beautiful deer, sheep, and lambs, and many delightful prospects ; but the thoughts of my beloved family often come in—your kindness on my departure and before it—you each come before me with so much love and unity. I often think of dearest sister Rachel, and hope her cough is better, and my children at Lynn. I feel grateful for your aunt Hoare's kindness to me, and to you ; let her know about me, and let me know how her dear little Richard goes on. I feel rather odd to be here, away from you all, but the duty which brings me here makes it easy, otherwise I should feel sadly out of my place; but I am bountifully provided for, much more so than I desire. Your uncle's kindness and attention almost unbounded, and your aunt also very kind. Farewell for to-night, my much-loved husband, children, &c., &c.

Sixth-day evening, Holy Head.—We arrived here about eight o'clock, after a beautiful journey: at least the greater portion of it. I never saw such scenery,—the rocky mountains with long icicles hanging from them, and sheets of ice over parts of them— the mountain torrents full and strong—and the sun just enlightening the tops of some of the mountains, whilst others were in deep shadow. You can hardly conceive the grandeur and beauty of the scene. As a work of art, the Menai Bridge exceeds any thing I ever saw, its principle being so simple, yet so wonderful.

Dublin, Second Month, 14th.

My dearest Children,

I told my tale up to First-day evening. On Second-day morning we visited the Asylum for the Deaf and Dumb, kept by Joseph Humphreys, a very interesting institution, well situated within sight of the Dublin Bay; his collection of Irish shells is beautiful, he means to procure me some of them, with their names, and some minerals. We made calls on the aged and sorrowful, came home, rested, and dressed; then went to dine and spend the evening at Robert Fayle's, where we met about seventy Friends, it was the place my dearest sister Priscilla stayed at, when she was here; it is very striking to me to observe, there, and amongst many Friends, the effect of her labours. We had an interesting evening with this large party of fine comely young persons; your uncle and I told them anecdotes that we thought useful and desirable. The Irish are a very interesting people. Religion has done much amongst Friends and others, and will I believe do yet more, and so regulate and further polish them, as to bring forth their bright, and overcome their darker qualities. I like the people, and always did; they are very kind to us. Engagements are thickening upon us: one Roman Catholic lady has called, a charming woman, and through her means we are likely to visit the Nuns on Sixth-day. This evening, we propose having a meeting for the youth; on Sixth-day, for older Friends in the evening, and for the public in the morning; next week we look to the prisons and public institutions. Farewell for to-day, in dearest love.

E. F.

Fifth-day, one o'clock.—We breakfasted at the Castle, at Major Sirr's, where we met a number of interesting people ; he is in office, one of the heads of police. In the cross, yet in the power, we had a religious time with them. Afterwards we saw a most curious and beautiful collection of antiquities found in the bogs, and other places in this country ; also minerals and shells, one a most rare specimen. Since I came home, many have called. Very striking is the work going on in this land, it appears the time for those who love the truth, to labour for it.

"Dublin, *Second Month*, 17*th.*

My dearest Husband,

*   *   *   *   *

After I sent off my letter on Fifth-day, we went to the castle to call on the gentleman, who, in the absence of the Secretary of State, is acting as such. He treated us with great kindness, and appeared really pleased at our visiting Ireland : he has invited us to dine with him next Second-day. We then went to A. Maginn's office, he was also truly kind, and says he will forward any letters for us. We dined with a valuable Friend, Sarah Phelps, and met several Friends. My dear sister Elizabeth all this time was completely poorly, and confined mostly in bed, at the house of our kind friends, Jonathan and Eliza Pim, where we are so hospitably entertained, when to my sorrow, my brother Joseph was taken in the same way ; in the evening, he felt himself really ill, so that what with our many guests, and my two patients, you may fancy me (more particularly as Joseph is in the next house, and Elizabeth up high flights of stairs), rather overpressed ; each had a medical attendant—however, the next morning, my brother was able to go to Meeting, it was a public one, he preached there as he generally does, much in the demonstration of the Spirit, and of power.

I had the comfort in the morning, to have both my patients better, and I hope it was not a want of resignation, anxiously to desire their recovery ; it reminded me of Paul, how much he wished for his companion's revival, lest he should have sorrow upon sorrow. We received afterwards many persons, not Friends, Lady Lorton and others ; Joseph and I went to wait on the

Lord Lieutenant (Lord Wellesley), by his desire, we had a very gratifying and satisfactory interview. His views and ours appeared perfectly to correspond on many things of importance, particularly the subject of punishment. Lady Wellesley was ill, or, he said, she wished to see me. I forgot to tell thee, that I paid a very nice visit to the nunnery of the Sisters of Charity, and heard many particulars of their institution and of their plans ; we also had some interesting conversation of a religious nature, with them. You all know how deeply I have felt being away from my beloved husband and children, but I think I never remember being any where, with such an opening for service in every way, religiously, morally, and in benevolent objects. Our being esteemed, as in truth we are, quiet and conciliatory in our views, and our being of no party in religion or politics, appears just now important. But if we are the least useful, we must remember that all our powers are gifts. Yesterday, we had crowded meetings, and we had all three in no common degree, to press the point of looking less to the ministers, and more to the Minister of ministers. More of Christian charity, and being all one in Christ, appears the thing wanted here ; there is certainly a great portion of light, and many individuals who seem to be very serious and spiritual.

The people are powerful, and warm-hearted, but not, I think, possessing more feeling, or sensitiveness, than the English. They appear to me formed, bodily and mentally, in a more hardy mould. This city is very fine, its houses and buildings above the mode of living, or the state of the inhabitants.

I feel (notwithstanding the illness of my dear companions) that we are rightly together, for with such a weight of various services, a treble cord was wanted for strength.

Dublin, *Second Month.*

My dearest Children,

To go on with our journal : on Fourth-day, after I sent my letter off, we visited four prisons—some of them in a most deplorable state, particularly those for debt—almost the deepest distress I ever witnessed. We hope that some remedy may be

found.   Should this prove the case, it will be a strong confirmation of our being in our right place ; as I find, that those, who
can help in these things, are willing to listen to us.

We dined at the house of the temporary Secretary of State.
We met there, the Archbishop of Tuam, and many connected
with him ; Lady Ann Gregory is his sister.   Highly valuable
and agreeable people, indeed.   I think I never, any where, saw
so many serious people ; surely, the true leaven, more or less, is
affecting the whole lump.

Yesterday was the week-day meeting; crowds attended, and
very solemn it was.   I forgot to say, that when visiting the
prisoners the day before, the judges were sitting in the court, and
sent for us to go to them there.   Picture your uncle, myself, and
some other Friends, in a crowded court, sitting beside the judges.
I could but be reminded of the difference of our situation, to that
of Friends formerly, taken into the courts in time of persecution,
and so cruelly treated ; but my belief is, that their standing their
ground as they did, prepared the way for even these services.
" They laboured, and we have entered into their labours."   May
the same power preserve us, in what may appear heights, as it
did them in depths.

After writing so far, we went to breakfast at a lady's named
Hoare, some relation to your uncle Hoare, many met us there.
After a religious time with them, we went to the Bridewell, to
meet a large number of ladies, to form and arrange their prison
committees.   This was a very arduous, but a very important
business ; I trust, things are now put in good training, so that
if we do nothing else, it appears almost worth while to have
come here for this day's work.

Almost as soon as we returned from the prison, we had to go
to the park, for me to see Lady Wellesley.   I paid her a very
interesting visit ; she is a sweet woman, and, I think, serious.
She is a Roman Catholic.   We next went to call on the Roman
Catholic Archbishop, and, as the Protestant one is now, I
believe, here I must stop.

My dearest Husband,

I feel that my journal was cut too short at Dublin, from a press upon me, which appeared unavoidable. I left off, I think, before we visited the House of Industry, almost the most interesting institution I ever saw; but, being accompanied by (I should think) nearly a hundred persons, added to the fatigue, and lessened the pleasure. Afterwards, we had quite an entertainment from the governor, as luncheon. Seeing the lunatics, gave me real pleasure; their order, comfort, and industry, appeared to be great. We then visited the Richmond Lunatic Asylum, and part of the great Government Prison. After one of the most crowded Meetings I ever attended, and I think, one of the most solemn, we paid another visit to the Government Prison, and then took our departure from our most kind friends, and the highly interesting city of Dublin; with, I believe I may say, thankful and peaceful hearts, under a deep feeling that "hitherto the Lord had helped us," and out of "weakness we had been made strong." We had a dark evening drive of many hours, to James Forbes', at Christianstown, near Rathangan, where we found every comfort. We had two Meetings the next day at Edenderry; nothing but turf-fires, and the aspect of things very different to England. The next evening we travelled again, and were not fully expected; but fires soon burnt up, and after a while, a nice supper refreshed us.

Armagh, *Second Month,* 28*th.*

My dearest Children,

We are here comfortably settled by a nice fire-side, in a good inn, and in what appears to be, as far as we can judge, rather a fine city. We left Lord Bective's yesterday, about twelve o'clock, and then went with Lady Bective, and others, to see her charities, and a sad little prison. After this, we set forward to Coote Hill, two stages, each about twelve Irish miles, which, I can assure you, was a fatiguing day's journey; we dared not stop to dine, and were about six hours on the road, or more, which was done with difficulty, with four horses, the roads were so very bad. The boggy country has a peculiar and desolate look; the generally miserable cabins, and appearance of the poor (though most of the women have cloaks, and the men great coats,) give a very different appearance from England. There is also a general want of order in the manner of cultivating the ground; the hedges half down, and badly kept, excepting near gentlemen's places, where things bear a different aspect. We observed a number of goats ; I suppose they use their milk. Pigs abound ; I think they have rather a more elegant appearance than ours, their hair often curled—naturalists perhaps may attribute this to their intimate association with their betters ! The turf-fires, mostly used in the neighbourhood of the bogs, are pleasant. We yesterday, met a true Irish funeral ; it was a curious sight, and really surprising to see how neat and clean the people turned out of their dirty cabins, some were really good-looking. The howl (if it was the howl) was like a dirge—melancholy, but rather pleasing. We have not lately had so much begging, as nearer Dublin, or the appearance of so much distress. We had a curious Meeting this morning of Friends, respectable persons, labourers, and the very poor people, many, I believe, Roman Catholics.

We have travelled again to-day, twenty-four miles ; more fatiguing, I can assure you, than to travel fifty miles in England ; but we have not been on the best roads. We visited a large prison at Monaghan, and to-morrow we hope to visit one here, and a Lunatic Asylum ; also, to form a committee at Lady Lifford's, to attend a Meeting some miles off, and then to go forward to sleep at Thomas Greer's. Our life is a busy one, certainly. So now, my much-loved family, I bid you farewell for this evening.

Thomas Greer's, Rhone Hill, Sixth-day morning.—Yesterday, we began our morning with some Friends to breakfast at the inn, and after reading, we set off to the prison. It was a fine day, and we had a pleasant walk to it. Several were waiting for us, both gentlemen and ladies. We had, for the first time, a religious opportunity with the prisoners ; first, Elizabeth and myself, with the women, then all of us, with the men. The Roman Catholics appear very hard to reach ; but with the poor men, I think, the power of truth reigned over all, and their spirits appeared brought down. We then went to the Lunatic

Asylum, which was in delightful order; then to Lady Lifford's, where we found an excellent committee. We had a religious time with this charming lady, and then went forward to a Meeting at Rich Hill, a curious place, and as curious a congregation, but we had a good Meeting. Afterwards, by some accident, I went into a private house, thinking it was the inn, and gave orders as if at an inn; I ordered tea immediately, and begged to be shown to a bed-room, for my sister to lie down, as she was but poorly. At last I discovered my droll, and at first, disagreeable mistake; but such was Irish hospitality, that the lady of the house made us stay, gave us some tea, comforted us up, and sent us off, not knowing whom she had received, nor do we know her name. We then had an easy drive here, horses good, roads better; but both my dear companions far from well. I feel we have much cause for thankfulness; we are daily provided for; and may, through unmerited mercy, say with the disciples formerly, to the query, "Lackest thou any thing?" "Nothing Lord"—except to be better ourselves, and more fit for such a service.

Lisburn, Third Month, 4th.

My dearest Husband,

I yesterday had the real comfort of receiving letters, in the evening, from home. I was made quite cheerful by it, and weighty as it is to begin upon a new field of service in these parts, yet I went light-hearted on my way, and, I trust I may say, thankful.

I am sorry to hear of our poor friend William Morley's state, and particularly wish to be affectionately remembered to him, and to have him told how much I desire that, as his flesh and his heart fail, he may know the Lord truly to be the strength of his heart, and eventually, through His unmerited mercy in Christ Jesus, to become his portion for ever; he must cast himself, just such as he is, on Christ his Saviour, the propitiatory sacrifice for our sins, whose mercies are unbounded.

Now for my journal—after I last wrote, we attended a large Meeting of Friends at Grange, where unbelief formerly, had made much devastation; we were enabled to preach Christ, I

10

trust in power, and it appeared a very solemn time. We find the Meeting we had at Coote Hill made a great impression in the place, particularly amongst the Roman Catholics; numbers have been since to the Friend's house where we slept, for tracts; he had given three hundred away. We arrived here, and had a most hearty reception from Jonathan Richardson and his brother; their kindness is very great to us poor travellers. Yesterday, we had Friends very much alone in the morning, and a very crowded Meeting for others in the evening, painfully so to me; I was so much afraid the house was not safe, and I believe one of the higher galleries creaked; it was however, well got through. What a day this is in Ireland! something of a shaking in religion, only there is such a field of service open, that it seems as if we hurried a little from the different places; but we desire to do our best. We have met with a delightful old minister here, John Conran, a most able gospel preacher, eighty-eight years old, he has stood through every storm in the time of heresy here; he was desired to quit the gallery, and no longer to preach, but he kept steady to his gift, and his sun is indeed setting in brightness; he is a man of good family, who came into our Society by convincement. I think such an instance of a lively spirit in old age, is a powerful evidence of the truth of religion, and that there is a principle above the natural part in man, which lives and flourishes when the other part declines. I must now go to breakfast, looking to the Quarterly Meeting to-day. May best help be with us, and grace, mercy, and peace with you. Amen.

Third-day Morning.—We had a very satisfactory Quarterly Meeting. We are now returned from a concluding Meeting of worship, one of the most solemn, and striking, I ever attended; the good power and anointing distilled as the dew amongst us, to the great refreshment, I believe, of all present. The ministry of the old Friend was wonderful—his experience of the power of light, life, and salvation striking; he overflowed with love, and the doctrine he preached a strong proof of the reality of that power which remains after all the rest is shaken. When the reality of these truths are brought home to us, how earnest becomes the desire for all whom we love, to be made partakers of such a benefit. May husband, children, brothers, sisters, and all near and dear to me, partake of this joyous, glorious, full salvation!

We have here delightful quarters at John Bell's. We dined and rested, then called on some of the sick and sorrowful; after which, we proceeded to our Public Meeting, to be held in a large school-room at the top of a high building. Feel for us —upon our arrival, the crowd was so great and the press such, that when we endeavoured to ascend the stair-case, I thought we must give up the attempt; however, after great pressing, we were driven into such an assembly, that my poor heart almost sank, I so extremely feared accident, whether the building or the floor would not give way under the weight, however, in tender mercy, after a little while quietness reigned; I had a few words to say, which appeared to tranquillize the assembly, and then your uncle was enabled beautifully to preach the glad tidings of the gospel of Christ. I did afterwards say something, but in weakness, as my voice nearly failed me. Your aunt spoke powerfully, and I had power given me to offer the sacrifice of thanksgiving and prayer at the end. All dispersed without injury, I trust peaceful and edified; but your dear uncle and myself had had such a shake, that we both passed very poor nights. I felt a little like Peter on the waters, as if fears got too much hold of me, and made me ready to sink; your aunt was sadly crushed. We set off after breakfast to the Bridewell, numbers with us; but we hope that good resulted, and we are to form a committee to visit it. We proceeded to Carrickfergus, a very interesting place, and a most beautiful drive to it; we passed a fine old castle by the sea. We visited a sad prison, and formed a Ladies' Committee; also committees for visiting different charities, and had a large meeting of ladies.

To her Son William Storrs Fry.

Londonderry, *Third Month*, 18*th*.

My dearest William,

I have now matter for a very interesting letter, if I can get time to write it. After my last communication, we went to a second Public Meeting, which was very large and satisfactory.

8

We dined at our dear hospitable friend's, and in the evening, thy uncle went to have a Public Meeting at Carrickfergus, whilst we had a Meeting with the benevolent ladies, to form committees to visit their different institutions, which had in Belfast answered well.

We met a cheerful party in the evening, when our labours were concluded, and set off the next morning:—a pleasant company, and the weather bright. We had with us, Thomas Wakefield, John Christy, and William Bell, all superior Friends, and highly esteemed. Our drive was beautiful, by the lake called Lough Neagh, one of the finest pieces of water, looking like the sea, without a boundary to the eye, in parts. Lord O'Neal's place is situated on its banks; we passed through its beautiful scenery. We slept at a Moravian settlement, where we were pleased and interested, and met a gentleman and lady, who said they knew thee, and had seen thee at Herrnhut, with Dr. Pinkerton. We had no religious time with them, but were interested by the whole thing, though I wanted them to do more good to the community generally, instead of confining their exertions so exclusively to their own body. We then set off to a curious little country meeting, dined at a public-house, in a small town, where we were almost mobbed for tracts; the energy for knowledge is great, very different to what we expected, great eagerness evident in the public mind for more religious light. Some think there is the beginning of a reformation here, but I believe this work will be very gradual; much is, however, going on, of a highly interesting nature. We had a meeting, in the evening, in an out of the way-farm-house, and slept there. Kindness and cleanliness made all pleasant. We went forward to Coleraine, and as we had a leisure morning, and were only ten miles from the Giant's Causeway, we thought that we ought to visit it; a fine expedition we had, and an adventurous one— two horses tumbling down, pouring rain, and so forth. However, we persevered, and first visited a very fine ruined castle, built on a rock projecting into the sea, called Dunluce Castle. There is a little bridge from one rock to another, without defence of any kind. It was a very fine scene—beautiful black rocks, forming a sort of amphitheatre on each side of it. We went on in pouring rain and violent wind, to the Causeway, and found, as usual, that we were quiet deceived in the distance. After walking over rocks, and at the edge of cliffs, nearly overwhelmed with wet, we opened upon this wonderful work of nature ; like an unfinished building, formed of stones fitted into each other, being concave and convex, and so rising in pillars of different heights. some with three sides, some as many as nine, of various colours, I am glad we saw it, as a fresh proof of the wonderful and various works of God.

I hardly knew how I should be able to get back, from the painful effect, walking up hill in the wind, has on me ; however, by the help of some poor working men, I at last effected it. Thy aunt was able to manage better than I did, being light, they carried her over all difficult parts.   Curiosities abounded, stones, spar, &c., &c.; but my excessive fatigue prevented my having wit to get what I ought, however, I did obtain some.   In a place like this, abounding with beauties, both grand and minute, I could delight myself for days with my beloved family.

I have almost ruined my cloak and bonnet, being nearly wet through.   We arrived in time at Coleraine, for a large Public Meeting in the town.   The next morning we set off for this place, passing by the beautiful Lough Foyle, partly a gulf from the sea. This is one of the most beautiful towns, as to situation, I ever saw, strongly fortified by a wall, so wide that there is a walk upon it ; a fine river flows before it.

We found, on our arrival, that all our letters had miscarried ; but we had not been long here, before the Bishop, his wife, the Mayor, Magistrates, and Prison Inspector, came to visit us, trying to help us in every way.   We dined at the palace ; but, for all this kindness from man, I felt low and sunk, under an awful feeling of service in the place.   To-day, we have had one meeting attended by all descriptions of persons.

Evening.—We are just come in after a very large meeting, held in the Presbyterian Meeting-house.   Since that, we have been reading to the prisoners, and forming a committee to visit the women.

Omagh, *Third Month,* 19*th.*

My dearest Children,

My letter of yesterday, was so far from giving a full account of some of our interesting proceedings, that, as we are stopped here from the want of horses (being assize time), I shall begin another letter.   I think you will be amused to hear, that upon our arrival at Londonderry, we were saluted by a peal of bells; some of the party thought they were for us, which proved true, as we found afterwards, by a very curious letter from the ringers.

The manners of the people in the north of Ireland and their dress much resemble the Scotch; most of them, even the poor, are neat, though without shoes and stockings.   I am sorry to say, the great numbers that we find in the prisons, prove an unsettled state in the country ; but, I think, there is a good deal to excite their bad feelings, and, in some parts, they are almost starving, though this is not by any means generally the case in the north.   We never go many miles without passing much bog which is valuable, as it affords such good fireing; and we see continually cabins made of little else than turf, with a hole at the top, for the chimney, much like those in Scotland.   We have this morning visited the Prison, the Lunatic Asylum, and Infirmary at Lifford; and the Prison, and Infirmary here.   We think that in their institutions, there is a great spirit of improvement; though some of them remain in a deplorable state.   The Infirmary we visited to-day, was so ; I found there a poor patient without any linen, laid between blankets, and in an exceedingly dirty state ; but this is not common, some are in beautiful order.

Boyle, *Third Month,* 22*nd.*

My dearest Husband,

Since I last wrote, we have passed a very interesting time. We got up about four o'clock.   On our way to Enniskillen, stopped at a curious public-house for breakfast, where we saw a good deal of the people, who flocked after us for tracts.   I wish I could picture to you the scene, in a mud-floored parlour, with a turf fire.   I took my seat some time in the curious kitchen, to talk to the family.   After a time, they sent out to buy us a little

bread, and some eggs. We fared well, and had a cheerful meal
in our humble abode. The roads bad, and horses bad; we got
on very slowly, going twenty miles in about six hours. The
roads, too, are often dangerous, many of them being raised very
high, without wall or hedge of any kind. In several places, a
precipice on each side. Much of it through bog; indeed, I
think, we have not passed a stage, since we left Dublin, without
part of it being through black bog. We reached Enniskillen in
time to visit the Infirmary and Prison, and to form a Ladies'
Committee. We are shocked to find so many bad cases of
murder and cruelty in the prisons; it shows an awful state of
things, proving extreme moral degradation in this part of Ireland. We saw six men, who had through enmity knocked a
man's head to pieces, and then put his body down a cave, where
it was found. Another instance of burning, nearly to death, a
woman, with whom they were angry.

With these impressions, as to the state of this part of the
country, we all felt a little alive to our own safety, but were
obliged to set off for our journey to Sligo, because we could not
otherwise accomplish all we had in view. We could have no
other horses, than those from Omagh. We went forward by the
side of a fine lake and beautiful rocks and mountains, till we got
to a house half-way from the place of our destination. We had
been nearly five hours going about fourteen miles, and had eight
or nine more to go ; the question was, whether to pass the night
in this solitary public-house, or go on with the same horses.
Our dear Irish friends were evidently unwilling that we should
remain; therefore, though close by the place of the sad murder
that had just happened, we took courage, and set off again.

A curious dark drive we had ; but our friends accompanying
us, and the belief that we were in our right place, took away
fear, on my part at least. We expected to arrive at a nice inn
to sleep; but, to our great disappointment, after our fagging
day, we arrived between ten and eleven o'clock at night, at a
miserable dirty public-house; and we did not get even eggs or
bacon, nor ourselves settled, some in one house, and some in
another, till one o'clock in the morning. You will not wonder
when I tell you we passed rather a nervous night. The next

morning, we went to Sligo, a highly interesting place. We found in that prison again cases of murder; but much as there is of fearful evil, there is great good also stirring, many Roman Catholics turning to Protestantism, several of whom we met this morning; they appear highly interesting, and to be a spiritual people. We spent the evening at the Rector's, met a very large party, and formed a fresh Committee, though two ladies have already done wonders here in the prison. The High Sheriff and the Clergy were most kind to us. The inn was so full, we had a private lodging, and were treated by the mistress of the house with no common attention. We had this morning, a large Public Meeting, which appeared to give much satisfaction to our numerous new friends. We parted in real love from the people of the place, and then set off here, paying visits to two cabins by the way. We have had no further adventure. Imagine us in the cabin round a turf fire on a mud floor, a hole in the top for a chimney, a little dirty straw on the floor for them to sleep, as the woman said, "up and down in the room." Some heath and turf for fireing, no windows, and two little dirty benches to sit on; the husband, wife, and children, round the boiling potatoes; they offered us "a prater and an egg;" though so poor, so hospitable!

Moate.—We slept at a tolerable inn at Boyle, and went on to Roscommon, where, in the prison (as usual in these parts) were murderers; and, at the county town of Westmeath, fifteen men, all to suffer death (I believe) for murder. The little Meeting was fully attended at Ballymurray. It is curious to observe the efforts made to attend these Meetings, by persons generally. After Meeting, it was late, and report said that stones were laid on the road to stop our progress, from some evil design, on our way to the farm-house where we were to sleep; but happily, this proved false. No fire in our room; still, I did well, and we had much to enjoy, and be thankful for. We are struck by the true kindness of the Friends, and with the effects of true religion, in changing the nature of this people; making them clean, courteous, and gentle.

We got up soon after five o'clock, and set off for Moate; in passing through a large town, we found an eager desire for tracts, before we were through the town, persons running after the carriage for them—when, out came a man from one of the houses, a sort of lay priest (we suppose), stopped those who were near us with an austere countenance, and made the people tear them in our presence. A priest did the same with one of Joseph's tracts; they delight in receiving them generally, when out of sight of their rulers. A want of horses made us late here, and in passing through another large town, we were requested to have a Public Meeting, the room all ready for us, which we did not accept. To-day, we begin the Quarterly Meeting, which is a weighty prospect.

Our dear friends, who are so kindly yet accompanying us; had a trial last night, in hearing that sixteen armed men had broken into a house very near theirs, where they have left their wives and children. A Friend, who would keep arms in his house, and did not keep to our peaceable principle, was murdered near where we were yesterday; and I hear that the woman Friend, who was murdered, was a strange person. The Sheriff of Roscommon said, "the sword of the Spirit was the best defence in this land."

Third Month, 30th. Galway, First-day morning.—Here we are, in the midst of what appears gross darkness; hardly any Protestants, and the Roman Catholics in a highly irritable state, so much so, that the Mayor has just called to say, he thinks a guard ought to attend us at our Meetings. This of course we cannot accept. We look forward with some anxiety to our day; but not without hope. I had meant to send this letter this morning, but shall now wait till we see how the day is accomplished.——Our Meeting is well over. In the first place, we had about three hundred persons in the Assembly Room at this inn, it was very much like being surrounded by those whom we should suppose knew little or nothing of religion; as for Friends, and women's preaching, it was a marvel indeed to them; I never was in a place apparently so dark. The Sabbath hardly at all kept, except in going to their places of worship; but to tell you of the meeting—there was one continued bustle until I knelt in prayer; then your uncle spoke at considerable length, and there was something like quiet; he enlarged beautifully on Christian love and charity, which appears so extremely wanted here, (there is so much contention). After he sat down, I rose and said, that when the women brought word that our Saviour was risen, the disciples believed that they were "idle tales," partly, probably, because the instruments were weak who conveyed the tidings, and so it might then be, but I hoped they would lay aside prejudice and not consider what we call "idle tales," because, we who spoke them were also weak instruments. The people were very attentive, and a solemn time we had, though so curious a one; this afternoon, we had another Meeting of about a thousand persons, different to any thing I ever witnessed. We had close exercise of spirit, and to our blessed Lord alone could we look for help. Such an assembly of Roman Catholics, for any such purpose, was never known to have met before; some were heard to say, that if we held them, they would attend them every evening in the week, for all their priests. The Stream gradually rose in the Meeting, until it overflowed its banks; but how do you think it ended? Those in the lower part of the room, showed their satisfaction by knocking with their feet and clapping their hands. We were followed by crowds to our inn, who looked upon us as quite a spectacle! However we are encouraged to believe such a visit was wanted, and is likely to be of use, in drawing Christians together; as well as leading them from outward profession, to the real inward work of grace. We enjoyed peace after this awful Meeting, and parted in much love, for we have been treated with kindness by Roman Catholics and Protestants. The Irish are a fine powerful people; I have been thus particular in relating the history of to-day, because it has been so important a one to us.

The preceding letter, was almost the last which Elizabeth Fry addressed to her family, during her journey in Ireland; she was becoming worn and overfatigued, and every day added to the difficulty with which she accomplished the work allotted to it. Happily, they reached the hospitable dwelling of John Strangman, at Waterford, before her powers completely failed her. It

was on Friday, the 12th of April, that she arrived there, and
for more than a week she needed all the care, and close nursing
which she experienced : then she gradually began to rally, and
they pursued their onerous work. Her own journal written upon
their return home, gives a sketch of the latter part of their
journey, and more is not required, as the publication of her
brother, Joseph John Gurney, gives so full an account of the
state of prisons and public institutions in Ireland.

Plashet, Sixth Month, 2nd.—We continued our journey
until the 11th of the Fifth Month ; we went on much the same
as I before described, with the exception of visiting some important towns, where no Friends resided; Londonderry, Sligo,
and Galway, particularly the latter, where we held important
Public Meetings, and saw many persons ; we also visited some
institutions—amidst serious difficulties, particularly from the
Roman Catholics, but our way was marvellously made. The
great numbers that followed us, almost wherever we went, was
one of those things that I believe was too much for me, no one
can tell but those who have been brought into similar circumstances, what it is to feel as I did at such times ; often weak
and fagged in body, exhausted in mind, having things of importance to direct my attention to, and not less than a multitude around me, each expecting a word or some mark of attention. For instance, on one occasion a General on one side, a
Bishop on the other, and perhaps sixty other persons, all expecting something from me. Visiting Prisons, Lunatic Asylums,
and Infirmaries, each institution exciting feeling and requiring
judgment. I endeavoured to seek for help from above, and for
a quiet mind, and my desire was, that such times should not be
lost upon those persons ; they ended frequently in religious
opportunities, and many came in consequence to our Public
Meetings, however these things proved too much for me, and
tired me more than any part of our service.

There were some, I believe, who feared my exaltation, and if
they judged from outward appearances, I do not wonder at it ;
but a deep conviction of my own unworthiness and infirmity was

so living with me, that these things appeared more likely to cast
me into the dust, than raise me up on high. We went on thus,
from place to place, until we reached Waterford ; we had visited
Limerick, Cork, and other places. I felt completely sinking,
hardly able to hold up my head, and by degrees became seriously
ill. Fever came on and ran very high, and I found myself in one
of my distressing, faint states, indeed a few hours were most conflicting, I never remember to have known a more painful time ;
tried without, distressed within, feeling such fears lest it should
try the faith of others my being thus stopped by illness, and lest
my own faith should fail. My pain too in being from home was
great. We were obliged to stop all the Meetings that we had
appointed for days to come, however, much as I suffered for a
short time, I had most sweet peace afterwards, my blessed
Saviour arose with " healing in his wings " delivered me from
my fears, poured balm into my wounds, and granted me such a
sense of having obtained full reconciliation with my God, as I
can hardly describe. All was peace ; I no longer hankered after
home, but was able to commit myself and those nearest, to this
unslumbering, all merciful, and all powerful Shepherd. By degrees
I was sufficiently raised up to attend Meetings, visit some prisons,
and see many persons, and we concluded our general visit to
Ireland, to my relief, peace, and satisfaction. The Yearly Meeting crowned all, as to our ministerial services in our own Society.
We left Waterford on the 11th of Fifth Month, after visiting
Wicklow, and Wexford, at that time remaining at Waterford a
few hours only. We entered the steam-packet, slept on board, and
left the harbour about three o'clock in the morning. I suffered
a little, but not from sea sickness, and enjoyed part of the voyage
which was most favourable, wind fair, sea calm, and many dear
friends on board, who were most kind to us. We arrived at
Milford about one o'clock, but I felt a want of due thankfulness,
at being once again on this side the channel. We had an exceedingly kind reception from the Starbuck family, and a meeting with them, and other friends in the evening.

The next day, we went to Swansea, where we slept ; we had
a meeting there, and also at Neath.

On Fourth-day, I met my beloved husband at Maidenhead,

with a good account from home ; I arrived there in the evening, and although far from well, yet able to enjoy the sight of my beloved family and sweet home.   I find things going on to my comfort and satisfaction, for this I desire to be humbly thankful.

The week following was much occupied by the interests of our own Yearly Meeting, and this week by a deeply anxious dispensation in the serious and sudden illness of my beloved brother Fowell Buxton, the shock was great, and our feeling for him and his dearest wife deep indeed.   We have now the inexpressible comfort of his being much better, and likely to recover ; we rejoice not only for our own sakes, but for the world generally, that it has pleased a kind Providence to raise up again such a dearly-beloved and useful member of our family, and of the community at large.

Sixth Month.—In reviewing our late journey, I may say of my brother Joseph, that he is one who delights my heart,—I think such true Christian conduct is not often manifested ; he so remarkably combines the gifts and graces of the Spirit, his constant kindness and humility were striking and exemplary. We are certainly united in a remarkable manner, not only by close natural bonds but in spiritual unity.

END OF THE FIRST VOLUME.

W. MOLKMAN. ?

PLASHET HOUSE.

MEMOIR OF THE LIFE

OF

ELIZABETH FRY

WITH

EXTRACTS FROM HER JOURNAL AND LETTERS

———————

EDITED BY TWO OF HER DAUGHTERS

———————

VOL. II

CONTENTS.

CHAPTER XV.

CHAPTER XVI.

CHAPTER XVII.

CHAPTER XVIII.

CHAPTER XIX.

CHAPTER XXIV.

CHAPTER XXV.

MEMOIR

OF THE

LIFE OF ELIZABETH FRY.

CHAPTER XV.

1827—1829. Illness of her sister Rachel Gurney, gradual decline and death—Birth of a grandson and nephew—Estimate of infant life—Foreign correspondence—Dr. Julius, Madame Potemkin, &c., &c.—Public engagements—Journey into Norfolk and Derbyshire—Ladies' British Society Meeting—Marriage of a daughter—Journey into the north of England—Heavy sorrows—Leaves Plashet—Letter to a daughter—Letter to a sister—Many letters of condolence—Winter in London—Settlement at Upton Lane—Yearly Meeting.

MRS. FRY's return from Ireland was clouded by the illness of her sister, Rachel Gurney, who was then at Brighton for change of air. Thither she soon followed her, and remained for a few days with her and one of her own daughters, who was staying at Brighton to be near her aunt. Threatening as had been the symptoms attending the illness of this most beloved sister; it was on this occasion, that the sorrowful conviction was first driven home to her heart, that the case was becoming so alarming, that but one termination could be expected. From childhood, from the happy days of Bramerton, and Earlham, when " one cabinet, one little set of tea-things, one small light closet," had

been shared between them, their love had flowed on, deepening
and strengthening with life, and its vicissitudes. The depth
and fidelity of Rachel Gurney's attachment to her sister had in
truth been " wonderful." Self sacrificing, considerate, and protecting—most sensitively alive to her interests, her cares and
her joys; but there were distresses approaching, from which
this devoted friend and sister could not have shielded her; and
the mercy was apparent, when little more than a year had passed
by, of her having been taken hence, without seeing one, so tenderly beloved, borne down by many sorrows.

Plashet, Sixth Month, 24th.—(*First day morning.*) The
commencement of this day always feels weighty to me; another
week begun, the awful and responsible situation of a minister of
the gospel in the services of the day, at home and at Meeting;
all weighs upon me. Grant, Oh Lord! I pray Thee, a little
help, that whatever Thy unworthy servant does, in word or in
deed, may be done, as in the name, so through the power of
Christ her Saviour. Bless this day, I pray Thee, Oh Lord! not
only to our house and family and to our religious body, but to
thousands and tens of thousands, that however outwardly separated, thy servants may unite in magnifying Thy name, and
that their spirits may rejoice in Christ their Saviour. Amen.

Worse accounts from Brighton induced Mrs. Fry again to go
to her sister there; after a few days sedulous nursing, she was
able to move the invalid as far as Plashet, on her road into
Norfolk.

Brighton, Seventh Month, 20th.—When I arrived here, I
found my beloved sister Rachel exceedingly ill, with a fresh
attack of illness, and no sister with her; so that I was greatly
needed, and much as I had feared, that seeing this beloved one
in a low and suffering state, would be almost more than I could
support, I have been wonderfully shielded, and I trust enabled
to be a real help and comfort to her, in a time of deep trouble.
This I feel cause for humble and renewed thankfulness, to be

able, however feebly, to return the unbounded kindness of one, who has been so much to me. May I continue strengthened in this most interesting engagement, and minister to the spiritual and temporal wants of this tenderly beloved sister.

Plashet, Eighth Month, 2nd.—At Brighton, I had a meeting with the members of the District Society, which was humbling to me, as such exposures always are, more or less, and a real effort of duty; but I desired only to do it as such, and was very much helped to keep to my point and go steadily on with the business, to my satisfaction and I trust to the benefit of the institution; which appears to have done much good to the poor of the place. Nothing of the kind appears to me to effect so much, as forming and helping these public charities, because so many are assisted by them. I understood that this Society last year induced the poor to lay by amongst them, about £1000. Numbers of the distressed had been relieved, and visiting the poor appears to have been blessed, both to the visitors and the visited. I also called at one of the Blockade Service stations, and found that the libraries I had sent to the Coast Guard stations, after my illness, three years ago, continued to be very useful to the men and their families. Out of deep distress, I formed these institutions, (if I may so call them) little thinking that an illness that appeared to myself, as if it would almost take away all my powers, should be the means of producing good to so many—surely out of weakness I was made strong. May it be a lesson to myself and others to bow under the Mighty hand of God, however mysterious His dispensations may be.

I was enabled to attend to my beloved sister, during the remainder of her stay at Brighton, and then brought her home here; she left us, for Earlham, on Second-day, the 30th.

Very peaceful was Rachel Gurney's return to the home of her childhood; her "flesh, and her heart," were, indeed, "failing," yet God was the "strength of her heart," and to Him she looked with unfaltering confidence, as about to become her "portion for ever." She wrote to Mrs. Fry, on her journey:—

" The quiet travelling has only been a luxury; both morning and evening have been delightful to me, as to weather and scenery. I have felt soothed and comforted, more than any thing else. I am most deeply sensible of the blessing, thou hast been made to me, I think it seems to have put me more in the right way of taking, bearing, and feeling, my present allotment; above all, I trust it has strengthened me in my *best desires*, and endeavours to walk humbly with my God!

" My kind and grateful love to all my affectionate attendants, and abundance of love to the dear children.

From Earlham. —" I have never wanted yet, and think I never shall want, the kindest of helpers. I can look around this morning upon the beautiful order of every thing, with something like pleasure. Thou wouldest be pleased with the beauty of my luxurious apartment; the window, to the south being opened, is a beautiful improvement to it. In short, it is something of a paradise here below, that Joseph brings his bride to take possession of! How differently we are led, and allotted, in this world. Some seem to be taught by trial and bereavement, and others by having all things ' richly to enjoy.' If the heart be turned the right way, and the eye be kept single towards God, I believe all may equally learn that great and most important lesson, that here we have no continuing city."

The sunshine of her mind, her christian spirit of contentment, coloured all around her, again she says in another letter : —

" It is almost beyond my power to describe to you the relief to my feelings, in being put into these two rooms of profound quiet, and wheeled from one to another, without an effort; looking from my bed, where I am only for some hours in the day, on the peaceful lawn, and green trees, surely, ' He maketh me to lie down in green pastures: He leadeth me beside the still waters.' "

Dagenham, Eighth Month, 15*th.*—Since my beloved sister's return home to Earlham, my dear William and two of his sisters have set off, on an expedition into Normandy. My feelings have been much excited, by the very serious account of my beloved sister Rachel, implying a sensible decline of power and health, which touches me in a most tender place. I may say, in the prospect of losing her, that I shall lose the person that has (taking life through) been more to me, than any other mortal, in constant, faithful love, and kindness, and in ministering to all my wants, according to her ability. Oh! gracious Lord! grant her a full reward here, and above all, hereafter; but, I desire to return thanks for her prepared state of soul, (as far as we can judge, one of another), and the many alleviations granted her. If she be taken,—my companion, my friend, near my own age, —I think it will in no common degree, bring death home to my view, and may it lead me to have my heart really more placed on things above, less on things below.

22nd.—It is hard very hard, a most difficult matter to know how to help those, whose welfare and salvation are past expression, near to us. We can only go to Him, who is willing and able, not only to hear our prayers on our own account, but on account of those most tenderly beloved ; and who does, in His tender mercy, so bear our griefs and carry our sorrows, that our souls can rest on Him. Oh ! may I ever have the encouragement of seeing those nearest to me, walking closely with God ; not doing their own pleasure, or walking in their own ways, but doing His pleasure and walking in His ways. I believe it would bring unspeakable joy, refreshment, and consolation to my soul ; and may I never cease to commend them to Him, who can work with, or without human instrumentality.

I went on Second day to Lord Lansdowne (Secretary of State) and the Under-Secretary, T. Spring Rice, on prison matters, and was received with the utmost kindness and attention. The prison cause appears prosperous. On Third-day, I attended the Monthly Meeting, and much in the cross with great fear, weakness, and nervousness, I was enabled to minister consolation to others. Peace and refreshment followed to myself, and although trials have since attended me, I feel the sweet balm remain—that balm which heals the wounded heart.

25th. —The evening before last, an account arrived from Normandy, from my beloved children there, to say that my Richenda had been very seriously ill. But I desired to be thankful that she was better, and that she had fallen amongst such truly kind persons, (though total strangers to us) who had treated our children like their own, assisted in nursing her with the utmost care, and paid her every attention.

I am at times reminded of these words in Job, chapter xxxiv., 29th verse—" When he giveth quietness, who then can make trouble? and when he hideth his face, who then can behold him? whether it be done against a nation, or against a man only ?"

How striking a proof of the truth of the Scriptures, and that of which they testify, is the way in which they speak to our individual experience. Oh, may I dwell nearer to the source of all good, and live in a more devoted, quiet, humble, watchful, dependent and resigned spirit.

Earlham, 30*th*.—On Seventh day, the 20th, my son John came with an express from town, to say that the accounts from Earlham were so much worse, that it was thought desirable that I should go as quickly as possible to Upton, to fix whether to set off that day or not; this agitated me and brought me very low, but on reading the different letters, and seeking for a quiet mind, I believed that there was no such hurry, and concluded to wait until after Meeting on First day, and an early dinner with my family before setting off. I find it very important in such cases as these, not to act upon impetuous feelings, but upon quiet and sober consideration ; hurried movements rarely answer to ourselves or others.

We set off, and were favoured with a quiet journey, and a hopeful one, as I could not believe that we should find any very great change had taken place, and so it proved. Our much-loved invalid was certainly sunk, since we were last together, and in many things gone some steps lower; but there appeared to me so strong a vital principle remaining, that I think weeks rather than days are likely to be her portion here below. Her mind is in a most favoured state, she appears to feel it wonderful how easy her circumstances are made to her ; all fear of death seems to be removed from her, she talks of it with ease, almost pleasure.

Last night she said, that, she wished not to be in other circumstances than she was, the way in which she had found the fulness of the power was quite beyond her expectation, and even her trials only appeared now to fit her for greater joys. At times her sinkings are great and also her sufferings, but in these states, though naturally low, faith always appears more than sufficient to sustain her, and she receives them only as a part of the present work of preparation. She said, they led her to desire to depart; but her wish was, to say from her heart, " Not my will, but Thine be done."

Surely, this is a fresh proof of the wonderful work and power of grace, and Christian redemption—what consolation it brings! and how much we see, even in these times of deep trial, the mercy of a kind Providence, in granting so many mitigations and alleviations. Surely, His tender mercies are over all His works.

I think, I never am brought into contact with many of my beloved brothers and sisters, without a very humbling feeling of my own infirmity, and short-comings; I find them such examples to me, and am ready to say within my heart—though I have come so publicly forward—though I have preached righteousness in the great congregation, what will become of me, and of my house? and where is there amongst us the same fruits of the Spirit?

My merciful Father has helped me, cared for me, sustained and provided for me, and in many ways blessed me; but I still see many hidden evils in my heart, and as for my family, fears often get hold of me, and for myself also, lest I should not walk worthy of my high and holy calling. I can only intercede for us all, that for the sake of Him who came to seek and to save that which was lost, our gracious God would have mercy on us. Oh, dearest Lord! Thou hast granted the petition of Thine handmaid, for her brothers and sisters, she now sees in them, in a great measure the travail of her soul, and is satisfied. Reject not her prayers for her husband and children; bring them by any ways, or by any paths, that Thou mayst see meet, but let them also come to the knowledge of the ever-blessed truth, as it is in Jesus, that they may be saved with an everlasting salvation.

And oh, gracious Lord be with Thy poor servant to the end ; and through the continued extension of Thy grace, Thy help, and Thy mercy, let nothing ever be permitted to separate her soul from Thy love in Christ Jesus, her beloved Lord, and all-sufficient Saviour.

" By any ways, or by any paths, that Thou mayst see meet ; but let them come to the knowledge of the ever-blessed truth as it is in Jesus.

Such had become the language of her heart.

More than twenty-five years had passed, of deepening experience and growing dedication, since the ministry of William Savery had been the means of producing so marvellous a change in her. Religion, for the first time presented to her view, through the medium, and under the aspect of Quakerism, was, for a length of time, associated in her mind too exclusively with the peculiar form in which she then had known it, and which had been so eminently blessed to herself. She appears now to have attained to the conviction, that the peculiar forms and scruples of sects may be mistaken and substituted for the cross of Christ, and that there may be faithful and devoted Cross-Bearers, who adopt none of these peculiarities ; having learned to recognize the vast distinction, between the diversities of forms in religious worship and the mighty mystery of religion itself ; even the " being renewed in the spirit of the mind, and born again from the death of sin to the life of righteousness."

Amongst her brothers and sisters, she saw much of the fruits of the Spirit, in dedication of heart, and labours of Christian love ; but it was not at first easy to her to believe, that the path that some of them had chosen, was for them as entirely right, as the one she had taken was for herself and others of the family.

To a mind so honestly seeking truth, and desiring to receive

it in simplicity, conviction could not fail in its effect, and she
became at last reconciled to these " diversities of administration." Her acquaintance with the excellent of the earth, beyond the sphere of her own family, tended to enlarge her boundaries, still, she clave to the peculiar form of Christianity which
she had adopted for herself; and for her children, it was long
the craving of her heart, her intense desire, that they might
become " Friends" from conviction—but even this strong desire
of her heart was to be, in great measure, disappointed. We
now find her, fully and unreservedly, petitioning Him who had
eminently proved to her a " prayer-hearing, answering God,"
" by any ways, or by any paths, that He might see meet," but
that they might " come to the knowledge of the ever-blessed
truth, as it is in Jesus." Here is no reserve, no holding back,
the surrender of will is entire, and the spirit of submission
complete. Very blessed it is to those of her children, who
have been unable to see as she saw, and to receive the views
which she entertained, to know, that it was given her by degrees,
without any wavering in her own opinions, without any diminution of her entire love for the principles of Friends, "to
recognise no distinction," provided "the narrow path was
chosen, and the cross of Christ borne."

Earlham, Ninth Month, 2nd, First day.—My sisters Catherine, Rachel, Richenda and I have had a very remarkable morning.
I thought it better to stay at home from Meeting, to be with my
beloved suffering sister. I had a desire for some religious time
with her. After she was dressed and removed into the dressing-
room on her couch, we read in the Bible; but so overcome was
she from weakness and sleepiness, that she could not keep
awake; however, we went on, till I knelt down in prayer and
thanksgiving for her and for us; this, appeared more than
to revive her, she prayed beautifully and powerfully for us then
present, for all her sisters, for my children, and for me and my
dearest husband. Afterwards, she sent a particular message to

some of the absent, her " dear love, and that they should be told, what a rich blessing she had found there was in seeking, *first*, the kingdom of God and His righteousness." The consoling effect of this time lasted for many hours, so that our beloved invalid remained in a delightful state all day.

First day, *9th*.—I was sent for express this morning from Lynn, where I had gone for a day or two to see my beloved daughter. This visit proved highly satisfactory. I had it in my power to make all arrangements for her, as to medical attendance; and what was more, in no common degree, I found the spirit of prayer poured forth on her account, so that, I believe, it was well to be there. But my dearest sister passed through so deep a conflict last evening, that I was sent for. The letters from Plashet conveyed the happy news, that my children were returned from abroad, and my Richenda better, though far from well.

10th.—My beloved sister appeared much sunk last evening, but awoke early, greatly refreshed, quite clear, and even very bright in her mind, and relieved from suffering. In the night I went to her, and seemed unable to endure witnessing her conflicts of body; but to my help and consolation, I found her thus relieved this morning. So it is, things too hard for us are not permitted; and my humble trust is that as trials come, so strength will be given to endure them. My strong confidence for my beloved sister is, that for her, way will in tender mercy be made through the valley of the shadow of death, and support granted to us also; though from the weakness of the flesh, fears at times overwhelm me on this subject. On seeing her so comfortable, I said to her, " brooks are granted us by the way; she replied, " yes, and more of them the nearer we approach the journey's end."

11th.—Yesterday, our dear patient passed through nearly constant conflict, from spasms on her breath, which was deeply affecting to us. We besought for her present relief; some mitigation was granted, and by degrees, during the night, she became more easy : she told me, this morning, it was " as though, the Ruler and Head of the people had been very near to her all night;" and mentioned what a conflicted day yesterday was, but added, " I leant on the beloved." Her apparent patience and quiet spirit were striking to witness.

13th.—A wonderful revival; she appears better than she has done for many days. This is extraordinary, after watching what has been thought her dying bed for some time past ;—last evening, almost all the symptoms of the near approach of death were apparent. I so deeply have felt it, that being in the room has been often almost more than I could bear ; indeed, it is a time of much self humiliation to me, my unworthiness is very present with me. I feel as if I did not fulfil my duties towards my loved sister, because I do not sit up at night, and remain constantly with her; I am afraid of being upset by it, my tender inexpressible sympathy is so great for her in her sufferings, though I cannot but thankfully rejoice for her blessed state of spirit. As for myself, these words seem applicable : " Oh Lord ! Thou knowest my foolishness and my sins are not hid from Thee."

15th.—Sitting opposite to my most beloved sister in the blue-room :—She appears to be gradually sinking into death, and may we not humbly trust and confidently believe, into the arms of her God and Saviour. Grant Lord, I pray Thee, if consistent with Thy holy and blessed will, that she may fall asleep in Thee, and that no painful struggles may attend her change; that quietly and imperceptibly, she may cast off this mortal tabernacle, having already testified to us her faith and her hope, and be landed on the other side of Jordan, awaking to joy and glory unspeakable. And do Thou, Oh Lord! sustain us also, in this time of trial, and enable us in our low estate to rejoice in Thee, our God and our Saviour, who yet giveth the victory over death, hell, and the grave.

I have been alone and quiet a little while, and I find in this awful time, that " help is laid on One who is mighty ;" for that, which ever since I came to an age of understanding has appeared almost impossible to bear, even the loss of *this* sister, who has been like " flesh of my flesh and bone of my bone," now I am enabled to receive, and bow under the dispensation with peace. I believe that she has done her work, and that we have nearly finished our work for her ; but, is there not an all-

sufficient Helper near, who is holding up her head above the
waves of Jordan, that they overwhelm her not!

17th.—About three o'clock this morning, our most tenderly-
beloved sister departed this life. Late in the evening she fell
asleep, from which sleep she never appeared to awake. They
came to let me know, about twelve o'clock, how she was going
on; but, at first, I felt unequal to going to her, and she did not
want me; but, gradually, I found my tribulated, tossed spirit,
calmed, animated, and strengthened, so that I joined the company round her bed, where I remained until the solemn close.
We sat some time in deep silence; then I knelt down, and asked
that mourning and lamentation might not be the garment of our
spirits, but thanksgiving, inasmuch as the warfare was accomplished, the conflict over, and through the unmerited mercy of
God in Christ Jesus, an entrance was granted through the gates
of the City, whose walls are salvation and whose gates are praise.
Then I prayed for ourselves, that the loss of such a sister, who
had in so remarkable a manner ministered to some of our necessities, might be made up to us by an increased portion of spiritual
blessings, and that her various labours of love to us and to our
children might receive such a blessing, as to produce an increase
to our lasting good. After returning to bed, natural weakness
much overcame me; the death of the body, and its terrors, got
hold of me, and the heavenly Inheritance appeared hidden from
my view, for a time. To-day, I feel able to partake of the repose
now granted us, in no longer having to travel through " the
valley of the shadow of death," with one so beloved; and, in
measure, to partake of her rest, as I believe I did, in no common
manner, of her sufferings, as if one with her in them.

19th.—Blue-room—with my beloved sister's remains. All
quietness, rest in comparison—over my own mind a solemn feeling of peace, and this truth impressed upon me, " There is a rest
for the people of God." Several important lessons, I think, I
have learnt by attending this most beloved sister. 1st, That
persons are apt to dwell more on the means of grace, about which
they differ, than its simple pure operation leading out of evil into
good. This I have long believed, but, seeing one who united as
she did with the good in all and could hardly be said to be of

any sect or body of Christians, so grounded in the Christian life and practice, proves experimentally ; that being united fully to any set of people is not essential, and all minor points of difference of comparatively little value. 2ndly, I learn to trust more, and be less afraid. She like myself was liable to many fears, particularly in her nervous sinking states—how little cause had she for these fears, and how were the things that she most dreaded remarkably averted ; also, That the last part of a death-illness gradually appears to diminish rather than increase in conflict, as with natural life and power, sensibility to suffering lessens. In short, the lesson taught us is, to seek to serve and follow our Lord, and He will be with us and make a way for us, even unto the end. 3rdly, That in passing through life, patience should have its perfect work, that we should seek for a more willing mind to suffer, as well as to do the will of God, looking for daily help in this respect; that we should endeavour in all things for an upright, circumspect walk before the Lord, speaking the truth in love ; above all, that we should seek after full understanding of, and reliance on, the work of salvation through Christ; and obtain (if possible) more knowledge of the Scriptures, and a better acquaintance with religious books.

Of my very many outward blessings, the brothers and sisters that I yet have are amongst the greatest. C—— with her simple, powerful, noble, yet humble and devoted mind. R—— with her diligence, excellence, cheerfulness, vivacity, willingness and power to serve many. H—— with her chastened, refined, tender, humble, and powerful character. Louisa with her uncommon ability, talent, expansive generosity, and true sympathy and kindness. S—— always my friend and my companion ; more or less my guide, my counsellor, and my comforter. His stable mind, his living faith, his Christian practice, rejoice me often. Joseph, the fruitful vine whose branches hang over the wall, my prophet, priest, and sympathiser, and often the upholder of my soul. D——, his uprightness, integrity, power and sympathy, and son-like as well as brother-like attentions to me, invaluable ; he has sweetened many of my bitter cups.

The various places, taken in our beloved sister's sick-room by the different sisters were very beautiful to see, how conscientiously they filled their different allotments. I have been struck in this, as in other instances, how much real principle is needed, to enable us to nurse and do full justice to the sick, particularly, in very long illnesses, and how much patience and watchfulness are required even with the most favoured patients. I should like to give a little account here of this most beloved sister. We began life very much together, she was a year and a half the elder. We were partners, as children, of almost all that we possessed, we were educated a good deal together, and mostly slept in the same room. She was also very strongly united in early life to Catherine. She was when young, beautiful, lively and warm-hearted ; she was very attractive, so as even to excite in some of us who were much less so, feelings of jealousy. She formed a strong attachment when quite young, under very painful circumstances, being contrary to our father's wishes. It eventually was broken off, although our father withdrew his opposition, when she reached twenty-one years of age. This produced a wonderful change in her, destroyed her naturally fine spirits ; brought her into deep distress, but I believe also led her to seek better consolation, and that love which could satisfy and would remain. She was a most constant, faithful, devoted friend to her own family, most particularly to myself, a companion and helper in illness and distress, such as is rarely met with or heard of, both before and after my marriage. Of her it might in no common degree be said, " self was of no reputation," she was able to give up her own will, her own way, and her own pleasure to others, in an extraordinary manner.

My becoming a Friend was in the outset a trial to her, she would weep over it, and endeavour to show me the folly of it, as at that period her own mind was only opening to receive religious truth; but on perceiving that my peace was concerned in it, and that my desire was simply to obey that which I believed to be the manifestation of duty, she soon became one of the foremost to make my way easy, in any sacrifice or cross that this led me into ; and so far from remaining a hindrance, she became a faithful, constant, steady, helper to me. Even to the last, she would in the spirit of love and truth, warn me or any of us, of such rocks as she thought our peculiar views would endanger our stumbling against; and I may truly say, I have for one, often found them watchwords in season—words, that I trust have taken deep root in my heart, and been blessed to me. In religion, her ground was expansive. As it respected worship, I think she united much with Friends, in some other matters with the Established Church, she had peculiarly the power not only to see, but to unite with the good of all persuasions ; and according to the ability granted her, to help all on their way. She was cheerful, hopeful, but very sensitive ; yet so remarkably grounded on the everlasting Rock, as not to be greatly moved by, though deeply sensible of, the various trials and fluctuations of this life. She owed much also to her well-regulated and self-possessed mind. Her heart was in no common degree affectionate, even so as at times to prove a trial to her, but deep and strong as was her affection for her own family and friends, her dependence was on higher ground ; and He who gave himself a ransom for her, and was her Lord and Master, had her first love.

Her sound mind, good understanding, and clear judgment were very conspicuous ; her patience and long-suffering, united with natural cheerfulness, very marked, particularly in her last illness ; amongst her minor virtues, her order, regularity, and punctuality were great. She had peculiar power over children, and possessed, in no common degree, the gift of training and educating them ; she was strict, though most kind to them ; she particularly cultivated habits of industry, and having whatever was done, well done ; she also early proved a teacher to bring them to Christ, and was able, not only to instruct them in the Scriptures, but general religious truth, and many bear testimony to her invaluable labours with them on these most important subjects. She not only sympathised particularly with the afflicted in her own family, but was a frequent and faithful nurse to many others in sickness, and a comforter to them when sorrowful. In short, she was greatly gifted by nature and grace, and what is far above all, she " gave diligence to make her calling and election sure ! "

The funeral of Rachel Gurney took place on the 23rd. An

7

occasion of very deep feeling, and one that wakened many
sorrowful recollections and associations.

On the 24th, Mrs. Fry went to Lynn, and the following evening wrote to announce the birth of a little grandson, thus rapidly
passing from the last, to the first scene in " man's eventful
history." She had been anxious to come to her child, and yet
could scarcely leave Earlham sooner. To her family at home she
says, "I cannot but thank a kind Providence for bringing me
here in the needful time, and thus guiding my steps aright."
One day later she was sent for to Runcton, in consequence
of the birth of a nephew; whose life, which hung upon a
most slender thread, was apparently saved through her unremitting exertions. She set an unusual value upon infant life ;
she was almost displeased at the death of little children being
lightly considered; "You none know how good or how great they
may live to be." Nor was it only in reference to this world that
she felt thus, for "Are there not ' many mansions ?' different
degrees of glory, in the heavenly inheritance." This estimate
of life, and the use to be made of it, was perfectly consistent
with absolute submission to the will of God, whenever it was
His good pleasure to take it. There were four lines of Sir
William Jones, which she greatly delighted in—often and of ten
has she recited them, with some little one in her arms, whose
soft skin, and meaningless expression, bespoke how lately it
had become an inhabitant of this world—

> " On parent knees, a naked new-born child,
> Weeping thou sat'st—while all around thee smiled,
> So live, that sinking to thy long last sleep,
> Safe thou may'st smile—whilst all around thee weep."

A press of engagements awaited her return to Plashet. Business and correspondence, public and private, at home and abroad.
Communications addressed to her had become increasingly
numerous, especially from the continent. Dr. Julius of Ham-

burgh, became a frequent correspondent. This gentleman had long devoted himself to the subject of Prison Discipline. During this year, he had lectured at Berlin, for two months upon the subject, the course being attended by above a hundred gentlemen of rank and fortune. From M. Ducpetiaux, at Brussels, a zealous advocate for Prison Reform, she had received communications. A long letter, of great interest, had reached her from Madame Potemkin née Galitzin, at St. Petersburg ; also, through John Venning, Esq. she received details of Prisons and Lunatic Asylums, by desire of the Empress Dowager of Russia. From another quarter, she had details sent to her, of the Grand Duke of Baden, having in his dominions, instituted inquiries as to the best method of constructing prisons. Again, from Paris she received communications of the state of prisons in France, with, amongst other matters, an account entitled, " Fragmens d'un compte rendu sur les Prisons de Lyons, 1827," &c. &c.; presenté à Monsiegneur le Dauphin, par M. le Baron De Gerando.

The era of advance was come ; and those who wished well to their fellow-creatures, marked the progress of good with intense satisfaction. Few and scattered as were the efforts made, the opinion was gaining ground, that preventing crime was of sounder policy than punishing it ; and the reformation of the culprit, the end to be sought in penal legislation.

Plashet, First Month, 3rd, 1828.—This year commenced with many interests. On the morning of the new year, we assembled almost all our large household, and many guests, principally young people. Before we began reading, I mentioned some of the striking marks of Providential care and mercy shewn to us during the last year. We then read, and afterwards had a solemn time, in which I returned thanks " for mercies past, and humbly craved for more." My dearest brother Joseph joined us, and under a serious, yet cheerful influence, our large party sat down to breakfast. This is often to me a most agreeable time of the day, after the repose of the night, and often some spiritual refreshment in our readings. I can hardly say how much I enjoy my family circle, and thankfully receive the blessings conferred on us.

31st.—During this month, my beloved family, husband and children, have occupied most of my time and attention, and in many respects I have had much comfort; but at their present age, when there is so much to excite the susceptible mind of youth, my anxieties are many on their account, and I feel that I have to watch with at times fearful care over them and their associates, and perhaps when they do not know it, sympathise with them in their passing troubles arising from such circumstances. I sometimes pour forth my prayer for them, that if they are to be united to others in life, their affections may settle on the right objects. How deeply, how tenderly, to be felt for, and watchfully to be cared for, are young people at this period of life; and how difficult for us, who apprehend ourselves, as Friends, to be bound by unusual restrictions in marriage connexions, exactly to know the right line to pursue. I have been, as usual, much occupied by public objects, and have met with both encouragement and disappointment. Encouragement, because the government has greatly aided us in the female convict ships; and disappointment, from not succeeding in more generally obtaining permission for ladies to visit prisons. In our own Society, I have had one important call to Birmingham, to attend a funeral; a very serious and weighty occasion it proved; numbers of the children and grand-children of the deceased, of various descriptions were present. There was a crowded meeting, and few ministers, so that the weight of the service appeared to devolve on me, there, and at the house. The help granted me was marvellous in my eyes; and I was enabled, at these different times, to preach the glad tidings, the liberty and the peace of the gospel of Christ. So it is, out of weakness, we are, when dependent on our Lord alone, made strong, and fear is removed in the most remarkahle manner—my dearest brother Samuel accompanied me—who has such brothers as I have, to help in the needful time? I think, as it respects the ministry, I am never so much helped as when without other ministers to look to, my dependence being then singly on my Lord and on His anointing. I yesterday went to see one of my sons at school, and attended Epping Meeting, which I thought a satisfactory time. I tried to make my visit pleasant to all the boys, by taking them a walk, and giving them oranges; I like that the instruments, who communicate religious instruction to the young, should be pleasant to them. I have had interesting, and encouraging communications from Ireland, as if, in some parts particularly, our labours there had not been in vain. I have once or twice been to see my sister Hoare, and have felt the value of the near union between us; my dearest sister Rachel is often present with me, the way in which I have been enabled to support this inexpressible loss, is surprising to myself; surely it is only the tender mercy of my God, that has thus healed my wounds and upheld me under it. Indeed, at the close of this month, I may raise up a fresh Ebenezer, and say—the Lord be magnified for His loving-kindness to me, His poor unworthy, yet dependent one. Oh! may He see meet to keep me in the way that I should go, and preserve me from right hand and from left hand errors.

Second Month, 2nd.—Yesterday, was a full day, and one humbling in its effect. In the first place, I earnestly desired preservation, that I might keep my eye single to God, and not bow to man in spirit. I then went to town, and to Newgate, under a feeling of rather deep concern, where I unexpectedly found numbers of persons, a magistrate, foreigners, a Jew, a clergyman, many ladies, some Friends, and my brother Samuel. Before I began to read, I in secret asked for preservation, at least it was my earnest desire to have my eye kept single to my God. But either the fear of man got too much hold of me, or the "unction" was not with me, for I did not feel the power of Truth over us, as it very often has been at such times. I am ready to believe, that if I had not looked at man, but dwelt yet deeper in spirit, I should have openly called upon the Lord, and should have found help and power in so doing. I went away humbled. My sister Elizabeth said something; but of late there has been so much felt and said about our doing too much in these things with the

prisoners, and going out of our province, that it makes me fearful, and consider that as far as the Spirit is rightly subject to
the prophets, so far, at this critical time, we ought to curtail in
these things. I then went with my beloved brother Samuel to the
Bishop of London, to talk to him about religious services with
prisoners, to inform him of our situation respecting it in Newgate,
and the extreme care necessary in the appointment of chaplains
for gaols; also to speak to him of the state of our parish. I
spoke, I trust, to the point, and that good and not harm will
result from the visit; but I always fear, after such times, lest I
should have said too much. We then made a call, where I pretty
boldly spoke my opinions of theatres and public places; and
in reply to the question, "How I went on, in reforming the
world?" I replied, that my zeal was strong in my declining
years to do what little I could towards reforming things. Afterwards, I feared that I might have said too much. We went
to the Secretary of State's office, and saw the Under-Secretary;
there, again, I had to speak my mind fully on many things,
prisons especially.

Now, during this day, my services were numerous—some of an
important nature, and such as might by some persons be supposed
exalting, to be admitted although a woman, to represent things
of consequence to persons of influence and power, and to be received as I am by them—but He who searcheth the heart, only
knows my humiliation, and how, in these services, fears for myself
get hold of me, lest I should bow to man and not to God; lest
any thing but the simple object of promoting " the thing that
is good," should influence me. This I certainly know, that
such engagements often bring me into deep exercise of spirit
before the Lord, that I may be kept as a clean instrument ready
for His service, and not become contaminated by the spirit of self
nor the spirit of the world. Truly, my desire is, to walk humbly,
faithfully, circumspectly, before my God in the first place, and,
secondly, before my fellow-mortals; but ever and in all things,
to seek to serve my Lord, doing His will and His pleasure, before
serving myself or others, or doing my own will or the will of
man. Lord, continue to be my help, my strength, my glory and
the lifter up of my head; and if consistent with Thy holy will,

bless my labours and the labours of others, in these works of charity, and keep us, the unworthy instruments employed in them, so, as to be fitted to perform them, or any other service Thou mayst see fit to call us into.   Amen.

25*th*.—At times, I have felt distressingly overdone in body and mind ; but in the midst of fatigue and bustle, I have sought the Lord for help and endeavoured to wait upon Him, that a quiet spirit might be granted me, which, in tender mercy, has frequently been the case, so that the storm has become a calm. Generally speaking, I do not think that I work too hard, for I am deeply sensible that we do not serve a hard Master, and that He will never require more of us, than we have strength to perform.   I think our health, strength, and life, are valuable gifts, that we have no right to play with, but should take all reasonable care to preserve; although, I am also of opinion, that active employment for body and mind is preferable and conduces to the health of both, whilst many suffer great loss for want of it ; sitting, as it were, in their " ceiled houses," taking undue care of themselves.   I also believe, that a portion of rest, quiet and recreation, is not only allowable but right, and in the ordering of a kind Providence for us all.   Surely, in a spiritual, as well as an outward sense, I may fully and heartily testify, that in unmerited mercy the " brook by the way" is often partaken of, sometimes in a large and overflowing manner, so that I may say, " my cup runneth over "   I am at times ready to exclaim, " Oh Lord ! our Lord, how excellent is Thy name in all the earth !" The works of the outward creation give me delight ; and I am enabled to perceive the beauty and the excellency of the spiritual dispensation, as revealed to us, through the unspeakable blessing of the gospel of Christ.

Third Month, 5*th*. —May I not say to Him, who seeth in secret, Thou hast known my soul in adversity ! but amidst these dispensations, is not the " Lord known by the judgment which he executeth ?"   What peace, what blessing, what fulness of help and consolation, have I also experienced.   How have gospel truths opened gradually on my view, the height, the depth, length and breadth of the love of God in Christ Jesus, to my unspeakable help and consolation ; principally, I believe, through the dispensations of Almighty wisdom, partly from the soundness of faith of some near to me, my brother Joseph, my sisters Priscilla, Catherine, and Rachel, as well as many others of different religious persuasions. I think that my general religious association, has delightfully extended my spiritual borders. I can, from my heart say, all one in Christ; all dearly beloved, as brethren and sisters, who love His name, and seek to follow Him. Although, I remain a decided Friend in principle, and believe for myself and for many others, that it is our calling, for I consider ours to be a highly spiritual dispensation, and that not only we ourselves, but others would suffer much loss by our not keeping to it.

27th.—On Second-day, I attended the Select Quarterly Meeting, and was appointed representative to the Yearly Meeting. The next day the meetings were satisfactory. How striking to me, and how humbling—here am I, that used to be one of the last, least, and lowest in this Quarterly Meeting, now obliged to be one of its foremost members in the Meetings of Discipline; partly, from so many vacant places being left amongst us, partly from my long experience of its ways, and many years in its service; and last of all, truly, deeply unworthy as I am, because it has pleased a kind Providence to grant me the unity of my beloved friends, and thus to raise me up. My spirit, notwithstanding my outward cheerfulness, was much bowed down within me, in earnest cravings to be washed, renewed, and more fitted for my Master's service.

In April. Mrs. Fry accompanied her husband on a short journey. To visit some meetings of Friends, and several Prisons, formed her chief inducement, but she also was glad to avail herself of the change of scene and travelling for some of her family. " To follow, and not force Providence" was a favourite sentiment with her, she had taken it from " Cecil's remains," a book in which she delighted. " To avail ourselves of the openings," was another expression to be frequently heard from her lips. Extracts from two of her letters, pourtray something of her various objects and interests.

Matlock, *Fourth Month*, 19*th*, 1828.

My dearest Children,

The beauties of this delightful place, even amidst pouring rain, are such, as to make me long to have you all around us, to admire them. I am sitting in a bower window; a sweet little garden, cut out of the side of a high hill, on one side, a deep valley on the other, the river Derwent at the bottom, full with the late rains, flowing over rocks; and very high rocky hills, covered with trees, beyond. We are in a quiet, comfortable hotel, kept by a widow, where we feel quite at home, and only want all of you, and a little fine weather, to complete the pleasure of our circumstances. We feel the comfort of quiet and rest the more, because we have had such a very full time, almost as much so as in Ireland. At Leicester, Nottingham, and Derby—Meetings, Prisons, Friends, other people, forming Prison Associations, and various engagements. I have hardly had time for rest or meals. We unexpectedly met my dear brother Joseph at Leicester, on First day; and the next day, he greatly helped me, as usual in the prisons and in endeavouring to form committees. He and I went forward to attend the Quarterly Meeting at Nottingham, which we were favoured to get well through. On Fourth day, I was very busy receiving visitors and taking care of your dear uncle (who was very unwell), until he left us. We then proceeded to visit three Prisons and a Lunatic Asylum; and in the evening there came about thirty ladies to form themselves into an Association, and to revise the Prison Committee now existing. We arrived at Derby on Fifth day, in time for Meeting; afterwards I set off with our dear friend Henrietta Newton and others, to visit the different prisons. The town one is vile, and the country one as beautiful; there, I think six, at least, of the principal magistrates met me, as well as other persons. I was sadly tired, and only returned to Leylands in time to dress for dinner with our charming host and hostess, and their dear children. The next morning there was a party to breakfast with us—after a solemn reading. About eleven o'clock, many ladies, Friends and others joined us, to form associations for the Asylum and Prisons. This done, I had to write to the magistrates, go and visit the Asylum and

Infirmary, then dine at a kind friend's, where we met several persons; and set off for this place about six o'clock.

Now, in the nearest love to you all, farewell.

Your mother,
E. F.

Uttoxeter, Fourth Month, 21st.

My dearest William,

We are just arrived here after a pleasant visit to Matlock, although it rained nearly the whole time we were there.

Yesterday was very interesting. We went eleven miles to sit at Meeting with some persons of the lower class, in a stocking-weaver's room ; a very striking scene it was, and very pleasant afterwards to see these poor people. But, my dear children, you know enough of mama's eye for the ludicrous, not to wonder that my fancy was tickled to see the mistress get up during our Meeting, to attend to dressing the dinner ; two Friends also sitting on the stocking-loom for want of chairs, and we believed that those chairs we had, were lent by the neighbours to help the party out. It is a very remarkable case—a poor man, a wheelwright, in a little out of the way place called Cowhouse Lane, about ten miles from Matlock became convinced of the principles of Friends at a public meeting, and it has spread to several of his neighbours, who sit down in silence together on First days. We were all much pleased and interested by them. We returned to Matlock about four o'clock, and spent a quiet pleasant evening, until a smell of fire excited anxiety in some of our party. We were sitting in our little parlour, at the end of a long passage, three stories high. I asked Foster Reynolds to go into my room, as there was a fire there, and see if anything was burning. What should he find all in a flame, but my cloak hanging up, a large packing-cloth, towels, towel-horse and side of the fire-place. Some how or other, from the window being open, part of the towel must have blown into the fire, and all the other things caught. We think that, as it was very near to the bed, and that the flames were up to the ceiling or nearly so, had we delayed only a few minutes longer, the whole large inn would have been burnt ; and what is more, we could not have passed the door, which it was necessary for us to do to go down stairs. Thus we have had a most providential escape. Foster gave no alarm, but began to put it out before we got to him ; then, with thy father's aid in throwing water on the flames extinguished the whole. We happened not to have begun reading, therefore, our attention not being occupied, we were particularly alive to what passed ; we were just going to read something very interesting. It made us think of thy escape at Bristol. What a mercy to be preserved from such awful dangers.

Thy nearly attached mother,

E. F.

Plashet, Fifth Month, 7th.—I am once more settled at home, after a journey to Lynn, and into the midland counties, with my husband, my daughter Richenda, and Foster Reynolds. In the course of it, I visited thirteen prisons, also some Meetings; often to my wonder that so unworthy an instrument should be so honourably made use of to minister to the spiritual state of others, and to visit and be the means of assisting so many in prison and in bonds. It is perfectly curious to me to observe how my way is made when I go to a place, hardly knowing a person in it ; how soon I am favoured to be surrounded by the serious and the good of different descriptions ; to partake of sweet unity of spirit with them, to encourage them in their good works, and often induce them to visit the prisons. Surely the hand of Providence is in some of these things, small and great ? It was strikingly manifested in many instances on this journey ; I was enabled to form three new Committees for visiting prisons, and to re-organise others, in a way that I hope will prove useful. Where my lot was cast among Friends, I also found the best help to be near. I attended the Derby and Nottingham Quarterly Meeting, as well as several other Meetings, and met my dearest brother Joseph at Leicester, where I was enabled to assist him in the needful time ; it appeared almost providential. I walked into the Meeting where he was at Leicester ; he did not expect me, neither did I know he was in that town. He appeared greatly in need of help, being fatigued and very unwell. Since my return home, the

British Society Meeting has much occupied my attention. It was on the last day of last month ; it was a very numerous assemblage of ladies, many of them of high rank. I had much to do in it from time to time, when the different reports were read ; I explained a little, and at other times poured forth much of my mind on the subject. However, I went away low and humbled at the conspicuous part I had to take, not doubting that it would bring me into evil report as well as good report, and fearing lest the Secretaries and other valuable members of the Society might feel my doing so much, and their doing comparatively little ; and yet my heart was so full of interest upon the subject, and my head so full of matter, that I did not nearly express all I had to say. The general impression I hear was satisfactory, and I trust good was done : but I may set my seal to this—that public services are fearful services, and none but those engaged in them, know how much those are spared who do good privately. Still, if the Master calls us into public duties, it is not only well, but honourable, and in them much more good is accomplished, because so many are concerned ; still I would have no one seek for them, but if rightly brought into them, preservation will I believe be granted. A watchful, humble spirit is called for ; one that is not exalted by the undue approbation of fellow-mortals, nor too much cast down by disapprobation or evil reports. There must also be a willingness to commit all these works to Him, who can prosper them or not, according to His own good pleasure.

For this meeting of the British Society, Mrs. Fry had prepared rough notes, or memoranda, which exist. They contain allusions to some facts but not the facts themselves, as illustrations of her opinions as to the proper treatment of female prisoners. They were much the same, as those contained in the little work published by Mrs. Fry in 1827. The same ideas are to be found in her evidence before the Police Committee of the House of Commons, and in letters to official persons. They include observations on the good effect of ladies visiting prisons, workhouses, hospitals, lunatic asylums and other public insti-

tutions ; the necessity of classification, female officers, regular
occupation ; enforced plainness of appearance, separation, and
where that cannot be enforced, absolute silence after retiring
for the night ; with many details that must present themselves
to every one who has entertained the subject of Prison Discipline, but above all, the infinite importance of religious instruction. She enlarged on the state of female convict-ships, the
need of better clothing for the women, the wretched condition
of their little nurslings, and various topics connected with the
peculiarities of a sea voyage. She finished by a heart-stirring
appeal to the many present, gifted with influence and talent,
wealth and position, on the subject of the increase of crime in
this country, the responsibilities of all, the sphere of usefulness
open to every individual, even to the tender and delicate
woman, who might be said scarcely " to have the air of Heaven
visit her face too roughly," as a wife to influence, as a mother
to educate and train, as the mistress of a family to guide, control, reprove, encourage. She touched upon district societies,
libraries for the lower classes, general education,—and concluded by urging upon her hearers in nothing to be discouraged ; but in humble confidence to go on, remembering that
the work is not ours—therefore, we may look to Him Who is
mighty, upon Whom help is laid, to be " stedfast, immoveable, always abounding in the work of the Lord, forasmuch as
their labour would not be in vain in the Lord."

Plashet.—Last Sixth day, we had a very interesting visit to
Newgate. Numbers were there ; clergy, some of the nobility, the
Sheriff, many ladies, gentlemen, and Friends. It was a solemn
time; the fear of man much taken away. After the reading I
had to speak for them, and pray for them. I have of late been
surrounded by my family, and deep cravings of spirit have been
my portion for them. Through all, I have at times almost
panted for a surer and a better resting place, more particularly

where there will be no more sin or responsibility. I see much
to enjoy here; but the temptations that are in this world, at
times make me feel, if not weary of it, at least longing for a
Heavenly inheritance ; although the fear of the passage to it
always makes me flinch from this great change, as well as the
knowledge of my unutterable unworthiness.

Since I last wrote my journal, death has been brought closely
home to me. I was unexpectedly called to attend my dear aunt
C——, in a violent illness, which ended in her death. I went
to her on Seventh day, and for some hours every day afterwards,
and one night, till she died. I fully believe her state was a
blessed one, and that in her trial she knew the Rock to be her
stay. Still, as far as I can judge from observation, death is
even to the righteous an awful conflict, generally attended with
distress of body, reduction of spirits, some obscurity of mind,
and great difficulty in communicating to others, either the wants
or the feelings. My aunt seemed in her distress to depend
much upon me; I appeared to be a comfort to her, and was
enabled, in measure, to minister to her bodily and spiritual
wants. The day after all was over, and after having had a very
solemn time with the family, I became ill myself; much as I had
been at Waterford, hardly able to hold up my head, or go on my
way. On Sixth day I was worse. It was a sudden, unexpected loss of strength, being brought down as to the ground,
when I was anticipating with no common degree of pleasure
the Yearly Meeting, and after it my child's wedding, looking
for rather prosperous days. As usual in my illnesses, I was
greatly cast down at times, and wonderfully reduced in a short
time. In the midst of my conflict and distress, I still thought
I could see the hand of God in it to keep me low ; may it be
at *His footstool.* I abounded also with outward comforts and
mitigations. My husband, my sister Buxton, my children, my
sister Elizabeth Fry devoted to me, I wanted no outward thing ;
but was plunged under a deep feeling of my infirmity and great
unworthiness before God. I am now much relieved, very thankful, full of love, may I not say to all ; sweetly in unity with my
beloved Friends at the Yearly Meeting; in degree overflowing
towards them all, still abundantly sensible of my unworthiness

before the Lord.　Oh! may He see meet further to fit me, to suffer as well as to do His will.

20th.—I think I am better, but am remarkably reduced for so short an illness.　If during such times of trial, or in the end,— I am supported, the whole glory must be given to God; for I think it impossible for any one to be more naturally distressed or overset by bodily illness.　Even if my sun sets under a cloud, all must be laid to my great natural infirmity in this respect.　With God all things are possible, but if He should see meet at that awful hour to hide Himself from me, may none be discouraged; but all look upon it as a dispensation permitted in some way for good.　In times of health, also at times in sickness, I have had to rejoice in His salvation, and frequently when most favoured with clearness of judgment, have perceived the wisdom and mercy of all His dispensations, particularly some of these afflictive ones.　Why he saw meet to permit sin to come into the world is not for us poor frail finite mortals to comprehend; but that we have an enemy to buffet us, I cannot doubt.　May we look to that blessed day, when God shall be all in all and shall put all enemies under His feet, even Death itself.　Dearest Lord, increase my faith more firmly, more fixedly establish me upon the Rock of Ages, that however the winds blow, the rains descend, or the floods beat against me, I may not be greatly moved; and let not any of the hindering or polluting things of this world lessen my love to Thee and to Thy cause; or prevent me from going steadily forward in heights and in depths, in riches and in poverty, in strength and in weakness, in sickness and in health; or prevent my following hard after Thee in spirit, with a humble, faithful, watchful, circumspect, and devoted heart.　Amen.

21st.—The day before yesterday the wedding was accomplished. The Meeting was solemn and satisfactory.　Our bride and bridegroom spoke well, and with feeling.　My dearest brother Joseph prayed for them and ministered to them, as did others; I prayed at the close of the Meeting most earnestly for them, for the other young people, and ourselves further advanced in life.　After a short solemn silence the certificate was read and signed.　In the morning we had a satisfactory reading with our children.

Thanks be to our Heavenly Father, there was, I think, throughout the day a great mixture of real solemnity with true cheerfulness. It was certainly no common day. William Foster Reynolds and his wife, my husband and myself, with nineteen of our own children in the two families, besides children-in-law and some grandchildren, and nine of my brothers and sisters. Through everything, order, quietness and cheerfulness were remarkably maintained. After dinner I returned thanks for our many blessings, and could with a few present feel how many outward deliverances we had experienced ; that we had had our heads kept above the waters, spiritually and temporally, and were able to have such a day of rejoicing. Our dear bride and bridegroom left us in the afternoon. The evening was fine, and our lawn looked really beautiful, covered with the large and interesting party. In the evening we assembled together, and had a solemn religious time; giving, I trust, the praise that was due alone to Him from whom all good and blessings flow.

This marriage was hailed by Elizabeth Fry with sincere pleasure : not only was the connexion highly acceptable to her, and one that she believed likely to promote the happiness of her child, but it also possessed what was, in her estimation, the peculiar advantage of being with a member of the Society of Friends. Whilst her hospitable and affectionate nature was gratified with the prospect of receiving the bridal party at Plashet, she craved spiritual blessings for the two most interested, and that the occasion, like the marriage at Cana in Galilee, might be owned by the presence of the Lord. It was a beautiful summer day, —the sun shone brilliantly,—Plashet was arrayed in all its verdure, gay with bright flowers, and sprinkled with groups of happy young people. After the bride was gone, one of the sisters crossed the lawn to speak to her mother, she said something of the scene before them, and the outward prosperity which seemed to surround that beloved parent. The reply was remarkable ; for, after expressing a strong feeling of gratification and enjoyment, she added, in words which have have rivetted themselves upon the memory of her, to whom they were addressed : " But I have remarked, that when great outward prosperity is granted, it is often permitted to precede great trials." There is an old rhyme which says,

> " When joy seemeth highest
> Then sorrow is nighest !"

Surely this was verified, in the contrast between that day and the scenes, which so shortly followed in that long-loved home.

Shortly after the wedding, the family removed to Dagenham for their summer retreat; and in the autumn Mrs. Fry accompanied her husband into the North of England, where he went on account of some business transactions. In this journey, her daughter Hannah was with her. She received at that time, as she had frequently done before, very great kindness from her valued friends of the Benson family. Nor was theirs the friendship which existed only in the day of sunshine; for when so soon afterwards the storm arose, and adversity prevailed, they were among those whose efficient kindness was singularly manifested.

Plashet, Eleventh Month, 4*th.*—I have been favoured to partake of very sweet feelings of peace, and refreshment of soul, since my return home ; that which I am ready to believe, in the most unmerited mercy, is something of the " Well of water springing up unto eternal life." But I find outwardly and about me there are storms, not at present so much in my very own borders, as close to them.

15*th.*—The storm has now entered my own borders—once more we are brought into perplexity and trial—but I have this consolation, " He will regard the prayer of the destitute, and not despise their prayer." To whom can I go in this time of emergency, but to Him who hitherto has helped me and provided for me and mine in a marvellous manner—made darkness light before me and crooked things straight. Lord ! Thou who remainest to be the God of my love, above all things, in this our sorrow and perplexity cast us not out of Thy presence, and take not Thy Holy Spirit from us ; keep us from evil and from the appearance of it, that through the help of Thy Spirit our conduct may be kept upright, circumspect, and clean in Thy sight, and amongst men ! that in all things, at all times, and under all circumstances, we may show forth Thy praise. Keep us in love and unity with. those whom we have to act, even if they do contrary to our wishes and judgment. But, oh, dearest Lord, if it be Thy holy will, make a way of escape for us, from the calamity we so much dread, and continue in Thy unmerited mercy to provide for Thy unworthy servant, her family and all concerned in this trial, that we may not want what is good and needful for us, and that others may be kept from suffering through us. If it be possible remove this bitter cup from us ; yet, if it be Thy will that we drink it, enable us through the grace and spirit of Him who suffered for us, to drink it without repining,—yet trusting in Thy love, Thy mercy, and Thy judgment.

But it was not at this time the will of God to remove " the bitter cup" from His servant, but rather to grant strength and grace to drink of it, as coming from His holy hand.

It is a marvellous thing to the natural mind of man, and wholly beyond the unassisted scope of his reasoning powers, why, eminent Christians are often so intensely afflicted. Faith's estimate is different, and holy writ solves the problem, by showing us that it is by this process they are fitted for the heavenly inheritance, the most fine gold purified, the diamond of the first water polished for the Master's use.

The failure of one of the houses of business in which her husband was a partner, though not that which he personally conducted, involved Elizabeth Fry and her family in a train of sorrows and perplexities which tinged the remaining years of her life. Nature staggered beneath the blow—but the staff on which she leaned could not fail her, and she fell not.

Eleventh Month, 25th.—I have been brought at times, into little short of anguish of spirit; not I think so much for what we must suffer ourselves, as for what others may suffer. The whole thing appears fraught with distress. When I look at this mysterious dispensation permitted by Almighty wisdom, I am ready to say, How is it Lord, Thou dealest thus with Thy servant, who loves Thee, trusts in Thee, and fears Thy name—and then I say this is my infirmity, thus to query. Need I not chastisement? Do I not deserve it? May it not be a mysterious dispensation of deep and sore affliction, laid not only upon us, but upon others, to draw us all more from the things of time and to set us more on the enduring riches of Eternity. I cannot reason upon it, I must bow, and only bow and say in my heart, which I believe I do, "Not as I will, but as Thou wilt." Well, if it be of the Lord, let Him do as seemeth Him good. Lord let Thy grace be found sufficient for us in this most awful time, and grant that we faint not when Thou rebukest us!

The following Sunday the question was much debated, as to whether she, and her family generally, should attend their Meeting for worship or not, but she felt it right to go, and of course was accompanied by her husband and children. She took her usual seat, bowed down and overwhelmed, with the bitter tears rolling down her cheeks—no common thing with her.

After a very solemn pause she rose with these words, her voice trembling with emotion: "Though He slay me yet will I trust in Him;" and testified in a short and beautiful discourse, that her faith and love were as strong in the hour of adversity, as they had been in the time of prosperity. Her friends were deeply affected, marking by their manner their sympathy and love.

To her only absent child she wrote.

Plashet, Eleventh Month, 27th, 1823.

My dearest Rachel,

I have at last taken up my pen to write to thee; but to one so near, and so much one with myself, it is difficult. I do not like to pour out my sorrows too heavily upon thee, nor do I like to keep thee in the dark as to our real state. This is, I consider, one of the deepest trials to which we are liable; its perplexities are so great and numerous, its mortifications and humiliations so abounding, and its sorrows so deep. None can tell but those who have passed through it, the anguish of heart at times felt; but thanks be to our God, this extreme state of distress has not been very frequent, nor its continuance very long. I frequently find my mind in degree sheathed to the deep sorrows, and am enabled not to look so much at them—but there are also times, when secondary things arise—parting with servants, the poor around us, schools, and our dear Place. These things overwhelm me; indeed I think naturally I have a very acute sense of the sorrow. Then the bright side of the picture rises, I have found such help and strength in prayer to God, and highly mysterious as in some points of view this dispensation may be, yet I think I have frequently, if not generally, come to be able to say, "Not as I will, but as Thou wilt," and bow under it. All our children and children-in-law, my brothers and sisters, our many friends and servants, have been a strong consolation to me; and, above all, a little refreshment to my tribulated spirit has been granted me at times, from what I trust are the well springs from on High.

To her Sister, Mrs. Buxton.

Plashet, *Twelfth Month*, 2nd.

My dearest Hannah,

I have received your valuable and excellent letters; and the advice, as well as consolation in them, I trust will do us all good. My desire is, that we may entirely and altogether bow under our circumstances and the various pains attached to them. I feel with thee, and have felt all along, that a still greater pain and trial might in many ways have been permitted us; but one of its deepest stings is from the peculiar and perplexing nature of it. It abounds with temptation, as my dear friend, Mary S——, so deeply felt under similar circumstances; but there is a power that can preserve amidst them all, and in this power I trust. I see that I have many blessings left, and do earnestly desire to estimate them as I ought. Your very kind offer for Hannah, I do not at present think it right to accept ; I think it better for her to drink the cup with us for a time, but I may be glad before long gratefully to accept it. I feel all your kindness, and trust I shall never be a burden to any of you. I expect our way will open—we must commit it in faith.

The tide of sympathy flowed in marvellously from all quarters. The mass of letters that exist, attest by how many, and how well, she was loved ; how highly she was valued, and upon how many hearts, she and her sorrows were borne.

Amongst such numerous communications, it is difficult to select, but a few of them ought to be known, to give some idea of the feeling excited towards her amongst persons of different classes and denominations.

FROM WILLIAM WILBERFORCE, ESQ.

" Farnham Castle, 29th November, 1828.

" My dear friend,

" Though my eyes are just now weaker than usual, I must claim a short exercise of their powers, for the purpose of expressing to you the warm sympathy which Mrs. Wilberforce, and, indeed, all of my family that have the pleasure of knowing you, as well as myself, are feeling on your account. Yet you, I doubt not, will be enabled to *feel* as well as to *know*, that even this event will be one of those which in your instance are working for good. You have been enabled to exhibit a bright specimen of Christian excellence in *doing* the will of God, and, I doubt not, you will manifest a similar specimen in the harder and more difficult exercise of *suffering* it. I have often thought, that we are sometimes apt to forget that key, for unlocking what we deem a very mysterious dispensation of Providence, in the misfortunes and afflictions of eminent servants of God, that is afforded by a passage in St. Paul's Epistle to his beloved Philippians ' Unto you it is given not only to believe on Him, but also to suffer for His sake.' It is the strong only that will be selected for exhibiting those

D 2

graces which require peculiar strength.   May you, my dear friend, (indeed, I doubt not you will) be enabled to bear the whole will of God, with cheerful confidence in His unerring wisdom, and unfailing goodness.   May every loss of this world's wealth, be more than compensated by a larger measure of the unsearchable riches of Christ.   You will not forget that the time is short; but there will be no end to that eternity of happiness and glory which, I doubt not, will in your instance follow it.   Meanwhile, you are richly provided with relatives and friends, whom you love so well as to relish receiving kindnesses from them, as well as the far easier office of doing them.   That you may be blessed with a long continuance of usefulness and comfort in this world, to be followed by a still better portion in a better, is the cordial wish, and shall be the prayer also, of (begging from you a frequent performance of the last-named office of friendship for myself and mine)

"My dear Mrs. Fry,
    " Your sincere and affectionate Friend,
                    " W. WILBERFORCE."

Mrs. Backhouse, daughter to her uncle Joseph Gurney, wrote to Mrs. Fry's sister Mrs. Samuel Hoare, finding it less difficult to express to her the earnest breathings of her heart for one united to her not alone by ties of consanguinity, but by a close agreement in religious opinions and spiritual experience than to address her afflicted cousin herself.

"26th of Eleventh Month, 1828.

"I have felt far too much for her (Elizabeth Fry), and for many of her family, not to acknowledge a little of the near and dear sympathy I feel for her and for them.   I hardly know how to express it to herself immediately; through thee I can do it more easily.   I think if ever I have known what sympathy is, it has been with her, and especially at times during the course of the last year or two, it has sometimes nearly melted all within me to come near her.   Well, I can make no doubt she is graven on His hands, who chooses his servants in the furnace of affliction,

and that in due time she will come out of this yet more pure.
Deep searchings of heart may be her portion, yet I trust the
enemy will not be suffered to prevail, so as to call her good evil,
either in her own estimation, or in the estimation of those among
whom she has stood so high.   I think I never loved her half so
much before."

FROM THE REV. JOHN W. CUNNINGHAM.

"Harrow, *November 26th,* 1828.

"My very dear Friend,

"I need not tell you, with what sorrow, I have received the
most unexpected intelligence which reached me yesterday.   It
is but a short time, since I was called to sympathize with a near
relative in similar circumstances, and now again I am called to
mourn as for a brother and a friend.   My experience in the
former case, has enabled me to take a more hopeful and cheerful
view of your heavy trial.   Perhaps, dear friend, this event may
be made a blessing to every member of your family; and we
must not complain of a little rough handling when the jewels
are to be polished for the treasury of God.   All that drives us
home to Him, and to the power of His spirit, for grace, and
strength, and joy, is beyond all price to the soul.   Is it not a
comfort to you, dear friend, at this moment, that you have spent
so much of your time and property for God and for His creatures.   Is not money given to the poor lent to the Lord, and to
be returned again in some form or other, "with usury!"   I beg
my very kind remembrances to Mr. Fry, and your dear children.
I have already been led to pray for them more than once, that
this affliction may be sanctified to them, and that they may more
and more seek the durable riches of the kingdom of Christ.

"My wife unites with me in very kind regards, and I am very
affectionately yours.

"J. W. CUNNINGHAM."

FROM HER BROTHER-IN-LAW, T. F. BUXTON, ESQ.
(AFTERWARDS SIR T. FOWELL BUXTON, BART.)

" Northrepps, *December* 1*st*, 1828.

" My dearest Sister,

" I have hitherto, I confess, shrunk from writing to you. Not surely, however, from any want of feeling for you, and with you; but from so deep a sense of your calamity, as to make all attempts at comfort appear almost idle. A very quiet day yesterday, and a long time spent over the 69th Psalm, from the 13th to the 17th verse, with peculiar reference to you, have given me more encouragement. I am more able to feel, that we may confidently commit you and yours to that most merciful Lord, from whom the dispensation has come, and I have been comforted by the reflection, strange comfort as it may seem, that you and all of us have not long to live; that in truth it signifies little how we fare here for a few years, provided we are safe in that long and endless journey upon which we shall soon enter. I think, however, I have in some degree followed you in the little mortifications, as well as the great ones, of this trial. I am not sure that the great and lasting disaster is so galling to my mind at the moment, as some of the little provoking and humbling attendants on it. But since the time I spent in heart with you yesterday, I have been able in some measure to get rid of these intruders, and to look upon you under the aspect of one beloved of God, honoured of men, and more than ever loved, cherished, and delighted in, by a large brotherhood. I never felt so keenly as now, the privilege of belonging to you, or so conscious of the honour and the benefit of such a sister; and I feel no distrust about your future lot. I cannot doubt that years of contentment and happiness await you. I expect that your light will shine forth more brightly than ever. You have ever been a teacher to the whole family, and now, I am confidently persuaded, you will instruct us with what humility, with what submission, and with what faith, we ought to bear the deepest trials. What comes from above cannot be bad for us; and under the sense of this, I adopt David's words, ' Why art thou cast down,

Oh my soul! and why art thou disquieted within me ; hope thou
in God, for thou shalt yet praise him.'

"Ever, my dearest Betsy,
"Your most affectionate brother,
"T. F. BUXTON."

The following extract is from a letter addressed by the
Marquis of Cholmondely to Mrs. Opie, inquiring after Mrs. Fry.
He had been acquainted with her for many years, and his friendship was highly valued by her ; he had supported many of her
benevolent objects, and had strenuously exerted himself in behalf of more than one wretched object, at the time when executions for forgery were so rife at the Old Bailey.

"It is a consolation to hear, that that exemplary woman Mrs.
Fry is enabled to look to her God in this hour of trial, and I do
hope that she may be yet made an instrument of much good ;
even if her own ability should unfortunately be lessened, she has
the comfort of knowing that she began the good work of Prison
Reform.   I have seen it suggested, in the "Record" newspaper,
that it would be grateful to Mrs. Fry's feelings, if additional
subscriptions were now made to one or two societies which have
lost so much, owing to the stop which has been put to her benevolent exertions.   I should be much obliged to you to let me
know if there is any truth in this suggestion."

FROM MRS. OPIE.

Twelfth Month 17*th,* (*First day morning*), 1828.

"Though I have not hitherto felt free in mind to write to
thee, my very dear friend, under thy present most severe trial,
thou hast been continually, I may say, in my thoughts—brought
feelingly and solemnly before me, both day and night.   But
I am now desired by thy sister Catherine to tell thee, that she
will be with thee to-morrow evening.   I must also tell thee, to
please myself, that two nights ago I had a pleasing cheering
dream of thee !—

"I saw thee looking thy best, drest with peculiar care and neatness, and smiling so brightly that I could not help stroking thy cheek, and saying, 'dear friend! it is quite delightful to me to see thee looking thus again, so like the Betsy Fry of former days,' and then I woke. But this sweet image of thee lives with me still, and I trust, that when this dark cloud has passed away from you (as it has passed away from so many, many others) I shall not only see thee in a dream, but in reality, as those who love thee desire to see thee always.

"Since your trials were known, I have rarely, if ever, opened a page of scripture, without finding some promise, applicable to thee and thine. I do not believe that I was looking for them, but they presented themselves unsought, and gave me comfort and confidence. Do not suppose, dear friend, that I am not fully aware of the peculiar bitterness and suffering which attends this trial in thy situation to thy own individual feelings; but then, how precious and how cheering to thee must be the evidence it has called forth, of the love and respect of those who are near and dear to thee, and of the public at large! Adversity is indeed the time to try the heart of our friends, and it must be now, or will be in future, a cordial to thee, to remember that thou hast proved how truly and generally thou art beloved and reverenced."

The committee of the Ladies British Society evinced their deep sympathy, in a letter from one of their members, Miss Neave.

Albemarle Street, *Tuesday Night.*

"I was deputed by our friends of the British Society Committee to address our dear absent leader, which under these circumstances will not be considered an intrusion. No answer is claimed. Your note was read, and its contents received with strong emotion; and ere it was read, prayer had been made orally and silently, I need not add fervently, for you and yours.

"The conduct of the Navy Board, and the account of the Penitentiary being completed for the convicts on their arrival, were cheering circumstances. How pleasant to find that text verified, ' They that wait upon the Lord shall renew their strength.' May you, my dear friend, under your present afflicting trial, find every part of this text verified in your experience. May you mount up as with eagle's wings above every earthly cloud, and be enabled to fix your eye solely on the Sun of Righteousness, who has arisen for you, with healing on his wings, who has received gifts, and laid them up for you. You may have need of patience, but may the Spirit, the Comforter, make you now to feel what He has indited—that afflictions are light, and the glory that awaits the Christian a weight; you have received the earnest, having been sealed with that Holy Spirit of promise, and the purchased possession is yours ; all things are yours, and all things must work together for your good, for thus saith the Lord. We have His oath and His promise, and nothing can separate us from His love.

" My dear friend, you cannot now trace God, but you can trust Him ; if you can no longer equally relieve the temporal wants of others, you may still minister to the spiritual necessities ; and your inability may open other sources, and teach those who before were inactive, to labour— be that as it may, the poor are God's creatures, not ours, and His will must be done in this also. I have continued still to place my Asylum women most advantageously ; there are now thirty-two, of whom we entertain no doubt, who have been many of them from one to four years in respectable service.

" And now, my dear friend, commending you, and all that are near and dear to you, to the care of the good Shepherd of the sheep—his own sheep, whom He knows by name, and with whom in all their affliction He is afflicted.

" I remain,

" Yours, with much esteem and affection,

" C. H. Neave."

A severe accident to her eldest grandson, for a few days detained his mother in Norfolk. She had last seen Plashet really and figuratively basking in sunshine. All the family had been assembled for her sister's wedding, all were again together ;

there was the same pleasant dwelling, the same expanse of verdure, the same beloved ones to receive her—but all was changed. The countenance and effect of her mother at that time, were emphatically her own—an expression of such intense suffering, and yet such immoveable peace. Her soft full-toned voice, saddened, yet sweet as ever ; her chastened smile, whilst she could point to better days, and hopes to be fulfilled, even in this life ; and then the wonderful judgment—clear, discerning, and practical—with which she would enter into details so little suited for women, and without minutely following their different points, from her ready quickness, arrive at true and just conclusions.

She had a quality difficult to describe, but marked to those who knew her well, the power of rapidly and by a process of thought that she could herself hardly have explained, arriving at the truth, striking the balance, and finding the just weight of a doubtful question ; nothing could be more valuable than this quality, under such circumstances.

Mr. and Mrs. Fry resolved upon at once leaving Plashet, and seeking a temporary home in St. Mildred's Court, then the residence of their eldest son. One immense mitigation attended this calamity, that the mercantile business formerly their grandfather's, and conducted by their father, remained to the young men of the family, who were enabled by the important assistance of their mother's brothers to carry it on, and by this means aided by their uncles to re-establish their parents in comparative comfort. With leaving Plashet came much that was sad—uprooting habits, long-formed tastes and local associations, parting with servants, and leaving many old pensioners and dependants.

The surrounding poor found a kind and judicious friend in the Vicar of East Ham (of which parish Plashet is a hamlet), to whom the living had very recently been presented. To him the schools hitherto supported by Mr. and Mrs. Fry, conjointly with William Morley, Esq., of Green-street House, were transferred, and in his hands and under his care, they have since remained and flourished.

It was no easy thing to arrange for a very large family party, accustomed to country habits, and liberty of space, when confined to a city dwelling ; and that under circumstances of such peculiar pain. Mrs. Fry had for many years displayed singular wisdom and economy in her household arrangements, as well as in her charities and benevolent objects, varying according to the various circumstances in which she had been placed. To "be just before generous," was a maxim often expressed to those around her. On this occasion, these powers were called into full action. As the winter advanced, her health greatly failed. Circumstances occurred to weaken her husband and children's attachment to the Society of Friends—truly the sorrows of her heart were enlarged. She exclaims in her journal (which was very irregularly kept), that her " soul was bowed down within her, and her eyes were red with weeping." Yet was she enabled to adopt the language, " I will hope continually, and yet praise Thee more and more ;" and also to acknowledge that she was much sustained inwardly, and that at times her heart was kept almost in perfect peace. But in addition to domestic trials, her tender feelings were at times grievously and unnecessarily wounded, and from without there was much of bitterness infused into her daily cup, which can only be appreciated by those, who have had to bear the brunt of a similar calamity.

Plashet, Twelfth Month, 16*th.*—I have had some quiet peaceful hours, but I continue in the low valley, and naturally feel too much, leaving this sweet home, but not being well makes my spirits more weak than usual. I desire not only to be resigned, but cheerfully willing to give up whatever is required of me, and in all things patiently to submit to the will of God, and

7

to estimate my many remaining blessings. I am sorry to find how much I cleave to some earthly things—health, ease, places, possessions. Lord, Thou alone canst enable me to estimate them justly, and to keep them in their right places. In thine own way, dearest Lord, accomplish Thine own work in me, to Thine own praise! grant that out of weakness I may yet be made strong, and through Thy power wax valiant in fight; and may I yet, if consistent with Thy holy will, see the travail of my soul and be satisfied, as it respects myself and my most tenderly beloved family. Amen!

Mildred's Court, First Month, 19th, 1829.—My first journal in this year! What an eventful one was the last! prosperity and adversity were peculiarly our portion. It has been in no common degree a picture of life comprised in a small compass. However, through all, in prosperity and in adversity, however bright or cloudy my present position or my prospects may be, my desire for myself, and all whom I love is this, so strongly expressed by the Psalmist, "I will hope continually, and yet praise Thee more and more!" So be it, saith my soul, and if it be the Lord's will, may light rise in our present obscurity, and our darkness become as the noonday, both as to temporal and spiritual prospects!

The deep discouragement passed through by Mrs. Fry at this period, is evidenced by the following letter from her kind and faithful friend, Mr. Wilberforce, to whom it would appear, by the reply, that she had expressed some doubts of the propriety of resuming her labours in the prisons.

"Highwood Hill, Middlesex, 30th *January,* 1829.

"My dear Friend,

"Though my eyes are just now so indifferent that I must be extremely sparing in the use of my pen, yet I cannot forbear or delay assuring you, that I do not see how it is possible for any reasonable being to doubt the propriety (that is a very inadequate way of speaking—let me rather say, absolute duty), of your renewing your prison visitations. A gracious Providence has blessed you with success in your endeavours to impress a set of miserables, whose character and circumstances might almost have extinguished hope; and you will return to them, if with diminished pecuniary powers, yet we may trust, through the mercy and goodness of our Heavenly Father, with powers of a far higher order unimpaired, and with the augmented respect and regard of every sound judgment, not merely of every Christian mind, for having borne with becoming dispositions, a far harder trial (for such it is) certainly than any stroke which proceeds immediately from the hand of God. May you continue, my dear madam, to be the honoured instrument of great and rare benefits to almost the most pitiable of your fellow-creatures.

" Mrs. Wilberforce desires to join with me in saying, that we hope we shall again have the pleasure of seeing you, by and by, at this place.   Meanwhile, with every kind regard and friendly remembrances to Mr. Fry, and your family circle,

" I remain, with cordial esteem and regard,

" My dear friend, very sincerely yours,

" W. WILBERFORCE."

Mildred's Court, Third Month.—It appears late to begin the journal of a year ; but the constant press of engagements, and the numerous interruptions to which I am liable in this place, prevent my having time for much writing. We are remaining here with our son and daughter, and their children, until there is some opening for having a settled home. However, my desire is, that we may in faith and in humility entirely bow. I have of late not visited the prisons, and been much occupied at home ; but I trust that I may be permitted to enter this interesting work again, clothed, as with fresh armour, both to defend me, and qualify me for fresh service, that my hands may be taught to war and my fingers to fight ; and that if consistent with the will of my God, I may, through the help of the Captain of my salvation, yet do valiantly.

During that mournful winter in London, there were periods of peculiar suffering and anxiety. Mrs. Fry's own health being so shaken by her severe mental distresses, as nearly to confine

her to her room with a bad cough. Her beloved and valued
son William was on the bed of sickness from oppression of
the brain, the result of an overstrained and exhausted mind.
Shortly afterwards, her daughter-in-law was in the same house
in an alarming state of illness, and a lady, who came to assist in
nursing, was taken ill with the measles. The measles in a
grown-up family becomes a serious disease. They were driven
from London in consequence, though too late to escape infection,
and took shelter in the vacant house at Plashet, which, for many
weeks, became a scene of anxious nursing.

Thence they removed, early in June, to a small but com-
modious dwelling in Upton Lane, immediately adjoining the
Ham House grounds, the residence of her brother Samuel
Gurney, Esq.

Upton, 10th.—We are now nearly settled in this, our new
abode ; and I may say, although the house and garden are small,
it is pleasant and convenient, and I am fully satisfied, and I hope
thankful, for such a home. I have at times been favoured to
feel great peace, and I may say joy, in the Lord—a sort of
seal to the important step taken ; though, at others, the extreme
disorder into which our things have been brought by all these
changes—the pain of leaving Plashet—the difficulty of making
new arrangements, has harassed and tried me. But I trust it
will please a kind Providence to bless my endeavour, to have and
keep my house in order. Place is a matter of small importance,
if that peace which the world cannot give, be our portion,
even at times, as a brook by the way, to the refreshment of our
weary and heavy laden souls. Although a large garden is not
now my allotment, I feel pleasure in having even a small one ;
and my acute relish for the beautiful in nature and art is on a
clear day almost constantly gratified by a delightful view of
Greenwich Hospital and Park, and other parts of Kent, the
shipping on the river, as well as the cattle feeding in the meadows. So that in small things and great, spiritual and temporal, I have yet reason to raise up my Ebenezers, and praise,
bless, and magnify the name of my Lord.

Sixth Month, 23*rd.*—I little expected to attend the Yearly Meeting, having of late appeared to be so much taken out of such things and such services, but, contrary to my expectation, way opened for me to attend every sitting, and to take rather an active part in it, to my real consolation, refreshment and help. The unity of Friends was remarkable. I certainly felt very low at its commencement. After having for so many years received dear friends at my house, and that with such heartfelt pleasure, it tried, not to say puzzled me, why such a change was permitted me. But I rest in the weighty import of the words, "That which I do, thou knowest not now, but thou shalt know hereafter."

CHAPTER XVI.

1829, 1830. Foreign Correspondence—Dr. Julius, Madame de Pastoret, Madame de Barol—Letter to a daughter—Summons to the sick-bed of a niece—Poor men by the road-side—Prepares her Text-Book—Anecdote—Letter—Attends Suffolk Quarterly Meeting—Visits Pakefield and Earlham—Letter to her children at home—Foreign prisons —Death of a connexion—Illness of a nephew—Visit to Brighton—Death of her uncle Robert Barclay, Esquire—Of a little grandchild—Of a nephew—Of her uncle, Joseph Gurney, Esquire—Attends his funeral at Norwich—Letter to her family from Earlham—Interest in prisons unabated—Capital punishment—Prison reform.

AMIDST her own personal sorrows and perplexities, Elizabeth Fry was cheered from time to time, by finding that the subject so near her heart continued to prosper. At Berlin, a Committee of Ladies had been formed to visit prisons. Dr. Julius had informed her a few months before, of the publication of his " Lectures on the improvement of Prison-discipline, and on the

moral amendment of Prisoners." Prefixed to them, was a long
and laborious intoduction on the causes, number, and different
kinds of crime, in most of the countries of Europe and in
America, with remarks on the most likely means of prevention.

The result of Dr. Julius' observations amounted to this—
that in those countries where the education of the people is
decidedly on a moral and religious basis, crime diminishes, but
where instruction aims only at the increase of the means of
wealth, and imparting human knowledge, there, crime increases.

From Madame la Marquise de Pastoret, she received interesting accounts of the efforts making in France, amongst pious
and benevolent individuals, to benefit the unfortunate. In a
letter addressed to Miss Fry, that lady mentions some of the
existing associations, and still further enlarges on the subject in
another communication to Mrs. Fry of later date.

Differing essentially, as do the Protestant churches from that
of Rome, they may yet learn from her, in the performance of
practical duties towards their fellow-creatures, for amongst
pious Roman Catholics, there is to be found eminent devotedness
of purpose, in the fulfilment of these self-imposed offices of
mercy. Knowledge and system, it is true, are wanting; for
combined endeavour is incompatible with the power of the
priest, and cannot exist while his will controls, directs, stimulates or arrests exertion. In countries as our own where the
laity have no human interposition between God and their own
consciences, where education freely flows forth to all, where the
Bible is to be found up and down in the lanes and streets of
our cities, what might not be effected, if the spirit of self-sacrifice and self-devotion that is to be met with in the prisons and
hospitals of Roman Catholic countries, more generally prevailed?

What is there in our Protestant institutions to prevent sisters
of mercy—devoted ones of the female sex—being wholly given

to such works ; or amongst the more busy part of mankind,
hours and periods taken from the needful occupations of life,
and devoted to good deeds ? In the patient teacher of the
ragged school, in the laborious district visitor, who threads his
way through the endless mazes and foul air of the worst parts
of our metropolis, we recognize the dawn of a better day ; nor
is this hope diminished by the fact, that it is not alone in the
middle classes, but amongst the sons of our nobles and our
statesmen, and amongst those nobles themselves, that may be
found the most resolute and persevering in these labours of love.
An immense stimulus is given to acts of charity, amongst the
members of the Church of Rome, by their favourite dogma, that
"good works" can be performed to the exceeding benefit of the
individual, and the covering of many sins ; but he who simply
takes the Bible as the rule of life, and receives the words of
scripture in their direct and literal meaning, there learns, that
from the moment he has received the Lord Christ into his
heart, his time, and talents, and powers, are consecrated to His
service—not to the exclusion of any relative or domestic duty,
nor to the neglect of his outward calling, but to the consideration of what may be required of him individually for the service
of God, and the good of his fellow-men. Were this spirit more
devoutly entertained, and more practically exercised in England—civilized, educated, reflecting as she is—how new an
aspect would her children wear ; misery and crime would stalk
no longer unchidden through the land, tenderness and sympathy would be offered to the afflicted, counsel and wise reproof to
the offender. The best regulated and well-planned institution is
but a body without a soul, whilst rules and regulations are enforced, unaccompanied by personal influence or individual communication. The prisoner, the lunatic, the hospital patient,
require these to touch the heart, to reach the mental malady, or
give confidence under suffering and painful treatment.

Prussia has shown what may be accomplished in various Protestant Institutions of extensive and increasing usefulness. Her recognition of the Diaconate has undoubtedly tended to this result, and taking in their full sense the words " Kings and Priests unto God," she has led the way in showing the practical benefits that must accrue from using the laity as agents for religious instruction as well as employing them in general education and the care of the helpless and suffering. Very frequently did Elizabeth Fry urge upon others the importance of these acts of benevolence. She believed that not merely were they blessed to the receiver ; but to the giver " twice blessed." Earnest were her desires, and strong her hopes, that English men, and English women, would increasingly awake to their responsibilities, that they would not rest content with subscribing of their abundance, or even of their penury, to refuges, to hospitals, and schools, but that they would give of that which is more precious—of time, sympathy, communion between man and man, and mind with mind. For how admirable would be the results, could the well-planned Protestant institutions of Great Britain be visited, and cared for, and watched over, by spontaneous benevolence and unpaid services, with something of the love, and of the zeal, which can illumine even the dark regions of Popery. A greater proof of this devotion, can hardly be found than is pourtrayed in the following letter, describing the Refuge established at Turin, by Madame la Marquise de Barol, née Colbert, for penitent females.

"Turin, *ce 1er Avril*, 1829.

" C'est avec beaucoup de regret que j'ai appris, Madame, la cause de votre silence ; le mien a aussi été l'effet d'une longue maladie, dont je ne suis pas encore guérie. Elle m'a empêchée, Madame, de vous remercier de votre aimable lettre et des inté-ressants rapports que vous avez eu la bonté de m'envoyer. Vous désirez que je vous rende compte des soins donnés aux prison-

E 2

nières, et moin je désire vivement pouvoir faire quelque chose qui vous soit agréable.

" Nous continuons à suivre la même marche pour l'amélioration des prisonnières. Nous sommes le même nombre de personnes, nous employons les mêmes moyens. Quelques heureux résultats nous soutiennent dans une entreprise qui, comme vous le savez mieux que personne, a souvent des moments pénibles. J'espère que cette marche que nous suivons avec uniformité et exactitude, a quelque chose de bon, car elle améne le repentir. J'ai pendant quelque temps, ainsi que je crois vous l'avoir mandé, placé dans différentes maisons des femmes repentantes et sorties de prison. Je croyais qu'il valait mieux les disséminer que de les réunir dans une maison de refuge ; mais l'expérience m'a prouvé combien j'avais tort. J'ai donc sollicité et obtenu de la bonté du Roi une maison peut contenir de 50 à 60 personnes ; elle est dans un bon air ; il y a un grand jardin, une chapelle. Elle a déjà vingt-sept femmes repenties. Quatre sœurs de St. Joseph (ou de la Charité) sont à la tête de cet établissement. Il y a un Confesseur, mais point de Directeur. Nous n'avons point de revenus : jusqu'à présent la charité fournit aux besoins de ces pauvres filles. J'espère avec le tems obtenir de la bonté du Roi un revenu fixe. Je tâche en attendant de réunir les fonds nécessaires. Je les remets à la supérieure qui ne rend qu'à moi compte de son administration. Je crois qu'il vaut mieux ici ne pas mettre d'hommes à la tête d'un établissement de ce genre. Et j'ai pensé à la manière de me faire remplacer quand la mort viendra interrompre mes soins. Le travail peut être compté pour quelque chose pour le soutien de l'établissement ; mais comme cette maison est un lieu d'éducation et non une manufacture, le travail ne peut suffire au payement de la nourriture et des vêtemens. Les femmes apprennent à faire de la toile et des étoffes en coton. Elles font des robes, des jupons de toute sorte d'ouvrage en tricot. L'administration du Bureau de la guerre leur donne à coudre des chemises de soldats. Plusieurs travaillent à faires des gants. La Supérieure de la maison sait bien blanchir et raccommoder les dentelles. Elles n'apprennent pas toutes tous ces différents ouvrages ; mais cependant chacune est instruite de manière à avoir plus d'une ressource au moment où elle sort de la maison. Elles apprennent toutes le Catéchisme, l'Evangile, et à lire ; les plus intelligentes, celles qui le désirent, apprennent aussi à écrire et à compter.

Rien n'est fixé pour le temps de la sortie. Il faut que l'on sache suffisamment travailler pour pouvoir gagner son pain, et que la conduite soit assez bonne pour que nous puissions espérer que ces pauvres femmes, se trouvant dans les mêmes occasions, n'y commettent plus les mêmes fautes. J'en ai déjà placé plusieurs qui jusqu'à présent se conduisent fort bien ; dans ce nombre il y en a eu de rendues à leurs parens ; une s'est mariée ; d'autres placées comme servantes ; deux, dont la santé n'était pas trop bonne et qui savaient bien travailler, se sont réunies dans une chambre : elles vivent du produit de leur ouvrage. Le repentir seul donne accès dans cette maison ; et lorsqu'on est renvoyé pour cause de mauvaise conduite, on n'y est jamais plus admis. Il y en a qui quelquefois ont voulu sortir dans un mouvement de colère ou d'inquiétude ; lorsque celles-là sont bien repentantes, on peut encore les recevoir : mais comme il est certain que dans la maison on fait pour leur amandement tout ce que la charité peut inspirer, et qu'on les renvoie parcequ'elles sont incorrigibles, il est nécessaire qu'elles sachent bien qu'une fois chassée de cet asile, il leur est fermé à jamais.

Les filles de la maison de refuge peuvent sortir quelque fois pour des choses nécessaires ; mais toujours accompagnées. Quand elles sortent, elles quittent leur costume. Ce costume, fort simple, est de toile blanche et blue. Dans les premiers mois elles adoptèrent avec peine ce genre de vêtement, et deux d'entr' elles se sont sauvées de la maison pour ne pas le porter. Maintenant être habillé aux frais de la maison, est une récompense que l'on n'obtient que lorsque l'on sait faire un alphabet en points de marque. Ce travail qui les applique beaucoup et qui est un peu minutieux, a été choisi exprès pour les obliger à l'application, et profiter du premier moment de ferveur qui les amène. Les pénitences sont toutes fort légères, La plus grande est de manger à genoux au milieu du réfectoire, de ne manger que du pain et boire de l'eau, et de garder le silence pendant l'heure de ses récréations. La manière d'infliger les pénitences était ce

qui m'embarrassait le plus, car, toutes ces femmes étant à peu
près d'un âge où l'on doit être raisonnable, il était très-embar-
rassant de les traiter comme des enfans. D'ailleurs elles sont non
seulement volontairement dans cette maison, mais y être admises
une récompense. Aussi ai-je pris le parti d' établir que ce soient
elles-mêmes qui demandent la punition. Je leur ai expliqué
qu'elles étaient ainsi plus utiles, plus méritoires, et cette méthode
a apporté beaucoup de calme et de paix dans l'intérieur. Quand
une fille a fait quelque faute, elle demande elle-même sa pénitence, et le plus souvent la Supérieure à qui elle s'adresse, est
moins sévère que la coupable ne l'est pour elle-même, et
retranche une partie de la pénitence demandée.

"Dans les premiers tems j'avais promis aux repenties de leur
donner, au moment de leurs sortie, le tiers de l'ouvrage qu'elles
auraient fait dans la maison ; mais j'ai trouvé à cet arrangement
un inconvénient. Elles calculaient l'argent qu'elles pouvaient
avoir, faisaient des projets, des plans qui nuisaient à la subordination. Maintenant elles se fient à moi, comme elles le feraient
à une mère occupée de leur bien. Comme je l'ai dit au commencement, il n'y a point de Directeur ou d'administrateur dans
cet établissement. Je vois dans la prison des jeunes filles qui
annoncent les meilleures dispositions. Je les fais mettre dans
une chamber séparée sous la tutelle d'une prisonnière, dont la
conduite est bonne et les sentimens religieux ; et après un peu de
temps d'épreuves, quand le terme de la condamnation est arrivé,
ou bien si je puis obtenir grâce, ce qui m'arrive quelque fois, je
conduis (le plus souvent moi-même) les repenties de la prison à
la maison du refuge. Quand l'une d'elles arrive, elle se met aux
genoux de la supérieure à qui on donne le titre de mère. Elle
lui demande de la recevoir par charité au nombre de ses enfants.
Elle lui promet obéissance : l'obéissance, le silence et la prière
sont le bases du régime moral de cette maison. Une
grand douceur est aussi indispensable ; c'est par elle que l'on
ramène au bon Pasteur ses brebis égarées. Quant au régime
physique, il est simple et entremêlé de mouvement et de travail.
On se lève à cinq heures, et on se couche à neuf. Il y a, outre
le temps des repas, deux heures de recréation par jour, pendant
les quelles on court dans le jardin. On joue à des jeux propres

à leur faire faire de l'exercice. Leur nourriture est grossière, mais saine et abondante. Elles ont du pain blanc à discrétion, deux soupes par jour, et à l'heure du diner des légumes et de la viande. Elles boivent du vin mêlé avec beaucoup d'eau, excepté celles qui travaillent à faire la toile et à qui l'on donne un verre de vin pur. La chaleur et l'humidité de ce climat obligent à ne point refuser cette boisson fortifiante.

Il me semble, madame, que je vous donne des détails trop minutieux ; mais votre amour du bien vous fera, j'ose l'espérer, prendre de l'intérêt à tout ce qui est essayé pour l'obtenir. Permettez moi encore avant de finir cette lettre, de vous faire part d'une bonne action d'une de mes prisonnières: elle était avec quatre de ses compagnes et une surveillante dans une chambre séparée où elles attendent leur sortie de prison pour venir au refuge. Mais comme il ne serait pas prudent d'en faire entrer un grand nombre à la fois, je les avais prévenues que je les prendrais l'une après l'autre, choisissant toujours celles qui se conduiraient le mieux. Elles se piquérent d'honneur ; et vraiment sans injustice, je ne pouvais faire un choix. Je fis tirer au sort leurs noms qui avaient été écrits sur des morceaux de papier. Le nom de Thérése Borat sortit le premier ; toutes les autres se mirent à pleurer, en disant : " au moins si ce n'était pas celle-là ! elle sait un peu lire et nous apprend, afin que nous ne soyons pas si ignorantes en arrivant au refuge." Je fis sortir Thérése un instant de la chambre, et je lui dis : Tu vois le chagrin de tes compagnes ; il ne vient point de jalousie ; mais elles regrettent de perdre en toi un moyen de s'instruire. Dans ta vie, mon enfant, tu as nui à ton prochain ; tu l'as aidé à mal faire ; tu lui as donné de mauvais exemples : veux-tu réparer cela, et céder ta place à une autre pour continuer à instruire celles qui restent ? Elle me répondit : " Oh ! oui, Madame, je veux faire tout ce que vous croirez bien, tout pour réparer mes fautes." Elle rentra, et dit à ses compagnes : ' je ne sortirai que la dernière.' Ce qui ajoute à sa bonne action, c'est que nous étions au milieu de l'hiver, et qu'elle était fort mal couverte par une vielle robe de toile. Je lui ai, comme vous pensez, donné tout de suite des vêtemens chauds ; mais elle est restée la dernière, et, depuis son entrée dans la maison du refuge, elle continue à se bien conduire.

Ces pauvres filles ont un grand esprit de prosélytisme : elles m'avertissent que, dans tel lieu, je trouverai un être faible, coupable, qu'un peu de secours aiderait à sortir du vice ; et, quand je puis suivre leurs conseils et amener, parmi les repenties, celles que leurs vœux ont appelées, c'est une grande joie ; mais ces événemens sont rares. En général toutes les habitantes du refuge ont été habitantes de la prison.

" Il faut cependant finir cette lettre : je voudrais, Madame, vour offrir encore l'assurance de tout le prix que j'attache à votre souvenir, à votre amitié. Veuillez me les conserver et croire à ma reconnaisance.

　　　　　　　　" La Marquise de Barol nee Colbert."

Eighth Month, 29*th*.—Our wedding-day! twenty-nine years since we married! My texts for the morning are applicable :— " Our light affliction which is but for a moment, worketh for us a far more exceeding and eternal weight of glory."—" We walk by faith, not by sight." As far as we can judge from external appearances, mine has not been a common life. He who seeth in secret, only knows the unutterable depths and sorrows, I have had to pass through, as well as at other times, I may almost say, joys inexpressible and full of glory. I have now had so many disappointments in life, that my hopes, which have so long lived strong, that I should see much brighter days in it, begin a little to subside, and my desire is, more entirely to look beyond the world, for that which can alone fully satisfy me ; and not to have my heart so much set upon the things of this life ; or even those persons nearest to me, but more set upon the life to come; and upon Him who is faithful, and will be all in all to His dependent ones. At the same time I desire faithfully to perform all my relative duties ; and may my heart be kept in tender love to all near to me.

Upton, Tenth Month, 21*st*.—Something has occurred which has brought me into conflict of mind; how far to restrain young persons in their pleasures, and how far to leave them at liberty. The longer I live, the more difficult do I see education to be, more particularly, as it respects the religious restraints that we put upon our children ; to do enough, and not too much, is a most delicate and important point. I begin seriously to doubt, whether as it respects the peculiar scruples of Friends, it is not better, quite to leave sober-minded young persons to judge for themselves. Then the question arises—When does this age arrive ? I have such a fear that in so much mixing religion, with those things which are not delectable, we may turn them from the thing itself. I see, feel, and know that where these scruples are adopted from principle, they bring a blessing with them ; but where they are only adopted out of conformity to the views of others, I have very serious doubts whether they are not a stumbling-block.

On First-day, we were rather suddenly summoned to Plashet House, to attend Anna Golder (aunt to my faithful Chrissy) who had charge of the house. She was one of the lowly, retired humble walkers before the Lord ; she was suddenly taken very ill, and died in half-an-hour after her niece got there. It was apparently a departure without sting, to mind or body; as far therefore as it respected her, all was peace. But to myself it was different. I arrived there after dark, drove once more into the dear old place—no one to meet me but the poor man who lived in the house, no dog to bark, nor any life nor sound, as used to be. Death seemed over the place, such was the silence— until I found myself up stairs in the large, and once cheerful and full house; when I entered the bed-room, there lay the corpse, in her gown, she having died in her chair, only our washerwoman and the woman who lived in the house in the room besides. Circumstances combined to touch some very tender feelings, and the inclination of my heart was to bow down upon my knees before the Lord ; thankful, surely, for the release of the valued departed—but deeply and affectingly impressed with such a change ! that once lively, sweet, cheerful home left desolate— the abode of death—and two or three watchers. It brought, as my visits to Plashet often have done, the hymn to my mind,—

" Lord, why is this ? I trembling, cried."

Then again I find I can do nothing, but bow, trust, and depend upon that Power, that has, I believe, thus seen meet to visit us in judgment as well as in mercy !

31st.—Since I last wrote I have been called to another death-
bed scene, our old and valued Roman Catholic friends, the
Pitchfords, have lost their eldest son, a sweet good boy. I felt
drawn in love, I trust I may say, Christian love, to be much
with them during their trial ; I felt it right to leave my family,
and spend First-day evening with them, when all hope of the
child's life was given up. I had not only to sympathise with
them in their deep sorrow, but to pour forth my prayer on their
behalf. The next day, I was with the poor child when he died,
and was nearly the whole day devoted to them. We had a
deeply interesting time after his death—my dear friends themselves, all their children, their mother, sister, and old nurse. My
mouth was remarkably opened in prayer and praises, indeed, all
day at their house something of a holy influence appeared to be
over us. A fresh living proof that what God had cleansed we
are not to call, or to feel common nor unclean. It surely matters not by what name we call ourselves, or what outward *means*
we may think right to use, if our hearts are but influenced by
the love of Christ, and cleansed by His baptism, and strengthened by His Spirit, to prove our faith by love and good works.
With ceremonies, or without ceremonies, if there be but an establishment upon the Rock of Ages, all will be well. Although I
am of opinion, the more our religion is pure, simple, and devoid
of these outward forms, the better and the safer for us ; at the
same time, I do earnestly desire a more full union amongst all
Christians, less judging one another, and a general acknowledgment, in heart, judgment, and word, of the universality of the
love of God in Christ Jesus our Lord.

To her youngest Daughter, who was spending the
autumn at Earlham—

My dearest Louisa,

It is rather too long since I wrote thee a full letter. Having
John Henry here is quite a pleasure to us, he is better, but I
am doubtful whether he will be fit for school next week ; we
moderately employ him, and I think the real quiet he has here
will be very useful to him. It appears to me, and tell thy uncle

and aunt so, that his mind has been rather overworked, a little above his years.   I see great advantage in children being well employed and industrious, but their minds, particularly at an early age, require a good deal of rest and recreation, which gives *power* in future to receive and retain knowledge.   Dr. Babington told me, he thought children in the present day suffered materially in body by over-study, particularly boys; and that Latin and Greek were too much pressed upon them.   But at thy age, my dearest girl, which is so much more mature, I think it the time to *work*, and that very diligently.   When the soil is prepared before, and a good foundation laid, which I hope in some degree is thy case, *real* accomplishment is easily received and retained from fifteen to eighteen years of age.   It is a time when good habits should be formed, and good seed thrown in, that will tell in a future day.

Farewell my darling girl.   Be sober, and watch unto prayer; and may the God of peace be with thee.

Thy loving, tender mother,

ELIZABETH FRY.

Upton, Eleventh Month, 18*th.*—The last few days have brought with them trials of faith, and humiliations.   I have for a little time past, looked to joining my dear brother Joseph at Chelmsford, to attend the Meetings there with him, on First-day.   On Seventh-day, I found my dear son's baby so very ill, that it was a great effort to leave it and its mother, but duty rather pointed the way to go, therefore I went, and certainly felt much peace in being there.   I believe that I was really helped to minister in the power, that is not my own, in the Morning Meeting, but before the evening, so sad an account of the dear child came, that I was brought into real conflict, to know whether to stay the Evening Meeting, or to return to London—however, outwardly and inwardly, the way opened most clearly to stay, although for some time, I felt unduly tried and tossed by it; but in tender mercy, after a while my spirit was quieted, and I again was enabled to minister, I trust, in the name of the Lord.   When I arrived in town, the poor babe was still alive, and has since revived.   In looking back to my distress for a time at Chelmsford, these words might have been applied, " Oh thou of little faith, wherefore didst thou doubt ?"

After the recovery of her little grandchild, she was called into Norfolk to attend the sick-bed of her most beloved niece, Priscilla Buxton, who was dangerously ill ; to her she administered spiritual help, and the most judicious nursing. Referring to this illness especially, she describes her aunt's skill in a sick-room as " peculiar indeed ; her very presence and aspect as perfectly calming—possessing an authority mixed with soothing tenderness, which gave her a most helpful power, quieting both body and mind by her judicious and always indulgent advice, and by her unfailing power of hoping, perhaps too well; yet under feelings of need and discouragement, what an instrument for good !" She speaks of her "as condescending to the humblest services," recalls " her soft hand, her exquisite reading, and delicious company," concluding, " Oh that we could hear her, feel her, see her once more!"

She slept at Earlham, on her road to North Repps, and there found her daughter Louisa, looking so ill that she could not make up her mind again to part from her, but took her with her.

On the road, they saw a man lying apparently at the point of death. Mrs. Fry immediately went to him, desiring her daughter to open her dressing-case and bring a vial of brandy, which, from her frequent attendance in sickness, she had learned always to have in readiness. She knelt down by the poor man, whose head she found dreadfully torn, she carefully replaced the scalp which was lying back, tied it down with her pocket-handkerchief, then gave him brandy, and he began to revive. After a time a cart came by, into which she had him lifted, and carefully conveyed to the next village. He had been driving a powerful team of horses—they ran away, and the waggon-wheel went over his head. He died in Norwich

Hospital, after lingering some weeks, apparently ready for that solemn change. Mrs. Fry returned by Lynn to visit her daughter and her family, and was accompanied by her, from Norfolk to her "comfortable little home."

Her return thither, was however clouded, from finding that her beloved son William, who had been under every circumstance a firm support and great comfort to her, now thought it best for himself, to lay aside the peculiarities of the Society of Friends in dress and manners; he having come to the conclusion, that unless conformity to them arose from personal conviction of their importance, however becoming in a very young person under the immediate direction of his parents, their practice was inconsistent with truth in one of more mature years.

Writing on this subject, she says :—

Upton, Twelfth Month, 24*th.*—I truly desire not to be unreasonable upon the subject, or to require of my dearest William, at his age, that which his own judgment does not dictate. Beyond a certain point, I have believed it right not to press it, and oh, if I thus take from him my yoke and my bonds, may the Lord take him up and put His yoke upon him. Oh! most merciful Lord God, hearken to the earnest prayer of Thy servant for this dear child ; make him Thine own, prepare him in Thine own way for Thine own service, grant that through Thy help and Thy power he may wax valiant in the Christian warfare, until all his enemies be wholly subdued before him; and if consistent with Thy holy will, make him in his own family an instrument to draw others nearer to Thee and Thy kingdom. Lord God make no tarrying, but visit and revisit my family, lead them more from the vanities of time, to the enduring riches of eternity; keep also Thy very unworthy servant alive unto Thyself, even yet make her joyful in Thy house of prayer, and more faithful in the field of offering, and let Thy grace continually rest upon us. Amen !

Early in 1830, we find this entry in Mrs. Fry's journal, "my

time has lately been much occupied in writing my text book."
She had long felt the difficulty of young people generally, and
older ones in active life, possessing themselves of any scriptural
instructions, before commencing the employments of the day.
The experience of life, had infinitely confirmed her value of the
written word. She deplored the feeling, wherever she met with
it, that the Bible was to be approached as a sort of sacred
mystery, to be applied to only occasionally, and with something
almost amounting to awe.

At the period of Mrs. Fry's early life, this was too much the
case amongst Friends, nor was a circumscribed use of the holy
scriptures, by any means confined to that body. How much
more general now, than fifty years ago, is the habit of reading
the word of God in families; how much more universal its
close and individual study. But Mrs. Fry considered, that
there was something more wanted, to enable those, who have
but a short period for a hasty toilette before an early breakfast,
still to taste of the spiritual manna provided, and to have a portion
of holy writ, however short, impressed upon their minds.

Amidst her numerous avocations, she found time to select a
passage of scripture for every day in the year. She endeavoured
to combine in it, that, which is " profitable for doctrine, for
reproof, for correction, for instruction in righteousness; and in a
little preface, she urged the importance of endeavouring to appropriate the truths contained in it, with a heart uplifted, that the
blessed Spirit might apply the word ; and concludes, " The rapid
and ceaseless passing away of the days and weeks, as well as the
months of the year, as numbered at the head of each day's text,
it is hoped may prove a memento of the speed with which time
is hastening on, and remind the reader of the importance of
passing it as a preparation for eternity, in the service of God and
for the benefit of mankind." As soon as her little work* was

* Text Book by Elizabeth Fry, published by Charles Gilpin, Bishop-
gate Street without

her Monthly Meeting, a concern, which had for some time rested upon her mind, to pay a religious visit to parts of Suffolk and Norfolk, and attend the Quarterly Meeting at Ipswich. Doing this, involved many pains and much effort; she considered herself called to go by her Great Master, but she had cause to believe, that there were individuals in that neighbourhood, to whom her visit would be scarcely acceptable. It was with fear and trembling, that she set forth on this errand of Christian love. Accompanied by her sister-in-law, Elizabeth Fry, and their valued friend Joseph Foster, they left home one Saturday, spent the Sunday at Bury; on Monday went to Needham, where "the kindest sympathy and hospitality was extended" to her by Thomas and Lucy Maw; that evening moved to the house of Dykes Alexander; and the following days attended the Quarterly Meeting at Ipswich. There Christian love and unity rose higher and higher, till "all obstacles were removed," and she permitted to partake of something like "joy in the Lord," and unalloyed communion with her friends.

She wrote, whilst on this little journey, to her children at home, upon their being invited to attend the consecration of a Church, and to be present at a party afterwards.

Earlham, Third Month, 23rd, 1830.

My most beloved Children,

The information received to-day, that you should any of you have admitted a serious thought of attending our kind friend's party on the 31st, surprises and pains me; not but that I am also fully sensible of your willingness fully to be guided by my judgment in it. With respect to those over whom I have authority, I feel it impossible to leave them in any degree at liberty about it—it is a thing that must not be. I look upon it not only as perfectly inconsistent with our views as Friends, but perfectly so for all religious professors, because if I did approve of *consecrating* a church for the worship of the Almighty, I could not possibly conceive it an occasion for amusement or gaiety, but one of real seriousness. I see the thing to be altogether inconsistent with religious truth, both as to the thing itself, and this commemoration of it, and I trust that none of you will be present. I am sure it was, in the first instance, your own view of the case, therefore do not, my dearest children, be shaken in your judgments about it; I believe it will be a cross that you will never repent taking up, but on the contrary, be glad you have done so, for, now and then, sacrifices must be made to duty. Can you approve sacred things and the world's pleasures, being thus mixed together ? Can you think the consecration of churches, as it is too frequently conducted, consistent with the purity and simplicity of the gospel of our blessed Lord ?

Upton, Fourth Month, 26th.—My Suffolk and Norfolk journey proved an interesting, instructive, and I think very satisfactory one. My way appeared to be remarkably made in Suffolk, where I almost feared to go. At Ipswich, when the Quarterly Meeting was over, I think for a time I partook of perfect peace ; my rejoicing was, I may say, in the Lord. It was well worth suffering, only to taste of such a brook by the way. At Pakefield, we had a highly valuable and edifying visit to my much loved brother and sister Cunningham ; although their religious path is certainly in many respects, very different to my dear sister Elizabeth Fry's and mine, yet it appeared, as if it pleased the great Head of the Church, in no common degree to bless our intercourse, Christian love breaking down all partition-walls ; —we were sweetly refreshed together. We indeed, have but one Lord, one faith, one baptism, and one God over all, above all and in us all. I have for many years felt much liberality towards those who differ from myself ; but I may say, with increased years and experience I know hardly any distinction, all one in Christ. Those in my own family, who have gone to the Church, are so very near to me spiritually. After our visit to Pakefield, we went to Earlham and met with a cordial reception ; but I think that we were all in a low place. My arrival at home was clouded by a party, to which my children were invited and rather wished to go. We had some pains about it—my path is a very peculiar one, and as to bringing my family up consistent Friends, a most difficult one. My husband not going hand in hand with me in some of these things, my children, in no common degree, disliking the cross of the minor testimonies of Friends, and from deeply sorrowful circumstances, often having had their faith in them tried, also their being exposed unavoidably, to much association with those, who do not see these things needful, renders it out of my power to press my own opinions beyond a certain point. I believe it best and most expedient for them in small things and great, to be Friends ; it has to me been a blessed path, and my belief is that it would be so to them, if conscientiously walked in, but it is not I, who can give them grace to do it, and if their not walking more consistently brings reproach upon me, even amongst those nearest to me—I must bear it. I cannot deny that much as I love the principle—earnestly, as I desire to uphold it, bitter experience has proved to me, that Friends do rest too much on externals ; and that valuable, indeed jewels of the first water, as are many amongst them, yet there are also serious evils in our Society and amongst its members. Evils which often make my heart mourn, and have led me earnestly to desire, that we might dwell less on externals, and more on the spiritual work ; then I believe that we should be as a people less in bonds, and partake more of the glorious liberty of the children of God. My desire is, only to do what is for the real good of my children, and for the good of the cause I love, and leave myself altogether out of the question, whether it bring me into evil report or good report. I have often been brought by these things, especially of late, into deep conflict of spirit, and out of the very depths can only cry, Lord, help and guide me ! and give us not over to the will of our spiritual enemies.

Sixth Month, 7th.—I had a difficult path to tread during the Yearly Meeting. I did not of course receive Friends, but went as I was kindly asked, to various houses. I could not but at times na· turally feel it, after having for so many years delighted to entertain my friends, and those whom I believe to be disciples of Christ, and now in considerable degree to be deprived of it. But after relating my sorrows, I must say, that through the tender mercy of my God, I have many blessings, and what is more, at times such a sweet feeling of peace, that I am enabled to hope and trust, that through the unbounded and unmerited mercy of God in Christ Jesus, my husband, my children, and myself, will eventually be made partakers of that salvation that comes by Christ. The state of our Society, as it appeared in the Yearly Meeting was very satisfactory, and really very comforting to me ; so much less stress laid upon little things, more upon matters of greater importance, so much unity, good-will, and what I felt, Christian liberty amongst us—love appeared truly to abound, to my real refreshment. I am certainly a thorough Friend, and have inexpressible unity with the principle, but I also see room for real improvement amongst us ; may it take place : I want less love of money, less judging others, less tattling, less dependence upon external appearance. I want to see more fruit of the Spirit in all things, more devotion of heart, more spirit of prayer, more real cultivation of mind, more enlargement of heart towards all ; more tenderness towards delinquents, and above all, more of the rest, peace, and liberty of the children of God !

I lately paid an interesting visit to the Duchess of Gloucester. Our British Society Meeting has been well got through. There is much yet doing in this cause ; Oh ! for a right and diligent, and persevering spirit in it, and may the grace of our Lord Jesus Christ be with all those who are engaged in it.

The accounts received at this Meeting from various Committees for visiting female prisoners in Great Britain, were very encouraging.

"Liverpool, *Sixth Month*, 5*th*, 1830.

"The Ladies' Committee who visit the House of Correction at Kirkdale, near Liverpool, beg Elizabeth Fry's acceptance of a counterpane worked by the female prisoners, and trimmed with a fringe of their making. This memorial of a class of her unhappy fellow-creatures, so eminently benefited and tenderly felt for by Elizabeth Fry, will, the Committee believe, be peculiarly grateful to her, as well as being a proof of their own affectionate regard.

"Signed, on behalf of the Committee, by

"REBECCA CHORLEY, *Secretary*."

A counterpane, elaborately embroidered, accompanied this letter.

From Hamburgh, Elizabeth Fry received an application that a copy of her likeness might be engraved for an Almanac published by Beyerink, entitled, "For that which is Beautiful and Good."

With this was sent to her a translation of some lines inserted in the "Almanac for the Beautiful and Good."

"1830.—Though faithful to her duty, as a wife and mother, into the night of the prison Elizabeth Fry brings the radiance of love—brings comfort to the sufferer, dries the tears of repentance, and causes a ray of hope to descend into the heart of the sinner. She teaches her that has strayed, again to find the path of virtue, comes as an angel of God into the abode of crime, and preserves for Jesu's kingdom that which appeared to be lost. Is not this, indeed, what may be called, loving our neighbour more than one's self?"

"Leenwaarden, *September*, 1829."

From Berlin, Elizabeth Fry had received letters from the Countess Von der Grœben, giving encouraging details of the results of Ladies visiting Prisons ; and there, and at Potsdam also, of the establishment of places of refuge for such liberated prisoners, as seemed anxious for amendment.

The effect of kindness and patient instruction even on the most abandoned characters, is beautifully exemplified in a letter from Madam Potemkin née Galitzin, addressed to Mrs. Fry, from St. Petersburg.

"Gastiletta près de Petersbourg, 12 *Juin*, 1830.

"En entrant dans la société des Prisons, Madame, mon cœur avait regardé comme un de ses devoirs les plus doux d'entrer en relation avec un être, qui a été d'une si heureuse influence dans son pays et à notre société des prisons, et qui est depuis tant d'années, l'ange consolateur des malheureux confiés à ses soins.

"Aujourd'hui, Madame, que trois années viennent de s'écouler depuis le jour où j'ai été associée au sort des malheureux, je viens, avec le même sentiment de confiance et d'affection chrétiennes, vous exposer l'état des choses telles que je les laisse en ce moment, où des circonstances de famille me forcent à quitter Petersbourg pour m'établir à la campagne.

" Nos prisons, établies à l'instar des vôtres, Madame, offrent l'aspect le plus satisfaisant quant à l'ordre et au bien-être qui y règnent. Tout ce qui peut légitimement s'accorder avec l'état de la recluse et l'adoucir, y est employé. Les mesures sévères et les chambres obscures n'ont pas été employées deux fois cette année, à notre grande satisfaction. Le nombre des prisonnières a diminué de beaucoup à partir des années précédentes. Nous n'y avons plus vu les mêmes individus qui souvent, dans le courant de l'année, se retrouvaient en prison. D'après ces résultats, j'en augure une amélioration bien sensible dans l'état moral de nos prisonnières. Leur attachement pour la Surveillante, nommée par le comité, la soumission, et l'esprit d'ordre et de docilité qui se maintient parmi elles, nous encouragent à persévérer dans un but où le Seigneur est notre seule espérance.

" Les prisonnières qui savent lire, en profitent pour faire la lecture aux autres ; et c'est dans un séjour de réclusion qu'on peut surtout apprécier le bonheur d'avoir reçu l'éducation première, et de pouvoir venir avec un bon livre au secours de sa misère et de sa solitude. Mon expérience m'a démontré ce bienfait plus encore en prison que partout ailleurs : car, les mauvais livres étant prohibés, et le choix des lectures se bornant uniquement à la parole de Dieu, celles qui s'en occupent, Madame, y puisent des consolations nouvelles, et un goût pour la lecture sérieuse qui naguères leur était tout-à-fait étrangère. J'ai eu la consolation de voir une prisonnière, dont le départ pour la Siberie était retardé par une maladie, se nourrir avec avidité de la parole de Dieu, lire avec une foi véritable et un cœur contrit les souffrances de notre Seigneur Jésus Christ, et puiser dans ces souffrances la force de supporter ses maux, et la douce resignation que donne l'espérance d'une vie future. Sa résignation contrastait fort avec le sort d'une de ses compagnes, qui, plus ignorante qu'elle, ne pouvait se soumettre à son avenir, et qui se tordait les mains de désespoir.

"Voici, Madame, en peu de mots l'état présent de notre Prison de ville. Espérons que le Seigneur daignera de plus en plus bénir le zèle et les charitables soins des Dames qui composent notre petit comité. Toutes, Madame, sont dévouées de cœur à l'œuvre du Seigneur, et la regardent comme le plus cher et le plus sacré devoir de leur vie. Je me suis séparée de mes chères compagnes avec tous les regrets qu'inspire leur charité ; mais je m'en sépare avec confiance et emportant la conviction, qu'il n'y en a pas une qui ne remplisse mieux ma tâche, et avec plus de zèle que je ne l'ai fait. Car, je vous parlerai en chrétienne, Madame : je n'étais pas digne de présider une-Société, dont la charité était l'unique bien ; mais mon cœur était à leur suite, et désirait faire comme elles.

"Adieu, Madame ; je n'ai pas le bonheur de vous connaître et pourtant je vous aime, parceque je sais que vous aimez Celui, que nous devons seul aimer, et qui réclame notre cœur tout entier.

"TATIANA POTEMKIN."

Woodford, Eighth Month, 14*th.*—Last evening, a Bible Meeting was held here, my brother Samuel in the Chair ; seeing my beloved sister and her lovely family all there, swimming in the current of full apparent prosperity, spiritually and tempo-rally, brought feelingly home to my mind days that are past, when I used to delight to take my family upon similar occasions, in some degree, I believe, to manifest my love to the cause of Him whom I most desire to serve.

Not one week had passed over, from the time of this entry being made in the journal, before a heavy blow fell, where prosperity had been so apparent. The only brother of Mrs. Samuel Gurney being called to endure the bitter affliction of losing his wife.

Dagenham, Eighth Month, 2*nd.*—Last First-day fortnight,

I was suddenly sent for to my much loved and highly esteemed
friend Lucy Sheppard. She had been very ill, however she
appeared nearly recovered, but was taken with extreme sinkings,
and from one of these she did not revive as usual. My beloved
sister Elizabeth Gurney was with her, and being alarmed, sent
for me. I had a deeply affecting scene to witness, no less than
the sudden and unexpected death of this dear friend : her husband leaning over her—her poor children—and our dear sister
in almost an agony of grief. I think so affecting a death-bed
scene I never witnessed, where there was the inexpressible consolation of believing, that the departed one was really ready.
She was in the very prime of her day, in every sense of the
word ; in the meridian of her power and usefulness, a person of
good understanding, uncommon disposition, and all sanctified
by grace. I believe that she not only knew, but loved her Lord,
and through the assistance of His grace, appeared to me in no
common degree to be fulfilling the relative duties as wife,
mother, mistress, daughter, sister and friend, and to the poor
particularly.—Indeed, I feel our loss to be very serious, and
very great, and that it should strongly stimulate us who remain
to seek to be ready, and whilst we live, to fill our right places,
and perform in love, meekness, gentleness and humility, all our
relative duties.   May this affliction be sanctified to all parties !
and may the blessing of the Most High rest upon those most
bereaved.

My dear Gurney has been to pay a visit to France with his
tutor, which proved a very interesting one ; he received great
kindness from many French persons, particularly my valued
friends the Delesserts ; it brought me into communication with
them, and I have felt much sweet unity of spirit with them.
What matters it to what nation or sect we belong, if we love the
Lord in sincerity, and our neighbours as ourselves ? Since my
dearest boy left France, there has been a most awful time there,
through the arbitrary and imprudent conduct of King Charles
the 10th. The people have risen—there has been a dreadful
battle between the opposite parties in the streets of Paris, and
the King has fled. I felt the mercy of having my boy safely at
home, but I may truly say, afflicted for the French. War in all

forms is awful and dreadful; but civil war worse than all, as to
its present effect, and future consequences.

*   *   *   *   *   *   *   *

Eighth Month.—In bringing up our children, it is my solid
judgment that a real attachment is not a thing to be lightly
esteemed, and when young persons of a sober mind are come to
an age of discretion, it requires very great care, how any undue
restraint is laid upon them, in these most important matri-
monial engagements; we are all so short sighted about them,
that the parties themselves should after all be principally their
own judges in it.   Therefore, unless I see insurmountable objections, I believe duty dictates leaving our children much at
liberty in these matters.   May a gracious and kind Providence
direct them aright.

Upton, 11th.—I felt it right yesterday, to lay before the
Monthly Meeting, a view that I have had of attending the
Quarterly Meeting of Sussex and some of its particular Meetings.
My sister Elizabeth Fry felt disposed to join me.   It appeared
to meet with rather unusual unity, therefore we are likely to go
forward in it.

Tenth Month, 12th.—We, (my sister E. F., my brother
Samuel Gurney, and myself,) returned home from our journey
on Seventh day evening, after being out a week and two days.
We were in the first place outwardly cared for by our dear
friend Joseph Foster, who is truly a helper, spiritually as well as
naturally; he accompanied us to Horsham, where, as usual
under such circumstances, I felt ready to query, why I was there,
and fears got hold of me.   Friends received us with much kindness and apparent openness.

At Brighton, Elizabeth Fry attended the meeting for Friends
on the Sunday morning, and in the evening held a Public
Meeting for persons of different persuasions.   She had at
the Pavilion an interview with the Countess Brownlow, and
through her communicated a message of serious import to Queen
Adelaide.

My prayer for the King and Queen was, that a blessing might rest upon them ; that they might be strengthened by the Spirit of God to do His will, and live to His glory, (or to that purpose); then for the Queen, I felt the great importance of her situation, that she was indeed like a city set upon a hill, amongst women ; and my desire for her was, that her light might so shine before men, that they, seeing her good works might glorify our Father who is in heaven.   I expressed my desire that, for the good of the community, she might promote the education of the poor, the general distribution of the scriptures, and the keeping the Sabbath seriously, by discouraging parties, &c. &c., on that day amongst the higher ranks, as I was sure the tendency of them was very injurious to the lower classes, and the community at large. Then I touched on the anti-slavery subject, and the abolition of capital punishment, and presented for the Queen, my brother Joseph's Essays, also his Peculiarities of Friends, and my little book on visiting Prisons.

On Fourth-day morning, after several calls and attending a Bible Meeting, we dined with some Friends very agreeably, and in the evening went to our kind friends the Elliots, who invited about seventy persons to meet us on account of the District Society.   It was truly encouraging to me, to hear what wonders it had done for that place.   We had a delightful meeting, a great variety of Christians present, and so much good-will and unity felt, that it comforted my heart.   At its close, our dear and valued friends Charles Simeon and Joseph Hughes gave us some sweet religious counsel ; I felt the power such, that I could not help following them, and found that " out of the fulness of the heart the mouth speaketh "—giving glory to the Lord.   As far as I can see, how much more marked a blessing has attended my benevolent labours for public good, than any other labours of love that I have been enabled to perform in my own house, or amongst my own people.

On Fifth-day, several of the higher classes were invited to Meeting, and to my own feelings, a remarkable time we surely had ; it appeared as if we were over-shadowed by the love and mercy of God our Saviour.   The ministry flowed in beautiful harmony, I deeply felt the want of local prayer being offered, but I did not see it my place upon our Meeting assembling together, when, to my inexpressible relief, John Rickman powerfully and beautifully offered up thanksgiving and prayer, which appeared to arise as incense and as an acceptable sacrifice. After a time of silence, I rose with this text: "There are diversities of gifts, but the same spirit; differences of administration, but the same Lord; diversities of operations, but it is the same God who worketh all in all." In a way that it never did before, the subject opened to my view whilst speaking; how did I see and endeavour to express the lively bond of union existing in the Christian Church, and that the humbling tendering influence of the love and power of Christ, must lead us not to condemn our neighbours but to love and cover all with charity. My sister E. Fry was rather closely and differently led, and I had to end the Meeting by praying for the King, Queen, and all their subjects every where; for the advancement of that day, when the knowledge of God and His glory would cover the earth as the waters cover the sea; for those countries in Europe that are in a disturbed state, and that these shakings might eventually be for good. After a most solemn feeling of union the Meeting broke up. We dined at our dear friends the Elliots, where were Charles Simeon, Henry Elliot, (valuable clergymen,) and others. A pleasant, sweet, refreshing time we had; I think I never feel so able to rejoice in the Lord, as when united with real Christians of different denominations. We went that night to Chichester, and slept at Maria Hack's, and were much interested by her and her family, some of whom have joined the Church of England, but they appeared to us truly valuable and serious, and we were much pleased with our visit.

I have been thus full in the account of this journey, because it is I think well, in this way, to leave some memorial of the tender dealings of my gracious Lord and Master with me, when engaged in His service.

Upton, Eleventh Month, 3rd.—We returned home yesterday from Bury Hill, where my brother Samuel and myself went on Seventh day, in consequence of the death of my dear uncle Barclay, whose funeral we attended the preceding Sixth day, when thirteen of his children and children-in-law attended. It was to me very affecting, following the remains of this dear uncle to the grave, who was such a kind generous friend, and helper to me. It is very striking to see one generation so nearly gone ; so many of us, now entering the evening of our day, and our children and children's children coming up after us. Life thus passing away, " as a tale that is told."

Twelfth Month, 7th.—May I be enabled so to give an account of the various dealings of the Almighty with me and mine, that it may be useful to some, at least to my most beloved children and children's children. I have to begin with rather a melancholy tale:—My beloved children, Foster and Richenda Reynolds, lost their sweet baby upon the 4th of last month, after a few days severe illness. Death is awful and affecting, come as it may ! and this I truly felt, when seeing the sweet babe in its coffin, still retaining its beautiful colour. I could not but feel the uncertainty of all our possessions, yet the comfort, that death had only entered our family and taken one for whom we could feel no fear for the future. At her grave, the desire was very strong within me, that we might all become like little children, fit to enter the kingdom of God, being washed and made white in the blood of the Lamb. Since then, my dear nephew Harry Buxton has been called hence. His end appeared in no common degree peace, if not joy in the Lord. He was about seventeen years of age— a remarkable instance of the care and religious instruction of parents being blessed ; he was greatly protected through life, from any evil influences, and more carefully and diligently instructed by his dear mother, particularly in all religious truth. He was a child, who in no common degree appeared to be kept from evil, and live in the fear and love of the Lord ; he was cheerful, industrious, clever, very agreeable, and of a sweet person —a very deep trial it is to his dear parents to lose him. Still I feel, as if I could give up all my sons to be in such a state, but I may be mistaken in this, and perhaps my Lord may yet be pleased, to raise them up to His service here below, which would be even a greater blessing, than having them taken in the morning of the day. I think the way in which the children of my sisters turn out, proves the efficacy of much

7

religious instruction, and not too much religious restraint. It certainly is a very serious thing, to put upon young persons any crosses in their religious course, that Christ does not call them to bear!

First Month, 11*th.*—When dressing, last First day fortnight, A—— came in to tell me, that my dear and valued uncle Joseph Gurney had suddenly dropped down dead at his house at the Grove, near Norwich, my aunt only with him at the time. It exceedingly affected me, for he was very dear to me, and more like a father than any one living; he was one in whom the religious life was beautifully manifested, more particularly in his humility, in his cheerfulness and in his obedience. He was a lively minister of the gospel, a valuable and a delightful man, and his loss is indeed very great to those nearest to him as well as to many others. I had a painful struggle to know whether I ought to go to his funeral or not. However, I decided to go, in which I felt peace, and then could leave it all comfortably. I have seldom of late felt more discouraged from a deep sense of the evil of my own heart, than when I first arrived at Earlham. There are times, when with my brothers and sisters particularly, the contrast of my circumstances with theirs pains me; the mode of my feeling these things oppressed me. I walked alone through some beautiful parts of Earlham, and how did it remind me of days that are past! The sun shone brightly, and hardly a tree, a walk, or a view, but brought interesting remembrances before me; how many gone! how many changes! and then how far was I ready for my great change? It was New Year's Day; little did I expect to keep it there. I returned home, wrote to my husband and children, and poured out a little of my heart to them. I went to the Grove—felt my much-loved uncle being *really gone*—all changed there. I went to Norwich to call on a few sick, &c.; the place the same, but again how changed to me! However, as my dearest family assembled, I became more comfortable.

She wrote to her family from Earlham.

First Month 1st, 1831.

My dearest Husband and Children,

I have withdrawn into my own room for a little quiet and retirement, and my attention has been much turned towards you. I have just returned from a solitary walk about this beautiful place, the sun shining upon it, so much of it bearing the same aspect as in my childish days, and circumstances so greatly changed ; my feelings were greatly affected. How many gone that used to delight in its beauties, and rejoice together in no common bond of love. Surely the passing scene of this life could hardly be more feelingly brought home to the heart. Then I was led to look at my family, and oh ! what love, what tender desire, what inexpressible travail of soul was and is excited for you all, that amidst all chamges, (and you have already known many) you may each for yourself have a real substantial hold of that, which can never be changed and will live through every storm, even death itself. On Second-day, I went with my brother Buxton and Priscilla to North Repps, and paid a very interesting visit to my dearest sister. I was truly comforted and edified by my visit to them; religious principle appeared very present to help and sustain them; nothing could exceed their kindness to me, it cheered me on the way, and helped me. Indeed, I may say, that the stream so rose on First-day, and Second-day, and the healing power was so near, that I experienced a little what it is to have "beauty for ashes, the oil of joy for mourning, and the garment of praise for the spirit of heaviness."

First-day, First Month.—I desire to remember a few of the principal events and some of the mercies and deliverances of the last year—an important one in the political world,—the French revolution, and its consequence in other countries, and in our own in measure. I think, I unusually see the hand of Providence in some of these things. I never remember my prayers to have been more raised by any public event, than on behalf of the French, during their revolution. Their conduct in it has given me great comfort, because it shows a wonderful advancement, at least in Christian practice, since the last revolution. I feel still deeply interested about the French, and have a hope that a great and good work is going on amongst them. I have a hope also that the general stirring amongst the European nations is for good, and I have the same hope respecting our own country. I see that it is in rather an unsettled state, yet, as I also see that many things want a remedy, and as the process of fermentation must be passed through before a liquor can be purified, so, at times with nations—such a process, though painful whilst it lasts ends in the good of the people. May it prove so with us, and with other nations, and may all these turnings and over-turnings advance the coming of that blessed day, when the "earth shall be full of the knowledge of the Lord as the waters cover the sea."

My interest in the cause of prisons remains strong, and my zeal unabated; though it is curious to observe how much less is felt about it by the public generally. How little it would answer in these important duties, to be much affected by the good or bad opinion of man. Through all, we should endeavour to go steadily forward looking neither to the right hand nor to the left, with the eye fixed upon that Power which can alone bless our labours, and enable us to carry on these works of charity to the good of others, our own peace, and His praise.

The excitement occasioned by Mrs. Fry's first visits to New-gate, the strangeness of ladies visiting prisons, the astonishment of the public mind at finding the sin engendered and the misery permitted, within the prison walls of christian and enlightened England, had indeed passed; but a steady, resolute spirit of improvement was making its way, and men from all classes and all parties, were coming over and ranking themselves amongst the labourers, or at least the well-wishers to progressive improvements.

Sir Robert Peel had been for years grappling with the difficulties of the criminal code respecting forgery, and had, during the last Sessions, presented to Parliament his acts for consolidating its various sanguinary enactments. The subject had become one of general interest; and after many discussions, a majority of the House of Commons voted for the abolition of the punishment of death, in all cases of forgery. These clauses were restored in the Lords, notwithstanding a petition signed by a thousand bankers, supporting the vote of the Commons. The effect, practically, however, of this assertion of public opinion was, that the extreme sentence of the law in cases of forgery was not again carried into execution.

Thus, the work was advancing—but much remained to be done. He who set fire to a stack of bean stalks in an outlaying field was still to lose his life, whilst he who burnt a helpless family in their beds, could have no greater punishment awarded him ; again, the half-starved peasant, who carried home the sheep he found fallen and bruised in a neighbouring ditch, was to endure the same fate as the man who might waylay the farmer on his return from market, despoil him of his well-earned gains, and then to prevent detection, leave him lifeless —weltering in his blood by the road side.

The Prison Discipline Society continued its exertions. The greater number of county prisons were either rebuilt or remodelled, and classification and occupation introduced. Amongst female prisoners, officers of their own sex were becoming increasingly general.

Many of the Borough gaols and Scotch prisons continued, however, in their former state of neglect, wretchedness, and promiscuous intercourse amongst the prisoners, but there were exceptions, as for instance at Derby and Leicester, where the Borough magistrates purchased the old County prisons after the removal of the prisoners to the admirable new County gaols erected there. At Penzance, a new town prison was built ; at Barnstaple, the old one had been rebuilt. A new gaol was erected at Norwich. The Yarmouth prison remained unaltered in cells, and yards, and hired management, but under the teaching of Sarah Martin, and her devoted labours of love, wonderful results were produced, and an admirable lesson taught to her country-women, of what may be effected by kindness, perseverance and discretion.

DAGENHAM.

CHAPTER XVII.

1831—1833. Journey to Lynn—Letter from Ely—Attends the Kent Quarterly Meeting—Interview with the Duchess of Kent and the Princess Victoria—Yearly Meeting—Interview with Queen Adelaide, and some of the Royal Family—Leave-taking on board the Mary Female Convict Ship—Dagenham—Public Meeting in that neighbourhood—Journey with her husband—Ilfracombe—History of Samuel Marshall—Death-bed of a converted Jew — Death of Mrs. Sarah Fry—Opinions on choice in Marriage—Cholera—Examination before Committee of House of Commons—Yearly Meeting—Ladies' British Society Meeting—Attends Half-Yearly Meeting in Wales—Crosses to Ireland—Marriage of a Son—Marriage of a Daughter—Visit to Norfolk—Yearly Meeting—Family assembled at Upton.

THE last day of January, brought Mrs. Fry accounts of the severe illness of one of her daughters, and the following morning saw her, through most inclement weather, setting forth to go to her.

To one of her Daughters.

Ely, *Second Month,* 1*st.*

My dearest Hannah,

Here I am shut up at the Inn at Ely, unable to go on. It was with some difficulty we arrived here, from the snow, and when we reached this place we found that the way to Lynn was quite obstructed, and that no person had come from thence to-day. But now I must tell you a little about our journey ; there was one Lynn gentleman, and two young men, no doubt students ; at first we were all flat and said little, but after awhile we entered into very interesting, and rather intellectual conversation, upon some important subjects. I found the Lynn gentleman knew me and called me by my name. I tried to make the conversation useful. We talked of the state of the Established Church, and much belonging to it, in England and Ireland, tithes, &c. &c., then we went to prophecy, then to theatres, and so on. At last, I felt free enough to give the young men each a text book, with which they appeared to be much pleased. My dear nephews met me at the Inn, at Cambridge ; they were most kind. Upon my arrival here, the coachman, the outside passengers, and one of the owners of the horses, came to consult my wishes as to what to do, but when a medical man who had been out, told us that six miles from hence, the roads were impassable and really dangerous, there appeared to be no doubt for us, but to remain quietly where we were. They were all very kind and attentive to me, and so are the landlord, landlady, and servants. I believed it right to ask my fellow-passengers to breakfast ; the outside passengers proved to be two very interesting clergymen, related to the Styleman family. We had a solemn reading together with part of the family here, and all felt (I believe) what a sweet bond Christians have with each other, and how truly they are friends to each other.

The coach is now come in from Lynn ; therefore, I hope to proceed there safely.

Farewell, in much near and dear love,

ELIZABETH FRY.

Upton, Second Month, 12th.—I returned last evening from
Earlham with my dear brother Joseph, having been suddenly
called into Norfolk, in consequence of my dearest Rachel's alarming illness. I heard of it late on Second-day week, and set off
to her on the Third-day morning : the snow so great, I was
stopped on the road, and slept at Ely. Upon my arrival at Lynn
the next day, I found my child going on favourably. The
pleasure is great of having with my children the double tie, not
only of mother and children, but a friendship formed upon its
own grounds. I certainly think, that in common degree my
children feel me their familiar friend.

Third Month, 19th.—I went on Second-day to attend the
Kent Quarterly Meeting, accompanied by my dear sister Elizabeth Fry and Joseph Foster. I was much engaged from Meeting to Meeting, laboured to encourage the low, the poor and
the sorrowful ; to lead to practical religion, and to shake
from all outward dependencies, and to show that our principles
and testimonies of a peculiar nature should not be maintained
simply as a regulation amongst us, but unto the Lord, and in
deep humility, in the true Christian spirit, particularly as to
tithes, war, &c. I felt much peace afterwards, and in going
from house to house, breaking, I trust, a little bread spiritually,
and giving thanks. It appeared *very* seasonable though long
delayed, as I have had it on my mind many months, but
hitherto have been prevented by various things, yet this appeared to be the right time, and I take the lesson home,
quietly to wait for the openings of Providence, particularly
in all religious services, and not to attempt to plan them too
much myself.

The kindness of Friends was great, and I received much *real*
encouragement from them ; some from the humble ones, that did
my heart good. Indeed I cannot but acknowledge, in humiliation
of spirit, however any may reason on these things, and however
strange that women should be sent out to preach the gospel, yet
I have in these services partaken of joy and peace, that I think
I have never felt in the same degree in any other.

30th.—Yesterday, I felt delicate in health and flat in spirits ;
however, I attended our large Quarterly Meeting, and kept silence,

perhaps unduly so, in our Women's Meeting. I felt (as I often do from numerous calls) driven two ways, whether to go to Devonshire Street, to see my dear brother Buxton, who I apprehended to be under much discouragement in bringing forward his slavery question that night in the House of Commons, or to attend the adjournment of the Quarterly Meeting; however, I made up my mind to go to Devonshire Street. I went, greatly exhausted,—my cough poorly, the wind cold,—and in walking and going in the stage, in my infirmity I was ready to query, why I had been permitted to lose my carriage, who so often wanted it, whilst others who appeared to have less call, were so much indulged.

Fourth Month, 16*th.*—Since I last wrote, very deep sorrow has been our portion in the illness of my dear nephew, John G——; my nights have been truly suffering; *very deep* has been the exercise of mind on his account. Oh, dearest Lord God! grant, that before this dear child goes hence, he may be fitted, through the blood of his Saviour, for a place in glory.

20*th.*—I have seldom witnessed earthly prosperity more clouded for a season, than by this illness in the family of my beloved brother and sister. Where the sun appeared to shine so *very* uncommonly—health, riches, houses, lands, in abundance; children amiable and sweet—indeed, in going to their house, I have been ready to tremble, because it is not in the general ordering of Providence that such a full cup should continue—and what a change—what an inexpressible trial, what a cloud over the picture; however, He who can dispel the darkest clouds, and quiet the heaviest storms, saw meet to arise in His own Almighty power, and manifest His mercy and love, by granting us deliverance from our great distress. I was reminded of these words on his account, "I have seen his ways, and will heal him, and restore comforts unto him and his mourners."

Fifth Month, 14*th.*—About three weeks ago, I paid a very satisfactory visit to the Duchess of Kent, and her very pleasing daughter, the Princess Victoria. William Allen went with me. We took some books, on the subject of slavery, with the hope of influencing the young princess in that important cause. We were received with much kindness and cordiality, and I felt my way open to express, not only my desire that the best blessing might rest upon them, but that the young princess might follow the example of our blessed Lord, that as she "grew in stature she might grow in favour with God and man." I also ventured to remind her of King Josiah, who began to reign at eight years old and did that which was right in the sight of the Lord turning neither to the right hand nor to the left, which seemed to be well received. Since that, I thought it right to send the Duke of Gloucester my brother Joseph's work on the Sabbath, and rather a serious letter, and had a very valuable answer from him full of feeling. I have an invitation to visit the Duchess of Gloucester next Fourth-day; may good result to them, and no harm to myself, but I feel these openings rather a weighty responsibility, and desire to be faithful, not forward. I had long felt an inclination to see the young princess, and endeavour to throw a little weight in the right scale, seeing the very important place that she is likely to fill. I was much pleased with her, and think her a sweet, lovely and hopeful child.

The Yearly Meeting begins next week; I am rather low in the prospect, having no house to receive my dear friends in London, continues to be a pain to me. I desire to attend it in all humility, looking to my Lord, and not unto man; I desire to be kept in the unity of those with whom I am in religious communion, for I am one with them in principle; but we must forbear with each other in love, and endeavour through every trial of it, "to keep the unity of the Spirit and the bond of peace." Be pleased, oh Lord! to be near to Thy most unworthy servant, defend her with Thine own armour from the various shafts of the adversary, keep her safely in Thy pavilion from the strife of tongues. If Thou see meet to call her into Thy service, be a light unto her feet, and a lamp unto her path.

Sixth Month, 3rd.—The Yearly Meeting concluded this day week. I was highly comforted by the good spirit manifested in it by numbers. I think I never was so much satisfied by the ground taken by Friends, leading us to maintain what we consider our testimonies upon a scriptural and Christian ground, rather than because our forefathers maintained them. My opinion is, that nothing is so likely to cause our Society to remain a living and spiritual body, as its being willing *to stand open to improvement;* because, it is to be supposed that as the Church generally emerges out of the dark state it was brought into, its light will shine brighter and brighter, and we, as a part of it, shall partake of this dispensation. My belief is, that neither individuals nor collective bodies should *stand still* in grace, but their light should shine brighter and brighter unto the perfect day. My dearest brother Joseph had a valuable Meeting for the youth, further to instruct them in Friends' principles, which delighted me ; he was so clear, so sound, so perfectly scriptural and Christian, and so truly in the spirit of charity and *sound* liberality, *not laxity.*

25th.—I must give an account of the British Society Meeting. It was, I trust, well got through, and I feel the way in which its objects prosper cause for humble thankfulness. Surely the result of our labour has hitherto been beyond my most sanguine expectation, as the improved state of our prisons, female convict ships, and the convicts in New South Wales. I desire to feel this blessing and unmerited mercy towards us, and those poor creatures, as I ought, in humility and true thankfulness of heart. The day before yesterday, I had a very satisfactory interview with the Queen and several of the Royal Family, in rather a remarkable manner. There was a sale on account of the Hospital Ship in the River, in which I was interested; and hearing that the Queen was to be there, whom I wished to see, I went; but was so much discouraged when I arrived, by the gaiety of the occasion, that I should have turned back, had not my sister Catherine made me persevere. We saw the Queen and her party, and quickly passed through the gay scene. When we got out, we found ourselves with a valuable friend of mine Captain Young, in a quiet airy place, at the head of the staircase; we were told by him, that the Queen would go down that way, and we should have an excellent view of her. We therefore waited until some of the royal family came down ; their carriages not being ready they withdrew into a private room, where Captain Young admitted us; the Duchess of Gloucester met me with her usual kindness, and presented me to the Duchess of Cumberland. The Princess sister to the Queen, Prince George of Cumberland and Prince George of Cambridge were

there with them.   The Duchess of Gloucester soon withdrew,
and the Queen's sister and I had rather a full conversation together with the Duchess of Cumberland and Prince George.
Then came the Duke of Sussex and the Princess of Hesse
Homburg ; the Duke appeared pleased to see me, and we had a
good deal of conversation, the Duke said he would present me
to the Queen, who soon came into the room, with the Princess
Augusta, whom I knew, he did so in the handsomest manner,
and the Queen paid me very kind and marked attention. I had
some conversation with the Queen, almost entirely on benevolent objects.   I expressed my pleasure in seeing the Royal
Family so much interested in these things ; my belief that it
did much good, and that being engaged in them brought peace
and blessing. I was enabled to keep to my simple mode of speech
as I believe right, and yet to show them every respect and polite
attention.   I did not enter religious subjects with any of them,
though I trust the bearing of my conversation was that way.
We spoke with the Princess Elizabeth, of Friends, of the love
her father George III. had for them, his visit to our great-grand-
father Barclay, my meeting Queen Charlotte in the city and
many other things.   My dearest sister Catherine's simple boldness certainly got me into the room, and made me go through
the thing ; her company was delightful, helpful and strengthening. It was a very singular opening, thus to meet those, some
of whom I so much wanted to see—it is curious, but for days I
had it on my mind to endeavour to see the Queen, and by night
and day seriously had weighed it, lest my motives should not
be right, but when I remembered, that from not having been
presented to her, I could never on any point communicate with
her in person, I felt that if there should be an opportunity to
put myself in her way, I had better do it. It was striking, how
the whole thing wss opened for me, I may say providentially ;
for already I believe some good has been done by seeing one of
the party, and I look upon it as a very important event in my
public objects for the good of others.   Afterwards, I felt as I
mostly do, after any thing of this kind, rather anxious, and extremely fearful for myself, how far it was safe for me thus to be
cast among the great of this world, how far it was even right to

put myself in the way of it, and how far others would judge me
for it; however, the next day, my mind was much quieted, my
fears much allayed, and my present sober view is, that it was a
remarkable opening, and my desire is, that it may please the
Most High to bless it that good may result from it. I lately have
had a deeply interesting visit to a female convict-ship, surrounded as I am at such times by poor sailors, and convicts, it
is impossible not to feel the contrast of the circumstances in which
I am placed. The last time I was in the ship Mary, there was
such a scene round me—parting from them, probably for ever.
So many tears were shed, so much feeling displayed—and
almost all present the low and the poor. Then, within a few days
to be in such a scene of gaiety, though the object in view was
good, surrounded by royalty and the great of this earth. The
contrast was striking and instructive. I ought surely to profit
from the uncommon variety that I see, and the wonderful
changes that I have experienced in being raised up, and cast
down. Oh! may it not prove in vain for myself and others.

At our last Monthly Meeting, I proposed to Friends to hold
a Public Meeting at Maldon in Essex, and some among the
lower classes around Barking and Dagenham. This is a weighty
service; may the Lord be with me in it, to my own help, and the
comfort and real edification of those I am thrown with, and may
my beloved family partake of it.

Dagenham, Seventh Month, 6th.—I have now before me,
some deeply weighty family matters respecting my children. May
the Lord in His tender mercy, be pleased to direct me in my
conduct towards them; keeping me on the one hand from giving them undue liberty, and on the other from using any unnecessary restraint. May I be enabled truly, faithfully, and humbly to do my duty towards them. Oh Lord! be Thou my helper
and their helper, my guide and their guide, my defence and
their defence, and whatsoever is right for them bring to pass;
whatsoever wrong, prevent by Thy power and Thy providence!
Amen!

Eighth Month, 1st.—Last evening we finished our Public
Meetings in barns. I passed a humbling night—even in our
acts of obedience and devotion, how evident is the mixture of

sin and infirmity (at least so it appears to me) and we need to
look to the great offering for sin and for iniquity, to bear even
these transactions for us.   I apprehend, that all would not understand me, but many who are much engaged in what we call
works of righteousness, will understand the reason, that in the
Jewish dispensation there was an offering made for the iniquity
of their Holy Things.   Humiliation is my portion, though I
may also say peace, in thus having given up to a service much
against my inclination, and I hope, thankfulness for the measure of power at times granted in them.

Notwithstanding many family cares, and the weighty objects
in which she was engaged, the summer of this year, which was
passed at Dagenham, proved a very happy one.   The two cottages were fully peopled ; the larger one inhabited by Mr. and
Mrs. Fry, and as many of their home party as it could be made
to contain, the smaller cottage was lent to a married daughter,
and received the overflowings from the other house.   The first
burst of the calamity in 1828 had passed away, the younger
members of the family had been transplanted sufficiently early, to
take root at Upton Lane ; this was never the case with their
parents, or the other children, but Dagenham was not new to
them, and though the arrangements were different, yet no charm
was lost by that.   Pleasant it was, to listen from the larger
boat, especially appropriated to their mother (and bearing her
name) in the quiet of a summer's evening, to the joyous voices
of the younger members of the party borne from the other
boats, as they rose and fell in cadence, singing the burthen of
some old song to the dipping of their oars.   The gentlemen
generally spent the morning in London, but about the time when
the heat of a summer day is beginning to abate, the ladies and
children looked for their return.   One of the little watchers
would announce that the boat sent to meet them was in sight,
and then the expectant party poured out of their cottages.

6

Foremost in the group and conspicuous from her stature, she might be seen—whose smile was ever ready to greet them, her gentle voice to bid them welcome.   An unbroken band, they met in love, abounding in hope, with life before most of them, coloured by the prismatic hues of youthful fancy; even she, who had suffered so much, and encountered so many disappointments would catch their tone, and join with delight in the feelings of the party and the scene around her.

Dagenham, Eighth Month, 24*th.*—Upon my return home to Dagenham this day week, in the pony chair, with little Edmund Gurney, there was a severe thunder storm the greater part of the way, but I felt quite easy to persevere through it.   But when I arrived at the Chequers Inn, I thought another storm was coming, and went in.   We had been there but a few minutes, when we saw a bright flash of lightning, followed instantaneously by a tremendous clap of thunder, upon being asked whether I was alarmed, I said that I certainly was and did not doubt that an accident had happened near to us.   My dear husband who was in it, arrived safely, but in a few minutes, a young man was carried in dead, struck with the lightning in a field close by.   I felt our escape—yet still more the awful situation of the young man, who was a sad character; he had been at the Meeting at Beacontree Heath.   This awful event produced a very serious effect in the neighbourhood, so much so, that we believed it right to invite all the relations of the young man (a bad set) and the other young men of the neighbourhood to meet us in the little Methodist Meeting House, which ended in one more rather large Public Meeting.   The event and circumstances altogether made it very solemn, it appeared to set a seal to what had passed before in our other Meetings.   My belief is, they have had a stirring effect in this neighbourhood, but they have been very humbling to me; the whole event of this young man's awful death has much confirmed me in the belief, that our concern was a right one, and tended to prepare the minds of the people to profit by such a lesson.   My dear brother and sister Buxton and their Priscilla were with us at many of our Meetings.

27th.—We are just about leaving this place. I have endeavoured to promote the moral and religious good of the people since the Meetings, by establishing libraries of tracts and books at different places, and my belief is, that my humble labours have not been in vain, nor I trust will they be. I have felt so strikingly the manner in which the kindness and love of the neighbourhood has been shown to me, after thus publicly preaching amongst them, and as a poor frail woman advocating boldly the cause of Christ; I expected rather to be despised, whereas, it is apparently just the reverse. The clergyman and his wife almost loading us with kindness, the farmers and their wives very kind and attentive, the poor the same; I felt how sweet it is to be on good terms with all—one day drinking tea at the parsonage, abounding with plate, elegancies, and luxuries, the next day at the humble Methodist shoemaker's, they having procured a little fresh butter, that I might take tea under their roof; the contrast was great, but I can indeed see the same kind Lord over all, rich to all, and filling the hearts of His servants of very different descriptions, with love to each other.

In the autumn, Mrs. Fry accompanied her husband into some of the South-Western Counties.

Sand Rock Hotel, Tenth Month, 9th.—This is the place in the Isle of Wight, where my most beloved sisters Rachel and Priscilla spent a winter. I may truly say, since coming to this beautiful and interesting spot, my heart has been much tendered, in remembering those so inexpressibly dear, feeling deeply, that their places here know them no more ; it has revived a very strong feeling respecting the past. Their course finished, mine not yet fully run ; and as I am deeply sensible that I cannot keep alive my own soul, oh may He, who remains to be our light and our life, keep me alive unto Himself, until He may fit me, by His own Almighty power and unmerited mercy, to enter a new life with all His saints in glory.

Barnstaple, 23rd.—First-day morning.—My distress is great this morning, owing to the steam-packet, with our dearest son Gurney, not arriving as we expected last evening. I have passed

10

a conflicting night ; my husband is gone to Ilfracombe, in hopes of hearing something of the packet, and seeing after our dear boy, if he arrives, I stayed, because I thought that duty pointed out attending the little Meeting here, but I feel nervous, afflicted, and desolate.   I believe it well, to be now and then brought to these trials of faith and of patience—may I not say, like the disciples formerly, " help Lord or I perish ;" may my experience be this day, that I cried unto the Lord in my trouble, and He delivered me out of my distresses.   Oh, gracious Lord ! quiet my troubled mind, increase my hope, trust, and full reliance upon Thee, upon Thy wisdom, Thy love, and Thy mercy, both as it respects myself and my most dear children, particularly this beloved boy—give me faith to do Thy will this day, and even to prove a helper to those amongst whom my lot may be cast, and if Thou seest meet, give me help from trouble, for vain is the help of man in these extremities.

Linton, 27th.—I heard before I went to Meeting (at Barn-staple), that the people of Ilfracombe were not much alarmed for the packet.   How far my mind was influenced by this I cannot say, but I was favoured with a sweet calm in Meeting, and was enabled, I trust faithfully, to attend to the openings of duty there, to my own relief and peace, and I hope to the comfort and edification of those present. I had hardly entered the Friend's house afterwards, when the glad tidings came of my dearest Gurney's safe arrival.   I have not for some time felt so much joy, I might almost say, that my heart rejoiced and leaped for joy; and I was enabled not only in heart, but on sitting down to dinner with my friends, to return thanks to Him, who in His tender mercy, granted me this deliverance.

Shortly after this anxiety, when at Ilfracombe, a woman asked me if I should like to see a poor man, who was wrecked, and had had a very wonderful escape, the night before Gurney was on the sea; of course I assented, and Gurney, the woman and I, set off to see him. When we arrived at his cottage, we found a very fine, rather tall young man, who appeared to have been much bruised, shaken, and wounded, with a nice looking young woman his wife; the house very clean, and a few books—but one particularly struck our attention—a Bible, with an inscription upon it

in gilt letters, to this effect, " In commemoration of the coura-
geous conduct of Samuel Marshall, in saving the lives of two
women (who had been out on a Sunday party, a third was
drowned) off the pier at Ilfracombe." It appeared by the short
history of this young man, that he had from his great courage,
good swimming, and kindness to others, been at different times the
means of saving eight lives at least; he had gone out to ships
in danger, near Ilfracombe, where, from the rocky nature of the
coast, there often are shipwrecks. His own simple story about
himself, was as follows:—He was fishing in a small boat with
two other men; about twelve o'clock at night, a sudden squall or
land wind blew from between the hills, he called out to his companions, " we are lost;" the boat capsized, they, poor fellows,
prayed for mercy and sank. Marshall knowing his great power of
swimming, would not give himself up, but caught hold of an oar,
which proved to be a good one, nearly new; and although he
knew that he was a mile from the shore, and the sea in consequence of this land wind very boisterous, he felt it right at least
to make the effort to reach land. He soon found that with all
his clothes on, it would be impossible, but how to take them off
was the difficulty; his presence of mind appears to have been
wonderful, he first got off his jacket, then his trowsers with
extreme difficulty, because they became entangled in his feet, but
by a violent effort he succeeded ; he then found he could not
well get rid of his shirt, nor swim with it on. He was driven
to great extremity, his shirt being a new stout cotton one—he
therefore once more made a violent effort, and tore it down in
front, but the hem was so strong, that he there stopped, this he
put to his mouth and bit it through; he then swam on until
he nearly reached the shore, where the breakers ran so high that
he lost his oar, once more, he almost entirely gave up hopes,
but resolved on one last effort, and found himself thrown upon
a rock very seriously bruised; he climbed beyond the reach of
the water, and laid himself down, cold, hungry and exhausted,
either to perish or to rest. He told me that, it being quite
dark, he could not tell where he was cast ashore, but he was
fully sensible that it must be where the rocky high cliffs could
be only here and there climbed by man—his anxiety was con-

sequently great, till day dawned, when he saw some sheep feeding up the cliff side. He was sure that wherever sheep could go, he could climb. As his poor feet were sadly cut, he took his stockings, (which he still had on) and bound them round his feet with his garters; with this exception, he ascended the rough cliff naked, his exhaustion and fatigue great indeed. After walking awhile, he arrived at a farm-house; the farmer took him for a lunatic, and at first spoke to him sharply, but soon finding his real case, he took him in, and treated him with the utmost hospitality. The farmer's wife prepared him a bed. I now stop my narrative to say, that from my conversation with Samuel Marshall, I took him to be a man actuated by religious principles, but not possessing an enlightened understanding on these subjects, one who endeavoured to do, as far as he knew it, his duty, which he had so remarkably shown in risking his own life, to save the lives of others, particularly in the instance of the women, who were poor and unable to remunerate him. I was strongly reminded in hearing of his deliverance of these words of Scripture, "with the merciful Thou wilt show Thyself merciful." The poor man said, also, that he prayed constantly when the salt water was not in his mouth, which showed on the one hand, his value for prayer, and on the other, his ignorance in supposing that when he could not speak, he would not be equally heard by Him, who knoweth the most secret desire of the heart. However, as I doubt not his prayers were offered in sincerity, they appear to have been accepted and answered. He was carried home to his sorrowful wife, who had heard of the boat being lost, and did not know that her husband was saved.

The mother of one of the other men, I found in the deepest distress, almost out of her mind. I tried to pour a little balm into her deep wounds, by endeavouring to lead her to look to Him, who can alone heal and help in our greatest trials.

Upton Lane, Eleventh Month, 16th.—I felt greatly helped in the quiet performance of my duties yesterday up to a certain time, when, I believe, I gave way a little to natural infirmity about a trifle, and found how soon a cloud may be brought over the best principle, and what care and watchfulness is needed; and if there be the least fall, how necessary immediately to have recourse to the justifying principle of faith, that no further separation take place from good. I fully believe, that our spiritual enemy remains the accuser of the brethren, and endeavours, when he sees those, who desire to serve the Lord give way, even in a trifle, to take advantage of it to discourage them, and further to insinuate himself into their hearts. It is I believe one of the most important points in the Christian life, if we find ourselves tripping in thought, word, or deed, immediately to fly to the fountain that is set open for the unclean, that we may at once be cleansed, and obtain peace with God, through our Lord and Saviour Jesus Christ. Oh! for a little help this day, to come to the living fountain, that I may be fitted for my Master's service, and enter it with a quiet mind. Lord let it be so.

Twelfth Month, 20th.—I am once more favoured, after being far from well, with a renewal of health and power, to enter my usual engagements, public and private. Yesterday, I went to town,—first attended the Newgate Committee, then, the British Society, which was very encouraging to me; there were many present, of different denominations of Christians, and a sweet feeling of love and unity pervaded the whole. Elizabeth Dudley spoke in a lively manner, and I had to pray. There is still much ground for encouragement in the prison cause, I believe a seed is sown in it, that *will* grow and flourish, I trust, when some of us are laid low. It is a work that brings with it a peculiar feeling of blessing and peace; may the Most High continue to prosper it! Afterwards I went to Clapham to visit a poor dying converted Jew, who had sent a letter to beg me to go and see him; my visit was highly interesting. I often wish for the pen of a ready writer, and the pencil of an artist, to picture some of the scenes that I am brought into. A man of a pleasing countenance, greatly emaciated, lying on a little white bed, all clean and in order, his Bible by his side, and animated almost beyond description at seeing me; he kissed my hand, the tears came into his eyes, his poor face flushed, and he was ready almost to raise himself out of his bed. I sat down, and tried to quiet him, and by degrees succeeded. We had a very interesting conversation; he had been in the practice of frequently attending my readings at Newgate, apparently with great attention ; latterly, I had not seen him, and was ready to suppose, that like many others, his zeal was of short duration, but I lately heard that he had been ill. He is one of those Jews, who have felt perfectly liberated from keeping any part of the Law of Moses, which some other converted Jews, yet consider themselves bound to observe. I found that when he used to come so often to Newgate, he was a man of good moral character, seeking the truth. But to go on with my story—in our conversation, he said, that he felt great peace, no fear of death, and a full reliance upon his Saviour for salvation ; he said that his visits to Newgate had been to him beyond going to any church—indeed, I little knew how much was going on in his heart. He requested me to read a Psalm that I had read one day in Newgate, the 107th. This I did, and he appeared deeply to feel it, particularly as my dear friends and I made our little remarks in Christian freedom as we went along, truly, I believe (as Friends say) in the life. The poor Jew prayed very strikingly ; I followed him, and returned thanks ; what a solemn, uniting time it was! The poor Jew said, " God is a spirit, and they that worship Him, must worship Him in spirit and in truth," as if he felt the sprituality of the Christian administration. His countenance lightened with apparent joy, when he expressed his undoubted belief that he should soon enter the kingdom, and that I should, before long, follow him ; then he gave me his blessing, and took leave in much tenderness, showing every mark he could of gratitude and love. He did not accept any gift of money, saying, that he wanted no good thing, as he was most kindly provided for by serious persons in the neighbourhood.

I arrived at home, about eight o'clock, peaceful, after my day's work, but humbled, because of the great imperfection even in what may be called our works of righteousness, and the need even in these, of pardon for the evil, that may have crept in, through the sacrifice that atoneth for all sin, even for the iniquity of our Holy Things.*

* After about two or three weeks, I received an account of the peaceful end of this poor Jew.

But a few days remained to the close of the year, filled as it had been, by incessant occupation and much bodily fatigue: but even in that short time, another call was to be made upon her time and feelings.

Mrs. Elizabeth Fry her sister-in-law, had continued to reside at Plashet, in a cottage which she had built on a part of the property many years before. With her lived an elder cousin, Mrs. Sarah Fry. She was one of kindly cheerful nature; the children, the poor, but especially any one in a scrape or difficulty, or a little in disgrace with the rest of the world, were sure to share her peculiar protection and kindness. Their pleasant pretty residence was a happy retreat to the tired and invalided—in so much peace and quiet did they pursue the even tenor of their way. In peace and calm emphatically, was the journey of one of them now about to terminate.

Last Third day, I went to Plashet Cottage to see my dear sister Elizabeth Fry, and my cousin Sarah Fry, both of them ill in bed with severe colds. Dear cousin Sarah was full of lively conversation, I much enjoyed her company, and waiting on them both, and left them tolerably comfortable, but on Fourth day morning I was sent for in great haste, understanding that dear cousin Sarah was much more ill. When my husband and I arrived at the cottage, we found her dead. It was a considerable shock, and very affecting, still not without strong consolation on her account, for my belief is, that she was one of the retired, humble devoted believers in and followers of the Lamb, that she was indeed one of his redeemed ones, ready to depart and be with Him for ever. It was particularly sweet to observe the work of grace appear to increase with her years, and her light to shine brighter and brighter, as her outward powers declined. This always strikes me as a sure mark of living faith, because it is natural, as infirmities of body increase, for infirmity of mind and temper to increase also, but it was very different with her; the gentle and sweet, cheerful and lamblike spirit, appeared to abound more and more as her years increased. I could hardly help desiring, if ready, to be favoured with such a translation from time to eternity. My dear sister is very unwell, but much supported under this trial; she says, that she has been shielded as on every side, and though unworthy of it, wonderfully upheld. This was one of those scenes I long to have pictured—the sweet appearance of dear Sarah Fry's remains lying by dear Elizabeth's side, who looked so wonderfully quiet and supported, though so very ill. It really was no common sight, the living and the dead thus together.

First Month, 2nd, 1832.—I think I have seldom entered a year with more feeling of weight than this. As the clock was striking twelve, the last year closing and this beginning, I found myself on my knees by my bed-side, looking up to him who had carried me and mine through the last year, and could only really be our Helper in this. We have had the subject of marriage much before us this last year, it has brought us to some test of our feelings and principles respecting it. That it is highly desirable and important to have young persons settle in marriage, particularly young men, I cannot doubt, and that it is one of the most likely means of their preservation, religiously, morally and temporally. Moreover, it is highly desirable, to settle with one of the same religious views, habits and education, as themselves, more particularly for those, who have been brought up as Friends, because their mode of education is peculiar; but, if any young persons upon arriving at an age of discretion, do not feel themselves really attached to our peculiar views and habits, then, I think their parents have no right to use undue influence with them, as to the connexions they may incline to form, provided they be with persons of religious lives and conversation. I am of opinion, that parents are apt to exercise too much authority upon the subject of marriage, and that there would be more really happy unions, if young persons were more left to their own feelings and discretion. Marriage is too much treated like a business concern, and love, that essential ingredient, too little respected in it. I disapprove the rule of our Society, that disowns persons

H 2

for allowing a child to marry one not a Friend—it is a most undue and unchristian restraint, as far as I can judge of it.

I see and feel the present to be a stirring time in our family, and in our country also. The cholera is an anxious thing; the stir about the Reform Bill, the general spirit of insubordination amongst people, and the clashing amongst the highly professing in the religious world, I consider also to be serious; but I do not take the violent alarm that some do, as to the state of the times, or as to any very great event being about to take place. Some are of opinion, that the second coming of our blessed Lord is just at hand. As we are sure at all events, that He will soon come to us individually, may we above all things seek to be found ready for that day.

Upton, Second Month, 21st.—We have lately been brought to feel very seriously the approach of the cholera to our own borders, as it is said to have been as near as Limehouse. I have not generally felt any agitating fear, but rather the weight of the thing, and desirous that it should prove a stimulus to seek more diligently after eternal things, and to be ready spiritually for whatever may await us; and outwardly to use all proper precautions. I have desired earnestly, that we should do our very utmost to protect our poor neighbours, by administering to their many wants. This led me to make some efforts with some of our women Friends, also with some other kind and influential people, and although perhaps thought by some a busybody in it, yet more has been already accomplished, than I could have looked for. The poor are likely to be really helped and cared for. In such works of charity, I always desire to be preserved from a forward spirit, or an over active one, yet on the other hand, when I feel any thing laid upon me, as I did in this instance, I feel much bound to work in it, even through some discouragement and opposition; I mostly find in such cases, that way has been made for me, as if He, who called me to the work was indeed with me in it. I was too poorly to go to our Monthly Meeting to-day, which I do not much regret, as our dearest son Joseph was to send in his resignation of membership; I so much feel it, that I think perhaps, I am better away. I believe he has done what he now thinks best; there I leave it, and though I certainly have much felt his leaving a Society, I so dearly love, the principles of which I so much value, yet no outward names are in reality of much importance in my view, nor do I think very much of membership with any outward sect or body of Christians—my feeling is, that if we are but living members of the Church of Christ, this is the only membership essential to salvation. Belonging to any particular body of Christians has, I see, its disadvantages, as well as advantages, it often brings into the bondage of man, rather than being purely and simply bound to the law of Christ; though I am fully sensible of its many comforts, advantages and privileges. Earnestly do I desire for this dear child, that his Lord may make his way clear before him, that he may be truly here a member of the militant Church of Christ, and hereafter of His Church triumphant.

Third Month, 21*st.*—To day is proclaimed " a fast-day" on account of the cholera; it is one of those occasions, in the observance of which we must each follow our own consciences. If the government of a country could make a people keep a day really holy unto the Lord, in real fasting, penitence and prayer, much good would result, but this, no government can do, and I fear that the present will rather be made a day of lightness and recreation. However, those who do keep it seriously, I trust will be blessed in so doing, and their prayers answered, and that this awful disease may be (if right for us) checked in its progress.

I rather feel having to go before the Committee of the House of Commons, on the subject of prisons. May any good to this important cause be done by it, and may I be helped to do my part with simplicity, as unto God, and not unto man!

The object of this Committee, was to ascertain the best mode of Secondary Punishment, so as to be the most effectual in repressing crime. The points Mrs. Fry earnestly insisted upon were these :—

The expediency of having matrons, and only female officers in female prisons, and as much as possible in convict-ships also.

The necessity of employment, and the advantage of its being suited to the sex, at all events with those least hardened, or who show symptoms of amendment.

The importance of separation, especially at night.

The good to be derived from compulsory instruction, where prisoners are unable to read.

That solitude does not prepare women for returning to social and domestic life, or tend so much to real improvement, as carefully arranged intercourse during part of the day with one another, under the closest superintendence and inspection, constant occupation, and solitude at night.

The value of the visits of ladies to prisons, as a check upon the matron and female officers, and an incentive to good conduct among the prisoners; but on this point her own evidence may be adduced.

Every matron should live upon the spot, and be able to inspect them closely by night and by day, and when there are sufficient female prisoners to require it, female officers should be appointed, and a male turnkey never permitted to go into the women's apartments; I am convinced, when a prison is properly managed, it is unnecessary, because, by firm and gentle management, the most refractory may be controlled by their own sex. But here I must put in a word respecting ladies visiting. I find a remarkable difference depending upon whether female officers are superintended by ladies or not. I can tell, almost as soon as I go into the prison, whether they are or not, from the general appearance, both of the women and their officers. One reason is, that many of the latter are not very superior women, not very high, either in principle or habit, and are liable to be contaminated; they soon get familiar with the prisoners, and cease to excite the respect due to their office, whereas, where ladies go in once or twice, or three times in a week, the effect produced is decided. Their attendance keeps the female officers in their places, makes them attend to their duty, and has a constant influence on the minds of the prisoners themselves; in short, I may say, after sixteen years' experience, that the result of ladies of principle and respectability superintending the female officers in prisons and the prisoners themselves, has far exceeded my most sanguine expectations. In no instance have I more clearly seen the beneficial effects of ladies visiting and superintending prisoners, than on board the convict-ships. I have witnessed the alterations since ladies have visited them constantly in the river. I heard formerly of the most dreadful iniquity, confusion, and frequently great distress; latterly I have seen a very wonderful improvement in their conduct. And on the voyage, I have most valuable certificates to show the difference of their condition on their arrival in the colony. I can produce, if necessary, extracts from letters. Samuel Marsden, who has been chaplain there a good many years, says, it is quite a different thing; that they used to come in the most filthy, abominable state, hardly fit for any thing, now they arrive in good order, in a totally different situation, and I have heard the same thing from others. General Darling's wife, a very valuable lady, has adopted the same system there; she has visited the prison at Paramatta, and the same thing respecting the officers is felt there, as it is here. On the continent of Europe, in various parts—Petersburg, Geneva, Turin, Berne and Basle, and some other places—there are corresponding societies, and the result is the same in every part. In Berlin, they are doing wonders, I hear a most satisfactory account; and in Petersburg, where, from the barbarous state of the people, it was said it could not be done, the conduct of the prisoners has been perfectly astonishing, and an entire change has been produced.

Upton Lane, Sixth Month, 3rd.—We have just concluded the Yearly Meeting. It has been in some respects a marked one, and I hope an instructive one. We had much advice, particularly from one Friend, upon the subject of Christian faith; holding up much more decidedly to our view, the doctrine of the Atonement, showing, that our actuating motive in all things must be faith in Him who suffered for us, and love for Him who first loved us. In this I quite agree, but I felt with her, as well as with some others, that they strain the point of all our

minor testimonies being kept to, as a necessary proof of this
love. I fully believe, that many of us are called thus to prove
our love ; but I also believe there are some, if not many amongst
us, to whom this does not apply, and that we cannot, therefore,
lay down the rule for others. I had to speak decidedly twice
in the Meetings ; once in the first Meeting, acknowledging the
loving-kindness and tender mercy of our God as manifested to
us during the year that was passed, and what an inducement it
should be to love and faithfulness. This appeared greatly to
relieve and comfort many minds, for they freely spoke to me
about it afterwards. I had particularly to make allusion to the
cholera not having made further devastations amongst us. I
had in another Meeting in a similar way to return thanks, and
pray for us, as a Society, and for the Universal Church. I also
had from a deep feeling of duty, to express my thankfulness,
that the Christian standard had been upheld amongst us, so
much encouragement given to read the scriptures, and attend to
their holy precepts ; but I felt a fear, whether the influence of
the Holy Spirit, as our guide, had been quite enough dwelt upon,
which, as a fundamental part of our principles, I trusted we
should ever maintain. I also expressed my desire, that the fruits
of the Spirit should be more manifest amongst us, not only in
our peculiar testimonies, but in the subjection of our tempers
and wills, which I thought to be much wanted, fearing that some
maintained our testimonies, more from expediency than principle,
which produced great inconsistency of conduct. I then added
my earnest hope, that individually and collectively, we should
stand open to improvement, making this our prayer : " That
which I see not, teach Thou me ;" that we should be willing to
be taught of God immediately and instrumentally, that our light
might shine brighter and brighter to the perfect day.

9th.—I yesterday was favoured to get through the British
Society Meeting. It was to me a very serious occasion ; our
different reports were highly satisfactory and encouraging ; but
I felt it laid upon me to speak so decidedly on some points, that
I could not fully enjoy it. After the British Society report was
read, I first endeavoured to show the extreme importance of the
work in which we were engaged, and the best means of producing

the desired effect, of reforming the criminal; but what most deeply impressed me was, considering the awful extent of existing crime, and the suffering and sorrow produced by it—how far the conduct of the higher classes may influence that of the lower, and tend in many ways to the increase of evil, by ladies not setting a religious example to their servants, nor instructing them in the right way; by not keeping the Sabbath strictly,— by very late hours, and attending public places,—by vanity in dress, and by hurrying mantua-makers and milliners, and so causing them to oppress and overwork their young women,— by not paying their bills themselves, or through some confidential person, but trusting them to young or untried servants, thus leading to dishonesty on their parts, or that of the tradespeople,—by allowing their maid-servants or char-women to begin to wash at unseasonable hours, and consequently to require ardent spirits to support them. Then I represented how much they might do to promote good and discourage evil, by educating the poor religiously in infant and other schools, by watching over girls after they leave schools, until placed in service, and by providing for them suitable religious, instructive and entertaining books; also, by forming libraries in hospitals, and workhouses, and by preventing the introduction of irreligious and light books. I also urged the establishment of district societies. These things I had forcibly and freely to express, showing the blessing of promoting good and the woe of encouraging evil.

Seventh Month, 14*th.*—I have just parted from my dear son Gurney, for a sojourn on the Continent, with three of his young friends, and their tutor. It has been a subject of serious feeling giving him up, but there has appeared no other opening so suitable for him. This has arisen in a very satisfactory manner, and as far as I can judge from his character, it appears the most likely means for his improvement; there are remarkable advantages likely to attend them, from my serious friends abroad being interested for them. I have been enabled, in faith, to commit him to the keeping of our Heavenly Father. In His mercy do I hope, above all, that He may keep him from evil, and if consistent with His holy will, bring him back again in

peace and safety. Gracious Lord! grant for Thine own sake
that it may be so, and that this beloved child may so grow in
grace, that he may be enabled to resist the temptations that are
in the world. My prayers have also been raised for the other
dear children, particularly —————— whom I have felt much for,
and taken much pains in reading with him and Gurney in the
morning,—may it take deep root in their hearts.

To the gentleman who accompanied her son and his young
companions, she presented a written sketch of her wishes and
opinions. Some of these hints, are as follow :—

Never allow the boys to be out alone in the evening; nor to
attend any public place of amusement with any person, however pressing they may be. I advise, thy seeing that they
never talk when going to bed, but retire quietly after reading a
portion of the holy scriptures. In the morning, that they be as
quiet as possible, and learn their scripture texts, whilst dressing.
I recommend the party accepting all suitable invitations from
German families, as an important means of improving their
general knowledge, as well as their German. It must be remembered that no study is equal to that of mankind, and nothing so
likely to enlarge the mind as society with the good and the cultivated of every nation. I advise their taste for our best poets
being encouraged, by occasionally learning some by heart, and
reading it aloud. Also, their being led particularly to observe
and admire all the productions of nature, and to study geology,
&c. &c., as far as their time will admit of it.

Above all things, and far beyond every other consideration,
mayst thou be enabled to teach them, that the first and great
object of life is, to seek the kingdom of God and to do His will.

Upton Lane, 19*th.*—I have been brought very low on
account of one of my dear children, who has since her return
home had a serious cough, united with great prostration of
strength, so as to excite our anxiety as to what it may end in;
besides this, the very important affair of last year is again

hanging over her. I deeply feel it, far more than I like to acknowledge to myself, or others, and am at times brought into deep conflict of spirit before the Lord. I must seek to have no will about her, much as I long naturally for her restoration; but, rather most earnestly pray, that, whatever our heavenly Father may do with her, He may keep her His own, that she may be a member of His militant church on earth, or of His triumphant church in heaven; and oh! may He be pleased to make the way clear for her and for all, that will conduce to peace here and happiness hereafter. Notwithstanding this weighty cloud, I believed it right to walk by faith, not by sight, and propose to my Monthly Meeting, to attend the Half Year's Meeting in Wales, next month, and ask also liberty for such other services as Truth might lead into; but I can hardly say how much it cost me.

Before leaving home for this journey, during which, she visited parts of Ireland, Elizabeth Fry, communicated her intention of visiting some of the county Gaols, to the Under Secretary of State, S. March Philips, Esq., and her wish to make arrangements by which ladies might be allowed to attend to the female prisoners confined in them. She received on this occasion, a highly gratifying communication, with permission to make its contents known, dated Home Office, August 10th, 1832, assuring her, that—" Lord Melbourne was fully sensible of the good which had been done by herself, and the ladies connected with her in many of the prisons; and of the great benefits derived from their exertions, by the female transports; and that his Lordship was anxious, that as far as it could be done, the Visiting Magistrates should favourably entertain and second her benevolent intentions."

Ninth Month, 18*th*.—We returned home from our journey last Sixth-day evening, having been absent just five weeks. We visited several places in the south of Ireland, a good many in Wales, and some in England. I think I never remember

8

taking a journey in which it was more frequently sealed to my own mind, that we were in our right places; through much difficulty, our way was opened to go, and to continue out. Though I believe we have scripture authority for it—still further confirmed, by the internal evidence of the power of the Spirit, and its external results,—yet, I am obliged to walk by faith rather than sight, in going about as a woman in the work of the ministry; it is to my nature a great humiliation, and I often feel it to be " foolishness," particularly in large Public Meetings, before entering upon the service; but generally, when engaged in the ministry, I find such an unction, and so much opening upon Christian doctrine and practice, that after a Meeting, I mostly say in my heart, " It is the Lord's doing, and marvellous in our eyes." Such was often the case in this journey. I felt, amongst Friends in Ireland, as if my service was to lead them from all external dependence, either on their membership in the Society, their high profession or their peculiar testimonies, and to show, that these things are only good as they spring from simple Christian faith and practice, and avail nothing, unless the heart be really changed and cleansed from sin, though I believed that these things would follow as the result to those who fill the important place in the church, that in my opinion, Friends are called to occupy. Above everything else, I endeavoured to lead all to the grand foundation of Christian faith and practice. My dear sister was much led in the same line of ministry.

On some occasions, I felt a far greater openness than others, I believe, in places, there was rather a jealousy over me, I apprehend that my believing it right, as much as possible, to avoid mysticism in my mode of expression, is not fully understood by all Friends; I desire to be sound, simple, and clear, and not to clothe anything in a mysterious garb, even if with individuals it might give it more weight. The unfeigned kindness shown me by several persons can never be forgotten by me.

We visited many Prisons, and had cause for deep humble thankfulness and rejoicing, to see how much has been done in this cause, and the effect of some of our labours when last in Ireland : it is marvellous to myself, how it has pleased my Lord

and Master to bless some of my unworthy labours. Now for the
narrative of the journey :—We set off under outward discouragement, more particularly two of my children being very unwell, but my dearest brother Samuel going with me, was a great
support, though I also felt the weight of taking him from his
family. We set off in his carriage, a very pleasant open one,
my sister Elizabeth Fry, my niece Sarah Gurney, Samuel, and
myself, the day fine, with all outward comforts and indulgences
—the Lord surely doth provide. We visited Cirencester on
First-day, Gloucester on Second-day, and so on to Brecon ;
taking Meetings, Prisons, &c., forming Committees as we went
in our way to Milford. There we had a most interesting time.
Crossing to Ireland, we all rather dreaded the weather being
stormy, and we much feared being ill ; however, by delaying
one day, we had a delightful voyage, and also a very satisfactory Meeting with the poor and the sailors, near Milford. We
met with a kind reception in Ireland ; I think I never felt more
in my right place, there appeared an indescribable evidence of
it. Now and then, a feeling of almost unmixed peace. Our
visit to Cork was highly interesting ; we were frequently in the
neighbourhood of cholera, and at times I felt fearful about it,
but generally was raised above it ; the weather was mostly fine,
and much of the country that we went through, lovely, so that
the journey was not without outward refreshment to me. We
saw grievous evils remaining in some Prisons, which we trust
that our visit may remedy, by bringing them to notice. At Car-
low, I had a deeply-interesting, and for a time, afflicting season,
hearing that my dearest Hannah had broken a blood-vessel on
the lungs, happily, the account did not arrive till a week after it
had happened, and with it came a second account much more
favourable. I was, in mercy, favoured with a trustful, hopeful
spirit ; happily, too, our steps were turned homewards. The
letters became more and more comfortable, so that we were
enabled to remain in Dublin the full time, to perform what we
believed to be our various calls of duty in that very important
and interesting place. We had a delightful passage from Dublin to Wales, of five hours and a half ; wind and all in our
favour, and a very satisfactory journey home.

Mrs. Fry returned, strengthened and refreshed by this journey. Matters of great import awaited her return, in the approaching marriages of two of her children. Her son William was now, almost for the first time, about to quit his parents' dwelling. His mother subsequently beheld his advance in the Christian life— from year to year she marked his exemplary fulfiment of all the relations of husband, son, father, master, friend, and lived long enough to see " the place that had known him, know him no more." With her whole heart could she then acknowledge, that God had led him, although by paths that she knew not, and by ways that she had not seen.

It is proposed, that my dear son William's marriage should take place in little more than a week. I cannot help feeling deeply giving him up. To have this dear child married, and not be able to be with him, is very affecting to me. With three children likely to marry out of the Society, and the life of one of them very uncertain, I have much, very much to feel; but respecting her and all of my children, if they do but get to the kingdom, I may be thankful! and shall I hold them back ?— My desires are unutterable, my prayers frequent and fervent, to be directed amidst all my difficulties, to do that which is right, —first in the sight of God, then in the view of my family, and lastly in that of the Society to which I belong.

Dagenham, Tenth Month, 3rd.—Here am I sitting in solitude, keeping silence before the Lord ; on the wedding day of my beloved son William.* As I could not conscientiously attend the marriage, I believed it right to withdraw for the day. Words appear very inadequate to express the earnestness—the depth of my supplications for him and for his—that the blessing of the Most High may rest upon them. I was yesterday enabled, when with him and his sisters alone, to pour forth my soul in prayer for him, and read such portions of scripture as I thought would be for his good and comfort; he was low, and so we were all, but as the day advanced, we brightened, and as dear William himself

* October 3rd.—William Storrs Fry married Julia Sally, eldest daughter of Sir John Hewry Selly, Bart.

said, there appeared a spirit of good over us. I stayed with him almost all day, and went in the evening with him to Ham House, where their kindness was almost unbounded. We then went to our dear friends the Pelly's, where I had a warm reception; they very sweetly bear with my scruples, for it must appear odd, very odd to them, my not feeling it right to attend the wedding of such a son—but my heart is full of love to them. Though I do not see as they see, I most deeply feel that all who truly love Him are one in Christ, yet the more simple and spiritual, the administration of religion, the more I believe we are enabled to abide in Him, therefore I feel zealous, perhaps too much so, to have my children thorough Friends; but of this I now see little or no hope, though I expect many of them to be serious in another line, and fully believe, that my striving and labours have been blessed, in leading them to a love of holiness and true righteousness, and beyond all of their Saviour. We concluded the evening in quietness, and strange to say, I slept well and peacefully. This morning, we almost all assembled before breakfast, with one or two valuable dependants and William Champion Streatfeild with us; I was enabled to exhort earnestly, and to pray fervently, not only for the beloved couple, but all the children, and those who were to be, or were already united to them, and for their children; for ourselves, household, &c. It was a very solemn time, and I humbly trust that the presence of the Lord was with us. I desired also to return thanks for this dear son in giving him up from my care, that he had been so much preserved from the evil which is in the world, that he had ever displayed such near love to me and to all of us, and had been so good a son to us. There is much to be thankful for respecting him, and though it has been a great disappointment his not marrying a Friend, yet there is also much to value in this connexion. I have a secret hope it may prove in the ordering of a kind Providence for his good. As for myself, I sit solitary in many things, but I thought to-day (from this wedding bringing these things home to me.)—Have I not my Lord as my friend, and my comforter? and is He not as a husband to all the members of His church? and am I not often satisfied and refreshed by His love? I may indeed say I am— so that I am ready to trust, that the great and curious overturnings that my family have met with, will in the end work for good, through the love and unmerited mercy of God in Christ Jesus ; and that we may more and more all become one in Him ! Amen.

A month afterwards, another child was married. Mrs. Fry considered that the case of a daughter was different to that of a son, and the wedding taking place at her own house, that it was for her to remain at home.

Upton Lane, Eleventh Month, 5th.—Last Fourth-day, the 31st of the Tenth Month, my dearest Hannah was married to William Champion Streatfeild. The morning was bright, the different families collected,—of course I was not present at the ceremony. The bride and bridegroom went to Ham House to take leave of their dear party ; they then came home, and we soon sat down to breakfast, about thirty in number. There appeared a serious and yet cheerful feeling over us. I felt prayer for them, but saw no opportunity vocally to express it. As we arose to leave the table, William Streatfeild the vicar of East Ham, returned thanks for the blessings received ; when, quite unexpectedly to myself, there was such a solemn silence, as if all were arrested, that I was enabled vocally to ask a blessing upon them, and to pray that the Most High would keep them and bless them, cause His face to shine upon them, and be gracious unto them, lift up the light of His countenance upon them, and give them peace ; and through His unbounded love, and unlimited mercy in Christ Jesus, that He would grant them enough of the fatness of the earth, and so cause the dew of heaven to descend upon them, that they might be fruitful to His praise, and live to His glory, and be His in time, and His to all eternity. After a short further pause, we withdrew, walked in the garden, or rested, until they left us. The tears often flowed from my eyes in parting from this beloved child.

The little band at Upton Lane was now greatly diminished. Mr. and Mrs. Fry, with the two daughters who remained at home, sought, after these events, the refreshment of a visit to their relatives in Norfolk. They first went to Lowestoft, and remained some days at the vicarage; there Mrs. Fry saw the schools just established, united in the cottage-readings, and entered warmly into the various interests of the place. Her sister, Mrs. Cunningham, wrote at the time her own impressions of this visit :—

"November 22nd.—We have had the treat and great advantage of a visit from our dearest sister. She was encouraged to come and assist us in the formation of our District Society, which, in this large place, we find to be essential for the right working of the parish. We are most thankful for the assistance of our dear sister (our brother and two of our nieces accompanied her); it is almost like having an angel visitor, so full of loveliness and grace is she. On Sunday, my dearest sister being at Pakefield with the Friends, induced my remaining all day there. She drank tea with me, at the Hawtreys. Mr. Hawtrey and she had some animated and delightful conversation, before we went down to the lecture in the school-room; my sister accompanied us there, and some of the other friends joined us. After the usual singing and prayer, Mr. Hawtrey read very impressively the latter part of the third of Ephesians; we then had silence, after which she arose, and beautifully addressed the meeting, on the necessity of domestic and private religion, and enlarged a good deal on the duty, spirit, and manner, in which scripture should be read and studied, it would not do to hear it only in public service. After the powerful outward means which had been granted to the people of Pakefield, how were they called upon, to examine, and digest for themselves, the written *word* of God. Then, in a full and beautiful prayer, she seemed to bring the blessing of heaven upon us. I hardly know any scriptural treat so great, as uniting with her in *prayer!* it is such a heavenly song —so spiritual—so elevating, enjoying glimpses, as it were, of the eternal world! Oh! may we long retain the power and the blessing of it! Her last short address was very impressive, that we should not come short of our rank in righteousness;

that we should follow our crucified Redeemer, in humility, meekness, and self-denial, that we should walk worthy of our very high calling, &c. Mr. Hawtrey ended with a very feeling prayer, and after taking an affectionate leave of the people, I drove our beloved sister home. On Monday, we were all in movement, in preparation for our District Society Meeting; this was held at our house, and well attended. Our dear sister displayed much of her tact and power, and gave us the *greatest* assistance; how marvellously gifted she is! Through her influence, all parties were brought together, and the District Society begun under most favourable auspices, the town was divided, and every arrangement made, according to her advice. Our meeting was highly satisfactory, and promised the most favourable results, every one seemed willing to yield to her wisdom and eloquence. What a power of communicating good she possesses! what a faithful steward in that which is committed to her! A very interesting party dined with us, which increased much in the evening. After the reading, our dearest sister prayed most beautifully to our comfort and edification. On Tuesday, we went off to breakfast with the Hawtreys. As usual, we met with a warm reception, and had a cheerful, pleasant talking breakfast with them; the family service afterwards was peculiarly edifying. Mr. Hawtrey read the fourteenth of John; our dearest sister's address to the children, and to the parents, and then to Mr. Hawtrey, as a minister, was most touching and edifying. Surely these times do leave a peculiar savour, which is not to be forgotten; adding to the precious seasons which are foretastes of heaven. Her mind appears to me in more lively exercise, and more gifted than ever, rich both in grace and gifts. She is indeed beloved of the Lord, and dwells in safety by Him. After this she paid visits to the Friends, and we did not return till towards the latter end of the morning; the evening was occupied by the Committee for the District Society. Wednesday was a full day, my sister and I walked about most of the morning, visiting the schools, making calls, &c. &c. Nothing can be more benevolent and beautiful than her spirit, overflowing with love and tenderness. Our dinner-party was not very large, but cheerful and pleasant; the first part of the evening was necessarily

devoted to the agreeable, after which, my little society of
women, and several others, assembled in the parlour, my beloved
sister went to them, and gave them a little sketch of her Newgate histories. We afterwards all removed into the drawing-room,
and had a beautiful meeting, very suited to the subject we had
been upon. My husband took the Prodigal Son as the subject
for reading, which my sister applied to herself, and to all of us,
as being led as penitents to return to our Father's house, and oh !
the display of mercy, and of goodness, and long suffering, in the
exquisite character of the God of Israel. The prayer at the conclusion was as usual, as like an air from heaven. Our large
party then broke up in much love. On Thursday, our beloved
sister left us, after again enjoying prayer together, and commending each other affectionately to the care and keeping of
the good Shepherd of Israel."

They then went to Earlham—that home of the past! afterwards to North Repps Hall. The all-absorbing subject of
Slavery was occupying Mr. Buxton's mind. It was to her most
interesting, to listen to his details of the struggle of the preceding
Sessions of Parliament, one replete with importance to this vast
question, now approaching the crisis of its fate. All but alone,
and nearly single-handed in the House, he had brought forward
a measure for emancipation, in opposition to the wishes of Government, at a cost of effort and self-sacrifice little known to
lookers on in general.

Her stay at North Repps Cottage delighted her; she visited
the schools, met the hardy fishermen of that boisterous coast, in
the school-rooms at Overstrand and Trimmingham, and partook,
as no common privilege, of social intercourse with the inmates
of that lovely retreat. Their journey concluded with visits to
Runcton and Lynn. The different administrations which they
had seen were very striking to her, and particularly cheering,
under the circumstances of her own family. To a sister she
wrote soon after her return home.

I think of your dear party with much interest, and feel the
sweet remembrance of having been with you, I hope that I
received profit, as well as pleasure, from it; indeed, I think our
journey was an instructive one in many ways. My desire is, as
I go along, to take a leaf out of every one's book ; and surely at
Lowestoft, Earlham, North Repps, Lynn, and Runcton, I might
do it. It is well to see the truth through different mediums ; for
however the colour of the glass that we see it through may vary,
the truth itself remains the same, and beholding it of many hues,
may be the means of throwing fresh light on diverse parts of
it. How does the knowledge of others often make us think
little of ourselves ! at least I find it so, and am much humbled
in most of your houses.

Upton Lane, First Month, 28*th*, 1833.—It has been a serious
time to the country, the cholera prevailing nearly throughout
England and Ireland. We were frequently where it was on our
journey, but were favoured to escape unhurt. A great stir in
the elections for the new Reform Parliament. Joseph Pease, a
Friend, admitted ; this opens a new door for our Society—to what
it will lead is doubtful. A war for a short time with Holland.
Much stirring in the world generally, religiously and politically
—great variety of sentiments. Notwithstanding all these things,
it appears to me, that the kingdom of God is spreading its pure,
blessed, and peaceable influence, and that the partition walls
that have been built up between Christians generally, are breaking down. The suppression of Slavery — the diminution of
Capital Punishment—the improvement in Prisons, and the state
of the poor prisoners—the spread of the Scriptures, also of the
Gospel to distant lands—the increase of education and knowledge generally, and many other such things, are truly encouraging. I do thankfully believe that there is a great and
glorious work going on, promoting the advancement of that
day, when the knowledge of God, and His glory, will cover the
earth as the waters cover the sea. For Thine own name's sake,
gracious Lord, hasten this day, when all flesh may see and rejoice in Thy salvation !

Fourth Month, 12*th*.—One of my near relations has died sud-

denly—my cousin Martha B——. I can hardly think why it
should have spread such an influence over me, as our spirits
were not particularly united here; but it may be so, for from
my own experience I am much inclined to believe in the
communion of spirits, both with those here, and those departed. I think it by no means impossible, that those who
remain a little longer to maintain the warfare, may sympathise
in spirit with those who have entered into their rest, and whose
warfare is accomplished. With my dearest and most beloved
sister Rachel, I have thought she has been as a ministering
spirit to me, and like one formerly, that her mantle has in
degree descended upon me, for I certainly have in some respects,
ever since that period, been under rather a different influence,
and have had different views and feelings. It may be only the
effect of her blessed example in life, and at last in death. I
desire neither to indulge imagination nor superstition on religious subjects; but some of these private views can harm no
one, and are a comfort to myself, and what is more, I think I
have scripture authority for them.

Sixth Month, 5th.—Yesterday, we finished the Yearly Meeting, as far as women have to do with it. I think, as it respects the
Society, it has been an important time; there is much stirring
amongst Friends, arising from a considerable number taking
apparently a much higher evangelical ground, than has generally
been taken by the Society, bordering, I apprehend in a few, on
Calvinism. This has caused strong alarm to some, far beyond
I believe what is needful, so great, however, as to produce something of two sets amongst us, and at times an uncomfortable
feeling. Still harmony has prevailed, and through all, real Gospel Truth appears to me to be spreading amongst us.

Seventh Month, 10th.—We have been favoured the last two
days, to have all our fifteen children around us, and the day
before yesterday, we had all to dine at our table, and our nine
grandchildren afterwards at dessert, our dearest sister Catherine
Gurney, the only other person present at table—(excepting our
sister Elizabeth Fry and Rebecca Sturges, for a short time), it
was a deeply interesting, and to me touching, as well as pleasing
sight. It is remarkable, their none fully seeing religious truth

with me, yet I cannot repine, if I may but see real marks of the Christian life. Outwardly, through all our difficulties, I could not but feel how all have been provided for, and a liberal table spread before us. The married children all provided for, some abundantly—the grandchildren generally bringing up so well, is a great cause of thankfulness—I could not rejoice or give thanks as I desired, at our many unmerited mercies, but I felt bowed in spirit under a sense of them. We had a cheerful dinner, Rachel, the only one really out of health at this time ; but she enjoyed herself. After dinner, we walked a little about, then had tea. After tea, we read the 103rd Psalm, and I spoke to my children, earnestly impressing upon them the importance, now most of them were no longer under our restraint, that they might be conformed to the will of God, and be faithful stewards of His manifold gifts, so that if we went by different ways, we might in the end meet, where there will be no partition walls, no different ways, but all love, joy, peace, and union of view, and of conduct—I blessed them, and most earnestly prayed for all—we then separated in much near love.

CHAPTER XVIII.

At this period, in consequence of the marriages which had
taken place, and other circumstances, the press of interests and
engagements had become greater than the family could bear. A
long absence from home appeared the best resource, and after
some deliberation, the Island of Jersey was selected as the place
of retreat. Its lovely scenery and fine air afforded strong inducements ; augmented by the interest attached to the peculiar language, government, and internal regulations of the Channel
Islands, that only remnant of Norman ducal power, still united
with England. Some of the party preceded the rest, to prepare
for their mother's reception with the second detachment. They
had a long and stormy passage, and their first encounter with the
rocky approach to the island, from a boisterous sea in the obscurity of twilight, gave an unfavourable impression of the navigation, which their letters conveyed home. Mrs. Fry naturally
dreaded the sea, so that after receiving their accounts, she felt
peculiarly alive to the mercy and indulgence of a tranquil voyage.

She arrived in the morning—the lovely bay of St. Aubin's smooth, full and blue—the rocks mostly covered by the tide—the verdant island before her smiling in sunshine. A profusion of flowers and fruit ornamented the breakfast table that awaited her in "Caledonia Cottage," which had been engaged and prepared for their residence, and charmed with the beauties that surrounded them, they could hardly believe the discomforts that had attended the arrival of the first party. They were supplied with a few excellent letters of introduction amongst the island families, with some of whom friendships were formed, which lasted till the close of her life. The circumstances by which she was surrounded, were very congenial to her. The beauty of the scenery, the luxuriance of the productions, the prosperity of the inhabitants, the refinement and intellectual cultivation of the upper classes, combined with simplicity of habit and in many instances with true piety and active benevolence, rendered the period of her residence in Jersey one of peculiar refreshment and pleasure. With her husband and children, and a few of her intimate friends, she would often spend the day in the remote parts of the island, amongst the secluded and romantic bays of its northern coast. The little party would picnic in the open air, or, as was then a very common practice, in one of the empty rooms of the small barracks scattered round the coast; left under the care of some invalided soldier and his family. On these occasions, the tract bag was never forgotten—whilst the rest of the party were sketching or walking, she would visit the cottagers, and making herself as well understood as their antique Norman dialect permitted, would give her little French books, and offer the kind word of sympathy or exhortation. Alive to the beautiful, especially to the picturesque, and with her quick eye for the droll, the peculiarities of the Jersey Cottage and its inmates were all observed and enjoyed by her; the fire of Vráck (sea-weed) burning on the hearth, with a large kettle suspended over it, in which the soupe à la graisse, or potage, was preparing for the family repast; the knitting of the women from the wool of their own sheep, occasionally with the fleeces of one or two black ones intermingled to produce the desired grey tint; the dairy, and their far-famed cows tethered in picturesque little enclosures; orchards rich in fruit, and gardens painted and perfumed by the carnation, picotee, hydrangia, and many brilliant flowers that so peculiarly flourish there. Amidst these scenes, the summer passed away, but higher and more important objects were not unheeded. There was in the island, a little band of persons, in very humble life, who professed the principles of Friends, one or two only however being members of the Society. They assembled for worship on the Sunday morning, in the cottage of Jean Renaud, an old patriarch residing on the sea shore, about a mile from the town of St. Heliers. There was a quaint old-fashioned effect about the low large room in which they assembled, whilst from large bundles of herbs suspended from the beams to dry, a flower or a leaf would occasionally drop upon those sitting below.

The appearance of the congregation was in keeping with the apartment, seated on planks, supported by temporary props. An antique four-post bedstead stood in one corner; when the mistress of the house died, which occurred during their sojourn in Jersey, she was there laid out, a circumstance which did not prevent the Meeting assembling as usual, the drawn curtains screening the corpse from view. High-backed chairs were prepared for the seniors of the assembly, the younger members of Mrs. Fry's family appropriating to themselves the window seat. The novelty of the occasion was increased, by the English ministry having to be interpreted to render it comprehensible to the greater part of the hearers.

Nor were the Afternoon Meetings much less peculiar. They also were held at a private house, situated in the suburbs of the

town ; but the heat in-doors being considerable, the congregation not unfrequently moved to the small walled garden, and
sat beneath the shade of some ever-greens. This, however, was
found practically so inconvenient, that a room in the town was
engaged for the purpose, and properly fitted up. There, until
Elizabeth Fry left the island, large congregations assembled,
including many of the gentry and principal inhabitants ; these
meetings were exceedingly solemn and instructive. In this important service, she was greatly helped by the company of her
sister-in-law, Elizabeth Fry, with her friend and companion,
Rebecca Sturges. Philanthropic objects also presented themselves to her notice, especially the state of the Hospital, including
the Workhouse and Lunatic Asylum, and the Prison. Acts of
the British Parliament have no power in the Channel Islands,
as part of the ancient Duchy of Normandy, they are governed by
their own laws and customs. To explain these would involve
an historical and antiquarian discussion, out of place in a work
like the present. It is sufficient here to bring forward the result,
that none of the recent improvements in Prison Discipline had
been effected in Jersey. After repeatedly visiting the Prison,
and communicating with the authorities—she believed it the
best course to have a letter which she had addressed to them,
printed for circulation.

To the Authorities of the Island of Jersey, who have
the Direction and Management of the Prison and
Hospital.

Gentlemen,

Having been requested by a number of persons of influence
and respectability in this Island, to make known to the competent authorities my views on the subject of your Prison and
Hospital: I have decided on the present method of doing so, as

the most easy to myself, and the most likely to be accurately understood; and I trust you will excuse me, if the interest I feel in the unfortunate inhabitants of those, and similar institutions, should induce me to take the liberty of offering some strong and decided observations on their condition and management.

Our protracted residence in this beautiful and interesting Island, has afforded me a full opportunity of observing the manner in which the defective system pursued in the management of the Prison, appears to operate upon its inmates; and I feel it to be my duty to represent to you the effects, which my experience has taught me, must necessarily result from its operation; as being nothing less than a gradual but certain demoralization of the lower, and some of the middling classes of society; and the increase rather than the diminution of crime.

I shall begin by remarking, that the great and leading objects of Prison Discipline are in a very material degree overlooked.

Allow me to state, that the proper purpose which confinement in a prison is intended to accomplish—is not merely safe custody, but a suitable, and (if the imprisonment be just) a decided, but well and legally defined measure of punishment, of a nature tending to deter others from the commission of similar offences, and to produce salutary reform in the prisoners themselves; of these objects the only one noticeable by an observer in your prison, is (with the single exception of cases of solitary confinement) that of the safe custody of the person.

In order to attain the salutary penal effect of imprisonment, together with the reformation of offenders, and to prevent the contamination of association and example, I beg to observe, that in addition to the restraint and confinement of a prison, the following objects are necessary, viz:—

I. A full sufficiency of employment, proportioned to the age, sex, health, and ability of the offender.

II. As much wholesome privation of those comforts and enjoyments, which they might be able to obtain when at liberty, as is compatible, with the preservation of their health and strength.

III. A proper system of classification; consisting, in the
first place, of a total separation of the men from the women,
(which latter ought always to be under the superintendence of
one of their own sex) and next, a complete separation of
debtors from criminals, and of the tried from the untried, (and
were your prisoners numerous) of great criminals from misdemeanants ; but in the present case, it might suffice to separate
any very bad offenders from the rest, and except at stated times,
and under the constant observation of the Gaoler, or Turnkey,
no visitors whatever should be admitted to the tried criminals,
but in cases of special emergency.

IV. A fixed and suitable dietary for criminals, under the
management of a Gaol Committee, who ought to contract regularly for the articles of food ; and in no case should the prisoner be allowed to supply himself, or be farmed out to the
Gaoler, or to any other person whatsoever.

V. An absolute and total prohibition of spirits, wine, and all
fermented liquors, with a penalty for its infringement, except
when especially ordered by the medical attendant, (or a moderate portion of beer or cider might be allowed daily to those
who work hard, or are not strong in their bodily health)—also
a prohibition of cards, and all other gaming.

VI. A suitable prison-dress, with sufficiently marked distinction, which has been found by experience to have a humbling
and beneficial effect on the mind of the prisoners generally.

VII. A complete code of rules and regulations, for the direction and government of the Gaoler and other officers of the
prison, of the nature of those contained in an Act of Parliament, lately passed in England for the Government of Gaols,
4th Geo. IV., cap. 64.

VIII. A law or regulation, that should be imperative on Visiting Magistrates, or Gaol Committees, regularly and frequently
to visit the prison, and minutely to investigate the details of its
management.

IX. And lastly, but of primary importance, the due and stated
performance of Divine service, and regular religious and other
instruction of the prisoners ; every criminal who stands in need
of it, being taught to read and write.

By the system at present pursued, nearly all the above regulations and restraints are wholly omitted.

The criminals, instead of being kept to employment, are constantly idle.

Indulgences of nearly every description, and money may be
introduced to those who can procure them.

Prisoners of all descriptions are mixed up together, or at any
rate allowed frequent intercourse, male and female, criminal and
debtor, the hardened offender with the unpractised youth ; and
all of them (with the exception of the cases of solitary confinement alluded to) exposed to communication with the public
through the grating.

And in addition to these serious evils, your Gaoler is only
remunerated according to the numbers his prison contains, and
the quantity of spirits, wine, and other fermented liquors sold
to the prisoners ; consequently, however conscientious the individual may be, it necessarily involves his own personal interest
to make the prison agreeable to its inmates, that their stay may
be prolonged, and others induced to come in ; and my observation has led me to conclude, that this circumstance powerfully
operates in increasing the number of your prisoners, and the
duration of their stay.

I wish to add, that after having carefully examined the building and the ground appertaining to it, I am of opinion that these
crying evils might be obviated, and the needful improvements
introduced, and a House of Correction (which I consider indispensable) superadded to the present Prison, without any very
considerable expense, especially with the assistance of a person
from the Prison Discipline Society of London : and further, that
if the Gaoler and his wife received a moderate salary for their
attention to the male and female prisoners, it would not prove
more expensive than upon the present plan, more especially if
coupled with productive labour on the part of the prisoners, and
that it would essentially contribute to its improvement.

I am well aware that your island is not subject to the Acts of
the British Legislature ; but as the important improvements in
Prison Discipline, which have taken place òf latter years in the
dominions under its control, are the productions of men of large

experience, and have also been substantially introduced into the most enlightened European States, and the United States of America ; I trust you will not object to adopt the progressive wisdom of the age, from whatever quarter suggestions may arise, and I have therefore taken the liberty of appending some abstracts from Acts of Parliament of the 4th George IV., cap. 64, and others, on the subject of Prison Regulations, and which bear upon most of the points to which I have adverted.

I am, &c., &c.,

ELIZABETH FRY.

The funds devoted to the support of the Jersey Prison being wholly insufficient for that purpose, rendered it impossible to carry out any plan for classification and instruction.   It was a case in which nothing could be done effectually, without a complete renovation of the existing system.   It became, with Mrs. Fry, an object of continued interest and exertion, though years elapsed, and she again twice crossed to Jersey, before the desired ends were accomplished.

The Hospital was an institution of mixed character, intended not only for the sick and for accident cases, but it served also as a place of confinement for persons guilty of small offences, or wilfully idle or disorderly.

The building was being at this time enlarged, with a view to classifying its inmates.   In this institution she urged the necessity of—

I. An entire separation of men and women, both in house and yard, &c.

II. A subdivision of each sex into classes.   First, the sick ; secondly, the aged and infirm ; thirdly, the children; and fourthly, those who are confined for idleness or small offences ; the latter description to be allowed no intercourse with the other inmates, not to have the same comforts and indulgences, as this class of persons being admitted for vagrancy or crime has a great tendency to degrade the character of the institution, in the eyes of the honest and praiseworthy poor, who are admitted here for causes for which they are in no way blameable, and to render the most deserving objects in necessity, unwilling to avail themselves of the benefits of the charity.

A woman having become pregnant in the prison, was afterwards, on her discharge, sent on this account, as a punishment, to the hospital, and as she tried to escape from this new imprisonment, she was compelled to wear a chain and a heavy log by night and by day for several weeks. No instance can more forcibly prove the absolute necessity of improvement in both establishments.

The Treasurer and Master of the Hospital have endeavoured to improve the state of the lunatic cells; but they are only suitable for violent, incurable, or outrageous patients. Upon this point, an entirely different arrangement and mode of treatment is indispensable. It is a lamentable fact, that in this enlightened age, there can exist a Christian country, possessing so many advantages, and containing a population of nearly forty thousand persons, in which there is no public provision for the treatment and cure of persons labouring under that most melancholy and humiliating visitation of Divine Providence, mental aberration, whatever their sex or condition, other than cells suited only for the worst of condemned criminals.

Mrs. Fry took great pains in establishing a District Society at St. Heliers. A gentleman of high standing and importance in the island, thus bears testimony to the results of her exertions:—

" I can only affirm, with perfect truth, that your dear mother's visits to Jersey were blessed, as a means of incalculable good. It was through her peculiar talent and persevering exertions, that a District Society was formed in St. Heliers. Mr. John Hammond and Mr. Charles Le Quesne very ably seconded her views, in connexion with this matter.

The Island of Jersey, Seventh Month, 30th.—We arrived here last Seventh day, after a most beautiful and favoured voyage, which I felt an answer to prayer, and a mark of Providential care towards us. I had a very great deal to accomplish before I left home, but was enabled to leave all in peace ; and now I desire as far as it is permitted me to rest in the Lord, at the same time being open to any service I may be rightly called into ; and in faith to do what my hands may find to do. There are a few interesting Jersey Friends, but I find the difficulty of communicating with them on account of the language ; I endeavour to do my best, and look to Him who can bless my feeble labours.

I think the island and country delightful ; I never saw so little poverty, no beggars whatever, which is to me a real relief. Few amongst the inhabitants appear to be in high life ; but as far as I have seen, all appear to be well off. I expect my sister Elizabeth and Rebecca Sturges soon to join us, which I trust may prove right for them, for us, and for the people here. May it please my gracious and merciful Lord God, to bless us in this place, preserving us from doing harm, and enabling us to do that which is right and acceptable in His sight, and what may be for the real good of the people.

Eighth Month, 12*th.*—We feel much at home in this lovely island, and in rather a remarkable manner, our way opens in the hearts of those amongst whom we are residing. A very extensive field of service appears before us in many ways. To try and thoroughly attend to the prisoners—to try to correct evils in the hospital—to assist in various ways the Friends and those who attend Meeting—to visit several in Christian love, and try to draw them nearer together—oh ! gracious Lord God, grant Thy poor unworthy servant the help of Thy Spirit, to do Thy will, and let not her labour be in vain in Thee, her Lord and her God ; but through Thy unmerited mercy in Christ Jesus, grant that her way may be made *very* clear before her, and ability given her to walk in it, to Thy praise, her own peace, and the real edification of those among whom her lot may be cast.   Amen !

To a daughter and son-in-law preparing to leave
England for Madeira.

Eighth Month, 25th, 1833.

My much loved Children,

I fully expect one more opportunity of writing to you, before
you leave England, but as our communications are now likely to
be very seldom, I mean to take every opportunity to pour out my
heart to you. I am, I hope, thankful to say, though truly and
deeply touching to me, peaceful and satisfied about your proposed
very important step. I remember Cecil's remark, " we are to
follow and not to force Providence," and as far as we can tell, the
openings of Providence for you appear to be, quietly, hopefully, and trustfully to go forward in your proposed plans. I live
much under the feeling that we are poor impotent creatures, that
we cannot save each other spiritually or naturally ; and though
nothing I believe can in feeling exceed a mother's love or lively
desire to serve her children, yet how little can she do ! in short
nothing, but as she is helped from above to do it, and the same
power that can help her, can also work with or without His
instruments ; this I most sensibly feel, therefore to Him, who
is the keeper of His dependant ones, (which I believe you are) I
entirely commit you, body, soul, and spirit. May He " do more
abundantly for you than we can either think or ask !" I desire
for you, amidst the ups and downs, the storms and calms, the
joys and sorrows that may attend your course, that your hearts
may be fixed trusting in God. It is most important to seek for
this fixedness of spirit, which sustains in trouble and sanctifies
our enjoyments. I have suffered from too deeply and acutely
feeling things, and from much undue fearfulness—I wish my
children to guard against these weaknesses, and to live more
constantly in the quiet and trustful spirit. You must expect
some little trials and difficulties in the voyage, but I trust they
will not be great. Pray try to be of use to the crew, have
tracts, testaments and psalters, to be got at for them, it might
be of real use to the men, and a nice object of interest for you.

That grace, mercy and peace may be with you both, is the
earnest desire and prayer of your most loving mother,

ELIZABETH FRY.

Jersey, Ninth Month, 10th.—I have much enjoyed and valued
the pleasant retreat we have here. I desire in deep gratitude to
acknowledge the renewed capacity to delight in the wonderful
works of God. The scenery, and feeling fully at liberty to spend
part of many days in the enjoyment of this beautiful country
and weather, with my beloved husband and children, has been
very sweet to me! What has not religion been to me! how
wonderful in its operation. None but He, who knows the heart,
can tell. Surely it has brought me into some deep humiliations;
but how has it raised me up! healed my at times wounded spirit,
given me power to enjoy my blessings in what I believe an unusual
degree, and wonderfully sustained me under deep tribulations. To
me, it is anything but bondage, since it has brought me into a
delightful freedom, although I had narrow places to pass through
before my boundaries were thus enlarged; so that from experience, I wish to be very tender over those still in bonds.

Since this time of rest on first arriving, my way has remarkably
opened to a tide of service of various kinds, as a minister of the
gospel, and in philanthropic concerns. The prison, hospital, and
the formation of a District Society, take up much of my attention, and visiting religiously the families who attend the Friend's
meeting. I have very much felt the weight of these meetings,
duty alone, and what I believe to be the help of the Spirit
could carry me through such services, for which I am so totally
unfit and unworthy. My dear sister and Rebecca Sturges have
lately been with, and I have valued their company.

LETTER TO HER BROTHER JOSEPH JOHN GURNEY, OCCASIONED
    BY HEARING OF THE DEATH OF HIS MOTHER-IN-LAW MRS.
    FOWLER.

Jersey, *Ninth Month, 5th,* 1833.

My dearest Joseph,

I received thy deeply interesting letter to-day, which has produced in my mind much mixture of feeling; for death, in its

most mitigated form, is awful, and to our natural feelings very touching. But on the other hand, to have the warfare of those we love accomplished, the good fight fought, and a membership in the church militant changed for one in the church triumphant, brings such a feeling of peace and thankfulness, that it heals the wounds. Amidst much engagement, I have dwelt with you to-day in spirit, and not only felt for *you*, but I have also been in measure afflicted at the loss of the poor female convicts in the "Amphitrite," on the French coast—a hundred and twenty women, several of whom we knew in Newgate, besides many children—it has brought death very home to us !

I am glad that dear Rachel Fowler thought of the poor French, for whom I feel much interested, and if attention is paid to her wish, which I doubt not it will be, I think that it would be better than sending the whole Bible, to give something to Captain Bazin for printing certain parts of the Testament, to be distributed as tracts. There is a fine field for service in many ways ; how sweet for us one day to labour together in it, if permitted. I feel myself so very weak, that if any good is ever done, it will be only by Him, who out of weakness can make strong. Our party are generally well and comfortable ; we deeply feel about the absent, our nephew dear Sam Hoare, our own Rachel, and Champion and Hannah ; but we can only commit them to the Everlasting Keeper of His people, whose tender mercies are over all His works. The danger of the sea has been painfully brought home to us here, many vessels having been in distress with these high winds.

I am, with dear love to all, particularly our dearest Mary,

Thy tenderly attached sister,

ELIZABETH FRY.

Captain Bazin, to whom allusion is made in the preceding letter, commanded the "Ariadne" steamer, which crossed from Southampton to Guernsey and Jersey, and during the summer months used to proceed thence to St. Malo's and Granville.

He was a hardy Jersey sailor, an experienced pilot, and a devoted Christian ; he had a missionary spirit, and without abandoning his calling, or changing those circumstances in which he was placed, he strove to occupy with the talent committed to him, and to turn opportunities to account. He distributed Bibles, Testaments, and tracts, in those French ports which he visited: nor was he satisfied with this, he established both at St. Malo and Granville, a sort of meeting for religious instruction, reading the Bible, singing and prayer, and when a minister was present for preaching also. These meetings were attended by numbers at Granville; the functionaries and soldiers were often present; occasionally the superior officers. The demand for books was curiously great—multitudes would watch for the vessel, to go on board and ask for them; and often, before the passengers and luggage could be cleared out, the quarter-deck was crowded with applicants.

These details greatly interested Elizabeth Fry. Captain Bazin, in the intervals of his voyages, often came to "Caledonia Cottage" to confer with her, and exceedingly confirmed the interest she long had felt in the religious state of France, and her wish to return home by that route. She had mentioned it in a letter to her brother Joseph John Gurney, who was staying at Melksham. He read it aloud in the sick chamber of his mother-in-law Mrs. Fowler, a devotedly Christian woman, of lovely and enlarged character, and a valuable minister among Friends. The subject occupied her dying thoughts. After her family had been for some time sitting silently by her bed, supposing that the slumber of death was upon her, and that she would speak to them no more, she suddenly roused, and seemed as though she had yet something to communicate. On going quite close, they could just hear her twice repeat the name of the vessel "Ariadne;" one of them caught her meaning, and said, "Money to buy Bibles." She faintly repeated, "Money to buy Bibles," fell back into an apparently unconscious state, and spoke no more.

The thirty pounds which her family sent for the purpose were of the utmost consequence at that time, in enabling Captain Bazin to circulate the Holy Bible, in whole or in parts, where the demand was so great and the power of meeting it so small. After some weeks in Jersey, the party crossed to Guernsey, they remained there about a fortnight, received with the hospitality of the " olden time;" Mr. and Mrs. Fry at Miss Le Marchants, their daughters at Castle Carey, and Mrs Elizabeth Fry and her companion at the house of a Friend, named Edmund Richards. The islands of Guernsey and Jersey have separate and independent legislative assemblies, and differ in some minor points of law. Mrs. Fry's time was divided between social enjoyments, objects of benevolence, and above all devotedly caring and labouring for the good of others. She visited the Prison, and found, that since the death of Sir William Keppel, the last Governor, it had been supported by the Board of Treasury out of the revenue of that island, formerly appropriated to the Governor, a portion of which was always expended on the maintenance of the prisoners, and the same proportion was still expended for the same object by the Treasury.—The building such, that debtors and criminals easily and freely conversed with each other, and the internal arrangement of the building bad in almost every respect. Tried and untried prisoners, as well as those convicted of almost every degree of offence, freely associating together, and even when sentenced to solitary confinement, too frequently placed in one small cell for want of room.—The gaoler, having little remuneration, except the profit to be obtained out of ninepence a day, allowed for the support of each prisoner, and upon the sale of wine and spirits to the prisoners; the latter checked in measure by an order limiting criminals to two wine glasses of spirits a day, besides other liquors.—No employment, nor any chaplain or religious service ; no instruction, except that, occasionally given by any charitable person

who might visit the prison. In short, she found the whole
system entirely defective, tending continually to promote and
increase crime among its inmates, which in a small island like
Guernsey was severely to be felt, counteracting the efforts of the
upper classes for the general good of the community. The
Hospital she considered in excellent order, though in a few
minor points capable of some improvement.

One most important work she accomplished in that island—
establishing the St. Peter's Port Provident and District Society.
It is spoken of at the present time in Guernsey, as being " a
real blessing to the poor of the community, not only in having
administered to their temporal wants in sickness or accidents,
but also in having greatly improved their domestic comforts
and moral character, by inculcating frugal and temperate
habits."

From Guernsey, Mrs. Fry crossed to Sark. This singular
island lays between Guernsey and Jersey, and is seen on the
horizon from both ; though rarely communicated with, from
the latter island, being distant twenty miles, and extremely difficult of access. The best approach, is by crossing the channel
called the Great Russell, from Guernsey, nine miles in breadth.
Sark is a rock, precipitous on all sides, about three miles long,
by one and a-half wide. It is divided into great and little Sark,
by a very curious natural bridge of rock, about eighty yards in
length, in breadth not exceeding four or five feet; it is very steep
on one side, but on the other absolutely perpendicular. They
went in an open sailingboat, but as they approached its rocky
shore, perceived no inlet, nor any indication of ascent to the
lofty table land. A small jetty, from a natural projection, formed
a little basin, where they landed, amidst impending rocks; it was
not till they were on the narrow shelf of pebbly beach, that they
perceived what appeared to be the mouth of a cavern, there a cart
was waiting, and in it were placed two high-backed chairs, this

7

was the carriage to convey the ladies. The cavern gradually
narrowed and at length the party emerged through a ravine on
the plain. A lodging had been engaged for them at a farm-
house. The island consists of a level plain, intersected with
valleys, well cultivated; there are woods, cottages, small gardens
and orchards, fields dotted with cattle, and a village collected
around the Manor House. Sark is a dependency of Guernsey,
but the legislative power is vested in the Hereditary Lord of
Sark, and his forty tenants; a curious remnant of feudal tenure.
They stayed three or four days there; they also visited Herm,
an islet between Guernsey and Sark, nearly four miles in cir-
cumference, but the population very small.

Jersey, Tenth Month, 12*th.*—Since I last wrote, I have visited
the islands of Guernsey, Sark, and Herm, accompanied by my
husband, and part of the time by my sister and Rebecca
Sturges; my children with us when in Guernsey, and my kind
and valued servant, C. Golder. It has been a full tide of engagements, with here and there, by the way, a little rest and
recreation, although but little. I have deeply and weightily felt
two very large Public Meetings in Guernsey, one by invitation,
one not. In both of them I think we were much helped to
express our concern towards the people; but holding such
Meetings, goes to the *very extent* of what I apprehend women
are called to in public service. I view it very differently from
ministering in their own assemblies, and I have often thought it
rather too lightly entered into; although at times, I believe it is
called for. I feel peculiarly bound, when I do hold these great
and important meetings, simply to preach the gospel and its
practice, more particularly the importance of the unity of all
members of the Church of Christ, of every denomination. This
I have much to press upon in these islands. In the small island
of Sark, with about five hundred inhabitants, they are quite
divided religiously, about half of them Methodists, and half
members of the Church of England. They will hardly speak to
each other. I tried to use influence, and trust it may not be in

vain. In the island of Herm, there is neither school nor place of worship ; but there appears to be there, a most providential opening for forming a school,—a young lady willing to live on this desolate island, and devote herself to educating the poor. May the Lord be with her, and bless her in this undertaking ! our visit appeared to make way for this opening. In Guernsey, I think some grievous evils are likely to be remedied in the prison, in time ; I have also recommended some alterations in the hospital, which is a very large and important institution. A District Society will be probably established, I trust to the great benefit of the poor.

26*th.*—On Seventh-day evening, in the midst of a very large party, our letters arrived ; some from our dearest Hannah, of a very touching nature ; she had suffered so extremely on her voyage (to Madeira) as to bring on her confinement on board ship. Her child died, and her sufferings appear to have been extreme. The whole account was exceedingly affecting to me. But I desire to look above the agency of man, to Him, without whom not a sparrow falls to the ground, who orders all things in love, as well as in wisdom. My trust must be complete, my reliance entire, my hope continual. Lord, as all my springs are in Thee, I pray Thee daily, hourly, minutely, increase and renew my faith, patience, reliance, and hope, that I never cast away my confidence, but that my soul may follow hard after Thee, even unto the end.

The time had now arrived to break up the pleasant Jersey party. The accounts from England were very anxious. Several of her children required her attention ; one of her daughters was dangerously ill, and her beloved sister, Mrs. Hoare, had just closed the eyes of her eldest son. To divide the party, renounce the route through France, and take the long sea-passage, with only her maid and her little boy, was not decided upon without great conflict. The season had been peculiarly stormy, and several vessels had been lost in the Channel; amongst others the "Amphitrite." Many of the poor creatures in her were personally known to Mrs. Fry, although she had never been on board that ill-fated vessel. The *Times* newspaper contained, however, a statement, said to have been made by one of the sailors named Owen, in a letter addressed to the editor of that journal, dated Boulogne-sur-Mer, October 7th. **Dr.** Whately, in his letter to Earl Grey on "Transportation," Appendix (No. 4,) speaking of the "Amphitrite," mentions this sailor's statement, and adds,—

"There is one passage, which I hesitated to publish, from the fear that it might wound the most excellent lady mentioned in it; not for her own sake, for ingratitude can wound her only, as an indication of failure in her benevolent attempts at the culture of virtuous feelings, but for the sake of the unhappy beings whom habitual vice has steeled against such cares as hers."

The passage in the sailor Owen's statement, to which the extract from the letter refers, is as follows; after giving a shocking account of the depraved habits of the prisoner women, and of the absence of all attempts to restrain or bring them under discipline, on the part of the surgeon-superintendent, this passage occurs:—

"There was no divine service on board. Each woman had a Bible given her at Woolwich by Mrs. Fry and two other Quaker ladies; most of them could read and write. Those from Newgate had been taught in the school there. Mrs. Fry and the other ladies came on board at Woolwich four or five times, and read prayers."

In reply to inquiries, as to the previous life and habits of the women, the sum of Owen's answers were as follows:

"Forty of the women were from Newgate—most of them were very young."

"Those who had been longest in Newgate were the worst."

It was Owen's place, as boatswain, to sling the chain for Mrs.
Fry and the other ladies when they came on board. He "*heard
the Newgate girls wish she might fall overboard and be
drowned.*" It is startling to find circumstances such as these,
asserted on authority, apparently unquestionable ; to be not only
incorrect, but wholly unfounded.

At this time the Jersey post had become quite irregular, from
the packets being detained by weather. The feeling of confinement in a small island, to those unaccustomed to it, and on the
eve of departure, was so uncomfortable, that, sad as it was to
separate, it was almost a relief, when the two parties found
themselves fairly embarked in the different directions they had
taken.

No date.—Before I left Jersey very serious accounts came of
our dearest Rachel; of such a nature were they, last First-day,
just before an important Public Meeting ; that it became necessary for me to decide to return home direct, and not by France,
with my husband and daughters. I felt greatly afflicted, and
earnestly prayed that I might be permitted to see my tenderly
beloved child again. I was brought into a state of deep conflict,
walking about the room, weeping bitterly, and hardly knowing
how to go to the Meeting appointed at the Hospital, for the
poor there, and the public generally : however, I went, and
power was present to calm my troubled spirit, and enable me to
preach the Gospel to the poor, the sinners, and the afflicted. It
was a very solemn parting with the people of the island; but,
through mercy, I felt so clearly in my right place, and such a
blessed calm came over me, in spite of myself, that undue
anxiety was taken away. I passed a calm night, and was
enabled to commit my dear child and my all, to Him who can
do all things for us. The next day I had many little matters to
finish off, and to take leave. On Third-day morning, after a
short solemn time in prayer, my husband set off for France with
my daughters, and I, with my maid and my little boy, for
England.

Lynn, Eleventh Month, 12*th.*—As related in my last journal, I left Jersey in the steam-boat for Southampton. Parting, with many beloved friends there, I felt much. It is a place and people in which I have taken great interest; I also felt the uncertainty of the prospect before me, and in what state I should find my beloved child. I was much cast down, the wind rather high, and evidently rising. My maid and child quickly became ill, as did even our little dog. The passengers, one after another, almost all, in the same state. The day gloomy, only now and then a ray of sunshine to enliven us. I remained, through mercy, quite well. We stopped at Guernsey, where I found, to my encouragement, some of my objects really prospering, and I was much pleased to hear that the School was established in the island of Herm. We dined whilst in the harbour there. Afterwards the weather became so boisterous, my cold so indifferent, and my poor boy so ill, that I remained in the cabin the whole evening, and a low time it was; fears got hold of me that I should never see Rachel again alive; but on the other hand I knew that I had a merciful Lord to deal with, who heard my prayers, knew my weakness, and I believed would not permit so overwhelming an affliction to overtake me. I desired humbly and patiently to trust. I felt the seriousness of our situation in the high wind, but was enabled entirely to leave it to Him, who orders all things well. We arrived at Southampton the next morning; I was much cast down and overdone, and during the journey to London, I had almost an inexpressible feeling of fatigue. I found rather a better account from Lynn, to my unspeakable relief.

From the accounts continuing better, Mrs. Fry was for a day or two able to remain in the neighbourhood of London. One day she spent at Hampstead, with her sister Mrs. Hoare; entering into the depth of her bereavement, and that of her widowed daughter-in-law—but cheered by the greatness of their consolation.

Then she pursued her way to Lynn, where her presence was greatly needed; for six weeks she remained devoted to her daughter, and to that devotion, guided by singular skill, was apparently to be attributed her child's gradual restoration to health. From Lynn, she wrote to her youngest daughter, then just entering life, to greet her on her return home.

Lynn, *Eleventh Month 9th,* 1833.

My dearest Louisa,

I feel inclined to write thee a few lines of salutation on thy return home. Thy sister and thyself have very important places to fill, although they may differ; and as I have told her my mind, I mean to do the same to thee—remember these words, " be sober, be vigilant," At thy important age much depends on not letting the mind *out,* if I may so express myself: it is a period of life when this is natural—various prospects in life may float before the view ; but how infinitely important to know the heart to be staid upon God, and to find it, meat and drink to be doing His will—how important to attend to *present* duties ; this is the best preparation for the future, whatever that future may be. I see that much devolves on thee ; thou hast not only to look to thy own soul, but younger ones are looking up to thee, whom, I believe, thou mayst be the means of winning to Christ. Thy friendship with the —— family I trust will be of use to thee ; but on no account let imagination wander upon it; this will do thee harm, and on the contrary, I wish thee to profit by it.

Farewell dearest Louisa,

In much tender love,

E. F.

To the daughter she had been so long nursing, she wrote con-tinually, for some time after her return home, offering the wisest counsel, as to the conduct both of body and mind. Amongst other things, she says, in one of her letters :—

The better accounts of thee are certainly very encouraging, and set me more at rest about thee, still, my beloved child, I feel thou needest my sympathy and prayers ; there is much to feel, even if it pleases Providence quite to raise thee up again ; there is much to go through. I have often found, in recovering from long and severe illness, and entering life again, that our enemies spiritually are yet lively and strong, and even, we may say, after the " Beast has had a deadly wound, it still lives ;" I know this has been my experience. Though thou thinkest I feel with the Psalmist about long life, yet I am deeply sensible of the conflicts and temptations it involves; still, if we are through grace enabled to live to a great and good purpose, and to promote the welfare of our fellow-mortals, it is well to have such an opportunity granted to us, of proving our faith and our love towards our Lord and Saviour. Mayst thou, my much-loved child, be raised up for this blessed purpose.

Her advice, under differing circumstances, was very discriminating. To another daughter she wrote :—

I feel in the first place, earnestly desirous that thou shouldest think as little as possible of thy nervous feelings. I know how extremely painful they are, but experience has taught me, the less I think of them the better. It is most important to look upon them as much as possible like the toothache—that it must be endured while it lasts, but is not dangerous in its nature. As for the discoloured view, the imagination may at the time give to things, nothing is more important than to set it down as a clear and fixed thing in the mind, that whilst this nervousness lasts it is not sound, and *must not* be believed or taken heed to. I would not have thee discouraged at this return of it. I believe I never had death brought home very closely, without being brought into a low nervous state, it is after all, so awful; though I increasingly see, that this is real weakness, and that those who are believers in the Lord Jesus, however unworthy, need not fear it, as through Him, its *plague* and sting will be done away. But it is folly in one sense to look ahead, we have enough to do to seek for help and grace for the present time to do our *present day's work*. When the day comes that we have to give up "this mortal life," we may and ought humbly to trust, that through the unmerited mercy and love of our Lord, His grace will be found sufficient for us. I observe, for my great encouragement, that what we call nervousness often proves no common blessing, if made a right use of, and not given way to. It so wonderfully humbles, prevents the creature glorying, and makes willing to do any thing to come to that peace, which quiets every storm. Thy uncles and aunts have nearly all been striking instances of this: and I believe, hard, very hard as it is to bear, it is a baptism to fit for a fulness of joy and glory rarely partaken of; but it in no common degree calls for patience. I always think both David and Paul largely partook of this sort of humbling experience. Therefore my dear child, if tried this way, possess thy soul in patience, and look upon it as a suitable, though bitter medicine, prescribed by the Physician of value to promote thy health and cure. Louisa is to add; therefore I must in the most near love say farewell.

I am thy most tenderly attached mother,

ELIZABETH FRY.

Upton Lane, Twelfth Month, 28th.—In my own Church, when at home, I have been rather unusually active, and in the present stirring and unsettled state of things had to take the quieting and hopeful side. I now feel as if the clouds rather over-shadowed me; but I desire to have my heart fixed, trusting in the Lord, that in due time the Sun of Righteousness will arise with healing on His wings. My dear son Joseph is likely to be married on the 1st of next year. Oh! may the Lord be with him in it: it has been a subject that has very greatly occupied my heart and mind lately. My brother Joseph has been labouring amongst us in the Gospel, with wonderful brightness; this I feel a deep cause for thankfulness. Ah! for a heart, a spirit, and a power more fully and more abundantly to praise the Lord for his goodness, and to show forth His marvellous works to the children of men!

31st.—The last day of this year! I much feel these epochs: time going so fast. Peace and quietness are my portion this morning. I have cause for thankfulness and a good deal of encouragement; I have certainly had many proofs that my Lord has been near to me and mine during the last year, and helped us in many ways.

Third Month, 2nd, 1834.—First-day. I only to-day heard of my unworthy labours being greatly blessed in the Island of Guernsey; and lately the same from Jersey and France. Not so much individual instances of reformation, as the various plans for the religious, moral and temporal good of the poor, &c., &c., really prospering. I have also in my home circle, my dearest son Joseph and his valuable wife living here, to my great comfort. Surely, several of my children are drawing near to good.

Fourth Month, 1*st.*—I am likely to leave home to-day for religious service in Dorset and Hants. Oh Lord! I pray Thee be with me and anoint me for Thy work, that it may be fully to Thy praise, the edification of those I go amongst, and to my own help and peace ; and be pleased to keep my children and family during my absence. Grant this, dearest Lord, for Thine own name sake. Amen.

12th.—I returned yesterday from my expedition, which I may thankfully say, proved very satisfactory.

She was accompanied on this journey by her friend William Forster, and her nieces, Priscilla Buxton and Priscilla Gurney. Her aunt's address and manners on that occasion, and the impressions made upon her own mind, are admirably described by one of them ; being at the time in very delicate health, she was, perhaps, the more sensitively alive to her aunt's peculiar powers of soothing—

" There was no weakness or trouble of mind or body, which might not safely be unveiled to her. Whatever various or opposite views, feelings, or wishes, might be confided to her, all came out again tinged with her own loving, hoping spirit. Bitterness of every kind died, when entrusted to her, it never re-appeared. The most favourable construction possible was always put upon every transaction. No doubt her failing lay this way ; but did it not give her and her example a wonderful influence ? Was it not the very secret of her power with the wretched and degraded prisoners? She always could see hope for every one; she invariably found or made some point of light. The most abandoned must have felt, she did not despair for them, either for this world or another, and this it was that made her irresistible.

" At Southampton, time and opportuninity were rather unexpectedly afforded for an excursion to the Isle of Wight. I think she undertook it chiefly for the sake of pleasing Priscilla Gurney and myself; but it had important consequences. We travelled round by Shanklin, Bonchurch, and the Undercliff. She was zealous as we, in the enjoyment of the scenery and the wild flowers; but the next day, on reaching Freshwater, she was fatigued, and remained to rest, whilst we went to see Alum Bay. On our return, we were told she had walked out, and we soon received a message desiring us to join her at the Coast Guard Station. We found her in her element; pleased and giving pleasure to a large group, who were assembled around her. She entered with the greatest sympathy into their somewhat dreary position, inquired into their resources for education for their children, and religious improvement for themselves,— found them much in want of books; and from this visit originated that great undertaking, of providing libraries for all the Coast Guard Stations in Great Britain—an undertaking full of difficulties, but in which her perseverance never relaxed, till it was accomplished.

From the long low inn upon the beach at Freshwater, when you look from the beautiful sea, the range of cliffs beyond, and the two lonely rocks in the foreground, you see nothing, but a few fishers' cottages and the dark gloomy-looking Preventive Service buildings beyond them, just where the hills which enclose the little bay begin their ascent. It was very early in the year; before the great metropolitan hive had thrown off its endless swarms of summer travellers. Something of gloominess and desolation rested on the place—her companions had left her, and

10

she sat and pondered the condition of the inmates of the dwell-ings before her. It was at Brighton, in 1824, that the idea first suggested itself to her mind, of the great need there was for supplying this class of men with employment, that would at once occupy the long intervals of time left to their own dis-posal, and furnish them with subjects for thought, during the weary hours of lonely watching, that they must of necessity pass. She knew idleness to be a fruitful source of ill, and that the human mind preying upon itself, becomes inert, if not vicious. Circumstances had precluded her making any general or systematic exertions to remedy this evil, yet it rested upon her thoughts. She waited long to see her way clearly, and to be convinced that the duty was laid upon her, but no sooner had the conviction arrived, than she set herself vigorously to the work.

The experience of life had taught her, that He, who rules as a God of Providence, directs as a God of Grace—that with duty comes opportunity, and that with outward circumstances, the inward call is sure to harmonise, where man desires to act only in conformity to his Master's will, and to occupy with the talents given him to use.

Upton, Fourth Month, 12*th.*—At Portsmouth, we paid an interesting visit to the Haslar Hospital, the Hulks Hospital Ship, and some prisons ; we also paid a delightful little visit to the Isle of Wight. I felt more able to enjoy the great beauties of nature, from having been owned by my Lord and Master, in my religious services. What a relish does true religion give for our temporal as well as spiritual blessings! I have still much to feel respecting the offer of marriage made to my dear Louisa. It is a very serious thing, my children thus leaving Friends, and I have my great fears, that in so doing, they are leaving that which would be a blessing and preservation to them. At the same time, I see there is no respect of persons with God ; nor in reality is there the difference some would make out in the different administrations of religion, if there be but a true, sincere love of our Lord, and endeavour to serve Him. What is above all to me, I have felt peace in it rather peculiarly—still, we at present are exceedingly feeling the weight of the affair ; it is also a considerable pain to me to go through the discipline of the Society respecting it—but in bearing it patiently and humbly, I may in that way be enabled to preach Christ. Lord be it so—Help me Thyself through all these rather intricate paths, and make a way for thy servant in all these things ; that she may do right in thy sight, and not offend even the weakest of her brethren and sisters in religious connexion with herself—Help, Lord, or we perish !

21*st.*—Yesterday (First-day) I attended Meeting, rather oppressed in body and mind. Ministered to by dear Elizabeth Dudley, but had such heaviness of body as to hinder spiritual revival. In the afternoon I went, accompanied by Elizabeth Dudley, Rebecca Sturges, and some others, to visit the female convict ship ; the sun shone brightly, the day delightful, the poor women rejoiced to see us, but my spirit was in heaviness, from the difficulty of leaving my family, even for a few hours, on that day. It was a fine sight to see about one hundred and fifty poor female convicts, and some sailors, standing, sitting, and leaning round us, whilst we read the scriptures to them. I spoke to them, and Elizabeth Dudley prayed. Surely to witness the solemn effect, the tears rolling down many cheeks, we must acknowledge it to be the Lord's doing ; still I felt flat, though the others thought it a very satisfactory time, but in the evening I became more revived and comforted and thankful that it has pleased the Lord to send me to the poor outcasts, although at times feeling as if I went more as a machine moved by springs than in the lively state I desire ; but at other times it is different, and there is much sense of light, life, love and power. To-day I expect to go to the Duchess of Gloucester, and amongst some of the high in this life. May the Lord be with me, that my intercourse with these, may not be in vain in Him. I feel it no light responsibility, having the door so open with the Government of our country and those filling high places, I am often surprised to find how much so ; and yet the

Lord only knows the depth of my humiliations, and how it has been out of the depths, that I have been raised up for these services.   At the Admiralty, I have lately had important requests granted ; at the Home Office, they are always ready to attend to what I ask ; and at the Colonial Office, I expect that they will soon make some alterations in the arrangements for the female convicts in New South Wales.

Who has thus turned the hearts of those in authority ? surely it is the Lord.   May He give me wisdom and sound discretion rightly to use the influence He has given me.   Be near to Thy servant this day, gracious Lord, in every place, and so help her by Thy Spirit, that she may do Thy will and not bow to man, but alone to Thee her God, doing all to Thy glory. We made several other calls, and dined at my brother Buxton's, where we met some gentlemen.   I felt, as I mostly do after such days, fearful and anxious, lest I had done any discredit to the vocation wherewith I am called, or in any degree, in my own heart or conduct towards God, done amiss. It caused me rather a watchful, fearful night.   I see it much easier, and in many respects safer in the religious life, to be quiet and much at home ; yet I also feel that in a more general association there are great advantages, enlarging our spiritual borders, and removing our prejudices ; and if we are really enabled to stand our ground as Christians, in the meekness of wisdom, and so adorn the doctrine of God our Saviour, it may be the means of promoting the good of others.

24th.—We dined at Lord Bexley's, and met Captain Mangles the great traveller, several clergymen and others.   I desired to maintain the watch, but the company of serious intellectual and refined persons, is apt to draw me a good deal forth in conversation and mind, and often leads me to many fears afterwards, lest there should imperceptibly be any thing of showing off, and being exalted by man ; but I may truly say, inwardly, I mostly feel reduced and humbled after such times, and fearful, lest I should have a cloud over me, so as to hinder my near communion with my Lord. A few words in the Proverbs rather encouraged me : " Reproofs of instruction are the way of life,"— (Proverbs 6th chapter 23rd verse) I see it well to be reproved ;

may I profit by it ! I often fear for myself, lest I am forsaking my first love, or becoming lax, because I certainly feel far more liberty than I used to do, in uniting with others in their prayers, grace, &c., &c., and less in bonds generally—in short my borders are greatly enlarged ; may this arise, not from my love becoming cold, but from experiencing the service of my Lord to be already to me, in measure, perfect freedom.   Oh dearest Lord ! make manifest in Thy own light, if this be in me laxity, that I may be reproved and amend my ways ; if, on the contrary, it be the liberty wherewith Thou hast made me free, cause me in Thine own power, firmly and fixedly to stand in it, even if some of my fellow-mortals, whom I love and esteem, appear to remain under a different dispensation.

A few days ago I visited Plashet—it was almost too much for my natural spirits. When I saw our weedy walks, that once were made and kept up so neatly—our summer-houses falling down, —our beautiful wild flowers, that I had cultivated with so much care, and no one to admire them —the place that had cost us so much, and been at times so enjoyed by us, the birth-place of so many of my children, the scene of so many deep and near interests—the tears trickled down my face, and I felt ready to enumerate my sorrows, and say,   " Why is this ?"   But I felt the check within, and desired and endeavoured to look on the bright side of the picture, and acknowledge the tender and unmerited mercy of my God, in Christ Jesus.   Mine has been, I fully believe, a very unusual course in many particulars; in some things known, in some hidden from the eye of man. Oh ! may all end in good and blessing.

Fifth Month, 5th.—Yesterday was the Sabbath. I can hardly say how deeply I feel these days as they come, first, as it respects the ministry of the word. It wholly resting on two or three women in our rather large assembly, is an exercise of my faith, and a real trial to my natural feelings ; then to believe, as I do, that some of our congregation are in an unregenerate state, how must their silent meetings be passed ?   And for the babes in Christ I have great fears, inasmuch as true, solemn, silent worship, is a very high administration of spiritual worship. I frequently fear for such, that more external aid is wanted, though I see not how it is to be given. I also feel the want of each one openly uniting in some external act of worship, for there is much in taking an absolute part in what is doing, to feel a full interest in it, but I see not with our views (in which I unite) how this can be remedied. Then for myself, as a minister of the Gospel, I desire to be very faithful, and give the portion of meat in due season to the household ; but even here, deep humiliation is my portion, in its appearing, that though I preach to others, I cannot manage my own—my children, one after another, leaving a Society and principles that I love, value, and try to build up. My Lord only knows the exercise of my spirit on those days. Then for my home hours, not having space as we had at Plashet, in which my boys can recreate in the way I consider advisable, during part of this day ; now, I have anxiously to watch where they go, and what they are about, so that I am not often favoured to know the Sabbath a delight, or day of rest; yet through all these things, and my too anxious nature, help is wonderfully granted to me. I find the spring within that helps, keeps, revives, sustains, and heals, but I feel that I am bound to seek, and to pray not to be so exquisitely anxious.

Sixth Month, 10*th*.—Since I last wrote, I have got through the Yearly Meeting, which I attended nearly throughout. There appeared to me much more apparent love and unity than last year, still it is a serious and shaking time, and some of the Leaders of our Tribes think they differ in some points of doc-trine ; but I believe it is more in word than in reality, and as they love the Lord Jesus, if they have wandered a little, they will be brought back. I was a good deal engaged, having to take a quiet view, neither on one side nor the other, but seeing the good of both, but I have a very great fear of ever being too forward, a thing I very much dislike and disapprove. May my Lord preserve me from it.

I was favoured to get well through the British Society Meet-ing, and could not but return thanks that our Holy Head had so blessed this work. With respect to my dear Louisa's engage-ment of marriage, I have apprehended that the hand of the Lord is in it, and oh ! saith my soul, may it prove so. The pain of her leaving our Society, and the steps attending it, have begun to the wounding of my spirit; for though I do not set much value on outward membership in any visible church, yet it has its pains, at times great pains to me, and I am ready to say, in my heart, How is it? When I have one after another of my family thus brought before our Meeting, it has its trials and humiliations. It would be to me a pleasanter, and I think a more satisfactory thing, if the discipline of our Society had not so much of the inquisitorial in it, and did not interfere in some things that I believe no religious body has a right to take a part in; it leads, I think, to undesirable results. Though I approve persons being disowned for marrying out of our Society, I had rather the act of marriage in itself forfeited membership.

Seventh Month, 21*st*.—I have been very busy trying to obtain libraries for all the Coast Guard Stations, and have had to see men in authority, who received me in a way that was surprising to myself: at the Custom House by Lord Althorp, as Chancellor of the Exchequer, also, about the District Society concerns at Brighton, by the Archbishop of Canterbury, the Bishop of Chichester, Lord Chichester, &c., &c. These things might probably exalt, had I not deep inward humiliations. I forgot also to add, that Lord Melbourne, as Home Secretary, and Spring Rice, as Secretary of the Colonies, received me lately in the handomest manner, respecting our British Society concerns.

Her objects at this time were almost overwhelming, even to her—indefatigable and earnest as she was.

Her desire was, to extend the plan of libraries to all the Coast Guard Stations in the United Kingdom; but the project was vast, there being about five hundred of these, divided into twenty-four districts, and comprising upwards of 21,000 persons, including the wives and children of the men.

The estimated expense was considerable. Mrs. Fry proposed that £1,000 should be raised by private subscription, and £500 would, she hoped, be granted by Government, for the advantage of so numerous and useful a body of its servants. Lord Althorp, then Chancellor of the Exchequer, received her proposal favourably, but considered his continuance in office too uncertain to undertake it, although he promised to recommend it to his successors.

Her communications with Lord Melbourne were upon subjects connected with the Ladies' British Society, chiefly that of transportation, female convicts on board ship, and their treatment upon arriving in the colony.

Nothing could be more courteous than her reception, or that of her friends, in an after interview with Mr. Young, Lord Melbourne's private secretary. These ladies strongly recommended that there should be a Dépôt for female prisoners, where they might be instructed, before being sent abroad, much on the plan that is now pursued at the Millbank Penitentiary. Mr. Spring Rice (Lord Monteagle), in the Colonial Office, gave Mrs. Fry and her companions, the Honourable Mrs. Upcher and Miss Fraser, a kind and patient hearing.

Lord Melbourne granted another interview, when the subject of matrons for convict ships was discussed with him. The first matron who undertook that office, with the joint sanction of Government and the Ladies' British Society, was Mrs. Saunders, the wife of a missionary, who went out in the " George Hibbert." Her passage was paid by Government, but she suffered so much from sickness, that her own exertions were continually impeded. Mr. Saunders supplied her place, as far as it was possible to do so, and very satisfactory were the results. They cannot be better described than by extracts furnished by Miss Fraser, from the books of the Convict Ship Committee, held September 12th, 1834.

" The ' George Hibbert ' convict ship embarked one hundred

and fifty female convicts, and *forty-one* children ; also, nine free women, and twenty-three of their children.   It was visited four times by members of the Convict Ship Committee, and the usual articles distributed.   The ship was found to be much crowded, and serious inconveniences were felt, and were to be apprehended during the voyage, from this circumstance.   It is however to be noticed, with thankfulness, that both the captain and surgeon-superintendent appeared to be peculiarly well qualified for the offices to which they were appointed. We have also to state, that a lady (who, with her husband, a missionary, had been accustomed to visit Newgate) had a free passage granted her in this ship, with the understanding, that they should assist in the superintendence and religious instruction of the convicts.

"Mr. Saunders writes on the 26th : — 'Two services last Sunday. I have seen great improvement in the women, arising, I believe, from the ladies' reading, and the remarks of the surgeon on the use of bad expressions.   Our present rule is, to read the scriptures, and pray with one half of the prisoners one evening, the other half next evening.   I believe soon, I shall be able to have morning service and school every day.

" ' December 12th.—The Convict Ship Committee have the satisfaction of laying before the British Society, some most interesting accounts from the ' George Hibbert,' written by the Rev. J. Saunders, to his brother :—Sunday : Church service at half past ten and two o'clock.—Sermon after each service. The remainder of the week : ten to twelve, children's schools.   We have four school-mistresses, and two give me great pleasure.   Two to three o'clock, adult schools, twenty-four scholars, the same school-mistresses. Three to four o'clock writing school, two classes, twelve scholars each day ; but I have not yet hit upon the right method for the writing school, the women are eager to learn, but I cannot, as yet, put them in the right way.   When I have set the schools at half-past ten o'clock, I meet a Bible class of about twenty, they are chiefly Scotch girls, and it gratifies me to see their attention. At a quarter past eleven o'clock, another Bible class of fourteen ; this contains better readers, and persons of more intelligence, and gives me great pleasure.   Monday   and   Thursday   are   washing days, and the Bible classes are intermitted : rainy weather will of course interfere, as all these services are on deck. The church and the schools are on the poop, the Bible classes on the quarter-deck ; but in the evening, when the women are mustered, I go between decks, into each of the two prisons, separately read the scriptures, and pray, always concluding with the Lord's Prayer, because that is familiar to all.' "

How marvellous a change within twenty years ! True, that much was only external : for the heart of man is not touched by outward order and observances. True, most sorrowfully true— that many restrained for a time, by circumstances and regulations, would return, when at liberty to do so, to their former depravity. But yet to those who desired better things, to those of the female sex, who, although they had fallen, were not utterly cast down ; who, guilty perhaps of theft or robbing an employer, were not utterly lost and degraded, there was now offered hope and encouragement, the decencies of life were preserved, propriety and industry could be maintained, and even some advance might be made towards restoration. Character might once more be earned, integrity and industry practised, and the opportunity given, to prove that sin was repented of, and amendment of life desired and chosen. Of course much depended upon the Surgeon Superintendent, and upon the Matron, when that appointment became general, but some good was effected, and much absolute evil was spared. Nor were these advantages confined to the voyage. hen arrived at their destination, a ticket of good conduct was given to such of the women, whose behaviour had deserved it, by the Surgeon Superintendent, which almost insured their obtaining a good situation in service, and for all, there was a shelter ; the horrors described by Mr. Marsden, in 1819, no longer existed. The factory of Paramatta, at least afforded an asylum, overlooked by the Governor, and regularly visited by the venerable Chaplain.

Upton, Seventh Month, 25*th.*—To-morrow I expect to set off on a journey into Scotland. I have taken an affecting leave of my family, praying, that we might again (if the will of God) be refreshed together, and my way has satisfactorily opened to go.

Her husband, and two daughters preceded her, and awaited her coming at Birnam Inn, near Dunkeld.

She arrived there on the 5th of August, and after giving her a few days' rest from her journey, the party set off for Loch Tay, taking a most delightful route by the Braes and town of Aberfeldy, so famed in Scottish song; up Loch Tay to Kenmore, a village at that end of the Loch, where the river Tay, a deep, clear, rapid sweeping current flows out of it. At Kenmore, they enjoyed a quiet Sunday, and tolerable Highland accommodation. In the evening, anxious to turn the day to some good account, Mrs. Fry invited the servants of the inn, to attend the reading she intended to have with her own family. Some ladies were polite enough to offer the use of their sitting room, as it was more roomy, a large congregation of barefooted chamber-maids, and blue-bonnetted hostlers, assembled. She read part of her brother Joseph John Gurney's letter to a Friend, on the Evidences of Christianity; the people were very attentive, and anxious each to possess a copy, that they might read the remainder of the book themselves. The next day, some gamekeepers who came to the inn requested a similar gift, having heard from the people there, all that had taken place.

By Loch Tay, Eighth Month, 9*th, First-day*—Not having a Meeting to go to, and not believing it right for me to attend any other place of worship, I desire to spend a time in solemn searching of heart before the Lord, and may I be enabled to hold communion with Him in spirit. On the morning of the 1st, the day appointed for the liberation of all the slaves in the British dominions, and on which my dear niece, Priscilla Buxton was to be married, I poured forth my soul in deep supplication before my heavenly Father, on behalf of the poor slaves, that a quiet spirit might be granted them—that their spiritual bonds might also be broken—that the liberty prepared for the children of God might be their portion. I also prayed for my beloved niece and her companion in life, that the Lord would be with them, keep them, and bless them. My son Gurney, accompanied me from Newcastle, and we arrived at Dunkeld on the 5th, where we met my husband and daughters. I ought thankfully to remember how my way has been made, where I could hardly see any opening to join them ; how difficulties have vanished, and how a kind Providence has been with me, and provided for me, and brought me to these dear ones ; may I be edified and refreshed by beholding the wonderful and beautiful works of God, and may I rightly attend to such little services as may open towards others. Lord be with me, and help me by Thy Spirit, to perform all my duties to Thy praise. I pray Thee be very near to us all; protect us by Thy providential care over us, and above all, further visit us by Thy love, power, and Spirit. Oh Lord! turn us, and we shall be turned; help us, and we shall be helped; keep us, and we shall be kept. Amen.

On Monday, the 19th, the weeping climate seemed to forbid their progress, and the mountains were enveloped in clouds; but departing when the rain ceased, they had a fine drive along the banks of Loch Tay to Killin. The clouds rose considerably, and the mountains seen to great advantage—heavy masses rolling over them, sometimes resting on them, sometimes leaving them bare, with Ben Lawers towering magnificently over all. At Killin, the troubles of real highland travelling began. The inn was small and full, and Mrs. Fry and her party were obliged to take up their abode in a cottage, in some little humble bed-rooms, without a sitting room ; the highland mistress and her family carding and spinning wool in the kitchen. Notwithstanding the want of accommodation, the party remained over the next day to enjoy the romantic scenery of this spot, especially where the river Dockhart, broad, rapid, and roaring along its headlong and resistless course, rushes round two rocky islets, and under a long bridge, to where it falls into the Loch. Whilst the gentlemen were fishing, Mrs. Fry and her daughters rambled with delight through this wild highland scenery. From Killin, the party proceeded to Mrs. Stewart's famous inn, near Loch Katrine. The inn was fuller than usual, but accommodation having been secured beforehand, they found comfortable apartments ready ; but they had not them long to themselves, for as travellers arrived, weary and hungry, for whom there was no room in the inn, Mrs. Fry could not resist sheltering them for a time. Just at the close of the day, a party of ladies drove up, extremely fatigued, and dreading the danger of the roads in the darkness of night ; the entreaties for admission were heard from without, they were invited to share their sitting-room, and with their maid passed the night on its floor. These traits of character may be considered trifles, but trifles in daily life often tell more than greater things.

Edinburgh, Eighth Month, 28*th.*—I left my dearest husband and two daughters in the Highlands, to accompany my boy on his way to England, and above all, to attend the Meetings, see the Friends, and visit the prisons here. I came under the belief that duty called me to do so. We experienced some danger in our journey, from an accident in a steam-boat, but the Lord protected us. I feel it to be a fearful thing to be here ; there are many ministers besides me. Lord, be near to Thy servant, who is here without one relation or companion, and has left all, for what she apprehends to be the call of duty. Guide, guard, and keep her, qualify her for Thine own service, of whatever kind it may be, to Thine own glory; keep her eye very single to Thyself and the direction of Thy Spirit.

Tarbet, by Loch Lomond, Ninth Month, 14*th.*—I have been more than a week returned to my husband and children, and have had, during that time, the real comfort of having Andrew

Johnston and my beloved niece Priscilla with us. They returned with me from Glasgow. In Edinburgh, I had much to be thankful for, in the help granted to me in such religious services, as I believe I was called into, in Meetings, families, and institutions. I had a very solemn religious time in the Gaol and large Refuge, also a shorter one in the Bridewell and another Refuge. The hearts of many appeared to be peculiarly opened towards me, and entire strangers wonderfully ministered to my wants, and upheld my hands, particularly the Mackenzie family. Our dear friends who knew me before were abundantly kind to me. May the Lord, in His love and mercy, reward them for all their great kindness to me His very unworthy servant ; and may He still soften and enlarge their hearts towards me, until the work that He gives me to do amongst them be accomplished. I find a field for much important service for the poor, and to make more arrangements for the ladies who visit the prisons. I desire, and earnestly pray to be preserved from an over-active spirit in these things ; and on the other hand, faithfully, diligently, humbly, and watchfully, to do whatever my Lord gives me to do, that may be to His glory, or the good of my fellow-creatures.

We have passed through very lovely country ; but the sun has not shone much upon us, and the atmosphere of my mind has partaken of the same hue, which is not so pleasant as more lively colouring over the mind, but I am ready to think more profitable, and perhaps more likely to qualify me for the weighty duties before me.

From Loch Katrine the party passed to Balloch, and Luss, and thence to Inverary and Loch Awe, from which place Mrs. Fry returned (her son with her) to Edinburgh. Whilst on the banks of Loch Awe, the party spent a few days at Inistrinich, under the hospitable roof of K. M. Mac Allister, Esq., enjoying the beauties of that fine district, and on their return, they passed a Sunday there. In the evening, Mrs. Fry had a solemn reading with a large party of guests and the assembled household. It was her invariable practice on this journey, even at the inns, to invite the servants to attend their Sabbath evening readings, and many of the visitors frequently joined them.

The party having re-assembled at Oban, with the addition of Mr. and Mrs. Andrew Johnston, remained quietly a few days, and then retraced their steps through Dumbarton and Glasgow to Edinburgh, where Mrs. Fry was again received with the most affectionate kindness by her friends. Her time and energies being devoted to the completion of those objects begun on her former visit.

But whilst many institutions of value directly or indirectly owe their existence to her exertions—and she sowed the seed of many a noble tree—she did not omit the smallest opportunity of benefiting others. Her's was a constant endeavour to leave some savour of good on all with whom she had any communication. The chambermaid and the waiter received the word of kindness and counsel, and a little tract or text book to impress it upon their memories. The postilion at the carriage window, or the cotter at the road side met with appropriate notice, and this mingled with the most unaffected enjoyment of the country, and spirit in all the incidents of travelling.

The result of her observations on the state of the Scotch Prisons, she forwarded to the proper authorities after her return home.

A Prison Discipline Society, at this period established in Edinburgh, composed of many gentlemen of position and influence, was carrying on its important work, in spreading information, and leading to more general interest on the subject. With them Mrs. Fry held much communication, and letters passed between her and the indefatigable secretary, Dr. Greville, on different matters connected with prisons; his enlarged and Christian view of the subject being very congenial to her.

Mrs. Fry's remarks addressed to the authorities, include many of the topics so continually urged by her.

The care of women, being intrusted to women.

Employment of some nature for all.

More instruction to be given, and that not only for the sake of the thing learned, but for the good effect of change of occupation, both for body and mind.

Proper books to be furnished to those who can read.

A uniform prison dress.

A proper and sufficient dietary—the purchase of food, or receiving it from friends, to be absolutely prohibited.

Water for all purposes, to be thrown up, on every floor. Officers to sleep close to the prisoners.

Arrangements for worship and instruction on the Sabbath-day.

She was also becoming anxious on questions then occupying much attention.—The solitary and silent systems ; imported from America, where in many respects, and under the closest and most careful inspection they appeared well to answer, but which were to her feelings both liable to grievous abuses.   She was always slow in forming decided opinions, and even more so in expressing them ; but on these points she became very clear, as to their uses and their dangers, and at a later period she believed it her duty very strongly to express her fears on the subject.

After her return from Scotland, Mrs. Fry resumed her visits to Newgate.   At that time, she went once a week regularly.   On a few rare occasions, she did not confine her ministrations to the female prisoners.   Her faithful coadjutors and valued friends, Mrs. (now Lady) Pirie, and Miss Fraser, were her frequent companions.   The journal of the latter lady contains many entries of interest, which, most kindly, she has furnished for the present work: amongst others—

"November 29th, 1834. —I spent an interesting time in Newgate, Mrs. Fry and I were there together for several hours.   She went with me to the cells, and read to the men just sentenced to death.

"Amongst them, there were two brothers, convicted, I believe, of housebreaking. The youngest was drawn into the commission of the crime by the elder brother. James, the youngest, could not read ; he was married to a very pleasing looking young woman, and had two children.

" I recollect Mrs. Fry told the poor men who could not read, that if they would try to learn whilst they were in Newgate, she would give those who succeeded, each a Bible. James took very great pains, and before he left the prison to be transported (which the whole of the men were, five in number) he could read very tolerably. On the 8th of January following, Mrs. Fry again went with me to the cells. James then read the 7th chapter of St. Matthew's gospel and received his Bible. He became a valuable servant to the gentleman, to whom he was assigned in New South Wales, and his wife, who had been assisted by Lady Pirie and some friends of her's, in obtaining needle-work, was sent with her children to him. It was a pleasing circumstance, that his master, as a reward for his good conduct, sent an order for a sum of money to defray the expenses of the voyage, in order that the family of this poor young man might join him. The letter with this order arrived after the wife and children were on their way. So remarkably favoured was this poor convict and his family, through the goodness of the all-seeing Father of mankind, that it is most probable his sojourn in Newgate was overruled for the good of himself and family, both spiritually and temporally. It was indeed a remarkable instance of the benefit of prison visiting."

Tenth Month, 7th.—I have had a note from the Secretary of the Colonies to say, that all our propositions for improving the arrangements for the convicts are forwarded to the Government in New South Wales. At the Home Office, they are forwarding my recommendations about Scotland.

After recording the birth of another grandchild, the first of a now numerous family, the journal contains the following remark :—

I feel it cause for deep and humble thankfulness to see the happiness of my son and his wife; I feel it also a fresh proof in the important step of marriage, how well it is for young persons to choose for themselves, provided there is no insurmountable objection. Indeed, I have unusually felt comfort in my beloved children of late—beginning to partake of that enjoyment in them that I have all along hoped would one day be mine. May I be encouraged, with a thankful heart, to persevere in training up my younger ones in the Lord, and to trust for them, when walking in the slippery paths of youth—not to be too anxious about them; but earnestly seeking for help, strength, and direction in doing my duty towards them, there commit it. I have been unusually discouraged the last day or two, by —— and —— taking a very decided part in things appertaining to our school at East Ham, and in our Newgate Committee. I have not felt them tender over me and my views, which were rather different to theirs; I felt a little roughly handled, but as I firmly believe they did not mean it, and as I attribute it much to the warm zeal of dear —— ——, I have truly desired to take all in a humble Christian spirit; I mean to seek to be doubly and unusually kind to those who have hurt me, and admit no other than kind constructions upon all they have done. —— —— cast reflections upon me for my " incorrigible love of the Church," as she told me she considered it.

I find in most things in the religious Society I belong to—in charities—in education—I am so much disposed, from inclination and early habit, to take enlarged liberal ground, that perhaps watchfulness is needed, lest Christian liberty degenerate into laxity; but, oh! the love, the enlargement I feel towards all, at times, inexpressible—the deep unutterable sense I have of the largeness of the foundation, the fulness and real freedom of the Gospel, how it brings glad tidings to all who love the Lord and His righteousness, how it breaks down partition walls, how it unlooses heavy chains, and unlocks prison doors, how it enables us even to bear with the prejudices of our fellow-mortals, and yield to them, if in so doing we do not hurt our own consciences. For my poor self, how do I desire, that however slack in the view of my fellow-mortals, I may not be slack in

the sight of the Lord. How I fear for myself, lest I should get
from under His cross, or in any way forsake my first love. Oh!
gracious Lord, be Thou my Judge and my Lawgiver ; examine
and prove me. Be pleased ever to preserve that freedom which
is of Thee—let me be in bondage to no mortal ; but, whatever
is not of Thee, manifest Thou it, that it may come under the
restraint of Thy cross. And if it be Thy will, keep me, I pray
Thee, in the unity of those who love Thee, and whom I love ;
or, if, for my humiliation, Thou seest meet they should in some
things set me at naught, let me ever rest satisfied in Thee and
Thy love. Amen.

Twelfth Month, 25th.—I returned from Brighton the day
before yesterday, having felt a drawing of love to visit the
Friends there, and to attend to the difficulties of the District
Society. I went quite alone, and yet not alone, because I believe
my Master was with me. I quite hope and trust the valuable
District Society will be continued. I had about a hundred guests
to meet me. We read the 90th Psalm, and I felt called to pray
for them and the Society. Afterwards I strongly pressed the
importance of Christians of different denominations working
together in unity of spirit, also of diligence in the work, and
the care of all the districts. I advised a diminution of the premium on deposits. I also saw some of their leading gentlemen,
and I think an ear was opened to hear what I had to say. It is
a weighty responsibility, the opening our Heavenly Father has
given me with different classes of persons—oh! for grace to
make a simple right use of it. I returned home well satisfied,
though, by remaining a little longer, I might have accomplished
more.

At the close of this year,—in public matters, I look upon
Slavery being abolished, as an unspeakable blessing ; Capital
Punishment much lessened, I also think cause for thankfulness ;
and that in the Prisons it has pleased my Gracious Master yet
to bless our unworthy labours of love. I have also had very
satisfactory accounts of the District Society formed in Jersey ;
and I trust the Scotch Gentlemen and Ladies' Societies will
prove the means of good. Oh! for a thankful heart, for
being in any degree enabled to be useful to our fellow-crea-

tures.   I have yet many things stirring, and what a favour to have health granted me, thus far to attend to these important duties; and I am informed, that though quite a new party is now in power, the members of Government are still ready to listen to my requests.

CHAPTER XIX.

THE close of the year 1834 was marked by the death of the Duke of Gloucester. He had been highly esteemed by Elizabeth Fry, from the time when quartered at Norwich, in the latter part of the last century His Royal Highness was amongst the few, who addressed words of friendly caution and sound advice to the young and motherless sisters at Earlham. To the Princess Sophia of Gloucester, she wrote upon the occasion—

Upton Lane, *Twelfth Month*, 13*th*, 1834.

My dear Friend,

I hope thou wilt not feel it an intrusion, my expressing my sympathy with thee in the death of the Duke of Gloucester. To lose a dear and only brother is no small trial, and for a while makes the world appear very desolate. But I trust, that having thy pleasant pictures marred in this life, may be one means of opening brighter prospects in the life to come, and of having thy treasure increased in the heavenly inheritance.

The Duchess of Gloucester kindly commissioned a lady to write to me, who gave me a very comforting account of the state of the Duke's mind. I feel it cause for much thankfulness that he was so sustained through faith in his Lord and Saviour, and we may humbly trust through His merits, saved with an everlasting salvation.   It would be very pleasant to me to hear how thy health and spirits are, after so great a shock, and I propose inquiring at Blackheath, where I rather expect to be next week; or if thou wouldest have the kindness to request one of thy ladies in waiting to write me a few lines, I should be much obliged.

I hope that my dear and valued friend, the Duchess of Gloucester, is as well as we can expect after her deep affliction.

With desires for thy present and everlasting welfare,

I remain, thy attached and obliged friend,

ELIZABETH FRY.

Upton Lane, First Month, 27th, 1835.—I yesterday went, by appointment, to visit the Duchess of Gloucester, after the death of the Duke.   She gave a highly interesting account of his death.   He appeared to depart in the full hope of a Christian. This I felt satisfactory and comforting, after having traced him from his youth up, and seen his conduct, and known his principles when a young man.   I observe how gently the Lord deals with His people, and how, under the most varied circumstances, He visits all, and how He bears with those that fear Him.   It appeared to me that the Duke desired to act up to the light received, and his faith was strong in his Saviour, which proved his stronghold in the day of trouble.

Second Month, 8th.—The way appears opening with our present Ministers, to obtain libraries for all the Coast Guard Stations, a matter I have long had at heart.   My desire is, to do all these things with a single eye to the glory of God, and the welfare of my fellow-mortals, and if they succeed, to pray that He, who alone can bless and increase, may prosper the work of my unworthy hands, and that I may ever wholly give the glory to Him to whom it is due, even my Lord and my God.

25th.—The affairs of our Society cause me real anxiety and pain, and reconcile me in measure to so many of my children leaving Friends.   Though it is painful and humbling, in my own Meeting, my children's names being on the books only for disownment, yet I deeply feel my Lord is still with me and mine, and my trust is, that He is working in a " mysterious way His wonders to perform" amongst us. I have a very strong sense of His mercy and pity towards us, and the wonderful loving kindness already shown us in heights and in depths, in riches and in poverty, in strength, and in weakness.

Third Month, 13*th.*—I returned yesterday from my expedition with my dear brother Samuel. I find much satisfaction and true peace, in now and then giving a portion of my time and strength to the service of my own Society; it is useful to myself, and in no service does the presence of my Lord and Master appear to be more evidently round about me. Upon going to the Custom House, on my return, I found Government at last had granted my request, and given £500 for libraries for the Coast Guard Stations; this I think cause for thankfulness, and my desire is, that the measure may be blessed by the Lord.

The beneficial effects of the libraries introduced through her influence into the Naval Hospitals at Haslar and Plymouth, and the testimony borne to their utility by Sir William Burnett, the highest medical authority in the navy, had confirmed her desire to extend this advantage to all the Coast Guard Stations, without further delay. It was brought under the notice of Sir Robert Peel, then first Lord of the Treasury, by means of a letter addressed by Mrs. Fry to his brother Lawrence Peel, Esquire, who had already ably seconded her views in the Brighton District Society. This application met with the approbation of Sir Robert Peel, by whom it was referred to Sir Thomas Freemantle—from him an assurance was received, that there existed a strong disposition on the part of the Board of Treasury to give effect to this object, and that as soon as the proposed plan was matured it should receive all the assistance in his power.

Captain Bowles, R.N., at that time Comptroller of the Coast Guard, gave the project his cordial support. Captain Sir Edward Parry united with Mrs. Fry in this movement, and under such powerful patronage it rapidly advanced. A formal application was made to the Treasury for a sum of money for this purpose, and the result was, the grant of £500. Large private subscriptions had still to be sought, and were obtained, chiefly through Mrs. Fry's influence. The details of the arrangement were almost entirely her own, and curiously adapted to meet the requirings of those she desired to benefit, having made herself mistress of the subject, and of the nature of the service, with surprising rapidity and exactitude.

Besides subscriptions in money, many liberal donations of books were received from some of the most eminent booksellers, which, with the grants from the Society for Promoting Christian Knowledge, the Religious Tract Society, and other similar institutions, amounted in value to upwards of a thousand pounds.

The selection of the libraries was a work of considerable difficulty, demanding much caution, and examiners were appointed to decide on suitable books for this important purpose. The gentlemen selected were the Rev. John W. Cunningham, Captain Sir W. E. Parry, and Captain Bowles.

The libraries, for the Stations alone, amounted in all to 25,896 volumes. Fifty-two different works were prepared for each Station, whilst a still larger and more important collection was to be attached to every one of the seventy-four districts, in order to afford the needful variety and change. The packages of books, the greater part carriage-free, were dispatched in the course of the summer from the Custom House, in Government vessels, to their different destinations, But all this was not done without much fatigue and exertion, many wearisome journeys to London, and a great deal of writing, though in the latter she was much helped by Mr. Timpson, a dissenting minister, who undertook the office of Secretary, and proved an efficient and useful agent to herself and those gentlemen who acted with her.

On the 22nd of May, Mrs. Fry was ordered to attend the Select Committee of the House of Lords, appointed to inquire

into the present state of the several Gaols and Houses of Correction in England and Wales. She was accompanied by Mrs.
Pryor, Mrs. Pirie (Lady Pirie) and Miss Fraser, who were likewise to be examined. Sir T. Fowell Buxton was with Mrs. Fry.
The ladies were conducted by him to an ante-room, where they
found the Duke of Richmond and Lord Suffield; the Duke of
Sutherland came in shortly afterwards. The Duke of Richmond,
as Chairman of the Committee, presided; Mr. Gurney, the
short-hand writer, was seated at the corner of the table, and
Mrs. Fry, Mrs. Pryor, Mrs. Pirie, and Miss Fraser, at the right
hand of the Duke. There might be from twelve to fifteen
noblemen present.

An eye-witness writes:—

"Never, I should think, was the calm dignity of her character
more conspicuous. Whatever her inward feelings might have
been, nothing like excitement was visible in her manner—nothing
hurried in her language. Perfectly self-possessed, her speech
flowed melodiously, her ideas were clearly expressed, and if
another thought possessed her, besides that of delivering her
opinions faithfully and judiciously on the subjects brought
before her, it was, that she might speak a word for her Lord and
Master in that noble company."

Perhaps the heads of a little strip of paper, prepared by her
to assist her memory, will prove the best guide to those subjects
she the most earnestly desired to press upon her auditors.

NOTES FOR EXAMINATION BEFORE COMMITTEE OF THE
HOUSE OF LORDS.

General state of female prisons.—Want of more instruction.
—Ladies visiting in female prisons.—Objections to instruction
being given privately and *alone* to women, even by chaplains or
ministers of their own persuasion.

The Tread-Mill—injurious for women, under many circum-

stances of health and constitution—often destructive to the
health of men, when too prolonged upon a meagre diet—unfitting for labour afterwards. Matrons, to be efficient, must be of
character and weight. Gaoler's daughter of sixteen, as in one
instance in Wales, acting in that capacity.

The state of most Borough prisons—instance, a woman alone,
for a considerable time in one prison, never seeing any of her
sex, in the power and under the care of men.

Equality in labour and diet in different prisons, though the
kind of diet must depend upon the local habits. Great need of
Government Inspectors in English and Scotch prisons, the plan
answering so well in Ireland. Chaplains, for general daily instruction, and the services of the Sabbath.

Convict ships—difficulties about choosing matrons—women
more competent to judge of the qualifications of their own sex
than men.

But far beyond all other topics, did she urge the vast importance of scriptural instruction for these poor fallen ones. Warmed
by her subject, with her voice a little raised, and a look of solemn
earnestness she went on to say, after replying to one of the questions addressed to her—

I believe the effect of religious and other instruction is hardly
to be calculated on—and I may further say, that notwithstanding
the high estimation and reverence in which I held the Holy
Scriptures before I went to the prisons, as believing them to be
written by inspiration of God, and therefore calculated to produce
the greatest good, I have seen (in reading the scriptures to those
women) such a power attending them, and such an effect on the
minds of the most reprobate, as I could not have conceived. If
any one wants a confirmation of the truth of Christianity, let
him go and read the scriptures in prisons to poor sinners ; you
there see, how the gospel is exactly adapted to the fallen condition of man. It has strongly confirmed my faith, and I feel it
to be the bounden duty of the Government and the country,
that those truths should be administered in the manner most
likely to conduce to the real reformation of the prisoner, you

then go to the root of the matter—for though severe punishment may in a measure deter them and others from crime, it does not amend the character and change the heart, but if you have altered the principles of the individuals they are not only deterred from crime, because of the fear of punishment, but they go out and set a bright example to others.

The quiet self-possession with which she delivered her opinions, won confidence and consideration, even, where they failed to convince; and she had the satisfaction to believe, that some points of importance were forwarded by the information she furnished.

The varying forms of the kaleidescope, change not more rapidly than the scenes in the life of Elizabeth Fry.

On the 22nd of May, she went before the Committee of the House of Lords; on the 28th, she went into Norfolk, to be with her daughter, and on the 29th, announces the birth of a little grandson.   She returned home on the 2nd of June; and on the 10th, in the retirement of her morning room, within sound of the burst of bells that announced the event, we find her before the Lord in prayer, during the celebration of the marriage of her youngest daughter Louisa, to Raymond, second son of Sir John Henry Pelly, Bart.

Upton, Sixth Month, 10*th.*—Alone in my little room, my whole family gone to Church to the wedding. I feel solitary, but I believe my Lord is with me.   Oh gracious Lord! at this moment be with my child ; pour out Thy Spirit upon her, that she may not only make solemn covenant with her husband, but with her God.   Help her to keep these covenants, be with, help, and bless her and her's.   Grant enough of this world's goods, but above all, far above all, grant them durable riches and righteousness ; that joy and peace, which the world can neither give nor take away.   Not that I am worthy, to ask for these blessings, but I ask them for the sake of Him, who is our rightousness ;

and through whom, Thou showest Thy tender mercy towards us. Amen, and Amen.

13th.—I can hardly express what the desire and prayer of my heart was on the wedding-day, that it might be rightly spent, and that a blessing might be with us, and all our mercies, remembered and acknowledged. I think this was a good deal the case; they returned from Church, soon after I wrote in my little room, the party appeared cheerful, peaceful and sober-minded; the dear grand-children, many of them with us, looking truly lovely, they had their wedding meal, a sweet group round a table with some other children. We sat down about fifty at our table, we had fifteen of our children, my sister Catherine, and my sister Buxton, the bridegroom's family, and a few of our dear and valued friends. I have seldom seen a more lovely party, or apparently in a sweeter spirit; really quite a delightful and beautiful sight. I felt that I could not let the party separate, without some expression of my deep feeling, my pleasure, and satisfaction in our table being so surrounded; my gratification at the interest shown for the bride and bridegroom, and ourselves—and my desire, that this fresh union with our friends and neighbours might be blessed indeed to us all; then my prayer for our dear young people, that they might walk with a perfect and upright heart before the Lord, that they might be of good comfort, be of one mind, live in peace, and that the God of love might be with them even unto the end. I also expressed, that I had remembered in my prayers, those members of the family that were afar off—that grace, mercy and peace might be with them! We then broke up, and wandered a little about until our dear bride and bridegroom left us. After which, our party dispersed, but an uncommon feeling of love, sweetness, peace, and blessing appeared to me to rest upon us, for which as a token for good, I desire, very humbly and reverentially to return thanks.

Some important affairs requiring her husband's personal attention in the south of England, Mrs. Fry and their remaining daughter accompanied him; it appeared a desirable opportunity for seeing the Commanders of the different Coast Guard districts, through which they would pass, and endeavouring to stimulate them, with the officers and men under their command, to a proper application of the books they were about to receive. This proved, however, almost needless, for in nearly every instance, these gentlemen warmly seconded her views, and approved of the plan. Her suggestions were received by them with the utmost attention and politeness, and greatly did the intercourse with the Coast Guard officers add to the interest of this agreeable journey, along the whole southern coast of England, from the Forelands to the Land's End.

She almost always visited the Stations, and conversed with those she found there; frequently the officers would follow her to the inn for further communication. At Portsmouth, she visited Haslar Hospital, speaking kind and pitying words to the sick and deranged. Admiral Garrett and his family paid her the most hospitable attention; with Miss Garrett she visited the Penitentiary at Portsea. While they went over the house, the unfortunate inmates were assembled in the parlour, where they were all standing, when Mrs. Fry, and the party with her returned to the room. Miss Garrett describes Mrs. Fry, as "sitting down, laying her bonnet on the table, and making some inquiries as to the arrangements of the place, and the conduct of the young women there. Two were pointed out to her as being peculiarly refractory and hardened—without noticing this, she addressed some words of exhortation and advice to all, but when she arose to go away, she went up to these two and extending her hand to each of them, said, in a tone and manner quite indescribable, but so touching:—'I trust I shall hear better things of thee.' The hearts that had been proof against the words of reproach and exhortation, softened at the words of hope and kindness, and both burst into tears."

The travellers made a three days' tour of the Isle of Wight; but at Cowes Mrs. Fry separated from her husband and daugh-

ter, believing it her duty to cross to Jersey, in the hope of effecting something towards remedying the crying evils which still
existed in the prison there.   She was accompanied by a young
Friend from London, who had kindly agreed to go with her;
they went in the "Ariadne," Captain Bazin's steam vessel. They
had a rough passage, but a warm reception at D'Hautrée, Colonel (now General) Touzel's. By him and his family were they
treated, not merely with hospitality, but with true Christian fellowship, as " beloved for their works' sake."

She had many interviews with persons in authority, but to
little immediate purpose. Her desire was, that such buildings
should be added to the prison, as should render it a House of
Correction, and make it possible to enforce classification and
needful discipline; but great difficulty existed from many perplexing questions between the States of the Island and its Governor, Field Marshall Viscount Beresford, as to who was to
pay the expenses that would be entailed.   She found the District Society flourishing, and a committee of ladies visiting the
Hospital.

On her return, she spent a few days in Guernsey, the prison
was in the same deplorable state in which she had seen it two
years before.   Thence she crossed to Weymouth, where she
rejoined her party, who were rejoiced to welcome her again in
safety.   She was laden with fruits and flowers, the rich produce
of those fertile islands.   Among other treasures, she bore with
her an enormous bunch of carnations and picotees of every
colour, scarlet, yellow and bizarre.

They were some days at Plymouth.   Occasional intervals of
rest, with the addition of sunshine and fine scenery, were thankfully received by her.   She prized the varied beauties in the
material world, not alone as in themselves good and pleasant,
but as types and emblems of the beautiful and good in the

spiritual creation, and above all, in the spirit of Heber, she
could appropriate his language—

> " If thus Thy meaner works are fair !
> If thus Thy bounties gild the span
> Of ruined earth, and sinful man,
> How glorious must the mansion be,
> Where Thy redeemed shall dwell with Thee !"

There was one day she often referred to with pleasure, when,
with the Coast Guard Captain of the District, in his cuttter,
they visited some of the Stations, crossing Cawsand Bay, and
landing at a romantic spot, where one of them is placed. At
the Breakwater, on their return, they were met by several naval
officers, their cutters or yachts, meanwhile, sailing about that
beautiful harbour.

The contrasts of her life were great. This was rather a fresh
variety—walking up and down the Breakwater, with her daughter, surrounded by naval officers of various ranks and different
ages, but the one great aim of her life not forgotten. The conversation between the Quakeress and those sons of storm
and strife, was of benefiting seamen, raising their moral condition, and the best methods of inculcating habits of piety and
virtue.

At Falmouth, they were warmly welcomed by Mr. and Mrs·
George Croker Fox, and by every member of that family. Mrs.
George Croker Fox, and Mrs. Robert Were Fox, were amongst
her oldest friends ; their mother Mrs. Barclay, was sister to her
father. In childhood and youth, the intercourse was frequent
and delightful between the two groups of sisters, seven in each
family, alike left motherless in early life.

Here she heard much of the packets continually sailing from
that port; she wished to have libraries for them also. In this

she was seconded by Captain Clavell, R.N., of the "Astrea" flag-ship, and by many of the commanders of the packets, and their families.   Grants from the Societies, and private subscriptions were raised, the Religious Tract Society gave their publications at half-price, and the Christian Knowledge Society presented books to the amount of ten pounds.   These vessels were supplied with Bibles, Testaments, and Prayer-books, by Government.   The library books were placed as a dépôt at the office of Captain Clavell; each packet, when she sailed, took out a box containing thirty books, changed from time to time, so as to produce constant variety.   The gratitude of the men was great, and the co-operation of their officers hearty—of fifty-one pounds, that this arrangement cost, twenty pounds were subscribed by them.   A few months afterwards, from one of Captain Clavell's family was received a communication, dated Falmouth, January 27th, 1835 :—

"I am sure you will be glad to hear our library is getting on with much success.   The men appear more anxious than ever to read.   *   *   I cannot tell you how much we all feel indebted to you for your great kindness, and benevolent exertions ; but particularly our poor sailors."

A second letter, of a later date, stated—

"I have delightful accounts from all the packets ; the men really beg for the books.   I wish I could show you a box just returned from sea, the books well thumbed, a proof, I should think, of their being read."

The writer of these letters was not the only person engaged ; Lieutenant Jennings of the "Tyrean," was amongst the warmest and earliest promoters of the plan, and so were the Fox family.

Accompanied by some of their relatives, the travellers proceeded, passing through the wild stern features of the Cornish coast, to Penzance and the Land's-End. The state of the lunatics at Penzance was very grievous. Elizabeth Fry could not permit such evils to remain without some endeavour to remedy them. She soon afterwards heard from a friend that " the comforts of the poor lunatics at Penzance are likely to be increased. A wall is now building round a part of the garden, which is made expressly for them to walk in, and I hope the internal arrangements are also improved."

A few days were passed among the romantic beauties of North Devon. Thence they turned their steps homwards; but at Amesbury she paused long enough to make arrangements for a library being established for the use of the shepherds of Salisbury Plain. An excellent individual, approved by the clergyman and Sir Edward and Lady Antrobus, undertook the care of the books, and their circulation. After a few months' trial of the plan, he wrote to Mrs. Fry——

" Forty-five books are in constant circulation with the additional magazines. More than fifty poor people read them with attention, return them with thanks, and desire the loan of more, frequently observing, they think it a very kind thing indeed, that they should be furnished with so many good books, free of all cost, so entertaining and instructive, these long winter evenings."

From the different officers of the Coast Guard Stations, she received letters that gladdened her heart; but far too numerous for insertion here, and to select would be most difficult, as all breathe the same spirit, and express their cordial approbation of the plan, and the pleasure felt by the men and their families. But something beyond pleasure was desired by her, with whom the idea originated, that advantage and edification should accrue, to those who read. The seed she sowed has in truth

10

wonderfully flourished, and now it is, that the fruits may be discerned If those, who visit our coasts for pleasure or duty, would make their way into the low-browed preventive houses so continually recurring, in some apartment, frequently the room where the arms are kept, they may see three or four shelves against the wall, filled with well kept, but evidently well read books. Let them enter into a little conversation, with the intelligent looking man, decently dressed, who sits reading, after a long watch, and they will find, whether or not these books are appreciated ; or let them address a few words to the wife, and hear her estimate of their value. Exceptions of course there are, and degrees in the estimate put upon the opportunity for improvement, but the former are few, and the amount of interest and pleasure afforded by the books far beyond any thing that was anticipated, even by the most sanguine supporters of the plan.

Upton, Tenth Month, 13*th.*—I returned home yesterday with my dear husband, from a very affecting and unexpected visit into Norfolk, in consequence of the severe illness and death, of my beloved sister Mary Gurney, my brother Joseph's amiable, devoted, and superior wife. She was in the prime of her day, only thirty-two years of age, a spiritually minded and lively minister, a very intellectual person, and highly cultivated, generous, and remarkably cheerful, a wonderful helper to my brother, adapted to his wants. When I heard how ill she was, I could hardly believe she would die, she had such an apparent call here below, but our ways are not the Lord's ways, nor our thoughts His thoughts. He took her, thus early to Himself, but we apprehend, as the shock of corn fully ripe. Our dearest Joseph's resignation and patience are great indeed, and his even cheerful acquiescence to the will of his God is instructive. The funeral was deeply affecting. After dinner we had an extraordinary time. Our dear brother Francis Cunningham prayed— his dear Richenda spoke. Joseph in the most striking manner enlarged on the character of the departed, on his loss, and his

consolation, the day went on and ended well, in a reading with
the poor neighbours; but words fail me, to tell of the solemn,
holy, loving feeling over us.   Oh! what a blessing is family
unity in the Lord—my children who were present, and many
others were deeply and powerfully impressed.   May it be lasting—may the same spirit that has so remarkably rested upon
us, rest on them, the same love, the same peace, the same unity
of spirit, the same freeness of spiritual communication.   Such
a day is almost like being raised above the things of this world;
all appeared sanctified, all blessed, even the very beauties of the
place.   How did I feel called upon to entreat, and to warn, how
did I seek to bear testimony to the very truth—and how did
dearest Joseph in his affliction beseech all to come to Christ, for
salvation.

23rd.—Since my return home, I have had very satisfactory
letters from the island of Jersey, saying that great alterations
and improvements are taking place in the Hospital.   The Prison
Committee have also acted upon many of my suggestions, I am
now in communication with Lord Beresford, the Governor of
the Island, in the hope of accomplishing an entire alteration in
the prison, new buildings, &c. &c.

In our home prison cause, it is really marvellous to me to
observe the openings of Providence, in the good effected by the
members of the Ladies' British Society.   I feel rather bound to
record these things—not by way of boasting, but as a proof that
all comes from the Lord, who blesses in the labour, and who
strengthens for the work.

Eleventh Month, 25th.—After a beautiful drive over the
Forest, to see Robert Barclay and his children, after their heavy
loss; I incline to express a little of the feelings of my heart.   I
have in my drive, admired the various works of creation.   I have
felt in missing dear Elizabeth Barclay at Knotts Green—how
many are departed from amongst us—how much we have in our
circle, seen, felt and known.   I have observed the marvellous
changes and various deliverances, and how some tenderly-beloved departed ones have been very gently dealt with, provided
for in time, and we believe redeemed, so as to be prepared for
eternity; and when I looked at the various difficulties, temporal

and spiritual, that some amongst us have passed through, the low places they have been brought into, and then again raised up ; provided for naturally, their sins, as we humbly believe, forgiven and blotted out, through the Saviour, and snatched as brands from the burning—my conclusion was, not to be too anxious, not to be too fearful, but to have my heart more fixed, trusting in God.

Twelfth Month, 11*th.*—I returned last evening from a visit to my dear brother Joseph, who was so very low and unwell, that I was unexpectedly sent for ; my visit was interesting, and I trust satisfactory.

To her youngest daughter, who was ill during this absence, she wrote.

Earlham, Twelfth Month, 7th.

I have thought of thee with much tender interest since we parted, and have felt being separated from thee in thy present delicate state of health.   In thinking of thee yesterday, it occurred to me, that this text would eventually apply to thy condition : " I was brought low and He comforted me ; return unto thy rest, oh my soul! for the Lord hath dealt bountifully with thee."   I believe it to be needful for us to be brought low, to know what it is to be really helped of the Lord.   I wish for thee and for myself, and for all of us, to have our hearts fixed, trusting to the Lord.   There is nothing like committing ourselves, and our ways, and our all, to Him, who is our Helper, and who orders every thing for us, in wisdom, love and mercy. I have not been very well since my arrival here, but I do not feel uncomfortable, and expect soon to be better.   I long to return to you all again, although I hope this little turn out is a right one.   I hope, my love, if a little better, that thou wilt get into the air in the garden.

I am, thy tenderly attached mother,
ELIZABETH FRY.

Upton Lane, First Month.—I have had a hope that the last year has, notwithstanding all our short comings, drawn some

near to God; but may we all remember, that we cannot stand
still in our religious course, and if we do not go forward, there
is very great danger of going backward. I have felt unusually
bound to encourage all my most tenderly beloved family, to a
full and entire surrender of themselves, to the service of the best
of Masters, to be willing to be taught of Him, by His Holy
Spirit, through the Scriptures, and through the dealings of our
Heavenly Father towards us. I want all my children to partake
of the same delightful spiritual union that we have partaken of,
as a family, that they may be each other's joy in the Lord. I
think there is much in the observation of Rogers—"It is a rare
thing for any man, so to use prosperity, as to have his heart
drawn by it nearer to God. Therefore we have need in that
state, to watch diligently, and labour to walk humbly." I desire in our intercourse with each other, that we should increasingly partake, not only of temporal enjoyments, but also of
intellectual pleasures, and above all, of spiritual communion,
which gives so lively a relish to all the gifts of God. As to
outward religious callings, at present, there appears some
diversity amongst us ; sweet as it would be to me, to have some
led in the same path as myself, yet I may in truth say, my first
desire is, that my dearest children may seek to be of God, in
Christ Jesus, (as it is easier to join ourselves to a sect than to
be joined to Christ) and may know their Lord's will respecting
them, may seek to be conformed to it, may be fully persuaded in
their own minds, and then hold fast, very fast, that which is
good; that here, they each may fill their ranks in righteousness,
as followers of a crucified Lord, and eventually through Him,
be saved with an everlasting salvation. Amen.

During the commencement of this year, Mrs. Fry encountered
some annoyance, not to say pain, from the animadversions of the
newly-appointed Prison Inspectors, on the state of Newgate.
She had long strenuously urged the necessity of appointing
Prison Inspectors for Great Britain, having seen the advantage
accruing to the prisons in Ireland from their superintendence.

At the close of the preceding year, the Rev. Whitworth

8

Russell and William Crawford, Esquire, were appointed Prison Inspectors to the Home District; Captain Williams to the Eastern; and Dr. Bisset Hawkins to the Southern.   Mr. Frederick Hill was named Inspector for Scotland.   Mr. Russell and Mr. Crawford commenced a searching investigation into the state of Newgate.   Having studied the subject of Prison Discipline, with the advantage of personal inquiry, on the part of Mr. Crawford, in his visit to America, and personal experience, on that of Mr. Russell, whilst Chaplain of the Millbank Penitentiary, they saw, without making fair allowance, the unavoidable defects existing in Newgate.   Mrs. Fry had always herself represented Newgate, as a most defective prison, allowing no room for proper classification or arrrangement.   She had never approved, as a permanent system, the admission of Visitors to the Readings there on Friday; but during the infancy of the question of Prison Reform, whilst public interest had still to be aroused, she believed it a useful and allowable means towards a desired end.

The Inspectors appear altogether to have overlooked the fact, that this was done for the purpose of making known how much might be accomplished by kindness and moral influence, without authoritative enactments, rather than to gratify any morbid curiosity on the part of the visitors, or love of display on that of the ladies.

It is not now worth while to dwell on what was deemed discourteous or unkind at the time, or the means adopted to rectify the inaccuracies which appeared in the First Official Report of the Inspectors.   The differences between them soon died away, and on subsequent occasions, the ladies felt themselves under obligation to these gentlemen for the attention paid to their requests on behalf of the Transports.   The reader may judge from the perusal of the following letter from Mr. Russell, how completely their minds were freed from all misapprehension of the motives or conduct of the Ladies' Committee.

Letter from the Rev. Whitworth Russell to the Secretary of the Ladies' Convict Ship Committee.

"26, Cumberland Street, 14*th July*, 1843.

" My dear Madam,

" As there was no Board of the Inspectors of the Millbank Prison until yesterday afternoon, your very valuable and interesting letter could not sooner be brought under their notice. I am commissioned by them to convey to you their best thanks, and to assure you, how much they desire to promote the objects to which your letter refers, and to carry out the many excellent suggestions it contains. I am going to-day to make inquiries of the different departments, in order to ascertain what has been done with reference to the fitments of the Woodbridge, and the clothing of the convicts who are to go out in her. I am almost afraid we shall not be able to alter the existing arrangements, so as to bring them to bear on the Woodbridge ; we shall, however, try what can be effected.

" We shall not only be anxious to communicate to Mrs. Fry any arrangements we may succeed in making, but shall also be glad to benefit by her advice and experience. As, however, Mr. Crawford is now absent at Parkhurst, and does not return until the afternoon of Monday next, the interview proposed for that day must necessarily be postponed. When our arrangements are more matured, we will ask Mrs. Fry to fix any time for an interview which may be convenient to her. We also beg to offer our thanks to the ladies of the Convict Ship Committee, for their kind co-operation in a work, for which they have already done so much, and in which they will prove such valuable assistants. Let me again thank you, my dear madam, and be assured, we shall gladly receive any communication you may be so good as to make to us.

" I am, my dear Madam,
" Yours very faithfully,
" Whitworth Russell."

Thus, through a measure of evil report, and through many difficulties, did Mrs. Fry pursue her way ; but her aim being singly to serve Him whose service she had deliberately chosen, wherever and however that service might lead her, she could not be " greatly moved." She dealt with Him who " looketh not at the outward appearance" but at " the heart." It was from within that she sought consolation, and there she found the Reward of peace, for her heart was " fixed, trusting in the Lord." From His hands she received success with gratitude—checks or impediments, she knew, were equally of His sending, and to be alike received with thanksgiving.

Upton Lane, Second Month, 16*th.* Yesterday, I had the real satisfaction of meeting our Coast Guard Library Committee; Government gave us £300 ; and Captain Bowles, who was present (the Comptroller of the Customs, or head of all the Coast Guard Stations) gave £20 ; through which grants, we paid for all the books bought for our District Libraries, about 20,000 volumes ; we gave our secretary, T. Timpson, a present of £50, and had £10 over. When I remember the many difficulties I had to encounter in it, first, at the Custom House, the wearisome walks to the top of that great building to see Captain Bowles, my protracted correspondence with various members of the Government, many committees, besides some rebuffs and humiliations to go through, I think hardly any public engagement has occupied so much of my time ; but, now, thanks to my Holy Head, and merciful Helper, I think my part in it is finished. I desire to be very watchful how I put my hand to any other fresh public work, for I see much care needful, lest my attention should be too much turned from my own heart, my own family, or even my duties to the religious community to which I belong, but on the other hand, if ever called again by my Lord, into fresh service of this kind, may I be enabled, promptly, diligently and faithfully to attend to it.

At this time, Mrs. Fry had the gratification of making the

acquaintance of Miss Anley,* then about to proceed to Australia, to reside for a time with her cousin, Mrs. Dumaresq. This lady entered warmly into Mrs. Fry's views; the observations she made during her sojourn in that distant land are highly interesting, though the picture she draws is very sorrowful, of the almost unavoidable crime and misery existing there.

Colonel Dumaresq, had as many as one hundred prisoners in his employ, and it was his aim in every way to promote their moral and religious welfare, but his difficulties, though great, could not have equalled those of his predecessor Sir W. Edward Parry, who, with his lady, spent some years at Port Stephen, devoted not more to the secular interests of the company he so effectively served, than to the good of the wretched convict population around him.

Upton Lane, Second Month, 25th.—On the 23rd instant, I thought it right to lay before my Monthly Meeting, my belief, that it was my duty to have some religious services in Sussex, Kent, and my own Quarterly Meeting. I can hardly express the sweetness and peacefulness I felt, in making this small sacrifice, to what I believe to be, the call of duty. The near unity and sympathy expressed with me by my friends, was also very encouraging and comforting. My dearest brother Samuel offering to take this expedition, was quite a help and comfort.

Third Month, 13th.—I returned from my journey on Sixth-day last, having been out a week. I felt low, in fact, almost ill with the serious weight of the prospect of the Public Meetings. The first Meeting I wished to have, was at Hastings, the second at Rye; a curious interesting place, towards which I had felt much attracted in my last journey. We found a meeting-house there. Grover Kemp, a valuable young minister joined me at my request, which was a great satisfaction to me.

At Hastings, several of the Coast Guard men and officers were at the Meeting. I had many proofs of the use and value

* Authoress of the " Prisoners of Australia," " Miriam," and other works.

of the libraries sent to them, to my comfort and satisfaction ; proving it not to have been labour " in vain in the Lord." Real kindness, almost affection, as well as gratitude was shown to me, by several of the men and officers and their families. We hope a Bible Society will be formed at Rye in consequence of our visit, and a Prison Society at Dover. But to come to one of the most interesting parts of our expedition, we went to Sheerness, to visit the women and children in the ships in ordinary. Captain Kennedy had them collected at my request ; it was a fine sight, in a large man-of-war, instead of bloodshed and fightings, to see many naval officers, two chaplains, sailors, soldiers, ladies, numbers of women and children, all met to hear what two Quakers had to say, more particularly a woman, and to listen to any advice given by them. We examined the children, as to their knowledge, then gave them advice, afterwards we addressed their parents, and lastly, those present generally—we were received with great cordiality by Captain Kennedy, and his wife.

23rd.—I laid before our Monthly Meeting on Third-day, my belief of its being my duty to go to Ireland, and take Liverpool and Manchester in the way. I had the unity of my friends —I say in my heart—unless Thy presence go with me, take me not up hence. May my Lord answer this prayer in His tender mercy.

Fourth Month, *12th.*—My beloved niece Catherine Gurney is to be married this morning, to my dear nephew Edward North Buxton. My prayers have been offered up on their behalf, may the Lord be with them, bless them, keep, prosper and increase them !

14th.—Just about leaving home for Ireland—oh dearest Lord ! bless I entreat Thee this act of faith, to my family, myself, and those amongst whom I go, and be, I most humbly pray Thee, my Keeper their Keeper, my Helper their Helper, my Strength their Strength, my Joy and Peace and their Joy and Peace, Amen ! Grant this for Thine own name sake, oh ! most gracious Lord God, cause also, that we may meet again, in love, joy, peace, and safety.

The motives of Elizabeth Fry for undertaking this journey were two-fold. To attend the Meetings of Friends in Lancashire, and be present at the Dublin Yearly Meeting ; and to visit the prisons at Dublin, and make a renewed effort for their amendment. She cared especially for the large female prison, in Grange Gorman Lane, then in contemplation, she had long earnestly wished to see a prison devoted to women. This being the first in the kingdom, it was likely to prove a sort of model, should the example be followed in other places, she therefore considered it of great importance, that the arrangements should be as complete and effective as possible. Lord Mulgrave (Marquis of Normanby) the Lord Lieutenant, she had reason to believe was anxious to carry out, a wise, and yet merciful system of prison discipline. Mr. Spring Rice (Lord Monteagle) kindly furnished her with a letter of introduction to him, but in a note to herself, assures her that any introduction to that nobleman was unnecessary, which indeed she found verified, for the attention Lord Normanby gave to her suggestions, was not greater than his personal kindness and courtesy to herself and her friends, during their stay in Ireland.

The Grange Gorman Lane prison was completed early in 1837. After the lapse of ten years, it is thus mentioned in Major Cottingham's Report. Appendix to Twenty-fifth Report of Inspectors-General of Prisons in Ireland.

"Visited, February 18th, 1847.—Although I made my annual inspection of this prison on the 18th February, 1847, as a date upon which to form my report, yet I have had very many opportunities of seeing it during the past and former years, in my duties connected with my superintendence of the convict department. The visitor may see many changes in the faces and persons of the prisoners, but no surprise can ever find a difference in the high and superior order with which this prison is conducted. The Matron, Mrs. Rawlins, upon whom the entire responsibility of the interior management devolves, was selected some years since, and sent over to this country by the benevolent and philanthropic Mrs. Fry, whose exertions in the cause of female prison reformation, were extended to all parts of the British Empire; and who, although lately summoned to the presence of her Divine Master, has nowhere left a more valuable instance of her sound judgment, and high discriminating powers, than in the selection of Mrs. Rawlins to be placed at the head of this experimental prison, occupied alone by females; and so successful has the experiment been, that I understand several other prisons solely for females, have lately been opened in Scotland, and even in Australia. In this prison is to be seen an uninterrupted system of reformatory discipline in every class, such as is to be found in no other prison, that I am aware off."

The following extracts are from a letter, written by the Matron, Mrs. Rawlins, dated September 1st, 1847.

"It is perhaps needless for me to tell you, that Mrs. Fry had long wished to have the trial made of an exclusively female prison. That Mrs. Fry's plan has completely succeeded, every authority, both city and government, have born ample and unqualified testimony, but I regret to say, she never personally saw the fruit of her labour, not having visited Ireland since my residence here, but to her wise, judicious, and maternal counsel (under Providence) I entirely ascribe the success that has attended our exertions. I never took any material step at the commencement, without consulting her, and at her own request, at least every week, I wrote an account of my movements; and many obstacles that at first arose, she settled in her own quiet way by her influence with the government."

There was another subject which occupied Mrs. Fry's attention in Ireland, the state of the National Schools there; she visited some and obtained minute reports of the state of many others. To effect this, she requested her friend James Doyle, who afterwards was examined before a committee of the House of Commons upon the subject, and another of her friends, to visit as many of these schools as they conveniently could, and to procure reports of others, which they could not personally inspect.

They accordingly visited all the Schools (as far as they could ascertain) under that system in the city and neighbourhood of Dublin, and some in the neighbourhood of Cork. From other parts of the country they received reports from creditable sources.

It appeared that in Dublin and the South of Ireland, there were in all 28 schools, containing 4400 children— 79 only of whom were Protestants.

Of the above—

9 were attached to Roman Catholic Chapels,
3 on Chapel Premises,
1 on Nunnery ditto,
3 conducted by Monks,
12 unattached.

In Belfast were two schools containing 800 children, of whom (in one) were 375 Protestants.

In most of the schools they found the scripture lessons recommended by the Board, but in very few instances, had they the appearance of having been read except in the Belfast School, where the Protestants were numerous. In all the other schools were found the Roman Catholic Catechism, and other books inculcating Roman Catholic doctrines, and in most of them they were daily taught. After hearing these details but one conclusion could be formed, that the schools were falling rapidly under the power of the Roman Catholic priesthood, and that instead of affording Scriptural instruction generally they gave but a fresh opportunity for inculcating the spirit of Popery. Even the Bible lessons so strongly recommended by the Commissioners were in most cases very little used, and then without the children being told from whence they were taken, or led to reverence the Bible as the word of God. It was not Mrs. Fry's wish to take a prominent part in any thing which she did not consider as an absolute duty, encumbent upon herself to perform. She communicated, upon her return to England, her observations to Lord Morpeth, but it was through her brother-in-law, Mr. Buxton, that she endeavoured, to bring forward the dangers which she detected, in the working of the system. That she was most liberal, almost too liberal, no one who knew her will deny; but this very liberality caused her to disapprove of the expenditure of public money in the support of schools, professedly intended for the good of all, and to favour no sect or party; but in point of fact, excluding by their practical arrangements and internal government, the children of pious Protestants, and the superintendence of pious Protestant ministers, of every name.

Upon, Lane, Fifth Month, 13th.—I returned home safely yesterday afternoon. I think I never had so happy and so prosperous an arrival—I wept with joy; the stream appears to be turned for a while, my tears have often flowed for sorrow, and now my beloved husband and children have caused them to flow for joy. I found not only all going on well, and having done so during my absence, but to please, comfort and surprise me, my dearest husband had had my rooms altered and made most comfortable, and my children had sent me nice presents to render them more complete. Their offerings of love quite gladdened my heart, though far too good for me; I felt utterly unworthy of them, I may say peculiarly so. I have seldom returned home more sensible of the hidden evils of my heart. Circumstances have unusually made me feel this. I fully believe in this going out, much help has been granted me in various ways; my understanding has appeared to be enlightened more fully to see and comprehend gospel truth, and power has been given me to utter it boldly beyond what I could have supposed. The fear of man was much taken away in Ireland, when I had to tell them what I believed to be home truths ———. I may say I am brought down under a very deep feeling of utter unworthiness ; and earnestly desire and pray, that whatever of our labours have been acceptable in the sight of our heavenly Father, they may be truly blessed to many, and not be in vain in Him; and that whatever may have been in any way not according to His will, that He would in His own power prevent any harm from it arising to others.

The kindness shown us by James and Hannah Doyle, Elizabeth Doyle, and their mother, is I think never to be forgotten, during our long stay with them ; also by our much valued friends Jonathan and Eliza Pim, and many others dearly loved in the Lord. My desires and prayers are strong, that being returned home, I may profit by the deep experience of this expedition. May my holy Redeemer cause me by His Spirit to walk very closely to Himself, keeping to the Truth in His Spirit, and by His power preserving me from impetuous zeal in holy things. In this Yearly Meeting, may very sound discretion be my portion. As for my home duties, my longings are indescribable that I may perform them in deep humility, godliness, holy fear and love ; that I may be a preacher of righteousness in all things and in all ways.

Sixth Month, 12*th,* (*First-day morning*).—We, yesterday, had our British Society Meeting, and it was striking to me to observe, how much our various labours had been blessed, and to hear how many poor women from various parts have been induced to forsake their evil courses, and are now either leading good lives, or have died happy Christian deaths.

18*th.*—I have felt a good deal pressed in spirit, these last few days. The day before yesterday I counted twenty-nine persons who came here, on various accounts, principally to see me ; there are times, when the tide of life is almost overpowering. It makes me doubtful, as to our remaining much longer in this place, which, from its situation brings so many here. I have several things which rather weightily press me just now. I desire to lay my case before the Lord, trusting in Him, and casting myself and my whole care upon Him. Dearest Lord, help, supply all our needs, through the riches of Thy grace, in Christ Jesus ! Amen.

I yesterday accompanied General Campbell, the Lieutenant-Governor of Jersey, to Lord John Russell, our Secretary of State, to settle the difficulties respecting the prison in that island. May our efforts be blessed.

23rd.—I much regret to say that last evening, I had an account that my dearest sister Louisa ruptured a bloodvessel on the chest and is very poorly, she had a similar attack, last summer. She has in addition, ever since the loss of her son, three years ago, been much tried by nervous depression, so as to cast quite a cloud over her, still she is lively in spirit, walking humbly and watchfully before the Lord ; but I consider her affliction to be a heavy one, and one that claims in no common degree, our deep sympathy and prayers—may our Lord, heal, help and sustain her ! whether her course here be for a longer or shorter time !

In June, Mrs. Fry had the gratification of receiving the printed Report of the Committee, acting under the sanction of His Majesty's Government, for furnishing the Coast Guard of the United Kingdom, with libraries of religious and instructive books; announcing the completion of the project with a short account of what had been effected.

" The committee, acting under the sanction of His Majesty's Government, for furnishing the Coast Guard of the United Kingdom with libraries of religious and instructive books, and also with school books for the families of the men employed on that service, having, by the blessing of Divine Providence, completed that object, it becomes their pleasing duty to lay before the subscribers a Report of their proceedings.

" In the commencement of this duty, it is proper gratefully to acknowledge, that the idea of furnishing these libraries first suggested itself to the benevolent mind of Mrs. Fry, whose active and charitable exertions on all occasions affecting the benefit of mankind are too well known, and too highly estimated, to need further remark on the present occasion, and who having previously succeeded in inducing His Majesty's Government to establish libraries for the use of the patients in the naval hospi-

tals, was induced by the observations she had made on the subject, to endeavour to extend the same beneficial measure to the
Coast Guard Service, and after several unsuccessful efforts,
arising from the expense which it would occasion, a sum of
£500 was obtained in 1835, from the first lord of the treasury
(Sir Robert Peel) for this purpose, which munificent donation
has since been followed by subscriptions from many charitable
individuals, and grants from several public book societies, but
as the whole of these funds were not sufficient to meet the object
in view, the present chancellor of the exchequer (Mr. Spring
Rice) kindly granted two further sums amounting together to
£460 to effect its completion.

"The means thus so liberally afforded, have enabled the committee to provide and forward to the coast,

498	Libraries for the Stations on shore, containing	25,896 vols.
74	Ditto	Districts	12,880
48	Ditto	Cruisers	1,867
School books for the children of the crews of stations			6,464
Pamphlets, Tracts, &c.			5,357 in Nos.

Making a total of 52,464 vols.

and thereby to furnish a body of deserving and useful men and
their wives and families, (amounting to upwards of 21,000 persons, with the means of moral and religious instruction, as well
as profitable amusement, most of whom, from their situation in
life, have not the means of procuring such benefits from their
own resources, and who in many instances, are so far removed
from places of public worship and schools, as to prevent the possibility of themselves or their families deriving advantage from
either."

This work was now accomplished; and dismissed from her
mind as a point gained, and a blessing granted.   But the undertaking had been a very onerous one, in some respects the
most remarkable ever accomplished by Elizabeth Fry.   It
had involved much bodily fatigue and moral effort.   It had

brought her into contact with a great variety of persons and had subjected her to some trials and rebuffs in the outset, which with her shrinking and sensitive nature would only have been borne because she believed it her duty to persevere in the object she had in view.

Her active exertions in behalf of the prisons of the United Kingdom generally, were drawing to a close. She had been an eminent instrument, in calling attention to the subject—but attention was now fully aroused, and the Prison Inspectors were pursuing their scrutinies with great and good effect.

Other matters, however, pressed upon her attention; nothing so much as the state of the Prisons in Guernsey and Jersey; in the latter prison, the difficulties of remedying the existing evils appeared almost insurmountable. Dr. Bisset Hawkins had visited both these gaols, and carefully investigated their state; he had also given his attention in Jersey to the points in dispute between the States and the Governor, Field-Marshal Lord Beresford. In his report to Lord John Russell, he describes the prison as in the most neglected state, exhibiting almost every defect in arrangement, which a prison is capable of displaying, and suffering under the absence of many common essentials, such as " clothing, suitable bedding, soap, washing, white-washing, while the keeper appears to be almost his own master, and is appointed by the Bailiff of the Island, although he derives his emoluments from the Governor,"

Dr. Hawkins recommended to have the question settled, of maintaining the prisoners, by an equal portion being borne by the Governor and the States. He proposed that a House of Correction should be built on the grounds on which the present prison is situated, which affords ample space for the erection of such a building, without disturbing the already existing gaol. With respect to the expense of building it, he shows, that the Grant of King Charles the Second, by which the States are

empowered to raise an Impôt on Liquors, expressly enjoins that
" Three Hundred Livres Tournois," out of the revenue so raised,
" shall be yearly employed for the erecting and building a convenient House, and for and towards raising and maintaining of
a Stock of Money, to be used for the setting to work, and orderly governing of Poor and Idle People, the relief of decayed
Tradesmen, and the Correction and Restraint of Vagabonds and
Beggars within the said Isle."

From this fund, he considers, that the States, by the payment
of £1000 for two successive years, could, without difficulty,
meet the expenses of erecting a building, in all respects sufficient for the required purpose.   He recommended a Prison
Board for the superintendence, not only of the work, but of the
prison afterwards, to consist of the following five high functionaries of the Island; namely the Lieutenant-Governor, the
Bailiff, the two Law-officers of the Crown, and the Sheriff or
Deputy Sheriff, (usually denominated Vicomte or Deputy
Vicomte) the Secretary and Treasurer to be the Greffier of the
States.

Dr. Hawkins' propositions met with the concurrence of Lord
John Russell, who recommended their adoption to the States.
By that body Lord John Russell's communication was very fairly
received, and the alterations they suggested were unimportant.
Mrs. Fry took a lively interest in the subject as it proceeded.
She was urged by many of her island friends, again to go to
Jersey, before the contemplated buildings were begun.

Lord John Russell had favoured her with an interview on
the subject, and she had frequently communicated with Lord
Beresford.   On this, as on many other occasions, her knowledge
of the subject, and her facility in devising expedients, occasioned
her not merely to be listened to with attention, but not unfrequently her counsel to be sought.   And it is due to men of
different parties, who successively guided the helm of State, to

acknowledge, that her remarks were invariably received with courtesy, and where (as was generally the case), the subject matter approved itself to their own judgments, her advice as invariably followed. How much of this was owing to her extreme caution in forming opinions, and her nice discretion in bringing them forward, will be discerned by those, who whilst they read the history of her life, observe and comprehend her mental qualities. She considered that her presence might prove serviceable in Jersey; she was earnest that the arrangements about to be made there should be as complete as possible, especially for women. She wished again to inspect the Hospital, and to see the working of the District Society. Similar objects attracted her in Guernsey. She believed also, that it was her duty to visit the island of Alderney, where hitherto she had not been.

To her husband and daughter the idea of a renewed tarriance in Jersey was entirely agreeable—but in her heart, an impediment existed, which occasioned her no little conflict, many doubts, and much distress, before she could determine upon the allotted path of duty.

Her sister, Mrs. Samuel Hoare had never rallied from the loss of her eldest son. She bowed in submission to the blow; but never recovered the shock, and though she was enabled to persevere in all her duties, with much true Christian cheerfulness, it was evident to those who loved her, that the serious injury her constitution had received, was slowly but surely undermining the powers of life. Never, perhaps, had a son been more to his mother than her first-born son, had been to Mrs. Hoare—never the tie of affection or sympathy stronger. She had reared him with a firm, but most tender hand; he had passed through the slippery paths of youth, and early manhood, singularly intact, and had distinguished himself at College, which he quitted with high credit, to enter with equal diligence a business-career

with his father in London. He had only left the home of his
parents, when united to one, as much their choice as his own.
Blessed as husband and father with all outward prosperity,
suddenly, the message came, " Thou shalt die, and not live."
He returned to his father's house, for a few weeks of deep illness
and sedulous nursing ; there, in perfect, acknowledged and
most simple reliance on the wisdom and goodness of God his
Saviour, in all His dealings with the children of men, he left his
father's house, on earth, for the eternal home, prepared for him
by his Father in heaven.

At the time that Mrs. Fry was preparing to leave England, it
became obvious that her sister was approaching that " country
from whose bourn no traveller returns." There are many who
believe that they " acknowledge God in all their ways," trusting
in Him, " to direct their paths ;" but there are not many who
carry this belief into the practice of life, or are from experience,
able to unite with Judge Hale in his assertion, that—

" They who truly fear God, have a secret guidance from a
higher wisdom than what is barely human, viz., the Spirit of
Truth and Godliness—which doth really, though secretly, prevent and direct them. Any man that sincerely and truly fears
Almighty God, and calls and relies upon him for his direction,
has it as *really as a son has the counsel and direction of his
father ;* and though the voice be not audible, nor discernible by
sense, yet it is as real as if a man heard a voice saying, ' This is
the way walk ye in it.'

" Though this secret direction of Almighty God, is principally seen in matters relating to the soul; yet it may also be
found in the concerns of this life, which a good man that fears
God and begging his direction, will *very often* if *not at all
times* find. I can call my own experience to witness that *even
in the temporal concerns of my whole life,* I have never been
disappointed of the best direction, when I have, in humility and
sincerity implored it."

Elizabeth Fry was one of the few, who sought this guidance, and there probably lay the secret of her strength. She watched for opportunity, she waited for occasion, she listened for the Father's voice, but when heard, unhesitatingly pursued her way.

She believed it her duty to go to Jersey, at any sacrifice of personal feeling, and this view was confirmed, by knowing that by her suffering sister she was not needed; every thing that love or skill could effect, being done for Mrs. Hoare, by her own family and her other sisters. Another circumstance tended to satisfy Mrs. Fry as to the rectitude of her decision, her sister-in-law Elizabeth Fry, then in very delicate health, having been advised again to visit the Channel Islands, where she had before derived much benefit from the mild sea air. She, with Mr. and Mrs. Fry, and their daughter, embarked at Southampton, on a calm fine evening, with every prospect of a favourable voyage, but these favourable appearances were not of long duration. About four o'clock in the morning, all on board were roused by the sudden stopping of the vessel. A dense fog had come on, when passing through the intricate passage between the Caskets and the Island of Alderney. They remained many hours entangled amongst rocks, with the fog so thick, that it was not always easy to see the length of the vessel; much apprehension was entertained by many on board, in which Mrs. Fry partook, though preserving her wonted calmness of demeanour.

Happily, may it not be called providentially, there was as passenger in the steamer, the old Guernsey pilot who had brought Lord de Saumarez, and two frigates under his command, into Guernsey, in the presence of a superior French force, by piloting them through a passage, generally considered impracticable. Of his advice and assistance, the Captain himself a skilful pilot, took advantage, and after a time of careful navigation, the joyful tidings spread among the passengers, that the jeopardy was over, that they were through the channel, and once more in the open sea. The spirit of Mrs. Fry's mind was exemplified by her remark to her daughter, when as they approached Guernsey the clouds drew up, the sun shone forth in brightness and the cheerful sounds of sabbath bells saluted their ears, " I have felt it very doubtful whether this was not to be for us the dawn of the eternal, instead of the earthly Sabbath; I thought it rather the Church above, than the Church below, we were to join to-day."

Jersey, Eighth Month, 6th.—My husband and I have been here rather more than a week. I left home on Fourth-day, the 27th, accompanied by my dear sister Gurney, leaving my husband and the rest of the party to follow on Sixth-day, because I believed it my duty to attend the Quarterly Meeting at Alton, in my way to Southampton. In tender mercy, I was permitted to part from my beloved family in peace, in love, and in good hope that our Heavenly Father would bless and protect them   On Second-day, before leaving home, we had our dear children and grandchildren, for a sweet cheerful evening, drinking tea and having strawberries, in the garden, a little farewell frolic—it was a lovely sight.   From Alton, I proceeded to Southampton, where we all met, and were favoured with a favourable passage till early in the morning, when so awful a fog came on, just as we were in the midst of the rocks, between Alderney and Guernsey, that the Captain and the crew appeared to be much alarmed.   We all felt it very seriously, and I experienced something of my own infirmity and fearful nature, still I was quiet, and I think trustful.   It was delightful once more to see land, and to have the sun shine upon us. .I can hardly express the feeling.   We were detained about four hours in this fog.   I must describe our arrival, the sun breaking out, showing us the Island of Guernsey, Herm and Sark.   Castle Carey, the place of our destination, on the top of the hill, surrounded by trees, looking beautiful, we met with the most cordial reception from our friends and their children—the place delightful— my room commanding the finest view of the sea and islands, our comforts abundant, far above our deserts.   I had appre-

hended, previously to leaving home, that I should feel it a duty
to visit the island of Alderney, but I became discouraged, the
danger of the sea having been so much brought home to me,
and the passage being very difficult. But I found upon weighing the subject, that I was not satisfied to omit it, and therefore if a favourable opening occurred, resolved to make the
effort, and to go on Fourth-day, the 11th. We tried for a
conveyance in vain, till the very morning, when we found a
vessel going. The sun shone brilliantly, the wind fair; every
thing prospered our setting off, and we appeared to have the
unity of all our party. My beloved husband, Edmund
Richards, Sophia Mourant, and myself. We had a very favourable voyage, though these little sailing vessels are unpleasant
to me, and give me an uncomfortable sensation. We arrived at
this curious island, which is rocky, wild, not generally cultivated, covered in parts with a carpet of lovely wild flowers, and
scantily inhabited by an interesting people. No inn of course,
but we had a very nice lodging, where we might truly say, we
wanted for no real comfort, so the Lord doth provide. I was
low and poorly, the first part of our visit; but like the fog on
the voyage, my cloudy state was suddenly dispersed, as from a
ray of the Sun of Righteousness. We held some meetings, we
also formed a Ladies' Charity to visit the poor, we proposed
sending a library, and Edmund Richards formed a temperance
society. We were received with great kindness, by numbers of the people, and by Major Baines the Governor, and
his wife. We found no opportunity for our departure at the
time we had proposed leaving Alderney, and were literally
confined there, until the end of the following week, when
the way appeared to be as clear to return as it had been
to go. A vessel to take us—the wind fair, and the sun
bright. We arrived safely at Castle Carey, on the evening of
the 24th of the Seventh Month, and found good accounts from
home, and from the party who had preceded us to Jersey; thanks
be to my Heavenly Father! My too anxious and fearful mind
having been disposed to much anxiety. I had not much public
service in Guernsey. Meetings as usual on First-day. I went
to see many families of Friends and others, and besides some of

the poor, visited the Hospital, and urged the great need of a Lunatic Asylum. The evening before our departure, I had a very solemn Public Meeting, with many interesting persons, afterwards several joined us at Castle Carey, where we had a time of much interest, pleasantly partaking of natural friendship; afterwards we were read to by a clergyman, and then I had a very solemn occasion of thanksgiving and prayer, greatly doubting my ever seeing most of their faces again. The next morning, John and Matilda Carey, their children, the clergyman, and our friends the Richards, all accompanied us to the shore, some went with us in a boat to the ship, which I entered in peace and comfort, under the belief, that I had been in my right allotment in that island, and Alderney. We had a beautiful passage here, calm, and lovely weather, and had the blessing of finding the party well.

Jersey, 19th.—In this place I find much to occupy me, in the Hospital, the District Society, and in the Prisons. We receive much kind attention from the inhabitants of the island. I had much to say in a large District Society Meeting, yesterday—I hope usefully. I entered it prayerfully, but not enough so. I have enjoyed some delightful expeditions into the lovely country, where we have sometimes taken our cold dinner, and spent the day in the rocky bays. We have also joined two large parties of the same kind, which were pleasant to me; my nature leads me to be social, and rather like general society, but I wish all to be done in the right spirit. Innocent recreation, I believe, is profitable as well as pleasant. Our Lord desired His servants to rest, and He evidently felt for them when they had hardly time to eat; (6th chapter of Mark, 31st verse;) but this rest was after labour. I believe our recreations are right, as far as they fit us for our Master's service, and wrong if they enervate and disqualify us for it. I have deeply felt my sister Hoare's state. I may say in measure, I bear her burdens with her,—she has my frequent prayers, and my tears often rise in remembrance of her. My heart is also much at home, most tenderly interested for all my children, more particularly my boys. I think I have cause for much thankfulness in the accounts from them.

23rd.—The letters on First-day brought us the affecting intelligence that my much-loved sister Hoare was worse; her decline has been rapid the last week or two. My sister Cunningham wrote to me to beg me to set off to her directly; this proved a stunning blow—the low estate of this tenderly beloved sister, the difficulty of getting to her, the doubts as to what I ought to do, the disappointment that we should again lose our time of refreshment and recreation in France, all upset me, as I say, stunned me. What could I do, but pray in this emergency to be helped and directed aright; that I might faithfully do my duty to all, and that my poor dear afflicted sister might be so helped immediately by her Lord Himself, that no other help might be really needful to her, yet the infirmity of my heart led me to pray also, that if right for us, I might see her again and be some little help and comfort to her in her last hours.

Mrs. Hoare was to Mrs. Fry a beloved sister, a faithful and unfailing friend, and often a wise counsellor—she being a woman of a large and comprehensive mind, excellent in judgement, and of very uncommon cultivation. Besides, it was again a lessening of the band; another taken of the seven sisters, who had entered life together, and, as such, an event to affect and alter it, to those who were left.

In the early days of Earlham, Louisa Gurney is described by one who shared with her their interests and pleasures, as " a noble girl, and the most talented of any of them, possessing a fine understanding, great energy, and a taste for excellence, which produced a high stimulus in her pursuits, and success, for the most part, in all she undertook, but, in case of failure, an equal degree of disappointment and vexation, a heart warm and generous, a glowing disposition, very benevolent, active and effective in her habits; rising early of her own accord, full of her own objects, and fond of learning and cultivation of every kind."

As a mother nothing more need be said of her, than that the

principles inculcated in her writings,* she carried out in daily practice, enlarging and expanding as her children advanced in life.

After the death of their son, Mr. Hoare's family removed to their residence at Cromer.   Thence she wrote to Mrs. Fry—

" How kind of you, my dearest sister, to write again so fully to us ! With your tender hand, never be afraid of touching us in our present low estate. You well know the secrets of real and deep grief—few have been taught like yourself to minister to the afflicted. I always feel a difficulty in describing our present state ; I do so long to be thankful, and enabled to acknowledge the mercies received, and the manifestations that have been vouchsafed to us, of the beauty and efficacy of grace received in humble faith and obedience ! such simplicity of faith, humility, meekness, fortitude, and deep resignation of spirit as we were permitted to witness !   But the loss is indescribable ; and the conflict has been greater and sharper than I was prepared for. There is a natural sinking too, after strong and continued excitement, and I believe I am suffering from the shake to the nerves, as well as the great trial to the feelings.   How do we need, in the season of deep trial, to refrain our souls and keep them low ! to be made willing to suffer, till the time of revival and refreshment is ordered for us ! ' He will command His loving kindness in the day-time, and in the night His song shall be with me.' May this be our happy experience, and your dear Rachel's too, in her long sickness !   What an exercise of long suffering day after day ! But what a provision for us—' Give us day by day our daily bread !' We must learn to live as little children, our eye continually fixed on our God and Saviour, seeking for nourishment from Him, and that precious anointing, which can heal our deepest wounds, and shed abroad in us the consoling and constraining love of Christ ! Oh, for more of that love, to elevate and sanctify our natural affections, and gradually to swallow up the sense of sorrow and mourning, in the view of the love and faithfulness of Him who hath promised

* Hints on Early Education, and the Workhouse Boy.

eternal life to all that believe in Him! How I long to drink more deeply of this living stream! for all our fresh springs are in Him, and our times of mourning and of joy in His hands."

The accounts of Mrs. Hoare becoming rapidly worse, and Mrs. Fry's objects in the Channel Islands being accomplished, she prepared for her departure.

A Committee of Ladies was established for visiting the Hospital in Jersey, with the Lady of the Lieutenant-Governor General Campbell at its head. The District Society was increasing in usefulness, the new House of Correction was likely to be established on the best principles; and she had the comfort of knowing, that all these objects were left under the skilful and efficient superintendence of her kind friend Major-General Touzel, who had been with other Jersey gentlemen, faithful coadjutors in her various labours. Her visits to Alderney and Guernsey had been accomplished to her own satisfaction.

Jersey, Eighth Month, 25th.—Since I last wrote, I have passed through much conflict—indeed I have been strongly drawn two ways. I now expect to cross to-morrow; but some discouragement attends it. I am about going to a Public Meeting of importance, to finish, as I suppose, such services here. Be pleased, most gracious Lord, to be with me in this straitened place, help me through this service, by Thine own Spirit to glorify Thee; edify, comfort, and help this people, and those dear to me. Show me, I pray Thee, for Thy dear Son's sake, this token for good in my low estate—and if it please Thee, make my way quite clear before me; if I am called to my beloved sister, oh, dearest Lord, be Thyself with me, and all of us, that we may part in peace, love, and joy, in Thee. Amen. In Thy love and pity in Christ Jesus, hearken to my unworthy cry.

Upton Lane, Ninth Month, 13th.—I was favoured to get through this Meeting well. By the close of that day, I had very much concluded the various duties that I was called to

7

perform in that island. My daughter was better, and the time to depart seemed come, though I minded having to get up in the night, for we had to be in the vessel before four o'clock, A.M. When the morning came the wind was favourable, and we, not the worse for getting up so early. I felt peace, in going at that time, and not waiting for the next post, and prayed for preservation for us all. We then set off, found a comfortable small vessel, a good captain, rather a moderate sea, at first the weather doubtful; but by degrees the day cleared, the sun shone upon us, and though the wind became high and the sea rough, yet it did not make us unwell, and we had altogether a pleasant and prosperous voyage. I left my sister Elizabeth Fry at Weymouth, and travelled on to London on First and Second-day, as in a case of this kind, I consider it allowable to travel on the Sabbath. I arrived at Hampstead on Third-day morning the 29th, and found my much-loved sister in a very affecting state; her malady, whatever it is, having made rapid advances. From extreme reduction, her mind appears unable to form more than one sentence at a time; she therefore can express but little of her mind religiously, but, even in this very low tried state, we perceive her high Christian principle. No complaining, no irritation; kind and grateful, yielding to our requests, whilst a word or two, now and then, show us her mind. When I said, "How suffering illness is," and "what it is to suffer"—she added, "to reign," referring to the text, those who "suffer with Christ will also reign with Him in glory." Being tried by pain, I expressed that "all was right" that was ordered for us; she replied, "perfectly right." I was plunged into deep feeling and conflict on entering the scene, the transition being great from the one in Jersey, and my foolish, fearful, doubting mind was full of misgivings at having left my husband and daughter, and not going with them to France; but, thanks to my Heavenly Father, my spirit became gradually more at rest.

I had the inexpressible comfort of being permitted a few days with her, and she evidently liked my company. I particularly observed, how gently I was dealt with, by her reviving a little after I arrived, so that I had not the bitterness of her at once sinking. The affliction was thus mitigated to me; I was en-

6

abled to show her some marks of my deep and true love, and to be with, and earnestly pray for her, in the hour of death. I was helped to be some comfort to many of her family, and (utterly unworthy as I know I am of it) I believe in my various ministrations, I was enabled to prove the power of the Spirit to qualify for his own work, and amongst them all, particularly with my dear nephew, who has just entered the Church, deeply to impress the necessity of the work of the Spirit being carried on in the heart; and of having Christian charity towards others of every denomination. My beloved sister Hoare's death has made a deep impression on me. I do not like to enter life or its cares, or to see many, or to be seen. I like to withdraw from the world, and to be very quiet. I have naturally much felt the event, though supported and comforted under it.

To her Sister Mrs. Buxton, and her Family then in Scotland.

Upton Lane, *Ninth Month,* 14*th,* 1836.

To the Dear Party at Rennyhill,

The accounts of you and from you, have deeply interested me this morning. I desire, my tenderly beloved ones, to hand you a few words of encouragement, more particularly my dearest sister. I feel our loss a deep one indeed ; but I also see much wisdom, mercy and love in the heavy trial,—in the first place, as it respects herself. Her very susceptible mind was so acutely sensible of the trials of life, that her Lord saw she had had enough ; more might have overwhelmed her, therefore she was taken in the accepted time. I see also, that her many preservations and deliverances, and her being kept as she was by the power of God, in soundness of faith through her sore conflicts, a cause for deep thankfulness, and then, to look upon her, really and fully at rest—in and with the Beloved of her soul, with her Lord, and also with the just made perfect—brings to my feelings, as well as to my mind, much rest, peace and refreshment on her behalf. Then I consider ourselves, and our great loss ; but I also see a something of gain, in her being taken in so much freshness, in the midst of her usefulness, it causes her death to speak so loudly, the very vacancy makes it stimulating. I have not unfrequently observed Christians being called away in the midst of their labours, much blessed to those who remain, in leading them to look more simply to Him, who can work with or without his instruments, in making them more diligent, seeing that the Lord is at hand. Again, by encouraging to pa-tience, hope, and trust, as we know not how soon the warfare may be accomplished with any of us; and further, the holy lively example of such, is so present with us, and so encouraging to strive to follow them, as they followed Christ. But after expressing so far, the bright side of the question, I know and feel the other but too well, to have one so tenderly beloved gone from our present view—to see her place vacant—to miss her delightful influence and tender watchful care over all, is bitter, causing many a heaving of the heart. I am very anxious for thee, dearest Hannah, that thou mayst be comforted; remember all our time is short, and that it is well, to have some safely landed beyond the reach of every storm.

Upton Lane, Ninth Month, 22nd.—On Third day, I dined with Joseph and Alice; thirteen of my children were there, and no one else. I have seldom enjoyed a visit anywhere more. We had a solemn reading and time of prayer, before we parted.

To her Daughter, Mrs. Francis Cresswell.

Upton Lane, *Ninth Month.*

My dearest Rachel,

I fancy you arriving to-morrow from Cresswell, and I write for a letter; in my quiet home it would be a treat to hear from thee. I much value and enjoy the true kindness I receive from all my married children. I have lately daily dined with one of them; it has made me think of thee, my loved child, and thy dear husband, particularly when the other day at Joseph's, on his birthday, I sat surrounded by all the married pairs. I am much disposed to pay you a visit. I deeply feel, in the loss of my beloved sister, the shortness of the time that I may be with you. No remaining duty has dwelt so much on my mind as my relative duties, that I may be enabled to minister to my beloved husband or children, brothers or sisters, as they may want it either spiritually or temporally. May we all do our part faithfully towards each other, seeing how little we know how soon we may part! I have written to Harrow, to ask your dear Frank to come and see me; I think it right he should do so after my long absence, I have requested him to ask Dr. Wordsworth to let him come on Seventh-day, to stay over the Sabbath. Our garden is lovely, and house pleasant; so our Heavenly Father deals very kindly with his unworthy servant.

I am,

Thy tenderly attached mother,

ELIZABETH FRY.

Tenth Month, 2nd, First-day.—On Second-day morning, when going into the Select Quarterly Meeting, with my brother Samuel, my son William came to tell us, that a serious accident had happened to my husband and daughter in Normandy. They had been thrown down a precipice, the carriage broken to pieces, and although they had experienced a very Providential deliverance, in their lives being spared, and no dangerous wound received, yet Katharine was so much hurt, and my dearest husband so much shaken, that they wished me to go to them immediately. I gave up the Quarterly Meeting of course, and set off with my much-loved son William to Dover, so as to cross by the first packet to France. I remembered my sorrow, and perhaps undue disappointment in not accompanying them to France. It seemed almost as if my Heavenly Father had heard my murmurings, as He heard the children of Israel in the Wilderness, and had taken me to France, when I did go— against my inclination, alas! I received it also as a lesson to have but one prayer and desire in all things, "that the Lord's will be done on earth as it is in Heaven." The accident was most serious; such an escape, I think I never heard of, the carriage, in the first instance, fell with one horse (the driver and the other horse being separated from them before) about four yards perpendicularly; then the carriage was dragged down about twenty-six yards more. The poor peasants came to assist, and fetched the village doctor for the body, and the priest for the soul.

Calais, *Ninth Month,* 26*th,* 1836.

My dearest John,

William and I reached Dover soon after twelve o'clock last evening. We were settled by one o'clock, and off about half-past seven this morning. Our journey was an anxious one, until as the evening advanced, I became more quieted, and trustful that all was ordered for us in mercy and wisdom. We had a very favourable passage of three hours; and to our great satisfaction, found your father looking for us on the quay. We found our dearest Kate exceedingly bruised and very grievously hurt altogether. Your dear father looks, I think, shaken and aged by all that he has gone through. Mary has been a very attentive nurse. She looks also jaded, but from her excessive fright, when they were going down the hill, she knelt down and put her head on Katherine's lap, by which means her face was perfectly saved. And so I have at last touched French ground. William and I have not been idle; we have already visited the Prison and Hospital. We hope it may please Providence, in tender mercy to permit us all to arrive at home next Seventh-day, probably by a packet that leaves this place that morning for London.

Upton Lane, Tenth Month, 15*th.*—William and I went one day to St. Omer, and stayed till the next. We had a very in-teresting expedition; his company was sweet to me.

I was a good deal instructed as well as interested, in visiting the Roman Catholic charities. The sacrifice that must be made to give up the whole life, as the Sisters of Charity do, to teach and bring up the poor children and attend to the sick in their hospitals is very exemplary; and the slackness of some Protestants and coldness of too many led me to think, that whilst on the one hand the meritoriousness of good works may be unsoundly upheld by the Roman Catholics, yet, that it stimulates to much that is excellent, and a fear arose in my mind, that the true doctrine that teaches that we have no merit in any thing that we do, is either so injudiciously represented, or so misunderstood, that in too many cases it leads to laxity as to sin, and a want of diligence in works of righteousness and true holiness. I was much interested in attending High Mass, but here I thought I saw something of the work of true religion under what appeared to me, the rubbish of superstition and show. But I also thought, that much of the same thing remained amongst Protestants. I long to see true religion in its purity and simplicity, spread more and more to the glory of God and the peace of men.

Eleventh Month, 6th, First-day.—It has pleased our Heavenly Father to permit much trial within the last two or three weeks. My dearest Richenda has had a very serious, I may say dangerous illness, one of great suffering. This day week her medical attendants were much alarmed, and wished to have a third called in; I deeply felt her state, but very earnestly desired to have no will in it, seeing I knew not what was best for her. My prayer was most earnest for her salvation, that whenever taken hence she might be ready, being washed and made white in the blood of the everlasting covenant.

During Chenda's illness, I had very affecting accounts from Lynn, of dearest Rachel: her little Willy and his nurse, all in the scarlet fever; the little boy very dangerously ill.

From amongst almost daily letters, written from the sick chamber of one daughter, to cheer and soothe the sorrow and sufferings of the other, the following extracts are taken :—

Upton Lane, *Eleventh Month,* 11*th.*

The very affecting account from you is just arrived; to think of that lovely boy laid so prostrate ! Still sweet babe it is good to remember " that of such is the kingdom of God," and the encouraging delightful idea that their angels or ministering spirits, are always before the face of our God. I am afraid of asking for his life, lest he should be contaminated in this evil world, but I can ask, if in the mercy of our Heavenly Father, He should see meet to keep him in the world, that He would preserve him from the evil; and that should he be raised up, it may be for purposes of His own glory. But it is a trial indeed, to flesh and blood—I have found it a bitter one, to see these little ones suffer—but as thy dear husband truly says, we must in all things learn to say, " not my will but Thine be done."

Eleventh Month, 15th.

Your time of trial has been a deep one, surely you must both have been deeply afflicted to see the poor little one's sufferings. I have a sweet hope for these little ones, that the Lord comforts and supports them by His Spirit in their afflictions, though their understandings may not be enlightened to know the hand that sustains, but that it is felt, though not known by them.

Twelfth Month, 17th.—I went to the Great Mill Bank Penitentiary, to meet a committee of gentlemen, with some of our ladies afterwards; and found, to our great satisfaction, that through the Secretary of State, Lord John Russell, our way was fully open to visit this prison, which we had long desired to do, but never before had gained access to it. Now I think, every criminal prison in London, is visited by us. I see much encouragement and cause for thankfulness, in our way thus continuing to be made in this work of Christian love. I went to Hampstead in the evening, truly affecting was it to find the real great loss in that dear family. I felt much love towards them, but did not see religiously or naturally, that I was very likely to be able to help them.

We had a very interesting Quarterly Meeting yesterday, though the ministry of our dear friend —— ——, tried me much in parts, more particularly her applying to us as a people, those blessed hopes and promises, that I apprehend simply belong to the members of the living Church of Christ, gathered out of all administrations and nations. I doubt not the living members of our body, from their first rise, have been in many instances bright and shining lights in their day, and have peculiarly had to uphold the simple pure spirituality of gospel truth; but I see no authority for our supposing ourselves to be more of a chosen people, the select few, than all who are redeemed by the blood of the Lamb, though I think our calling a high and important one, in the Militant Church of Christ. May our Holy Head establish by His own power, all that is true and of Himself, amongst us, and entirely bring to nought all that is contrary to His will. This I earnestly desire, and may I not say pray for myself individually, as well as others.

31*st*.—Late in the evening, alone,—I feel it rather a solemn close to this year, not a time of brightness though abounding with causes for thankfulness—which I desire more deeply to feel. May my Lord grant for His dear Son's sake, that the Holy Spirit may more abundantly rest upon me and mine, as our Guide, Sanctifier and Comforter. May I more faithfully, watchfully, and humbly perform all my duties to my Lord, my family, my friends, the church generally and the world, and to myself —in afflictions may my soul be possessed in patience and watchfulness! and may every day draw us nearer to God and His kingdom!

CHAPTER XX.

Earlham, First Month, 4th, 1837.—It is rather striking to begin my new year here. The drawing of my mind led me this way, and I ventured to leave all, in faith, after offering many prayers for their help and preservation during my absence. My prayers have been expressed in public, in my family, and in private, upon entering this new year. There are cries from the depth of my heart, unutterable; but He who is my advocate with the Father, will, I trust, availingly present them before the throne. I may say, Help, Lord, or I perish! Grant through thy love, pity and grace, that I may know Thee always, in all places, and at all times, to be my Defence—my Help—my Counsellor. Enlighten my darkness, cause me, in all things, to choose the good and refuse the evil; lighten mine eyes always lest I sleep the sleep of death, and Satan in any way blind mine eyes. Pour forth more fully, and more freely, Thy Spirit upon me, that I may be qualified for Thy work, in my family amongst my neighbours, in the church, and wherever Thou mayst call me.

5th.—I am much struck, by observing in my spiritual course, how different are the lines we are led in, even those, who may be under the same outward administration. We observe in nature both animal and vegetable, there are different classes, orders, genera, and species; so I think, I see it spiritually, as

the flowers of one species differ a little in colour or size, so in
the Church of Christ, those who may be said to be of one
species, differ in some small things, no two quite alike.   May
these differences in no degree separate us from each other.

Upton Lane, 25*th.*—My heart and mind have been much
occupied, by my brother Joseph writing to inform me, that he
apprehends it will be his duty to go to America this year, upon
religious service.   The subject is deeply important and weighty,
yet I desire to rejoice in his willingness to give up all for the
service of his Lord.   Though some fears have arisen from a sort
of floating apprehension I have had for many years, that I
ought or might go with him, if ever he visited that land.   Upon
viewing it, as it respects myself, I believe I may truly say, I do
not at present see any such opening.   As far as I can see,
home has my first call of duty, what the future may produce, I
leave ; but as far as I know my own heart, I very earnestly desire
to feel continually that I am not my own, but bought with a
price, therefore I am my Lord's servant, and must do as I am
bidden, even if the service called for, appear to me unreasonable.   But I must further observe, that in condescending mercy,
I have generally found in services really called for, there has
been a ripeness, that may be compared to the fruit come to
maturity.   For this service for the present, I see no way.

29*th.*—The present time of sickness and death is almost un-
precedented.   We hear of one or other continually.   Two of
our dear friends are taken.

Second Month, 11*th.*—Yesterday, when I went to town to
visit Newgate, I was stopped by Foster Reynolds, saying, that
he had sad tidings for me—which proved to be, that my beloved sister Harriet was most suddenly taken, leaving eight
young children and my poor dear mother.   Still, I trust not
"left," because surely his Lord will be near, to help him in this
very deep sorrow.   Of course, we are brought very low by this
fresh family affliction. Deeply do I desire, that it may be sanctified to us all.   The same post brought yesterday, the account
from my brother Joseph, that he had laid his concern to visit
America before his Monthly Meeting.   So one brother is called

to do, the other to suffer ;—may our Lord's will be done, by and through them both.

15th.—The funeral of my much loved sister takes place to-day. What a scene of unutterable sorrow at Runcton, where, a few days ago, all was in no common degree, joy, peace and great prosperity. Oh ! what occasions are these, where families meet together for the affecting and solemn purpose of committing the remains of a beloved one to the silent grave !

May the Lord Himself lift up the light of His countenance upon them, bless them, and keep them in a sound mind and sound faith. Be pleased, oh gracious Lord ! to help, pity, and comfort these afflicted ones this day.

No event could be more startling or more touching than this. Lady Harriet Gurney had entered the family, when many of the elder members had reached the meridian of life. She had come, not alone to gladden her own domestic hearth, but to diffuse of her bright, loving, hopeful spirit amongst her husband's relatives. For fourteen years she had in an exemplary manner, fulfilled the duties of wife and mother, friend and mistress—

"A spirit, yet a woman too."

Her brother-in-law, Mr. Buxton, wrote on the day of her funeral :—" In seeing her coffin committed to the vault, I could not but feel, that it contained all that remained of as much beauty and true loveliness of mind, body, and spirit, as we ever saw removed from this world !"

Upton Lane, Third Month, 12*th.*—I, yesterday, went to the Colonial Office to meet Sir George Grey, on subjects respecting New South Wales, and the state of the female convicts ; to the Irish Office, and saw Lord Morpeth respecting National Schools and Prisons, and then to the Home Office, about Jersey Prisons, &c. In every one I met with a most cordial reception. So the Lord yet makes my way with those in power.

Sixth Month.—The King died last Third-day, the 20th. Our young Queen was proclaimed yesterday. My prayers have arisen

for her, that our Heavenly Father would pour forth His Spirit
upon her, guide her by His counsel, and grant her that wisdom
which is from above.   I was with Lord ——yesterday, who told
me, that she behaved with much feeling and remarkable propriety when meeting the Privy Council.   She was supported by
her uncles the new King of Hanover, and the Duke of Sussex.
I have received a long letter from the Duchess of ——, containing a very interesting account of her, and the death of the
late King.

25th.—Being wounded in spirit, the grasshopper becomes a
burden,—still my causes for thankfulness much more abound.
Yesterday, I went to my son John's and saw his lawn, sprinkled
over with my lovely grandchildren and their parents, so as to
remind me of these words, " The Lord shall increase you more
and more, you and your children.   Ye are blessed of the Lord
which made heaven and earth."—Psal. cxv. 14, 15.   I believe
that the blessing of the Lord is with us ; blessed be His most
holy name, for this gracious and unmerited mercy !

Seventh Month, 20th.—I returned home yesterday evening
from Lowestoft, after having accompanied my brother Joseph to
Liverpool, in his way to America.   Our time at Earlham was
very interesting ; I believe I was helpful to my brother in a large
Meeting that he held, to take leave of the citizens of Norwich.
It was a highly interesting occasion, and I trust edifying to many.
I am very sorry to say, my mind has too much the habit of
anxiety and fearfulness.   I believe this little journey would have
been much more useful to me, but from an almost constant cloud
over me, from the fear of being wanted by some of my family.
I think it would be better for myself and for them, if they did
not always cling so closely round my heart, so as to become too
much of a weight upon me.

My beloved brother's leave-taking of Earlham and the family
there, was very affecting ; still there was peace in it, and joy in
the Lord, inasmuch as there is delight in doing what we believe
to be His will.   Of this, I think we partook with him.   We
went from Earlham to Runcton, there we dined.   Shall I ever
dine with my three brothers again ? the Lord only knows—my
heart was tendered in being with them.

I rejoice that I proceeded with Joseph, for I did not before that feel that I had come at his mind, he had been so much engaged, but on the journey I did so very satisfactorily. Samuel, Elizabeth, Joseph and myself, thus had a time together, never to be forgotten. We had much interesting conversation respecting things spiritual and things temporal, ourselves and our families. We proceeded to Manchester, where we met our dear Jonathan and Hannah Backhouse, their children, and Eliza P. Kirkbride; also, William Forster. We were a very united company. That evening, William Forster read the 54th chapter of Isaiah, expressing his full belief, that our dearest Joseph would experience the promises contained in the last few verses. The next day we went to Liverpool, and spent much of the morning in his very comfortable ship; we felt being in it, for it was very touching parting with one so tenderly beloved. We made things comfortable for him, I attended to the books, and that a proper library should go out for the crew, passengers and steerage passengers. However occupied or interested, I desire never to forget any thing that may be of service to others. We had a delightful morning with Joseph, but the tears often rose to my eyes; still, I desire to be thankful more than sorrowful, that I have a brother so fitted for his Lord's service, and willing to give up all for His name's sake.

That evening again we had an interesting religious time in prayer. The next morning there was a solemn calm over us— the day of parting was come. After breakfast we all assembled with some of our friends. We read the 4th of Philippians, our spirits were much bowed and broken, but the chapter encouraged us to stand fast in the Lord, to help one another in Christ, even the women who laboured in the gospel, and, to be careful for nothing, for that the Lord would supply all our need.

After her brother had ministered to them, and prayer had been offered, she adds:—

Soon afterwards we went to the ship. I saw the library arranged with some others to help me; then went and devoted myself to my beloved brother, put sweet flowers in his cabin, which was made most comfortable for him. It was announced that the ship was going—we assembled in the ladies' cabin, I believe all wept. William Forster said, the language had powerfully impressed him—" I will be with you always, even to the end of the world;" therefore we might trust our beloved ones to Him who had promised. I then knelt down with these words—" Now, Lord, what wait we for, our hope is in Thee," and entirely committed him and his companions in the ship, to the most holy and powerful keeping of Israel's Shepherd, that even the voyage might be blessed to him and to others. In short, our souls were poured forth before and unto the Lord, in deep prayer and supplication. Joseph almost sobbed, still a solemn quiet and peace reigned over us. I believe the Lord was with us, and owned us at this solemn time. We left the ship, and walked by the side of the Pier until they were towed out, then we went away and wept bitterly—but not the tears of deep sorrow, far from it ; how different to the grief for sin, or even disease, or the perplexities of life. It appeared the Lord's doing, though long marvellous in my eyes, yet I now trust and believe it is His call, and therefore it is well, and there is more cause to rejoice than to mourn over it. We remained at Liverpool till Second-day morning ; went by the railroad to Birmingham, meeting with an accident by the way which might have been serious, but we were preserved from harm. I became at last very poorly, and one morning nearly fainted. I was much sunk, and brought once more to feel my deep infirmity in illness or suffering. By the time we arrived at Lynn, I was too ill to go on to Earlham, and there remained to be most affectionately cared for by my beloved son and daughter, and their servants. I afterwards went to Earlham, and from thence to Lowestoft. I much valued my visits, only my foolish nature was too anxious, to enjoy them as I might have done, fancying I was wanted at home. We truly partook of the unity of the Spirit in the bond of peace. I am favoured on returning home, to find my children unusually well, and receive good accounts from my husband and sons on the Continent ; so that, once more it has pleased the Lord to permit me to rest as beside the still waters. He restoreth my soul !

Upton Lane, Eighth Month, 6th.—I am much occupied about the great Female Prison in Ireland, also the one at Paramatta. Government is wonderfully kind, and I believe much good likely to be done by the steps now being taken.

The Factory at Paramatta, in the first instance was intended as a prison for women, and arranged for the reception of refractory as well as unassigned prisoners. It was well disciplined, and the inmates divided into three classes; a distinction being very properly made in the treatment of the different classes. Gradually, the establishment, from mismanagement fell into great confusion; so that from being a place of punishment, it had become a home and refuge for the idle and profligate, preferred by them to service and hard work. In the Factory they were fed and clothed, and lived in idleness amongst congenial companions, and having once incurred the disgrace of being sent there soon lost all sense of shame, and after being released, again offended, for the express purpose of returning thither. It was a great satisfaction to the ladies of the British Society, to learn, that a system so subversive of every hope of moral improvement had been altered. By the introduction of hard labour and strict discipline, the Factory was re-converted into a place of punishment, and other measures were in progress likely to conduce to the reformation of the prisoners. Sir Richard Bourke endeavoured not only to reform the Factory arrangements, but to induce ladies suitable for the office, again to visit it. Immense advantage had accrued to the institution, from the regulations and occasional inspection of Lady Darling, supported by the authority of Sir Ralph. Lord Glenelg and Sir George Grey paid the subject every attention, not meeting the case as one merely of business routine and political expediency, but with kindness of heart and real philanthropy they entered into details, and endeavoured to obtain information from every available source. Mr. Clapham as Superintendent, and Mrs. Leach

as Matron, were sent out to take the charge of the Factory, with
full and minute directions for their own conduct, and supplied in England with every thing required for the occupation
and instruction of its inmates, or furnished with orders for them
on the Government stores there.

About the time that some improvement appeared likely to
take place amongst the wretched inmates of the Paramatta
Factory, the long debated question of the Jersey Prison was
brought to a close, by the accession of the States to the proposals
of Lord John Russell; and arrangements being entered into
for commencing the building without further delay.   Mrs. Fry
never again visited Jersey, but she had the pleasure of cheering
reports, from time to time, of the alterations effected there.

Upton Lane, Eighth Month, 18*th.*—I have believed it right
to have the poor invited, to attend the Evening Meeting at
Ratcliff to-morrow.   These are weighty engagements; may the
Holy Spirit be poured forth, for the comfort, help, and encouragement of the hearers, and to my own peace.

Second-day, 20*th.*—Yesterday, we were favoured to get well
through the Meeting, the people were very attentive, and some
appeared in tears.   Christ was preached as the " Way " to the
Kingdom of Heaven, the sacrifice for our sins, and the healer of
our wounds.   He appeared to me to be exalted through the
power of the Spirit.   May I be faithful in every call of duty,
trusting in Him who can qualify me by His own power.

Ninth Month, 2*nd.*—Since this Meeting, the interest that
others have taken with me in the poor of Ratcliffe, has led us to
look into their deplorable state.   We have formed a committee to visit them at their houses, see their state, provide a
library for their use and probably an infant school.   So one
thing springs out of another!

Last Seventh-day, my brother and sister Gurney and I went
to Crawley to attend the little Meeting at Ifield, to go to
William Allen's, and to Linfield.   My brother said, that any
serious persons who liked to attend the Meeting might do so,
and to our surprise, we found a large congregation of the

labouring classes; I should think nearly a hundred men in smock-frocks; it was quite a sight. I felt low, empty, unworthy and stripped in spirit, but my Lord helped me. We certainly had a solemn Meeting, the people were very attentive; we also had a very satisfactory reading with the people at the inn. In the evening we attended another Meeting at Linfield, in which William Allen very acceptably united. Other Friends were there. We also called upon some poor, sorrowful, destitute ones. This little excursion appeared blessed to our comfort, refreshment and peace, and I believe had the same effect on those whom we visited. I observe, with those who may think they differ in sentiment, there is nothing like bringing them together; how often it is then found, that the difference is more in expression than reality, and that the spirit of love and charity breaks down the partition walls.

I have for many months past, deeply felt the wish for more religious intercourse with my children, and more uniting with them upon important and interesting subjects. I have turned it in my mind again and again, and at last have proposed making the experiment, and meeting this evening—first, to consider different subjects of usefulness in charities, and then to close with serious reading and such religious communication as way may open for.

Thou Lord only knowest the depth of my desire, for the everlasting welfare of my children. If it be Thy holy and blessed will, grant that we may be truly united to Thee, as members of Thy Militant Church on earth, and spiritually united amongst ourselves, as members of one body, each filling his different office, faithfully unto Thee. Grant that this little effort may be blessed to promote this end, and cause that in making it, we may experience the sweet influence of Thy love shed abroad in each of our hearts, to our real help, comfort, edification and unity!

Upton Lane, *Eighth Month*, 15*th*, 1837.

My dearest Children,

Many of you know that for some time I have felt and expressed the want of our social intercourse at times leading to religious union and communion amongst us. It has pleased the Almighty to permit, that by far the larger number of you, no longer walk with me in my religious course. Except very occasionally, we do not meet together for the solemn purpose of worship, and upon some other points we do not see eye to eye, and whilst I feel deeply sensible that notwithstanding this diversity amongst us, we are truly united in our Holy Head, there are times when in my declining years, I seriously feel the loss of not having more of the spiritual help and encouragement of those, I have brought up and truly sought to nurture in the Lord. This has led me to many serious considerations, how the case may under present circumstances be in any way met.

My conclusion is, that believing as we do in one Lord as our Saviour, one Holy Spirit as our Sanctifier, and one God and Father of us all, our points of union are surely strong, and if we are members of one living Church, and expect to be such for ever, we may profitably unite in some religious engagements here below.

The world and the things of it occupy us much, and they are rapidly passing away—it would be well if we occasionally set apart a time for unitedly attending to the things of Eternity. I therefore propose that we try the following plan, if it answer, continue it, if not, by no means feel bound to it. That our party in the first instance, should consist of no others than our children, and such grandchildren, as may be old enough to attend. That our object in meeting, be for the strengthening of our faith, for our advancement in a devoted, religious, and holy life, and for the object of promoting Christian love and fellowship.

That we read the Scriptures unitedly, in an easy familiar manner, each being perfectly at liberty to make any remark or ask any question ; that it should be a time of religious instruction by seeking to understand the mind of the Lord, for doctrine and practice in searching the Scriptures, and bringing ourselves and our deeds to the light, that it may be made manifest if they are wrought in God. That either before or after the Scriptures are read, we should consider how far we are really engaged for the good of our fellow-men, and what, as far as we can judge, most conduces to this object. All the members of this little community are advised to communicate any thing they may have found useful or interesting in religious books, and to bring forward any thing that is doing for the good of mankind, in the world generally.

I hope that thus meeting together may stimulate the family to more devotion of heart to the service of their God, at home and abroad to mind their different callings, however varied ; and to be active in helping others. It is proposed that this meeting should take place once a month, at each house in rotation.

I now have drawn some little outline of what I desire, and if any of you like to unite with me in making the experiment, it would be very gratifying to me, still, I hope that all will feel at liberty, to do as they think best themselves.

I am indeed,
Your nearly attached mother,
ELIZABETH FRY.

The plan was tried and found to answer exceedingly well. Some of the collateral branches of the family afterwards joined these little réunions, they proved occasions of stimulus in " every good word and work." Some important good has resulted from the combined exertion consequent upon them, they continue to this day under the name of " philanthropic evenings ;" and are always concluded by a scripture reading, and occasionally by prayer.

One of the first subjects brought forward, was the condition of the Coalwhippers in the port of London. Lieutenant Arnold, of the Navy, had long advocated their cause, at great expense to himself, and at length applied to one of Mrs. Fry's sons to assist him in carrying forward a plan for their benefit. In visiting the poor in Ratcliffe, Mrs. Fry found the wives of some of these men, who were nominally in receipt of large wages, not only in a condition of abject poverty, but resorting to most undesirable means to obtain a living. Their husbands bringing home little or no money in consequence of the system

by which their occupation was regulated. The Coalwhippers
work in what are called gangs, of nine men in each. They
are remarkably athletic and their labour is very severe.
They require baskets and tackle ; which in those days were the
property of the publicans along the banks of the river Thames,
to whom the captains of the colliers applied when they
wanted to discharge a cargo. The publicans let out the tackle
to the coalwhippers, always giving the preference for employment to those who owed them most money for beer. They
supplied them whilst at work with enormous quantities of
porter, and expected them to drink at other times also, by
which means their wages fell entirely into the hands of the
publicans, whilst their families at home were left in great distress. The evil appeared so great that several of the gentlemen of Mrs. Fry's family exerted themselves and were at considerable expense to assist Lieutenant Arnold in his benevolent
views, until finding it impossible to accomplish by their object
private means, three of them appeared as petitioners on behalf of
the coalwhippers at the bar of the Common Council of the
city, applications to the Government were also put in form.
The result was a most favourable reception of the subject, and a
Bill has since passed, by which the coalwhippers are registered,
have a public office of their own, where their tackle is kept,
and are completely emancipated from the thraldom of the publicans ; rendering numerous families respectable and independent who before wanted the commonest comforts of life.

This redress of their grievances excited in their minds a strong
feeling of gratitude and attachment towards the Government,
as was evinced when hundreds of them desired to be enrolled as
special constables during the period of the late excitements.

Twelfth Month, 20*th.*—I have laid before my Monthly Meeting my prospect of visiting France for a few weeks, and ob-

tained the concurrence of Friends. Oh! for help, daily, hourly, —and may a sound mind, love and power be granted to me and to others, to our own peace and the glory of God.

First-day, Afternoon, 24th.—An accident about carriages keeps me from Meeting, which I much regret. The Morning Meeting was solemn. After it, my certificate was read in our adjourned Monthly Meeting, which was exceedingly encouraging to me, it expressed great unity with me as a minister, and much concurrence in my concern to go to France. It appeared to be signed by nearly the whole of the Meeting.

TO A NEAR RELATIVE.

North Repps Hall, *First Month, 2nd,* 1838.

I have trusted that if right for thee, this year may bring thee some deliverances from thy trying and exercising states. At the same time we must not desire the fire to cease burning, until the dross is burnt up ; but we may ask, that it may never be heated so as to hurt the pure metal. I have a strong apprehension that all the ordeals thou hast lately had, are sent for a purpose, I am ready to believe to fit thee to receive more of the enduring riches of Christ, and not only so, but to fit thee to enrich, comfort and help others. I can assure thee that it is deeply interesting entering the new year with my only three remaining sisters. We much value and enjoy being together ; but we feel like a few remaining autumnal fruits, at the close of no common summer, of family love and unity. We had a very solemn time together this morning, in which our children and our children's children, with ourselves were remembered at the throne of grace. The day is very fine, and all looks bright. May happy accounts from home complete the brightness of the picture.

Upton Lane, First Month, 6th, 1838.—I yesterday returned from a visit to Norfolk. Before going there, I laid my concern to go to France, before our large Quarterly Meeting, and had the very great encouragement of such a flow of unity, as I have seldom heard expressed upon any occasion.

24th.—I expect to leave home to-morrow for France. My spirit has been very much brought down before the Lord; some causes of anxiety have arisen, still in this my going out, love abounds in no common degree, and a portion of soul-sustaining peace underneath. These words comforted me this morning, 2 Timothy i. 12. "I know whom I have believed, and am persuaded that He is able to keep that which I have committed unto Him against that day." I, therefore, in this going out, commit myself and my all to my most blessed and holy Keeper, even to the Lord God of my salvation, my only hope of real help and defence, and of eternal glory.

Mrs. Fry was accompanied in this journey, by her husband, their friend Josiah Forster and Lydia Irving, the same young friend who had kindly gone with her to Jersey, in 1835.

Abbeville, *First Month,* 28*th.*

My dearest Children, and Brothers and Sisters,

As I know your kind interest in all that concerns us, I go on whilst I can, with our journal letters myself. We left Boulogne yesterday morning, in a very comfortable French carriage after some delay in our departure, from various difficulties with luggage, we enjoyed our reading and conversation, until we arrived at Montreuil, where we were refreshed by a little bouillon, and then proceeded to this place; but the cold was bitter, and neither French fires, nor tea, nor any other means proved sufficient to warm us. As the following morning advanced, my sense of mercy and peace was great. I remembered what some devoted Christian expressed, "where the God of peace is, there is home." After breakfast we read as usual, then Josiah Forster went out; but he could hear of no Protestants nor of any place of worship for them; nor of any place desirable for us to visit, excepting one hospital, one convent, and one prison. These we visited, after having had a very solemn and sweet meeting in our own room. That text was feelingly brought to our minds, "where two or three are met together in my name, there am I in the midst of them."

VOL. II.   Q

I find my small knowledge of the language very valuable, I can read to the fille de chambre, and in some degree convey my feelings and sentiments, enough to produce sympathy and interest. In our visit to the prison, convent and hospital, I found this the case.

To go now to minor points : picture us,—our feet on some fleeces that we have found, generally wrapped up in cloaks, surrounded by screens, to keep off the air; the wood fire at our feet. We have just finished an interesting reading in French, in the New Testament, with the landlady, her daughters and some of the servants of the hotel, they appeared very attentive, and much interested.

Farewell, my dearly beloved ones. May the Lord be with you, and keep you, and bless you !

Your tenderly attached,
E. F.

In Paris, comfortable and commodious apartments were prepared for them at the Hotel de Castille, by the kind attention of M. François Delessert. They arrived there very tired and very cold, on the 30th of January. The morning of the 31st was opened with solemn united prayer, offered for wisdom from on High to direct, and strength to perform whatever might be called for at their hands. Then came a visit from Madame François Delessert, two notes from Lord Granville, our Ambassador at Paris; a call at the Embassy, and in the evening the company of M. and Madame de Pressensé, the Secretary of the Bible Society.

In a letter to her children at home, Mrs. Fry not merely describes their rooms at the Hotel, and gives a plan of them, but sends a little sketch, drolly characteristic of the femme de chambre and the waiter.

February 1st, they attended the small Friends' Meeting held in the Faubourg du Roule, and afterwards called on La Baronne Pelet de la Lozere. In her Mrs. Fry found a friend and sister in Christ. They then paid a visit to Count Montalivet, Minister of the Interior, by whom they were most kindly received, and promised all needful admissions to the different prisons.

Afterwards, at the Hotel, they received visits from the Duchess de Broglie and other ladies.   The following day found Mrs. Fry oppressed and feverish, and evidently suffering from the cold she had endured on her journey.   Her new friends all displayed the liveliest sympathy, whilst Madame Pelet, in particular, neglected no kindness or attention that could add to her comfort.

The 3rd, though too unwell to go out, Mrs. Fry received in the evening M. de Metz, Conseiller de la Cour Royale, and had the pleasure of much important conversation with him on the subject of Prisons, in which he was greatly interested.   On the 4th, she paid pleasant visits to Lady Granville and to Madame Pelet.   On Sunday, the day began with seeing a school conducted by M. de Pressensé, for two hundred children ; a most cheering and delightful sight.   At twelve o'clock they attended the Friends' Meeting, there were assembled French, English, a Pole, and Americans.   Among this motley group might be found Roman Catholics, Presbyterians, Episcopalians, various Dissenters, and Quakers.

Monday, the 5th, they visited the St. Lazare Prison for women, containg nine hundred and fifty-two inmates, a very melancholy sight.   An American lady invited the party to her house in the evening, where she received about fifty individuals mostly English and American.   The conversation turned upon the general state of society in Europe, but especially in France, and what would be the most likely means of benefiting its polished, refined, but dissipated and irreligious capital. The fearful writings of the day, " many too bad to read," were discussed, and what might be the root of a tree, the branches of which bore fruit of such deadly nature.   There was present, on that occasion, a young medical student, who addressed him-

self to Mrs. Fry on the fearful contamination to which young
men in his position were exposed—no domestic home to retire to,
none of that indefinable but potent influence around them of
public opinion, in favour of virtue and morality, their studies all
tending to materialism, and to the lessening of that dependence
upon an unseen superior Power, which lingers even in the
unregenerate heart of man ; and, above all, little or no opportunity afforded them for the commonest religious advantage. This large gathering concluded by solemn exhortation
and prayer.

On the 6th, accompanied by Madame Delessert, the travellers
visited a French Protestant school, for two hundred children, on
the British and Foreign system, admirably conducted by a valuable committee of ladies. They dined at M. Pressensé's, where
was a large party afterwards. Many of them active members
of the Société Evangélique. Mrs. Fry entered deeply into
their labours of love, and spoke of this occasion as very encouraging to her, when she compared it with the state of things in
France during her youth, and how unlikely it then seemed, that
such a dawn of better things would ever appear there.

The 7th, they received many guests both morning and evening, and in the course of the day accompanied the Duchess
de Broglie to the Prison des Jeunes Détenus, a good new building the inmates well ordered, but still capable of improvement.

The following day was occupied by attending their Meeting
in the morning, and in the evening receiving a party of ladies
to consider how they might, in the best manner, promote good
in the city, in Prisons, Schools, District Societies, and similar
objects. The evening was finished by reading the 15th chapter
of St. Luke.

On the 9th, the Prison for men (La Force) was visited.
A dinner at M. Pelet's, and a very large party there in the
evening.

The 10th, they inspected the Military Prison at St. Germains which appeared to them to be upon the whole well conducted, and in tolerable order; books they found to be greatly wanted. Afterwards they saw the Central Prison at Poissy, but whilst they admired its good order, they considered it not sufficiently penal, too much like a large manufactory for different trades, instead of a place of punishment.

The following day—the Sabbath was indeed welcome, for its rest was greatly needed by Elizabeth Fry. She desired that it might be free from company, and prove a season of refreshment, the press of people being so great and the subjects for consideration so many and so exceedingly important. The Meeting was not a very large one, in it their certificates were read. They appeared much to interest those who heard them, and opened the way for a little explanation of Friends' principles. There were a few callers in the evening, amongst others, a gentleman interested about prisons, who remained during their Scripture reading, at which some of the servants of the Hotel were also present.

On the 12th, they visited the Prison of the Conciergerie. There they saw the room where the unhappy Marie Antoinette was confined. They took tea at Mr. Toase's, successor to Mr. Newstead, the Methodist minister, and passed an interesting evening with a large party of his congregation. At this time and in her subsequent visits to France, Mrs. Fry's sympathies were much drawn forth towards the French Methodists, who appeared to her to be an earnest and spiritual people.

The next morning they went to some schools; one, an Infant School, was particularly attractive, the superintendents appearing well adapted for their important post; money was given to purchase the little creatures each a bun, which highly delighted them, their happy faces showing how pleased they were. Also an Hospital, and the Enfans Trouvés, were visited. Mrs. Fry's maternal experience, led her to give some advice about the poor babies' dress, that it might be less complicated, and afford them more liberty of movement. The nuns appeared kind. The Hospital they found very close, and wanting ventilation. In the evening to Mr. Lutteroth's, where between fifty and sixty persons were present, a "charming company," "many amongst them truly serious."

On the 14th, another visit was paid to the Women's Prison of St. Lazare. There, after going over the building, the women were collected at Mrs. Fry's request, that a portion of Scripture might be read to them. She chose the parable of the prodigal son. It was beautifully read by a French lady, from the Roman Catholic Prayer Book. A pause ensued, then Mrs. Fry commented upon it, the same lady translated for her, sentence by sentence. It was exceedingly well done, losing little or nothing of its solemnity. The women were touched and impressed. She then asked them whether they would like ladies to visit them, read to them, and sympathize with them. The offer was eagerly accepted. " Oui, oui," " Eh, moi, aussi!" came from all sides; nor was it only these poor outcasts, or those accompanying Mrs. Fry who wept, the jailor and turnkeys who had entered the room, contrary to her wishes, were so affected that tears ran down their cheeks. " Elles ne sont pas pire que nous, ces pauvres femmes," (said an excellent lady for the first time brought into contact with such as these,) " seulement les circonstances sont toutes pour nous, et toutes contres elles."

This reading occasioned quite a sensation in Paris, for it had been said, that the wonderful effect of Mrs. Fry's readings in Newgate arose from her peculiar voice and manner, her skill in arresting the attention of her auditors, and her power to touch their hearts. She and others attributed it to the simple indwelling power of the word of God, and asserted that it would be found the same whatever national differences might exist, or by whomsoever the inspired word might be presented.   The result on this occasion was decisive.

They saw on the 15th, a school for about forty-five Protestants, many of them training for servants.   To find attention paid to this class afforded them much satisfaction.   In the evening, Mr. and Mrs. Fry dined at the English Embassy.   Throughout their stay in Paris the kindness and attention of Lord and Lady Granville were unfailing.

The next day, some more " delightful schools" were inspected, and a prison for debtors.

In the evening, the party for the promotion of philanthropic objects, which had been adjourned the preceding week, again met; much interesting conversation took place.   As on the previous evening, the party concluded with reading a portion of the Holy Scriptures, and solemn prayer.

On the 17th, Mrs. Fry had an interview with the prison officers, and obtained much information respecting the state of St. Lazare Female Prison.   Madame Pelet and Madame Jules Mallet intrepreting for her.   They saw M. Toase on the subject of fitting up a room as a library for the benefit of English and American students, and in the evening they went to Mr. Baird's, the American clergyman, to meet some of them, who are invited there every Saturday to read the Scriptures, &c., &c.   A young Englishman present expressed himself strongly; warning his cotemporaries, first, on the awful prevalence of taking the sacred name in vain, secondly, the desecration of the Sabbath, and thirdly, against the literature of modern France, poisoned as it is with infidelity and licentiousness.

The 19th, was devoted by Mrs. Fry to writing observations on the prisons which she had seen, to making some calls; and in the evening receiving several gentlemen to consider and talk over prison subjects.

On the 20th, they visited the Salpétrière, an Hospital for the old, infirm, epileptic, idiotic and insane. The building stands on nine acres of ground, and the whole establishment occupies ninety-eight. There are five thousand inmates. They were exceedingly struck with the kindness manifested towards them, particularly towards the insane, so much liberty being given them. Formerly, these unhappy creatures were chained and cruelly treated; many of the inmates followed the party about, pleased at being noticed. One thing, however, occasioned real pain to the visitors amidst the good order which prevailed, the absence of all religious instruction. Proved, as it has long been, that this unfortunate class of persons are helped and soothed by the blessed promises of Scripture, and capable in many instances notwithstanding their mental infirmity, of feeling and appropriating the Christian's hope.

A third visit was paid on the 21st to the St. Lazare, in company with Lady Granville, Lady Georgiana Fullerton, and two other ladies. From what was witnessed in these visits, it was obvious, that great good would result from the regular attendance of a Ladies' Committee, though no easy matter to arrange it. In the evening, went to M. De Metz's. Great had been the kindness of this gentleman and his brother-in-law, M. Piron, in going about with them to the different prisons.

On the 22nd, M. Berenger came to breakfast, when the conversation was almost entirely on subjects referring to prisons. The Friends' Meeting that morning was an important one, the ministry leading all to Christ, and many strangers and persons of different denominations being there. Afterwards, Mrs. Fry met several ladies at the Duchess de Broglie's, to consider the possibility of forming a Committee for visiting prisons. They dined at M. Rumpff's, Minister of the Hanse Towns. The Duke Decazes was there, with whom Mrs. Fry had much conversation, the Duchess Decazes, and the Duke and Duchess de Broglie.

The 23rd, they breakfasted at Mr. Mark Wilk's at Passy, where they had the gratification of meeting M. David, the sculptor. Afterwards they called on Madame Pelet and Madame de Pastoret, concluding the day by a dinner at the Duke de Broglie's.

The following day they visited a convent, and some schools conducted by Sisters of Charity. Dined at M. Jules Mallet's, about twenty to dinner, and saw nearly a hundred in the evening ; a most interesting company—several hitherto unknown to them—many young people, which was " delightful" to Mrs. Fry.

On the 25th, was their last Meeting at Paris, a very large and solemn one it proved.

The 26th was devoted to the discussion of prison subjects with the Prefect of Police. They dined at M. Dutrone's, the Deputy for Amiens.

The 27th, they paid some important calls, and had a large Committee of Ladies to consider prison subjects, though there were too many present to effect much. The party that day dined with the veteran philanthropist, the Baron de Gerando.

During the 28th they received many callers, paid leave-taking visits, and dined at the Duke Decazes'.

The 2nd, was the day appointed for them to wait upon the King and Queen, and the Duchess of Orleans. They dined at M. de Salvandi's, Minister of Public Instruction, and were quite delighted in accompanying him to see a large library and room fitted up for the use of the middle classes.

Their two last days in Paris were occupied by winding up their different objects, and preparing to depart.

The result of her observations on the state of the prisons, Mrs. Fry embodied in a letter addressed to the Prefect of Police, but

10

as it contained little beyond her opinions so frequently stated, as to arrangements, classification, female officers for women, and instruction, it is not inserted here.

She also addressed a memorial to the King, touching on the subject that so deeply occupied her thoughts, but beyond every other thing, urging a more extended circulation of the Holy Scriptures, and their free use in all public institutions in France.

From St. Germains she wrote to her children.

Third Month, 5th, 1838.

We arrived here last evening, after quitting the most deeply interesting field of service, I think I was ever engaged in. My first feeling is, peace and true thankfulness for the extraordinary help granted to us ; my next feeling, an earnest desire to communicate to you, my most tenderly beloved children, and others nearest to me, the sense that I have of the kindness and goodness and mercy of my Heavenly Father, who has dealt so bountifully with me ; that it may lead all to serve Him fully, love Him more, and follow more simply the guidance of His Spirit.

I mean now to tell you a little of my reflections upon this important period, the last month at Paris. I was at first very poorly, very low, and saw little opening for religious usefulness, though some for charitable and benevolent objects. Soon my health revived, and we had full occupation in visiting prisons and other institutions, and saw many influential persons. This opened a door in various ways, for close communication with a deeply interesting variety of both philanthropic and religious people, and has thus introduced us into a more intimate acquaintance with the state of general society. Religiously, we find some, indeed we may say a great many, who appear much broken off from the bonds of Roman Catholic superstition, but with it, I fear, have been ready to give up religion itself, though feeling the need of it for themselves and others. To these I think we have been helpful, by upholding religion in its simplicity, and most strongly expressing our sense of the necessity of it, and that nothing can alter and improve the moral character, or bring real peace, but true Christian principles. To this we have very faithfully borne testimony, and most strongly encouraged all to promote a more free circulation of the Scriptures, particularly the New Testament, and a more diligent reading of the Bible in institutions and families. I have, in private circles, introduced (frequently by describing what poor criminals wanted in prisons) the simple truths of the Gospel, illustrated sometimes by interesting facts, respecting the conversion of some of these poor women prisoners, and have been thus enabled in numerous parties, to show the *broad, clear,* and *simple* way of salvation, through our Lord and Saviour, for *all.* It has been striking to me in our dinner visits, some of them splendid occasions, how curiously away has opened without the least formality, or even difficulty in conversation, to " speak the truth in love," especially one day, as to how far balls and theatres were Christian and right; the way in which Roman Catholic priests appeared to hinder the spread of the Gospel—the importance of circulating good books (this has been a very common subject) and above all the New Testament. At our own Ambassador's Lord Granville's, several were in tears during the conversation. I think our dinner visits have been an important part of our service, so much has been done by these communications after, and at them. In many instances, numbers have joined us in the evening, particularly the youth. With these, it has pleased my Heavenly Father to give me some influence. Last First-day evening, I had a very large party of them to a reading, which appears to have given much satisfaction. It has been a most curious opening with persons of many nations. Many have lately flocked to our little Meetings; I wonder how I could feel easy to go away from such a field of service, but I did, and therefore went. On Third-day, when we went to the King and Queen, and therefore could not attend our little week-day Meeting, they said eighty persons came to it who went away. I have found unusual help at these times, to speak the truth with power; my belief is, that there are many unsettled and seeking minds in this country.

8

We have had much intercourse with the Minister of Instruction, and he gives me leave to send him a large number of books from England, to be translated into French. My full belief is, that many Testaments and valuable books will circulate in consequence of our visit.

The efforts made to form a Ladies' Society, to visit the prisons of France, and particularly Paris, (whether they succeed or not) have been important. First, by my taking many ladies to visit the great Female Prison of St. Lazare, and there reading, or having read, small portions of Scripture, and my few words through an interpreter, producing (far beyond what I could have expected) such a wonderful effect upon these poor sinners. The glad tidings of the Gospel appeared to touch their hearts, many wept exceedingly, and it was a fresh and striking proof of the power of the truth, when simply told. In the next place, the large number of ladies that have met at our house upon the subject, has afforded so remarkable an opportunity to express to them my views of salvation by Christ alone, of the unity that should exist amongst Christians, and must do so, if sanctified by the Spirit, and deeply to impress the simplicity and spirituality of true religion. I think something important in the prison cause will eventually come out of it, but it will take time.

We have had very large parties of English and Americans, and some French, at the houses of the Methodist minister, the American minister, and at another serious person's. Also we joined the French Wesleyan Methodists in their chapel, and had a precious meeting with them. Of the highly evangelical Episcopalians and Independents, we have had very large parties at different houses. In all these, we have had solemn religious service. The Episcopalians have been brought into very close union with us. In our own house, we have had two large parties of a philanthropic and religious nature, attended by many. Lady Olivia Sparrow has often been quite a comfort to me; and many others I may say have proved true helpers, French and Americans, and more than these—the Chargé d'Affaires of the Hanse Towns and his wife, also Russians and Swiss. The Greek Ambassador, Coletti,* came to me for advice on some points in

* Afterwards Prime Minister to King Otho.

the state of Greece, in which I believe I shall be enabled to assist him. A Captain B—— thinks of having my sister Hoare's "Hints for the Labouring Classes" translated, for the parents of the children who attend the schools upon the mountains in India. We have also seen many of the medical students, English and American, and are anxious to have some efforts made for their moral and religious good, in Paris, where so many come.

Our visit to the King and the Queen was interesting; but alas! what in reality is rank? The King I think in person like the late Lord Torrington, the Queen a very agreeable and even interesting woman. I expressed my religious interest and con‑cern for them, which was well received, and we had much con‑versation with the Queen and the Princess Adelaide, before the King came into the Room. We strongly expressed to the Queen our desire to have the Sabbath better kept, and the Scriptures more read. She is a sweet minded merciful woman. There were present Madame Adelaide, the King's sister, one of the young Princesses, and the Marchioness of Dolomieu, principal Lady of Honour to the Queen.

We then proceeded to the Duchess of Orleans'; there we had a delightful visit, the sweetest religious communication with her and other interesting conversation. We found her an un‑common person—my belief is, that she is a very valuable young woman.

The Queen appeared much pleased with my Text-book; and the Princess Adelaide said, she should keep it in her pocket and read it daily. Indeed no books have given the same pleasure as the Text-books, both in French and English. I think we have given away many hundreds of them, and next in number my sister Louisa's books on Education; they delight the people; also a great many of Joseph's Letter to Dr. A——, of which we have a beautiful edition in French, and his Sabbath; of these we expect to give many hundreds, and one or two other tracts, upon Christian Duties, and the Offices of the Holy Spirit. Our various books and tracts have had a very open reception, but we have been very careful when, where, and what to give; although in some of the newspapers it was stated that I distributed con‑troversial tracts, which is not true.

I began in my letter to say what a variety we have seen, but
I did not say what deeply interesting and delightful persons we
have met with; amongst the Protestants particularly, some first-
rate ladies, who have been as sisters to me, so abundant in
kindness and love.   One has truly reminded me of my sister
Rachel, in her person, her mind, and her excessive care over me;
she has felt me, I believe, like her own.   We have indeed increased our dear and near friends by this visit, much as it was
in Jersey and Guernsey, only in far greater numbers.   I think
nothing could be more seasonable than our visit; as it respected
the prisons, and I believe the influence of our advice has been
very decided, with many persons of consideration.   The schools
we have also attended to, and I have encouraged a more scriptural education; some schools of great consequence, kept by
serious Protestants in a district of Paris, much want help.
There are seven hundred children, and we hear that the Head
of the Police in that neighbourhood, says the people generally
are improved in consequence.

The want of the language, I have now and then much felt,
but not very often, so many speak English well, and many
understand it who cannot speak it.   Also I blunder out a little
French.

The entreaties for us to stop longer in Paris have been very
great, but my inclination draws homeward; I am a very great
friend to not stopping too long in a place.   And as I believed I
saw a little light upon our departure, we thought it best to leave
all for the present, and go, if we even have, before many months
more, to return for a short time.   We have been a united, and
often a cheerful little party.   At times I have carried a great
weight, never hardly having my home party out of mind for long
together, however full and occupied. At other times our business
has been so great, as almost to overwhelm us—callers almost
innumerable, and most of them on important business, and out
and in almost constantly ourselves, so that I have sometimes felt
as if I could not long bear it, particularly when I could not
obtain some rest in the afternoon.   Through all I must say, He
who I believe put me forth, has from season to season restored
my soul and body, and helped me from hour to hour.   This day

week I sat down upon my chair and wept, but I was soon helped and revived. I long for every child, brother, sister, and all near to me, to be sensible how very near my Holy Helper has been to me, and yet I have exceedingly and deeply felt my utter unworthiness and short coming, and that all is from the fulness and freeness of unmerited mercy and love, in Christ Jesus. I can hardly express the very near love I have felt for you all. My prayers very often have risen for you, and if any labour I have been engaged in has been accepted *through the Beloved,* may you my most tenderly beloved ones, partake of the blessing attendant upon it. My dearest husband has been a true helper; and Josiah Forster and Lydia Irving, very kind and useful companions.

I forgot to say, I think the few Friends in Paris have been greatly comforted and stimulated by our visit.

I end my account by saying, what I trust is true, " The Lord is my Shepherd, I shall not want." We are now quietly at St. Germains. We hear most interesting accounts of the state of Normandy, and have many letters of introduction to the places where we propose to go, if not wanted home, I shall be glad to go there. We propose being at Rouen to-morrow.

I am,

Your most tenderly attached,

ELIZABETH FRY.

At Rouen they were much interested by meeting with a respectable woman in humble life, who had lived nurse fifteen years in a gentleman's family, a Roman Catholic but his wife a Protestant. There she had been so much impressed by religious truth, (though still a Roman Catholic herself) that she felt it her duty where she resided to circulate the Scriptures and religious tracts. Her master told them, it was surprising the great influence she had obtained in the neighbourhood. Mrs. Fry supplied her with six Testaments and a Bible, from the Bible Society Dépôt. From the same Society she obtained Testaments for the school in the prison, where the Testament was habitually read, but the supply very inadequate. This school was under the care of the Abbé Gossier, M. Du Hamel and other religious gentlemen, who themselves daily instructed the young prisoners.

At Caen, they found some excellent and devoted Methodists amongst the French, and, that through the efforts of one young English lady, an orphan residing in a gentleman's family as governess—many copies of the Scriptures had been purchased ; and at the shop of a Roman Catholic, more than a hundred of de Sacy's Testaments sold since the beginning of the year.

The Prison of Beaulieu near Caen they visited with much satisfaction, nearly a thousand prisoners were confined there ; they found it admirably regulated, and a serious Roman Catholic clergyman devoted to the good of those under his care. He gladly welcomed the gift of fifty Testaments.

At Havre, the Ladies' Bible Society had sold during the former year four hundred and twenty-six Testaments, and thirty-three Bibles, and had given to soldiers fifty Testaments, who were in the habit every evening of reading them to their comrades in barracks.

At Boulogne, they made arrangements for the sale of the Holy Scriptures, and took a lively interest in the District Society, thence crossed to Dover, and the following day Mrs. Fry had the comfort of finding herself again with her family at home.

The effect on her mind, of this her first introduction to France was very powerful. She was greatly attracted by the life and facility of the French character; in a letter she speaks of them as "such a nation—such a numerous and superior people—filling such a place in the world—and Satan appearing in no common degree to be seeking to destroy them—first, by infidelity and so called philosophy—secondly by superstition, and the priesthood rising with fresh power—thirdly, by an extreme love of the world and its pleasures—fourthly, by an unsettled, restless, and warlike spirit—yet under all this, a hidden power of good at work amongst them, many very extraordinary Christian characters, bright, sober, zealous Roman Catholics and Protestants, education increasing—the Holy Scriptures more read and valued, a general stirring to improve the prisons of France. The Government making fresh regulations for that purpose, but great fear of the priests prevailing, from the palace downwards—and they alas! resisting all good wherever or however it may arise."

Upton Lane, Fourth Month, 27th.—Yesterday was the largest British Society Meeting I ever remember, partly collected to hear my account of our French journey, there must have been some hundreds of ladies present, many of them of rank. In the desire not to say too much, perhaps I said too little upon some points, although I do not feel condemned, yet I am ready to think if I had watched and prayed more, I should have done better—my prayers have arisen, that however imperfectly or unworthily sown, the seed scattered yesterday, may be so prospered by His own free power, life and grace, that it may bear a full crop to His praise!

Fifth Month, 8th.—I have just had a serious faintness for a short time, at times I think I may be suddenly taken off in one of these attacks—they appear to have so much to do with the heart. If perfectly ready, by being washed and made clean in the blood of the Everlasting Covenant, then, I think that a rapid translation from time to eternity, may save much pain and sorrow. But all these things, I am disposed to leave wholly to the Lord, who has through His unutterable mercy, been remarkably with me in life, and will I believe, be with me in death. So be it Lord Jesus, when Thou comest, even if it be quickly, through Thine own merits receive me unto Thyself!

20th.—To-morrow I am fifty-eight, an advanced period of what I apprehend to be not a very common pilgrimage, I now very earnestly desire and pray that my Lord may guide me continually, cause me to know more of the day of His power, that I may have my will subjected to his will. What He would, have me to do that may I do, where He would have me to go there may I go—what He may call me to suffer for His name sake may I be willing to suffer. Further, may He keep me from all false fears and imaginations, and ever preserve me from putting my hand to any work, not called for by Him, even if my fellow-creatures press me into it, as I think some are disposed to do about America. Be pleased to grant these my desires and prayers for Thine own Holy and Blessed name's sake.

Two days later on hearing of the death of Mrs. Clarke of Crimplesham Hall, Norfolk, an old and valued friend with whom and her daughters, Mrs. Doyle and Mrs. James Doyle, she had so lately been staying at Dublin, receiving under their roof boundless hospitality, she thus addressed them :—

Upton Lane, Sixth Month, 8th.

My dear Friends,

Dear E. B.'s letter is just arrived containing the account of the departure of your beloved mother, you are much to be felt for in so great a loss, for she was a mother indeed to you, and a dear friend to many. I not only loved her but highly esteemed her also, she appeared to have about her much of the Israel indeed in whom is no guile, partaking of the blessed state of those whose transgressions are forgiven, and whose sins are covered, unto whom the Lord imputeth not iniquity, and in whose spirit there is no guile. I should much like to be with you upon the affecting occasion of the funeral, but I do not see how I can properly leave all my concerns and duties at home; but (I think) I shall be with you in mind. Pray write to me as soon as you either feel able, and tell me all about yourselves and particulars of your dear mother's bodily and mental state previous to her departure.

*   *   *   *   *   *   *

Seventh Month, 8th.—This day I enter with much fear and trembling, as we are looking forward to a very important Meeting to be held at the Westminster Meeting House, at the request of

Hannah Backhouse, to which foreigners of rank and our own nobility are invited. The weight is great—very great from various causes, partly from my fears and doubts as to women's holding Public Meetings.

14*th.*—The Meeting was attended by many high in rank. Soon after we assembled, William Allen spoke for some time, then I knelt down and felt much unction and power in prayer for the Queen. After Hannah Backhouse had spoken, in a lively, simple, powerful manner, preaching the truths of the gospel, several went out. I then rose, first endeavouring to show that truth must not be despised, because it came through weak instruments. I mentioned, how Anna in the Temple spoke of our Lord to all who looked for redemption in Israel, how the women first told of our Lord's resurrection, and that their fellow-disciples called it " idle tales." After thus showing that the Lord might see right to use weak instruments, I expressed my feelings towards those present. First, from Scripture, I showed that God is no respecter of persons, that from the palace to the very dungeon, I continually saw this. Then I showed, the important and responsible situation of those who fill high places in the world. Either they would be blessed themselves and be a blessing to others, as a city set on a hill, their light shining before men ; or they would be of the number of those, through whom, offences come, and therefore with the " curse of the Lord" resting on them. I showed them some of their peculiar temptations, in being clothed in purple and fine linen, and faring sumptuously every day ; and warned them, seeking to lead them to Christ, and to eternal glory through Him. At the close, I had a few words to express in the way of exhortation, as to their example in their houses, amongst children and servants, reading the Holy Scriptures, family worship and other points.

On the 12th of July, an event took place in her family, which afforded Mrs. Fry peculiar satisfaction, the marriage of her fourth son at Frankfort-sur-Maine, to the daughter of her valued friend, Dr. Pinkerton.

But there was another and a very different subject weighing

at this time heavily upon her mind, one which she turned again and again before she dare dismiss it, and then, it was more that other calls of duty appeared immediately required of her, than that she deliberately abandoned the idea. Her brother Joseph John Gurney was pursuing his labours in America, as a minister of the Gospel; and she doubted, whether it might not be her duty to cross the Atlantic, in order to join him for a time in his visits in the United States, and to accompany him to the West Indies. There were those who thought she ought to go; but, on the other hand, she knew how entirely it would be against, not only the wishes, but the judgment of her own family. She had learned to trust very little to the opinions of any of her fellow-mortals, and these conflicting views only served to bring her in deeper dependence and more entire self-resignation, to the footstool of her great Master to learn His will, that she might fulfil it. Whilst she pondered these things, a strong conviction arose in her heart, that there was a present duty for her to fulfil—once more to visit Friends and their Meetings in North Britain, again to inspect the prisons there, and to communicate with the magistrates and men in authority, whilst the Bill was still pending, which had been brought before the House the preceeding Session of Parliament, to improve prisons and prison discipline in Scotland.

She laid this concern before her friends, and receiving the assurance of their unity, she left home the 11th of August, with her constant companion, her sister-in-law Elizabeth Fry, and her husband's old and valued friend, John Sanderson. They stayed a night at Birmingham, and on the 14th of August, arrived at Glen Rothay, in the vale of Rydal, where the kindest reception awaited them; but the kindness of their host and hostess ceased not here. Elizabeth Fry's onerous and multiplied objects requiring more assistance, William Ball, a minister amongst Friends, though not at the time travelling in that character, and peculiarly suited for the undertaking, was prepared, upon her particular request, to leave that beautiful home and accompany them on their way. They left Glen Rothay on the 15th, Mrs. Ball going with them the two first stages.

As Mrs. Fry's occupation and great fatigue made it almost impossible for her to write fully to her home party, or to keep a journal of their proceedings, Mr. Ball undertook both offices. He had never travelled with, or known her so intimately before, and his journal is interspersed with observations on her objects and habits. From it, the account of this journey is chiefly taken.

"After being kindly received at G. H. Head's, Rickerby Hall, we left Carlisle, posted four stages to Hawick, attended a Meeting that was appointed for that afternoon, in which our dear friends were enabled to 'labour in the Gospel;' went on two stages to Torsance Inn, where we slept.

"On the 17th, left Torsance about nine o'clock; arrived at Edinburgh to dinner, at our dear aged friend Alexander Cruickshanks; came on to Kinross to tea, and arrived at Perth in the evening. A fine drive this day; the approach to Edinburgh very striking, also the neighbourhood of Perth; but the free course of interesting and profitable conversation on the part of our beloved friend, the chief charm of a charming journey. How instructive is her regard to the comfort and the feelings of others, even in little things!

"18th.—In the carriage about half past six o'clock. From Perth to Cupar Angus to breakfast, in the hope of being at Aberdeen, in time for the Meeting that is held the evening previous to the General Meeting of Friends of Scotland. At Forfar, visited the prison—it is in very bad order. Changed horses at Brechin, but did not allow ourselves time for dinner, which we took in the carriage. At Stonehaven, finding it vain any further to attempt to reach Aberdeen by six o'clock, we rested awhile, and had tea at a very pleasant inn. The drive from Stonehaven to Aberdeen over hills in view of the sea, is very fine. But we had no time to stop at Ury, (the seat of the Barclay family,) which is passed on this route. Arrived at Aberdeen at eight o'clock, and took up our abode at the Royal Hotel.

" These journeys are, I trust, not lost time ; we have two Scripture readings daily in the carriage, and much instructive conversation ; also, abundant time for that which is so important, the private reading of the Holy Scripture. This is very precious to dear Elizabeth Fry, and I have thought it a privilege to note her reverent ' marking and learning' of these sacred truths of divine inspiration. Often does she lay down the Book, close her eyes, and wait upon Him, who hath the key of David to open and to seal the instruction of the sacred page. Truly, it helps to explain how her ' profiting appears unto all,' when she is thus diligent and fervent, in ' meditating upon these things, and giving herself wholly to them.' "

The first two days at Aberdeen were devoted to attending the Meetings, and visits to Friends. Amongst others, one to a very old and valued friend, John Wigham. He had been to her as " a nursing father" in the early part of her religious course.

" It was much like the meeting and interchange of parent and child, after long separation and many vicissitudes; and these last, as they had affected our dear friend in the interval, were freely spoken of by her, with that deep feeling, chastened into resignation, which so remarkably covers her subjected spirit, in relation to these affecting topics.

" Some of the serious inhabitants, a clergyman and others, called on us this evening.

" 21st.—An agreeable breakfast-visit to Principal Jack, of Old Aberdeen College, and his amiable family ; where we were privileged to partake both of friendly hospitality and Christian fellowship. Visited the prison, in company with our friends A. and M. Wigham, the Provost, Sheriff, Town Clerk, and Baillie Blackie. The Baillie is a valuable man, who has done a great deal for the improvement of the gaol, which Elizabeth Fry finds

very materially mended ; in fact, in excellent order. The authorities here, are most anxious to facilitate Elizabeth Fry's inspection, and to forward her views, well knowing them to be
the result of the enlarged observation, and long experience of
a practical judicious mind, as well as of close and heartfelt interest in the subject:

"A meeting with the ladies of Aberdeen this evening at our
Hotel, when prison matters were discussed, and things put in
train for forming a regular association, ere we leave the city.
Elizabeth Fry's capacity for various successive engagements, all
of an important nature, is astonishing. Surely, it is because she
dwells mentally in the 'quiet habitation,' to which she continually resorts, for the renewal of that calming influence of the
Spirit, which purifies the heart, clears the understanding, and
rectifies the judgment, bestowing upon the truly devoted follower of the Lamb, ' the spirit of love and of power and of
a sound mind.' She is both lovely and wonderful on close acquaintance ; such energy, combined with meekness, and so
much power with entire teachableness, are rarely found.

" 22nd.—We went to Kinmuck—setting out quite early ; had
much satisfaction in being among the Friends there, who seem
a kind, serious, simple-hearted people. Returned to Aberdeen
late.

" 23rd.—After a morning engagement, we were occupied with
the principal officers of the gaol who visited us, desiring to have
some private conversation with Elizabeth Fry. Then came on
the large meeting of ladies ; nearly two hundred assembled. She
had only meant to receive them in our drawing-room, but they
flocked in to such degree, that a large assembly-room in our
Hotel was got ready on the spur of the moment. There was
much reading from reports, &c., as well as valuable communication from Elizabeth Fry, to this interesting assembly. Her
excellent tact and remarkable facility on these occasions, are
admirable. A society was formed for the prisons of Aberdeen
and its vicinity. The Countess of Errol is Patroness ; the Lady
of the Provost, President ; very respectable persons take the
other functions. The Provost, Sheriff, and many other gentlemen were in attendance, but, to their evident disappointment,

were most politely dismissed by our dear friend, who feels it important, as a woman, not to overstep the line which restricts her public addresses to those of her own sex, excepting only in the exercise of the spiritual gift of the Ministry.

" Between the formation of the association, and proceeding to select the various officers, Elizabeth Fry read a psalm, spoke very nicely upon it to the ladies, and was then engaged in prayer. This meeting satisfactorily over, we went, accompanied by a large party of gentlemen, magistrates, and others, and many ladies also, to visit the Bridewell. A thorough inspection was made, indeed this visit employed an hour and a-half; all met afterwards in the Committee-room, to hear what Elizabeth Fry had to remark upon the state of this large and important establishment; she made an excellent address."

Embodied afterwards in a letter,—

To the Provost and Magistrates of the City, and Sheriff Depute, and Sheriff Substitute of the County of Aberdeen.

On visiting the prison of your city, I had much satisfaction in observing the great improvement in the construction of the building, and the arrangement of the yards, since I was last at Aberdeen. The diet also is improved; but I am of opinion, that the addition of a portion of animal food once a week, is very desirable, and likely to conduce to the preservation of the health of the prisoners.

I observe, that the separate system is adopted for tried and untried prisoners, that attention is paid to their instruction, that some employment is provided for them; and that, upon their dismissal from prison, they are allowed to partake of their earnings.

It is satisfactory also, to learn, that a medical man and a chaplain attend the prisoners, but above all, that it is intended to appoint a female officer to have the oversight and care of the female prisoners. This arrangement is, under any circumstances, important, but peculiarly so when the prisoners are separately confined. There is an obvious impropriety, in women so circumstanced, being under the sole care of men, both as it respects the prisoners and the persons who have the custody of them. The indelicacy and moral exposure are great, and have been found from experience, to lead to injurious consequences to both parties ; so much so, that by the last Prison Act, of George the Fourth, in England, no male officer, not even the Governor or Chaplain, is allowed to visit a female prisoner except in company with a female officer.

The appointment of women to the care of prisoners of their own sex, would moreover prove an economical arrangement inasmuch as the salaries of women are less than those of men, but one female turnkey will prove insufficient for the gaol. A Matron will be wanted to instruct the prisoners daily, and to have a constant superintendence over them ; and one female turnkey under her. They should both reside in the prison, and no male officer, except the Governor and Chaplain, should ever enter the women's side. The choice of these officers is of the utmost importance ; they should be women of good principles, should possess good sense and discretion, and combine gentleness with firmness. The system of separate confinement, although it has many advantages, requires great care in its administration, in order to make it productive of good effects on the mind of the prisoner, who should frequently be visited by serious judicious persons, to read the Scriptures, and carefully mark and cherish any returning good impressions. This practice of regular visiting has been adopted in America, as well as our own country, with great advantage.

The opinion that I had previously formed, as to the peculiar care required in applying this system, was confirmed by learning, on visiting your prison, that no less than two of the prisoners, now in confinement, had attempted self-destruction.

With respect to untried prisoners, several months of separate confinement before trial and before conviction of any crime, is certainly severe discipline. These prisoners therefore, besides having the above-mentioned advantages, should be allowed to receive food from their friends, and occasionally to be visited by them.

The introduction of a prison dress has my entire approbation.

It tends to promote the comforts of the prisoners during their confinement, and they have the advantage of taking away their own clothes in an unimpaired state, when they are discharged. Without this provision, they frequently leave the prison in a most destitute condition.

In the Bridewell of your city, I was much satisfied with the general order that prevails, and especially with the very desirable provision of two cells for each prisoner. The want of female officers appears the great and important deficiency of this institution.

I beg to press on your attention, in conclusion, the great benefits that I believe will result to the female prisoners (and to the community at large) from the visits of respectacle and discreet ladies, who have formed themselves into a Society for this purpose, and who will be subject to regulations, which will be submitted to you for your approbation. The good that has been produced by similar associations in England, and also in some places in Scotland and Ireland, is so great and obvious, and so fully acknowledged by persons in authority, that I need not enlarge upon it; but respectfully entreat you to extend to the ladies, who have undertaken this work of charity in the city of Aberdeen, your kind assistance and patronage.

I feel greatly obliged by the kind attentions which I have received from you in my visit to your city, for which be pleased to accept my thanks.

I am, very sincerely,

Your Friend,

ELIZABETH FRY.

"On our return from the Bridewell, the Sheriff, Dr. Duar, Principle of Mareschal College, and another gentleman of influence, came to attend at a private discussion of certain points, especially of the new Prison Bill for Scotland."

From Aberdeen, Mrs. Fry and her companions went to Rennie Hill, and remained for three days with Mr. Johnston and her niece. A large party of magistrates, lairds, and their ladies, met on Saturday at Rennie Hill, when prison subjects were discussed. The history of the Sunday must be told in Mr. Ball's own words :—

" First-day, 26th.—Our little party sat together after the manner of Friends this morning. Dear Priscilla Johnston joined us. I felt afresh, that it is a privilege to know that the worship of God is in spirit and in truth ; and may be rendered acceptable, wherever contrite hearts are reverently turned toward Him, in dependence on the mediation of His beloved Son, who is ever near to those, if only 'two or three,' who are met to offer this worship in His name."   *   *   *   " Elizabeth Fry and her sister had desired to meet with the fishermen about Anstruther this evening ; but we were all taken by surprise on going down to the town, to find that this simple, religious gathering, turned out to be a very large and crowded Meeting. The room we had arranged for, not having proved nearly capable of containing the people, they had flocked to a chapel near, the service of which (and of some others I believe) was put off to give place for a Public Meeting of Friends. We had expected to sit down with the poor fishermen in a much more private way. John Sanderson stated to the assemblage that we began with a pause of silence. Then Elizabeth Fry explained our views on worship, rather in the way of an affectionate introductory address. Her sister E. Fry bent the knee in prayer. After which, Elizabeth Fry was strengthened, in a very striking manner, to proclaim the glad tidings of the gospel of life and salvation—truly an awakening ministry ! Her sister followed, enlarging on the nature and fruits of true repentance !—then Elizabeth Fry addressed the sea-faring men, most appropriately and feelingly, warned the sinners emphatically, and was afterwards engaged in fervent prayer. At the close of this memorable Meeting, Andrew Johnston briefly addressed this large assembly of his neighbours, acknowledging the kindness of the minister and attention of the people, and enforcing, with great seriousness, his desire, that the novelty of the occasion, might in no degree be suffered to divert solemn attention, from the infinite importance of the Gospel truths delivered."

" After primary attention to religious engagements among

Friends in Edinburgh, on the 28th, 29th, and 30th; there was
a party assembled to meet Elizabeth Fry, at the house of our
valued and hospitable host, the late Alexander Cruikshank, on
the evening of the 30th, when her conversation on the important
subject of the condition and care of prisoners, greatly interested
a large company, including some distinguished individuals and
some foreigners.

"31st.—Having arranged on our arrival, in concert with the
active members of the Scottish Society, for a large meeting of
ladies at the Royal Hotel, it took place this day, Andrew and
Priscilla Johnston having joined us the evening before It was
a good and serviceable Meeting. The ladies of the Scotch Committee proved their efficiency in conducting business, and developing the state of prison affairs in their city, as well as their
diligence in the details of self-denying exertion on behalf of
the cause; and the leading objects of this meeting, in extending
the sphere of interest on behalf of poor prisoners, through the
personal communications of Elizabeth Fry, among the ladies of
Edinburgh, seemed to be fully obtained.

"Afterwards, in company with Elizabeth Fry's much valued
coadjutors, the sisters Mackenzie (of Seaforth), Eliza Fletcher,
and others, we visited the Refuge; also a house, where they
think of establishing a Penitentiary, to see if it met Elizabeth
Fry's ideas of the requisites for such an institution. There was
an interesting reunion at the dinner-table of Lord Mackenzie
at Belmont, this evening; where continued interchange of sentiment upon the subjects so near to the heart of our devoted
friend, was pursued and enjoyed.

"Ninth Month, 1st.—A party of about twenty, at a *déjeûner*
at Augusta Mackenzie's, where the same profitable conversation
freely flowed. Elizabeth Fry opened out on the prison objects
of her journey, very instructively, and was listened to with deep
attention. Visited the Sessional Schools, among other engagements this morning; and Elizabeth Fry, with the sisters
Makenzie, went to inspect the solitary wards of the prison,
where no gentlemen are admitted. In the evening we received
at the Royal Hotel, a number of gentlemen, magistrates, and
others, when the new Scotch Prison Bill, in particular, and the

general subjects of Prison Discipline and Reformation were fully discussed."

Mrs. Fry was at this time extremely anxious as to the extent to which Prison Discipline was carried in Scotland. She greatly feared the enforcement of solitary confinement, and felt it her duty to make a sort of appeal against its possible abuses.

She had therefore invited this large number of influential gentlemen, whose attention had been given to the subject, magistrates, lawyers, members of the Prison Discipline Society, and others, to meet her on this occasion—an appalling audience —as they all sat round, to the number of fifty. She gently engaged in conversation with some, who were seated at the most distant part of the room, and, by degrees, fell into an account of her experience, and a full exposition of her mind on the subject.

As an abstract principle, she doubted the right of man to place a fellow-creature under circumstances of such misery, if his offences were not of a very heinous or aggravated nature. She could not believe that it was accordant with reason or religion, thus to isolate a being, intended for his great Creator for social life, unless necessary for the safety of the community at large ; nor did she consider continual solitude the best method of reforming the offender. Very many hours, she thought, might be passed alone with advantage, and the night always ; but she recognised a vast difference between useful and improving reflection, and the imagination dwelling upon past guilt or prospective evil. Her conviction was, that with the greater number of criminals left to feed upon their own mental resources, the latter state of mind was highly probable, the former very unlikely. Confinement, that secluded from the vicious, but allowed of frequent intercourse with sober and well-conducted persons, would have been in her view perfect. But where could funds be obtained to raise the prison, or maintain its discipline on such a system? Some intercourse for a few hours daily, among prisoners carefully classed, diligently employed, judiciously instructed, and under most vigilant and unceasing superintendence, with the remaining hours of the twenty-four passed in separate, but not gloomy seclusion; was in her opinion the best and the most likely method of benefiting the criminal, and thus eventually diminishing crime. She shrank from the abuses to which the solitary system is liable. How soon might the cell become an oubliette—how short the transition from kind and constant attention, to cruelty and neglect;—how entirely the comfort, nay the existence of a prisoner, must depend upon his keeper's will; and what was human nature, to be trusted with such responsibility? With an active magistracy, a zealous chaplain, and careful medical attendant, all might be well; but who could ensure the continuance of these advantages? and were the activity and benevolence of the present day to pass away, why might not the slumber of indifference again cover the land? Nor was this her only fear—" They may be building, though they little think it, dungeons for their children and their children's children, if times of religious persecution or political disturbance should return." Cell within cell, as in some prisons, in others the light and air of heaven admitted through a crooked funnel, but the glorious sun shut from their eyes; with no sound to reach them, and,—but a keeper withdrawn, or a wire broken,—no sound to be heard *from* them, however deep the need of assistance.

" On the evenings of the 2nd and the 3rd, large Public Meetings for religious worship were held; the former at Edinburgh, the latter at Leith, in which Elizabeth Fry was greatly strengthened to declare the truths of the everlasting gospel of our Lord and Saviour Jesus Christ. Many calls were made on distinguished persons, and some visits also received, on the 3rd; especially one from the late Dr. Abercrombie, which will long be remembered with interest.

"4th.—We came to the George Hotel, Glasgow, and on the 5th and 6th, Elizabeth Fry and her sister were occupied in their religious engagements, amongst the Friends of that city. Our valued friends and most efficient helpers, the sisters Augusta and Helen Mackenzie, arrived to our aid on the evening of the 6th, and joined us at our Hotel. The Lord Provost and other gentlemen visited Elizabeth Fry, and she went to the Bridewell. At seven o'clock the same evening, a large number of the ladies of Glasgow met at our Hotel, a very crowded, but as usual interesting occasion.

"7th.—The whole party went to Greenock. Elizabeth Fry and the sisters Mackenzie had a very important meeting with the ladies of Greenock this morning; about one hundred were assembled, and it proved highly satisfactory; Elizabeth Fry and these experienced companions entered into many particulars in regard to the visiting of prisons, a subject generally that excited lively interest. She was also engaged strikingly in prayer, with, and for the large company of ladies thus met together. We visited the Greenock gaol, when the women were collected, who were very affectionately addressed by Elizabeth Fry; we were glad to find this gaol a good one, and capable of much usefulness. A large Public Meeting for religious worship was held in the Seaman's Chapel this evening, it proved satisfactory, and was intensely crowded; the doctrine of the gospel was fully set forth, in the love and power of the truth, by our dear friend. An interruption by an advocate of the temperance movement, who embraced the occasion for speaking in favour of that cause, and was applauded by the throng, seemed to threaten the service of this Meeting. But Elizabeth Fry soon resumed, and the seriousness and weight of her manner happily restored solemnity.

"8th.—Invited the landlord of our Greenock Hotel, and his wife, and servants, to our Scripture reading this morning. They came in and we were favoured with an instructive season; another large Meeting of the Greenock ladies afterwards, who seem thoroughly desirous to render their aid to the poor imprisoned ones, too often tied and bound also with the chains of sin! Elizabeth Fry much interested, in arranging to bring into communication with the Religious Tract Society, a man who sells books to sailors on Greenock quay, and in visiting a large factory on the hill, where the work people were assembled and addressed by her. Returned to Glasgow, and visited the Bridewell the same day. The inspection there was truly satisfactory. It is an excellent institution.

" 9th.—Our usual Meeting for worship at Glasgow this morning, almost like a public one, so many of the inhabitants who were aware of Elizabeth Fry's presence, came in. We went to a very satisfactory Public Meeting for worship at Paisley, seven miles from Glasgow, this evening.

" 10th.—The ladies' large Glasgow Prison Meeting was held in the Friends' Meeting House, and an association was formed which we hope will work well. We received company this evening at our Hotel, some ladies as well as gentlemen of Glasgow, who were disposed to give their interest to our objects,—conducted as usual. The Scotch Prison Act and similar matters discussed.

" 11th.—Our party made a hasty visit to Paisley, and there inspected the gaol. Here the magistrates met us and showed every attention to facilitate Elizabeth Fry's inspection, as well as in listening to her suggestions, which she was requested to leave in writing."

How sincerely these gentlemen desired to profit from her suggestions, was proved a few months later, when a local newspaper was sent to her, containing the following paragraph.

" PRISON REFORM.

" On Tuesday, the 1st, Janet Stewart of Glasgow was unanimously appointed by a committee of the Commissioners, Matron of the Paisley gaol and Bridewell. The duties of this office are new in the prisons of Scotland. The object of the appointment is, to put the whole of the female prisoners exclusively under the charge of one of their own sex, who is to perform the duties over them of teacher, turnkey, gaoler, &c. In fact, they are not to be seen by any other person but the female keeper, unless it be by persons visiting the establishment, and as far as possible these

visitors are to be exclusively females also. It was at the suggestion of Mrs. Fry, at her late visit, that this plan of appointing
an instructress and keeper for the females of their own sex, who
should be constantly beside them, was adopted ; and we have the
pleasure of adding, that several of the other improvements which
were then in contemplation, and which had been recommended
by that lady and the Government Inspector, Mr. Hill, have now
been carried into effect."

From Glasgow by Carlisle, Penrith, and Patterdale, where
meetings for worship were held, this united little band travelled
on, till again at Glen Rothay. There, they passed a day of rest
and refreshment. With Mr. Ball's account of it, must close the
extracts from his narrative.

" 15th.—A day of unwonted quiet. After writing and such
restful avocations were done, Elizabeth Fry enjoyed a ramble
into the mountain air of Loughrigg Fell, though she did not
reach the summit. Amidst many secret exercises of soul, and so
much laborious exertion for the temporal as well as spiritual
good of others, our dear friend largely shares in the sweet experience that " He giveth all things richly to enjoy." Her love
of nature, from the mountain to the field-flower, is signal ; and
admirably preserved through atmospheres unfavourable, in
general, to the maintenance of a taste for simple and retired
pleasures. Yet, where the love of religious retirement is
in lively exercise, probably such a taste is less endangered ; it
harmonizes with that frame of spirit, which seeks the valley
where the dew remains. Precious indeed, is a childlike and
watchful spirit, submissively eyeing the chief Shepherd, and
waiting His leading."

They attended some meetings appointed for them, in West-
moreland and Lancashire. Mr. Ball accompanied them as far
as Liverpool ; from whence Mrs. Fry and her sister returned
immediately home:

Upton, Ninth Month, 26*th.*—We arrived at home last Seventh day, and to my great comfort I found all my family going on well and comfortably. I ventured to ask, or at least to desire, if my goings out were acceptable to the Lord, and if I were to be called to further, and perhaps still more weighty service, that I might find the blessing of preservation extended to those most dear to me at home, as well as to myself in going. Through mercy, this sign has been rather unusually granted me. What can I render unto my Lord for His tender and unmerited mercies ?

After leaving William Ball's (Glen Rothay), we spent First-day at Kendal. This meeting is in the most critical state, some of its most valuable members, young and old, leaving the So-ciety. I can hardly express how much I felt in attending it ; fears got hold of me ; however, I experienced much help. I had simply to preach the Gospel, until the close of the After-noon Meeting, when I believed it my duty to express my convic-tion, that we, as a Society, fill an important place in the Church of Christ ; and having found it myself a blessed adminis-tration of the truth as it is in Jesus ; I felt that where so many seeking minds were about leaving the Society, I was bound to bear my testimony to that which I believed to be true. We afterwards attended some very interesting Meetings at Lancaster, Yelland and Ulverston. These places had been long on my mind, I think at least ten years. So things rest with me, until I see the time come to work in them.

Tenth Month 28*th.*—I have been a satisfactory visit with my husband, and partly accompanied by Peter Bedford and John Hodgskin, to Croyfield and Ifield. Our Meeting in Sussex was a very satisfactory one ; and a reading we had the next morning at a cottage on a Common, belonging to a dear Friend, where we had been before. The libraries we established, appear to have been much read and valued. It is cause for much thankfulness, to find that our labour has not been in vain in the Lord. How sweet are His mercies! May all become His servants, saith my soul!

I have also left home accompanied by my beloved husband and my sister Elizabeth, to visit a few Meetings in Essex.

Twelfth Month, 6*th.*—This morning I felt deeply the seriousness of laying before my Monthly Meeting, my belief that it may be my duty again to visit France and some other parts of the Continent of Europe. It is after much weighty consideration that I have come to the conclusion, that it is right to do this. I have long thought that this summer my course might be turned either to my dearest brother Joseph in America, or to the Continent of Europe; after much weighing it, I have believed the latter to be the right opening for me. I laid my prospect before the Friends of our Monthly Meeting, this morning. Several Friends were there, not members of it. We had a very solemn Meeting—for worship first. My sister and I returned our certificates for visiting Scotland, and then I asked for one for Europe ; having very earnestly prayed for help, direction, and protection. When under a fresh feeling of its being right to do it, I simply informed Friends that I looked to paying a visit to Paris, then to the Friends in the South of France ; and should probably in returning visit some other parts of Europe. Much unity and sympathy were expressed with this prospect of religious duty, by our own members and those who visited us. There certainly appeared to be in no common degree, a seal set to this serious prospect of religious service.

I now desire to leava lle to the further openings of Providence, as to when to go, who is to go with me, and where to go. I desire to leave it all to my most holy and gracious Head and High Priest, my All in All, my Lord and my God. Although I am very deeply sensible that it is only through the fulness and freeness of unmerited mercy, love and grace, that I dare call or feel my Lord thus to be my Head and my Helper. I may acknowledge in faith, my belief that through the help of the Holy Spirit, my Lord has been and is unto me " Wonderful, Counsellor, the Mighty God, the Everlasting Father, and the Prince of Peace."

28th.—Yesterday, excepting our dear Frank and Rachel, all our beloved children dined with us. It really was to me a beautiful sight. Sixteen round our table, happy in each other, a strong tie of love amidst the brothers and sisters ; and much united to us their father and mother. I felt the occasion serious as well as sweet, and very earnestly prayed to the Lord that I might be very faithful, if He called me to any religious service amongst them ; whether it were to pray for them, or speak to them of His goodness. When the cloth was removed after dinner, I believed it my duty to kneel down, and very fervently to pray and to return thanks to my God, for all these most tenderly beloved ones. Great help and deliverance has been granted to some of our circle ; the Lord has been very gracious, He has added to our number and not diminished them. I did from my heart return God thanks, earnestly asking in faith for a continuance of His mercies ; more particularly, that our souls should be satisfied more abundantly with the unsearchable riches of Christ ; and that we might be still more closely united in our Heavenly Father's love. I asked the Lord that it might please Him to grant us peace and prosperity, through his tender mercy in Christ Jesus ; and that wherever we might be, His blessing might be with us ; and that when the end came, it might crown all.

After this solemn time, thirteen of the sweet, dear grandchildren came in. We missed dearest Frank and Rachel, and their lovely group; but they were not forgotten by us. We passed an evening of uncommon enjoyment, cheerful yet sober, lively yet sensible of the blessing and peace of our Lord being with us. I seldom if ever remember so bright a family meeting, it reminded me of our Earlham days ; but I could not but feel it a blessing, when a mother as well as a father is spared to watch their family grow up and prosper, and to see and enjoy their children's children.

When I remember all that I have passed through on their account ; above all the exquisite anxiety about their spiritual welfare, and now so far to see what the Lord has done for me and for them, What can I say ? What can I do ? ought I not to leave them all to His most holy keeping, and no longer "toil and spin" so much for them?

CHAPTER XXI.

First Month, 12*th.*—I returned from Lynn last evening. I was a good deal with my beloved sister Catherine, who was there. Before parting, we had a deeply interesting time together, when the spirit of prayer was remarkably poured forth upon us. I prayed for them each separately, and believe that access was in mercy granted to the Throne of Grace. My dearest sister offered a solemn prayer for us before we rose from our knees. I felt, as I have often done, an earnest desire, that we may none be in spiritual bonds. I think Satan, in hardly any way mars the Lord's work more, than in putting persons in the stiff bonds of High Churchism. He attacks all professors in this way, and leads them to rest in their sectarianism, rather than their Christianity. I do not mean that this is the case with those I was amongst, but I see it a frightful bait, thrown out to all professors of all denominations. Few things I more earnestly desire, than unity in the Church of Christ, and that all partition walls may be broken down. Lord, hasten the coming of that day, for Thine own name's sake !

16*th.*—I have had the pleasure and satisfaction of meeting at dinner, at my son Foster Reynolds', my beloved brother Gurney, three of my sons, one of his, and my nephew Edward Buxton, previous to attending a Bible Meeting. Surely it is a cause of deep thankfulness to have my children, and others so near and dear to me, engaged in so excellent a cause. I consider it to be an honour of which we are all unworthy, to promote in this or any other way, the knowledge of the everlasting Gospel. On Second-day, I laid my concern to go to France, before the Morning Meeting. I feel encouraged by all the testimonies from the Lord's servants, and the real help and excellence of the arrangement, that we should thus, in such weighty and important duties, have the sanction of that section of the Church to which we belong.

I have received very encouraging accounts from Scotland as to the results of our last journey. Several refuges are likely to be formed, and women prisoners to be visited. The accounts from France have also been in many ways encouraging. My dear and valued friend, the Duchess de Broglie, who died some little time ago, expressed that her faith had been strengthened by our visit. Many important alterations have taken place in the prisons; the New Testament is now circulated in some of them, and the hospitals. So I may take courage, and return God thanks.

There was one subject of anxiety pressing upon the mind of Elizabeth Fry, which she knew to be so important, that with all the preparations for her long journey, and arrangements to make for her family at home, she resolved to remove it if possible— the low state of the funds of the British Ladies' Society.

Money was not only wanted in carrying on the Prison Visiting, to furnish employment in many cases, and to supply books and little rewards as encouragement for good behaviour; but there were also to be assisted the valuable Refuges that had been established; one for little girls at Chelsea, and another for young women at Manor Hall, in the same place. There were, besides these demands, heavy and continual calls upon their funds, to meet the melancholy cases of liberated prisoners, or accused but destitute females, who could not be received into either of these institutions. A sub-committee had been formed, under the name of the Patronage Committee, and at this time was actively at work, to assist such cases; once a week the ladies met (and continue to meet), to receive applications. Fearful details of misery and guilt are constantly brought before them—frequently may be seen a prison officer with some poor creature in her custody, (or voluntarily under her care,) come to implore shelter and opportunity of existence, without living in sin. Besides this, the Convict Ships continued a heavy demand upon the funds of the British Society. Some expedient to meet these emergencies was become essential. Mrs. Fry had no taste for Bazaars and Repositories; but, conducted in a sober quiet manner, she did not believe them wrong; under these circumstances, therefore, and after full consultation with her friends and coadjutors, she determined upon having a sale for this purpose.

There is an ancient building in the city of London, called Crosby Hall, still beautiful, though fallen into decay. It had become the property of a lady, desirous of restoring it; she had already begun the work, and willingly granted the use of it, as a means of carrying on some of the repairs. A few days, however, before the sale was to take place, the needful preparations were found not even commenced. Twe rooms, formerly part of the ancient palace, absolutely necessary on this occasion were still a ruin. Skilful workmen were called in; a magical change passed over the scene, the worm-eaten timbers were covered and floored, the arched windows through which the wind had howled, and the rain beaten three days before, were glazed, and where cobweb waved upon ruined walls, hangings were suspended, with at intervals armorial bearings, to enliven the whole. By the day of sale all things were ready to receive the public.

Paris, Third Month, 17th.—Before leaving home, we were much occupied by a very large sale, for the British Society, held in Crosby Hall. I felt it an exercising time lest any should be exposed to temptation by it, and I see that there are two sides to the question respecting these sales, as there is an exposure in them that may prove injurious to some. However, I think I saw in this instance many favourable results, and particularly in the kind and capital help my children gave in it, and the way in which it occupied them. One day I had fifteen children, and several grandchildren helping me to sell. A sweet and Chris-

tian spirit appeared to reign in the room: There were more than
a thousand pounds obtained by it, clear of all expenses, which
will be a great help to the British Society. The marks of kindness shown to me by numbers, in the things sent to the sale,
were very encouraging to me. My brothers and sisters, my
nephews and nieces, were also very kind, in aiding me in many
ways.

Previous to our departure, I had the servants of our different
families meet me at Meeting ; it proved quite a large number,
almost filling our Meeting House. I believe it was a time of
real edification and comfort to some who were there.

Josiah Forster, an elder among Friends, accompanied Elizabeth Fry on this journey. Her husband and a daughter were
also with her ; her youngest son to join them at Paris. Difficulties attended their first starting, which gradually yielded,
and they left home on the 11th of March.

Scarcely had Mrs. Fry reached the Hotel at Boulogne, before
so many came to seek her, that with difficulty she found time to
breakfast or change her dress. She visited the prison, which was
in a very deplorable state ; and in the evening received about
forty at the Hotel, chiefly the ladies of a little district Society
she had been instrumental in forming on her previous visit. The
results of their labours were very satisfactory ; many of the poor
French were subscribing for, or buying New Testaments, as well
as eagerly reading the tracts circulated amongst them. The state
of the resident English poor was also considered as decidedly
improved, through this means.

On retiring to her room at night, Mrs. Fry's maid could not
refrain the expression of her astonishment, at the eagerness of the
servants of the Hotel for Testaments, " The people here are
craving Testaments Ma'am ;" it appeared that they lent them
to their friends, who carried them into the country, where they
were so eagerly read and re-read, that it was difficult for the
rightful owners to regain possession of them.

On the 14th, en route to Abbeville, the party stopped at Samer for an hour, to give Mrs. Fry the opportunity of visiting a poor sick Englishman in great affliction. At Montreuil-sur-Mer, she gave a tract to a man whilst changing horses; the carriage was soon surrounded by people begging for books; it was curious to see their energy to obtain them. The same thing occurred at the Hotel at Abbeville, where those, to whom she had given them on her previous visit, begged for more, and came creeping up to her apartment to prefer their request. Her Text-books, "Les petits livres de matin," were the decided favourites. In the morning, the people of the Hotel again gathered round her. The Sunday she had spent there on her former visit to Paris—the reading they had in the evening—the prayer she offered for them, had made a deep impression. They beguiled her into the kitchen, where she told them in broken French, which however they contrived to understand, a little of her wishes for them as to faith and practice ; then all would shake hands with her to the portly " chef de cuisine."

Paris, Third Month, 17th.—Here we are once more in this most interesting city, after a favourable journey, and calm passage. Leaving home was very touching to our feelings ; I never saw my children feel a separation so much.

I am not high in spirits on my arrival here. At Meeting, and in a time of prayer with some of my dear friends, I felt the springs very low, but I trust through the tender mercy of my Heavenly Father, they will rise by degrees. It was sweet on our arrival, to see some beautiful flowers and other things all ready for us, provided by our dear kind friends as marks of their love, particularly from the Baroness Pelet, it cheered my heart ; sweet visits from Sophia D—— and Emelie M——, were also comforting. How earnestly do I desire and pray, that my Lord would clearly point out my work in this place; that He would enable me by His own Power and Spirit, to perform it in sim-plicity to His praise, the good of others, and my own peace.

Lord, regard Thy servant in her low estate, and if it be Thy holy will, give some token, by Thy presence, Spirit and Power, that Thou art with us ; and more abundantly fit and prepare for Thine own work, as Thou hast often blessed and abundantly increased that which may appear small in the eyes of man, to the help of numbers : so, oh Lord ! bless, prosper, and increase the weak labours of Thy unworthy servant, to the good of numbers, and the promotion of Thy cause in this place ; where " the world, the flesh, and the devil," appear so powerful.   Answer this cry, I beseech Thee, and give Thy poor servant a quiet, patient, trustful spirit, only dependent upon the fresh pourings forth of Thy Spirit, and the incomings of Thy love.   Amen.

24th.—In mercy my cry was heard.   We went to our little Meeting, where were some seeking minds ; and to my own feelings, we were remarkably bound together by the presence of our Lord. I also may thankfully say, that I was enabled to preach the word and to pray.   I felt it an encouraging, edifying time, and an answer to prayer.   After Meeting, we called at our Ambassador's, and met with a very cordial reception.   In the evening, we went to an evangelical party which I was glad to be at, although I thought part of the service flat.   I had a few words only to say.

On Sixth-day, we visited a large French Methodists' school ; it was a very encouraging sight : there were about a hundred children, who appeared well taught.   I had a good deal of advice to give them and their parents, and felt peace in the service ; but the place was so exceedingly cold, that I left it with severe tooth-ache, which lasted all day, and brought me down in body and spirit.

Having invited a large company for philanthropic and religious objects for the following evening, I felt anxious ; but when the time came, I was enabled, though the party was very large, to speak a little on the subject of Negro Slavery : Josiah Forster also expressed himself very agreeably upon the subject.   We finished with a short, lively Scripture-reading, and to my own feelings, strength was in a remarkable manner given me in the needful time.

The morning, I paid a most interesting visit to a Roman Catholic lady,—a young widow,—her little children, and her friend.   I have seldom seen the Christian life more exemplified.

So we see and "perceive that God is no respecter of persons ; but in every nation, he that feareth Him, and worketh righteousness, is accepted with Him."—Acts x. 34, 35.

Thus began this second sojourn in Paris : the same friends gathered round her, the same institutions were revisited, with some others which she had not seen before; the same objects of interest occupied her attention. The mornings were thus spent; the evenings generally at the houses of their many kind friends, or in receiving guests at the Hotel. No one was more capable than Mrs. Fry of appreciating the enjoyment of social intercourse or society, such as these occasions afforded, but it was not from this motive she united in them. She considered it her duty to avail herself of the opportunities thus afforded, for the diffusion of knowledge on those subjects which had brought her to Paris, and the introduction of topics of a philanthropic and religious character.

Mrs. Fry had not before visited the hospitals generally ; now she did so, accompanied by the Baron de Gerando. The enlarged religion and benevolence of this excellent old man was delightful to her : his being a member of the Roman Catholic Church in no way preventing their Christian unity. He was endeavouring to found a Penitentiary, or Magdalen, in Paris ; but complained that people are so easily influenced through their senses, that it was comparatively easy to induce them to feed the starving, clothe the naked, and administer to the sick ; whilst moral reforms, the benefit of which are less immediately obvious, but of such infinitely greater importance, are too often neglected.

The first visit was to the Hospital of the Hôtel Dieu, a vast pile built on either side of one of the branches of the Seine, over which is a communication by a covered bridge. It is an extremely ancient foundation, and contains 1260 beds, of which a hundred or a hundred and fifty, are placed in each of the immense wards. These, notwithstanding their size and the cleanliness of the beds,

linen, and floors, were offensively close. The mortality in this
hospital is at all times great: partly to be attributed to the
severity of the accidents and other cases brought to the Hôtel
Dieu, but even more to the defective ventilation. This is proved
by the singular fact, that the greatest number of deaths occur
on the third or highest story, less on the second, and the fewest
on the ground-floor.

This hospital is under the care of a lay director, and nuns of
the Order of St. Augustin ; there are forty of them divided
between the Hôtel Dieu and the Hospital of St. Louis.

The Superior spoke feelingly of the trials to which they
were exposed, in fulfilling their arduous and distasteful labours;
that only as a duty to God could they endure it. The nuns
appeared very kind to the poor creatures under their care, but
take no part in ministering to their mental necessities and
religious state.

The following day, accompanied by the Baron de Gerando
and M. Valderuche, Mrs. Fry visited the Hospital of St. Louis,
founded by Henri IV., for plague, leprosy, and other contagious
complaints. It was entirely built in his time, and contains all
that was then considered necessary to prevent or check contagion ; it is now used for cases of cutaneous disease. The Hospital of St. Louis is a noble pile of buildings, placed amongst
gardens, in the outskirts of the town. It encloses within itself,
five large courts laid out in gardens ; the wards each containing
as many beds as those in the Hôtel Dieu, but being lofty,
vaulted, and with the finest ventilation from a double tier of
almost unnumbered windows, they were perfectly fresh and
pleasant. The nuns said the rate of mortality was very small.

A poor English maid-servant was amongst the sufferers ; she
had been there for months, having been left by an English family
with whom she had been travelling. She spoke of the kindness
she had received in the Hospital as great. Her heart bounded

at the sound of her native tongue; nor was she left without arrangements for her future comfort.

The establishment of baths of various descriptions is very complete, and available for out-door as well as house patients. The appearance of the hospital was highly gratifying as to every outward arrangement, but not so as to any opportunity for moral and religious improvement. Before quitting the establishment, Mrs. Fry asked to see the Chaplain (L'Aumônier.) After some general discourse on the state of the institution, she addressed him on the subject of her concern for the souls of these poor people, the reply was, " Nous avons les sacremens de l'Eglise," which closed the conversation; the priest accepting a Text Book, and parting from his visitors in a friendly manner.

Two days afterwards, the same party went to the Hospital des Enfans Trouvés. This monument of St. Vincent de Paul is an affecting sight, from the miserable state of the wretched infants, and the fearful mortality that prevails among them. Their sufferings must be greatly increased by the unnatural practice of swaddling, from which thraldom they are only unloosed once in twelve hours, for any purpose ; the sound in the ward could be only compared to the faint and pitiful bleating of a flock of lambs. A lady who not unfrequently visited the institution said, that she never remembered examining the long array of clean white cots that lined the walls, without finding one or more dead. In front of the fire was a sloping stage, on which was a mattress, and a row of these little creatures placed upon it to warm, and await their turn to be fed from the spoon by a nurse. After much persuasion, one that was crying piteously, was released from its swaddling bands, it stretched its little limbs, and ceased its wailings. Mrs. Fry pleaded so hard for them with the Superior, that their arms have since been released. The Sisters of Charity professed to be desirous of doing justice to the children ; but the conduct of the whole institution wanted vigour and deliverance, from the prejudices which consigns infancy to so much suffering and untimely death.

The medical attendants were alive to the defects of the management, but professed themselves unable to effect any change in the old-established usages of the place.   These appeared to Mrs. Fry and her party to be almost confounded in the minds of the Sisters, with the regulations of their religious order ; at all events, if not belonging to it, very naturally arising from the "invincible immobilité" of monachism, as a strict Roman Catholic lady, but a keen observer of all around her, expressed it to Mrs. Fry many years before.

If these infants survive the first few days, they are sent into the country to be nursed.   There is also a sort of Orphan Asylum attached to the Enfans Trouvés for children of all ages, but they are seldom there a month before removal into the country to be brought up by the ignorant peasants to whom they are consigned.

Mrs. Fry saw at a glance, how vast an opportunity of national good was here lost; multitudes of children belonging to the State, and ignorant of any other parentage, would if properly trained and educated on scriptural principles, act as a leaven amongst the mass to raise the tone of good feeling and principle, and increase the attachment of the lower classes to their country and its institutions.

From the Enfans Trouvés they proceeded to the Hospice de la Maternité, this building is full of recollections, being the Porte Royale of Paris—now so changed !   The cells used for the patients still retain their cellular divisions, so that complete privacy is enjoyed by each poor woman, with all the convenience of wards.   Mrs. Fry thought this, the best Lying-in Hospital she had ever seen; the Matron and the Superintendent appeared enlightened and intelligent, the whole condition of the place vigorous and sound.   It is entirely under secular care.

In this as in all the other Paris hospitals, no tickets of admission are required, a person has only to prove herself poor and ill, to be admitted as a patient.

Third-day.—Visited an hospital, and dined at Lord William Bentinck's, I trust to some good purpose, but I fear for myself in many ways on such occasions.

Fifth-day.—A very solemn Morning Meeting, numbers there, mostly women, some ladies of rank, some very interesting persons, I was afresh enabled to pray and to minister.

Her ministry on this occasion was wonderful, chiefly addressed to the afflicted, and seemed to find an echo in many hearts. She afterwards called on Madame Guizot, mother of the Minister; a charming old lady eighty years of age, taking charge of her three little grandchildren.

Mrs. Fry again visited the St. Lazare prison. She found some improvements effected, and female officers introduced. Many of the prisoners knew her again, and seemed delighted to see her. In one ward (Salle) they told her that since her last visit, they had thought and talked so much of religion, that they had subscribed to purchase " Ceïle-là," pointing to an image of the virgin placed against the wall.

The St. Lazare Prison is only for women, and often contains 1,200 at one time; to it is attached a sort of compulsory Lock hospital.

She also saw La Roquette, or the prison for " Les Jeunes Détenus," a very fine establishment for boys. By the laws of France, a boy is not held responsible for his actions under sixteen years of age, and therefore if he commits a crime, he is detained and confined, but not sentenced. Fathers in France have the power of confining sons under this age.

La Roquette is built upon the plan of a prison, and contains between five and six hundred inmates; there is a regular school

7

for their instruction in reading, writing, and arithmetic. Several of the classes were reading the New Testament, (De Sacy's translation). Each boy has a copy, and they may have the book to read if they wish it in their hours of recreation. There are various workshops where they learn trades. Of their earnings they receive one-third at the time, one-third when they leave the prison, the remaining third goes to the establishment. They have no other punishment than solitary confinement. The boys under " Correction Paternelle" were in cells, where their education was carried vigorously forward, according to their rank in life, no other difference is permitted—the same little bed, table, chair, and shelves in each, and the same diet and costume. It was to Mrs. Fry's feelings a highly interesting and satisfactory establishment. Not so the prison of La Force, into which she ventured, and saw six hundred untried persons crowded together in a state of total idleness, vice and neglect, without even Sundays, or fête days, the service of the Roman Catholic Church being performed.

About this time the party was joined by several of Mrs. Fry's family, it was highly interesting to them, thus to be together under such novel circumstances, and to be permitted for once to witness and partake in the scenes, incident to their beloved mother's labours in the cause of benevolence and religion.

Fourth Month, 7th, First-day.—One day we dined at our dear friends the Mallets', where we met a large family party, and had much interesting conversation. There was a blessed feeling of the love of God over us; I believe this service was called for, and was blessed to many present. Last evening about a hundred persons spent the evening with us. The subject of prisons was brought forward, Newgate, &c., I endeavoured to show the state of prisons formerly, and many of their improvements. But above all, to inculcate Christian principle as the only sure means of improving practice. I sought in every way, in the cases brought forward, to uphold the value of the Scriptures, and to show the blessed results of faith and repentance. We finished by reading in a solemn manner the 15th of Luke, as the chapter so greatly blessed to poor prisoners. I made little comment, there was very great solemnity over us. There were Catholics and Protestants, and I believe some of the Greek Church. There were Greeks, Ionians, Spaniards, a Pole, Italians, Germans, English, Americans and French. Several of the English and French, persons of rank ; the Marquis de Brignolles Sardinian Minister, and Prince Czartorinski. Thus this week has run away ! may it have been for the real good of others, and the glory of God. Most merciful God, I perfectly know that I am unworthy to present myself before Thee on the bended knee of my soul. But I come boldly to the throne of grace, through the merits of Thy dear Son, our Mediator with Thee our God. Grant Holy Father, that the iniquity of my holy things may be blotted out, and that in my efforts to serve Thee, and promote the cause of truth and righteousness, my infirmities and the unworthiness of the instrument may not have cast a blemish on Thy truth. Grant also, Holy Father, that the word spoken may through Thy blessing, comfort, strengthen and edify Thy followers, and be a means of bringing many to repentance and faith in Thy beloved Son Christ Jesus our Lord. Dearest Lord, be near to keep, to help, and direct all my steps, as I go on in this cause, for Thy glory, the good of others, and my own edification and peace. Permit Thy servant also to commend to Thy special keeping, all most near to her, left in her own land, and all everywhere, beloved by her, and for whom she travails in spirit, and spread the knowledge of Thyself, and of Thy Son, and Thy righteousness, through the Holy Spirit, everywhere on this earth. Amen !

Paris, 21st.—I feel that, under a lively sense of peace and rest of soul, I may record the mercies of the Lord this last week.

Our First-day was very satisfactory, a large Meeting, five of our children with us. I now mention the events of the week without stating the days.

I had a very serious, interesting, and intimate conversation with the Duchess of Orleans.

I visited and attended to some prisons, formed a Ladies' Society to visit the Protestants in prisons and hospitals, met a very influential company at dinner at Lord Granville's, much interesting conversation in the evening; the same twice at Baron Pelet's, and we had an agreeable dinner at Lord William Bentinck's. I have paid some very interesting private calls, spent one morning with my children; our great philanthropic evening largely attended, about a hundred and forty present. Josiah Forster gave a concentrated account of our former evenings, and added other things very agreeably. I strongly impressed upon them the extreme importance of the influence of the higher, on the lower classes of society, by their example and precept; mentioned late hours, theatres and other evils. Then advised; giving the poor, Christian education, reading the Holy Scriptures in their families, lending Libraries, District Societies and other objects: we finished with a very solemn Scripture reading, the greater part of the third chapter of Colossians, and 20th and 21st verses of the last chapter of the epistle to the Hebrews, " Now the God of peace that brought again from the dead our Lord Jesus, that great Shepherd of the sheep, through the blood of the everlasting covenant, make you perfect in every good work, to do His will, working in you that which is well pleasing in His sight, through Jesus Christ; to whom be glory for ever and ever. Amen."

Previous to reading this, I had expressed some solemn parting truths, and our party broke up in much love and peace.

May the Lord of the harvest Himself cause that some of these may be gathered into His garner, and may He bless, prosper, and increase the seed so unworthily scattered.

On Fifth-day, we dined with some sweet, spiritual, and delightful people, the de Presensés and de Valcours; in the evening to Mark Wilkes', to meet a very large party of ministers from different parts of France, come to attend the Meetings of the various Societies.

Fontainbleau, 28th.—The day before our departure from Paris we visited the Prefét de Police, took in our report of the state of the prisons, and obtained leave for the Protestant ladies to visit the Protestant prisoners ; we had much interesting conversation. We have the great satisfaction of hearing, that a law is likely to pass for women prisoners throughout France, to be under the care of women.

In the evening and during the day, numbers came to take leave of us ; a good many Greeks, who appeared to feel much interest in and for us, as if our labours with them had not been in vain.

On parting with my beloved children, (to return to England,) I could not refrain from many tears. Our beloved friend Emilie Mallet joined us very early in the morning, also our kind friend John Sargent, our friend de Béranger, and one or two others. My soul was particularly humbled within me, and, before parting we assembled with our friends, and poured forth deep prayer and thanksgiving unto the Lord ; thanks for the help granted to us, and for the kindness shown us by our Christian friends, and the love and unity we have partaken of with them ; prayer that our labours might be blessed, and the seed scattered, prospered and increased, and that no reproach might have been brought by us upon the cause nearest to my heart ; earnestly did I ask a blessing upon our friends, ourselves, the tenderly beloved ones just parted from, and those at home. After this we took an affectionate leave of all, including our host, hostess, and the Hotel servants.

Among other topics connected with penal legislation, the solitary or separate system was frequently debated in the conversations at Paris. Mrs. Fry was continually called upon to give her opinion. M. de Béranger and she discussed it frequently, and on leaving Paris she employed her husband to address to him the following letter :

The subject of separate confinement is one presenting many difficulties, from the diversity of views taken by so many persons of talent and humanity ; and my wife has thought that I could not better convey her ideas than by simply stating the arguments that appear to her to bear with the most weight, favourably or unfavourably, on the question.

The following she considers the most prominent reasons in favour of separate confinement:—

First,—It prevents, with the most certainty, all contamination from their fellow-prisoners.

Secondly, —It prevents the formation of intimacy, or acquaintance, with persons who may prove highly injurious associates in future life.

Thirdly,—It affords more opportunity for serious reflection, and should any become religiously disposed for prayer and meditation, and being much cut off from their fellow-mortals, it may lead to a greater dependence on God, and to having their hearts more devoted to Him.

Fourthly,—The privacy of the confinement may prevent that loss of character, in the estimation of the world, which is the general consequence of imprisonment, as now inflicted.

The following reasons may, on the other hand, be strongly, adduced against the system being generally adopted :—

In the *first* place, the extreme liability to its abuse, and to its being rendered an unduly severe punishment, *or the reverse*, according to the will or caprice, partiality, dislike, or neglect, of the persons who have the management of them.

Secondly,—The very great difficulty of obtaining a sufficiency, of either men or women officers, of that high and upright principle, as by their impartiality and firmness, with proper kindness and due attention to the welfare of the prisoners, would be *fit* persons to be entrusted with so weighty a charge. This opinion is strongly corroborated by that of the experienced Governor of the Great Central Prison of Beaulieu, also by the Governor of the House of Correction, in Cold-Bath Fields, in London.

Thirdly,—Prisoners so confined are rendered almost *irresistibly* subject to the moral contamination of officers, which is the case only in a very limited degree, when allowed to associate daily with their fellow-prisoners.

Fourthly,—Although, when the moral good of the community is concerned, expense ought to be a very secondary consideration, yet it ought not to be overlooked. The expense of providing proper cells, and a sufficient number of properly qualified officers, for so large a number of prisoners, would be enormous; and the difficulty, of so building as to prevent the communication of sound, very great, and its attainment uncertain, besides the liability of the prisoners not being able to make themselves heard, in case of necessity, arising from sudden illness or accident.

Fifthly,—Although for short periods, neither the powers of the mind nor body might suffer essentially, yet after a long and too solitary confinement, there is *unquestionable danger for both.* Too much silence is contrary to nature, and physically injurious both to the stomach and lungs; and as regards the faculties, we are credibly informed of the fact, (in addition to what we have known at home,) that amongst the monks of La Trappe, few attained to the age of sixty years without having suffered, an absolute decay of their mental powers, and fallen into premature childishness.

Sixthly,—That whilst, on the one hand, it affords to the penitent an opportunity for salutary reflection, there is reason on the other hand to fear, that a large proportion of those who are confined in jails, are so deeply depraved, that when left to themselves they would be *more likely* to consume their hours in ruminating over past crimes and exploits, and in devising and planning schemes for the commission of new ones; the heart becomes more hardened, the character and temper more sullen and morose, and better prepared for fresh crimes upon their dismissal from prison.

The *seventh* and most weighty objection of all, is this, that as the vast majority of those who enter a prison, are likely to be returned into the bosom of society, it is a most important and paramount consideration, that as man is a social being, and not designed for a life of seclusion, such a system of prison discipline be adopted, as may best prepare those under its correction, for re-entering active life, and all its consequent exposures and temptations. This can never be effected in solitude or separation: it can only be achieved by such regulations, brought to bear upon every day prison life, as may most easily, and with the best chance of success, be afterwards carried out and realized in daily practice, upon their restoration to liberty. Of course, this view embraces all useful labour, and excludes such as (like the Tread-wheel) can in no way facilitate the future means of an honest livelihood.

Having thus briefly stated the reasons for and against the separate confinement of prisoners in the day-time, and the result of which is the conclusion, that it is inexpedient to bring it into general practice : I will endeavour to represent Mrs. Fry's opinion, as to the best line of conduct to be adopted towards untried prisoners, not only with a view to prevent the commission of such offences, as would subject them to punishment, but fundamentally to improve their principles, and regulate their whole future conduct and life, which is the one grand point to keep in view.

In this first place, from the instant that any individual is placed under restraint, charged with the commission of an offence against the law, the grand preliminary object ought to be, to preserve, by every possible means, the morals of the person thus detained, from being *deteriorated* by the process; and that, at all events, the *law itself* should not become the instrument of the most cruel and fatal of all injustices,—that of demoralizing, by every species of exposure and contamination, the wretched being whom it sooner or later may have to consign, as the consequence of its own action, to infamy and punishment.

A man,—a youth, perhaps,—is charged with a crime. He may be innocent, he may be a trembling beginner : his education, his previous habits, may have been good. He knows little of crime, and has few or no associates in it. He is now turned loose into a den, amongst the most hardened criminals, and in one short month, all remaining scruples, all remaining tenderness of conscience, are gone too probably for ever. But it is not only one short month ; but in France, and in most English counties, it is many months' opportunity which is thus afforded to the profligate villain, to harden, to season, and to embue the mind of his unpractised victim, for re-entering society depraved, debased, and ripe for the commission of crimes, at which he would have shuddered, when the act of the law, by placing them in public detention, first exposed him to irretrievable degradation and ruin.

But let us suppose the case of those, wholly innocent of the crimes laid to their charge, the victims of false accusation, malice, or mistake. Suppose them, by the aid of religious and moral principle, to have withstood all the baneful influences to which a cruel and unjust law has exposed them; and to go out of prison justly acquitted, and worthy to be replaced in the esteem and confidence of their fellow citizens. What follows? why, they go forth blighted and blasted. Their involuntary association, with the companions the law has chosen for them, has for ever destroyed their characters; they are shunned, and become the objects of most reasonable suspicion; they have no means, no hope left, of gaining an honest living,—the law has effectually prevented that, —they are driven to dishonest, dishonourable, or violent means, of obtaining a morsel of bread; they are again arrested, and the same law that made them what they are, pours forth its heaviest judgments on the victims of its own injurious policy.

Heartily, therefore, should every friend to humanity hail the day, when arrangements are made for the separate confinement of all untried prisoners, with liberty, daily to see some of their own friends, to consult their legal advisers, to improve their own accommodation in their bedding or their diet, to be visited by such benevolent persons as may seek to promote their present and everlasting welfare; and, joined to this, every practicable arrangement made by the Government of their country, for the shortest possible period, elapsing, previous to their trial, both for the good of the prisoners and its advantage to the country, by lessening essentially the prison-room required, and the many expenses attached to the confinement of prisoners.

If found guilty on their trial, and if their first offence, Mrs. Fry's views are simple, and are given in her own words :—

I believe nothing so likely to conduce to the real improvement of principle and conduct in delinquents, and to render them fit for a return to society, as a limited number of them being regularly instructed, and working together in small companies— say, from ten to twenty—under faithful, constant, and strict inspection by day, and at night always sleeping in separate cells. The mode of instruction and its subjects, should be very simple, and if possible, be rendered agreeable to them. The Scripture-readings, (and reading the Scriptures ought never to be omitted) should be short and well-selected, adapted to their generally dark and very ignorant state, and calculated to give them a taste for something superior to their former low and depraved habits. Books of a moral and religious tendency, that amuse whilst they instruct, are also very desirable, and especially so, in the cases of separate confinement. I consider religious instruction, given in a kind and judicious spirit, the most powerful and efficacious means of deterring from crime, and inducing good conduct, resulting from improved principles. Some advantage may occasionally arise from this instruction being given privately; but it is more generally likely to be well received in companies, because, very close and cogent advice may be thus given, without danger of hurting individual feelings, as they receive the advice, without supposing it directed immediately to themselves. I consider, also, that employment in companies, is more likely to be well and industriously performed, as there is a stimulus in trying who can do the best, and, who can do the most, in the shortest period of time.

If, after the plan of being associated in small companies has been tried on any prisoner, he returns to undergo the penalty of a second condemnation, a more rigorous system had better be adopted. I think, they should then be confined separately, having instruction and employment, and a certain number of visits daily, from the officers of the prison, or persons allowed or appointed for this special purpose; thus preventing the (now) old offender from associating with the novice in guilt, and suitably proportioning the punishment to the offence. But it is necessary to add, that in no case should women be separately confined, unless placed under the care of officers of their own sex; nor should any man, not even the Chaplain or Physician, be allowed to visit them under any pretext, unless accompanied by a female officer.—I remain, &c.

Just before Mrs. Fry left Paris, she was informed that the Archbishop was annoyed at her proceedings, that he had expressed dissatisfaction at the alterations she had recommended in the St.

Lazare Prison, and had gone so far as to speak with regret, if not displeasure, of the Baron de Gerando's having accompanied her in her visits to the hospitals. But the secret of the Archiepiscopal opposition lay not here—it was the more general knowledge of the Holy Scriptures which he dreaded. It was, that the reforms, Mrs. Fry recommended, were all based upon Scriptural authority, that it was to those sacred writings she referred for rules of active obligation, as the only source from whence to learn all that is due from man to man; and above all this, that she lost no opportunity in all companies, and on all occasions, where it could be done with propriety, to urge their perusal and general circulation.

But whilst she did this, believing it to be an absolute duty, she had no tendency, where she deemed the great foundation of religious truth secure, to oppose the opinions of others, or introduce her own.

The party left Paris on Saturday, the 27th of April, and proceeded through Melun to Fontainbleau. Mrs. Fry was furnished with a letter from the Minister of the Interior, granting her, Mr. Forster, and her husband, permission to visit all the prisons in France. This important document was first made use of at Melun, and on this occasion, as on every succeeding one, Mrs. Fry was received with respect, and every facility afforded her and her party, for inspecting the prisons.

The Prison at Melun contained upwards of a thousand men, thirty of whom were Protestants, and visited by their own minister, who supplied them with copies of the Scriptures; but on inquiring of the Chaplain (l'Aumônier) whether the Roman Catholics were allowed to possess the Bible, he evaded the question, by replying, " They have religious books."

An accident to the carriage detained the party for the night at Auxerre. During the afternoon, Mrs. Fry went to the prison, where she found that a benevolent woman in humble circumstances, had for many years daily visited and read to the prisoners, and still persevered in her work with vigour, although eighty years of age.—At Chalons-sur-Soane. The evening was occupied by a visit to an hospital under the care of nuns, which had the effect of comfort greater than ordinary. The beds having clean white curtains, and each patient a little table by his side.

The next morning they embarked on the Soane before six in the morning, and had a delightful voyage to Lyons with the mountainous districts of Auvergne, and the Puis-de-Dome full in sight. The change of climate in steaming so rapidly southwards was very remarkable—it was spring in the morning at Chalons, at Lyons in the afternoon it was summer. Many tracts were distributed among the passengers on board the boat; some refused them, some returned them, but one man not only kept the " Letter on the Evidences of Christianity" by J. J. Gurney, but insisted on Josiah Forster's acceptance of his wine flask; an ancient and grotesque specimen of china which the donor considered of Sevre manufacture and upwards of two hundred years old. There did not appear to be the same desire for books as in the North of France; partly arising from comparatively few of the people being taught to read.

In Lyons, where they arrived on the 4th of May, many objects of interest presented themselves. In the Prison of La Perrache, they saw a hundred and thirty-two lads under the care of fifteen of the Brethren of St. Joseph.

They also visited the Maison d'Arrêt or La Roanne, where they saw with pleasure, the beneficial effects of women being placed under the care of persons of their own sex; ten or twelve Sisters of St. Joseph are here devoted to this work. Mrs. Fry expressed a few words, through an interpreter, exhorting them to repentance and faith, and speaking of the joy in heaven over one sinner that repenteth, which appeared to touch them.

They saw an institution under the care of the same Order of nuns, called La Solitude, where, as in the former instance, they were pleased with the Superior. The women were out for recreation; the young persons " at a simple dance, for their amusement." The building commands a very fine view, and extensive garden, and orchard attached to it. The inmates, about eighty in number, are either discharged prisoners, or vagrants; they are employed in washing, spinning, &c. Some were being trained as novices, eventually to enter the Order. The whole effect was neat and orderly. With M. Cordes, the Protestant Pasteur and many members of his flock, their intercourse was valuable and encouraging.

Avignon, Fifth Month, 9*th.*—We had no particular calls of duty until we arrived at Lyons, where there was a great press of engagements—prisons and refuges to inspect, besides many schools, of which I only had time to visit one—a woman's adult school. We had a large company of the poorer French Protestants on two different evenings, when we read with them. We also visited several of their houses; but it was more for serious conversation amongst them, than absolute religious engagement. We had one *very* important Meeting of influential people, in which I desired to speak the Truth in love. It was introduced by the Prison subject. I endeavoured to show, that change of heart could only be produced by Christian principles, as revealed to us in Holy Scripture, through the power of the Holy Spirit. This, I very boldly attested, and then strove to impress the importance of Christian example, and of religious duties being faithfully performed, both public and private. Then I entered upon useful societies, charities, and schools, with Christian instruction. We had much attention paid to us, much kindness shown to us, and I humbly trust, an impression made on many minds, and some humble valuable Christians comforted by our visit.

LETTER FROM ELIZABETH FRY.

Nismes, *Fifth Month,* 12*th,* 1839.

My much loved children,

I have been considering which is best, to write one full letter to you, or several notes, and I am come to the conclusion, now we are so far from home, and have so much to do, that it is better to write to you collectively: . . . . We thankfully say, we feel peaceful and in our right place, although separated from many so very dear to us.

We paid a very interesting visit to Lyons, and found a good deal new in the Prisons and Refuges. An order of Catholics, called the Brethren and Sisters of St. Joseph, believe it their duty entirely, to take care of prisoners and criminals generally. They do not visit as we do, but take the entire part of turnkeys and prison-officers, and live with the prisoners night and day, constantly caring for them. I thought the effect on the female prisoners surprisingly good, as far as their influence extended. But the mixture of gross superstition is curious, the image of the Virgin dressed up in the finest manner, in their different wards. I feared, that their religion lay so much in form and ceremonies, that it led from heart work, and from that great change which would probably be produced, did these Sisters simply teach them Christianity. Their books appeared to be mostly about the Virgin ; not a sign of Scripture to be found in either prison or refuge. I felt it laid on me as a weighty, yet humbling duty, before I left Lyons, to invite Roman Catholics and Protestants, who had influence in the prisons, to come to our Hotel, and there, in Christian love, to tell them the *truth* to the best of my belief, as to the *only* real ground of reformation of heart, and the means likely to conduce to this end. It was the more fearful, as I had to be entirely interpreted for. My heart almost sank within me as the time approached. It was about three o'clock in the day, about sixty people came of the very influential Catholics and Protestants, and I was enabled, through a most excellent interpeter, to show them, that nothing but the pure simple truth, as revealed in Scripture, through the power of the Holy Spirit, could really enlighten the understanding or change the heart. My husband and

Josiah Forster also, took a very useful and valuable part. *Much* satisfaction was expressed. We afterwards dined at a gentleman's, who lived in a lovely situation, on the top of a hill near Lyons. Our invitations began to flow in, and we should, I doubt not, had we stayed longer, soon have been in as great a current as at Paris, or greater. We met with some very interesting, devoted Christian characters—a cousin of the Baroness Pelet's almost like herself, her notes and flowers coming in every morning. The last day was most fatiguing ; we had to rise soon after three in the morning for Avignon, to go a hundred and fifty miles down the Rhone.

We have passed through the most delightful country I ever saw. Lyons, with the Rhone and Soane, is in its environs beautiful, and the passage from Lyons to Avignon really lovely; mountains in the distance (parts of the Alps,) their tops covered with snow ; vegetation in perfection, the flowers of spring and summer in bloom at once, grass just ready to be cut, barley in the ear, lilacs, laburnums, syringas, roses, pinks, carnations, acacias in full bloom, yellow jessamine wild in the hedges. It is a sudden burst of the finest summer, combined with the freshness of spring. The olive groves, intermixed with abundant vineyards and mulberry groves, all beautiful from their freshness. The ancient buildings of Avignon, the ruins on the banks of the Rhone, the very fine and wonderful Roman remains of the aqueduct, called the Pont du Gard, really exceed description. This place also abounds in curious buildings. Here, or in the neighbourhood, we expect to remain some time.

We find the poor Friends delighted to see us, and the Protestants give us a hearty welcome. All these interests do not prevent our hearts being with you, and I am longing to know all about you . . . .

I am,

Your most loving mother,

E. F.

At Avignon, Mrs. Fry's order to see the prison, did not avail with the gaoler, when first presented to him. The guard-room was reached, but no further was she permitted to enter. But in the evening, at the Hotel, the Préfet was announced, with whom it was arranged to visit the prisons on the morrow. Mrs. Fry was accompanied by him, the Mayor, the Procureur du Roi, and several gentlemen. The prison once formed a part of the Papal palace : it is only one of passage for untried prisoners, or before removal to the Maisons Centrales. Like all old prisons, especially those not originally intended for the purpose, it is ill adapted to its present use, but the rooms clean, large, and airy. Excellent cells, for separation by night, were in process of construction. In the work-room, every operation of picking old rope, was being carried on, carding, spinning, and weaving it, until it became a coarse strong wrapping-cloth, used to pack the madder grown in Provence for the English market.

From Avignon, the party proceeded to Nismes.

Nismes is perhaps more the centre of Protestantism, than any other place in France. There, Mrs. Fry made a longer tarriance than usual. For a week, she remained exceedingly interested by the various objects that presented themselves to her notice, and by the persons she met with. There exists at Nismes and in the neighbouring villages, a scattered body of people professing the principles of the Society of Friends. She and Mr. Forster visited with much interest all who resided at Nismes, and attended their Meetings. This simple, but interesting body of people are the descendants of the Camisards, who took refuge in the mountains of the Cevennes and fought valiantly for their faith, during the persecutions subsequent to the revocation of the Edict of Nantes. The Camisards were of the old stock of the Albigenses. The continual loss or imprisonment of their ministers, induced their ministering one to the other. At the cessation of hostilities, many of them persevered in a system, which, in the first instance, had resulted from circumstances. Towards the close of the last century, a man, named Paul Codognan, formed the project of giving a positive form to the belief and customs of this his little community, and prepared a work, though very imperfectly, on the subject. It was taken by one of the body to Holland, to be printed, and there he heard, for the first time, that in England and America there existed a people, who entertained many of the same opinions as himself.

He proceeded to England, and became acquainted with the Society of Friends, to whom the existence of this little body of fellow-believers was thus made known. Since that period, but more especially of late years, the community at Congenies has become an object of much interest to Friends in England, and has been visited from time to time by ministers and other members of that Society.

The Protestant pastor at Nismes, M. Frossard, with his lady were to Elizabeth Fry as providential helpers, such excellent interpreters, such true sympathizers! Much kind attention was paid them by Dr. Pleindoux, who entertained them sumptuously, in his kindness of heart thus marking his welcome. After dinner, a still better entertainment awaited them, in interesting, important, and edifying conversation, amongst a large party of excellent persons. Mrs. Fry took a lively interest in the great Maison Centrale at Nismes, containing about one thousand two hundred prisoners. It is built on the site of the old citadel, from which, in the time of Louis XIV., the Protestants were attacked whilst holding their assemblies for divine worship. In her first visit, besides Mr. Forster, Mrs. Fry was accompanied by M. Frossard the Protestant chaplain, and M. Castelnau the Surgeon of the prison. The men were employed in vast workshops, in which silence was maintained. In passing through two or three of these, she expressed her interest for the prisoners, her pity for them, and her desire for their repentance and amendment of life. She particularly desired to see the Cachots. In the first were eight men, placed there as a punishment for

6

exacting usury of their fellow-prisoners ; for instance, lending them a franc when they came out of the infirmary, or when, from any other cause, they were without money, and receiving eight sous weekly as interest. This practice had existed to a great extent, and is one of the many evils resulting from the cantine system. These men were discontented and clamorous, their appearance fierce and depraved, Five armed soldiers were introduced into the cell with the visitors, to protect them from their violence. In the second cell, were eighteen men without employment. Into this, the visitors requested to be admitted alone. In the third, which was entirely dark, were two placed for refractory conduct ; one was chained both hands and feet. Mrs. Fry said to them, that she had sometimes, when she had seen men thus circumstanced, pleaded for their liberation, on the promise of future good behaviour, if she believed their promise to be sincere. The fettered prisoner immediately volunteered this promise, and was promptly released.

In this prison, besides the Roman Catholic chapel, served by the Aumônier, who resides in the prison, there is a Protestant chapel, in which daily service is performed by a pastor of that faith. This is attended by any prisoner who desires it ; besides the professed Protestants, about a hundred among the Roman Catholics, from preference, worshipped there. On occasion of Mrs. Fry's second visit, she was accompanied by her family party, as well as some of her particular friends ; the object being, to attend the religious service of the Protestant prisoners. The chapel was small, and the middle filled by depraved-looking men in their rough prison dress. At the top, in a semi-circle, sat the party of ladies and gentlemen, six or eight in number, with the Governor (Directeur) and Protestant Chaplain. At the bottom of the room, and around the door, clustered the gens-d'arms and gardiens (turnkeys) in their smart, soldier-like costume, to the number of ten or fifteen. The service com-

menced with singing a hymn. Then M. Frossard read beautifully the 24th Psalm ; after which, Elizabeth Fry spoke to the
audience in one of her most impressive strains—translated for
her by M. Frossard, with such spirit and force, that it hardly
lost in the change of language. She began in the most touching tone of voice, on the conversion of poor Mary Magdalene,
her loving much, because forgiven much, her washing her
Lord's feet, her being with Him at His death, watching at His
tomb, and permitted first to see Him after His resurrection. It
was the strongest encouragement to the repentant sinner. She
then turned and spoke in a strain of awful entreaty and solemn
warning to the hardened and profane. The listening expression of all countenances showed how deeply her words impressed them. Many tears were shed ; and she heard afterwards,
that among these hardened men, a few instances of real repentance and amendment of life had occurred. On leaving the
chapel and crossing a corridor, a gendarme brought two men
out of a workroom to Mrs. Fry; they began to speak eagerly
to her, one told her that he should never lie down in his bed
without praying for and blessing her, whilst the other echoed
the sentiment. They were the two men for whom, on her previous visit, she had interceded, that they might be liberated
from the dungeon.

After that, she again visited the cells, accompanied by M.
Frossard and a venerable grey-headed pasteur, one of the fathers of
the French Protestant Church. They went without guard. The
visit was interesting and satisfactory, and ended in a condign
apology being offered by the culprits, and forgiveness granted by
the governor ; though so desperate were these men, that the
governor of the prison had thought it prudent, unknown at the
time to them or to the prisoners, to place soldiers in conceal-
ment near.

A few days afterwards, Mrs. Fry received this letter from one
of the prisoners :—

"Nismes, *le* 19 *Mai*, 1839.

" Ttrès-honorée Dame,

" La visite que vous avez bien voulue faire a de malheureux prisonniers, a été pour beaucoup de nous un grand sujet de consolation. Les paroles, pleines de bienveillance et de bonté que vous nous avez adressées, se sont profondément gravées dans nos cœurs.

" Nous sommes si peu accoutumés à voir des personnes étrangerès et jouissant d'une considération si distinguée, et en même temps, si bien méritée, plaindre notre sort et nous offrir des consolations, que nous regrettons bien vivement de ne pouvoir souvent être honorés de vôtre visite.

" Ah ! s'il vous était possible, madame, de nous voir encore une fois, et d'assister dimanche prochain au service divin, vous nous combleriez de joie. Car nous pensons que vos prières, jointes aux nôtres, ne pourraient manquer d'être agréables à Dieu, et qu'il nous donnerait la force et le courage nécessaires pour imiter nôtre Sauveur Jésus-Christ, qui s'est immolé pour nous en supportant les plus affreux tourmens avec patience, et en priant son Père de pardonner à ceux qui le faisaient mourir.

" Daignez, honorée Dame,

" Recevoir mes humbles respects,

" Vôtre très-obéissant serviteur,

" M———."

Congenies was the next place visited by the travellers, it is a retired village, to the west of the road from Nismes to Montpellier ; about four leagues from the former place. The inhabitants are almost all Friends ; a simple and serious people.

To abandon hotels, towns and high-ways, and diverge amongst lanes and cross roads, to spend a fortnight in a country village in France, amongst its simple inhabitants, was an event not without its great interest, and even amusement. As it was considered necessary to take provisions, hampers well stocked with coffee, sugar, candles, &c., were piled upon the carriage, or the attendant van, which was also the Congenies and Cordognan diligence. The country became less and less interesting, although well cultivated, till a group of grey flat roofs in a little hollow amongst the hills, marked the first appearance of Congenies. After passing some distance through the village street, the carriage stopped at the door of a large, dull, prison-like house, the windows barred with iron and the door at one side up a flight of eight or ten steps. This was the house prepared for the reception of the travellers. A hall with no one single article of furniture ; an ante-room containing a buffet, a fire-place, and a couple of chairs; and a saloon with white curtains to the windows, a table, and some rush-bottomed chairs—all these vaulted, whitewashed, and floored with stone, formed the suite of reception rooms.

Other rooms of the same character, communicated with the hall of entrance, from which ascended a dark, wide stone staircase, leading to suites of rambling comfortless chambers. Various needful articles were willingly supplied by the friendly peasants—spoons were lent by one, by another a bed-side carpet for Mrs. Fry. A second table, was arranged in the saloon, and after a day or two, a sort of homely comfort prevailed. The finest anchovies from the neighbouring Mediterranean, a cask of olives of the village produce, and sweet wine, made expressly at the last year's vintage, were prepared by these kind people.

The hostess had good store of white household linen, and her kitchen was in high activity, though provisions were uncertain and had to be obtained from Calvisson. The Savoyard waiter, who had accompanied them from Nismes, superintended the cooking. The day's bill of fare, hung by him on a nail in the kitchen, was an inexhaustible source of amusement to the village women, who were perpetually gossiping with the hostess, and watching with curiosity the proceedings of her foreign inmates. There was one peculiarity in this ménage, the usual operations of a scullery being carried on in the entrance hall! where an old woman and girl had established themselves, with a broken-down table and chair, perpetually flooding it, in process of cleansing all manner of pots and pans, iron and copper, and earthenware, red, yellow and green.

The Friends, in Congenies and the neighbouring villages, appeared to be a respectable well-conducted body of people. Louis Majolier was a valuable minister amongst them. Accompanied by her friend Josiah Forster, Elizabeth Fry regularly attended their Meetings for worship and discipline, by which she became exceedingly interested in their welfare. Their Meeting House was neat, and abundantly adequate to the needs of the congregation, she also visited them all in their families.

The houses were mostly entered by cartgates, under an archway, into a court-yard, filled with dust and straw, with chickens and rabbits running about. On one side of this court or yard was the sitting-room, with a vine covered porch, under which the women sate and knitted silk gloves and mittens. An open outside flight of stairs led to the chambers. A stable opposite the entrance, a well in one corner, and a cart under the gateway,—such was the style of most of their buildings. These cottagers all possessed abundant supplies of table linen, and in every house where Mrs. Fry dined, she found dinner napkins provided. Soup, one or two entrées, a roast of lamb or a fowl, salad and vegetables composed the dinner.

Although there are no horned cattle, the villagers possess a good many sheep and some goats, which gather a scanty subsistence from the herbage of the rocky hills, where the vine cannot grow. Their milk is excellent, and so is the butter made from it. The flocks are invariably attended by a shepherd and strong dogs, to protect them from the wolves of the Cevennes mountains; after watering them at the fountain in stone troughs, a most picturesque sight, they are folded in the village at night.

The women Friends wear their cap and peasant costume with, perhaps, a graver shade of colour over the whole. The men the usual peasant dress. In all the villages round, there seemed to be a most eager willing ear to hear the truths of the gospel. The Meeting held at Congenies, on the last Sunday evening, was crowded —the people clustered up to the top of the doors, in all the open windows, and on the walls outside, yet in perfect quietude and order. At Calvisson, on the following Sunday, it was the same, the Meeting there was held in the Protestant Temple. The party broke up from Congenies on the 27th, and after again partaking of the abounding hospitalities of Doctor Pleindoux, at Nismes, proceeded by the ancient city of Arles to Marseilles.

Congenies, Fifth Month, 22*nd.*—Yesterday was my birthday, and it pleased my Heavenly Father in His love and pity, to cause it to be a day of remarkable peace, from the early morning to the evening. I felt it was not for works of righteousness, that I had done, but of His grace and His mercy, that I have thus known my soul to be refreshed in the Lord. Lord, continue to be with us! lift up the light of Thy countenance upon us, and bless us all, absent and present; and particularly at this time, I ask Thee to bless our labours among this people, to their solid good and Thy praise, Amen!

Sixth Month, 2*nd.*—We found a great deal of what was highly-interesting in Congenies. A peculiar and new place to us. The country remarkable, much cultivated in parts, and planted with vineyards, mulberry, olive, and fig-trees, with but little corn. There is a very delightful air; the hills rather barren and singularly grey, with fine ruins upon some of them, and here and there a peep at the Mediterranean. The little dull villages, much strewed about, thickly inhabited, mostly by Protestants, who appear generally in a low neglected state; we visited some of these villages, and had larger or smaller Meetings in them. We found a great inclination in the people to hear the truth, and I believe there is a real thirst after it. I humbly trust that the blessing of the Lord was with us, as I have seldom felt more peace or more sense of this blessing, than when engaged in these labours of Christian love at Congenies, or a more clear belief that I was in my right place.

At Marseilles, Mrs. Fry visited several of the institutions. The first of these was described to her, as a refuge for female penitents.   It was not without considerable difficulty, that she obtained permission to enter.   She was accompanied by a Roman Catholic lady, a stranger to her, who consented to be the medium of her introduction, and was called one of the Directresses.   It proved to be a regular convent, under the control of nuns of the strict monastic order of St. Charles, who, in addition to the three ordinary vows, add that of converting souls, and therefore admit poor young women, under the name of "Pénitentes," into the convent.   The lady Directresses were no longer permitted to see the penitents, or even to enter the building, with the exception of the one charged with its repairs.   She is allowed to see the dilapidations, but not any of the sisters or inmates.   Mrs. Fry and her companions were introduced into a large, comfortable parlour, plainly furnished—on one side was a close double grating, painted black, with black shutters behind, extremely gloomy looking.   Chairs had been placed for them in front of the grating.   After Mrs. Fry and her companions had waited some time, the shutters were opened by the "Supérieure," a handsome woman of about thirty years of age.   The object of Mrs. Fry's journey was explained to her, which led to a long and interesting conversation, in which the talents of this lovely Abbess were abundantly displayed, and she proved herself thoroughly mistress of her subject.   She informed them, that the number of penitents admitted are a hundred and five, that they are not permitted to become Nuns in that Order, but when the vocation is very strong, they may do so in others—

that more than half are converted, that most become servants, and if well-behaved, are still cared for by the nuns. None are compelled to enter or are retained against their will, although encouraged by every means to stay. Some have remained nine years.

They are not taught to read or write; neither is the least morsel of paper, pencil, pen, ink, or any other possible material for writing, permitted, from the fear of their communicating with people without. The day is spent in a perpetual round of work, embroidery, recreation, recitation of prayers, psalms, &c. The nuns were in number forty. They came from Tours about eighteen months previously, to take charge of this establishment. Upon Mrs. Fry's speaking of the importance of the Gospel for such persons, she informed them, that it was in parts read to them, and admitted that the history of Mary Magdalene, and the parables of the prodigal son, the piece of silver, and the lost sheep, were fit and good for them; she added, that she found parts of Isaiah and all the Psalms suited to them; but then went on, as Roman Catholics are wont to do, to urge the unsuitableness of the Scriptures, as a whole, especially parts of the Old Testament, for people in general. Mrs. Fry spoke of the sufferings of Christ for sinners, and salvation through Him: all which the nun united in. Indeed, to judge from her report, nothing could be better conducted than this institution.

The Abbess related a long history of one of the Pénitentes, who had died, only an hour before, the " death of an angel and a saint." The narrative is given as nearly as a translation will admit of it in her own words.

The young Pénitente was eighteen years of age, and bent upon leaving the Asylum. The abbess gave her a month to consider her determination. At the end of this time her wish was unchanged, and the abbess informed her that in a week she should go. This week she was made to spend in penances, and prayers to the Virgin, and such was the effect that she decided to remain in the convent, although she declared that she should surely die if she did so. Shortly afterwards cough and expectoration came on, to which hemorrhage from the lungs succeeded. The very day that Mrs. Fry visited the institution she died. During her last hours she shewed much consideration for others ; on the night preceding her death she begged the nuns to retire to rest, assuring them that she should not die till the morrow. She retained her senses and her speech until within five minutes of her end. On the abbess presenting the crucifix, the sufferer exclaimed, " J'y suis cloué en cœur, je le sens dans mon cœur."

Surely this tale is capable of two constructions, and rather plausible than satisfactory ; for who that has read the human heart, or traced the history of mankind individually or in collective bodies, has not detected a love of power, and an abuse of that power when obtained, which renders a system of secrecy and seclusion, with absolute authority, an evil liable to terrible abuse. Nuns directed by churchmen ! Woman always extreme for good or ill, guided by superstition—herself a slave, employed to enslave others. If prisoners or penitents are committed to the care of monastic orders, justice assuredly demands the oversight and superintendence of the magistracy, and that these unhappy persons should be never placed beyond the reach of the secular arm.

From this establishment of darkness and mystery, Mrs. Fry went to a very different one, called " La Maison des Orphelines du Choléra." It was under the especial care of the Abbé Fisseaux, an active, intelligent young man, apparently devoted to doing good. The children were in excellent order. He accompanied the party to an interesting and prosperous little institution, founded by himself, called " La Maison des Jeunes Détenus, or Nouvel Pénitentiaire," for twenty-eight young delinquents, boys. They had all been committed for theft, and collected from the different prisons of the department. They appeared very kindly cared for by the Abbé; they sleep separately at night, with the exception of some, who, for good conduct, are permitted to be together in one apartment. The town prison contained more than sixty prisoners; the women in a separate part of the building; but there was no further classification, not even the tried from the untried, nor any employment. After this, Mrs. Fry visited a large Hospital, in which were four English sailors from ships in the port. One of these recognised her, having seen her on board a female convict-ship, in the River Thames, and greeted her as though she were an old and valued friend. He informed those, who accompanied her, who she was, which they had not previously understood. This fatiguing day was concluded by dining at Monsieur Rabaut's.

Hyères, Sixth Month, 2nd.

My much-loved Children,

I now mean to sit quietly down and communicate with you. Orange groves in flower, with here and there a little fruit, in abundance around me, and a lovely blue sea with hills and islands before me. We are at a small pleasant hotel, where we walk out of our bed-room and saloon upon a sort of brick terrace, part of which, has vines and roses over a lattice-work, and an awning. Here we take our meals, and with the abundance of fruit and vegetables our tastes have been rather uncommonly gratified. The beauty of the scene, the fragrance of the orange flower, the niceness of the fruit; the air also, so warm, fresh and delightful—that we could not but wish that you could have taken a peep at us when seated round our table. This is the farthest distance that we expect to be from home, therefore, I hope to-morrow, that we may feel we are turning our faces thitherward.

On Monday, June 3rd, Mrs. Fry returned from Hyères to

Toulon. The next morning, accompanied by the Protestant pastor and a naval captain, appointed to do so by the Préfet de la Marine, she and her companions visited the Bagnes; on their way seeing the Arsenal, at one extremity of which is the Bagnes, or prison for the galley-slaves (galériens) ; they work hard, sleep on the boards, eat only bread and dry beans, with half a bottle of wine to those who work. Many of them die. The returns are considerable, as from the close communication, the contagion of evil is fearful. A man who is vicious when he goes in, inevitably comes out more so. They sleep in vast galleries, a hundred or two hundred in each, chained to a long iron rod which runs the whole length of the foot of the sleeping board. There is a salle, which contains four hundred, for those who have improved in conduct, and to them mattresses are allowed and rugs. In their leisure hours they are allowed to make and sell little carved toys and netting. Their look is generally unhealthy. The dress—a red cap and jacket, and the greater number fastened two and two by heavy chains ; notwithstanding this, they often escape. One Englishman, taken on board a slaver was amongst them.

This was a day of extraordinary fatigue. Mrs. Fry went in the afternoon to see the town prison. Some poor Algerine women were confined there. She was accompanied by the Sous Préfet and his lady, who is a regular prison visitor.

From Toulon to Aix,—once the centre of Provençal song, and where King Réné held his court surrounded by his Troubadours. There, her heart was attached by a lively little Protestant congregation, under a zealous and apparently spiritual pastor. A great contrast to the scene which met her view, on turning into the Course on her arrival,—the procession of the Fête Dieu in all its tinsel finery.

From Aix, the travellers returned to Nismes. The subject

10

of a District Society was much discussed.   Sunday, the 10th,
was passed there.

Sixth Month.—Our First-day at Nismes was deeply weighty
in prospect, so that I rested little at night, as I had ventured to
propose our holding one meeting in the morning, in the
Methodist chapel, that whoever liked might attend it; and in the
evening, to do the same in a very large school-room, that all
classes might attend, as I believed that all would not come to a
Methodist Meeting.   I went prostrated before the Lord, to this
Meeting in the morning, hardly knowing how to hold up my
head; I could only apply for help to the inexhaustible Source
of our sure mercies, feeling that I could not do it, either on
account of myself, or because it was the work in which I was
engaged; but I could do it for the sake of my Lord, and that
His kingdom might spread.   Utterly unworthy did I feel myself,
but my Lord was gracious.   My dear interpreter, Charlotte
Majolier, was there to help me in a very large Meeting, and I
felt power wonderfully given me to proclaim the truths of the
Gospel, and to press upon the point of the Lord Himself being
our teacher, immediately by His Spirit, through the Holy
Scriptures, and by His Providences and works; and to show,
that no teaching so much conduced to growth in grace, as the
Lord's teaching.   There was much attention; at the close, I
felt the spirit of prayer much over us, longed for its vocal expression, and felt a desire some one might pray, when a Methodist minister, in a feeling manner, expressed a wish to offer
something in prayer, to which, of course, we assented—it proved
solemn and satisfactory.

We dined at our dear friends, the Pasteur Emilien Frossard's;
he and his wife have been like a brother and sister to us; we
were also joined by a Roman Catholic gentleman and his
daughter.   He has, I think, been seriously impressed by our
visit, and it has led him to have the Scriptures read to his workmen.   There were also Louis Majolier, his daughter, and a
young English friend.   I think I have very seldom in my life
felt a more lively sense of the love of God, than at his table.   I

may say, our souls were animated under its sweetness. I think we rejoiced together, and magnified the name of our God.

In the evening, we met in a large school-room that would contain some hundreds, where numbers assembled, principally the French Protestants and some of their pastors. There, again, I was greatly helped, I really believe, by the Holy Spirit, to speak to them upon their very important situations in the Church of Christ, and the extreme consequence of their being sound both in faith and practice. I also felt it my duty to show them, as Protestants, the infinite importance, not only in France, but in the surrounding nations, of their being as a city set upon a hill that cannot be hid. I showed them how the truth is spreading, and how important to promote it, by being preachers of righteousness in life and conversation, as well as in word and doctrine. There was here also much attention; and our dear and valued friend and brother in Christ, Emilien Frossard, prayed beautifully, that the word spoken might profit the people, and particularly, that the blessing of the Lord might rest upon me. It was no common prayer on my behalf. Thanks to my Heavenly Father, the Meeting broke up in much love, life, and peace.

The next morning Josiah Forster and I held a large meeting, partly in the open air, at the village of Codognan. I was pleased to see many of our dear friends from Congenies and the neighbourhood, at this our last meeting in this part. We separated from them under a lively feeling of true peace and much love, and concluded our services under a strong confidence that our feet had been rightly turned amongst them—a pastor, a stranger to us, closed the Meeting in solemn and beautiful prayer.

After this, we proceeded on our journey to Montpellier, where important service opened for us. A Protestant Ladies' Committee was formed to visit the great Female Prison there; much important advice offered to the Governor upon the changes now being made in the prison, and female officers being appointed; we appeared to go in the very time wanted, and obtained the liberation of several poor women from their very sad cells. The

Préfet was most kind to us, and thus, our way was easily made, the Mayor and all with us. Help was given me to speak religiously to the poor women, before all these gentlemen.

This was a Maison Centrale, and contained five hundred women, for whom it was exclusively used. The prisoners were employed in work-rooms; some resistance had been shown on their part to the introduction of the female officers, so that this visit was useful and timely. Mrs. Fry visited this prison again the following day, and had a long conversation at her Hotel, with the Director and the new Matron, on their important duties. After this, she met a number of Protestant ladies at the Pastor Losignol's, who had waited for her arrival to form themselves into a Committee for visiting the Protestant women, both in the Prison and Hospital; this Committee was then regularly organized, and was, as well as that formed at Marseilles, to correspond with the Committee in Paris. In the evening, she returned to the Pastor Losignol's, as she supposed, to spend a quiet social evening, but found instead, a large congregation assembled for a religious meeting. There were rich and poor, all ages, and the place so crowded, that the windows were lined with listeners, and boys perched upon the trees beyond.

The day the party left Montpellier, Mrs. Fry diverged to Cette, and crossing the Lagune of Thon, in the boat of an English merchant's vessel, rejoined her companions at Meze, a little fishing village on its banks ; the British Consul and his lady came with her, and the captain of the merchantman. It was a temperance ship, and he a serious man. Whilst waiting at Meze, to avoid the mid-day sun, Mrs. Fry wrote to her friend John Carey, Esquire, in Guernsey, to interest him on behalf of the British seamen frequenting the port of Cette.

To JOHN CAREY, ESQ., CASTLE CAREY, GUERNSEY.

Meze, South of France, *Sixth Month*, 13*th*, 1839.

My dear and valued Friend,

In a tour that my husband and myself, accompanied by our friend Josiah Forster, are taking, we have had the satisfaction of meeting with Richard Ryan and his amiable wife ; he is British Consul at Cette ; I understand that they are friends of yours, therefore the application I am about to make appears to be almost needless, as they could represent the case better than I am likely to do it. I understand that there are several ships from various countries that call at Cette, in which many of the crews speak English, therefore it would be highly desirable for them to be well supplied with English Testaments and Bibles, and tracts ; and it is so difficult to get them here from England, that I venture to propose, a few of our Guernsey friends inducing their different Bible Societies each to send some copies of the Holy Scriptures, and I also thought, with your usual kindness, some of you would give some English tracts. I believe my dear friend Sophia Mourant would do her part, and by several others, each doing a little, much would be accomplished. I thus apply to my dear friends, because I find that ships not unfrequently visit Cette from Guernsey.

We are deeply interested in our visit to France, where we find many devoted characters, and we do believe that truth is spreading in this interesting land. We find the weather very warm, and are rather oppressed by it, but we are generally favoured with health.

I think of our dear Guernsey and Jersey friends with much gratitude and love, and desires for their present and everlasting welfare. I wish to be affectionately remembered to those in Guernsey.

And am, with dear love to thy wife and family, and also to Sophia Mourant, and affectionate remembrance to all thy brothers and sisters whom I know,

Thy affectionate and obliged friend,

ELIZABETH FRY.

In the evening, of this fatiguing day, whilst resting and refreshing themselves at the Hotel at Béziers, the Sous-Préfet was announced, he having been requested by the Préfet at Montpellier, to show Mrs. Fry attention during her visit to Béziers. He was anxious she should see the prison and hospital, but all arrangements had been made to set off again at five in the morning, and therefore, fatigued as she was, she and her companions consented to accompany him to the prison. It had become quite dark as this little band threaded its way through the narrow winding streets of Béziers,—how altered since those streets ran blood, at the time of the first crusade against the Albigeois when the papal legate gave order to the Roman Catholic chieftains " to kill all, for God knows those who are His."

The astonished gaoler, candle in hand, followed by his myrmidons, answered the thundering rap of the Sous-Préfet, and the mastiffs which were prowling in the yards having been chained up, the prison, (a badly constructed and ill-arranged one,) was inspected.

In returning to the Hotel, they paid a visit to the Cathedral, a vast, lofty, gothic building of one aisle and transepts, which had been lighted up to receive them. The effect was magnificent, illumined by a glare of partial light from the various altars, and the lamps carried by the attendants.

Saturday the 15th, was a cloudy day and travelling comparatively easy. Quiet, cool rooms at the Hotel de France, at Toulouse, afforded the travellers a most welcome retreat, for the heat had become extreme, the sun pouring down his rays, with overwhelming intensity, and adding greatly to fatigue, whilst the nature of their engagements forbade rest during the midday hours. The early morning, or cool of the evening being unsuited for visiting prisons and hospitals.

On Sunday evening, Mrs. Fry and her party went to the Scripture-reading, held at the house of M. Chabraud the pasteur, which is attended regularly by many of his congregation. Amongst others, a captain in the French army, a captain in the British navy, and a sergeant belonging to one of the regiments quartered there—all devoted Christian characters. They heard with pleasure of many really serious soldiers in the regiments then in Toulouse; so many, that at the Scripture-readings which took place, two evenings in the week, at the house of the Messrs. Courtois, two long benches were often filled by them; three or four more being occupied by young men inquiring after religious truth.

There are about six hundred Protestants at Toulouse, in the midst of a population of seventy thousand Roman Catholics. So lately as 1760, a Protestant was martyred there having first been broken on the wheel. The sentence and report of his execution are still to be seen in the archives of the town.

M. Chabraud considered, that from the time the British army occupied Toulouse in 1814, the Protestants had been held in higher estimation. Instead of taking possession of the Cathedral, as was generally anticipated at Toulouse, the victorious army worshipped in the humbler temple of their Protestant brethren, those hours being chosen when the French service was not going forward. The English regiments were seen marching to the Temple, headed by their officers, where the service of the Anglican Church was performed for them, by the chaplains of the army.

JOURNAL RESUMED.

We proceeded from place to place until we arrived at Toulouse, on Seventh-day evening, the 15th of the Sixth Month. On First-day evening, we met a large number of Protestants at one of their Scripture-readings. We took part in the service; at the close, a solemn prayer was offered for us by Francis Courtois, one of a very remarkable trio of brothers, (bankers there) all three of whom are given up to the service of their Lord, and appear to have been instruments greatly blessed. Their kindness to us was very great. In Toulouse we visited two prisons ; had one important Prison Meeting, and one exceedingly solemn and satisfactory Scripture-reading and time of prayer, with the Courtois family, one or two pasteurs, and other religious persons.

I left my husband who was unwell from the heat at Toulouse, and went in faith and somewhat in the cross to Montauban ; the place, where the ministers of the Protestant Church of France are educated ; but I believed it right to go—Josiah Forster accompanied me.

To her Children in England.

Bagnères de Luchon, *Sixth Month,* 23rd.

Here I sit before breakfast, with a most lovely scene before me. On entering this solemn Sabbath morning—my soul and body refreshed, not only in admiring the wonderful works of the outward creation, and being revived by the delightful air, fresh from the snowy mountains before me; but what is more, my soul refreshed. I have been enabled to lift my heart to my Heavenly Father, for every brother, sister and child individually, and for my dear husband ; and collectively, for my many beloved ones; committing all to His holy keeping. I feel rest. And now my beloved children, I will tell you a little how we go on.

My attraction homewards grows stronger and stronger, but I desire patiently to wait the right time :—the openings for religious service are greater than I expected, more particularly amongst the Protestants, at Montpellier, Toulouse, and Montauban. At Montauban, without expressing any other wish, than to have an evening party at one of their houses, to meet some of the professors and students of the College (the only one in France for educating Pasteurs for the Reformed Church). We found, to our dismay, all arranged to receive us in the College ; and on arriving there, imagine how I felt, when the Dean of the College offered me his arm, to take me into the chapel. There, I believe, the whole of the collegians were assembled, in all at least a hundred. It was fearful work. There were also numbers of the people of the town ; we thought about three hundred. Josiah Forster spoke first, explaining our views at some length. Then I rose, with an excellent interpreter, one of their pasteurs; I first told them something of my Prison experience, and the power of Christian principle and kindness; then, I related a little of the state of their prisons in France; then, my ideas as to the general state of France; and afterwards, endeavoured to bring home to them the extreme importance of their future calling, as pasteurs in their church. I reminded them of that passage of Scripture, " the leaders of the people caused them to err." I endeavoured to show them how awful such a state of things must be, and the extreme importance of their being sound in doctrine and practice. Simple duty led me to Montauban. Josiah F. was my kind and useful companion. We were united in much Christian love to many there I forgot to say, that at the close of the occasion, the pasteur who interpreted for me, prayed beautifully and spiritually, that the words spoken might profit the people; he also prayed for us: this has frequently occurred at the close of some of our interesting meetings, a pouring forth of the spirit of prayer has been granted. My not knowing the language has obstructed my offering it, and it has appeared laid upon others instead. I have seldom felt sweeter peace in leaving a place than Montauban. At Toulouse, we were deeply interested by the Courtois' brothers : they appear, body, soul, and spirit, devoted to the service of their Lord , quite a bright example to all of us. The world appeared as nothing to them. I have seldom seen men so wholly given up to good and useful objects ; they were most kind to us. We had various calls of duty in that town, and I had a most excellent interpreter in François Courtois. We arrived here yesterday evening, after serious consideration, believing it the best to pursue this course. A certain time of quiet appears really needful to make representations to the French government, and to those in authority, of the various evils that want remedy in prisons, &c. We understand there are many seeking, serious minds, to whom we may be of some comfort, which helps to reconcile us to the measure.

Mrs. Fry's determined perseverance had surmounted every

obstacle as long as her physical powers permitted ; but they were beginning to fail. Rest, and some cessation from mental and bodily labour, had become indispensable, and she yielded, though not without reluctance, to her husband's wish for a short tarriance in the cooler atmosphere of the Pyrenees. Speaking of this retreat, she says,—

We went from Toulouse to Bagnères de Luchon, a most lovely place, where we had a sweet, quiet lodging. I went two wonderfully fine excursions with my husband and children, (Josiah Forster partly with us,) which I rather enjoyed, particularly going into Spain.

One of these expeditions was to the Lake D'Oo. The gentlemen of the party, who were on horseback, having gone on, Mrs. Fry and her daughter found themselves, when about half way up a steep ascent, on a little level of green sward, shadowed by a huge rock. They left their chairs for the carriers to rest themselves. A group of wild-looking peasants were reposing near. Mrs. Fry sate down by them, and entered into conversation, they assured her they " adored the Virgin in those parts ;" she took out her French Text-Book ;—the eight bearers joined the party. She read some words of Scriptures, then drew their attention to the wonderful works of God in creation, in the beautiful scene around them ; from thence, she led to His infinite mercy in giving a Saviour to die for them. They listened with earnestness and respect, and thankfully received the little books she offered.

After a day's rest from the excessive fatigue of the excursion to the Lake D'Oo, Mrs. Fry accompanied her family in another into Spain. A cool wet night followed by a cloudy morning gave hopes of less heat ; after leaving Luchon, the party passed through the forest and valley of Bourbe, defiling along the most exquisite mountain path, higher and higher it led

x 2

them, till, on a mountain crest, the path turned suddenly downwards at a point called the " Postillion," where a small rock marked the boundary, and the guide exclaimed, " Nous voici en Espagne." They continued their descent for about half an hour to where beech trees and oaks again grew amidst small patches of cultivation. Two Catalonian peasants were there in their brown costume and scarlet sashes, and caps with long depending peaks. Mrs. Fry, through the kind agency of Mr. Forster, was well supplied with extracts from Scripture in Spanish; to these men she gave several of them. Whilst the party dined on the grass, they observed one of them reading attentively as he sat under the shade of a spreading chesnut, surrounded by his flock of goats. When rested and refreshed they continued their descent to a spot where they found several scattered cottages. Desiring to sow as " beside all waters," she left the little scripture extracts at all these ; in the manger of a cow-house, or on a nail of the door, for she had heard that the Spaniards, including the priests, were eager for books, and carefully preserved them. Then from a rocky height she looked down on the valley below, through which the Garronne, here no wider than a brook, flowed like a silver thread, whilst Spanish fields, villages, and roads were spread at her feet. Some days afterwards the guide who had accompanied her on this occasion, came to request some of these little books to carry with him on the following day, when he was to conduct a gentleman into Spain—for that he should certainly be asked for them. Many had been by Mr. Forster consigned to an intelligent custom-house officer, who was often stationed at an advanced guard-house, high up amongst the mountains on the Spanish passes. When about to leave this part of the Pyrenees, upon entering the first little town of the plains, their carriage was stopped by this man. Their first impression was, that some regulation of the Customs was the cause

of their detention, but they found the motive to be a very
different one. He was anxious before they went away to
obtain any of the little Spanish books that might remain. He
assured them he should have many opportunities when his
turn came to be again on duty at the out-posts, to send them
into Spain. In this, as well as in the instance of the guide,
the intention was probably to sell the books; but the object of
disseminating scripture in the vernacular tongue would be as
well, if not better accomplished, than if they were gratuitously
distributed.

During this recess, Mrs. Fry, assisted by Mr. Forster and her
husband, prepared a long memorial for the Minister of the
Interior, and a shorter one for the Préfet of Police, embodying
her observations on the state of the prisons she inspected, and
her recommendation for their improvement.

The evils of the Cantine system, and the large sleeping apartments, affording every facility for evil and unrestricted communication, were the points on which she most strongly insisted;
though she also entered into various details of particular prisons
requiring alteration.

From Bagnères de Luchon, they went to Bagnères de Bigorre.
There in an ancient tower, they found a curious ill-constructed
prison, happily with but few inmates.

Wednesday the 3rd, they left Bagnères de Bigorre, entering
the gorge that leads to Luz and St. Sauveur. They passed the
ruined castle of St. Marie, built by the English, the Templar's
Fortress-church at Luz, and pursued their way to St. Sauveur.
There they remained some days, amidst the shadowy mountains which surround the town, and the rushing waters not alone
of the Gaves, or rapid rivers of the district, but of the hundred
little riviulets which feed them, tumbling and foaming from the
heights above.

St. Sauveur, Seventh Month, 4th.—We left Bagnères de Bigorre, on the 3rd of the Seventh Month. I had a painful journey, having met with rather a serious accident, falling backwards, from a stool slipping from under me; besides this, my throat was very sore, but I desired to be patient and thankful that I was not worse. We arrived at this most beautiful place in the evening, I felt better, and to-day am quiet, peaceful and in great degree refreshed.

Very little service opened in the last places we were at. I formed a fund to assist the poor afflicted persons who come to the baths at Luchon, and at Bagnères de Bigorre, visited the prison;—two poor sick prisoners were liberated in consequence, and placed in a comfortable hospital. I also had a serious reading of the Holy Scriptures, with many English who came to see us at our hotel, and a time of prayer, but the openings for service were small, which was a discouragement to me. I may however say, that through every discouragement, I commit myself, my all, and my work to the Lord, and believe that I may go on quietly and hopefully, trusting that day by day, and hour by hour, my Holy Head will not forsake me, but be my Guide and my Guard, and be with us all even unto the end. Our returning home through Switzerland, I still view very doubtfully. Unless Thy presence go with us, oh Lord! take us not there or to any other place.

Grenoble, 22d.—We remained a few days at St. Sauveur, which was refreshing and satisfactory, with some sweet Christian friends. We visited the great military hospital at Barèges, and obtained leave to introduce the New Testament, and I hope a library also. The men appeared much pleased with our visit.

By permission of the Directeur, the party distributed about two hundred tracts that day amongst the patients. They remained over the following Sabbath at St. Sauveur, holding a little Meeting in their room in the morning, whilst an English clergyman had service in his parlour. In the evening most of the English (two clergymen among the number), assembled in Mrs. Fry's rooms and a very solemn religious meeting was held. Meanwhile at the Catholic Chapel, a sermon was preached, warning the people against the books that the Protestant visitors might distribute, especially " one lady, who went up even into the mountains to give them away." These were all to be given to the priest, or committed to the flames, unread, on pain of excommunication. This allusion, probably, did not relate to Mrs. Fry, as it so happened, that she had not distributed books there or ascended the mountains.

I felt best satisfied to stay over First-day, that such of the English as might incline, should join us in our worship in the evening, a good many came, we were I believe really helped together ; and I was enabled to speak the truth to them in Christian love. We set off the next morning for Cauterez, another of these beautiful places, taking it in our way to Pau. There we were much interested and pleased, visited three little bodies of Protestants, serious, agreeable people, who appeared glad to see us, and we trust, are a little helped by our visit. From Pau we returned to Toulouse, where we spent a Sabbath, and had a farewell Meeting with the Protestants. We parted with them in uncommon love and unity, and the prayers offered for us in this Meeting, and on other occasions have been to me very encouraging and comforting. May our Lord in His love and pity answer them !

On the 8th, they departed for Pau. The drive was beautiful, the country familiarised by Froissard's descriptions, through the valley of Argellez, and by the old castle of Lourdes. Pau delighted them. In the birth-place of one, for a time the hero of the Protestant Faith, there is still a small body of Christian believers, untainted by the errors of Romanism, and adhering to the pure and simple faith of their forefathers. A few Protestants were found at Tarbes. With them Mrs. Fry had a Meeting, and was exceedingly interested by them and their pasteur M. Doudret.

We left Toulouse last Second-day, and have been travelling rather hard through the South of France, the heat very oppressive. Little religious service opened on the way. But at Montpellier and Nismes, we again met some of our dear friends, and there appeared reason to believe that our labour had not been in vain in the Lord, particularly at Nismes and Congenies. Oh, may our Heavenly Father, bless and prosper the seed scattered by us His unworthy instruments; and may He in His tender and unmerited mercy, guide and guard us to the end! Answer I pray Thee, the deep cries of Thy servant for Thine own name sake, and cause Thy love and peace to abound in our little circle until we separate.

Bönigen, near Interlachen, Switzerland, Eighth Month, 11th. —I believe that my gracious Lord has guided our steps to this place, blessed be His name. Now to go on with my journal. At Grenoble, where I felt rather pressed in spirit, to spend a First-day, I had a curious opening for religious service, and I believe an important one with several enlightened Roman Catholics, several Protestants, and a school of girls. It was a time of spiritual refreshment, by which many appeared helped and comforted. The next day was occupied in important prison visits, and in the evening a Meeting with influential Roman Catholics.

The prison at Grenoble, is an old and ill-constructed building, but kept very clean, and its defects and the wants of the prisoners as much remedied as possible, by an active Committee of ladies and gentlemen, who pay much attention to the bodily wants of the prisoners. Their moral and religious instruction did not appear so well cared for, although they saw one man reading de Sacy's New Testament. The funds of these Committees are chiefly derived from money dropped into a box at the gate, by the peasants and lower class of persons, to obtain the prayers of the prisoners, which are considered by them peculiarly efficacious in releasing souls from purgatory: these alms often amount to as much as eighty francs in a fortnight, which is chiefly expended in linen for the prisoners' use. The chaplain occasionally employing some of the better sort of prisoners, to say the prayers for the souls.

The Government and authorities have tried to put this system of the " tronc" entirely down, but have been successfully opposed by the Committee, on the ground that they have neither power nor right to interfere with private almsgiving, its purpose or appropriation.

Josiah Forster having left us to go by diligence to Geneva, we travelled alone through Savoy, and had a pleasant journey through a lovely country; but the darkness of the Roman Catholic religion, and the arbitrary laws not allowing even a tract to be given away, were painful (we found that a Swiss gentleman had lately been imprisoned for doing it, and confined with a thief.) We arrived at Geneva, the 25th of the Seventh Month, in the evening. Here we passed a very interesting time, from various and important openings for religious service, in large parties, in prisons, &c. My belief is, that we were sent to that place, and amidst some trials from different causes there was a pouring forth of spiritual help, and spiritual peace. Many of the pasteurs came to us, and not a few expressed their refreshment and satisfaction with our visit; before we left, several of the most spiritual, in a very striking and beautiful manner preached to us, particularly to myself, and prayed for us all, a time, I think, never to be forgotten by us. We had one of the most beautiful entertainments I ever saw, given by Colonel Tronchin, at a lovely place, a few miles from Geneva, the fine snowy mountains about us, the lake within sight. In an avenue, in the midst of a fine wood, we had a handsome repast, to which above a hundred persons sat down. The gentleman who gave it, is a devoted Christian, a man of large property, and this blessing sanctified by grace. I visited a delightful institution for the sick, established by him, and on his grounds ; to return to our entertainment, grace was very solemnly said before our meal, and very beautiful hymn-singing afterwards. Then we withdrew into the house, where I believe the anointing was poured forth upon me, to speak the truth in love and power. I had an excellent spiritually minded interpreter (Professor La Harpe); many appeared to feel this occasion. A young English gentleman came up to me afterwards, and expressed his belief that it would influence him for life ; and a lady came to me, and said, how remarkably her state had been spoken to. Much love was also shown to us and unity. Indeed, I felt how our Lord permits His servants to rejoice together in love, and even to partake of the good things of this life, in His love and fear, with a subjected spirit rejoicing in His mercies, temporal and spiritual. We had very great kindness also shown us by many, among others, by our dear friend Mary Ann Vernet and her family, including her daughter the Baroness de Staël, with whom we dined at Coppet. The Duke de Broglie and his family were with her; we had a very interesting visit. We went from Geneva to our dear friend Sophia Delessert, her husband was out; they have a beautiful place on the banks of the Lake of Geneva, near Rolle; here we had the warmest reception, and were refreshed and comforted together, she is truly loved by me.

It is thus that she has described her own impressions of Geneva : but the circumstances of the visit are well worthy of remembrance. In Madame Vernet, Mrs. Fry found a congenial friend, a mother in Israel. At Coppet lived Madame de Staël, her daughter, and with her the Duke de Broglie, the brother-in-law of the Baron de Staël. One evening a very large party assembled at Madame Vernet's. It had been Mrs. Fry's most earnest wish to enjoy some conversation of a decidedly religious character with her Genevan friends on points forming the common ground of faith and hope, with all who look only to one Mediator between God and man, Christ Jesus our Lord, but the occasion proved somewhat different to her expectations, for in the evening came in a Sardinian, Count Pettiti, a kindred spirit in works of benevolence and philanthropy, and soon the conversation turned upon prison subjects, on which both the

Count and Mrs. Fry spoke at considerable length. She handled the subject in a manner peculiar to herself, and to the opportunity she then possessed. Some were present that evening belonging to the National Church of Geneva, a Church fallen from her first love, whose doctrines have become tinctured with vital error, and her faith corrupted and mystified.

Mrs. Fry felt the opportunity to be one given her to *use :*—a solemn responsibility lay upon her, and it was with trembling earnestness that she called the attention of her hearers to her experience in Prisons. She spoke of her firm conviction that no human means of Reformation amongst Prisoners can avail aught, except God's word be brought to bear upon their own condition, their daily life, their past sins, their future improvement. Earnestly she told of the one way open alike to the weary-hearted guilty captive, and to " whosoever will," among men : that way, the precious Blood of the Lamb slain, whereby alone the sinner can be reconciled to God, and be cleansed from the power and guilt of his original and contracted transgression. The impression she made was deep and permanent. Many remember the edification and instruction they there received, and recall with grateful emotion her clear earnest statement of the way of Life. At Beseinge, the beautiful place of Colonel Tronchin, a few miles from the Lake, Mrs. Fry met above a hundred persons at an entertainment given by the hospitable owner of the domain. The repast was laid out in the avenue, and after its conclusion, Hymns were sung, and thanks returned, and then they withdrew to the House, where Mrs. Fry appears to have spoken with peculiar power and wisdom. M. La Harpe, of the "Société Evangelique," and Theological Professor of the Genevan School acted as her interpreter. The occasion was one of deep interest and improvement. " I can never forget Mrs. Fry, at Beseinge, or her words of faith and earnest counsel," says one there present, M. Anet secretary of

8

the Belgian Société Evangelique, " they were burned like words
of fire on my heart and brain."

" We had half expected a philosophical discourse upon subjects
of a philanthropic and general interest, but every thing that
fell from her lips was characterized by delicacy, extreme
simplicity, and an ardent desire to draw our attention to
our own happiness, in being permitted the opportunity for
meditation on the one subject which seemed always present in
her thoughts, Christ Jesus crucified for the expiation of our
sins. At this distance of time I have an actual realization of
the opening of her exhortation—' I think it is impossible for us
to be more profitably employed than by occupying the next few
moments, with the contemplation of the love which the Lord
Jesus has for us;' were her arresting words. I was at that
time a young student at the Genevan school, under M. la
Harpe, and much absorbed with my studies preparatory to my
entrance into the ministry, but those words can never leave my
memory as long as I retain any power of recollection. After a
little time spent at the large table, with the host, the magistrates, chief people of the Republic and others, Mrs. Fry
joined us, a cluster of students and others under a wide spreading
tree, and through her interpreter spoke to us all, with kindness
and much judgment. In order a little better to understand the
circumstances of that déjeuner, I must premise that above fifty
persons having arrived at Beseinge, uninvited by Colonel
Tronchin, but drawn there by an irresistible impulse, to see and
to listen to Mrs. Fry, the tables spread out in the avenue were
found insufficient to accommodate all those assembled. The
students, therefore, and the younger portion of the guests had
retired to a little distance, to a beautiful spot under one of the
finest trees in the place, surrounded by flowering shrubs, and
carpeted by a soft moss of the richest green ; there we made
for ourselves a sort of eastern banquet, each reclining in
the position the most convenient for the repast, and supplied
with provisions by Colonel Tronchin's care, the mossy bank
became our banqueting hall, the rough rocks, which rose here
and there from that verdant covering, our tables. Thus placed

we chaunted our hymns at Mrs. Fry's request, and then all
returned to the house together.   The rooms were full to
overflowing; my fellow-students and I took up our places in
the passage, on the stair-case crowded round the open door,
eagerly hanging on such parts of the beautiful exhortation, as
we could catch by the most breathless attention; after she had
concluded, she kindly came out among us, and expressed her
regret that we should have been so inconvenienced.   I can see
her now, her tall figure leaning on Colonel Tronchin's arm,
M. la Harpe at her side, her dignified, animated, yet softened
countenance bending towards us.   I can never forget it.   Such
occasions are rare in life, they are very green spots in the garden of memory—more, they are opportunities given for improvement, solemnly increasing the responsibility of each who parti-
cipates in them.   May I never lose the impression of that day
at Beseinge, nor the holy lessons, I there heard and learnt."

It was on the same day that Mrs. Fry accompanied by Colonel
Tronchin, visited the institution which he had founded on his
grounds, for receiving convalescents during that trying period
of debility and weakened energy which so commonly follows
severe illness, and requires such judicious and tender treatment.
All admitted into this valuable institution were under spiritual
instruction.

On another occasion, at the hotel, a party of above eighty
met in the evening, expressly to discuss the state of prisons.

The Sunday morning the travellers sat down in their room as
usual, to worship after the simple manner of Friends.   Some
of the Vernet family, and a few others were present, and it
proved a very solemn meeting.   In the evening, their scripture
reading was attended by several pasteurs and a very numerous
company, some belonging to the evangelical section of the
church, and others to that national church, whose creeds

and catechisms, alas! but too clearly show the fearful un-
soundness of their doctrine and faith. On this occasion she
read the 58th chapter of Isaiah, and spoke at length on some
parts of it. She prayed solemnly for those present; for the
pasteurs that they might be endued with wisdom and strength,
for all who love the Lord, everywhere and of every name, and
for the inhabitants of Geneva in particular.

Mrs. Fry was much struck with the completeness of the
"Maison Pénitentiaire" at Geneva. There were only fifty prisoners under a Directeur, Sous Directeur M. Grellet, brother of
Stephen Grellet, and many guardians. The prisoners are divided
into four classes, perfectly separated from each other, and their
treatment varying in severity. They work and eat in common,
each class in its own atelier; they also recreate each in the yard
of the class, but sleep in separate cells; in every cell is a bed,
a chair, table, shelf and some books. For the Protestants,
Ostervald's Bible is provided; for the Catholics, the Manuel du
Chrétien: they are here for long terms of imprisonment. The
returns, average fourteen to the hundred; but the health fails
after the first or second year.

The second time she visited it, the prisoners were assembled
in the chapel, for Mrs. Fry to have a religious opportunity with
them. The Catholic priest however did not allow his flock to
be present.

The same thing occurred at the Evéché, an old bad prison,
about to be pulled down; the priest was there, purposely to
prevent the four or five Roman Catholic women being present,
should Mrs. Fry speak to the women, unless she would promise
only to enforce "morality," and not touch on religion or Christian faith. She assured him she never touched upon the
"dogmes" of religion, only on the great principles of faith and
practice. This would not do, and the Roman Catholic
women were withdrawn!!

At Lausanne, we met with a kind friend, Charles Scholl, whom we knew in England, a valuable pasteur, We visited the prisons; and with the women I had a religious time, one that appears to have made a considerable impression upon some of them. I have had very comforting accounts since I was there. A good many ladies and some gentlemen, met Josiah Forster and myself at a lady's house, where the subject of prisons was entered upon. In the evening we met a very large party, numbers of pasteurs, &c., at a gentleman's beautiful place on the banks of the lake ; here again we had a deeply interesting time. I had to speak for some time, showing the effect of Christian principle and kindness on prisoners. I was well interpreted for, by my friend Charles Scholl. In conclusion, one valuable pasteur read, and another prayed; and prayed much for my preservation in my peculiar situation, and that I might not be entangled by the many snares that surrounded me. Much love and real unity we felt with many of these dear people. We then proceeded to Berne by Friburg ; at Berne I again visited the Prison. These Penitentiaries at Geneva, Lausanne, and Berne, interested me much, as excellent; still there are some things wanting. At Berne, I had also a religious time with all the female prisoners. We visited the large and interesting institution of Dr. Fellenburg for boys, with which I was much pleased ; but I desired more reading of the Holy Scriptures, and spoke and wrote to him on the subject. We had a very hospitable reception to dinner, invited for half-past eleven, from a gentleman and his lady. At the prison, I was at first badly interpreted for, when a young lady, Sophia Werstemburger, came forward, as she has since told me, from believing it a duty, and offered to assist me. It was striking to me to observe, how remarkably she appeared helped to do it, and to convey my meaning.

The subject of this address was afterwards embodied by Miss Werstemburger in a German tract, and has been extensively used in Prisons. Notwithstanding the disadvantage of having to restore it from its foreign medium, the substance of

it is presented to the reader, for although after a double translation, the language can scarcely be considered her own,
it embodies the topics she was wont to urge so faithfully and
yet so tenderly upon her hearers, and is almost if not the only
record of the kind in existence.

In the fulness of my heart I desire to express to you poor
afflicted ones, my sincere and earnest feelings of commiseration
and sympathy for your condition. You are now as sinners
tasting some of the bitter fruits of disobedience to God; you
have now had experience of the anguish of heart and distress
of mind which sin brings with it, and as the result of your evil
deeds, you have to endure the painful inflictions of human
justice.

Your situation affects my heart deeply, even in the present
view of your outward state. But how much more does the
consideration afflict me when I survey the awful prospect before
you, should you unhappily persevere in the same evil courses;
then indeed I can see nothing for you but disgrace and ruin in
this life, and afterwards the judgments of a Holy and offended
God.

On one side, therefore, there is no hope to be held out to
you, but on the other, it still remains. Yes, I see it even for
you, that solid and undoubted, that only true and infallible
hope for us all, the glorious privilege of the children of God,—
who loosed from the bondage of their own evil nature, through
the mercy of God in Christ Jesus, abide with Him in a state of
blessed peace and holy freedom.

A new prospect for you dawns upon my mind at the
thought of which my heart rejoices, involving as it does, not
only your restoration to the esteem of your fellow mortals, but
peace to your own souls, and a well-founded hope after this
life is ended of your participation for ever in that eternally
blessed state to which we are all called by God.

Although ignorant of your language, I feel as if I had a
special mission to unfold to you, my poor afflicted friends this
prospect, to explain the ground of this hope, and to announce

the message of tidings of great joy which are still open to you. I not only wish to tell you that which I myself believe, but the reasons of that belief, grounded as it is on what I have myself seen and witnessed during a long life. I have known many as sinful as yourselves in other respects situated as you are; I have closely observed them and their course of life, and I have marked their onward path to its termination. I have seen such as these, prisoners like yourselves, who have been by the blessing of God on the labour of his servants, aroused to the consciousness of their sad and forlorn condition, and to a deep sense of the bitterness of their sins, addressing themselves with penitent and sincere hearts to the mercy of God in Christ Jesus, and I have witnessed the fruits of their repentance, so that it could not be doubted but that they had received mercy, and obtained that peace which the votaries of this world so ardently though vainly wish to attain. I have seen such as these enter the prison as you have done, and leave it altogether altered characters; and I have seen them die as Christians die, for whom death had lost its sting and the grave its victory. Let me then, my friends, in few words assure you that I entertain the sweet hope that there are many amongst you who have still desires after the way of Salvation, and oh, may this day realize the blessed Hope.

Begin then you elder ones, who have known a long career of bitterness and disappointment, and who must be well aware that your old course of life leads to destruction; do not remain behind you younger ones, who now hear this admonition at an earlier period of life. That day will be a blessed day, when any of you, old or young, abandon the road to destruction, and being sanctified by the Spirit of God, become as his pardoned children.

Take courage therefore, and accept this invitation as from the Lord; confide in the promises of your merciful Saviour, who can yet save you, who entreats you by His word to come unto Him. Then will the true peace of God be with you, and joy on your account before the angels of God. There are many present who take a deep interest in your happiness and

well being. Let our caring for you be to you a pledge of that
Heavenly joy of which the Gospel speaks. And now I bid
you all a hearty farewell in the Lord, beseeching Him that you
and we all may be sprinkled with the Blood of Christ, the im-
maculate and holy Lamb of God, and sanctified by the Holy
Spirit unto eternal life. May you be so born again as to
become the children of God, and so thoroughly sanctified by
the Holy Ghost as to become more and more subject to the
will and law of God ; and may you through the mercy of God
in Christ Jesus our Lord be admitted into that city, " whose
walls are salvation and whose gates are praise." What a
prospect for poor sinners (as we all are) to be permitted to meet
again through the love of the Father, the mercy of the Son,
and the blessed power of the Holy Ghost, in the mansions of
eternal glory, and to join in the hymn of the redeemed multitudes out of every language, and nation, and people who sing,
" worthy is the Lamb that was slain, to receive power, and
riches, and wisdom, and strength, and honour, and blessing,"
for He has " redeemed us to God by His blood," and " made us
kings and priests" unto God.

Elizabeth Fry then proceeded to give various striking and
most affecting narratives, from her own intimate knowledge, of
the conversion and happy end of several prisoners, who had
been under the care of the ladies, adding—

Let me impress upon you now, that which I then told them—
let me explain to you somewhat concerning your Hope, concerning that which saved them, and can alone save you. This hope
of salvation is founded only on the infinite mercy of God ; but
if we would find and experience this mercy for ourselves we
must seek it in His name, by whom alone we can be saved,
Jesus Christ our Redeemer, for " we have," says the Apostle,
" not a High-priest who cannot be touched with the feeling of
our infirmities, but was in all points tempted like as we are,
yet without sin." He came down on this earth for the

salvation of sinners, and lived amongst sinners. Do you remember those consoling words in the 15th of the Gospel of Luke, in the parable of the Prodigal Son, who in his utmost need remembered his father's house, and arose and came to his father, and when he was yet a great way off, his father saw him and had compassion on him, and came and fell on his neck and kissed him, and the words the son spoke to him, " Father, I have sinned against Heaven and in thy sight, and am no more worthy to be called thy son;" and how his father upbraided him not with his sins, but received him as his beloved child. This is left on record for all sinners. Some of you, perhaps, poor, forlorn, and abandoned, have been left without earthly parents, dependant only on your heavenly Father; and will you not with the prodigal son, go to Him, remembering what is further written, that there is more joy in the presence of the angels of God over one sinner that repenteth than over ninety and nine just persons who need no repentance,—only consider this, that there will be joy amongst the angels of God over one sinner that repents. This you have no doubt heard and even within these walls, but have you also thought and considered, how this love has been already proved to you? do you bear in mind how you have been spared until now, and how different it might have been with you had you been taken away in the midst of your sins, that time has yet been allowed you to repent and return to the Lord,—yes the Lord, He is the Father who wills not that the sinner should perish, but that he may be converted and live.

You believe that in His displeasure he had suffered you to be brought here for punishment, but oh, I entreat you above all things to believe that your souls are still precious before the Lord, and that it is not His anger but His love which has brought you to this house, that you may learn His will, and know of His doctrine. Understand, that He desires that the important time you remain in it, may be a blessed time for you, a time for reflection and of returning in heart to him. Even this day He invites you by me to accept his free mercy, pardon, and eternal well being. Every one who is weary and heavy hearted, and truly laden with the burden of their sins, is in-

vited to come to the compassionate Redeemer, to Him who
despises not, nor abandons the most forsaken penitent. Hear
what the Gospel says of him who calls himself the good shepherd, The good shepherd left his ninety and nine sheep, in
order to look after the one that was lost, and when he had
found it he carried it home, rejoicing that the sheep that was
lost was found again.

I will now turn to the way by which to lay hold on this
hope thus held out to you; it is by sincere contrition, earnest
belief, and thankful love which will be bestowed on all who
seek it through the merits of their Saviour. This is the path
in which they of whom I have told you walked; those who in
prison found their Saviour, and with him true liberty,—this
was their uniform experience, and as we are all children of one
and the same God, it cannot be otherwise with you. They
were all brought to feel and experience that there is no
bondage so grievous as the bondage of sin; no misery equal to
the servitude of Satan. They had to partake of the bitter fruits
of their sinful doings, and experienced how hard to be borne
are the chains of the evil one. Fearful of that eternal condemnation, which they acknowledged themselves to have deserved, they were brought with an alarmed conscience, and a
contrite heart, to look to their Saviour for deliverance—" Lord
have mercy upon me a sinner." They learned to hate their
sins more than they formerly hated their punishment, nay
more, they learned to kiss the rod wherewith their heavenly
Father chastised them.

Remember Mary Magdalene, the sinner, may her example and
her repentance and faithful love influence your hearts. Remember
how she cast herself at the feet of the Redeemer, kissed them,
anointed them, and washed them with her tears; how the
Lord forgave her sins and accepted her in mercy. Throw yourselves therefore like Mary Magdalene at the feet of your Lord,
and in earnest prayer implore his pity and reconciliation
through his blood. I will conclude with the words of the
prophet: " Seek the Lord whilst He may be found, call ye
upon him whilst He is near, let the wicked forsake his way, and
the unrighteous man his thoughts, and turn unto the Lord, for

He will have mercy upon him, and to our God for He will abundantly pardon."

After this visit, we parted from our dear friend Josiah Forster, in love and unity, and I may add, grateful to him for his constant kindness, and faithful and industrious endeavour to help me in my various duties. May it please the Lord to grant him his reward, in a further knowledge of Himself, and of the rest, peace and liberty that He gives His children and people. We went from Berne to Thun, and then to this beautiful, delightful and interesting country, where I have almost entirely devoted myself to my dearest husband and children. We have had some sweet and refreshing times together. I have rested as beside the still waters, at times refreshed in body, mind, and spirit, so as to be able to rejoice in my Lord, and glory in the God of my salvation.

In the midst of mountains and waterfalls.

Eighth Month, 18*th.*

My dearest Hannah,

We are come here for my companions to see one of the finest waterfalls in Europe. After a curious walk with a boy, my guide, who only spoke German, I have come to our pretty Hotel, where we are to have luncheon, and happily I have found ink and paper. I often long for you to see some of my droll and entertaining communications with those to whom I cannot speak. By small papers and little tracts, that I have in German, I manage to show some interest in those around me; at least a certain degree of pleasant feeling is excited, and they bring little presents of flowers in return for tracts and marks of kindness. I was amused just now in my walk, at being joined by three girls, as well as my boy guide, who began to chatter to me in German, and some things we at last made each other understand.

Switzerland is certainly a wonderful country, and very attractive, but I think not more so than the Pyrenees. Sweet as it is, the flats of East and West Ham look to *us* sweeter.

I have much felt on this journey, that life itself is but a journey, and how important to feel it so much so as to keep the end constantly in view; not over anxious respecting the changes to which we are subject, but going steadily forward through clouds and sunshine, ups and downs, trusting to the wisdom, love and mercy of our Guide, and His power to aid us when walking through dangerous places. I also desire to commit more constantly our "fellow-pilgrims" to the same holy and sufficient Helper. I want to be more without carefulness and to have more hopefulness.

But in the midst of rest and relaxation, Mrs. Fry did not forget her objects; she called on the pasteur at Grindenvald, found his flock large, scattered, and she feared, ignorant. The Bible Society's operations did not appear to have reached this place; Bibles being scarce amongst them, and so expensive as to be unattainable by these poor people, especially from their preference for folio Bibles with clasps, which they consider a sort of heir-loom.

One Sunday was passed at Brienz, where they had the unexpected pleasure of meeting some of Mrs. Fry's excellent friends of the Mackenzie family from Edinburgh, and of spending a quiet day together, concluded by a reading in the evening. The pastor of this place was also visited, and the condition of his flock inquired into. On a previous occasion when on the Lake of Brienz, a poor boy who rowed the boat, told her that his mother lay sick in a cottage he pointed out. It rested on her mind, and in crossing the lake to return to Bönigen, she landed not without difficulty, accompanied by the wife of the pasteur of Brienz. They found the poor woman very ill on a mattress, spread in the gallery of her cottage, with her Bible by her side; she was an afflicted discouraged Christian woman to whom the few words of encouragement offered were very timely, to strengthen that which, through bodily suffering, seemed almost ready to die. The temporal wants were not forgotten, and the case was left under the care of the pastor's wife.

Whilst at Bönigen, the landlord of the little inn and his family attended their Sunday evening readings. On one of these occasions a peasant girl was with them who appeared pious and afflicted ; her name was Madelina Kauss. She came from a neighbouring village to seek council of Mrs. Fry. Madelina and her mother had joined themselves to a little body of pious people, Pietists, somewhat resembling Methodists, seceders from the National Church. The father, a coarse igno- rant man, vehemently threatened his wife, and turned his daughter out of doors to earn her own livelihood, which she did by weaving for nine French sous a day. Good people from Berne had interfered on their behalf, but had only made mat- ters worse. It so fell out that about this time a certain small old-fashioned black-letter German newspaper reached the little inn at Bönigen, the host and his household were startled therein to find a long account of his guests, a history of Mrs. Fry, " her works and labours" of love, concluding with her visit to the Oberland of Berne and residence at the Herr Mitchell's country inn. After careful perusal, it occurred to the worthy host that in his inmates he had found the very people to rectify the wrongs of poor Madelina, and restore peace in her parents' dwelling, persons in his opinion not to be resisted by Henrich Kauss, the peasant of Wildersewyl, to whom he advised that a visit should forthwith be made. When the carriage came to convey the party, he insisted on driving it himself arrayed in his holiday costume. The interview with the family was quite pathetic. The father laid the fault of his violence and severity on the grandfather, and he on the schoolmaster; but a little kind and wise conciliation sufficed to bring them all to tears; they wept and kissed, and Herr Mitchell wept for sympathy. After which Mrs. Fry had a religious time with Madelina, her mother and a few of their neighbours, leaving them with the thankful belief that they had been permitted to act the blessed part of peacemakers.

After leaving Bönigen, Mrs. Fry was met at Thun by Miss Werstemburger, and in the evening Mr. Felemburgh, the chaplain of the prison at Berne arrived there also, a few important hours devoted to prison subjects was beautifully concluded by reading and prayer, in which Mr. Felemburgh took part.

Zurich, Eighth Month, 25th.—We left our sweet little home at Bönigen, on the banks of the Lake of Brienz, last Fourthday. I felt refreshed by our visit to this lovely country. I think my prayers have been heard and answered, in its being a very uniting time with those most tenderly beloved by me. We have had some interesting communications with serious persons in the humble walk of life, who reside in that neighbourhood. We have desired to aid them spiritually and temporally, but the difficulty of communication has been very great, from want of suitable interpreters; still, I trust, that some were edified and comforted. I also hope our circulation of books and tracts has been useful, and the establishment of at least one library at Brienz, for the use of the labouring classes. We have travelled along gently and agreeably by Lucerne, and through a delightful country.

The state of things at the time of their visit to Zurich, both religiously and politically, was very peculiar. A few months before the government had appointed Professor Strauss to the Theological chair, an avowed unbeliever. This appointment was so violently opposed by the majority of the population, Protestant as well as Roman Catholic, that the Professor was obliged to withdraw, and the chair remained vacant. Those in power finding themselves thus thwarted in their intentions, resorted to the expedient of placing masters, unsound in matters of faith, in the national schools. The pastors of the evangelical section considered it their duty to institute a society, or central committee, to counteract so fearful an evil. The very day before Mrs. Fry arrived in Zurich, orders had been issued by the government to prohibit and put down all meetings in their districts. To convene and hold meetings is one of the fundamental rights of the Zurichois, which the magistrates on taking office are sworn to maintain inviolate. Some of them declared they would not break this oath. During the travellers' tarriance these parties remained in this position, but a few days after they left the place, a civil war broke out, and a fearful struggle ensued before, by the interposition of the more moderate, even external order could be established.

The morning of their departure from Zurich, the venerable Mr. Gesner (Antistes, or Prelate of the Canton), and many others, called to take leave. This apostolic old man pronounced a wonderful blessing on Mrs. Fry, to which she replied in terms that caused the bystanders to weep aloud. A tedious journey of four days, through very wet weather, brought the travellers to Stuttgard; here the impediment of the language was great, few of those to whom their letters were delivered speaking either French or English. They proceeded to Ludwigsburg for Sunday.

Ludwigsburg, (a few miles from Stuttgard), Ninth Month, 1st.—On the evening of the day that I wrote at Zurich, we went with our very dear friend La Baronne Pelet, afterwards joined by the Baron, to the house of that ancient devoted pasteur, Gesner. His wife was the daughter of that excellent servant of the Lord, Lavater. We met a large number of persons, I believe generally serious. I had proposed to myself speaking on the Prison subject, but my way opened differently; to enlarge upon the state of the Protestant Church in France, to encourage all its members to devotedness; and particularly in that place, where deep trials have been their portion, from their Government upholding infidelity and infidel men. At the close of the Meeting, our venerable friend, Gesner, spoke in a lively, powerful man-

ner, and avowed his belief that the Lord Himself had enabled
me to express what I had done, it was so remarkably "the
word in season." I paid, also, a satisfactory religious visit to
the female prisoners in the afternoon. The next morning I
visited the head magistrate, represented the evils I had observed, and saw some ladies about visiting prisons. We afterwards went a sweet expedition on the Lake, with our beloved
friends the Baron and Baroness Pelet. Early in the evening,
I set off with a dear girl—great grand-daughter to Lavater, and
grand-daughter to Pasteur Gesner—Barbara Usteri, in a curious
little carriage to pay some visits, and to spend an evening at
the house of the aunt of Matilda Escher, another interesting
young woman, with whom I had become acquainted, I believe
providentially, at an inn near Interlachen. I had no one with
me but strangers, as my dear family stayed with the Baron and
Baroness Pelet at my desire ; but I felt not among strangers,
because those who love the Lord Jesus are dear to me, and in
our holy Head we are one. I can hardly express, on this
journey, how much I have found this to be the case. The
love, the unity, and the home feeling, I have had with those I
never saw before ; and I have also found how little it matters
where we are, for " where the God of peace is, there is home."

A letter to Mr. Klett, resident Inspector of the Prison at
Ludwigsburgh, was delivered, and half-past seven o'clock the
next morning, appointed for her visit to that place. There a
Swiss lad of eighteen years of age, was in waiting to act as interpreter. The women, though it was Sunday, were engaged
in needlework by order of the King,—a sad sight in a Protestant country. They also visited an Orphan Asylum ; and in
the evening again went to the prison. The women are well instructed, by a devoted lady who spends her life in this service.
They appeared in a tender, feeling state of mind, and a solemn
reading of the Scriptures impressed them much.

Cologne, Ninth Month, 8th.—At Frankfort, we met with a

most cordial reception from our dear friend Dr. Pinkerton and his family, they treated us in the most handsome manner, and with true Christian kindness. Their warm-heartedness, their piety, and their cultivated minds, rendered their society delightful. We had one evening a large party at their house, where much passed of an interesting nature, and I fully believe that we were blessed together. I also visited the prisons—all sad, (with one exception). I hope the prisoners will be visited in consequence, and a stall opened in the town for the sale of Bibles and tracts.

A rapid journey from Frankfort brought the travellers to Ostend. They landed at Dover on the 12th of September.

Upton Lane, Ninth Month, 22nd.—We arrived here in the evening of the 13th, in health and peace, and found the numerous members of our beloved family generally well and prospering. Nothing appears to have suffered from our absence; for this, we may reverently return thanks.

Lynn, Tenth Month, 20th.—I am sitting in Rachel's little sitting-room, on the Sabbath morning. I am thankful it has pleased my heavenly Father to direct my steps to this place at this time. I did desire and pray to be directed, as to the time of coming here.

First-day, Eleventh Month, 10th.—My time at Lynn was spent very satisfactorily with my beloved children and grandchildren, and my attention particularly occupied by the intention they had, of our dear eldest grandson going into the army. My prayers were first offered in secret, that my Lord would open some way of escape from a life, that I felt to be so unchristian and fearful a one. At first I said little, but kept my heart much lifted up on his account; but afterwards, I fully represented my views to him and to his parents, and I found they had great weight with them. I partook of rather unusually sweet spiritual unity and intercourse with these dear children, much as they outwardly differ from me in many things, still we are, I believe, united in some most essential points of religious truth. My dear grandson Frank and I visited Earlham together, where I highly

7

valued the company of my sisters, Catherine and Richenda, also of the rest of the party. I travelled home with my dear niece, Catherine Buxton.

Upton, First-day, Twelfth Month, 8th.—I, yesterday, had some intimate conversation with Captain ———, who has just joined, or is about to join the Plymouth Brethren; with a young lady, a follower of Edward Irving; with another lady, a high Church woman; and with Josiah Forster, an elder in our portion of the church: I cannot say, but that it is at times an exercise of my faith, to find the diversities of opinions existing amongst the professors of Christianity, and not only the professors, but those who I believe really love their Lord; but my better judgment tells me, that there must be a wise purpose in its being so. These divisions into families and tribes may tend to the life and growth of religion, which, if we were all of one mind, might not be the case. But whilst I see these differences, I perceive that there is but one Christianity, one Body, one Spirit, one hope of our calling, one Lord, one faith and one baptism, one God and Father of all. All true members of the Church of Christ are, and must be one in Him, and the results we see the same everywhere. Love to God and love to man, manifested in life and conduct; and how strikingly proved in death, as well as in life, that victory is obtained through the same Saviour, that in the dying hour death loses its sting and the grave its victory. Therefore, if we believe and know our hearts to be cleansed by the blood of Christ, and through the power of the Holy Ghost live to His glory, bearing the fruits of faith, it matters little, in my estimation, to what religious denomination we belong, so that we mind our calling, and fill the place our Lord would have us to fill, in His Militant Church on earth.

I have had very satisfactory letters from the Continent, in which it appears, in various ways, that our visit has been blessed in many places—Committees formed to visit prisoners —Prisons improved. The minds of prisoners appear to have been seriously impressed, encouragement given to some who wanted it, and, I trust, by what I hear, many stimulated in their progress heavenward.

I visited Lord Normanby, our Home Secretary, a few days since, and met with a most cordial reception; and found, in consequence of some suggestions that I had offered, a material improvement likely to take place in the arrangements for our female convicts; that they are to be sent from the country, after trial, to the Milbank Penitentiary, to be employed and instructed, previous to their going abroad. He also very kindly attended to some other things of secondary importance, about which I was anxious to communicate with him.

CHAPTER XXII.

First Month, 26th, 1840.—An eventful time in public and private life. Our young Queen is to be married to Prince Albert. She has sent me a present of fifty pounds for our Refuge at Chelsea, by Lord Normanby. Political commotions about the country—riots in Wales—much religious stir in the Church of England, numbers of persons becoming much the same as Roman Catholics—Popish doctrines preached openly in many of our churches—infidel principles, in the form of Socialism, gaining ground.

The prospect of returning to the Continent, with my brother Samuel Gurney, is rather bright to me. William Allen and Lucy Bradshaw's company will be very desirable, and I fully expect to find them all true helpers in the Lord. The only real drawback, that I know of, is the state of health of some of my children; but I leave it all to my Heavenly Father, who governs all in Mercy, according to the purpose of His own will; and I desire, as Leighton advises, to roll all my cares upon Him, more particularly the cares appertaining to duty. We have many and very great causes for thankfulness; and surely our latter days are our brightest days. In the midst of dark and heavy trials, I used to believe this would be the case.

Under a sweet feeling of Thy merciful and providential care over us, and Thy gentle dealings towards us, most gracious Lord God, I humbly return Thee thanks, and ask Thee in faith, and in the name of our Redeemer, to continue to be with us, to keep us, and bless us, and more abundantly to bestow upon us the gifts of Thine own Holy Spirit, that we may faithfully fill the office Thou mayst call us into, to Thy glory, the good of others, and the spreading of the Truth as it is in Jesus; also, be pleased, not only to bestow on us the gifts, but also the graces of Thy Spirit, that in meekness and deep humility, and much patience and long-suffering, we may walk worthy of Thee, who hast called us to Thy kingdom and glory. And now, Holy Father, under a fresh feeling of Thy love, Thy pity, and Thine unmerited mercy towards us, I commend my husband, my self, children, grandchildren, brothers, sisters, and their children, and all my beloved friends at home and abroad, and all who love Thy name and fear Thee, particularly the afflicted and tempted, to Thy most Holy keeping; and I also pray Thee, for the sake of Thy beloved Son Christ Jesus our Saviour, who tasted death for every man, to regard for good the world at large, especially those who yet sit in darkness. Lift up the light of Thy blessed and holy countenance upon these and all wanderers, that they may behold Thy beauty and excellency, and come to the knowledge of Thyself and Thy dear Son. So be it, most merciful Lord God, that the day may hasten forward, when the knowledge of Thyself and Thy Christ, through the power of Thy Spirit, may cover the earth, even as the waters cover the sea ! Amen.

Mrs. Fry had not returned the certificate which she had received from the Meetings of Friends for her Continental journey in 1839. She had, when she asked for it, some expectation of prolonging her travels into Germany, but her objects in France occupied so much more time than she had anticipated, that she was under the necessity of returning to England. But she did not abandon the idea, and the time seemed now approaching, when she might again leave home with satisfaction. Her brother Samuel Gurney, his daughter Elizabeth, and her friend William Allen, with his niece Lucy Bradshaw, accompanied her.

Upton, Second Month, 1st.—I am called to visit our young Queen to-day, in company with William Allen, and I hope my brother Samuel also.

We went to Buckingham Palace, and saw the Queen. Our interview was short. Lord Normanby, the Home Secretary, presented us. The Queen asked us where we were going on the Continent. She said it was some years since she saw me. She asked about Caroline Neave's Refuge, for which she had lately sent the fifty pounds. This gave me an opportunity of thanking her. I ventured to express my satisfaction that she encouraged various works of charity; and I said it reminded me of the words of scripture, " with the merciful Thou wilt shew Thyself merciful." Before we withdrew, I stopped and said, I hoped the Queen would allow me to assure her, that it was our prayer that the blessing of God might rest upon the Queen and her Consort.

Our beloved daughter Louisa was confined on Fourth-day. The babe, a lovely girl, breathed for twenty-four hours, and then died. They had the child named and baptised. I happened to be present, and certainly some of the prayers were very solemn, and such as I could truly unite with; but part of the ceremony appeared to me superstitious, and having a strong savour of the dark ages of the Church. I have for some time believed that duty would call me to have a meeting in London and the neighbourhood, previous to leaving home. I see many difficulties attached to it, and perhaps none so much, as my great fear of women coming too forward in these things, beyond what the Scripture dictates; but I am sure the Scripture most clearly and forcibly lays down the principle that the Spirit is not to be grieved, or quenched, or vexed, or resisted; and on this principle I act, under the earnest desire that I may not do this, but that whatever the Lord leads me into by His Spirit may be done faithfully to Him, and in His name; and I am of opinion, that nothing Paul said, to discourage women's speaking in the Churches, alluded to their speaking through the help of the Spirit, as he clearly gave directions how they should conduct themselves under such circumstances, when they prayed or prophesied.

In a letter written a few days afterwards, a lady who was present, not a Friend, described that Meeting: " It was really a most impressive occasion—the large fine circular building filled—not less, I should think, than fifteen hundred present. She began by entreating the sympathy and supplications of those present. I cannot tell you how mine flowed forth on her behalf. After her prayer, we sat still for some time, then William Allen spoke, and then she rose, giving as a text, ' Yield yourselves unto God, as those that are alive from the dead ;' and uncommonly fine was her animated yet tender exhortation to all present, but more especially the young, to present themselves as living sacrifices to the Lord,—to be made of Him new creatures in Christ—the old things passed away, and all things become new as those alive from the dead. This change she dwelt and enlarged on much ; its character, and the Power that alone can effect it ; the duty demanded of us—' Yield yourselves ;' and its infinite and eternal blessedness. I was astonished and deeply impressed ; the feeling was, ' surely God is amongst us of a truth.' "

In the carriage on board the steam-boat going to Ostend :—

Second Month, 26th, 1840.

My dearest Husband and Children,

Here I am by myself, none of our companions liking the carriage ; my brother Samuel and Lucy Bradshaw near me on the deck. The sun shines brightly,—the wind and tide quite contrary to us,—the sea not very rough,—Calais in sight,—the birds delighting themselves on the waves, and I feeling much refreshed.

I desire to recount my mercies to you, inasmuch as at this moment separated from so many so dearly beloved, I am quiet, peaceful, hopeful, and well in health, neither faint nor sick with the sea, but my quiet time alone in the carriage refreshing and pleasant to me.

I think I must not say more, therefore farewell for the present. Surely goodness and mercy have thus far followed me.·

Ostend.—Here we may thankfully say we are, after a not unfavourable voyage of eleven hours. I feel the water separating
us, but we are united in heart, and I may gratefully say I believe
I am in my right place ; every thing most comfortable for us.
I send what I wrote in the packet, hoping you can read it.

Farewell in nearest love,

ELIZABETH FRY.

Ostend, Second Month, 27th, finished Ghent, 29th.

We are favoured with a bright morning, and we may thankfully say that our spirits are permitted to partake of the same
brightness. I have a sweet feeling of being in the right place.
An order is come from the Belgian Government for us to visit
their prisons. So the way opens before us ; and though I give
up much to enter these services, and feel leaving my most
tenderly beloved ones, yet there is such a sense of the blessedness of the service, and the honour of doing the least thing for
my Lord, unworthy as I am, that it often brings a peculiar
feeling of health, (if I may so say) as well as peace to my body,
soul and spirit.

My brother Samuel is a capital travelling companion, so
zealous, so able, so willing, so generous; and I find dear Elizabeth
sweet, pleasant and cheering. Bruges is a delightful old town;
such exquisite buildings—they delighted my eye. Here we
visited the English Convent, where, to our surprise, we could
only speak through a grating. We had a good deal of conversation with dear S. P——'s sister and the Superior. They
appeared very interesting women. We talked about their
shutting-in system. I expressed my disapprobation of it as a
general practice, and one liable to such great abuse. I sent
them some books, and mean to send more. We also visited a
large school, to the great pleasure and amusement of the
children, your uncle gave them all a present. They could not
the least understand our language, as they speak Flemish.

We have been much interested, this morning, in visiting the
Maison de Force ; it is a very excellent prison of considerable
size, but wants some things very much. We have since been

occupied with the numerous English here. They are without pasteur or school, and quite in a deplorable state. We propose having a meeting with them of a religious and philanthropic nature, and hope to establish some schools, &c., amongst them.

May the blessing of the Most High abundantly rest on you all. Yours, in a close bond that I trust will never be broken.

E. F.

Brussels, Third Month, 1st.

My dearest Husband and Children,

We left Ghent on Seventh-day, about half-past two o'clock, after visiting a most deplorable prison, where we found a cell with the floor and sides formed of angular pieces of wood, so that no prisoner could stand, lie down, or lean against the wall, without suffering. We also visited a lunatic asylum, so beautifully conducted, that I more took the impression of how happy such persons may be made than I ever did before. They are cared for by the Sisters of St. Vincent de Paul. After rather a slow journey, we arrived here to dinner, at six o'clock.

Ghent, Third Month, 3*rd.*—Here we are once more—we have visited another large prison for the military; and had a very interesting Meeting with the English workmen, their wives and children. I am glad to say, they conclude for us to send them schoolmasters. We had flocks after us last evening, English and Belgians—I suppose about seventy : they appeared to be touched by our reading. I observe how much the English appear impressed on these occasions. Our little party are very comfortable, and each has plenty to do.

Farewell, yours indeed,

ELIZABETH FRY.

Antwerp, Third Month, 6th.

My dearest Husband and Children,

Upon our return to Brussels from Ghent, we visited the great prison of Vilvorde, where we were met by Count Arrivabene, a very interesting Italian, who has been our most kind and attentive friend in Brussels. He is a great philanthropist, and is likely soon to visit England. We gave many of our little Scripture extracts to the prisoners. We got home to dinner, and spent the evening at the Baron de Bois', where we met several pleasant persons. The pictures were beautiful: the Dutch and Flemish masters are to me very attractive. The next day we visited many large institutions. We had company to dinner; and a considerable number of Belgians, poor and rich, came to an Evening Meeting at our hotel. The next day was one of no common interest. After some engagements in the morning, breakfasting out, &c., we visited the King, who held out both his hands to receive me with real kindness, and appeared quite pleased to see me again. Our party were William Allen, my brother Samuel, J. Forster, and myself; and before we left, Lucy Bradshaw and dear Elizabeth were admitted to see him. We first had a very interesting conversation on the state of the prisons, and your uncle read the King our address to him upon the subject; when the part was read expressing our desire for him, the Queen and his family, he appeared to feel it. We had open, interesting communication upon many subjects. We remained nearly an hour. The Queen was unwell, and the children asleep, therefore I did not see them. We gave the King several books for himself and the Queen. After we returned home we had engagements until near dinner-time. We were invited by Count Arrivabene to dine with one of the first Belgian families. I felt it rather fearful, when, to my surprise after dinner, I was seated by the Dean of Brussels, surrounded by the company, and told that I was permitted to speak openly upon my religious views. Indeed, I think the wish was, that I should preach to them. This was curious, because I was warned on going to say nothing about religion. Preach I did not—as I do not feel that, at my command; but I spoke very seriously about the Scriptures not being read in the prisons, and endeavoured to show in few words what alone can produce change of heart, life, and conduct, and the danger of resting in forms. We parted in much good-will, and we sent the Dean and the ladies books. In the evening we had a philanthropic party at our hotel. The next morning, a large,

6

very solemn and interesting religious Meeting, also at the hotel. We left Brussels in much peace (*rejoicing* would not be too strong a word). In nearest love,

E. F.

From the journal of her niece, Elizabeth Gurney :—

"Brussels, March 6th.—We expect to end our very interesting visit in this place to-day. Had I a hundred times more power of writing, I could not initiate you into our life here. A great Meeting is now assembling in the Table d'Hôte salon, fitted up by our landlord for the occasion. This is to be our farewell Meeting. We have had a very full morning, partly employed in distributing books. The servants at the palace sent an entreaty that they might not be overlooked. I wish you could have seen us looking out a good variety for about sixty of them.

"Yesterday began with a full tide of business. They were to see the King at twelve o'clock. My aunt looked beautifully. He is a particularly pleasing-looking man, rather older than I expected. The Duchess of Kent had kindly written to the King, to say, that my aunt was likely to visit Brussels.

"I must tell you about our dinner at M. le Comte de ——, the first Roman Catholic family here. We were taken there by our kind friend Count Arrivabene. The party consisted of fifteen persons, only two speaking English. Amongst them was the Dean, the head of the Church here, under the Bishop of Malines. Much that was interesting passed. The Dean and our aunt seated themselves in a corner of the room, and by degrees the whole party gathered round; the Count and Josiah Forster interpreting by turns. It was a critical thing to know what to say, as the conversation became more and more of a religious nature. She began on the prisons—prevention of crime —how much the upper classes are often the cause, by example, of the sins of the lower; related a few of her prison facts as proofs, and finally ended by saying, ' Will the Dean allow me to speak my mind candidly ?' His permission being given, and that of the Count and Countess, she began by expressing the sincere interest that she felt for the inhabitants of this city, and how much she had been desiring for them, ' that as a people, they might each place less confidence in men and in the forms of religion, and look to Christ with an entire and simple faith.' The priest said nothing ; but turned the subject, and asked what the views of the Quakers were ? upon which Josiah Forster gave them a short account in French, which appeared to interest them all."

Amsterdam, *Third Month*, 14*th*.

My dearest Husband and Children,

I think you have not heard of our departure from Brussels, and of the great kindness of our dear friends, who shed tears at parting. At Antwerp we visited a prison in a deplorable state, where much evil, I fear, is going on ; and two excellent institutions, one for old women, under the care of Sisters of Charity. Their comfort, order, and cleanliness, were great indeed ; and I think I never saw so much appearance of religion in a Roman Catholic institution. One poor old woman took up her rosary, and pointed to the beads that were to be prayers for me after I was gone ; they almost all appeared to be meditating, praying, or working. My dear brother and myself then visited a Refuge for poor girls, in the most beautiful order, kept by ladies (not nuns) who give up their time and fortune to attend to this Christian duty. Such perfect arrangements for moral good, I have seldom, if ever, seen in a Refuge. It is inspected day and night by the ladies. The girls are well employed, and receive some instruction, but, sad to say, the Scriptures forbidden.

Our journey to Rotterdam was over one continued marsh ; the road raised considerably above the level. Rotterdam appears half water and half land ; it has a curious effect. John Mollett met us, a valuable, cheerful and bright old man. On Third-day we visited a large Prison for boys, capitally taught by gentlemen, who daily visit them, and by an excellent school-master. Your dear uncle and I gave them an exhortation, to which they were very attentive.

Mrs. Fry's observations on this prison were as follows :—

It contains about two hundred and forty boys.

The building not suitable.

An excellent school, and good master.

Visited daily by a gentlemen's committee.

Proportion that returns to the prison small.

They appear to be well fed and clothed.

A hammock for each boy, two rows one above another.

No inspection by night, except an officer watching round, and looking through a grating into the lighted rooms.

Divided into three classes.

Three courts for them to walk in.

Good employment when not at lessons.

They do not go to bed until nine o'clock.

Medical attendant and infirmary we thought not very good.

Attended by Protestant and Roman Catholic chaplains.

There was another prison, under the same roof, for women, but solely under the care of men. A considerable number of highly-respectable Dutch gentlemen and ladies came in the evening, and a few English; amongst them a delightful clergyman. We closed our evening much as at Paris, with a short reading.

The next morning Sir Alexander Ferner, our English Minister, visited us. We then went over land and water to a great female prison, about twelve miles from Rotterdam. Such country not only I never saw, but hardly could have imagined; small pieces of land, evidently raised out of a bed of water by the art of man ; a field, perhaps fifteen or twenty yards square with water round it, perhaps four yards wide, and a little further off a body of water quite a large lake on one side, and a river on the other. They have good farm-houses on these pieces of land, and bridges made to turn round ; so they are thrown across the water by day, and turned on to the land by night. I really liked the perfect novelty of the scene. Gouda, the place of our destination, is a curious old Dutch town, with a church of great beauty and celebrity, said to contain the finest painted glass in Europe. We went to the female prison ; there were three hundred prisoners under the care of two women, lately introduced, and five men, and never watched at night by any one.

They are visited by two very interesting ladies, (Madame veuve Van Meerten, and Madlle. H. M. de Graves), and some gentlemen. We were received, by about six gentlemen and these two ladies, with the greatest kindness; coffee ready for us at the prison. Such a curious place I never saw; we had to ascend story upon story, by stairs little better than ladders, and at the very top we found three great rooms in the roof, where the women worked; two were attended by a female officer, the other was without. We spoke to them, which they appeared to feel, their tears running down their faces. It was most evident, through every disadvantage, that great good resulted from the ladies' visits, and their labours had been much blessed. The next morning we went to the Hague, and dined that day at the English Minister's Sir Edward Disbrowe. We became acquainted with a very superior Dutch family, and a good many other persons. We visited a sad prison, in company with several gentlemen, in the morning; and a considerable number came to us in the afternoon, trying to form committees to visit prisons. The Secretary of the Interior came in the morning, and we had a thorough prison conversation with him. In the evening we went to a large religious party, at the house of the French pasteur; here I took a part which appeared to be very well accepted; the pasteur prayed for us. We then drank tea in a very beautiful Dutch house, with a rich, but excellent gentleman, his wife, and some other choice persons. The next morning we set off for this place, visiting the large military prison at Leyden, where we saw the excellent effect of the Scriptures being freely read. Our Sabbath ended highly satisfactorily; we had a very large Dutch company, an English clergyman and Scotch minister; after our reading, and William Allen and myself had spoken, a gentleman got up, and in a powerful, encouraging and beautiful manner, expressed his unity with us, and satisfaction in our visit. He is, they say, a very pious, devoted and learned man, a merchant here. We then ended in prayer.

I am yours, in tender love, and desire that the best of blessings may be with you.

E. F.

Although so many circumstances occurred to encourage her, Mrs. Fry often went heavily on her way, feeling delicate in health, and oppressed in spirit. A letter from Dr. Bosworth, with whom she had become acquainted at Rotterdam, was very consoling to her.

"Before I answer your questions, let me discharge a debt of gratitude, which I and my wife owe to you and your friends, for your benevolent exertions in Rotterdam. You have excited amongst us, and have left, I trust, an abiding Christian affection. We feel we are brethren, unite in the same good cause of our adorable Saviour, that of promoting 'peace on earth, and good-will to men.' How soon will the wood, hay, and stubble of party be burnt up, and what is built on the Rock of Ages remain, &c., &c. We are here in a parched wilderness, but your visit has brought a refreshing dew, and may it abide with us."

To her Youngest Son.

Amsterdam, *Third Month,* 19*th.*

My dearest Harry,

We find this a very interesting place. How amused you would all be at some of our curious Meetings. The other evening we went to drink tea at the house of a converted Jew, where we met numbers of the Pietists; he read the 14th chapter of John in French, I spoke, and gave a little advice on Christian love and unity; then the Jew spoke, and another Jew prayed, and afterwards William Allen. The serious, the sweet, the good, and the ludicrous were curiously mixed up together. Yesterday was very full: first company, breakfast and reading, then preparation for two meetings, one for prisons in the afternoon, and one in the evening for philanthropic objects, &c.; at three o'clock about twenty gentlemen came to discuss with us the state of the prisons of Holland, an excellent meeting. A gentleman named Surengar was present, who has followed us from Rotterdam, and has kindly invited us to his house in the North of Holland. Your uncle is very clever in his speeches, and real knowledge of the subject. I received blessing and thanks from many, far too much ; our visit appears most seasonable here, so much wanting to be done in the prisons, and other things.

Fifth-day morning.—We went to our Friends' Meeting, when we arrived the numbers round the door were so great that we doubted whether we could get in, however, way was soon made for us, and we found a large and highly respectable congregation needing no interpreter. We had certainly a flowing Meeting in every sense, I think the cup flowed over with Christian love. I believe it has been a most unusual thing the way in which hearts have been opened towards us. I then went off to the prison to launch the Committee of Ladies in visiting it, several gentlemen also with me. I had just time to go home, rest and dress, and set off to a dinner at our friend Van der Hope's, where there are the most exquisite paintings by the Dutch masters. I think I never saw any so much to my taste.

I can assure thee, my dearest Harry, when I see how ripe the fields are unto harvest every where, I long and pray that more labourers may be brought into this most interesting, important, and, may I not say, delightful service, but there must be a preparation for it, by yielding to the cross of Christ, and often deep humiliations and much self-abasement are needful, before the Lord makes much use of us, but above all, we must yield ourselves to God, as " those that are alive from the dead ;" He will then fit for His own work in His own way.

Dearest love to all of you,

I am, thy most tenderly attached mother,

ELIZABETH FRY.

Zwolle, *Third Month,* 22nd.

My Dearest husband and Children,

Since I sent my long letter to Harry, we have visited Utrecht. We had invited different persons to the hotel, but as none appeared likely to come, we sat down industriously in our travelling trim to our employments, when to our surprise, gentlemen and ladies began to assemble, and we had quite a large party,

who were so much interested that we agreed fully to open our
doors the next evening to any one who liked to come. We had
indeed a very full day in prospect, and could only look upwards
for help, mentally and bodily. First we visited a Lunatic Asylum, a very interesting and superior one, then we went to Zeist,
a large Moravian settlement, about five miles from Utrecht; here
we remained some hours, and had some weighty business to lay
before the elders; my desire for them is, that they may turn
their powers to more account. In the evening we went to tea
with a lady and found about twenty to meet us. When I followed my brother and Elizabeth to the hotel about eight o'clock,
you may suppose I felt scarcely equal to encounter a party of
eighty-two persons, whom I found assembled in the large room.
My heart was almost ready to sink; however we began by a
capital speech of my brother's on slavery, showing them the
importance of liberating the slaves in their colonies; then John
Mollet spoke in French; afterwards my poor self, first upon
prisons, with all appertaining, then their schools, little or no
Scripture being allowed in the public ones, about this I spoke
most strongly. We ended with Scripture reading and exhortation : there was great attention paid, and much love shown
to us.

      Believe me, your most tenderly attached,

                            E. F.

From Zwolle, the travellers went to Minden, to visit a small
body of Friends resident there, as well as the larger congregation at Pyrmont.

Minden, Third Month, 28*th.*—We left Zwolle on Second-
day, the 23rd, and slept at a true German inn—neither carpet
nor curtain. Our night was disturbed, still we did well. The
next day we set off in good time, and travelled until twelve
o'clock ; we did not settle till two in the morning. I think I
have not yet recovered the fatigue, not having slept well one
night since. We have been interested by the Friends, who are
much like those of Congenies, but more entirely Friends ; we
have visited them in almost all their families, and had two Meetings with them. We have been brought into much sympathy with

them, for they are tried, and I believe a Christian people. We have this evening had three pastors with us, two of them I think spiritual men. Our Meeting was largely attended this afternoon, and I can assure you my heart almost failed me, being interpreted for in German is so difficult, but we have in Auguste Mundhenck, a well educated young Friend, a capital interpreter. The Meeting ended well. In my wakeful nights I feel solitary, and have you very present with me; but I humbly trust He that sleepeth not is watching over you with tender care.

Pyrmont, 29th.—In our way here we visited at Hameln, a large prison, under the King of Hanover, almost all the poor prisoners, upwards of four hundred in number, heavily chained. I told them a little of my deep interest for their present and everlasting welfare; they appeared to feel it very much; one poor man, a tall fine figure, with heavy chains on both legs, sat weeping like a child. I am just come in from visiting the families of Friends; they are really a very valuable set. I longed to take a picture for you of an old Friend with a plain skull-cap, either quilted or knitted, a purple handkerchief, a striped apron, and the whole appearance truly curious; but she was a sweet old woman full of love. I am really amused, the old and young are as fond of me as if I could fully speak to them; the little ones sitting on my lap as if I were their mother, and leaning their little heads upon me. A little child about four or five said, what happy days they should have when we went to see them. We expect a large party this evening.

30th.—We had our party, and understand there were present some of the first persons of the town, besides the master of the hotel, his wife, the doctor, the postmaster, the bookbinder, the shoemaker, &c., &c., &c. ! We discussed the state of their poor, their not visiting them, or attending to them; for it appears that visiting the poor is not thought of here. I hope and expect our coming will be useful in this respect. How curious is the variety we meet with, and the different things there are to occupy our attention !

Hameln—ended Hanover, *Fourth Month*, 2nd.

My Dearest Husband and Children,

Whilst stopping at a small inn, I mean to finish my account of our visit to Pyrmont. After I wrote we went shaking on such bad roads from house to house, to see the Friends, that I almost feared we must break down. We twice dined with them, in their beautiful spot at Friedensthal, (or the valley of peace,) surrounded with hills, and a river flowing through it. Roebucks wild from the woods abounding. We were very pleasantly received. I must describe the dinner. Many Germans were present, young and old, and our English party ; the table was well covered with cakes, and dried and stewed fruits, the produce generally of their grounds. The soup on the table, and one large Westphalia ham. We had veal handed round afterwards in different forms ; and plum-puddings, of course for us, in the middle of dinner. I much liked the true German hospitality, and also seeing the mode of living in the country. Our visits were very satisfactory to these very valuable and agreeable people. Tears and kisses abounded at our departure. I must tell you of an interesting event :—I went to buy something for little John at a shop, where a very agreeable lady spoke to me in English, and I was so much attracted by her, that I requested her to accept a book, and sent a work on the rites and ceremonies of the Jews. I asked her to attend our Meeting on Second-day morning. She proved to be a Jewish lady of some importance ; she came to Meeting with several other Jews, and truly I believe her heart was touched. I invited her to come and see us the next evening, when we expected several persons to join our party. The following day we agreed to form a District Society, to attend to the deplorable state of the poor. The Jewish lady capitally helped us, she then appeared in a feeling state ; but this morning when the ladies met to finish our arrangements, and I felt it my place to give them a little advice, and my blessing in the name of the Lord, the tears poured down her face. I then felt it my absolute duty to take her into my room to give her such books as I thought right, and to tell her how earnest my desires were that she should come to the knowledge of our Saviour. I think in our whole journey no person has appeared to be so affected or so deeply impressed ; may it be lasting, and may she become a Christian indeed !

Your much attached,

E. Fry.

Hildesheim, Fourth Month, 6th.

My much beloved Family,

We left Hanover to-day about five o'clock, after rather a singular visit. We arrived there on Fifth-day evening. On Sixth and Seventh-day our way did not open quite so brightly as some times. We saw a deplorable prison ; poor untried prisoners chained to the ground until they would confess their crimes, whether they had committed them or not, and some other sad evils. Several interesting persons came to see us. Seventh-day evening we spent at a gentleman's house, where we met some very clever and superior persons, and had much important communication upon their prisons, &c., &c. On First-day we had our little Meetings ; such a tide on a Sabbath I think I hardly ever had ; it was like being driven down a mighty stream ; we had allowed persons to come to us, supposing it would be the last day there. I made some calls of Christian love. The principal magistrate came for an hour about the prisons, and very many other persons. In the evening we had also a party of a select nature to our Scripture reading, and after a very solemn time we represented many things wanted in Hanover. I forgot to tell you, amongst other visitors, the Queen's Chamberlain came to say that the Queen wished to see our whole party on Second-day at one o'clock. We had proposed going that morning early, but put it off on this account. I think I never paid a more interesting visit to royalty—my brother Samuel, William Allen, and myself. In the first place we were received with ceremonious respect, shewn through many rooms to a drawing-room, where were the Queen's Chamberlain and three ladies-in-waiting to receive us. They showed us some pictures of the family, until Prince George and his half-sister came in to us ; he appeared much pleased to be with me again. His sister appeared a serious and interesting

young lady. After some little time we were sent for by the
Queen; the King was too ill to see us. She is a stately woman,
tall, large, and rather a fine countenance. We very soon began to
speak of her afflictions, and I gave a little encouragement and
exhortation. She was much affected, and after a little while
requested us to sit down. We had very interesting and important subjects brought forward: the difficulties and temptations
to which rank is subject—the importance of their influence—the
objects incumbent upon them to attend to and help in, Bible
Societies, Prisons, &c. We then read our address to the Queen,
wishing her to patronize ladies visiting the prisons; it contained
serious advice, and our desires for her, the King, and the Prince;
then I gave the Queen several books, which she accepted in the
kindest manner. . . . .

I am indeed,

Your most tenderly attached,

E. F.

At Berlin the travellers found a cordial welcome from all
ranks of persons. A wonderful field of usefulness appeared open,
and many hearts ready to receive them. Much service of various
descriptions awaited them, some of a peculiarly interesting
nature. Her gracious and cordial reception by the Royal
Family was very gratifying to Mrs. Fry, and in the Princess
William, sister to the late King, she found a zealous co-operator
in her labours on behalf of the prisons. This eminent and
truly Christian lady had been as a mother to the younger members of the Royal Family after the death of Queen Louisa, and
in her exalted station she was an example of every good word
and work.

From a letter written by her niece :—

Hotel de Russie, Berlin.

"Our dear aunt's first evening for philanthropic purposes took
place on the 13th. There is a splendid room in the hotel,
capable of containing two hundred persons, where we have our

réunions. At one end is raised a low platform ; on this platform sat my aunt, William Allen, Lucy Bradshaw, papa, and
Professor Tholück (a very noted scholar) as interpreter. A fine
company of the higher classes filled more than half the room.

" It would be impossible to describe the intense interest and
eagerness which prevailed when our aunt rose. Papa having
introduced her to the assembly, she commenced with the deplorable state of the London Prisons when she was young—her
own first entering these horrid abodes—the clamour that was raised
by all parties on her venturing to go in alone and unprotected —
the shocking state of filth and depravity that the prisons were
in, and the violence of the prisoners, the females especially, so
great, that even the turnkeys hardly dare venture amongst them
then; she related the quiet way in which she and her companions were received, their taking clothing for the children, and
the respect with which the prisoners treated them. She went on
to express her own feelings about introducing Christian doctrine
amongst them. ' Could it be possible to touch their hearts by
religious truths ? Shall I venture to read the Holy Scriptures
to them ? What effect will it produce ?'

" The attention of the whole assembly seemed completely
rivetted by her address. Those that could not understand a
word, could at least watch her and listen to her voice. She then
mentioned a few instances of the good that had been effected, and
the changes that had been brought about through the means of
the visiting ladies; such as, commencing public worship amongst
the prisoners, and instituting matrons over them, &c. She
ended with a most earnest and eloquent appeal to all to come
forward in the work, and lend their aid to seek to turn these
poor sinners from the error of their ways, and to take an interest
in their everlasting welfare. William Allen had previously told
them the object of their mission, and a little of what they had
been doing since our arrival in Berlin. Every one wants to
know about our aunt's history. ' Where does she live ?' ' Is
she married ?' And their astonishment is great, when I tell them
of five-and-twenty grandchildren ; this seems to add to the respect paid to her.

" The Princess William has been very desirous to give her

sanction, as far as possible, to the Ladies' Committee for visiting the prisons that my aunt has been forming; and to show her full approbation, had invited the Committee to meet her at her palace. Imagine about twenty ladies assembling here, at our Hotel, at half-past twelve o'clock to-day, beautifully dressed; and further, fancy us all driving off and arriving at the palace. The Princess had also asked some of her friends, so we must have been about forty. Such a party of ladies, and only our friend Count Gröben to interpret. The Princess received us most kindly, and conducting us herself to the top of the room, we talked some time whilst waiting the arrival of other members of the Royal Family. The ladies walking about the suite of rooms and taking chocolate, for about half an hour, waiting for the Crown Princess, who soon arrived. The Princess Charles was also there, and the Crown Prince himself soon afterwards entered; I could not but long for a painter's eye, to have carried away the scene. All of us seated in that beautiful room, our aunt in the middle of the sofa, the Crown Prince and Princess, and the Princess Charles on her right. The Princess William, Princess Marie, and the Princess Czartoryski on the left. Count Gröben sittting near her to interpret, the Countesses Bohlen and Dernath by her, I was sitting by the Countess Schlieffen, a delightful person, who is much interested in all our proceedings. A table was placed before our aunt with pens, ink, and paper, like other Committees, with the various rules that she and I had drawn up, and the Countess Bohlen had translated into German, and which she read to the assembly; our aunt then gave a clever concise account of the Societies in England, commencing every fresh sentence with 'If the Prince and Princesses will permit.' When business was over, my aunt mentioned some texts, which she asked leave to read. A German Bible was handed to Count Gröben, the text in Isaiah having been pointed out, that our good aunt had wished for, 'Is not this the fast that I have chosen,' &c. The Count read it, after which our aunt said, 'Will the Prince and Princesses allow a short time for prayer?' they all bowed assent, and stood, while she knelt down and offered one of her touching, heartfelt prayers for them—that a blessing might rest on the whole place, from the King on his throne to the poor prisoner in the dungeon, and she prayed especially for the Royal Family. Then for the ladies, that the works of their hands might be prospered in what they had undertaken to perform. Many of the ladies now withdrew, and we were soon left with the Royal Family. They all invited us to see them again, before we left Berlin, and took leave of us in the kindest manner."

Amongst other most onerous matters, Mrs. Fry felt it her duty to inquire into the actual state of the Lutheran Church, in the Prussian dominions, and whether it was still exposed to persecution. She found, that although more leniently dealt with than it had been, great oppression existed; confiscation of property and imprisonment being not unfrequently resorted to, to compel submission. Mrs. Fry could not feel justified without endeavouring to bring the subject before the King. Lord William Russell, our Ambassador, her kind and constant friend, and the Baron Humbolt, discouraged her attempting to do so. She had a strong inclination to consult the Crown Prince, when the unexpected meeting at the Princess William's, afforded her the desired opportunity. After earnestly petitioning the best Help, and wisdom from above, she opened the subject. His Royal Highness gave her most attentive hearing, and entirely encouraged her to act as she believed to be right. A petition had been beautifully drawn up by William Allen, this was translated into German, and presented through the official channel to His Majesty. It was no light matter doing this; but in faith she committed it to Him, who had put it so strongly into her heart, to bless the measure. The following day the King's Chaplain was the bearer of the delightful intelligence, that the petition had been graciously received, and that the King had said that 'he thought the Spirit of God must have helped them to express themselves as they had done." She told this gentleman what a subject of prayer it had been with her; to which he rejoined, that, " like Daniel her petition had been answered before she had ceased praying."

To a Daughter.

Leipzig, *Fourth Month*, 30*th*.

My dearest Louisa,

The deeply weighty exercises at Berlin had so much expended all my powers, that I concluded to remain here alone, with my maid and our young friend Beyerhaus, whilst the rest of our little company went to Dresden. I have had a quiet time, and am much refreshed. I enjoy this fine weather. How beautiful is the breaking forth of spring! It is almost hot in the middle of the day, and the country very pleasant.

We have been particularly interested in visiting Luther's abode at Wittemberg, being where he was, and sitting where he sat by his table. Though in an old monastery, he appears to have had very comfortable apartments. We saw a beautiful painted ceiling in his sitting room, though now much defaced. I hope you have all read Merle D'Aubigné's History of the Reformation, we have found it so very interesting, we expect to visit many of the places mentioned in it, and to see the castle in which Luther was confined.

When left alone here I really was amused to find how kind friends gathered round me; one brought me beautiful flowers and oranges, another books, another a very fine print of prisoners in their place of worship. In the morning of Second-day I took a little recreation, accompanied by two gentlemen, and drove about to see this pretty town and environs, the longest excursion for pleasure I have had. I spent the evening at the house of one of these gentlemen where were many to meet me. Two or three spoke English, some French, I am absolutely obliged to communicate my ideas in French, when by myself, and visitors come to see me, who cannot speak English, I manage to hold much communication with them, although no doubt in a very blundering manner. It often surprises me how little real obstruction the want of knowledge of languages has proved to me ; but it makes me long for my children and grandchildren thoroughly to know the modern languages. What should I have done, had not numbers here known English? Indeed, every well-educated person abroad appears instructed in English and French. As to French, our young people ought to know it as well as they do English, for it is a passport everywhere. I hope the greatest pains will be taken with it, with all the grandchildren, both girls and boys. I must now say, in much near and tender love, farewell.

Farewell in the Lord, every one of you,
Your most tenderly attached,
E. F.

Frankfort, Fifth Month, 4th.—I felt very unwell yesterday, and low in spirits. My dearest brother and sweet niece were most kind to me; all that I required I had, so, " the Lord doth provide." I almost dreaded my night; but through tender mercy the Comforter was near to comfort and help my great infirmity, so that I rested in my Lord, and feel revived in body and soul this morning. This text has been present with me, " I am the Lord that healeth thee."—Exodus xv. 26. Such fears presented themselves. How could I get home? How could I bear the sea? should I not be much burdened, not having finished what I thought I ought to do? and so on; but now my most gracious and holy Helper delivers me from my fears. Thanks to His most blessed and holy Name.

At Düsseldorf, Mrs. Fry was able to ascertain many particulars she wished to know, of the Association for the improvement of prisoners in the Prussian Provinces of the Rhine and Westphalia. She found it to be composed of nine connected societies: those of Düsseldorf, Aix-la-Chapelle, Cologne, Cleves, Coblentz, Treves—in the Rhineland; of Münster, and Herford —in Westphalia.

The society of Düsseldorf is the principal or leading society (Haupt-Gesellschaft), the other are of second rank. All these societies are established in places in which there is a larger prison, and the object of their activity, is principally to maintain the order of this prison; the classification of the prisoners; to furnish work; to procure the spiritual assistance of chaplains, and the use of the holy Scriptures and other religious books.

A General Meeting is annually held at Düsseldorf, where matters of common interest are discussed, and the reports of the different societies read. The general report is printed and distributed to the members of the association.

To every one of these nine societies are subjected Auxiliary-societies (Hülfs-vereine) in every place of the country, where a sufficient number of men, who are interested in the subject, are to be found. The care of those Auxiliary-societies is to provide work, and assistance of every kind, for the discharged prisoners of their neighbourhood. The society of the place, in which he has been imprisoned, gives a notice of his dismission to the Auxiliary-society, in whose compass he is likely to reside.

From Düsseldorf the travellers visited the establishment of Kaiserworth under the care of M. Fliedner for training Deaconnesses, to tend and nurse the sick, and to aid their spiritual necessities, whilst providing for their temporal wants. At that time this admirable institution had existed only four years, but its utility was generally acknowledged and information upon the subject earnestly desired. M. Fleidner, in a letter of a very recent date, has kindly furnished his recollections of the visit. He says—

" The 8th of May, 1840, was a great holiday to us; Elizabeth Fry of London visited our institution. Of all my contemporaries none has exercised a like influence on my heart and life : truly her friendship was one of the ' all things,' which God in sovereign mercy has worked for my good. In January, 1824, I had had the privilege of witnessing the effects of Mrs. Fry's wonder-working visits among the miserable prisoners of Newgate. On my return to my father-land, my object was to found a society entitled the ' Rhenish Westphalian Prison Association,' having ramifications in all the provinces of Germany. In this I was greatly assisted by the advice and experience afforded me by this eminent servant of God. During my second stay in England, in 1834, I had the happiness, in common with Dr. Steinkopff, of spending a day with Mrs. Fry, at her own home, and also of accompanying her in one of her visits of mercy to Newgate. By this means, I was enabled to see and admire her, in her domestic as well as public character. Thus may my happiness be estimated, when in 1840, Mrs. Fry, accompanied by her brother John Joseph Gurney, her young niece Eliza- beth Gurney, William Allen and Lucy Bradshaw, came in per- son to see and rejoice over the growing establishment of Kaiser- worth. She saw the whole house, going into every room, and minutely examining each detail, and then delivered to the in- mates a deeply interesting discourse. Many were the tears shed, and I have a bright hope, not in vain. To the ' helping sisters' of the institution she gave much motherly advice, and told the results of her own labours, showing that truly she estimated the great difficulties in educating those aright who are hereafter to have the care of the sick and suffering. It was a particular matter of rejoicing to that dear mother in Christ that so many of those trained at Kaiserworth were earnestly desirous of filling places of trust in other institutions of a simi- lar nature. She examined thoroughly the 'Mutter Haus,' and the wards for the sick, which contained at that time between forty and fifty, and was much interested in the infant school connected with the institution : she assembled the twenty work- ing deaconesses, and those who were undergoing their time of probation also, as well as the twelve young people training up for female teachers in infant schools, and with her accustomed gentle and dignified eloquence, she pointed out to them that alone through earnest love, through faith in Him, who has done all for us, could they find acceptance in these their works of mercy. In particular she urged upon the deaconesses the delicate, responsible and onerous duties of their vocation, and besought them to take for their pattern Jesus Christ, the healer and physician of mankind, in all their treatment of the bodies and souls of the afflicted ones under their care.

After dinner, and a short interval of rest, she permitted us to share with her the rich fruits of her varied experiences, thus giving us counsel and help of the most valuable kind. She examined with me the rules and regulations of the household, with which she expressed herself greatly satisfied. Truly God was in the midst of us, and the remembrance of that spirit of active self-denying love is one of the sweetest consolations which I possess, amid the trials and difficulties which every such institution must afford.

"THOMAS FLIEDNER.

"May 26, 1848."

Düsseldorf, Fifth Month, 10*th.*—Here we are, and thanks to my Heavenly Father I am much revived : my cough better; unfavourable symptoms subsided ; sufficient strength given me for the various duties as they arise. I feel my prospect weighty; first, going to the prison to visit some prisoners whom I did not see yesterday. And then, we expect a large evening party to read the Scriptures and for worship, and this amongst strangers who know little or nothing of us or our ways, and our interpreter not accustomed to us; but our holy Helper can, through His own unmerited mercy and Almighty power, really so help us as to touch the hearts of those who come to us, to their true edification. O gracious Lord ! be with us; help us and bless us. Thy servants have come in much fear, much weakness, and under a belief that it is Thy call, that has brought them here. Now, be Thyself present with us, in this our last occasion of the kind, to our help, consolation, and edification ! I can only cast myself on Thy love, mercy, and pity !

In the afternoon I visited the prison, accompanied by my dear brother, William Allen, and Lucy Bradshaw. We first collected a large number of men in a yard, and I was, in my low state of body, strengthened to speak to them in the open air. Unexpectedly, a valuable man, the Pastor Fliedner, met us, who interpreted beautifully for me. We then visited several wards, and the prisoners appeared to feel a great deal. May its effect long remain. I also visited a very valuable lady, a Roman Catholic, who has visited the prison many years. We

partook of Christian love, and, I believe, of Christian unity.   In
the evening we had a very large party to our reading and worship; I should think nearly a hundred persons.   My Lord and
Master only knows what such occasions are to me, weak in body,
rather low in spirits—amongst perfect strangers to us—not able
to speak to them in their own language.   To whom could I go ?
I could say, "With God all things are possible ;" and so I found
it.   My brother Samuel read the 7th chapter of Matthew.   One
of the pastors read it in German.   I soon spoke, and unexpectedly
had to enlarge much on the present and past state of Germany :
how it was that more fruit had not been produced, considering
the remarkable seed sown in years past; the query, what hindered
its growth ?   I expressed my belief—first, that it arose from a
lukewarm and indifferent spirit ; secondly, from infidel principles
creeping in under a specious form ; thirdly, from too much
superstition yet remaining ; fourthly, and above all, from the
love of the world, and the things of it, beyond the love of Christ.
After showing the evil and its results—the seed obstructed, as
in the parable of the Sower, bringing no fruit to perfection ; I
endeavoured to point to the remedy—to look at home, and not
to judge one another; to ask for help, protection, and direction
to walk in the narrow way ; to be doers and not hearers of the
word; and to devote ourselves to His service, who had done so
much for us. William Allen followed with a satisfactory sermon.
I then prayed very earnestly for them, and afterwards exhorted
on reading the Scriptures, family worship, keeping the Sabbath,
&c., and ended with a blessing—the attention was excessive; the
interpretation excellent, by my dear friend the Pastor Fliedner ;
hearts much melted, and great unity expressed by numbers.   It
was a very solemn seal, set to our labours in this land, and one
not to be forgotten.   So our Lord helped us, and regarded me
His poor servant, in my low estate ; afterwards, peace was in
no common degree my portion.   Blessed be the name of the
Lord. All my dear companions, William Allen, my brother, and
the younger of the party, Lucy Bradshaw and my dear niece,
appeared happy and cheerful. I returned thanks on sitting down
to a refreshing meal, after the labours of the day ; and I think
I may say we ate our " meat with gladness and singleness of
heart."

We had a pleasant journey through Liege to Antwerp, where we were cordially received by some of our dear friends in that place, who appeared to have been deeply impressed by our last visit. We had a solemn time after our reading in the morning, at Ostend, the last reading we had of this kind, in which I very earnestly and fervently prayed for my most tenderly-beloved brother, that the sacrifice he had thus made in his Lord's service, and all he had so liberally done for us, as His servants, might bring blessing to his own soul, and a large portion of the unsearchable riches of Christ. I prayed for his dear daughter, that the experience of this journey might be greatly blessed to her soul. I prayed for William Allen, that now in his latter days, he might more and more be filled with, and spread the glorious truths of the Gospel in their fulness, freeness, and universality. I prayed for Lucy Bradshaw also, and for the servants, that the journey might be blessed to them ; and lastly for my poor unworthy self, that I might be kept by the Lord, humble, faithful, trustful, and more devoted to Him and His service. It was as a spiritual farewell, and break up of this most interesting expedition. Our voyage was calm and beautiful. I return in a delicate state of health, and very weak in spirits, but deeply feeling my Lord's mercies towards me.

In the course of this journey, Mrs. Fry had experienced less difficulty than she anticipated from her entire ignorance of the German language, partly from the assistance of her companions, but even more from the excellent interpretation of like-minded persons, who arose for her help, as she passed on from place to place. She had also been furnished with a document most useful and important to her, by the Chevalier Bunsen, at that time Prussian Minister at Berne. She had requested him to furnish her with letters of introduction to such of his country-women as were likely to interest themselves in the objects of her journey. Instead of this, he proposed to provide her with a printed address to the women of Germany, written as in the name of Elizabeth Fry. He informed their judgments, whilst he enlisted their sympathies on those matters which Mrs. Fry desired so earnestly to recommend to their attention. The pamphlet opens with a sketch of her prison labours, of the success which had attended them, and of the Christian principles from which she derived her strength and power to accomplish the varied and arduous works which she undertook—it touches upon the workings of the Prison Discipline Society ; explains the various measures enacted by the British Government for the improvement of prisons and discipline amongst the prisoners themselves ; alludes to societies formed on the Continent with a similar intention, and afterwards enlarges on the general principles involved. A spirit-stirring appeal to woman on her duties and capabilities, her high and holy mission, and her dependant yet helpful position, follows. But this part of the work, though serving to illustrate the views of the gifted author on so important a subject, scarcely belongs to this memoir. But there are passages which so well describe the results of Mrs. Fry's experience, and present so true a view of the condition of the fallen, and the most likely methods within human reach of again raising them to usefulness and happiness, that the lessons they inculcate ought not to be omitted here.

Chevalier Bunsen, after detailing Mrs. Fry's Experience in Prisons, and the methods she found the most beneficial and satisfactory in her intercourse with their inmates, enlarges on the important subject of their education and training, giving it as his matured opinion, that voluntary and unpaid exertions are essential to success :

" To serve for love and nothing for reward !"

The mere fact of instruction being offered on the free principle of a loving interest in the scholar, prepares him to receive it. Especially is this the case, where the instruction to be received may be deemed in some measure compulsory, as then kindliness and sympathy of feeling, and earnest interest of manner on the part of the teacher, are *essential* to the improvement of the pupil.

In this address Mrs. Fry recommends that reading and writing should be taught, and even if these branches of education are already acquired, that instruction should be continued, especially in the knowledge of the Holy Scriptures : she ever considered moral improvement as the end of all education, and the means to be employed to produce the desired result, to be, not alone an intimate knowledge of the truths of the Bible, but the having those truths so presented as to touch the feelings and win the heart. Whilst, on the one hand, she desired that the attention of the fallen should be called to the infinite mercy of God, in Christ Jesus, the fulness of that mercy, the freedom of that grace ; she aimed carefully at avoiding the danger of representing sin as other than exceeding sinful and offensive to a just and holy God, who is of " purer eyes than to behold iniquity." That they need never despair, but that they must never presume. Not alone that sinful habits, but the love of sin, the taste for past scenes of guilt and depravity must be eradicated before repentance could be considered sincere. It is not enough for sin to be dreaded for its consequences, it must be hated as offensive to a loving Father. Thus did she desire to have them instructed. Elizabeth Fry could almost invariably trace the first impressions made upon prisoners to some expression of warning, reproof, or invitation spoken by the Saviour, some appeal to their fears, to their hopes, or some word of divine compassion, as an arrow winged by love, which had reached the captive's heart. Besides the Gospels, she recommended the Psalms, and selections from the Epistles, such parts especially as bring before the mind the holiness and justice of God, in combination with the blessed doctrine of man's redemption, through the death of Christ. She recommended also simple exhortations and short admonitions, judiciously and not too frequently offered. Urgently did she press the importance of the deportment of ladies visiting prisons and other institutions, where they come in contact with suffering and sin. M. Bunsen has well described her own appearance and effect, in depicting that which she recommended to others—a quiet dignity, avoiding the slightest appearance of anger or impatience, a look more in sorrow than in wrath. When reproof was required, Elizabeth Fry counselled its being always administered in private ; she recommended the circumstance, whatever it might be, being clearly stated, tenderly urged home to the conscience, but no allusion made that could bring recollections of former vices or mode of life. She found such recitals an invariable temptation to falsehood, which was rarely entirely resisted, and even in cases where the prisoners did apparently tell the whole truth, the effect upon their minds of recurrence to scenes of unhallowed and desecrating tendency, always deteriorating ; recurring to past acts of wickedness, often awakes a sleeping fire, and disturbs the quietness and peace of the soul. Committing portions of Scripture to memory, she considered as highly advantageous, instructive and occupying, and in cases of sickness or solitude an invaluable resource. Hymns also she liked them to learn by heart. As the character and knowledge of the prisoner advanced, she approved placing in their hands suitable works of biography, or anecdotes illustrative of the power and efficacy of religion.

Whilst Elizabeth Fry appreciated to the full all that government can effect in the erection and regulation of prisons she considered that little would be accomplished unless those set in authority were actuated by a lively sense of duty and responsibility. Daily witnessing the wickedness, obduracy, and misery of the human heart, must act as a depressing weight upon the spirits, even where the desire to serve is strong and sincere. To find persons suited for the onerous post of controlling, directing, and influencing prisoners, appeared to her as difficult as important,—nor did she believe full perseverance in these heavy duties to be possible without the support and stimulus of unpaid superintendence and participation. She knew that strict discipline and constant occupation are essential to prevent the contamination of evil ; but to soften the hardened heart, to bring the sinner to acknowledge his desert of punishment, and the use and necessity of discipline, something more is required.

To accomplish this, the spirit of love must so impregnate all the regulations, so manifest itself in every arrangement, and be so avowedly the guide of all persons connected with the prisoners, whether officially or as visitors, that they cannot fail to recognize the source in the streams which flow from it, and learn from the daily conduct and habitual temper of His followlowers, that their heavenly Father's name is Love. Elizabeth Fry was not unmindful of the part allotted to the Church, or the importance of the influence and superintendence of ministers of religion, but after government had done its best, after the Church had furnished her instructions and consolations, she still considered that a sphere of most important usefulness remained unoccupied, especially with prisoners of her own sex. Woman has a voice for woman, to which she only can respond. Strongly did she desire to urge this upon the women of Germany, and persuasive is the language in which M. Bunsen clothes her desires, enlarges upon them, and presses them upon the attention of his countrywomen. Emphatically does he use those words of lofty and solemn import which the last great day shall echo in the ears of every immortal soul—either " I

was sick and in prison and ye came unto me ;" or " I was sick
and in prison, and ye came *not* unto me." He urges that it
is not to the prison officer or the salaried chaplain that the
query is confined, but that it is spoken for all, an inquiry to
be answered by all !

In another part of the address, M. Bunsen shows that ignorance can no longer be pleaded as to the misery, the corruption,
and the vice existing in prisons. The " wall has fallen" which
concealed the hidden wretchedness, the secrets of the prison
house. Light has penetrated, and enough has been done to
prove how much may be accomplished were efforts made
more generally, more perseveringly to enlighten the darkness,
to instruct the ignorance, and soften the hearts of their unhappy indwellers.

The address was widely and beneficially circulated by Elizabeth Fry, both during this and her next journey.

Upton 19*th.*—I attended the first Select Meeting yesterday.
My lot was to sit in silence. I saw many 'much loved by me.
May my most gracious Lord help me by His own Spirit this
Yearly Meeting fully, simply, and clearly to lay what I think
and feel before this people ; that which is right for the aged, and
more experienced before them, and that which is for the youth
before them. Gracious Lord, help me to do it in faithfulness, in
love, in truth, in deep humility and godly sincerity. Amen.
We have had altogether a favourable reply to our letter from the
King of Prussia ; he justifies the measures pursued towards the
Lutherans, but I believe our address will not be in vain. We
have had satisfactory reports, of the Government already acting
on our suggestions respecting the prisons in Prussia. The
prisoners are to have more religious instruction, and more inspection. I have had also a very interesting letter from the
Queen of Denmark, expressing real regret at our not going
there, and not only great desire to see me there, but much unity
with my views on many subjects.

There certainly is the most extraordinary opening in the hearts of those in authority on the Continent, to receive me. I felt much drawn to go to Denmark, but the way did not open for it; if I am called still to go, may my Lord make my way plain before me, though I do not see it now. My present position is this—I consider my health has been almost in a precarious state for many months; I have not recovered my usual strength, and there is a feeling of delicacy throughout, I do not think that I am nervous, but my spirits are low, I am, however, so much revived and strengthened by generous living and a little care and quietness, that I rather look to a general revival of health. On the other hand, I query whether a step downwards is not taken, that I shall never fully recover—at all events, I have been poorly enough to have the end of life brought closely before me, and to stimulate me in faith to do *quickly* what my Lord may require of me; but above all, it leads me to desire to cast myself more entirely on the fulness of His love, mercy, and pity, and to entreat his care over me, not permitting more to be brought upon me than my extremely weak and infirm nature can bear, and that He will undertake for me at the last, and through the freeness of His grace, and the fulness of the merits of His dear Son, grant me a place within the gates of His city. I long, before I go hence, to have a clearer and more certain view of the Heavenly inheritance.

25th.—Before breakfast—I am in a strait. O, my gracious Lord! be Thou my Helper, my Guide, my Counsellor, and my Defence, keep me, I pray Thee, from the most weighty service before me, unless it be really and truly Thy call, and if it be Thy call, fit me for it by Thine own Spirit, and Thine own power, and touch my lips, as with a live coal from Thine altar, that I may be qualified to speak the word in season to those who need it. Anoint Thou the tongue to speak, and the ear to hear. Grant this prayer for Thine own sake.

Fifth-day, morning, 28th.—The Yearly Meeting has cordially united in William Allen and myself having a Meeting for the young people. It is appointed for this evening, which I much regret, as my children cannot attend it, but I must commit all to my Lord.

I received this morning a most encouraging letter from the
Crown Prince of Prussia, expressing great kindness and unity,
his belief that a blessing had rested on our visit to Berlin, and
requesting us to go again; it contains an affecting account of
the King's health.

In great weakness, in much lowness, and under some real discouragement, and yet not without a sweet hope and feeling of
Thy love, most gracious God, and even Thy peace. I do ask
help of Thee this day, that through Thine own power, and Thine
own Spirit, Thou wouldest help me so to speak the truths of the
everlasting Gospel, that sinners may be induced to turn from
their evil way, the wavering may be confirmed to give up all for
Thy Name's sake, the mourners may be comforted, and the
weak strengthened. Take from me the fear of man, and help
me to do all singly and simply to Thy glory, and for the good
of others, for Thine own Name's sake answer this petition.
Amen, and Amen.

First-day, Sixth Month, 14th.—The King of Prussia died
this month, and his son the Crown Prince, our dear and valued
friend in the Lord, has succeeded him.

Our young Queen and Prince Albert were shot at, a few days
ago, by a man with two pistols; but we may thankfully say not
injured.

I desire to commend those in authority, gracious Lord, to Thy
most Holy keeping. Be Thyself their Helper, in their very
difficult and dangerous circumstances, and grant them wisdom
and sound discretion, to reign over the people with equity, with
judgment, and with mercy.

21st.—Our British Society Meeting was, I think, well got
through, our reports, &c., &c., occupied so much time, that I could
not properly say all that I wished to say; but I trust that the
short account I gave of our journey was satisfactory. I pressed a
few points about prisoners, also on having Patronage Societies for
discharged prisoners, and Sisters of Charity. I enlarged a little
on the great good the Bible Society had effected in Europe, and
the sweetness of Christian unity, as we had been enabled to maintain it in the British Society, and how I desired that the Lord
Himself might preserve this unity, for with advancing years

and increase of experience, I more and more feel myself a member of the Church Universal, and am less disposed than ever to any sectarian spirit.

28th, First-day.—Since I last wrote I have called upon the Duchess of Beaufort, and the Duchess of Sutherland. The Duchess of Beaufort received me with much true Christian friendship; the Duchess of Sutherland, in a remarkably kind manner: soon after I entered the room, the Duke and his daughters came in. We had much interesting religious conversation. I felt the spirit of Christian love and prayer arise in my heart for them, that the blessing of God might rest upon them, that as He had given them so liberally of the fatness of the earth, He would also cause the dew of Heaven to descend upon them. The next day, I wrote to ask the Duchess whether she wished to attend a Meeting, on account of the Anti-Slavery Society, at Exeter Hall, as I fancied she might like it, I had a cordial answer, saying that she would go. We sat near the Duke of Sussex and the French Ambassador. To find my poor unworthy self thus placed in the face of this immense assembly (I think three thousand persons) was rather fearful, and yet very interesting, from the cause we were engaged in, the numbers interested in it and the honour of appearing on the side of the afflicted slaves.

On the following, Mrs. Fry encountered one of those days, of extreme fatigue and overwhelming interest, which unquestionably were sapping the springs of life. The morning began with a meeting of Friends in London; afterwards she waited upon the Duchess of Gloucester, had a short interview with the Duke of Sussex; and returned to Upton to meet, at Ham House, the residence of her brother Samuel Gurney, the American Delegates, who had come to England on the subject of slavery. She describes her drive from London, with the Duchess of Sutherland, and Lord Morpeth " as pleasant and interesting."

We had much conversation on deeply important subjects, I endeavoured to show them the blessedness of the Lord's service, and its excellence ; and the beauty of the work of grace in the heart, how it strengthened, regulated, and gave power to enjoy the blessings of this life.

Upton Lane, Seventh Month, 7th.—We had the French Ambassador, and a large party to dinner here yesterday, these occasions are serious to me. The query comes home, how far the expensive dinner is right to give, and further, whether good results from it, and whether, if death was approaching, we should thus spend our time ; on the other hand, after the extraordinary kindness shown us in France, and even by the French Government, some mark of attention was due from us. Also, to show hospitality to strangers is right and Christian, and in some measure to receive them as they are accustomed to live, does not appear wrong. My fear is, that the time was not turned to account, by the most important subjects being enough brought forward, I tried to do a little in this way, but I fear not enough. May my Lord keep us from in any way lowering the cause we love, may He help us by His grace more continually to exalt it, and may neither our omissions or commissions injure it. Grant gracious Lord that this may be the case.

15th.—I am just come from, what we believe to be, the deathbed of my dear cousin Agatha C——, and a very remarkable scene it is. After a long illness of much suffering, and the birth of a child a few days ago, and after much deep conflict of spirit, and humiliation of heart, she appears, through grace, to have experienced entire pardon and reconciliation with God, which she has most clearly expressed ; besides, in the most remarkable manner, having exhorted her husband and children to serve the Lord with purpose of heart. She says, the world is a cruel, hard master, but the Lord our God is a most merciful Master, it appears as if spiritual things were in a very remarkable and powerful degree opened to her view. She wished once more to see W. Wigram the clergyman and me, but she added " I have ceased from man." When I went to her she said " I am washed." I replied, in the blood of the everlasting covenant. "I see my Saviour, and wish always to look to Jesus." I said, I believed I might say, thine eye will see the King in His beauty, and behold the land that is very far off ; she replied, " Yes, I shall see the golden streets and the pearl gates of the city." I said, eye hath not seen nor ear heard, what the Lord hath prepared for those that love Him; she replied, " God is love." I said, I believed that through mercy, the blessing of the Lord rested on her, and would rest on those nearest to her; she added, " if they cleave to Him, and entirely serve Him without compromise."

First-day, 19th.—My attention much occupied by poor dear Agatha, and all nearest to her. To have extreme illness, suffering and death, brought so closely home, touches me and makes me feel my weakness on these points.

I also spent part of the afternoon with dear Sarah Sheppard, reading the Scriptures with her and her sisters, desiring, in her suffering state, to lead her to look to the Saviour simply and unreservedly; so that my day was nearly devoted to the sorrowful, at the same time that I felt myself encompassed with infirmity.

26th.—I paid a very interesting visit to Lady Granville, and found the Duchess of Beaufort with her, that dear devoted spiritually-minded lady.

Eighth Month, 6th.—There has been some fear of a war with France, which has been really sorrowful to me; I could have wept at the thoughts, so dear are the people of that country to my heart, and so awful is it to think of the horrors of war, whichever way we look at the subject, religiously, morally or physically. The longer I live, and the greater my experience of life, the more decided are my objections to war, as wholly inconsistent with the Christian calling. O may the Almighty grant, that through His Omnipotence and unutterable love and mercy in Christ our Saviour, the day may not be very far distant, when the people shall learn war no more,—when peace and righteousness shall reign in the earth.

16th, First-day, morning.—After being unwell for some days, I set off with my dearest husband and Harry for Sea View, a lovely little spot on the Isle of Wight, where Foster, Chenda, and their children are staying. We met with the kindest, and warmest reception, and were, I may truly say, cherished and comforted by them. How the tide turns; my dearest children, for whom I have felt so deeply, are in their turns becoming my helpers and comforters,—thanks be to my Heavenly

Father. The place beautiful—the sea air very refreshing, and I almost like another person. On First-day morning we had a very solemn Meeting together; and in the evening, a large number came to our reading, the gentry, sailors, &c. One day I visited Parkhurst, an interesting new prison for boys, which gave me much satisfaction. It was curious to see some of the very things that in early life I in part begun, carried out in practice. I have lived to see much more than I expected of real improvement in prisons. We are expecting our dearest brother Joseph home this week from America, and I mean to accompany him into Norfolk, if it be my Lord's will. May a blessing rest upon his return! I am increasingly of opinion, that these long separations are liable to serious objections; I think, where it is clear that the great Head of the Church calls any of us far off for a long time, it is most important to have those nearest to us, join us for part of the time, and I believe it would be according to the will of our God.

Earlham, 21st.—My dearest brother Joseph is safely returned home, after his absence of three years, on his religious visit to America and the West India Islands. I think I never saw any person in so perfectly peaceful a state ; he says, unalloyed peace, like a sky without a cloud, and above all, enabled thankfully to enjoy his many blessings. He arrived at Liverpool on the 16th, and I first met him at my son Gurney's, as he called there for me. We all went together to Upton, after our visit to Gurney and Sophia, and a delightful time we had together. The next morning our dearest brother Joseph returned God thanks for his unspeakable mercies ; his many deliverances, his great preservations spiritually and temporally, his labours of Christian love being blessed and prospered, and many fruits of it seen. He then returned thanks for my brother Samuel and his family, and earnestly prayed for them, that the windows of heaven might be opened, and blessings be poured forth upon them; he also returned thanks for our brother Fowell, and for his having been prospered in his work of Christian charity for the poor slaves, then for me, and for the blessing attending on me and mine ; and lastly, for his own children, wholly giving them up to the Lord and to His service. After dinner the same day, he made a beautiful and striking acknowledgment of the mercies shown him ; and what delighted me, he appeared to stand fast in true gospel liberty, and to feel true unity of spirit with all that love the Lord Jesus in sincerity. I also returned thanks for these innumerable mercies. We left home the next morning, and I had a very interesting journey here with dearest Joseph, Fowell and Hannah; but I was fatigued.

Twelfth Month, 31*st.*—I deeply feel coming to the close of this year, rather unusually so, it finds me in a low estate, and from circumstances, my spirit is rather overwhelmed, although I am sensible that blessings abound through unmerited mercy. I think the prison cause at home and abroad much prospering, many happy results from our foreign expedition, and much doing at home. Among other things, the establishment of a Patronage Society for prisoners, by which many poor wanderers appear to be helped and protected, and a Society for Sisters of Charity to visit and attend the sick. I have had much to do with those in authority, in other countries and our own; and have been treated with great kindness and respect by them.

I have been really interested for our Queen in her marriage with Prince Albert, and lately in her confinement with a little girl.

Mrs. Fry's habitual acquaintance with the chamber of sickness, and with scenes of suffering and death, had taught her the necessity that exists for a class of women to attend upon such, altogether different and superior to the hireling nurses that are generally to be obtained. Her communications with M. Fliedner, and all she learned from him personally, and by letter, of his establishment at Kaisersewerth, and above all her own visit to that remarkable institution, stimulated her desire to attempt something of the kind in England. Her own occupations being too urgent and numerous to allow of much personal attention, the plan was undertaken, and on a small scale carried into effect by her sister, Mrs. Samuel Gurney, with the assistance of her daughters, and some other ladies. The

Queen Dowager kindly granted her name as Patroness. With Lady Inglis as President, and an effective Committee to conduct the management of the institution, it has steadily advanced and prospered. The plan of proceeding is this : suitable women are selected with great care, and their characters minutely inquired into. They are regularly trained for a certain time in one of the public hospitals, in order to prepare them for their important duties. At the expiration of this period of probation, if their conduct and qualifications be found satisfactory, they are received as sisters. They are allowed an annual stipend of £20, (which is raised to £23 after three years' service,) supplied with an appropriate dress, and maintained in a home provided for them during the intervals of their engagements.

There are at the present time twenty-six sisters belonging to the institution, but the demands for their assistance are so numerous and pressing, that it is highly desirable this number should be gradually increased by the addition of women of decided piety, whose bodily and mental powers are such as to qualify them for the undertaking.

The income of the Institution for 1847, was between nine hundred and one thousand pounds. There is also a small distinct fund under the name of the " Superannuated Fund," for the assistance of such of the sisters as may after long and faithful services be disqualified for labour.

By the rules of the institution, Christian women of various denominations are admitted to join its ranks. No direct system of religious instruction is pursued, although the Sisters are required to attend family and public worship regularly when in the house. They are encouraged to read the Scriptures to their patients, and to endeavour to promote their spiritual welfare, as well as to labour for their bodily comfort, and there have been instances in which their efforts have appeared blessed to

the souls of those under their charge. Whilst at the Home
the sisters visit and nurse the sick poor in its neighbourhood.
But there is another class of persons to whom their services
are invaluable, persons of comparative refinement, but who are
in circumstances of great limitation, perhaps wholly dependent on their own exertions for support. To such as these
the boon is great indeed, of a careful, experienced conscientious
nurse ; not one who squanders the little substance of the sufferer,
not one who watches harpy-like for perquisites and profit, nor
" snores the sick man dead," but carefully and with fidelity
discharges her onerous duties. In cases of this kind a large
proportion of their time is occupied often entirely gratuitously,
at other times, on terms proportioned to the means of the
patient, but which are very far from repaying the institution.
The lowest sum which is considered to cover its current expenses is £1 1s. a-week, but when circumstances claim a
pecuniary sacrifice, the Committee on their part are ready to
make arrangements accordingly, as well as to render assistance
entirely gratuitous, in cases of great necessity.

The sisters are not permitted to receive mourning or presents
directly or indirectly, from the patients or the families on whom
they attend. The funds of the Society depend partly upon
subscriptions, and partly upon the liberality of those who have
benefited from the institution.* The help of the nursing
Sisters has been sought and greatly valued, by persons of all
classes, from royalty to the poorest and most destitute.

Mrs. Fry could imagine a still higher calling ; one of a more
spiritual nature, in which love to souls should be the leading,
compassion to the suffering body the secondary motive for action.
Perhaps the nearest thing in England, to that which she would
have desired to see, is to be found in the German Hospital,

* Institution of Nursing Sisters, No. 16, Broad Street Buildings,
Bishopsgate Street.

established at Dalston, where Deaconnesses from Kaiserswerth perform their arduous duties in a spirit of meekness, perseverance, and love, that ensures, not only the tender and judicious care of the patient, but has been marvellously blessed, in leading many to the Fountain opened for sin and uncleanness.

Earlham, First Month, 3rd, 1841.— I found my spirits much overwhelmed yesterday, by a very serious account from Champion Streatfeild, of an accident that they had met with in the Mediterranean, by a vessel striking against their steamer, but in mercy they were saved by the hand of the Lord (we may say) though in the greatest danger. From the ship that ran against them, a man fell into their vessel; and as he came direct from Constantinople, they became, in the eye of law, infected, and were therefore obliged to perform quarantine for weeks, in a small dirty steam-vessel, in the harbour of Civita Vecchia. Hannah being so extremely tried by the sea, I consider it an affliction; and yet so far greater an one has been averted, that I have only cause humbly and reverently to return thanks to Him, who has answered my prayers for them, that they might be kept safely in the hour of danger. Twice they have thus been exposed in steam-packets already; once in going to Havre, and now again.

Second Month, 21*st., First-day.*—Our dearest son Joseph had been poorly a few days with influenza, and on Third-day last, Alice sent for me, saying he was very unwell. I walked over with little delay, and found him, I thought, really ill. We sent for Dr. Elliot, who said his lungs were highly inflamed, and evidently blood constantly flowing or oozing from some vessels. Our eyes were suddenly opened to see this most tenderly beloved one in a state of real danger. My heart almost sunk within me, and with the exception of leaving him for a few hours to see the Queen Dowager, an appointment which I did not think it right to break, I have been constantly nursing him since, except sitting up with him at night. He has, at times, suffered a good deal; at others, not so much as might be expected. I have felt deep anxiety, but generally a quiet and hopeful spirit has been my portion. His dearest wife has been greatly afflicted, and latterly much overcome, but the evident amendment of yesterday and to-day has comforted us much. It has closely brought home to the heart, the need of knowing Christ to be our Refuge, our Help and our Salvation ; it will not do to wait until the day of sickness comes upon us, when perhaps, the least excitement might cause danger and death, when the most solemn truths are felt, but must not be spoken ; when subjects of the deepest interest ought not be named in the sick room, and often, if they are, the mind is not in a state to receive them.

Third Month, 12*th.*—A few days ago, I went to meet the gentlemen going to Africa in the Niger expedition. Several naval officers, Sir Edward Parry, Captain Trotter, Captain William B. Allen, Sir Robert Inglis, Sir Thomas Acland and many others. After our luncheon, my dear brother Buxton asked me, if I wished for a pause, when almost without my consent, there was silence. I had not a word on my mind before, although deeply concerned for them. I however felt then enabled, to recommend all to keep a very single eye to their Lord ; not to depend on the arm of flesh, but continually to look upwards ; not to be discouraged at any difficulties or opposition, for I had found it good to meet with these things, because they led us more constantly to Christ, as our Help, our Refuge and our Guide. There was a very solemn feeling over us, and I think, much unity of spirit felt. They wish me to go to see their ships, and meet the officers and men to have some religious time with them, previous to their departure for Africa.

28*th, First-day.*—This has been a very important week, and very exercising in part. In the first instance, our dearest Louisa was taken very ill last First-day afternoon, not having been confined a week. I went to her after going to Tottenham Meeting, and I was very weightily engaged in ministry and prayer there ; and the same in our Afternoon Meeting, so that, in addition to my anxiety and fatigue with our dearest Louisa, I felt really overdone. The next day, I closely nursed her until the evening, when I went to Ham House to meet again most of the naval officers going out on the African expedition, to endeavour to suppress slavery and promote free trade and missionary labours in that land. There were many naval captains, and a considerable

7

number of other interesting persons. I should think, sixty or seventy. I felt it laid upon me to have a religious time with them, and spoke to them and prayed for them—to me a very deeply humbling service, much, very much in the cross; but my Lord helped me. I have to-day a very weighty prospect of duty, to go to the ships to see those who were not with us the other evening, and some who were. May my Lord be very near to me, fitting me for His own service, out of weakness making me strong. May He freely pour forth His own holy anointing upon me, and be unto me Himself wisdom, that His own praise may be really shown forth, and the people edified, comforted and helped, before they leave for their great undertaking.

Upton, Fourth Month, 4th, First-day.—On the afternoon of last First-day, we went to the ship Wilberforce, my dear brother Buxton, my brother Gurney, and several of our young people. We found our valuable friend Captain Cook, and his wife there, Captain Bird Allen and many other officers, also the chaplain going out with them. After a while, we all met together in a great hulk, as there was not suitable room in the ship. First, a considerable portion of the Church Service was read. Then Captain B. Allen opened the way for any present to speak;— my brother Buxton rose and addressed all present, officers and crew. Further, he said, on behalf of any there of the Society of Friends, he wished all to know that they did not come prepared, but entirely trusted to the teachings of the Holy Spirit, and how earnestly he desired, that on that occasion the Holy Spirit might be poured forth upon some present, and help them to speak. He said to those going the expedition, how he prayed for them, and should pray for them day and night, that their Lord might be with them, keep them and bless them, (or to that effect) ; we then sat in silence awhile, then I arose and ministered. I think the first text I had to speak was, " Put on as the elect of God, holy and beloved, bowels of mercies, kindness, humbleness of mind, meekness, long suffering." I had to show the wonderful power and efficacy of the influence of a true Christian spirit, and however humble a situation any might fill, they would be preachers of righteousness if they were thus governed by the spirit of Christ. I showed them how our Lord

8

made use of humble instruments, such as the poor fishermen ; then I endeavoured to encourage the most peaceable conduct towards the heathen. I had some advice for the officers, and afterwards knelt down, and had a very solemn time in prayer. My brother Samuel spoke very acceptably, and then gave them all a text-book, and we parted in love. Captain Bird Allen accompanied us to the convict ship, where we found the poor women on deck singing hymns. I spoke to them as a fare-well exhortation. I had been with them some time the day before, several of the poor women have become delirious, from the excitement of the change from separate confinement to the bustle of the ship. This must lead me to make further and stronger efforts for an entire change of the system adopted with them.

Mrs. Fry's dread of the solitary system was only augmented by further knowledge of its consequences. As permanent and a punishment for life, she considered it was too cruel to con-template, even for the most heinous crimes. As a preparation for returning into society, she could only suppose it desirable for very limited periods to be followed by greater enlargement, and gradually extended intercourse with their fellows. The eye after being accustomed to total darkness is not more fitted for a burst of light, than, in her opinion, was the inmate of the solitary cell to be again exposed to temptation and unrestricted intercourse with his fellow-men.

Nor was the silent system, when carried to an extreme, approved much, if at all more by Mrs. Fry, than the solitary or separate one—though her objections to it were on different grounds. She knew, that it was not liable to the same abuses, from neglect or cruelty, but she considered it little likely to benefit the criminal, and particularly adapted to harden the heart. Who that has reflected much, or marked the workings of the mind of man, has not found that without word or action, a spirit may pervade any collection of persons, either of resistance, op-position and defiance, or of comparative kindliness and subordination. No delusion did she consider greater, than that man can be treated as a machine, and remodelled, through having his conduct bent to obedience by strong coercion and dread of punishment. To benefit a sentient being, his sympathies must be as much as possible enlisted on the right side, the spirit of opposition never needlessly excited, nor his displeasure roused against the circumstances he is under, and the authorities over him. Perhaps no scheme could be contrived by the ingenuity of man, more likely to petrify the little remaining softness of the heart, or aggravate his already rebellious passions, than to consign an individual to the companionship of others similarly circumstanced, submitting to in act, but resisting in spirit, the influences they are under. He and they may be so placed, as habitually, not even to see one another. But who will believe, that there are not moments and opportunities, when the evil glance can pass from man to man? When the concentrated malice that burns within, will show itself in the countenance? When the mighty power of the human eye can convey meaning, or circulate a watchword of mental resistance, without a sound escaping the lips? Men are not likely to abhor evil from being driven to abhor the *method* by which it is purposed to bring them to good. The more hateful the restraints of virtue in the aggregate become to any one, and the stronger his dislike of the authorities by which they are enforced, the more ready is he for the commission of fresh crime; for no mere dread of punishment, because a little more or less severe, or under somewhat different modifications, in the hour of reckless temptation will deter from guilt. To induce an inclination to do better, something of a taste for better things, a glimmering of light shed on the darkness of former depravity, were in Mrs. Fry's estimation the great objects to be obtained. As a loving parent mixes tenderness with unflinching and even stern severity, so would she have had the State, the " Powers that be," deal with the offender as,

"A father, whose authority in show
 When most severe, and mustering all its force,
 Is but the graver countenance of love."

With these views, she could not fail as occasion presented itself, to urge her opinions upon others, and deprecate the attempt at enforcing absolute silence amongst prisoners—for though she approved of only partial and guarded intercourse, varying with their guilt and character, and in no case without the presence and oversight of the officers of the prison ; the endeavour absolutely to close all avenues of communication where personal contact remained, was in her estimation, in its practical working as delusive, as the system in itself was harsh and untenable.

Upton, Fifth Month, 23rd, First-day.—The last week has been a serious one, attendance of the Yearly Meeting difficult, from Louisa's serious illness and other causes.

25th.—Yesterday, I accompanied Hannah Backhouse into the Men's Meeting. When she had spoken, I rose, saying, that I feared to make any addition, but that I had a few hints to offer. After expressing my earnest desire that they might all be washed and sanctified, and justified in the name of the Lord Jesus, and by the Spirit of our God, I began with my hints. I said my views of the state of the Society were not so discouraging as those of many others. I remembered, that our first Friends were gathered out of various religious denominations, and from the most spiritual of these, therefore they were a spiritual and seeking people; but in our day, most were Friends from birth and education, and not conviction, though I believed there were really spiritual ones amongst us ; but I saw much wanting, arising partly from these causes, first, the tendency to be a formal people, resting in a high spiritual profession, like the foolish virgins with lamps but no oil in them, this did much harm. Then I feared, being so much a commercial people, that there were too many who bowed to the idols of gold and of silver, and this hindered their serving only the living God ; but above all, I apprehended that too many grieved, quenched and resisted the Holy Spirit of

God, and this was most injurious to us. I feared an unwillingness to be taught the first simple lessons of the Spirit, because
humbling to the human heart, and that this hindered arriving
at greater knowledge. I thought our deficiencies in faith and
practice much to arise from this quenching the Holy Spirit. I
believed if there was more faithfulness at all times and in all
places—in the Market place—in the Counting-house—they would
be preachers of righteousness, and there would be judges raised
up as at the first, and counsellors as at the beginning, that we
should as a people, arise, shine and show that the glory of the
Lord had risen upon us, and that we should uphold our important
testimonies in the spirit of wisdom and meekness. I also showed
those who were young, how gently our Lord dealt with us, how
He fitted us for His own work, how He gave us, not the spirit of
fear, but of love and of power and of a sound mind. I also
expressed my desire for all those engaged in the discipline, that
their spirits might be covered with charity, that they might
seek to restore the offender, remembering themselves, lest they
should also be tempted, and that they might be enabled to
strengthen the things that remain that were ready to die. I
concluded by expressing my desire, that all might fill their
places in the militant Church on earth, and eventually join the
Church triumphant in Heaven in never-ending rest, peace, joy
and glory.

To the daughter who was so ill, whom she was sedulously
nursing, in a moment of agitation and distress, she administered
a lotion by mistake for a draught, which was likely to be seriously injurious, unless the measures resorted to proved entirely
successful.

Upton, Fifth Month, 30*th.*—In the very depths of affliction.
O Lord! I apply unto Thee, in faith, for help. Leave me not,
nor forsake me in this awful time, and enable me to thank Thee
for the mitigations permitted. Our dearest Louisa being again
extremely ill, I in my hurry gave her a wrong medicine of a
poisonous nature—my fright at first was inexpressible. We sent
for the Doctor. who gave an emetic. It was thought that she
did not suffer materially from it, but in addition to her other sufferings and afflicted state, it was bitter to me, almost past ex-

pression; but I sought to endure as seeing Him who is invisible. The conflict of my mind is great indeed; not I think so much in giving up this beloved one, if the Lord saw meet to take her to Himself into His kingdom, though it would be very hard to part, as I have perhaps too much encouraged her with the expectation of recovery. Still she has had a long time of preparation; for many months past, she has, I know, doubted her living, and I do believe that a very precious work of grace has been going on in her heart, and that through infinite wisdom, mercy, and love, that she has, through a Saviour's blood, obtained pardon and reconciliation with God.

Permit me, gracious Lord! in this deep emergency, to entreat Thee to save my beloved child, with an everlasting salvation, and if it be Thy blessed will, grant her a little revival, that I may never have the weight of believing that her end was accelerated by my carelessness. Be very near to her, granting her Thy peace, and the joy of Thy salvation, and be very near to help her beloved husband, whose tender care over her is wonderful. Keep also, merciful Lord! Thy poor servant, from losing her faith or her power of mind in this close trial of faith and patience.

Near one o'clock.—Our sweet Louisa revived wonderfully out of a sleep, that looked almost death-like, and she has been quite lively ever since.

Sixth Month, 5th.—Our dearest Louisa decidedly mending, her state of mind highly favoured, so entirely resigned to her Lord's will. My spirits also are revived, and my bodily health much restored. I have seen the tender mercy and faithfulness of my Lord, in keeping my understanding clear and my faith alive during that awful night, when I made so sad a mistake.

The query now comes closely home, Am I called again to the continent or not? Gracious Lord, I earnestly pray Thee, for Thine own name sake, to make my way plain before me, and through the power of Thy own Spirit, to make me perfectly willing to go or to stay, to do or to suffer, to be something or nothing, exactly as Thou mayst see good for myself, or on account of others. I do commit myself, my all, and Thy cause which I love, to Thy most Holy keeping and direction.— Amen.

CHAPTER XXIII.

FROM the time of Mrs. Fry's return from her journey the preceding year, she had continually received communications from
the Continent, urging her to visit places, where she had not
been, or to return and complete her work where she had already
commenced it. When she heard of these openings for usefulness, her heart responded to the call. Her daughter, whose
fearful illness had caused her such extreme anxiety, had nearly
recovered it effects, and another daughter, who had passed the
winter in Italy with her family was again in England. Her home
party was provided for, having arranged to spend the autumn
at Ramsgate; whilst her beloved brother, Joseph John Gurney,
offered her the great advantage of his society and support—he
believing it his duty to visit several places on the Continent, for
various religious and philanthropic purposes, especially, to impart the observations he had made during his lengthened tarriance in America and the West Indies, on slavery, and slave-
holding, to those potentates, who still permitted this evil to
exist in their dominions. Mrs. Fry shrunk from the great effort
of leaving home, and encountering the fatigue of travelling, from

the shaken state of her health; for her sensations and symptoms induced the belief, that her life of exertion and effort had told irremediably upon her vital powers. But it was not because the shades of evening were gathering round her, that she would slacken her labours for the good of others. Whilst it was yet day she desired to work and accomplish all that her great Master might have for her to do, before the night should come in which no man can work.

(*Previous to Ratcliff Monthly Meeting*), *Sixth Month, 22nd.* —I most earnestly desire the direction of my Lord and Master, through the immediate teaching of His Holy Spirit, that I may really know and do His will, and His will only. For Thy Name sake, O Lord! lead me and teach me. Am I once more to lay before the members of our little portion of Thy Church, my apprehended call of duty to go abroad? I earnestly pray Thee, if it be Thy call, make it very clear; if it be not, let me certainly know it, gracious Lord, that not my will but Thine be done. Amen.

27th, First-day.—After most deeply weighing the subject, and after very earnest prayer for direction, I felt best satisfied to inform my friends of my belief that it might be right for me to accompany my dearest brother Joseph to the Continent, and to visit some of the more northern countries of Europe. I had very decided encouragement from the Friends, particularly the most spiritual amongst them, which I felt helpful to me; but I was surprised at the degree of relief and peace that I felt afterwards, as from a voice before me, saying, "this is the way, walk in it."

28th, Second-day.—I had, on Seventh-day, letters from the Queen of Prussia and the Princess William. The first expressing much satisfaction at our proposed visit; our way is clearly open in her heart, and that of the King.

My sister Gurney, and our dear friend Charlotte Upcher, went with me to the Bishop of London on Sixth-day, on the subject of the Sisters of Charity. It has been a great pleasure to me the Queen Dowager giving her name as Patroness.

Before leaving home, Mrs. Fry addressed this letter to Captain (Colonel) Jebb, on the subject of the Model Prison, at Pentonville :—

Ramsgate, *Seventh Month,* 22*nd,* 1841.

Esteemed Friend,

Thy letter, explaining the cause of our not having the pleasure of meeting thee at Newgate, followed me to this place. But not being willing to give up seeing the new prison that is building before I went abroad, my brother Gurney and two of his sons accompanied me there, after having waited some time at Newgate, in the hope of seeing thee there.

We were much interested by our visit to this new prison. We think the building, generally, does much credit to the architect, particularly in some important points, as ventilation, the plan of the galleries, the chapel, &c.; and we were also much pleased to observe the arrangement for water in each cell, and that the prisoner could ring a bell in case of wanting help.

The points that made us uneasy, were first, the dark cells, which, we consider should never exist in a Christian and civilized country. I think having prisoners placed in these cells a punishment peculiarly liable to abuse. Whatever restrictions may be made for the governor of a gaol, and however lenient those who *now* govern, we can little calculate upon the change the future may produce, or how these very cells, may one day be made use of in case of either political or religious disturbance in the country, or how any poor prisoner may be placed in them, in case of a more severe administration of justice.

I think no person should be placed in *total* darkness; there should be a ray of light admitted. These cells appear to me calculated to excite such awful terror in the mind, not merely from their darkness, but from the circumstance of their being placed within another cell, as well as being in such a dismal situation.

I am always fearful of any punishment beyond what the law *publicly authorises,* being *privately inflicted* by any keeper, or officer of a prison; for my experience most strongly proves, that there are few men who are themselves sufficiently governed and regulated by Christian principle, to be fit to have *such power* entrusted in their hands ; and further, I observe, that officers in prisons have generally so much to try and to provoke them, that they themselves are apt to become hardened to the more tender feelings of humanity, they necessarily, also, see so much through the eyes of those under them, turnkeys and inferior officers, (too many of whom are little removed, either in education or morals, from the prisoners themselves,) that their judgments are not always just.

The next point that struck us was, that in the cells generally, the windows have that description of glass in them that even the sight of the sky is entirely precluded. I am aware that the motive is, to prevent the possibility of seeing a fellow-prisoner ; but I think a prison for separate confinement should be so constructed that the culprits may at least see the sky ; indeed, I should prefer more than the sky, without the liability of seeing fellow-prisoners. My reason for this opinion is, that I consider it a very important object to preserve the *health of mind and body* in these poor creatures, and I am *certain* that separate confinement produces an unhealthy state, both of mind and body, and that, therefore, everything should be done to counteract this influence, which, *I am sure*, is baneful in its moral tendency, for I am satisfied that a sinful course of life increases the tendency to mental derangement, as well as bodily disease ; and I am as certain, that an unhealthy state of mind and body has generally a demoralising influence, as the mind in an enervated state is more liable to yield to temptation, than when in a lively powerful state ; and I consider light, air, and the power of seeing something beyond the mere monotonous walls of a cell, highly important. I am aware that air is properly admitted, also light, still I do think they ought to see the sky, the changes in which make it a most pleasant object for those closely confined.

When speaking of health of body and mind, I also mean health of *soul*, which is of the first importance ; for I do not believe that a despairing or stupified state is suitable for leading poor sinners to a Saviour's feet for pardon and salvation.

I remain, with regard,

Thy friend,

ELIZABETH FRY.

C C 2

Upton, Seventh Month, 30th.—All difficulties and obstructions, which have been serious and numerous, are removed, as
far as I can see ; the way is made plain and open before us, to
set off to-morrow for our visit to Holland, Germany, Prussia,
and Denmark. My brother Joseph, his daughter Anna, my
dear niece Elizabeth Gurney, and my own maid go with me,
with the prospect of every comfort this life can afford ; and, I
humbly trust, the Lord Himself calling us into His service,
that His blessing will be with those who stay, and those who go.
Grant, gracious Lord, through the fulness of Thy love, that this
may indeed be the case.

The travellers arrived at Rotterdam, July the 31st, and
passed a tranquil Sabbath there. In the evening, they held a
large Meeting in an apartment of the Hotel; the following
day visited prisons; and on the 2nd of August proceeded to
the Hague.

Returning a second time, they neither felt themselves, nor
were received as strangers. They again visited the prisons, and
urged upon the proper authorities the means of remedying the
evils existing there. The gracious reception given to themselves and the objects of their mission, by the Royal family,
Mrs. Fry describes in a letter to her home circle.

You will like to know that, through tender mercy, I was
favoured to feel much rest, refreshment, and peace, at Rotterdam,
and much evidence that I was in my right place. Our visits to
the boy's prison at Rotterdam, and to the women's prison at
Gouda, were highly interesting. I find a second visit to a
place much better than a first. We had two meetings—one
philanthropic, one religious—both well got through, and a large
attendance. I felt in leaving the place much comfort and
satisfaction.

When we arrived at the Hague, our kind friend Lady Disbrowe,
(the wife of the British Minister), and Sir Alexander and Lady
Malet, received us cordially. We divided our evening between
Sir Edward Disbrowe and our hotel, having a party for us by

C

accident in each place; on the whole both passed off very well, and many appeared to be very glad to see us again. We sent our letters to the King from Prince Albert. On Sixth-day, a message came to desire that we would wait upon the King and Queen the next day, at half-past one o'clock, accompanied by Lady Disbrowe.

We remained with the King and Queen, and their daughter the Princess Sophia, about an hour. As rather an interesting event in my life, I mean to tell you particulars of this interview. Before we went, we had a solemn, short Meeting for worship, with our dear and valued friends of this town; afterwards we prepared to go. I was decorated by my best garments outwardly, and I desired so to be clothed with better ornaments spiritually, as to render attractive that which I had to recommend. We all felt very weightily our serious engagement, as we had much to represent to the King respecting the West Indies, prisons, and religious education for the people in his own country. The King, a lively, clever, perfect gentleman, not a large man, in regimentals; the Queen (sister to the Emperor of Russia), a fine, stately person, in full and rather beautiful morning dress of white; the Princess much the same. After our presentation the King began easy and pleasant conversation with me, about my visiting prisons. I told him in a short, lively manner, the history of it; he said, he heard I had so many children, how could I do it? This I explained; and mentioned how one of my daughters now helped me in the Patronage Society. He appeared much interested, as did the Queen. I then said, my brother had visited the West Indies, and would be glad to tell the King and Queen the result of his observations in these islands. This he did capitally, shewing the excellency of freedom, and its most happy results; he represented, also, the sad effects of the Dutch enlisting soldiers on the Gold Coast, and how it led to evil and slavery, which so touched the King, that he said he meant to put a stop to it. I then began again, and most seriously laid before the king, the sad defect of having no religious education in their Government Schools, and the Bible not introduced. He said he really felt it; but what could he do when there was a law against it? We then endeavoured to explain how we thought it might be obtained. Our very serious conversation was mixed with much cheerfulness. I felt helped to speak very boldly, yet respectfully; so did my brother. I concluded by expressing my earnest desire that the King's reign might be marked by the prisons being so reformed, that punishment might become the means of the reformation of criminals; by the lower classes being religiously educated; and by the slaves in their Colonies being liberated. The King then took me by the hand, and said he hoped God would bless me. I expressed my desire, that the blessing of the Almighty might rest on the King, Queen, their children, and their children's children. We gave them books, which they accepted kindly. It certainly was a very pleasant and satisfactory interview, that, I humbly trust, will not prove in vain in the Lord.

On Sixth-day, with my brother, I visited the Princess of Orange. We had open, free, pleasant communication on many important points. The same morning, I visited the Princess Frederick, sister to the King of Prussia, just out of her confinement. I found her like the other members of that superior family. My brother, also, had very satisfactory intercourse with the Princess of Orange. The Ministers of the Interior and of Finance have been very kind, and we hope and expect that real good will result. The Princess of Orange has a lovely little boy about two months older than our Princess. The girls went to see him; they accompanied me to the Princess Fredric, who wished to see them, from her knowledge of us through the Prussian Court.

The 7th, they reached Amsterdam, where they remained four days, visiting the prisons and various public institutions, and holding meetings for philanthropic and religious objects. The Lunatic Asylum they found in a deplorable condition.

Among other miserable objects, one unhappy woman unclothed lay grovelling in straw. Whether the look of compassion or the voice attracted her, cannot be known; but she dragged herself, as nearly as her chains would admit to her visitant, and endeavoured to reach her: the hand she desired to touch was yielded.

she kissed it again and again, and burst into an agony of tears. Will any one venture to assert that this poor creature was past all touch of human feeling, or the reach of gentle control ?

It was a question, on leaving Amsterdam, whether to take the usual route to Bremen or to go by Wilderhausen, over desolate country, by a shorter, but not so good a road.   The one which was chosen proved extremely rough and fatiguing, in places, the sand reaching to the axle-tree of the carriage; scarcely a bird or an insect, or any living thing to be seen ; miserable accommodation by night, and wearisome travelling by day.   Mrs. Fry became much indisposed, and scarcely able to proceed, when, in the middle of the last day's journey, a sudden jerk broke the mainspring of the carriage, but happily, not far from a small inn, where rest and refreshment could be obtained.   On Saturday, the 14th, they had the happiness of finding themselves in excellent quarters, in the pleasant town of Bremen.   The early part of Sunday was tranquil, but in the evening there was a very large Meeting held in the Museum, a noble building near the Hotel. Long before the appointed hour, well-dressed persons proceeded to secure places. Several of the pasteurs were present. One of them at the close arose and beautifully addressed the missionary brother and sister, expressing his desire that what had passed might be blessed to the people, and that they might be themselves blessed.   To Mrs. Fry he said, your name has long been to us "a word of beauty." A Christian gentleman wrote to them afterwards, " Now I am more than convinced that you are sent to us by the Lord, to be and to become a great blessing and a salt to our city." The following morning they went to see the prison. Bremen being a Hans Town, the address afterwards forwarded by Mrs. Fry and her brother to the authorities necessarily varied in some respects from one intended for a sovereign power.

When the carriage came to the Hotel door, for their departure, crowds of the lower classes surrounded it, wishing them a prosperous journey, "bon voyage," thanking them for the good Meeting they had had the evening before, and begging for tracts; whilst numbers could not be persuaded to move till Mrs. Fry had shaken hands with them.

Their little transit across the Elbe would have been delightful, with a glorious setting sun, but for a mob of persons returning from Hamburg market, who having discovered Mrs. Fry, and her tract bag, so pressed upon her that she was glad to take refuge in the carriage, whilst their clever and devoted courier (François) harangued the people, on his lady's various excellencies, but carefully prevented their approach. The time at Hamburg was extremely full; work was ready for them before their arrival. There she found Miss Sieveking, with whom she had long communicated, and whose active energy had been the means of establishing an association, termed the "Society of the Ladies' Committee," in the well-being of which Mrs. Fry was deeply interested. In the foundation of this Society for "Succouring and Nursing the Sick and Helpless Poor," various objects were had in view. The Committee designed to establish "District Visiting," by which the wants and peculiar circumstances of the indigent might be made known to those able and willing to relieve them: it specially aimed at providing the sick poor with medicine, medical attendance, nurses, and other temporal relief, whilst the most earnest attention was paid to the spiritual necessities of this class, and prayer and reading, formed a specified part of the visitor's duties. It also strove to find employment for such as were out of work, by furnishing them with implements and materials for continuing their various trades, for which they were remunerated at the average rate of wages in Hamburg and the neighbourhood. Connected with this association is an Hospital for children, whether orphans or the children of those who from having large families, crowded dwellings or other causes, are unable to take such measures as are conducive to their restoration to health. The superintendance of this "Children Hospital," is in the hands of Deaconnesses, who also visit and nurse the poor at their own houses, and are employed in testing the merits, and inquiring into the necessities of such applicants as desire to be placed on the books of the Society. Each family thus enrolled is visited *at least weekly*, and the peculiarities, illness, wants, with remarks upon each is reported by the deaconness or visitor to the Committee. It is an invariable rule of the Society that all members of it, should as far as possible themselves personally visit the poor, and individually succour them temporally and spiritually. It should be understood that a distinction is drawn in favour of the honest and industrious poor over those who are wilfully idle and guilty.

Much difficulty in obtaining work for the poor is often experienced even when they are able and willing to do it. The plan pursued is to employ such mechanics as are without work or the means of obtaining it, in working for those poor persons under the care of the Society who are unable to obtain the articles they require ; for instance, a poor shoemaker makes shoes, at the expence of the Society to be given or sold at reduced prices. Women work for the disabled, or nurse the sick and helpless, whilst an infirm aged upholsterer quilts the sea-grass mattresses for those who require them.

In speaking of the public institutions of Hamburg which came under Mrs. Fry's notice, it will be necessary to bear in mind the peculiar constitution of all public bodies there, in common with the other Hans Towns ; generally under a board of control, constituted of members elected much on the same system as the directors of Insurance and other companies in England. Individuals retiring in rotation from year to year, and new persons nominated in their places, thus bringing new minds and fresh thought to bear upon the improvement of the system, so that whilst new intellect is continually evolved *within* each body, there still is ever an equalizing and conservative spirit pervading the whole, from the presence of the old and experienced members of the Board, who are hence always in a larger proportion than those *recently* elected. It must be remembered too, that the Boards, thus individually changing, and yet as bodies always remaining, are elected from the whole class of burghers, of which the wealthier part of the population of the Hans Towns consists. And it is a beautiful and interesting phenomenon to contemplate these unsalaried men of business devoting time, money, talent and thought to objects so conducive to the moral and physical improvement of their fellow-creatures : self-constituted into their guardians, ameliorators, and friends ; bound by no compulsory engagements, but on the principle of faith and love, each in his own peculiar self-denial, fulfilling the law of charity to his poorer neighbour. Thus, through the whole mass of wealthier citizens, there exists a knowledge and experience of the condition and wants of the poor, of which we in England can scarcely form an adequate idea. To the effect of the government of these boards on the public institutions, and to that so generally diffused spirit of earnest helpful love, are to be attributed much of the beauty and wisdom of their internal management, which cannot fail to strike the mind, as it arrested the attention of Mrs. Fry. The many infant schools which exist in Hamburg are similarly conducted. In these schools, the wives, daughters and sisters of the members of the board, take a strong personal interest ; they examine, direct, in many cases themselves teach the children, which supersedes the necessity, as in other institutions, for committees or female visitors. In these schools, the infants remain during the day, having there the mid-day meal, and being provided with little beds, for the mid-day sleep. The average rate of payment is 8*d.* per week, and it is a remarkable feature in the condition of the lower orders in Germany, that they rarely if ever shrink from the burden of this payment, though under cases of great poverty it is remitted by the Board.

The " *Orphan Asylum*" is regulated on the same principles and receives children who have been deprived of their natural protectors gratuitously ; they are carefully brought up until of an age to be apprenticed to a trade, or sent to service as circumstances or inclination dictate.   Since the fire at Hamburg this institution has been placed some way out of the town ; and it may be here remarked, that throughout the city the healthiest situations are invariably chosen for all charitable institutions.

Mrs. Fry inspected another establishment of a nature deeply instructive, even beautifully sublime in the objects which it has in view, and in the means in use for the attainment of those ends.   This is the Asylum known by the name of the " Rauhhaus," because at its foundation in 1833, Herr Wichern led his first band of young men and boys into a small thatched house, which has formed the *nucleus* of a colony, and has still preserved its original and accidental name.   At its establishment the great object of the founder Wichern was to form a species of house of reformation for children from the earliest age to their eighteenth or twentieth year ; chiefly children whose parents and instructors had hitherto laboured in vain on their behalf, or whose neglected education had led them to the commission of crime, or whose moral and spiritual life had been perilled by the contamination of vice in their families and neighbourhood.   The design became gradually enlarged whilst the general point remained the same. This Refuge, unconnected in any way with the police, thus offered its services of helpful love, aiming at the restoration of such youths to society and the church of Christ, by the mere effect of the Gospel on the heart, and the winning example before them of a virtuous and industrious life. The children labour in a variety of workships built in the colony (and chiefly by themselves), shoemakers, tailors, joiners, bakers, printers, bookbinders, &c.; they are besides engaged in spinning and in agricultural and garden work. One point aimed at being to enable each individual as far as possible to provide every necessary for himself. Gradually from the first thatched house the " Rauh-haus " has been increasing in size. The old cottage remains, and around it have been grouped eleven other houses, which are clustered about a central hall for prayer, the whole situated in an extensive garden and surrounded by many acres of arable land. Every year a new house has been added, and fresh members admitted into a participation of like advantages.

The great aim of this institution is the restoration of the fallen, but there is another object held constantly in view, raising up within the church young men, who shall be strong in faith, active in charity, and habituated to guiding and directing the youthful mind. The adoption of a *family* life in this institution in lieu of a more generally scholastic or even military one, has been found of the greatest utility, forming the character to domestic life and the fulfilment of family charities without destroying individuality or healthy self-dependence. Thus at the " Rauh-haus," the inmates are divided into groups of twelve, living together each in one of the little houses; they share their meals, pleasures, instructions, play, and daily labour, meeting only in the central hall for morning and evening prayers.   Each of these families is under the superintendence of young men, called " Brethren of the Rauh-haus," who in fact partake of everything with their families. And this brings us to a most important and valuable part of this truly church regenerating society.

The " *Brotherhood of the Rauh-haus* " is now in fact a training school for labourers in home missions ; it is an elementary regiment, so to speak, of an active militia to the church of Christ, who after serving a time of apprenticeship as the heads of their small families in the " Rauh-haus," it is hoped will fix on some interior mission in the church, and there by pure conduct and earnest will to serve the cause of God and to propagate His faith, form another regenerating nucleus " in the whole temple knit together," which is truly of God and from above.   Each of these heads of the " Rauh-haus " families in entering the institution must prove himself thoroughly acquainted with some one trade or profession ; and these Brethren (whom you might indeed call masters) themselves, during the space of from two to four years, go through a theoretical and practical course of instruction.   They are of the same class, operatives, all desirous of giving themselves to the service of God in His church, by such orderly and free exercise of love, " for the building up the kingdom of God both in Church and State, in all such places where the Church and State have hitherto lacked the powers needful for the work," as the leadings of Providence and the individual circumstances of each point out.   Some have been employed in the foundation of other similar institutions in the northern part of Germany, in the German provinces on the Baltic, and even in France and Sweden.   Others amongst them are occupied in the care and visiting of prisoners, and in various works of Christian activity.

Such is the bond of sacred love which pervades the whole "Rauh-haus" establishment, an earnest, improving, regenerating training up of young minds, by the beautiful examples of holy industry and loving faith, by the constraining power of the love of Christ in the Gospel, acting as an expulsive force in the heart, and driving thence the accumulated dregs of original and contracted transgression, filling up the vacuum with holy activity and earnest desires after a Christian life here and hereafter.

Connected with the " Children's " and the " Brethren's " institutions, are the " *Printing office* " and the " *Agency*," subservient to the former, and which may indeed be considered as a ministering help towards their support, otherwise dependent on voluntary contributions.

The *Printing office* employs about twenty persons, its first object being the employment of a rather superior class of the inmates of the " Rauh-haus." Twice a month is published at the Agency of the Rauh-haus, and in the Printing office there,* a newspaper called the " Fliegende Blätter," or Flying Leaves, which reports the state of Christian and benevolent institutions, and of the success of the interior missions of the Church, and is of much interest and general instruction.

The " Agency " comprises in fact, an independent *publishing establishment* for the publication of such works as belong to the literature of the people ; a *bookbinder's* shop also employs twelve workmen under a master ; lithography with colours, a *foundry for stereotype*, and it also furnishes *woodcuts*. This whole business is connected with the suitable employment of the children-pupils.

---

* Fliegende Blätter Berichte über Vereine Austallen kurz alle Bestreluregen auf deu Gebrete der *innern Mission Agenter des Rauhere Hauhes*, Horn bei Hamburg, 1845, 1848.

Whilst prisons and public institutions occupied the mornings, the evenings were devoted by Mrs. Fry and her party to social intercourse, when subjects of benevolence or religion were discussed, or to appointed Meetings for worship. They held two of this nature, the last, a very large one, took place in the Assembly Room, a splendid apartment fully lighted and well arranged with seats. Many of the authorities and principal inhabitants of the place were present, the English Chargé d'Affaires, the French Chargé d'Affaires, their friend Colonel F——, and many others. They were conducted into the Meeting by the Syndic Sieveking, an eminently good man, who led them to a small platform. Mrs. Fry rose to explain her experience in prisons, and the principles upon which she had acted. The results of Gospel truth being taught, Christian kindness, change of habit and many similar topics ; she then spoke of the institutions of their city, and all she had remarked in them of a desirable or an undesirable nature. Mr. Gurney addressed the assembly upon what he had seen in the West Indies, Abolition of Slavery, Religious Liberty, &c. Great attention was paid, and the interpretation was excellent. At the conclusion, about fifty of their friends attended them to their apartment, when after partaking of refreshments, they parted with regret and affection on all sides.

The following afternoon saw them embarked on the Baltic, they had a brilliant moonlight night and an easy pleasant voyage to Copenhagen, where they remained a week.

On board the packet after leaving Copenhagen, Eighth Month, 30th :—

My dearest Husband and Children,

We have been favoured to leave Denmark with peaceful minds, having endeavoured to fulfil our mission as ability has been granted us ; a more important one, or a more interesting one, I think I never was called into. On First-day morning, when

10

we arrived in the harbour, we were met by Peter Browne the Secretary to the English Legation, to inform us that the Queen had engaged for us apartments in the Hotel Royal. The appearance of the Hotel was, I should think, like the arrangements of one of our first-rate Hotels about a hundred years ago.

The next morning the Queen came to town, and we had a very pleasant and satisfactory interview with her, she certainly is a most delightful woman, as well as truly Christian and devoted character: she is also lovely in person, and quite the Queen in appearance. She took me in her carriage to her infant school, it really was beautiful to see her surrounded by the little children, and to hear her translating what I wished to say to them. After staying with her about two hours, we returned to our Hotel; and that evening took a drive to see the beautiful Palace of Fredericksburgh in a most lovely situation, the beauties of land and sea combined, with fine forest trees around it. The following morning we regularly began our prison visiting, very sad scenes we witnessed in some of them. We saw hundreds of persons confined for life in melancholy places ; but what occupied our most particular attention, was the state of the persecuted Christians. We found Baptist ministers, excellent men, in one of the prisons, and that many others of this sect suffered much in this country, for there is hardly any religious tolerance. It produces the most flattening religious influence, I think more marked than in Roman Catholic countries. We were much devoted to this service of visiting prisons. Third and Fourth days, we received various persons in the evenings, but saw as yet but few Danes. On Fourth-day we dined at Sir Henry Watkyns Wynn our ambassador, and here we became acquainted with several persons, they live quite in the country, and we saw the true Danish country-house and gardens. The King and Queen were kind enough to invite us all to dine at their palace in the country, on Fifth-day, this was a very serious occasion, as we had so much to lay before the King —slavery in the West Indies—the condition of the persecuted Christians here—and the sad state of the prisons. I was in spirit so weighed down with the importance of the occasion, that I hardly could enjoy the beautiful scene. We arrived about a

quarter past three o'clock ; the Queen met us with the utmost
kindness and condescension, and took us a walk in their lovely
grounds, which are open to the public. We had much interesting
conversation, between French and English, and made ourselves
understood; when our walk was finished, we were shown into the
drawing-room to the King, who met us very courteously, several
were there in attendance. Dinner was soon announced : imagine
me, the King on one side, and the Queen on,the other, and only
my poor French to depend upon, but I did my best to turn the
time to account. At dinner we found the fruit on the table ; first
we had soup of the country, secondly, melons, thirdly, yams,
anchovies, cavia, bread and butter and radishes, then meat, then
puddings, then fish, then chickens, then game, and so on. The
fashion was to touch glasses ; no drinking healths. The King
and Queen touched my glass on both sides; when dinner was over
we all rose and went out together. The afternoon was very entertaining, the King and Queen took us to the drawing-room window,
where we were to see a large school of orphans, protégés of the
Queen. I took advantage of this opportunity and laid the state
of the prisons before the King, telling him at the same time, that
I had a petition for him which I meant to make before leaving
the palace. After an amusing time with the poor children, my
brother Joseph withdrew with the King into a private room,
where for about an hour he gave him attention, whilst he
thoroughly enlarged upon the state of their West India islands.
I stayed with the Queen ; but after awhile went in to them, and
did entreat the King for the poor Baptists in prison, and for religious toleration. I did my best, in few words to express my
mind, and very strongly I did it. I gave also Luther's sentiments upon the subject. We slept at our friends the Brownes',
a beautiful place by the sea-side. An agreeable serious gentleman,
Julius Schesteed, was our interpreter, and remained with us,
helping us to prepare our document for the King, he has become
our constant companion, and is now with us in the packet, going
to Lübeck, to interpret for us there. On Seventh-day one of
our fullest days, we drove into the country to visit the King's
sister the Landgravine of Hesse Cassel, the Prince her husband
brother to the Duchess of Cambridge, and the lovely Princesses

her daughters. We endeavoured to turn these visits to account, by our conversation. In the evening, we held one of our very large Meetings, I may say a splendid one, as to the company, room, &c. I trust that we were both so helped to speak the truth in love on various and very important subjects, as to assist the causes nearest our hearts, for our poor fellow mortals; it did not appear desirable to allude to the persecuted Christians, as we had laid their case before the King, we might have done harm by it; but I feel the way in which Protestant Europe is persecuting, to be a subject that cannot and must not be allowed to rest.

Where we now are, the same old Lutherans whom we found persecuted in Prussia are persecuting others. The way in which ceremonies are depended upon is wonderful, no person is allowed to fill any office civilly or religiously, until confirmed, not even to marry; and when once confirmed, we hear that it leads to a feeling of such security spiritually, that they think themselves at liberty to do as they like, sadly numerous are the instances of moral fall! These very weighty subjects so deeply occupying my attention, and being separated from so many beloved ones prevent the lively enjoyment I should otherwise feel, in some of the scenes we pass through; but I see this to be well, and in the right ordering of Providence. I have the kindest attendants and everything to make me comfortable.

On First-day morning, we had a very interesting Meeting with the poor Baptists. We then again went into the country, to lay all our statements before the King and Queen. I read the one about the prisons and the persecuted Christians; and my brother read the one about the West Indies: we had had them translated into Danish, for the King to read at the same time. After pressing these things as strongly as we felt right, we expressed our religious concern and desires for the King and Queen. I read a little to them in one of Paul's Epistles; after that I felt that I must commit them and these important causes to Him who can alone touch the heart. We had a very handsome luncheon, when I was again seated between the King and Queen. I may say their kindness was very great to me.

On Second-day morning, we formed a Society for attending to

poor prisoners—gentlemen and ladies ; and then paid a most delightful farewell religious visit to the Queen and Princess. I forgot to mention a very interesting visit to the Queen Dowager.

We arrived at Lübeck, after a calm voyage; but I do not like nights in steam-packets. I believe that we were sent to Copenhagen for a purpose. May our unworthy labours be blessed to the liberation of many captives, spiritually and temporally.

May the God of peace be near to all of you and to us, as our continual Keeper and Helper.

Farewell, in most tender and near love to all.

Yours indeed, and in truth,
ELIZABETH FRY.

By Lübeck they returned to Hamburg; thence Mrs. Fry wrote to her family :—

"Hamburg, Ninth Month, 3rd.

. . . .

We last night finished our labours in these Hans Towns. We have laboured in them in various ways, particularly in this large and important town. We have boldly set our faces against religious persecution, and upheld religious toleration and Christian unity in the Church of Christ. We also have laboured about their prisons, and expect to have many evils mitigated. It is extraordinary, the good fellowship and love that we have enjoyed with numbers. In a spiritual sense, fathers, mothers, brothers and sisters given to us, and helpers most curiously and constantly raised up from place to place. . .

. . . . ,

From Hamburg, by Minden and Pyrmont, they pursued their way to Hanover.

TO HER YOUNGEST DAUGHTER.

Hanover, Ninth Month, 9th, 1841.

My dearest Louisa,

I cannot express the fulness of my love and interest for my children in their different allotments, and how often I think of

you and your families before the Lord, in my quiet meditations.
We arrived here, after finishing our interesting and satisfactory
visits to our dear Friends at Minden and Pyrmont. I felt it
refreshing, being again with these dear simple-hearted people,
and I do think they are useful in their allotment. How much
I should like you to have seen us dining with them at Friedensthal; such a numerous family, grandmother, children, grandchildren in a large room, and a beautiful and most hospitable
German dinner. We not only were favoured with outward
refreshment, but it reminded me of the disciples formerly, who
went from house to house breaking bread and giving thanks ;
and I desired that we might do as they did, " eat our meat with
gladness and singleness of heart." I hope there was something
of this spirit. The country lovely. I retired for rest on a little
German bed, whilst my companions took a ride on horseback
over the beautiful hills. We had a very interesting Meeting,
largely attended by the company who come here to drink the
waters and the Pyrmontese. At Minden, the Friends are in
more humble life. I could not but be struck with the peculiar
contrast of my circumstances; in the morning traversing the bad
pavement of a street in Minden, with a poor old Friend in a sort
of knitted cap close to her head, in the evening surrounded by
the Prince and Princesses of a German court; for, to our surprise, Dr. Julius' sister followed us to Minden, to inform us that
in the town of Bückeburg, that we had passed through, there
was a desire expressed that we should hold a Meeting, and that
the reigning Princess wished us to go to the palace. After some
consideration we agreed to go, and upon our arrival in the town
found a large Meeting of the gentry assembling; some time afterwards the Prince and Princess and their family came in. They
rule the state of Lippe Schonenburg, one of the small rich
German states. I endeavoured to speak the truth boldly in love,
drawing results from my experience in prisons, and seeking,
as ability was granted me, to bring it home to the hearts of those
present. Your uncle also spoke to the same purpose. Afterwards we had a very agreeable visit to the palace, where we
were most cordially received, and had tea at five o'clock ; there
were many to meet us. After this singular visit, we proceeded

here, but did not arrive till past twelve o'clock at night, having had two Meetings at Minden, and one at Bückeburg. We were completely tired; almost too much so. To-day we are busy here, and I am delighted to find the dear late Queen really had the chains knocked off the poor prisoners at Hameln; it was a delightful sight to see their happy grateful faces. They looked as if they knew that we had pleaded for them. I think it was one of the pleasantest visits I ever paid, and to find that the prisoners had behaved so well since, and that the kindness shown them had had so good an effect. We are now much occupied in answering an interesting letter from the King of Hanover to me, and as I have many weighty things to say to him, I fear I must leave off, being very tired, and expecting a large party this evening.

The party in the evening proved particularly satisfactory. Mrs. Fry and her brother, also met both the gentlemen and the ladies' Committees for visiting prisons. A day of very hard travelling brought them to Magdeburgh, and a second, by railroad diverging to visit Wittenburg, to Berlin. Numerous objects awaited their attention in that city, not the less weighty to Mrs. Fry, from having been there before and made so many acquaintances, besides the additional interest she felt in Institutions already known to her.

The state of the prisons was of course her chief object of attention. Mrs. Fry and Mr. Gurney prepared recommendations to lay before General Thile, Minister of the Royal House, embodying their observations and opinions, and urging the necessity of many alterations before real improvement could be effected. The Prussian Royal Family were at the time in Silesia; thither the travellers had been invited to follow them, for there were those amongst them who considered that the retirement and tranquillity of that place would be well suited for the consideration of Mrs. Fry's objects. It was not a light prospect to Mrs. Fry; she had naturally the fear of man deeply implanted in her character. Religion had changed its direction, but not eradicated it. It was no longer for herself that she was afraid, it was for the cause sake to which her heart was given, for amongst these royal and noble personages she dreaded in either herself or her companions, any thing that might not adorn the doctrine of God her Saviour : but she soon discovered that she had come amongst Christians, many of them devoted as herself to the service of their Maker. Amongst the members of the House of Brandenberg, she found many intellectual and excellent persons. In the noble head of that royal House, one, who with a spirit indomitable as the great Frederick's, showed equal moral courage in carrying out all that he believed likely to conduce to the temporal and eternal good of his subjects, as his predecessor had displayed in self-aggrandisement and war. In the beautiful retirement of the Reisenberg, she saw Royalty retaining all the grace and finish that appertains to it ; but freed from the encumbrances of a city court. Her reception was more than kind, honoured for her "works' sake," she found herelf by all and on all occasions, treated with Christian affection and consideration.

No record of this time, singular and important as it was, exists of her own writing, but a letter to her grandchildren. But the deficiency is well supplied from the journal of one of her companions.

It was on the 10th of September that the party arrived at Hirschberg ; a beautiful little village, inhabited by a clean and very respectable class of peasantry. It is situated about eight miles from the Royal residences of Erdmansdorf, Fischbach, and Schildau ; and is nearly equi-distant from Buchwald, the home of the Countess Reden, of whose Christian character and benevolence Mrs. Fry had often before heard. The King and Queen were at that time residing at Erdmansdorf. At Fischbach lived Prince and Princess William (the uncle and aunt of the Queen), with their sons Prince Waldemar and Prince Adelbert, and their daughter Princess Mary, now Queen of Bavaria. Prince Charles, brother of the King, was also on a visit at Fischbach. The sister of the King and her husband, Prince and Princess Frederic of the Netherlands, with their daughter Princess Louisa, were then residing at Schildau.

To many of the Royal family, Mrs. Fry had been presented the previous year at Berlin, and the Princess Frederic of the Netherlands she had visited at her own beautiful home near the Hague, some time before. It was a lovely spot in which Mrs. Fry now found her tent pitched for a while. Of its rare beauty she had heard much, and from a painting of Schloss Fischbach, presented to her by Princess William during her stay at Berlin, she had formed some idea of the wild mountainous scenery and picturesque loveliness of the neighbourhood. To a mere passing traveller there was much to delight and to please; but even still more of deep interest to those who could in any degree enter into the Royal domestic circles there assembled, and this was Mrs. Fry privileged to do, with much enjoyment and an earnest desire to be permitted to be useful and faithful in all her intercourse with them. To enable her to be more accessible to the opportunities thus furnished, the pleasant little Goldenstern Hotel in the village of Schmiedeberg, had been exchanged for the equally agreeable and commodious inn at Hirschberg. The mornings were usually passed in writing and preparing important documents on the Prison, Slavery, and other questions ; and the afternoons were commonly spent in some visit to one of the palaces, which had been previously arranged. The Sunday was a day replete with interest. In the early part of it, it was necessary to finish an address to the King on Religious Toleration and on matters connected with Prisons.

Mrs. Fry was at that time suffering from great debility and fatigue ; but a power not her own seemed granted her to rise above her infirmities, and meet the various duties, which on that Sabbath were given her to fulfil. It is only those who held intimate communication with her at these times, who can in any measure understand the extreme nervousness of her constitution on the one hand, or on the other, the amount of strength granted her—granted doubtless in answer to fervent constant prayer, offered to the very moment of her entering a large assembly, or sitting down to commence some document, or engage in some important conversation. She prayed that in nothing might she seek herself, in *all* Christ Jesus ; and that all which He laid upon her for His glory, and the good of her fellow creatures, she might rightly and faithfully perform. Such was the spirit in which that Sabbath morning found her. Marvellously were her prayers answered :—most remarkably was her strength upheld. The long and interesting papers which she and her brother Joseph John Gurney had prepared for the King, were again perused during the drive to Princess William's Palace, which they reached about one o'clock, having called on the way at Buchwald for the excellent countess, whose ever ready aid was given to support and help her, and who in the present instance, interpreted Mrs. Fry's words for the Princess. Many other ladies were assembled at the Palace, and after some conversation of a general nature, every one remained in silence to listen to what she might have to say to them. This opportunity of addressing Gospel truth to such a company, she dared not pass by ; every word was listened to, every expression of her countenance watched, during her discourse. She spoke of the importance of upholding a religious standard in the world ; of making a final and decisive choice in these important matters ; of taking Christ as the only portion, and rejecting all besides. She impressed upon her hearers the duties incumbent on persons of a higher class of using their influence with others for good, and not for evil. She spoke of the privilege of possessing such means of usefulness. Very solemnly she urged upon all heads of large establishments the vast amount of responsibility entrusted to them ; the prevention of crime, and the good to be derived even by silent example : still more by the daily reading of the Holy Scriptures to the assembled family. She added an account of the experience of many prisoners, as to the blessings of being placed in professedly religious families, and the awful temptations presented to the servants of those who take no care for their souls, and are neglecting their eternal interests. Many tears were shed on this occasion, and all seemed anxious to share her sympathy and love.

During her stay in Silesia, Elizabeth Fry had opportunities of intercourse with the poor Tyrolese, who having fled from their native Zillerthal, on account of the religious persecution which they endured from the Austrian Government, had thrown themselves under the protection of the late King of Prussia, and by him had been placed under the care of the Countess Reden, who had proved herself indeed a nursing mother to them. It will be necessary to take a hasty review of the history of these Zillerthalians, in order rightly to estimate the deep interest excited in Mrs. Fry's mind in their behalf. For much information on the subject acknowledgments are due to an able article in the ' Quarterly Review,' of June 1839, as well as other important and interesting documents.

On the high road between Saltzburg and Innesbruck, after advancing more than two-thirds of the way, there lies between two majestic masses of rock, a wide and lovely valley. It is watered by a clear stream which, issuing from the Southern Alps, falls into the Inn a little below Strauss. Very nearly in the middle of the valley, stands the town of Zill, the seat of a

Landgericht, and the residence of a dean. The locality presents alternately rich meadows and heavy arable land; and here and there are dotted about villages and pretty white cottages, farm-houses, chapels and churches with lofty towers and spires. The population, amounting to from 15,000 to 16,000 souls, get their living chiefly by agriculture and the rearing of cattle. The poorer class emigrate yearly to Styria and Carinthia, where they are employed in felling trees, and in some of the manufactories of the country. Extreme poverty is nowhere to be found, and a common beggar is a rarity. The people are strong, healthy, and well made, and are chiefly distinguishable by extreme good-nature and honest simplicity. Their religion was without any exception (until a few years back) Roman Catholic; and the ecclesiastical jurisdiction lay between the bishops of Brisen and Saltzburg. In this valley, and amongst this simple people, did Protestantism suddenly appear. Not a single Protestant place of worship could be found for many miles around. A century before, the Archbishop of Saltzburg and his soldiers had crushed in that pleasant land the simple worship of Almighty God, which they deemed heresy, by the strong arm of power, and had robbed every Protestant of his possessions, driving them into perpetual exile. But in their haste to expel the heretics, they had left the cause of heresy behind,—their Bibles and other religious books; thus it came to pass that, after many years the good seed again sprung up and took deep root in the hearts of the Zillerthalians. Bound up with some of the old Bibles, was the Augsburg confession of faith. The Zillerthalians read, learnt, applied to themselves the fruits of their study. They found in this compendium of Protestant doctrine a uniform system; they became of one mind, and were enabled to give a clear answer to their enemies. Many amongst their number, in their yearly migrations, visited Bavaria, and formed acquaintances among the Protestants there ; they returned home with their faith strengthened, and their knowledge enlarged, and in possession of fresh books on these subjects. They began to scruple at assisting at the celebration of mass, or paying homage to images, and some determined to take legal steps for a public profession of Protestantism. The storm long gathering, now burst with fury on their heads. The " six weeks' instruction," in Popish doctrines necessary by law in Austria, before any person leaves the pale of the Romish church, on the plea of preventing any one from changing their religion in ignorance, was *denied* them !—an unworthy shuffle, a mean trick of might against right ; as by the edict of Joseph the instruction is dependant *solely* on the will of him who wishes to abjure Popery. This gross injustice, however, neither shook the resolution of the applicants, nor prevented others from imitating their example. On the arrival of the late Emperor Francis in the Tyrol, he determined on personally informing himself of their wrongs and their wishes. Though most amiable and courteous to their deputation, this interview with their Emperor in nowise improved their condition. Doubtless the keepers of the royal conscience, exercised not their influence in vain. They were allowed no place of assembly, were compelled to send their children to the Romish priest for baptism, (who claimed them as part of his flock,) and were plunged into the greatest difficulties, and exposed to all sorts of petty vexations, as well as violations of their consciences. The only answer they could obtain to their complaints, was a letter from Vienna, dated April 2, 1834, informing them that the Government saw no reason for acceding to their request, but that if they wished to secede from the Roman Catholic Church, they might migrate to some province of the empire in which a Protestant congregation existed. Determined, however, if driven from their homes, that they would go to some country where they might enjoy the free exercise of their religion, they applied for passports to leave the Austrian dominions ; but this privilege of voluntary exile was denied them.   In the course of about two years, however, an ungracious permission for so doing was accorded them, in the form of a command, to leave Austria within four months.   The late King of Prussia had warmly sympathised in their sorrows, and at this juncture sent from Berlin his chaplain Dr. Strauss, to Vienna, to entreat from Prince Metternich, permission for the emigration of the Zillerthalians into Prussia, as he was willing to receive them all.   About the time that the royal chaplain left Berlin on his embassy of mercy, arrived there Johann Fleidl, the Zillerthalian deputy, with the following petition drawn up by himself, on behalf of his fellow sufferers.

" MOST ILLUSTRIOUS, MOST MIGHTY KING, MOST GRACIOUS KING AND LORD.

" In my own name and in the name of my brethren in the faith—whose number amounts to from four hundred and thirty to four hundred and forty, I venture to address a cry of distress to the magnanimity and grace of your Majesty, in your high character of defender of the Gospel.   With my whole soul I desired to have advanced this prayer personally and orally, though I am content, too, if it be permitted to me to do so only in writing.   After the lapse of one hundred years another act of persecution and banishment is perpetrated in our fatherland.   Not for any crimes that we have committed, not for any misdemeanour of ours, but because of our religion, we are compelled to forsake the land of our home, as the accursed certificate from the Lauderícht Zell, dated the 11th of this month, will show.   It is true that we have the alternative of transportation into another Austrian province, or emigration ; but in order to spare ourselves and our children all further vexation, we prefer the latter.   Once before, Prussia granted our forefathers an asylum in their time of need—we too, put all our trust in

God and in the good King of Prussia. We shall find help, and not be confounded.

"We, therefore, most humbly petition your Majesty for a condescending reception into your states, and kind assistance on the occasion of our settlement. We pray your Majesty to receive us paternally, that we may be able to live according to our faith. Our faith is built entirely on the doctrines of Holy Scripture, and the principles of the Augsburg confession. We have read both with diligence, and have arrived at a full knowledge of the difference between the divine word and human additions. From this faith we neither can nor will ever depart: for its sake we leave house and land, for its sake we abandon our native country.

"May your Majesty graciously permit us to remain together in one congregation—that will increase our mutual help and comfort. May your Majesty most graciously place us in a district whose circumstances have some resemblance to those of our own Alpine land. Our employments have been agriculture, and the breeding of cattle. Two-thirds of us have property—one-third live by day labour, only eighteen have trades, of whom thirteen are weavers. May it please your Majesty to give us a pastor faithful to his Lord, and a zealous schoolmaster; though at first we shall most probably not be able to contribute much towards their support. The journey will be expensive, and we do not know how much we shall bring to our new home, and we and our children have been for a long time deprived of the consolations of religion, and the benefit of school instruction. If want should anywhere make its appearance among us, especially amongst the labourers, and those who are better off be not able to give sufficient relief, inasmuch as here they have to begin life over again, may it please your Majesty to be a father to us all. May it especially please your Majesty to intercede that the allotted time of four months, from May 11 to September 11, may be prolonged until next spring. The sale of our farms, which has already begun, but which cannot be ended in so short a time without loss—the approach of winter—the infirmity of the old people, and the children—make this prolongation of the term highly desirable. May God repay to

your Majesty any good that your Majesty does to us.   Faithful,
honest, and thankful, we will remain in Prussia, and not put off
the good features of our Tyrolese nature.   We shall only increase the number of your Majesty's brave subjects, and stand
forth in history as an abiding monument, that misfortune when
it dwells near compassion ceases to be misfortune, and that the
Gospel, whenever it is obliged to fly from the Papacy, finds
protection near the magnanimous King of Prussia.

"The Tyrolese of the Zillerthal, by their spokesman, Johann
Fleidl, of Zillerthal."

Whilst Fleidl, was thus urging his suit at Berlin, Dr.
Strauss was successfully advocating the same cause at Vienna.
The Austrian ministers, ashamed of their eight years perfidy
and injustice consented to all that was proposed.   The
Zillerthalians hastened to complete their preparations ; and
fourteen days before the expiration of the four months the first
division of the wanderers commenced their journey, old age, and
infancy, manhood and gentle woman, alike leaving their beloved
homes and turning their faces to the asylum opened for them by
the compassion of their noble protector. Very touching was the
detail of their pilgrimage, most affecting and instructive their
patience, their courage, their simple faith.   Their new home
lay in the domain of Ermansdorf, where each obtained a house
and farm suitable to his means, and his former position in the
Tyrol. The colony itself has received the name of their old
home, Zillerthal.   The countess of Reden was appointed to
attend to their necessities.   She had them cottages built in the
true Swiss style, with large balconies and long roofs, and
established for them schools, and in every possible way employed
and instructed them.   Ever thoughtful of their interests, the
countess invited them to come to Buchwald that evening to
receive encouragement and comfort from Mrs. Fry; she having
expressed her anxious wish to hold with them some communi-

cation in Christian love. The King and Queen and other members of the Royal Family were present at the service, and before the evening closed Mrs. Fry had much close and heart searching intercourse with them. At length arrived the exiles from Zillerthal, forming a curious and picturesque group, dressed in the costume of their country. Both men and women in the dark green cloth clothes, and high-pointed hats, many of the latter ornamented with garlands and nosegays of flowers. A long table was placed at one end of the room at which the Zillerthalians sat, and in front of which was a Moravian brother, for whom the good Countess had sent forty miles to act as interpreter. On the right hand of the table were seated the Royal family and others, and many persons stood crowding round the door. It would be scarcely possible to describe the deep interest of that whole group, or the solemn silence which prevailed when Mrs. Fry began to speak.

After Mr. Gurney had in a few words prepared the way for her, she rose with much solemnity and earnestness. Never did she address any assembly more beautifully, with more unction, or more truly from the depths of her heart, and no audience could have given more profound attention to every word she uttered. She invited them all to a close dependence upon Jesus Christ, and urged a full, firm, and constant trust in Him as their Lord and their Saviour, their King and their God.

With her usual tact and power, each individual, each class present seemed included in her address. It was the first occasion on which she had seen the King since his accession to the throne, and she knew too that it was the first time of his meeting many there present, as their sovereign. Her words of sympathy to him, on the death of his father, and her estimate of his present important position in Europe, which she spoke for herself, as well as for those about her, were beautifully adapted to the occasion. Mr. Gurney added a few words ; afterwards a hymn was sung, led by the Moravian Brethren ; and then the Tyrolese departed. Every one flocked around her with a word of love or kindness, but none expressed more interest or more gratitude than the King himself.

The following day the travellers dined at Fischbach, where she again met the King, and then came the leave-taking, always so sad when the probabilities of life afford little expectation of meeting again on this side the eternal world.

Fischbach.

My much-loved Grandchildren,

Instead of writing my private journal, I am disposed to write to you from this very lovely and interesting place. I am not very well in health, but I may thankfully acknowledge, that although tried by it for a while, such sweet peace was granted me that I was permitted to feel it sleeping as well as waking; so that I may say, my Lord restored my soul and I fully expect is healing and will heal my body. I think a more interesting neighbourhood I never heard of, than the one we are in. These lovely mountains have beautiful palaces scattered about them. One belonging to the King, others to Prince William, Prince Frederic, and other Princes and Princesses, not royal, besides several to the nobility ; but what delights my heart is, that almost all these palaces are inhabited by Christian families—some, of the most remarkable brightness. Then we find a large establishment, with numerous cottages in the Swiss style, inhabited by a little colony of Tyrolese. They fled from Zillerthál, because they suffered so much on account of their religious principles, being Protestants. The late King of Prussia allowed them to take refuge in these mountains, and built them these beautiful cottages. We therefore rejoice in the belief, that in the cottages as well as the palaces, there are many faithful servants of the Lord Jesus Christ. This evening we are to hold a Meeting for such as can attend, at the mansion of the Countess Reden, who is like a mother in Israel to rich and poor. We dined at her castle yesterday. I think the palaces, for simple country beauty exceed any thing I ever saw ; the drawing-rooms are so filled with flowers, that they are like green-

houses, beautifully built, and with the finest views of the mountains. We dined at the Princess William's with several of the
Royal Family, the Queen came afterwards, she appeared much
pleased at my delight on hearing that the King had stopped
religious persecutions in the country, and that several other things
had been improved since our last visit. It is a very great comfort to believe, that our efforts for the good of others have been
blessed—may we be thankful enough for it. Yesterday, we paid
a very interesting visit to the Queen, then to Prince Frederic
of Holland and his Princess, sister to the King of Prussia, with
her we had much serious conversation upon many important
subjects, as we had also with the Queen. Dined early at the
Countess Reden's. The Princess William and her daughter the
Princess Mary joined us in the afternoon, with several others.
How delighted you would be with the Countess and her sister ;
they show the beauty of holiness. Although looked up to by
all, they appear so humble, so moderate in every thing. I think
the Christian ladies on the Continent dress far more simply
than those in England. The Countess appeared very liberal,
but extravagant in nothing. A handsome dinner ; but only one
sort of wine, and all accordingly. To please us, she had apple-
dumplings, which were felt quite a curiosity, and they really
were very nice. The company stood still before and after dinner, instead of saying grace.

Afternoon.—We are just returned from Prince William's,
where we have had a Meeting of a very interesting nature. Many
ladies were assembled to meet us, that I might give them some
account of my experience in prisons. Your uncle added some
account of his journey in the West Indies. We expressed our
desire that the blessing of God might be with them. Great love
was shown us, indeed, they treat me more like a sister than a
poor humble individual as I feel myself to be. On our return,
we met the King, we rather expect he will be at our Meeting
at the Countess Reden's this evening.

Second-day morning.—We returned from our interesting
Meeting at the Countess' about eleven o'clock in the evening.
The Royal Family were assembled, and numbers of the nobility ;
after a while the King and Queen arrived. The poor Tyrolese

flocked in numbers. I doubt such a Meeting ever having been held before any where—the curious mixture of all ranks and conditions. My poor heart almost failed me. Most earnestly did I pray for best Help and not unduly to fear man. The Royal Family sat together, or nearly so ; the King and Queen, Princess William, Princess Frederick, Princess Mary, Prince William, Prince Charles, brother to the King, Prince Frederick of the Netherlands, young Prince William, besides several other Princes and Princesses not royal. They began with a hymn in German. Your uncle Joseph spoke for a little while, explaining our views on worship. Then I enlarged upon the changes that had taken place since I was last in Prussia, mentioned the late King's kindness to these poor Tyrolese in their affliction and distress ; afterwards addressed these poor people, and then those of high rank, and felt greatly helped to speak the truth to them in love. They appeared very attentive and feeling. I also, at the close of my exhortation, expressed my prayer for them. Then your uncle Joseph spoke fully on the great truths of the Gospel, and showed that the prince as well as the peasant would have to give an account of himself to God. In conclusion, he expressed his prayer for them. They finished with another hymn. It was a solemn time. We afterwards had interesting conversation for about an hour. When the King and Queen were gone, we were enabled to pray with the Countess, for herself and her sister, that all their labours in the Lord's service might be blessed. Now, my much-loved grandchildren, let me remind you that we must be humbled and take up the cross of Christ, if we desire to be made use of by our Lord ; " He that honoureth me, I will honour." May you confess your Lord before men, and He will then assuredly confess and honour you. I can assure you, when surrounded by so many who are willing to hear me, I feel greatly humbled.

I wish dear Frank to read this, as my eldest grandchild, and one in whom I take so tender an interest. Indeed, my beloved grandchildren, you dwell very near my heart ; may the same Holy Spirit who has helped and guided your grandmother, help and guide you !

May the Lord bless you and keep you, and raise you up for

His own service, for it is a most blessed service.   Dearest love
to your fathers and mothers,

I am,

Your most loving grandmother,

E. F.

It was on this occasion the Princess William gave an account
of the great prison at Jauer, and the King expressed a strong
wish that Mrs. Fry should see it, though considerably out of her
route.   This visit was afterwards accomplished.   It proved one
of great interest.   In one cell was a murderer, in another a
man of well known desperate character; they were both most
cruelly ironed to prevent their escape through the window;
each was fastened to an iron staple in the floor, with a heavy
iron bar across the shoulder, to make any movement irksome.
Their condition was afterwards represented by Mrs. Fry to the
King, who ordered their chains to be lightened, and insisted on immediate attention being paid to their health.

Many of the prisoners on this occasion were assembled in
the chapel, when both Mr. Gurney and Mrs. Fry addressed
them at considerable length.   Their discourses were interpreted
by the Moravian brother from Buchwald, whose attendance
at the prison had been commanded by the King for that purpose.

Erdmansdorf, <i>Ninth Month,</i> 20th.

My dearest Harry,

I wish thee, as my beloved youngest son, to have the account
of the conclusion of our visit to the beautiful mountains and
valley of Silesia.   I wrote a long letter to the grandchildren,
which I hope thou wilt see, as it gives an account of our adventures yesterday and the day before.   This morning we visited
the King and Queen, after our very interesting Meeting last
evening which they attended, at the Countess Reden's ; a
Meeting never to be forgotten.   This morning we went with a
long document to the King and Queen about the prisons, and

E E 2

various other subjects; we were received with the utmost kindness, and remained with them nearly two hours and a half. We had also a reading of the Holy Scriptures, and I prayed for them. We parted in love. We then went over the lovely country, past the little beautiful Swiss cottages built for the Tyrolese by the late King, and proceeded to Fischbach to dinner, to take leave of our much valued friends in these parts. We had a cheerful pleasant dinner, and afterwards, when thy uncle and the girls went a drive, I sat down with Prince and Princess William, and the Countess Reden and her sister, and told them the history of all my children. When your uncle and the girls came in with the young party we had a serious time—afterwards I prayed for them. With many tears we parted, and left this lovely country and family and friends. I go on with my letter—This morning we left Hirschberg between six and seven o'clock, and sad to say, our careless postilions ran us violently against a cart, and broke our pole; we were none hurt, as it was on level ground. Here I am in a little German pot-house, disposed to finish my history to thee. I wish thou couldest see us, I think it would make thee smile—having a sort of breakfast in the same room with the poor labourers, and such a singular set of people. Thy uncle would have me get into a cart to come here; picture me laid down in a curious German waggon made of basket work, lying on sacks and straw, but the jolting rather trying, as I am very far from well. I wish I could fully describe the deep interests we have had in this journey, and how marked has been the kindness of Providence towards us in many ways, and how blessed His service is. I certainly think the inhabitants of the mountains of Silesia the most interesting and curious assemblage of persons that I ever met with. We from this place see those beautiful mountains the Reisenberg, in their splendour, the morning being very fine and bright; probably the last time I shall ever see them—though the King and Queen begged me to return; but this I never expect to do, for I find the roughs of the journey are, with all my numerous indulgences, far too much for me, and I often feel very nearly ill. I think through all, I have seldom had more reason to believe that I have been called to any service, but we have been so much limited for time, as to make the press in travelling too great for my strength.   We hope to be in England next Seventh-day week.   How often and how tenderly I think of thee, my dearest youngest son.

I am thy loving mother,

E. F.

Cassel, Ninth Month, 26th.

My most tenderly beloved Husband and Children,

I am glad, and I trust thankful, to be so far on our way homewards, and I hope and expect that we may this day week have the inexpressible consolation of being once more in England ; my longings for it are almost inexpressible, and I have to pray and seek after faith and patience not to be too anxious, or in too great a hurry.   I have continued very far from well, with latterly a considerable stiffness in my limbs, so that I am obliged to be assisted to walk up stairs, and helped into the carriage, sometimes by one or two men.   I might have had the same attack at home ; but one thing is certain, we may fully trust in our Heavenly Father, who is constantly protecting us under the wing of His love, and who knows what is best for us.   I have sometimes thought that after being so helped on my way, from the palace to the prison, it was likely that the poor instrument should need a little further refining and purifying, for our works are to be tried as by fire.   I have very earnestly desired not to repine, or to be unwilling to drink the cup that may be given me to drink.   We travel with six horses to make the greatest speed home.   I have a board in the carriage, that when your uncle and Anna are outside, I can quite rest and make a real sofa of it, when I need it, which I do for one or two stages in the day. Mary and François are very attentive and kind ; indeed how differently am I cared for to many poor missionaries.   I wish you to feel for me, but not to be two anxious about me ; commit me entirely to Him who only knows what is best for me Your aunt Elizabeth's letter was very seasonable and acceptable.   I wish her and all my children to know how it is with me, for I need their sympathy and prayers, at the same time that I feel best help to be near, and the Power that says to the waves, " So far shall ye go and no further."   Often in my wakeful and at times distressing nights, a sweet peace comes over me to calm my troubled spirit. We hear from newspapers, that the poor Baptists in Copenhagen are to be released from prison, a small sum being paid by way of fine. What a comfort! and the poor Lutherans in Prussia say they are now so well off, that they do not wish us to ask for any more liberty for them of the King.

I am indeed yours most faithfully and lovingly,

ELIZABETH FRY.

From Cassel they pursued their rapid journey to Ostend, and landed at Dover on the 2nd of October. There Mrs. Fry was met by her husband, who was little prepared for the sorrowful state in which she was brought back to him. At Ramsgate, where her eldest daughter awaited her, she remained, till she could be moved without material suffering. Her son William was at that time residing at Upton Lane, whilst his own house, (Manor House) was undergoing some alterations. She stayed a few days with him and his family, and then, with great difficulty, she was conveyed into Norfolk, where for many reasons, she was particularly anxious to go.

Lynn, Tenth Month, 21*st.*—At Ramsgate, I met with the utmost love and kindness, constant and faithful care, which were very useful to me until the time of my departure.

My visit to Upton Lane, to our dearest William and Julia, has really been cheering to my heart; the day appears come, that my beloved children for whom I have passed through such deep travail of spirit, and for whom I have exercised such tender care, and felt such wonderful love are to take care of me; indeed, their kindness has been delightful and very comforting, quite enlivening and consoling. I see in this an advantage in coming home so broken in health, I have fallen upon them for care, first at Ramsgate, then at Upton Lane, ministering to my wants in the kindest way, Katharine doing all she can for me; and now Frank and Rachel are abundantly kind. I already feel better for their care over me, and that my suffering is more than made up to me, by the tender love and sweetness it has drawn forth from my most beloved ones.

I yesterday received a letter from my husband, saying, that my dearest brother Joseph was married to Eliza P. Kirkbride, on the Fifth-day the 21st. On the morning of their marriage, my heart was poured forth in prayers and tears on their behalf, that the blessing of the Most High might rest upon them.

Earlham, Eleventh Month, 1st.—We had a very delightful reception here. This is our son Harry and grandson Frank's birthday,—nineteen. We have cause for deep thankfulness on behalf of these dear sons ; they have known many deliverances, and are, I trust, alive unto God as well as alive naturally. I humbly trust they may this year grow in grace, in the knowledge of God and of Christ our Saviour. Grant, gracious Lord ! for Thine own name' sake, that it may be so.

Warley Lodge, 5th.—We had a most satisfactory visit, and parting from Earlham and my beloved brother Joseph. His dear wife met me as a sister, and was most kind to us all. We had a very interesting Sabbath. I accompanied them to Meeting in the morning, wishing to be with Eliza at her first entry to Norwich as Joseph's wife. Our Meeting was very solemn, many very dear to us there. My brother spoke first, after I had knelt down and poured forth my heart in thanksgiving and prayer, for surely we had deep cause for thankfulness for his marriage, our remarkable journey, &c, ; and indeed, we may say, our many great and wonderful deliverances. I also prayed for a continuance of blessing. Joseph's was one of his excellent and instructive sermons, particularly on the certain guidance of the Holy Spirit of Truth. Mine was rather a song of praise to our Lord as the Lamb of God who taketh away the sins of the world, the Physician of value who healeth all our diseases, our Guide through this wilderness, as a cloud by day and a pillar of fire by night, who had brought some of us through very dark places, so that through the fulness of His love, " the wilderness" had become at times as " Eden, and the desert as the garden of the Lord, joy and gladness being found therein, thanksgiving and the voice of melody." I also impressed upon

all, how we were encompassed with so great a cloud of witnesses
of the redeemed ones, who were gone, and of those who remained here; and how we ought to accept and rejoice in so
great salvation, "laying aside every weight, and the sin that so
easily besets us, running with patience the race set before us,
looking unto Jesus the author and finisher of our faith." My
sister Eliza followed in very solemn thanksgiving to the same
purpose. In the evening we had another very interesting religious time together, in which our dear friend Robert Hankin-
son, prayed for our brother and sister and all of us.

On Second-day, our sister Catherine, our brother and sister
Cunningham, and others dear to us, joined our party, and we
had a large wedding-dinner, being refreshed together. We parted,
and no common parting it was.

I much enjoy my beloved children of this place, and desire
to be enabled to minister to them spiritually before we part, according to their needs. I leave them, as I have done the other
places, in much love and peace.

Upton, Twelfth Month, 5th, First-day morning.—I have
been favoured to be much better the last few days,—far more
easy,—thanks to my Heavenly Father: though I suffer still at
times. I look upon this late indisposition as a very privileged
one, and have felt, and deeply feel, the mercy extended towards
me, in all my wants being so wonderfully provided for. The
luxuries of life and generous living that I have had, I accept as
gifts from a gracious and merciful Providence, that have been
greatly blessed to my help, and, I believe, have greatly promoted
my recovery. I exceedingly regret what I consider the intem-
perate and unchristian views some take of these things, judging all who feel it right to take stimulants in moderation. I
believe Christians may use and not abuse these outward blessings, and that we have the highest authority for doing so; as
He who set us a perfect example, and exactly knows our wants
spiritual and temporal, certainly took wine. May He guide me
in this and all other things, and guard me from being injured
myself, or injuring others. Grant that this may be the case,
gracious and most adorable Lord God and Saviour!

The infirm state of Elizabeth Fry's health precluded at this period much active exertion ; but her time was fully occupied, and her interest not at all diminished in those subjects to which she had so long devoted her attention. Her correspondence was extensive, both at home and abroad—the latter especially, much of it arising from her late journeys on the Continent. She had the happiness of hearing of the beneficial results of her exertions in different places ; from others, she received details of the obstacles which had occurred to delay or preclude improvement. To the Minister of the Interior in Holland, she wrote :—

Upton Lane, *Twelfth Month, 7th,* 1841.

Dear Friend,

I hope thou wilt excuse the liberty that I take, in communicating a little further with thee, on the subject of your prisons in Holland, and making some observations on the state of your lunatic asylums, as I presume such objects all come under thy notice, as Minister of the Interior. Since my return home, I have felt such a strong interest in the welfare of your prisons and lunatic asylums, that I cannot be satisfied without again addressing thee, respecting these important subjects.

I feel that our time is short ; I therefore am very anxious that whilst the present King reigns, and whilst thou art filling thy important post, such measures should be adopted as may conduce to the real welfare of the community, in the reformation of criminals, in the prevention of crime, and in mitigating the sorrows of the poor lunatics. One point I feel peculiarly bound to press, that women in all your prisons should be under the care of their own sex ; and that no men, not even the governor, chaplain, or medical man, should be admitted, unless a female officer be present, as experience has proved to me the absolute necessity of this measure, for the moral preservation of the female prisoner. I consider this a most important point. I am also very desirous that ladies should visit your prisons wherever women are confined, as their influence is highly beneficial, both to the prisoners and officers, and tends greatly to raise the standard both of religion and morals amongst them. I have been gratified to observe, the beneficial results of such visits at Gouda and Amsterdam ; I have also had favourable reports from the ladies who visit the prisoners at Zwolle. Excuse my reminding thee again, that the number of guardians (turnkeys) in most of the prisons in Holland is not adequate to that of the prisoners. I have sometimes thought that Gouda is not the best situation that might be found for a female prison, and that if the one which it has been proposed to build, near Amsterdam, were large enough, it might accommodate a considerable number of women. One or two more prisons are much wanted, and it is very desirable that all these new prisons should have separate night cells. I also feel it very important, that men and women should be placed in separate prisons entirely. The building of prisons for women is less expensive than those for men, as they need not be so strongly constructed ; and the expense of female officers is also smaller than that of men. I think it best to inform thee, that I was greatly shocked by the state in which I found the lunatic asylum near Amsterdam, as its inmates appear grievously neglected ; and such humane measures are not adopted, as experience has proved not only tends to the comfort, but to the recovery of patients thus afflicted. I am rather anxious to know whether the King has attended to the subject of Scriptural education of the lower classes, as I believe the greatest advantage would result from the Holy Scriptures being daily read in your different public schools, at the same time I am not a friend to the Bible being used as a common class-book, in which children are taught to read. If thou thinkest me very urgent on these subjects, I am inclined to hope the deep interest I take in the present and everlasting welfare of of the people of the Netherlands will plead my excuse for being so. Pray present my kind regards to thy wife ; and with true desire that wisdom from above may be granted thee, to direct all thy steps in thy important position, I remain, with regard and esteem,

Thy obliged friend,

ELIZABETH FRY.

Count Schimmelpennick.

From her beloved and valued friend, the Countess Reden, she received heart-cheering communications ; the King of Prussia having urged upon General Thile, Minister of the Royal House, the necessity of effecting various reforms in prisons The Countess Reden's letter enclosed an extract from a Prussian newspaper, giving an account of Mrs. Fry's visit to the great prison at Jauer, translated by one of her nieces with so much feeling and simplicity, that although retaining something of the German idiom, it is presented here.

" Jauer, *the 8th of October.*

" Our town has been rejoiced soon after the presence of the many military persons assembled here on occasion of the great review, by the visit of a stranger, whose object was very different, but well worth our attention. This was Mrs. Elizabeth Fry, who has for more than twenty years given her chief attention to try how the poor prisoners, who are almost all sunken so deeply, could be saved from the wretchedness of their souls, and rendered useful again in common life. Having found, during many years, that the doctrines of the Bible, of the sinfulness and corruption of mankind, and of the salvation through the bloody death of Jesus Christ, were the only means of arriving at it ; she has now been driven by Christian love, to make known her experiences in Germany. After having been last year at Berlin, where she directed the attention of several persons in high stations to this point, she visited our prisons, coming from Berchwald, where she stayed during the sojourn of His Majesty the King, at Erdmannsdorf, on the 21st of September, accompanied by her brother, Mr. Gurney. She went through the work, and bed-rooms, as well as through the isolated rooms, and the other apartments of the house, and denoted by her questions, her deep knowledge and acquaintance with everything which tended to the welfare of the prisoners. The female prisoners, and a great part of the men, were now assembled in the praying-room, and after singing some verses, and a speech of the clergyman of this institution Mr. Feldner, Mrs. Fry spoke to them with the aid of a very good interpreter, Mr. Wïrnsahe from Nisky. The impression this made was extremely deep and striking; not only the women wept, but even a great number of the men could but ill conceal their emotion produced by her appearance. Several stories of female criminals who had been converted in prison, and lived now (being set at liberty), a christian and honourable life, seemed to make great impression upon all. This very remarkable meeting was finished by a very serious address by Mr. Gurney; and we may hope that this visit will be blessed, and made useful in many respects to our prison."

A few weeks later, a delightful account came from the Pasteur Feldner, chaplain to the prison at Jauer, of the improvement amongst the prisoners. A hundred and three Bibles, and a hundred and twelve Prayer Books, had been purchased by them, at the price of much self-denial, out of their small earnings, besides many copies of the Scriptures and tracts having been distributed amongst them. M. Feldner, amongst other cases, instances " a poor female prisoner, who, longing to possess a Bible, took the firm resolution to lay apart her very small gains till she was able to procure one by them. On the birth-day of our beloved King, the Director delivered to her, as a reward for good behaviour, a fine Bible: I have seldom witnessed a more touching emotion of joy than she manifested, when stretching out her hand she received the precious treasure. Another prisoner, careless and ripe in sins, who had long ago repulsed all my warnings, by assuring me that he was not worse than other persons, and hoped for eternal blessings as well as they, came on a sudden to beg for a Bible; when I asked him what he intended to do with it, he answered, that he wished to compare himself, if what he heard in my sermons and lessons was really so. I gave him a copy, with the serious advice, never to read in it without praying God fervently, to bestow on him the grace to understand what he was reading, and if he found difficulties, to come and beg me to explain them to him; and I can but state the most satisfactory result in his behaviour and feelings. He is persuaded now he is a sinner, and implores grace. One prisoner acquainted me with surprise, that in the beginning, he could read whole chapters without interruption, but that now a single verse could put him in so deep a reflection, and in such thankful adoration for the divine grace shown him, a poor sinner, that he frequently could not read further."

A letter from Mademoiselle Nauti told her of admission being obtained for ladies to visit the prison at Lübeck, though not without difficulty, and under strict regulation. The permission to visit prisons at Hanover was not so readily granted; but whilst awaiting the desired leave, several ladies there—amongst the most active—Lady Hartman, with Miss Ida Arenhold as President, established a Society for visiting and relieving the sick poor.

Mrs. Fry had also almost endless letters, asking for assistance or advice, and requiring more time and thought than she had power to give. The liberality of her brothers, and some of her other relatives, enabled her to administer to the claims and distresses of many persons, in a manner which would have been otherwise impossible. She was at this period much with her own family, welcoming them to Upton Lane, or paying little visits at their respective houses. A small but commodious close carriage, given to her by her faithful brother Joseph John Gurney, and kept for her own particular use, afforded her the power of moving easily about, and greatly added to the comfort of her declining years.

Sir John Pirie had been elected, the preceding autumn, Lord Mayor of London. Lady Pirie had been one of Mrs. Fry's most indefatigable helpers in Newgate, and in all her public objects. Sir John and she, being both persons eminently devoted to the service of God and the good of their fellow men, resolved to use their year of power in doing everything within their reach to benefit others, and exalt the cause of truth and righteousness on earth. Amongst other things, they were bent upon assisting the cause of prison reform; and in their partial kindness looking upon Mrs. Fry as a sort of impersonation of the subject, they desired to bring her into communication with such persons as were likely to forward her views, for they believed, that her persuasive arguments were founded on such indubitable truth, that they required but to be understood, to carry conviction to the minds of those who heard them. With this object they urged her being one of the few ladies invited to the banquet given at the Mansion House on occasion of the laying the first stone of the new Royal Exchange.

Upton, First Month, 11*th*, 1842.—The Lady Mayoress has been here again to-day, to see if there is any prospect of my going to the Mansion House, according to the warm desire they have expressed to meet Prince Albert, the Duke of Wellington, and our different Ministers. I feel it a very weighty matter for my body, mind, and spirit, and do very earnestly crave direction and preservation in it, that if I go, my way may be made very plain, and that my Lord may be with me there.

14*th*.—As the time approaches, I much feel this prospect. Gracious Lord, for Thine own Name's sake, keep me from doing anything in this, or any other thing, that is not right in Thy sight; and if right, be with me Thyself in it, clothing me with the beautiful garments of Thy righteousness and Thy salvation, touching my tongue as with a live coal from Thy altar, so to speak the truth to those around me, that it may tend to good and edification. Grant me wisdom from above, to do all in wisdom and discretion.

The last week I have been generally better. We had an interesting visit from the Chevalier Bunsen, (the Prussian Minister), and his wife, in which I was enabled to relieve my mind, by speaking to him on some weighty subjects after a solemn Scripture reading, and in prayer. I felt relieved by it, as I had borne him much in mind, believing him to be a sincere and Christian man.

17*th*.—Be pleased, oh Lord, to be very near to us this day.

and help us to adorn Thy doctrine, and to speak the right thing in the right way, that the cause of truth, righteousness, and mercy may be promoted !

18th, Third-day.—Through condescending mercy, I may say I found this prayer answered. I had an important conversation on a female prison being built, with Sir James Graham our present Secretary of State, upon the Patronage Society, &c. I think it was a very important beginning with him for our British Society. With Lord Aberdeen Foreign Secretary, I spoke on some matters connected with the present state of the Continent. With Lord Stanley our Colonial Secretary, upon the state of our penal colonies, and the condition of the women in them, hoping to open the door for further communication with him on these subjects. Nearly the whole dinner was occupied in deeply interesting conversation with Prince Albert and Sir Robert Peel. With the Prince, I spoke very seriously upon the Christian education of their children, the management of the nursery, the infinite importance of a holy and religious life; how I had seen it in all ranks of life; no real peace or prosperity without it. Then the state of Europe ; the advancement of religion in the Continental Courts. Then prisons; their present state in this country—my fear that our punishments were becoming too severe—my wish that the Queen should be informed of some particulars respecting separate confinement, &c. &c. We also had much entertaining conversation about my journeys, the state of Europe, habits of countries, mode of living, &c. &c. With Sir Robert Peel, I dwelt much more on the prison subject; I expressed my fears that gaolers had too much power, that punishment was rendered uncertain, and often too severe—pressed upon the need of mercy, and begged him to see the New Prison, and to have the dark cells a little altered.

To her Sister, Lady Buxton.

Upton, *First Month,* 22nd.

My dearest Hannah,

I feel really grateful for thy letter, for deeply as we feel for the Niger expedition, no one lets us know any particulars, or sends us any document respecting it. Last evening the report we heard was, that all the captains were dead; this, I trust, is false. We have deeply felt with our beloved brother in this close exercise of faith and patience, but we poor short-sighted mortals cannot see the end of it; the whys and where-fores, we cannot as yet comprehend. We trust it may please our Heavenly Father to permit Captain Trotter to return; but after all, we must leave it to Him, who does all things well. With respect to my Mansion House visit, it appeared laid upon me to go, therefore I went: also at the most earnest wish of the Lord Mayor and Lady Mayoress. I was wonderfully strengthened, bodily and mentally, and believe I was in my right place there, though an odd one for me. I sat between Prince Albert and Sir Robert Peel at dinner, and a most in-teresting time we had; our conversation on very numerous important subjects. The Prince, Ministers, Bishops, Citizens, Church, Quakers, &c. &c., all surrounding one table, and such a feeling of harmony over us all. It was a very remarkable occasion; I hardly ever had such kindness and respect shown me, it was really humbling and affecting to me, and yet sweet, to see such various persons, who I had worked with for years past, showing such genuine kindness and esteem, so far beyond my most unworthy deserts.

I am,

Your tenderly, loving and sympathizing sister,

ELIZABETH FRY.

23rd, First-day.—I find that the newspaper report of the dinner at the Mansion House has excited some anxiety at my being there, from the toasts, the music, &c., &c.; it is thought I set a bad example by it, and that it may induce others to go to such dinners, and that my being present appeared like approv-ing the toasts. I quite wish to be open to hear all sides and to be instructed, and if I had erred in going, to do so no more, should such an occasion occur again. At the same time, I felt so much quietness and peace when there and afterwards, and until I heard the sentiments of others, that I fear being now too much cast down or tried by these remarks. I desire to keep near to Him who can alone help me and defend His own cause,

that no harm should be brought upon it through me. I desire
and pray to be kept in unity with those who love the Lord Jesus,
and particularly with the people with whom I am in religious
connexion. May I be guided at this time through what I feel
a difficult place, by my Lord Himself, through the fulness of
His love, mercy, and pity.

The King of Prussia's arrival in England, to stand in person
as sponsor to the infant Prince of Wales, was an event of much
interest to Mrs. Fry. She could not be insensible to the kindness
he had shown her, and the gracious reception afforded her in his
dominions ; she admired the magnanimity with which he maintained the right on all subjects that approved themselves to his
conscience, and greatly wished to see His Majesty again, but it
was not for her to make any overture; it was therefore with
much pleasure, that she received an intimation of the King's
desire to meet her at the Mansion House.

First Month, 29*th.*—To-morrow, the King of Prussia has
appointed me to meet him to luncheon at the Mansion House.
I have rather felt its being the Sabbath ; but as all is to be conducted in a quiet, suitable, and most orderly manner, consistent
with the day, I am quite easy to go. May my most holy, merciful
Lord, be near to me as my Helper, my Keeper, and my Counsellor. My dearest husband and Katharine are to go with me.
Oh ! may my way be made plain before me as to what to do,
what to leave undone ; when to speak, and when to be silent.

30*th, First-day.*—I felt low and far from well when I set off
this morning for London ; but, through the tender mercy of my
God, soon after sitting down in Meeting, I partook of much peace.
I was humbled before my Lord in the remembrance of days
that are past, when I used to attend that meeting (Gracechurch
Street), almost heart-broken from sorrow upon sorrow, and I
remembered how my Lord sustained me, and made my way in the
deep waters. He also raised me up, and then He forsook me
not. I was enabled very earnestly to pray to my God for help,
direction and preservation.

After this solemn and refreshing Meeting, we went to the
Mansion House. We waited some time in the drawing-room
before the King arrived from St. Paul's Cathedral. I have
seldom seen any person more faithfully kind and friendly, than
he is. The Duke of Cambridge was also there, and many
others who accompanied the King. We had much deeply interesting conversation on various important subjects of mutual
interest. We spoke of the christening. I dwelt on its pomp
as undesirable, &c.; then upon Episcopacy and its dangers;
on prisons; on the marriage of the Princess Mary of Prussia;
on the Sabbath. I entreated the Lord Mayor to have no
toasts, to which he acceded, and the King approved; but it was
no light or easy matter. I rejoice to believe my efforts were
right. I told the King my objection to any thing of the kind
being allowed by the Lord Mayor on that day; indeed, I expressed my disapprobation of them altogether. I may at the
end of this weighty day return thanks to my most gracious Lord
and Master, who has granted me His help and the sweet feeling
of His love.

At the Mansion House, the King of Prussia arranged, to meet
Mrs. Fry the following morning at Newgate, and afterwards to
take luncheon at Upton Lane.

Second Month, 1st, Third-day.—Yesterday was a day never
to be forgotten whilst memory lasts. We set off about eleven
o'clock, my sister Gurney and myself, to meet the King of Prussia
at Newgate. I proceeded with the Lady Mayoress to Newgate,
where we were met by many gentlemen. My dear brother and
sister Gurney, and Susannah Corder, being with me, was a great
comfort. We waited so long for the King that I feared he would
not come; however, at last he arrived, and the lady Mayoress
and I, accompanied by the Sheriffs, went to meet the King at
the door of the prison. He appeared much pleased to meet our
little party, and after taking a little refreshment, he gave me his
arm, and we proceeded into the prison and up to one of the long
wards, where every thing was prepared; the poor women round
the table, about sixty of them, many of our Ladies' Committee,

and some others; also numbers of gentlemen following the King, Sheriffs, &c. I felt deeply, but quiet in spirit—fear of man much removed. After we were seated, the King on my right hand, the Lady Mayoress on the left, I expressed my desire that the attention of none, particularly the poor prisoners, might be diverted from attending to our reading by the company there, however interesting, but that we should remember that the King of Kings and Lord of Lords was present, in whose fear we should abide, and seek to profit by what we heard. I then read the 12th chapter of Romans. I dwelt on the mercies of God being the strong inducement to serve Him, and no longer to be conformed to this world. Then I finished the chapter, afterwards impressing our all being members of one body, poor and rich, high and low, all one in Christ, and members one of another. I then related the case of a poor prisoner, who appeared truly converted, and who became such a holy example; then I enlarged on love, and forgiving one another, showing how Christians must love their enemies, &c., &c. After a solemn pause, to my deep humiliation, and in the cross, I believed it my duty to kneel down before this most curious, interesting and mixed company, for I felt my God must be served the same every where, and amongst all people, whatever reproach it brought me into. I first prayed for the conversion of prisoners and sinners generally, that a blessing might rest on the labours of those in authority, as well as the more humble labourers for their conversion; next I prayed for the King of Prussia, his Queen, his kingdom, that it might be more and more as the city set on the hill that could not be hid, that true religion in its purity, simplicity, and power, might more and more break forth, and that every cloud that obscured it might be removed; then for us all, that we might be of the number of the redeemed, and eventually unite with them in heaven, in a never-ending song of praise. All this prayer was truly offered in the name and for the sake of the dear Saviour, that it might be heard and answered. I only mention the subject, but by no means the words. The King then again gave me his arm, and we walked down together; there were difficulties raised about his going to Upton, but he chose to persevere. I went with the Lady Mayoress and

the Sheriffs, the King with his own people. We arrived first,
I had to hasten to take off my cloak, and then went down to
meet him at his carriage-door, with my husband, and seven of
our sons and sons-in-law. I then walked with him into the
drawing-room, where all was in beautiful order—neat, and
adorned with flowers: I presented to the King our eight daughters
and daughters-in-law, (Rachel only away,) our seven sons and
eldest grandson, my brother and sister Buxton, Sir Henry and
Lady Pelly, and my sister, Elizabeth Fry—my brother and
sister Gurney he had known before—and afterwards presented
twenty-five of our grandchildren. We had a solemn silence
before our meal, which was handsome and fit for a King, yet
not extravagant—every thing most complete and nice. I sat
by the King, who appeared to enjoy his dinner, perfectly at his
ease and very happy with us. We went into the drawing-room
after another solemn silence, and a few words which I uttered
in prayer for the King and Queen. We found a deputation of
Friends with an address to read to him—this was done; the
King appeared to feel it much. We then had to part.

The King expressed his desire that blessings might continue
to rest on our house.

Two very diverse interests shortly followed: the departure of
a grandson for the China seas, in H. M. S. Agincourt, and preparations for a sale for the benefit of the Funds of the British
Ladies' Society. The Lord Mayor had offered the use of the
Egyptian Hall for the purpose, and Lady Pirie had volunteered
to make every possible arrangement to lessen the fatigue of
Mrs. Fry, and render it easy and agreeable to her coadjutors
and friends.

Upton, Third Month, 15*th.*—My son and daughter Cresswell, and several of their children are staying here ; their little
Gurney just going into the navy. It really oppresses me in
spirit, I so perfectly object to war on Christian principles; it is
so awful in its devastating effects, naturally, morally, and
spiritually.

Fourth Month, 17*th*.—I feel the prospect seriously of our dear grandchild's going to sea ; he leaves us to-morrow ! It is no light matter. May our God, through His tender mercy, bring good out of this apparent evil. I have exceedingly regretted his going, but I am now more reconciled.

This week we have a very large sale at the Mansion House for the British Society. Although, on the whole, I approve these sales, there are many difficulties attached to them. I earnestly desire and pray, that through the tender mercy of my God, no harm may come of it, but in whatever we do, that the cause of truth and righteousness may be exalted.

Oh Lord hear ! Oh Lord help ! Oh Lord protect and forgive, for Thine own Name's sake ; and I pray, gracious Lord, that Thou wouldest be very near to me this day and this week, and help me, in deep humility, godly sincerity, and faithfulness, to do Thy will. And be near, I pray Thee, to all my children and friends, as their Helper and Keeper, and to my dear little grandson in this his most serious going out. I ask Thy protecting care over him, and if it be Thy will, make him feel the dangers, temptations, and difficulties of the line he has chosen, that he may never be one to promote war, but rather peace upon earth.

24*th, First-day*.—We commended our dear little grandson in faith to the keeping of his God, this day week in the evening, ourselves, my brother Gurney and some of his family, his father, mother, and brothers. I read first a solemn portion in the Proverbs, most applicable to him and his state. I spoke to him and prayed for him. He left us the next morning for Devonport with his father.

On Third, Fourth, and Fifth-day, we were fully occupied, principally by the Sale. It was very largely attended ; quantities of things given and sent to us ; extraordinary kindness shown to us by numbers, and the Lord Mayor and Lady Mayoress treating us with almost unbounded hospitality and kindness. One day they gave dinner and luncheon to three hundred persons, and I should think nearly as many another day or days. We sold things to the amount of about thirteen hundred pounds, still many things were left on hand ; when I consider the great

10

trouble, the enormous expense, the time taken up, the obligation we put ourselves under to so many persons, and the fatigue of body, I think I never can patronise another Sale.   However, in mercy, I was carried through without much suffering.   I think I was rather humbled than exalted by the great kindness I received ; but my Lord only knows my real estate, and to Him alone can I go to have my heart kept humble, watchful, and faithful.   These public events bring me into care about myself, and a fear lest like Ephraim, I should be mixed amongst the people, and lose my strength.

About this time she addressed to her eldest son the following letter, on his becoming a magistrate :—

My dearest John,

Ever since I heard of the prospect of thy being a magistrate, I have had it on my mind to write to thee ; but, alas ! such is the press of my engagements, that in my tender state I cannot do what I would.   I now, however, take up my pen to tell thee a little of my mind.   I think the office of magistrate a very weighty one, and often, I fear, too lightly entered, and its very important and serious duties too carelessly attended to ; and this I attribute to a want of a due feeling of the real difficulty of performing any duty ; particularly one where much true wisdom is required in doing justice between man and man, unless governed and directed by that wisdom that cometh from above, which is pure, then peaceable, gentle, easy to be entreated, full of mercy and good fruits, without partiality and without hypocrisy.   I believe it is thy desire to be governed by this wisdom, and to do justice, and love mercy ; but remember this requires a very watchful and subjected spirit, and those who have to sit in judgment on others must often sit in judgment on themselves : this fits the mind for sympathizing with the wanderers, and adopting every right measure for their reformation and improvement.   I think it is of the utmost importance to enter the duties attached to a magistrate in a very prayerful spirit, seeking the help and direction of the Spirit of God, and that the understanding may be enlightened to comprehend His will.   I am perfectly sensible that a justice of the peace must keep to the laws of his country in his decisions, and further, that he should be *well acquainted with these laws;* but I also know much rests with him, as to leaning on the side of *mercy,* and not of *severity;* and I know from my experience with so very many magistrates, how much they do in the prisons, &c., &c. to *instigate* or *increase* suffering; and also how much they may do for the improvement, and real advantage of criminals.   Much is in their power; they may do *much* harm or much good : too many are influenced by selfishness, party spirit, or partiality, both in individual cases and where public good is concerned; but the simple, upright, faithful, just and merciful magistrates, are too rare, and they are much wanted.   Mayst thou, my dearest John, be of this number; but remember it can only be by grace, and being thyself directed and governed by the Holy Spirit of God.

I advise thy reading Judge Hale's life—I know a judge and a justice are different things ; but the same wise, truly impartial spirit, should govern both.   I wish to remind thee, that in petty offences, much is left to the magistrate's own judgment, and the utmost care is needful that crime is not increased by punishment, and the offenders become hardened, instead of being brought to penitence.   I fear for young people.   Our prisons in Essex generally only harden ; therefore, try any other means with boys or girls : get them to Refuges, or try to have such measures adopted as may lead them to repentance and amendment of their ways. My very dear love to thy wife, and all thy children ; and with deep and earnest desires that through the grace of God thou mayst perform all thy duties, domestic and public, to His glory, thy own peace, and the good of mankind.

I am,

Thy very affectionate mother,

ELIZABETH FRY.

I forgot to say that a late Act of Parliament gives very great liberty in not sending young offenders to prison, but much rests with the judge or the magistrate, as to what is to be done with them ; this Act was I think about two years ago.   Many of the late Acts of Parliament respecting persons need much studying,

accompanied with the reports from the different Inspectors, these
give such an excellent knowledge of the subject. I believe I
could send thee most of them. The prisons in Essex are considered to need much improvement. I hope before very long to
visit you at Warley Lodge, and to enter upon many particulars
with thee.

How delightful the weather is, quite summer like; I think your
country must be very beautiful.

Upton, Fifth Month, 8*th.*—On Third-day, the Lady Mayoress
and I paid interesting and satisfactory visits to the Queen
Dowager, the Duchess of Kent and the Duchess of Gloucester.
I went with my heart lifted up for help and strength and direction, that the visits might prove useful, that I might drop the
word in season, and that I might myself be kept humble, watchful, and faithful to my Lord. I have fears for myself in visiting
palaces rather than prisons, and going after the rich rather than
the poor, lest my eyes should become blinded, or I should fall
away in any thing from the simple, pure standard of truth and
righteousness. We first called on the Duchess of Kent, and had
interesting conversation about our dear young Queen, Prince
Albert and their little ones. We spoke of the sale—my foreign
journey—the King of the Belgians, and other matters. I desired, wherever I could, to throw in a hint of a spiritual kind,
and was enabled to do it. I gave the Duchess some papers, with
a note to Prince Albert, requesting him to lay the suffering
state of the Waldenses from their fresh persecutions, before the
Queen. We next visited the Queen Dowager, and met her sister,
and the Duchess of Saxe Weimar, and her children. We had a
delightful time, much lively and edifying conversation upon the
state of religion in Europe, particularly amongst the higher
classes, and the great advancement of late years in the conduct
and conversation of the great of this world.

"How blind are we to ourselves, so that neither nations,
churches, nor individuals, see in themselves the symptoms of
decay visible to all around ! the pride which leads to break the
law of God, leads to this self-flattery." I have felt much warning and instruction in these words, they lead to the prayer, O

Lord, open Thou mine eyes, lest I sleep the sleep of death! and lest the light that is in me become darkness!

Mrs. Fry's health continuing in an infirm and suffering state, although better than during the winter, some change appeared necessary, and absence from the continual tide of London engagements, which reached her at Upton Lane. Her brother-in-law Mr. Hoare, offered the loan of his house at Cromer, a commodious and agreeable residence on the top of the cliff, commanding fine sea views. The little village of Cromer and its beautiful church in the foreground, and at the back, the Light-house hills, their easy ascent and smooth short turf, dry in even the wettest weather, affording a delightful resort for one whose failing powers could no longer encounter exertion. Cromer, too, was associated with the days of happy childhood. She greatly enjoyed this time, and was cheered by the singular kindness and affection of many whom she had long loved, and others with whom she then for the first time became sociably acquainted. Her sister, Mrs. Catherine Gurney, was with them at the Cliff House; she saw much of the beloved residents at Northrepps Hall. Northrepps Cottage, Sherringham, and Cromer Hall, were also points of light on the landscape —two months thus passed pleasantly and rapidly away.

(*On the journey*), *Seventh Month.*—I have been poorly part of every night, or early in the morning, since I left Upton, so as to feel discouraged and flat at being so far from home; but I desire to trust entirely. I have sought to have my steppings directed by Him, who knows what is best for us. I have not felt a will in these arrangements, and I desire to leave all to Him who orders all things well. I at times feel, particularly at night, so sunk, that I am ready to apprehend my natural powers are really failing. I occasionally ask in prayer for passing revival from my states of suffering, which prayers are often remarkably granted; but I am not disposed really to ask for prolonged life, because I fear lest, like Hezekiah, I should live to transgress before the Lord. I have probably an undue fear of an imbecile or childish state, and becoming a burden to others ; at the same time the idea of life being continued to me is pleasant, and the fear of death and the grave, to my nature great ; not that I fear for the everlasting state, although this confidence arises from no trust in any thing in myself, but faith in the mercy of God in Christ, who tasted death for every man ; and a full belief that the tender mercy of my God is over all His works ; and, unworthy as I am, that through His mercy, He will not cast me out of His presence, (which I delight in), nor shut up His tender mercies from me.

Cromer, 6th.—Here I am, in what was my dearest sister Hoare's little room, looking on the sea, but poorly after my journey, feeling the air almost too cold for me; but I am favoured to be quiet and trustful in spirit, and desire to leave all things to Him, who only knows what is best for me. My sister Catharine being with us, and my brother Joseph and his Eliza and dear Anna near to us, is very pleasant, and our dear brother and sister Buxton and Richenda being still at Northrepps.

Every week was marked by slow but sure increase in strength. But her amendment was retarded by anxiety on account of a daughter, then very ill in the Isle of Wight. To this daughter, who was under much trial, she wrote—

I am not very well to-day, but have not by any means lost the ground I had gained, though your trials appear to have brought me some steps back. If, in the ordering of Providence, things shall be brighter, I think I should rally again ; but I desire to have my will given up to the will of Him who knows what is best for us all, and earnestly desire to be very thankful that our trials are not of a deeper dye ; and being as far as I know, brought on us by Infinite Wisdom, I do not feel them like those produced by the exquisite suffering of sin.

I am, thy loving, sympathizing, and yet hopeful mother.

E. F.

She was also distressed by her eldest grandson entering the army, having a strong objection to war, and grieved that any belonging to her should directly or indirectly promote it.

First-day, Eighth Month, 14*th.*—I have deeply and sorrowfully felt our grandson Frank determining to go into the army. I truly have tried to prevent it, but must now leave it all to my Lord, who can, if He see meet, bring good out of that which I feel to be evil.

Mrs. Fry, with her brother Joseph John Gurney, who, with Mrs. Gurney and his daughter, had been staying at Cromer, endeavoured to establish a reading-room and library for the fishermen, to draw them from the public-house and its attendant evils. Some good was effected, but circumstances precluded permanent benefit. The affection many amongst them evinced to her was, however, extraordinary; as one of her German friends had expressed it, her very name was a " word of beauty " amongst them.

Eighth Month, 14*th, First-day.*—I have felt the weight of undertaking to establish a library and room for the fishermen, and something of a friendly society, as in my tender state the grasshopper becomes a burden. I was encouraged however in the night by these words, " Stedfast, immoveable, always abounding in the work of the Lord." In weakness and in strength, we must, as ability is granted, abound in the work of the Lord. May our labour not be in vain in Him ! I have had very comforting accounts from Denmark—our representations attended to respecting the prisons, and likely to have much good done in them ; also from Prussia. Surely our Lord has greatly blessed some of our poor efforts for the good of our fellow-mortals.

In Denmark, the King had given his warm sanction to the measures proposed by the Royal Danish Chancery for adding new buildings to the Police Prison, for the purpose of affording

more space and the opportunity of classification, for employment to be provided, and the cells heated in winter. Endeavours
also were to be made to place the female prisoners under the
care of women. In the House of Correction at Christianhaven
this was to be attempted immediately, and continued, if found
to answer. Bibles, New Testaments, Psalms, and other religious books were to be fully supplied to all prisoners, also works
of general information and instruction. Moreover, that the
opportunity was to be given them for attending public worship
—a chaplain was appointed expressly for the House of Correction. On the same occasion, His Majesty received a petition
from Pasteur Raffard and several others for permission to form
a Prison Society, and was graciously pleased to resolve with
regard to it as follows :—

" We have heard with the greatest satisfaction of the desire
of benevolent individuals to unite together to form a Prison
Committee, whose object should be the moral improvement of
the prisoners, and their employment, and return to society on
obtaining their freedom.

" Therefore, we gladly give an opportunity to the members of
this Committee, by means of visits and the distribution of religious and other fitting books, to exercise a good influence on
the prisoners. But it must be remembered that these visits, and
the distribution of books, must not take place without speaking
beforehand to the Chaplain and Director of the prison ; they must
be told which of the members of the Committee are going to
undertake the visiting. To them it must also be left to decide
which of the prisoners are to receive the benefit of these visits.
They must also fix the time and place, when and where these
visits are to take place.

" To visit the prisoners in the House of Detention is not
allowed by the rules ; but at any rate, these visits must be entirely
dependent on the inquiring judges. The defects in the internal
arrangement of the Stock House, will also cause difficulties in the
way of visiting this prison ; but the useful activity of the Society

may best be practised in the House of Labour Punishment and Correction, where particularly female prisoners may be visited by those ladies of the Committee, who, submitting to the annexed conditions, will turn their attention and care to this suffering and depraved part of mankind.

" It is our will that those authorities who have the chief superintendence of the prisoners, should weigh with attention any proposition for a change in the treatment of the prisoners, or in the arrangement of the prison, considered as desirable by the Society.

" Finally, we acknowledge the usefulness of the Society's object to endeavour to procure situations and work for the liberated prisoners, in order to secure them a maintenance, and to prevent their return to their former courses; and to this end would consider it desirable that the Society should act in concert with the police, and the Poor-Law Commission."

From Berlin Dr. Julius, who was then there, wrote to her that the construction of the four new penitentiaries was to be begun immediately. One at Berlin; one at Münster, in Westphalia; one at Ratibor, in Silesia; and another at Königsberg. " Two of the penitentiaries to be exactly like the Model Prison in London, according to the express will of His Majesty. In the two other penitentiaries, three of the wings to be on the plan of separate confinement by day and night; but in the fourth wing to be only nightly separation, and by day the convicts to be kept at work in small classes of picked men, as much as possible in silence."

The Countess Reden gave her a most gratifying account of the successful labours of the devoted chaplain at Jauer, adding, " he has established a sort of refuge or asylum for those who leave the prison, and have no home where to return, and need observation and religious instruction longer. An excellent, simple man, preparing for a missionary station, resolved to begin at Jauer for this purpose, and has taken into his lodging, five of the prisoners. It is a beginning, and from the very small income of this man and the chaplain all that could be expected."

From Düsseldorf she heard, through Miss Golstein, of the continued exertions of the Ladies' Committee for visiting female prisoners; also, that from the great prison at Werden all the female prisoners were to be removed to Cologne, to a separate prison. Miss Golstein also mentioned, that at Ratingen, a borough not far from Düsseldorf, an Asylum had been established "for young girls dismissed, and showing repentance, where, under the guidance of an excellent monitor, they obtain instruction in every work required of a good servant. This establishment is in such good repute, that as soon as they are able to go into service the opportunity is never wanting for it. We hear many instances of their behaving well, and leading a good life. The best proof of the good effects of our Asylum is, that in the two years of its existence, none dismissed from thence have been committed again."

The scenes which had occurred in the "Surrey" and "Navarino" female convict ships, and in the "Rajah" the preceding year, increased the conviction long felt by Mrs. Fry and her coadjutors, of the necessity which existed for the presence of female officers to receive the convicts on board, and remain in charge of them from the time of their embarkation until they reached the land of exile.

Under this impression, no sooner were the Ladies of the Convict Ship Committee informed that the "Garland Grove" was chartered for the conveyance of two hundred and five female prisoners to Van Diemen's Land, than they exerted themselves to find suitable persons to accompany them as matrons; having first applied to Sir James Graham, then principal Secretary of State for the Home Department, for his sanction and aid in effecting this object.

The following note addressed to Mrs. Fry, who was at this time at Cromer, much out of health, will show the readiness and kindness with which Sir James listened to her request, and that of her colleagues.

Whitehall, *August 9th,* 1842.

" Madam,

" I am directed by Sir James Graham to assure you, that he will, to the utmost of his power, procure every accommodation for the two ladies (matrons) proceeding with convicts in the ' Garland Grove.'

" The favourable consideration of the Board of Admiralty will be requested to the subject this day.

" The heavy pressure of business attending the close of the Session, prevents Sir James addressing you himself.

" I have the honour to be, Madam,

" Your most obedient servant,

" D. O'BRIEN, Private Secretary."

Some difficulty occurred, after this kind permission on the part of Government had been granted, in procuring a matron in the room of one of two who had been fixed upon by the Ladies' Committee, and who afterwards declined the proposal made to her.

Mrs. Fry's anxiety on this subject was evinced in the notes written by her to her friends in London. She longed (to use her own expression) for health and power to come and aid them.

The conclusion of one of these notes is so characteristic, that it is inserted.

I truly feel for you all, my beloved friends, who have now to bear the burden and heat of the day. May grace be granted you, and help from above, that you may be strengthened for your important work, and may your way be made plain before you ; and may our Heavenly Father undertake for us in this weighty matter, and lead us to the right parties to send abroad, who may be a blessing to those they go amongst, and be kept and blessed themselves! I long to hear from thee, or one of you, again, and hope I may one day be enabled again to take a labouring oar. Farewell, in much true love and sympathy, to thyself and all thy fellow-labourers.

I am,

Very affectionately, thy friend,

ELIZABETH FRY.

This letter is dated Cromer, Eighth Month, 20th, 1842.

Two very suitable persons were subsequently recommended by the ladies, and appointed by Government to the arduous and important office of matrons in the " Garland Grove." Before their embarkation the following admirable letter was written by Mrs. Fry to Miss Fraser :—

Cromer, *Eighth Month*, 27th, 1842.

My Beloved Friend,

Thy note received to-day has been a real comfort to me; the post brought some sorrows, and thy note brought weight in the other scale; but I have sat at home weeping, as I did not feel much inclined to meet a delightful party of brothers, sisters, &c., at my brother Buxton's, but rather to sit alone, and look to my own vineyard, and my own very deep interests in my family and my beloved friends, and for the causes that are near my heart. I humbly thank our Heavenly Father, who has regarded our very unworthy prayers, and raised up those that we trust may be suitable in the convict-ship, and helpful in the colony; may grace and wisdom from above be poured forth upon them; may they remember that the servants of the Lord must prove their faith more by *conduct* than word or profession; they must avoid anything like religious *cant*, if I may so express myself, and in an upright, holy, self-denying and watchful deportment, be preachers of righteousness, and prove who it is that they believe in, serve, and obey. I am often inexpressibly bound and brought low in spirit when I look at the standard and holy example of our blessed Lord, and then behold my own shortcoming. I long for a closer walk with God, for myself, and all that I love; and that, through the help of the Holy Spirit, we should more constantly prove our love to Him who died for us, and hath loved us with an everlasting love. Pray impress on these matrons the extreme importance of their prudent and circumspect conduct, as it respects the gentlemen on board ; and towards the women, the need of sound discretion, and the meekness of wisdom ; and amongst all, to be wise as serpents, harmless as doves, and to be pitiful and courteous. I quite feel my indulgent life, and am very ready to work when my Lord may enable me. I do not desire to save myself unless duty calls me to do it ; indeed, dear friend, I have always felt it an honour I have been unworthy of, to do anything for my Lord, and to be made an instrument of good to my fellow-creatures. I have been thankful for thy letters, because they have encouraged me to hope that you are not discouraged, but that the Spirit of our God is poured forth upon my beloved friends, to help them in this weighty and important work, and to make them willing to labour in this service, and for the good of their poor fellow-mortals. My dear love to all our sisters in this service ; and I am truly, in gospel bonds,

Thy attached friend,
ELIZABETH FRY.

The appointment of these matrons was justly regarded by Mrs. Fry, and her fellow-labourers, as a step of the utmost importance. It mitigates most materially the evils attendant upon the transportation of females. Objections had been urged to the measure in former years, but now it was clearly admitted that none were so fit to have charge of these unhappy women, as persons of their own sex, if such could be found who, influenced by right motives, and possessing the requisite qualifications, were willing to encounter the privations and perils of a long voyage in such society.

Northrepps Hall, Ninth Month, 18*th.*—I exceedingly value the company of so many of my most tenderly beloved brothers

VOL. II.   G G

and sisters, and other near and dear relations, so many nephews
and nieces, and others also. How I wish that I upheld amongst
these tenderly-beloved ones a more holy example. I do not
often apprehend it my place to speak much of spiritual things ;
but I most truly desire constantly to uphold the Christian
standard in an humble and watchful walk before the Lord, and
before my fellow-mortals.

25th, First-day.—I have not enough dwelt upon the extraordinary kindness of our dear brother and sister Buxton and
their children to us at this time, truly humbling to me, a poor
unworthy worm of the dust, also my dear brother Hoare, and all
that family—such a sweet renewal of love amongst us. How
blessed and how sweet is love, and how delightful to believe that
it has in measure the Heavenly stamp upon it. Our dearest
sister Catharine left Cromer yesterday,—quite a loss to us ; her
kindness has been great indeed.

Cromer, Tenth Month, 23rd.—Perhaps the last journal I may
ever write in this place, as to-morrow we mean to depart for
Lynn. Yesterday, I was very much affected and touched by
something that occurred—it was almost overwhelming. We paid
our farewell visit to Northrepps. My brother Hoare and his
family went also ; and at our beloved Fowell and Hannah's were
Andrew and Priscilla Johnston, Edward, and Catharine, and
Richenda Buxton. After dinner, Gurney Hoare brought me
a beautiful piece of plate, a silver inkstand, and my husband a
Testament, of fine paper and print, most beautifully bound.
They gave these presents in the kindest way, expressing love
and gratitude to us, and saying that dearest Anna Gurney and
those absent of their families united in the present. I felt before
receiving it, that I had been unduly loaded with gifts and kindness. My spirit was humbled, and really bowed within me
under a deep feeling of unworthiness at these proofs of love.
My Lord only knows my sense of it ; a poor, weak, unprofitable
servant as I am, that He should thus put it into the hearts of
His servants to show so much love and pity to me in my poor,
low, weak and unworthy estate before Him. Gracious Lord !
Thou knowest how little I can do for all these beloved ones. I
pray Thee reward them with spiritual and temporal blessings,

and if it be Thy will, let the sickly in body be more strengthened and restored, the sickly in soul healed, that all may be more
filled and satisfied with the unsearchable riches of Christ.

On her way home, she stayed at Lynn for a few days, her last
visit ! Never was she more bright or lovely in spirit. She had a
wise, kind word for all—children, servants, dependents. All
loved her, all felt that her message was not from herself, nor of
man's invention ; but that in her Master's name she invited
others to "love and to good works." How she condescended
to all ; listening to the minutest details of their cares and pleasures. How ready in devising means for helping others, not
merely in the great, but the little things of life : for who so
prompt in expedients ? in the sick room ? in the nursery with
an unmanageable child, or a froward servant ? She returned
home the end of October, but great pains and anxieties encountered her there !

CHAPTER XXIV.

A heavy family affliction awaited Mrs. Fry's return home—
the illness and death of her lovely little grandaughter, Harriet
Streatfeild, between seven and eight years old. She was much
with her children during their sorrowful nursing, and a close
participator in their grief.

To an absent daughter she wrote thus from the house of
mourning :—

Although I know that thou art written to fully, I add a line
of most tender love ; and to express my earnest desire, that as
our Heavenly treasures are increased, we may all more diligently seek the city which hath foundations, whose maker and
builder is God. Grace appears all-sufficient here.

Thy most loving mother,

E. F.

Her bereaved daughter having decided upon attending the
funeral of her child, Mrs. Fry accompanied her. It was
a bright clear winter's day ; besides her parents, nearly
twenty of their children and grandchildren followed to the silent

tomb, the first with the exception of their own little Elizabeth, of their forty-six descendants, who had been taken at an age of understanding.   The solemn procession arrived at East Ham Church, when with no spectators but the weeping villagers, the Vicar the Rev. William Streatfeild, commenced that most impressive service, which from this time was to be so frequently heard in the family circle.   Mrs. Fry went in the carriage with her daughter, and stood by her at the grave—when the service was ended, an impressive pause ensued, then, as the mourners prepared to move away, might be heard the tone of her gentle voice, " a solemn breathing sound " as she addressed the bereaved mother—" It is the Lord, let Him do what seemeth Him good."

A family party gathered in the evening : after the fifth chapter of the 2nd of Corinthians had been read, Elizabeth Fry addressed a heart-searching exhortation to her " children, grandchildren, and all the dearly beloved ones present," to be ready " when the next summons should come—thanksgiving that the lamb taken was a believing child, one rather peculiarly impressed with the fact of redemption, and forgiveness of sins through Christ ; and in practice, an obedient gentle-spirited creature, and according to the measure of so young a child, unusually full of good works and alms deeds, for she gave much to the poor, whose tales of woe, (whether true or false, she did not stop to inquire,) always touched her ; and her *good mark* money, which she saved till it amounted to a pound, she had given to the Ceylon Mission. Thus, even in so young a child, did the good tree bring forth little blossoms of good fruit ! gone to mature and fructify in Heaven ! through Christ who died for her, and in whom she truly believed." Many other things were spoken by her. Then she prayed for all the three generations present, a soul-touching prayer, committing all to God.

Upton Lane, First Month, 1st, 1843.—Another year is closed and passed never to return. It appears to me that mine is rather a rapid descent into the valley of old age.

Second Month, 6th.—I am just now much devoted to my children and all my family, and attend very little to public service of any kind. May my God grant, that I may not hide my talents as in a napkin ; and on the other hand that I may not step into services uncalled for at my hands. May my feeble labours at home be blessed. Gracious Lord, heal, help, and strengthen Thy poor servant for Thine own service, public or private.

Third Month, 19th.—It has been a week of various interests. On Second-day we met Lord Ashley at dinner at Manor House (my dear son William's), to consider the subject of China and the Opium Trade. Lord Ashley is a very interesting man, devoted to promoting the good of mankind, and suppressing evil —quite a Wilberforce I think.

Fourth Month, 2nd, First-day.—I entered the last week very low in my condition, bodily and mentally, so much so, that some of my family could hardly be reconciled to my attending the Quarterly Meeting. In the select Quarterly Meeting of Ministers and Elders, the subject of unity was much brought forward ; several spoke to it, and I had to express rather strongly, my belief that there is a great work going forward in the earth, and Satan desires to mar it by separating the Lord's servants. I warned Friends upon this point, because there are diversities of gifts, differences of operation and administration, they should not sit in judgment one on another, or condemn one another, or suppose they are not of the same spirit, and one in the same Lord and the same God.

With somewhat of restored health, Elizabeth Fry believed it her duty once more to visit the Continent. Her attraction was peculiarly to Paris. Matters of importance that she earnestly desired to have completed, awaited her attention, and there appeared an opening beyond any thing she had known before, for usefulness in that great capital. There were Christian and benevolent persons whom she desired to see again " in the flesh," and build them up, if enabled, in faith and hope. She had retained her certificate, granted her by Friends for her last journey. Her brother, Joseph John Gurney, also believed it his duty to visit Paris, as part of a more extended journey. Mrs. Gurney accompanied him, and Josiah Forster consented to join their party. In addition to these three participators and supporters in the various religious and philanthropic objects which might open before them, her eldest daughter went as her mother's especial companion, to watch over and care for her health.

They landed at Boulogne. The voyage had been so trying to Mrs. Fry, from a heavy rolling sea and the weather being cold and unfavourable, that her fellow-travellers doubted the practicability of her pursuing her journey. By setting off late, and resting an hour or two in the middle of the day, she seemed revived, when at the end of two days they arrived at Amiens. Here the Sunday was passed. In the evening they were permitted to worship in the simple mode of Friends, in the room used by the Protestants as their chapel, where a venerable pastor, eighty years of age laboured among a small flock in the midst of a large Roman Catholic population. Many of these were present ; their hearts appeared touched and animated by the ministry on this occasion, which tended to console the discouraged, and strengthen the feeble-minded.

At Clermont-en-Oise, the ladies were permitted to inspect the Great Central Prison for women, calculated to contain twelve hundred, although nine hundred only were in confinement when they were there. It is under the charge of a Supérieure and twenty-two nuns, no men being allowed to enter. The Supérieure was an intelligent, powerful-minded woman, greatly afraid of the abuses to which the solitary system is liable, and the silent system also, when carried to extremes. The prisoners work in

large cheerful rooms, a hundred together, under the closest inspection of the nuns, who relieve the monotony by not unfrequently uniting in singing hymns.   But a splendid prison extremely well managed, is not so rare a scene as that which concluded the visit. On first arriving, Mrs. Fry had expressed a great
wish to see all the nuns, but the Supérieure considered it impossible, as they never leave the women; however, just before quitting
the prison, Mrs. Fry was conducted into an apartment around which
sat, some on chairs, some on extremely low seats, some apparently
on the floor, the twenty-two nuns in their grey dresses, and the
lay sisters in black ; placed in the middle were Mrs. Fry and her
sister, Mrs. Joseph John Gurney, the Supérieure between them,
holding Mrs. Fry by the hand, whose daughter was requested by
the Supérieure to interpret for them. It was no light or easy task
to convey exactly her mother's address, on the deep importance of
maintaining not alone good discipline amongst the prisoners, but
endeavouring to lead them in living faith to Christ, as the only
Mediator between God and man, and through whom alone they
could be cleansed from the guilt and power of sin. At His name
every head bowed.   She then went on to tell of Newgate, and the
effects of the Gospel there ; many tears were shed at this recital.
She concluded by a lively exhortation to these devoted nuns,
whom she could " salute as sisters in Christ," to go forward in
their work, but in no way to rest upon it, as in itself meritorious.
Here the Supérieure interposed, " Oh non, mais il y a un peu de
mérite, l'homme a quelque mérite pour ce qu'il fait :" an old nun,
who probably understood English, rejoined, " Ma mère, Madame
thinks that if the love of God does not sufficiently animate the
heart to do it without feeling it a merit, or desiring reward, it
falls short."   " Ah, c'est bien ! comme elle est bonne !" replied
the Supérieure. Mrs. Fry concluded by a short blessing and
prayer in French. It was a curious scene, and a solemn feeling
pervaded the whole.

Mrs. Fry had strong hopes of effecting much during her stay at Paris, another spirit prevailed there. M. Guizot in fact head of the Cabinet, though the Duke of Dalmatia was President of the Council, having proved himself ready to support any measure for the moral benefit of the people, and their advance in sound knowledge and civilization. In 1833, when Minister of Public Instruction, he had shown his genius for education, and lively interest in the good of his countrymen, by the ordinance which, prepared by himself, and promulgated as law, raised in an exceedingly short space of time, in nine thousand Communes, the village school-room, for the instruction of the village poor.

Mrs. Fry believed that she should find in him the enlightened philanthropist, and the prudent yet fearless politician ; one who taught in the school of the French Revolution, had marked and comprehended its horrors, without being blind to the benefits it had conferred upon his country and mankind, in sweeping away the accumulated tyranny and bigotry of centuries : one who, whilst he shrank from changes for the sake of novelty, was as capable in devising expedients for the remedy of real evils, as he was resolute in carrying them into execution. Unblemished in personal character, exemplary in private life, and professing the Reformed faith in religion, Mrs. Fry looked to him as eminently calculated to receive and respond to her own opinions and experiences.

Paris, (Hôtel Meurice), Fourth Month, 22nd.—We are favoured to be very comfortably settled here, and I may most thankfully say, feel in our right place, after a time of unusual conflict to my own mind.

I was little fit to enter Paris ; the day was hot, and the rooms at the hotel oppressive ; the noise of the street so great, that I feared, in my poor state, I could not support it, and was frightened about myself and felt as if it were altogether too much for me, but I revived towards evening, was favoured with a peaceful night, and awoke much refreshed and comforted. Our beloved friend the Countess Pelet has been a real helper to me, quite a spiritual comforter ; so encouraging as to the time of our visit. She expresses her belief of our being surely guided by a spirit within, safely leading us to places at the right time. Others really dear to me show much faithful love, and they appear delighted to have us with them. On Fifth-day, we attended the little Meeting of Friends in the Faubourg du Roule. The next day, some of our serious friends came to us in the evening. And the following, we spent a very agreeable evening at the Mallets', where there was, to my feelings a sweet sense of love and peace over us, with the numerous members of that interesting family.

I may thankfully say, I now feel greatly healed and helped and encouraged, although it appears but little I have done for my Lord in any way ; but I must wait His time and His putting forth, and not enter anything in my own way and time.

Lord be pleased to grant, through Thy tender mercy in Christ my Saviour, that our visit to this place may be really profitable to ourselves, and to those we are come amongst, and that it may promote love and charity amongst Christians generally ; help to remove dependence on the arm of man, and to have it placed on Thy arm of power, and stimulate many more diligently to seek Thy kingdom and Thy righteousness—that some worldly-minded and wanderers may be led to return, repent and live—that some that are dead may be made alive again—and that those that are lost may be found in Thy fold of peace and safety. Grant also, gracious Lord ! that the great blessing of preservation may be with my tenderly beloved family at home.

On the 25th, Mrs. Fry waited, by appointment, on the Duchess of Orleans, at the Tuileries ; but finding some difficulty in fully conveying her meaning, her daughter was sent for to interpret. In a letter to her sisters, she describes herself ushered into an immense drawing-room, the size, and heavy crimson and gold magnificence of which exceeded any room she had ever seen. On a sofa, about half way up the room against the wall was seated her mother ; by her side a young lady, in deep mourning, over whose white and black cap hung a large long crape scarf or veil that reached the ground on either side, her figure tall and elegant, her face and features small and delicate, her eyes blue and her complexion very fair,—a lovely blush came and went as she spoke. From her dress and appearance no one could for a moment doubt, but that it was the widow of the heir of France. Opposite to her on a chair was an elderly lady the grand Duchess of Mecklenburgh, her step-mother, who had brought her up from childhood.   These three were the only occupants of that vast saloon : its walls were hung with crimson velvet, embroidered in heavy gold columns, with vine leaves twisted round, and all things magnificent in proportion.   The conversation at first was upon the Duchess of Orleans' affliction.   They had each a Bible in their hand, Mrs. Fry read to them a few verses, and commented on them, on affliction and its peaceable fruits, afterwards.   They then spoke of the children of the House of Orleans, and the importance of their education and early foundation in real Christian faith ; the grand Duchess of Mecklenburgh, an eminently devoted, pious woman, deeply responded to these sentiments.   It was an hour and a half before this interesting conversation came to a close.

The following Sunday, after attending their own little Meeting, a large public one was held in the Methodist chapel. Mr. Gurney spoke well in French, Mrs. Fry through an excellent interpreter.

The evening of the next day, they gathered round them a very singular party, about thirty persons of colour, chiefly from Hayti, the Isle of France, and Guadaloupe, principally students of law or medicine ; one a painter, who had some good pictures in the exhibition.   Several of them spoke excellent French, and were intelligent-looking young men.   Mr. Gurney was desirous of obtaining from them any information he could on the state of the different West Indian Islands.

The evening concluded with reading in the Bible.   Mrs. Fry

addressed her auditory on the words of St. Peter, " I perceive that God is no respecter of persons ;"—Acts x. 34—going on to that glorious passage in the Revelation, which tells of the company that cannot be numbered, gathered out of every nation, kindred, tongue, and people.

Speaking of the close of the day, she says: " I laid me down and slept in peace."

Wednesday was a dinner at Count Pelet de la Lozère's. Thursday, at M. Guizot's : seated by their celebrated host, this dinner was felt by Mrs. Fry to be an occasion of great responsibility. She was encouraged by his courteous attention, unreservedly to speak to him on the subjects which had so long been near to her heart. It was no common ordeal for woman, weak even in her strength, to encounter reasoning powers and capabilities such as his : their motives of action arising probably from far different sources, but curiously meeting at the same point, her's from deep-rooted benevolence, directed by piety in its most spiritual form ; his from reflection, observation, and statesman-like policy, guided by philanthropy, based on philosophy and established conviction—yet in the aggregate the results the same, an intense desire to benefit and exalt human nature, and arrest the progress of moral and social evil, and an equal interest in ascertaining the most likely methods of effecting the desired end. They spoke of crime in its origin, its consequences, and the measures to be adopted for its prevention ; of the treatment of criminals ; of education and of Scriptural instruction. Here Mrs. Fry unhesitatingly urged the diffusion of Scriptural truth, and the universal circulation of the Scriptures, as the most potent means within human reach of controlling the power of sin, and shedding light upon the darkness of superstition and infidelity.

The following evening, Mrs. Fry and her brother received at their hotel a large party of Greeks ; amongst others, their Ambassador, M. Coletti. The Duke de Broglie was kind enough to interpret for Mrs. Fry. Before the party separated, Mr. Gurney read the account of St. Paul's visit to Athens ; his comments on this portion of Holy Writ were luminous, powerful, and appropriate.

When in Paris in 1839, Mrs. Fry had become interested in a large party of Greeks who met at her hotel one evening. On the present occasion that interest was confirmed. The want of books in Greece, even those of elementary instruction was fully discussed, and it was decided to form some regular plan to supply this want. That this might be done effectually, a second evening was appointed for the purpose. There were assembled on this occasion some very superior men, among others M. de Comnène, who though not " born in the purple," was one of a family, recognized as lineally descended from the Emperors of Constantinople. A committee of Greeks, French and English, was formed to draw up rules, and endeavour to raise subscriptions, though not till after much animated discussion ; the young Greek students in Paris undertaking to translate some works of elementary instruction. A spelling book with pictures was to be the first thing attempted, a desideratum not existing in that country. There was reason to expect that, through influence with the Government at Athens, these books would be dispersed into every Commune for the use of the schools and poor. Mrs. Fry had before been interested on the subject of female education in Greece, and in this important movement for supplying that country with elemental literature, she believed that the women also would eventually partake in the benefit.

Paris, Fifth Month, 7th, First-day.—Second-day last was a very great festival called the Fête du Roi, when it was striking to observe such great crowds of people so orderly and well conducted. There is something in the French very attractive to

me,—their lively yet sober habits—their politeness to one
another—indeed they are to me peculiarly agreeable.   During
the day we had various calls of duty, and an evening of rather
quiet recreation with a family who spent it with us.   From our
windows we saw the most beautiful fireworks, which was pleasant; as perfect order prevailed, I rejoiced that the poor should
partake of such innocent refreshment and recreation, for there
appeared no drunkenness or dissipation.   I wish we had more
innocent recreations for our poor at home, to keep them out of
the public-houses.

Fifth-day evening, the 1st.—We had a most weighty and
serious time.   We met at our friend Mark Wilks' about a hundred persons, perhaps forty of them pasteurs and missionaries.
They had a religious service of their own—first singing a hymn,
then reading the Holy Scriptures, afterwards prayer; which when
concluded, Mark Wilks said any brother or sister present was
at liberty to speak.   I ventured in fear to open my mouth ; an
interpreter at hand.   First, on the state of Protestant Europe,
the religious persecutions in it, and dependence on forms. I also
expressed my desire that they might stand fast in the liberty
wherewith Christ had made them free, and not be again entangled
with any yoke of bondage ; my hope that they might arise and
shine, manifesting that their light was come, and that the
glory of the Lord had risen upon them ; and further said that I
believed this would be the case.   I then addressed the pasteurs
only, desiring that the Spirit of God might be poured forth upon
them, that sinners might be converted, mourners comforted, and
the weak strengthened.   I felt humbled afterwards, ready to
hide my head from the sight of man ; yet I returned home, laid
me down and slept, for the Lord sustained me.   But He only
knows the deep exercise of my spirit at such times.

On Sixth day, we paid a long visit to the St. Lazare Prison,
with both Catholic and Protestant ladies, spoke to the women at
different times, as did my sister, through much difficulty in being
heard, or properly interpreted for ; yet the truth did appear to
reach many hearts, and I believe this visit was not in vain in
the Lord.

Several very large parties succeeded each other, in which religious communications were blended with social intercourse.

Mrs. Fry again saw the Duchess of Orleans; with the grand Duchess of Mecklenburgh, she was permitted several interviews, in which the intercourse between these eminently Christian ladies assumed a deeply religious character.

It being the period of the annual religious meetings, many pasteurs were assembled in Paris; about thirty of them were invited by Mr. Gurney to breakfast, at the Hôtel Meurice.

Paris, 14th.—On Second day, about thirty pasteurs to breakfast, from different parts of France, a very interesting set of men. First we had a Scripture reading; Joseph and myself had much to express to them at the time; a most weighty concern it was. My brother prayed, and one of the pasteurs spoke. We then breakfasted, and had really a delightful meal. I remembered that our Lord condescended to attend feasts, and this was a feast offered to His servants, of which we partook in love and peace. The pasteurs afterwards gave us an account of the religious state of the people around them; a good work certainly appears going on amidst many obstructions. We then spoke to them. I particularly recommended religious unity with all who love the Lord, and kindness to the Methodists as a valuable body of Christians.

One evening M. Guizot dined with Mrs. Fry's party. The topics before discussed were then resumed:—the state of Protestants in France, La liberté des cultes, and Negro Slavery. Mrs. Fry entreated M. Guizot's attention to the state of the Sandwich Islands. She had received from Kamehameha III. the King, a letter a few months before, entreating her good offices to second his endeavours to prohibit the importation and use of spirituous liquors in his kingdom, the baneful and demoralizing effects of which he stated to be lamentable.

Much had been done for the improvement of prisons since

10

Mrs. Fry was last at Paris. The importance of the subject had been fully recognised, and a bill brought before the Chamber of Deputies.

The following extract from the opening speech of the Minister of the Interior, shows by what means he contemplated concili- ating the requirements of humanity with the interests of the community at large.

" Our object," says the Minister, " is not entirely to seques- trate the prisoner, or to confine him to absolute solitude; such is not the object of our bill, and this is what makes it differ from the American system.

" We want to exclude convicts from the society of their fel- low prisoners, to keep them free from bad examples, and wicked associations ; but we want at the same time to multiply around them moral and honest connexions. Besides their being visited by the Director of the Jail, they will be in frequent communi- cation with the teacher and the medical attendant. The chap- lain, or the ministers of the several denominations acknowledged by the State, will have easy access to the cells at.the hours ap- pointed by the prison regulations. It is to be the more effica- cious, as the infection of bad example and contaminating influence will be removed. Some of the provisions of the bill will mitigate the principle of solitary confinement, in a manner which has been suggested by the commission of 1840, and should not pass unnoticed by the Chamber. Convicts sentenced to more than twelve years hard labour, or to perpetual hard labour, after having undergone twelve years of their punish- ment, or when they shall have attained the age of seventy, will be no longer separated from the others, excepting during the night. Prisoners sentenced to " réclusion" or undergoing a correctional punishment, when seventy years of age, will not be subject to individual confinement."

The bill laid down as a principle that the " Bagnes " were to be ultimately replaced by houses of hard labour; that houses of " réclusion" were to be erected, to take in all convicts sentenced to " réclusion " now detained in central houses. It introduced considerable improvement into the management of houses of imprisonment, especially those supported by Departments. In conformity with the principles of the system adopted, the bill had also for its object, to bring under the direct authority of the Minister of the Interior, as a centre, all the prisons in the kingdom. M. de Tocqueville was a strong advocate of the separate system, although he desired to see some modification in the manner of its execution. M. Carnot, also a member of the commission for the improvement of prisons, entertained rather different opinions, and was less favourable to the entire separation of prisoners.

With this dawn of promise for the future, and so much improvement already effected, it was sad to think of the St. Lazare prison and its twelve hundred inmates, still in a state of wretchedness and neglect.

The institution for Deaconnesses, or Protestant sisters of Charity afforded an asylum for such female penitents of the Protestant faith as desired to seek shelter within its walls, after their liberation from prison. Mrs. Fry visited and inspected the institution with M. Vallette, a devoted pasteur who has shared with its founder, M. Vermeil, the spiritual care of the association. M. Vermeil of the Calvinist, M. Vallette of the Lutheran Church, have represented the two divisions of Protestantism, by which the society has been jointly and most amicably nurtured.

Although then only in its infancy, Mrs. Fry was deeply impressed with its promises of usefulness, and heard of its progress from time to time with lively pleasure. A letter from M. Vallette to a daughter of Mrs. Fry, very lately written, recounts the circumstances of her visit, and gives a clear and succinct report of the present state of the institution, its steady advance and extended usefulness.

Madame!

Vous avez bien voulu me demander quelques détails sur la visite que feu Madame votre mère fit à la maison des Diaconesses, lors de son dernier voyage à Paris, Je m'empresse de répondre à votre désir, mais je dois le faire en toute hâte au milieu des derniers préparatifs de mon départ.

Cette femme si vénérée aussi parmi nous, se porta dans toutes les parties de la maison des Diaconesses et après avoir tout examiné elle exprima son approbation du but, et de l'arrangement. Mais ses plus longs instants furent réservés aux repenties ; elle les vit, leur parla et leur adressa en commun une exhortation. Nous les avions réunies dans la salle où se fait la prière ; plusieurs autres personnes de l'établissement et plusieurs Dames du Comité étaient présentes ainsi que moi. La locution de Mme. Fry fut sérieuse et simple, forte et émouvante quoique traduite phrase par phrase de l'Anglais en Français, ce qui diminue toujours un peu l'effet.

Ces paroles firent une profonde impression sur l'esprit des pauvres femmes qu'elles avaient principalement en vue. Plusieurs des Repenties exprimèrent, ce jour même et beaucoup plus tard encore, leur reconnaissance et les sentiments sérieux que cette visite leur avait inspirés.

Madame Fry paraissait heureuse elle même de ce qu'elle avoit ou, l'œuvre qu'elle avoit sous les yeux lui inspirait de l'espoir pour l'avenir sous la bénédiction du seigneur.

Si elle la visitait aujourd'hui elle y trouverait les grands changements qu'elle a desirés et pressentis. La maison qu'elle visita alors (rue des Trois-Sabres) n'est plus habitée que par les élèves institutrices et par les Diaconesses que leur charge ne force pas à demeurer ailleurs ; il y demeure aussi quelque jeunes personnes qui désirent acquérir sous la Direction d'une Diaconnesse, la pratique des différentes œuvres de Charité Chrétienne. Mais à côté de l'ancienne maison s'en élève une beaucoup plus vaste (rue de Reuilly 93,) que Madame Fry n'a pu voir, c'est la maison de service proprement dite. Elle contient dans des locaux parfaitement séparés, et pourtant unis dans un plan commun :

1. *Education.*—Une crèche pour 8 berceaux, une salle d'asile pour 100 à 150 enfants.   Une école pour 100 à 120 jeunes filles un ouvroir d'apprentissage pour 30 apprenties.

2. *Refuge proprement dit.*—Un refuge avec 25 cellules pour femmes et filles repentantes.   Une retenue pour 14 jeunes filles mineures sequestrées.   Un disciplinaire pour 28 à 30 plus jeunes filles en correction.

3. *Santé.*—Trois salles de malades pour 30 personnes, hommes, femmes, enfants.   Une infirmerie de 20 lits pour des enfants scrofuleux.   Six chambres de convalescence.

Il y a aussi deux écoles du dimanche de plus la maison offre au public de ce quartier un oratoire très commode pour 300 personnes ; mon ami le pasteur Vermeil et moi nous avons assumé la charge d'y célébrer un cutte public tous les dimanches et jours de fête, outre les autres soins que nous donnons à cette maison.

Íl y a journellement aussi des vaccinations et des consultations gratuites par le médecin de l'établissement pour les gens du quartier, et les Diaconesses visitent les pauvres des environs pour leur porter des secours temporels et spirituels.   Au reste il a dû paraître dans la Revue d'Edinbourg un article puisé à la source qui vous donnera d'autres détails ; j'ai voulu seulement, Madame, vous faire remarquer quelle différence heureuse il existe entre ce que nòtre amie vénérée a vu, et ce que pourront voir les personnes qui visiteront l'etablissement.   J'ose appeler sur cette œuvre qui est conduite d'après les principes du pur Evangile, votre intérêt et vos prières ainsi que la co-opération chrétienne des personnes à qui vous auriez la bonté d'en parler.

Je joins à ces lignes un exemplaire du Rapport que d'ailleurs on peut se procurer chez le Rev. Martin, pasteur de l'Eglise Française à Londres, 241, Oxford Street.

Agréez, Madame, l'assurance de mon respectueuz dévoument.   Que le seigneur soìt avec vous !

Votre serviteur en Christ,

L. VALLETTE, Pasteur.

P.S.—Je sais que vous devez connaître les principes sur les

quels repose toute l'œuvre des Diaconesses, mais je désire vous répéter que nous désirons en tout, enseignement, exhortations, instructions, consolations, visites, voir à la base les inébranlables vérités du salut gratuit en Jésus Christ et la Charité, fruit d'une foi-vivante.

In the Penitentiary department there are some admirable arrangements which Mrs. Fry considered singularly judicious, and likely to be of great benefit to the penitents. Each inmate has a small sleeping room, plainly but comfortably furnished. In this room the first fortnight after her reception, is passed, her solitude being relieved by walks in the garden, under the inspection of one of the Sisters, and by the visits of the pasteurs and the ladies. This measure is intended as a test of the sincerity of her good resolutions. It is not regarded as a hardship by these poor young women, one of whom said, " that she should prefer passing twenty years in her cell, to remaining two months in the prison of St. Lazare." Another excellent rule is, that after attending public prayer in the Chapel of the Refuge, each penitent retires to her cell for an hour; thus affording time for quiet meditation on the truths just brought before her. From Paris, her brother and his family proceeded to the South of France, and Josiah Forster having returned to England, Mrs. Fry was left alone with her daughter to spend a peculiarly interesting fortnight in Paris.

Paris, Fifth Month, 21st, First-day.—My birth-day, sixty-three! My God hath not forgotten to be gracious, nor hath He shut up His tender mercies from me.

The last week has been an interesting one. We were first sent for by the King. My brother, sister, and I paid rather a remarkable visit to him, the Queen, and the Princess Adelaide. To my surprise and pleasure yesterday, there arrived from the Queen a most beautiful Bible with fine engravings, without note or comment, given me as a mark of her satisfaction in our visit.

Boulogne, 28*th.*—Through the condescending mercy of our Heavenly Father we are safely and peacefully arrived here, after a quiet journey with my dearest Katharine. We were near meeting with a very serious accident, but through mercy, we escaped without injury. Our leaving Paris was no common occasion. The morning before, several of our beloved friends were with us ; they literally loaded us with presents, indeed, it appeared as if they did not know how to show their love to us enough. Before we parted from each other we had a most solemn time in prayer, little knowing whether we should see each other's faces more. I hardly knew how to accept all their generous kindness. What can we say, but that their hearts being thus turned to us must be " the Lord's doing, and is marvellous in our eyes ?"

The previous evening many of our dear Friends, English and French, came to take leave of us; we read together the 121st Psalm. In the morning I visited a Roman Catholic Refuge and finished well with the Greeks in the afternoon.

On Third-day, we visited the great military prison at St. Germain, accompanied by a French general, an English colonel, our excellent friend Count Pelet, and Moreau-Christophe. We were received very kindly by the Colonel Governor of the Prison, and his wife, and took our *déjeûné* with them.

In the evening we went to a large Meeting in one of the Faubourgs with the French Methodists in humble life. How curious the changes in my daily life !—what a picture they would make !—In the morning surrounded by the high military and the soldier prisoners—in the evening in a Methodist meeting-house, with the people and their pasteurs, and afterwards by poor little French children, hearing them read.

Another day I was at a large Prison Committee of Protestant ladies. I think they have been greatly prospered in their work of Christian love, in which they have persevered ever since my first visit to Paris ; there have been many instances of great improvement in the prisoners under their care. After prayer for them I left them.

The afternoon of the Sabbath, I paid a distressing visit to the St. Lazare Prison ; such a scene of disorder and deep evil I have seldom witnessed—gambling, romping, screaming. With much difficulty we collected four Protestant prisoners, and read

with them. I spoke to those poor disorderly women, who, appeared attentive, and showed some feeling. I have represented,
to many in authority the sad evils of this prison, and have
pleaded with them for reform, for religious care, and for Scriptural instruction.

In the evening the dear Countess Pelet was with us, and we
had a large assembly mostly of English, it was thought ninety
or a hundred. I was tired and poorly, my flesh and my heart
ready to fail, but the Lord strengthened me, and I felt really
helped by a power quite above myself. With this company I
had a most satisfactory parting time, and a sweet feeling of love
and unity with these servants of the Lord.

A quiet resting day was spent at Passy with her old and
valued friends of the Delessert family, with whom she had some
solemn religious communications on this, the last day she spent
amongst them.

On returning home, she was able to attend one or two sittings
of the Yearly Meeting in London, and for a short time to
encounter the current of life better than she had done before her
journey.

Sixth Month, 25th.—A week of considerable occupation.
Second-day, the British Society committee, an interesting meeting with those beloved ladies; so much oneness in heart and
purpose, a delightful evidence of the sweetness of Christian
unity, and how those who differ in secondary points may agree
in the most essential ones, and be one in Christ. We have cause
for thankfulness in the excellent arrangements made by Lord
Stanley for our poor prisoners in Van Diemen's Land; he
appears so carefully to have attended to the representations we
made respecting the evils existing there, and to have proposed
good measures to remedy them.

The attention of Mrs. Fry and her friends in the Prison
Committee, had been awakened anew to the condition of the

female prisoners in Van Diemen's Land, the only colony to which they then were sent. She had received letters from Lady Franklin, and Miss Hayter, (the late matron in " The Rajah,") depicting in lively colours the various evils to which these banished ones were exposed. The assignment of men had nearly ceased, but female convicts were still disposed of in that way to which the term " domestic slavery" had been so successfully applied, that the whole system, so far as male prisoners were concerned, was at an end.

But the assignment of women continued. When a convict ship arrived from England, as many or more persons than there were prisoners on board, were immediate candidates for their services. These candidates were not bound to shew any qualification of their fitness to be the employers of convicts. Publicans or ticket-of-leave holders were not permitted to take them into their employ, but with these exceptions, they might immediately on landing from the ship be located in the families of the colonists. Those supposed to be the best, were assigned to the best masters and mistresses, whilst the refuse fell to the lot of the lower ranks of society ; the word "best" being applied to the upper classes. As a great proportion of the tradesmen are emancipated convicts, a fair estimate of the chances of improvement (so to speak) of the prisoner servants may easily be formed.

" The Cascade Factory is a receiving house for the women on their first arrival (if not assigned from the ship,) or on their transition from one place to another ; and also a house of correction for faults committed in domestic service, but with no pretension to be a place of reformatory discipline, and seldom failing to turn out the women worse than they entered it. Religious instruction there was none, except, that occasionally on the Sabbath the Superintendant of the prison read prayers, and sometimes divine service was performed by a chaplain, who had also an extensive parish to attend to.

" The officers of the establishment consisted at that time of only five persons—a porter, the superintendent and matron, and two assistants. The number of prisoners in the Factory, when first visited by Miss Hayter, was five hundred and fifty. It followed, of course, that nothing like prison discipline could be enforced or even attempted. In short, so congenial to the taste of its inmates was this place of custody, (it would be unfair to call it a place of punishment,) that they returned to it again and again when they wished to change their place of servitude; and they were known to commit offences on purpose to be sent into it preparatory to their re-assignment elsewhere."

This brief account, drawn from the letters already referred to, may be summed up with a passage extracted from one of them :—

" Yet after visiting the Factory, and hearing every body speak of its unhappy inmates, I could not but feel that they were far more to be pitied than blamed. No one has ever attempted any measures to ameliorate their degraded condition. I felt that had they had the opportunity of religious instruction, some, at least, might be rescued. I wish I could express to you all I feel and think upon the subject; and how completely I am over-whelmed with the awful sin of allowing so many wretched beings to perish for lack of instruction. Even in the hospital of the Factory, the unhappy creatures are as much neglected in spiritual things as if they were in a heathen land; there are no Bibles, and no Christians to tell them of a Saviour's dying love."

On the receipt of these letters, Mrs. Fry lost no time in communicating their contents to Lord Stanley the Secretary of State for the Colonial Department, accompanying the large extracts which she sent to his Lordship, with a detailed account of the plans adopted by Sir Ralph and Lady Darling at the Factory at Paramatta, which was, on their arrival in New South Wales, in almost every respect in the same state as that at Hobart Town.

It was necessary there to alter the building, so as to admit of a perfect separation into classes.   Employment was supplied by the Ladies' Committee ; daily religious services were performed, schools brought into operation, and by degrees the whole establishment conducted, as far as was found practicable, in the manner recommended in Mrs. Fry's work on visiting prisons, and according to the Rules of the British Ladies' Society.

The state of the prisoners of Van Diemen's Land was already occupying the attention of Government, and measures were taken, which have since much changed the circumstances in which female prisoners are placed when transported.   An account of the alterations which have been made, would occupy more room than can be devoted to the subject ; but it may briefly be stated that a man-of-war, fitted up as a temporary prison, was shortly after this period sent to Van Diemen's Land, and moored in the Derwent, the river on the banks of which, Hobart Town is built.   A large staff of officers, male and female, was sent out, and Dr. and Mrs. Bowden were placed at the head of the establishment.   In this ship (the " Anson"), all females transported from the United Kingdom are received on their arrival in the colony.   They remain under systematic instruction for six months, and are then placed in the service of the colonists. An opportunity of testing their characters is thus afforded.   If they are well disposed, they are recommended to situations where they are not exposed to temptations, too strong, for their newly-formed resolutions of amendment to resist.   But the factories are as yet the only receptacles for prisoners who leave their situations, whether on account of incompetency for the fulfilment of their duties, or in order to be punished for offences committed in servitude.   A new prison is in progress of erection, and it may be hoped that when completed it will be placed under such regulations, as to remove some, if not all the evils which still exist.

On the 21st, Elizabeth Fry attended the Quarterly Meeting

at Hertford, accompanied by her brother Samuel Gurney and one of his daughters ; it was the last time she left home on a mission of this character, expressly for religious service.

The following evening a large party of the Delegates from different parts of the world, assembled in London to attend the Anti-Slavery and Peace Society Meetings, came to Upton Lane ; the evening was closed by Scripture reading and prayer.

JOURNAL RESUMED.

Last First-day was not one to be forgotten ; much of the morning without clouds. My dear brother and sister Buxton were at Meeting. I felt it my duty to encourage the weary, and enlarged upon our foolishness, yet how the Lord is made unto His people wisdom, righteousness, sanctification, and redemption. There were some who appeared much impressed. Through the whole of that day and into the next, renewed peace rested on my spirit.

I feel that I am pressed rather beyond my present power of mind or body, and I really forget things—my desire is lively and strong to serve all, one omission has been a real pain, and led me to endeavour afresh to bring myself and my deeds to the light, that they may be reproved, or be made manifest, that they are wrought in God.

In July, Mrs. Fry showed increasing symptoms of illness, partly the results of over fatigue and stress upon her body and mind, and partly as she always considered from a chill, when sitting one evening in the garden at Upton Lane. In this increased state of indisposition she went to Sandgate, chiefly for the sake of her sister-in-law, Elizabeth Fry, whose declining health induced her husband and herself to wish to be near her, much being due to his own and only sister. The only house that could be obtained was on the lower road to Folkestone ; this part forms a complete undercliff, and from its southern aspect is extremely hot, which was obviously unfavourable for Mrs. Fry.

Sandgate, Seventh Month, 29th.—We arrived here yesterday. I have been permitted to pass through rather an unusual time of late, I think ——— (alluding to a painful circumstance), hurt me, bodily and mentally, and discouraged me. Our house was rather too full for me, and I got too anxious (my easily besetting sin), about some nearest to me. I was uncommonly pressed by other people, and then business of various kinds, and from a fine state of health, such as I have not enjoyed for a long time, and the most excellent refreshing nights, I have lately frequently been awake nearly all night, and from some cause become in so irritable a state of constitution as to be for hours in the day really distressing. It particularly depresses, and flurries the spirits, and this with an extraordinary press of engagements has almost overwhelmed me. I have very earnestly prayed for help and patience, night and day, and it has been hard to come at a resting place, bodily or mentally. I find myself here in a lovely place by the sea, the air delightful, and the house pleasant. Thus the Lord provides for me in this my tried estate. If it please my Holy Helper, may He soon see meet to heal me.

First-day afternoon.—No one of the family at home but myself; how very unusual a circumstance. I have at times passed through a good deal of conflict and humiliation in this indisposition, and it is a real exercise of faith to me, the way in which I am tried by my illness. I suppose it arises from my extremely susceptible nerves, that are so affected when the body is out of order, as to cast quite a veil over the mind. I am apt to query whether I am not deceiving myself, in supposing I am the servant of the Lord, so ill to endure suffering, and to be so anxious to get rid of it; but it has been my earnest prayer that I might truly say, "Not as I will, but as Thou wilt." Lord! help me. I pray that I may be enabled to cast all my burthen and all my care upon Thee, that I may rest in the full assurance of faith in Thy love, pity, mercy and grace. I pray Thee help me, that my soul may be less disquieted within me, and that I may more trustfully and hopefully go on heavenward. Increase my faith in Thy faithfulness gracious Lord, whilst I believe that those who are once in grace are not always in grace ; yet help me ever to feel that faithful art Thou, O Lord ! who hast called us out of darkness into Thy marvellous light, and Thou only canst do it ; therefore be pleased to hearken to the prayer of Thy poor servant, increase her faith, and be Thyself, for Thine own name sake, not only the author, but the finisher of it. Amen.

First-day.—Again alone, or nearly so ; the rest gone to Meeting. 1 have passed a humbling week, still poorly by day and night. I think a place so remarkably void of objects does not suit my active mind, but it is well to be brought where I may rest on my oars ; for there is a danger of depending on active occupation for comfort, and even for a. certain degree of diversion. I feel this when at the sea, at night in my wakeful hours ; generally in the day I have something to occupy me ; but this place has been unusually dull to me, though I have the sweet company of several of our own dear family. Dear Edward and Catherine Buxton, and their children, my sister Elizabeth Fry, and her companion, have been here, and their company has been acceptable, but I think the lowness has been very much from my bodily indisposition. I think I mend a little, but it is very slowly. But truly do I pray night and day for mercy and help. I feel so peculiarly in need of it, seldom more so ; however, perhaps when we feel most in danger we may be more safe, than when we apprehend ourselves in a place of safety. Gracious Lord, keep Thy poor servant by Thine own power and Spirit, who cannot keep herself even for a moment !

Sandgate, Ninth Month, 4th.—Oh Lord ! in Thine own time deliver me from my fears, enable me patiently to bear this chastisement, until Thou seest it has accomplished that which Thou sentest it for, and deliver me out of it, and cause, in Thine own time, that I may return Thee thanks on the banks of deliverance.

It was at Sandgate, that she recived the account of the death of her lovely niece Harriet C——. Nine weeks before, a beautiful and blooming bride, she had been united to the object of her especial choice ; one of whose principles and character, Mrs. Fry entertained a high estimate, and whose affectionate attentions to herself ceased not, till the last sad duties had been paid to her memory. In the state in which she then, was, these tidings were very grievous to her, and very sorrowfully she writes respecting the event.

In how many ways the Lord teaches us ; surely the present is no common lesson.

Three days later she says—We live with you in spirit; (and after naming the most bereaved, adds,) and all most dear to the beloved departed. It is sweet to remember that help is laid on One that is mighty, who, blessed be His holy name, is ever near to His dependent servants. I feel, as if I could write to one or other of you more than once in the day, I have such a drawing towards you. How curious, that the only place in the world I have longed to be in, since my indisposition, has been West Norfolk. Had I not had others to consider, and only followed my own inclination, I believe, that I should have been amongst you through this deep trial.

After several distressing weeks, Mrs. Fry was moved to Tonbridge Wells, closely and faithfully nursed by her two youngest daughters.

Tonbridge Wells, 10*th.*—We are favoured to be settled here in a comfortable house, where many accommodations abound, which, in my delicate state, I find a real help. I have been favoured to partake of sweet resting sleep ; thanks to my Heavenly Father for His own great mercy.

Third-day.—My case has been rather increasingly distressing, from an almost total loss of appetite, and at times great lowness. Many fears creep in for my natural health, more particularly, as it respects the nervous system. Hitherto my Lord has said to the waves that would overwhelm me, " so far shalt thou go and no further." And, merciful Lord, if it be Thy holy will, continue to keep them from overwhelming Thy poor unworthy servant, in this time of weakness and of frequent distress.   Let not the waterfloods prevail.   When my spirit is overwhelmed within me, enable me to look to the Rock that is higher than I, as a "refuge from the storm, a shadow from the heat, when the blast of the terrible one is as a storm against the wall."

24th.—I desire in this my sorrow and suffering, to cast myself and my whole care on my Lord.   I know that I am poor, miserable, blind and naked, and I look to my Lord for every thing.   The kindness of all around me is great, indeed wonderful to me, and their pleasure in being with me comforting, for I feel as if I must be burdensome to them.   Most gracious Lord, if it be Thy will, let not this be the case, but bless this trying, humbling illness to them, as well as to myself; and may it please Thee to grant me grace, minute by minute, to hold fast my confidence, stedfast unto the end, that continuing faithful unto death, I may through Thy merits receive a crown of life !

She returned to Upton the end of September, and very reluctantly renounced the hope of spending part of the autumn in Norfolk.   Her eldest daughter, who had been awaiting her there, returned home on the 2nd of October, joining her aunt Lady Buxton on the road.   She found her mother very ill, more so, she thought, than she had ever seen her.   She was laid very low, her illness had its fluctuations, but she did not come down stairs after October the 5th.   She however often told those around her, in her great bodily suffering—that the everlasting arms were always underneath her—that the under current was peace and comfort, though the surface was so much tempest-tossed.

In a letter, dictated October 2nd, she thus expresses herself.

I have been very much struck in this illness, with the manner in which my children have been raised up as my helpers, and when I look back upon the deep and unutterable travail of spirit I have had on their behalf; and now that it has pleased the Lord that His hand should, in some respects be heavy upon me, how it has pleased Him to enable them to minister to my support and

10

help, I think it should be to all of you who are parents, an encouragement to do your best, and commit the rest to God. I think this more especially to be felt as respects our sons, that our first aim must be (in asking for a blessing on our endeavours) that we bring them up for the kingdom, and little can we calculate, how the Lord may bless and deliver them, and make them a blessing to ourselves.

Lady Buxton remained near her for some time, visiting her continually, and frequently uniting in reading and religious intercourse with her and her daughter Louisa, who was then, and continued to be for several succeeding months, peculiarly devoted to her as her personal nurse. On one occasion, after having read the 7th chapter of St. John, she remarked how injurious the spirit of priestcraft had ever been to the progress of true Christianity in all ages and under all forms. She went on to express her longing desire, that the day of grace might come, when all nations would be filled with the knowledge of the Lord. In reference to this, the first twelve and two last verses of the 47th chapter of Ezekiel were read, so beautifully descriptive of the gospel rising and spreading as waters, and covering the earth to fructify and bless.

On hearing the 8th chapter of St. John, she commented upon the freedom of the gospel, remarking that she had known much of it, but that her prayer had been to obtain liberty, not laxity. She also said, she had felt a portion at times of that peace which passeth understanding, but, that this life was a state of warfare and would be so even to the end.

Upton, Tenth Month, 10*th.*—My God hath not forgotten to be gracious, or shut up His tender mercies from me; it appears to me that all of nature is to be brought low, for all that is of the Lord only, can stand the day of humiliation. I may thankfully say, I am quiet and sustained in spirit, but do not often know peace to flow as a river, as at some former times; still help is constantly near from the sanctuary, though I abide under a sense of deep unworthiness before the Lord; but what can I do but wait in faith, until He be pleased fully to clothe me with the garments of His righteousness and His salvation. I feel I can do nothing for myself.

The only daughter who had not been with her, since immediately after her return from France, came to her at this time; she found her in a singular state, one of great natural depression, but unshaken in faith. The complaint being so much upon the nerves, produced sensations of irrepressible distress and discomfort. Yet never under any circumstances could the chord of religion be touched, but it immediately vibrated.

One afternoon, when one or two members of her family were reading with her, she was unable to attend to a very interesting religious biography, saying, it was "too touching to her—too affecting." She added, after a pause, "How I feel for the poor when very ill, in a state like my own, for instance, when 'good' ladies go to see them." "Religious truths so strongly brought forward, often injudiciously." She went on speaking on this subject, and then dwelt on "the exquisite tenderness of the Saviour's ministrations;" "His tone and manner to sinners!"

Soon afterwards she resumed, in the most impressive manner, saying, that "religious truth was opened to her, and supplied to her inwardly, not by man's ministration, but administered according to her need;" adding, "if I may so say, it is my life."

She constantly spoke of not being called to active service now, and that she had no desire as to recovery; on the contrary, she was "able quite to leave it." Frequently she repeated to those about her, "I feel the foundation underneath me sure."

One evening she opened her heart on her deep and earnest desires for the good of her children. Of her "great sufferings"

—" greater than any one knows"—that if they were to last, no one could wish for her life; but soon added, " there is one thing I would willingly live for—the good of my husband and children, and my fellow creatures."

On the night of October the 25th, she poured out a wonderful stream of rejoicing after she was in bed, a perfect flood of faith and hope, quoting many passages of Scripture, to prove that faith must work by love, and that faith, if true, must produce works. She said, " with the text, ' He that keepeth my sayings shall never see death,' take this one also, ' He that believeth on me shall never die.' " She afterwards expressed in a tone of the deepest feeling her " perfect confidence, her full assurance, that neither life, nor death, nor angels, nor principalities, nor powers, nor things present, nor things to come, nor height, nor depth, nor any other creature, should be able to separate her from the love of God which is in Christ Jesus our Lord;" adding, " my whole trust is in Him, my entire confidence."—" I *know* in whom I have believed, and can commit all to Him, who has loved me and given Himself for me, whether for life or death, sickness or health, time or eternity."

In the course of the same day, she said very emphatically, " My dear Rachel, I can say one thing—since my heart was touched at seventeen years old, I believe I never have awakened from sleep, in sickness or in health, by day or by night, without my first waking thought being, how best I might serve my Lord."

Mrs. Fry had greatly wished to attend the marriage of her niece Anna Gurney; but as the time approached, all hopes of accomplishing this passed away. With the promise of a family Bible, (her favourite wedding present), she sent this note (dictated) : —

My dearest Anna,

I was very glad to receive thy note. I hope the Bible will be ready in a few days; the one I had ready for thee, I sent to Lady ——, hoping that it would induce Lord —— and her to have family reading. It is a great and unexpected disappointment to me, to see no probability of being able to attend thy wedding, but " it is not to him that walketh, to direct his steps ;" the humiliation of my suffering may be better for me than going to the house of rejoicing, and if so permitted, we cannot doubt it. At all events, I think thou art sure that few more earnestly desire thy peace and prosperity than I do, in spirituals and in temporals—that thyself, and thy companion in life, may be enabled to serve the living God faithfully, through the power of His Holy Spirit; and that through the faithfulness of the Saviour's love, His richest grace and peace may be with you, in heights and in depths, in sickness and in health, in riches and poverty, in life and in death. My very dear love to my sister Catherine, thy father and mother, and the rest of your circle, also to thy dear intended husband. Thy much-attached and well-wishing aunt,

Elizabeth Fry.

At this time, her regular attendants were her daughters; her youngest, Louisa, with her husband and children, remaining for many months at Upton Lane, to assist her eldest sister in devotion to their mother; the other daughters and daughters-in-law resident in the neighbourhood, taking their regular days to spend in the sick-room.

Her eldest son also, leaving his family at Geneva, paid her a particularly acceptable visit, remaining for several days with her.

On Sunday, November the 6th, her son William remained from church to be with her, and her daughter Louisa. After reading a chapter in Job, and the 3rd of St. John, she prayed in a very striking manner, that after all the sorrows and fluctuations of time were ended, " We might behold His face in glory, that whilst here we might not deceive ourselves, but be true and decided followers of Him, who in His own good time would arise with healing on His wings to deliver us from all our pain."

The following day, a very beautiful note being read to her, from one who preceded her to the heavenly mansions, a few days after writing it—in which, with reference to her, the three first verses of the 41st Psalm were quoted. She lay quiet for a short time, and then calling one of her daughters to her bedside said, " May they not be deceived!"   " One thing is certain, I have desired and sought to serve the Lord."

11*th*.—When suffering from intense thirst, and drinking Seltzer water with some wine in it, which much refreshed her, she observed, " what a beautiful provision of nature and blessing of God, is water—natural waters to heal the body, and ever-lasting waters to heal the soul"—adding, " when awake and distressed with thirst, a few nights previously, this thought of the natural and spiritual waters springing up, made the night almost pleasant."

13th.—Her nephew, the Rev. Edward Hoare, came to see her. He sat down by her sofa and said to her, " My dear aunt, what a consolation to know you to be of the church of God, which He hath purchased with His own blood." After a little pause she said with great humility, " But we must avoid false confidence." He replied, that there could be no false confidence, when our hope is fixed on Christ alone. She said with emphasis, "There, indeed, is no false confidence ;" and added, that in this illness she had entirely felt without carefulness ; so able to commit every person and every thing, and leave them in His hands ; that she felt no service now called for from her, only to endure, as seeing Him who is invisible.

Her nephew reminded her, how St. Paul had to endure the thorn in his flesh, and how encouraging it was to remember that he had prayed three times for its removal, which prayers were not answered by removing the thorn, but by giving grace to bear it, quoting the Scripture, "My grace is sufficient for thee." He then moved to go away, but she detained him, saying, "Dear Edward, if thou hast anything on thy heart for me, do not fear to express it." His answer was, "Yes, dear aunt, I have a few words of prayer much on my heart for you." It was, however, rather an earnest giving of thanks for the assured hope he entertained concerning her. When he ceased, she added, as she laid on her sofa, an intercession, "For this beloved nephew and his work of the ministry, and that in these difficult times he may have wisdom and judgment to act, and power to stand fast in the liberty wherewith Christ had made him free, and not be entangled in any yoke of bondage."

To her Children in Norfolk.

Upton Lane, 20*th.*

My dearest Frank and Rachel,

Often, in the night especially, I feel the pain of the difficulty of communicating with those I love at a distance; I therefore thought I must express a few words to you myself, to tell you how deeply I feel all your kindness. Thy gifts and loans, dear Rachel, are truly useful, and so often bring thee pleasantly to my remembrance. At present, I think we are well off for help; I may thankfully say that I am well cared for in every way, and my opinion is, that this care which has now been extended to me for so many weeks has not been in vain in the Lord. Although yet in a state of serious illness, I feel in some degree raised in myself, of course amid great fluctuations. I may thankfully acknowledge, I not unfrequently partake of hours of rest and peace, through the tender mercy of Him, who is touched with a feeling of our infirmities, and is our ever-loving Advocate. Times of sore conflict are now and then permitted, but I have been sooner delivered out of them, than I was. As to outward help (with regard to medicine), I believe little can be done, but as it respects sympathy and care, much; but as I abound in these latter, in such a remarkable degree, I trust, if it be the will of my Heavenly Father, they may tend to raise up, if not that they may be blessed to my soul. My particular love to dear Frank in Edinburgh, Addison and Gurney, when you write. All your dear children dwell much in my heart, with earnest desires for their present and everlasting welfare. I remain, with dear love to the little boys, and much to my brother——,

Your tenderly attached mother,

ELIZABETH FRY.

But the degree of amendment described, slight as it was, did not continue.

On Sunday, November 26th, one of her sons, a daughter, and her little grandson Walter being by her bedside, she prayed nearly as follows, after the 18th chapter of St. Matthew had been read to her :—

Gracious Lord, grant that the promise to those, where two or three are gathered together in Thy name, may be fulfilled in our experience; and that Thou wilt look upon our whole circle, as well as the little group now present. Heal as far as is consistent with Thy will, and grant patience and submission to whatever Thou mayest order. Lord, enable us to cut off the right hand and pluck out the right eye, if they are likely to lead us into temptation. For ourselves, and those especially who are nearest to the little one whose spirit passed to Thee yesterday, enable us to give thanks, that he is among those innocent ones, whose angels redeemed by the mercy of Christ Jesus, are for ever in Thy presence; and for all who are in affliction, we would ask Thy support.

This alluded to a lovely infant of her nephew and niece Sir Edward and Lady Buxton ; they had been her near neighbours, and much with her at Sandgate. The loss of this child, to which she had attached herself, afflicted her very much.

In one of the remaining entries in her journal she thus expresses herself :—

Upton, Twelfth Month, 7th.—Lord ! undertake Thyself for me ; Thy arm of power can alone heal, help, and deliver ; and in Thee do I trust, and hope, though at times deeply tried and cast down before Thee ; yet O Lord ! Thou art my hope, and be therefore entreated of Thy poor sorrowful and often afflicted servant, and arise for my help.   Leave not my poor soul desti tute, but through the fulness of Thine own power, mercy and love, keep me alive unto Thyself, unto the end ! that nothing may separate me from Thy love, that I may endure unto the end ; and when the end comes, that I may be altogether Thine, and dwell with Thee, if it be but the lowest place within the gate, where I may behold Thy glory and Thy holiness, and for ever rest in Thee.

I do earnestly entreat Thee, that to the very last I may never deny Thee, or in any way have my life or conversation incon- sistent with my love to Thee, and most earnest desire to live to Thy glory ; for I have loved Thee, O Lord, and desired to serve Thee without reserve.   Be entreated, that through Thy faith- fulness, and the power of Thy own Spirit, I may serve Thee unto the end.   Amen.

On the 28th, she said to one of her sons, " I see the gates of mercy open, and rays of light are shining from them."

A few memoranda from the journal of her son William, are here introduced, not merely as illustrative of her state, but as descriptive of his communication with the tenderly-beloved mo- ther, whom he was to precede by so short a period to that land, where there is no more Death !

" ' The evening of the 29th, was one of the greatest suffering and distress, such as I never remember to have witnessed. But, through all, her faith was triumphant, and her confidence un- shaken. I endeavoured to remember a few of her expressions, and have succeeded in calling to mind the following :—

" I believe this is not death, but it is as passing through the valley of the shadow of death, and perhaps with more suffering, from more sensitiveness ; but the rock ' is here ;' ' the distress is awful, but He has been with me.'

" ' I feel that He is with me, and will be with me, even to the end. David says why hast Thou forsaken me ? I do not feel that I am forsaken. In my judgment I believe this is not death, but it is as death. It is nigh unto death.' Her agony appeared almost unbearable ; but she frequently expressed fears of being impatient. ' May none of you be called to pass through such a furnace ; but still my sufferings have been mitigated through mercy and grace ! fulness of grace ! Now, my dear William, be stedfast, immoveable, always abounding in the work of the Lord ; and then thy labour shall not be in vain in the Lord. O ! the blessedness of having desired to be on the Lord's side ! (not that I have any merit of my own). I cannot express, even in my greatest trials and tribulations, the blessedness of His service. My life has been a remarkable one ; much have I had to go through, more than mortal knows, or ever can know ; my sorrows at times have been bitter; but my consolations sweet ! In my lowest estates, through grace, my love to my Master has never failed, nor to my family, nor to my fellow-mortals. This illness may be for death, or it may not, according to His will ; but He will never forsake me, even should He be pleased to take me this night."

February 1st.—Her son William, her brother Samuel Gurney, and two of her daughters, being around her bed, she prayed in a low voice, and at broken intervals, to the following purport :—

For help for this poor afflicted servant in her deep tribulation, that in passing through the floods they should not overflow her, and through the fire she should not be burned ; that these trials in the hands of the great Refiner might tend to more perfect purification and refinement, and preparation for His service, whether in time or in eternity ; but she wholly left this to His will. That if raised up, she desired it might only be to more entire devotedness to His service, and as an instrument to spread the knowledge of Christ and His truth amongst her fellow-mortals ; and that mercy might be granted in body, soul, and spirit, to her husband, children, brothers, and sisters, and all

beloved by her, even by Him whom she had steadily loved and
desired to serve from childhood, though, through sore temptation
and tribulation.

The evening of the same day, holding her husband's hand in
one of her's, and her son-in-law, Raymond Pelly's, in the other,
she burst forth into a most remarkable and triumphant expression of her faith ; her certainty of the truths of Revelation, " I
know my foundation to be sure, I feel the rock *always* underneath me."

The following morning, on her son William's reading an
expression of love and sympathy from her eldest grandson, who
was at Edinburgh with his regiment, she said, " My very dear
love to him ; tell him to be stedfast, immoveable, always abounding in the work of the Lord, for in *whatever circumstances*, it
will not be in vain in the Lord."

Her only absent daughter was at this time, again summoned
from Norfolk.   Her mother had suffered some days before with
most painful neuralgic symptoms, but just then there was a
degree of respite ;   the change, however, since she had seen her
before was sorrowful indeed to witness, and could but lead to the
most alarming apprehensions. She spoke of her own recovery as
a thing hidden from herself, and concerning which she had no
desire.   One day it was said to her, " that many a Christian
had slept in this world and to their own surprise awakened in
glory;" she exclaimed directly, with most striking emphasis,
" Oh ! what a sweet thought." She spoke occasionally of her
" timid nature ;" of her " natural fear of death;" but on Monday night, the 19th, when very low in body and spirit, she said
emphatically, " should I never see the light of another morning,
remember I am safe !"

Her dependence on her Saviour, and utter rejection of every
merit of her own, was entire.   On one occasion, she breathed

forth, when under deep illness and distress, " I am nothing, I have nothing; I am poor, miserable, naked, helpless. I can do nothing, but my Saviour is every thing, all-sufficient—my light, my life, my joy, my eternal hope of glory.''

One night, her husband sitting by the fire, she said, " I have never felt before so sunk and faint as I have to-day ; never so like one whose ' feet draw nigh unto the gates of death;' " he not distinctly hearing her words, she asked some one to repeat them to him. She appeared not to desire to know what was before her, continually saying, " I wish to leave it in better hands."

To one of the " nursing sisters " who was attending her, she thus expressed herself, " I am of the same mind as Paul, I can say, ' to me to live is Christ, but to die is gain.' What a grand thought it is ! everlasting to everlasting, without trouble and without pain ; to meet there, and together be for ever with Christ."

Her gratitude to all about her was unbounded, continually saying, " How am I cared for ! I am fed surely on the finest of the wheat." This, particularly alluded to the innumerable little gifts and tokens of love, that she received in every form that could be devised to tempt her appetite, and induce her to take more nourishment. "Love ! all love ; my heart is filled with love to every one," was amongst her frequent expressions. Her delight was great in the attendance of her husband and children : "they minister to my wants; my children's attendance upon me is perfect !"

Towards the end of February her sufferings became most afflicting ; how unutterably awful then appeared the curse of sin and death, when a servant so devoted was thus permitted to endure. Night after night a sorrowing band was mustered for the conflict. Fervently was prayer offered in her behalf, far and near it rose for her help ; but though it pleased her God and

Saviour eminently to abide with her in the furnace, yet the time was not come for Him who watches over His people, as a refiner and purifier of silver, to conclude the process and to quench the flames.

She was comforted, as were her attendants, by occasional visits from members of her own religious persuasion and other Christian friends. Prayer was offered from time to time in her chamber. The visits of her sister, Lady Buxton, were a true solace to her, she clung to her with inexpressible tenderness. She also was very dependent on the services of her faithful attendant Christiana Golder. On one occasion she was heard to say, "Dear C., how little I thought when thou wast a little girl, what a comfort thou wouldest become to me! how many are my mitigations!" She often repeated these lines :—

> " Come what, come may,
> Time and the hour run, through the roughest day."

She had letters frequently of much value ; some addressed to herself, others to her family. One from her brother Joseph John Gurney addressed to one of her daughters was very consoling to her :—

"Earlham, *Second Month.*

     " My beloved Niece,

" Thy truly interesting and affecting letters are both received this morning. Had the first come yesterday, we should, of course have answered it, as we are all here together, thy uncle and aunt Buxton, thy uncle and aunt Cunningham, my dearest wife and I. It is a favour that the letters of yesterday's date are more comfortable, as it regards our tenderly beloved sister's sufferings, and the bright gleams of a spiritual nature which have been permitted to penetrate your gloom, are hailed by us all with humble thankfulness (I trust) to the Author of all our sure mercies. I need scarcely tell thee how heartily and nearly we all sympathize with her and with you. Prayer on her account has flowed from more than one mouth amongst us this morning,—may I not say the prayer of faith and sweet assurance —that He who sees meet thus to bring into the furnace, is, and ever will be, near to her, for her support, consolation, and final deliverance. I have been afraid of writing to her, lest it should not be proper for her to receive letters ; but our tenderest love is with her, and in the midst of the deep tribulation of having her brought so low, we would wish her to know that we feel a precious serenity of mind in thinking of her, and in mentally visiting her bed of sickness and sore affliction. There is a holy hand stretched forth, which is holding up her head, far above all the boisterous waves; and we think we can, in some measure, not only submit to being baptized with her, with this baptism of pain and sorrow, but rise with her in faith, and hope, and love, above the billows. It appears to us that the faithfulness of Christ, and the eternal stability of His truth, are manifested in no common degree on this most trying occasion. On that faithfulness and stability we must all endeavour quietly to repose, in the full belief that every passing day will bring its own support and alleviations, as well as its own appointed measure of conflict; what a blessing it is that none of these things move us, and that the things which cannot be shaken, are not only still in full force, but are more than ever developed to our view.

As March advanced, there was perceptible improvement, less severity of pain, and rather more appetite ; she was moved now and then into another room, in a wheeled chair, and she began strongly to wish to be taken to Bath for the benefit of the waters. St. Paul tells us of body, soul and spirit, in 1 Thessalonians v. 23 ; and again in Hebrews iv. 12 ; he tells us of soul and spirit ; her state was a curious illustration of this—the body suffering and infirm—the natural powers of mind enfeebled—but the immortal and renewed spirit rising superior to it all, and shining but the brighter for the surrounding darkness.

To a son and daughter, who had left her two days before.

Upton Lane, *Fourth Month*, 1*st.*

I felt so poorly in body, and low in spirits, there was very little I could say when we parted; but I thought I must tell you without delay, how peculiarly acceptable your visit has been. Though parted, I hope you will hold me in remembrance, in this my low estate. It has been very precious to find the best of bonds strengthening with our years, which I humbly trust we may acknowledge to be the case, that being united in Christ, and bound together under his banner, we may all fight the good fight of faith, until we obtain the victory through our Lord and Saviour Jesus Christ, and join that company which cannot be numbered, gathered out of every nation, kindred, tongue, and people, who have washed their robes, and made them white in the blood of the Lamb, and are for ever at rest. But then we must press towards the mark, faithfully, diligently and watchfully, until we obtain the prize of our high calling in Christ Jesus. I must tell you, that when you left me, dear Louisa came to me almost immediately, which was acceptable and very seasonable, and William soon after brought a Christian Missionary to see me, and we had a sweet time in prayer, which refreshed my spirit.

I am your tenderly attached mother,

ELIZABETH FRY.

After many weeks of difficulty and doubt, the decision was come to, and her husband accomplished her removal to Bath. Sir Fowell and Lady Buxton were already there; and, though he, like Mrs. Fry, was bowed under infirmity, yet the closeness of the union, natural and spiritual, which existed amongst them, rendered their being near one another an important solace to them all. Various members of their families successively joined them; amongst others, her son William, and his little Emma. How merciful is that arrangement in God's government of the world, which denies to His frail, feeble creatures, the knowledge of the future! Much of sorrow and infirmity had they to endure, but they could not foresee how soon the brightest and the best were to be laid low—the most pleasant pictures marred.

During the sojourn at Bath, her husband's only brother Mr. William Fry with his family, resident in the neighbourhood, were frequently with her. Their almost entire absence from London, since the death of his wife in 1821, rendered this opportunity of intercourse particularly agreeable to her, as she always entertained much affection towards him and his children.

She gained strength at Bath, and was unquestionably in better health on her return home. But she was closely touched by the rapid decline of her sister Elizabeth Fry. They had been affectionately united for a long course of years. They had travelled together as ministers, amongst Friends, they had, year after year sat side by side in the meeting-house at Plaistow, and now in her low and weakened condition, the severing of this tie was to her very painful.

Her sister died on the 2nd of July; rejoicing that the hour of her deliverance had arrived, to lay down her frail tabernacle, and appear in the presence of her God and Saviour.

There was an extraordinary weight upon Mrs. Fry's spirit, she dwelt much and often on the invisible world, her sleep partook of these impressions. Did not coming events cast their shadows before? And was not she thus, in some measure prepared for the woes that were to follow? Her little grandson Gurney Reynolds was an especial object of interest to her; he was frequently with her, delighting in her gentle tenderness, and the pursuits she provided for him, so well suited to his feeble health. He left her not more unwell than usual. Tidings came of his being worse, and three days afterwards that he had breathed away his patient, lamb-like spirit, as he laid upon the sofa in his mother's room. This was the 18th of July.

On the morning of his funeral she wrote to his parents,—

My dearest Foster and Chenda,

I deeply feel my separation from you this day; I long to be present with you to minister to your consolation. You have my earnest prayers that the best help may be with you, sustaining, healing, comforting you; enabling you to behold your beloved child at rest in Jesus, consequently that death has lost its sting, and the grave its victory. In the midst of this sore trial, may grace, mercy and peace continue to be with you, and in His own time, may the Lord grant you " beauty for ashes, the oil of joy for mourning, and the garment of praise for the spirit of heaviness."

Your tenderly attached and sympathizing mother,

ELIZABETH FRY.

A change of scene and air seemed so important for her, that her son William's success in obtaining a very suitable house at Walmer, was a real matter of gratulation ; but there was another office of love for that beloved one to perform by his mother, singularly suited to the bond of love and sympathy which had so long united them, and eminently fitted to be his last.

She had long and earnestly desired again to attend the Meeting for worship at Plaistow. It was proposed from Sunday to Sunday, but the difficult process of dressing was never accomplished till long after eleven o'clock, the hour when the Meeting assembled. An attempt was made on the 28th of July, but totally failed. Her disappointment was extreme, and the hold it took of her spirits so grievous, that it was resolved to make the effort at any cost the following Sunday. Her son William undertook to carry out her wishes—drawn by himself and a younger son in her wheeled chair, she was taken up to the Meeting, a few minutes after the Friends had assembled, followed by her husband, her children, and attendants. Her son William seated himself closely by her side, and the rest near her. The silence that prevailed was singularly solemn. After some time, in a clear voice she addressed the meeting. The prominent topic of her discourse was " the death of the righteous ;" she expressed the deepest thankfulness, alluding to her sister Elizabeth Fry, for the mercies vouchsafed to " one who having laboured long amongst them, has been called from time to eternity." She quoted that text, " Blessed are the dead who die in the Lord, for they cease from their labours, and their works do follow them." She dwelt on the purposes of affliction, on the utter weakness and infirmity of the flesh ; she tenderly exhorted the young, " the little children amongst us," referring to the death of little Gurney Reynolds. She urged the need of devotedness of heart and steadiness of purpose; she raised a song of praise for the eternal hope offered to the Christian, and concluded with those words in Isaiah,—" Thine eyes shall see the King in His beauty, they shall behold the land that is very far off." Prayer was soon afterwards offered by her in much the same strain. He, joined her in that solemn act, who never was to worship with her again, till, before the throne and the Lamb, they should unite in that ineffable song of praise, which stays not night nor day for ever !

Her removal to Walmer was accomplished without much difficulty, from thence she wrote :—

I walk in a low valley, still I believe I may say the everlasting arm is underneath, and the Lord is near to me. I pass through deep waters, but I trust, as my Lord is near to me, they will not overflow me. I need all your prayers in my low estate ; I think that the death of my sister, and dear little Gurney, have been almost too much for me.

Thus was this servant of God permitted to go sorrowing upon her way. But the storm had not blown over ; again the thunder clouds rolled up. On the 15th of August, the lovely little Juliana, the second daughter of her son William, one of the

10

sweetest blossoms that ever gladdened parents' hearts, was cut off after thirty hours' inexplicable illness. One day, however, but too fully sufficed to solve the doubt, three of the servants at Manor House being attacked by scarlet fever. But all preceding sorrows seemed light in comparison, when the beloved and honoured head of that happy home, was himself laid low by the tremendous malady. He had written on the death of his aunt shortly before: " Yesterday, we followed the remains of our dear aunt to the grave. We have the comfort of feeling assured, that she has entered into the joy of her Lord. May such be the case with us all!—but if we would ' die the death of the righteous,' as the righteous we must do our day's work in the day."

All stood aghast at these fresh tidings, and with breathless suspense awaited the accounts from hour to hour, and day to day.

" He surely will not be taken—so fearful an overthrow, so terrible a blow cannot be coming," thus spoke hope and natural affection ; but there was a response from the inmost heart of those who had watched his life and conversation, his growth in religion, the simple earnestness of his piety—Is not his Master calling for him ?

The children were removed to Plashet Cottage, vacant from the death of Mrs. Elizabeth Fry. As one and another showed symptoms of fever, they were carried back to Manor House. The servants continued to sicken successively, and were conveyed to a ward prepared for them at Guy's Hospital. The help of the nursing sisters became invaluable, two or three being in constant attendance. For about a week, strong hopes were entertained that the most precious life would be spared to his family but the fiat was gone forth, and the summons given. On the day of the funeral of his little Juliana, he had asked to have his door open, that he might see the coffin as it was borne by, when, to the nursing sister by his side, he exclaimed, " I shall go to her but she shall not return to me."

The fever ran its course, the excitement attending it came and went, but there was no recovering; all seemed to depend upon his powers of taking nourishment. He was calm, even cheerful; there appeared to be little, if any suffering; he perfectly knew his danger, he said that he " should like to recover, if it were right, but he was quite willing to leave it in God's hand." When remarked to him, how great the mercy that sustaining patience had been granted him, he held up his hand with a great effort, and most emphatically replied, " God never has forsaken me, no not for a moment, and He never will." As his last day commenced upon earth, his window wide open by the bed-side, and the sweet morning air blowing freshly in, he spoke of the fair view to be seen from it, and listened with interest as the scene was described to him, the grey tints passing from the garden and terrace, and leaving them in light and sunshine. He spoke of his place, of his family, of his many blessings. Some little effort exhausting him a stimulant was given, as he recovered, with a bright smile he exclaimed, " God is so good !" and they were his last words. Never was a dying-bed more favoured—more wonderful the evidence that " God was with him of a truth :" a most solemn calm prevailed ; beautiful was the smile which lingered on his dying features. Unseen realities were felt and understood then ; it had been heard before, but now was known, and appropriated, " Blessed are the dead who die in the Lord."

" Can our mother hear this and live ?" was the natural exclamation of her children. Thus wrote one of her sisters :— " We are perfectly thunderstruck ! What a wonderful dispensation of sorrow and loss ! The loss of him in life so entire ; the fever so alarming ! How will your precious afflicted mother bear it ? I fear she will not live under such calamity ; but let no one dare to murmur." No one need have feared her enduring the blow, for He who sent it bestowed His Holy Spirit with it.   The Christian's faith proved stronger than the mother's anguish.   She wept abundantly, almost unceasingly, but she dwelt constantly on the unseen world, seeking for passages in the Bible which spoke of the happy state of the righteous.   She was enabled to rejoice in that rest, upon which her beloved ones had entered, and in a wonderful manner to realize the blessedness of their lot.

Her natural affections and interests were, moreover, occupied for his widow and children, all his little ones having the fever.

The medical men insisted on the necessity of every one quitting the house.   The little children were carried back to Plashet Cottage, where the others had become ill, and with the exception of three servants in one corner of the basement story, the house was deserted.   There are minutes which burn themselves into the brain, from which there is no recovering to be the same again. It was such an one, to the two, who standing on the steps had seen all depart, and remained themselves but to give one last look and follow.   They traversed the empty apartments where the light struggled to force its way through the closed shutters. They turned the key and stood in the chamber of death ; and as they went away, they remembered that one fortnight before, the " voice of joy and mirth had been within that dwelling."   Two days later, the family carriages assembled under the trees, near the Lodge gate.   The day was glorious—the house in the dis- tance all in light ; the heavy sound of wheels was heard, and the black plumed hearse was seen advancing from it, as it passed, to be followed by the different carriages ; and the pro- cession wended its way to Little Ilford church.   A flood of light fell on the old grey tower, and the rich masses of foliage of the noble trees around it.   Never was the funeral service more deeply needed, or its force and its beauty more entirely to be felt.   Here he had come from week to week to worship with ·his family ; here he had joined with child-like humility in the services, and knelt in meek reverence to partake of the Sacraments of his Church. Here he was again come, for his beloved remains to be deposited, " in sure and certain hope of a joyful resurrection."

Mrs. Fry was earnest to hear everything, and to have all particulars given her. The illness of her grandchildren occupied much of her thoughts; the accounts from them continued to fluctuate; but on Monday the 2nd of September, Emma, the eldest, was worse. She had been intensely anxious about her father—her inquiries continual; and after his death and her own illness begun, he was still the object of her thoughts. She was a child of strong feelings, and very sensitive nature. At first, some endeavours were made to divert her, but they wholly failed, and it was the truth and all the truth which alone had power to soothe her, she responded to the glorious hope set before her, and partook in the assured confidence of his eternal happiness.

Early on Tuesday morning, she followed him to that Saviour whom her young heart had loved, and desired to obey, just one week after his departure, and eighteen days from the death of her sister. One grave contains all that is mortal of the father and his daughters. " They were pleasant in their lives, and in their death they were not divided." The tidings were conveyed to Walmer the same day by some of her children, others of them had been with their mother from the time she went there.

Her eldest son was with his family in Switzerland, when he received accounts of the alarming illness of his brother; they travelled rapidly home, but before they could reach England had letters announcing his death. On landing at Dover, they turned aside to Walmer, and joined the large family party already assembled there.

The following Sunday was a memorable one; the two last chapters of the Revelation were read, and then some memoranda concerning the beloved departed and their closing hours upon earth. The service was concluded by solemn thrilling prayer, offered by their mother for those who remained, and for herself in her " low estate :"—for such as had fought the good fight, kept the faith, and obtained the victory, thanksgiving and praise!

Her own journal, but written before the last blow fell, tells her feelings :—

Walmer, Eighth Month, 29*th.*—Sorrow upon sorrow! Since I last wrote, we have lost by death, first, my beloved sister, Elizabeth Fry; second, Gurney Reynolds, our sweet, good grandson; third, Juliana Fry, my dearest William and Julia's second daughter; and fourth, above all, our most beloved son, William Storrs Fry, who appeared to catch the infection of his little girl, and died on Third-day of scarlet fever, the 27th of this month. A loss inexpressible—such a son, husband, friend, and brother! but I trust that he is for ever at rest in Jesus, through the fulness of His love and grace. The trial is almost inexpressible. Oh! may the Lord sustain us in this time of deep distress. Oh! dear Lord keep thy unworthy and poor sick servant in this time of unutterable trial; keep me sound in faith, and clear in mind, and be very near to us all—the poor widow and children in this time of deepest distress, and grant that this awful dispensation may be blessed to our souls. Amen. This tenderly beloved child attended me to Meeting the last First-day I was at home, and sat by me on the women's side. Oh! gracious Lord, bless and sanctify to us all, this afflicting trial, and cause it to work for our everlasting good; and be very near to the poor dear widow and fatherless; and may we all be drawn nearer to Thee, and Thy kingdom of rest and peace, where there will be no more sin, sickness, death, and sorrow.

EARLHAM HALL.

CHAPTER XXV.

1844, 1845.—Return from Walmer—Death of a Niece—Visit to Kensington—Visit to her brother Joseph John Gurney—Parting with some of
her children for Madeira—Marriage of a Nephew to a Niece—Death of
Sir T. Fowell Buxton—Visit to Norfolk—Earlham—North Repps—
—Runcton—Yearly Meeting—Ladies' British Society Meeting—Marriage of her youngest Son—Marriage of a Niece—Removal to Ramsgate—Successive parties of her family—Sudden increase of illness—
Death—Funeral—Conclusion.

" SORROW upon sorrow " was the language of her wounded
spirit. In an unusual manner was this devoted servant permitted to partake of the Master's cup, and through much tribulation to enter the Kingdom. Nor was it only in the greatness,
but the character of her afflictions, that so deep a lesson is to be
read. Possessing extraordinary natural powers, with extraordinary gifts in grace, she obtained a marvellous influence over the
spirits of others, to control the will and win the affections. She

could not but know her power, and be conscious of the love she
inspired, and the strength she imparted. She was proportionably
to be emptied of self, and furnish a striking exemplication of
the truth of the scriptural assertion, that "no flesh shall glory
in His presence." It was permitted that she should endure, till
they who had felt that life would be a dull blank without her,
dare no longer desire her tarriance. The habit of dependence
was to be altogether broken, and she who had been as a tower
of strength, was to require and depend upon all that human
tenderness could invent, and cherishing love bestow, for her
daily and hourly comfort.

Her own desire after these heavy calamities was to return
home; but she yielded to the wishes of those around her to
continue a short time longer at Walmer.

The regulation of her mind, and her established self-discipline,
were at that period very instructive; her health infirm, her
natural spirits broken, she persevered as much as possible in
regular habits and certain hours for different occupations; in no
degree refusing to be comforted, willing to be diverted, driving
out in the carriage, or on fine days drawn in the beautiful little
pony chair that her son Joseph had given her, whilst some of
the party walked by her side. But after a little while she
became irresistibly desirous of returning to Upton, principally
that she might see her bereaved daughter, before the birth of
her expected little one.

The return home was sorrowful indeed; all outwardly the
same—but the void—the want so great, of a member of the
circle, who, whilst he was the tried friend and faithful counsellor,
was wont to bring with him an atmosphere of cheerfulness and
love. His habit was to go by Upton Lane on his road to
London. His mother and her attendants would watch for the
glad tone of his voice, as he hastened in, for his little morning
visit. It is long before the heart realises, that a pleasure daily

repeated at a given time, and for a lengthened period, can
never recur.

Another beloved son, William Champion Streatfeild, had
taken the fever, one of her "married children," as she desig-
nated those, not by birth belonging to her. The day of the
return from Walmer, all hope of his recovery was abandoned.

It is possible that her intense anxiety, whilst the life of one
so dear hung suspended on a thread and then the gradual
deliverance from it, tended to withdraw her thoughts from the
afflictions which had preceded it. Her mind was also occupied
by her bereaved daughter-in-law.

Upton, Tenth Month, 13*th.*—We returned from Walmer on
the 17th of the Ninth Month. We first went to my dear
brother Gurney's at Ham House, where I was received with
every kindness. Our beloved daughter Julia was here when we
came home, and stayed a few days afterwards. She was then
removed to her sister's, where she (I may thankfully say,) has
since been confined. She has a sweet little girl, and is doing
well. So we see that the "Lord gives and the Lord takes
away, blessed be his holy name."

A few days later, to her sister Mrs. Samuel Gurney who had
been from home, she wrote,—

                              Upton, *Tenth Month,* 21*st.*
My dearest Elizabeth,
I must thank thee before thy return home for thy sweet
letter, but as we hope soon to meet, I will not say much. I also
received one from our dear sister Eliza, which I hope to answer
in a day or two.

I cannot give a very bright account of us, as I feel very
poorly, very low and flat, and that we have many causes of deep
sorrow—the effect of William's loss is hardly to be told. But
I desire always to feel that our God is able to supply our needs,
through the riches of His grace, in Christ Jesus our Lord.

I long to visit Earlham, but I fear that the season is too far advanced.

May you all feel for, and remember us, in our very low estate, and hoping soon to see your party home, I am, with dear and tender love to all of you, including John and his sweet wife,

Thy much attached sister,
ELIZABETH FRY.

On the 1st of the Eleventh Month she addressed her last written communication to the Committee of the Ladies' British Society.

My much-loved Friends,

Amidst many sorrows, that have been permitted for me to pass through, and bodily suffering, I still feel a deep and lively interest in the cause of poor prisoners; and earnest is my prayer that the God of all grace may be very near to help you to be stedfast in the important Christian work, of seeking to win the poor wanderers to return, repent and live; that they may know Christ to be their Saviour, Redeemer, and hope of glory. May the Holy Spirit of God direct your steps, strengthen your hearts, and enable you and me to glorify our Holy Head, in doing and suffering even unto the end; and when the end comes, through a Saviour's love and merits, may we be received into glory and everlasting peace.

In christian love and fellowship,
I am affectionately your friend,
ELIZABETH FRY.

As might be reasonably expected, Mrs. Fry's health suffered from all her sorrows, and there were threatenings of the return of some of her most painful symptoms; but they were in mercy averted. She went for a few days to Kensington, to be with her son and daughter—mourners like herself for a beloved child; this little change suited her, and on her return she was rather cheered by a visit from her brother, Joseph John Gurney, and her sister-in-law.

But a new sorrow awaited her. On the 1st of December, Catherine H——n, the daughter of her late beloved sister Louisa Hoare, died—a few days after her infant son. Though young in years, she was not young in religion: devoted in heart and life, she was apparently ripe for glory, when God took her.

Eleventh Month, 2nd.—The accounts of to-day are deeply affecting—to have the grave once more (and so soon) opened amongst us. What can we say but that " it is the Lord," for the flesh is very weak, and these things are hard to our nature. I have felt the pain of this fresh sorrow, but desire that all most closely concerned may find Him very near to them, who " healeth the broken in heart and bindeth up their wounds." My love and sympathy to all most nearly interested. We have our poor dear Julia and her children here, and very touching it is to be with them. I am I think just now very poorly, and much cast down, but I remember the scriptural words, " cast down but not destroyed."

This " fresh sorrow" involved much personal loss and grief to one of her daughters, which occasioned her writing to her two days later.

A few lines of most tender love to thee and thine. My spirit is so much broken within me, and bowed down, that I cannot write much. As the body so much affects the mind, I feel the more sunk under our trials from my state of illness, still the Lord sustains me in mercy and in love. I need all your prayers in this time of deep affliction, and you need mine. May our Lord sanctify our deep afflictions to us, that they may work for us here, the peaceable fruits of righteousness, and hereafter a far more exceeding and eternal weight of glory.

The increasing illness of her brother-in-law, Sir T. Fowell Buxton, occupied much of her thoughts, and excited her tenderest feelings.

To her Niece Priscilla Johnston.

(*December,*) 1844.

My dearest Priscilla,

Thanks for thy kindness in writing to me at this time of deep sorrow; but strange to say, before thy note came, I had been so much with you in spirit, that I was ready to believe thy dearest father was sinking. I have felt such unity with him spiritually. My text for him in my low state this morning, was, "The sun shall be no more thy light by day; neither for brightness shall the moon give light unto thee: but the Lord shall be unto thee an everlasting light, and thy God thy glory!" I believe this will be his most blessed experience, whenever our Lord takes him to Himself. I write with difficulty and in haste, but my heart is so very full towards you, that I must express myself. My dear love to every one of your tenderly beloved party, particularly thy mother. I feel as it respects thy dearest father, whether a member of the Church militant or the Church triumphant, all is well—and we may through all our tribulations return God thanks, who giveth us the victory, through Jesus Christ our Lord! Most near and tender love to you all.

I am,

Thy much attached aunt,

E. F.

To the same, on the last day of the year.

Upton, *Twelfth Month,* 31*st.*

My dearest Priscilla,

Thy mother's and thy letters have been truly consoling. I dwell much with you in spirit, and I feel near sympathy and unity with your beloved invalid, and with you all. How weighty to come to the close of this year, wherein so much has passed! The Lord has given, and the Lord has taken away, but through all we may say, blessed be the name of the Lord! I desire your prayers, for my estate is a very low one, for myself, for my husband and children, as we have all been brought very very low before the Lord. May our afflictions be sanctified to us, not leading us to the world for consolation, but more fully to cast ourselves on Him who died for us, and hath loved us with an everlasting love. I write sadly, as it is difficult to do it, my hands are so much affected by my general state of health. With thy dearest father I have felt in life no common religious bond. How sweet, how blessed to feel, that we have one Lord, one faith, one baptism.

Though of a different character, another trial awaited her. Her son-in-law William Champion Streatfeild, had not rallied from the effects of the fever, and he was now ordered without further delay to Madeira. To part from him, and especially from her daughter, was very grievous to her. It was not merely the pain and sorrow of losing the society of this beloved child, which she felt so acutely, but the peculiar and protracted nature of her own illness had rendered her exceedingly dependent on those who like her daughter Hannah had so largely shared in the attendance upon her. Two of their children remained near their grandmother, the others with their parents took their departure on the 16th of January. She committed them in earnest supplication to Him, " who holdeth the winds in his fists" and with whom are the issues of life—and so they parted, never to meet again on earth.

As the winter wore away there was some revival; her widowed daughter, with her broken band, returned to Manor House; she resumed some of her former pursuits, she wrote more letters, took more part in the daily interests of life. For the sake of her grandchildren, in whom she was anxious to encourage a taste for such objects, she endeavoured to re-arrange her collections of shells, minerals, corals, and other natural curiosities.

She was generally carried down stairs in a chair about noon, and wheeled from room to room ; she was dressed as usual, sometimes joining her family at table, and was able to look occasionally at a book. She now generally attended Meeting once on the Sabbath, her ministry often very beautiful and not at all par-

10

taking of the sort of infirmity which clouded all earthly matters. She enjoyed occasional visits from her friends, and conversed upon various topics.

On one of these occasions to a friend who found her very ill and low, and who expressed a hope that she might yet be better, she said, " I have not yet seen how it will terminate. Sometimes I have thought that perhaps I may be partially raised up, but I lay no stress on it." Afterwards she said with tears, " Oh, He is a covenant-keeping God! He keepeth covenant and mercy. Oh, may I ever keep hold of His mercy!" On the 29th, the same friend being again with her, and perceiving that she was much depressed, remarked, " I believe there is an open door set before thee, although thou mayest not always be able to perceive it open." The precious invalid wept much, and after a time said, " Oh, yes! it is an open door." Presently she continued, " The Lord is gracious and full of compassion; I believe He will never leave nor forsake me;" and after a solemn pause, she added, "I have passed through deep baptisms of spirit in this illness, I may say, unworthy as I am to say it, that I have had to drink in my small measure of the Saviour's cup, when he said, ' My God! my God! why hast Thou forsaken me!' Some of my friends have thought there was a danger of my being exalted, but I believe the danger has been on the opposite side, of my being too low." She afterwards said, with much sweetness, " I feel that He is gracious and full of compassion, and that He will not leave me destitute; and I trust He will never suffer me to dishonour His holy name." And on another occasion, the same friend being again with her, she dwelt, in a very clear and instructive manner, upon her own state, bodily and mentally. She expressed her belief that her illness was permitted for some special purpose, as it regarded herself, her family, and perhaps many others; said she could not see what the termination of it was designed to be, adding, " I have had to look over all my life, and to review all the engagements which I have been led into." She spoke of her visit to the Mansion House, and of her meeting the King of Prussia there, and said she had never known a more deeply humiliating occasion ; adding, " I cannot doubt that I was rightly led there, and none can think what I went through." Soon afterwards she said to the same friend, " My life has been one of great vicissitude ; mine has been a hidden path, hidden from every human eye. I have had deep humiliations to pass through. I can truly say, I have wandered in the wilderness in a solitary way, and found no city to dwell in ; and yet how wonderfully I have been sustained. I have passed through many and great dangers, many ways ; I have been tried with the applause of the world, and none know how great a trial that has been, and the deep humiliations of it ; and yet I fully believe that it is not near so dangerous as being made much of in religious society. There is a snare even in religious unity, if we are not on the watch. I have sometimes felt, that it was not so dangerous to be made much of in the world, as by those whom we think highly of in our own Society. The more I have been made much of by the world, the more I have been inwardly humbled." She added, " I could often adopt the words of Sir Francis Bacon, ' When I have ascended before men, I have descended in humiliation before God.' " At another time, she expressed to some of her near connexions, that she " felt comfort in having given up, to do what she had believed to be her duty." One of her daughters remarked to her, that she had " made great sacrifices ;" to which she replied, she " could not call them sacrifices, it was her delight."*

---

* Annual Monitor, or Obituary of the members of the Society of Friends for 1846.

She was much interested in the engagement of her nephew Fowell Buxton, and her niece Rachel Gurney. She knew from former experience, the pain that her brother and sister had to encounter, in the marriage of their daughter leading her from Friends, and yet for them as for herself, she desired to take the highest ground of Christian liberty. She was present at their wedding breakfast, she gave them her blessing, and offered prayer on their behalf.

In February, she paid her first visit to Manor House since all was so changed there. She greatly shrunk from the pain of this visit in prospect, but in fact bore it far beyond expectation. The children won her attention; their delight at seeing her gave her pleasure, and, to a certain extent, her thoughts were occupied. The touch of infirmity which had attended her illness, certainly had its effect, as to the manner in which she felt her afflictions. She was more easily diverted by little things, and for the moment became interested in them; but those reasoning powers were enfeebled, which would have enabled her to grasp the causes of her grief, to encounter its circumstances of pain, and arrange them in her own mind. Sorrow is an enemy that can never be escaped by flight or evasion—it must be grappled with to be subdued.

The 19th of February, her brother, friend and early coadjutor Sir Fowell Buxton quitted this world,

> " To be a glorious guest
> Where the wicked cease from troubling,
> And the weary are at rest."

These successive departures could not but have their effect, not only in weaning from earthly things, but in making it of small import, whether a little sooner, or a little later, summoned to join the band which was mustering so strongly on the other side Jordan. In the mind of this way-worn traveller it was very perceptible. She dwelt more in spirit with those who were gone. Unseen realities increasingly opened upon her view. Many so near and dear had been gathered round the throne, that her heart and soul continually ascended thitherward.

There was one thing which rested upon her mind,—an intense desire again to visit Norfolk, and stay once more at Earlham. With great difficulty it was accomplished, her husband and daughter Louisa taking her there. She remained at Earlham many weeks; often able to partake of enjoyment, and highly valuing the communion with her brother Joseph John Gurney, his wife, and her beloved sister Catherine. There were also familiar faces, whom it gladdened her heart to see, and friends of every grade who came to visit her, and were all welcomed. Occasionally, her sufferings overcame her, and weighed her down ; and when her young relative, John Birkbeck, sank and died, she was afflicted for his family, and her own wounds bled afresh ; the close communication between Keswick and Earlham rendering it impossible to shield her from the daily alternations of hope and fear.

She went frequently to Meeting at Norwich. She was drawn up the Meeting, seated in her wheeled chair, and thence ministered with extraordinary life and power to those present; her memory in using Scripture in no degree failing her, or her power in applying it.

What a history had hers been, since the time of the scarlet riding habit—since she sat and wept under the ministry of William Savery. Her ardent aspirations had been strangely granted ; she had passed a long life of blessing to others, but by a path of singular sorrow to herself. She had been eyes to the blind, and feet to the lame—when the ear heard her then it blessed her. She had trodden regal halls to plead for the afflicted and the destitute ; she had not withheld unpalatable truth when the language of warning was called for at her lips.

She had penetrated, nothing daunted, the gloom of the felon's dungeon, nor had she shrunk from the touch of the unclothed maniac; she had nourished and brought up children, and they had risen up to call her blessed; and now, helpless and suffering in body, enfeebled in memory, all that could be shaken tottering to its base—she came again, to take a last look at the home and the haunts of her childhood.

She went for ten days to North Repps; the atmosphere of that place was very genial to her. Her sister and she were fellow-mourners, close participators in the greatness of their sorrows, and the vastness of their consolation. They held sweet counsel together; they dwelt on the blessedness of their departed ones, and together sought and found comfort in the Book of Life.

Whilst there, upon one occasion, Elizabeth Fry spoke of her prayers as constant for those she most closely loved. Being asked how this could be, with other occupations and hindrances; she replied, " It is always in my heart;" adding, " even in sleep I think the heart is ever lifted up," (putting it as no uncommon experience) ; "it is, if I may venture to say it, living in communion with Christ,"—"in Him."—" What! should I be without Him ?"—" Where should I stand ?"   She continued, " I never have known despondency; whatever may have been my depths of suffering in mind or body, still, the confidence has never left me that all was and would be well, if not in time, in eternity—that the end would be peace."   " I never lose the feeling of this, and am always on the rock—that conviction never leaves me."   " I have been so comforted by the sense of the glory and happiness of those taken, that it has proved a preparation for the sorrows."

Whilst at North Repps, hearing of the dangerous illness of her little grandson, Oswald Cresswell, she wrote to his parents :—

I have indeed drunk the bitter cup with you: perhaps I may say in my low estate I am too much disposed to drink it to the dregs ; but I desire to look upwards to Him, who not only can heal and raise up, if it be good for the beloved child and those nearest, but can also, through the fulness of His love, mercy, and merits, fit this sweet lamb of the flock for a place in His kingdom, if it be the will of God that the work should be cut short in righteousness. Our Lord's words are very sweet respecting these little ones : " Suffer little children to come unto me, and forbid them not, for of such is the kingdom of heaven." I understand by this, that we must not be too anxious for their lives ; but I know it is hard, very hard, to human nature, to have no will in it. My prayer is for the darling little one, that whatever awaits him, he may be the Lord's child and servant; and if it be His holy will, that he may here fill a place in the militant church of Christ, to the glory of God, the good of mankind, and the peace of his own soul ; and then join those who " rest from their labours and whose works do follow them," and who " for ever rejoice in the presence of our Lord and our God !" but I desire to leave all to Him, who knows what is best for us and for him.

I am your tender, loving, and sympathising mother.

The last letter she ever addressed to her husband was from North Repps, dated Fourth Month, 10th, 1845 :—

My dearest Husband,

I am anxious to express to thee a little of my near love, and to tell thee how often I visit thee in spirit, and how very strong are my desires for thy present and thy everlasting welfare. I feel for thee in my long illness, which so much disqualifies me from being all I desire to thee. I desire that thou mayst turn to the Lord for help and consolation under all thy trials, and that, whilst not depending on the passing pleasures and enjoyments of this world, thou mayst at the same time be enabled to enjoy our many remaining blessings. I also desire this for myself in my afflicted state, (for I do consider such a state of health a heavy affliction), independent of all other trials. I very earnestly desire for myself, that the deep tribulation I have had to pass through for so long a time may not lead into temptation, but be sanctified to the further refinement of my soul, and preparation for eternal rest, joy, and glory. May we, during our stay in time, be more and more sweetly united in the unity of the Spirit, and in the bond of peace.

We have much to be thankful for in Harry's prospect; I must write to him; I long to see him.

We have been deeply anxious about dear little Oswald, and I long to return to Lynn to see him and his father and mother, yet rather fear the exertion may be too much for me; still, I should feel more easy and happy to have seen them; but I wish for thy opinion on the subject.   *   *   *   *

After she left Earlham, she came for a few days to Runcton, as it was thought better than her going to Lynn. Her children met her and stayed with her there. She had not been at Runcton since death had last entered that pleasant dwelling; she had greatly loved the mother and the daughter who had successively gladdened and adorned it, she had deeply mourned their loss, and in her weakened state of spirits, sorrowful associations mingled with the enjoyment she experienced, in being again with her brother and his children. She liked their cordial glowing welcome, and the affectionate attentions of that young party. It was pleasant, to see them occupied alternately in performing for her the little offices of love. The old servants vied in attention to her, whilst those who were married away, or lived in the village, pressed to see her, and obtain a word of counsel or kindness. Before she left Norfolk, she heard of the intended marriage of her youngest son. Nothing could be more agreeable to her, than the prospect of this event; towards this, her last-born child, her motherly care had been peculiarly extended. She very much liked her future daughter-in-law, and her being a member of the Society of Friends afforded her no small gratification. It was indeed a boon for all who loved her, to feel that she returned home under a ray of sunshine, and that the brightness of this event to her

feelings, was permitted a little to enlighten the last few months
of her home-life.   Whilst the various arrangements and preparations connected with it, occupied, without wearying her mind, and
her attention was in some degree withdrawn from dwelling upon
her sorrows and deprivations.   In her eldest granddaughter, the
first-born of her eldest son, and bearing her own name, she had
during this spring a helpful cheerful companion, who, with the
elasticity of youth (which is so pleasant to the infirm and
declining), cheered, whilst she cared for her grandmother.   She
had also many visitors, who came to her in their abundant kindness, for the hearts of all who had ever loved her, were drawn
out towards her in tender compassion.

The Duchess of Sutherland and her daughters, the Chevalier
Bunsen and his family, and many others, besides her own relatives and connexions, and the excellent of the earth of various
denominations, would drive down to Upton Lane, and sit awhile
by her side, to mark that " love," which George Herbert desig-
nates " a present for a mighty King. '

The latter part of May, accompanied by her granddaughter
Elizabeth Fry, she attended two sittings of the women's Yearly
Meeting of Friends in London ; the women being wholly separate from the men in all matters of business.   A person not
a Friend, would scarcely credit the order and regularity with
which women Friends carry on a system of discipline, extending
in fact through all the ramifications of the Society.   The desired
information is elicited by a list of queries, which are answered
by the Monthly or Particular Meetings, with reference to the
individuals composing the Meeting.   The Quarterly Meetings
answer the same queries to the Yearly Meeting, with reference to
the Monthly Meetings composing the Quarterly Meeting ; and
thus a condensed view of the state of Society is brought before
the Yearly Meeting.—The information to be obtained relates to
the regular attendance of Friends at their meetings for worship

and discipline—their frequent reading of the Bible and religious books—their punctuality in money matters, and in the fulfil-ment of engagements—the sober temperate and orderly conduct of themselves and their families—their not frequenting places of amusement, nor joining in vain sports, and their adherence to the simple garb and language of Friends.   A summary of these answers having been prepared, was to be laid before the Meeting on the day of Mrs. Fry's first attendance.   A sitting of the women's Yearly Meeting must be seen to be imagined.   It is a singular and striking sight, and may vie with any of the deli-berative assemblies in which men are convened throughout the world, in gravity, in absence of display, and in steady attention to the business before it.   Many hundred woman, arrayed, with but slight variation, in the same peculiar attire, seated in a large lofty apartment, preserving entire silence, their countenances bespeaking unusual good sense and power of attention, listening to, and weighing the matter laid before them.   Those who, from being " ministers" or " elders " of the Society, take a more pro-minent part, rising, one at a time, to give information or offer an opinion ; but the person of least account in the Meeting equally at liberty to address the assembly, and equally sure of being heard with kind and courteous attention .   Elizabeth Fry had for many years, been regular in her attendance upon these Meetings, and had taken a lively interest in their proceedings. After an illness so critical, and still in a state of such great infirmity, to see her again amongst them, was scarcely less grati-fying to many of the Friends there, than it was interesting to herself. On this occasion she spoke of the Saviour's declaration, " I am the true vine,"—" ye are the branches,"—" as the branch cannot bear fruit of itself, except it abide in the vine, no more can ye, except ye abide in me." She alluded, in the course of her observations, to the day that is " fast approaching to every one ;" but urged the blessed truth on her hearers, that those " who loved,

served, and obeyed Him, who alone is worthy of all glory and
praise, would find death deprived of its sting, and the grave of its
victory." The second Meeting she attended, was one when a
Friend named Edwin Tregellis, gave a relation of his missionary
labours in the West Indies. This recital drew from her, some
account of her own travels on the continent. She afterwards
enlarged upon the various instruments, by which God accom-
plishes His own work in the world.—She referred to the simile
of the different living stones, which compose the temple of God.
—She addressed those of every age who heard her, especially
such as might be compared to the hidden stones of the building.
—She encouraged them to go forward fearlessly in the path of
righteousness and good works, for though they might not be so
much seen and known, as the more polished stones in the orna-
mental parts of the structure — though perhaps not so fitted to
shine, or to occupy a conspicuous situation—yet were their
places each equally ordered, equally important, and equally
under the direction and all-seeing eye of the Divine Architect.
She expressed her doubts, as to whether she should again be
permitted to meet her beloved Friends in that place.—She offered prayer, her rich full voice filling the house ; and concluded
with that sublime passage, " Great and marvellous are Thy
works, Lord God Almighty, just and true are Thy ways thou
King of saints."

On the 3rd of June, Mrs. Fry was present at the Annual
Meeting of the Ladies' British Society. To spare her fatigue,
the Committee kindly arranged, to hold it in the Friends'
Meeting-house at Plaistow, instead of the one at Westminster,
which hitherto had been the place chosen.

At the Committee of the Society, held on the 3rd of the
November following, there was drawn up by its members, a
touching memorial of the feelings they entertained towards her.

In it they speak of this Meeting :—

" Contrary to usual custom, the place of Meeting fixed on was not in London, but at Plaistow in Essex; and the large number of friends who gathered round her upon that occasion, proved how gladly they came to her, when she could no longer with ease be conveyed to them. The enfeebled state of her bodily frame seemed to have left the powers of her mind unshackled, and she took, though in a sitting posture, almost her usual part in repeatedly addressing the Meeting. She urged, with increased pathos and affection, the objects of philanthropy and Christian benevolence with which her life had been identified. After the Meeting, and at her own desire, several members of the Committee, and other friends, assembled at her house. They were welcomed by her with the greatest benignity and kindness, and in her intercourse with them, strong were the indications of the heavenly teaching, through which her subdued and sanctified spirit had been called to pass. Her affectionate salutation in parting unconsciously closed, in regard to most of them, the intercourse which they delighted to hold with her, but which can no more be renewed on this side of the eternal world."

When Mrs. Fry attended for the last time the Meeting of the British Ladies' Society, she had the happiness of knowing that Newgate, Bridewell, the Millbank Prison, the Giltspur Street Compter, White Cross Street Prison, Tothill Fields Prison, and Cold Bath Fields Prison, were all in a state of comparative order; some exceedingly well arranged, and the female convicts in all, more or less visited and cared for by ladies—varying according to their circumstances and requirings. The prisons generally throughout England much improved, and in the greater number, ladies encouraged to visit the female convicts.

Let the state of prisons and female prisoners be recalled as it existed thirty years before—not, that to Elizabeth Fry alone this vast improvement is attributed—much has resulted from the spirit of the day, and the tone that has pervaded and increasingly pervades the upper ranks of society. She was but a

7

type of her times, an illustration of the benevolent and enlarged philanthropy, which is diffusing its influence throughout all classes.

Though unquestionably, she accomplished much, and above all had the joy of knowing, that the principles she had so long asserted were universally recognized—that the object of penal legislation is not revenge, but the prevention of crime ; in the first place, by affording opportunity of reform to the criminal, and in the second, by warning others from the consequences of its commission. But there was one thing she was not permitted to see accomplished,—a refuge for every erring and repentant sinner of her own sex ; the opportunity of reformation for all who desired to reform. There are those, who have striven to connect the memory and the name of Elizabeth Fry, with such a shelter for the outcasts of our great metropolis ; the arrangements are not yet matured, nor has the call for funds, to carry the measure into effect, been hitherto responded to, in a manner at all commensurate with the greatness or the importance of the undertaking ; but the need of such an asylum is too obvious, and the evils which it would remedy too sorrowful, to doubt of its final accomplishment.

On the 26th of June her youngest son was married. She described the Meeting as " a very solemn one, something like a token for good;" and spoke of the connexion as a " ray of light upon a dark picture."

There was through all the real brightness of the occasion a deep feeling of the past; when dear Julia's children joined us in the afternoon, then the miss of dearest William was keenly to be felt. Champion and Hannah too so very far off, that there was much to cloud over the scene, as well as my poor state of health, making it more difficult to estimate my many present blessings, as I ought and desire to do.

As the summer advanced, sea air was considered desirable for her, and after some difficulty her husband obtained a house at Ramsgate, exactly suited to her necessities. She went for a week to see it, and to make her own arrangements, accompanied by her husband and her daughter Richenda. The day before leaving home, she wrote to her brother and sister Gurney.

My dearest Samuel and Elizabeth,

I have rather longed to bid you farewell before accompanying my husband to Ramsgate for a few days. My heart is much with you and our dear brother Joseph also, just now. I particularly feel for you in your conflicts, as well as your joys. Humiliations we must expect to pass through, if we are to drink of the cup our Lord drank of, and be baptised with the baptism that He was baptised with ; therefore we must not fear, but when our spirits are overwhelmed within us, we must look to the "rock that is higher than we, as a shelter from the storm, a shadow from the heat when the blast of the terrible one is as a storm against the wall."

From Ramsgate, was written the last letter, her eldest daughter ever received from her mother.

Ramsgate, *Seventh Month, 5th.*

I much desire to be at our own Meeting on First-day with dearest Harry and Lucy, and hope it may please a kind Providence to enable me to do so.

I have felt very poorly here in the morning, more so than usual, which has been rather discouraging. I much like the house as far as I have seen it, but I have not been up stairs. I have felt unusually low, and am sensible of my poor condition, as it is most feelingly brought home to me in almost every fresh effort. I desire in heart to say, " Not as I will, but as Thou wilt." I think none of my friends need fear (as I believe they used to do), my being exalted by the good opinion of my fellow-mortals. I think my state is " cast down but not destroyed." May my Lord, whom I have loved and sought to serve, keep me alive unto Himself, and may He clothe me with His armour that I may " stand in the evil day and after having done all, stand."

*   *   *   *   *

I am, in most tender love, thy much attached mother,

E. F.

The return of her son and his young bride, to Upton Lane, she wished to make as cheerful as under existing circumstances was possible, and in celebration of the event, a large family party was arranged for the garden. She asked the company of her brother and sister from Ham House, in the following note.

My dearest Samuel and Elizabeth,

In true love, I advise your joining our simple evening party, which I humbly trust will be conducted on Christian grounds. The fact is, in my low estate I felt much indisposed for a large dinner ; I then wished for our dear little children to have some innocent pleasure, and also to show some mark of the deep interest we feel in the bride and bridegroom here, and in the bride and bridegroom elect. We wish to do it in the most simple manner. Remember our most blessed Master attended the wedding feast.

Your most loving sister,

E. F.

She received her guests in a room opening into the flower garden, and thence was wheeled to the end of the terrace ; a very large family circle surrounded her, many connexions and others of her friends. It was a beautiful scene,—the last social family meeting at which she presided ; and although infirm and broken in health, she looked and seemed herself.

In an easy chair, under the large marquee, she entered into animated discourse on various and important topics with the group around her, the Chevalier Bunsen, M. Merle D'Aubigny, Sir Henry Pelly, Josiah Forster, her brother Samuel Gurney, and others of her friends.

An event of great interest shortly followed: the marriage of her faithful niece, Elizabeth Gurney, to Ernest Bunsen. This connexion was one, which her aunt liked inasmuch as she valued the individual and highly esteemed his excellent and gifted parents, though not unmingled with regret that the children of her brother and sister, as so many of her own had done, should leave the Society of Friends by marriage, and thus separate themselves from that body of Christians, to which their parents were so warmly attached. The wedding took place on the 5th of August. She joined the party afterwards at Ham House. It was an occasion of singular interest—Christian love, unity and good feeling prevailing over " diversities of administration," yet all owning " the same Lord."

The week following, she was moved to the house on Mount Albion at Ramsgate, which had been prepared for her. A spacious bed-chamber adjoining the drawing-room, with pleasant views of the sea, in which she delighted, adding to her hourly comfort and enjoyment. She found objects there well suited to her tastes. She distributed tracts when she drove into the country, or went upon the Pier in a Bath chair. Seafaring men have a certain openness of character which renders them more easy of access than others. They would gladly receive her little offerings, and listen to her remarks. She was also anxious to ascertain the state of the Coast Guard Libraries—whether they required renewing, and were properly used.

The party were scarcely established at Ramsgate, when the family of her beloved son William came to them, and remained for some weeks. She delighted in them all ; but little Willie Fry was something to her, almost beyond anything left in the world. He read the Bible to her every morning on her awakening. She strove to impress upon his young mind the value and beauty of the Christian life ; she endeavoured to cultivate in him a taste for natural objects ; she encouraged drawing and similar pursuits. Partly his name—partly his character, so much resembling his father's in early boyhood—excited her tenderest love.

Her prayer for her daughter and her children, the evening before their departure, was beautiful, comprehensive, and touching; and so she commended them, whom she was to see no more in the flesh, to Him, who has promised to be a " Husband to the widow, and a Father to the fatherless." Her eldest son, and her daughter Mrs. Foster Reynolds, with their families, were near her in the town ; and the daily intercourse with them, was also a source of much comfort and pleasure to her.

On the 27th of August, in a hand almost illegible, she thus wrote in her journal :—

Ramsgate, Eighth Month, 27*th.*—It still pleases my Heavenly Father that afflictions should abound to me in this tabernacle, as I groan, being burthened. Lord, through the fulness of Thy love and pity, and unmerited mercy, be pleased to arise for my help. Bind up my broken heart, heal my wounded spirit, and yet enable Thy servant, through the power of Thy own Spirit, in everything to return Thee thanks, and not to faint in the day of trouble, but in humility and godly fear to show forth Thy praise. Keep me Thine own, through Thy power to do this, and pity and help Thy poor servant who trusteth in Thee. Be very near to our dear son and daughter, and their children in Madeira. Be with them, and all near to us, wherever scattered, and grant that Thy peace and Thy blessing may rest upon us all. Amen and Amen.

On the 13th of September, she thus wrote to her son Joseph.

First-day, Afternoon.

I am rather blanked to hear that we cannot see thee and thine this week. I rather particularly long to see a dear son again, as it feels long since John left us, and you are sure your beloved wives have also a true welcome. I feel myself *much* broken, and finding that neither sea air, nor any other thing appears much to raise me up; I do feel that while *here* (I mean in this life,) a great desire to be as much as I can with those most dear to me. My heart overflows with love and most earnest desire for your present and everlasting welfare, particularly that all may be of the number of those who " die in the Lord," " who rest from their labours, and whose works do follow them."

      *   *   *   *   *   *

I feel certainly very poorly and unless there be some revival more than I now feel, I think that you cannot expect, that you will very long have a mother to come to, but I know the Lord can raise me up again, and I should not be surprised if it should be His holy will, but into His hands I commit my body, soul and spirit, humbly trusting that He will be my Keeper, Guide, and Guard, even unto the end; through the fulness of His love, pity, mercy in Christ our Saviour! I know this is a low letter, may it lead to your sympathy, love, and prayers. I think I am low from parting with Julia and the children; my heart is so bound to you all. I am encouraged by remembering the 13th chapter of the First of Corinthians, because I feel that I may humbly trust that that love or charity there spoken of lives in my heart, and is as the apostle John says it is, a mark of having passed from death unto life, " because ye love the brethren." (1 John iii. 14.)

The following day she wrote to her brother Samuel Gurney as follows:

I was very low when I wrote to thee yesterday, therefore do not think too much of it. There is ONE only who sees in secret, who knows the conflicts I have to pass through. To Him I commit my body, soul and spirit, and He only knows the depth of my love and earnestness of my prayers for you all. I have the humble trust that He will be my Keeper even unto the end, and when the end comes through the fulness of His love and the abundance of His merits, I shall join those who after having passed through great tribulation, are for ever at rest in

Jesus, having washed their robes, and made them white in the blood of the Lamb.

I am in nearest love,

Thy grateful and tenderly attached sister,

E. F.

Pray remember the books for the poor old women, we must work whilst it is called " to-day," however low the service we may be called to, I desire to do so to the end, through the help that may be granted me.

On the 16th of the following month, she again, and for the last time, recorded her feelings there, but written in a firmer hand, and with apparently more power.

Ramsgate, Ninth Month, 16*th.*—My dearest son Harry was married to dear Lucy Sheppard last Sixth Month, 26th. We had a very solemn Meeting; peace appeared to rest upon us at the Meeting, and at her father's house afterwards. My humble trust is, that the blessing of the Most High God is in this connexion. They spent some very satisfactory time with us before we left home. May grace, mercy and peace rest upon them, and neither the fatness of the earth, nor the dew of heaven, be withheld from them, through the fulness of the love, mercy and pity of our God, in Christ Jesus our Lord.

Our dearest niece Elizabeth was also married the latter end of the Seventh Month to my dear young friend Ernest Bunsen. May the blessing of the Most High God also rest upon them naturally and spiritually. I pray the same for them as for Harry and Lucy.

Here the journal ceases ; the above being the last entry.

Her sister Lady Buxton, with her daughter Richenda, went to her on the 17th of September. There was much opportunity for intercourse, after her waking in the morning, and especially during her lengthened toilet ; her sister generally read the Bible with her at these times. She found her mind clear and

powerful in spiritual things, enlarging upon them with comprehension of their import ; her heart entirely in the things of God,
choosing him and his service solely, seeking first the kingdom
of God, with deep earnest constant desires (beyond words to
express) for her husband and children, grandchildren, brothers
and sisters, nephews and nieces, and all who were dear to her.
She was wonderfully alive to all good things going on in the
world, receiving with thankfulness any instance of this, without partiality or distinction.   After her sister went, her youngest son and his bride stayed a few days with them.   Different
members of the family came also to see her.   Her son Joseph
and his wife left her a grandchild when they went away.

The 14th of September, with a large party of her children,
she attended the small Meeting at Drapers, about four miles
from Ramsgate.   On this occasion she preached a most powerful and remarkable sermon on the nearness of death, and the
necessity of immediate preparation and repentance, for she
believed to some of that small congregation it was the eleventh
hour of the day.

Her ministrations were much of the same character the two
following Sundays.   Her brother and sister Gurney stayed near
her for some days, and some ladies from Zwolle did the same ;
she also valued the near neighbourhood of her kind friends, Sir
John and Lady Pirie.

On the 29th, the large family party dispersed.   The Meeting
of the preceding day had been one of great solemnity, and
though little imagined at the time, well fitted to be a parting
occasion with so many dear to her.   The next day she was left
with only her husband and eldest daughter, but the nursing
was too arduous for them to bear alone, and it was a great relief to them when her daughter Rachel and her family arrived
from Norfolk.   At the Pier gate, awaiting them in the carriage,
they found their mother.   Her daughter had not seen her, since

her visit to Runcton, six months before, a great change was perceptible. There was a look of heaviness and weight; she rarely smiled, but on the other hand, far less often looked distressed; she walked rather better, her appetite was improved, and her nights not so disturbed; but there was a new symptom—occasionally severe pain in the head. It had first appeared ten days before, and had often been acute, but then was better.

The next Sunday she went as usual to Meeting. On her return, she asked some of the party, who from circumstances had been precluded from accompanying her, and had attended their own place of worship, if they had had "a comfortable church;" her general question when she met any of her children under similar circumstances. Then without waiting to be asked, she said, they had had "a very remarkable Meeting, such a peculiarly solemn time;" that she had been so impressed by the "need of working whilst it was day, to be ready for the Master's summons come when He might." Here the subject dropped, but she reverted to it more than once during the day. Those who were present described the occasion, as a very peculiar one. She had urged the question, "Are we all now ready? If the Master should this day call us, is the work completely finished? Have we anything left to do?" Solemnly, almost awfully reiterating the question, "Are we prepared?"

Her habits at this time were apparently those of former times. She was a good deal occupied by writing. She arranged and sorted Bibles, Testaments and Tracts. She had applied to the Bible Society for a grant of foreign Bibles and Testaments, which was liberally acceded to, and in the distribution of which, amongst the foreign sailors in the harbour, she took great delight. She expected intelligence on subjects that interested her, and was more disposed to carry on objects continuously. She liked having her grandchildren with her; one of them read her a Psalm invariably before she rose, and whilst dressing, a

younger one was in her room, sorting shells under her direction
or looking at the many prints and picture-books, which she had
collected for their use.

On Tuesday, when driving out, her lively interest for the good
of others appeared if possible greater than ever. Her natural
character, acquired habit, and Christian duty, alike combined
to strengthen this, but the judgment and power to direct it had
in measure passed away.

On Wednesday she was grievously distressed by her little
grandson Oswald encountering a fearful accident, one knee
slipping through the area bars of a window. It was at least ten
minutes before help could be obtained to extricate him. The
child's cries, and her knowledge of the fact, though at the time
borne apparently well, occasioned a severe return of pain in the
head at night, and she was very unwell the next morning, though
through the day she had appeared but little the worse for it, and
was perfectly self-possessed and judicious in giving directions.
The same morning, her friend Mary Fell paid her husband and
herself a religious visit, she derived much comfort from it, as
she had done from the society of this long known and valued
Friend for some weeks preceding.

Generally, whilst she dressed, one of her daughters sat with
their mother. On one occasion, the Bible was opened at the text,
" Beloved, think it not strange concerning the fiery trial which
is to try you, as though some strange thing happened unto you."
She entered with lively interest into the subject, and mentioned
other passages of somewhat similar import, which were sought
for and read. The participation of the disciple in the sufferings
of his Lord, was dwelt upon. She expressed herself with peculiar
power, in a manner startling to the hearer. She had, through all
her conflicts, seemed to cling to something, like the hope, almost
expectation, that the western sky would be bright, that her sun
would not set behind clouds ; but now there was no allusion to

any idea of the kind. The high privilege of suffering as a member of Christ, was the point she the most dwelt upon. The world, even in its beauty and pleasantness, even the renewed regenerated aspect which it bears to the Christian, appeared to have lost nearly all attraction. She had long done the will of God, to her active mind comparatively an easy duty, she had now completely learned the far harder lesson of being willing to endure it.

There was another wonderful change. Her powerful understanding and great capacity had given her the habit of control—she was accustomed to power. During her long illness, this continued more or less to show itself, and it was not always easy to distinguish, how far her opinions about her own treatment and capabilities were well founded or not. This feature of her character had disappeared. The will seemed wholly broken, the inclination to resist, or even strongly to desire any thing, passed away ; and she was content to leave little things and great to the direction of others. It was inexpressibly affecting to see her look of meek submission, to hear her plaintive answer, " Just as you like," to those about her.

One morning of acute suffering, the remark was made to her, How marvellous it was that she never seemed impatient to depart, believing, as there was good ground to do, that she had been fitted for the great change. Her inherent fear of death had probably prevented this, for there was something in her mind, which, whilst she desired " the kingdom," caused her to shrink from the encounter with the great enemy — the last grapple before the victory can be won. But this too was altered ; she expressed her entire " willingness to stay the Lord's time ;" that whilst " there was any work for her to do, she wished to live," but beyond that, expressed not the smallest desire for life. She added, that she had come to an entire belief, that any remaining dread would be taken away from her, when the time came, or that

in " tender mercy to her timid nature," she should be permitted
to pass unconsciously through the dark valley.

On Thursday, she wrote to her youngest daughter :—

                                    Ramsgate, *Tenth Month,* 9*th.*

My dearest Louisa,

I think that a visit from thee and thy dear husband would be
highly acceptable to us ; but much as I should like to see the
dear boys, I fear that the house is now too full to take in more
than we should have with Raymond and thyself.

I feel so shaken and so broken down, that I wish to see as
much of my beloved children as I can ; my love is very strong,
and my flesh is very weak, I think increasingly so. I wish dear
Christiana Golder to know how much I miss her. Pray tell
Gurney and Sophia also how much I should like to see them ;
indeed, my heart is drawn very near to you all, and deep are
my desires for your present, and above all, your everlasting
welfare.

     *   *   *   *   *

I am, with dear love to Raymond and the boys, and love to
all the dear Plashet family, our dear Julia and the children, thy
tenderly attached mother,

                                    ELIZABETH FRY.

On Friday morning, though very languid and feeling uncomfortable, she addressed this note to a lady, an old attached
friend, with some texts for a young person, who desired to
possess her autograph.

                                    Ramsgate, 11*th.*

My dear Friend,

I have copied thee, these valuable texts, that prove salvation is
open to all, through a Saviour's love and merits, who believe in
Him, who no longer live unto themselves, but unto Him who
died for them and rose again. May we all be of this blessed

number. I should much like a nice long letter from thee.
With true desires for thy present and everlasting welfare,

I remain,

Thy affectionate friend,

ELIZABETH FRY.

"We trust in the living God, who is the Saviour of all men,
specially of those that believe," 1 Tim. iv. 10. "And I, if I be
lifted up from the earth, will draw all men unto me." John xii.
32. "Therefore as by the offence of one judgment came upon
all men to condemnation; even so by the righteousness of one,
the free gift came upon all men unto justification of life."
Romans v. 18.

After finishing this note, she brought out some sheets of
Scripture selections, which she had prepared with a view to
eventually publishing another Text-Book on the same plan as
her former one. She turned over the leaves of her small travelling Bible, without spectacles, to look for others; she had also
written the note in a firm, clear hand, with no glasses. On this
being observed to her, she replied, "Oh yes, my eye-sight is
so much better;" which was corroborated by her own maid, for
many years her devoted attendant. This was not a symptom
to pass lightly by.

Later in the morning, whilst driving out, she was strangely
oppressed—scarcely noticed the lovely views of the sea which she
generally so much enjoyed; but the most unusual thing was,
that when her grandchildren were eager to give some tracts, she
scarcely noticed their request till repeated two or three times.
On passing some open country, where a ruddy farmer's boy was
keeping cows, he told the children that he was there all day,
that he had nothing to do, and should very much like to have
"some reading." Their grandmother took no notice, nor until
her tract-bag was put into her hand did she attempt to choose

M M 2

any for him ; then she did it with a slow distracted air, as if her
thoughts were far away. That evening she was heavy and
oppressed, and complained of suffering from the light.

These many circumstances, each trifling in itself, brought and
weighed together, gave such cause for uneasiness, that her husband and daughters resolved the next day to send to Broadstairs, to learn if Dr. Paris was still there, for they had heard
of his being at that place a short time before, and call in his
assistance ; but he was gone.

On Saturday morning she awakened, suffering severely in her
head. One of her grandchildren went to her at half-past seven
o'clock : he read the 27th Psalm, which she asked for. Half an
hour later, another went to her. She in no way referred to his
brother having been there before, but again asked for the 27th
Psalm. Her dressing was very slowly accomplished ; she leaned
her head upon her hand, and spoke very little. A text or two out
of " Great and precious promises," that excellent selection for
the sick chamber, seemed all that she could receive. She had not
asked for a child whilst she was dressing, the only morning she
had omitted to do so, nor did she remark their absence. She had
invited the children of Lady Arthur Lennox, to take their dinner
at her luncheon. It was proposed that their coming should be
deferred to another day, as she was so uncomfortable, but this she
would not allow : when they came she was scarcely able to notice
them, and sat looking very ill, leaning her head upon her hand.
Afterwards Lady Arthur Lennox, and her sister Mrs. Langford
Brook came for the children ; she received them in the drawing-
room and conversed a little, but they thought her unwell, and
made a very short visit. They had been frequently with her
before, they had paid her much kind attention, and their society
had been very pleasant to her.

About five o'clock, whilst her husband and daughters were consulting as to the best method in which medical help might be

obtained, her bell rung. She was in her own room, according to her usual custom in the afternoon, lying on the sofa, whilst an attendant read to her. She had nearly fallen, in moving from the sofa to her chair by the fire, and help was wanted, to accomplish it. After being placed in her chair, she leaned to one side, as if unable to hold herself upright. Her own maid, who was accustomed to her, was alarmed and uneasy, but the little dressing before dinner was completed without difficulty, and she was wheeled into the drawing-room, where it was proposed that she should dine, being nearer to her room than the dining-room. After her dinner, on attempting to move to the sofa, she twice sunk to the ground, though entirely assisted by two persons. With extreme difficulty she was removed to her bed, where she lay with a calm, almost a torpid expression of countenance. She was quite willing to see a medical man, and answered his questions correctly. The attendance of one so kind and skilful was a great help and comfort, but her worn-out constitution forbade stringent remedies, so that little was attempted either by him or the physician, who twice saw her in the course of the following day. As no fresh symptoms appeared, and she was herself very anxious for it, it was arranged that she should settle as usual for the night. Even at that period, the real seat of the complaint appeared doubtful. Diseases of the nerves are so various in character, that they often, when quite unaccompanied by danger, bear the semblance of fatal maladies. A few texts were repeated to her, and her daughters left her to her husband's care, who throughout her lengthened illness attended her by night; but scarcely had they reached their rooms, when her bell rung loudly. Throughout the night, though occasionally for an instant confused, the mind was there. Some passages of Scripture were read to her, which she appeared to comprehend, and she entirely responded to any observation made to her. This was favourable, but other symptoms were not so—she lay so heavily, and the limbs appeared so wholly powerless. The morning broke at last, but it brought no comfort. About six o'clock, she said to her maid, " Oh ! Mary, dear Mary, I am very ill !" " I know it, dearest ma'am, I know it." " Pray for me—It is a strift, but I am safe." She continued to speak but indistinctly, at intervals, and frequently dosed, as she had done through the night. About nine o'clock, one of her daughters sitting on the bed-side, had open in her hand that passage in Isaiah, " I the Lord thy God will hold thy right hand, saying unto thee, fear not thou worm Jacob, and ye men of Israel, I will help thee saith the Lord, and thy Redeemer, the Holy One of Israel." Just then, her mother roused a little, and in a slow distinct voice uttered these words, " Oh ! my dear Lord, help and keep thy servant !" These were the last words she spake upon earth, she never attempted to articulate again. A response was given, by reading to her the above most applicable passage ; one bright glance of intelligence passed over her features, a look of recognition at the well-known sound, but it was gone as rapidly, and never returned. From this time, entire unconsciousness appeared to take possession of her—no sound disturbed her—no light affected her—the voice of affection was unheeded—a veil was between her and the world about her, to be raised no more.

As the morning of Sunday advanced, all hope became extinguished. A messenger was dispatched, to summon such of her absent children, as might be able to come to look upon her once again in life. Whilst those who were with her, made ready for the conflict, to go down with her as into the valley of the shadow of death, for they whose lot it has been to watch the dying-bed, must be conscious, that there is generally a given moment of anguish, when the tremendous conviction pierces the heart, that the " inevitable hour " is come.

The difficulty of breathing, with convulsive spasm, increased; at first occasionally, but after midnight it became almost con-

tinuous.   From three o'clock there was no pause, but such
absolute unconsciousness to every impression, as satisfied those
around her, that the anguish was for them—not for her.   Yet, as
they marked the struggle, the irresistible prayer of their hearts
became, " How long, Oh Lord !—how long ! "

Suddenly, about twenty minutes before four, there was a
change in the breathing ; it was but a moment.   The silver cord
was loosed—a few sighs at intervals—and no sound was there.
Unutterably blessed was the holy calm—the perfect stillness of
the chamber of death.   She saw " the King in His beauty, and
the land that is very far off."

The night had been dark and lowering, but the morning
broke gloriously, the sun rose from the ocean, commanded by
her chamber windows, and as a globe of living fire,

" Flamed in the forehead of the morning sky."

The emblem was too beautiful to be rejected—one of the
types and shadowings furnished by the material world, to illustrate and adorn the Christian's hope.

Before evening, the greater number of her children were assembled at Ramsgate.   There was much kindness and attention
shown by the inhabitants.   Sir Moses Montefiore was deputed
to call upon the family, to propose that the hearse bearing her
remains should when taken from Mount Albion, be followed
through the town by such gentlemen of the place as inclined to
do so, with the shutters closed, and other marks of respect.
Arrangements made in Essex prevented the proposal being accepted ; but it was none the less gratifying, as a token of the
estimation, in which, though so lately come amongst them, the
departed had been held.   The different members of her family
successively quitted Ramsgate, till none remained but her eldest
son and one of his brothers-in-law, who stayed to share with
him the sad office of following the hearse to Upton.   They travelled through the night.

Monday at noon was fixed for her funeral. In the grey of the early morning, the loved, the revered, was brought for the last time, for a few short hours to her home of many years. Vast numbers of persons attended the funeral. The procession passed between the grounds of Plashet House, her once happy home, and those of Plashet Cottage. In the Friends' Burying-ground at Barking, her grave was prepared, close by that of her little child, whom she had loved and lost, and tenderly mourned so many years before. There is no appointed funeral service amongst Friends. A deep silence prevailed throughout the multitudes gathered there. Her brother Joseph John Gurney was the first to address the assembly, and by him solemn prayer was offered. A Meeting was held afterwards; but her immediate family were thankful to withdraw, and seek the shelter and recollections of Upton Lane.

Conclusion.—There may be some, who expect a sketch to be here given of the character of Elizabeth Fry—but a little reflection will show, that in the present case to attempt doing so would be presumptuous. Neither is it necessary. Her actions and conduct in life have been narrated. Her letters to her family and friends, pourtray her domestic feelings and her powers of loving. Her communications to others, supply the knowledge of her opinions upon the subjects, to which she gave her attention. In her journal may be found the outpourings of her heart, the communings between God and her own soul.

But there is a voice from the Dead—and the living are called to proclaim, before their work is concluded, and the memory of the departed committed to the stream of time—something, of her earnest desires for the well-being of her fellow-creatures, especially for that of her own sex. She was willing to spend and be spent, in her Master's service. She considered herself, called to a peculiar course. She was very young when she first saw a prison ; she had an extraordinary desire to visit one, and at last her father yielded to her wishes, and took her to see a bridewell—when and where is not exactly known ; but not long before her death, she narrated the circumstances to a friend, and how powerful an impression it had made upon her mind. It must be a question whether this visit was occasioned by, or led to the peculiar bent of her after career ; that it tended to strengthen it is indubitable, and that it was one link in the chain of Providential circumstances, which produced in the end, such signal results. But she would have shrunk, from urging the same course upon others. She feared her daughters, and

young women generally, undertaking questionable or difficult or
public offices; but she believed, that where one erred from over
activity in duty, many more omitted that, which it behoved them
to perform. " Woman's Mission" has become almost a word of
the day. Elizabeth Fry was persuaded that every woman has
her individual vocation, and in following it, that she would
fulfil her mission. She laid great stress on the outward
circumstances of life ; how and where providentially placed—
the opportunities afforded—the powers given. She considered
domestic duties the first and greatest earthly claims in the
life of woman ; although in accordance with the tenets of the
Society to which she belonged, she believed in some instances
her own amongst others, that under the immediate direction of
the Spirit of God, individuals were called to leave for a time their
home and families, and devote themselves to the work of the
ministry. She did not consider this call to be general, or to
apply to persons under an administration different to her own.
But it was her conviction, that there is a sphere of usefulness
open to all. She appreciated to the full the usual charities of
gentlewomen ; their visits to the sick and aged poor, and their
attention to the cottage children, but she grieved to think how
few complete the work of mercy, by following the widow or disabled, when driven by necessity to the workhouse ; or caring for
the workhouse school, that resort of the orphaned and forsaken,
less attractive, perhaps, than the school of the village, but even
more requiring oversight and attention.

A fearful accident, or hereditary disease, consigns the mother
of a family or some frail child to the hospital. In how many
cases does she lie there from day to day, watching the rays of
the morning sun reflected on the wall opposite, tracing them as
they move onwards through the day, and disappear as it advances; and this perhaps for weeks and months, without hearing
the voice of kindness and sympathy from her own sex, save

from the matron, or the hired nurses of the establishment. What might not, and when bestowed, what does not, woman's tenderness effect here ?

She heard of thousands and tens of thousands of homeless and abandoned children, wandering or perishing in our streets. She knew that attempts were made to rescue them, and that unflinching men and women laboured and toiled, to infuse some portion of moral health into that mass of living corruption ; but she mourned that so few assisted in this work of mercy, compared to the many who utterly neglect the call. She saw a vast number of her own sex, degraded and guilty, many a fair young creature, once the light of her parents' dwelling, fallen and polluted,—many who had filled useful situations in business or domestic service, sunk and debased. The downward road open wide before them, but no hand stretched forth to lift them the first step up the rugged path of repentance, or assist in their hard struggle against sin. She encountered in the prisons every grade and variety of crime. Woman bold and daring and reckless—revelling in her iniquity, and hardened in vice—her only remaining joy to seduce others, and make them still more the children of Hell than herself;—the thoughtless culprit, not lost to good and holy feeling, nor dead to impression from without ;—and lastly, the beginner—she who from her deep poverty had been driven to theft, or drawn by others into temptation. Elizabeth Fry marked all these, and despaired of none amongst them. Here again, in her estimation, a crying need existed for influence, for instruction, reproof, and encouragement. But it was not to all, she would have allotted *this* task, though she could never be persuaded, but, that in every instance, women well qualified for the office might be found, to care for these outcasts of the people.

These were the things that she saw, and bitterly deplored. She believed that a mighty power rested with her own sex to

6

check and to control this torrent of evil ; a moral force, that
the educated and the virtuous might bring to bear upon the
ignorant and vicious.   She desired to have every home duty
accomplished, every household affection met; but reason and
Scripture taught her, that each individual has something to
bestow, either of time or talent, or wealth, which spent in the
service of others, would return in blessing on herself and her
own family.   In the little parlour behind the shop, in the
suburban villa, in the perfumed boudoir and the gilded hall,
she saw powers unoccupied, and time unemployed.   She lived
to illustrate all that she enforced.   She wore away her life, in
striving for the good of her fellow-sinners.   Does she now regret these labours ? or find any service to have been " in vain
in the Lord ?"   When our great Redeemer declared, that in
feeding the hungry, and giving the thirsty drink, receiving the
stranger, clothing the naked, and visiting the sick, it was done
unto Him ; He added, "I was in *prison* and ye came unto
me."   She was one who felt the force of this commendation,
and she took it in its largest sense ; not as applicable to those
alone, who " suffer for conscience sake," but to the guilty and
the wretched—in the spirit of Him, who came to seek and to
save that which is lost.   Through weariness and painfulness,
she laboured to fulfil it.   And now, that her conflicts upon
earth are ended, and her work done, may it not be confidently
believed, that for her, and such as her, are those words of marvellous joy—" Come ye blessed of my Father, inherit the kingdom prepared for you, from the foundation of the world."

THE END.

INDEX

INDEX.

In this index the initials E.F. stand for Elizabeth Fry. A relationship in parentheses following an individual's name indicates, except where stated otherwise, that individual's relationship to Elizabeth Fry.

PATTERSON SMITH SERIES IN
CRIMINOLOGY, LAW ENFORCEMENT, AND SOCIAL PROBLEMS

1. *Lewis: *The Development of American Prisons and Prison Customs, 1776–1845*
2. Carpenter: *Reformatory Prison Discipline*
3. Brace: *The Dangerous Classes of New York*
4. *Dix: *Remarks on Prisons and Prison Discipline in the United States*
5. Bruce *et al.: The Workings of the Indeterminate-Sentence Law and the Parole System in Illinois*
6. *Wickersham Commission: *Complete Reports, Including the Mooney-Billings Report.* 14 vols.
7. Livingston: *Complete Works on Criminal Jurisprudence.* 2 vols.
8. Cleveland Foundation: *Criminal Justice in Cleveland*
9. Illinois Association for Criminal Justice: *The Illinois Crime Survey*
10. Missouri Association for Criminal Justice: *The Missouri Crime Survey*
11. Aschaffenburg: *Crime and Its Repression*
12. Garofalo: *Criminology*
13. Gross: *Criminal Psychology*
14. Lombroso: *Crime, Its Causes and Remedies*
15. Saleilles: *The Individualization of Punishment*
16. Tarde: *Penal Philosophy*
17. McKelvey: *American Prisons*
18. Sanders: *Negro Child Welfare in North Carolina*
19. Pike: *A History of Crime in England.* 2 vols.
20. Herring: *Welfare Work in Mill Villages*
21. Barnes: *The Evolution of Penology in Pennsylvania*
22. Puckett: *Folk Beliefs of the Southern Negro*
23. Fernald *et al.: A Study of Women Delinquents in New York State*
24. Wines: *The State of Prisons and of Child-Saving Institutions*
25. *Raper: *The Tragedy of Lynching*
26. Thomas: *The Unadjusted Girl*
27. Jorns: *The Quakers as Pioneers in Social Work*
28. Owings: *Women Police*
29. Woolston: *Prostitution in the United States*
30. Flexner: *Prostitution in Europe*
31. Kelso: *The History of Public Poor Relief in Massachusetts, 1820–1920*
32. Spivak: *Georgia Nigger*
33. Earle: *Curious Punishments of Bygone Days*
34. Bonger: *Race and Crime*
35. Fishman: *Crucibles of Crime*
36. Brearley: *Homicide in the United States*
37. *Graper: *American Police Administration*
38. Hichborn: *"The System"*
39. Steiner & Brown: *The North Carolina Chain Gang*
40. Cherrington: *The Evolution of Prohibition in the United States of America*
41. Colquhoun: *A Treatise on the Commerce and Police of the River Thames*
42. Colquhoun: *A Treatise on the Police of the Metropolis*
43. Abrahamsen: *Crime and the Human Mind*
44. Schneider: *The History of Public Welfare in New York State, 1609–1866*
45. Schneider & Deutsch: *The History of Public Welfare in New York State, 1867–1940*
46. Crapsey: *The Nether Side of New York*
47. Young: *Social Treatment in Probation and Delinquency*
48. Quinn: *Gambling and Gambling Devices*
49. McCord & McCord: *Origins of Crime*
50. Worthington & Topping: *Specialized Courts Dealing with Sex Delinquency*
51. Asbury: *Sucker's Progress*
52. Kneeland: *Commercialized Prostitution in New York City*

* new material added

* new material added   † new edition, revised or enlarged

PATTERSON SMITH SERIES IN
CRIMINOLOGY, LAW ENFORCEMENT, AND SOCIAL PROBLEMS

* new material added   † new edition, revised or enlarged

PATTERSON SMITH SERIES IN
CRIMINOLOGY, LAW ENFORCEMENT, AND SOCIAL PROBLEMS

* new material added   † new edition, revised or enlarged